Hometown Memories . . .

Cold Outhouses and Kerosene Lamps

Tales from the Good Old Days in Southeastern Ohio

A TREASURY OF 20TH CENTURY MEMORIES

OTHER BOOKS FROM HOMETOWN MEMORIES

Claremont Tales
Taylorsville Tales
Burke County Tales
Catawba County Tales
Cleveland County Tales
Blue Ridge Tales
Foothills-Piedmont Tales
Memorable Tales of the Smokies and Blue Ridge Mountains
Caldwell County Tales
Albemarle Tales
Lincolnton Tales
Montgomery Tales
Lee County Tales
Rowan County Tales
Cold Biscuits and Fatback and other Richmond County Tales
Skinnydipping in the Mule Trough and Other Rockingham County Tales
Lunch in a Lard Bucket and Other Cabarrus County Tales
Rooster in a Milkwell and other Moore County Tales
It Always Rains When Old Folks Die and other Tales from Davidson and Randolph County
A Prayer for a Baby Goat and other Tales from Alamance County
The Mill Village and the Miracle Bicycle and other Tales from Gaston County
Wilmington Tales
Guilford County Tales
Asheville Tales
The Class of '47 Was Me and other Tales Along the North Carolina Coast
The Elegant Tarpaper Shack and other Tales from the Heartland of North Carolina
Outhouse Spiders and Tin Tub Baths Tales from the Blue Ridge Mountains
Wringer Washers and Ration Stamps Forsyth County
Front Porch Stories, Back Porch Bathrooms Tales from Alexander, Davie, Iredell, Rowan, and Yadkin Counties
Crank Victrolas and Wood Cook Stoves Tales from Green, Lenoir, Pitt, Wayne Counties
Mules, Mud and Homemade Soap Tales from Anson, Stanly Union Counties
Life in the Good Old Days in Alamance, Caswell and Rockingham Counties
Life in the Good Old Days in Catawba, Lincoln and Gaston Counties
Life in the Good Old Days from Buncombe and Henderson Counties
Two Holers and Model T Fords and other Randolph County Tales
Ham Biscuits and Baked Sweet Potatoes and other Montgomery, Richmond, Scotland County Tales
Possum Hunters, Moonshine and Corn Shuck Dolls and other Memories from Wilkes County
Chasing the Ice Truck and other Memories from New Hanover County and Wilmington
Steam Whistles and Party Line Phones and other Memories from Roanoke
Squirrel Gravy and Feed Sack Underwear Memories from the Tennesse Mountains
Miners' Lamps and Cold Mountain Winters Memories from Southwest Virginia
Brush Brooms and Straw Ticks Memories from Northwest Georgia
Coal Camps and Castor Oil Memories from Southern West Virginia
Lessons by Lamplight Memories from Southeastern Kentucky
Memories from Upstate New York
Memories from the Texas Panhandle

Hometown Memories . . .

Cold Outhouses and Kerosene Lamps

Tales from the Good Old Days in Southeastern Ohio

A TREASURY OF 20TH CENTURY MEMORIES

Compiled and edited by Bob Lasley and Sallie Holt

HOMETOWN MEMORIES PUBLISHING COMPANY
Hickory, North Carolina

COLD OUTHOUSES AND KEROSENE LAMPS

Senior Editor: **R. T. Lasley**
Design and Graphic Arts Editor: **Sallie Holt**
Assistant Editors: **Shannon Lasley, Todd Blair, Ashley Buchanan, Larry Dale, Jenny Denny, Robin Desrosiers, Nancy Geiger, Christina Harris, Maurice Hord, Carl Jost, Wesley Nichols, Sarah Robinson.**

ISBN: 978-0-9799199-7-8

Published by:

Hometown Memories Publishing Company
1030 15th Avenue N.W.
Hickory, N. C. 28601
(828) 324-7446

Printed in the United States of America

ACKNOWLEDGMENTS

To those southeastern Ohio old-timers (and to those few who "ain't from around here") who took the trouble to write down your memories and mail them in to us, we offer our heartfelt thanks. And we're sure you're grateful to each other, because together, you have created a wonderful book.

To encourage participation, the publisher offered cash awards to the contributors of the five most appealing stories. These awards were not based upon writing ability or historical knowledge, but rather upon subject matter and interest. The winners were Charles Augenstein, Myrtle Hammons, Larry Kirk, Joanne Mathias and Margaret Smith. It was extremely difficult to choose these winners because every story in this book had its own special appeal.

Associate Editors

Irma Ankrum
Norma Jean Antill
Betty Arbaugh
Blanche Armstrong
Betty Bagent
Ellie Behman
Ruth Bowman
Willard Bryan
Bertha Burkhart
Dorothy Bussemer
Norval Camp, Jr.
Betty Lou Campbell
Carol Conrad-Moore
Tammy Crom
Esther Dailey
Danny Easterling
Marilyn Foster
Lester Gadd
Robert Gatten
Jeannine Gaumer
Doris George
Sally Hale
Curtis Harper
June Hickman
Joyce Hill
Loretta Kay Hillis
Harry Hinkle
Ralph Hollingsworth
Marcie Hunter
Betty Ischy
Trudi Joseph
Arlie King
Virginia Lee Kinney
Larry Kirk
Jeanette Kirkbride
Ida Labaki
Linda Lahmon
Martha Lasure
Linda Laughlin
Ruth Liggett
Rosemary Masteller
Ruby Masterson
James Mayhugh
Suzzanne McAfee
Ona McCarty
Carol McIntire
Elva Miller
Donald Moore
Barbara Osburn
Donna Pirolozzi
Helen Ray
Judith Rockwell
Donald Rodabaugh
Phyllis Shreve
Amanda Slabaugh
Delbert Snell
Jean Starr
Zelda Stephens
Ray Straub
Ruby Swihart
Wilma Thompson
Kathryn Weber
Norman Zimmerman
Gladys Zimmerman

TABLE OF CONTENTS

INTRODUCTION

We know that most folks don't bother to read introductions. But we do hope you (at least eventually) get around to reading this one. Here's why:

First, this is one of the last books that Sallie and I will ever produce. We're turning over what began as a retirement hobby to a youngster who has much more energy than we, and who will continue saving even more of these wonderful old tales from the good old days. So, after over fifty books, we're saying goodbye.

Second—and far more important—is the who, what, where, when, why and how of this book. Until you're aware of these, you won't fully enjoy and appreciate it.

This is a very unusual kind of history book. It was actually written by 478 southeastern Ohio old-timers who remember what life was really like back in the earlier years of the 20th century in that part of Ohio. These folks come from all walks of life, and by voluntarily sharing their memories (which often include their emotions, as well), they have captured the spirit and character of a time that will never be seen again.

Unlike most history books, this one was written from the viewpoint of people who actually *experienced* history. They're familiar with the tribulations of the Great Depression; the horrible taste of castor oil; "outdoor" plumbing; kerosene lamps; and countless other experiences unknown to today's generation.

We advertised in newspapers all over southeastern Ohio to obtain these stories. We sought everyday folks, not experienced authors, and we asked them to simply jot down their memories. Our intention was by no means literary perfection. Most of these folks wrote the way they spoke, and that's exactly what we wanted. We tried to make only minimal changes to their written contributions. We believe that an attempt at correction would damage the book's integrity. (Sadly, however, when we sent out the first draft to story contributors for correction, many were returned with grammar and usage "corrected," and the original tone was lost.)

We need to include a few disclaimers: first, many important names are missing in many stories. Several folks revealed the names of their teachers, neighbors, friends, even their pets and livestock, but the identities of parents or other important characters weren't given. Second, many contributors failed to follow instructions in submitting and identifying pictures and making corrections to their first draft copies. We're sure this resulted in many errors (and perhaps lost photographs) but we did the best we could. Third, each contributor accepts full responsibility for his or her submission and for our interpretation of requested changes. Fourth, because some of the submitted photographs were photocopied or "computer printed," their quality may be very poor. And finally, because there was never a charge, "fee," or any other obligation to contributors to have their material included in this book, we do not accept responsibility for any story or other material that was left out, either intentionally or accidentally.

We apologize for the many typographical errors you'll undoubtedly find. We don't have a proof reading staff and our eyes are old.

Bob Lasley and Sallie Holt
August 2009

Dewberry Telephones in Frog Holler
by Shirlee D. Mencer of Coshocton, Ohio
born in 1935

My name is Shirlee and I am the sixth child down, and three to go, nine children in the family. My mother lived in Indiana, Elsie Marie Talbot, and she married my father, James D. Milhoan. My mother was adopted and very rich; my father was what would be known as a "poor farmer." She, my mother, was disowned when she married my father. They came to live on a farm of one hundred and five acres called "Frog Holler."

Here are my stories. Now go with me down memory lane, about ten miles south of Newcomerstown, Ohio on old Route 21, turn right onto a county road, and about a mile down the lane you will come to an old log cabin on the right, nestled in the hills around it. A place called "Frog Holler," that was my home. I was born in that cabin in August 1935.

We had outhouses (toilets), pots for inside (chambers) and we used catalogs for toilet paper. There were floods, with water all around our house—we would sit for hours on the hillside until the water went down. We had hard winters with not enough clothing.

In the log cabin, times were hard there, but the child in me did not know it. It got really cold in the valley and we had a fireplace and a cookstove for heat.

I remember on the log mantle sat two little brown sacks. My oldest brother reached up and grabbed a handful of hard cinnamon balls and put them in his mouth. All of a sudden, he was screaming, yelling and spitting out the candy! (Or so he thought.) One of the sacks just like it had carbide in it! WHOOPS! That was for the carbide light! Who would have known any difference, with the sacks looking the same?

I looked in the closet one day. I was three or four years old maybe, and I saw a box in there. I opened it up and there was beautiful wavy and curly long blonde hair cut off and laying in paper in the box—where Mom was trying to keep it (a memory from her rich days in Indiana, where she had it cut). Also in there too was a creature with lots of long fur and a small head with teeth and eyes! I was scared to pieces and ran out of there fast. Later I found out it too was from Mom's rich days (a fox fur). She sure must have loved my dad to go from "riches to rags."

One winter day, my dad couldn't get the old car started and he put a bucket of oil or grease on the cookstove to warm it up, to start the car. Through all the commotion the oil was left on the stove too long and it

Log Cabin where Shirlee Mencer was born. Left to right: Bonnie, age seven; Uncle Harry Milhoan and son, Billy; Cousin Marg, age thirteen; and Shirlee, age two.

poured over the hot stove and that burned the log cabin down! All were safe.

I don't know where we stayed for a while until a house on down the bottom was cleaned up. All the doors were left open on that old house and the sheep used it for a barn. They scrubbed it with lye after they got all the manure off the boards and we moved in (happy day). We had a stove in the middle of the living room floor and a cookstove in the kitchen—it was cold as ice in the winter. There were nine of us kids so we slept at the top and the bottom of the beds. We hardly had any covers so we would put coats on us to keep warm. The window was boarded over upstairs; you could see out the cracks. In the morning we would have snow on our blankets or whatever covered us. We carried water from a spring and water from the creek. It ran right beside the house, a few yards out. Saturday night was a bath in the big round tub. Yuk!

My mom never ate a thing until all of us were fed; then she would sit down and eat. Saturday night we would usually have chili with spaghetti in it. (It went further that way.)

A small memory I have from the log cabin is all of my brothers and sisters would go play on the hill and we would take dewberry vines and hook them together to be our telephone lines. Mom would call, "Yoohoo, come and eat!" and we would ask, "What are we having?" She would say biscuits and gravy, and since we either had gravy and biscuits or biscuits and gravy every meal practically, we would go eat, or some would just stay up there and play with the dewberry wires. Ha, ha. We had a good imagination, for sure.

When we moved to the sheep house, my sister, Crystal, and I was hungry. It was a frosty morning and we went over by the hill where there was a small building built back in the hill to keep things cool. We found a broken jar of applesauce and we took two forks and the bottom of the broken jar and took it on the hill, eating applesauce out of that broken jar; kinda dangerous but it was good!

We had a gray pony all of my life until I was grown. His name was "Pal," and he was so gentle. We rode him without even a bridle. We would use a switch and tap him on the neck with it. Tap him on the left and he would go right, tap him on the right and he would go left. All six of us would ride him, lots of times, and sometimes at the same time.

I want to tell a story about my grandma. My brothers made a snake out of clay and they put its head on a small stone and then called out to Grandma, "Grandma, snake!" She grabbed the hoe and came running and chopped it up into pieces. The boys laughed their head off. She didn't see that well.

Another time when my brothers were swimming in the creek (skinny dipping) my grandmother came up the field to check on them and Vernie, my brother, put a lot of clay on his naked bottom and it looked like he had swimming trunks on, especially if you couldn't see well, like Grandma. She said, "Look at you boys. Why Vernie is the only decent one of the bunch!"

I went to a one room schoolhouse called Prohibition. In the first grade, I got very sick and I thought the potatoes I was eating out of a cup with no handle was what made me sick.

Next memory, I rode Pal the pony in front of Vernie, my brother, all the way up our lane about a mile to catch a ride to the hospital in Cambridge, Ohio. It was snowing and very cold; I had double pneumonia and I had to go and stay with my aunt in North Salem to get well because our house was too cold. My first grade teacher brought me grapes, fruit and coloring book and crayons. I never had grapes before and they were heaven.

An embarrassing moment for me was when in the second or third grade, I wore a pair of my mother's underwear to school. I pinned them with a small safety pin. (*Safety* pin my eye.) We all had to stand at the front of the children in a one room schoolhouse to do any of our lessons. As I was standing there in front of a room full of kids, first through eighth grade, I felt a "pop." (Uh-oh.) My pin opened up and down came the bloomers! I tried to hold my legs together so they would not fall but they were too big and down they came. The boy in the front row was an ornery brat and he just grinned. I was so mad, so I just stepped out of them and left them on the floor where I was standing and took my seat. The teacher saw them and got a piece of paper from her desk and picked them up. She held them up and said "Whose pants?" The boy in the front row, Billy McFarland, said, "Shirlee Milhoan's!" The teacher put them on her desk and said they could be picked up later.

Another story on snakes. I was with Bonnie and Crystal and they were picking berries. I was eating berries. I was barefooted and while I was eating the berries, I felt myself rocking back and forth, up and down. I looked down and both feet were on a huge, curled up blacksnake! I called to my sisters and they killed it. It was as long as my sister was tall!

Another time I was eating berries and I was in a den of copperheads in my bare feet. I screamed and my brother shot them. Snakes like berries too. I hate snakes. I cut one up and put him in a jar—I canned him!

A game we used to play was the boys set a piece of roofing made of wavy metal up in the yard and was jumping over it. I was little and I tried to jump it but I didn't get across it and I cut my leg badly. I went down to the creek and let the blood flow away; we didn't have a doctor. I have a scar on the front of my leg to this day.

Getting back to this beautiful valley that we called

Frog Holler—lots of frogs there—we could hear them every spring. We would play with them. My brother Gene would make little harnesses out of string and put them on two bullfrogs and make them pull little sticks!

One time on a warm summer day it was raining (we were outside, all us kids) and little frogs were everywhere. We couldn't walk or we would step on them! It had to be raining frogs because they were in the wagon bed, they were on the pony's back, they were on everything and they were too little to jump on anything. Wherever the rain hit they were there—hundreds of tiny, tiny frogs! I've never seen anything like it since.

We were poor, had one pair of shoes in the winter—barefoot in the summer. We had secondhand clothes and not enough of them. In the winter, my sisters Bonnie and Crystal would wash me off in a frozen mud puddle because I had dirt on my face and legs when I went to school. We had kerosene lamps and sometimes Delco lights run by a motor outside and it wasn't always easy to keep this kid clean in those lights. We bathed in the creek all summer and swam. We would take a gunny sack (feed for horses came in it) and we would hold it on both sides and put it under the water and bring it up and we would have fish in it—it's called "seining."

Hogs would be shot in the fall and they would build a fire and tilt an iron barrel filled with water and when it got hot they would put the pig in the barrel to get the hair off of it. They would scrape the skin. Then they would butcher it for pork chops, bacon and ham. Winter was coming and we were a hungry bunch.

We also had two groundhogs and one squirrel. My sister Bonnie shot at the groundhog and grazed the top of its neck, but it was ok. So we took it and its brother home with us. They were half grown. We petted them with sticks and finally we petted them with our hands and tamed them. We cut a square hole in the wooden porch and "Sunny" would stay there. They would hibernate and in the spring come back. "Buster," the one that got wounded on the neck, went away and he was gone. About two years later my sister Crystal and I went walking up two pasture fields and saw this grown groundhog eating grass. We said, "I bet this is Buster." He did not run away and I picked him up in my arms and we took him home! When we got home we found out he was blind! Probably from the bullet that grazed him. (A wild groundhog will bite you to pieces and won't let go!) Thank God it really was our tame groundhog, Buster.

Our squirrel would sit on my dad's shoulder and try to get the Prince Albert can of tobacco out of his pocket. We tried to make everything a pet.

Again when Crystal and I went walking over the hills to eat berries or whatever we carried home baby skunks by the tails! Our mother was not pleased. "Turn them loose and get a bath in the creek!" I think she wasted canned tomatoes on us. The good ole days!

In the spring, we would go to a huge slippery elm tree and we would pry the bark off in small pieces. We would eat the white, thick part of the bark. It is used for medicine today. We ate the bark year after year and we skinned that poor tree up as far as we could reach. It tasted like food to us and was very chewy. The old elm died because we skinned off the bark.

My sister Crystal and I went up to milk the cow in the winter; we had to walk a very long way. We got a big bucket of milk but we were so cold and the milk was so warm, we drank a lot of the milk. We knew we could get into trouble so we put snow in the milk to fill it back up (would be 2 percent today).

Old Prohibition School was a small building and that is where my three brothers, five sisters and myself attended, first grade through eighth grade, all in one room. When I was around 10 years old and my sister Crystal was around 12, we were given the opportunity to memorize 500 Bible verses. It was given to the whole school. Crystal, myself and Laura Jean Wilson (a classmate of mine) every morning would learn the verses. As a prize, we got to go to two weeks of Bible school in Elyria, Ohio at a campground. It was a highlight in our life.

Long summer days to do our chores and to walk for miles or ride "Pal" the pony and play "Annie over" or "Red Rover" send somebody over. We had days to fill with all the precious memories we have today. Depression, black bread, and stamps, not much to go on except love. I wouldn't trade it for anything! Thanks, Mom and Dad, for the best of times.

One Night and No Tomatoes

by David S. Winston of New Philadelphia, Ohio
born in 1937

Halloween in the late forties was more than just one night; the fun could last for weeks. Our neighborhood was no different. Keith and Ken Van Epps, twins and my best friends, spent many evenings throwing corn, rapping on windows and being as mischievous as any ten year old boys.

One night we decided to throw tomatoes at a neighbor's house until they came out and yelled at us. When we got no response, we kept on throwing, pausing to gather more ammo from our garden. Boredom set in; we ran out of tomatoes and still no response. The next day it didn't take long before there was a knock on our door and an even shorter time to discover the culprits. We had to clean the house and apologize and then were punished; I didn't go outside to play after supper for many months.

Our mothers anguished over what would become of us and decided that some time at the YMCA camp could only help. That summer we were sent to Camp Nelson Dodd for several weeks to learn some proper behavior. Everything was going well until the fourth day of camp when one of the campers came down with polio. The camp closed; we were sent home AND quarantined! We could only play with each other for three weeks. We were so sick of each other that it is a wonder we are still friends today.

Our parents would be happy, because we turned out pretty well despite our misspent youth. We settled down and became doctors; the Van Epps twins in medicine and I became a dentist. Our children and now grandchildren still have fun on Halloween but it is only one night and there are no tomatoes.

Neighbor Kids in the Buzza Living Room

by Miss Mirem Rose Buzza
of Zanesville, Ohio
born in 1935

There was six of us: Mother, Daddy and four siblings; Bill, Joy, Jay, and Mirem Rose, better known as Sissy. We moved into this big two story home on the hill with this big yard and a fence went around the entire property. I was almost 11 years old. It wasn't long before the neighborhood kids came around to investigate who or what moved into this big home and it didn't take long to make new friends, plus we were close to schools to make friends, but our true friends were in our neighborhood in Zanesville, Ohio.

William A. and Rosa Buzza (daddy and mother), Bill Jr., Mirem Rose, Joy and Jay Thomas.

We started to congregate on different porches but soon we and they all gathered at the big home on the porch in the yard. Hanging on the fence with their bicycles to the point where we had to take the front fence down. My parents didn't complain. All open space now and we continued finding more things to do.

First was the comic book craze. We traded our books then, but a few came here to read in the living room for hours while the rest of us were outside playing kick the can, hop scotch, hide and seek, mumbly peg, and just play simpleness. It was a joke among relatives who came to visit that not one of the Buzza kids were in the living room, just neighborhood kids. There were so many friends coming and going into our home that they wore a path in the rug from the front door to the bathroom door. They didn't even go home for their personal things and my parents didn't complain again.

Then we got this upright piano and a wind up record player. Boy, were we hot—and musically inclined. We would use the "wand" of the Electrolux sweeper as our microphone and belt out the music.

Donald Bryan, brother of Willard Bryan, learned to play our old upright. He was really good and couldn't read a note of music but he picked and played the songs by ear, as the saying goes. Eventually he was taught by a professor and I guess piano music was his profession for years and it makes me feel good that he started on our old upright.

We passed this stage to junior high school and our attention went to sports, boys, and girls and sneak a little kiss now and then. We would lay on the bank in the back yard and look for objects in the clouds and in the evening we would tell ghost stories.

Then came high school. Things changed. We were searching and thinking of the future and kind of drifted apart and rarely saw one another. Mainly because we had to work four summers in a concession stand and not much time for fun. Some of these friends are gone or not well and not around here now.

I moved and did my thing after graduation but now back in the "old big home" on the hill taking care of my 97-year-old mother.

There were so many adventures and stories, but...

I miss those good old days. You don't know what life will hand you, so you had better enjoy what you can, if you're able, when you're young, but the "things that probably wouldn't happen today" is also true.

Most young people today don't know the objects you can pick out of clouds, ghost stories, good comic books, and all those games you can play that don't cost a lot and having and living life. This is a new ballgame. Hours of computers, hours of TV, texting, different cell phones, video games, drugs, gangs, you name it. Their face and nose is stuck in these things and don't see what's around them. We had TVs since the early 50s, but it came with family, friends, popcorn, and Kool-Aid. The only thing I wanted was the piano and organ, which I had; and a printer so I wouldn't have to write so much—just type it in—push the button—print—of which I never got.

I'm not saying all kids missed a lot, but a majority has or there wouldn't be all these problems. There is a lot of problems out there now, and we had better help one another and give thanks for what we have and pray for better things to come.

I'm glad we had the parents we had. We didn't have a lot of things, but we had the material things and were rewarded for what we did.

Several memories in my life—some sad—some good, and funny, but this was the good times while very young when we didn't know yet what life had to offer and what was going to be on your plate.

Airplane Watching and Dough Snitching

by Alice Shirer of Zanesville, Ohio
born in 1934

As I was growing up in my hometown of Sonora in southeastern Ohio during World War II, I thought I knew the type of warplanes that flew overhead. You know—the B24, B25, P28, Mustang, etc. Since I had five brothers in the military during the war and one joined after high school graduation at the end of the war, I was very fascinated. We were glued to the radio for news reports.

I was the youngest of nine living children of Wilmer and Ina Shirer, having seven brothers and one sister. As the brothers went off to work or war, I was given more responsibility. As their baby sister, I wanted to prove I could do the same work as my brothers, like milking cows, building fences, etc.

We always had a large vegetable garden and a larger truck patch of sweet corn. Mom did a lot of canning. I remember helping Mom peel lots of peaches and apples. We dug the potatoes by hand and stored them in the cellar during the winter. Dad raised Berkshire hogs and butchered from two to four each fall. That was quite a chore. One of my jobs was to keep the fire going under the large kettle of fat to be rendered for lard. Of course, the smoke always found a way to my eyes, but after the rendering, that meant cracklings I could eat as I walked to school. They were so good. After the sausage was ground, we would spend a whole evening in the kitchen frying sausage patties and putting them in large crocks to be stored in the cellar for winter. Boy, you talk about good eating! We sometimes stuffed sausage into links.

The kitchen coal-fired cook stove served many uses. It not only heated the kitchen, it had a water reservoir and was the perfect spot for a small child to be given a bath with the oven door down. Mom used to set her bread dough on top of the stove bread warmers to rise. One time after school I pulled a chair to the stove, reached up and took a large handful of dough to eat. I loved all kinds of raw dough. You know what happened. The large, puffy partly risen dough went completely flat. I patted and patted, but the dough still showed a scar. It sure tasted good though.

I completed my first eight years of schooling in a two story wood frame school house. Four grades down, four grades upstairs. Since our house was a short distance from the school across an open field, teachers could easily observe all things going on there. Especially when I was home sick, teacher would often question why I was outside. I had the usual kid diseases, like whooping cough, measles, colds, sore throat, sore throat, and more sore throat. My two youngest brothers and I have discussed how important we felt when we were quarantined with a large red sign reading "measles" or some other disease. Of course, the county health nurse was the one to order and remove the quarantine. I never forgave my youngest brother though because he did not get the whooping cough and I did, even though we both had shots. I was six years old at the time. My teacher came to visit me.

At this time we had two general stores, the "upper store" and the "lower store" in a village of around 350 people. We had a large feed mill with a railroad siding and the B&O Railroad buzzed through town with two passenger trains and numerous freight trains each day. We had a railroad station where people could get on or off and the mail was dropped and carried to the post office for delivery every day.

The Methodist church played a vital role in most lives at that time. Santa was a regular visitor and treats were given to each child attending Christmas services. Promotion or Children's Day was special because children went to a higher grade Sunday school class. Awards were given for perfect attendance. Revivals were held and lots of good meals served for whatever reason. A large board listing all the men and women in the area who had gone to war was erected in the churchyard.

Movies were shown on Friday nights at the school house. Cowboy movies of Tom Mix, Crash Corrigan and other with many serials that required coming back next week to see "who got'em." There was popcorn of course and I think the cost was like 10 cents, which in those days, was sometimes hard to come by. I can remember how good a five cent bottle of Whistle orange pop tasted after pushing a lawn mower over our big yard.

In the late 1940s the two story school house was torn down and a metal one floor building was erected. Then Friday nights produced square dancing. The school was closed in the early 1960s and children were bussed to Perry Elementary on the East Pike, Route 40.

Mrs. Esther Slenker was my teacher from second through fourth grade. We said the pledge of allegiance, the Lord's Prayer, and John 3:16 every day before school.

We drank well water and had two toilets. We had no playground equipment, but made up our own games. In nice weather we played softball, jump rope, marbles, crack the whip or Red Rover. In bad weather we played jacks, pick-up sticks, or other inside games. All kids went home for lunch.

I did not like Mrs. Slenker. She was strict, spied on me when I was home sick and had eyes in the back of her head. She would be at the front blackboard and we at the back blackboard behind the large furnace but she always knew when we were playing tic-tac-toe. But I came to admire and love her. She lost a son in the war. She was very fond of my mother. She said she always knew when it was Monday because Mrs. Shirer had a washing out. One of my jobs was to help take the sometimes stiff, frozen clothes into the house to thaw and iron. We corresponded and visited Mrs. Slenker until her death a few years ago.

There were favorite radio programs like the Lux Radio Theatre with Pam and Jerry North, The Shadow, Inner Sanctum, Mr. District Attorney, The Hit Parade, Fibber McGee and Mollie, The Grand Ole Opry, and many more.

I thank God I was born when I was, in the family I was and where I was. Blessings abound then and now. I wish everyone could say the same. My mom lived past 101 years. Life was hard but good in the good ole days when a village helped raise this child.

Itinerary of a Feed Sack

by Charlotte W. Abels of Byesville, Ohio
born in 1933

When I was a young girl around five to seven years, we lived on a farm with a lot of animals, so feed was a necessary item. Daddy, Thomas C. Rogers, would go to the feed mill and bring a large sack of feed home and soon the flowered feed sack was in the old Maytag washer, washed and dried to send back with Daddy to the mill to match up to get another just like the first. We sometimes would get three alike. Then came the new dress for me or aprons for mother. I was so proud of that new dress.

Feed sack quilt with pictures from a coloring book.

Then the scraps went to Grandma, who lived with us, to cut and sew blocks for a beautiful flower garden quilt.

The plain sacks were washed and pillow covers made or sheets and sometimes blocks 12 inches in diameter were traced with beautiful pictures from our coloring books so my brother and I could embroidery them to make a full size quilt which I still have at age 75 and is still in good shape today. Nothing went to waste in those days.

Jonas's Raccoons and the Hat Eating Goat

by Menno N. Miller of Sugarcreek, Ohio
born in 1936

I was raised on a farm of 105 acres. Living on the farm with Dad and Mother, nine brothers and four sisters, life was never bored. There were always plenty of children chores to keep us Miller youngsters occupied, both mind and body.

If there was any time left over after chores, we learned quickly to busy ourselves with our own imagination.

Fishing in the creek bottom was very exciting. Breaking of a branch from a tree, whittling it down to a little boy's size, wrapping a string, which had been used to sew feed bags, on the one end of the branch. Attach a bent-over straight pin found in Mother's sewing basket. This was just perfect for fishing hook. For a sinker, we used a rusty machinery nut found in Father's old shop. For the bobber we used an old bottle cork. Oh, the excitement running for the creek bottom. How exciting to have our first nibbles or caught a wiggle fish, some even seven inches long. No matter how small the fish, my mother always fried it. Oh, how good it tasted with a piece of Mother's home baked bread.

I had the responsibility to show a young calf how to drink milk out of a bucket by pushing the calf's nose down into the milk. All that happened was I got a face full of milk when the calf pulled its head out of the bucket and snorted in my face. I wiped my face on my shirt sleeve. I soon learned to have more patience and try all over—putting the calf's nose down into the milk, putting my finger in the calf's mouth, and sure enough the calf started sucking on my finger, drawing milk from the bucket. All went well until the bucket was nearly empty, then the calf butted, knocking the bucket out of my hands looking for more milk. What a challenge to see this same calf grow to be a big mother cow, bringing more baby calves and milk for family use or to sell for money to provide for the family.

My brothers and I spent many a spring and summer day "herding" the big milk cows. Fences were few, and it would not do to let the cows wonder in the corn or hay fields. The small acreage under fence was reserved for

Saturdays or holidays. What a frustrated feeling if we didn't pay enough attention to the cows. They would find their way into the corn field with heads and tails up running, and we could hardly get them out of that good tasting green corn. Sometimes tears went down our dirty faces in frustration till we had them all gathered together again. While watching the cows we would play a game of hide the glove in the ground and my brother would try and find it. This was a great pastime.

We always looked forward to come evening to bring the cows in for milking time. Oh, how good it tasted to go to the spring and dip in for a fresh tin cup of clean sparkling water.

My brother, Jonas, raised raccoons, which was so interesting. To watch the small baby raccoons coming out of their nest. As I was watching the cute babies I laid my new straw hat on the ground. We also had a very mischievous milk goat tied nearby. While I was enjoying the cute baby raccoons, the goat got a hold of my brand new straw hat and had eaten everything but only a very small piece left over to show my father. What a disappointment for a six-year-old.

My father also raised lots of white Muscovy ducks. This was a very beautiful duck, snow white with a bright red head. On the farm we had a creek bottom with large water holes which gave the ducks lots of room to swim in the water. One day the ducks were very frightened and disturbed…a loud squawking flapping noise.

My brother, Ben, and I quickly went to investigate. To our surprise a big 12 pound turtle had one of the ducks, holding it by its beak trying to pull this big white duck under the water. With Ben's quick motion, jumping in the water to pull the duck from the turtle. The turtle had pulled the top part of the beak to the side. Ben caught the turtle and sold it to the mailman for 50 cents. The beautiful Muscovy duck got along fairly well with the damaged beak.

Who Was Poorest?

By Bonnie Milhoan of Kimbolton, Ohio
Born in 1930

In the late 1930's a new family moved into the area, and the kids went to our school at Prohibition. They lived here for only a few months, and didn't get to finish out the school year. This was a disappointment, because they would spend time playing with my brothers. We never knew where they located from here.

More than fifty years passed, and I was living back at the old home place. One summer day, I was out working in the garden in front of the house. A car came down the lane, slowed down, then pulled over and stopped. The man inquired about a family that used to live here; "Or I think they lived here," he added. "Everything changes a lot in fifty years."

I asked his name and he said simply, "Harold." Then, "I used to play with some boys here, I think."

"Your last name is Harold, isn't it? Not your first?" He confirmed that, and instantly, I knew who he was—Garland Harold, one of the three who played here many years ago. He was surprised that I remembered him.

I invited him in, and we spent the next two to three hours just reminiscing the time he spent with my brothers, and his brief stay at our school.

I was raised in a family of nine kids, caring parents, and an extra strong bond of love to keep and sustain us. Hold us together. We lived in an old, old house with only meager necessities. This man had lived in a big house while here, and a nice house. I'd soon detected that they were better off than we were, even at that tender age. But now he tells me of circumstances as to why they moved, both of sharing our hearts of when we were poor.

Gene, on left; Har; brother, Vernie, and Bonnie Milhoan.

"We didn't have warm coats," I told him.

"We didn't either."

"Maybe others didn't know it, but we had snow in our shoes when we got to school," I said.

"We did too."

"Yes, but I mean because the soles were coming off our shoes."

He insisted that they were still poorer than we were. Can you believe that? Why would he insist he's right when all the evidence is so clear? Very sincerely, he looked straight at me and said, "We were poor. We were very poor. You were rich, very rich." So simply stated, and I was a bit bewildered, hearing this.

Then he paused, and continued, "Do you know why you were rich? I'll tell you why. You had a pony. We didn't. You had a pony, and you had everything!"

He was right. It took me over fifty years to come to the realization that I was indeed rich when I was a child. I was rich because I had a pony. And there isn't enough money in all of God's creation to buy the happiness, the joys, and the pleasures that were mine for thirty-one years; and all because I had a pony.

Note: When I was around two years old, Daddy got me a two year steel roan gelding pony. We called him "Pal." Daddy had traded something for him to a neighbor, because he had no money. Pal was the best investment my daddy ever made. He was the family pet. Everybody's friend; Pal died at a good old age of 33.

As a small child, I remember seeing hundreds of wee brown frogs, some less than an inch long. They would appear only after a rain. My theory is that they came down with the rain. Why? Because they were found in some most unusual and most unlikely places. They were on the roof of our small buildings, in wagon beds, on top of the house, and on the backs of our big work horses. Another oddity; they would all disappear immediately after a rain.

My cousin and my brother Gene were asked to go to the store for spaghetti. "And hurry!" they were told. They took the shortcut through the cow pasture and the woods. They hurried. However, coming home through the cow pasture, they laid the spaghetti on a small rock and played for a time.

Finally, they realized time was passing, and they'd better get home. "Oh yeah, we can't forget the spaghetti!" They go to the rock and...they can't remember. "Whose turn is it to carry the spaghetti, anyway?" Well, fun time's over, and the argument began. They were both so stubborn and refused to carry it home. They left it laying on the rock.

"Where's the spaghetti?" my aunt asked. Each angrily blamed the other for leaving it. Two angry parents said, "Go back and get it. And be quick about it!" So they did. Err...they went back to get it. But it seemed the cows got it too. And they were almost finished when two bewildered boys came on the scene.

Woe be unto those boys when they get home!

Brenda Was Worth the Beating

by Larry Morris of Caldwell, Ohio

born in 1950

This is a true story that happened in 1967, when I was a junior at Shenandoah High School. Shenandoah High School was named after the USS Shenandoah that crashed near Caldwell, Ohio.

The week was not a good week at all. We were under Marshall law in study hall, which meant no one was to leave study hall without permission, or talk. To leave the study hall, you had to sign your name on a paper to go to the bathroom or your locker.

Well, I was on the front seat in front of the teacher's desk, doing my geometry lesson. I was minding my own business until this beautiful young lady came up to sign her name to leave the study hall. As she bent over to sign her name on the paper, my ruler that I was using to do my math with just slipped off the end of my finger and cracked her hind end in her tight skirt. Well, it all broke loose. She screamed, and the kids all roared.

She (Brenda Clark) begged the teacher, Mr. McCullogh, not to beat me, but that was vain, being so much interruption had happened. I bent over the desk, and our teacher—six feet, six inches and weighs 295—beat my hind end and brought both my feet off the floor! I never forgot the day or what happened, but like a fool, I would do it again. Ouch! For Brenda, she was worth it.

Softball, Tombstone Math and the New Oxfords

by Claire J. Thompson of Stafford, Ohio

born in 1943

I grew up in southeastern Ohio near the small village of Sycamore Valley, Ohio in a family of seven children and a baby sister who died in infancy.

My father and mother, Joe and Ida Day, and our grandmother, Janie Yoe, were truly an inspiration to us and taught us the value of hard work and respect for one another and our friends and neighbors.

I was born at the end of World War II, the youngest of eight children. We didn't have very much money or material things, but as I look back on my childhood, it was truly a happy time in my life. We were very rich indeed with family, love, respect, hard work, and fun times.

Our family is a story of struggling, hard times, and hard work. We lived on a farm and raised most of our food. We hoed corn in the summer and helped our father in the hayfield. He had two horses and a wagon. We kids used pitchforks to put the hay on the wagon. It would be so hot, but I remember Dad saying, "You kids have to get all of your work completed before you can go swimming." Needless to say, we worked real hard to get that hay on the wagon and into the barn.

We raised chickens and pigs. We kids would have to gather the eggs twice a day. We would try to see who got the most eggs in their pail.

We also had a cow named Lil. My grandma milked her every day. We drank the milk and churned our own butter.

By the time we got our chores finished the day would be almost over. We would go swimming almost every day in the hot summer months. I remember those little bugs that got between our toes and stuck there. I hated those bugs, but went swimming anyway. After a hot day in the hay field, it was such a relief to jump into the water and go swimming.

In the same hay field during the summer we would have softball games. All of us had a name referencing one of the famous Cleveland Indians professional players, such Bob Feller, Bob Lemon, Larry Doby, and so on.

I remember the neighbor kids, John, Robert, Larry, and Donnie Burkhart. They lived in the next house down the road. Also the Curtis family, Ruth, John, Gard, and Carole who lived on the farm next to them. All of us would get together and have a softball game almost every afternoon. My sister Hazel or, as we called her, Bubby, was one of the best players. She could hit the ball hard. Everyone always wanted her on their team. My brother Dennis was always the boss. He and Ed Bode, a neighbor kid, would pick and choose sides. That was always so much fun. There would be twenty kids playing.

Claire, Rosemary, Hazel and Harry Day.

Sometimes in the evenings we would build a fire and go fishing with all the kids. Our fishing poles were made of long skinny tree branches we got out of the woods. We also had to dig our own worms before we went fishing.

We made most of our toys. There wasn't a Wal-Mart to purchase these things. We could not have been able to afford to buy those things anyway. With myself being the youngest, my bother Dennis would sometimes say, "Chummy, you and Carole (that was my neighbor friend) can play doll babies while we have our softball game." Now I realize why he said that; we were younger and couldn't hit the ball very well.

We siblings all had nicknames. My oldest brother Emerson's name was Sir, because he would also boss us around. My brother Ellis's name was Dunk. He was the quiet one in the family. My brother Dennis was Buzz, my sister Rosemary was Chip, my sister Hazel was Bubby, my brother Harry was Bawler, because he would cry when was up to bat and couldn't hit the ball. I remember he would throw the bat down and go somewhere and cry. My nickname was Chummy. My siblings still call me that once in a while today.

In the springtime we would help our grandmother, we called her Granny, plant and take care of the big garden. We would gather all the vegetables and help our mom can them. It wasn't unusual to have two hundred cans of vegetables and fruit in our cellar. Mom also made her own jellies. We mowed our yard with a push mower; there were no power mowers. Mom would make her own flower pots. She would save empty tin coffee cans, paint them in pretty colors, such as yellow, red, green. My sister Rosemary, she was the gardener of the family, would help plant geraniums, which she saved from one season to another. We didn't go to the nursery and get flowers; I do not think that there were places like that to purchase flowers back then. Anyway they were very pretty and Mom would set them on the front porch.

In the summertime, we kids went barefoot most of the time. We only had one pair of shoes and they had to last all year. We each got a new pair before school started.

We would go berry picking with our granny. We took our buckets up over the big hill and would find big patch of berries. Our granny would carry a hoe, just in case there would be a snake to deal with. We would eat some of the berries we picked and then go over to the spring that flowed through the hill and drink the springwater. It would always be crystal clear. Probably much better than the water available today.

We played in the woods. I remember there was an old cemetery, probably a family plot, which really stole our interest. We would read the old tattered tombstones and figure out how old the people were when they died. I would always be scared to be there and would hang on to my sisters.

I remember the abandoned log house on the other side of the hill. That old house was so intriguing to us. Mom and Dad never wanted us to go up there, but we didn't tell them and went anyway. We would take our flashlights with us and go inside. There was spider webs everywhere, bugs of all kinds and snake skins. When we saw the snake skins we got spooked out and would run back home.

Our mother did the laundry with a tub filled with hot water and a washboard to help clean the clothes. It would take her all day. At the end of the 1950s she was able to get a wringer washer. I remember she purchased it at the Montgomery Ward store. It made me happy to see my mother not have to work as hard to do the laundry. There were no automatic washers back then. My mother never had an automatic washer until somewhere in the 1980s.

My grandma did most of the ironing. She would sprinkle the clothes, wrap them in a sheet, and keep them until ready to iron. She used an iron which was made of cast iron. Imagine how heavy that must have been. It was heated on the cookstove, which made it ready for ironing our clothes. At the end of 1950, we were able to get her an electric iron.

My brothers worked in Canton, Ohio, at Timken Roller Bearing Co. after graduating from high school, and helped buy things for the rest of us at home. I remember our first television set. My two brothers, Dennis and Ellis, bought it for us. It was black and white with a seventeen inch screen. It was so snowy you could barely see the picture. This was sometime in the 1950s. The antenna was at the top of a big hill behind our house. The wind would blow hard and turn the antenna, and then we couldn't get reception. We would climb the big hill and turn it in the right direction. We were pretty exhausted by the time we got back. This happened quite often.

I also remember our first telephone. We were on party line with six other families. Everyone's phone would ring into your house, such as two rings, three rings, four rings, and so on to signal which ring was yours so to answer. Needless to say there was plenty of eavesdropping on your conversation. I can't imagine that happening today.

I remember Easter time, when we kids would gather our own moss to put in our Easter baskets. We gathered the moss in the woods and put it in our baskets. Our mother would hide our baskets in the house and we would have to find them. Later in the day we would hide the eggs outside and try to find them.

At the beginning of fall, when school started, we got to wear our new shoes. I remember going to Woodsfield, Ohio, that was the town nearest to buy clothing, to purchase my new shoes. Mom purchased those dull brown oxfords. I didn't like those and I wanted the popular black and white oxford shoe like the other kids had. I started to cry and Mom took me back into the store to get the kind I wanted. They were more expensive but she sacrificed and got them for me. I was so proud the first day of school with my new shoes.

Our mother made most of our clothes. We each had a new outfit for the first day of school. She even made my brothers' shirts. Our mother was a beautiful sewer. By the way, she passed that trait down to me because I sew now and have made most of my two daughters' clothes for them when they were in school.

We couldn't afford to buy the hot lunches at school, so Mom packed our dinner pails. We usually had a sandwich, homemade canned peaches, and homemade sugar cookies. Mom would stay up late and make those sugar cookies so we could have them for our lunch pails.

Our granny made homemade bread. When we got home from school, I could smell the hot rolls as they came out of the oven before I would get into the house. How delighted we were to have one of those rolls with homemade butter and jelly on it.

I also can remember before there was electricity in our home. We had gas lights in every room. It wouldn't be very bright, so we did most of our work and playing before dark. We didn't have electricity until the early 1950s.

The wintertime was a special season for us. The creeks would freeze over and stay frozen until February or March. We played ice hockey all winter long. My brothers Dennis and Harry would make our hockey sticks out of tree branches. We used a canning lid for the hockey puck. Denny was the boss of these games also. I guess we thought he was older than us and we had to listen to him.

Denny, Rosemary, and Harry would set traps along the creek banks with hopes of trapping a muskrat or a mink. They would get up early before school, put on their boots and check their traps. One time my brother Harry caught a mink and thought it was a strange animal and wanted to throw it back into the water. He took it up to the house and our dad said, "Son, you just caught a mink." Needless to say it was worth much more money than the muskrat.

Christmas was always special to us. We went to the woods to get our tree. We bundled up with extra layers of clothing, hats, and gloves, put boots on, and tracked through the snow to get our tree. One Christmas Harry cut a tree that was so tall we had to cut it almost half off to get it into our living room. For Christmas we each got one toy for under the tree. I usually got a doll baby. What a thrill it was to get that one big toy. Our mother probably had to save all year long to buy us each that one big toy for Christmas.

We always had a big Christmas dinner. Usually chicken and homemade noodles. Our mom could make the very best homemade noodles. I only wish I would have inherited that special talent.

As I look back on all of these memories, I am truly delighted, proud, and thankful for having the opportunity to grow up in that era. All of us have been successful in our lives today. We did not have the opportunity to get a college education, but after graduating from high school, all of us went to the city and were able to get a job and work our way up to be successful.

My two oldest brothers have passed away now but their families still live in northern Ohio. My brother Dennis and Becky live in Carrollton, Ohio. They have a lovely home. Their children and grandchildren live in Ohio, Georgia, and Florida. My sister Rosemary and her husband Lou live in Columbus, Ohio. They have a beautiful stone house near the Scioto River. Their daughter and son-in-law live in Missouri. My brother Harry and his wife Donna live in Sardis, Ohio. They have a lovely home, and three grown children and several grandchildren. My sister Hazel, who works for the state of Ohio, and myself, who is retired from the state of Ohio, lives in the same town not far from where we grew up. My children, granddaughter, and son-in-law live near Marietta, Ohio. We are still a close family and keep in touch whenever we can.

Sliding Away From Home

by Carol A. Shook of Blue Rock, Ohio
born in 1948

The icy winter of 2009 reminded me of another icy winter when we lived on the farm near Rural Dale. My brother, Ed, and I were sleigh riding when we discovered a giant sheet of ice down the valley behind the barn. We slid and fell several times when to our surprise we realized we had gone all the way to State Route 376 between Rural Dale and Gaysport. We really thought we would be in trouble for going so far from home. Hurry as we might, we soon realized it was easier sliding down than trying to get back up.

My Birth Procession and Mrs. Taylor's Pen

by Joy L. McGrath of Crooksville, Ohio
born in 1940

My name is Joy McGrath, and I am sixty-eight years old. I will write a brief description about my life. I married George McGrath, and we had two sons. Their names are Randy and Kevin McGrath, and they both live in Crooksville, Ohio, near me. George had lung cancer and died three years ago. So now, I live alone in my big house with my two cats. I have four grandchildren and four great-grandchildren. And I am happy that I have a great family and a happy life.

I will now tell you about my childhood. From the time that I was born on August 18, 1940 until I was in the seventh grade.

I was one of the five daughters born to Helen and Joe Thomas. We lived in a place called Deavertown. There was a Methodist church that we all attended, a school, a store, three cemeteries, and a voting place.

I had four older sisters, who were still in school when I was born. They were all very pretty and very popular. Their names were Marjorie, Jo Ann, Monabell, and Patricia. We lived about four miles from our small village away back in the country.

The day Mom gave birth to me was quite an event. I was born at home, as my sisters were, and Dr. Lawrence, who was to assist my mother, had to drive from Crooksville, about ten miles from where we lived. He made the statement that he had never seen so many boys and girls walking along the road waiting for me to be born so they could see me. It was a very hot day on the 18th of August, but that did not stop my sisters' friends from coming to our house.

I weighed ten pounds when I was born. Of course, I was a beautiful baby girl with a lot of long black hair, and all of the kids wanted to hold me. And so my life began on that hot August day on August 18th, 1940. I was such a lucky little baby to be so loved by my dad and mom and my four sisters.

Of course, I had to be named, and everyone in my family put a little piece of paper with the name they wanted in a hat, and then my mother held my little hand in the hat, and the first name that I touched was the name that my mother had chosen. That name was Joy Lynn Thomas, and I have always loved my name. I was such a happy baby and had so much love. I was so lucky.

Some of my fondest memories was our big family dinners on Sunday. On Saturday, Mom would always bake a cake or make pies. Then cook all morning on Sunday. A lot of the times, she would have Dad kill and butcher two chickens, and we would have fried chicken and mashed potatoes and chicken gravy and sweet potatoes, candied, and all delicious food that went with fried chicken. Fresh killed chicken is so much better than store-boughten chicken. My sister, Marge, was married, as was Monabell, and they would all come for Sunday dinner with their husbands and their kids, and I was so excited because I would have someone to play with.

My mom was the best cook in the world, and when Dad was working in the mine, she would have to go out in the barnyard and kill two chickens. I remember that I would hide under the bed until the chickens were dead and had quit flopping around with their heads cut off. Then I would come outside and help Mom pluck the chickens' feathers. Mom would bake on Saturday, usually pies, or bake a cake. She would always bake me a little cake that I could eat warm or bake me cinnamon rolls from the leftover piecrust. Those cinnamon rolls and my little cake would get done first, and those goodies were my treat for being a good girl and helping my mother. I was so happy, and my mom and dad were so good to me.

I also remember that in the spring, Dad and I would clean out the chicken house with creosote and water and spray the walls and floor and their nest. Dad said that would kill the lice. We would go to a town called McConnelsville, about thirty miles from where we lived. Dad would buy one hundred little fluffy chicks (we called them biddies).

Joy Lynn Thomas McGrath in 1946.

Dad always let me pick out two chicks for pets. I would get a black one and a red chicken. I wanted a rooster and a hen. The nursery could tell the difference in the male and female chickens. He would raise the chickens for their eggs and also for the table. Dad would fix lights in the chicken house so they would stay warm. They were so tiny, I don't know they lived, but survived they did.

I started to school when I was six years old, and I was in the first grade. I would ride on the big yellow school bus to and from school. I had a dog, named Rusty, and he knew when the school bus would stop in front of my house to let me off for the day. And Rusty was always there to meet and greet me. the other kids would say, "There is Rusty waiting for you," and I was so proud of him and how I loved that dog. He was my best friend.

I also loved school, and my first grade teacher's name was Mrs. Taylor. She was middle-aged, and she was the kindest, nicest teacher. And I learned so much and how I loved Mrs. Taylor. She had a pen that she always wore around her neck. She would pull that pen down from her dress, where I think it was pinned with a small brooch. Then she would grade my paper when she came around to each of our desks. I think it was a retractable pen. I never forgot Mrs. Taylor or her pen.

The Grease Lamp and the Flying Granma

by Helen E. Bates of Zanesville, Ohio
born 1924

It was in the fall, and Mom and Dad had gone to the sorghum mill to pick up the sorghum. My two older brothers took the lanterns and went skunk hunting and left me and my younger brother without any kerosene for the lamps. It was getting dark and we was afraid, so we made a grease lamp. We took a pie pan, put a piece of cloth in it, and spread it with lard and set it on fire. We had light, but getting it out the door before it burned the house down was another problem. We never tried that again.

* * * *

Grandad was moving a grain building by rolling it on poles. One of the poles came out and let it down, and he had to jack it up by putting one end of a pole in the center of the building and a block in the center. Then Granma, Grandad, and three of us lifted up the building and Grandad said to her, "You hold it and we will put the pole under the building." When we let go, the building went down and she went flying up in the air. It was not funny at the time, but we sure have had some good laughs about it every time someone brings it up about Granma flying up in the air.

The Olney Experience

by Ray W. Stanley of Sebring, Ohio
born in 1922

I was born on a 23 acre "poverty farm" just east of Fairhope, Alabama, the youngest of seven children. Four of my older siblings were born in Whittier, Iowa, before my parents moved south in 1916. My twin sisters, Lillian and Louesa, born at Fairhope, were four years old when I was born. Papa was a seventh generation Society of Friends (known as Quakers) recorded minister, as well as an excellent carpenter. My mother was a Methodist from Kansas, who had "converted" to Quakerism at age 21 before marrying my father in 1897.

Now enters Barnesville, Ohio—The "Olney" Friends (Quaker) Boarding School—where our Stanley patriarchs and matriarchs for six generations have received a "college-prep" or "life-prep" education. My father had graduated at Olney in 1896 and he wanted his children to have that same experience, so in the fall of 1936 my twin sisters were seniors at Olney. He had run out of family help on the farm, and it was Ray's turn to go to Barnesville, Ohio and enter the "Olney" experience.

I had attended a one-room Quaker school at Fairhope, just east of the Mobile Bay a couple of miles—about 100 feet from the Friends' Meeting House. Our teacher was usually a graduate of "Olney" school, sometimes with credentials also from Westown Friends School near Philadelphia.

We had owned a 1925 Model T three-door Touring Ford, which Papa had driven to Ohio to take a load of boarding school students at least twice. It must have had over 100,000 miles on it, when during the Depression we ran out of funds to buy gas and license for it. In 1930 Papa made a farm wagon out of the frame and wheels, and he mounted the engine on big steel wheels, for power to run a feed and corn meal grinder and to saw wood. Many neighbors and friends, both black and white, would carry a bag of shelled corn or grain out to our place to grind in Will Stanley's gristmill, to keep family and stock alive.

All through the Great Depression Papa found carpentry and repair work after hurricanes, and time to plant a few acres of sweet potatoes, Spanish peanuts, corn and pecan trees. When the Lord called him to preach the gospel among Friends across the United States, Canada, Central America or the British Isles, he took the "concern" to his Friends' meeting for approval. He never received pay for his ministry, though he sometimes returned home with more finances than when he left home. However, many people spoke later of the edification and encouragement he brought.

So when Papa left on a "religious" visit, Mama (who had handled many horses as a young girl in Kansas) and

I would hitch up old black Frank to the recycled "T" wagon and trot uptown to the stores, where credit was always available to the Stanleys—until William returned.

One hundred percent tithing seemed appropriate in our home. By the fall of 1936 we had sold the farm, I had graduated from Quaker one room elementary school, Papa worked steadily in maintenance for Dr. Jordon's two clinics. It was my turn to go to Barnesville to Olney Boarding School.

Ray, in the center front, at the Olney Belfrey in 1936.

I rode north to Barnesville with a carload of Mendenhalls in their shiny black 1934 Chevy Deluxe. I thought it a marked improvement over the '25 Ford "T." We stopped in North Carolina to visit brother Clayton and Mable (Mendenhall) Stanley. Mother had sent along money to buy me my first double-breasted suit, which we found in Greensboro, N.C. Then on to southeast Ohio—and Barnesville.

Now here I began to see the great attractions I had heard my family talk about all my life: the beautiful village of Barnesville, surveyed and laid out in 1808 by Quaker James Barnes. We entered Barnesville on Route 800 from the south and thrilled at the Olney School sign. Among the rolling hills of Belmont County, just east out Sandy Ridge Road, stood the impressive huge Stillwater Friends' Meeting House, a 60 foot by 90 foot high domed worship center and headquarters for Ohio Yearly Meeting of Friends, built in three months in 1878 by Aaron Frame and his two sons and many laborers. (Now a state certified historical building.) Back a side lane a quarter mile south stood that Olney Friends School which had effectively schooled four generations of Stanleys before me—and now at last it was to be my turn.

We arrived at Olney late at night, during summer vacation, found a small button switch at the east entrance, pushed it and soon slippered feet were heard coming down the steps—Gilbert Thomas, superintendent. Soon others were up preparing refreshments and sleeping arrangements in the "nurseries." What a glorious welcome!

By arriving two weeks before school opened, we had time to help about campus in preparation for arriving students. Soon a carload arrived from North Carolina with a classmate, Kathleen Barker (later Tullis). We all lodged at Olney and found school preparations to do to help with our board. My first and lasting impressions of Olney are largely the same.

Greatly blessed and fortunate are those teenagers who attend Olney. By so-doing they establish a "second home" which brings them and their families back to Olney for homecoming and other important occasions—year after year. Soccer and field hockey both flourish on Olney campus.

Huldah (Starr) Stanley of Newmarket, Ontario, Canada, and Raymond W. Stanley, of Fairhope, Alabama, were classmates at Olney four years, graduating together commencement day 1940. We were married September 30, 1944 while I was serving God and country at University of Rochester, School of Medicine & Dentistry, under the Office of Scientific Research and Development, selecting the best food for rehabilitating starved concentration camp inmates in Europe. I had left a management job with The Deming Pump Co. of Salem, Ohio and Huldah had prepared for family life by earning an LPN in Canada. After our marriage she had worked at Strong Memorial Hospital in Rochester.

Since our service days we have raised four boys and two girls of our own who are Olney grads. In addition we have parented eight foster children and a few foreign students. I have practiced a fun hobby which helped with Olney and college expenses—antique cars and clock restoration. We restored a 1914 Model "T" Touring car for 55 years. It is now under the care of grandchildren in Marietta, Ohio.

We entered Copeland Oaks Retirement Community, in Sebring, Ohio on November 1, 1997. This lovely place is truly a blessing to hundreds of seniors. A pool and hot tub are provided for our enjoyment. We are both slowing down somewhat; however, we are yet able to enjoy the "little bit of heaven" which is here at Copeland Oaks.

Huldah and I have been married 65 years. My retirement hobby is antique clock restoration. Our second grandson recently graduated from Olney Friends School.

Rooster Revenge and Chocolate Pudding

by Lillian Shaw of Zanesville, Ohio
born in 1924

In 1936 we moved from the city to a farm. We got the usual animals and some Dominic chickens. One rooster was as big as a small turkey. He thought he was a real "cock of the walk." We children carried a towel or something similar to use bull fighting style and when we were outside looked to see where he was.

One day he attacked my nine or ten-year-old brother. I don't remember how but we got him off. Dad shot him. Mom cooked him in a huge canning kettle. We all ate lots of chicken for a week.

We got a team of Clydesdale work horses. They had lice in their manes. Grandpa said to mix lard and snuff for a cure. One evening we had chocolate pudding for supper. Mom left the leftover bowl on the kitchen table. Later Dad put the cure bowl on the same table. My brother took a big bite of the cure.

The Hobo and a Small World

by Betty Adams of Mineral City, Ohio
born in 1932

In the early spring of 1945 I was 13, raised on a mini farm. It was my job to mow the grass with a push mower. I had made several rounds with my pattern. I was almost finished when I looked up towards the railroad tracks, and the trestle to spy a tramp (bum or hobo). They were very plentiful at the time—hard times—and I was very much petrified of them. My dad was sitting by the kitchen window, smoking his after supper cigarette. He said for me to be calm. He was watching him.

Betty Adams with her dad, Bob Deubner, in 1935.

Within minutes the bum was at my side. He asked me in a real polite manner if my parents were home. By that time my dad made his appearance. Shook hands with him. Asked him if he'd like a bite to eat, what little bit we had left. There was five in our family. Of course, the bum said yes. He wanted to know if my dad could give him some chores to do to repay. So my dad asked him to stay a few days, to paint fence and to spade up a garden.

Within this stay they visited, talked in the evenings after my dad come home from work. My dad was a heavy construction worker. By the time the three days were up, they discovered they knew one another by working together on a road job out in Indiana.

The moral of my story: It's a small world.

King and the Thanksgiving Snow

by John K. Schmelzer of Junction City, Ohio
born in 1932

November 25, 1950. I remember it well. Many will remember this same day as the "Snow Bowl" when Ohio State played Michigan in a blizzard with winds reaching 29 miles per hour. Michigan ends up winning this game 9 to 3 of mostly fumbles and missteps by both teams.

The day before on the farm, my dad, brothers and I had been shredding corn on the neighbor's farm. It was Thanksgiving weekend and we had worked all day and went home to do the evening chores and milk the cows. When we woke up the next day, there was snow everywhere. I had never seen anything like this.

Everyone was having problems traveling because of the snow. That evening, one of my classmates from Harold High School was coming home from work and was having trouble getting home passing through the road because the snow was too deep for driving. He stayed with us, but after a while, he got restless and tried again, but he did not make it any further on this second attempt.

The next morning was Sunday and we made it to the barn to milk and do the morning chores. My dad asked me to use the big truck to make a path down the lane. The truck was a 1 1/2 ton flatbed with chains on the back wheels. I took the truck and started out the lane to make a path. With the back wheels flying through the deep snow, I made it to the highway, but it was impossible to go any further. The highway was full of snow, so deep it was almost covering the fence posts. Putting the truck in reverse, I backed up all the way back to the truck garage and told my dad the road was impassible and no one would be traveling. I told him the highway was full of snow and we won't be going to church this morning.

After breakfast, I went to the barn and decided to put the saddle on my horse, King, and I started for town. Nothing was moving and it was deafening quiet.

When I got to town about one mile away, I ran into a buddy [Ralph?]. He was trying to dig out his big black Cadillac car away from the curb. He did not have boots but had put on several brown paper bags on each foot to keep the snow out of his shoes. I asked him why he was trying to dig out his car when he could not drive anywhere. I told him to get up on my horse with me and we would go to church for the 9:00 Mass. Finally he agreed and we headed off to church.

I had always been an altar server and today was not different except for my clothes. I was dressed in bib overalls and gumboots. There were not many people in church. I was glad that I made it to church that day and will never forget that trip. We tied the horse to the rectory clothesline.

After I got home, my dad and I talked about how would we take care of the cows on our second farm, which was about four miles away. I told my dad that I could make the trip with King. I got ready and started out for the other farm. During that trip, we ran into snow so deep in some places that King could not step forward. In those spots, I would get off, put my arms around my horse's neck and we went step by step with each other until we were through the worst of it and then I would get back in the saddle and travel on to the farm. This trip took almost five hours and it was exhausting for both King and me.

Along the way I came upon a state highway truck with a snow blade that was broken down in the middle of the road. It had burned out the transmission during the night trying to plow a path through the snow. The truck was left disabled in the middle of the road and no one could get past it.

I finally made it to the lane to the other farm. Down that lane about 100 yards was an old house where an old man [maybe Bill Woodis?] lived all by himself. He was somewhat crippled, walked with a cane, always had a hard time getting around, so I went to the house to check on him. I yelled for him a couple of times and after a short while he opened the door and asked me in. We talked for a while and then he asked if I would take his bucket down to the spring and get him a bucket of water before leaving. I agreed to help, but this was not an easy task because the spring was about 100 yards away and the snow was waist deep. After I returned with the water, he asked if I would be coming back tomorrow. When I told him yes, he asked me to bring him a loaf of bread, a gallon of kerosene and a pouch of tobacco the next time through. I told him I would do that for him.

The barn and cattle where about another half mile up over the hillside, so I got back on King and we started out for the barn. Once I got there, I had a hard time getting the big doors open large enough for King and me to get in and out of the snow. In the barn there were about 30 head of young cattle. I filled all the hay mangers, not knowing when I would be able to return. I was not worried about getting them water, because there was a running spring below the barn.

After a short rest, King and I got ready for the return trip back home. I arrived back home late in the afternoon. I was cold and King was tired. I took good care of my horse that night, knowing we would probably be making that same trip tomorrow.

The next day, I got King ready and we went to town to get the mail and groceries for my mom and also the supplies I promised for the old man at the other farm. King and I made this trip for the next four days until Thursday when a large bulldozer came down the road and pushed the disabled state highway snow truck to the side of the road and then made its way on through to town so people could get out and travel.

Over the next couple of weeks, I received calls to help pick up mail and groceries for the older friends and neighbors who lived off the main road.

I remember the snow being so beautiful and the temperature not too bad at about 30 degrees, which was not so severe, but the amount of snow was just too much to handle in such a short period of time.

[Apologies to author—inserts weren't marked in left column. Ed.]

Grape Juice and the Summer Grippe

by Rose Mary Founds of Somerset, Ohio
born in 1929

My name is Rose Mary Founds. I am 80 years old. Born in Perry County, Somerset, Ohio June 1, 1929.

My parents, three sisters, and I lived on a farm in Perry County, Ohio. My dad raised all types of farm animals. Having no sons, we girls helped with field work, milking cows, feeding hogs, sheep and chickens. I especially loved caring for the newborn lambs in springtime. After grazing in fields during daytime, we drove the sheep into the barn at night. Little lambs that couldn't keep up, we carried to the safe place for night as wild dogs were out at night looking for easy prey: the baby lambs.

Rose Mary Founds carrying two baby lambs in spring of 1934 at Gilmore Farm.

The morning and evening milking time was just one of my daily chores. I got so attached to "my cows," and when Dad decided they were past their prime, he would send them to market. As the truck went out the lane I was in tears to see them go, knowing they would be going to a butcherer. But there was always a new cow to replace the old one. Then once again I had a new pal.

I had three sisters, no brothers; so much of the farm work, gardening, and housework was divided between we four girls.

For most of the summer I was helping my mother planting, hoeing, and harvesting vegetables from our big garden. Those were the years of the Great Depression, so our food came from the land. Vegetables, berries, beef, pork, and chickens were all homegrown.

It seemed every summer we all came down with the summer grip. We didn't go to the doctor often. Mother healed us with castor oil for every ailment. If you had constipation, you got castor oil. If you had diarrhea, you got castor oil. I don't understand the logic in that.

Well, one day, Mother put castor oil in a glass of grape juice for one of my sisters who was ill with the dreaded summer grip. Mother also had a pitcher of grape juice for the rest of us. Well, Sister was not fooled by the set-up. She quickly poured her glass of doctored juice into the pitcher. My story ends here as I do not remember if we all drank the doctored juice or if it got thrown out. I think Sister probably got a "jawin'."

The Unappreciative Lunch Skunk

by Harold George of Birmingham, Ohio
born 1934

Lunch time started like they usually did at Birmingham School in northern Guernsey County: you grab up your lunch pail and run outside to find a shady place to eat your peanut butter sandwich, your apple and a couple of cookies.

Well, this particular sunny day the routine got quite changed. A little furry black and white striped creature decided to join our noon activities. Having it around was not quite the game we had in mind to do this noon. But, several of us daring boys decided to take the challenge and see who could get close enough to grab the skunk by the tail, pick it up and not get sprayed. This went on for quite a while until it was almost time for the noon bell to ring for us to go back inside for class.

I felt I had to try just one more time. I got into what I thought was a good approach and angle to be the big winner by picking it up and not getting sprayed. Everything went well but on my last grab for that tail I found out how fast that skunk was. It let go with a blast of stinky skunk oil that really covered me. I got a nice round of applause from the students, but that didn't help my situation.

Now, the bell rings and it is time for us to go back in for class. As I approached the door, the teacher said, "Where do you think your going?" It was obvious I was not going inside. So the teacher wrote a note for my mother and told me to go home.

Walking home was no big deal because we walked the mile and a half to school anyway. Upon arriving home a frustrated mother met me at the back porch door. Again, "Where do you think your going?" I had to explain how it happened, and it was obvious Mother was not happy, but amused, and that I was not going inside. So on the back porch a little elementary school boy was instructed to strip bare and receive a midday scrubbing. But, after the bath I was at least allowed to go inside, and I spent the rest of the day smelling like soap.

A Tribute to Irvie and Mom

by George Sidwell of Englewood, Ohio
born in 1923

My mother's parents were Irvin Clarence Masterson (1880-1941) and Autie Lauretta (Curry) Masterson (1884-1941). I was the oldest and only grandson. As a youngster, I went everywhere with my grandfather. Everyone called him "Irvie," so I did too. He always wanted to be called Grandpa but when my sister, Lou, came along she picked up Irvie from me. And our grandmother we called "Mom." To others she was Autie. They were married in 1904.

Irvie was the seventh of nine children and Mom was the youngest of three. Irvie taught school briefly at McCluny School, just outside Crooksville, Ohio. This was before you had to have college to get a teaching certificate. Mom did stay with her brother, Edgar, when he was at college at Ohio Wesleyan University and studied piano. We would spend many an evening around the piano singing the old familiar songs as well as hymns.

Because Mom's two brothers had left the farm, Elbert moved to Bowie, Texas. Edgar was a Methodist pastor in Massachusetts. Irvie and Mom took over the Curry family farm. It had been in the Curry family for generations, the original deed being signed by President Adams. Their three children, Freda, Brice and Kathryn, were born in the old, two-story log house. Kathryn died of diphtheria at seven months. A new nine-room house was built in 1920. The farm was sold after their death, though Brice had built a home on five acres on one corner and it had been deeded to him.

Though a farmer, Irvie had been a teacher and continued to be well read. He kept up with the latest farming methods and in the 1930's worked part time for the Morgan County Extension Service. In the early days there was no telephone system in the area, so he got some other people together and they formed a telephone cooperative, set in poles, strung the lines and installed a switchboard in Portersville operated by the Allens. He had an early crystal radio set, operated by an automobile battery. I can remember listening through earphones to the broadcast of the take-off and later arrival in France of Charles Lindberg's flight across the Atlantic. When they built the new house, he determined that the strong spring beyond the old house was enough higher that gravity would give running water in the kitchen, so he installed a water line. Unfortunately, the spring was not high enough so that water would reach the second-story room that had been set aside for a bathroom.

Another of his progressive innovations was the installation of a carbide plant in the 1930's. There was still no electricity in that rural area, but the carbide plant, contained in a huge tank buried in the ground, provided a gas which worked like natural gas for lights. When the house was built, he installed a large dumbwaiter between the kitchen and the basement. This not only served as a place to keep food cool when lowered, but saved my grandmother unnumbered trips carrying things back and forth to the basement.

In farming, he had one of the first tractors, a big lumbering Fordson. But he still had horses at his death. He planted an apple orchard on the top of the hill, called the "knob" above the house. He fenced it in for hogs and let their rooting cultivate around the trees. They also could feast on the dropped apples. He had several varieties, but as a kid I especially liked an old-fashioned sweet apple. His apple orchard was written up once in the Morgan County paper. He told them he had two trees of lopsided apples, "so they wouldn't roll off the hillside." He used to sell apples at the former coal mining town of San Toy in Perry County. He would also catch the blood when he butchered hogs and rush it to Corning where it was prized by the Hungarian miners for blood pudding. Early on, he began raising White Leghorn chickens because they produced more eggs.

Left to right standing: Autie Curry Masterson, Irvin Masterson, Rev. E.J. Curry. Seated: Ella and William Curry. Front: Brice Masterson, Norman Curry, Freda Masterson circa 1912.

He also was one of the first to raise alfalfa for hay, a high, legume hay that you could cut three times a year. He also was a pioneer in raising hybrid corn, which increased the yield dramatically. I remember being pressed into service to de-tassel the male (or was it the female?) rows. Before hybrid corn, he would pick out a number of his best ears of corn, number them, and put three or four grains from each ear in small, numbered pockets in a specially constructed piece of canvas. He would then keep the canvas moist for a period of time to see if the grains sprouted properly. Those that sprouted were the ears that provided his seed for the next year. Of course, back then, you still had to hoe corn...and did those rows seem long, especially on a hot day.

He also decided to diversify his cattle operation. He purchased about a dozen pure-bred Jersey heifers; Jersey for the high cream content of their milk. Then he used a separator to skim off the cream. After keeping enough to make their own butter, he sold the rest. I remember how hard it was to turn the handle to get the separator going around. Then you would see the cream slowly running from one spout and the skim milk pouring from the other. It was quite a trick to get an empty bucket under the skim milk spout and remove the full one, all without spilling any or stopping the separator. The skim milk went to the hogs. And though Irvie was not a large man, he could somehow carry four buckets, two in each hand.

The other part of his cattle enterprise was raising cattle for beef. But Jerseys didn't make good beef cattle. So he purchased a purebred Hereford bull. The combination provided cattle suitable for their beef. Also, additional income as neighboring farmers brought their cows to him for breeding.

Since one of his horses was a mare, he decided to breed her and raise a colt. He had purchased Queenie from another farmer who had not set about breaking her properly and she ended up kicking until she got all her harness off. Irvie managed to break her to harness. You had to keep an eye on her because she could still let fly, unexpectedly, with those hind hooves. Later, he purchased another mare and I would sometimes ride them about three miles to where there was a stallion for breeding. Queenie produced a fine colt, black with a white star in his forehead. He grew to eighteen hands, a measurement for the height of horses. Irvie had never had a matched team and now he set his heart on finding a young horse to match Prince. He traveled all over the countryside, even going as far as St. Clairsville, over toward Pittsburg. Finally in New Lexington he found a young mare who was a perfect match for Prince. We tried her out and she seemed fine. But when he got her home, he found her stumbling as if she couldn't see properly. However, he noticed that when he took her out for watering at dusk or after dark, she didn't have any problem. He called in the veterinary who determined she was "moon blind," not seeing well in bright light. The horse dealer he had purchased her from at first refused to take her back. But Irvie, giving up his dream of a matched team, talked him into giving him another plain brown mare instead.

Another horse project was the purchase of a half-dozen western mustang colts. They were wild! Mom worried about my quiet, docile pony, Betty, being in the same pasture with them. That is until one day we saw the western colts begin to nip at Betty. She let fly with her hind hooves, swinging in a circle at the same time. Those colts never bothered Betty again.

Irvie missed WWI because of a horse. The horse he was riding reared and fell over backward on Irvie, breaking his leg. He spent a long time in bed with sand bags tied to his leg to keep it from healing shorter than the other.

Being a farm wife meant that Mom's work was not confined to the house. While I never knew her to work in the fields, she did work in the garden and worked some with the chickens. She also helped with the milking. In fact, my grandfather admitted that she could milk a cow faster and get more milk than he could.

She was a great cook. The kitchen was large with a large table which served as her work counter. There were two stoves, one a kerosene stove and the other a wood burning cookstove. It had a large water tank at each end which served to keep warm or hot water on hand. On stormy days, when I couldn't work in the fields, and there was no other inside work for me, she would get me to help her bake...never pies, but cookies or cake. She made the best molasses cookies and a delicious marble cake from her mother's recipe. I would also help churn butter in a gallon glass churn. It was hard work and it seemed as if the butter would never come. Then came the job of pressing all the buttermilk out of the butter. But was it good. I wouldn't eat margarine until after her death.

Butchering was always a busy time. Thanksgiving was when we butchered hogs. After a painless rifle shot, the hog was sluiced up and down in a 50-gallon barrel of boiling water until the hair was soft enough to be scraped off. The first thing we kids got was the bladder, which we blew up as a balloon. The lard was cooked out over a hot fire in a large iron kettle. Then we feasted on the cracklings which remained. That night, we always had fresh fried pork loin for supper. Nothing tasted better.

There was no freezing of meat then. Irvie would cure the hams while Mom would fry sausage and can it. She did the same with beef that was to be kept. I miss that unique flavor still. And, of course, she used some of the pork to mix with apples and raisins to make mincemeat for pies. She also canned produce from the garden, as well as berries, peaches, cherries, etc. Irvie would wrap the apples in newspaper and store them in the basement.

In July came the binder to cut wheat, followed by the threshers. In the fall, in later years, was the corn shredder to husk the corn. These all required extra hands which meant Mom was busy preparing huge meals...two or three kinds of meat, huge tureens of mashed potatoes, three vegetables, and pies and cakes.

Irvie's family had come from Ireland in the early 1800's and were Irish Catholic, though his mother had been Methodist. Mom's grandfather had been a Class Leader and a founder of the Portersville Methodist Episcopal Church. They were in church every Sunday and often as not, brought the pastor home for Sunday dinner. When they remodeled the church, Irvie was the main contributor and did the major share of the work. In those days Methodists didn't dance. And the only cards in the house were Old Maid, Authors, and Rook.

Both were active in the Portersville Grange, a farmers organization. Both held offices at various times, locally as well as in the Pomona or County Grange. Mom was often in charge of the program and kept a huge collection of poems, readings, jokes, etc. When I was about five, they took me along when their Grange presented the program at a neighboring Grange. One skit had people disappearing behind a curtain where a noisy machine transformed them. Mom was rather plump. She disappeared behind the curtain, the machine groaned and humphed and out came two young, slender girls. I started crying and calling for my grandmother and wouldn't stop until Mom came out from behind the curtain and showed me she was all right. One time they were delegates to the State Grange Convention in Columbus. Mom was hesitant to go because her Night Blooming Cirrus, which she had been nursing along for years and had never bloomed before, had buds. Sure enough, it bloomed it's one night while she was gone.

Their home was frequently home to additional family members. We lived with them a couple of times during the Great Depression in the 1930's when my dad couldn't find work. My Great Grandfather Masterson lived with them and they took care of him for seven years after he was immobilized by a stroke. Also, later, my Great Grandmother Curry made her home with them until her death.

Irvie's youngest brother, Basil, lost his young wife and was left with two young children. Uncle Almer took in the little girl, Eileen, while Irvie and Mom took the boy, Carl. Carl finished high school and, since the Depression meant no jobs, he joined the 3-C's, a federal work camp program for young men. When my grandfather's new young Jersey heifers calved, Irvie wrote Carl in California that he was now milking fifty-six. The first thing Carl wanted to do when he got home was see those fifty-six cows. Irvie told him to divide by four. Since he had been a cook in the 3-C's, Mom asked him one day to bake a cake. When he said he needed fifty pounds of flour and a half-case of eggs, Mom decided she'd better do it herself.

They were both always ready to help others. But Irvie nearly balked when a man came to him from twenty miles away in Perry County with an unusual request. His little boy was ill with diphtheria and the doctor said that mare's milk was essential. He had heard Irvie had a new suckling colt. Now, Irvie had never milked a horse before. Furthermore, the mare was Queenie and you never knew when she would let fly with her heels. But he couldn't say no in this desperate situation. With great trepidation, he approached Queenie and began to milk her. She stood quietly. He repeated the operation daily for over two weeks. The child recovered nicely. A horse will give twenty or more gallons of milk.

My mother and Brice attended a one-room school, Peeper Run. I think they were the third generation of the family to attend there. I also attended the second grade there, the last year before it closed because of school consolidation. When my mother finished the eighth grade, my grandparents didn't want her to walk alone to the high school, which was about two and one half miles away at Sayre. Irvie was on the school board, so he had my mother held back a year. The teacher at Peeper Run had a free assistant that year.

I loved the farm and spent my summers, as well as Thanksgiving and Christmas vacations, there. Irvie was a good teacher; from him I learned responsibility and a number of skills. I learned to milk, plant a garden, teach a new calf to drink from a bucket, hunt rabbits and squirrels, shock wheat, handle a team of horses, and load a square load of hay. He was patient as well as persistent. One day when I was only four or five, he had to replace some slate at the ridge of the barn roof. I begged to climb up with him, but he told me it was too high and dangerous. Finally, he said I could climb up with him on the low shed roof at one end of the barn and wait for him there. He was carefully scooting along the high ridge, halfway across, when he heard a noise behind him. He nearly had a heart attack when he turned around and saw me right behind him. He finally got us both turned around and me back down on the ground. There I got a stern lecture.

Just before my senior year of high school, feeling grown up, I accepted a job on a farm in Guernsey County at $1.00 a day plus room and board. I had injured my back and was back at home and not at Irvie and Mom's when the telegram arrived the morning of July 31, 1941. It informed them that Uncle Edgar, then pastor of the Methodist Church at Vineyard Haven on Martha's Vineyard Island, was dying. If they wished to see him alive they should come immediately. Hurriedly, they made arrangement for the farm chores and left just after lunch for Massachusetts. Two hours later, having driven only seventy miles, their car was hit by a semi-truck and they were both killed instantly. The driver claimed he was driving slowly, but they were clear off the pavement on their side when he hit them and dragged the car 120 feet, before stopping a truck length ahead of them.

Because they had been so active in church, Grange and community affairs, hundreds of people came to the house. (In those days, visitation was usually in the home.) As the funeral procession was turning in at the Portersville Church, I looked back and cars were still coming over the rise above their house, one mile away. They were buried in Zion Cemetery, Portersville, in the Masterson family plot.

A special regret was that they missed the birth that fall of Brice and his wife Ruby's daughter, Arlene Kay. This, also, was the summer before Pearl Harbor and the family always thought this was one blessing, for they would have been greatly distressed at the war.

The Old Fox

by Nora G. Bash of Zanesville, Ohio
Born 1937

Clarence and Wavelene Cottrell raised chickens. Tildy Cottrell, Clarence's mother, wanted to buy a fresh chicken for a Sunday dinner. Tildy asked Wavelene if she could buy a chicken to butcher. Wavelene said no, that she didn't want to get rid of any.

Clarence told his mother to wait, for the "old fox" would be out tonight after dark. Clarence went to the chicken coop after dark and scooped up a chicken and ran it up to his mother for free.

Next Sunday, Clarence and Wavelene went to Tildy's for Sunday dinner. Wavelene was very happy with her dinner and said, "That's the best chicken and dumplings that I ever had!" Wavelene had no idea that it had been one of her own chickens.

Dreamsville, USA

by Joyce Ann Roush Boren of Newark, Ohio
born 1942

My fondest childhood memory took place in the latter years of the 1940's, while I was a child living in Dennison, Tuscarawas County, Ohio. My parents, brother and I lived in the small village of Dennison until I was nine years old, when we moved to Pleasant Valley, about five miles outside the village.

I began my formal education at Dennison Elementary School in 1948. Our home was located about two blocks south of the school, and I walked to and from school each day, also going home for lunch.

At that time, which was just after the close of WW II, the railroad station in our little village was a major hub of activity. There were many sets of train tracks and in order to get to school or return home, it was necessary that I cross those tracks each time. The trains were constantly coming and going; engines were starting and racing to their next stop, or screeching to a stop as they pulled into the station. As a child in the first and second grade, it was very scary to be crossing the tracks and to see a train moving in any direction. I just knew I wouldn't make it across in time. I was afraid to go forward, and it seemed so far to go back; so I made sure that I kept my eyes on the crossing watchman who stood there with his big STOP sign until I was safely across.

The war was fresh in everyone's mind, and my own father had recently returned safely after serving aboard a Destroyer Escort in the Pacific. The days were dark and no one knew what the days following the war might bring.

My most beautiful memory of those years and one that I will forever cherish was to see the train cars full of soldiers, leaning out the open windows of the many passenger cars as I waited for the train to pass. They were smiling, laughing, waving and calling out to us as they passed through our tiny village on their way home to their families. Most had been injured in the war and wore bandages around their heads, arms, and faces. Some were missing limbs, and the scene spoke starkly of the pain that they had endured.

Joyce Ann Rous Boren in front of a photo of the Dennison Railroad depot as it was in the 40s.

But what impressed me the most, were the smiles on their faces. I was so caught up in the sadness of the moment and the excitement that they were experiencing, as they returned home to the ones they loved. I smiled and waved back to them, feeling very special that I was able to share in that one moment in their lives, and to photograph it in my mind's eye.

You see, our little village railroad station was the site of the famous WWII Canteen, known to the soldiers as "Dreamsville" that served 1.5 million soldiers as they passed through our tiny village on their way home.

Things That Must Remain in the Past

by William Oliver of Byesville, Ohio

When I was young we lived in the country. When WWII started, we moved to town because of gas and tire rationing. I did start to school in the country at a one room school, but only for two months.

I have listed many of the radio programs and newspaper comics I remember from years past. Once I did get my arm caught in the wringer washer while helping my mother with the wash. When my elbow reached the rollers, they each released my arm causing only a small bruise. It sure scared me!

As I grew, I got a paper route, which I enjoyed very much, especially at Christmas. My customers gave me many tips.

In 1948 some of the older boys had built a tree house in a large field at the north end of town we called the cow pasture. One day while playing war games, one group of guys I knew got up in the tree house with BB guns. We, with BB guns, attacked them, and I was shot in the eye. It ruined my sight permanently. It kept me out of sports in school and later, the military.

At one time in Cambridge, where I lived at the time, there were three movies: Liberty, Strand, and State. Usually went to the Strand. It showed the most Westerns and double features with a serial all for 12 cents when I first started, but over the years they raised the price to 25 cents and etc. Later the State was the only one left. It is sad even to this day.

I guess I was about 15 when my mother had to go to Columbus, Ohio to have some surgery. For some unknown reason, my father went to see her but rode the bus instead of taking our car. I told my younger brother we would go out to eat. He said, "How?" I said we would take Dad's car, but he knew I had no license. "Don't worry," I told him, "just watch when I back the car out of the garage," because Mr. Smith's garage was right opposite ours. Well he didn't watch very well because I hit the door, breaking it. Needless to say, I paid for that one many times over.

Speaking of the garage, in earlier years, I must have been about eight or nine, is when I kissed Patty L. I still remember doing it, but I don't remember any after effects.

The snowstorm of 1950 was a bad one, two to three feet of snow in many places. Dad worked for the State Highway Department. The men plowed snow for days. Would take naps in their trucks when they could. Mom would have things ready for his lunch bucket when he could stop.

I had a fox terrier named Sparky. That little sucker would take on any other dog. Size didn't matter.

Mom's cooking, what can I say? Fried chicken, beef and pork roast, homemade pies, and cakes. They were great.

Mischief you asked; speeding in Dad's car, underage drinking, and other things, at Halloween mostly, that must remain in the past. Skinny dipping, sure did. The girls, some of them, liked it too. Too many fishing and hunting trips to mention. Great times, even when we got skunked.

All of my friends from my younger days are dead or live away.

Lastly, I mention my skipping school. In my senior

year, I already had all the credits I needed to graduate, so I thought. I and my friend, Dick, decided we needed some time off. We didn't go to class for two weeks. As both my parents worked daytime, they didn't know. Then one day they received a letter wanting to know if I had quit school, if we had moved, if I was sick. Well, when I got home I was fairly sure I would die. Things were hot then cold, quiet then loud. I walked a lot that summer.

About five years ago, I had to have a bowel resection with a cholostomy due to colon cancer. Now I can't stand or walk, so I live in my recliner and move around in wheel chairs. I've had a pretty good life. I am with wife number three. She's a good woman. When I started, I didn't think I'd have this much to say. There is more, but this is the end.

Profitable Horns and a Burning Effigy

by Adrian F. Nader of Allendale, New Jersey
born in 1914

Dad made me do it. As the 1900s dawned in New Lexington, Ohio, my father, Lewis Nader, graduated from playing a fife in the local fife and drum corps to learning to play the saxophone—novelty instrument at that time. Soon he and three other sax players formed a quartet that was in demand to entertain at church and lodge affairs and other special events. He then learned to play a clarinet in order to join the local band.

When we three children came along five years apart, Dad determined that each of us should experience "The joy of making music." Money was scarce, but Dad had saved enough to buy a sax for his first son, Harold. The next child was a daughter, so she was taught to play the piano, "a proper instrument for a girl." Finally it was my turn.

At age 14 I was too busy with school and Boy Scout activities to waste my time practicing on a horn an hour or more each day, but Dad insisted. I learned to play on his horns, and after a year I was good enough to play with other musicians at country dances, earning enough to buy my own sax and clarinet. By the time I graduated from high school I had saved $300, which could pay for a year's tuition at Wittenberg College in Springfield, Ohio.

Today, loans are easily available to help with college expenses. Not so at the beginning of the Great Depression. Also, part-time work for college students was scarce. My horns were my Magic Carpet. Each summer they provided enough work to pay for my next year's tuition plus spending money.

That first summer I played for dances throughout Perry County as a member of the Irene Irvine/Mac McQuade Combo from New Straitsville. The second summer a booking agent connected me with Pete Wilson's Band, playing at Clear Lake, Indiana. The third summer I lucked out again and was accepted by Les Sheppard, playing at Russel's Point, Indian Lake, Ohio. I earned my room in historic Myers Hall at Wittenberg by doing janitor work for the college. Local dance-band engagements provided for my meals and spending money.

Adrian Nader, first row far left, playing with Les Shepard's Band.

A few readers may remember me as the English/Journalism teacher at NLHS where I taught for seven years. When World War II broke out, I received a commission in the Navy and served for three years in the Pacific. After my return home, I learned of a faculty opening at Marietta College in Ohio. I applied and was accepted. That ended my dance-band career, for it wasn't proper at that time for a faculty member to play with jazz musicians—at least anyone on the MC faculty. (Privately, I was beginning to get a bit too old to depend on that uncertain lifestyle.)

Today I still have Dad's fife and clarinet. I get them out occasionally to reminisce and tootle a tune or two. And I always give thanks for the interesting years my music provided—all because "Dad made me do it."

A World War I memory. It was the 11th hour of the 11th day of the 11th month in 1919. The Armistice had been signed.

This glorious news had just been received in New Lexington, Ohio, and the townspeople had gathered before the county courthouse to celebrate. I was just five years old, so my father held me astride his neck and shoulders so I could see what was happening.

A straw-stuffed dummy representing the German king was hanging by its neck from a lamppost. The people shouted, "One, two, three!" and the town mayor held a match to the dummy.

Germany had been defeated! "The War to End All Wars" was finally over! Soon our New Lex soldier boys would be coming home!

Yesterday's Teachers

by Carol Lyons Foster of Bethel, Ohio
born in 1943

When I look back to my school days in Kentucky, it is always with fond memories and a grateful heart for the care they showed which helped influence our lives.

They put their hearts and souls into their jobs. If that failed, out came the "ole paddle." Then, when we got home, our parents always found out about it and they gave us a licking also.

One particular time stands out in my memory. Our principal, also our eighth grade teacher, took us on a picnic at Pine Mountain State Park. It was supposed to be an end of the year treat. He loaded the whole class in the back of his old coal truck, and off we went. When we got there we were told to stay close to the shelter house. As eighth graders, we were old enough to ignore him, or so we thought.

When he missed us, he sent out his well-behaved students, I think there were two, to find us. After rounding us up and loading us up in the old truck, he brought us back to the ole school.

There he lined us up and the line began in our classroom and out the door and down the hall. He brought out the homemade paddle with holes burned in it, so it would sting our bottoms, and gave us each a hard swat.

Well, as we departed grade school to enter Bell High, we took with us a very valuable lesson: respect your teachers, or else; one that is missing in our classrooms today.

The Queen of Lower Main Street

by Sally Seaton of South Zanesville, Ohio
born in 1939

On a hot day in August 4, 1939 Carl and Betty McCoy Woerner became parents of a baby girl weight six pounds nine ounces and 19 inches long.

Betty McCoy Woerner Huffman in front of Square Deal Market in 1945.

I was born at Good Samaritan Hospital. I was taken home to 811 Clay Street. On the north side of Clay Street was houses where the bank and the parking lot are now.

On the south side was all fields where Carl would take his hound dog and hunt for rabbits and squirrels. I remember watching him clean them even though I was small.

When I as about two-and-a-half, my dad went into the service. He was in training at Alabama. My mother and I took the train down to Alabama to see him.

During the year I was two, my mother was washing clothes. While she was sorting clothes and I managed to get my right arm caught in the wringer. The washer had a release on it. My arm was not broke, but all that was left was my elbow bone and a piece of flesh on it. Dr. Eliott and Dr. Faircloth grafted skin off my legs to graft on to my right arm.

My days in Norval Park was good. While we lived there, my mother worked at Mosaic Tile Company till she made enough money to open a grocery store. I was about five years old. My grandparents had a pawn shop on Lower Main Street. Our grocery store was next to the Army Navy Store on Second Street by the railroad tracks. My grandparents' pawn shop was directly across from our grocery store.

I was queen of lower Main Street. If I wanted something I just go into a bar and ask for whatever I wanted. I'd get candy bars or a soft drink at La Salle. If I wanted a Coney Island hot dog, I'd go to Coney Island Bar to Tony and get it. At the Question Mark on Third Street they had an apron and a stool with steps and I'd pretend to be waiting on customers.

Down by the bridge on the southwest side of Main Street was Goodwill and American Light. Then you come to Second Street by the railroad tracks was Army Navy Store. Next to that was our grocery store called Square Deal Market. There was some other stores at the southwest corner was Krogers or A&P store or a hardware store. Cross Third Street on the north side was Sanitary Meat Market. Go north on third a place that sold popcorn, candy, soda, etc. Continue north was the Weller Theater. Several other stores. Going west you'll come the Coney Island Bar then one or two other stores. I don't remember what they were. Then my grandparents' pawn shop. Next is the La Salle. Cross the tracks there was a pool hall, a hotel, Nate's Bar. Across from Goodwill was Shervises. They really had good milk shakes. I guess it could be considered a drug store.

We go back to third and main on the north east corner was Bintz's. Continue east I know Singer Sewing Center at Fourth Main was Starz. On the northeast corner is the court house. That has changed some. Across the street was the Claradon Hotel which faced Fourth Street. Go down Fourth south was Lee's Restaurant. Next was and still is the newspaper. Before the newspaper I believe may have been Red Cross and later a doctor's office. Cross South Street I cannot remember what was there cross Fourth Street to the west side is the police station. Then cross south and go north there was a church there. Then the Rambo Center. Up the street by the alley Montgomery Wards. Then a state liquor sales and on the corner of Fourth and Main was The Spot restaurant a cab company. Underneath the restaurant was a pool hall.

I started my schooling at Norval Park School at the age of six. When I reached seven, my mother and I moved into my maternal grandmother's house on Nancy Avenue. On the corner of Pine and Nancy was the gas company.

I went to Wilson School while we lived there for a year. At the age of eight, we moved to Marietta Street. A year later Mom married Albert Huffman. She later opened a grocery store in the basement of the building we lived in. There was four bars from Eighth Street to Sharon Avenue, and three grocery stores including ours. We had one drug store.

Because of my mother marrying Albert Huffman, I got to do and learn things I probably wouldn't have learned. Like square dancing, working with horses and working in restaurant at the auction at the age of 14.

All Clear on Finley Avenue

by Marilyn McCarty of Zanesville, Ohio
born in 1935

I grew up in Zanesville and was the youngest of five children. There wasn't much money for toys, but we had lots of fun anyway. Some games we played were Hide and Seek, Tag, Hopscotch (with pretty colored glass bits). When we didn't have a ball and bat we played baseball with sticks and tin cans. I have a scar on my head to prove it. We played Jacks and Jump Rope. I especially liked "Bounce." You bounce a ball against the side of the house and catch it. I could play this alone also. We also played Trust. You fall back and someone catches you. We had real trust back then. I saw a Geico commercial the other day for that (please don't try this at home).

When it was cold and snowy, we would go sled riding, usually down Finley Avenue on to Moorhead Avenue. One person stayed at the bottom of the hill to tell if a car was coming or "All Clear." Had to take turns.

Some evenings, we would play "I Spy" in the living room. Mom played too. What you spied would be red, blue, etc, or could say beings with A-B-C. Others guessed.

When we were allowed, we went to McIntire Park to swing, teeter totter, or just climb bars. They had a tennis court, but we didn't have tennis rackets, so we just played in there. On Friday evenings my Mom and I would go up hill to Band Shell and hear Zanesville Memorial Band play. They were wonderful.

All of us liked to roller skate on sidewalk and later at Municipal Auditorium where we skated in the basement until Lind Arena opened. What fun!

Another memory was sewing class at Roosevelt Jr. High. Our aunt saved her feed sacks from chickens and we made skirts and shirts from them, especially broomstick skirts. These were real full and gathered. They turned out pretty and got good grades on them.

Our dad cut our hair when we were young. He shingled it, which was real short and shorter yet in the back. I hated it, but seems now the trend is back some and cute.

More Kids than Beds

by Margaret Parker of New Lexington, Ohio
born in 1915

Back in the '20s to '30s as I remember, my grandfather, like many others, made bootleg whiskey which they sold. One trip my sister Dorothy and I visited the farm. When we were ready to leave to go back to our home, Grandmother asked us if we would do her a favor. So she had a shoebox wrapped. She asked us if we would deliver it to a country store for her. We were happy to do this for her.

When our father come home from work that evening, we told him we had done his mother a favor. When he learned what we had done, he knew what we had delivered. We got our orders never to let that happen again.

January 1976. For some time I've pondered over the thought of writing down the things I remember about my childhood. The good memories about my grandparents, my parents. Even though I've told some of these things I remember, it's good to remind the grandchildren and great grandchildren of things and events in a generation or two back.

As a child, as far back as I remember, we first think of grandparents, Grandmother Ellen McIntyre, Grandfather Jack McIntyre, Grandmother Anna Charles Hammers, grandparents on my mother's side of the family. So different now.

Visiting Poppy and Mommy, as all the McIntyre family would say, was not on weekends but every night. Yes, every night, two miles or more on foot for the few of us, who had no car. We hopped and loved every minute of it.

My Grandmother and Grandfather McIntyre were two of the most warm-hearted people I can think of. They were the parents of George, Frank, Howard, Edna, Mayre, John, Charlie, Phillip, Ralph, and William.

There were no pets or special ones in that family as every one was respected as an individual and loved for what they were. Howard and Edna died one week apart of Black Lung Diphtheria. Uncle George never married, but the rest were all married and thinking of the grandchildren by name. There was Thelva, Delvin,

Margaret, Dorothy, Howard, Caroline, Evelyn, Norma, Ellen, Ardella, Genieveve, Cleve, Gloria Jean, Dolly, Frankie, Margaret, Donna, Jack.

To go to our grandmother's was a delight. The farm has many memories. The parlor with the velvet rug, with pink roses. The portieres that hung in the doorways. Lace curtain that she would say, "Mustn't touch," and would smack our fingers if we needed it. We loved her for it.

Very pretty, dainty statues that were on the dresser in the bedroom and lovely quilts by the dozens she would piece in the winter. What she couldn't make out of the feed sacks, beautiful curtains with drawn work by pulling threads. Lace by the yards, all the kitchen curtains had big wide lace, tablecloths with embroidery work. Made all her slips to go with her good dresses that she had tailor made.

Her dress-maker, or the one that I remember in particular, was Minnie Wiley. To go for a fitting she would get on the train at Misco and come to McLuney, which at times we made this trip with her. Her choice was wine and green crepe which were made very flattering.

Grandmother Ellen was a very hard worker. Never was there a time when the stone jar in the pantry didn't have a fresh supply of sugar cookies.

Churning day was fun for us. We would take turns turning the crank on the churn, which we always was treated with a glass of buttermilk with chunks of butter.

There were always a variety of six or more pies to choose from, homemade jelly was poured in quart jars instead of small ones that we use.

Breakfast consisted of two or three dozen eggs fried, skillets of fried potatoes was served to the men who were at home early in the morning before daylight as the miners left for work, using carbide light to light the way for their long walk to the coal mines to work eight hours in the mine then the long walk back home to enjoy the comforts of home for the evening.

Evenings were all of the children coming home with their little ones staying two or three hours each, and when leaving, receiving everything that was loose or she could spare to each family; milk, eggs, butter.

Weekends were still more company on the farm. Grandpa and Grandma's brothers and sisters coming with their children.

Shopping was done at the Big Shopping Centre or the kitchen table – the Sears Roebuck Catalogue, Larkin Orders. All of the women, daughters-in-law enjoyed this.

Jack and Ellen McIntyre (Poppy and Mommy) in 1917.

The daily mail was the Mail Buggy, pulled by a horse. Packages were picked up at the depot, Misco and Sayre being the closest ones.

The amusement of the day was the Sunday ballgame which everyone was involved. Refreshments was the homemade ice cream. Tubs were filled with chunks of ice with pop bottles in the icewater, back in the days of five cents for a bottle of pop.

I remember Thanksgiving at Grandma's house. What I remember is everyone being together, a day of butchering for the meat to be used all year, fires burning, wood being piled under huge iron kettles of boiling water, a large drum of water being heated to scald the hogs. How we dreaded that moment when they shot the hogs with a rifle. We would run and hide, hold our ears. Then, curiosity getting the best of us, we would run back just in time to see them shot. We would take off running again.

They would work late into the night cleaning and cutting meat. That day Grandma was really happy knowing that all of her family would leave with fresh meat. Days followed with stuffing sausage, making head cheese, mince meat, lard, smoking meat.

My grandad, I'll never forget. All the boys called him Poppy. Grandma had a way of talking to him by saying, "Jack," like no one else did. He listened.

He was very small, quiet. He found a corner beside the kitchen stove on the floor where there was always a bushel of corn on the cobs. He would sit there between chores shelling corn in the gallon dinner bucket. He kept it full to throw out in the back yard when he would go out and yell, "Chick-ee-ee!"

I don't ever remember them attending church. But whenever we would go in the parlor she always asked my mother to play "The Pearly White City," a song that was played at her mother's and father's funerals. She would always stand in the doorway and raise her apron up to her face and wipe tears from her eyes.

Later in her life, she enjoyed the Cadle Tabernacle program very much. "Ere you Left Your Room This Morning Did You Think to Pray," as sung by Mrs. E. Howard Cadle.

She passed from this life at the age of 65, loved by one and all. That farm home was never the same again without Mommy.

Years went by after the children, Howard and Edna, died without the loss of anymore in the immediate family until my father, John, passed away in 1932. My grandmother began to fail then, never got her health back. Granddad lived to be 85 years old.

While her life was lived on the farm performing all the duties connected with a big family, besides loving the ball games, she dearly loved to dance. She gracefully whirled around and round on the floor square dancing. Even her own family could hardly believe it was Mommy, so young at heart.

My last visit with her was after she had suffered a hemorrhage. She knew me but was not able to talk much. She drew my hand close, pressed it to her, smiled, and was glad that I had come.

Our childhood days were spent in the Misco, Rose Farm area, all the school days were walking to school, which we enjoyed. One of the things I remember that I enjoyed the most was whistling, walking in the rain, all going to and from the groceries, walking to and from. Except for the times we went from the Rose Farm area to Crooksville for our mother on the train, carrying a split basket, a note, coin purse. We had one hour and 15 minutes to leave the depot platform, go to the A&P Store to purchase food, go to the Tedrow Variety Store (which was operated by Dr. Tedrow's mother). Having purchased all we were sent for, back to the depot and what a thrill to hear that train coming, a high step, but we would get on. Now I wonder if that conductor that helped us on that train didn't wonder if we was like "Topsy," just growed, that our mother would let us do the "family business."

The first and only car my father ever had was a new Graham Page, purchased off the showroom floor, which is now the Lamb's Laundry. I was 15 years old when that car was bought.

On my mother's side was Charles and Anna Hammers. Lived at Misco for a beginning. Their children were Hazel, Pearl, Rolland, Charlie, Sam, Harry, Olive, Margaret, Helen, Jesse, Mary. Jessie and myself were the same age. Dorothy and Mary were also born in the same year. So when we went to visit the Hammers grandparents that was "No Vacancy." More kids than beds, but they were always glad for the McIntyre girls to visit and stay overnight.

Then our grandmother Anna would see if there were any clothes around, outgrown, that she could pass on to us, and see us back home, which, when we left, we always coaxed her to let Helen and Mary return with us.

Grandmother Hammers, like Grandmother McIntyre, was a total stay-at-homer. She was always at home to be found in the kitchen working, cooking for a large family. I guess these mothers didn't shop. The family of children did it for them. She was very jolly, real witty, fun to be around. She could always make a joke out of any situation. Then she was very stern. What she said they knew she meant it. Wonderful grandparents.

You talk about the style shows we see now on television. They are nothing to be compared to what we saw live. Our grandmother Anna trying on hats, she would pose and strut and have us laughing. She enjoyed it more than all.

Grandma McIntyre called the miner's life feast and famine. She stocked the shelves with all types of food: jellies, lard, potatoes, beans—because there was no work in the summer.

It is fun to remember the good things from the past, but as we go back and realize the things that has slipped away, especially all this wonderful family, we don't realize what we have today is going to change and our children and grandchildren will look back [portion of manuscript cut off by copying machine] and we hope they too will say they enjoyed a few things about growing up. What wouldn't we give of what we have to be able to go back to Mommy and Poppy, to Dad and Mom just for one hour.

Free Popcorn and Nickel Dances

by Harlan Ted Hodder of Indianapolis, Indiana
born 1924

I am one of the "Greatest Generation," 1924-present.

My fondest memory of Cambridge is, while growing up, I could walk anywhere I wanted to go: the City Park, swimming pool, downtown, and the movie theater. We once had five theaters; the State was the largest and every Monday night a new release was shown. I and several classmates worked there for 50 cents an hour plus all of the popcorn we could eat. Of course, we could also get our dates in free.

There was a lot to do in Cambridge in the late 1930s and early 1940s and much was free. Every Thursday and Saturday nights there were dances at the park pavilion. Music was provided by the Johnny McCracken Band and dances were 5 cents a dance. We could also dance to a jukebox in the Masonic building. Both locations were very popular.

Another popular activity was sledding down N. 8th Street hill when we had enough snow. The city closed the street to traffic and we had the street to ourselves. We spent many hours sledding down and walking back up the hill.

Cambridge had one municipal pool (the Big Pool), the twin wading pools, seven outdoor tennis courts, and three softball fields. Before the pools were built, we swam in the pond. On the Fourth of July there was a big swimming competition at the pool, followed by medal presentations at the town fireworks display at the ball field.

Bicycles and legs were the accepted mode of transportation in Cambridge. One summer day, I was walking through Greenwood Cemetery and saw a snake lying in the sun. Thinking it had been run over by a car because the head was so flat, I reached out to pick it up. Imagine my surprise when it struck at my hand! Fortunately it missed, since it turned out to be a copperhead.

I could tell you more about growing up in Cambridge, but my memory is sketchy. My wife was four years behind me in school and we met during the war. We've been together for 61 years!

The Nicer Outhouse

by Diana Lowe of Tecumseh, Michigan
born 1972

My Grandpa and Grandma Koon had twenty acres of land in Proctorville, Ohio. They lived off Rt. 775 up on Tick Ridge. The land had belonged to my grandpa's dad and mom. I would get to go visit them during the summer.

Icie Hosey Garvin, Ada Hosey Koon, Ralph Koon and Ginger the dog.

Grandpa and Grandma had no running water or inside plumbing. They heated their home-with kerosene heaters.

Time there seemed much simpler and I loved it. For fun we would play dice games or cards. We also did a lot of front porch sitting.

I remember hating to have to use that old outhouse. Oh that smell was enough to make you run. I would always check the hole for snakes and other creatures that could be lurking around before sitting down. Then while I was sitting I was sure something was fixin' to bite my bottom.

Then the day came when Grandpa and Grandma could afford a nicer outhouse. Grandpa built one twice as big as the old one. Grandpa painted it white with a pretty blue toilet seat. Then he ran an electrical cord, so we could have light. Grandpa had it set up, so when you turned on the light an electric heater would come on. Then there was a new empty coffee can to store the toilet paper in.

At nighttime we didn't have to go outside to the outhouse. Grandma had a five gallon bucket with a toilet seat on it, set up in a little room. She didn't like us going out at night. I was just thankful it was Grandpa's job and not mine to empty it out come morning.

There were big tubs around the house to catch rain water in. At times my grandparents would get water down the mountain from a neighbor who had running water. My grandpa didn't like to ask them for such a favor, but they were always obliged to do so.

I would wash my hair in the front yard and let the sun dry it. The rain water made your hair feel so soft. Grandma said it was free from all the chemicals they put in city water and wouldn't dry out your hair.

One of my favorite things to do was going flower hunting with Grandpa. He'd say he'd have to go get Grandma some flowers and off we'd go. We would find morning glories, tiger lilies, black eyed Susan and many others. We'd dig them up and plant them around the house. They sure did look pretty.

My grandparents grew a garden every year. I loved all those fresh vegetables. My grandpa would always say to eat onions everyday and you wouldn't have to see the doctor.

Sometimes, Grandpa and I would go out raspberry picking and Grandma would make us raspberry dumplings. Grandma was the best cook! She'd cook hush puppies, mush, potato cakes, and fried green tomatoes. It makes me hungry now just thinking of all that good food.

In the evening we'd set out on the front porch drinking sweet tea, watching the sun go down and into the night. Sometimes, if I was lucky, Grandpa and Grandma would tell stories of when they were growing up. I'd just sit there, listening to every detail and try to imagine what life was like back then.

The Old Outhouse and My Daddy, Dennis Earl

by Velma J. Cochran of Dover, Ohio
born in 1927

Not many older people talk about the outhouses some had to use. It was a needed thing before the modern bathroom. They were usually built on the back of the lots.

Our dad built a new one and it wasn't so stinky at first—but that changed soon enough.

You would never believe how many things that outhouse could be used for, but many things did happen there.

When playing hide and seek, you could slip in there and just sit and wait and who would guess you would go there to hide? Or, how many times when jumping off its roof did our homemade parachutes of old newspaper just flop and you hit the ground with a thud.

After Halloween, you may even see an outhouse perched on some nearby roof. There were several older boys in our neighborhood, but of course no one ever fessed up to anything at Halloween time!

If you were in that outhouse very long, you were probably looking through the old catalog. It was a far cry from toilet tissue of today, even though the center section was the softest to use.

One incident happened in our ole outhouse that could have been a tragedy, and I am sure the whole neighborhood heard the story and it would bring a smile to their face. My two sisters and a neighbor girl (about the age of four or five) went into that outside toilet, and my sister accidentally dropped her dolly down into the miry mess down below. They couldn't reach far enough to get it, so the older two girls each took a leg of the sobbing sister and lowered her, head first, down towards that dolly in the messy dark until she could catch hold of the doll. They had already screamed for help.

I don't remember if Mom scolded them or was just thankful. It was just one of those "what if" things. I'm sure the story got all around our neighborhood.

Mom did a nice job of cleaning up that dolly and thanking God for the safety of her little girl.

My Daddy. My father was an extra hard working man. Our family kept growing—a new baby every two years—and it took a lot of groceries to feed nine kids. We always had plenty to eat. Daddy had a very large garden and Mom canned 1,000 quarts of vegetables and fruits each summer.

Daddy worked in a coal mine about 15 miles down the road. After being a mile back under the hill, he would wind up in a little shanty and drive the fifteen miles home. When he got home, he would give Mom a long hug and kisses and then lie down on the dining room floor on his stomach and take a short nap while Mom prepared supper. After eating, he would work in the garden until sundown and then milk the cow and set the bucket of milk on the table to be strained while cooling. Then several days a week he walked across to a garage/store front next door and several other men would come and they would have a table or two that played yass. They had a good time after a hard day's work.

Daddy did have an accident in the coal mine. A cave-in sent a large rock and it fell on his back and he ended up with a broken back and was off work several months over that.

He always kept a neat straight-rowed garden and kept the long grape arbor trained and has many groups of rhubarb plants. What a variety the garden showed to the neighbors. He kept a large berry patch with red raspberries and blackberries. As each food started ripening, he would bring them to the grape arbor and have all of us kids help Mom snap beans and things and wash all the many fruit jars. She always had 100 jars filled of each vegetable. So Daddy was a good provider for his large family.

Daddy chewed tobacco in the mine to relieve the black coal dust that was always in his mouth. When he walked into the house he would take his tobacco out of his mouth and throw it far out into the garden area, claiming it was good for the lettuce patch.

When Daddy walked in from work and set his lunch bucket down, we kids would quickly open it to eat the double butter sandwich and hunk of cheese. It seemed like a good treat, like he had kept it just for us kids, but when I got a little older, I learned that all coal miners left food from lunch in their buckets and also water in the bottom section every day. It was a thing of preparing for the worst, that is, a cave-in that would take days to dig out of.

Daddy raised the largest berries. We even had some to sell to neighbors and friends. He would buy a half a beef at the beginning of winter and Grandma would fry us all steaks. She could fry them so they melted in your mouth, they were so tender. Daddy would fill the large boiler with the meat and place it up on our flat roof over the add-on kitchen to be there all winter for no one had deep freezes back then.

Everything my dad did was done accurate and well organized, just like his garden, house painting, and even mowing the grass with his old push mower in those perfect rows. On Saturday, he and Mom got all dressed up and went to town. Mom would shop and get a supply of groceries and set in the car and wait on Daddy who was playing cards with the guys and having a beer also.

Coal mining was hard on pants, and he patched his own pants, us kids watching his every move. Even his long johns, which were a must in the cold coal mine, had holes in the knees, and you had to scrub them. We couldn't imagine how he could work on his knees all day and then come home and go to work in the garden or mow the yard.

Weekends were special to us. On Saturday morning, Mom never got up early. Daddy did though. He would make a large bucket of scrub water and go into the kitchen and scrub every high chair, table, cabinet and floor. They were all white and he made everything shine. Then he would stir up a batch or two of pancakes or corn cakes and fry a platter of bacon or sausage. That smell always got all us kids downstairs to the table. He would sing and also tease us with his jokes. It was a happy time.

My job was to help take care of the little ones, since I was the oldest girl. But one Saturday morning, things changed. I was sitting in a chair, warming my feet on the floor register. Daddy came to the dining room door and said, "Come here." He was holding a scrub rag in each hand and gave one to me. "Come, I want to teach you how to scrub." So we started with all the white cupboards and chairs and table and floor and I learned what my dad had done so faithfully all those years. After I left home and was married, he did the same procedure with the next oldest girl. He used this same tactic with the third girl. He called her early on a Saturday morning and took her with him down the road about a third of a mile to a lot he rented to plant extra vegetables. He showed her how to plant things accurate and neatly. She has always had a beautiful garden herself each year.

Oh, we certainly had a loving father, but we didn't know it. We did know that he loved our mother. When he would take her in his arms and hug and kiss her, all of us really kept our eyes glued on them.

Daddy sang little songs. His main instrument was an accordion. When I was very small I had a rocking chair and each evening I would rock as he played songs and sang to me. When I would fall asleep, he would carry me to the bedroom. What a pleasant remembrance of him.

The Lonely House on Bean Ridge

by Edna Brown of Ava, Ohio
born 1928

My name is Edna Brown. I was born May 3, 1928. My parents were Aaron and Nellie Everly. I had ten brothers and sisters. Their names were Chester, Harry, Paul, Herbert, Walton, Iva, Verna, Clarice, Rosa, and Bertha.

We were a big family living in a small log house that my dad fixed up. Our house was between the small towns of East Union and Carlisle. We lived on a ridge which was called Bean Ridge. We were the only house for miles. The school bus could not pick us up, so we had to walk one mile to get on it. In the wintertime the snow was almost up to our waist. I remember being very cold.

Aaron and Nellie Everly in 1909.

I was told that when I was born, my dad took the horse down to get Dr. Cain. My dad had made a saddle out of a groundhog's hide. Dr. Cain said, jokingly, that was the first time he had ever ridden on a groundhog.

We never had electricity in our house. We did our homework by kerosene lamps. Our radio was played by using a car battery. I couldn't listen to it for very long because the battery would go dead. I loved staying up on a Saturday night listening to the Grand Ole Opry.

We had sleds my dad made himself, and our swing was a grapevine we used to swing over a creek. We also had a teeter-totter, which was a board over an old stump.

Our toilet was an old outhouse with a catalog for our toilet paper. We had no running water in the house so we had to walk to the spring, which was down over the hill, and carry water in buckets to heat on a coal and wood cook-stove. That was for our bath and to wash our clothes on a washboard. We had to hang our clothes outside on a clothesline to dry. In the wintertime our clothes would freeze as soon as they were hung. That's what you call "freeze dry."

Mom and Dad raised a garden to feed all of us. While Dad ran the plow, I would ride on the horse. We picked a lot of berries, so Mom could make us pies and jelly. Dad would hunt. We always had rabbit, squirrel, or young groundhog to eat. We were too poor to buy our meat.

Also then in the Depression, we had to have a stamp to buy a pair of shoes and they would have to last all winter. My mother made most of our clothes. She also made quilts and dad cut our hair.

We also went swimming in the creeks. The water was muddy and we weren't allowed to get our clothes dirty, so we went skinny dipping.

These are some of the memories of my childhood—memories of the "good old days."

Skinnydipping at Dowdy Holler

by Bill Hammond of Cambridge, Ohio
born in 1934

Back in the 50s, my father ran a large orchard—apples and peaches. The peach crop began ripening in August, the hottest time of the year in southeastern Ohio. I had three brothers ranging in age from 16 to eight years old, me being the oldest. We all shared in the picking duties. That meant hauling the fruit from the orchard to the picking shed and sorting. Even my youngest brother, Dick, was expected to drive and operate all machinery. Every once in a while as quitting time was drawing near, my father would holler, "The last one to the pickup drives." We all knew what this meant, we were going swimming.

About one mile from our farm was a place called "Dowdy Holler" which had a couple of ponds which were spring fed with clear, cool water. The part that makes this story interesting, as we were driving down this dusty country road, all of us were stripping off our clothes so we would be ready when we got to the water.

If this would happen in today's society, couldn't you see the headlines in the local paper: "Sex crazed man and his four sons terrorize the neighborhood."

This is written in memory of our loving father, Russell Hammond. My three brothers are John, Ed, and Dick.

Refreshing Cold Mornings and the Heated Outhouse

by Blanche Kinney Baker of Woodsfield, Ohio
born in 1933

My name is Blanche Kinney Baker. I was born in 1933 near Graysville, Ohio, Monroe County. This was the latter years of the Great Depression.

I was born the fourth child in a family of seven. My parents were Harold and Viola Kinney. Both taught school for several years. My dad taught in one-room schools of the area.

Most people lived on farms and raised most of their food.

Clothing for our family was made mostly by our mother. When Dad went to the country store to buy needed staples such as sugars, flour and lard and feed for the cattle, Mom would tell my sister and I to pick out at least two matching feed sacks for a new dress each.

Everyone around us lived much the same way.

All of the family had chores to do and was made to do them. It is very refreshing to get up on a cold morning and have to go milk a cow, feed chickens, and then get ready and walk two mile up a hill to attend the one-room Thompson School.

Just like the country singer, Loretta Lynn, all seven of us children were born and lived up a valley, or as some would say, a holler. You could drive in when the creek was almost dry. So we had to walk a foot bridge and walk at least a mile up to our house. We had a rather large house and were raised by loving caring parents.

We were all born at home. The local country doctor, Dr. Heber Latta, came and helped bring us into this world. He then took care of all illnesses and even pulled a tooth if you needed it. Our youngest brother was born on October 31, Halloween. We didn't even know what was happening. We just wanted to go to Woodsfield for the parade. We never let him forget it was his fault that we didn't get to go.

In a family like ours, we made our own ways to play and amuse ourselves. We would meet our neighbor kids at the nearby creek and swim or fish. We played together, attended the one-room school, and some of us walked to the Graysville, Ohio Church of Christ where my parents were members.

Our house was lit by natural gas lights. We had a well on our property to supply free gas. We didn't get electricity until the late 40s. Our water was supplied by a spring running out of a pipe in a nearby hill. We kept our milk and home churned butter in a homemade spring house which the cold water ran through.

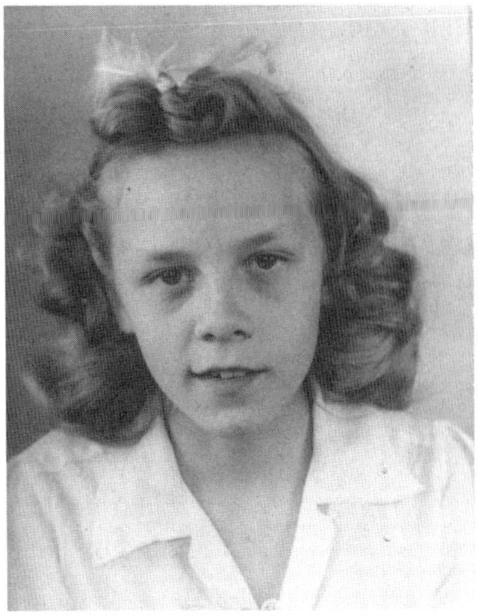

Blanche Kinney Baker in the 4th grade.

Our outhouse with a path up behind the house had the very latest style: a two seater and a Sears Roebuck catalog. It was also heated by a small gas stove. This was extremely nice if the snow or rain was coming down and you had to go. Man, we had luxury.

We washed through the week with a small basin of water, homemade soap. On a Saturday night the large wash tub was pulled out, filled with water, carried and heated on the nearby gas stove. This was done and then to bed to get up early and get off to church.

Kids today would probably feel sorry for us, but I wouldn't trade one single memory of my childhood.

My parents moved to a property on a paved road when I was in the fourth grade. They worked hard and loved us always. I thank God for my brothers and sister.

My husband also came from a large family: nine boys and one girl. When he was a small boy, his parents were forced to leave the town of Woodfield, Ohio and move to a small farm. There they managed to raise crops, cattle and eke out a meager living. His father had previously been employed by the narrow gauge railroad which ran from Woodsfield, Ohio to Bellaire, Ohio on the Ohio River and the other way to Zanesville, Ohio. M. J. Mooney owned the bank and railroad. He lost everything. The railroad was done away with.

My husband's father later went to Steubenville, Ohio and became an engineer on the Pennsylvania Railroad.

Although times were hard, this family always remained close.

Doctor Hornbrook and the Knobby Tires

By Emerson Straub of Sardis, Ohio
Born in 1930

It was the spring of 1950 that our neighbor was very sick. They called the doctor and he agreed to come over. He still made house calls at that time.

This time of year the roads got pretty muddy, they just had a layer of gravel. He got back to our ridge, but it was about half mile back a lane and he couldn't get back that road. The doctor came to our house. Dad told him we had knobby tires on the old car and said Emerson would take him back to see the sick man.

So I took Doctor Hornbrook back to see John Bowery so he could give him some medicine that he needed. I didn't have any trouble getting through that mud with the 1932 Chevy with the knobby tires.

The Whole House in Proctorville

by Rose Lowe of Tecumseh, Michigan
born 1952
submitted by Diana Lowe

When I was a kid we moved to Proctorville, Ohio to live with my Grandpa and Grandma Koon. Dad had to stay in Michigan to work, but he would come down on weekends to visit my Mom, brother and me.

My grandparents had a three bedroom house on twenty acres. My grandpa took used lumber and built the whole house. You'd never know by looking at the house. We didn't have running water so there was an outhouse out back, over the hill.

On Sundays, my grandma, brother and I would walk down the mountain to church. This is where I first started singing in a choir. In fact people would request us to come sing for them.

I loved when Grandpa would come back from the store with syrup to make pop and fresh bologna. It was a real treat to have a bologna sandwich and a glass of pop.

Rosa Lowe in 1958.

In the winter when it would snow, Grandpa and Grandma would take fresh snow and mix it with heavy cream, vanilla, eggs and sugar to make us homemade ice cream. It was so good! I miss those simple times.

Freckles and Lemonade

by Katie M. Miller of Sugarcreek, Ohio
born in 1938

I was raised on a farm in Ohio with Father, Mother, six brothers, and five sisters, Maryann, Ada, Levi, Daniel, Ida, Iva, Amos, Betty, Jr., Moses, Delbert [Last names not given]. My parents raised pigs, cows, chickens, ducks, and geese. Father had large powerful work horses named Rock and Tom, watchful farm dogs named Rover and Queene, also a family milk goat. Father raised corn, oats, wheat, had large hay fields.

We learned at a very young age to milk by hand. It was so much fun to send a streak of milk toward the farm cats, how the cats enjoyed this licking the milk which had missed their mouth.

Mother had a large garden, raising all kinds of vegetables. We had a large watermelon patch. Oh, what fun to hitch old faithful Pete to our old farm wagon and gather watermelons. Oh, how sweet and tasty. We also had an orchard of apples, cherries, pears, peaches.

It was fun for us girls to help with the haying time. The grain binder cut the wheat and oats put in sheaves tied with twine. We would help with shocking, or setting up the bundles to dry. We got all excited when we came across a nest of field mice or baby bunnies. My mother got us girls new big straw hats to keep the sun off our faces. The sun brought out freckles on my face and arms. Mother would make big pails of lemonade, made from real big lemons.

We girls and the younger brothers helped with the haying. My father at that time didn't have a hay bailer. We put all the hay in the barn loose. A hay loader was pulled behind the hay wagon, picking up the hay. We smaller children would walk behind the hay loader with hay forks and pick up what the loader didn't pick up. Then again, we would come into excitement. Snakes, big snakes, were sometimes picked up by the hay loader. Once a snake would be picked up everybody would scream, "Snake!" It would be slithering up the hay loader. My father and older brothers would soon take care of it. We also met up with baby rabbits and field mice running desperately in all directions. Sometimes we tried to make pets of the rabbits. Summertime was always so enjoyable.

I remember so well one day back in late May when I was 13 years old. We had a dangerous afternoon hail storm. Our family dog, Queene, laid around lazy. The birds seemed uneasy. In the distance we heard a low rumble of thunder. Heavy dark billowy clouds gathering in the west. It started to get windy. Lightening flashed, followed by a loud clap of thunder. We jumped slightly as we children looked at each other. We were taught at a very young age to trust in the almighty God. Mother had already started supper and was poking at the fire in the black and white qualified wood cook stove with the lid lifter, pushing the hot embers together. Mother was cooking noodles in a kettle. The wind and thunder claps were frightening. It started to hail. It looked in a distance like a white sheet—hail the size of hickory nuts. With the strong wind against the windows, they started to break, with wind so strong pieces of glass started to fly in the kitchen over the cook stove and into the kettle of noodles. It was frightful. The storm soon died down leaving 14 windows for Father to fix. How thankful we were to God we still had a roof over us. Life was never boring on the farm.

My mother was a very creative cook. Good food and exercise went with the role of farm life.

One evening in late May everything was a most luscious of green with a beautiful sun set. The birds were having quite a commotion. There was a hollowed old fence post along a row of fence beside the roadway close by the house. The beautiful blue birds had built a next in this old fence post. The blue birds were diving down toward the hollowed out post, even the black birds, starlings, and sparrows. As darkness set in, the birds settled down. The next morning was another most beautiful day. Mother and Sister Ada were cleaning eggs which were sold for weekly income and for us to eat. The morning dew was so sparkly on each blade of grass. After breakfast at age nine I went to investigate, stepping on the rickety old rusty fence, stepping up so I could see in the hollow of the post. No, there was nothing, or was it? Shading my eyes from the bright morning sunshine, I jumped back seeing two black eyes, a mouth wide open and a red tongue moving. I quickly stepped back from the fence, running to tell Mother. Mother was puzzled how to get the snake out. She decided to take a corncob dipped in kerosene, light with a match, put in the hollow of the post. Sister Ada was standing on the other side of the fence post with the garden hoe. Mother put one lit corncob inside. With a bellow that big snake with mouth wide open came straight for Mother. Mother screamed with Sister Ada trying to hit the snake, the hoe got stuck in the old wood post and missed the snake every time. The snake went down the only side of the post, as tall as the post and crawled away, never to be found anymore, never to pester the blue birds anymore. We had lots of excitement on the farm.

When we were small children, my father and mother had ten or twelve milk cows. They put the milk through a milk strainer to remove any dirt or impurities. They had a cream separator. They separated the milk while still warm. The milk was put in the top container, then turn a handle giving power so that the cream came out one spout and the skim milk out the other. Mother made delicious smear cheese with the skim milk. The rest of the skim milk was given to the pigs, cats, and dogs. The cream was cooled and churned into butter. We children taking turns turning the butter churn. It sometimes took a long time till finally little lumps of butter gathered into large lumps. Mother would take a wooden paddle and put the butter into a big bowl and work the buttermilk out, then washed the butter with cold water, put in a rectangle-shaped pan ready for use. The buttermilk was waiting to be used making pancakes and buttermilk crumb cakes. Oh, how delicious it tasted.

The Made Over Doll and the Cadillac School Bus

By Martha F. Perkins of Barnesville, Ohio
Born in 1925

I was born in 1925, the youngest of four children. We lived on a rented farm near Somerton, Ohio. It was a small farm, but it allowed us to keep a horse, one cow and some chickens. We raised a garden with strawberries and sold cream and eggs.

My mother was a school teacher and taught in a one room school. She returned to teaching after about a year's absence when I was born. Approximately two years later, she became ill and eventually died. I was only 3 ½ years old with my oldest sibling only eight years old.

My brothers went to live with Aunt Elsie and Uncle Leo. My father, sister, and I stayed with Grandpa and Grandma Dallas in Barnesville.

I remember taking baths in a large galvanized wash tub.

After Dad remarried, all six of us lived together between Tacoma and Spiedel (about 1932). We walked a mile and a half to and from a one roomed school each day.

These were Depression years. Dad erected a sign in the front yard advertising his services as available for painting and paper hanging, "Work done cheap." But times were hard. People didn't have money.

That winter, Dad didn't buy car license until spring when they could be bought for a reduced price. A few times he walked the three miles to Barnesville and carried home a twenty-five pound bag of flour for my stepmom to bake bread. We ate lots of homegrown and canned foods—also berries that we picked. We really didn't celebrate Christmas beyond having a special dinner. When I was seven, however, my grandpa "made over" an old doll for me.

The next year we moved to Perry County to be closer to my stepmom's parents. She wasn't well, and remained there with them, while my sister and I went to stay with Aunt Elsie and Uncle Leo. (Dad and my brothers went back to Barnesville to live with my widowed grandpa.) While Virginia and I lived

Left to right back: Martha's dad, Grandpa and Grandma Dallas. Front: Brothers, Jim and Bob; sisters, Virginia and Martha, and cousin, Paul on bicycle.

there, our [cousin?], their only child, Paul, died. He was fifteen, but caught pneumonia.

In 1935, Dad and Mom and my brothers moved to Egypt Valley. We girls joined them in 1936. We attended the Groves No.3 School, and were transported in a school bus which had been converted from an old Cadillac auto.

The old farm house had no electricity or running water. We cooked on an old coal fired stove and heat was provided by a coal fired heater in the living room. The upstairs where we slept was mighty cold.

For entertainment we had a guitar, a wind up Victrola, an old pump organ, and ourselves to sing. We sang at church and the Farmer's Institute.

Infrequently, we went roller skating in Barnesville, and sometimes there was a square dance to attend. There was no telephone, but our neighbors, the Groveses and the Smiths would take us with them to church, 4-H, and other places. They were very good to us.

We did farm work for the neighbors. When I was eleven, I began helping with the cow milking. Sometimes, I rode the horse which pulled the rope to lift the hay into the barn. I worked all day—milked, hoed corn, and pitched hay. The pay was fifty cents. My sister helped the farmer's wife in the house, while I helped with the outside chores.

After high school graduation, my brothers, Bob and Jim, joined the CCC's. They sent a portion of their paychecks home to help support the family. Dad began working for the WPA on road projects, and later at a stone quarry. I also worked some at the M-K Grocery in Barnesville, during my senior year at Barnesville High School. After graduation, I worked for a brief time at Hercules, in Canton. But I came home and married a farmer in 1943.

Horse Handling and the FBI

By Carol Snopel of Barnesville, Ohio
Born in 1935

I was born on my grandparents' farm in 1935. My dad worked on WPA, a government sponsored program. This paid very little, so finally he went to Canton, Ohio and got a job in the steel mill.

When I was around eleven years old, we moved back to Belmont County, and worked a farm on the shares. This meant the owner of the farm got half of whatever we made, and we got half.

By this time, I had a sister and two brothers. Being the oldest, I worked in the barn and fields. By the time I was 15, I was driving the horses and hauling in hay. I also raked hay with the team of horses.

Our school at Mt. Olivett was a one room school, with all eight grades in one room with one teacher. I remember she would take a Friday afternoon off from school work about once a month, and we would do something besides school work. One winter, she taught us girls to knit. I still have the mittens I knitted that year. In the spring, we would take one Friday afternoon and go on a hike through the woods looking for wild flowers, and try to name them. Now, everybody that owns land where we hiked has "No Trespassing" signs up.

We milked the cows by hand every morning and night. I had usually about five to milk, and that meant before I went to school. It was my job a lot of the time to go get the cows at milking time. In the winter, they stayed pretty close to the barn, but in the summer, they went as far as they could go down in the hollow. We had one cow that I would keep back and after I got the other ones headed for the barn, I would get on her and ride back.

For me, the best part of farming was the horses. I rode one when we marked out ground for the garden and the corn fields. I learned to drive the team for hauling in hay, and used the rake to rake the hay into windrows. I was never allowed to use the mowing machine.

When I graduated from high school, I got a civil service job at Goodyear Atomic Corporation near Portsmouth, Ohio. The FBI did a background check. When they talked to one of my neighbors at the farm, he told the FBI man that I could handle a team of horses better than any man around there. I imagine that went a long way for my job as a secretary!

Now, sixty odd years later, I am back living at Mt. Olivett. The farm was sold, and is now being sold off for people to build homes. The house we lived in is gone along with the barn and other outbuildings, and a nice new modern house sits there. But I still have my memories.

A Nosy Christopher and the Rusty Cup

By Jeanne Hlavac of Seven Hills, Ohio
Born 1923

Christopher Robin is a horse who acts like a dog. A tall handsome fellow, he is half Arabian and half thoroughbred. Thirty-year-old Chris is friendly and frisky. Although a herd animal, he has no animal friends. Alone for many years now, he spends daytimes in the pasture and nights or bad weather in the family barn.

Christopher is in the pasture today when Jeanne comes and calls him. "Here Chrissy! Christopher! Come here."

Although no longer young, Christopher races around like the thoroughbred he is. Here he comes at a hundred miles an hour, aiming for Jeanne. She runs behind the nearest tree so she won't be trampled. But Chris slows down and then follows her around and around the tree, until she stops.

Chris loves Jeanne. He's been with her family since he was eighteen months old. Jeanne and her father are his caretakers.

Sometime ago, Christopher Robin had a friendly horse companion. Then that one left him for greener pastures and Chris is again alone. Chris follows Jeanne like a puppy follows his mother. Today she opened the gate to the pasture and let Chris come into the yard. When the phone rang, she disappeared into the house. Nosy Chris ambled over to stare in the kitchen window. He had to see what she was doing. Jeanne returned outside and again Chris followed her around the yard.

That evening, Dad collected all the dry brush in the area and piled it in the center of the pasture. After setting the brush afire, he sprawled on the ground nearby to watch it burn safely.

Nosy Christopher came over to inspect the fire. This project could take some time so Christopher reclined on the ground next to Dad.

Jeanne wanted to ride Chris, but a novice rider wasn't the best one to try out Christopher. No one had ridden him for years. Her friend Karen, an experienced rider, owned and worked with horses. Karen offered to take a trial ride on Chris and came there with her dog, Dakota.

After saddling Christopher, Karen mounted and gathered the reins. At her direction, Chris walked and then trotted nicely, impressing the onlookers. Next, Karen had to see if he would canter. But Chris would not canter; instead he bucked. Karen flew off and landed on the ground. Disregarding her bruises and the raucous laughter from the onlookers (her former friends) she again mounted Chris.

Again Chris walks and then trots nicely. Now will he canter? No way! Again Karen picks herself up off the ground. Puzzled, she had to think more about this before she tried cantering again.

Later, pictures taken the day she rode Christopher gave her the answer. Her protective dog Dakota kept dashing at Chris's feet. Dakota wanted Karen OFF that huge beast. Next time she saddled Chris, Dakota stayed home and a happier Chris cantered nicely.

* * * *

The Rusty Cup. In 1934, Jean and Rosemary were nine and ten when they came to live with their dad. Separated for a year, they joined their father and brother at the fourteen room farm house where Dad grew up.

Kuenzer family picnic in 1927. Jeanne Kuenzer, age five, in the center with her aunts and uncles.

Besides Dad and his three children, two spinster aunts, a widowed aunt and a bachelor uncle lived there. Dad, at fifty-three, was the youngest sibling; his oldest sister was sixty-three.

After dinner almost every Sunday, another uncle came with his wife and their grown son. If it was a nice day they drove the 1926 Buick sedan, but if it rained or snowed Uncle Joe drove the 1933 red Chevy coupe with the rumble seat.

The first thing Uncle Joe did was pump water from the family well on the east side of the house. After stashing the jugs in his car, Uncle Joe was ready for the usual Sunday walk through the woods to the quarry. The four men and three children crossed the road and took the well worn path up the hill. In the late 1800's the family cows took this path to the pasture for the day, returning again in the late afternoon.

We didn't stop, but all observed the old round wooden table with built on seats circling it just off the path. In 1927, fifteen family members gathered around the table for a picture and a picnic lunch. That was probably the last picture taken there. Originally it was built for the Family Reunion their father held in the early 1900s.

This walk was a Sunday tradition and it was traditional to first stop at the spring. One of the men pulled back the large flat sandstone cover. Another fumbled in the nearby weeds for the old rusty cup. Year after year the trusty old rusty cup was left there. Then one by one, men first, everyone dipped the cup in the water which was near the surface. After all had a drink, the spring was recovered and the rusty cup set nearby. We continued our walk until we reached the quarry.

The quarry was a pleasant sight as it was filled with water. From 1848 to the early 1900's the men in the family cut sandstones. The larger stones were the basis for a nearby bridge while others were cut for grindstones and flaggings.

Several times during the summer Aunt Laura would call, "Come along girls. We're going to the quarry."

We heard shouts from the woods. Teenage boys were likely skinny dipping on this hot summer day. We didn't want to go. Those boys were most likely in our classes at school. Although she carried a gun, Aunt Laura didn't want to go there by herself.

I should describe the gun: at one time it was a gun. Now it was held together with strips of rags. Of course Aunt Laura had no intention of getting close enough for the boys to view her weapon. Nevertheless, she waved it around as she shouted for the boys to get out of the water. It was enough to scare them. They jumped out at the far end, grabbed their clothes and ran.

We were told that a young boy drowned there while carrying a lunch pail to his dad. I don't believe that. When men worked the quarry, the water was removed.

Back at the house the table was set in the kitchen. A bowl of canned peaches or maybe pears was passed; coffee was poured and buns, followed by German kuchens, either apple, grape or maybe plum. This was a traditional Sunday supper.

The dishes were put away and we left for the porch or the lawn swing. Soon Uncle Joe and his family returned to the city.

We three children left the farmhouse after we married. At that time another widowed aunt moved in there. No wonder it was referred to as the Aunt House. The house, built in 1883, is listed in the National Register of Historic Places.

Burying the Evidence

by Iva M. Hoff Wise of Barnesville, Ohio
born in 1934

These are some of my memories of growing up on a farm, from the early 1930s to the early 1950s.

The farm was located high on a hill, not too far from Lewisville, Ohio, Monroe County, about one mile south of Route 145.

I was born the second daughter of Ernest and Marcella (Weber) Hoff. I was one of five daughters, having no brothers.

Farming was hard work at this time. We girls had to fill the role of sons our parents didn't have. We learned to do anything involved in farming, while also learning to cook, clean and keep house.

The farm consisted of about 235 acres. Daddy raised beef cattle, hogs, chickens and nine milk cows. Having this many animals meant raising all kinds of crops, including corn, wheat, oats, hay and sugar cane (the sugar cane was made into molasses), and sometimes just planting something for the pleasure of trying it, which once included peanuts. We put up a lot of hay and the other crops. We ground our own feed for the cattle—corn, wheat and oats.

We planted acres of corn, which had to be hoed to keep it free from weeds. We girls had to do the hoeing, and we were sure the rows of corn became longer as the day, under the hot sun, wore on.

A large field of potatoes was planted and also needed hoeing and spraying for bugs. We carefully planted the potatoes and dug them up when they were ready. We had bushels of potatoes that were sorted and stored in the cellar, with any excess sold or given to those in need.

We were "allowed" to help a neighbor with his corn. His family was grown and no longer at home. We girls hoed his corn for twenty-five cents a day. He warned us not to chop off any of the stalks of corn, so if we accidentally chopped one out, we buried the evidence. We were sure the wrath of God would rain down on us if our neighbor discovered our misdeed. What can you expect for twenty-five cents a day? But he and his wife were good neighbors. They always fed us a good lunch, with thick slices of ham and fresh strawberries.

We raised hogs as well and enjoyed the little piglets. These hogs were butchered in the fall, and Daddy "sugar" cured the meat, curing it with hickory smoke in a smokehouse near the house.

We had many good neighbors and were helped when we needed them with butchering, making hay or threshing the grain, and in return, we helped them. When we worked together, everything seemed to go smoother, and the women always fixed wonderful lunches for the workers.

In the early days, we didn't have a tractor, but instead used a team of mules, Maude and Dick. Daddy also did some logging in our large forest. The mules came in handy for this big job. We also cut down locust trees to be made into posts and sold. I remember being on the other end of a "crosscut" saw while cutting a tree and Daddy saying, "Don't lay on the saw." Hard work.

We girls learned to do most anything that needed done on a farm—we were Daddy's "boys." We loved trailing along after him, having fun while we worked.

Mother always had a couple of large gardens. We helped her with growing the garden, canning the produce or freezing it after we got electricity and could have a deep freezer.

Mother also raised chickens, having several hundred, selling eggs and fryers. Sunday after church, we often had relatives for company and lunch with a big chicken dinner.

I remember Mother's having an ugly-tempered large rooster, who loved to chase us and flop us. He would throw his whole body at you and sink his claws into your legs. One day, he followed me to the "outhouse," which was down over the hill beside the chicken house. He would not let me leave the outhouse, attacking me when I tried to leave. I guess he finally gave up.

Along with the hard work came the freedom of living on a large farm and enjoying having sisters to play with all the time. We loved nut hunting in the fall, wading barefoot in the creek on Sunday afternoons, catching "lightning bugs" at dusk on warm spring evenings, riding down a long snow-covered hill on a bob-sled our daddy made for us in the winter.

We loved to play card games around the kitchen table while Mother made popcorn balls for us to enjoy on winter evenings.

We didn't have electric lights until 1946. Before that, we did our lessons by the light of oil lamps. We studied our lessons while Daddy sat nearby, listening to a battery radio. He loved the "Green Hornet," "Gangbusters," "Amos and Andy," and a radio show which opened with a phone ringing and a man answering with, "Duffy's Tavern; Duffy ain't here." Was that the name of the show?

We had loving parents, who worked hard training and teaching us many good things. Church attendance was very important to us. We loved the fellowship singing of hymns and sharing happy memories with close friends and relatives in our community.

We girls all grew up, married and had families of our own. We gave Mother and Daddy ten grandsons and four granddaughters. The grandchildren loved staying with Mother and Daddy.

It is good to remember good times, good parents, and sisters that are still close. Life growing up on a farm was hard work but very rewarding.

The Five Dollar Bill and the Dynamite Cap

by Donald Cable of Dennison, Ohio
born 1930

I was born during the Great Depression, March 20, 1930. The youngest of five children, my mother died in July of 1931, leaving my dad with a heavy burden to carry. He was a coal miner who was unable to work anymore because he was afflicted with black lung disease.

Thanks to President Franklin D. Roosevelt my brother, Ralph, went to Utah to work in a CCC camp which Roosevelt created to help families. My oldest brother worked at the taxi office next to the Pennsylvania Depot in Dennison, Ohio.

There are several memories from my childhood that stick out.

I went for a walk with my dad when I was 5 years old and he found a $5 bill which he used to buy a big order of groceries.

When I was 7 or 8 I found a dynamite cap in the old Dennison railroad yards. I put it on a brick and hit it with another brick. I could have lost my hearing or eyesight but fortunately I did not. I never told my dad.

As a boy my first experience with faith came when my dear sister would take me to church.

There was a railroad bridge a few hundred yards east of the Dennison Depot. The bridge made it possible for people to cross the train yards to the south side of Dennison. When I was five or six years old, my brother took me on the bridge to fly a kite with the other kids. My brother always looked after me and tried to help me find fun things to do.

Father, Clinton Cable, and son, Donald, in 1937.

As a little boy growing up on the south side of Dennison I would walk to school in the winter and stop in Jim Cahaney's tailor shop to get warm. Jim Cahaney was a kind Irish man who loved children.

I remember when my 2nd grade teacher Glenna Wells, who would lose a son in World War II, gave me a note to take home stating that I should get a diphtheria shot. I never gave the note to my dad because I was afraid of a shot.

Speaking of my father, he never remarried.

As a child we would sled ride and skate (if you had skates) on the Little Stillwater Creek when it was frozen. In January of 1940, I fell through the ice and nearly drowned.

There were no local swimming pools so kids would skinny dip in the creek in the summer. Kids would also swim in the water tanks used to fill the steam engines. Their fun was usually cut short by the railroad detectives who would chase them off.

Many times we would eat groundhogs, being that they only ate clover.

My brother Frank would trap muskrats and sell the hides to buy food. He later went to war (1941) in the 8th Air Force in the B-17 Flying Fortress stationed in England. He was a waist gunner who was awarded the Distinguished Flying Cross and the Air Medal.

We always had an outhouse and I would get cardboard boxes at the furniture store to put inside during the winter to keep the wind out.

We would also listen to radio programs like Fibber McGee and Molly, Jack Benny, the Hermit, Fred Allen, and the Hit Parade.

I also saved baseball cards of players like Babe Ruth, Lou Gehrig, Charlie Gehringer, Met Ott, Lefty Grove, Carl Hubbard, Jimmie Foxx and many more. I no longer have any of these cards.

On Saturdays I would go to the movies (two people for five cents) at the Palace Theater and the Lincoln Theater in Dennison, and the State Theater and Ohio Theater in Uhrichsville.

I also remember when my dad would whittle bean shooters out of elderberry branches for the kids. We would also make "rubber guns" out of a piece of wood and inner tubes from car tires.

I once mowed a lawn with an old push mower and the lady gave me an Edison record player that had cylinder records that would be worth a lot today. The record player is gone now.

My favorite dog was Theodore. He was a wire haired terrier and Airedale mix who would kill rats on sight.

The town of Dennison was known as the Altoona, P A of the west. It was the halfway point between Pittsburgh, Pennsylvania, and Columbus, Ohio, as the Pennsylvania Railroad sent trains through it east and west.

Now when World War II came in 1941, the Dennison, Ohio Canteen was established to serve sandwiches and coffee to the thousands that came through on the ''troop trains." Dennison was referred to as "Dreamsville" by the troops.

Being 11 or 12 years old I would go to the railroad station. The soldiers would ask me to get them cigarettes from across the street as they were not allowed off the trains. They would give me a nickel or dime, and the store would give me the cigarettes because they knew they were for the troops.

FDR came through Dennison when I was ten years old on "The Sunshine Special," a passenger train operated by the Pennsylvania Railroad.

Also when the coal cars were parked on the siding, I would pick up coal off the ground to take home to burn in our pot-bellied stove.

The biggest snowstorm occurred in November 1950, on the day before Thanksgiving. This was also the year I got married, 59 years ago. I also shared my first kiss with that same woman with whom I continue to share the rest of my life with.

Where the Flowers Grew

by Clarence D. Armstrong of New Philadelphia, Ohio
born 1944

I lived in a small house with my parents, three sisters, and one brother. Our first house had no indoor plumbing. Needless to say we all took turns taking our baths on Saturday evening, sharing the same water which was heated on the ole pot belly stove and poured into a galvanized tub.

We all shared the "chamber pot," which was my job to empty; a job I hated so much especially when it was freezing cold out. Our outhouse consisted of two holes. Every couple of years we would always have to dig a new hole and move it. You always knew where the old one sat because that was where the flowers would grow the biggest and prettiest.

We lived there until I was 16 years old. We then moved across the "holler" to a much better house. It had running cold water and a toilet in it. My mother still lives in it today at 91 years of age, and it has been modernized.

There was never much money back then for extras. My little brother was sick all the time living until he was eight years old. So it took all my dad's money to take care of us and pay the bills. He worked in Barnesville at a foundry known as Watts which made mine cars until the late 50's. He then got a job working for Tri-State Asphalt, operating heavy equipment, mainly a roller—big money so we thought.

The little country school where I would've started first grade closed that year, so I had to ride the bus to the big school in Barnesville. I graduated high school class of 1962.

I spent a lot of time turtle hunting with my Granddad, Dad, and other relatives; walking the creek beds, reaching under the banks for turtles. Lots of times the turtles would go in backwards, biting you when you tried to pull them out. We would usually get a sack-full by the end of the day; bring them home to clean and make turtle soup, which was delicious!

I would also walk the creek banks in the spring of the year to snag the "Red Horse Suckers" with a tremble hook. They were big fish and "good eaten," although there were a lot of bones in them.

We also spent a lot of time making homemade ice cream in the summer with the ole hand crank maker. It really got tiresome, but the eating of it when it was done was wonderful. Now they use the electric ones. Not much fun to make these days, as it was back then.

I remember the Ole Cider Mill that was at the end of our lane. I used to watch the men press the apples into cider, waiting to get a cup of cider for tasting. It was good. One time I was waiting for the school bus, jumping from one apple sack to another, when I fell to the floor and broke my shin bone.

I worked as a janitor for our little country church making $15.00 a month cleaning it and building the ole coal furnace fire on Saturday; keeping the church warm for Sunday Services. I saved my money and bought my first .22 rifle for $19.99, which I still have today.

Summers meant I would help the farmers putting up hay making 50 cents an hour working long hours just waiting to go the strip pits to swim and cool off after a hard day's work. When I wasn't helping put in hay, my buddies and I would head for the woods for camp outs, packing our snacks and Kool-aid and spending the nights. We would swing from grapevines, climb the trees and wait for one to cut the tree down with us in it, falling to the ground; lucky we never got hurt.

I joined the Army after graduating high school in September, 1962, spending a year in Thailand before the Vietnam War started, returning home to marry my high school sweetheart, Blanche Clark. We just celebrated our

45th wedding anniversary. Our family includes three daughters, three sons-in-law and eight grandsons, one of which is deceased.

Changing Conditions on Ancestral Land

by Dean Miller of Uhrichsville, Ohio
born in 1922

I was born in 1922 at home on Plum Run Valley, a few minutes before my twin brother Charles. I always thought my name was Dean Brown Miller. When I retired and signed up for Social Security, we discovered that grandmother Brown had pulled a fast one on us all. Apparently, she had wanted me named after my grandfather; and as she gave the information to the officials at the time, she named me as she wanted, McClellan Miller, and she carried that little secret to her grave. So after 65 years, I officially had my correct name for the first time.

My mother was a Brown of English and Scottish descent. They lived nearby at Tunnel Hill, so named because of the trains. When my great-grandfather first came there in the early 1800s, there were still Indians in those days. They built their house with the well inside so the Indians wouldn't poison them. The story goes that future generations were not allowed to play under the grape arbor as there were Indians buried there.

He owned a lot of land, and together with a couple neighbors donated the land and built Tunnel Hill Church, which is still there with the cemetery, part of which is designated Brown Cemetery, reserved for our family and still in use. The house was finally torn down just last year.

My paternal grandmother's family, Crumrine of German descent, first came to Plum Run with a land patent in 1820. My paternal grandfather's family, Miller, also of German descent, came here in 1885 after leaving Ohio to try farming in Kansas. Bad weather and locusts made life hard there, so he came back to Ohio and settled here on Plum Run. The two families lived next door. The last of the Crumrine land was sold in 1920s after being here 100 years, as most of them moved west. The Millers are still here. The ones who came and went before have their memorials in Plum Run Cemetery on the hill behind my home.

House on Plum Run. Back row: Isaac Miller and James Crumrine, great grandfathers; Mary Crumrine Miller, grandmother. Front row: Charles B. and Clyde Miller, grandfather and father.

I grew up in the house my great-grandfather built. A two-story farmhouse package made by Sears Roebuck, built in 1906. There were four rooms up and five down. The house was built with two kitchens, two living rooms and two front doors. A double wooden door pulled out of the wall to separate the two areas, perfect for two families. On the back porch was an attached building for doing laundry and other work, and a springhouse with the best water, three cisterns full, cold and clear. There was a garage where we kept our 1929 Buick. There was me, my twin brother, an older sister, our parents, our grandmother and her mother, who was the last of a family of 16 children from Ireland, and the first born in the USA in 1855.

We had gas piped through the house for heat, lights and cooking, which came from one of six oil wells on the land. We also used coal to heat. There were several mines on the land where we went in the tunnel and dug our own coal every three months. The tracks, cars and a lot of tools are still in those old mines, though the entrances have been covered up for safety. One mine went under the cemetery and some of the graves fell through. The men would never go back in that one and it was closed.

There were other mines up the road, which was then a dirt road, and Dad often went out with the horses to pull a coal truck over the hill that was stuck in the mud.

We had four barns for hay and animals, various other buildings for grains and a smokehouse for the meat. The blacksnakes grew big here and were always in the hay and barns. Copperheads were always around the oil wells and in the cemetery. We had three horses, 18 head of milk cows, 30 chickens and four pigs every year, and we used to have sheep in the early years. Mom got a big box of chicks in the mail every spring to start out her chickens for the year. We made our own butter, milk and buttermilk and had eggs and butchered our own meat. There were apple and peach orchards on the farm plus various berries, all of which were eaten, cooked, canned, and cider made from the apples. Dad would shake the apple trees until the apples rolled down the hill to a wooden stop he made, where we loaded them on the wagon and took them to the cider mill. We kept the cider in barrels in the cellar, adding wintergreen to keep it fresh. Mom canned a lot of peaches. The peaches then were big as a baseball. We hand picked those to keep from bruising. We also had hickory nuts, walnuts and chestnuts, which were a treat. We hunted squirrel and rabbit. There weren't many deer in those days, but the men would always carry a gun in some parts of the woods, as they said there were still panthers around. With all this and the gardens, we had lots of good fresh food, and Mom was a wonderful cook.

We had 160 acres of land. We grew corn and wheat, oats for the horses, hay for the cattle, and barley which we took to the mill and had ground up for chicken feed. We took the wheat in to the mill to be ground up for flour. Mom would make six big round loaves of bread at a time, which would last for about two weeks. Hot fresh bread with butter she churned. Imagine, when we were older we thought it was a real treat to have store bought bread. We didn't know how good we had it.

The work was hard. We used two horses to pull the plow. A person would walk behind to guide it. It would take all day to plow two small fields and we had eight fields to plow. We made hay with a hay loader. One person cut the hay as the loader threw it onto the wagon; then one pushed it up front to the person that would rake it and stomp it down. The corn was harvested in the fall and had to be hand picked. Barley had to be cut. Oats and wheat were harvested with a thresher. A neighbor would go around to local farms with his thresher. Neighbors would get together and help with the work. Mom loaded a table full of food for the workers and everyone would enjoy a great meal and visit. The three of us worked hard for two months cutting grain and getting ready for threshing in September.

When we were sick they would give us hot honey or castor oil for cough or sore throat. Once I had a bad chest cold and they smeared pig fat all over my chest and wrapped me up. Great-grandmother had asthma. Not sure what it was, but they would burn something in her room and she would breathe in the smoke for that.

The church we went to was across the road. We went to a one room school a couple of miles up the road. Grades one through six were up front with seven and eight in the back. We sometimes rode our ponies and sometimes our teacher would pick us up in her car. They used to move the schoolhouses around to where the kids were. Later in high school Dad drove the bus to Bowerston where we attended. You knew all your neighbors, went to school and church with them. Everyone worked together to help each other. It was a real community. Family and friends visited a lot and had big meals together for different occasions or no occasion.

We sometimes all piled in a big sleigh in the winter and the horses would pull us over the hill to a neighbor's house for a get-together. We would go visiting in the 1929 Buick. There were no heaters in cars then and they would wrap us up in big thick blankets when it was cold. A cousin had an airplane which he would land in the field when he came for a visit. He got a surprise when the phone and electric wires appeared.

On Saturday night the family would go to town. While Mom and Dad shopped we would go to the movies which only cost a dime. This was a big thrill for us kids. When we reached our teens we would go roller skating every Saturday night. As twins, my brother and I sometimes got into some mischief. They say we had our own language for a long time and talked to each other before we talked to anyone else. We also played a few tricks on the girls, as not everyone could tell us apart.

This was our life growing up. We were entirely self-sufficient, working hard, eating good and enjoying the community social life with family and friends. It was a good life. We didn't have electric, TV or telephone until after we got back from the war. We enjoyed a simple life, and when you did go to town or to see a move, it was really a thrill and something special.

When World War II broke out, Charles and I were called to serve and were away from home for three years and three months. We did basic training at Fort Riley, Kansas, where we worked as groundskeepers for actress Gene Tierney and husband Oleg Cassini the famous designer. We were in 88 straight days of combat in the freezing cold in the deep snows of the forest of the Ardennes as Trailblazers in the 274th under General Patton. We were on a ship headed for the Pacific when they turned us around as the war had ended. We spent some time repatriating in Europe. Charles escorted some reporters to Berchesgaten, Hitler's famous hideout. I escorted an officer to his wedding in Italy and toured Rome then on to Austria. On the way home our ship hit an iceberg in the North Atlantic and we barely made it back.

It was especially hard on Dad, as he was in World War I and knew what war was like. We even landed at Marseilles where he landed years before. He was gassed over there and sick the rest of his life because of it. He was able to keep up the farm with the help of Mom and my sister and then he got a job with the clayworks to keep busy and keep his mind off of his worries about us. We made it back home safely, returning to Dreamsville by train, the Dennison depot near our home. This famous depot has been renovated and they have a museum and yearly festival with events honoring all soldiers. People come from all over the country. The trains were a really relaxing way to travel and see the country. On long trips sleep came easy listening to the clickety clack of the wheels.

When we came home life was changing. The farm was scaled down. We put in our own electric, got our first television. The old roads followed the bottom of the hills and were being rerouted so it didn't take so long to get to town. The nearby village of Tappan was turned into Tappan Lake. When my sister married, they tore down a house at Tappen and moved it to our land to rebuild it for her. Later my brother and I built our homes on the family farm. Mine was built from good sturdy oak that will last forever from a house torn down at Clendening when that was made into a lake.

A lot of the old homes that were here when I was young are gone or abandoned. The fields are all grown up and it's reverting back to a wilderness with wildlife in abundance. People had always kept their land clear and their fence rows mowed after the hard work of clearing the land to use for farming. The small towns are quiet and the businesses all gone. There used to be several stores, restaurants, theaters and even colleges in all these small towns. They were all alive with business and society.

We are still here on the land of our ancestors since 1820 with our memories. Charles and I will be celebrating our 87th birthday in May. Our sister Helen will be 89 in September.

Fire Drills, Penny Candy and Spit Balls

by Karen Saylor of Wintersville, Ohio
born in 1943

I was five years old, first grade. Miss Russ was my teacher. We had our first fire drill. I knew we were supposed to get in a single file out of the school. I didn't know we weren't supposed to empty out our entire desk and carry it out in my dress all pulled up and showing all my worldly goods. I did get a good scolding.

Bowestown, Ohio, fifth grade I had a real long walk to school and had to pass a store with penny candy in it every day, so in my mom's kitchen she had a change purse with a lot of change in it because she sold Avon and kept it on the china closet. I thought she wouldn't miss a few coins as I helped myself to it every morning on my way to school to get my penny candy until she caught me red handed with my hand in the cookie jar. From then on the change purse was never in my reach.

Sixth grade we had a teacher Mr. Smyth and he was always falling asleep, so a couple of us kids decided to throw spit balls, but as soon as one left my hand he happened to wake up and catch me, so I spent the rest of the day in the corner.

I remember fourth grade and I was supposed to say my speech "In Flanders Fields" for Memorial Day at the cemetery. I had a real pretty sleeveless dress to wear. Well it happened to snow that day and I had left my only coat at school, so I had to say my speech while my teeth chattered because I had no other coat to wear. Every time I go to that cemetery I think about it snowing in May.

I remember my mom taking me and my sister to live in Steubenville. We had moved from Bergholz. We found an apartment in someone's attic. My mom fixed us our Thanksgiving dinner. We sat down to eat. We tasted it and none of us could eat any of it because we were not used to the water and it tasted like chlorine. What a waste of a good dinner. I guess we eventually got used to it.

Everything But Coffee

by Ruth E. Wahl Russell of Columbus, Indiana
born in 1927

Peter Wahl, born near Miltonsburg, Ohio, married Magdalena Letzelter, who was born in Alsace Lorain, Germany. They loved on a farm in Woodsfield, Ohio and had nine children.

After the kids were grown, Magdalena Wahl was sickly and they needed someone to move in and help care for her. Thus, after the youngest son Roman (my father) was married to his bride Clara, they moved into the family farm to help care of his parents. At that time, Roman and Clara bought the Wahl Farm from his parents.

After Magdalena passed away, her husband Peter asked Roman and Clara if he could stay with them for the rest of his life, because he said that he had built the house and he would be so lonely living anywhere else. Roman and Clara agreed and thus Peter lived with them for 18 more years which was the rest of his life.

Roman and Clara's four daughters always felt honored to have been born in the same house their father was born in. And the girls were also privileged to grow up knowing their grandfather who lived with them as they were growing up. This is one of the differences in family living in the early 1900s and today.

To me, my grandfather was more than a grandfather; he was my buddy. I have many, many fond memories of him. One of my favorite memories is that every evening he had a special chair he retired in and I got to climb on his lap and he would sing me songs in German and tell me memories of his childhood.

One of my favorite stories from my grandfather was about his father, Conrad, and Conrad's brother, John, who came to America from Germany. They got on their ship in New York City and they got separated from each other and were never reunited.

Knowing this, as I went through my own professional and personal life, I always kept an eye open for the unique German spelling, "Wahl," and also looked out for the male family trait of early baldness. Not many young girls were attracted to bald men as I was, but I had this reason. In fact, when my husband and I were on own honeymoon in Florida in 1956, the gentleman who checked us into our motel in Miami was bald and his last name was Wahl. I will always think that he was a descendent of John Wahl and one of my long last relatives.

When I worked for a subsidiary of Proctor and Gamble in Dayton Ohio, a salesman once called on me and I am sure that he too was a long lost relative. His name was also Wahl and he was bald and when I met him, I said, "You have to be a cousin of mine!" He found the family history very interesting and said no one had ever said anything like that to him before.

On the Wahl family farm we had several oil and gas wells drilled. Most of the wells were drilled in my father's time and Dad would pump the wells about once a week. We felt very fortunate that we had our own gas for heating our home, when most people at that time had to use coal or wood. My dad sold the oil to Texas Eastern; and I recently found out that Texas Eastern has a pipeline that runs through the city where I now live, in Columbus, Indiana.

My father attended a one-room schoolhouse for eight years. As a child, I also had the privilege of attending the same one-room schoolhouse for my first years of school. We walked a mile each way to this schoolhouse in all kinds of weather. Then, after four years, the one room schoolhouse was closed and I had to walk another mile to the highway to catch a school bus and attend St. Sylvester's School in Woodsfield. By the time I was in high school, the bus came by our house and I got to take the bus to Woodsfield High School, where I graduated in 1945.

We had a cast iron cooking stove. My father converted it to gas but my mother preferred to cook with coal and wood; so every morning she would get up early and start the fire in the iron stove and when it was heated up, would cook us breakfast of biscuits or flapjacks or oatmeal. The stove also had a water well that would heat the hot water we needed to do dishes and use for our baths.

Growing up on the farm, we all had chores to do and animals to care for and crops to plant, care for and harvest. I loved being outside on the farm and working with my father on the farm. I was a real tomboy and worked side-by-side with my dad, just as a son would have done. I started off driving a team of horses and I had a special old white horse named Mac. Mac was also my buddy. Our farm ran one mile in every direction. If I was working in the field with my family, and I got real tired working, Dad would put me on old Mac and no matter where we were on the farm. Mac knew just how to take me home. My dad built a wooden block of steps for me to get up on old Mac. When Mac and I would return to the barn, Mac would stop at the steps, let me off and then turn around to the watering trough and I would pump him water to drink. When he got through drinking, he would go into the barn and walk by himself into his stall and then I would go in and get him hay from the barn to eat. Only when my father returned to the barn, sometimes hours later, Mac would stay in his stall and wait for my father to tie him up.

Party line phones: Being in the country, we had a party line phone with 12 homes on our party phone line. Every family had a different ring and you had to be able to identify whose ring was whose. The Wahl family ring was "half of ring." Ours was the first in a series that went by half ring increments. The phone was long and box shape, about three feet long and one foot wide. It hung on the kitchen wall. It had a large bell inside that made the ring. On the side of the phone was a crank handle. There was a mouthpiece and two bells about the mouthpiece that looked like dinner bells. The phone rang on a big battery. I feel very fortunate that in my home today, I still have that phone I grew up with. My children enjoyed playing "old fashioned days" with it when they were younger and making the bells ring.

Wind-up record player. When I was a young girl, in our parlor we had a wind-up record player. The records were heavy vinyl. We had to wind up the record player with a handle and then place the record on the turntable and bring the arm down onto the record with the needle. Each "wind up" lasted about 30 minutes. It was listening to these record that we learned how to dance—first the waltz and then the fox trot. Our partners for the prom would come over to our house and learn/practice how to dance before the prom. Our parents taught us.

Square dancing with callers (people who would tell the dancers what moves to make) were common and popular at wedding receptions. Our father was often the "square dance caller." It was a skill passed down from parent to child. When growing up, at each square dance it was customary for a girl's father to have the first dance with his daughter; and then it was OK for a young man to ask the daughter to dance. But only after she had danced with her father!

Feed sack dresses. Feed sacks came with different prints and in different colors. When my father would buy feed from the feed store, he would try hard to get as many sacks as possible with the same pattern and color. Because, after he used the feed, my mother would use the sacks to make my three sister and I dresses. My mother also used scraps left over from the feed sack dresses to make quilts.

We also used and re-used everything for anything my parents could think of. Nothing went to waste on the farm. We rarely had any new clothes. Although we did have to buy new shoes. When our shoes wore out Dad used his tools to re-sole our shoes so our shoes could last us a year. For example, my mother used her wedding gown to make first communion dresses for us four girls. We passed along our clothes until they were worn out. Hand-me-down were common, welcome and enjoyed. Used coffee cans were used to store dried beans and dried fruit. My grandmother, who was a seamstress, would cut down adults' winter coats to make coats for us children. She was also a milliner and would re-create Easter bonnets for us from old hats.

Ruth Russell driving the tractor and her father, Roman Wahl, loading hay in 1956.

Being farmers during the Depression, there was only one thing we bought from the store and that was coffee. We collected honey from the bees for sweetener. We raised cane and pressed and cooked the stalks to make molasses. We tapped the maple trees for syrup each spring. We grew fruits and vegetables and those were canned and stored for the winter months. We butchered a hog per person yearly and one cow for beef each year. We also raised chickens, turkeys and ducks. So we had fresh eggs. From the cows we had fresh milk and made butter.

I really enjoyed hog butchering the best because there were so many things to do. We cut the lard and cooked the lard and rendered the lard, pressing it to small squares to make cooking lard for the year. When we pressed it down. We had cracklings which we loved to eat and Mother loved to add to the cornbread for extra flavoring. We also ground and stuffed the sausage from the butchered hog.

We also had a smoke house on the farm and smoked the hams, shoulders and bacon there so it did not need to be refrigerated or frozen. After a while we smoked the sausage and then Mother canned the smoked sausage in crocks filled with lard. To this day, it's still the best sausage I've ever tasted!

In the summertime we had a lot of thunder and lightening. My father had Hereford cattle. In my time, there were three of the cows struck and killed by lightening. When that happened, we lost a valuable farm asset. Dad would have to call a man to haul the dead, burnt cow away and the only use for it was to take it to the factory to make dog food. Sometimes, if we didn't find them quick enough, we had to bury the dead burnt animals. We also had two barns burned to the ground and destroyed by lighting. Both of the barns had to be rebuilt for the cattle and storage.

Making flour. We raised several acres of wheat and we had a threshing machine that would travel from farm to farm helping to harvest the wheat on each farm. Farmers from all around would follow the threshing machine from farm to farm to help harvest the wheat at each place until threshing was over. My father took 25 sacks of wheat to the mill in town and had it ground into flour. Then he would return home with 25 sacks of flour. We put the sacks of flour in a big flour bin and that was enough flour for a year for our family. Mother baked everything possible bread, biscuit, rolls, pancakes, donuts, cakes, pies, cookies, gravies. My father also had a hammer mill which was used to grind corn into meal. From the meal, Mother would make mush and cornbread.

Christmas time. At Christmas time we always had snow. Father would hook up the team of horses to a sled and we would all bundle up under Indian blankets. We would travel from house to house to visit all of our neighbors, taking them something Mother had cooked or baked. I guess that was an early version of a progressive dinner party! Fathers would make wooden toys for the children and other neighbors would come visit is in the same fashion. It was our tradition of sharing the holiday spirits with our friends and neighbors.

My father would also make us wooden sled for playing in the snow. One year he also made us a wooden wagon complete with metal wheels and wooden tongue. For years we used that wagon to haul vegetables from the garden to the house for meals.

We also cut our own pine tree from the farm for our Christmas tree and each year we would make decorations for the tree. We would string popcorn. We had all kinds of nut trees on the farm. All year long we would save the shells and then color them and hang the colored shells on string and yarn to decorate the tree. We also used colored paper to make ornaments and icicles for the tree. Everything was homemade for the tree. Dad even made the tree stand which we kept and re-used from year to year.

During less busy season, when the men would go hunting, women would get together at one or another farm and all quilt together. Women would travel from house to house and quilt once a quilt top was ready to be quilted.

Neighbors all pitched in and helped one another. We never had to hire help to do these sorts of things. The only time Dad would hire on extra help was for the harvest.

My parents were farmers in every respect of the

word. They respected and tended the land which in turn provided food and nourishment for them and their family. They lovingly planted each seed into the ground and, in return, Mother Nature rewarded them with harvest. At the same time, they sowed a background for their children that created the fabric of our future lives.

As their children have now grown old, we cherish the lessons taught by them and often yearn for the good old days on the farm, when work was hard, but life was simple. When family meant the most, and neighbors were always close by and caring when the earth provided all you needed—except coffee

These thoughts and memories are lovingly dedicated to my deceased parents, Roman and Clara Wahl.

Neighbors and Winter Wood

by Myrtle Hammons of Brinkhaven, Ohio
born 1932

I was born in December of 1932 so the first half of the Depression never affected me at all.

My father was a tenant farmer and my mother was a housewife. As a tenant farmer, Dad would get a house to live in and sometimes he would get around $32.00 a month. He had to work from daylight to well past dark on the farm, milking, feeding, plowing, planting, harvesting. Just regular farm work day in and day out.

My mom had her own chickens, a cow, and a sow pig that had a litter of pigs each spring. She always raised a good sized garden and canned or dried most of what we ate.

We moved about every two years or so but basically the farms were all the same in the area of Ohio where we lived then (Knox County).

The people that lived around us were all in the same situation that we were, but almost all of them were good, caring friends. If one family had a need, others jumped in to help. Say a man broke his leg at corn cutting time. The neighbors would come and take care of the corn and most often get his winter wood in too. They would pitch in and do his chores and when he got well he would repay by helping out others when he could.

I started school in 1938, and there wasn't much difference between any of the children. We all had the same clothes and shoes. The boys and girls all dressed pretty much the same and none were mean or stingy. And no one made fun of anyone else as far as I knew.

I was very, very bashful. I had learned to read a little before I started school and I loved to hear others read. My dad would read to us sometimes in the evening. The first school I attended was at Millwood, Ohio.

We lived beside a highway, Route 36. I loved to ride the bus and go to school. The ride to school was on a road that was (and still is) a winding, curvy road. The road ran parallel to a river. There was a long, rocky drop off between the road and the river. I was afraid the bus would go over the bank into the river so in the mornings I would set on the right side of the bus and in the evenings I would set on the left side of the bus.

Because Route 36 was a major highway a lot of hobos (or tramps) came by our house; most were men who were out of work and hunting for a job. Some would stop and ask if Mom would give them something to eat. They would be so hungry that they would eat anything. Almost all of them would offer to do any kind of work for food.

When I was five years old I had a little sister. One day my sister was asleep and Mom had to go to our landlord's who lived just a short ways away, across a little field but within shouting distance of our house. My mom worked for our landlord who took in boarders that worked putting in the Mohawk Dam about 3 or 4 miles from our house. For the first time ever my mom left me to watch my baby sister. She told me to stay in the house and watch sister and she would be right back. I was satisfied, I had a picture book and sister was asleep. Suddenly there was a loud knock at the back door. I opened the door. A BIG man was standing there! He said, "Is your mother home, little girl?" I said, "No, but she will be back in a minute, she is over at that house." I pointed to the landlords. "What do you want?" He said, "I thought I'd ask her for a little bite to eat, I'd cut some wood for her or something, but she isn't here." I said, "I will give you something to eat." He said that he would wait on the porch for my mother. I said, "Okay."

Now I thought that my mom baked the best bread in the world and I loved catsup. I pushed a kitchen chair over to the cabinet and climbed upon the top of the lower half of it. I opened the bread box and got out a loaf of bread and climbed down. I put the bread on the table and got into the cabinet drawer and got out the big long knife that Mom cut bread with. I went to the "ice box" (no ice in it) and got out the bottle of catsup. I got on my knees on the chair by the table and took the bread and knife and cut off a big slice of bread—about 2 inches thick and then I cut another piece about the same size. I got the catsup and put it on one slice thick, real thick! I did the same with the other slice. I took the first slice over to the door and said, "Hey Mister, here is you a sandwich!" He was setting over on the last step on the porch. He came to the door and I held out the bread with the catsup. (He had to reach in the door because I wasn't allowed to go outside.) He said, "This looks real good and I sure do thank you." I said, "That's okay, I like these sandwiches too." He ate his on the porch and I ate mine at the table.

Just then my mom came. He stood up and thanked her. Mom wasn't happy I could tell, but he went out to the wood pile and chopped wood for awhile. Mom fixed him a plate of food and got him a glass of milk; he ate and then left.

Mom was so scared and sorry that she left me and sister alone that she didn't yell at me for getting the bread, catsup, and knife out.

We moved that March closer to Tiverton Center, Ohio (in Coshocton County). From the house I had to walk across a field, up a small hill, across a rock fence, down the other side of the hill and up the road a short distance to catch the bus at the new landlord's house. I wasn't scared on that bus; the boys sat on one side and the girls sat on the other side. The bus would get very crowded by the time we got to school and I was very scared I'd touch one of the boys.

Two boys were in a quarrel one evening on the way home. The bus driver stopped the bus and made both boys get off.

The Tiverton School was three buildings. I was in the building that had first and second graders in it. The second graders read the story of "Hansel and Gretel" out loud and I thought it was an interesting story.

There wasn't a cafeteria at the school in those days; each person took their lunch in a bag or pail. Sometimes my dad would give me a dime to buy my lunch at the store in town. I would only go if my cousin that was in high school would walk with me. At the store, Smith's, I could get a bottle of malted milk for a nickel and five cents worth of cookies which was a little brown paper bag full. The cookies and crackers were in glass containers in front of the counter. So were big jars of dill pickles.

Between the school and the store was an old house that was surrounded by flowers. Some of the kids said that the old woman that lived there gave them cookies sometimes. Her house set just a short distance from the road. One day I was slow getting with my cousin and friends; they were just a short ways up the road and I thought I could catch up with them. When I got to the old woman's house there was a large puddle of blood in the road in front of her house. The old woman came out on her porch. She had on a pretty print dress and an apron. In her hand she had a big plate of cookies. She said, "Hello, come on over here little girl, you can have some cookies!" I could not answer, I could not run, I eased one foot in front of the other until finally at last I could run. I knew that old lady was the Old Witch from the "Hansel and Gretel" story.
Later, much later, I found out that she was a sweet friendly person, Mrs. Ridenbaugh was her name. And the blood? I found out later that some men had butchered a cow in that spot.

I miss hearing whippoorwills in the evenings. One evening I told Dad and Mom that the whippoorwill was saying, "Sprinkle Rain, Sprinkle Pain.

I miss hearing hoot owls hoot. One would hoot close and soon one would answer from up the hollow or other hill side.

I miss having the wood cook stove in the kitchen and wood heating stove in the living room; the stove pipe generally went up through the ceiling and then up through the roof.

I miss having the ole battery radio that we all would listen to the Grand Old Opry on and at times we would listen to "prize fights." Joe Lewis was generally the favorite.

When I got home from school I was allowed to listen to one program before I had to do chores. One evening would be "Just Plain Bill." The next night would be Bobbie Benson at the B-Bar-B Ranch. Sometimes in the morning there was a program that came on all the way from Chicago, Illinois! The station told the news and advertised "Hot Ralston" which was a cereal. The little ditty that went with the advertisement went like this: Start the morning with hot Ralston and you surely will agree, this warm bang up breakfast gives you cowboy energy. It's delicious and nutritious made of golden western wheat. So take a tip from Tom, go and tell your mom hot Ralston can't be beat!

Almost every spring my mom would order a hundred baby chicks from Murray McMurrey Hatchery. It was such a surprise and a treat when the mailman would honk (or leave a message to come and pick up the baby chicks). There would be 3 or 4 extra in case any had died. They were in cardboard boxes about 2-by-2 foot. Each big box had 4 little separate compartments inside. Each box had little round holes cut in them for ventilation.

Danville, Ohio had outdoor movies on Saturday evenings. It was so exciting to be there. You had to bring your own blanket to set or lay on. As soon as it got dark enough the movie would start. They only had the movies in the summer.

There were also Indian medicine shows that came to Danville, Ohio each year. They usually stayed for two weeks in the summer. All the Indians would sing while an Indian girl played a guitar. A couple of the Indian boys would perform with "blacksnake" whips. One boy would put a cigarette in his mouth, the other would crack the whip and the cigarette would be cut in half. I never knew if the whips were real snakes or not but the whips were black. The old Indian told about their medicine and you could go up on the stage and buy some. They also sold little boxes of stuff, that was like cracker jacks and if it had a coupon in the box you could get a designed silk pillow cover or dresser scarf or other stuff. One of the medicines I remember was "Rattlesnake Oil" and it was good for a lot of ailments! Even toothaches.

I remember one night in 1941 my mom and dad along with my Uncle Earl had gone to Danville to get groceries. My sister and I got to stay with my Aunt Myrtle and her sons, Kenny and Jimmy. We all enjoyed that. We played games and Kenny was working on making a radio. He was 16 or 17. About 9 p.m. I had to go to the outhouse. I was almost to the outhouse when I looked up at the sky. It was red and terrible to see! I screamed and ran back in the house crying. I tried to tell my aunt what I had seen but was crying too hard. I finally told her the sky was on fire. We all went outside to see. We stayed out until Aunt Myrtle said it was too cold and she couldn't tell us why the sky looked like that. I asked her if the world was coming to an end; she said she didn't think so. Kenny brought his radio into the kitchen and put it on the table. He fiddled with the knobs and buttons and it cracked and buzzed. All at once a man's voice said, "The Northern Lights can be seen over this area of Ohio." And the radio quit and Kenny couldn't get it to work any more. Mom and Dad and Uncle Earl came home soon after that and said people in Danville were kneeling in the streets praying, and the dogs were barking and howling.

One month later Pearl Harbor was attacked!

The sky that night was red all over with red rays flowing out from the center which was a red ball. Gigantic! And the red rays waved and circled. It was terrible and scary. Seemed to me like Heaven was on fire.

Oil Lamps in Vinegar Valley

by Betty Schoeppner of Powell, Ohio
born in 1932

Sitting here in front of a fireplace that burns on gas, that I turned on with an electric switch, is a far cry from the old fireplaces and coal stoves we had growing up in the country of what was known as "Vinegar Valley," between Barnesville and Fairview. Also, the day is rather cloudy, but there is still a brighter light than I used to do homework by, with the old oil lamps. Those old farmhouses, neighbors, and even the hills and woods are no longer there because of the strip mining that was done in the area.

The old farmhouses did not have all the modern conveniences; we did not have electricity until I was in high school. We had oil lamps and coal stoves.

Outhouses and chamber pots were two of the things that do not hold good memories, but they were a necessity. Who wanted to go to the outhouse in the dark or in the winter, so therefore the old chamber pot came into the picture. The bad part about them was you still had to go to the outhouse the next day to empty them. This could now be known as one of the "dirty jobs" the TV show talks about. Although, in elementary school the outhouse was a good spot to go and talk and share secrets with your best friend; there could be a few wasps and other bugs there, but I never found any snakes there. It is a good thing as that is not one of my favorite things.

Several old radio programs hold very fond memories. I can still hear the mellow voice of Lowell Thomas, Grandpa's favorite program. He would begin his world news show with "Good evening, everybody" and end with "So long until tomorrow." Grandma and my mom would listen to what we now call "the soaps," so named because they were usually sponsored by soap powders. The two I remember were "Ma Perkins" and "Mary Noble, Backstage Wife." Family favorites were "Grand Ole Opry," "Amos and Andy," "The Lone Ranger," and who could forget "Death Valley Days," with the clip clop of the mule's feet at the beginning of the show. The show was sponsored by 20 Mule Team Borax. The radio often had a lot of static, but it gave us news of the world, music and a taste of make-believe lives we never could imagine.

Party line phones, oh what fun. You could always tell when your neighbors got a phone call and, of course, they knew the same about you. You always recognized your calls by long rings and short rings. I remember ours; it was two longs and two shorts. You were never allowed to talk long, because someone else might want the line, and you also watched what you said because they could listen in on your conversation. If you picked up the receiver and someone was on, you always hung up quietly and waited until you thought it were safe to try again. You could not move it around and take it with you; it was mounted on the wall. Can you imagine a teenager of today living with that type of phone situation?

Then there was the windup record player. I remember going into what was known as the parlor in my grandparents' house and winding up the old Victrola, as it was also known. Some I remember were "Red River Valley," "Hello, My Baby" and "Go Home and Tell Your Mother." I probably wore the records out, but I was always allowed to go in and listen to them. It seemed to be a special place because it was seldom used. I was really amazed to go online and find that all of those songs are still available. I'm sure they would not sound as good to me now as they did then.

Saturday night baths, how can I forget those? I don't know if it was only on Saturday, but I do remember them in the old washtub in the basement and when we were very young, out in the back yard on a warm day. We did live way out in the country, and no one could see our back yard.

My grandchildren still cannot believe the way we used to live, but when I look back, it was a good life and people did not have half the worries we have today. Can you imagine letting two little girls walk out on a dirt road, which went through the woods? My friend and I often did that to visit each other and never thought a thing about it. We spent lots of spring afternoons walking in the woods and picking wildflowers, such as trilliums, violets and Dutchman's breeches.

Wringer washers, what a great invention. Mom and Grandma were much happier with that than with the old washboard. I remember going to Grandma's house and doing the laundry there; we lived close by. We would heat water in an iron kettle outside over a wood fire and carry it to the washer, hot to wash and cold water in the "Saturday night bathtub" to rinse. I remember even having a wringer washer when we were first married. It was fine until one day I went to the basement to do laundry and saw a mouse. I would not go back down by myself. We soon got an automatic washer and dryer and put them in the kitchen.

Saturday movies, a wonderful way to spend the afternoon, while Grandpa and Dad went to the Saturday auction. Roy Rogers, (my favorite), Gene Autry, Hopalong Cassidy, Johnny Mack Brown, Wild Bill Elliott, and many more were always there on Saturday, along with a cartoon, news and a short continued serial story, usually about a cartoon hero. Bohandy's restaurant was the first stop to buy a bag of potato chips for a nickel and a huge homemade coconut candy bar, also a nickel. A whole wonderful afternoon and it only cost twenty cents; the movie was only a dime. Dad would pick us up afterwards and home we would go to "Mom's home cooking," no eating out in the restaurants back then.

Bill Patterson, Betty's younger brother, taking his Saturday night bath in 1943.

Mom baked bread, pies, cookies, cakes that could not be equaled anywhere in the world, as far as we were concerned. Her vegetable soup and chicken potpie are among my best memories of home cooking.

A lot of us wore homemade clothes, often made from feed sacks. A feed sack was exactly what it says, a sack that held feed for the animals when you bought it at the store. I loved helping to pick out the sacks, because I used a lot of them for 4-H projects and made a lot of my own clothes. My aunt liked to sew and made all of my clothes while I was real little. My mom often said she spent hours ironing all the frills and ruffles my aunt liked to make. She was an excellent seamstress and I am very grateful that she passed her skill on to me.

Snowstorms in the country always meant lots of sled riding and often riding in my uncle's sleigh. I remember one snowstorm where he took me to old Route 40 to meet a friend's father, who was taking us back to college at Muskingum after the big snowstorm of 1950. It seems the school bus always made it through, even though the sides of the road were piled high with drifted snow. The drifts were so prettily sculptured and white. I remember one particular day the snow was so high one of the older boys at the bus stop had to lift me over the pile of snow by the side of the road to get to the bus.

The school bus reminds me of my favorite teacher, Grace Walker. She taught all eight grades at the No. 9 schoolhouse on old Route 8. She was my teacher during all of my elementary years. She was the teacher, janitor, nurse, activities director, and our friend. She was always willing to be on the playground with us, as well as teach us all we needed to know academically.

There were five of us in the same grade, four boys and me; one other girl came in about the seventh or eighth grade. Age did not seem to matter much then; we all had recess together and were friends with everyone. We went on to high school in Barnesville and did well. It was a wonderful experience in the old one room school, another thing my grandchildren cannot even imagine.

I had never played hooky from school and the days of our senior year were going fast; a friend and I decided we should not miss out on that experience, so what did we do about it? We took off one afternoon and went to my aunt's for the afternoon; we did get caught, got a talking to from the principal and that was it. I guess he knew we were too chicken to try it again.

I always heard stories about funny things happening at one of the houses across the hill from us. The lady who lived there often said she heard footsteps on the stairs and doors closing. The story she told that I never liked was about seeing a hand appear in the window at night while she was sitting in the room. I guess I must have been at the "impressionable age" when I heard that one, because I still prefer to have the drapes closed at night. I'm sure that's not why; it just seems cozier. I don't think the house was really haunted, but that's a story I always remember. It did not seem to scare my brothers and I and our friends away.

One of our favorite things to do was go over behind their barn and swing on the grapevines that went out over the ravine between our houses. Our parents did not know we did that at the time. I can see now how really dangerous it was.

We did not really get into a lot of mischief; we just seemed to have a lot of fun. We also had chores to do as we got old enough, like helping with the milking, going after the cows, feeding animals and my job was often doing the supper dishes. Going after the cows was always one of my favorite things to do. It was so peaceful walking in the back fields to find them and head them back toward the barn. Of course, there was always a big collie dog to go with me.

My childhood playmates were my brothers and my cousin who lived with my grandparents. Neighbors would visit some and children always came with the parents. Wiener roasts were always fun when we were junior high age. That was probably where a lot of us got our first kiss, while playing "Truth or Consequence" or "Post Office."

There was always Sundays at my other grandparents' who did not live as close. Aunts, uncles and cousins would come and enjoy being together. My mom and dad liked to fish and we would often take my mom's parents and go to Seneca Lake and fish for the day. Grandma cooked the fish over an open fire; it was a fun day for all of us.

With all the technology today, I'm sure this sounds like life back then was a real bore. But thinking about all of it makes me wish the world we live in today could be a little more like it used to be. I don't want to go back to the no electricity, outhouses, no TV, no cell phones, no computers and e-mail. I must admit I enjoy them all now; I didn't miss them when I did not know about them, but I would miss them now. It would just be nice to have things a little more relaxed and not so rushed. But, let's admit it, all those things made a lot of good memories, and that makes growing old worthwhile.

A Normal Way of Life

by Mamie Lykins of Bullhead City, Arizona
born in 1923

From the oldest of the Clark Clan, age 85, I am Mamie. I have lived in Bullhead City, Arizona for the past 25 years.

I moved to Barnesville in 1931 with my mom (Mabel), pap (Gene), brother (Robert) and baby sister (Della). She was my "Baby Doll." We moved into a partially finished house on Dutch Ridge (Wiley Avenue). Our house was small. Pap and Uncle Earl lived in the garage as they built it. I remember Mom sealing the walls with cardboard boxes and then wallpapering over them. It took a very long time, never did finish a bathroom. We did have a very nice outside privy with two high holes and one low one for us little ones.

In the middle of one night, at age nine, Mom woke me to go get Eve (last name unknown) and the Doctor. She lived a long way across town toward Somerton Road. Eve called for the Doctor. By that time we got back to the house, I had a brand new baby brother, Russ.

We didn't have a lot of luxuries as we grew up. We had a garden, chickens, rabbits and a pig. On Thanksgiving weekend, Pap butchered the pig. Sometimes 2 or 3 of the neighbors would have a pig to do, too. I hated those times as I didn't like washing the greasy stuff, but it was worth the reward of having good meat in the winter months.

We had a lot of chores, but we all just thought it was a "normal" way of life. I was always busy helping with the babies, the garden, feeding the animals, getting coal or kindling in, washing jars and helping to prepare the fruits and veggies for canning.

My brother Robert and I walked to school with all the other kids who lived in the area. We'd walk the railroad tracks by the Watt's Foundry, and then pass the railroad station, sometimes stopping to get a drink or use the potty. We always got chased out! Next it was past the M&K Warehouse. Sometimes we'd be so lucky to find cookies, fruit or what a jackpot if we found CANDY! That surely made our day.

I recall some of our neighbors. Grandma Heines lived next door. I helped Gene with her paper route sometimes. The Bowersocks lived across the street, Chuck, Walter and I fought all the time. The Pittman family had twin girls, Alta and Alma that were a little older than me. The Wheelers and their old maid daughter lived next door and they were very crabby.

In June, 1934, we got another baby girl, Elizabeth. Brother Charles came in March of 1936. I was nearly 12 at this time.

We moved from Barnesville to Neffs, Ohio. While living here, Brother, Eugene, the twins Elroy and Leroy and another sister, Mable was born.

I graduated from Martins Ferry (Ohio) High School in 1941. I started my adult life by getting married. My folks and all my siblings moved back to Barnesville shortly thereafter. Two more sisters, Blanche and Esther, were born in Barnesville to complete the family.

Life was hard, the love was good, and the memories are many.

The China Doll, a Shrunken Daddy and Maywood's Dog

by Bettie Roe of Salesville, Ohio
born in 1942

I grew up in the beautiful rolling hills of Appalachian

Ohio in the small village of Batesville in Beaver Township in Noble County. Although I no longer live there my heart will always belong there in many wonderful memories.

I was born April 2nd, 1942. How could you be born at a better time with being a teenager in the 1950s and '60s and still be above the ground in 2009 to be watching so much history on television.

My first memories was when I was about three years old in 1945. We were living at the ancestral farm in Beaver Township with my father's parents while he was away in the Army. I am sure it must have been a very big change in my grandparents' lives with my mother, brother and me moving in with them in their small house. My father had been an only child and they hadn't had a small child around for many years. I only remember them being very good to us.

My grandparents were very poor, but I didn't know that. Their house inside didn't have color like we have today with paint and wallpaper. But every year for my grandmother's birthday my mother would make crepe paper curtains with big ruffles for her. They were very colorful and cheery.

Our meals at the farm consisted of chicken, eggs and big square dumplings cooked on an old black coal stove. There was no refrigerator so for a special treat now and then when she could afford it Grandma would give us a quart jar of Jell-O to put in the water at the spring. What a thrill it was when she told us to go get the Jell-O. All the water for the house had to be carried up a steep hill from the spring. In the summer we ate wild raspberries and in the fall we ate pawpaw, which we called the wild bananas. After my daddy got his own home he said he would never eat another piece of chicken or an egg again. And he never did.

My mother would tell my brother and me to go out to the chicken yard to watch for the chicken hawks in the sky. We weren't to let them come down to carry the chickens away. We spent many hours out there waving our arms. I think Mother really just wanted us out from under foot.

During our time at the farm my mother was mixing up whitewash to paint around the tree trunks. My mother later said I must have thought it was food and swallowed some. So I had my first experience with a country doctor, who told my mother that I might not live, but I fooled him. My second experience of a county doctor was more enjoyable. It was in the form of a journal that was written by another country doctor about home births. My great-grandmother was one of the babies listed. He wrote that it was an uneventful birth as most were recorded except for one lady he wrote, "She was cantankerous, but she was always cantankerous."

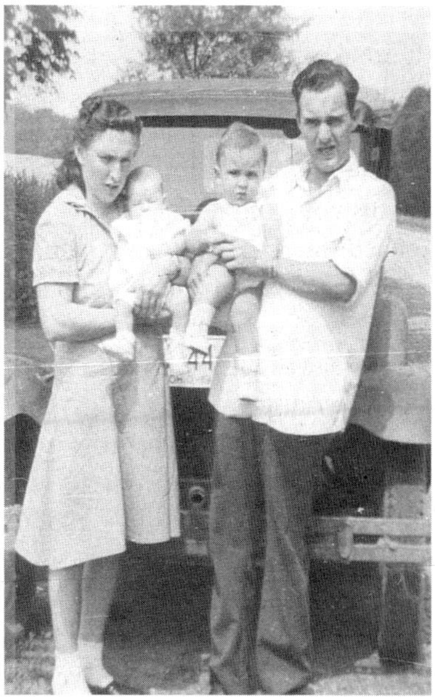

Mother, Isabella Dingus, holding Betty and father, Ernest E., holding Herman in 1942.

Grandpa had the last family owned licensed, running, Ford Model T in Noble County. He would take us to Batesville a couple of times in the summer to the Red & White grocery store. He would buy us a package of cookies that was like an oblong thick graham type cookie with pink and white hard icing on them. They really weren't very tasty, but we never had cookies at the farm so it was a real treat.

When I was about nine years old we moved to Batesville. My parents had bought their first home, which was nothing more then a shack. It had four rooms heated with two coal stoves. It was very hard to control how hot the stoves would get. If you weren't careful the stove and the stovepipe would become cherry red from too much heat and that was very scary wondering if the log house would catch fire, but luckily it never did. Once we had a small round kerosene heater. It ran out of fuel one night while we were all in bed. It filled the house with a thick black soot. When we woke the next morning all you could see was the whites of our eyes. We had a great laugh seeing each other covered with soot, but what a terrible mess we had to clean up.

In the early 1930s Daddy had what was called a Delco Power Plant. It was a sort of generator that ran on gasoline. It provided us with the first electricity in the area. It had enough power to light a few light bulbs and people would come to our house just to marvel at seeing the lights. Later when electricity came to the area Daddy would wire homes in the area, and some of the house are still using that original wiring.

When we still lived at the farm Grandma gave me her most prize possession, which she had had since she was a little girl. It was a china doll with a beautiful hand-painted face and homemade clothes. I loved the doll so much, but one day I dropped the doll and her head shattered into pieces on the ground. I cried and cried. My mom gathered up the pieces and glued them back together. I still have my Grandma Becky's doll and it has a special spot in my bedroom for 62 years now and when I am gone it will be passed down to my niece Becky, who was named after Grandma.

My most scary event that happened to me while living at the farm was when I was six years old and they brought my baby sister home for the first time after Mom had given birth. I couldn't wait to see her and rushed to see what was in the blanket. The poor thing looked exactly like my daddy and I really thought they had shrunk him somehow. But she grew out of looking like Daddy and is today a pretty woman.

When I was sixteen and my youngest brother was fourteen Mom told me to drive the family car down to an older relative's house to see if he was all right. His name was Maywood Dingus and he would always drive his team of horses and wagon to Batesville two or three times a month to visit us. We noticed that Maywood had not been around for a few weeks. As we were getting in the car to go check on Maywood my grandpa said very seriously, "I want to tell you two something. Maywood might have died and you know he has that old dog that lives in the house with him and if the dog got hungry enough he might have ate some of him so don't be surprised at what you might find." Grandpa really put the fear in me and my brother but off we went to see what we could find. We drove as far as we could then had to get out and walk the rest of the way. We were almost to his house, scared to death and yelling as loud as we could, over the hill came three huge Army transport planes flying very low and very loud. Our hearts nearly stopped because we had never seen anything like them before. The whole day was very scary but thank goodness Maywood came outside to see what all the commotion was about. We were so happy to see him and his old dog was still alive and kicking.

I never knew my grandparents on my mother's side of the family as well till I was a little older. Mom told us her parents were very poor when she was growing up. They had first lived in a little house on a creek named Rock River just over the county line in Belmont County. Mom told me many times of how when her mom would go to work in the fields she would sit her in an opening in a nearby rock that had been made by years of wind and weather to hold a baby just perfectly. She used the rock as a sort of crib so she could keep an eye on her as she worked.

One time when Mom was about five years old Grandma left her at the house to babysit her two younger sisters. Grandma always got about 25 chicks in the spring to raise for eggs and meat. On this day while grandma worked in the fields Mom and her two sisters decided to help their mom out. They decided it would be helpful to kill the chickens and clean them like they had seen their mom do time and again. When Grandma got back from the fields and saw what the girls had done she was devastated because she could not afford to buy more chicks to raise.

Mom often said that things were so bad back then that Grandma made Grandpa a big coat with big deep pockets inside so that he could go to the local stores and steal food so the family wouldn't go hungry. Years later he made moonshine whiskey to sell to buy food for the family.

Many people back then had a hard life. Some more than others just like today only worse because they had no help from welfare food stamps and charitable organizations.

We always looked forward to Christmastime around our house. My brothers would trap animals for fur and sell the hide to buy Christmas gifts for the family, and Mom would make a few gifts. One year an old man who lived out the ridge from us said that he would give us a Christmas tree if we would come out and get it. So my brother Herman was all excited to go and get it. Someone had given us an old horse a year or so before so Herman hitched up the old horse to a sled that he made and off we went. The horse was old and didn't move very fast anymore but he pulled us along. But when we went down the first little hill the sled my brother had made broke from the harness and ran into the back legs of the horse and he fell, sitting up on the front of the sled. We kids were getting off the sled a lot faster then we got on, but with some ingenuity and determination from my brother we were soon on our way again and brought the tree home without any further mishaps.

I really loved going to Sunday school as a child. We had a wonderful teacher, named Martha Eagon. She was so good to us. She even had her sons drive all of us kids to Pittsburgh, Pennsylvania. One of her sons lived there and his family fixed lunch for us. Then they took us to the airport to see the airplanes taking off and landing. Mom gave me a few cents to spend on the trip. I spent it on a big beautiful swirled sucker. I took it home so everyone in the family could see it, then I broke it up into pieces to share with everyone.

Mrs. Eagon made Sunday school so much fun for me. She told us Bible stories; we colored pictures and played games. I just loved being there with her. Then came the part I didn't like. Someone would open up the big door and lead us into the main church service. There was the preacher man talking to the congregation about things that I didn't understand. Then he would give all the adults a cracker and some juice to drink and there I sat hungry, wondering why I didn't get anything to eat. I didn't understand they were having communion until a couple of years later.

I also loved going to grade school, mostly to be with friends and play at recess. We would bring our dolls to school. We played marbles or jacks and had games like Red Rover. That game was not my favorite because it hurt my hands and arms so much when the other kids would come running to break through the line.

High school was another fond memory of mine. I did my lessons, but once again I was there more to enjoy my friends and recess. We had an old record player and we would dance at recess to our favorite Elvis songs and whoever else had a good song at the time.

For a school of our small size we had a wonderful home economics room. We had four nice complete kitchens set up and they looked so modern compared to what we had at home. One kitchen even had a garbage disposal, which caused a lot of fun one day in the school at our teacher, Mrs. Stevens' expense. At our first period class she had us make up cookies. We didn't have enough time to get them baked so she was going to take them out of the ovens when they were done. At our second period class we were going to clean up the kitchens from the cookie baking. We had all decided we would sneak a cookie or two. There was no cookies to be found. I was running the garbage disposal when it started making a strange noise. I thought, "Oh, I hope I didn't break it." I looked down into the disposal and saw something that looked like black round rubber things. My first thought was I would be in trouble for breaking it but on further inspection we saw that it was the burnt cookies. Mrs. Stevens had forgotten to take them out of the ovens and had burnt them black. Of course the word spread through our little school of our teacher's mistake. All the boys came into the room to tease her. They teased her so much that they brought her to tears.

She may not have been the best cookie maker, but she was a wonderful sewing teacher. We had rows of very modern sewing machines that came with a table and little stool. She had the patience of a saint with us girls and showed us how to make very nice clothes. And if you didn't do it right she would have you take out the stitches and do it all over again till we did get it right.

One day we had some excitement when an airplane came flying up the valley straight for the windows of our home economics room. We were all seated at our sewing machines when we saw the small plane coming at us. We were all screaming and running for cover when at the last second the pilot pulled the plane up and it buzzed just over the schoolhouse roof, much to our relief. We never knew who or why the pilot did such a thing but if he was trying to scare us he accomplished his mission.

During my high school years I worked at what was called The Beaver Valley White Egg farm. They supplied eggs to many of the area grocery stores. We sorted and packed the eggs and whatever else needed done at such a business. I made pretty good money for a teenager at that time I had money to go places with friends. We went to dances everywhere in our area. We went to movies, we would go to a restaurant in nearby Barnesville to hang out and drink Cokes, and I had enough money to buy gas so we could go cruising. On Sunday afternoons we would drive miles around one small city block in Barnesville. We just went around and around. We thought it was a lot of fun and it really was back in those good old days.

Sometimes a bunch of us kids would get together and go to Seneca Lake at night to swim and have fun. A couple of the boys would go out somewhere and steal a few chickens and we would have chicken to eat. One night one of the boys went and stole his own mother's chickens. We decided he didn't have the hang of being a chicken thief if he had to steal his own mother's chickens. I didn't go to the lake at night as much as some of the kids because one night I was ate up by mosquitoes. I had well over one hundred bites on my body.

We had a swimming hole in Beaver Creek at Batesville. For a while I was always at the back of the line of kids as we went down the path to the water, then one day I was first. I could not believe my eyes when I saw how many snakes dove in the water. I never went swimming in Beaver (snake) Creek again.

In the early 1950s we would go ice skating on Seneca Lake on the weekends. People came from everywhere to skate. The ice was so thick they even drove cars on it to pull skaters holding on to a rope. I had a pair of new white ice skates. A lot of the people that came didn't have skates; they would just run and go sliding across the ice. Forty years later I was telling my two sisters that I wish I would have kept my beautiful skates. My sister Bonnie said, "If you want them I will give them to you. They have been hanging in my building for years." I told my brother John about getting my skates back. He laughed and said he had worn them to skate at the old slew at Batesville many times. I couldn't believe he wore my beautiful white skates. I told him he must have looked really strange with girls white skates on. I now have my skates to hang up at Christmas. They hold many wonderful memories for me. Although they are worn looking now I still see them as they were when they were new.

In the 1950s they made paper dresses for a short while. I bought one. They were just sort of plain and you threw them away after wearing them.

My mom used to make many crepe paper dresses for me and my friends to wear in the Quaker City Folk Festival parade. Crepe paper in the '40s and '50s was made in beautiful colors. Today at the festival's Kiddie Parade the local newspaper, *The Daily Jeffersonian*, sponsors a special category in her honor. She was known for making costumes out of newspapers for us as it was very inexpensive. Today they even make all kinds of floats for the newspaper category.

We were so lucky to have a drive-in theater in the '50s and '60s. It was out in the country near Barnesville.

On Saturday night cars would be backed up down the road to get in. It took time to get all the cars in as they would look inside our cars at times and make you open your trunk to make sure we didn't have anyone hiding in there to get in without paying. Then a man would be out in the drive-in lot watching to see if anyone got out of the trunk. There was two movies every might with a break in between. You could stay in the car to watch the commercials and eat and drink what you brought yourself, or you could go down to the concession building to buy a snack and pop. The kids called it the confession building

They would have a buck night once a week. It would cost one dollar for a carload of all the people that could get in the car. So once my uncle who lived nearby brought his farm tractor and wagon loaded with as many people that he could haul. He paid his dollar and drove his tractor in and parked. That was a fun night.

In the late '40s and '50s the kids around Batesville did a lot of what we called Halleveing, some now call it halloweening but it was a time to go out and cause mischief in the days leading up to Halloween. The favorite thing to do was to walk though town and upset outhouses. My dad and grandpa got tired of this every year because they would have to work to set the little building back up and repair whatever was damaged. The last time they rebuilt it, they built it very strong. They set big posts in the ground so this upsetting would not happen again. Once we saw a group of high school kids coming out the road, marching bravely toward our house to upset our privy. They didn't even try to sneak onto our property to upset the building like our group always did when we were out doing the same thing to other people. When the kids got there, Dad and Grandpa were hiding just down the bank behind the outhouse with their guns and a lot of shells to shoot in the air. Just when they touched the building the guns started firing into the air. Kids were running everywhere. We heard one of the girls scream as she ran straight through the neighbor's manure piles and lost her shoe. What a crazy night that was, and the kids never tried to upset our outhouse again. But one night a bunch of kids put a neighbor lady's farm wagon on the roof of her barn. I imagine she was shocked when she saw that the next morning. When my mom would take us kids trick or treating she would take a long stick with her and anyone who didn't treat the kids she would attach soap to the end of the stick and soap their upstairs windows.

When we first moved to town there would be hobos or a truckload of gypsies go trough town and Mom always made us kids hide because it was thought that they would steal kids and take them with them. We also had men known as hucksters come to our house in trucks loaded with dishes, pots and pans, food of all sorts and various other treasures. They would have a bell they would ring and we would go out and look at all the stuff, but hardly ever had money to buy anything.

I remember that there was lots of home demonstration parties that we had in our houses. We loved them. It was things like Stanley products, Tupperware, Fuller Brush and Watkins. They gave away door prizes that were just little gifts. We would play little games on paper and the lady having the party would make some homemade goodies to eat. We seemed to find a little money to go to those parties but was never able to buy much.

My mother made many quilts. Some she would quilt and others she would knot. I would sit under the quilting frame and push the needle and yarn back up to make it faster and easier for her to knot them.

One time when my future husband, Willie, and I were dating, my brother John, who was always pulling practical jokes on people, really pulled one over on us. Willie and I were going to St. Clairsville to eat at an Elby's Big Boy restaurant. It was a trip of about 30 miles each way. When Willie came to the door to pick me up, John snuck out to Willie's car and put our old dirty yard dog on the floor of the back seat. The dog had been out running around that day and had run across some old dead animal so he stunk to high heaven. When we got in the car we didn't see the old dog but we sure could smell him. After we had gone about five miles Willie got to thinking that it was me that smelled and I thought it was him and things were starting to get very uncomfortable between us. Willie finally pulled the car to the side of the road and said, "I can't take this any longer," and started trying to find the smell, and there sat our old Jake, on the back seat just as big as you please riding along with us to Elby's. Needless to say we took old Jake back home. John denied knowing anything about the incident for years, insisting that the dog must have got into the car while one of us had the door open.

I was a senior in high school when I first met Willie. He was four years older than I was. I don't remember seeing him until one Sunday afternoon when I was walking down the street with my girlfriends and he was sitting in his turquoise and white '56 Chevy talking with some of his friends. He was a very cool '50s guy, and I was a 17 year old teenager dressed in '50s clothes. I was wearing a flared skirt, ruffled Cancan slip, sweater, Bobbie socks, and black and white saddle shoes. While he was talking I stupidly jumped up on the right fender of his car and said, "Take me for a ride," never thinking he ever would. But he fired up the car and I still thought he was kidding like I was, but he was serious. As the car started off I grabbed the right fender where it stuck out a little over the headlight and grabbed the big hood ornament with my left hand and planted my heels firmly on the big chrome bumper and held on for dear life. We were gone like greased lightning when we went over the hump in the road in front of the Legion Hall. I didn't know how far we were going but I knew I couldn't hang on much longer as we raced through the lower end of town. He finally pulled into the grade school yard and I fainted dead away as I tried to get off the car and fell into the grass. At that time he was probably as scared as I was. As we thought back on the incident years later we asked ourselves what we were thinking because both of our lives could have been ruined, but when you're young and looking for love and excitement there's no telling what we might do; but can you believe that was the start of a relationship that lasted through almost 40 wonderful years of marriage.

Although my life has not been as exciting as many people, my life has been rich with the simple pleasures that go along with living in these foothills of Appalachia in southeastern Ohio. Family, hard work, the beauty of the countryside and the wonderful family and neighbors who live here. I wouldn't have missed it for anything.

The Recess Kiss

by Helen E. Heston of Kimbolton, Ohio
born in 1933

Our community had a one-room school about a mile from our home. When I was five years old, my dad went to the teacher and asked if he could send me to school with my brother Dwight who was three years older than me. He told him when he got all the fall work done he would take me out of school and take care of me. When that time came I cried and didn't want to quit going to school. My dad went to the teacher and he told my dad why not leave her in school, she is top in her class and is not causing any trouble at all. I got my own way and got to stay in school. I graduated at sixteen years old. I tell people that I got smarter than the teacher and they had to let me graduate. Not true, but I get a laugh out of them.

During my eight years at grade school, I had a great time. I got my first kiss at school. A boy, during recess, just jumped up and kissed me. The teacher saw it and made us both stay in the next recess. I didn't think I should of stayed in. I didn't ask him to kiss me. He only went one year at the school. He lived with his mother and stepdad who ran a little country store.

The boy brought a box of rice to school and several of us helped him throw rice during school. The teacher never walked to the back of the school but I am sure she saw what was going on and took a stroll back where we sat. We all stayed in at recess and swept the floor. That wasn't as much fun as throwing it was.

When Dwight got older he took the job of being the janitor. In the winter, his job was to get there early and get the potbelly stove started to get the school warm before the kids got there. He had to walk because we didn't have a car. It was dark when he arrived at the school. He got the fire started and took the coal bucket out to the coal house to get a bucket of coal. At the coal house he thought someone had put a pile of stuff at the door to scare him. So he took the shovel and hit it and a man said, "Hold it, I move on." It was a tramp who had slept there to try and keep warm. I'm sure my brother's hair stood on end. He was really scared.

One cold day our neighbors both had cars and had children in school, so when it was really cold, they would take turns taking us all to school and bring us home. This day there was a mixup; each thought the other was going to pick us up. It was so cold that when we got to our house we couldn't open the door because our hands wouldn't work. My dad got us inside and got pans of water to put our hands and feet in to thaw them out. Our neighbor came to see where the children were. They felt so bad about what happened.

I thank God I got to go to a one-room school. I got a good education and made a lot of friends and memories.

The schoolhouse was sold and people made it into a house. Several years later, my brother bought the house and lived there for several years.

Those that are still living wish we had a picture of the schoolhouse but none of us could afford a camera.

We all had a lot of great memories and love to see those of us who are still around.

Spelling the Word "Apple"

by Sara Rose Moore of Barnesville, Ohio
born in 1920

I was born and grew up in a beautiful little town, Woodsfield, Ohio, county seat of Monroe County about eighteen miles from Ohio River—part of county called Switzerland of Ohio. As I was born 1920, by age nine 1929 depression was on.

I went all eight grades at old Woodsfield School—been torn down for years—a new one there. I attended all grades in one room for two grades two years in each one first to second grades and on.

If I remember correctly, I was in the second grade and we were having a spelling list. I couldn't spell the word apple. I puked in my spelling book and teacher caught me. She sent me to the cloak room. That is where all the coats were hung. I probably had to stand in there for a while. When it was okay to come back to my grade, I remember keeping my head down on desk rest of school. I never was more embarrassed and miserable in my life. After that I have always been a good speller. Today, if I'm not sure the correct spelling, I still look in the dictionary to see the correct way. Never told my parents this till I growed up. I expect I would have received a bit of a spanking.

Mother was a beautiful sewer, so my sisters and me always wore dresses she made. Were pretty and in style of what was back then. We always had what we called our good dresses and good shoes and wore to church and other doings. Always thrilled when we got a store-bought dress, as that didn't happen often. When I was nine, one of my aunts bought me a dress that cost 98 cents and I always called it my 98 cents dress. Now, the print for dresses wasn't color fast so it'd fade. Mother would soak it in salt water to set the color, rinse them, hang up to dry. It'd shrink quite a bit too. Then I'd be ready for the dress making. I wore black satin bloomers and petticoats she made—she'd embroidery orange on petticoats—they looked like Halloween, but I wore them as that was what I had to wear. Believe me, no one dressed fancy. I have worn patched long stockings to school which I hated. Re-soled soles on my shoes my dad did. He had all the tools to do it with. He did a neat job but at school in fourth grade when I had to walk to the blackboard those new leather soles would squeak. Boy, I hated that squeak. It was cheaper for Dad to do that than buy a new pair. I did get new shoes and some were pretty when Dad took me he'd let me have the pretty ones. Now, with Mother, it'd be the practical ones, so I guess back then kids worked their parents. Ha!

Sara Moore wearing a velvet dress her mother made.

As I would have been nine, I remember Monroe County Bank failed—heard the grown ups talk about people losing all their savings. Later years was W. P.A. and C. C. Camp this was for boys. They'd get paid some and part went to all their families to help out. So my dad, as a truck driver, had work on a lot of the W. P. A. Works. Was always glad when Dad was working. Everything was quite different. He wasn't abusive, but I could sense the difference. He had worries I didn't quite understand till I growed up.

Now back then a lot of storekeepers would carry their customers when they couldn't pay. One nice one did for my dad so in later years. Dad paid it all off. Told the store keeper his family would have gone hungry if he hadn't done this. I never went hungry and always had warm winter clothes. But a dear little friend of mine told me in later years if my mom and my grandma hadn't given her breakfast, she'd gone to school hungry. I heard Mother saying to her, "Come in and have some pancakes." Mother knew that little girl hadn't had any breakfast.

I think the most is her sour milk corn cakes and oh, those buckwheat cakes shemade from a starter she'd make. Her molasses syrup she made for them. We'd call it sugar. Always had cookies. I remember the big sugar cookies with pink icing and raisin filled ones I'd scoop out the raisins, didn't like them. Her homemade bread and vegetable soup she always made when we were sick. Wonder how these mothers cooked and didn't have everything to cook with. Good cooks I'd call them.

Taffy pulling after my older sister made it. Farm family playing dominoes and all eating popcorn Mother would pop. Cards—Rook and Flinch. Radio in the evenings, picnics, swimming, sled rides with sisters. I had a good family life. My older sister said a few years back we were all poor but happy.

My mother told this by hers. During the Civil War news wouldn't be heard by some. She said that I suppose her grandparents saw these battles fought in the sky so knew the outcome. Had never heard anyone else tell this till back in good ole days. Imagine a lady told the same thing. Strange things happen that is hard to understand let alone believe it but I believe it.

On my dad's side, when my grandpa was just a baby, he had an older brother, Frank, about eighteen, a Union soldier encampment at Marietta—his parents in a roadwagon took him to Marietta and his soldier brother named him Abraham Lincoln. Grandpa always went by name Abe.

Grandpa's House

by Dr. Marilyn S. Murphree of Zanesville, Ohio

I remember Grandpa's house: a two story brick house out in the country. When I was growing up, he was a very old, white-haired man with a white beard. I was told that when he was younger, he had red hair and that he played the fiddle for square dances. I was only nine years old when he died, and I don't remember anything he ever said to me. I don't remember Grandpa ever talking about anything. In fact, I don't remember the sound of his voice, or ever talking with Grandpa. But what I remember was the house and the chair he always sat in. Sitting in his lap every time we visited, I squirmed to get down. I think I was afraid of this old man with white hair and a beard.

His chair was located in the corner of the dining room; a huge room with a very long table. The floor was worn down, unvarnished wood that always had a clean, scrubbed look. Grandpa's chair was by a window, and under the window was an old treadle sewing machine with a pot of red geraniums sitting on it.

My aunts were very particular housekeepers. There

never was a time when there was clutter in their house. It was rather bare and plain as I remember it. There was a library in the parlor, but we never got to go in there very often. There were books, but I never saw magazines or stacks of junk mail anywhere in the house. Their motto was, "A place for everything and everything in its place."

Although the house was rather plain—a no frills house—there were nice crisp white curtains at all the windows, and there were some nice Victorian figurines on the mantle. The house had a clean, scrubbed, fresh smell. Even though there were cats and dogs on the farm, they didn't dare come into the house. No cats sleeping on a pillow in Grandpa's chair. No dogs curled up by the many fireplaces throughout the house.

My aunts were good cooks and they always served bountiful meals. I remember a big family dinner one time when all of the cousins were there, along with my aunts and uncle. There was an abundance of food on the table, including homemade baked beans. We soon discovered, to our dismay, that there were bugs in the beans and no one had noticed until the beans were on our plates.

The house has long ago been torn down. It was a nice, solid house with free gas heat from gas wells on the farm. No high energy bills to pay during the winter, and no water and sewage bills, either. They didn't even have running water.

What did I learn from Grandpa's house? How has it shaped me over the years? Grandpa's house was a peaceful house, not chaotic in any way. I don't ever remember hearing a harsh word spoken there. It was a clean house where possessions were cared for, and food was always plentiful, but never wasted. There were some of the finer things of life—such as the figurines on the mantle, the library books in the parlor, and the marble topped stand.

Looking back, I don't think they had a stressful life in spite of a lack of some conveniences that we take for granted. Grandpa, my aunts and uncle, and my Dad are all gone now; but I remember Grandpa's house in the country, and the people who helped shape me into the person I am today.

The Engineer and the Tootsie Rolls

by Harriette E. McBride Orr of Cambridge, Ohio
born in 1939

I grew up on a farm located on U.S. Route 40 two miles west of Cambridge, Ohio. Our house and barn were located between the old National Road (West Pike) on the north and Route 40 on the south. The Baltimore and Ohio Railroad ran east and west to the south of the highway. In the '50s our barnyard was sold for the Fairdale Truck Stop and was the site of my father James McBride's truck repair garage.

My grandpa R. Price Lanning had a potato patch between the highway and the railroad. Grandpa would load up my little red wagon with the tools he would need to work the garden and off we would go. Blondie the cocker spaniel and Yippie the beagle and usually a calico cat that hopped on Grandpa's shoulders as we passed the last fence post.

I held tight to Grandpa's hand as we crossed the highway for I was only three or four years old. Needless to say there was not the heavy traffic on U.S. 40 that we experience today. Mother must have had great confidence that Grandpa would get us all across safely.

Once down in the garden the animals were off to hunt critters. I usually took along my favorite doll Nancy Jeanne or Teddy Bear for my entertainment. I had a hoe and rake but soon tired of "working."

I loved the trains and we were very close to the tracks. You could hear the trains coming miles down the tracks for they blew their whistles to warn people they were coming to the crossing. Some of my first words were, "Here it comes and there it goes."

This was the early forties, World War II time, and many of the passenger trains would be full of soldiers in uniform. Train cars would be loaded with jeeps, tanks, big guns and army supplies headed for the East Coast and overseas. There were passenger trains, freight trains, cattle cars, tankers, boxcars, flatbeds all pulled by huge steam engines.

The man running the train was called an engineer and it seemed they all dressed alike in blue denim bib overalls, blue stripped billed caps with a gathered crown, denim jackets with red kerchiefs tied at their neck, and great gloves whose large cuff came up over the wrist to midarm.

One day when we were in the patch the train came to a stop right at our crossing (Frazier's Crossing); there was a lot of steam and hissing and clanging and banging as the train slowly screeched to a halt.

The engineer hollered down at Grandpa and they exchanged hellos. Then low and behold he climbed down from the great steam engine and came over to talk with us. I was awestruck.

This was almost like God coming down from Heaven. I hid behind Grandpa and peeked around staring up at this great man who ran the train. He tried real hard to get me to talk to him but I was shy and would not say a word. "Cat got your tongue?" He then said, "I bet you like candy." Of course I answered with a nod of my head. He climbed the ladder into the cab of the engine and came lumbering back down with what he called chocolate "Tootsie Rolls" for Grandpa and me. The gift of candy forced me to say a polite thank you. The only words I spoke the whole time.

I had never seen a Tootsie Roll but chocolate was my favorite food so I knew I was going to like this. I began taking off the paper wrapper which was the color of chocolate with white letters or maybe it was the other way around. Inside was another white wax paper wrapping that held one of the biggest pieces of chocolate I had ever seen. It was a huge round loglike bar, divided into sections by indentations and resting on a cardboard tray. Because it was chocolate I had thought the candy would be soft. It was tough and proved to be nougatlike candy.

The engineer laughed as I tried to get a bite sized piece into my mouth. Grandpa finally had to help me by pulling and twisting the log until a piece pulled loose. The candy became softer as it melted in my mouth and the great taste of chocolate hit my taste buds. It was wonderful.

After that I always looked for "my engineer" when ever the trains passed by. He always gave us a special whistle and a wave. I never to this day eat a Tootsie Roll that I don't think about that great engineer and my first Tootsie Roll.

During the '40s there was always something of interest happening on Route 40. We had a great water well with a hand pump.

My Grandpa Price Lanning was known for witching water wells. He would find wells by holding a forked peach limb and walking along until the limb turned in his hands pointing down towards the water. It would turn so hard that it caused the bark to peel off the limb as it found a vein of water underground. People came from all over and hired my grandpa to find them wells.

Our well was one of the best around, fresh and sweet. It came from deep in the ground so it was cool even in the heat of summer. Motorists would stop to get a cool drink and sometimes fill their car radiators that often overheated in the summer.

There were many hobos that walked or rode the rails. They would stop and rest under the shade of our large maple trees and drink water from the well and freshen up by pumping water into their hats and pouring it over their head. Mother would usually fix them a sandwich. If she didn't have leftovers to use she had peanut butter and her homemade jam and home canned fruit. Some offered to do work to pay for their meals. Grandpa was always on the lookout for markers the hobos would leave to let the next ones coming down the road know they could get a meal at our house. The highway workers often ate their lunches in our yard and used the privy and filled their water cans before starting back to work.

Some of my favorite people to travel the road were the caravans of gypsies. They traveled in large open cars with everything they had packed onto or in the vehicles. Kids and dogs hung out all over. They would stop up in front of our house on the National Pike and seek out my grandpa, asking for permission to camp on our bottomland next to Crooked Creek. They would pull off the side of the road and pitch their tents. They used the creek for their water needs, drinking and bathing. They would spend several days camped there catching wild game and roving chickens to roast over the open fire. The kids would walk up the road past our house on their way to the little store at the top of Fairdale Drive.

Mr. and Mrs. John Parry ran a tiny store out of the front room of their house. They sold Cambridge Dairy milk, ice cream bars, bottled soda pop, Kool Aide, Omar bread, candy bars, chewing gum, penny candy and potato chips in five cent bags. The gypsy children would walk up the road to the store passing in front of our house. I hid behind a tree and watched them wishing that I could be a gypsy and wear dangly earrings and travel with them to see the USA. They were always made to look so glamorous in the movies, dancing around the fire to the beat of the tambourine. I thought this should be the life for me.

My mother, Leota Lanning McBride, was raised in Kipling, Ohio and when the gypsy caravans came there they traveled in wagons pulled by horses with bells jingling. Mother often told me this story.

When she was very small the older kids told her stories about the gypsies and how you had to watch out for them for they were known to steal and how one day they had tried to steal Archie Symes right from in front of his house. Lucky for him the other boys heard his cries for help and pulled him free of the wagon.

One very hot day Leota was playing with her dolls when she heard the gypsy wagons coming up the street. This story was fresh in her mind. Off she went running into the house crying, "Gypsies! Gypsies!" Up the stairs into Grandma Lanning's bed, diving head first between her feather ticks. Grandma was ninety years older than Leota and not very strong. She tried tugging and pulling with all her might but for the life of her she could not get Leota out of the bed. Leota's cries were becoming muffled and Grandma knew she was going to suffocate. She cried out, "Please someone help me; this child is dying." Harriette Lanning, Leota's mother, and the hired girl came running up the stairs and between the two of them they got Leota out of the bed and got her revived with a pitcher of water that was on the nightstand.

Needless to say my mother did not have the same feelings toward gypsies that I had. Her story about gypsies did not change my mind. I carried a suppressed desire to run off with the gypsies into my adulthood. A love to travel and beautiful dangly earrings are my only tie to the gypsy life but the strains of a gypsy violin can still stir my heart.

At our house and in every other household, Monday was wash day. It was a big production. First all of the water used for washing clothes had to be pumped by hand outside at the water well. It was pumped into galvanized buckets and carried into the house. My Dad, James Mc Bride, always did this for Mother.

The reservoir on the back of the kitchen cookstove was filled the night before so it would be hot by morning. A large tub of water in which the whites would be soaked was added to the stovetop.

The washer would be filled with the hot water on Monday morning. Mother used home made bars of lye soap or Fels-Naptha bars which she shaved into the washer. There they dissolved making suds. After the war she used only Oxydol to get her clothes white and spot free. Her washer was a Sears Kenmore electric wringer washer, her pride and joy. If your hair or fingers got caught in the wringers it had a sudden release mechanism that kept the fingers from being smashed or you from being snatched bald. It was important that clothes were folded with the buttons inside so that they would not break or pop off as they were fed through the wringer.

Harriet McBride Orr pumping water at the well, source of water for the farm and house, which her grandfather, R. Price Lanning, witched.

Mother took great pride in her white whites and spotless clothes. The first items placed into the washer were the dish towels, these were made from feed sacks, then came the bed sheets, pillowcases, white shirts, Aunt Margaret Lanning's white cotton nurse's uniforms and then the underwear. While they were washing mother made up a pan of "Argo" starch. The starch was a powderlike substance that was mixed with boiling water until it was smooth and lump free. Bluing was added to this. It came in bars divided into squares like Hershey's chocolate. It was the same kind of bluing that was used by women to whiten their hair, thus the term "blue haired ladies." Mother always had to make a special batch of very stiff starch for Aunt Margaret's nurse's caps. They were dipped into the starch and lay to dry on waxed paper.

After all the whites were washed the light colors were put into the machine and then the darks. By then the water had cooled down and would not fade the colors. Dads work clothes and greasy coveralls were washed last. They had been soaking in a tub of warm soapy water. Dad had the cleanest mechanics clothes around. No spots on him when he started out for the day.

When the clothes left the washer they were wrung into a warm bath of rinse water. The next rinse was cold and from there they were wrung into an oil cloth lined bushel basket. They were ready to hang to dry or they were placed into the starch bucket and wrung through the wringer again. The rinse tubs were two large galvanized tubs sitting on a large board that was held up by sawhorses. Mother felt really modernized when after the War she got a new set of rinse tubs from Montgomery Ward that were on wheels and fastened together with drains at the bottom of each tub. The water was caught in buckets and used to scrub the back porch where the washing took place, the steps down to the yard and the summer kitchen, a room off the porch where the washer was stored.

While the clothes washed, Mother went down to the yard to prepare the clothesline. It had to be wiped clean with a soapy rag and Clorox and then dried so that the line would not mark the clothes.

The whites were hung on the line first with wood clothes pins. Things were hung just so because people driving by would see them. If they were hung in a sloppy manner what would they think about who lived there. After the lines were full, the clothesline props were put into place raising the clothes high off the ground. A prop was a long narrow board with two nails in the end. You placed the wire between the nails and lifted the line, raising the clothes high off the ground. Whites were hung in the sun and colors in the shade so they would not fade. Delicates were hung on the porch on a wood clothes rack. In the winter when it was too cold to wash on the porch this was all done in the kitchen. Clothes were hung to dry on ropes strung around the kitchen or on racks placed around the potbellied stove.

I remember eating supper with a pair of Grandpa's red flannel underwear hanging in the doorway.

After Mother emptied the wash water and scrubbed the porch she always got us the same Monday supper. It was my favorite meal, meat loaf, baked potatoes with the jackets on and baked corn and bread custard for dessert.

Mother spent the rest of the day taking down the dry clothes and bringing them into the house. After supper she would sprinkle them down using her hand and water from a pan. She then rolled them up and placed them in the basket to be ironed on Tuesday. In the bottom of the basket went the dark clothes and then the whites were placed on the top and covered with the bedsheets, underwear, hankies, and socks. Yes, these were ironed also; it made them softer. I learned to iron by practicing on dish towels, hankies and underwear. Mother's ironing board was a "Rid Gid" ironing board. Very sturdy with iron legs and a wood top covered with an ironing board pad and a heavy cloth cover made to fit with a drawstring. The electric iron was very heavy and I dropped it a few times on my fingers and hand. I soon learned to be very careful with the iron. Mother always said, "The way you iron your clothes is the way you will look in public." Everything had to be just so. The starched items took more time. You had to be careful not to get the iron too hot so that it would scorch the clothes but hot enough to dry them. This was not a steam iron. That is why you had to sprinkle the clothes. Mother always covered the floor with newspaper when she started to iron so that the sheets and especially the nurse's uniforms would not touch the dirty floor. The nurse's hats were dampened and ironed between white rags so that they would not scorch.

Starched shirts were ironed the collar first, back and front, and then the yolk in the back of the shirt and then the sleeves and cuffs, the facings on the inside of the front of the shirt and then you finished the body of the shirt and creased the collar. It could not vary, that was just the way you did it. Mother loved to iron and her favorite thing was embroidery work. She did a lot of cutout work and loved to starch and iron these things. Ironing them wrong side up on a terry towel made the needlework stand out. Mother's approach to the ironing board was that of an artist. She loved making things look beautiful and she did this with her iron every week.

Blackouts, Fence Walkers and Courthouse Climbers

by Richard E. Patterson of Zanesville, Ohio
born in 1938

My memories of World War II are few. I remember my dad telling me that he was old enough that he probably would not be called. Hearing my parents talk about the war scared me. One evening the air raid sirens sounded. This was a practice "blackout" for the real thing should that ever happen. So during this practice exercise all house lights were to be turned off. The street lights were turned off as well. At this particular time, Mother was baking cookies in a gas stove. She used a flashlight to see when the cookies were done baking. There was no attack and I'm sure I enjoyed the cookies.

An area in front of the courthouse, fenced with wire, was used to collect donated metal for the war effort. I remember seeing lots of pots and pans that people had donated and dropped over the fence. I remember people using the ration stamps and "pressed cardboard" coins to buy certain foods.

The sad time was hearing about my school friends' fathers and uncles that were killed in the war. The happy time was hearing that the war had ended and knowing my uncle came safely home. The happy celebration that went on in our town filled the downtown streets with people to watch the victory parade that included many military personnel and equipment, as well as the bands and other groups that were part of the celebration.

When I was three years old and shortly after my sister was born, my mother had difficulty holding my baby sister. She went to the doctor and was diagnosed with lateral sclerosis (Lou Gehrig's disease). I'll relate to this again later. Six years later we moved from Zanesville, Ohio to Rokeby Lock, Ohio, a small town my maternal grandparents helped develop by subdividing their farm. We moved into a small four room house next door to them. This proved to be a different style of living for us. We heated with a small oil stove in the living room and a coal stove in the kitchen which my mother and dad cooked on. There was no indoor plumbing, which meant that we went to the outhouse out back. Then at night, we had the chamber pots under the beds that saved a lonely trip to the outhouse at night. We had a hand pump for water just outside the back door. Cold linoleum floors with small throw rugs on them made for cold feet most of the time. Occasionally we ate at my grandparents' house. During the summer, potatoes and other vegetables came right from the garden, cooked, and served for us to eat. Any leftovers were put in a bucket with water and then carried out to the hogpens to "slop" the hogs. The hogs made that food sound good all over again as they smacked their lips while slurping the food. I use to hang around the barn when my grandpa and two of my uncles would milk the cows. I tried milking but never learned it very well. But for some strange reason the hoe handle fit my hands so I helped with others hoeing the large field of potatoes.

When Grandma would ask if I wanted milk to drink, I would say, "Yes, but I wanted the milk in bottles, not the cows milk." Everyone would tell me it's all the same. It all comes from the cows. But they couldn't convince me.

Our house was located directly across the highway from the lock tender's house. We watched many boats go through the locks while the lock tender pushed a long handle attached to a gear, that as he walked around it, it would open or close the lock gates. The water flowing over the dam created a low roar which we initially worried about the noise keeping us awake, but instead, it became one of the best "sleeping pills" before there were sleeping pills.

Every day at a certain time my sister and I would listen for that special whistle sound from across the river. It was the colorful two or three car train called the "Doodle Bug." It traveled from Zanesville to Marietta and back, I believe, twice a day. One car carried freight and mail and a second carried passengers. People could flag the Doodle Bug to pick them up just as one would flag a bus to stop.

My grandparents had the battery operated crank telephone that one would crank the long or short rings to the person they wanted to call. The phone was on a party line and people would listen in from time to time.

Another piece of furniture my grandparents had was the hand crank record player. I wasn't allowed to crank it up but had to have one of the adults crank it. It wasn't played that often but when I heard it I would come and watch and listen to it.

One day my dad showed me something he made as a child. Using white tissue paper, he would make a hot air balloon about five feet high. He would bend coat hangers into a circle, then adding two more across the circle forming an "x." He inserted the two wires through a paraffin soaked ball of string so that the ball of string would be at the two wire intersect. With my uncles holding the paper balloon in an inflated position, my dad lit the ball of paraffin. Soon the balloon was filled with hot air and began to rise. They let it go free and it flew for a few hundred feet before hitting some wires that collapsed the balloon, catching it on fire and falling to the ground. My dad said this is why it's against the law to make and fly them, because they are a great fire hazard.

In the 1940s, it was big news that traveled on the hand cranked telephone, that another farm had received electricity for the houses. It was some time later that electricity was extended to the barns and other outbuildings, replacing kerosene lanterns. The houses in Rokeby Lock had electricity but not the outbuildings. I can still remember the "aroma" of the kerosene lanterns, that many did not care for.

Our family lived in Rokeby Lock for only one year. We moved back to Zanesville and lived one block from the fairgrounds, but more importantly for my dad, we lived within walking distance from his place of work. The house was a nice two-story framed house with three bedrooms and a bathroom upstairs.

It was during the next several years that my mother became worse and was unable to walk. My dad had only an eighth grade education but was blessed with a mechanical mind. He was a maintenance supervisor at the former Line Material Company. It became difficult to take mother up and down the stairs each day. Using mostly scrap materials, my dad built a two person hydraulic elevator in our house that went from the kitchen to the upstairs bathroom. The design and operation was basic and worked great. It would not have a chance with today's codes and restrictions. This was for my mother's convenience and served its purpose well.

Four years later, when I was thirteen, my mother died. But while she lived my dad saw to it that she would go with us whenever possible. One such time was when "Holiday on Ice" came to Columbus, Ohio at the state fairgrounds arena. We went as a family and my dad parked the car at the front of the arena and went in and bought tickets. He came back and carried my mother in his arms to her seat. Before joining us he parked the car. Following the show, the process for getting my mother to the car was reversed. We never had a wheelchair. After the passing of my mother, my dad renovated the house again by removing the elevator and restoring the bathroom and kitchen to their original conditions.

While in grade school, we played marbles during recess. I always carried a few marbles in a bag along with my favorite shooters ready to play. After school we would play in the alley by drawing a circle in the cinders. I never learned to shoot marbles using the knuckle of my thumb like my friends could do. So I seemed to be on the losing end many times. Once in a while I was able to shoot my opponent's favorite marble out of the circle, adding it to my collection of marbles.

Living near the fairgrounds, two of my friends and I spent a lot of time using this as our playground. One of our challenges was to walk the fence around the half mile race track without falling. After many attempts, a day came when the three of us accomplished our goal on both the inside low fence and the outside high fence. We considered this "mile walk" a "record fence walk" since we never heard of anyone else doing this and the fences are now no longer there. We did have to get down at the gate openings.

Eight or nine of us neighborhood boys went camping in the woods on the far side of the fairgrounds. We spent two nights and most of three days. Part of two days was spent just hauling camping gear in and out of the camp site. This was a time before plastic containers or anything convenient to carry liquids, especially on a campout. Just about all the boys had at least one army backpack bought at the local Army-Navy store. Our pup tents were purchased there as well. We used the backpacks to carry fifteen quart mason jars of water to the camp site. So after two or three trips we had all of the "gear" at the camp site.

Our "refrigerator" was a sulfur stream where we set the jars of water to keep them cool. Some of us were Boy Scouts and practiced some of what we learned as Scouts, such as proper cleanup after breaking camp for the hike home.

On Saturdays during school and during the summer weeks, I would go to the Zanesville Country Club's caddy shack. I knew nothing about golf. I didn't understand the game or the purpose for the different clubs. But I knew I could earn a few dollars as a caddy. There were three classes of caddies, "A," "B," and "C," with "C" earning the beginners pay and "A" earning the experienced pay. I caddied for a couple of years and never moved above the "C" grade caddy.

I also was a pinsetter at a bowling alley. This was an exciting experience, learning to hold your feet and arms so a pin wouldn't bounce up and bloody your nose. I remember watching bowling on TV and hearing the announcement of the automatic pinsetter that could reset the pins back in the position they were initially and then reset them properly for the next frame.

The street where I lived was divided with a narrow park in the center. A pastime for me and a couple of friends was to cut the cover off of a battered golf ball and unwind the inner rubber string winding and stretch it across the street and tie it to a tree on either side. Sometimes we put a tissue on it that gave the appearance of hanging in midair. We wanted to see what people's reaction would be driving down the street. Traffic was scarce on this street. At that time there was less than one car per family. But it was worth the wait to see them slow or stop as the "rubber band" stretched across their windshield and then break. We would retie it and wait for the next victim. Having little or nothing in our families, the imagination was and is a great tool to have.

As a sophomore, I attended Lash High School located downtown. This was the last year for this school to be used as a high school. Lunchtime was a half hour and staggered so only half of the school would flood the downtown restaurants, 5 & 10 cent stores and the drugstores at one time. My friend Jerry and I would run four blocks to the YMCA cafeteria to beat the crowd. We most always had meat, mashed potatoes, a vegetable and coffee—all for just under a dollar. With dessert it was around $1.15. We would finish eating and have about fifteen minutes left, so we could roam the streets. We would venture into the county courthouse and roam around, riding the elevator to the second floor. Elevators back then had operators to run them. We noticed the operator in the courthouse elevator took a lunch break about the time we arrived.

One day we decided to take the elevator to the third floor, which was used as a storeroom for old files. The third floor was unfinished and dimly lit. We weren't interested in these items but to continue climbing up past the clock and on up to the very top, which we did. The last section to the top was on a ladder. We took turns climbing the ladder and lifting the hatch and stick our heads out to look around Zanesville. We accomplished this self tour without being caught, returning down the elevator before the operator returned. The down side to this adventure was that we were afraid to tell anyone about it!

Twelve years or so prior to our courthouse venture, there was advertised in the newspaper that a husband and wife team would perform on the top of the courthouse. They would do so on a platform 24 inches in diameter. The newspaper had a wide lined circle 24 inches in diameter so people could lay it on the floor and imagine trying to perform on it. The other thing was that they were performing on roller skates! The platform was on a pole ten feet or so above the top of the courthouse. My dad took us to see this performance. I recall the sidewalks and streets being crammed with people there to watch them, but don't remember much of their performance other than the man holding his wife by a foot and a hand and slowly rotating on his skates on this small platform.

Another courthouse feat that I barely remember was a man from Coshocton, Ohio. He called himself "Mad Man Jacobs the flagpole sitter." He offered to come to Zanesville to climb the front of the Muskingum County Courthouse. I learned later it was to help raise money for a charity. Once again my father took us to town one evening to watch him climb the wall of the courthouse. And again the streets were jammed with people. After climbing to the top, Jacobs asked how much money had been taken in for his climb. He stated that that wasn't enough so he climbed it a second time.

Past events advanced us to today's world and the wonders of the future.

Sharing on Paper

by Ellen Schlimm of Strasburg, Ohio
born in 1929

My letter will probably be different as I haven't actually sat down and put on paper the things in my life that all add up to make a full, blessed life. I have shared with my children, grandchildren, friends and many times when the occasion arose, so I will try to share on paper. I remember mostly what my parents told me how they met and I will go on from there.

My dad was one of eight children, the oldest from English/German parents. He, at a young age (12), worked beside his father in a coal mine under ground. He would turn his wage over to his mother. He grew up loved but very busy as he had seven siblings younger. As he grew up he married very young to a young lady. They divorced. Even back then that happened. When I became old enough to understand, my mother told me Daddy's story about what happened. Daddy was a private person about his past, but sometimes he would sit and talk, telling me he went on the rebound.

He hoboed to Saint Louis, Missouri. He would say he hopped a train and would be sure to say, "Ellen, There is a difference between a hobo and a bum. A hobo will work for his food and a bum won't." So he made it to Missouri by doing that and went to a rooming house where my mother lived with three siblings and her mother, my grandmother. He fell in love with her and married her then moved back to Ohio, as Daddy was from here.

My mother had polio at the age of seven with an affliction of one leg, so she walked with a crutch. What a wonderful mother she was and how she loved my daddy. Daddy was nine years older than her. She was 19 when they married. They rented homes and Daddy found work in coal mines. They had first a daughter, stillborn, then my brother Bill in 1917, sister, Dorothy, in 1922, brother Art in 1927, me in 1929 and a stillborn son, Jerry, in 1938.

Ellen with kittens; brother, Art, in center; brother, Bach, right, Bill and "cousins."

We mostly lived on farms after I was old enough to start remembering. Before that it was told to me as I said earlier. I have often thought of what that put my grandmother through seeing my mother move 500 miles away, leaving in the cars we had back then, Model Ts, and with a man they didn't really know. But my mother loved him and, talk about faith in God, that was it. Because of their choices, my life was and is.

Back to the rented farms, which sometimes where on the shares. Me and my brother closest to me, Art, would help Daddy. We had livestock, so that meant cows to milk, hay to mow and bring to the barn for winter, gathering apples and peaches from our trees, picking blackberries, which as a family we all worked together. It didn't stop my mother. She was inside the house preparing for the fruit (fruit jars to wash). Berries, we would bring for her. Then we all would help. We had bins in the basement for potatoes, one for apples, as the shelves lined with canned vegetables from our large garden.

We had our own milk which we would process to have our own butter which I would go to the Dennison Dairy with my dad with metal milk cans to sell part of our milk. That was before the milk trucks gathered it up. I always enjoyed going to the dairy as Daddy would get us a five cent cone. They were large. He had held down a full time job at Blue Shaft and later Number Seven Coal Company in Midvale, Ohio.

My mother washed on the washboard and hung clothes on the line to dry. I would help bring the clothes out and in, even in cold weather. My memories are bringing the frozen clothes inside. My mother ironed, heated irons on a coal cook stove and everything was ironed to perfection and put in the drawers that way.

At this date they had electricity in towns, but we were poor-rented and still had oil lamps in several houses we lived. But it was a fact we were happy. We didn't have or had even heard of a TV then and had a battery radio that Daddy loved to listen to Amos and Andy and Boxing on, Joe Louis. We had popcorn, apples to eat as our evening treat and bed early to keep warm upstairs with a lot of comforters, homemade quilts my grandmother mailed to us from Missouri. My mother, for her enjoyment, would write to them and anxiously look for the letters they sent to her.

We had a piano also, which she played and sang. Taught me and my brother Art the words of many songs. She enjoyed and loved that we could harmonize those songs from the time we were seven and eight years old and would sing at special times at our one-room school and for fun at home.

My older sister, Dorothy, helped Mother with the house work. Art and I did the tasks outside when Daddy was working at the coal mine. My older brother Bill was in poor health, didn't help very much, but sat around and played his guitar that he had a God given talent for and played without a teacher or music notes, but that was enjoyment for him. The rest of us knew he couldn't carry the responsibility of helping us much.

My daddy's side grandparents passed away, but aunts, uncles, cousins loved to come and visit our farm and thought of us probably as poor, but not really. We had everything, parents that loved each other and us.

They are all gone now but me. I lost Brother Art September 10, 2008 after a full life. He was married 62 years and had five children.

I was married very young. My first daughter, Lila Kay, passed away at the age of ten months. Then I was blessed with three sons. I wasn't as fortunate as my parents and my brother Art to share my life with one marriage. We divorced after 21 years of marriage, but God gave me a wonderful family. One son is a minister. I remarried to a wonderful man (37 years) with a son and a daughter that I considered as my own that we raised into adults. My second husband passed away in 2004 on Christmas Day, so I am widowed.

I can look back over the years and see where God had his hand on my daddy to let him go to Saint Louis, Missouri to meet my mother, come back here a lot of rough times for them, but happy times. And to work in my life through a lot of people to bring me to the place in my life where I am now, 80 years old, healthy, trying to do all His will. And a story to write and could have written much more, but I am new at this.

The Castor Oil Martyr

by Marjorie G. Milligan of West Lafayette, Ohio
born in 1919

My story takes place in the Depression days. I came from a poor family in Coshocton County, Ohio. There were seven of us kids, of which I am the oldest. I am 89 years old. My mother had us within 15 years and we are all still living. The baby of the family is 74 years old. We had the best Mommy.

When we all got the summer flu (or back then it was called "the complaint"), it was castor oil she used to get us all better. There was a big stump in our back yard close to the porch. Mom would fix 6 1/4 cups full of hot black coffee and put one big tablespoon of castor oil on top of it. It looked like an egg, floating in the cup. The reason for the six cups was my baby sister was too young. She was taking Castoria.

We were all sitting on the back steps, waiting to drink our cups. All of my siblings were crying and did not want to drink it. I felt so sorry for them that I quietly went and downed all six cups. They all cried some more and thought I'd die. Well, I didn't, just got a little sick.

The good news was the castor oil was all gone and the bottle was empty. We never had to face that again, at least I didn't.

Being the oldest, I was the first gone from home.

Editor's note: we believe the author's parents were Brice and Verna Scherer Dreher.

Chickens, Tramps, and Navy Tattoos

by Phyllis Smyth Stocker of Gnadenhutten, Ohio
born in 1931

Chickens—we always had chickens when I was little. We had them for meat and eggs. We never sold any.

My dad bought new peeps in the spring. Rhode Island Reds. We called the babies pee pees. Along with them came a quart jar with dark colored water for them.

My mother usually killed an old hen for Sunday dinner. We had a stump behind the chicken coop. It had two spikes about two inches apart on the top. The hen's neck was placed between the spikes and *whack*! One fast blow with a hatchet.

After it hung on the clothesline to bleed, she dipped it in a bucket of boiling water. It was then plucked of all the feathers (my brother and I helped), then she singed the hair off over a burner of the gas range. Terrible smell.

If by chance there were eggs inside the chicken, we had homemade noodles. Nothing wasted.

Everyone in our neighborhood had an outhouse. I had a banty rooster as a pet. It fell down the hole in the outhouse, and I cried. My dad got it out, cleaned it, and I loved it just the same.

We had a small radio on a stand and loved radio programs. My favorites were Mr. Keene—Tracer of Lost Persons, The FBI in Peace and War, and especially The Inner Sanctum, complete with an opening that sounded like a spooky, squeaky door.

One night, just as the door was opening, the lights went out. My brother took one giant leap and landed right in Dad's lap. So funny. We usually had a big pan of popcorn made with bacon drippings. Delicious.

We had a coal furnace in our house. In the winter, my mother or Dad would get up early and fire the furnace. We only had registers on the first floor. The bedrooms were so cold that you could see your breath in the morning. I spent a lot of time standing on the register in the kitchen.

When my four children were small, I owned a Dexter double tub washing machine, a wringer type. I loved it, and it got my clothes so clean. But—when I was trying to hurry, sometimes the clothes got tangled in the wringer. I would have to take it apart, untangle the mess, and put it back together again. My third son told me he was ten years old before he knew the brand wasn't a bastard.

My grandfather visited once in a while. We weren't close. He always changed my radio programs to the news. No one ever complained, but he was not my favorite visitor.

My dad developed scarlet fever. At the time, it was customary to be quarantined. No one came in, and we weren't allowed out. It lasted two or three weeks, I think. There was a sign nailed to our front door that said "Quarantined, Scarlet Fever." My dad was blood red, and later, his face peeled like an onion. My mother's family brought us sacks of food and left them on the front porch.

We always had a big garden. I helped by picking off tomato worms and killing them and by putting dust on the potatoes to kill the bugs. I also helped weed the garden. Not my favorite job.

My friends and I loved paper dolls. We had boxes of them. We also cut them out of the Sears catalogs.

Homeless—that was not a word you heard when I was young. My mother never turned away anyone who was hungry. None of our neighbors ever did. We called them tramps. They usually came through the town on freight trains. They usually asked for a bite to eat. Usually, it was a piece of bread and butter and a cup of coffee. It wasn't much, but they always thanked her and offered to work. That was the Depression.

My brother joined the Navy when he was seventeen. Just out of high school. When he came home, he sported two large tattoos. One was a Destroyer (his ship), the USS Cotton. The other—a large eagle with USN on it.

Both on his forearms.

You would have thought he did something terrible. My mother had a royal fit. Cried and yelled. It was terrible. I thought the tattoos were kind of special.

Babe Only Batted Once

by Robert E. Avon of Dover, Ohio
born in 1922

It was announced that the YMCA had tickets to the Indians game in Cleveland and any boy who wanted to go could get a ticket at the Fairgrounds. On that day, my dad walked with me to the fairgrounds. There were flatbed, semi-trucks that you could ride on. There was also a school bus from Midvale; you could ride for 50 cents. Dad said Cousin Max and I should ride the bus, although we wanted to ride the trucks.

We left for Cleveland and had to stop several times to get water for the radiator. We arrived on time and there were boys waiting for spare tickets. We sat in the left field bleachers. This was the last year that Babe Ruth played for the New York Yankees so that was very special to us. He only batted once and played one inning. He was replaced by George Selkirk. We enjoyed the game and the trip home was uneventful.

Glen Francis, Bob West, and I got into my 1934 Chevrolet one Saturday morning to go see Jerry Francis, who was in business school in Columbus. We wanted to go to the Ohio State game with Jerry, but he had to study, so we went by ourselves. We saw the Ohio State/Missouri game. Ohio State won 7 to O. This was the first game Paul Brown coached at Ohio State.

On September 29, 1933, I went to the County Fair to see an exhibition game between the Indians and the county All Stars. Back then, we got two afternoons off for the fair and we got in free. I arrived at the ball field, in the center of the racetrack. The teams were warming up and no one was sitting on the All Stars' bench. So I sat down with an older gentleman in a suit. I didn't know who it was, but I later found out it was Cy Young. He wasn't as famous then. But he was an ex-major-leaguer, so he was well known. I don't remember much about the game, but Cy Young pitched for the all stars and Walter Johnson pitched for Cleveland, each for one inning. It was great. I got to see some of the Indian star players up close.

I used to go to the Basketball Games at the Welty Gym. There was a four-foot wall around the court. There were steps from the court up to the top walk. That is where the visiting team sat. I liked to sit under the visiting team at the corner of the steps, on the top of the four-foot wall.

Once we played Massillon and Paul Brown sat on the top walk. Therefore, I was under Paul Brown during that game. Massillon won. That year, Massillon beat both New Philadelphia and Newark, who played for the State Championship.

Rex, the Snake Dog and River Skinny Dipping

by Judith A. Rockwell of Mount Perry, Ohio
born 1940

In the fifties, we lived on a farm in Morgan County. I was number six of seven children.

We had a black and white border collie named Rex. He was a great dog with a unique quality: he hated snakes and when he met one, they died instantly. He would grab them in the middle and shake them to death.

My mom also hated snakes and whenever she saw one, she would yell for Rex and he came to her rescue. The funniest time I can remember is when she was in the chicken house washing windows. She came flying out the door, the pan of water came first, and she was screaming for Rex. Again, Rex came to her rescue.

One time, our grandpa, Mom's father, was visiting. We were all in the yard talking under a pear tree and a blacksnake hung down out of the tree over Grandpa's head. Mom told Rex to get the snake and he jumped up, grabbed the snake, and it was soon history.

Mom never worried about us kids as long as Rex was with us. And we spent a lot of time in the woods, swinging from grapevines, etc. Even did some skinny dipping in the neighbor's creek.

Judy Rockwell and younger brother, Butch.

We were a close knit family. Never had much money growing up, but had a lot of love. I was the first of the seven to finish high school and beyond. I became a registered nurse and worked for 32 years. My older sister, Marge, should have been the nurse, 'cause she was the one who nursed us when something happened 'cause Mom couldn't deal with the blood or injuries.

When I was in the third grade, I got scarlet fever and I was quarantined in at my grandparents' house for two weeks and still my younger brother, Butch, got it.

My dad was a hard worker, a carpenter and a farmer. My oldest brother, Don, was in the Navy in Japan when my youngest brother was born. There is a 20 year span between the two. I had two other brothers who served, one in the Army and one in the Navy. My older brothers told Mom, after they were grown, of times when they were younger, of riding on the Muskingum River, naked on railroad ties, and of course she could not believe her boys would do such a thing.

I once cut my leg on a piece of broken glass sticking up through the ice while skating on a creek. I never got stitches and to this day have nasty looking scars.

Lima Shovel and Coshocton Girls

by Frederick E. Wendling of Newcomerstown, Ohio
born 1934

I've had a lot of good days. I'm 74 years old and I was born on a small farm in Dover, Ohio on May Ninth, 1934. But the down-home story close to my heart is at the age of twenty-six.

I stripped coal in Coshocton County for several years on Number Six. At this time, 1960, fuel for equipment was fifteen cents per gallon, and the coal price at the mine was two dollars and twenty-five cents per ton loaded. We paid the State fifty dollars cash bond. The good old farmer got six to fifteen cents a ton royalty and the local workers around three to four dollars per hour.

We had one operator of the 1201 Lima Shovel, and he chewed Mail Pouch. And in the wintertime he wore a coonskin hat and boy, could he uncover coal.

Our company worked two ten-hour shifts, seven days a week. We loved the outdoors and all the strange noises at night. Since I owned the mine I'd go at night and sit in the truck and watch Curvey swing the big 1201 Lima Shovel.

Yes, we sold coal to the local Coshocton Coal Company, which they picked up at the mine location and always paid us on Friday.

So to sum this up, Friday nights was the club night in Coshocton. A few beers and food, and there was always a good old Coshocton girl to date.

Ah, what a life.

The Flood of 1950

by Linda L. Sims of Crooksville, Ohio
born in 1940

Our family lived in a little village called Crooksville, Ohio, Perry County, southeastern part of the state.

This all happened in 1950 during the big flood. We lived on South Buckeye Street, and I was ten years old at the time this story began.

It had rained for three days and nights, with no sign of letting up. Moxahala Creek went through Rosefarm, south of Crooksville, and also Roseville, Ohio, north of our little village.

My dad built our home when he came from World War II in 1945. Our home was in the southern end of Buckeye Street and a little higher than most. Still the water kept getting higher, so we went to a neighbor's home. Their home was on still higher ground, so we went where our family would be safe.

My dad decided to go back to the house to shut off the electric to help prevent fire. He went in the back door, down the steps to the north wall, shut the electric off, turned, went back up the steps, and before he could get out the back door, the north wall caved in. The water rose within one foot of the ceiling of the basement. The weight of the water and a concrete bridge had hit against the outside.

My dad was saved. I think he had a guardian angel, maybe two or three were with him.

Dad had just made me a playroom on the northeast corner of the basement. This was my playroom for the wooden cradle, highchair, and table and chairs he had made me for Christmas in "1949." My dolls, dishes, and playroom were gone.

I cried because I lost all my playthings, but I had a more precious gift, my dad until 1973, when he passed away. We never forget our parents, the greatest friends we have here on earth.

He was fifty-eight years young when he passed, a good Christian man. His name, Wayne S. Whitehouse. I'm his second daughter, Linda (Whitehouse) Sims, still live in our little village of Crooksville. My husband Herbert and I have raised our three children, Scott, Erin, and Erik.

The flood devastated a lot of families in those three areas. We were very lucky!

The Lamp Made From an Altar

by Laura Kirkbride of Nashport, Ohio
born in 1922

I was born in 1922 on October 31, which is Halloween. My grandsons say it is their favorite day, and they tease me about needing a new broom. I am from a large family, five sisters and two brothers. We were always close and looked out for each other. We had lots of good times together.

We went to a one-room school, and to say it was interesting would be putting it mildly. Seems we were able to get away with lots of things behind the teacher's back. One was shooting paper wads, and another was eating popcorn out of a bag we had in our desk until the teacher caught us, and we were given a lecture. I loved going to school. Many of my happiest memories are of my school days.

We also attended church in a little country church. The church is still standing, but the altar and pews were sold at auction last summer. I was fortunate enough to buy one of the pews, and later, a good friend of mine, who had bought the altar, had a lamp made from it and gave it to me for Christmas. I feel so lucky to have both of these treasured items from my childhood.

My brothers were both hunters and trappers, and I loved to go hunting with them. Squirrel hunts was my favorite, but rabbit hunts was fun too.

There was no radio or TV, so we found our own entertainment, such as getting together with our friends and neighbors and going for long walks in the country. We would walk for miles and enjoyed every moment of it. Another thing we would do was swing on dried grapevines until the vines broke, and we would fall and get bruised up, but we never tell our parents we did that, as they knew about how dangerous they could be.

I could write pages about my childhood memories, and I enjoy living them over again in memory.

Twelve Loads and Ten Loaves

by Mary Lou Miller of Dover, Ohio

born in 1944

The ten of us were raised on a 100 acre farm outside of Winfield, a very small town near Dover, Ohio. The farm was a half mile from the road. We would walk the half mile lane to catch the bus to Winfield School (now the Winfield Methodist Church), Dover High or Dover St. Joseph High School.

Dad, Charles, worked at Shenango Penn Mold in Dover for 42 years. He helped on the farm in the evenings. Mom, Mildred, worked at home. Her week started with Monday, the laundry, with a wringer washer and at least eight loads of clothes. They were all hung out to dry, because there were no dryers at that time. If it rained, somehow, she managed to hang them in the basement on temporary lines. She ironed a lot and used the mangle on the rest. The girls had the chore of ironing their own blouses. Friday was another wash day, usually 12 loads.

She baked 10 loaves of bread, plus cupcakes, coffee cakes, cookies, pies and flounders (cut slabs of bread when it raised and then fried).

Kuemerle family: Top row, left to right: Patricia, Vickie, Larry, Tom, Nancy. Bottom row: Carolyn, Charles, Jr., Charlotte, Mary Lou, Judy.

The rest of her time was spent getting us, the ten, up for school or work and making lunches to go. Supper was at all times, starting about 4:30 to 6:30, till everyone got home from work, school, wrestling practice, band practice, bowling, etc. When supper was over, two of the girls did dishes while the boys did the barn work. We had our own milk, beef, chickens and garden items. Mom canned everything that she could.

Dad got most of the groceries before he came home from work, the rest were gotten between taking someone to Dover for practice and home.

Our kitchen table sat 12 people, so after supper out came the homework! Mom knew what we each had to do, math, reading, spelling, shorthand and Latin. While some did their homework, others practiced the accordion, tap dancing, clarinet, violin or piano. Mom was very smart and could play the piano and violin. Most nights, it seemed, you went from the sink to the table, then possibly to the television—black and white. We did not get a television until Christmas of 1957. Up till that time, we entertained ourselves on the farm.

During the summer, we had lots of Winfield boys come to the farm. They were usually warned "not to eat at the Kuemerles' because they had enough to feed!" Mom always invited them to eat and they seemed to enjoy it.

Mom made a lot of pancakes for lunch. I know all the boys appreciated her cooking. Someone was always baking. We did not know what "came in a box" meant! We went through 25 pounds of flour, 10 pounds of sugar and 50 pounds of potatoes in two weeks. We used lard for all the shortening. We would butcher a beef in the fall and have meat all year.

Mom kept a diary for most of our growing-up years. She typed her notes on the back of any paper she could find, even our church bulletin. We all love to read the things that happened. We all roll with laughter at what she wrote and wonder how she survived raising the ten of us. When Mom was sick with cancer, we, in turn, kept a diary. When I read the diary, I certainly did not remember all the things that happened. Everyone that came to visit wrote in the book. I recently copied it (about 300 pages) and gave it to the others. We all ten were involved in her care. Mom died in 1993 and Dad died in 1995.

We attended St. Aloysius Catholic Church in Strasburg. Mom would go to early Mass, and then Dad would take us to late Mass and stay for instructions (now called PSR). Dad did not want the younger kids going to Mass and making any noise. That was one thing that really bothered him.

Saturday night was chicken cleaning night. Everyone had a chore to catch the chickens, kill them, pluck them and cut them up. My job was cutting them up. When that was done, we could watch Lawrence Welk. I really enjoyed that because I played the accordion. Sunday Mom usually pan fried the chicken then roasted it. She always made a white cake, with pink sea foam icing. That was her favorite.

I have so many happy memories growing up on the farm. We were never rich, but we had plenty to eat and we always had clean clothes. We grew up to appreciate what we had.

At this point, we are all still living, ranging in age from 66 to 46. All ten of us have been fortunate enough to work. Two are now retired and the rest are still working. We had caring and loving parents and we are so thankful for that. We all agree that we would not be the persons that we are today without our loving and caring parents.

How Zanesville Came to Be

by Leroy Cranz of Zanesville, Ohio
Born 1937

Let's start at the beginning, or as near as possible.

Two rivers came together; from the north, the Muskingum, and from the near west, the Licking. American Indians traveled these rivers and camped in the flat lands where they met.

Immediately after the European settlement, American explorers itched to travel west. And so they came, traveling across the Appalachians, following animal and Indian trails. They were attracted to the land at the juncture of the two rivers.

One of the early searchers blazed a trail by cutting and marking the trees as they went west. This became known as the Zane's Trace. It was led by one of the earliest settlers from Wheeling, West Virginia, Ebenezer Zane, although, it was not yet "west," but still part of Virginia. He brought his brother, Jonathan, a seasoned frontier explorer and Ebenezer's shoemaker son-in-law, John McIntire. They were complimented by an Indian guide and several men to mark the trail.

Immediately they saw the need for a ferry to cross the rivers and carry the stream of explorers west. Thus, John McIntire began the design for the town called Westbourne, but the postmaster in Washington, charged with sending the mail west, used the name of the trail marker, Ebenezer Zane. And so it became Zanesville.

By 1796 settlers had built a group of cabins to house the travelers and the ferrymen. By 1813 the need for a bridge across the two rivers brought forth the "Y" bridge. And so it was that a town was built from the McIntire plans and became a major crossroads for travel east and west as well as north and south. The early use of the river system gave rise to the steamboat traffic from Zanesville down the Ohio to the Mississippi.

Zanesville became Ohio's capital in 1810 and a major staging area for parts west; with brickyards, steel mills, newspapers, hotels and gardens. So, from its founding in 1797 and through the 1800's, a major city grew and it is that story we plan to tell here!

The Horse Thief and Potato Pitcher

by Norma Jean Borojevich of Uhrichsville, Ohio
born in 1932

My friend of at least sixty-nine years. I get on the telephone and start laughing at each other about the times we shared together while growing up. We still enjoy each other's company and comments, although we live in separate states. She in Michigan, I in Ohio. About six and a half hours apart.

In grade school is when we met. Connie (Wallace) Moore came to my school in second grade, lived a block from me, and we became instant friends.

At the back of my house and the front of Connie's house was an old shack with a small barn boarding a (nag) horse. The owner wasn't home, so Connie decided she would take a ride on the horse bareback. She got on and, holding onto the mane, the horse takes off—me—yelling her name, "Connie, Connie." The horse wouldn't stop. Up the streets it went, across a bridge, and into our town. Me right behind still yelling for them to stop. Finally, a teenage girl, who did ride horses, got the horse Connie was on, and we walked it back to its barn. We say now she would have been hanged for horse stealing if we'd have lived out west.

Another "incident"...we were coming home from a movie and heard this prancing behind us and a large German Shepherd dog jumped on Connie's shoulders, and she began running, yelling, "Ma-ma," which was her grandmother. I jumped on a porch and hid until they were gone. I guess she made it home, 'cause we still chat about that.

My parents sent me to a grocery store (neighborhood) for a sack of potatoes. Of course, we weren't wealthy, didn't have enough money for goodies, but a boy the same age as we were got some groceries and a big ice cream cone. I guess we were jealous—Connie said, "Give me a potato."—took it and pitched it at him, but it missed him. Took the ice cream right off the cone. He saw us, started crying, and said, "I'm going home and get my dog after you guys." Boy did we run.

I missed a lot of school in grade school, 'cause my mom said I was her baby of seven other children, and she would have me sleep in. As I got older, I would tell Connie to come over early—call my name so I could hear her. I'd get up and get ready for school—off we'd go. When I got in seventh grade, I didn't miss a day of school through twelfth grade.

These are a few of my stories Connie and I shared—There were many more. We still enjoy each other's company. Both have been married many years. Connie, fifty-nine years and two children, five grandchildren. Myself, fifty-five years, five children, and twelve grandchildren. Our families all get along and are great friends.

Thank you for letting me share a few of our memories.

P.S. I'm going back in time. I also remember standing in our yards waving at the troop trains going east and west on the Pennsylvania Railroad and slowing down to stop at the Dennison Depot Canteen (also known as Dreamsville, U.S.A.), where young and old ladies fed the troops sandwiches and sweets (rolls, donuts, and cookies) with coffee. This was during World War II.

Connie and I both lived beside the Pennsylvania Railroad. On the other side of the tracks was a small creek, which emptied into the Tuscarawas River, and Connie, some other friends, and I would go to play. A small boat was tied to a tree. We'd get into the boat and pretend we were sailing to all parts of the world. Never a dull moment for us.

After high school, Connie, her boyfriend (husband), and I went fishing at Tappan Lake one Sunday afternoon, and I was the only one that caught a fish.

I could go on and on but want to get this in the mail. Thanking you kindly.

Two Flats Per Trip

by Richard D. West of Zanesville, Ohio
born in 1930

I was born in December 1930. I can remember when I was two, three, four years old, my mom and dad would go to Grandma's and Grandpa's on a weekend about the first of the month. Their farm was in Perry County, New Lexington, Ohio.

Dad had a 1934 or 35 Teroplane car. He would get the car ready to go. We lived in Newark, Ohio about 32 or 34 miles, about an hour drive. He didn't drive fast and before we left, he would strap two spare tires on the front fender, plus the regular spare tire on the rear. Then we would go and sometimes we would use two of the spares before we got back home.

Thank God he worked for Pharis Tire Company. In World War II we had tires, but flats came real easy. Boom!

Paper Wad and Hanky Grab Romance

by Mae Thomas of Wooster, Ohio
born in 1911

I am Mae Thomas and I am from Woodsfield, although my address is Wooster, Ohio for now. I still receive the paper and keep up on the news.

One day there was a blacksnake (which I of course found) in our washhouse, which was an extra room attached to the house made especially for the laundry; it was the same one used for the summer house. The purpose of a summer house used primarily to keep the house clean after we had house cleaned and also we did our canning in the summer house to keep the heat out of the house.

I remember when the neighbors went together and paid to have a private telephone line laid. I was eight years old. There was only one party who could call out but we could all call her. We also could talk among ourselves. We were the first ones to have a phone service.

We had to take a bath on Saturday night. I remember the old blue washtub as if it were yesterday. We had a stovepipe in one room and it was very hot. We all took turns. At our house we all got clean water.

Mae Thomas, age ten.

Fishing with my dad was a highlight. We fished along the water stream and took them home to clean them.

My dad had a deadfall, which was a stone made purposely to use in trapping; it somehow was a one way trap.

We had a man teacher one year. His name was Oliver Dailey; he was the best teacher I ever had but he only taught one year. All the other years I had Faye Railey, who was good also.

If you would ask me how I found my partner I would have to tell you that we had a game of paper wads. The boy who was interested in a girl would sail his paper wad in her direction. She treasured his paper wad.

Also we had the hanky grab in my day and age. We

wore our hankies under our watches. A boy would watch for the chance to swipe our hanky if he was interested in my friendship. At 97 I still have the hanky my boyfriend, later my husband, Royden, had for a keepsake. He always wore it in his suit coat lapel. I still have his suit and it is still in his pocket.

The Literary was the name of the Friday evening gathering. It was at the school and everyone could go. That's where I had my first date.

Separating milk and cream was a big job. Our separator came from Sears; those days you could buy almost everything from Sears, even a complete house to build.

Spring was the time to make new homemade soap. Everyone tried to make the whitest soap. After the butchering was done then came the soap making. We would soak our dirty and stained clothes the night before. We used Oxydol soap only for our special washings. First I remember the wash scrubboard; later we got a wringer washer. It was a Kenmore. It had a double tub.

Evenings were spent playing dominos, checkers and fig mill. We quilted evenings by the lamp. Our regular bedtime was 8:30 to 9:00.

How to Get Out of School With a Snake

by Phil A. Barker of Grand Rapids, Michigan
born in 1926

I remember wearing a sailor cap to school in Detroit, Michigan. The teacher told me to take it off and I refused to do it. *She* did it and I had a garter snake under the cap. I got out of school for a week as I remember.

When I was a little kid, my grandpa lived with us. He had the upstairs bedroom and every morning before school I had to go upstairs and get the chamber pot and bring it downstairs, dump it, rinse it out, and take it back upstairs.

I remember listening to Jack Benny, Red Skeleton, Fibber McGee and Molly on a little radio I had next to the bed.

I never got any spankings in school, but if I misbehaved, I sure caught hell when I got home.

Saturday afternoon baths were for me and I liked them. I had every toy that would float in the tub with me and I stayed in the tub for over an hour.

My mom had an old wringer washer and the motor kept shorting out every little while.

Saturday movies were a must for me and my friends. If it was a good picture, we would stay and see it twice and then catch hell when we got home for being late.

I can just remember the Depression. We were lucky. My dad had a good job, but even with that I can remember having oatmeal for Sunday dinner a few times. I remember my mom making me short pants out of my dad's old suits.

I didn't have any favorite teachers. I never liked school to start with.

I had a little fox terrier when I was a kid and when I went in service in World War II, he didn't know me for several days when I got home.

Tin Skins and Exploding Bottles

by Robert Brokaw of Cambridge, Ohio
born 1933

I was born January 27, 1933. The time period from the late 30's to the 40's. It will include sanitation, pollution, poor living conditions, entertainment, bad economy, and some dumb things I did as a kid.

We lived in a small house in Zanesville that was actually a double garage that was converted into a house. It was heated with a coal stove. It had two small bedrooms, a living room, and a kitchen, with no bathroom. We had no hot water, just cold water in the kitchen. There were six of us that lived there. I had two brothers and a sister that was older than me. It was very crowded.

Money was scarce and wages were low. My dad made 50 cents an hour and kept four kids on his wages.

We didn't eat anything that was expensive. We had plain food such as oatmeal, pancakes, soup, beans, and homemade bread. We never went hungry.

I was very young when we lived there and I didn't have much in the way of toys, but I don't have any bad memories of that time. We were a close family and sometimes I think we lived on love.

My dad was handy and I always thought there wasn't much he couldn't do. He used to half sole our shoes, cut our hair, make our toys, and anything else that needed done.

Mom had an old wringer Maytag washer. In the winter she would string up clotheslines all over the living room. I tried to stay outside on those days because you could hardly sit down without wet clothes in your face.

Garbage was dumped into a metal garbage can without any bags. In warm weather you could smell the garbage truck coming from a block away. The flies were terrible due to the poor sanitation. We had fly paper hung up in the house, but it didn't catch all of them.

We had an icebox and I remember an iceman came around periodically. I used to bum a small chunk of ice from him and thought it was a real treat.

The air was polluted with soot in the winter because just about everyone burned coal. I remember the snow wouldn't stay white very long.

For entertainment we had an old radio. I remember listening to programs like Amos and Andy, Mr. District

Attorney, Life of Riley, Baby Snooks, Fibber McGee and Molly. The sound effects were so good you could almost see what was happening. I remember hearing Joe Lewis fights and President Roosevelt declaring war on Japan. We used to listen to the radio and crack hickory nuts and walnuts that we had gathered and that was about all we did for entertainment.

In 1943 on my tenth birthday we moved to an eight room house on Corwin Avenue, and thought that we were in a palace.

I had a lot of friends there that were around my age.

I had quite a few chores I had to do. We, and just about everyone, had a coal furnace back then. In winter it was my job to clean the ashes from the furnace and pile them in the back by the alley. I also burned trash and helped Mom with the dishes. I still had a lot of time to play with my friends.

We used to play army where some of us were Germans and some Americans. We played marbles, basketball, and baseball; we played touch football with an empty tomato juice can since no one had a football. We called ourselves tin skins.

When it snowed they didn't clear the streets like they do now. Cars had bumpers back then and we would hook on the back of cars with our sleds and they would pull us up to the top of the hill. If you hit a bare spot the sparks would fly, but we didn't let go.

Comic books were the craze back then. I would read mine then look up the other kids and we would trade. That would keep us in plenty of reading material.

I was a caddy at the country club and I rode the bus as far as Harding Road, the end of the line, then I walked to the golf course. I usually made around ten dollars a week by working Sunday, Wednesday and Thursday. Back then ten bucks was a lot of money for a kid.

Things were cheap back then, for example, a pop was a nickel a bottle, also candy bars, chewing gum, and potato chips. I used to go to the Imperial Theater for twelve cents and watch the old cowboy heroes, like Gene Autry, Tom Mix and Hopalong Cassidy.

I finally saved enough money to buy a bicycle. We often pushed our bikes to the top of Ridge Road and coasted back down without hands on the handlebars; you could really fly by the time you reached the bottom.

One warm day in March, my friend and I pushed up to the top of the hill and decided we would follow the road to the end. We ended up on Route 40 and turned the wrong direction thinking we were headed for Zanesville. We got to Hopewell before we realized we had made a mistake. The weather had changed and started snowing. We about froze before we got home.

That was just one of the dumb things I did with my bike. One day I was riding my bike to school on Brieghton Boulevard and was reading a comic book and ran into a parked car. I bent the forks so bad I had to push the bike home with the front wheel turned.

Another time I pushed my bike across a railroad trestle that went over the river. A train started coming and I really had to beat my feet on those ties to get across before I was creamed by a train.

One time we kids decided we would make root beer, so we mixed up some kind of a potion from a recipe. We poured it into some beer bottles and corked them up. I took mine home and put them on shelves in the basement. A couple of nights later we were sitting in the living room and we heard noises similar to gun shots coming from the basement, and lo and behold my root beer was shooting corks out and spewing root beer all over the basement.

Another time we decided to have a talent show. We set up a stage using an old rickety table and made benches from planks and cement blocks. None of us really had any talent but we were all supposed to do something. I was dancing on that old table and it broke. I grabbed the rafters and kept my feet moving and the kids about fell off their bench laughing.

There are too many memories of the good old days for me to list all of them but these are some of my favorites. That old gang of mine was Gene Bryan, Paul Smith, Bill Baughman, Gene Smith, Bill Buzza, Jim Hooper, and Leonard Bready. Someday I would like for us to get together and talk about the fun we had back then.

Bovine Memory at Work

by Robert Groves of Belmont, Ohio
born 1935

My dad told this true story.

Dad worked on a threshing crew in the early 1900's. One time after they had finished threshing a farmer's grain they were moving the threshing machine to another farm. The machine was pulled by a team of two oxen. There had been a recent rain that made the dirt road very slippery.

The team approached a hill on the road and the team slipped and could not complete the climb up the hill. A second team of oxen was brought in, hooked to the threshing machine ahead of the first team, and the four oxen managed to pull the machine up the hill. They moved on to the next farm.

The following year the same team of oxen was pulling the same threshing machine and approached the same hill. There had been no rain, the hill was very dry. The oxen stopped at the same place where they had stopped the previous year and refused to go on. A second team was brought in front of the first team, was NOT hooked to the thresher and the first team proceeded up the hill with no difficulty. They moved to the next farm.

A note from my early years. Our farm had thirteen Jersey cows that supported a family of five. We raised corn, oats, wheat and hay; raised most of our own cows and had time for church, school activities, 4-H clubs and Farm Bureau. I still use the 1951 Farmall M tractor for bush hogging at the home farm.

No Mixes, Hard Work and Muffin

by Margaret Bole of Mt. Perry, Ohio
born in 1912

My name is Margaret Bole and I am 96 and-a-half years old. I have lived around the Zanesville, Ohio area all of my life. I was born in 1912. When I was 10 days old, my mother died of complications from childbirth.

In March 1913 a flood took place that was known as the greatest natural disaster in Ohio history. Zanesville was hit very hard. The Muskingum River at Zanesville crested 27 feet above flood stage and the water was 20 feet deep at several downtown intersections. Only the lamp posts were visible from the famous Y Bridge. Rainfall over Ohio totaled six to eleven inches and no area was spared. The death toll from this flood was 467 and more than 40,000 homes were flooded. I was six months old in March, 1913 and was told by my dad that I was dropped out of a second story window onto a sheet held by two men standing in a boat.

When my mother died, there were six children in our family including me. Two years later my dad married a wonderful lady that had two children. Together they had one child. That made nine children in our family.

Our parents moved to a farm close to Zanesville. My sisters, brothers, and I had to walk one and-a-half miles one way to school each day. I can remember that in extreme cold weather that when we got to school our hands would be so cold that our teacher would heat a pan of water on the coal stove and we would put our hands in the warm water to warm up. On our way home from school, I would get so cold I would cry and my older sister would carry me on her back to get us home.

Nine sisters and brothers. Row one: Carrie, Freda, Thelma, Ann, Margaret, Marie. Row two: Cokie, George, Eddie.

My stepmother made all of our clothes on a treadle sewing machine. She baked our bread and made delicious pies, cookies, and cakes. These were made from scratch. We didn't have mixes back then.

My dad and my stepmom milked cows, churned butter, made cottage cheese and whipped cream. They had a large garden and butchered our own meat. The whole family helped with the preparing of food for the next winter. We bought very little groceries—coffee, tea, sugar, salt, and flour and a few other items. We all had chores to do. Our whole family went to church every Sunday.

I am still in good health and contribute that to all of the hard work I have done in my lifetime, along with faith in God, my family, and my little dog, Muffin (she is my best friend) keep me pushing onward and upward each day. I hope to reach the 100-year mark real soon.

The Teacher's Drawers, the Bumblebee and Glass Eggs

By Joyce Ortt of Kimbolton, Ohio
Born in 1944

One room schoolhouse. Growing up in a one room schoolhouse was really unique. There were grades one through eight. The teacher had to be at her best to teach all these grades. Someone in the neighborhood had to be the janitor, and get to school early to start the wood (coal) burning stove. It seemed like the schoolroom in winter was always cold, even with the pipe red on the stove.

One day our teacher was walking back and forth in front of the room when the elastic gave way on her underwear, and fell to her feet. She just bent over, picked them up, put them in her desk drawer, and kept right on teaching.

Bumblebee in the eye. In 1948, I was four years old. The old house we lived in had lots of areas where varmints and insects lived. One warm day in August, my mom and dad were sitting on the front porch cleaning green beans. I sat there and watched this huge bumblebee come and go. After awhile, I decided to stuff a green bean up the hole where the bee had been entering. When nothing happened, I peeked in to see where he went. Much to my surprise, he decided to come out at the same time. I wound up with a huge black eye after he stung me.

Grandma's hen house. When I was six years old, and my sister Carol was eight years old, we went to visit Grandma several times a month. She lived a long way away, or so I thought, when I was six. In all actuality, she lived in Gnadenhutten. It was a twenty minute drive.

Grandma always wore her silver hair up in a bun in the back. She always made dinner for us. I especially remember her wilted lettuce.

But the one thing I really remember about Grandma was she always told Carol and I, "Don't go near the hen house!"

Now, being six, I really, really liked her glass nesting eggs. So of course the minute Grandma wasn't looking, off we went to visit the hen house and the glass nesting eggs.

How It Was Then

by Bernice Yakley of Sugarcreek, Ohio
born in 1916

The following was written by Bernice Yakley, a former member of the Union Hill Homemakers.

Looking back over the years, I have often thought of how it was then. We walked to our one room school with a potbelly stove in the center of the room. We had no snow days. When it was really cold most of the students kept their coats on. Water was carried daily from a neighbor's house in a two or three gallon bucket by two students. Most schools had two outhouses. Where there was no bus for high school students, the school board allowed 50 cents per day for transportation.

Most rural homes had an outside bake oven built very near the house. This was used in the summertime to bake bread and to dry vegetables and fruits. I loved dried corn.

Every home had a summer kitchen which we moved into in the springtime for cooking and eating. That was to keep the main house comfortable during the day and night.

Wood and coal burning stoves were used for cooking before electric came our way, which was around 1926. Most homes had no bathrooms. Outhouses were very prominent.

How to Wash Clothes

by Margaret Jones of Dover, Ohio
born in 1943

I was born and raised in Dover, Ohio, raised my children here and still live in Dover. Two of my sons are also raising their families in Dover. I had an outstanding childhood which continues to be great as an adult.

Party lines—this was our entertainment on rainy or very cold days. There were five families on the line and we were the only children—there were three of us. It infuriated the other people, which we knew, on our line because we would giggle and make comments while they were talking. My mother pretended not to notice and there were times when I caught her listening. My father was a different story! He thought this pastime was awful.

Wringer washers—I used to sit on the basement steps and watch my mother wash the clothes. We would have wonderful talks during these times. She would use a hose and put water in the washer. She would start with the white clothes, washing them until she thought they were clean, using the wringer to wring out some of the soap and water. Then put them in twin tubs filled with clean water. She would swish them around with her hands and wring them out again using the wringer on the washer. The whites were then ready for the clothesline. Using the same water, she would continue with the colors, finishing with the darks. I was frightened of the wringer because my mother had a story about a girl getting her long hair caught in the wringer. She would push it over to a small drain and using a small hose on the washer, drain it and get the washer cleaned up for the next wash day.

Snippets From Sugarcreek

by Wanda Croft of Sugarcreek, Ohio
born 1941

Claudia, Brenda, Ruth Ann, and I made up the cast, producer and writers of the plays produced in our backyard playhouse. Creativity flowed from our hearts as we designed our outfits of flat paper plate hats, Mom's old dresses and high heels, hung our stage curtains and rehearsed our lines. We sang, danced, cried, and laughed. Yes, the boys from up the street were kind enough to attend at least once. Free productions!

With the production over, the playhouse turned back to a home for our dolls and imaginary friends. They were all well taken care of and put to bed nightly.

Left to right: Ruth Ann, Wanda, Brenda, Tim, Wanda's brother, standing by the playhouse.

Life in the small town of Sugarcreek was simple. When walking down the street of town, all knew where I lived and who were my mom and dad. One could not get lost if you tried.

One day my brother Jim and Ruth Ann were going to walk to Baltic to her grandparents. They walked in the field so as not to get hit by cars. They only got a good start when Mom got the call. Did she know Jim and Ruth Ann were walking along the major highway (two lanes) out of town?

Aunt Elva worked in the Douglas-Mishler IGA. When I wanted to get candy, she simply wrote it on the note at the cash register for Dad to pay at the end of the week.

The Blue Bird soda fountain had coffee cups hanging on wooden pegs belonging to men and women who met each morning. Coffee and news of the morning were shared.

Every Saturday morning a western movie was shown in the community center which now houses the fire station. Jim needed to take me, his younger sister. I got to sit in the front row with all the boys.

Evening neighborhood games were "Hide and Seek," "Kick the Can," "Andy Over," "badminton," "croquet" and story telling while sitting on the big front porch. Often popcorn and grape juice (homemade) was offered to all.

When Mom was not home at end of school there was always Grandpa and Grandma Olinger. They really were not my grandparents, but the greatest neighbors one could have. Grandpa always had stories to tell. He sat on the back porch swing and mooed like a cow. He was a great "Rook" player, always starting his bid with more then I ever could get by the end of the game.

Snippets of the great small town life of Sugarcreek could go on and on. Stop by some day and see how the town has survived.

Linden Avenue and the Movie Star

by Ruth (Harmon) Bowman of Zanesville, Ohio
born in 1933

Here is my account of growing up on Linden Avenue in Zanesville, Ohio during the 1930's, 40's, and early 1950. We lived in the 1000 block of Linden Avenue, which was not unlike many older streets in other towns. The houses on Linden Avenue, when I grew up, were tree-lined and the streets were brick (later they paved them). We lived at 1067 Linden Avenue. My grandmother, Bessie Schenk, owned our home until her death, at which time my mother, Bertha, and father, Forest Harmon, bought it.

I grew up there with my brother, Bob, in the six room, wooden frame house which always seemed in need of paint and repair. Out front, were two of the three linden trees, which the two-mile street had been given its name. Our 1000 block of Linden Avenue was just a notch below middle class in the years before and during the Great Depression, World War II, and the Korean War. There were some retirees and businessmen living there, but most of the men were either in the armed services or blue collar workers in the potteries, tile works, or steel mill.

Our Linden-Avenue neighborhood was special. Our next door neighbor was Ralph Wall, who sold monuments. He lost an arm above the elbow in a newspaper press when he was a young man, but it did not stop him from becoming a top-flight cartoonist. For many years he drew a weekly full-page, Southeastern Ohio Highlights, for both the Columbus and Zanesville newspapers.

In the early 1920's, a young boy lived with his aunt in our Linden Avenue neighborhood and spent many hours playing with my uncles David, Albert, and Earl in the Schenk's backyard. The young man later worked for a short time as a cub reporter for the Zanesville newspaper. Then he left town and several years later, Richard Basehart was starring in movies, such as, "Moby Dick," "Time Limit" and as Admiral Nelson on "Voyage to the Bottom of the Sea."

As a young girl in the early 40's, I remember an incident about my parents, Bertha and Forest Harmon. My grandmother, Bessie Schenk, died in 1943 when I was nine years old. I remember it was right after the Depression, and at the time, there were my parents, an uncle, his two young daughters, my brother Bob, and I, all living in my parents' home. My father was working in a pottery and he wasn't making much money at the time.

My parents bought our groceries at a little store on the corner of LaSalle and Linden Avenues. Charles McCadden owned the grocery. He would allow my parents to buy groceries and charge them. When my father got paid, he would give Charlie McCadden some money to pay our bill. One evening, my mother and Dad wanted to go to a movie but really didn't feel they should spend the money to do so. At that time, the Imperial and the Quimby Theatres would have a weekly drawing called "Bank Night." My mother went to one theater and my father to the other one. When they drew a person's name for the drawing, they would announce the winner in both theaters. They drew my father's name for $350.00! My mother heard it at the Imperial Theatre and they were so excited. When Charlie McCadden heard my father had won the money, he knew he would be paid the next day.

In those days, we had no TV's, so my aunts, uncles, and cousins would come to visit often. My brother, Bob, and I and our cousins would go sled riding and build snowmen. One summer, my cousin took me on her bicycle up North Linden Avenue and we had a picnic up in the woods along the road.

When I was a little girl, my parents, brother, and I would sit in our living room and listen to our radio. My mother would listen to "Stella Dallas" and "Ma Perkins."

On Wednesday evenings, we would all listen to "I Love a Mystery," "The Shadow Knows" and "Mr. District Attorney." Saturday evenings we would listen to "The Hit Parade." After Thanksgiving, Bob and I would listen for Santa Claus to read our letters.

In the summers, my father drove us down to our Grandmother Harmon's farm in Olive Green, Ohio, not far from Caldwell, Ohio. Bob and I would spend two weeks on the farm. Grandma cooked on a coal stove and her phone was one which she cranked to call someone. Outside of her farmhouse, she had what they called a cold cellar which was in the side of a hill. It had a door which she opened and inside this door was a cave-like, cold room where they hung their meat and kept cold milk, butter, etc. My grandfather was older and blind. My grandmother milked cows in order to get milk. There were also chickens and I believe horses on the farm. The only thing we didn't like was the outhouse on the farm. In the summer, there were flies and bees and in the winter it was so cold. On Saturday evenings, we would drive into Caldwell to the square in the middle of the town. There, they were playing music by a country band.

When I started first grade, I went to Lincoln School, which was located on the corner of Euclid and Sheridan Streets. My mother attended that school when she was a little girl. I met my best girlfriend, Pat (Offenbacher) James in the second grade. She also lived on Linden Avenue close to Forest Avenue. We rode bicycles, took piano lessons and went everywhere together. We are still best friends today and we are both 75 years old.

When I still lived at home, my mother had a wringer washer and I would help her do the washing and hang the clothes outside on a clothes line to dry in the backyard.

In 1948, when I was 15 and my brother, Bob, was 13 years old, our father died. He was 48 years old. My mother did a wonderful job raising us until we were old enough to be on our own.

I attended Roosevelt Junior High School and the summer between 9th and 10th grade at Lash High School, I met my first boyfriend. He was a wonderful boy and we dated three years (all through high school) going to all the proms, etc. We broke up in my senior year.

I graduated in 1951. Shortly after, I met my husband, Ed Bowman, whom I had known when I was in junior high school. He worked after school in a grocery store on McIntire Avenue. My girlfriends and I would stop in for ice cream cones every day after school, walking home from Roosevelt Junior High. Shortly after he graduated high school, he went to the Army and served in the Korean conflict. Just before he left for the service, I talked with him and I wrote to him while he was in Korea. We started dating steadily after he returned and were married in October of 1953. We have been married for 55 years and have five wonderful children, six grandchildren, and one baby, great-granddaughter.

My brother, Bob, was a columnist who wrote items of growing up in Zanesville and also wrote weekly columns in the *Advertiser-Tribune* in Tiffin, Ohio, where he lived most of his life after graduating from Lash High School in 1953. He played baseball in Zanesville while he was growing up and right out of high school. In February of 2000, Bob was inducted into the Muskingum Valley Baseball, Old Timers Association's, Hall of Fame, even though he had not played for 46 years. He also became a talented artist.

I have wonderful memories of my childhood and my life in Zanesville, Ohio.

Another Farm Story

By Lisa D. Larey of Royal, Arkansas
Born in 1960

Growing up on a farm near Woodsfield, Ohio in the 1970's was a great life for me. I loved the outdoors and the farm animals. On our farm, females and males alike did the same chores.

I was a strong teenage girl. When challenged to an arm wrestling match, I could beat the older, bigger town boys. Each of them was surprised about it every time.

One event I'll never forget was the challenge of feeding the barnyard hogs. Up to 25 big sows and a boar, restless, whining and slobbering at the gate, anticipated their food. Accurate timing was the key. I would throw three to four ears of corn over the fence, onto the concrete slab about 150 feet away. As the hogs ran for the ears, my sister and I had just enough time to complete the chore. She opened the gate as I slung the sack of ear corn onto my shoulder and ran as fast as I could, often through deep mud, to the concrete slab to empty it before being approached and knocked down by the voracious herd. Sometimes a boot or two would get sucked off in the deep mud resulting in completing the job in socks, which of course added to the challenge.

Another unforgettable time was when our dad had bought a brand new hay elevator. It was on a set of two wheels with bars extending to each end. Because my dad and brothers had not finished assembling it, the conveyor was not inside. With one end resting on the ground, the other inclined upward, and a smooth inside, it resembled a long slide. So, my sister and I began climbing up and sliding down. What fun! Each time climbing up, we felt more daring, getting closer to the top end. At one point, as I slid down and jumped off the bottom end, it began to rise with the weight of my sister at the top end. Mom, watching from a window, ran out just in time to grab the end but to our surprise, it took her up with it. Dangling from the end, she yelled for me to get Dad. However, with my frightened sister moving towards that end, and the weight of our mom, it returned to the ground without anyone getting injured. Following that event, the elevator was reserved for putting up hay.

Ohio During the Depression Years

by Mary Annabell Archer of Cottonwood, Arizona
born in 1923

I was born in April, 1923. So now I am almost 86 years old, but my memory is still good. Just ask my neighbors.

I guess my memory goes back to 1927 or 28, and my most memory of the Depression was that my uncle and aunt lived with us. My aunt took care of my brother and myself. I remember she would open a can of soup and add enough water and seasoning to make it tasty. Along with that, bread and butter and whatever else was available fed six people—four adults and two growing children.

Then in 1932 or 33 my parents were out of work and no money to pay the rent, so we moved 50 miles to live with my father's parents. At that time I attended school in a one-room school house. One of the eighth grade students would come early and build a fire in the stove so that it would be warm for when the other students got there, and to dry off when we walked through snow.

I attended two different one-room schools before we moved to a different place and there we had grades one through four in one room and grades five through eight in another room. My mother drove us to and from school for which she got a small sum of money.

I really don't remember when we got our first radio. I do remember my brother and I hurrying home so we could listen to the Lone Ranger and Tom Mix.

We were on a party line and everyone knew everyone's ring. If you had to go through the central operator you would barely turn the crank, hoping no one but central would hear it. That's the only way you could have privacy on a party line. I have one of those old phones in my house today.

The kerosene lamps were the only lights we had to study by and when we finally got an Aladdin lamp, it was a lot better. My father gave it to my mother for her 34th birthday.

Thanksgiving Day was a special holiday because it was always butchering day at my grandparents' home. Early in the morning my father and grandfather would build a big fire under the big iron kettles. They were filled with water, later poured into a steel drum. In this they would lower the dead hogs to scald them. They were easier to scrape the hair off.

They would proceed to cut the meat, including saving the heart, liver, and entrails. The entrails were scraped clean and then later stuffed with sausage. The job of the cleaning was my grandmother's chore.

I guess our trips to town were exciting, because we only got to go on rainy days; days that we couldn't work on the farm, because the motto was, "Make hay when the sun shines." We didn't go to a restaurant. We couldn't afford it. So my mother would buy some sliced bologna and a loaf of bread and we would have sandwiches. No mayo, no lettuce, and no soda to wash it down—but it was good.

Lots of memories, some good and some not so good.

Saturday night baths were a must have. Church on Sunday called for a body cleaning. The youngest got in the old galvanized tub. Then I got mine. Then Mom and then Dad. Same water for all of us. An extra bit of hot water after each bather, so the water would warm up.

Since we didn't have a bathroom, it was the old two-holer outhouse. Usually quite a way from the house and a walk there at night was quite scary.

Good Guys and a Ride Named Sugar

by Sandra J. Dobson of Newcomerstown, Ohio
born 1940

I was born the daughter of Joe E. and Therma Hickenbottom, in Guernsey County in Ohio, in March of 1940, which I referred to as the "old country." I guess I called it the old country because it seemed so far from a town. The closest one being Newcomerstown, which was about 15 miles travel time.

We moved when I was about four or five into Tuscarawas County, just out of Newcomerstown. We lived on a farm about a mile from town and I attended Newcomerstown schools. We still live on the family farm with two more homes on the property, lived in by two of our four grown children. This is where I grew up and spent all but the first five years of my life.

Things were so different then, partly because of the times and also I'm sure I saw things through a child's eyes. Since we lived in the country, I didn't have very close neighbors to play with. I did have friends from our rural church, Hartwood, as it was and still is called. I also made friends in school, so I would occasionally invite friends to visit for the day or overnight.

My life growing up seemed rather simple and happy. Our family, mom and dad and an older sister by ten years, Betty, and an older brother by three and a half years, Billy and myself made up our immediate family. My sister was my protector and close friend growing up and still is.

It was just part of our family life to pitch in and help do work on the farm, whatever needed to be done. We helped in the hay making, planting corn, getting the fields ready for planting, feeding and milking the cows, feeding the chickens, gathering the eggs, helping in the house and anything else that needed to be done. We didn't have to be bribed, paid or harassed into helping. We actually wanted to help most of the time because we realized our parents worked very hard to support the family and we felt that since we were part of the family, we were needed to help.

My dad worked five days a week at Hellers Tool Company in town and had many days he should have been at home because he suffered with ulcers. He also was an agent for Eastern Ohio Fire and Tornado Insurance Company and a Director for Guernsey Muskingum Electric Company. My dad, Joe, passed away in 1968 from cancer. He was only able to attend school to the eighth grade because he had to quit school to help with the family income. He was the oldest of nine boys and two girls.

Kate and King pulling a mowing machine with Sandy riding the mower in 1945.

It always amazed me how much he could do and how intelligent he was for only seven years of school. He did a lot of reading, especially the Bible, and helped teach himself He knew many people in our area and never seemed to meet a stranger he couldn't walk away from knowing on a personal level.

Our mother worked on the farm raising and dressing chickens for people. She also made money from selling eggs. She went to work for an attorney when I was in the seventh grade. About two years later one of the bank managers asked her if she would consider working at the bank. She started with Peoples National Bank in Newcomerstown. She retired from there after twenty years. That bank is now known as Bank One. I took over some of her household duties at that time learning how to do laundry, clean the house, and cook the meals for our family as well as sometimes for men who would come to help us with the farm work.

My brother and I used to spend a lot of time together finding something to do when we weren't helping on the farm. We had a pony or a small horse that we could ride named Sugar and we could trust her not to hurt us. We spent time creating games to play with only one pony such as cowboys and Indians. The one of us that agreed to be the "good guy" would always get the horse. Then the other one of us, "the bad guy," would steal some pretend money or steal some cattle or something terrible we had learned from comic books or radio or library books as television had not been invented yet. Naturally the "good guy" would always get his horse stolen and then the other of us would get the horse for a time until the story would take a new turn which we made up as we played and created. One of us, of course, was always on foot, and the one with the horse always had to, part of the rules, tie Old Sugar up someplace, to a tree, fence, barn or wherever and miraculously the "good guy" ended up with her.

We used to climb small sheds and buildings around the farm. I learned to be a pretty good climber and jumper onto the horse to make my getaways.

We also liked to ride Sugar to a neighbor's house that was about 3 miles from us and we would then go riding together with our friend near our age.

We also rode our pony to a nearby property we owned, about 4 miles from us to feed more cattle we had. We had a barn on the property with hay stored in it for feeding. It was usually only done when the snow was so deep it was impossible to get to them with a vehicle. We dressed warmly and I can remember the snow being very deep, but we seemed to enjoy it and it was simply a way of life.

During hay making time we used a wagon, with one person on each side of it pitching the loose hay onto the wagon, pulled by a team of horses as we went by. My job was to stomp down the hay and rearrange it as the others pitched the hay on the wagon.

Another job I had was to ride the horse to pull the hay up into the haymow or loft attached to the hayfork and pulley. I knew exactly when to stop the horse named King.

As time went on we did get a tractor and then I was trained at a young age to drive the tractor to do all the jobs we had previously done with a horse. We eventually got a hay loader, which automatically brought the loose hay onto the wagon without men pitching it onto the wagon. Then from there we started using a hay baler. I have seen the changes in a lot of the farm machinery from the mowing machines to the corn planters to the plows and pickers. So I have experienced the changes in progress and have lived through some and have learned along the way.

We also played in the barn, and hid in the loose hay, which is what we harvested at that time Corncob fights was also a great fun way to get into a serious battle. We really had more fun when we had cousins or friends come and get in on the corncob fights. Every once in a while we will be reminiscing with friends and relatives and the memory of the fun we had with the corncob fights would come up. We did have to set some safety rules to keep the injuries down, such as aiming at the waist down. We had a few minor injuries, but all was handled with a cold wash cloth and a break with something homemade from my mother. Maybe bread and jam or fresh cookies and a glass of milk from our very own cows, right from the cow. No milk from the store back then!

We also enjoyed sled riding with the steel runners on the wood sleds, sometimes inner tubes or toboggans were used. We had a pond on our farm as well, and often we would come down the hill and out onto the ice...so much fun. We also used the pond for ice skating when it was solidly frozen. My dad was the ice inspector and we were never allowed on it until he drilled into it to see how deep the ice was.

Thinking back to our pond, that is where my brother and I learned to swim not the correct way, but what we called dog paddle. Our friends would even come from town to swim with us and didn't seem to be afraid of turtles, fish and other pond life. It was a treat because there just wasn't places to go swimming in our town in those days.

We even liked wading in creeks just to get our feet wet and cool off, which we did quite often when we visited our cousins and they did not have a pond.

I remember visiting our relatives in Barnesville; seven or eight of us would end up in their farm creeks having a blast, usually covered with mud looking like drowned rats. None of us were really worried about the impression we made on anyone else. We were simply having fun!

It seems there was a lot more creative thinking going on back when I was growing up. My brother and I always looked for things to do to have fun.

We had a part German shepherd dog named Nippy and she went with us to do many things. One day we got an idea to build a tree house around the hill from our house. We found two trees separated by a creek that came through our farm. We must have decided that to build a ladder was too common and our idea was also to get Nippy in the tree house with us. We knew she was too heavy for us to carry up a ladder anyway. So we constructed a cable from one tree to the other which held the tree house. Then we attached a pulley, which we were familiar with how they work from pulling hay up into our barn loft. The next job was to attach a big washtub to the pulley with a hay rope. Nippy was so used to us that she would stay in the tub and ride-up to the tree house in the washtub. We of course spent hours designing and building our tree house and tub elevator and many more hours in the tree house with Nippy. I cannot imagine our grandchildren spending their time doing that today. They are too much into ipods, videos, television, computer games, and all other electronic devices to get them involved in so many worldly activities. . I am all for technology, but today it is overused, overrated and abused. It can cause so much long term harm to all of us in various ways if not used properly and monitored.

My mother went to work when I was in the seventh grade, so my brother and I took over the care and milking of the cows. We fed and milked about 12 cows morning and evening. We did all the work involved in getting it from the cows to the cans to be picked up by the milk truck. We would get up in the morning early enough to get it all done, get dressed and catch the bus for school. We did the same process in the evening, and had to work around any school activities or practices we might be involved in, such as band, sports or drama.

We often rode our bikes to band practice in the summer, which was about a 2 mile ride for us as we lived out of town. Most kids today would not put themselves out to do that and would not always be safe. With the work and responsibility also came the money we received from selling the milk. It taught us to be responsible, to understand good work habits, and to earn our own money.

My sister, Betty Hickenbottom Ward, was out of the home by this time as she was ten years older than I. My brother left home after high school to pursue a career at Bliss Business College in Columbus. He had a great job with Western Electric.

I was a senior in high school when my brother, Bill Hickenbottom, got killed in an automobile accident at the age of twenty-one. It was very tragic and unexpected, but we do know that he is in Heaven with our Lord Jesus as he was a witness to Him and testified of his belief and acceptance.

His death changed the outcome of my life as I had been accepted to go to Connecticut to Airline School. I could not leave my parents alone to go so far away. My sister lived in North Carolina at the time. So with the help of friends from high school, I was still able to take the entrance test for Kent State University and was accepted.

My first year was very shaky and I was quite miserable. However my mom asked me to stick it out for one year and if after the first year I couldn't handle it, I could drop out. But I praise the Lord; He changed my attitude and gave me the strength to continue. God proved to me that Romans 8:28 is so true. "And we know that all things work together for good to those who love God, and are called according to His purpose." I graduated from KSU with my degree in Early Childhood.

I started teaching at Plainfield Elementary, Coshocton County, in the second grade. It was a small rural school and I loved it. I taught there for three years making a salary of $4500.00 for the first year.

In February of the next year, we bought our first home, a bungalow, one floor, five rooms, bath, sunroom, full basement, and garage for $7500.00. It was a very nice home in a very nice neighborhood on the outskirts of West Lafayette, Ohio.

When my dad passed away in March of 1968, my husband and our two-and-one-half-year-old son moved to the farm where we presently live and where the story of my life growing up took place.

Things have changed so much. Salaries for teaching have gone up and so have the prices of our homes.

I did teach school for 32 years and retired out of Newcomerstown, Ohio schools.

I also taught for part of a year in a third and fourth grade classroom in Bakersville, Ohio. I remember letting the kids go out the fire escape door to the playground while I usually stayed in to catch up on some work. That sure would not happen like that today.

Yes, life has certainly changed, but it does go on, as we must too. I sure could write much more about all the changes and incidents in my life, but it would turn out to be a book of memories rather than a short story. I hope you enjoy these few short episodes in my life as I have enjoyed reminiscing about the "good old days."

Cat's Paw Kits and Knickers

By Terrence Shaw of Coshocton, Ohio
Born in 1926

I almost never knew my father. On the night I was born, Dad was rushing home on Chestnut Street, and back then, railroad crossings had a shanty for the watchman to lower the gates when a train came through. But he had fallen asleep. Suddenly, waking up, he ran out in front of the car. Dazed, he would have stopped Dad right on the tracks. By swerving and speeding past him, Dad got off just in time.

I was born in the house where now the radio station WTNS stands. We lived on Sixth Street directly across from the Sixth Street Theatre, and I used to sit with friends and listen to the piano music accompanying the silent pictures. The pianist, by the way, was my future wife's Aunt Elda. Also, my uncle and her uncle were partners in show business. They produced medicine shows.

I remember you only got a pair of shoes when they were needed, which were in long intervals, because when your leather soles wore through, Dad would purchase a kit called "Cat's Paw" containing glue, a scraper, and two rubber patches. It was like patching a tire inner tube.

This brings to mind what was popular in clothing at this time that we wore, trying to emulate our heroes in aviation. These were knickers, argyle knee socks, leather high top boots with a pocket on the side, which contained a pen knife, aviator helmet goggles, and all, and an imitation leather jacket.

We made our own toys such as a scooter made from a wooden orange crate nailed to a two by four from a construction site, disconnect a roller skate, and attach one piece to the front, one to the back, and two tin cans for headlights.

We also made zip guns from a block of wood, a thin piece of wood for the handle, a nail for a trigger, and two slices of an old car inner tube, one to hold the gun together, one to shoot.

We moved from Sixth Street to Wilson Avenue. I remember our old 1929 Chevrolet, blue in color with black fenders, a running board and rich blue corduroy upholstery. Sitting inside, who had climbed through an open window, was my old dog Betty who, whenever she would hear words indicating going somewhere, would make sure she would be a passenger. And if by chance we would leave without her, she would run following behind till we let her in.

Betty, a fox terrier was quite mischievous. Behind our backyard was the Country Club golf course. One day while in the yard, my father and I saw two angry golfers chasing her, swinging their clubs. The last glimpse of her was hiding under the porch behind the trellis surrounding it. There, we discovered over a hundred balls! Thus ending her career of crime.

Some things I recall are Saturday matinees at the "Pastime," and the Sixth Street theaters with cartoons, weekly serials. "Flash Gordon," "Dick Tracy," "Red Rider," a western, and the feature movie. Every week there would be a drawing; if you had a ticket to match the number drawn, you could win a bike designed to look like a motorcycle. Each week I would honestly believe it would be mine. Then some kid whose dad could afford to buy one would win it.

Every Tuesday would be dish night. Mom would take us. Eventually, she had a whole matching set. After first grade we had moved to Chestnut Street to a house below a bar called "The Bucket of Blood." It was pretty noisy on hot summer nights.

Every afternoon we would rush home from Bancroft School to turn on the radio to listen to "The Adventures of Jack Armstrong, the All American Boy." Of course we had to eat our "Wheaties." We also would follow "Little Orphan Annie," and mail in the foil seal from "Ovaltine" for our decoder pins. A secret code was stated at the end of each episode.

I lived in Coshocton from 1926 to 1937. My dad was transferred to Philadelphia, Pennsylvania.

One day I was home with the measles. Mom and I heard extra loud engine noises above our house. Rushing out, we saw directly and low overhead, the airship "Hindenburg" circling to moor in Lakehurst. A few minutes later, listening to the radio, I heard them reporting the crash.

In 1946 after the War, we still yearned for the good years of life in a small town of Coshocton, Ohio. We moved back where our hearts have always been.

Not Your Usual Chewing Gum

By Shirley Wilhelm of Morristown, Ohio
Born in 1935

I was in the fourth grade in my hometown in 1945. World War II was going strong and many, many necessities were rationed. There were not many pleasures or treats for anyone.

There was a diner across the street from the elementary school and occasionally, we school children would get the opportunity to buy our lunch at the diner. We had no cafeteria at the school. Money was scarce so it was a great privilege when our parents gave us a quarter to buy a hot lunch at the diner.

One wall in the diner had a display of articles that were for sale such as razor blades, pain relievers, eye drops, something for upset stomachs—nothing that really interested the school children; but something caught my eye: "Chew like gum."

Chewing gum wasn't available very often. If you were at the diner or store when a shipment came in, and if you had a nickel, you could purchase a pack.

I had a little extra change the day I saw the package that said "Chew like gum," so I asked the waitress for a pack of gum on the wall. She got it down, gave it to me, and advised me to chew a small piece at a time—it would last longer.

I went back to school and announced to my friends I had just bought chewing gum at the diner—of course the word spread quickly on the playground, and everyone came running asking very politely for a stick. I told them I only had one pack so I could only give a small piece of gum to each one, which everyone agreed to. I very carefully broke off a small piece for everyone who had lined up.

By the time I had come to the end of the line, I had no gum for myself—oh well, that was okay. It was really fun watching each one chewing and enjoying my treat.

I think several of my friends saved their precious, delicious, used chewing gum for recess—it was too good to throw away after chewing it for such a short time, and several friends still had their used gum when it was time to go home—couldn't throw it away yet.

The next morning as the students got off the school buses I noticed some of my friends looked very sleepy, haggard and not bright eyed and bushy tailed as they usually did.

After they had hung up their coats and put their lunch buckets and books away, one by one my friends came to me and said they had not gotten much sleep the night before. I said, "Why?" I had slept fine. They said they had been going an awful lot outside to the outhouse. One friend said her mother wanted to know what kind of chewing gum I had given her.

Oh dear, mercy me, what had I given to my friends?

It was not your usual chewing gum; but—you guessed it, a chewing gum laxative.

Now the students were sleepy and not too sharp that day—but they still considered me as a friend—one who would share all the gum and have none left for me.

I had no idea what kind of chewing gum I was passing out to my friends. I just read "Chew like gum," and that they did!

Sailing to America

by Mary Ellen Wheeler of Zanesville, Ohio
born 1914

My name is Mary Vousdon Wheeler. My birth date is 7-9-14. I am ninety-four years of age and have lived in this little village called Licking View on the outskirts of Zanesville, Ohio. Hope you can read my story of most of my life.

To start my story with my grandma. I just can't remember dates so good. In the early 1800s, my great grandma made up their minds to come to America. They were Germans and lived in Nurenburg, Germany. They made up their minds to come to America. They had a chance to come and made it happen. She was pregnant with my grandma and they had to come across on one of those big old sailboats. My grandma was born in France on their way over. The woman at the hotel where she was born wanted to keep her. Said she would educate her and raise her. She said, "You will never get her across that ocean alive." But they took a chance of getting her to America. There were eight other babies that started with them on board the big sail ship. What a trip!

One night her mother awoke her dad and said that the baby had wet, so when he got out of bed, his legs went into water up to his knees. The ship was sinking. Made the call to awake the men. They pumped the ship with pumps. Hung on the rock for almost two weeks when they made it. I never knew how they did get help.

Of nine babies, the mothers had to wash their babies

in sea water and they got big boils on them and were gone. My great grandma saved a portion of the water rationed out to them to drink and washed her in it. They had to bury them at sea because the big sharks and whales could smell the bodies and if there were many could upset the ship. They traveled a lot to get to Zanesville.

When my mom and dad got married, they moved in with her and she lived with us all my life. When I grew up, she was still with us to Looking View. When I graduated from high school in 1932 (the very worst year of the Great Depression), I stayed home to care for her and she told me so many stories of her life and since I was the oldest girl and my mom had to work because it was the Depression, men couldn't get a job, but women all worked because they had to pay men higher wages. Old people who had a little money and the banks were going under and they were closing. The banks were going under and they lost everything. All the railroads were closing. Men losing their jobs. There were six kids and my grandma, mother and dad in a three room house.

Zanesville has the only Y bridge in the world and we were named the Clay City. Lots of potteries and tile companies. So most of the women were able to get work so my mom worked and walked five miles to work and five miles home at night.

My mom only went to the sixth grade of school but was a hard worker.

In my graduation class there was 280 graduate because we walked about five miles into town and went to the big high school. We went to a two room school to get to the eighth grade.

My life has seen everything. The first airplanes, the first electric, the first running water, the first radio and TV. We saw circus parades with the beautiful wagons with the bands on top. The pretty band members had beautiful clothes on. The big animals in cages.

Then the big dirigibles that flew over our house. The Von Hendinberg (German made). The Shenandoah. It went down in Ohio, not too far from where we lived.

Now I am almost 95. Will be in July 9. I live in the same place. My brothers are all gone. We lost one boy (John, 28 years old) in World War Two. Plane went down over Himalayan Mountains. Never was found. Another brother was in England five years, Air Force. My youngest sister is eighty-three and still living.

The thing that seemed to stick in my mind most, my dad had gone to a neighbor's house that had the first radio. When he come home and told my mom that he even heard the ball hit the bat and the whole game, I never heard anyone get so excited.

Then one day we kids and neighbor kids found a snake was going under our summer kitchen. My grandma yelled us to fetch her a hoe. We couldn't find the hoe. And there she was, getting it by the tail and throwing it back so she could kill it, so she just picked it up by the tail, used it like you would a rope and snapped its head off. The way you would a horse whip.

The summer kitchen that people would build close to your back door and in the hot weather, we would have a coal stove to cook with and we would move our table, chairs and have the coal stove out there so our houses wouldn't be so hot to live in. We were the pioneers.

Things are so much different now. One could never believe the differences unless you went through it. These are the small things we went through to live.

Now I have two daughters. The youngest daughter is fifty-seven and has worked at the two hospitals in Zanesville, Ohio and has worked in surgery for thirty-five years. I worked in the lab in Bertham Hospital for twenty years and got her on when she was twenty-one.

I have a granddaughter that is a R.N. Nurse in the big Riverside Hospital in Columbus, Ohio and the other daughter Vonda Lu was sixty-seven in August. She helps me so much and has two sons grown. One who just retired from the Air National Guard and was a lieutenant colonel and was able to raise his own son into the Air Force. In college now. My other daughter has three sons, all graduated from Ohio State University. Two graduated from Kent State University. My only granddaughter from Ohio University. The boys that graduated from Kent married girls who went there and are teachers.

If this is too long, throw it out. Maybe you won't be able to read it. My hands are so crippled with arthritis. At one time I was a pretty writer, but now all my good things are gone. Only memories. But I'm lucky to be able to write at all. I have two walkers and was able to drive my car up until last year and had no power steering. I finally gave it up at the age of ninety-three. I now have six grandsons, three granddaughters, two great-greats.

Running and Sacking at Campbell's

by Norval C. Camp, Jr. of Zanesville, Ohio
born in 1937

In 1947 at the age of ten years, I lived in South Zanesville, Ohio, an incorporated village. There were four grocery stores – Campbell's Super Market, George's Grocery, Smith Grocery and Maysville Super Market. My family dealt at Campbell's. I would sometimes walk to the store to get milk, bread, eggs, etc. Campbell was owned by Paul Campbell. His wife Gladys, son Paul Jr., daughter Lou Ann, niece Donna Fitch and meat cutter Earl Dale worked there.

One day I went to get something for my mom and I asked Mrs. Campbell for a job. She said, "I don't know,

The store in 1950.

I'll look around." While I was returning home, she called my mom to see if it would be alright, and behold I got my first job. Now there were no work permit laws. So I started working two hours after school for twenty-five cents an hour. When summer came and no school, I got four hours a day.

Now in 1947 there were no shopping carts. The customer would stand at the checkout and tell the cashier what they wanted. I was a runner and sacker. Now I also sacked potatoes in 10# sacks, cartoned eggs from thirty-six dozen boxes into one dozen egg cartons. I ground coffee for customers and stocked shelves. I cleaned up messes. Took out the trash and at that time there were no collectors. We had barrels out back that we burned the trash in.

At the age of twelve I was doing checkout work. Now when you checked people out you wrote down every item on a pad, put the price and added it up on an adding machine. Only certain customers paid by check, all others were cash. Then you punched the amount in on the register, pulled the handle to open the register and counted out the change.

I worked there until I was seventeen. At this age, six years later I was up to fifty-five cents an hour. I saved enough money to buy my first car. The car was a 1951 Ford Custom at $450.00.

Some of the prices at that time – coffee nineteen cents and twenty-nine cents a pound – soap eight cents a bar – Coke five cents a bottle in the machine and twenty-five cents for a six pack – apples a dollar a bushel.

When I quit at seventeen, I was in charge of the produce case. Many of the customers were very nice but once in awhile, you might get a hard to wait on customer. One comes to mind. When I waited on this older man, if I weighed his produce, I had to weigh it on the scale and then put it in the sack. He said he was not going to pay for the sack.

Now one day at Christmas season, I had cleaned the produce case and had thrown all the old rotten apples, oranges, etc. into a box. When I finished I trimmed the Christmas trees we were selling and threw all the broken branches on top of the garbage. He came in. He said, "What are you going to do with those pine boughs?" I said, "Throw them in the trash." He said, "Just set that box on the back seat of my station wagon." I said, "I sure will," and did (get even).

Now of the business that has been in South Zanesville, Campbell's Market is still there being managed and owned by Paul Campbell Jr.'s sons, Paul Campbell's grandsons. It is still doing well. I still deal at Campbell's Market 61 years later.

The Hobo Under the Cherry Tree

by Pauline Wilson of Barnesville, Ohio
born in 1922

This funny story continues to be repeated with laughter every time some of the family gathers together, many, many years after the actual event. The story happened in the early 40s on a country road in Belmont County, Ohio.

Times were hard in the late 30s and early 40s. Many families did not have enough to eat. Sometimes the man of the family would go out across the county to find some kind of work, or even food to take care of his family. Sometimes this man would be gone from home for days or weeks. He would stop at homes and ask for food or even extra clothes. He would sleep in farm barns and sometimes along the road under a tree. Being raised on a farm, we would occasionally see one of these men when they stopped to ask for something to eat.

One summer evening a neighbor lady and her small children came for a short visit. We were all sitting on the front porch, as was common on hot summer evenings, talking about these men going around the countryside begging for food and sleeping along the road. It was now getting real dark and our neighbor lady asked me and my two brothers to walk her and the children home. She only lived a short distance away, and we were glad to help her out.

It was so dark we had trouble seeing where we were going. After getting our neighbors home, we turned around and headed back toward our house. We were holding hands and talking as young people do. About half way home as we came upon a small cherry tree, we heard something move under the tree. Then we heard a low moan, followed by a loud groan. The hair on our necks stood up and we froze in our tracks. That is, except for my youngest brother. He took off like a shot. My other brother and I stood in the middle of the road shaking and screaming, wondering if this could be one of those men searching for help.

All of a sudden a man jumped up and came at us. He was laughing so hard he could barely talk. To our surprise, it was my husband. Once we realized what and who it was, we began to laugh along with him.

After we arrived home, Mother and Dad, who were aware of what happened, joined in on the laughter as well. A dark summer night that stayed with us all our lives.

Bats in the Bedroom and Pennies in the Bed Pipes

by Linda C. Warne of South Zanesville, Ohio
born in 1937

My mother's milk was not adequate and I was not gaining weight. The good Doctor suggested cow's milk, that was poured into bottles with a nipple for suckling. I had broken every baby bottle they gave me by pitching it out of the crib. Eventually, they were stretching rubber nipples over catsup and beer bottles. By the time I was three years old, I was still drinking milk and not taking any food. Soon, I was falling down when I tried to walk. Doctor Bateman said I had a bad case of rickets from malnutrition and they would have to get food in me anyway they could. Elbow macaroni was the only thing I would eat. If I picked up only one at a time and swallowed it, he said this was progress and to stick to it and build me a pair of legs. Mother and Grandma took turns feeding me mashed potatoes and they didn't stop 'till they had built me a pair of legs like the doctor wanted.

My older sister, Shirley, was the favorite of Grandma Z. (short for Zimmerli) and this was because she was the first grandchild and was rather frail. Grandma said that my mother was spending all of her time caring for Marilyn, my middle sister, and me, and was neglecting little Shirley. Daddy came in and found Mother crying and upset because of it and he immediately went up to Grandma and told her to mind her own business. After that, we didn't stay in the house behind hers. We moved to another house further away, in South Zanesville, where my mother could no longer be bothered. At the new house, Shirley really got sick with typhoid fever, so bad she almost died. My only memory of living there was the time a bat got into our bedroom. Daddy had a broom and every time the bat made a pass over our heads he would swing at it to try to kill it. We three girls were scared and hiding under the covers of our bed.

Our bed was made of pipes and we could save our pennies and nickels for Christmas by dropping them into the bed pipes. I always wondered how we would get the money out but Daddy said it would be no problem. We would need to have chewing gum and put it on the bottom of a long stick and pull the money up. We always saved our chewing gum overnight by sticking it on the bed pipes. When Christmas came, we had plenty for pulling the money up.

My older sisters started to school from this house and Daddy got a good job at the Line Material Company, a company that made transformers for electric poles. It was necessary work, so he didn't have to be drafted into the war. We moved to a house on Arch Street in Norval Park, a residential area with a really nice elementary school where we all attended.

Whenever we had a blackout, Daddy would pile us all into the car and go down the hill to the main highway, sit in the car and wait for him to come back. He wore a band on his arm and his job was to stop all traffic and have them turn off their lights. This would make it impossible for us to be spotted from the air if we had an air raid attack. This was very important. I was proud of my Daddy who served our country in this way.

The bungalow-style house was small, but adequate for our family of five. It had two bedrooms, living room, kitchen, and a room that was later converted to a bathroom. A full basement and two porches made it quite comfortable. Big elm trees flanked the backyard, a creek in the side yard for playing in, and an open space on the other side for a garden. The house was purchased from my father's grandparents, who were elderly, and by their own choice, living in the basement of the house. At five years of age, my family said I was Dutch, which meant that you couldn't talk plain and nobody understood anything you said. When I saw the old folks living in the basement I said the "uptays" is the downstairs and the "downtays" is the upstairs.

There was a door lying flat at one end of the kitchen and it had to be raised to go down to the basement. If you were in the basement, you would have to raise it overhead to come upstairs and Daddy changed this right away. It made the kitchen look smaller, but it saved us all from falling down the hole There was an open well out back which he closed over before we ended up in there.

My sisters and I played in the creek, built roads and houses on the banks for little play cars and jumped across to the street, just on the other side. The Norval Park School was across this street and sat at the top of the hill. We made a crude path up to the top and spent our summers playing on the school ground equipment. There were teeter-totters, monkey bars, a sliding board, and swings, besides lots of levels of rooftops and fire escape stairs to climb. The two-story schoolhouse had a series of rooftops from which you could climb up and jump off. There were secret hiding places just perfect for hide and seek games and from the outside, concrete steps, leading down to the basement where we would all gather once a week for an educational film. The janitor was Mr. Carr and his quarters were there in the basement where the furnace room was located. Because I lived close by, Mr. Carr and I became good friends. He was a grand elderly man who allowed me to pull the long ropes to ring the school bell for school.

My father became the president of the PTA while my two sisters and I attended the school. I vividly remember him playing Santa Claus for the children at the meeting and candy was passed out to everyone.

Each day, for lunch, I would bound out the door and down over the hill to our house. I listened to the Jack Birch Show on radio and always ate a hot dog sandwich and a Hershey bar for lunch, every day the same. My mother helped me to write to Jack Birch and tell them about Mr. Carr and what a good janitor he was at the Norval Park School. We dedicated a song to him. Years later, the building was raised and the only thing I have are my beautiful memories of my childhood in grade school and a dear man who loved me as much as I loved him.

I learned to ride a bicycle on the street below the school, Oseola Street; named after an Indian tribe. It was a cinder street and our knees were skinned up numerous times. The cinders often remained in our knees for years to come. In the summer, we rode our bikes and Mother would pack us a picnic and hope that when we went for the picnic in the woods, we would stay for awhile. But, we never stayed for long. Just the same in the wintertime, when we would take hours to dress for outside and only stay out for five minutes.

During summer, we spent hours playing in the ditches above our house on Arch Street in Norval Park. Beyond the ditches, we picked berries and wildflowers. Violets grew in abundance, and Trillium and Sweet Williams as well. We brought to our mother huge bouquets of our bounty.

Deeper in the woods, we followed well-worn paths to swing and hang precariously from an old but solid grapevine, which swung us out over a ravine and creek beyond.

Childhood days came to an end too soon and the old schoolhouse was demolished. But the memories remain long after the wrecking ball. The erosion of ditches where we spent time playing have disappeared and a row of houses now stand on the site. The old adage that time changes everything is true, indeed. But, scenes from our childhood will never fade from our minds. They will live in our hearts forever.

The Little Gray Outhouse

by Pam Winland of Woodsfield, Ohio
at Graysville, Ohio
born in 1948

I remember when I was a lot younger than I am now, living back home with Mom and Dad. We didn't have any bathroom in the house. Just the little gray outhouse out back. Every evening after dark, I always had to go out back. Yes, we had a pot in the house, but it was for number one. So Mom would always go with me, and I would always ask her if she was still there, and she said yes.

So one night, she left me there, and I said, "Are you there?" She didn't answer, because she left me, and she was really laughing. She said I always had to wait 'til dark to go. She passed away at eighty-four, and she always remembered it. I'll be sixty-one in June.

Another story I remember is about my brother and I. I was the youngest of seven kids. We had our well outside. We drawed our water out of the well with a big rope tied onto a long bailer. It had a hand crank on it, so you just cranked the bailer down in the well, and when it hit bottom and filled up, you turned the crank and brought it up to the top and let it out in a bucket.

So one time, I was bringing up a bailer of water, and the crank slipped out of my hand, and my brother said, "Grab the rope," and I didn't know any better, so I grabbed it, and I got bad rope burns. But them was the good ole days.

This is another story I remember. Our dad always smoked, so my brother and I got us a cigarette. Back then, out behind the house was where we planted a big garden. So this was after the garden was all done up. The weeds were all growed up. So my brother and I went out there to smoke. We were setting down in the weeds, smoking away, when our dad came out the back door.

My brother said, "Put out your cigarette." And I said, "He can't see us in these deep weeds." Back then, I didn't know the smoke was rising, and he seen it. Boy, did we get a talking to. They was worse on you than the peach switch we got used on us sometimes. We lost our dad when he was fifty-nine.

A Journey of Joy and Even More

by Elaine Isselstein Farie of Warsaw, Ohio
born 1941

A lot can be said about being the youngest child in the family, the "end of the line" so to speak. But who would ever let that thought occur at all? My golly, there's just too much to be excited about!

I overheard we might get to go down to my aunt and uncle's, who had a family of 11 children, and live on a farm near Lancaster. Of course, that will depend on the weather and especially if Dad is pretty sure the tires on our 1944 Chevy will make the trip. He always carries one of those tire patch kits and a tire pump if we go very far away. On a Sunday afternoon in the summer of 1948, there may be someone who could help us, if needed, along the way, not to worry.

So, finish your dinner, clean your plate, go to the

bathroom, wash your face and hands, it's a long way to Lancaster, and we don't stop. There are no McDonald's, that's why we ate at home and took care of necessities.

I noticed Dad had put some twine and a bushel basket in the car trunk, what for? I already forgot to ask, let's go!

So, even as we leave the city and enter into the rolling hills of the countryside, the air blowing through the open car window (air conditioning?) doesn't mess up my hair. Mom, of course, has my long blonde hair braided, in pigtails, with pretty blue ribbons tied at the end of each pigtail. Actually, my two sisters don't wear braids. They "did" their hair last night in "rags and pincurls" resulting in some soft curls. But, since hair spray and mousse hasn't been invented yet, they'll wish they wore their hair in braids by the time we get there, with all this August humidity.

"Are we there yet? We must be getting close to the farm because…there it is!" The barn I remember is the one at my cousin's house, at least I think so, but something is painted on the side. In big letters it says, "Chew Mail Pouch Tobacco." Since I'm already in the third grade, I can read signs, even the "Burma Shave" signs along the road. They are in sequence and I can hardly wait till we pass all four of them, to know what the rhyme really says.

So then my dad answers my questions about why "Chew Mail Pouch Tobacco" is written on my Uncle Virgil's barn. Something about "being paid some money for such a big sign that the whole world could see," the money really helps with the large family he and Aunt Mary have.

It then occurs to me, Oh, what if they aren't home? But Mom assures me she had mailed them a penny post card over a week ago to let them know of our proposed visit. Oh, thank goodness for the mailman and a way to talk to someone far away.

"We're here!" Lots of hellos, hugs and laughter. It's been a long time, at least six months, since we've been able to visit. We all settle on the big front porch, the swing, a glider, a couple of rocking chairs, the porch railings, and best of all, three of my girl cousins and I can play jacks by sitting on the porch steps. By now, my big brother Joe—he's twelve—is already playing pitch and catch in the backyard.

Before long, one of my cousins, Kathy, whispers that she saw her mom setting out a big cardboard box with "stuff" for us to take back home, and, for sure, some of the things are some hand-me-down dresses that she is sure will fit me. Oh, joy of joys! Can we go and look?

By this time, my mom and Aunt Mary are already in the kitchen with the box on the long plank table. "Come here Elaine, let me hold this dress up to you." Well, needless to say, the game of jacks, and looking at the new book of paper dolls, my cousin Sue had just received for her birthday, were quickly put aside.

Oh, how beautiful! Aunt Mary said all her girls had outgrown their dresses. "Elaine can probably fit right into them. Maybe let a hem up or down? If too short, a little ruffle would lengthen them just right." My aunt, a very good seamstress, had made some lovely clothes out of very colorful and sturdy feed bags. The colors are just so pretty and adding a new collar or changing the buttons down the front will make it look like new.

Needless to say, my heart beat even faster as Mom agreed to take the box home, with grateful appreciation.

The kitchen of their farmhouse smelled so good. I just knew a treat must be awaiting us. Sure enough, the most delicious spiced oatmeal cookies I've ever eaten were on the counter, covered with that familiar blue striped towel I always remember. And because of such a special occasion, homemade, fresh squeezed lemonade was added to our treat. My mom had brought some jars of homemade blackberry jam they would enjoy this winter.

After a wonderful time of playing and swapping family stories, everyone eventually walked around the farm. My dad and Uncle Virgil talked about crops and animals, Mom and Aunt Mary were comparing vegetable gardens and grape arbors. All of us kids had a great time skipping stones across the pond near the pasture field. My brother said he skipped one 12 times, but I don't believe him.

The sun was beginning to cast long shadows, so that meant we would have to be getting ready to start our journey back home, about 60 miles, but it was a journey I loved to take.

About this time, I realized why the twine and large basket had come down with us. It was now the temporary pen for a rooster, who Aunt Mary said "had chased the kids just one time too many." Oh, golly, we don't have fried chicken to eat very often, but now? Next Sunday's dinner?

It's funny! I never ran out of energy running around with all my cousins. But now, sitting in the backseat, wedged in with my sisters and the great box of clothes, I felt so sleepy. But what a great day, today, and just think, tomorrow will be Monday.

That means wash day! So fun helping Mom run the clothes through those two rollers on our wringer washer. In and out of the rinse tubs and then, carry the wicker basket up the basement stairs to hang everything on the clothesline. But, I remember Mom said I could have two of her wooden clothespins to make the "hollyhock dolls" my cousins had shown me how to make. We had a lot of hollyhocks, pink ones, growing back by the fence.

Oh, yes, I forgot, Mom said she is going to wash

Joe Isselstein and Elaine Isselstein Farie in 1945.

the lace curtains from our living room. That means making the starch in a special pan she uses, and stretching the lace curtains on the special frames till they dry in the sun. It's fun to help loop the material over the tiny little tacks on the stretchers. "Just don't prick your finger and get blood on the clean curtains." All the clothes smell so fresh blowing in the breeze, and I like to match the socks and fold the towels when they're dry.

And, another great thing! Tomorrow is the day three of my neighborhood friends and I are going to finish building our "fort" back in the honeysuckle vines in our back yard. Now, all I'll need to get will be that cardboard box after we take all the new clothes out. It will make a great chair to sit on in our fort.

But, I sure hope Dad doesn't let that rooster can't get out to chase me, Oh, I'm just so sleepy...

Stores and Snakes in Beallesville

by Mary Pool of Canton, Ohio
born in 1928

I was born in Jerusalem, Ohio but lived most of my life in Beallesville (Monroe County).

I remember Swallows Confectionary. They had "white house" ice cream. It was vanilla ice cream with cherries and it came in a big yellow truck that said Zignafelder on the side.

There were two Hudsone stores. One was like a department store and the other was hardware and feed. I went in and bought my first slack outfit for gym class. It cost $1.98. The feed was in colored feed sacks that we made clothes, curtains, dish towels and etc.

Blowers and Campbell Funeral home was on a corner. Bill Blowers was the owner. Whenever anyone died and they took the body back to the house, they put a wreath on the front door. And I didn't know that so I knocked on the front door to get our newspaper. I was so embarrassed when I found out about that.

Right next door was Dr. Pugh's office. There was a lot of jokes about that. The first time I was at the doctor was when I was 18 and had to get a blood test to get married.

There was also Milligan's store and restaurant. Charlie was the owner and he had trouble walking.

The Beallesville Post Office was in the main part of town. Harry Hamilton was the postmaster.

A Snake, Who Needs It? I lived in Beallesville most of my life till I was married and moved to Canton, Ohio.

When I was 16, my two brothers tried to scare me so bad, and they did. They were helping my dad put the hay in the barn. They would bring it in on a farm wagon and put it in the hay mow. They brought it all in but two stocks, so my brothers each took a pitchfork up and carried each shock to the barn. Under one of the hay shocks was a four-foot blacksnake. They played around with it and put the pitchfork in the middle of it and brought it down to the house and called for me to come see it. They knew I was so scared of a snake, but I wouldn't go see it. Later, I went out on the porch to get some water from the pump and there the snake was lying on the porch. I fell back in the house, about knocked my mother down as she had just come home from the hospital. I'm over 80 years old and still scared of snakes.

Learning Experiences, Outhouse Snakes and Gas Caps

by Mrs. Sue Barlow of Edgewater, Florida
born 1936

My husband and I, both city people, moved to a 25 acre farm. With the help of John, our neighbor, he took us under his wing to teach us farm life. We had a cow that was ready to give birth any day; when she went down, we couldn't get her back on her feet. The neighbors said we would have to cut the calf out in order to save it and naturally, the cow would have to die.

Up to this point our daughter and twin sons had seen a new born calf right after birth and saw the mother licking it to clean it up. I explained to them what we had to do to save the calf and they asked it they could stay home from school to observe. We said yes since this would be a learning experience that they probably would not have this opportunity again. I told them we would have to do what normally the mother would do when we brought this calf into the world. Trevor, one of the twins, said, "Yuck, I'm not going to lick up this calf."

Before they got home from school the next day, Trevor's teacher called to tell me what a beautiful job he did telling the class what they had witnessed. I questioned if it was Trevor, since this type of story telling is not his thing. She said he told it as if it was one of God's many miracles. I couldn't wait for them to get home to hear his story. All we heard was how upset he was that she took him to every classroom to repeat the story.

Friends of ours bred riding horses. One of the horses was due to give birth and their three-year-old son asked if he could watch the birthing. His mother, a school teacher, felt this would be a wonderful learning experience about the many miracles of life. When the colt was born, the three-year-old looked up at his mother and said, "I didn't know they came in baggies."

When I was young, I would visit my aunt and uncle in the country. Their outhouse was behind the main house and had a lattice in front of it with vines for privacy. I told her I needed to go to the bathroom but was afraid of snakes out there. She assured me there were no snakes. Just then we saw my older brother going to the outhouse and about five minutes later heard him screaming. We ran to the back door to see him standing outside the outhouse, one hand trying to pull up his pants and the other hand yielding a hoe, trying to ward off a big snake. I just looked at my aunt and said, "See, I told you so."

My husband bought a country store and filling station. He worked at a steel mill so his father, also a steel worker at the same plant, helped him run the business. My mother-in-law and I would go down and run the station for a few hours when our husbands were changing shifts and one of them would come and take over.

In those days, you never knew where to find the gas tank, sometimes under the license plate or either side of the car. We always wanted to hide when a car came up to the tanks so we wouldn't have to pump gas. One of our regular customers felt sorry for me as I was trying to find the gas tank and offered to pump it himself. I thought the least I could do for him would be to clean his windshield. I had seen my husband pull back the windshield wipers to do the job and figured this would be a piece of cake. As I pulled the first wiper up, it broke and came off in my hand. I felt terrible and handed it to the customer and apologized over and over. I figured we had just lost a good customer. My husband said he came back the next day, laughing so hard and feeling so sorry for me. There are good people in this world!

My Very First Memories

by Margaret "Jean" Roenbough Kilchenman
of New Philadelphia, Ohio
born in 1921

Now I lay me down to sleep,/ If I should die before I wake/ I pray thee, Lord, my soul to take./ God bless all your children everywhere. Amen—good night.

Yes, my very first memory of my mother teaching my brother (one year seventeen days older than I) this prayer to us by kerosene lamp. She also read to us from the book, "The Little Shepherd of Kingdom Come," a Civil War book that my father's siblings read over and over to their father as he never learned to read. I had the book, but in the move to New Philadelphia house, it became missing, and I've been brokenhearted.

Another book Mama read from was Aesop's Fables. I still have the remnants of that book. We never had children's books. We would swing in a large porch swing, and Daddy would sing hymns, and that's how we learned them.

But when I was about four, Mama got sick and was hospitalized. When she came home and got well, she had baby after baby, and story reading and singing was no more.

I remember my dad's first car. It was a Ford Touring, two-seater, that had to be cranked to get started. We had lap robes in the car to cover with in cold weather. Also side curtains had to be snapped on to keep out the rain and cold.

We did not have electricity, running water, inside plumbing or any modern appliances. Kerosene lamps were lit, and every morning, chimneys had to be cleaned and bottoms filled with kerosene. Outside kerosene lanterns lighted our way to the outside outhouse. At night, we had what we called "slop jars" that needed brought in every night and emptied every morning—all children's chores. Also the "water bucket" had to be filled. In the late twenties, we got an Aladdin lamp, which really lighted brightly, and we felt we were in heaven.

The first stove in the kitchen that I remember was a "Kate Olive" stove. It had oven doors on both sides and a hearth on the front. It put out a good bit of heat. The only other heat was a potbelly stove in the other room.

Often we kids had to take buckets and walk the railroad tracks to gather coal that had dropped when firemen were firing the engines. We did pretty good. This was during the Depression. To start fires in the stoves, corncobs would be soaked in kerosene after we had shelled the corn for the chickens, which ran wild during summer. We always went barefoot and had to step carefully to avoid their droppings. The gardens had a fence around it to keep them out, and it also served as a drying place for clothes when the clotheslines were full.

The first way Mama washed was a washboard and tubs. Then she got a wooden washer with handle that we pulled back and forth to agitate the clothes. It had a hand wringer, and there were always two rinse tubs. Water was heated in a copper boiler on the kitchen stove. Water had to be carried on Sunday nights from a spring in the pasture field as the pump would only put out four buckets of water before going dry, and it took a half-hour to refill. In the wintertime, Mama still hung out clothes, and they'd freeze as fast as they were hung, but in the breeze, they would thaw and did they ever smell good. Of course they had to be hung over chairs and rack to dry out seams, etc.

We usually had two hogs. Butchering day was early rising to get the large barrels of water hot to put the hogs in so they could get the hair scraped off. Then they would be hung on strong frames cut open, intestines had to be scraped to make casings for the sausage (women's work) and the stomach lining taken out to make schwortama. It was made of pig ears, snout, liver, kidney, some sausage and head meat—then tied shut and boiled in water for three or four hours and then put between two boards with a long rock on top for a couple of days. It was really good.

Krepples were also made in a big kettle. This was broth, ground meat and thickened with flour and buckwheat flour—stored in crocks and fried in skillets. I still like it. Lard had to be rendered from the fat, meat ground for the sausage, and there was always a huge chicken dinner with potatoes and gravy, usually circled endive from the garden and several pies and homemade bread, butter, and jelly.

The butter was churned form the cream Mama had skimmed from the crocks of milk kept on the porch where it was cool. When there was enough, we had an old wooden churn about two and a half feet high with a plunger on a handle, and we'd push it up and down until the butter separated from the buttermilk. I never drank regular milk, but I sure drank that buttermilk. Mama then would take the butter and put it in a bowl with water, and she could turn it over and over until all the milk was out. She would set a crock of milk on the back of the kitchen stove, and when it reached a certain temperature, the curds would separate from the whey, and she'd put the curds in a sugar sack (sugar came in cloth bags) and have it hang from the cupboard until all the whey was out. Then she'd salt it, add some cream, and we had schmercase cottage cheese. We had one cow named Daisy.

There were six children in our family. I was number two and the oldest girl. Mama had the six and two miscarriages in thirteen years and then had surgery. I learned to cook quite young, bake bread, bake, canned food, wash, sew, clean, and scrub.

We got electric in 1929. Each room had a cord hanging down with a light bulb and a pull chain for turning it off and on. A requirement to get the electric was to get an electric stove. It wasn't very fancy but baked good. We took our baths in the kitchen. Someone always was a lookout, as people always came to the kitchen door. I do want to go back a little and tell about Mondays after school.

As I said, we had to carry water for laundry on Sunday nights, and then on Mondays, the water had to be used. We had to wash the "slop jars," scrub the outside toilet, the back porch, the stepping stones from the house to the outhouse, and I always had to scrub the kitchen. Every bit was utilized.

Mama made our dresses, petticoats, aprons, sheets and pillowcases, sheets, baby diapers, all from feed sacks. The plain unbleached were the sheets, tea towels, petticoats, diapers, and curtains. The printed ones were dresses, pillowcases, aprons, skirts, and blouses. And they were pretty. I still have an apron.

We kids rode the school bus for our twelve years of school, and we all graduated and did well, as education was encouraged.

We wore a lot of hand-me-down clothes. Lots of times, we wore old ladies' clothes and would get teased at school. When we were young, we had to wear long underwear, one piece, with a pin at the waist on each side that had a piece of elastic fastened to it and then two supporters—one for the front and one for the back to hold up our long cotton stockings. The underwear also served as our nightclothes. We must have really smelled bad. We were forced to brush our teeth using baking soda for our toothpaste.

During the Depression, we were hungry. Daddy would not sign up for relief as he didn't want to embarrass his sisters. They always criticized him for having a big family. But a neighbor, who was township trustee, knew the situation and took pity on us. He also was in charge of the relief for our area, and he would bring us cornmeal, soup beans, and side meat at night. We never knew how he reconciled his records.

When my older brother and I were the only kids, people would always give us pennies. We had a Prince Albert Tobacco can full, but when things got bad, the pennies were used for food. Daddy and we kids would pick blackberries, and Mama canned them. One year, she did a hundred quarts. I remember the Crash—1929. Daddy was devastated. He lost all his money in the local bank.

The Coldest Spot in the Winter

by Shirley Welty of Carrollton, Ohio
born 1936

My family moved from Stow, Ohio to a farm, which had 88 acres, in Carroll County in April 1937. I was the youngest child of six. My parents figured they could raise the food to feed us on this farm. They were in the Depression and my father couldn't find any work.

My mother worked at "Motor End" restaurant for 15 cents an hour. Father was keeping house for us kids. He did work on W.P.A. some then also.

We got a cow from an older man who had a farm.

He paid us a visit one day and asked my mother what she'd think if he came one day leading a cow. My mother said, "Well, Sir, I'd take her in and milk her!" Back in these days neighbors were neighbors, not like today. He was sure a nice man. His wife had burned up in a house fire and he had a son.

We didn't have electric in this farmhouse or running water, much less, we had an outside "john." That was a cold pill!

My father eventually got a job and became an iron worker. He was gone a lot to other states or working in towns that was too far to drive. Then he would come home on the weekends.

Shirley's mother, Verdie Westfall, with some of her 700 chickens.

My mother started the farming with the help of the older brothers. She mowed down hay with a team of horses, then she'd turn it, and rake it. She planted corn, wheat and oats, as well as the many gardens for food we had. We had chickens, cows, and horses to feed.

All of us kids worked in the gardens and the crops. We hoed corn, put the hay in the barn. My job was to ride the work horse to pull the fork of hay up into the barn. We shucked the wheat, and carried it to the barn on wagons to be thrashed.

We had many chickens, like 500 to 700. We gathered eggs two to three times a day. They all were washed and cased in 30 dozen cases to sell to restaurants and individuals. My mother took the eggs every Wednesday to Canton to sell.

I had a beautiful collie dog, Rex, that stayed with me all the time outdoors. We had to go a long way to get the cows every evening for milking, and Rex went with me and helped to bring them in.

When we went to school, we walked a long way to wait for the bus. It was the coldest spot in the winter waiting for the bus. It was always late in the winter.

School was hardly ever called off like today. Sometimes we'd get to school an hour or two late, but the school started with whatever children that was there.

When we were kids and didn't feel good, my dad always gave us castor oil. He said that was the best way to get rid of colds etc., to take that, ugh!

We didn't have telephones until about 1950, then they were the kind that you had to ring by hand to get "Central," then she would get the call through for you.

When we moved to the farm, there wasn't electric in the house. There wasn't even running water in the house. We had a nice spring, which we carried by buckets to the house. We had an old wood coal cook stove in the kitchen. It had a reservoir for hot water. By the late 40s, we got things a little more modernized. Sure beat what we had before.

On the weekends we got to go to the movies in Carrollton. It cost 14 cents for a ticket. Then we'd go to "Isaly's" for a seven cent skyscraper cone, or a tin roof sundae for 14 cents. We really enjoyed that.

We had a wringer washer. You could put out a lot of clothes. We washed every Monday, for clothes, and Friday for sheets. We hung the clothes outside, or in the winter, we had lines in the basement.

We didn't have any heat in the upstairs, only what went up from a heat stove in the dining room. The cook stove in the kitchen helped to keep it warm too. Eventually, we got a coal furnace in the basement.

I remember Dad sitting by our big floor model radio every evening about 6:00 PM to listen to the news with Gabriel Heatter. We had to be quiet. We got a TV when I was in seventh grade. We were one of the first to have a TV, and everyone came to our house to enjoy it.

When I was in high school, my friend that lived next farm to us and I would skip school on Mondays after lunch time and go to the Carrollton stock sale. It was seven miles from school. We would find someone who was headed to Carrollton and get a ride there. Then we were always lucky to find someone heading back to Dellroy, and made it there on time to catch the school bus home. I never figured out how we never got caught. This wouldn't happen today.

When I was in high school, my brother and I milked 14 to 18 cows before school, and in the evenings. We had lots of chores to do. Kids today have no idea what it would be like to do this today.

I dated pretty young too, and I got married in my senior year of school. I still had to milk the cows before and after school, though.

I only had two months of school to finish after I got married. After graduation, my husband was in the Air Force, and we left for Dover Air Force Base in Delaware. My parents sold all the cows then. No more farming, all six kids were married and gone. My parents sold the farm and then moved to town. I'm sure I had things better than my older sisters and brothers did because of the times.

When I was little, Mother made a lot of my clothes. She was a great seamstress though, and they were nice. She would tear up old clothes that were good and make new ones for us. Back then, if you bought some kinds of feed for your animals, they used printed feed sacks. She would make curtains and aprons and clothes out of them.

We had good parents. We had strong discipline, and

we were taught respect. I guess those were the good old days!

A Good Time for Growing Up

by Joyce Hill of Nashport, Ohio
born in 1937

In early 40's, we moved to Lewis Drive. Our dad was in the army. There was three of us. Our little brother was just a baby. Our grandfather and aunt both worked at Mosaic Tile Company. They moved in with us to help pay the bills since at that time our mother didn't work. We got along pretty well.

We walked to Monroe Street School and home for lunch and back at night. Back then, no one was afraid to walk alone, day or night. We played baseball in the alley and did a lot of sled riding down Mitchell Hill. We would have it so slippery, cars couldn't get up to their homes. We would build a big fire and stay out well after dark. We loved it and never worried about getting cold. Also, we had a hood off of an old car we used as a sled. That thing would take you down a hill in nothing flat. What fun!

In 1948, the Lind Arena opened. Andy Foster was the owner and a guy named Ozzie took care of the skate room. We always got clamp-in-skates since there wasn't a fee for them. Then in later years, we got our own shoe skates. What a nice change! They had skating every night except Mondays and Tuesdays. There was skating also on Saturday and Sunday afternoons. What a good time we had going every chance we could.

In 1950, I started Hancock Junior High School on Sixth Street. That was an experience all its own, changing classes, going across the street for gym, home economics, and choir. Ninth grade graduation was a nice event. Also in 1950, we had a bad snowstorm. No taxis were running, no city buses, and people couldn't go to work. Pretty much everything was shut down. We were out of school for days which was okay with us. We ended up having fifteen inches of snow! What a mess. It seemed like everyone stayed home.

I believe in 1951, they began building Zanesville High School on Blue Avenue. The first class started there in 1954 and first graduating class was1955. That was the year the Zanesville basketball team won the state championship. That was a great time, parade and all. Things we will never forget. What memories! After school we would go to Jakes Sandwich Shop or Katsampes Ice Cream Parlor. We would meet with friends to eat, laugh, and have a good time.

Also in the 50's, they had square dancing at Valley Gem and out at Norwich. So Friday and Saturday there was also a good time. On Saturday afternoon, some of us would meet in downtown Zanesville and go to Kresges, dress shops, shoe stores, Newberrys and buy records and maybe a new outfit. There was so many places in downtown that aren't there now. There was also a portrait place up over Kresges. We would go up there and get our pictures taken for next to nothing. What fun we had trying on drapes and all; they draped around your shoulders for professional looks. We loved it!

Pioneer Electric was another place we would go in downtown Zanesville. On Saturdays, we would go in there and play records before we bought them. That was great! Then it was time to look for a job. Especially in 50's, you could get a job at Essex Wire on Sharon Avenue. Assembly work was fast and a lot of tape on fingers. They would cash our checks on Friday in the cafeteria which was nice. You could pretty much get a job there anytime. I could ride the city bus to and from work. That's when Pepsi still came in bottles. We could stop at Powells market on Putnam, and get six bottles of Pepsi to take home.

There was a flood in late fifties. We walked down on West Main Street. What a sight!

All in all it sure wasn't a bad time to be growing up.

The Miracle Sand Bar

By Richard Martin of Zanesville, Ohio
Born 1948

I was born in 1948 and raised in Philo, Ohio. Situated on the banks of the Muskingum River, Philo could be called a river town. Growing up so close to the river, it became our playground.

My brother, Dale, (now deceased) was nearly four years younger than I and we learned to swim in a creek we called Waxlers. Actually it is Duncan Run Creek, but an old lady named Louise Waxler owned a lot of land around the hole we swam at.

It was the last day of school and we were dismissed early. My brother and several others of us Philo boys headed for the river just south of Philo. There is a gravel bar located near an island there known for clams and a pretty fair fishing hole. There was one fellow in the group that day named Ray (not his real name) whom I didn't know very well. He had tagged along with the other boys and, as I came to find out, couldn't swim.

Except for Ray, we all were acquainted with this part of the river, having swam to the island and back many times. Being closer to the Philo side, there was a relatively swift waterway between the shore and the island. We could judge the current and swim downstream at an angle to get to the sandy beach of the island; a fascinating place for us kids. Going back was much harder. The river level was relatively low on that early June day, but there is always somewhat of a current at that particular place and the water was over our heads in depth.

It must have been 1962 because I was 13 and had just finished the 8th grade. My brother would have been 10 in August of that year and was a very good swimmer for his age. I was the best swimmer of the group and always swam near my brother. Dale and I lit out for the island first. The new guy was supposed to stay over on the gravel barge and the other guys set out to swim to the island after a short while.

Sitting on the sandy beach of the island, watching the others swim to us, Dale and I saw that Ray had waded into the water and was being carried out by the current. My brother and I yelled at the others to go back and help him, but they just kept swimming towards us. Probably best for everybody concerned that they did because (thinking back) they were only good enough swimmers to make it to the island. I told my brother that no matter what happened to stay on the island and not to leave it until I told him to.

I dove in and swam to Ray, passing the others on the way. I swam with all my might and got to him pretty quickly because the current was pushing him towards me. I started to talk to him, to describe how I intended to get him out of the river alive, but he surprised me how full of panic he was. Suddenly he lunged at me and grabbed me in a frantic "death grip" bear hug.

I was young and dumb, had no lifesaving training whatsoever and had only my skills as a swimmer to rely on. Plus, he was bigger than me. Not in height, but he was husky and a lot stronger than I'd anticipated.

Under we went! I panicked at that point too because I was exhausted. I had just swam a couple hundred yards to the island and about the same distance back through the current. I knew if I didn't get loose we were both going to drown. I raised my feet and got my knees between our chests and kicked us apart. I don't know where that strength came from, maybe from heaven. I bobbed to the surface gasping for very much needed air and started to swim away.

Ray was nowhere to be found and in another type of panic than before, I swam searching for him. In a desperate attempt to find him I decided to dive for him. Once, twice, three times I went into the now dark terrifying water with no luck. I knew I barely had enough strength left to make it to shore and started to swim away when I felt something touch my leg. I reached down and it was Ray's hand!

He had no fight left in him as I pulled him to the surface. He coughed, gasped and made funny gurgling sounding noises. I pushed and dragged Ray as best I could towards the shore as the current pushed us downstream.

I vividly remember to this day the despair I felt because I was exhausted beyond my limits. I was holding Ray's head above the surface but was going to have to turn him loose. I was so frightened; I knew he would die and somehow I would be to blame; how would I live with myself?

A thought came to my mind. As every "river rat" knows, there are sand bars throughout the river and I let my foot down to see how deep the water was. Like a gift from above, my toe touched bottom. I could feel solid sand, but it was sloped and I had to force myself and Ray uphill to get to where I could touch bottom and keep my head above water.

I lost track of what the others were doing, but they had swam back from the island and were almost to a river cottage boat dock downstream from the gravel bar. The current had pulled me and Ray down stream to just a little upstream of the dock the others had now climbed onto. Ray and I rested a while on that miracle sand bar. He was giving me no trouble at all at that point. He seemed to trust me entirely and after a while I moved around on the sandbar to find its highest point, which left the water to about chest high.

I still had a ways to go to get to the dock; and the water between us was over my head. Gary, Larry and, my brother Dale were on the dock and they all stretched out their arms and hollered, "Shove him the rest of the way!" I got my feet under me and pushed Ray as hard as I could, meanwhile kicking my feet in the water. With the help of the current they were able to catch him and I floated a ways downstream and had to swim back to the dock where they pulled me out too.

Once on shore Ray seemed to go into fits. None of us knew any type of CPR whatsoever. He gagged, coughed, puked and carried on something awful. He was ashy looking, but was alive and so was I.

After a while he kept saying thank you to the other guys and that they'd saved his life. They told him the truth, but he didn't seem to understand or didn't acknowledge it at first. On the way back to town I could tell he was aware of who had pulled him from the river and he made us all promise not to tell his parents, which wasn't hard for us; he rode the bus to school and we didn't know his folks. I never did know where he lived nor much else about him.

I have long since quit, but we all smoked cigarettes in those days. We were allowed to leave school for lunch and we'd puff up on our lunch break. I remember the next school year I ran into Ray at lunch and asked him for a cigarette. He turned me down! He said, "I only got a few left." I thought to myself, I didn't pull him out of that river for him to be beholden to me. I did it on instinct. I know if it were the other way around I would have obliged him at least one cigarette.

Thirteen years old, 130 pounds and I know even as an adult I don't belong in the river. Harrison Township built a pool in Philo in 1966. Best thing that ever happened to that town. If we'd had it back then I know we wouldn't have been swimming in the river.

Confessions of a BB Shooter

by Betty Lou Campbell of Cambridge, Ohio
born in 1938

I remember we lived on a small farm. My two younger brothers was playing at the end of a long driveway. They came home running. One of the boys got shot with a BB gun. Russell got shot, Ervin the shooter. My parents had policemen running all over the hill, but they couldn't find no shooter or gun. My whole family was afraid to go outside or walk in front of a window, except the two brave boys. We couldn't understand why they was so brave, because they should have been the ones that was scared.

We didn't find out who the shooter was until our parents passed away, and the brother that got shot. Then our younger brother told us it was him, and the reason they couldn't find the gun is they hid the gun at the end of the lane, and no one had a reason to look there.

Another experience was my parents had a rooster, and every time we went to the outside toilet, the rooster would slap us, and we would lock ourselves inside the outside toilet until our mother found us.

Another experience I had was we was poor, so my mother would get old ladies' coats and have her friends (Mary Jane—sister) to make me and my sister winter coats and put the fur on our coats too, and then make a hat of fur. But our hats always got "lost" on purpose.

I am in my 70s and to this day, I am afraid of roosters, chickens, ducks, birds, even down to canaries.

Four Bags the Same and the Music Roll Baby

by Margaret D. Smith of Barnesville, Ohio
born 1915

I was 94 on January 8, 2009. My son took 11 of our family to a local restaurant for lunch. What he paid for this lunch would have paid for seven or eight months of groceries in the mid 1930's.

That was a time of no money, no rest homes, no credit cards, no paid babysitters, no disposable diapers, no paper towels, and no throwaways. Most people did not have cars, electricity, bathrooms, and not much trash. There were some good things, some not too good.

It was a red letter day when the feed companies started putting feed into pretty printed bags, flowered, striped, and polka dots. We'd tell our husbands, "Get four bags the same." We could make a dress from four bags, made curtains and all clothes. I still have the tablecloth, purple and green, that my grandma crocheted around a feed sack for me when I got married. It's still pretty after 74 years of wear and tear. Things were made to last then.

A neighboring farmer sold ground chicken sandwiches on two slices of bread for five cents. If we had two nickels, we would go get them in the evening. They were so good.

And the movies, extra super, 25 cents each. We could sell a dozen eggs for 25 cents each at a local grocery. We would take two dozen eggs and sell them to go to the movies. They showed a small cartoon, news of the world, and the main movies. Roosevelt was in the news, later on, Hitler and the wars and Japan.

No one liked the oleo. It came in a white block with a tiny yellow capsule to mix in. If it was hard, it did not work. If runny it was terrible. Several years later we could buy yellow oleo and sliced bread.

Another bad job every morning, fill the lamps with smelly kerosene, wash the glass globes, and trim the wicks.

My pet peeve was ironing. No permanent press! We had "sad" irons to put on the stove to heat, one handle.

Roosevelt was elected in 1932 and took office in March 4, 1933. I graduated from high school that year and later worked at a small department store in our town of 4,000 people. I made $6.00 a week for 57 hours of work. F.D.R. put the blue eagle NRA sign in the window, then I could only work 40 hours a week for $13.00 pay. I was rich! I was in heaven. I showed Grandpa my check, he said, "You are making more than me!" He made $10.00 working in a planing mill.

Then F.D.R. put in the W.P.A. My dad got a job guarding shovels on Main Street at night. It was a cold winter. He could work 30 hours a week at 47 cents per hour. Now our family of four had two paychecks. I started me a bank account.

When I was 20, my intended, Mom and Dad and I got in his 1935 Studebaker coupe and I went to the courthouse for them to sign papers for us to get married. I sat on Dad's lap. For five dollars the minister married us at the parsonage.

My husband's family always had a car. My dad never owned a car. We went to Niagara Falls for our honeymoon and built a two room house on the farm. A large living room and a small kitchen, we had a studio couch opened into a bed and an open fireplace, and a little coal cook stove. It burned out in a year, but we could buy a new one at Sears for $5.00. So each year we did. No money, but very happy.

Then we found out I was "in the family way." His family had a player piano so we started rolling $1.00 bills in a roll of music. When I went to the hospital for our son to be born on September 25, 1936, he played the roll of music, we had 75 $1.00 bills, 25 for the doctor, and 50 for the hospital. My son and I stayed ten days in bed.

Margaret Smith, on the hood, with school friends in 1932.

Nobody threw anything away. Every family had a ball of string, a box of buttons, a Prince Albert tobacco can, and nails and screws, material scraps, etc. You repaired, made over, and re-used.

We had homemade Christmases. You could get an orange crate (30x18x18) free or for very little at the grocery. My husband made airplanes, trucks, and end tables. They were made of strong, thin, wood lengths. With hard work and sanding and paint, you had a long wearing gift. I made aprons for parties; they were welcomed gifts, also, pj's, pillows, and clothes.

Nobody was bored. We all worked hard, but had a satisfaction of seeing the results of a day's work, a garden, canned food, fences built, and clothes made. At night, too tired to need a sleeping pill, just went to sleep, children too.

We saved and used everything. All rubber tires had inner tubes. Sometimes, a boot, too, for extra safety. After the inner tube was patched too long, and no longer useable, they could be cut into strips and woven for pocketbooks. The ends could be fringed. They lasted forever. The rubber tire could be turned inside out and planted with flowers for the front yard. A little time and water. We would paint fences, old buildings, and trees, white in the spring.

All kids had kites, slingshots, all homemade. We had no TV or radio. People talked to each other and listened to each other. We exchanged ideas and plans. We valued our families. If a member was left alone, he or she was welcomed into another home that could use an extra pair of hands.

Grandma had an old brother, Uncle Ed, he just sat and rocked. Visitors brought him candy and they would tell him to "keep an eye on the children." We never minded. He shared his candy. We all loved our grandparents and liked to hear their stories.

We had a colored family on the next farm. They went to the city to find work. One day, my husband brought the prettiest white crockery chamber pot, painted with lavender violets and green leaves. "Pearl" had left it in their outdoor privy. We cleaned it up and forever more, "Pearl's chamber pot" was a conversation piece.

Everyone worked to think up new things to make or reuse what we had and we shared our ideas. Mum cushions were the fad. You needed a form for those. The tin foil on a stick of gum could be folded into a tiny strip and woven into an inch wide belt. I made dozens of those belts, beautiful crepe paper to make artificial flowers. My grandmother made enough sweet peas to cover an entire float for a parade.

We crocheted or braided rag rugs, used scraps for quilts. Our things were pretty and made our homes attractive with little money spent. We used newspapers to put under the rug.

My mother always put a clean tablecloth on the table when we ate. She'd put newspapers over it. I never liked that.

We had coffee cups and saucers, no mugs. Dad always poured his coffee into his saucer and he'd tip his chair so he balanced on the back two legs, never went over. They used canned milk in their coffee. I never drank milk until I married my former.

All my childhood years, and 11 years of my married life, we spent Christmas at my grandparents. My mom was one of nine, so there were lots of aunts and uncles and cousins. They always lived in town, but had a big garden, chickens, pigs, and a cow. They sold dressed white leghorn chickens; three for $1.00, rhubarb and green onions, three bunches for $1.00.

Everyone took the grandparents a gift, but no other exchange. Grandma loved gifts. Grandpa would cry and say (illegible) you shouldn't. He furnished the food. A bushel basket of donuts. Everyone sat at the table. The first table was the grandparents, the sons, in-laws, and my elegant aunt. The second table was the grownup grandchildren, third table was the younger children, the fourth table was the daughters and in-laws. It was a happy time.

I've rambled on here, but 94 years is a long time. I can't believe it has gone so fast. I have one son and three grandsons, six great grandchildren, and three great-great grandchildren. We are all close. I try to tell them, more to life than money. It just buys things.

Now I am alone, my home of things were not that important. I have never been sorry we didn't have more money. We did the things we wanted to by saving and planning. Wanting sometimes is half the fun. People today are missing a lot by being too busy.

I can't stop. When I was little, Grandpa saved buffalo nickels and bought a model T Ford car for cash. He and Grandma never could learn to drive, but whoever could would, and we'd all pile in the car to go visiting. At the bottom of the hills, we'd all get out and walk up the hill, except Grandma and the driver. They'd wait for us at the top of the hill. Most farmers had a tobacco field and a tobacco house for a cash crop. When the tobacco was ready to get in, everybody would go help stem the tobacco. It was fun. The farmer always planted some watermelons around the field. No money involved, just a tired, but happy day. The plantain weed that grew in the yard was my tobacco. I would stem the leaves, and take out the center leaf.

My dad was a cigar roller by trade, and later became manager for Roby Cigar Company. They later moved to Tampa, Florida, and my mother refused to move "out of the world."

The girls broke bunches by taking a number two tobacco leaf and putting scraps of tobacco in it, rolled to a rough form of a cigar, put into forms, then the roller, mostly men, on a board with a clip, cut a fine leaf of tobacco and rolled it on the form, a fine cigar. Tobacco finally phased out of here.

Who and Where They Are

by Frances Euman Snider Baughman of Somerset, Ohio
born in 1927

I've lived in Perry County all my life, 80 plus years and loved the area. My home is in Somerset. You hear folks say they live in the shadow of the church—I truly do. Holy Trinity Catholic church on Piety Hill, as they call it. I appreciate the fact that I can start my day by attending mass at my parish church. I volunteer each week at Holy Trinity School.

I am happily married to a wonderful man, Max Baughman. It was second marriage for both of us. I was a widow for 10 years when I married Max. His wife, Alice, was deceased too.

I have three children from my first marriage to my first husband, Bob Snider. He was a veteran of World War II, and proudly served our country. Bob was a young man when he passed away, age 43. Bob was just graduated from high school when he volunteered or the U. S. Army. He served four years—returned home and later he and I were married. We lived our married life in Somerset. Bob worked at Belden Buick until it closed and later was a talented carpenter. The war took a toll on Bob and the aftereffects weren't good. His death was attributed to heart problems.

My children, Stephanie Lynn Seifert, Catherine Jean DeRolph and David Snider were young adults when Max and I married. Lynn lives in Lancaster with her husband, John. They have two children; Dustin, who lives in Postales, New Mexico and Mollie Jean Seifert. Dustin is a professor of music at a small state college in Postales, New Mexico. I say God gave him his musical talent, because he didn't get it from his mom's or dad's family. Their daughter, my only granddaughter, was killed in an auto accident at age 25. Jeanie and Dale live in Glenford. They have two sons, Nathan and Christopher. Nathan and his wife, Leslie, live in Newark and have 2 children, Luke and Grace. Nathan is in the banking business, and Leslie enjoys the pleasure of the rare experience of being a stay-at-home mom; a busy mom though.

Christopher and Natalie live in North Carolina and they area both environmentalists. They are in the process of adopting a fine young boy, Nick.

My son David lives in Somerset. He and his wife, Anne, built a lovely home on the plot of ground that was where my childhood home was. They have three sons, Joseph, Robert, and William. I feel blessed that my children live close by.

We have family gatherings often and can spend all the holidays together. We go to Lancaster to Lynn and John's for Easter—to Glenford and Dale and Jeanie's for Thanksgiving and David and Anne's for a Labor Day celebration. Everyone comes to Max and my home Christmas Day.

Max's parents, Herb and Wilma Baughman both lived to be over 90, as did my mother, Bertha Euman. Good hard work never hurt that generation. They thrived on it.

As you can see—as you can read my life—it's been pretty ordinary. I haven't reaped any great (either awards or rewards), climbed any mountains, written a book, etc, etc. I'm pretty average for my times. I'd say I'm happy and content and I hope to have a few more good healthy years with Max. Thank you for taking the time to read.

Cultivating Corn With Grandpa

by Leslie C. Polen of Mineral City, Ohio
born in 1934

As a child, I was born in the depths of the Depression. I was raised on a dairy farm by my grandparents. My mother passed away when I was five days old. My grandparents on my mother's side of the family raised me the same as their own children.

As I grew up to the teenage level, I would go with Grandpa to the fields. During World War II, we would cultivate the cornfields with the mules and one row cultivators. After the war was over, my uncle came home from the U.S. Air Force, and in 1945, bought a John Deere tractor and next year bought another John Deere. Grandpa and I could really cultivate corn. I loved that part of my life.

When I was sixteen years old, Grandpa passed away. I was there for him as he went to be with the God. As I like at the time of my childhood, it was a great time in my life, which I carry with me forever.

"Casey Jones," the Robin Hood of Moonshining

by Dianna Kay Bobb of Corning, Ohio
born in 1944

I was born December 7, 1944, three years after Pearl Harbor was bombed. The war was just ending. There was two foot of snow on the ground. My mom and I had to be carried to the house on a stretcher. We lived back on a hill.

I can remember my mom cooking on a coal cook stove, buying ice at the ice plant in Glouster for our icebox, and we had a round table with one leg, three or four spider legs off from it. When I started school, Mom and Dad both got modern. We got electric, a gas cook stove, a refrigerator. We still heated with a coal "Warm Morning" heater and a grate (now known as a fireplace) to heat the house.

We listened to stories on the radio, Roy Rogers and Dale Evans, Gene Autry, The Lone Ranger and Tonto, Hopalong Cassidy. Television didn't come out until I was about eight or nine years old. We only had one channel, channel three out of Columbus. I remember my dad reading to me and telling us stories, which I would like to tell about my dad and mom.

My dad was a coal miner and a moonshiner. Back in the Depression days, he had to support my mom, three sisters, and two cousins. My mom's sister died, so Mom took her daughter, four years old, and son, eighteen months. I was born fifteen years after my youngest sister. I was more the age of the grandchildren.

My dad made and sold whiskey when he couldn't find a job in the mines. He helped the neighbors with food and other things they would need. Moonshine was illegal, so the revenuers were always looking for stills. My dad's real name was Haskell Paul, but somehow, he got the nickname "Casey Jones." He was a very honest person, never stole or lied. He always said he'd pay five dollars if anyone caught him lying. He was telling someone he only had to pay off one time, because this person asked my mom's age, so he just handed them five dollars, because Mom would have been mad, so I told Dad I wanted my five dollars because Mom told her own age. He said, "Anything you could turn into a joke was a fib, not a lie."

We lived down Scienic Road on the Athens and Perry County line in Athens County, which is now Oakdale Road. Dad was busted in 1962. The federal judge gave him three years in the pen (jail). The judge was from Perry County but worked in Columbus because he was federal. The judge told my dad, "You are like Robin Hood, steal from the government to feed the poor." After Dad went to jail, Glouster people took up a petition to get Dad out sooner. He was released in a year.

Dad didn't do too much after that. But he was fixing a still for a friend, and the revenuers came in on him again. He was in the woods above where we lived. The road is now named "Corn Still Road."

My dad never learned to drive. He tried two times and wrecked both times. Back in those days, you learned to drive and then got licenses. You had to take a driver's test but not a permit. My mom always drove Dad wherever he wanted to go. Mom died in 1975, so Dad would set on the bridge until someone came along to give him a ride. It was five miles to Glouster, where he shopped and socialized.

Everyone for two counties knew Dad and liked him. Ask anyone if they knew or heard of "Casey Jones," but not very many knew his real name.

We lived at the end of "Indian Run Hollow" in Athens County. The other end of the road comes out by "Miller High School." The road goes out toward "Beech Grove" Cemetery. Anyhow, my mom, dad, grandparents, aunts, uncles, and family is buried there.

My dad is a moonshiner legend. My dad also taught his brother, Eddy, to box. My Uncle Eddy taught his son to box, which Sam Jones is also well known. He brought the Golden Gloves to Glouster for a few years. He trained a lot of boys and girls. He (Sam) was also "Bondo Champ" of the United States in 1972. He has his gym in Glouster yet. Sam is four years older than me. He could probably tell a lot of stories about Glouster, which that is my hometown also, but things have really changed since I was a teenager.

There was twelve bars, a skating rink, a Charlie's (a kid hangout). I almost forgot, the ice plant had an ice cream parlor in the front. Then the Dairy Queen came about and the ice plant went out of business. The ice plant turned into a garage in one side, a fruit stand and then a pizza place. The ice cream parlor became a laundry mat. The A&P turned to a Key Market. Now everything is torn down. We now have "Happy Cat Junction." There is only one bar left, The Moose and Eagles. Charlie's is gone, a new post office and its parking lot in place of Charlie's and at one time, the old building had a wallpaper shop and shoe repair shop in one side. The skating rink and the bar in front of it burned down ten years ago.

I had five sons and one daughter. All my boys trained and boxed for Sam, but only for fun. I have a grandson Sam trained. Jeff won Tough Man Contest when he was sixteen, National Kick Boxing when he was seventeen.

Then he lost a few, now he cage fights.

Yes, when I was a kid, we had a Victrola, which I think I still have a few of the thick records somewhere. I would use a wringer washer, yet today, if I had one, where I grew up, snakes were everywhere. My two nephews got bit by copperheads.

I remember going to movie theaters, the silent movies, Maw and Paw Kettle and all their kids and animals.

Fred and the Thunder Mug

by Barbara Mead Garrett Ward of Barnesville, Ohio
born in 1929

My late husband, Frederick Lee Garrett, known to all his friends as "Fritz," was raised in the small town of Malaga, Ohio. Malaga was a typical crossroad town that boasted of a filling station, beer joint, and grocery store. Malaga boasted of a community church that had a very loud bell to call the faithful to church each Sunday morning.

As fate would have it, Fred lived across the road from the church with five sisters, mother and dad. In the center of the living room stood a huge pot-bellied stove above which was the register to heat the one big bedroom and at the bottom of one of the beds sat a chamber pot, also known as the family's "thunder mug."

Garrett family: Anna, Charles Garrett, Helen, Jesse Garrett, Eleanor. Picture on left: Fred; Picture on right: Ray Stegner.

As it so happened, the gentleman who rang the church bell would come over to Fred's home to visit until time to go back across the "street" and ring the second bell.

On this particular cold morning, Fred's dad got up, stoked the potbelly stove to a red hot temperature. Someone moved the "thunder mug" close to the register above the pot bellied stove, and when Fred jumped out of bed, his foot landed in said "thunder mug." The contents (you know what they were) sailed down on the red hot pot-bellied stove!

His mother was frantic. The gentleman was coming to the house before ringing the bell the second time: disgrace, disgrace for poor little Freddie.

This same little fellow grew up to become one of the 551 Lost Battalion members. He was in the first group to jump into enemy fire during daylight hours. The battalion was so scattered, it became known as the "lost battalion." After his death, the medals, ribbon, and certificate from the French government arrived to testify to the little fellow who stumbled in the chamber pot. He was a decorated defender of his (and our) country.

Raised on a family farm in Belmont County, Ohio, I was privileged to grow up with Grandpa, Grandma, Mother, Dad, Sister, and Brother in one house, and Uncle, Aunt, and five cousins in a small adjoining house.

Tobacco was the money crop, with a log cabin tobacco house where the women would string the tobacco.

Another great day was hog butchering. Talk about a football! We kids would get the bladder, fill it with water, and so the game began.

Threshing, another great day. Grandma baked for days ahead and neighbor ladies came to help feed the men who came to thresh.

All summer days were endless: water to pump, eggs to gather, hoping there was no blacksnake in the nest, haymow to play in, warm milk squirted in your mouth by Uncle George with the aim to match the best pitcher any ballgame produced. Nights to catch lightening bugs, listen to whippoorwill birds and each to take your lamp oil light, make sure the wick was trimmed, and like The Ten Virgins in the Bible, you made sure your lamp was full.

Across the cornfield, a swimming pool was dug out where neighbors gathered at dusk with their cakes of Ivory Soap to wash off the cares of the day.

You cannot imagine my surprise when I realized we were poor people. Only as I grew older did I realize we were as rich as Rockefeller. As a matter of fact, Dad always told me the stork carried me with a label, "To the Rockefellers," but he let me fall over the Mead farm and I fell out. Yes, a Rockefeller taste on a Mead budget.

Oh, by the way, the outhouse had a Sears Catalogue. We knew a new one was due when we got to the farm implement section.

Always hoping you'd get the first bath on Saturday night. The kitchen became the bathroom with the wash tub brought in from the wash house.

I was not very old when I was given 10 cents on Saturday and went to B&O Station, where a friendly porter would help me on the train and I would go by myself to Grandma Peddicord's. No one thought anything bad would ever happen, and Dad would joke, "Don't worry. If they get you under the street light, they'll let you go." So much for child protection. Wish a child could feel that safe again.

My personal opinion is that TV changed our lives completely. My aunt went to the 1936 World's Fair and told us she saw things filmed in one room, shown in another room. We all laughed and knew it was a trick. In a few years, this same aunt had one of the first TVs in Barnesville. Everyone visited for just the night when reception was possible to crowd into her dining room to watch. Actually, we couldn't believe our eyes.

Henry: Setting the Record Straight

by Ruth Crosier Jones of Freeport, Ohio
born 1945

It was a Sunday afternoon in late November 1960. I was a sophomore at the old Freeport High School and I was sitting in our living room completing homework for the following day. My sister (Donna Crosier Bower) and my father were enjoying a jam session in the dining room directly behind our living room. Donna was playing her accordion, and Dad was accompanying her on his guitar. My mom was enjoying an afternoon nap.

Suddenly I heard a loud roar outside. I rushed to look out the window and was amazed to see a small plane pulling up into our side yard. I called, "Dad, Donna, there's a plane in our yard!" They immediately came running. Dad rushed out the door. Mom joined Donna and me to see what was causing the commotion.

A short time later, Dad came back in with the young man who was piloting the plane. His name was Henry Rupert. I cannot remember whether he said he was flying from or returning to Dayton. He had run out of gas and somehow managed to put his plane down on Route 8, now Route 800, just about one-fourth mile south of the Harrison/Tuscarawas County line.

My dad called the New Philadelphia Highway Patrol to report the situation. While we waited for them, Mom fixed Henry something to eat. I remember our sitting around the dining table while Henry told us his story.

Henry was a Hungarian refugee. In October 1956 the people of Hungary revolted against the Communist regime. Unfortunately for them, the Soviets quickly put down the revolt in just a few short days. Henry was one of some 200,000 citizens who fled Hungary. He told us he had swum across a wide river to escape. It was possibly the Danube or Tizza River. Neither my sister nor I can recall. He had become an American citizen and settled in Dayton, Ohio where he had been able to find employment.

By this time the highway patrol had arrived. Since it was late in the day, they took Henry with them to New Philadelphia and arranged for him to stay the night there. The next morning after I had gone to school, they returned with Henry and gasoline. Route 800 was closed both north and south a ways to allow Henry to take off. The event was reported in the newspaper the next day. It may have been in *The Daily Times*. I do recall the article incorrectly stated that the plane landed in our neighbor's field. It never mentioned our family. This greatly distressed me, of course. Here was my one chance for fame and the paper nixed it.

Henry corresponded with our mom every Christmas for many years after his brief visit with us. We always looked forward to getting his card and hearing about his marriage and family.

I have no idea whether Henry is alive, or if he still lives in Dayton. He would probably be in his seventies now or even early eighties.

Rubadub

by Sandra J. Daniels of Quaker City, Ohio
born in 1938

I was born into a single parent nest, but my gramma taught life is only what you make of it. I was more or less a dreamer, taking myself out of my situation, however dull, and pretending to be a famous dancer (applause, applause) or another little Shirley Temple star (how we loved Shirley Temple), then Monday morning was upon me before I was ready for it. Wash day – and time to gather up all dirty clothes from eight people, plus bed clothes, maybe blankets or quilts, depending on the weather!

Financially we were very poor; blessing-wise, we were quite rich. We worked from sun up to after sun down helping keep this crazy bunch together and healthy, learning to be happy with what life passed our way, each one looking after the other, sort of.

Monday morning was early and cold – can't recall winter wash days whether it was done outside, but most likely, or did we somehow move the old wringer washer and the two rinse tubs and stand inside the kitchen because of the cold? But I, somehow, have the feeling it was done outside at the washhouse and we wore heavy scratchy sweaters, scarves, and gloves, at least for a while.

There was a gray and white speckled cook stove out there which probably kept us from freezing and was also used to "cook" dirty clothes and our supper. We knew soup beans, corn bread, or soup was our Monday night menu. Grandma always had a small penknife in her apron pocket. This was used to chip up small pieces of homemade soap – lye soap – but that is another story.

Back to the laundry: depending on how dirty we had

managed to get our white clothes – they would either be put to boil with lye soap, bleach and sometimes borax (20 mule team) when Grandma determined the clothes were as white as they would come, she yelled for me to get back and with a big wooden stick, she lifted the clothes from the boiler to the washing machine to wash as long as she determined.

When the kettle was empty it had to be washed out, wiped out, and refilled with water. We pumped and carried buckets of water heated for the next washer load. We also had to change the rinse water.

Now it was time to sort through the beans, pick out the stones and rinse and cover them with fresh water; add the seasoning and put them in the bean pot on the stove in the washhouse to cook for our supper. Depending on the amount of soiled clothes, pumping and carrying water and heating some of the water to wash with and rinse in the ice cold water—after lunch we might be bringing out pie or cobbler to bake in the oven for supper, and closer to suppertime, a big pan of Johnny cake (corn bread) to bake for supper, sometime biscuits.

Clean clothes were hung outside on long lines to dry. Our bed sheets were made from bleached out Ben Franklin sugar sacks and hemmed very smoothly. On special occasions she would receive a set of store-bought sheets, which she cherished, by not boiling or bleaching every week.

Today we do our laundry in minutes, throw the clothes in the dryer and complain about how tired we are from doing laundry. I'm glad I learned to work and do laundry the old time way. This was laundry in the good old days, but I prefer today's laundry.

Falling in Love at Milking Time

by Alice R. Clark of Barnesville, Ohio
born in 1938

I was raised on a small farm in southeast rural Ohio with my parents and three brothers and two sisters. We attended a rural one room school for eight grades with one teacher. We had a big pot bellied stove for heat in the school. I was janitor for three to four years. We raised our own gardens, canned vegetables, and fruits, raised our own beef for meat, milked cows, and had our own chickens. My dad butchered beeves, hogs, etc. for a local slaughter house. We did our own farming. Haying with horses. Our area did not get electricity until the 1950s.

My dad hauled cream from the local farmers to a dairy about 20 miles away. He would also pick up grocery orders for these people and bring back to them. Sometimes I went with him on these days. Other times I would stay home, help in the gardens with the chickens, hang out the clothes on wash day, watch my brothers and sisters. Before electricity, we had to take our milk, butter, etc. down over the hill to the spring house. This had to be done three times a day before and after meals. My two older brothers were either working away or in the military.

Our area had a local high school in the country about 12 miles away. But our town closest to our area had a high school. The one in the country closed in 1954 and we all had to go to the one in our local town.

We had a lot of neighbors near and far. A family of parents and 13 children moved just below our place. One of these boys was always at our place at milking time. I was always telling him to go home, but he still stayed around. We started going with each other when I was a senior, fell in love with him, married, live not far away from my home place and his. We live on a farm. My husband did public works for about 15 years and then he and our second son dairy farmed for around 20 years. We have two boys, Steve and Scott and one girl, Sharlein. We have two grandchildren, Brianne and Brian. Bri is in college in Ada and Brian is in seventh grade. Our oldest son, Steve, and wife live not too far away from us. He is employed by the county. His wife also works. Our second son is employed by a mining company, not married, and owns the farm where we live. Our daughter lives in Fort Worth with her husband. We have two step grandsons. We now have beef cows. My husband and son do several farms and put up hay for other people and for resale. We see our son and family almost daily and also we go to the same church. We don't get to see our daughter and son-in-law as much as we would like, but we do talk every day.

I worked public works—different positions, mostly office work. I retired in 2002. We are now into a whole different business. We raise Heeler dogs and sell puppies, also have border collies and sell the puppies. We also have chickens (around 500) and sell eggs to local businesses and also sell from our home. We keep busy. We enjoy what we do. We don't have the time to visit like we would like to do.

Both of our home places have been purchased by relatives, so we can say it is still in the family. We got to Fort Worth to visit our daughter and son-in-law. We also go out to eat on Saturday night and also to the local mall about 20 miles away. We also go to church on Sunday.

We hope our readers enjoy our story as much as we enjoyed writing about it. There is a lot more to our story, but you have here the high points. By the way, we have been together 52 years.

My husband has helped out during the pumpkin festival which is held in our local town. There is always a big parade and a lot of people visit our town during this time.

My husband has played the local Santa Claus for our town and also for the local Christmas Parade until this last year (2008) because he had surgery on his back and couldn't do it, but he is recovered very nice and looking forward to doing the pumpkin festival and Christmas parades in 2009

I am looking forward to spring and warm weather, also to working in the flowers and garden. We are members of the Church of Christ along with our son, daughter-in-law, and grandchildren.

I could write on, but there is always a stopping place. I hope you like my story.

Bad Bread, Pumpkin Pie and Ginger Tea

by Stanley J. Gatten of Gahanna, Ohio
born in 1940

My family lived on a farm in the 1940s, and we didn't get to a store too often, whereby my mother would bake her own bread from scratch. We bought most of the food products in bulk 25 to 50-pound bags. Flour, salt, sugar, etc.

There was five of us children. Four boys and one girl. We also had a young girl that lived with us through an agreement between our family and her family. She was older than us children by a few years, but was still a kid in her middle teens. She has always been a sister to us, since she helped raise us. She loved to help Mom with cooking, etc.

On one occasion, she asked my mother if she could make the bread by herself, to which my mother agreed. She normally would make up some 10 to 12 loaves of bread at one baking. Since she had helped before, Mom let her go ahead and do the complete batch on her own, which she did without the need of Mom's assistance.

Stanley Gatten's mother's birth house. The building in the front is a crank up water well.

The mixing, raising and re-raising went just fine, and all the loaves were baked in the old iron wood stove, and when finished (which took several hours), the bread smelled and looked great. We all were just happy as could be with her.

Naturally, we had to sample the bread as always was done immediately after baking. Upon doing so, we were totally shocked. The bread tasted just terrible. We didn't want to tell her and tried to hide it, but she and Mom saw our faces and tried it too. We didn't want to hurt her feelings, and tried to tell her we liked it and would eat it.

We couldn't, of course. Our dogs wouldn't even eat it.

Mom knew what the problem was pretty quick. The bread was very, very salty. Our sister had gotten the wrong bulk bag and had used Epson salts instead of regular salt in the bread mix. Our sister cried for an hour, even though all of us kids tried to comfort her and tell her it was just a mistake.

The bad part was, of course, we had to throw all that bread away. The chickens and the dogs wouldn't even eat it.

Our sister is almost 80 years old now, and we will tell that on her at our reunions, and we all have a good laugh about it.

As a kid in the 1950s, I was very fond of pumpkin pie, and my mother made the best. The problem was I had three older brothers and a younger sister, plus we always had a bunch of visitors (relatives and friends). It seemed I never was able to get the share of pumpkin pie I wanted. With research, though, I was able to find a perfect hiding place for one whole pie.

We had an old spin dry washer (one with two tubs). One tub, Mom used to wash the clothes. It also had a hand wringer, which she used since the spin dry tub didn't work. Well, the spin dry tub would fit a pie pan perfectly in the top and it also had a lid that would come down and cover it to hide the pie when placed there. At the time I didn't think about why Mom didn't question about a missing pie, but in later years I knew she just knew where it had gone and didn't let on.

I'm sure she knew where my hiding place was. I think she would just make an extra pie, knowing where it was going and have a good laugh to herself about it.

One summer in the late 1940s, my three older brothers and cousin and I decided we would go hand fishing in Bendfork Creek, leaving from my cousin's and ending up at our grandfather's, which was up the creek about a mile or two apart. Hand fishing was going into the water and reaching under rocks and banks to catch fish in your hands.

About three fourths of the way, we decided we were not doing so well and decided to walk through a grass field (about ankle deep or a little higher grass) the rest of the way. We were walking in a straight line with me on the end of the line.

All of a sudden I felt something hit my trouser leg and looked down to see a copperhead snake. I was fortunate enough that I had kept walking before he could strike again. I yelled snake! to my brothers, who fixed that critter real quick. That was one of the luckiest days of my life without a doubt, but we never could figure out how no one had gotten bitten in front of me. Fortunately for me, the snake was far enough away or late on the strike, or a combination of the two, and my jeans were just heavy enough to prevent the bite.

When I was a kid in the 1940s to 1950s, my mother had a home remedy for treating the croup, since we couldn't get to a doctor's office, nor afford to. One remedy was a spoonful of lamp oil (kerosene) and sugar. The other was ginger tea. Both were terrible to take. I could stand the lamp oil and sugar, but not the ginger tea. I remember saying, "It's down," after drinking the whole cup straight down, and then saying, "It's back up," after vomiting it right back up. Both the above must have worked, because I always seemed to get through the croup, and I am still going. I also have not had the croup for some 60 years now.

In the 1940s/50s, red and blackheart cherry trees grew in abundance along the roads and everywhere else in Belmont County. There are few left these days for some unknown reason. It was very common for me and my brothers to find a tree to climb and enjoy our fill during the summers.

On one occasion, my next older brother and I decided to climb our neighbor's tree just up the road from our property, which was along State Route 147. Being the young and ornery kids that we were, it somehow was decided that we would throw a few cherries at an occasional car passing by. We probably missed most of those that we threw at. Unfortunately for us, one car that we threw at stopped, and a very irritated, older, ex-teacher neighbor of ours got out. He had seen us in the tree. Several cherries had hit his windshield. He was not happy about it and immediately demanded we come down and clean the cherries off his windshield.

My brother was a kid that did not cater to anyone, and immediately said no way. An argument followed between my brother and neighbor to the extent he was going to climb up the tree and bring us down. I didn't want him to attempt that, so I finally climbed down and cleaned off the windshield. My brother stayed in the tree, of course. He still brings that ordeal up from time to time, and we have a good laugh about it.

Finally, Another Girl to Play With

by Sandra Russell of Hebron, Ohio
born in 19??

Unlike today—I grew up in times when we felt safe and secure. It was a small town along the Ohio River, a small little house with Mom, Dad, and three brothers. But when I was a senior, my mom had another baby (girl). Finally, I had a sister, and three years, she had another little girl.

But back to growing up. The neighborhood was all boys, so for many years, I didn't have anyone to play with. I would go with my brothers to a neighbor's, and we would all play in the sandbox, building roads and pushing our little cars and trucks around. I can even remember the smell of the nice summer day and the *arsama* around that house.

Then one day, a family built a house in the neighborhood, and guess what—there was a girl my age. And she had a brother and sister that was younger. We all spent a lot of time together. We talked on the phone some, but back then, you couldn't stay on a long time, because you shared your phone line with others. It was called a party line. People could listen to your conversation.

We didn't stay in the house because we didn't have TV or computers. I remember the day we got our first TV. The picture wasn't real clear, and I remember one of the first shows was Captain Video. We thought that was the greatest thing ever. I remember before TV, my one brother rocked on his rocking horse, listening to polkas on the radio.

My girlfriend and I spent a lot of time playing in the woods. We would go up this little creek and play in the creek, and there was grapevines we would swing on across the creek. We would build houses out of big sticks in the woods and play house. Our dogs would follow us. We could go out and play, go into the woods with no fear of anyone bothering us. My friend and I spent many hours playing jacks, marbles, and roller-skating.

We also walked around the neighborhood with our dogs and our parakeets on our shoulders. People would take a second look—like, "Did I see what I thought I saw?"—Those were such carefree times.

I didn't have designer clothes. I remember going to a lady's house, and she would measure out material made out of feed sacks and make my dresses.

The man next door had horses, and I love to stop, pet, comb, and braid their manes. Sometimes he would see me and get mad, because I was paying attention to them.

I remember my friend and I would walk down to the store, which was probably over a mile (never had to worry about someone taking us), and we would go buy penny candy and five-cent Popsicles and five-cent Sugar Daddies.

I remember we had an old corncrib, and me and my friend cleaned it up and hang pictures on the wall, and it was our playhouse.

Sundays were special, because we spent a lot of them going to Grandma's for dinner, and our cousins would be there, and all got to play, and Grandma always and a good meal and all the goodies to go with it.

Floating Cake, Bag Holding and the Celebrity Sis

by Mavis Young of Woodsfield, Ohio
born 1930

Mother sat by the phone on the wall and shushed us as she listened to her neighbors gossiping about their neighbors. As she took her hand from the mouthpiece, she chimed in to tell the ones on the phone, "That's not the way it really was."

Our ring was one long and three shorts. But that didn't keep everyone else from listening in on other people's conversations.

My sister, Joy, swears that she had to be the last one to get a bath in the wash tub every Saturday night after our brother, who was the oldest, and me ,who was the middle child, of course in the same soapy water. The water was heated on the kitchen wood stove and then poured into the wash tub

This is the same wood stove that I made my birthday cake in when I was about nine. I had no trouble reading and following the recipe, but, as the stove had no thermostat on it, I could not tell when it was hot enough to bake. All I could remember was that it was hotter than hell when Mother baked. So I fired the stove till it was that hot and carefully put the full cake pans in the oven.

The cake burned to a crisp in about five minutes. Then I had the problem of how to get rid of the evidence that I had been trying to bake while Mother was out at the barn milking. I put it into the slop bucket where all our scraps from the kitchen went to give to the pigs. Then I hurried and washed everything and thought I had it made. I did until Daddy wanted to know what that thing was that was floating in the slop bucket.

My aunt used to burn wood outside to make lye to add to lard to make homemade soap. When the wood was down to ashes, she would pour water over the ashes slowly and gather it up with a wooden spoon. I do not know what kind of wood that she burned, but the ashes were white.

Mother had it easier. She bought her lye in a blue can at the hardware store. I have a recipe for soap from an 1865 cookbook.

Feed sacks used to be printed cotton. Each one had a different print. When we got two or three alike we had enough to make a dress. Mother would wash and dry them so that they were pre shrunk. I used to love to pedal the sewing machine as fast as I could.

When I was nine years old, I pledged my head and heart, my health and hands and joined 4-H Club where I learned to sew. So as soon as Daddy bought the chicken feed, the sacks were used for my sewing rampages. Mother and my grandmother pieced quilts for years out of the sacks that I ruined.

My uncle and aunt and their son and wife used to go to town on Saturday night in their white shirts and fancy clothes to have a beer and watch the crowds of people. We didn't get to go, so we were very jealous. In front of our house was an old bridge where one side had fallen down and another had been built over it. As elderberries grew beside the old bridge in abundance, the plan was developed to hide down by the fallen down part and throw elderberries at them when they drove by. So when the relatives drove by with their windows open, we got them good, all over their white clothes.

Our dog, Jack, was with us as always. He was a snake killer. He slung them back and forth till he tore them to pieces. Well, that day Jack caught a big one and did what he did best and slung it all over Joy and me. We had on our little pink elephant dresses. We ran screaming home. Mother and Daddy each took one of us and pumped water from the cistern and washed us off. They laughed at us all the time.

Brother Kenneth was trapping and caught a skunk. We could smell him before he came into he house. Mother made him come in the cellar door, take off his clothes and put them outside. Then he had to take a bath two times. Mother had to soak his clothes in tomato juice to get rid of the smell. Luckily we had lots of it canned in the basement.

Snipe hunting was a favorite game or trick played on any unsuspecting kid. My first time was when my famous brother offered to take me. He took elaborate precautions to get ready. We had to get a big burlap sack to hold the snipe. He carried the bag till we got to the woods, then he told me it was my job to hold it while he went out and caught the snipes.

I waited and waited on him to bring in the snipes. It seemed like hours and I finally got scared and ran to the house. Guess what? There was my brother sitting in the corner of the couch listening to his favorite radio station, WJJD Chicago. Then I knew what "left holding the bag" meant.

We had a neighbor whose grandson came to stay with her every summer. We were the only kids in the neighborhood, so he came to our house most afternoons. Joy, my sister, and I convinced him that we could nail a cup of water up in the cherry tree. So we pumped a cup of water from the well where we got our drinking water, got a nail from Daddy's supply and climbed the tree by climbing up the fence then to the lowest limb.

Then I had Joy hand me the cup of water and then Robert was supposed to hand up the nail. But when he looked up with the nail in his hand, naturally I poured the water in his face. We thought it was a great joke. This is the same boy that we got to lay on his back in the grass and spit up in the air.

Daddy made a keg of wine every fall. He had

company every evening all winter. Mother used to keep a little pitcher of it by the old wringer washer. She said it made washing day go so fast.

When we were in 4-H club, my brother and sister and I each had a pig for our project. As butchering and selling them was part of the project, that day soon came. Bro was to shoot them and stick them to bleed. He did mine and Joy's sure enough, but his he only wounded and it ran around the yard screaming. Daddy had to do the deed. We had, of course, made pets of them and I couldn't watch but the sausage was good.

Years later when I had two little kids, I raised two pigs. When I weaned the kids from the bottle and they screamed, I told them that the pigs ate their bottles. When those two pigs were butchered we had a big snowstorm. It was 1948 or 1949. The butcher shop left the pigs cut up on the table for my husband to pick up when he got of work. The snow was too deep to drive in so he got a sled and brought what he could and the rest spoiled. Of course he had stayed too long at the tavern talking about the snow. No one could move for two days.

The most memorable person that I have known was Kay Young, my sister. Kay was born to be a star. On the day she was born, October 3, 1945, I was almost fifteen and her other sister was thirteen. Her older brother was in the Merchant Marine. She was everybody's pet.

Mother always raised a big garden. When anyone came to visit, Mother took them out to look at it. One Sunday afternoon we had visitors and Mother didn't get them out there fast enough for Kay and Kay went to the garden and gathered all of the tomatoes and brought them into the house. The only thing wrong with that was they were all little green ones.

She thought she was the only person in the world. One time she pulled a little chicken to pieces because it belonged to her sister. She stuck a bean up her nose and it had to be removed by a doctor after it sprouted. I don't believe she ever got spanked.

As a teenager she was head majorette. She had to perform with her hand in a cast because she had hit a cow on the head with her hand.

She graduated from Skyview High School in the first class to graduate there. She took harp lessons from the music teacher there and performed at weddings. She had to be the best at everything.

She saw a bodybuilding show once and said, "I could do that. I already have big calves." And she did, from chasing her pony over the hillsides. And she caught him too. She practiced on uneven parallel bars that Daddy made for her. She went to Kent State where she graduated with a degree in Physical Education. She met her husband there, Craig Baxter, and they moved to Toronto, Ontario.

She kept his last name throughout her career. She ran a health spa In Toronto. She wrote a booklet on physical fitness, diet and nutrition for the Canadian Women's Army. She began to compete in amateur fitness contests and began to win.

When her marriage became untenable, Mother went to Toronto to help her bring her things home. Kay moved to Colorado with her sister. They planned to open a health spa in Joy's home. They neither one had any money so that didn't work out.

Kay went to San Francisco and continued to work on her bodybuilding. In 1982 in the competition in Austria, she was best in the world. She competed in Caesar's Palace in Las Vegas and came in third. She competed in the Miss Olympia in Madison Square Garden where the crowd went crazy for her but she did not even place. The judges were still looking for the cutesy girl for their ads in Muscles and Fitness magazine. Atlantic City was the same result.

She moved to Los Angeles, the center of the body building industry. She trained with Arnold Schwarzenegger and was a personal trainer for Sybil Shepard and Richard Simmons among many other of the rich and famous, and advised them on nutrition.

She met and married Bill Wick who was a judge for the body building industry. He convinced her to join the Army which she did the day before she turned 35 years old. She said the Army was for 18-year-old men, not 35-year-old women. But at least she did not jump off the barracks roof like so many of the men did.

She divorced Bill Wick and met a Colonel in the British Navy. She bought a long crochet dress in which to be married to the Colonel. She was buried in it instead.

In 1987 she bought a house in Laguna Hills. She paid $75,000 down and took her martial arts teacher as a co-buyer as he promised to make the payments. The first month he paid the payment. The second month he gave her a bicycle. The third month he took in a "student" of his. That student was from Texas and his money came out of the ground. He "disappeared" and left his red corvette for the "teacher."

Joy and I went to visit in October of 1988. We advised her to get out of there as there was something fishy going on. The teacher had another friend living with him. So there were three adults living there in the same house and no one got up and went to work.

Kay bought another house in Laguna Hills and moved into it. A few weeks later someone trashed her house, poured bleach on her leather clothes and couch, and scratched her new TV, etc. It was the "teacher" as he was losing control of her and her money. He had been trying to promote a martial arts movie with him as the star. The "teacher" had imported some "stunt men" from England to help with his movie.

Kay called me from her home and said someone was trying to kill her. We talked about it for a while. The next day, I got a call from Joy who told me Kay was dead. One of the "stunt men " had taken her for a ride in the Corvette convertible, driven the wrong way on Milholand Drive and went over the *only* bank on the drive. He had contusions to his buttocks and she was dead. The "stunt men" went back to England the next day.

She is buried in Middle Church Cemetery, Lewisville, Ohio, with her mother and father. It was May 1989. Kay was 43 years old.

Disclaimer: Mavis Young, the contributor of this story, accepts full responsibility for its content.

Forty Cents the Hard Way

by Phyllis Patton Luke of Clayton, Ohio
Born 1936

Grandpa Hillis bought a farm outside Moxahala from the coal company. There was a small house on the property that he and his sons dismantled. They moved it by team and wagon seven miles to New Lexington, where they rebuilt in on Harrison Street. I was born in that house in 1936 and it is still there today.

Growing up in that era was fun as there were two movie theaters, the same school that my dad and uncle attended and lots of good friends and family. The janitor at school used to put the cinders from the old furnace on the playground which made for some scraped knees. When I took a hard fall on them and cut my leg, Dr. McDougall said he would give me five-cents for every stitch that I didn't yell. It was a hard way to earn 40-cents.

The war was on of course, and everyone was doing their part. We looked forward to a day off from school to go all over town to collect tin cans and newspapers and sales tax stamps.

The star hung in everyone's window that had someone in service. I was very proud of my dad, but we missed him.

Grandpa Patton was a foreman at the tile plant and he would sometimes take me to see the pottery; mostly cookie jars, that was being made in the 40's. My children surprised me last Christmas by finding three of the jars on E-bay for my present. They are a treasure to me.

It was a thrill to have my first communion breakfast at the Park Hotel on Main Street in New Lexington. It was very classy in its day.

Everyone had a victory garden and fruit trees and lots of sharing with each other so the rationing didn't seem too bad.

Quarantines were common as was the dreaded fear of polio. We were blessed to only have two cases in our area.

Many pleasant memories were from sitting on the porch in summer, waiting till the house would cool off enough to sleep. We would get a half pint of ice cream that had to be eaten before it melted. The iceman, egg man, and the Omar man were all welcome sites with their wares when they came each week to the house.

Thank you for allowing me to share a small portion of lots of memories in a not forgotten era.

In the 50's we lived on Main Street in New Lexington and this very handsome boy from Columbus came to visit me. For parking in front of the house that Sunday, he got a ticket and had to pay 50 cents. Fortunately, it didn't discourage him, as we just celebrated our 50th anniversary.

Spelling Detroit and the Trombone Player

by Janet Ann Kear Ramage of Byesville, Ohio
born in 1926

I must go back many, many ears in my memory and jot down a bit of background before I get to the escapades of Janet Ann.

Being the youngest of three children, a brother eight years older and a sister six years older, whom I surprised by coming into this world on my sister's first day of school in 1926. Neither of them had any idea that a new baby sister was coming to live with them.

I grew up in a happy home in the very small town of Lore City, Ohio. We were surrounded by Dad's family of Grandma and Grandpa Kear, his three sisters and families and Dad's Uncle Jack. I felt as much at home in any of their homes as I did my own. Often being there at mealtime, it was just expected to have another plate placed on the table. My cousins felt the same way when they were at our house.

Dad worked in a coal mine and I realize now it was a back breaking job with very little pay. I would venture to say that around 80 percent of the men and older boys worked in the mines if they had a job at all. Being very young, I would run to meet Dad on his return home from work to see what he had left in his lunch pail for me. It was never very much, but I thought I had hit the jackpot when the lunch pail was opened.

Mom was a very hard worker, having a reputation of "You could eat off of Mary's floor," not that anyone would want to, but she cleaned and scrubbed with a place for everything and everything in its place. During the summer and into fall, she canned everything that Dad could grow in his garden.

We didn't have a change of clothes for every day, they were sometimes worn two or three days, with a different set of clothes for Sunday only. Laundry, or "the washing," was done early every Monday morning in the kitchen using two round galvanized tubs, one with hot soapy water and the other with cold water for rinsing. This was done with a bar soap, that I remember as Fels-Naptha, and a wash board made of a wood backing and covered with ridges of tin to scrub away any stains. This was done only after the white clothes had been boiled on top of the stove in what was called a "boiler" mostly made of brass. Mom's washing was something that she was very proud of, because when it was hung on the clothesline, they fairly sparkled. They were also hung on the line in order, with the sheets first and graduating to the smaller pieces.

Janet Ann Kear and Richard Ramage's wedding picture in 1945.

My Grandma Kear was a short, round, loving lady that was sick most of the time that I knew her. It was probably her last Christmas with us that I received a red bracelet from her and Grandpa. To me it was the most beautiful bracelet that I had ever seen.

One day while in the first grade I wore the bracelet to school. Having to go outside to the outhouse, the only convenience that any of us knew, it sometimes caused big problems, and that was the day I thought my world had come to an end. I didn't fall through the hole in the seat, but during the shuffle of pulling up or pulling down my clothes, my beautiful bracelet fell in. I can remember the horrible feeling of seeing it, but I couldn't reach it. I saw our janitor, Mr. Jordan, who was deaf, and some way I got the message across to him what had happened. With a stick and a nail in the end of it forming a hook, he went fishing and retrieved my bracelet. I dearly loved him all the years that he was there.

Grandma and Grandpa lived near us and one day on one of my trips to see her as she had now become bedfast, I stopped in the Presbyterian Church yard and gathered a handful of Johnny-Jump-Ups to take to her. You would have thought they were the most beautiful flowers ever. She passed away shortly after that.

I was always a happy-go-lucky, friendly kid that knew everyone in town by name. I wasn't one of the top students, but probably one of the most liked. I had too many things to do and people to see to worry about getting all A's.

My fourth grade teacher was Miss Redd. I thought she was the most wonderful teacher in the world—so pretty, young, and always dressed in stylish clothes. She had made some rules to keep her classroom quiet by using demerit marks. She made a graph on the blackboard and added names as needed. Five demerit marks and you got paddled by leaning over the front seat.

Some way the name Janet Ann made it to the blackboard—not just one mark, but four. On occasion, Ms Redd would erase all the names and start over, giving you another chance, but not this day! As I leaned across the aisle to ask Dickie Hunt how to spell Detroit, there she was, looking straight at me. Up went the fifth demerit mark and down came the paddle with my invitation to join her at the front of the class. That was my most humiliating experience, but I still loved her.

Like everyone else, I was blessed with homemade clothes. They were sometimes made by taking clothing that an older person no longer wore. They were taken apart and remade into something new for kids. I was around eight years old, but my memory, it is so clear when Easter came and I had a new brown velvet dress that I was so proud to wear.

Mom could mend, but did not make anything from scratch. Our next-door-neighbor was our seamstress, making a dress for $2.00. Only on one occasion was I allowed to go to Miss Becker's drygoods store and choose a pattern and material all by myself. Big mistake! I chose a plaid cotton fabric and a pattern with an eight gore skirt. It had to be a nightmare to try to put together.

By the time I was in high school in 1940 to 41, the economy had changed and everyone was more comfortable. Dad even bought a car that I learned to drive.

I was often chosen to sing a solo at PTA meetings and/or at church, which was a big part of my life. Three friends and myself were also asked to sing at funerals. Our favorite song for that occasion was "Beyond the Sunset" and often accompanied by an old organ that squeaked with each push of the pedals. We sometimes got so tickled it was difficult not to laugh, but someway we kept our composure.

My friend Joan and I were elected to be cheerleaders for our basketball team and also majorettes for our school band. We did keep busy and loved every minute of it.

As the band was being organized and students purchasing instruments, Richard Ramage chose to play a trombone which lined up right behind the majorettes. He later said his motive was because he was right behind me.

We didn't really pay much attention to each other, since he was rather shy, but one night after some kind of entertainment at our school gym, he walked me home. It was possibly two blocks and when we got there he gave me a light pat on the rear and said good-night.

That small token of affection resulted in us becoming high school sweethearts, marriage, four children, ten grandchildren, and eight great grandchildren. Richard passed away shortly after our 63rd wedding anniversary.

Still Holding the Record

by Roman Miller of Sugarcreek, Ohio
born 1937

I grew up on a farm. There were fourteen children in the family. There were ten boys and four girls. There were seven boys in a row. I was the seventh one. We used to cook with coal and wood stoves.

We used to milk by hand. I still know the names of the cows. There were nine cows. I know their names. Beauty, Belly, White, Rose, Sheck, Sandy, Minney, Jenny and Fern. That was in about 1944.

We had about 250 chickens, about fifty sheep. We had about 110 acre farm at that time. In 1946, we moved to a bigger farm. About 220 acre farm. In one summer, we made 125 load of loose hay.

We had an outdoor toilet. We used tin tub to take our bath in.

When we went to school the one school we walked about mile and half, the other school we walked about a mile. When I was in the seventh grade we had a contest. Softball and baseball throw. I won that. Seventy-four yards. And in the eighth grade I threw the softball and baseball for 86 yards. I won that. I still hold the record as of today.

When I grew older I used to help our neighbors. I think there's not a one that I didn't help.

We used to take eggs to the store and trade for grocery.

I left home when I was twenty-three and went to Sugarcreek, Ohio. That is where I met my wife. We got married in 1961. We have six girls. My wife's name is Ora Lena Yoder Miller.

This morning when I got up, it was seventeen cold, February 20th, '09.

Glenford Before and After The Great Depression

By Carl L. Cooperrider of Glenford, Ohio
Born 1915

Glenford is a small town with a pretty name. The name conjures a picture of a stream and in that stream is a rapid over which one can easily cross by wagon or by foot. The ford is surrounded by a grove of native, ash, sycamore, or willow trees. The sound of the waters rushing across the stones in the rapids induces a feeling of peace, serenity, and pensiveness. Such a sensation must have caused one of the early settlers to give the name of Glenford to the crossing of Jonathan Creek.

The town is shaped geometrically as a script. The north and east branches (streets) unite at the railroad property. They continue southerly across the ford - now a bridge. They separate; one leading to the west and the other to the high country to the south. Over the years the street location between the railroad and the creek has moved, especially in the vicinity of the creek. The ford gave way to a covered bridge, the covered bridge was replaced by a steel beam structure near the turn of the 20th century; the steel frame bridge in turn was superseded by a wider bridge in the 1960's. Each time the replacement bridge was upstream from the ford and at the present there is little or no evidence that such a peaceful, pleasant site as the original ford in the glen ever existed.

My memory begins at about 1923 when I was eight years old. Like all small towns of the period, Glenford was the business center for the community. The two railroad lines; Baltimore and Ohio and the Zanesville and Western ran passenger trains on almost precision schedules. Each company had its own depot and depot agent. Interspaced in the train schedules was the shipment of crops and stock by using the railroad freight cars. The B & 0 had been built to haul coal from Shawnee to Newark and Sandusky on Lake Erie. The Z & W was a transfer or connecting line between Zanesville and the Pennsylvania Railroad at Thurston in Fairfield County. Since both lines were short, the movement of the coal from Shawnee to Newark and the transfer of freight from Zanesville to Thurston could be scheduled with a minimum effect on the passenger trains. The express car on the passenger trains delivered such items as bread, mail, baby chicks and other perishables. At train arrival time, the depot was a busy place with friends to greet arriving visitors and concerned people saying goodbye to those leaving. In my opinion, the most interesting feature of life in Glenford during the twenties was the railroads.

So with the train depots being the center of movement of life in the village let me try to recall the layout of the village. Along both main lines there was a siding on which the boxcars, stock cars or gondolas were set for loading or unloading. The holding pens and loading site for stock were only about fifty feet square, but they held cattle for a minimum of time because of the additional cost for food and water for the animals.

Continuing on the north road was the general store known as Shangles. The building was a two-story frame structure with the owner's house attached. The building and supplementary sheds are in use as a general store to this date. The remainder of the three or four houses on this side of the street and those on the other side are occupied as private homes.

Across from Shangles store stands a relatively new structure. It is the Glenford Bank. The shape is round and patterned on the concept that the customer is in the open rotunda and the tellers and bookkeepers are in offices located around the inside of the perimeter of the bank. The bank was locally owned, financially sound and large enough to serve its clients.

Between the bank and the railroad, a two-story frame structure stood. This building was quite important to the townspeople because one side of it was the Glenford Post Office with a small general store owned and operated by the postmaster as a supplement to the relatively small stipend paid by the government. This is one of those early instances of one stop shopping - one could get the mail and a loaf of bread while visiting one store.

Turning to the left and starting around the street leading to Glass Rock is Shafer's Hardware Store. The building is larger than some of its neighbors because it was the original Glenford High School having been built about 1875. The hardware included sales and parts for farm machinery. The remainder of the structures along this street were residences except for the public school located about a dozen houses east of the hardware.

Adjacent to the railroad and opposite the hardware store is the house, barn and outbuildings of the Frank King farm. He and his wife had the opportunity to engage in general farming and live in town at the same time. The railroad shipping yards were about 500 feet from his barn.

The south or west side of the tracks belong to the B & 0 Railroad. Their siding serviced a stock holding lot and a large lot over 100-feet square on which molding sand was stock piled. This pile of sand was a real play place for the kids. The sand was hauled in wagons by horses from a quarry near the south edge of town. Periodically a gondola was loaded and shipped to the steel mills. The loading was done by manpower - a shovel load at a time. When the area was not used for sand, coal was unloaded to fuel the stoves and furnaces of the community during the coming winter.

At the south corner of the street, beginning at the railroad, stood Hazlett's Grocery Store. This grocery was quite popular because the cream station was next door. On the right side of the street going south is the building housing the local garage.

There are no new car dealerships in the village now, the last one closed shop about 1920. The reason I know that year is because my grandparents lived in the property formerly occupied by the owners of the Chevrolet and Oakland agency. There were enough greasy spare auto parts to keep a kid dirty for weeks.

The last building on the street before approaching the bridge was the blacksmith shop. There were many farm horses and a few buggy horses that required shoes, although, most of the roadwork was being given to trucks and motor driven vehicles. So the village blacksmith became the community machinery repairman. This was before the days of the welding torch so the blacksmith's forge had to do the heating and his hammer the shaping of the repairs for broken machinery.

On the south side of the bridge there was only a general store owned by S. R. Johnson and the cabinet making shop of Mr. Helser. Except for these businesses, this part of town was entirely residential.

In the early 1920's the town was an unincorporated village with an elected constable policing Hopewell Township as the local law enforcement officer. There were no public utilities. Drinking water was pumped from private wells. Electricity and natural gas was not available and each property owner was responsible for his own waste disposal. There was very little trash to throwaway; perishable goods were delivered to the stores in returnable crates or boxes. Milk was sold in returnable bottles; food wrapped in paper was removed for a meal and the wrapper was used as kindling to start a fire in the kitchen cook stove. Canning in reusable glass jars preserved fruits and vegetables. The parlor stove or the coal furnace became the incinerator for any other combustible waste.

Topographically, Glenford lies mostly in a flood plain. The southern side of Jonathan Creek at the ford is a steep hill and bluff. As a result the whims of the creek as expressed by the regular flooding of the bottomland meant very little to the resident on the high land. The residents of the ten houses between the railroad and the creek had to be hardy (or foolish) to endure the nuisance caused by the periodic flooding of their part of the town. The creek was simply reclaiming for temporary use that land it had always used to contain the runoff of waters after a few inches of rain. I have no way of knowing, but I suspect that the railroad embankment and trestles north of town did more to stabilize the flow of water through Glenford than has ever been acknowledged. Let me explain. About one mile upstream from Glenford there is a fork in the creek. At this junction, Jonathan Creek coming from the Thornport area is joined by Popular Fork Creek carrying the drainage of many square miles of hill land south of the National Road and Brownsville. About one half mile south of this junction the railroad engineers designed and built trestles across the creek. The roadbed itself is on ballast to an elevation above flood stage. Thus the rail bed acts as a dike and the trestle clearance acts as a water gate and controls the volume of the floodwaters in the plain below the trestle.

As the residents of the flood plain learned, the water could be kept from their house floors if the foundation were raised above these high water marks. After this was done no one seemed concerned about the floodwaters surrounding their houses because there was nothing to be disturbed. The water well casings were extended upward to a point above the high water mark. A platform above flood level connected the back porch to the well top. The heating and cooking was done on coal stoves; there were no electric lines to foul or gas lines to leak. For all practical purposes the house was immune from the flood. The high water was a nuisance, but it was gone in a day or so and life went on as before.

The settlers of Glenford and Hopewell Township were mostly of German and Protestant decent and consequently the four churches in and adjacent were: Lutheran, Reformed, Methodist and United Brethren. Their respective memberships were in that order. There were two medical doctors in the town during the 20's and they were respected members of the community. One local undertaker handled the burial of the deceased.

The Great Depression hit Glenford in 1929 and 1930 as it hit the whole nation. With the collapse of the economy came a complete change in the character of the local businesses in the village. By the year 1935 the doctors were gone, the funeral parlor closed, the hardware store was out of business and there was only one general store. The bank was closed in 1933 because it did not have the assets that the Federal Government decreed as being necessary. The railroads tore out the stock pens and closed and razed the depots. Railroading had been reduced to strictly freight service. The entire business section of this once flourishing village was undergoing the transition from a self-contained community to the status of a satellite serviced by larger towns. The automobile was responsible for this change.

Employment in the community was furnished mostly by the Central Silica Company, a sand processing corporation which quarries the native sandstone, crushes, and refines the resultant silica for sale to glass companies and pottery glazing plants. Some of the sandstone rock strata in the quarries are 30 to 35-feet thick. With the discovery for a method for making fiberglass by Owens Corning Glass Company in Newark, Ohio about 1930, the future of the Central Silica Company was almost assured because of the high quality of glass sand it produced.

At the south edge stands the hill known as the Glenford Fort. The plateau atop this hill contains about thirteen acres. The rim of the hilltop is ringed with sandstone, which at one time formed some type of defense (or so it is presumed) of this vantage area. The purpose of the Glenford Fort has never been discovered. There are many theories, one of which ties the Glenford Fort with series of mounds northerly from it. The latest supposition seems quite reasonable and that is the concept of an era when the land contained no trees and the mounds were quite visible as a line of communication across the country. The landowners who have title to the land would possibly like to deed the land to the State of Ohio for preservation, but to date, the state has shown no interest. Personally, I think the Glenford Fort should be made into a historical park operated by a community organization. The 13 acres could be used as a setting for an outdoor stage production during the summer. A travel trailer campground could be established near the base. In order to get such a program off the ground a good writer is needed for the drama, a director is needed to put it together and a determination is needed by the community to make it succeed. (A generous philanthropist would also help.) In any event, the hill should be made a historical site; preserved, made accessible to the public and retained as a monument to some part of our predecessors.

The events of the year leading to the 1920's are lost to the writer except for a few bits of data relayed to me by my grandfather during fishing trips up and down Jonathan Creek. The sawmill of the 1800's was located about a half mile north of Glenford and the remnants of the dam provides a deep swimming hole for the boys and girls within a several mile radius. On hot July and August weekend afternoons the deep water below the former stone dam rang with young people swimming, diving and splashing in the cool waters of Jonathan Creek.

The community supported a baseball team during the 20's and rivalry with teams from nearby towns was displayed on weekend afternoons. Today Glenford is a quiet little community of about 200 residents; it is incorporated because the utility company had to have someone to pay the bill for the streetlights. Gone are the railroads and their whistles, the one general store and the bank building is four empty walls. There is still a post office and garage and Central Silica provides some employment, but the era of commuting is evident and many of the young wage earners are employed at factories in Newark, Zanesville and even Columbus. The town is no longer a real community but like so many other villages it is simply a residential section for larger cities.

Perry County had fourteen public high schools in 1933. Today it has four public high schools. Snow and ice days were unheard of 50 years ago, but today no board can afford chains for all the buses. Gradually a few houses have been removed from the flood plain until there are only about six or seven left. The town sponsors a steam engine show in mid-August each year and it's amazing to see the impact of the presence of 1000 to 2000 visitors upon the usually uncrowded streets of the town.

This story describes Glenford, Ohio "as I recall the town" from 1923-1976.

Annie Bando's Secret Garden

by Marlene Richcreek of Coshocton, Ohio
born in 1938

Two things I remember when I was very small. One, my teenage uncle taking me skating at the skating rink (where the American Legion is now), skating all afternoon with me on his shoulders. And number two, I remember my dad every night after supper taking me to Al Renner's Pool Room and me sitting in one of those high chairs like a shoe shine chair. He would carry me over and back on his shoulders. On Sunday, all the men in the neighborhood played horseshoes in the alley.

As I grew a little older, I remember my aunt going to work on the railroad. She wore a red bandana on her head, bib overalls and high heels, but 'til the day she died, I never seen her wear flat-heeled shoes. Of course, that was the beginning of wartime.

I remember going to the store and ration stamps for foods like flour, sugar, vegetables, beer, meat. Everything was rationed! My father was drafted, and he had three children under school age.

As I grew a little older, I remember going up to Wright's Bottling on Second Street right by Meadow Gold Dairy. Where Mr. and Mrs. Wright would always give you a bottle of soda pop and a fresh cookie, and we would set on the porch and talk about when they were young.

We lived on West Chestnut Street, where the new bridge is now, and it was a beautiful street! With big oak trees growing on each side. Annie Bando lived straight across the street from us. She owned the VFW 1330 Stage Coach Tavern, which was built back in the times of the stagecoach. They said many famous people and presidents stayed there. They also owned Bando's Bar, but in the back of the stagecoach on Second Street, in the alley, there was a stone wall yard, and it was beautiful on the inside.

She had a gardener to take care of it. There was every kind of flower you could think of and beautiful little trees and a pond with fish in it. About once or twice a week, she would holler at us and tell us she would unlock the gate and we could go over and play in the yard. It was like our own secret garden where no one else could go. We would sit and soak our feet in the little pond and play all day in that magical place!

I remember scarlet fever. My cousins were quarantined for fourteen days with a big sign on the door (Do Not Enter). I remember polio and how it struck so many children and how my mother worried continually about it striking home. But two of the things I really remember the most are:

Mr. Stipes owned a fur-trapping store right next to the stagecoach tavern. He sold trapping equipment. People would bring their pelts in to be sold. And the back of his store, clear to the alley he owned.

He owned a big, big vegetable garden, and every year, when the green tomatoes was ready and primed on the vine to be fried, my mother would say, "Marlene, you go over to Mr. Stipes' garden and borrow three big green tomatoes." She would do that about once a week through the summer. She never wanted ripe tomatoes, just the three big green ones when I went. If Mr. Stipes ever saw me take them, which he probably did, he never said a word!

My father was very playful and youthful all the time we grew up, and one day, they made a bet with him at Bando's, where he tended bar, that he couldn't swipe his Christmas tree off the man across the street, named Schaffer, who owned a whatnot shop and sold Christmas trees at Christmastime, and not get caught. Schaffer said it was impossible. That started a Christmas tradition on West Chestnut Street.

My father stole the tree that year and every year after, but around Christmas, all the neighbors would ask us if we got our tree yet, and they would ask Schaffer if my father had got his tree yet. The whole neighborhood watched very carefully but never seen Dad get a tree. But every year, we had a nice tree! Schaffer and my dad spent many hours laughing about the Christmas tree tradition on Chestnut Street.

I was born 8-30-1938 at 4:00 PM in the house below the Walnut Street Inn, upstairs in the front bedroom, in Coshocton, and I was never vaccinated!

Childhood Confessions from Maple Heights

by Dianne Porter of Caldwell, Ohio
born in 1954

I grew up in a small neighborhood just a hop, skip and a jump from downtown Caldwell, called Maple Heights. I was born in 1954, fifteen minutes behind my twin sister, Joanne. I'm fifty-five this year, that is, we're fifty-five this year. We were born in a small hospital right here in Caldwell, where the Senior Citizens Center is now. Mom didn't even know she was getting two for the price of one until she had us. Dad and Grandma were in the waiting room when the doctor carried in to them the new baby girl he had just delivered, then returned to the delivery room, just in time to deliver the second one. When he showed Dad that one he told him, "And here's the rest of your deal!"

Grandma was overjoyed, two little girls! She had raised seven boys and had prayed for a little girl. I know how she felt, too, because having five boys myself, I just flipped out when my first grandchild was a girl. Now I have four granddaughters and four grandsons.

It's unreal how much things have changed since I was a child. For instance, it's rare now for a new parent to be surprised by twins. Back in my time, the ultrasound was far in the future and prenatal care wasn't a big deal either. I don't think Mom had any kind of prenatal care at all and she carried two buckets of coal at a time from the coal house out back, she mowed our big yard and washed clothes on a wringer washing machine after carrying the water in from a pump on the back porch, heating it on the stove and filling washer and rinse tub.

Then between washing and wringing and rinsing clothes, she carried load after load out to the clothesline to hang up. Summer and winter. I remember how freezing cold her hands would be when she came back inside. And when she brought them back inside they were frozen stiff and had to thaw out! I can still remember how much I hated "wash day" because it was so messy and took up Mom's whole day.

Mom cleaned houses for people and when I was seven or so, she got a brand new clothes dryer by saving what she could for a couple of years. It was rough. Of course disposable diapers were a thing of the future, they were "new" when I had my first baby at seventeen. So Mom had to wash tons of cloth diapers between my two brothers and my sister and I.

When babies were born back then, the older women (at least my grandmother did) would make belly bands to wrap around the baby's belly after they had placed a quarter on the navel to prevent the belly button from protruding. This was necessary until baby was a few months old. So, when I had my first baby, Grandma got busy and whipped up some flannel belly bands for me. Well, I thought it was kind of a silly thing to do but being young and dumb, I didn't know any different so if Grandma said I must use belly bands or my kid would be deformed, I paid attention.

Well, when I took the baby for his first checkup all decked out in a belly band, with a quarter neatly nesting on his navel, the doctor had a fit! "What is this?" he screamed. I had no idea why he was so bent out of shape about it. He educated me pretty fast and then wrote, No Belly Band! on it and told me to give it back to Grandma. She wasn't amused. "Well, you can do what you want to," she sniffed. I was happy to know I didn't have to use them anymore.

Well, getting back to my childhood, another privilege we didn't have was an indoor bathroom. We had an old outhouse next to the alley at the edge of the backyard – right next to the coal house. Now, we weren't the only ones who had outdoor toilets, there were a few others. I sure did envy the kids I played with who had nice houses with running water and a bathroom. I thought they were rich. Compared to us they were! We didn't even get running water until I was eight or nine. We had a pump on the back porch, and when we moved I was twelve and we still didn't have an indoor bathroom. Yes, we used a chamber pot or a "posy pot" as I call it now, at night and in the wintertime.

Diane; baby, Donnie and Joanne sitting in the neighbor's yard.

I remember an incident when I was about seven, one summer day, the neighbor boy who was about my age and I were playing together, and we about had half a little crush on each other, so when we both had to pee we decided we'd use the toilet at his house across the alley because it was a two-holer, and we could go pee together. They never used it, it was in a deplorable condition but we disregarded that, beat the cobwebs out of our way and sat down on our respective holes to pee. We were just sitting there blabbing away when his dad heard us. Well, he had a conniption fit and yanked Danny out of there and thrashed him, and sent me home crying. Needless to say, we didn't do that again.

Back then, we could play all over the neighborhood and be gone all day and nobody thought a thing of it. We also never locked our doors. Especially in the summertime at night. We'd leave the big doors open and let the night breeze blow through the house, and leave all the windows up, too. Those days are long gone. Now, even when we lived out in the country, I was afraid to leave screens in the windows at night. I just didn't feel safe. It's become a dangerous world we live in now.

Back when I was a child, was a time of innocence. Children were children and we played outside unless we were sick or it was very cold outside. Mom would send us out to play and lock the screen doors Couldn't get back in until ten or eleven o'clock. Then Mom made us come in to wash up before we went to bed.

Many evenings, some of the women in the neighborhood would sit around in lawn chairs and talk. All the kids would catch lightening bugs in jars and play group games like Red Rover, Red Rover and Swing the Statue and Hide and Seek and Freeze Tag. It was great. Kids don't play anymore. And are allowed to see and hear things they have no business knowing.

Anyway, even though I didn't know a lot of grown up stuff I got into plenty of trouble. I was ornery. And I liked to get attention, unfortunately it was usually the negative kind. One time I told my teacher a joke that I heard my dad tell. I didn't understand it but all of his friends laughed so I wanted to make my teacher laugh. She didn't and I got in trouble.

I didn't do well in school at all, it was down hill from the first grade. I had a learning disability, which, back then they didn't recognize actual learning disabilities and have special programs for kids. They mostly just considered you stupid and gave up on you.

The only thing I did have going for me was that I could read and write before I started school. And that just got me in trouble. If Mom and a friend or my grandmother were talking and wanted to say something I wasn't meant to hear, they spelled it. Imagine Mom's surprise the first time I said what she had spelled. I also liked big words and used them liberally.

The writing got me in trouble at school too, my first grade teacher demanded that I print and I was forbidden to use writing. That was hard for me, because I loved to write, and read. I read everything I could get my hands on. We had a neighbor who got the Reader's Digest and the Grit newspaper. Popular in the late fifties and sixties. She always passed them down to me. If you wanted me, you'd find me somewhere reading usually.

We went blackberry picking once with an aunt and uncle and some cousins who lived out in the country. Uncle Cliff raised a lot of animals too. We drove to a good berry picking site on Uncle Cliff's farm, way up on top of a hill above a creek. I had brought a book with me, because whenever I got bored I would read.

Well, after a while picking berries and getting all scratched up and hot and sweaty, I went back to the car to sit in the backseat and read. I was soon all wrapped up in my book and not a bit aware of what was going on around me, until I noticed that the car was rolling down the hill, the door was open and I was scrunched down in the backseat with my feet up reading when I noticed the car was moving and picking up speed. Uncle Cliff's grandson, it turned out, had gotten in the car and put it out of gear, and we ended up in the creek.

Well, back in those days, kids got whuppings. And that boy got a good one. I thought his dad was going to beat him to death. That scared me more than the ride into the creek.

In the spring, Dad always put in a garden, it was my sister and my job to wash dozens of canning jars. Mom filled a galvanized wash tub with hot soapy water and set it in the backyard, and we got to wash and rinse all those jars because we had small hands that fit easily into the jars.

One summer, my sister and I got into very bad trouble. It all began when the neighbor boy hit our little brother in the face with a board that had a nail in it. It really busted his face and when we told his mom, she basically said, "So what." She couldn't have cared less. So my sister and I took it upon ourselves to get justice.

No one around there ever locked the door if they ran to the store or something, so a few days later when we knew they were gone, we went in and absolutely trashed their kitchen. We dumped and poured out everything we could get our hands on. It was awful. Then we scurried back home and waited, very nervously I might add, for the great discovery. Oh we were scared, and actually wished we hadn't gone to such extreme measures.

Well, when they got home and saw catsup and mustard and dish liquid and flour and sugar and whatever else we found, dumped all over the kitchen, they called the sheriff. We hadn't thought about that! Of course they sicked him on us and of course we fearfully denied knowing anything about it. And Mom didn't know what we had done or she would have worn a switch out on us. The neighbors of course suspected us from the start but of course had no proof. That was the worst thing we ever did. Well, almost, but that's another story.

Our next door neighbor had an apple orchard and a couple of cherry trees and she was a grumpy person. She didn't allow kids in there and if she caught us she'd raise a ruckus. That, of course, just made her apples and cherries all the more desirable. Seems like just about every day she chased us out of there. Once we gathered up a mess of rotten apple and put them in her mailbox.

We had a friend who lived in a little community across the railroad tracks. Her name was Becky. She was tragically killed in a car wreck when she was only fourteen. She lived beside this little Mom and Pop store where we went to trade in pop bottles for a nickel each and buy penny candy.

The old woman who owned the store liked to cheat kids. I think it was her policy or something, she did it every time. I remember the time the other kids dared me to swipe a six pack of pop. I did it and she chased me with a big stick, screaming her head off in Chekoslavakian. I dropped the pop and kept running. I didn't go back for a long time, and Mom grounded me from going to Becky's too. On top of that she made me apologize to Mary, the store's owner.

As long as I had known her, Mary seemed very old to me. She moved all bent over like and she wore long old worn out dresses, an apron and kerchief tied on her head. She ran the business all by herself. Her husband stayed upstairs. He was strange, sometimes we saw him walking on the railroad tracks that ran between Florence and Maple Heights. He believed that the world was in a peanut shell and there were aliens. He was pretty scary.

Back then the trains were running on a regular schedule, we would lay pennies on the tracks and get them flattened by the train. With our grandmother (Mom's mother) we took long walks on the railroad tracks looking for greens for Grandma to cook with bacon ends.

Every summer, Dad would get us an inner tube from a truck tire and fill it with air so we could jump on it. A homemade trampoline. We spent many hours playing on that. One year when hoola hoops came out, Grandma got us one; we loved those too.

We had hardly anything compared to some others, but we always had something to do.

Maple Heights was a great place to live. Everyone minded his own business. Men didn't go to jail when they beat their wives and kids. We knew one poor woman who walked the neighborhood at night crying because

her husband would beat her.

And if a man wanted to take his little kids to a bar and let them sit outside in the car half the night by themselves while he sat in the bar and drank, it was OK. If a man brought his two small boys into a bar and got drunk and forced them to fight to the finish, it was overlooked. Everyone thought it was awful and sad, but nobody did anything. Now that sort of thing wouldn't be tolerated but that's how it was then. Yes, things were sure different then in every aspect, and not for the better in many ways.

Evan the weather was different. In the summertime, every time it rained we played outside. Mom would give soap and a wash cloth and we would stand under the eve spout at the corner of the house and play and wash up. It rained more often than it does now. I loved those summer thunderstorms. And when it flooded, we played in the floodwaters. Unheard of now.

Germs and bacteria. Why, we didn't know what a germ was. We never got sick! We had immune systems, nowadays, kids don't have them. Everything makes them sick. Everything is antibacterial. No, it doesn't rain and thunder like it did when I was a kid, or snow either. And we went to school no matter what. They put chains on the busses and we went!

Our neighbor had a cow in the field beside of her house. The lady who gave me books and papers to read. And she had a real ornery grandson too. They didn't live close, so they didn't come very often, thankfully. As far as I was concerned, anyway. Tommy thought girls were only good for one thing: playing dirty tricks on. I'll never forget the time he jumped out from behind the outhouse with a cow pie in his hand and hit me smack in the face with the sloppy side of it. Oh I detested that boy.

I dearly loved Ethel, his grandma, though. Everyone loved her. She was honest and kind. She treated everyone the same. She made her own butter and lard and canned sausage. It was so good! I put in a lot of time at her house watching her. She had lots of cats and some dogs too and she knew what to do to get them better when they were sick or hurt. I thought Ethel could make anything okay again.

So one day I was holding one of our dog's newborn puppies while sitting on the piano bench after Mom said they were too little to hold and I dropped it on its back. It was hurt pretty bad, having trouble breathing. I ran to Ethel of course, sure she could make it all right again. But the puppy died.

Ethel had twin sons who lived with her, Frank and Fred. Frank had never gotten married and he was a great help to her. There was no household chore he wouldn't or couldn't do. He cooked, cleaned, baked, canned, washed clothes. One thing he did really interested me. He would sit at the dining table and make tapers out of newspaper for lighting kerosene lamps and the gas stoves. And he kept a big jar filled on the table. I just thought it was so neat. Funny the things that impress a child.

His brother Fred never talked to anyone. He just walked all the time or sat on the sun porch by himself. He had been in the war and I was told that he was shell shocked. He walked almost constantly and talked low to himself so fast you couldn't make out his words and he walked real fast too. Sometimes he would spin in circles and look at the sky and yell for every body to get down! Hide! It was very sad.

Then when I was about twelve, Ethel passed away suddenly. She just dropped to the floor in her living room. After that the twins lived there until they too passed away. I took it very hard when I lost Ethel. A huge part of my life was gone.

Well, I could probably write a lot more but this isn't supposed to be a book! Not mine, anyway. I did write a book though, but never got it published. I'm not sixty or older but I hope you can use my memories too because five years don't make much difference in a life.

The Memorable Truant Officer

by Charles Lee Ruff of Lancaster, Ohio
born 1932

I was in the summer of 1949. I was working as a farm hand on a neighbor's farm, earning three dollars a day. I have always enjoyed being outside. I was going to be a sophomore that fall, and although I disliked the studies, I did get to participate in sports which made going to school tolerable. So I would say I was having a good life.

Then in August we were threshing clover seed, a process which removed the seed from the plant. I decided to ride on the wagon load of clover. As the tractor made the turn from the field unto Schwilk Road, I fell from the wagon. My employer was unaware that I laid at the hill crest in the road, and continued on. Once he arrived at the threshing machine and noticed I was missing, he came back for me. He took me home from where I was laying to the hospital.

I spent the next thirty days in the hospital and sent home where I spent many more days recouping from a skull fracture. The days I missed school where many, but the day eventually came when I was able to attend classes. I was told I would no longer be able to participate in any sports and I had to make up my lessons. So I decided to become a dropout.

After a number days of absence the truant officer paid my parents a call. However, Dad was at work. Mom had a lot to say, but I kept my decision. No more school for me. The truant officer said I would need a working permit. I told him I had no way to town since Dad was at work. He did not take me to school, but to town where I got my working permit. At the age of eighteen, was hired by Anchor Hocking where worked for forty years.

A Good Day for Fishing

By Herbert "Dwight" Davis of Zanesville, Ohio
Born 1943

When I was about ten years old, a friend and I decided one Friday afternoon it was just too nice a day to be stuck in school, but a perfect day for fishing. I don't recall his excuse, but I told the teacher I had a toothache and asked to go home. We had a good time and caught a few fish.

It just happened that my Boy Scout troop was going camping that Saturday night and lo and behold I woke up about 2 A.M. Sunday morning with the worst toothache I had ever had. Needless to say, I paid for my little fib and never used that excuse again.

When I was a youngster we lived in the country and did not have indoor plumbing, so like most families we had an outhouse and used to say we had five rooms and a path. During the winter season we used a white enamel chamber pot. I had two older sisters and we had to take turns carrying it to the outhouse each morning to be emptied.

One winter morning we had snow and ice on the ground. It was my oldest sister's turn to empty the pot, and she was wearing a new purple velvet dress and was ready for school. As she stepped off back porch she slipped and fell and she and the pot went flying. You can only imagine how that turned out.

My 7th grade English teacher was my favorite and my first love. I thought she was the most beautiful woman I had ever seen and could not believe she was married and had not waited for me. I used to cringe every time she mentioned her husband's name.

My uncle raised pheasants at this time and she wanted to buy a couple, so we arranged for her to drive me home after school to purchase them. Some of my friends and classmates just stared in amazement when I waved to them as we pulled out of the school parking lot. I thought I was in heaven.

I became interested in hunting when I was about 10-years-old and being that young could only hunt with my dad or another adult. When I turned 16 and I was allowed to hunt by myself. I got a good lesson after I killed my first squirrel while hunting alone. Being a teenager and having to show off a bit, instead of putting it in my hunting bag, I tied it to my belt loop.

As I was walking up the driveway with my prize kill, my uncle came running out of the house screaming at me. "Boy," he said, "don't you ever do that again. There are some hunters who will shoot at anything that moves in the woods and that squirrel tail swinging back and forth and seen through the brush could have made an easy target." I never did that again.

In my preteen years we did not have the luxury of owning a TV set so we depended on the radio for entertainment. Our local station, on Saturday morning had a program called Roundup Time and played country music with the likes of Hank Williams, Webb Pierce, Stonewall Jackson, Kitty Wells and Flatt and Scruggs, to name a few.

Every Saturday I would listen to this deep voiced DJ and in my mind picture him as over 6-feet tall; with boots and a big cowboy hat.

Later on the station began doing remote broadcasts from the county fair, and as I was walking around the fairgrounds on a Saturday morning they were airing Roundup Time and I went flying over to the broadcast booth to see this big cowboy, and got quite a shock. He was about 5-feet 4-inches, no hat and probably didn't weigh 120 pounds soaking wet.

Later in life and to this day when I hear a voice on the radio, I try to imagine what the person looks like and remember that experience

As far back as I can remember I have been scared to death of anything reptilian. Whether it be live, a picture, in a movie or any other form. In the area where I grew up we had two mine reservoirs where we fished and swam.

One day I was watching a friend fish and wearing shorts and felt what I thought was a weed brushing against my leg. As I reached down to brush it away, I saw Godzilla on my leg. I made a beeline for home scared to look behind me for fear it was chasing me. Another time I was fishing with an artificial lure and as I was reeling it in I saw something swimming behind it. As it got closer to the shore I saw it was a water snake which to me looked the size of an Anaconda.

I threw down my fishing pole and ran home. It was several hours before I got up enough courage to go back for my pole. I just knew that snake was waiting for my return to attack me.

My kids and grandkids are all aware of my phobia about reptiles, so this was my most recent experience.

One of my grandsons was recently at Fort Sill, Oklahoma for US Army basic training. I received a letter from him and could tell from the envelope that there was something besides a letter inside I anxiously opened it expecting maybe an Army patch or something of that nature only to find a plastic bag containing a Diamondback Rattle snakeskin. I screamed and threw it across the room and wrote and told him he was off my Christmas list.

A few days later I received from him a t-shirt that says, 'My Grandson Defends Freedom in The United States Army' so all was forgiven.

When my dad was a youngster his parents, like a lot of families in the 1920's and 30's, farmed and grew a lot of their food and raised livestock for their meat. Almost everyone had a smokehouse for curing meat. Grandpa told me of the morning he went to the smokehouse to get some meat only to discover that a couple of hams and some other meats were missing. He called the family together and told them no one was to say a word about the missing meat and eventually they would find out who broke in.

Later a neighbor stopped by and asked grandpa if he ever found out who broke into his smokehouse and grandpa told him not until right now. The neighbor denied it saying someone had told him about it, but wily old grandpa was not buying that. He told the neighbor he would gladly have given him what he needed, to leave and all would be forgotten, but he was no longer welcome in their home.

Corncob Bananas and Other Stories

by Laura Fulton Wigert
of Mount Pleasant, South Carolina
born in 1919

My sister-in-law, who lives near Warnock, sent me the application to write experiences about southeastern Ohio. For fifteen years, I have written a chapter about my remembrances of growing up on a farm near Warnock, Ohio during the Depression years, before rural electricity in 1937. I had my ninetieth birthday February 8, so you see I have a lot to remember!

How many of you remember the store, Community Market? I do not recall what year we opened the store or how many summers it was reopened. It is my recollection that all of the younger children were involved at one time in running the store.

Outside of the fenced back yard, there was an old building, in which one half was used as a smokehouse to cure meats, and the other half had been a wash house for clothes. In this half, we opened our store. This building had two windows and two doors. The sign outside said COMMUNITY MARKET, and the phone number was 407-J.

To stock the shelves of the store, we salvaged and saved boxes such as butter and oatmeal boxes and coffee cans. For many of our products, we certainly used our imagination! We used corncobs for bananas, sand for brown sugar, and weeds such as burdock for rhubarb and wild carrots for carrots. We even rolled weeds and corn silk to make cigarettes in paper and sold them. All products were weighed with an imaginary scale and brown bags were used, refolded and reused many times.

The bakery was well supplied with cakes, cookies and candies. These were made from mud and decorated or iced with wild flowers such as daisies or Queen Anne's Lace. I must say that the baked goods looked very pretty and *almost* tempting to be eaten.

Our money, both bills and coins, were meticulously made and marked after cutting them from old wallpaper books. Walk-in customers would enter the door and pick an old purse hanging on the wall, and with the enclosed money, they could shop for groceries.

One of the big features of the store was our charge account customers who called on the phone to place orders. We used familiar names such as Mrs. Garden, Mrs. Apple or Mrs. Tree. The phone would ring, a clerk would answer, "Community Market, 407-J. How are you, Mrs. Grass? Do you wish to place an order?" We kept accurate accounts, putting the order through a nail pounded on a wall. The order was placed in a large bag or box, put in a little red wagon to be delivered to a customer. Later, the younger children would return these groceries to the store through a window, and the clerks would put them back on the shelves, ready to be sold again.

Later, we opened a drug store counter. We found many, many old cobalt and brown bottles under the old shop and in the dump. We also had milk of magnesia and other medicine bottles. All of these bottles would be collectibles now!

Before school started in September, everything was carefully packed away to wait for the next summer's grand opening!

An interesting sequel to our play store occurred while my sister and I were in college. At Christmastime, we applied for a job with Woolworths five and ten cents store. Martha was interviewed first, and I did not have a chance to talk to her before I went into the office. I did notice she was giving me a concentrated stare or frown. I wondered, "What's up?" The first thing the interviewer said to me was, "I suppose you worked in your father's store too?" Wonder of wonders. I knew he meant Community Market, and I said, "Yes!"

We both got our first paying job. I worked in men's wear in the basement. I remember asking one man, "What size necktie do you wear?" This was the year 1937, and my total pay was twenty-one dollars in cash.

I am trying to write about my childhood memories of the wonder, imaginative life we led during all those Depression years.

* * * *

Whitney School, a one-room school housing grades one through eight, was important to us in the Fulton family. It is located in Marbletown, where there was a Whitney post office until 1904. There were a few houses, the school, and an open-front railroad station. The Baltimore and Ohio passenger train picked up people, milk and other things. The freight trains hauled lots of coal, probably to the open hearth steel mills along the Ohio river.

Two schools earlier, a hewn log building that was torn down to be replaced by a brick building which in turn was also removed. Eventually, a neat brick building was built at 7 Mount Olive, Whitney, in the Smith Township.

Growing up on the farm, I remember the wooden forms long enough to make three bricks. I was told that these were the forms to make the bricks for Whitney School. William tells me that there is one in the museum in Belmont, Ohio.

Dad attended the school. He was born in 1874, so it was built before that date. Mom taught in the school, and all of us attended it over the years. After leaving Whitney, Dad attended Muskingum Academy in New Concord, Ohio. At seventeen, his father died, so he came home to take over the farm.

Later, Dad, James Fulton, was on the school board, and they hired a new teacher. He drove a horse and buggy to Whitney Station to meet the new teacher, Mattie Hensley. He took her to his sister Mary's house, a stone's throw from the school, to room and board. The rest is history! Mom and Dad were married and moved to the Fulton farm on the top of the hill, where all of us children grew up.

Whitney School was well built with one large, high room and four tall windows on each side and two in the front. From the porch, we entered the front door into the cloakroom, where the boys and girls used different sides to hang their clothing and store their lunches. We also used different doors to enter the classroom. The wide board floor was black from being oiled every year.

There was a row of seats in different sizes for each grade. The first graders were seated next to the eighth graders, who often helped the younger ones. I think we absorbed knowledge by osmosis from hearing the other grades recite. In the front was a platform, one step up, where the teachers were, with the blackboard and a bookcase for books and supplies. We also held our Christmas programs on the platform.

The room was heated by a coal burning, pot bellied stove with the stove pipe going through the ceiling. I remember that the room was usually nice and warm. I don't know who started the fire in the morning or who fired it all day long. I imagine it was the older boys.

We attended the school eight months of the year, so we had one less year of school compared with the nine-month year. We received a basic education in reading, spelling, arithmetic, geography, history and penman-ship. At the end of the eighth grade, one had to pass a test given by the state of Ohio to enter high school.

It is interesting that during the late twenties, Mom taught again for three years while the younger children were in school. She was a good teacher and made her own tow the mark.

In 1928, I remember everyone in school walking up to the farm to hear Herbert Hoover's inaugural address. We must have listened on earphones or a battery-run radio, because we did not yet have electricity.

It is interesting to note that Mom had to quit teaching because she was married. Some, especially one woman, felt that because of the Depression, the job should go to a single woman or man. How times have changed!

When Whitney School was closed, the younger siblings went to school in Warnock. Aunt Mary and Uncle Bob Coen bought the property and made it into two rental properties. Sometime later, the school was torn down. I wish that I had one of the bricks.

Over the years, our own Fulton family produced teachers, lawyers, engineers, ministers, farmers, nurses and secretaries. This is the evidence that we had good elementary education.

Thanks goes to brother Bill for historical help and to Betty and Charlie for the picture of Whitney School.

* * * *

The first car that the Fulton family owned was an Oldsmobile touring car purchased in 1919, the year that I was born. There were front and back seats and two folding seats that rested against the back of the front seat, making room for two more people. When our family outgrew this car, Dad bought a Model T Ford. I still remember our family going to church with both cars. Someone from the church likened this procession to "a calf following the mother cow."

I recall one incident with the folding seats. Martha smashed her big toe while closing a seat. Mary went to see how she did it and smashed her toe too!

One trip in the Oldsmobile that I remember was going to visit Grandma and Grandpa Hensley, who lived in Meigs

County, Ohio. James and George were the drivers in the front seat. Mom and baby William, Mary, and I rode in the back seat. William was probably six months old, and Mom held a blanket to keep the wind from blowing on him. I am sure we were not traveling at a very high speed. Rain started, so the boys stopped the car to snap on the side curtains, which had several windows, which were probably made of celluloid, an early plastic.

Due to impossible roads during the winter, we stored the car in a shed in the cow barn. How did we travel in the wintertime? Although I do not remember riding in the buckboard wagon, we probably did.

When there was plenty of snow, Dad used a large wooden sled with runners and drawn by two horses. He used it on the farm, but occasionally, when the snow was very deep, he would come down the hill to pick us up at Whitney School. I really liked that!

Another recollection was all of us riding in the sled to a Ridge Club meeting held at our Uncle George's. The night was a very cold, moonlit night, and we were all snuggled in blankets on the straw in the sled. I remember Dad put the jingle bells on our horses that night. No wonder I remember the event! There was a one-horse sleigh in the barn, but I never saw it used.

In early spring, on Sunday, we were returning home from church, riding in a two-seated buggy. Along the Warnock-Whitney Road, the buggy hit the side of the road, which had slipped over the bank, and the buggy overturned. Nobody was badly hurt, but Anna Lee and I still have dark scars in our knees from the cinders on the road. Albert told me that Dad had added a second seat to the buggy, and it was top heavy. He did it so more of us could ride to George's eighth grade graduation held in Centerville.

Dad also had an Oldsmobile truck, which had slatted sides in order to haul animals or hay. These sides could be made into benches. Sometimes we went to picnics in these seats.

We kept our first Oldsmobile until 1930, at which time Dad bought an Oakland. This company was later bought by Pontiac, General Motors.

Albert used the Model T to haul milk to Glencoe to be put on the train. He did this until the transmission quit! It is interesting that Albert drove all three of these first cars. During the war, Dad gave the Model T and the truck as scrap for the war effort. I wish we still had the Model T and the Oldsmobile!

Sometimes we walked to church, either by road or on the Baltimore Ohio Railroad. I used to feel scared crossing the trestle, as I could see the water flowing way below in the creek. Occasionally in the summer, we would walk two miles to Warnock just to buy a five cents ice cream at Delaney's Store. Of course, we walked about a mile to Whitney School. Going down the hill was easy; walking the mile up a very steep hill was slow going. When we hit the level of "the panhandle," we felt that we were home.

The trains of the Baltimore and Ohio Railroad were important. We would take the train at Whitney Station to go into Bellaire to go to high school, shop or go to the dentist. The train stopped at Glencoe, Stewartsville and Neff, and went on into Bellaire. We also used the train to carry our dairy products to markets. I was very excited every time I rode the train.

I thank my sister, Anna Lee, for suggesting this topic, and my brother, Albert, my historian, for so many details.

Getting Me Ready for the Army

by Donald Cottrell Sr. of Roseville, Ohio
born in 1941

The blizzard of 1950 was bad; but it was getting me ready for the snow and severe cold in the military in a machine gun nest at six below.

Also, the little coal mine across the creek was getting me ready. We hauled coal to the farm house. We used black powder to loosen up the coal. A keg of powder exploded. It was getting me ready for the white [AZ? A2?] hand grenades in the army. The hit plastered me.

Also on the farm I was hunting quail. The head of 12 gauge shotgun blew off and hit me in the face. It was getting me ready for the rocket launcher in the military. I fired two rounds 3.5 rockets and the third one was bad. I couldn't hear nothing for two weeks. Boom!

Also, the Boy Scouts came on to the farm. Camping for two weeks in the valley. That got me ready for tents in the military and taught me [to?] -survive a week when I was lost and to find my way back.

Football and working on the farm got me ready to jump over machine gun bullets. Sports are good for you. You operate in military like a team.

This farm is located on Route 555 just south of Zanesville-Roseville, Ohio.

I served with second and fourth in the Vietnam era and [illegible]. I guarded Roulph [Rudolph?] Hess in Berlin, Germany occupation.

There is some things I don't like to talk about. They happened on the farm and in the service of my country.

I hope you can get something out of this story of a farm boy from Southeastern Ohio.

Picture submitted by Donald Cottrell.

Streetcars and the Black Bear

by Mildred Andreas Houy of Beach City, Ohio
born in 1926

The new brick high school had just been finished with 1926 in the cornerstone where Route 93 goes past in Beach City, Ohio. That year the streetcar tracks still went down the middle of Church Avenue, past our front porch. That year I was born upstairs in the room where my sister, Ruth, was born in 1924.

Apparently our three older brothers kept her in tow, and off the street. The hired girl or Mother had to snatch me off the street because the streetcar came past from Strasburg, turned around and went back. Photos show us playing in the fenced-in side yard with dolls. The fence kept me off the street.

By then our older brothers spent more time at the creek nearby where Dad had a boat tied. The pet black bear had been returned to where it came from. Instead of a deer—venison for the table—he came with the little bear.

Now Ohio has too many deer. Motorists are being killed on the highway. Back in Model T days, when Dad was the local Ford car dealer, deer were as scarce as hens' teeth in Ohio, as the saying goes. Chickens do not have teeth, in case city children don't know.

By the time I was big enough to sit in the backseat with little brother, Bob, and Ruth, few Model Ts or Model A cars were on roads. At least I remember bigger better cars, a new one each year in which to ride to church. A D-1 or D-2 was on the license tag. That meant demonstrator car.

We always had honey on the table from little up. That happened because when Model T cars came out there was no anti-freeze, so honey was added to the radiator. Many men put the family car up on jacks over winter.

Sister and I played with dolls, made windows and doors in the carton boxes the half-gallon fruit canning jars came in. We played with kittens. Bob's little dog, Mickey, followed small Bob all over the farm. My years in town were only two before we all moved to the farm. The farmers had kerosene lamps and many a farm wife pumped water from a well in the lawn or carried buckets full from a spring house. It didn't matter if Amish or not. Then a congressman got the Rural Electrification Act passed and, for a price, families in the country could have electricity.

Dad fixed up the abandoned farmhouse and barn. Made it more modern than the neighbor's before the R. E. Act. A crystal chandelier hung half way down from the 10-foot ceiling.

Cars were selling, the older sons could learn to farm with the aid of hired day workers. Then the 1929 crash, then bank closings. An older brother told me one day they had corn meal mush for cereal with milk. That noon, mush with honey. Makes me wonder if they had eggs or a hen for supper.

When the church bells were rung two miles away in Strasburg, we could hear the ringing float across the valley. The World's Largest Country Store was located there and run by the Garver brothers. They sold stripes and floral prints by the yard, good for clothes, and solid colors to the Amish. Furniture was on the third floor. Farm machinery and dresses and hosiery, etcetera on the main floor, and best of all—candy.

Washing Pink Baby's Face

by Juanita (Dolick) Wilden of Plainfield, Ohio
born in 1937

A farm is the best place to raise children, and while I do not live on a farm now, nor did I when my children were growing up, that is still my belief.

My first memories are from the early 1940's, living with my parents and brother on our farm in Coshocton County, Ohio, near the little town of Plainfield.

I had a very happy, secure childhood, although I did wish at times for someone to play with more often. Having no sisters and only one neighbor girl living close enough that we could play together, I learned to play by myself. My dolls were my joy and my companions. Oh, yes, I had a brother. He was a very good brother to me, and still is, but he was always out with Dad doing farm work...and he certainly had no interest in dolls!

My mother was always there. While she would spend a lot of time talking with me, she was too busy to actually take time to play. She helped with the cows and the milking, raised chickens, grew a wonderful garden every summer, did a lot of canning, did some sewing and made quilts, was a very good cook, and did a lot to help her parents because Grandma became disabled. My mother was very busy. So, what did I turn to? My dolls. I don't believe any little girl ever spent more time with her dolls or loved them as much as I did mine. Let me tell you about them.

Well, actually, I guess I can't tell you much about the first two, because I really don't know much about them myself. You see, they were short-lived. All I know is what my mother told me about them. They were little twin dolls, evidently made of some breakable material... not a good choice for a very young child and especially not good for a child with a quick temper and a tendency to throw things when she became angry. Although I find it hard to believe I was ever like that, I was told that I was, too. It seems that one day, however, something must have irritated me. I threw my dolls, they hit the brick fireplace, and that was the end of my twins!

After that, there were several others whom I loved and cared for more carefully. The next one was a rag doll and while I still have her, I must have been very young because I do not remember playing with her.

Next was Pink Baby. Yes, Pink Baby. All of my dolls had names, and hers was Pink Baby. As time went by, I felt she should have a better name, so I tried various ones. I remember trying Bonnie, for example. But no name ever seemed just right, so she was always Pink Baby. The funny thing about her, however, is that in caring for her, I washed her face and hands so many times that much of the paint wore off. This was before the time when dolls were made of material meant to be washed. But I liked my dolls so much and tried so hard to pretend that they were real, so I washed Pink Baby and did all the other things that I thought a mother would do with a real baby.

I played with Pink Baby a lot and I still have her, although she is no longer very pink.

In fact, even though I am now past 70 years old, I still have all of my dolls, except the little twins and one other doll whose name was Janey. Near Christmas one year, my mother was gathering things together to give to a needy family with several children. She must have prevailed upon me to give Janey. I'm surprised I was willing to part with her because I liked my dolls so much. Evidently, the Christmas spirit was having an effect on me.

But I had other dolls. I probably acquired a new one each Christmas. There is Linda Lou, Nancy Ann, and Betty Ann. Notice how the choice of names would seem to show the era in which I was playing with dolls. Those names were popular in the early 40's. Linda, Nancy, and Betty all looked a lot alike, just somewhat different in size. They all had brown "painted-on" hair, eyes that opened and closed and a pretty smiling mouth, showing a couple of teeth. They all came dressed in pretty dresses. A couple of them even had coats and bonnets.

Nancy was the largest of the three. I was very fond of her, but she met with an unfortunate accident. We had a nice yard with big shade trees. One summer day I had taken my dolls outside to play and had spread a blanket on the grass and had them lying there. My brother happened to come by, and even though he would never have consented to play with my dolls, he asked if I thought he could jump across all of them. I don't remember how I answered, but he proceeded to jump. He evidently didn't jump far enough, because he landed on Nancy and broke her leg. I was devastated. I ran to my mother, crying and brokenhearted. She told me to save the pieces and she would glue them back together. I guess that quick temper showed up again, and instead of doing as she suggested, I took the pieces somewhere and threw them away. Using the ingenuity with which mothers seem to be blessed, she took a baby sock, stuffed it with cotton, and sewed it onto Nancy's cloth body. Nancy again had two legs. They didn't match but I still loved her.

Betty Ann may have been my finest doll, having the prettiest coat, hat and dress. All of my dolls made a crying sound when turned from front to back, but Betty did even better. Turned one way, she said "Mama." Turned the other way, "Papa." The sounds were quite distinguishable and I thought she was wonderful! That was before the era of dolls who talked by pulling a string or pushing a button.

My last doll was a Christmas gift when I was nine years old. I named her Judy Lynn, and she was the only doll I had with what I called real hair. She had blond curls, and to protect her hair, I kept a bonnet on her all the time. Remember, my dolls were very special to me and I wanted to take good care of them. For many years now, Judy has had to spend her time in an upstairs closet with the other dolls. But she still wears a bonnet to protect her hair.

Every Christmas, the main gift I hoped to receive was a new doll. On Christmas Eve, in order to show Santa how well I was caring for my dolls, I put them out on the couch for him to see. I thought he would be impressed and leave me another one! And he must have approved, because I don't believe I was ever disappointed.

For many years I gave all the credit to Santa Claus but I was to learn later that my Grandma Kline was quite concerned that I would receive a doll, and she and Santa worked together.

My other grandmother, Grandma Dolick, had been a good seamstress. I have some dresses that she made for my dolls, complete with dainty little tucks and pretty buttons. One of my aunts, for Christmas one year, made an assortment of dresses and bonnets and had them arranged in a miniature cedar chest with that enticing cedar aroma. I still have the cedar chest and all of the clothes.

Back in the era of my childhood, we didn't have quite so much as children have today. I believe that's the reason that what we did have was so special to us.

As stated earlier, I tried to make playing with my dolls as real as possible. I dressed them, rocked them, gave them their bottles, took them for buggy rides and put them to bed for their naps. When I was old enough to start to school, I loved school almost as much as I loved my dolls, so I played school with my dolls. I lined them up on the couch and pretended they were on the school bus. I used my story books and my easel blackboard and I taught them. (Preparation, perhaps, for when I later became a schoolteacher.)

My doll crib, the baby buggy, a little rocking chair, a

little stove and kitchen cabinet, table, dishes, doll bottles...all of these enhanced my many hours of playing and pretending.

For a little girl with no one else to play with, those dolls became constant, special and loved playmates. The only thing that could have been better would have been that they were real.

Years passed, my dolls were laid aside, I married. My husband and I were blessed with three precious children and eventually, grandchildren. And all the little girls have been introduced to my dolls, learned their names, and have taken their own dolls for rides in my baby buggy.

A Family by the Name of Shannon

by Donald E. Moore of Zanesville, Ohio
born 1930

I feel very proud to have been born and raised on a small farm just outside of present day Mount Olivett in Belmont County. Long before this town ever existed, a family by the name of Shannon pioneered into this region. George Shannon, being a Revolutionary War veteran, settled on a piece of government land in Warren Township just a few hundred yards northwest of what is now called Mount Olivett. He started to clear land and built a cabin. The year was 1801.

Later that year, my great, great, grandfather, Thomas Moore of Virginia purchased the rights to this land and rented it to George Shannon for a term of years. Unfortunately, George Shannon met a tragic death while hunting one very cold winter afternoon. In a driving blizzard, he got lost and froze to death. He was found the next day just a short distance from his cabin. Mr. Shannon was the first person buried in what became known as the French Cemetery located close to the town of Tacoma, Ohio in Warren Township.

In 1806 the Thomas Moore Family moved to Belmont County and settled on the land that they had rented to George Shannon. The Shannon Family moved about two miles west to a new farm.

George Shannon left five sons that became very well known for their dedication to public life. One son, Wilson Shannon, (1802-1877) attended Ohio University, studied law in Kentucky and practice law in Ohio. He was elected as the first native born Governor of Ohio from 1838 to 1840 and was reelected from 1842 to 1844. He resigned to accept a presidential appointment as minister to Mexico. Later he was elected to Congress in 1852. President Pierce then later appointed him territorial governor of Kansas, where he died in 1877.

George Shannon (1785-1836) scouted for the Lewis and Clark Expedition and served as a Kentucky judge and senator. A lot of what is read today about the Lewis and Clark Expedition was written by George Shannon. Thomas Shannon (1787-1843) served in the War of 1812. Later in the US Congress and the Ohio Senate.

James Shannon (1791-1832) was appointed US charge d' affaires to the short lived Federation of Central America in 1832. David Shannon (1793-1823) served as General Jackson's private secretary and as acting territorial Governor of Florida.

George Shannon also had a nephew; Isaac Charles Parker (1838-1896) was appointed Federal Judge of the west district of Arkansas in 1875. This was a notoriously lawless area now part of Oklahoma. His commitment to law and order earned him legendary status as the "Hanging Judge of Fort Smith." Footnote: George Shannon's cabin in Warren Township stood very close to where Thomas Moore built his home. Many people in Mount Olivett remember this as the Smith place. Today after many years and many owners, some of this land has returned to the Moore Family. Mount Olivett and its people can be proud of one distinction and that being the birthplace of the first native-born governor of Ohio, Wilson Shannon. In 1949 Governor Lausche the governor of Ohio came to my home town of Mt. Olivett and erected a tablet to mark this birthplace. In later years, the tablet was moved to the Belmont County Museum in Barnesville, Ohio where it resides today.

A memorable day. This event happened back when the United States was trying to contain Communism. I had just entered in the army and was at Fort Meade, Maryland. We had received our shots, our clothing issue and had taking numerous tests.

On about the seventh day our group was called out for instructions as to where we would be sent to take our basic training. The officer at the head of our group informed us that if our name was called out to form a line at the right. In a short time my name was called and I moved to the line to my right. The officer addressed us by telling us we would join a larger group to be sent out of the country to take basic training. We were not told just where this would be. We were told to get our gear and be ready to move out within an hour. After riding buses to the airport we boarded aircraft and took off to the west. After we took off we were told we would fly to Camp Stoneman, California. At this camp we would join more groups, get more shots and then proceed by ship to Schofield Barracks in Hawaii.

I knew the civil aviation traffic lane pasted over our farm traveling east to west or west to east. The route was pretty much over Wheeling W.V. into Ohio and west into Columbus. I was sitting by a window, so I could see out pretty well. As time went by, all of a sudden the Ohio River came into view. It was then I realized we might pass over the old farm place. As we flew west over Saint

Clairsville I started watching more closely. Sure enough we flew over the farm where I had spent my youth. I was hoping to see my dad working in the fields. However, this did not happen. I will never forget, as I looked down I felt a little sick at my stomach. Would this be the last time I will ever see home. Sometime that night we arrived in California.

When I got time, I wrote home and explained where I was and that I had flown over our farm. Some six months later I was home for a short leave.

Belmont County, Ohio in the 1930's. Just recently, on a cold snowy morning in January, as I was about to wash my face and shave, I thought about how things have changed since my boyhood days. Most people today have a warm bathroom with plenty of hot water. As I was growing up on a farm in Belmont County near Mount Olivett, Ohio things were not so convenient. We did not have a bathroom, nor did we have running water in our old farmhouse. Our water came from a dug well outside of the house about thirty-feet away. In order to get water we had to go outside, day or night, in warm or cold weather, to the well and use a hand pump to siphon water up and out into a two-gallon bucket. On a cold day one had to be very careful, because the metal pump handle could be so cold one's hands could freeze in place. Once the bucket was full one had to carry it back into the kitchen.

Most farmhouses at that time had a wood or coal burning kitchen stove. This stove served three purposes. One to heat the room. Two to warm water. And three to cook food.

In order to wash one's face, take a bath or shave, water had to be heated on the stove. Most farmers kept a coffee pot and a teakettle on the stove at all times. This teakettle held perhaps a half-gallon to a gallon of water. This was mostly the main source of hot water. Hot water would be poured into a wash pan, which held a couple of quarts, then this would be placed on a table, generally in front of a mirror, where one would proceed to wash or shave. After washing or shaving the water would be thrown outside on the ground.

Most people during the thirty's were very poor, people done the best they could with what they had. No electricity, no central heating system, no running water and no inside toilets. How did we make it?

I remember my father shaving with an old double edge blade razor. In order to keep the blade sharp, he would take the blade out of the razor, place it inside an empty water glass and slid it around the edge of the glass. Unbelievable how sharp an edge this put on the blade.

Since no water was pumped into the house, one could not have inside toilets. Most farmhouses had what was called an outhouse. This was built out of lumber and measured somewhere around four by six feet and possibly eight feet tall. Inside was a bench seat with two or three holes. These holes were eight or nine inches around. Imagine no fancy toilet paper was available. Usually a page of paper torn from a Sears catalog was used for this purpose. Needless to say, most trips to the outhouse was made very quickly, especially when the temperature was down around freezing or below.

I often wonder if we could survive today if we had to go back and live as we did back in the thirty's and before.

Troop trains, Kick the Can and Marching Bands

by Dianne Wallace Peffer of Dresden, Ohio
born 1939

Ah, the good old days of my youth. Ask any older person about the times of his or her youth and you're sure to get a large variety of stories and facts. America had gone through a dire and bleak decade of depression in the 1930's, only to be thrown into the worst war the world had ever known. In spite of the rationing during the war, that decade and a half truly showed what Americans were made of and how they endured the hardships of those difficult and trying times.

I was born and raised in Coshocton, Ohio, a small town of around 12,000 plus population. Coshocton got its name from the Indian word Cushogwenk, which means Black Bear Town.

I was only six-years old when the war ended. I can still see the troop trains that ran through the middle of town, often blocking the traffic and pedestrians from crossing when they were loading or unloading boxes or passengers. I remember looking up at those small windows, each one filled with a sad or expressionless face that stared back at me. I would wave to them and the faces would then smile as they waved back to me. I knew they were going far away to fight in the war.

I can also remember my mother sending me, at age five or six, to the small grocery store around the corner from us with a ration stamp gripped firmly in my small hand. She would lay the stamp on the palm of my hand, close my fingers into a small fist and make me promise that I wouldn't open my hand until the man at the store asked for it. I never did, because, even as a small child, I sensed the grave importance of that small piece of colored paper. Several years ago at an auction, I was able to buy several partially used Ration Stamp Books. As I looked through those pale-colored pages and read what product they were for, I thought of all the people whose lives had been so severely affected, how they made due with such small amounts and how they would have used each and every bit of that product, never wasting anything.

As a child, I would lie on my stomach in front of the radio listening to those wonderful old shows like The Shadow, Mr. & Mrs. North, The Lone Ranger and others, as I could actually see the heroes solving mysteries, capturing the bad guys and putting them in jail. My parents liked them too, but my dad especially loved the comics; Jack Benny and Spike Jones. Sometimes he would bend over in his chair from laughing so hard at them.

Christmases were very special. Dad would set up the live tree and then we would all decorate it. Mom and Dad had a small metal ornament that was shaped and looked exactly like an English walnut. I loved that little nut and always got to put it on a low branch so I could see it better. Years later, Mom gave it to me. I cherish it deeply and hang it near the top of our tree where it will be safe. The nut is now about sixty-years old. On Christmas morning, my sister and I had to drink a glass of tomato juice before we were allowed to open our presents. That was a tradition I carried on with my own two sons.

Dianne Wallace Peffer, wearing cowboy boots, with friend, Bill, in 1949.

When I was a little older, on Saturday mornings, my girlfriend and I would go to what they called The Saturday Kiddy Show at the Sixth Street Theater. For 20-cents we would see the weekly Movietone Newsreel, two cartoons, previews of coming attractions, the next chapter of the on-going serial, a western show and another main feather. Wow! All that! One Saturday, my girlfriend and I fixed a large bag of French fries to take to eat during the shows. Back then no one cared what you carried inside. Of course, by the time we ate them, they were cold and a bit greasy, but we didn't care. They were still good. Usually we ate candy and popcorn, and drank Coke Cola. Funny, but we never got sick from all the junk we ate.

In those days, before television and all the electronic gadgetry that everyone has to have now, children actually went outside and played for hours on end. One of the most popular games was Kick the Can, which was more fun when played in the early evening hours near a streetlight, or just plain old Hide and Seek. After several minutes, if not all the players could be found, the person who was 'It' could yell out, "oly-oly-in-free" and the rest of the kids would get back to home base free. Other favorite activities were roller skating, using skates that you tightened around your shoe with a skate key, walking or riding our bikes to Lake Park to swim all afternoon or going out to the farm the man next door owned. He had three ponies and we were allowed to grab the bridle from the barn, go into the field to get 'our' pony and then ride until early evening when he was ready to come back home. I dare say most of us were thin children because we were very active all summer long. In the winter, we would get all bundled up and go sleigh riding, usually at one of the grade schools where there was a hill. If there were enough snow, we would make snowmen, build forts, and have snowball fights. Such fun!

With other games, if a mistake was made, we could yell out, "Do over!" and no one seemed to challenge it. Other decisions were made by going "eeny-meeny-miney-moe." We kids knew how things were done. We didn't need adults cramming a bunch of rules into us. Halloween was such a favorite time for us kids. On Beggar's Night, as it was called then, we would go all around our own neighborhood, knocking on every door and yelling out "Trick or Treat." When our bags were at least half full, we would take them home and then go back out again and hit other neighborhoods close to ours. Some of the older people even asked us to come in so they could see if they could guess who we were. Such innocent fun, not like it is today when Trick or Treating has to be done in the daylight, and parents have to check the candy to make sure it's safe.

When it rained and we were sitting down for a change, we actually talked about what we wanted to be when we grew up. If they were like me, and many were, they changed their minds often. Depending on what stage I was going through, I wanted to be many things before I finally metamorphosed into a young lady. One of the careers I had chosen for myself was to be a cowgirl. I had a western shirt, a cowboy hat, cowboy boots and a gun belt that holstered two guns. I really thought I was something! I was very much a Tomboy then. (I even wore jeans and flannel shirts to school a few days a week, and that was back when girls weren't supposed to look or dress like boys.)

I finally turned myself around and became a sweet young lady in the summer of 1953 when I made the Senior Band at Coshocton High School. Oh, how proud I was, just knowing that I was good enough to play in that marvelous band! It was patterned then after the now-famous Ohio State Marching Band. Getting to wear that uniform and march in parades and on the football field were some of the most memorable and enjoyable experiences of my life! To this day, I still have a deep love of marches and beautiful music. I play in the

Coshocton County Community Band and the Walhonding Rube Band and thoroughly enjoy it! In a different way, it's like going back and enjoying some of my youth again.

Many people in the Coshocton area will remember a man named Marshall Jacobs. He would become known later as "Mad" Marshall Jacobs, not because he went mad, but because of his antics. While he was a man of many talents, he was by trade, a mechanic and carpenter. After the canal town of Roscoe Village, west of Coshocton, was restored in the 1960's and 1970's, he built the first canal boat known as The Monticello, a replica of the original canal boat during Roscoe's early history. One of Marshall's antics was climbing up the side of the Court House using just his hands and feet, using no ropes or hooks. But he is probably best remembered for building a platform on top of a flagpole at the Coshocton Fair Grounds in May 1946. He lived on the platform for several weeks and was even married on it. People came from all around to see him.

The house I grew up in was just a couple blocks around the corner from the fairgrounds. It was during the time Mad Marshall was on his flagpole, with hundreds of people coming and going in the area that a big white Samoyed dog appeared on our porch. My parents, realizing that she had probably gotten lost from her owners, who were here to see Mad Marshall, put an ad in the Coshocton Tribune to try to find her owners. No one ever showed up to claim her, so we kept her. She was the most beautiful dog we had ever seen. She was not only all white, with hair four to six inches long, but she was also an albino. Instead of having black pads on her feet, a black nose, and black eyes, hers were pink. She was not only gorgeous, but she was very well disciplined. Because of that, we named her Lady. She lived into the early 1960's and had three litters of puppies.

Both of my grandfathers died when I was pretty young, but I was very close to my grandmothers. My dad's mother lived straight through from us on the next street over and my mother's mother lived just out the street from us in the next block. Because they were so close, I visited them almost every day, especially during the summer when I wasn't in school.

My paternal grandmother loved to embroider, sew and crochet. It seems like when she wasn't in the kitchen cooking, she was making something. I still have a set of three white doilies with red roses in them that she crocheted. They are nearly sixty years old, still in tact, and being used on my vanity. Before she died, she made my sister and me each a hand-sewed quilt. I treasure it deeply, but will not use it. She was the sweet lady who patiently taught me to sew and embroider. She was never too busy to help me.

My maternal grandmother was just as dear in her own way. She was always dressed, had her lipstick on and was ready to go somewhere should someone come by and ask. I don't think anyone could fry an egg like she could. She used a small iron skillet; melted the butter, and at high heat, presented the best tasting egg you ever ate. She didn't like to sew or embroider. Oh no, not her! Playing cards and telling fortunes with the cards were more to her liking. In her younger days, I was told she loved going to the movies. As I grew older, and after I had seen a movie, I would have to tell grandma all about it.

She and I would sit and talk for hours. One of the most memorable stories she told me was about the 1913 flood. The water had raised quite high, flooding cellars and all low levels. Knowing how I loved horses, she told me about their horse raring up on his hind legs in the barn and putting his front legs on some kind of fixture in order to keep his head above water. Grandma said he had stayed that way for two or three days until the water receded.

I had a fantastic childhood, free to run and play, to dream about tomorrow and to enjoy each day as it came. We didn't have an abundance of money, but we had what we needed and made the most of it. When I hear an old song, smell a familiar fragrance or see an old picture, I am reminded of a time in America when the pace was slower, the people friendlier, the streets safer, and morals and beliefs more intact and secure. As much as I love the modern conveniences we have now and the tremendous strides that have been made in all aspects of life, there are times I still miss the wonderful, laid-back, easy-going life of yesteryear.

Good Neighbors and a Mysterious Apple Tree

By Betty J. Milligan of Coshocton, Ohio
Born 1929

I would like to tell you about a place called Zerbe. Sometime in the early 1900's a man whose last name was Zerbe bought several acres of bottom land along the Muskingum River in my home town of Coshocton, Ohio. In just about the center of this property he built a modest two story house. It was the first house that was built on the property. Soon after this, he sold lots reasonably priced for the times. The people that built there were low income people that lived from payday to payday. As you can guess it was the poor end of town.

I was born Betty Smith, April 28, 1929 in Coshocton, the youngest of four children. I had a sister and two brothers. We lived on South Third Street in 1936. There was a flood at that time. We had to leave the house for a few days until the water receded. Shortly after the flood, our landlord told Mom and Dad that he had sold the house and we had 30 days to move. Dad heard about a corner lot with a frame of a two room house that was already started for $150.00. Dad borrowed the money and bought this corner lot in the Zerbe Addition, as it was called then. Dad worked at the paper mill on day shift and worked on the house until about dark. He had to have this done before 30 days was up. We had the roof and sides on, but didn't have all the floors done; just part of the living room floor. We moved in and slept on the partial floor. Then Dad built a very large room for the bedroom. When we put in the floor he had me to help him. It was tongue and groove pinewood. It was easy to do and of course Dad checked everything to make sure I did it right.

Shortly after we got moved in, we had another flood in 1937. Dad put a few things in the attic to keep dry. We waited until the water was over the banks before we left. Dad had a pushcart that he had made and they put me and my sister in the cart with blankets, pillows and some clothes. I remember the water coming right behind us as we left our home. Dad didn't have much money at the time, so he went to this small grocery store and got some bologna and bread and some cookies to snack on. Mr. Gilmore, the man who owned the store, gave Dad some credit at the store. This was the first time that Dad and Mom dealt at that store and they stayed his customers for 39 years until he retired. We made some sandwiches and ate them in the Court House Square. We went to the cemetery on North Sixth Street and stayed there that first night. Later we went to an empty building on 15th Street and stayed until time to go home. We sure had a mess to clean up when we came back home. The Mohawk Dam was built after this and we didn't have any more floods. The water got high, almost over the banks a few times, but no more floods.

The reason for writing about Zerbe and my growing up there is that it was the happiest years of my life. I felt truly at home from the very first. I can remember a lot of things from the time I was between two and three-years-old and the places we lived, and there was no place like Zerbe. We made friends with the kids there and we all got along really good. We all got together and played games on our corner under the streetlight. Sometimes some of the parents got in the games too. We had some very good times and a lot of memories. In the winter time we had snowball fights and played fox and geese. The neighbors were good people that helped each other in times of need. We had some tough times, but we got by with the help of friends and neighbors. Mom and Dad would do wallpapering or anything they could to help out. People just helped neighbors out. I don't see much of that today. We had a big garden and we shared with someone that needed a little extra for their meal. When someone would pass away there was always someone to take up a collection for the family or for flowers.
We had some large families also. One had 13 children and another had 10 children. We had plenty of kids for our games. There was always something going on. We never got bored. We swam in the river, but not when it was up. The current was too swift. But we spent a lot of time in that river. One woman who lived across the street from us used to bake bread two or three times a week and would always invite me in to have some fresh baked bread with skillet gravy. Sometimes that's all they had to eat. They had five boys and three girls. All five boys were in the service in World War II and the father was in the Merchant Marines. There was a family that lived down by the river and they had a cow and some chickens. Every time I went to their house to play with their daughter she made me drink a large glass of milk. She baked bread a couple of times a week too. I think most everybody in the neighborhood baked their own bread. I've read about people who said that when they were kids and were poor, they didn't know that they were poor, because everybody was in the same position. Believe me, I knew we were poor. All the kids in our neighborhood were teased and harassed by the kids at school. We didn't have real nice clothes or shoes, just the basics. I ignored it a lot of times. I was easily hurt and went home crying several times. One boy was pretty brazen about his remarks to me. One day on the way to school, I was frustrated because we were going to be tardy and it started to rain. This boy was hurrying along too. He was late also. He took the time to call us some nasty names and I saw red right then. Me and that boy had a confrontation right then and there. He went back home. We went on to school. My 6th grade teacher was also the principal. She asked me why I was dirty and I told her. The boy's mother sent him on back to school with fresh clean clothes on. When he came in the room, the teacher took him into a large closet and questioned him and then we heard him getting the paddle. Needless to say he never called me and my sister any more names, at least to where we could hear him. His mother gave him a paddling too when she got the story.

I was kind of a tomboy at that time. I could out run most of the boys in the neighborhood and could out wrestle them too. Me and my sister used to climb some of the biggest trees down at the river. By the age of 14 I decided to act more ladylike. My dad finally got our house wired for electricity and he paid $40.00 to have it done. We were glad to be able to play our floor model Majestic radio. Every Saturday night we would listen to the Grand Ole Opry. I sat on the floor with my ear right up to the speaker. I didn't want to miss a thing. Dad would have fresh roasted peanuts and popcorn and root beer for us kids and some homemade beer for himself. I always thought my life was complete when Saturday came and I could hear the Grand Ole Opry. Mom listened to her soap operas every day. I never got hooked on soap operas, but on Tuesday nights we always listened to "Lights Out" or "Inner Sanctum." They had real scary shows on. We usually had a room full of kids who wanted to listen to "Lights Out." We made the room dark and took our places. Most of the time right where a real scary part was coming on, some girl would let out a scream because someone touched her and said "Boo!"

We had a lot of fun making candy and popcorn balls. Mom would make taffy and some neighbor kids would come to the house and we'd pull the taffy. That was something to see, but it always turned out good. We made peanut brittle too. One thing that stands out in my memory is whenever someone was sick or had a new baby the neighbors would come in and clean house or do laundry. They would bring in food already cooked or cook for you in your house. If someone had a money crisis people would help out with money or groceries. It was just a good place to live and grow up.

One thing I wanted to tell about happened when I was 11 or 12-years-old. My sister and I and another older girl borrowed a rowboat from Mr. Tatten and we went across the river to get some walnuts on the Hoop's farm. We had done this many times in the past. When we started up the small hill where the walnut trees were, I happened to look over to my left and I saw an apple tree. I had never seen this apple tree before in all the times we had went over there. The limbs on the tree were hanging to the ground with the most perfect red delicious apples you ever saw. We had two large burlap bags with us and we filled them full. It took all three of us to take one bag at a time down and load them in the boat. When we got back across the river my sister went to get Dad to bring a wheelbarrow to haul these apples home. Dad took the older girl's apples to her house first. This was quite a boon to us and to her family as they were quite needy. They were the best tasting apples and are still my favorite. Mom made some applesauce and we had fresh baked bread and it was a real treat. The most puzzling about all of this is when we went back over to get some more because we shared with some others. When we got over there on that hill, we couldn't find that tree. We looked all over even in some places where we knew we had not been and we never found that tree again. The Lord does provide, doesn't He? We did get our walnuts that time. They were good too.

When I got married in 1951 at the age of 22, I lived in a small house that Dad had built on his property. He added to it as my family grew. My husband was killed in an accident at work and left me with four children. I remarried and bought a house two doors up from Mom and Dad. I had two more sons. I was there 13 years. I divorced my second husband in 1972 and moved out of Zerbe in 1973; too many sad memories at that house. I sold out and moved on the other end of town on a hill. I don't have to worry about floods where I'm at. Nevertheless, I regret very much moving out. I wish with all my heart that I had stayed now. My kids, every one, did not want to move. They pleaded with me, but I was unhappy and thought I would be better off my moving and starting over. It's been 35 years now since I moved and this does not feel like home to me as Zerbe did. Whenever my kids get together there is always something said about Zerbe. They said there will never be another place that they liked as well as Zerbe. They had a lot of friends and good times there and won't ever forget it. Two years ago at Christmas, I gave four of my boys a tee shirt with "made in Zerbe" on the back and they loved it.

Zerbe is just about all gone now. They tore out a lot of houses to make way for a high rise for the elderly and handicapped. It's a business zone now. But there are two houses down by the river and four more up by 2nd Street; one small one and two house trailers in the middle. There were 70 houses when I lived there; and also a greenhouse and a mom and pop store. There was an open field with some young trees that separated us from the football field. We used to pick clover for the rabbits and blackberries from the bushes down by the river. The field is now the shopping center. From 2nd Street to the River is three blocks long. We had two streets: West Vine Street and West Pine Street, and also two alleys. It was Route 4 before they named the streets. We had dirt roads, no sewer, no city water and no sidewalks. They finally paved the streets in the early 1950's; put in the sewer and city water, but still no sidewalks. My sister and I packed water from the neighbors until Dad drilled for water and put a pump in the kitchen. What good water that was. We had some tough times, but so did a lot of people in the Depression. As Mom used to say, "We have a little more than some and a little less than others." We just made do with what we had. I remember one time Dad couldn't find a job. He had worked for the county for a time. So he went to one of the county commissioners who he knew personally and told him he needed a job bad. The man hired Dad to come and work on his farm for $1.00 a day. Dad stayed on the farm from Sunday night until Friday afternoon and came home for the weekend. This went on until Dad finally got a job at the Pope-Gosser Pottery. My dad was a very hard worker. He took any job he could get and whoever hired him got his money's worth. He passed away at age 92 and still lively. He had a stroke and went quickly. Well, I know my kids have some very good memories of Zerbe and so do I. There were some bad memories, but good ones outweigh the bad ones.

A Model T Confession

by Mary Kelley Kosar of Langhorne, Pennlylvania
born in 1928

I spent most of my childhood in Dresden. Our family—Mae, Sam and Ruby—last resided on 8th Street, next door to the Butler family and a few doors from the Longaberger family. I currently reside in Langhorne, Pennsylvania, just outside of Philadelphia.

My favorite teachers were Asa Thom (6th grade) and Margaret Penney (junior high).

I couldn't live one day without hanging out at Jerry's Dairy Store (Jewel's) with my girlfriends, Kay, Gloria and Whiss.

One of the things my parents never found out was the time my sister Ruby took me for a ride in my father's Model T. We almost ran into a deep ditch. I had to get out and push. Lesson learned: never again!

I still have ties in Dresden as my cousins Tom and Rita Cannon and Dick Frick still reside there as well as my first boyfriend, Bob.

Surviving the Snow of 1950

By Dana Clark of Chesterhill, Ohio
Born 1950

The following is a letter written to Dana Clark, on his fiftieth birthday, by his mother, Betty Clark.

Dear Dana,

I thought you might like this book because it's about the snow storm that took place when you were just five weeks old. Dad, the girls and I lived off State Route 377 near Pennsville on what was known as the Lester Terry place. It was an old one story house with a large living/dining room with two bedrooms off on one side and a long narrow kitchen the entire width of the back of the house. Of course it sat down under a hill at the foot of a lane.

The morning that things really turned bad was Friday the day after Thanksgiving. My dad came at about 10:30 to see you (his first grandson) and bring a present for you from Irma and him. I don't remember what the present was, but I do remember that he brought a bushel of red apples, an eight pound bag of oranges and two or three pounds of mixed Christmas candy. He also brought a box of Darla's used clothes and another box of used toys. Later we would be glad to have all of these things. He stayed and held you and visited until about noon. I ask him to stay and eat, but it was snowing pretty much so he said he'd better head back to Philo, but he did stay long enough to eat a piece of the pumpkin pie that Madge had given us when we had dinner with them for Thanksgiving. He said it was the best pie he ever ate. When he went out to leave, the ground was covered with wet snow and his new car wouldn't pull the hill so your dad put chains on our car and pulled him up the lane. They tore the lane all up and dad boiled all his anti-freeze out so he left our car backed in the end of the lane thinking he would put water in it and drive into Almendingers the next day for anti-freeze. Little did he know that he wouldn't see that car again for almost two weeks.

Dad was working at Malta Manufacturing on the afternoon shift. He had been bringing some kindling wood home whenever they had some out so we had that stored in the top of the barn. He had also been working for Morris Townsend some mornings and on Saturday cutting firewood. We were lucky that they had hauled two or three wagon loads down and dumped them in our front yard. Dad had started to split some of it to put on the porch. The only bad thing was that he left the axe out by the wood pile and had one heck of a time finding it in all the snow. Dad had a coon hound so had kerosene and a lantern and I had a lamp in the house so we had light after the electricity went off. It was off for an awful long time. It got so cold that we shut the two bedrooms off and slept on the mattress off our beds, one on each side of the stove. You were in the baby bed, but we took you into bed with us to keep you warm. In the day time we put one mattress on top of the other and the girls played there close to the stove. Thanks to my dad they had a lot of "new to them" toys.

Everything in the kitchen was freezing so we carried in all the food and what dishes and pans I would need and then nailed some plastic and a blanket over the doorway. The only warm place in the kitchen was inside the refrigerator. There were little snow drifts inside the kitchen windows and under the door. We put rugs and feed sacks down to try to stop the air, but the wind was just too strong. It came in everywhere.

We had a few chickens so dad got out to feed them and the dogs every day. He carried water from a spring down over a hill back of the house. Then he would split wood and pile it on the porch. The snow was so deep that everything he did took longer and was harder to do. It wasn't any easier inside the house either. We would build the fire up in the mornings to fix breakfast and heat water for dishes and baths. I only did the dishes up once a day in melted snow water because I had to use the stove to cook on the rest of the time. We were pretty lucky when it came to the food part. We had eggs on hand from our chickens, but of course they quit laying when it turned so cold. I had oats for breakfast and we used canned milk back then. Dad had killed some rabbits on Thanksgiving Day and had them hanging frozen on the porch. We ate them, but it took all afternoon to get them cooked. The dogs got the hot broth and I made them cornmeal mush and gravy too or they would have frozen. Dad had them fixed in the barn in the straw, but I know it was cold for them.

I had canned some that year so we had tomatoes, green beans, peaches and I had made some berry jelly and canned some berries in juice. Dad had killed some squirrels and I had some of them cold packed too. The rabbits and squirrels were our main meat, but two or three chickens froze their feet so dad butchered them the second week. We ate the apples, oranges and candy at night while we sat around the stove. I made a lot of applesauce too. We ran out of bread so we would have corn cakes or pancakes for lunch then I would make extra and we'd eat them cold with butter and jelly in place of bread for supper. I couldn't wash any clothes so the girls wore a lot of the things dad had brought down. I did wash out diapers every morning and hang them behind the stove to dry.

After more than a week Dad ran out of cigs and Prince Albert Papers and was down to his pipe so he walked up over the hill to where the county road was then out to the state road. They had just gotten one lane open on 377 and he got a ride into Malta to the A & P and back, but had to walk in from the state route. He got his tobacco, some canned milk, coffee, oats and since there was no bread in town he brought home some crackers. They were a treat. He got some other things too, but couldn't get much because he had to carry them so far in a feed sack and walk in the deep snow. We were lucky he didn't get sick from that trip.

After several days Dad heard some men up on the road. They had an old tractor and some horses and were trying to get the road cleaned out. Dad came to the house and got his heavy clothes on and went and helped them. He worked with them for several days, then it took two or three days to dig his own car out of the drift. When he finally did get to drive to town for food and supplies, he went to Almendingers and my dad had been there and left a case of anti-freeze for him. We couldn't use the lane for most of the rest of that winter, but we got along okay. You were just a baby, Dixie was 20-months-old, Donna was three-years and one-month- old and Diana was one month short of four years old. I doubt if they can remember any thing about that time.

I was 19 years old at that time and Dad was 25. Sometimes I wonder how we made it, but at that time it was just the way it was and you had to deal with it. I wonder what people would do if we had a storm like that now? Of course they have more to work with now so the roads would be opened quicker and the electricity back on sooner I expect.

Don't judge this on spelling or writing.

Love, Mom

There's Something in the Water in Dogpatch

by Maurice D. Henery of Lake Forest, Illinois
born 1923

Harold Finley calls McConnelsville "hillbilly Ohio" and I call it Dogpatch. I knew him way back then and we differed in more ways than the names we used for our hometown. Harold was a child prodigy too sickly to attend public school. He was taught at home by his mother, Kate. No way could he be "one of the boys" and look where it got him! I, however, was "one of the boys" and breathed lime dust most of my life. Harold marched off to Northwestern at age 13; I marched off to W.W.II at age 19. Harold was from the "good" side of the tracks; I was from the other side of the tracks. Harold was more intelligent and had a photographic memory; I was not as intelligent. Harold set his sights for the top; I was looking for a steady job, doing anything, anywhere and for whatever pay I could get.

Picture contributed by Maurice Henery.

But we both drank the same water and there may be something in the water found in Dogpatch. On a per capita basis (the county population totals 10,000 people) Dogpatch has produced more successful people than any area I know about. By Dogpatch standards, even I am considered successful and I could name quite a few more who are much more successful.

I suggest sending candidates for a college education to Ohio University in Athens, Ohio. Even if they flunk out, they will drink enough of the local water to succeed anyway!

The Buck Sheep and the Rock Pumpkins

By Daniel T. Burkhart of Marion, Ohio
Born in 1949

My grandfather, George M. Christman (1875-1957), told that he and his young teenage friends teased a buck-sheep. One boy pushed a long pole into the sheep pen with his hat on its end. They boy held the outside end of pole in front of him. The buck-sheep backed away and running fast, butted the hat, sending the pole hard against the boy's stomach.

The boy lost consciousness. The other boys

were scared. The injured boy revived and they all went home, promising never to try that trick again.

Grandpa and his brothers were instructed to plant pumpkin seeds. With a large bag of seeds, they planted many seeds, but they were tired! They didn't think anyone would know if they threw the remaining seeds into a rock pile. The rock pile revealed their secret, when it became covered with pumpkin vines and later, pumpkins!

Mother's Pet Snake

By Isabel Benington of Carrollton, Ohio
Born in 1926

I was born in 1926 to Beulah and Arthur Millhorn, and they lived near the small village of Tappan, Ohio. Of course, my growing up years were during the Great Depression, but we really did not realize we were poor.

We lived on an 80 plus acre farm which was paid for, and our life was mostly self-sufficient as we had our own cows, pigs, chickens, sheep, horses, and of course cats and one dog. My parents also had a large garden and "truck patch." So, we bought only necessaries at the general store in Tappan, Ohio, like pepper, salt, sugar, bananas, an occasional orange, kerosene for lamps (no electric) and gasoline for our model T Ford.

My father took wheat to the mill, had it ground into flour for bread and "middling" (wheat germ/bran) which we gave to the pigs. Pretty good eating for them!

We tried to use as few eggs as possible as my mother sold them, and with the money, she ran her household and bought clothes and sewing supplies. She made a game out of everything, trying to make do with as little as possible. We were happy. She made many things out of feed sacks including dresses, curtains, sheets, etc., and the prettiest appliquéd and embroidered pillow cases.

Our farm had a beautiful grove of trees and sometimes it was used for church picnics. For at least two summers, Dad allowed the Afro-American Boy Scouts of Cadiz, Ohio to camp in the grove. They were wonderful people! My mother got food poisoning and got very sick for a couple of days. The ladies from the Boy Scouts stepped in and cooked for my dad and me, and helped out wherever they could.

I remember those days in summer when I would go out the side porch door and there stretched across the grassy lawn would be a big blacksnake. Made going to the outhouse a little risky for a little girl. One summer a small garter snake seemed to be hanging around. It liked to lie on the walk just outside the porch door. Mother called it her "pet" snake. Later, it was found dead on the road in front of our house.

I was an only child so a dog was my playmate and companion. I had a beautiful collie, but he came up missing. I begged and begged my parents if they knew where he was. Finally they told me they found him stretched out dead in the yard. Someone had poisoned him. I cried and cried. Of course my father got me a new puppy but I'm still sad over losing my friend.

The general store in Tappan carried a full line of merchandise. Gasoline was five gallons for $1.00. I always got candy when we went to the store. A sack of assorted candy for ten cents. I thought never in my lifetime would I get all the gum or ice cream that I wanted, but now I do.

The store bought eggs and cream from the farmers. It also ran a "huckster" route every week out through the surrounding area to buy the eggs and cream from people who couldn't make it to the store, and selling essentials to the farm women.

Ralph Warren drove this route was very well liked, and a great cut-up. In the summer, he would take some of the local boys with him on the route. One time he stopped the truck, pretended he was having a seizure, and rolled around on the ground and into the ditch. It scared the boys—but it was all in fun.

My girlfriend asked me to go with her on the route. Guess what? On the day I was to go, the huckster showed up without her. My parents assured me it was okay, and I got brave enough to go alone, I had a wonderful time—no seizures!

My father was an excellent farmer and provider—always interested in anything new in the agricultural line. The top of the hill behind our house was saucer-shaped and ideal for an orchard. My dad planted fruit of all types: pears, apples, quinces, peaches, plums etc. Our fruit was always good—no bugs or worms and we did not have to spray.

He had a large sledge with side boards which he filled with fruit and brought to the house. The pears went into the washhouse with a cement floor to finish ripening, the apples into the cellar house which was half way underground with the walls filled with sawdust.

Mother canned everything she could from the garden and orchard and these were stored in the cellar house too. Father always gave out of this bounty to anyone who needed—friends/relatives.

My father was a gentle man—good and kind to his animals. He must have been very trusting and sure of his horses. He mowed hay with a mowing machine pulled by horses. He hitched my sled (for snow) behind the machine and pulled me over the swaths of new mown hay. What fun, except when I would see a snake slithering away in the grass!

There was no money to pay school teachers, so different families in the school district would give them their room and board free. My father was president of the school board and we had teachers stay with us two winters. One winter when I was seven, I had a severe illness. I slowly recovered with good care and many prayers. No antibiotics then! I was given lots of oranges, bananas and cod liver oil (ugh!). When the weather got warm the doctor ordered me out in the sunshine with only my underwear. In those days, we didn't have shorts. So even then, they were pushing Vitamin D!

In the early thirties along came F.D.R., the New Deal etc, and talk began to come to us about building dams to prevent flooding. Our community was typical, interacting with each other and not eager for change. My parents were the first to move when the government bought our farm. Many moved, but there were a few who opted to stay and fight the government for more money, etc. They ruined their lives and went to their graves bitter people.

The women of the community met once a month to quilt—making quilts for missionaries in Tibet, and other faraway places. They called it "Missionary Meeting." It was based in the Christian Church at Tappan, Ohio but many times they met in the different homes with a covered dish dinner at noon. Delicious food!

When the Tappan dam (a part of the Muskingum Watershed Conservancy) was being built, the women decided as a parting memory, they would exchange quilt blocks. The pattern chosen was "Dresden Plate" or "Friendship" quilt. Thus, each woman had enough blocks to make a quilt which would forever bring fond memories of friends far away.

I could write of many more things—like we lived on U.S. Route 250, the coast to coast highway. One night a truck had locked brakes which set fire to the tires. It was carrying a load of pigs. They opened the doors and many of the pigs escaped. The next morning the pigs were scattered, the truck burned, and the asphalt in the road melted.

But now it's time to say "good-bye" and get back to my memories another time.

A Town No More

by Stephen E. Hooper of Woodsfield, Ohio
born 1949

About one mile southeast of Antioch, Ohio, off State Route 800, there was a town called "Mechanicsburg." Because there were so many Hoopers living there lots of people called the town Hooperville. Hooperville grew up along the little Muskingum River. My brothers and I lived there with Dad and Mom.

Grandfather had a farm there and we lived right beside them. I was always working on the farm. There was always something to do. I don't even remember being bored. We had something to do all the time. There were coalmines and oil wells, a store, a church, a one-room school and a hotel. There were farms up and down the little river, on top of the hill, on the hillside houses and everywhere.

There were other people too besides Hoopers. I can't remember all the other people. In one of the coal mines, a horse lived there. He pulled the wagon of coal outside, but he seldom got to stay outside. He lived in the mine. He had his own hard hat. The cows had bells around their necks so that we could find them at milking time.

We had a good swimming hole in the summer time; there were always someone there swimming. After putting in the hay we would hit the swimming hole. We had rocks to climb, caves to explore, thousands of acres to roam and wild grapevine to swing on. We spent hours in the woods. Sometimes we would cut a stick, put on a line and hook and went fishing. From my house or the farm I could threw a rock and hit the creek. What a great place to live.

Hooperville and Muskingum River.

When I was eighteen we moved to the city of Woodsfield. Now I am about 60 years old. Often I think back to Hooperville and the great times we all had there. I can still smell the scent of fresh cut hay and other farm smells. There is no more Hooperville. Most of the people were dead and most of the land there and around has been sold to the government which is part of "Wayne National Forest". What lands that are left have "no hunting and trespassing" signs everywhere. Sometimes my family goes for a ride to Hooperville in my mind. I can see what it used to be there. There is still one Hooper living there and there are still some people here in Woodsfield that still remember Hooperville.

We had an old crank phone. Each one on the line had a ring tone assigned; long or short ring. Ours was long and a short ring. You were not supposed to listen to any conversation, but I think everyone were listening when they were not supposed to.

The hunting was very good. When we wanted to go hunting we never asked our neighbor. Everyone just went wherever they wanted to. We all knew each other.

The Deepest Snow Ever!

by Marlene Singhaus of Dover, Ohio
Carole Sweasey of Winston-Salem, NC
born 1934

Although the 1978 blizzard is recorded as the worst in Ohio's history, the Thanksgiving snowstorm of 1950 is considered the deepest.

By late on the second day, much of the state had snow depths of 20-inches and there were drifts of 25-feet. The OSU-Michigan game went on (haphazardly) as planned. It was referred to from then on as the "Snow Bowl." The state was at a standstill.

Surrounding the New Philadelphia Square, the snow was piled so high that the storefronts were not visible. There was no traffic. Troop trains could not get in or out of Dennison. Everyone was snug in their homes. Well, that is with the exception of two high school juniors who still to this day, talk about their glorious adventure. We climbed those drifts and slid back down over and over. Finally when we were tired, we found that the Union Opera House was open. We went in to rest and watched a movie. There was no trouble finding a seat.

Memories of Grandma Mildred

By Gail Workman of Lore City, Ohio
Born 1949

I first got to know the Dodds when my ex-husband worked for Bill in the garage on the school buses. This was in 1967. Mildred and Bill stood up for us when we got married. After we got married we had no place to go and no money to get started. So we stayed with Mildred for a short time until we got our first trailer in Winterset. We didn't have a phone so a flashlight signal was developed when Bill wanted John to work or go coon hunting.

I remember Mildred going to IGA with us to get groceries the first time. I didn't know very much about shopping back then. $25.00 was what the bill came to and Mildred helped pay for the groceries and supplied whatever we had forgot to buy to set up the cupboards in the trailer. Mildred gave me lots of cooking, canning, and washing clothes lessons

Rhonda and Duane were about five and 10 at this time. Mildred got a job at the State Hospital and she had to start the same time Bill went to New York coon hunting. That was the only fight I can remember them having. Bill didn't want to go to New York without her, so I was the next in line with Jo Ann Patterson, but I got a job at NCR and couldn't go either. Hershal, Bill, John, and Sam went on this hunt and came back just a little bit skinner without their cook.

Mildred's job the next year was the chief cook and camp fire handler. We canned coon. What an experience. We also barbecued coon to eat. This was my first experience at the good old life of a hunter wife. We were shot at by the caregiver of The Nicholas Plantation, checked by the state troopers and searched on this trip! Boy, I didn't know if this was such a good vacation by this time or not. We all made it back to Ohio alive with the grace of God showing us the way.

Rhonda and Duane and Bryan Richard became our ready made family while Mildred worked and Bill hunted at night. Someone even asked me who baby-sat my husband's kids while I worked. It didn't take me long to know who they were talking about.

One day my mother was visiting the Dodds when we figured out Mom and Bill were both from West Virginia and were distant cousins. Now we were officially in the family. I remember I felt it was an honor. Mildred was already my second mother and my kids' grandmother. When ever Mother's Day came. Larry had to have three flowers for all his grandmothers in Winterset: Grandmother Mildred, Grandmother Bates and Grandmother Lodge. He always came home from his walks with something from Mildred. The banana ice cream was a favorite. Larry set on the ice cream freezer while someone cranked; then came the electric freezer so much faster. Only Mildred could make ice cream to suit my kids. Still to this day it doesn't taste like Grandmother Mildred's.

I can remember being afraid to stay by myself when the men went hunting so it was Mildred's turn to baby sit me. That meant stuffing a chicken and eating about midnight and laughing for hours with a good old back scratch from Mildred. Mildred learned me to can white cling peaches for Helen Games who was sick at this time. Mildred also mothered me through Larry's birth. I always said he was a New York seed baby from all the grapes we would eat in New York.

I remember when the coon wouldn't look at the lights to be shot at Mildred could squall just like a coon to get them to look at the light.

Only Mildred's crochet house slippers were good enough for my family. Of course Grandma made them with special love. At each graduation everyone could count on getting a special afghan from Mildred. At the birth of each baby a special afghan. My mother and Mildred made the pot scratches by the hundreds. I don't remember who taught who, but they had fun visiting while doing this and selling them.

Along came the grandkids of the Dodd's and I grew attached to Jo Ellen who use to go out on the hill above the house and give a Tarzan call for me to meet her to cross the road and visit. The twin brothers, Kevin and

Keith, were my beauticians back then. Dough and Dee Ann were the hot rod kids with Mildred praying no one hit them in the back alley.

Home comes Carl from Vietnam and really brought joy to Mildred; and the old white 56 Chevy was hot on the road. The Birmingham road had just been re-topped and Carl laid the first set of black marks.

Mildred was such a beautiful person to know and love; she was just like my mother to me. I never moved more then an eyesight from her. I just know I could call anytime I needed her: she was there for us all the time.

These are only a small amount of memories that I have of Mildred; all very good and no bad ones; so Lord, please look after her now. We will truly miss you Grandma Mildred.

Ten Kids and No Grass

by Eleanor Roosevelt Hicks of Philo, Ohio
born in 1940

I was born on Election Day when F.D. Roosevelt was elected for his second or third term. We wasn't a rich family, but we had plenty to eat. We had an outside toilet and sometimes we had a catalog or newspaper for use as toilet paper. We have ten kids in the family, so we didn't have much grass in the yard. I don't remember even having a lawn mower. Our yard was all dirt.

My dad would play the guitar and mouth harp and I would sing "You Are My Sunshine." There was always neighbors at our house. We lived on a gravel dead-end road and my friend's dad, John (my friend was Dorothy), would come up to our house and tell stories from a long time ago. Then he would walk back home after dark. Nobody ever bothered you back then.

I used to put on my mother's high-heeled shoes and run up and down the hills, and us kids would go in the woods and play on trees. We had them bent over so we could get on them and bounce up and down.

I remember when I was in the third grade me and a friend, Joann, started laughing in school and couldn't quit, so the teacher took us out in the hallway and gave us a few cracks with the paddle. Then when I was in the seventh grade, me and a friend and the whole class went to a movie, "The Robe." It was a great movie. When it was over, all the kids and teacher went back to school, except two of us. We went and got on the city bus and went to my friend's house. When we got there, her mother said the school called and she took us back to school. I never did that again.

We lived in the city limits, but it was like the country. I used to walk to grade school in big snows up through the woods for two or three big hills. I walked to school in the morning and at noon, home for lunch and back to school and home again after school. I wore rubber boots and would have red rings around my legs where the boots would rub my cold wet legs.

We didn't have city water, just a dug well, and the water wasn't good. It was sulfur. It would turn everything red and was hard water, so we had to get water in town to drink and cook with. We had some 55-gallon barrels at the ends of the house to catch rainwater, which my mother used to wash clothes with in a wringer washer. The water would be kind of black because of the soot on the roof from the coal stove we had in the kitchen.

Eleanor R. Hicks' dad, Richard (Barney) and sister, Helen, in 1953.

We just had the one coal heater in the kitchen. It got really cold in the other rooms. When we got up in the mornings, we would bring our shoes and socks in the kitchen behind the stove and finished getting ready for school. By the way, Mother had to wait till it rained to wash clothes.

There was a family that lived down the road from us. The two boys used to come to our house all the time. The younger one was about eighteen years old, and he was kind of scared of his own shadow. Anyway, my dad was out in the yard and Fred, the boy, went to the outhouse. Dad put a white sheet over his head and threw a rock at the outhouse, and Fred ran out of there and ran all the way home yelling, "Mommy! Mommy!" all the way down the road.

My brothers and sisters and neighbor kids would be out after dark in the summertime playing hide-and-seek. That was a lot of fun. We had a lot of good times. We had a swing between two oak trees made out of rope. We had a good time swinging on it, but if one of the smaller kids got in front of someone swinging and got knocked down, my dad would cut it down.

Letting Ruth Get Ahead

by Charlene Scott Lenser of Rocky River, Ohio
born in 1931

I was a member of the class of 1948 at Lewisville High School. All twelve of us—probably the smallest class *ever* from anywhere.

On VE Day, some of us decided to skip the afternoon

classes—not just my class, but anyone in the high school. We had fun, didn't do anything but walk over back hills and valleys, some smug, thinking we had pulled off the greatest prank.

All through school, I (in my mind only) was competing for honors with a girl named Ruth. If I scored 100% on a test, Ruth scored 100 ½%. I was doomed!

Well, on our getaway, we (sneaked?) back to school. We took turns running across streets, peering around the post office and other buildings to be sure the coast was clear, and then we would all run to the next corner. How dumb, I think now, as everyone in town knew most of us. Finally, we're back at school, and ones who didn't go got to help clean up the cafeteria—wash dishes, etc. No one yelled at us or paid any attention to us, so we thought we were getting away with something.

Wrong! The next morning, our principal, Mr. Philpot, called on the P.A. for all who were gone the day before to report to the gym immediately. Well, he said they didn't know how to handle this just yet, but he suggested there might be a lowering of grades. Drats! Foiled again! I skipped, Ruth didn't—Oh well, I had fun.

I guess I did have fun, because this little getaway was the one I chose to write about.

Green Sandwiches and Frog Legs

by Harry J. Hinkle of Barnesville, Ohio
born in 1924

I was born in Bethesda, Ohio on September 13, 1924. The Depression came along during my childhood. We had a total of seven children in our family—four sisters, and two brothers and of course myself. Our mother was killed in an auto accident when I was eight years old. My two brothers were older than me by six years and eight years. Our grandmother came and tried to take care of us. I remember we had a lot of bean and drop dumplings in those beans. We kids called them "sinkers," but they did fill our little bellies.

I always tried to follow my brothers and a neighbor boy wherever they went. They would throw stones and green apples at me to make me go back home. One day they let me go fishing with them in a creek. We took our lunch with us. The only thing we could find in the house was some bread and some greens cooking on the stove. We made green sandwiches. That was all we had to eat at that time. We went fishing and my brothers fixed me up with a pole and a hook made out of a safety pin. They left me at a nice spot and they went on around the bend. I got a good bite and gave a big jerk. The sod gave way and I slid down the bank, went under a root and was half way in the water. I hollered for Help! Help! —They came and saved me! Built a fire, hung my clothes to dry over the fire.

It came time to eat our lunch, so my brothers caught some frogs and put the legs over the fire. We had green sandwiches and frog legs for lunch. Not bad back then.

Another time myself and a neighbor boy did something bad. I had to go in front of the mayor. I didn't know what was going to happen to me. Well my dad got me cleaned up and put my best clothes on and took me into Bethesda. We were sitting on the steps in town. We were waiting for the sheriff to come and take me to the "reform school." Scared the hell out of me. The sheriff never showed up! Finally, I got the message and was a better boy after that scare.

My grandmother could not take care of us, so we were taken to the Belmont County Court House to see Judge Albright. The judge decided to put the five youngest of us into the children's home at Tacoma, Ohio. That turned out to be the best thing that ever happened to us. I was there for three years, then placed out to Mr. and Mrs. Alvin Phillips' farm. I was there for seven years at which time I went into the army.

My two brothers were living in an old car behind Shepherd Chevrolet Garage. One evening my oldest brother told Earl that he was hungry for salmon. He told Earl to go to the M.K. Grocery and steal a can of salmon. Earl went and put a can of salmon down in his shirt and headed for the door. The lady clerk asked Earl if he would like to have some crackers with that salmon! Earl kept on out the door. He went back when he got some money and offered to pay for it, but the lady would not take the money. My brothers later went into the 3-C camps.

Another time a local man was delivering flour to a bakery in Bethesda and my brothers were loafing close by and the driver asked them if they would like to help unload it. They helped unload it. One brother was inside and the driver asked him if he had locked the window. He said yes, but he had not done so. That night they robbed the bakery, got a big sack of pink icing cakes. On the way out Earl said, "Look AG, the register drawer is open with change in it!" AG says, "Don't touch it." Earl says, "why not?" AG says, "Because that is stealing!"

After all of these hard times, all of us kids grew up and had decent jobs and became good American citizens. That's a big plus.

The Old Log House and Other Memories

By Judy M. Brown of Lower Salem, Ohio
Born 1958

This story is about my great grandparents. They did not have a lot of money and lived in an old log, two-story house that had originally been built to be a barn.

My father, who is 78, lived these memories that I have written.

My father was a boy when everyone in the valley would gather every weekend at his grandparents' place to eat, have fellowship, sing, and play music.

Eventually, my grandparents bought the old log house and property and lived there for many years. After they passed away, my husband and I bought the old two story log house. Because of termite damage, we dismantled the old log house and built a house on the property.

When my grandparents lived in the old log house, it was a place of comfort and warmth for me and my siblings.

The pink and white flower bushes are still in my yard and Grandma always had little purple flowers around the perimeter of the house.

Edna Day Love, paternal grandmother, in the early 1900s.

Even though my writing is in a story format, it is non-fiction. As a family we could fill a book of our own with memories from several generations. My ancestors were one of the first settlers in this part of Noble County.

My father has recounted the story of how the government gave the land to farmers who were willing to settle and farm the land.

My grandfather's grandfather was the first owner of this tiny corner of Noble County and even today the steep hill beside us is known as "Old Joe Love's Tater Hill."

Nestled at the feet of three rolling hills was the rustic two-story log house. Tiny purple flowers surrounded the gray tinted house, while red roses and large leafy pink and white flower bushes emphasized the perimeter of the yard. The green moldy slate roof of the weathered house had seen better days, but no one seemed to notice. A brook gurgled beside the lush green lawn, as a big maple tree in the front yard majestically beckoned the visitors under its cool umbrella of green leafy branches. Horse-drawn wagons full of friends and neighbors leisurely made their way toward the inviting home.

As usual, the men, after a long day in the fields, gathered to relax in the shade, compare tales, and discuss their long and difficult week. The children's laughter could be heard as they raced in circles around the yard, stopping occasionally to dip their toes in the cool water of the nearby stream. Succulent aromas escaped the small kitchen where the women bustled, laughing and talking, hurriedly preparing just-picked garden vegetables and ham from last winter's butchering. This was the gathering place on a summer evening for all the neighbors to come and relax.

Everyone knew they were welcome at Willard and Carrie's home. Somehow, no matter how many friends and neighbors came to visit, there was always enough food to feed everyone. "Come and get it," Carrie would call from the kitchen door, as soon as the vittles were done. Children stopped in their tracks and men ceased to tell their tales as they gathered to eat the delicious food that was about to be served. There was silence as one of the men offered thanks to God for all His blessings and for the wonderful meal they were about to receive.

With empty plates, people began to line up at the kitchen door. As the single-file, group of friends and neighbors entered the kitchen, the women doled out generous portions of food. Because of the smallness of the kitchen, the group continued through the back door and outside to find a spot under the cool shade of the maple tree. There was not much talking as everyone enjoyed the delicious food, which included warm homemade bread and pies.

As the evening wound down, musical instruments suddenly appeared and everyone joined in the festivities of the evening. Guitars, harmonicas, and strumming banjos sounded as voices harmonized.

Darkness came quickly to the little valley as the neighbors and friends said their goodbyes and farewells, thanking Willard and Carrie for another relaxing evening of wonderful fellowship. Morning would come soon enough and the hardship of manual labor would once again be a reality. Horses neighed and wagons creaked as they made their way out the narrow dusty road. The Loves stood in the dusk of the evening bidding farewell to their friends and neighbors. "See you next week, if the Lord is willing."

* * * *

When my father was a boy, castor oil was a cure all. He recalls an event his mother told him. As a very small child he had been outside all day and when evening came and he went in for supper, he started crying. His mother could not figure out what in the world was wrong, so she brought out the castor oil. After my father took the "medicine," his mother removed his shirt and noticed his very red back. My father was sunburned and that was the reason for his crying.

* * * *

As a fifteen-year-old, my maternal grandmother, as we found out later, liked to play hooky from school. She was meeting a neighborhood boy (my future grandfather) behind the barn. A few months later my aunt was born.

* * * *

Finally, the phone line reached the country, but unfortunately, four or more people had to share the line. My great grandmother loved to eavesdrop and hear the neighbors' gossip. This irritated my great grandfather. So, one day, when he entered the house and my great grandmother was eavesdropping, he bellowed, "Hey, Zilla, I emptied the piss pot!"

* * * *

People that lived in the country recycled long before it was popular. I can remember going to the old country store in our neighborhood with my grandmother to pick out the cattle feed. The feed was put into feed sacks that were made of colorful cloth that could be sewn into aprons, dresses, dish clothes, etc.

* * * *

My father, who is now 78 years young, had many first cousins around his age. There were two in particular that got into mischief.

My father's extended family was going to the "homecoming," which was an all day meeting at a local church. When the family got to the church, the churchyard was full of neighbors. The parking area in front of the church was parked full, so grandfather dropped off everyone in the front of the church and he drove off to find a parking place. As he drove off in front of all in attendance, a huge burlap bag and rope was dragging behind the car. Grandmother was mortified. She turned to the family and said, "Our reputations are ruined." When everyone got home that evening, the two cousins weren't laughing anymore.

That's a Lot of Pork

by Harry Warner of Quaker City, Ohio

This happened on Thanksgiving Day and night, 1950. I was nine years old at this time, now sixty-seven. Our family and friends butchered ten hogs that weighed between six and seven hundred pounds and cut them up, trimmed out the hams that weighed between fifty and sixty pounds each and shoulders weighing forty-five to fifty pounds and bacons that was at least thirty pounds each. Cut the lard to render the next day, also sausage to grind the next day also.

Everyone went home to do chores and rest the night to come back next day to help render lard and grind sausage and stuff it. The temperature was in the fifty to sixty degree range. This day was a nice winter day.

We went to bed about eleven PM, wake up about six AM, and there was between thirty-six and forty inches of snow on the ground, wind blowing it into drifts as high six to seven feet.

No one could get out to go anywhere on Friday, so we had all the work of taking care of all the lard and sausage and curing of the meat in meat house.

For three weeks, Dad, when we needed things from town, had the tractor and trailed to get the stuff. The neighbor had a milk route in town of Belle Valley that he and Dad delivered the milk to his customers then picked up the things that we needed at the store in town. We lived where the research farm is now at Belle Valley.

I graduated from Belle Valley High in May, 1960.

Chasing Tommy and Switchblade Jealousy

by Georgia A. Moore of Cambridge, Ohio
Born 1944

My earliest memories is living with my Grandma and Grandpa Tennant and Uncle Bud at their farm when I was about three or four-years-old. It's just a few miles from where I live now, Fairground Road, close to the small town of Old Washington, Ohio.

I went to first grade from there, a two room schoolhouse in Antrim, Ohio. First four grades in one room; fifth through eighth in the other. Mrs. Estalene Law taught the first four grades. I have her picture that I cut out of *The Daily Jeffersonian* on her 97th birthday a few years ago. She is still living. We had the "water bucket" and we brought our own cups from home, thank goodness! There was a potbelly stove and an outhouse. There was a boy in my grade that kinda liked me; he got me a small Christmas present. His last name was Bean; mine was Duck!

There was a big snow in 1950. About the only thing I actually remember was my mom and future stepfather came and got me at the farm, for me to spend the holiday vacation with Mom in Cambridge. Some days later they took me back out to my grandparents' in case we soon had school. We didn't! They took me out in the old-fashioned green jeep.

We went to Cambridge every few weeks for groceries and whatever else they needed. We went in an old Model T or A, I'm not sure which, and it seems we pretty much made a day of it. I remember Grandma always got salt-water fish out of the barrels, to eat, of course. We always ate at Coney Island; it seems we always got two Coney dogs, custard pie and chocolate milk. It is one of the few restaurants still there. We go a good bit. I still, on occasion, get Coney dogs and custard pie, but rarely, if ever, chocolate milk. Coney dogs aren't quite as good as years ago, but the pies are delicious.

My family was very prejudiced. My grandma had told me that people were black because they drank black coffee. As we were strolling the street on one of our outings, we saw two black men walking. I was quick to point out to Grandma Tennant what they had been doing and she just as quickly shook me and told me to be quiet. They remained prejudiced to their dying day, but never again told me such a tall tale.

In second grade one time, Mom got home from work a few minutes after I got home from school. One evening I brought a little colored girl home to play for a while. Mom got home, took one look, took me aside and gave me a little money and said, "Go to the store, get a box of crackers and lose her on the way!"

Also in second grade, I went to Garfield School. My best girlfriend, Jeannie Dickson, and I about chased Tommy S. to death trying to kiss him, but the three of us were buddies.

When I was in third grade Mom married my stepdad and they built and opened a restaurant, Prouty's Drive Inn. We even had curb service. For the next few years I spent a lot of time working at our restaurant; for the most part I enjoyed it. Hamburgers were 25-cents, cheeseburgers 30-cents; real meat, real potatoes, real food. Also they built and opened a Shell filling and service station.

A few years later, my step dad and Joe Losego opened a small airport across the road from the other two businesses. Around the same time him and Dean Long had ownership in the Casa Loma just down the road a ways, one of the nicest nightclubs around.

Unfortunately, my stepfather and another guy got killed in one of Dad's private planes when I was 15. He was only 41. His death devastated me, so I quit taking flying lessons. Really, he wouldn't have wanted me to quit. He is my memorable person, "The Best."

I did more than my share of playing hooky and goofing off. In seventh grade, Mr. Oliver was the teacher and down the hallway they had a sick room. Some of us girls would fake being sick. Usually by lunch, two, three or four of us were pooling our money for one of us to go across the street to the grocery store to buy lunch supplies.

Mom and Grandma's cooking and baking were so good! Years ago, I took my recipe box to see if Grandma wanted any of my recipes. She reminded me that most of mine were hers.

You ate what was fixed, no questions, no arguments; you tried everything. I would take the smallest piece of liver and largest piece of homemade bread to help the liver go down a little easier. My daughters still remember all my instructions when we went to Mom and Grandma's to eat. We all ate every meal at the kitchen table, passing the food, etc.

As for pets and toys, I had a female Chihuahua. Her name was Fannie. And I had a tricycle, a Raggedy Ann doll and cut-out dolls and clothes.

Remember I said my maiden name was Duck? Well, one time we had a class hayride and for some reason, at one point, I was standing and some of the kids hollered, "Georgia Duck!" As I turned and said, "What?" a tree limb hit me! That was funny, but this next story is embarrassing. When I started eighth grade, I had an upper partial plate; my front four teeth and one on each side in the back. I was at a basketball game, standing off to the side talking to a guy. I don't know what I did, laughed or something, and those blame teeth flew out of my mouth onto the floor. I quickly leaned over and picked them up and put them back in my mouth. Talk about embarrassing! You would have thought the old-fashioned wiring would have kept them in place. The hayride incident was funny, as I said, the next was totally embarrassing, but I don't know how to label this next one, as you will soon understand.

One of my best friends was Karen Bugos. When we were in our early teens, in the late 50's, we went to a basketball game at our school in Old Washington. They were playing our most rival school, Madison. It had been like that for years. Her and I stopped at Ozzie's Restaurant, just a short way from the school. We met a guy in there, Carl Voorhies; we got to talking and he wanted to know if we would do him a favor when we went up to the ballgame. Would we do him the favor of making his girlfriend jealous? They were all from Madison, so we agreed. First mistake! So we were all on the Madison side with Karen and I rooting for Old Washington. Second mistake. We were just talking to Carl, and these three girls (one was the girlfriend) was getting madder by the minute, especially when Karen and I got our famous giggles and couldn't stop. They thought that we were laughing at them. Really we weren't. Of course, they didn't believe us and the arguing began. Well, Karen and I decided to go back outside and headed towards Ozzie's again. Third mistake. They followed us and caught us where the buses parked. That's when the small silk-like neck scarves were popular. One grabbed Karen and another grabbed me by our scarves and pulled switchblades on us! Talk about scared; and to top it off we got the giggles again. By now, I'm sure it was nervous hysteria. Tried to explain; to no avail. I had on one of those totally straight skirts and I hiked it up and kicked that girl as hard as I could and ran to the schoolhouse to find Dave, Karen's brother, and some of his buddies to go rescue Karen. We swore we wouldn't tell anyone of the incident.

Well, the following Sunday when Karen and her mom was in church, Karen got really nervous and sick and ended up telling her mom. Our parents got together and all of us kids had to talk to the principal. We all ended up in court. As it was ending, the judge told the girls he never wanted to see them in there again regarding switchblades. And if you can believe this, they told the judge, "Okay, next time we'll use ball bats!"

One more unique experience: Joanne Treherne and I were good friends since third grade. On our senior trip, Joanne got together with Oral Frame and I got with Bill Moore. We all got married. They had one son, Gary, and Bill and I had two daughters, Teresa and Patricia. In 1983, Gary and Teresa got married and had two sons, Justin, and Kyle. Justin and Stacy now have Zac, three and a half years old. So, you can see, Joanne and I are grandmothers and great grandmothers of Justin, Kyle and Zac. Bill and Oral have both passed away. Bill never got to see any of our great grandchildren. He passed a few days before Brooklyn was born. She's five, Wyatt is three, Zac is three and a half, Sawyer will be one year in May and his little sister is due the middle of June.

Labaki's Market

by Martha West of Zanesville, Ohio
born 1929

My name is Martha Labaki West. I am seventy-nine years young. I have many fond memories about living next to the day nursery on Linden Avenue. There was Well's Drugstore on the corner, a day nursery and then my dad had a grocery (Labaki's Market) on the other side with some houses and Combs Lumber Company on down.

I remember looking through the fence that separated us from that day nursery. They were serving homemade ice cream to the little kids and I was wishing they would gave me a little bit. They didn't!

I used to walk from home to over the 5th Street Bridge (which was torn down later) to St. Thomas school (rain or shine). There were no school buses in them days and you had to go in the church to wait for school to open. The nun told us we had to start wearing a hat or scarf in church from now on. Of course I never wore a hat or scarf in my life and of course I forgot to do that. I really paid for that. We had some tough nuns back then.

Front row: Eddie, Martha and Mary Labaki. Back row: Emil, Charles, Shaheed (father) and Nancy (mother) Labaki.

My brothers used to swim across the Muskingum River many times. There is still a railroad bridge by the Y-bridge and my brother, Eddie, used to walk over it every once in a while on his way to school. One day he was on it and a train was coming. He had to hang on under the railroad bridge. He made it! God was looking out for him.

Later my family bought the old Merrick mansion on the corner of Maysville and Merrick Avenue. My dad added Labaki's Market on the front of the house. It was a big house. We had nine bedrooms. We were told this was one of the stops for the Underground Railroad.

After many years, our store and house was tore down and a car lot and body shop replaced it. It's now changed to a pizza shop. Across the street from it is the Clock Restaurant which has been there for many years.

The Skunk Under the Schoolhouse and Yellow Snow

by Jenny Slosky of Cambridge, Ohio
born in 1926

I'll start my story by telling about our wonderful dad and mom [names not given]. Us kids had that. There was eleven of us. Not one got a spanking. Dad told us what to do and that was it. He read the Bible to us a lot.

Oh yes, we had a chamber pot. The last one up emptied it and rinsed it out. Had kerosene lamps and had to clean them every morning, not my job.

Oh we had the party line phone. Dad said the first time he caught us nibbing, out would go the phone. We were lucky. We were all pretty good in school and had to keep our grades up.

We all got a bath on Saturday night. The cleanest got in first and it went down the line. I was last, as I was a tomboy dirty.

Mom washed clothes on a washboard. I think now how hard she worked raising us, but never complained.

My favorite teacher was my first grade through fifth grade teacher. He was a man. He was super man. At recess he would go out and play with all the kids. Sled ride, play ball, all of it. He was strict and we all knew to have our lessons.

We found a skunk along the road and took it up and put it under the schoolhouse (it was a two room school) and poked it good with a pole. We got two days out of school because it gave you a headache.

We had a lot of friends. Dad and Mom made us stay home. All the kids came there. They liked Mom because she would bring us stuff to eat.

Mom was the best cook in the world. She made bread twice a week. She was an old fashion cook. She taught us girls to cook, and we are good too. One brother also learned.

My first date: I was a clerk in a grocery store and he was the ice boy that brought ice in for the cooler. He was cute and about my age. So I gave him the eye. Two days later he asked me if I would go to the movies. We did. I dated him till he went to the navy. All the boys were in the service then. We would meet the train every night to see if any of our boys got off. It was real sad. We would cry every night.

Oh yes, we went trick and treating. There was no age limit on it then. Mom told us not to soap windows, but we upset toilets. That was fun. We would sled ride every night after supper and dishes were done and our homework was done.

We went skinny dipping in the reservoir and the sheriff came along and stopped, but he had to go. We got out and dressed on the hill. Another sheriff came but we were in the clear.

Our aunt made us baby doll cradles out of big Mother Oats boxes. She would put a little doll in it, take orange crates and make a little stand and put pretty curtains around them for our playhouse.

Mom made us ice cream out of snow. She would say no yellow snow. Two or three of the ladies would get with Mom and they made candy, taffy, and popcorn balls at night. We had fun, oh boy did we.

We helped the older people. There was this old man. He drank after shave lotion. Mom was not too crazy about that. He was a nice old man. He told us a lot of stories.

We picked strawberries for a penny a quart. I got the hives every day because I ate my share.

We had a covered bridge up the road and we would go up there at night and get on top of the bridge and wait on the lovers to stop. We sure was lucky we never got hurt. Fast runners.

Every night before Dad would go to bed, he would ask if any of us kids were hungry. Never hungry. Mom baked every day, cake, pie, or something. They were super to us kids. Never heard them argue.

We were to so good kids. They made a church out of the schoolhouse. I could write the whole book, but I'll close for now.

Milkmen, Too

by James Allan McBride of Cambridge, Ohio
born 1944

Waiting for the iceman's wagon so I could get a sliver/chip. Watching the trolley go by and hearing him ring the big brass bell. Playing tag on top of the 6th Street Bridge and Railroad Bridge. Outhouse M and W, S and R catalogues and corncobs "Ow" sometimes. The Shadow on radio, Tom Mix, Lash Larue, Whip Wilson, Twenty Mule Team Borax on TV.

Blizzard of '50, '51. Serials at the State Theater on Saturday. Sarge, German Shepherd and Cindy, cocker spaniel. Shinin' shoes at the courthouse for movie money. Scott's [Nu?] Shop. Shopliftin' pocket knives with scaling backs at Kressee's. Flippin' coins—odd man wins. Gettin night crawlers at the cemetery. Runnin' two trot lines, "ours" and others if they weren't there. Playin' euchre at Poor Paul's and learnin' 'bout educated elbows.

Pitchin' closest to the line. Going to the drugstore and gettin' Curt Paragoric. Appropriating a Zundap and MoPed to go to Buckey Lake one afternoon. Rehabbing a sunk, big rowboat and gone across the river to steal water melons. Shootin' dice on the gym walkaround at Hancock Junior High.

Bus skin—from Putnam to town—winter grab the bus bumper at a light and [illegible]. Puttin' the two pound carp in the fat girl's desk in science class. Gettin' shot rock with salt in the butt with stealin the biggest watermelon I ever saw.

P.S. Oh yeah, we had milkmen.

Instead of a Turkey

by Patricia Hildebrand of Zanesville, Ohio
born in 1937

My name is Patricia Ann Slatzer Hildebrand, born November 25, 1937 in New Lexington, Ohio on Thanksgiving Day. My sister thought she was getting a turkey and got me!

There was three girls, five years apart. We had good parents. My dad was a body and fender man, but he had a bad drinking problem. My mom was a wonderful Christian who believed God would provide, and He did. But Mom worked hard out in the Lambs Laundry eight hours, come home and wash and iron for other people. All the same, we were poor.

I remember a lot of things you mention. As a young girl, I remember going to Grandma's on the bus from New Lexington to Zanes. That was a big deal for someone my age. Grandma always had candy and goodies. At night, I would sit upon her bed a stack quilt blocks together or count sale tax stamps. Grandma would make us girls slips to keep us warm and P.J. She sent Mom money in the mail. If the letter had a stamp upside down, it meant there was money in it.

If Dad would go to town to get drunk, I had to get the coal in and chop the wood. Sometimes the boy next door felt sorry for me and helped.

We always had a big garden and also picked berries for jelly. In the winter, my sister and I had to hang out the clothes. They would freeze in the basket before you could get them hung. Thank you, Lord, for clothes dryers.

I remember the old outhouses. I hated them. The neighbors had bathrooms. One time my sister and I went down to empty the chamber pot late at night. You go late so the neighbors didn't see you. We both were scared. She heard something and took off running for the house. I threw the pot at her. It's a good thing I missed! Thank you, Lord. More on the outhouse: we never had nice soft paper, always newspaper or catalogs.

My Grandma, baby sister and me.

One time my dad hurt his arm and he couldn't roll his cigarette, so he asked me to do it. As I rolled them, I wondered what they tasted like, so I took one and went to the outhouse. I lit it up, and it was not long till I heard my dad holler, "Patty Ann, come out of there now. Was you smoking?" Oh no, he seen smoke come out of the cracks. I got the belt for smoking, lying, and stealing. I do not smoke today.

Best teacher: Mr. Conn, but one time he kept me after school. It was winter. I had to walk one and-a-half miles home with no boots or gloves. When I got home, Dad wanted to know what happened. I told him. He looked up Mr. Conn in the phone book. Soon as the man answered the phone, Dad started hollering. You guessed it, wrong number!

Saturday night baths: Big old wash tub and every one of us girls used the same water. I always tried to be first. It didn't always work.

In my Mom's busy schedule, she always had time for us. On Sunday morning she would roll out homemade noodles before going to church. My sister called them shoestring noodles. On Saturday night, when Dad went to "town" if Mom had sugar she would make fudge and pop popcorn while my sister and I would listen to the "Grand Ole Opry" and dance.

Games we played then are hardly heard of today, like whistle the hollower, marbles, and jump rope. Dad made a game out of wood, put nails in it, numbers, used Mom's rubber jar rings. Whoever got the most won. We played hopscotch too, hide and seek. Them was the days. Toys was a nickel. Christmas was slim. We got a new outfit and paper cutout dolls, warm slips from Grandma.

Grandma was scared of storms. She always pulled the blinds down. I guess she thought it wouldn't get through.

Kids today have it made. We didn't have sweepers. We had to get on hand and knee to mop, hang out clothes till they froze on the line, run in, stand a little while by the old potbelly stove, get a little warm and run back out and hang more.

We used to have coffee toast with a little sugar and cinnamon while waiting for the school bus. Our bus came no matter how deep the snow, not like it is today. An inch of snow and school is closed. I do remember a couple of the blizzards. The one of '78; my kids really liked that one.

Party line phones: That was a good name for them, because everyone partied. You knew who did what on Saturday night, who was pregnant before they knew, who died before they did. My sister and I always listened till we got caught.

Not many people can today, but it may come back. They will have to. Mom taught me to when I helped her. She canned everything and we picked berries to make jelly and Mom would can berries for pies in the winter. When I got home from school I had to put the big tub on the stove, get the water ready for Mom, till we got rich and Mom bought an electric water heater. You dropped it in the water and it heated the water. We had to iron everything back then too, and Mom cooked the starch. One time, she got burnt on it. She dropped the pan on her foot.

It is a wonder my sister or I didn't get killed. Talk about mischief. If Dad knew this, he would come out of his grave. We used to walk on the railroad track from our town. Way down the road was a tunnel where trains came through. My sister, a couple of friends and I was in the tunnel. Here comes a fast train. We got up against the wall. Some lied on the ground. We never did that again. God was surely watching over us. We also used to hitchhike from our town to the next town. Boys were cute over there.

One time we were riding on motorcycles. Well, one went through the light, and the other one didn't. I thought she went home, so I had my friend take me two streets below my house. I got home, no sister. My dad started yelling at me. He heard the bike, "If your sister gets killed, so will you." She walked in the door, and Mom and Dad was so glad to see her. So was I. My dad took off his belt and beat me so bad till blood ran down my legs. Mom had to stop him.

I played hooky a lot in junior high school. I hated school. Kids made fun of me and my hand-me-down clothes; letting me know when they seen my dad drunk. He was a good dad, he just had a problem.

I could never swim, but a bunch of us did go skinny dipping a few times, till I about drowned, then that was enough for me.

I got married young and had my first baby at 19. I'm getting ahead of myself. I must tell you about my babysitting days, which there isn't much of that anymore. All kids today have to go to the mall.

I watched five children; a set of twin boys, two other brothers, and their sister, who had cerebral palsy. Her name was Joyce Ellen. I named one of my girls after her. She was so sweet. She could not walk or talk. The boys would tease her. I was getting supper for them one night. She started to holler, and I went to see what was going on. She liked the "Howdy Doody Show." It was on, but she was having a fit and kept looking at the boys. I went back to the kitchen, and it started again. I peeked around the corner and they had changed it to their cowboy show. She was so glad I caught them.

She and I used to do a lot together. She liked going to the movies with me. Her dad would take us and come and get us. She could hardly hold her head up. I took her to the fair, to my Mom's when I went home for the weekend. She died about a year ago; one brother got killed in Vietnam. I wish I had stayed closer to the family. They were the best thing that happened to me.

I got married in 1956. I have seven grown children, 17 grandchildren, and a lot of great grandchildren. My first husband died at the age of 45 with cancer. But all-in-all, God has truly blessed me. I almost lost one son. He was 11 and got hit by a car riding his bike. They said he would not live through the night, but God had other plans, and He is our healer and He is boss. My son is living because of the Lord and is 36 years old, works every day making baskets at a local company. He has three children.

It has been fun for me to write this. I really don't care if I win my husband now that I laugh and laugh about my throwing the pot at my sister. Mom, Dad, Grandma are gone now. Someday I will see them again. I hope and pray you will be joining us.

Bare Shelves in a Blizzard

by Wilda Emily Bender of Caldwell, Ohio
born in 1938

I will be 71 this July, so I have lots of good old days "stories." The one that I want to tell about was the big snow in 1950. We lived between Jerusalem and Beallsville, Ohio on a farm. Now it is called the Country Club where people golf and have fun. We worked with a black team of horses.

Well, the snow started by the time the shelves were getting bare. With one brother and five sisters, that never took long. So my dad said, "Wilda, you get your pony ready, and I will ride the one black work horse. We will go to Jerusalem and get what your mother needs from Vernon Ricky Grocery Store."

I was scared, but back then you never questioned what a parent said. So we tied our burlap sacks to the pony and horse.

My dad said, "Stay in my tracks." The snow and wind was cold. The pony, "Danny Boy," had to jump from one track to the other.

Once we got to the store, we stayed and got warm. The phone rang at the store while we were there. The farm down from us, closer to Beallsville, they were stuck in another state. They had a chicken farm. So, Vernon called out, "Anyone can help feed chickens? You get the eggs free." With all of us kids, my dad said, "Oh yes! The Warner children would be happy to."

We made it back home and took care of the chickens. We ate eggs a lot, baked, made homemade taffy, and built a sled. It was so heavy it sunk, so we tied Danny Boy to the sled.

I must say, with all the snow and work, we got to eat good, have fun, and days to remember forever.

Dressing Chickens and Baling Hay

By Carol Cooperrider Smith of Fairborn, Ohio
Born 1954

I grew up in the rolling hills of northern Perry County in a small town of Glenford. The family farm was about a quarter of a mile from the town limits. Actually the farm was listed on some maps as the Glenford Fort. There was an Indian mound on our property. People would come to see the mound year round.

Living close to town was nice. It was convenient as I attended both elementary and junior high school in Glenford. Both school buildings have since been torn down.

Life on the family farm involved a lot of hard work, but yet there was time for fun. Farm life always gave us plenty of things to do to occupy everyone's time. The words, "I am bored" were never heard nor said by either myself or my brother.

During the spring, my parents, Don and Elizabeth Cooperrider, would order 150 baby chicks. Oh, were they cute. Plus made a lot of chirping noise. As they grew we knew that dressing day was nearing. It was usually on Memorial Day Weekend that we did the first day of dressing. Everything was set up outside for the whole process from start to finish.

My father was declared the "rabbi" as he would be the one that would cut the heads off the chickens once they were hung up by their legs across a long hanging board.

After they drained, they were dipped in a large black kettle, used for butchering hogs. A fire had been built under the large kettle as it sat on a three legged stand so to bring the water to a boil. After all the feathers were plucked off, the assembly line started. The chickens were drawn and cleaned. Once this was done, we put them in large tubs of ice water to chill before packaging for the freezer. After all the chickens were dressed that day then they were bagged and ready for the freezer. It made for a long day. We started early and was usually done by lunch time depending on the amount of help available. It would take two to three Saturdays to dress all the chickens.

This was a lot of work, but we had plenty of family there to work and to visit. I always remember these times and the fun we had even with all the work involved.

There was plenty of other work on the farm. Mother not only taught school, but had 1800 laying chickens. We sold the eggs from the farm on an honor system. Any excess eggs were taken to Newark to a grocery store on Friday evening right after school was out. We always looked forward to the trip as we knew it would be a chance to eat out. The place to eat was the BBF in Heath, Ohio.

Dad was a full time farmer. He had a herd of beef cattle and also a flock of sheep. There was always something to be done with the animals. Winter was a fun time as the calves and lambs were being born. I would often go out and just sit in the barns among the livestock and enjoy the quiet and peacefulness of animal life.

My favorite work in the summer was to bale hay. That's hard work and always during the hottest time of the summer.

Life on the farm was very educational. Yes, it was hard work. But it had many benefits. It's the life experiences that I would not trade for anything.

I have since moved off the farm and into the city. I sure have miss being where it's open and the chance to appreciate nature is greater. There are moments that I wish I could relive those days. But, since that isn't possible, at least have some acreage to raise a few cows and sheep and to remember those 'good ole days' gone by.

Early Memories

by Freida Phillips of Zanesville, Ohio
born 1922

I don't remember riding in the buggy, but saw it stored in a section of the barn. Never drove the Model T Ford. Remember it being put up on the blocks in the winter as the roads would fill from bank to bank with snow, no ditches back then. I got my drivers license before you had to take a test and drove the Model A Ford. My father, Thornton Alexander, liked the open touring type and when coming home from the state fair in August, we had to stop and put on the winter curtains as the air was too cold.

Walked a mile to a one-room school. The schoolyard had many trees that were used as home bases when the game blackman bluff was played. The older children made sure the little ones got to ride the sled with them down the hill during winter recess. All the children were in the church and school programs. The only one I remember was a school recitation about arithmetic. I held my red arithmetic book and a line was, "No old Mr. Arithmetic will get the best of me."

I was born in a brick home 11-7-22 in the southeast part of Meigs Township in Muskingum County, Ohio. This home was built by the Lett family, who were a part, at that time, of a Negro settlement. The bricks were made close by. The walls were double bricks wide. Inside and outside. This made for wide window sills. A good place for me to sit. A good place to grow flowers in the winter.

The back room was used for a courtroom in the early history of the Township. The hall was 10 feet wide with open stairs all the way to the third floor attic. Nice in summer, but so cold in winter. On my wedding day, I came down those stairs to music from the family picture album music box.

This area is all gone, being a part of the coal strip fields; close to the "wilds," but not a part of it.

Those were the days of threshing machines going farm to farm. You always had a neighbor wife or two coming in to help feed around twenty-four men, maybe two meals. Things happened as a lady not used to another's oven rack. That's how a filled pie browning the meringue landed upside down on the floor.

Another gathering time was butchering in the fall. I remember sitting in my old high chair, cutting up cold pork fat into small pieces so Mother could render it, making lard. This was used to make those homemade pies, cakes, bread and cookies. Mother, Hazel Alexander, won 1st place with her white cake at the local Farmers' Institute held at the centralized school. Yes, bus time.

Do you member incubators? We had progressed from putting chicken eggs under setting hens. I don't remember how many eggs could be placed on the large tray. It was heated by an oil lamp. The eggs had to be turned each day. At the proper time, the incubator was set up in that large hall.

Before radio in our area, it wasn't unusual for neighbors to walk half a mile or more to visit and let the children play, then walk home by lantern light with Dad carrying me on his shoulders.

What wonderful time when we got the Rural Electric.

I was a senior in high school. The brick home was hard to wire as the plaster had to be chipped down to the bricks to conceal the wires. I was very upset that they wouldn't move the line a little so they wouldn't cut down the best apple tree in the orchard.

I always had cats, outdoor mousers. I had a pen to put the weaned kittens in at night so they wouldn't be killed by the big tom cats. I had a turned upside down bucket under a pear tree to sit on when I fed my kittens milk. I had a Mason jar zinc lid to fill for each kitten. They would eat till their little sides were fat. Usually a big cat waited to finish any milk and lick each lid clean.

Frieda Alexander, born November 11, 1922.

A neighbor teased me when he saw me for a long time. He had asked me what I weighed. I said I had gained five pounds. He later found out I had been holding one of my cats. You got weighed on the barn scales that would weigh from a quarter pound to 500 pounds by using different weights.

One summer storm I had been upstairs putting down the windows and had gotten back downstairs when lightning struck the house coming in through a window in my room, went across the room and tore an actor picture to bits.

On our farm we had chestnut, walnut and hickory nut trees. It wasn't hard to get me to take out nut meat for a nut cake or candy. We had apples, pears, peaches, plums, grapes and berries, but you sure didn't want to eat a green persimmon. With all this fruit, apples were made into cider and then let go into vinegar. We made peach brandy, grape wine. Well I knew where the keg and hose to siphon you a drink. Of course grape juice was good before it became wine. I put the tube too low in the keg and got some sediments. Mother wanted to know if I was okay. "Yes I'm just sleepy." She sure knew what was wrong when I got sick.

When company came, Dad had a glass pitcher that he used for cider or wine. Small glasses were given out. No, I never got the hard stuff. And no one left having too much.

Always went to fairs and circuses that came around. I remember a man and his organ grinder and his dressed up monkey walking the midway. Don't know where or when but a whale was on exhibit. What a thrill for a child.

One summer day a blacksnake was climbing up the screen door. I was ordered to stay put. Mother always knew where the hoe was and no snakes survived. Never saw many around the home, but always watched in the berry patch and hayfields.

One hot, sultry summer, we had bad electric storms each night for a week. About each night you could see a red glow somewhere in the distant. A barn was burning. One burned in our area. I never liked storms after that. The brick home stayed cool until the bricks got warmed through, then they stayed hot. That is when I slept downstairs on the floor.

I don't remember how a fire started, but it got out of control and was heading for one of the barns. We were on a phone line with several other homes. Our ring was four long rings. If you needed help you went to the phone and made extra long rings. Someone would answer and stay on the line to tell others you needed help. There were no secrets on a party line. After a storm, the men would walk the line to find where it was broken and fix it themselves.

We had progressed from washboard to a wooden tub washer. It had five round wooden pegs to move the clothes. This was run by a motor that made a putt putt sound. We had bar soap cut thin and melted in hot water. We had progressed to a more modern cook stove. It had a water tank beside the firebox so we had warm water. We always had a teakettle on the stove for hot water unless you let the fire go out.

I was not good at milking cows, they said too slow. It was my job to start breakfast while they milked. Breakfast was a meal, hot fried potatoes, mush with hot homemade syrup, bacon or sausage, oatmeal, eggs or pancakes and always plenty of milk, homemade breads, butter and jelly.

In the fall, some wheat was really cleaned of chaff and taken to mill and made into flour, enough to use until the next fall. Wires were hung from attic rafters to a board so no stray mouse could find the flour. Corn was sorted and shelled by hand and ground so to make mush, cornbread and roll fresh fish before cooking. We didn't have a creek with fish, but was always welcome to try our luck at friends that did. I never fished from a boat on the river.

This is something I remember from when I started to school at five years old to when I got married in 1942. My husband was in the service and I was at four of the six bases where he was stationed during the over three years of service. I had never been on a train or places on my own. I worked at all the places. A candy factory, on bases, a welder, operator of heat treating ovens, typist and office clerk. At the last base it was changed into a discharge base. I had access to the list of those being discharged. One morning I looked at the sheet and my husband's name (Marion) was on it. The excitement must have been loud as every head in the large room, including the brass at the end of the room, looked my way. My embarrassment didn't last very long as the excitement of going home was too important.

I am doing genealogy, first families of Muskingum County, D.A.R., hoping to learn our history for my great grandsons. Think I'll leave a copy of this among the records.

Home Runs and Flat Dives

by Willard E. Bryan of Zanesville, Ohio
born in 1934

"Those were the days my friends, I thought they would never end."

I grew up in a neighborhood with many kids, we were never lonely. Picture this: It is late May or early June; three boys are walking out Ridge Avenue to clear off a field to play baseball. This field was once used by the Hazel Atlas Glass factory. A league of area teams (industrial) played during the 1920s and 1930s.

Gene Smith, Paul Smith, and I were equipped with a vintage lawn mower, two sickles, and of course, a bat, some gloves, and a ball. I don't remember how long it took us to clear the field. I'm sure it was several days.

We played until dark many times. All the boys did not have gloves. We would leave the gloves in the field when the side-out changed.

The field was improved each year. We lined the outfield and placed line posts. The bases were homemade. We engineered a pitcher's mound. A backstop was built with railroad ties stacked about six high. A two by four form was erected to hold the ties in place. These ties weighed a ton. They were disposed of in a swampy area alongside the field.

I found my first ball glove in this area. It was soaked. I took it home, cleaned it up, soaked it in linseed oil, placed a baseball in it, and let it dry.

In 1945 two WWII veterans came to play ball with us. They were local guys, and they missed those ballgame days. We were excited and honored to have them.

This trick to clean off the field went on for a few years. We got tired of the hard work. Playing ball took on another form. We played a street game called soak-um. The ball was made of paper and wrapped with tape. The game was started with three batters. Outs were made by hitting a hitter trying to reach base. When you were hit, you were replaced with someone in the field. Sometimes all three batters were on base with no one to bring them in.

Summertime was not just for baseball; swimming at the local pool when we had the money, 35 cents. However, Timber Run, a creek that ran along Route 40 West, was a popular place to swim. The pool of water under the Route 40 Bridge was six feet deep. We would dive off the bridge abutment, making sure you used a flat dive; otherwise the bottom came up to greet you!

I learned to swim in the creek pool. I would go up to my neck, and then shove off towards shore. I learned the basics in one day.

This creek provided another adventure. We put on our tennis shoes to protect our feet. We walked the creek picking up rocks, watching baby water snakes scatter. On another day, we got the idea to catch some of those small snakes and take them home in a bucket. My mother was not very amused. Of course, we had to scare a few girls before we got rid of the snakes.

An Elephant in Bristol

By Kenny Deavers of New Lexington, Ohio
Born 1942

I was born in 1942 in southeastern Ohio in a little town called Bristol. Bristol is located on State Route 93, five miles south of New Lexington, Ohio. Bristol was always a quiet little town. But that all changed in the summer of 1956.

My sister Evelyn's husband worked swing shift and when he worked at nights I would stay with her. Her husband was a very fun loving guy and was always pulling little jokes on us.

One morning as we were eating breakfast Gene said he heard an elephant. Evelyn said, "Yeah, right, like you want us to believe there is an elephant in Bristol." He insisted he heard one.

So we walked out of the house and there on the curve was a circus truck. Some men were trying to get an elephant back in the truck. We talked to them and they told us the truck upset and the elephant got out and headed toward the pits where it could smell water. They weren't having much success getting the elephant back in the truck.

Someone brought in a farm tractor and hooked a chain to the elephant. The elephant planted its feet and the wheels on the tractor just spun. Finally the men got big steel bars and beat on the elephant till it went back in. The men's language was the worst I had ever heard.

The news traveled fast. A local photographer from New Lexington (Mr. Flowers) came out and took pictures.

Later that day I was talking to my good friend Don Hollingshead. He told me that he and his mom and his little brother Jerry were picking berries along the road that runs from the schoolhouse down through the pits. Jerry was sitting on the bank waiting for them to get done. Jerry heard a noise and yelled at his mom that an elephant was coming down the road. They dropped their buckets and spilled their berries and ran for home as fast as they could go. Later that day when their dad came home, he went down and got the buckets and berries.

My good friend Don passed away over twenty-five years ago. But to this day his brother Jerry and I remain great friends. Many times we have talked about the day an elephant roamed the hills of southeastern Ohio.

Reading and Singing Champion

by Owen K. Hicks of Uhrichsville, Ohio
born in 1920

I was born in Uhrichsville on November 28, 1920. At that time, my father was working at the Robinson Sewer Pipe Company. We lived there until 1923 and we moved to Roanoke, which was at the north end of Uhrichsville, which is know[n] as McCauley Drive today.

About the time I was to start to school in 1927, my Grandmother Stone passed away. My father rented our house out and we moved in with my grandfather. We didn't get moved back in time before school started, and my father didn't want to start me in another school while they got moved back in their own house. It was three months before we got moved back, and my mother wanting to get me in school, wrote a note to the teacher and sent me to school with some other children.

The teacher stopped by that evening to talk to my dad and mother. She reminded them I was three months behind. She told them if they would help me, she would do all she could to help me catch up with class. By February, I caught up with this class.

At that time, they had reading contests in schools, and my teacher chose me as the best first grade reader. She stopped and talked to my dad and mother and wanted them to help me. Every night after school, my dad and mother had me reading. In March 28, 1927 was the contest started. My mother asked the teacher how many schools I would be reading against in Uhrichsville. She told my mother I would be reading against three schools in Uhrichsville. The day came. I went to read, and I won the first round.

Back row, left to right: George Swaney, William Gambs, Ralph Bender. Front row: Ethel Graham, Thelma Fowler, Evelyn Graham.

When the teacher brought me home, my mother asked the teacher how many schools I would be reading against the next time. She said it would be held in New Philadelphia, Ohio and would be reading against twenty-two schools. In two weeks, my teacher took me to New Philadelphia. Before I went in to read, an older boy told me not to get rattled. I went in, and I read and came back out. Later on, they called me back in, and I read against a girl from Newcomerstown. It was different. They put her in one corner of the room and put me in another corner of the room. We read at the same time. We had read something different. In the afternoon, everyone met in the auditorium. When they called the winner, I was lifted up on the stage. I was announced as the best first grade reader in Tuscahowas County. I still have my artifice. My teacher received a pennant to put up in the schoolroom. I received 100% for reading for the year.

In October, 1929, the Depression came along, and it was a very hard time for our family. There were approximately twenty clay plants in our area, and they were all shut down. There wasn't any food stamp programs at that time. There was a relief office in town where you could get a little help, but that was rare. My father worked for the farmers wherever he could find work. They paid sometimes twenty-five to fifty cents a day.

My father worked out the water bill so we could have water in the house. The electric company shut the electric off, so we had to use oil lamps. My mother did the cooking on a three-oil-burner oil stove. She did the washing on the washboard and did the ironing by using sad irons heated on the stove.

I remember I would go to the soup kitchen two or three times a week to get a gallon of soup. With red stamps, we were able to get skim milk at a dairy farm, known as Bouler's Dairy. I picked blackberries and was able to sell some of those for five cents a quart. My father always put in a very large garden, and my mother canned everything she could get her hands on.

One time, after my grandmother died, my grandfather stopped by one day and told my mother when she got ready to do her canning to send my brother and me over to his place, and he would give her the vinegar she needed. One day, my mother asked my brother and me to go over to our grandfather's to get her vinegar. We went, but we didn't tell her what we were going to do.

We had a little coaster wagon a friend gave us. It was made of wood. It had wooden wheels with steel rims. My grandfather lived on Indian Hill Road. It was steep, it was gravel road at that time. We decided to pull our wagon with us that day. It was about three miles to my grandfather's place. There was a left-hand curve with a barn located on that curve. You couldn't see around the curve.

When we got to the top of the hill, I told my brother to put the jug between us, and I would do the guiding. We started down the hill, and the handle got to vibrating so bad that I couldn't hardly hold on to it. I saw this curve coming up, and I began to wonder if I was going to make it or not. We made it, and we almost coasted to my grandfather's house. I look back at that once in a while and think if we would have met a car on that curve, I wouldn't be writing this today.

In 1937, we had a flood. This was in February, and we still lived at Roanoke. We lived two houses from a Standard Oil pumping station, and this night, the warehouse caught fire. The fire department came out but didn't stay because there was a chance of the big storage tank exploding. The only thing coming out of the Town of Urichsville that night was the fire truck and police cruiser. My father was working midnight shift and wasn't home, so the chief of police came out and took my mother and my brothers, my sister and me to stay at the mayor's office that night. They brought us back home at five o'clock the next morning.

There was also a medicine show come to our town every summer, and we would go about every night. This one night, they had an amateur contest. My father said we couldn't unless we got up and sang. My brother and I practiced a song and we sang. They chose one winner by handclaps. Everybody knew us, and we won. We received seventy-five cents. They didn't have much money to give away. I have a lot of fond memories of those times in my life. They were called the good old days.

Me, My Girl and My Whizzer

by Joe Shotts, Sr. of Zanesville, Ohio
born in 1932

A WHIZZER is a regular bicycle with a Whizzer gasoline tank and motor kit added. I wish I still had it or could locate one. Jim had one and I bought what was left of it from him for $50; then I combined the best of his bicycle and mine into one neat outfit. I was 16 then. I rode it to high school and work and it was stolen from school only once.

I first met my girlfriend just as my friend Danny and I were leaving the ball field and we saw this farm truck loaded with hay and girls. We asked where they were going. They said Buckeye Lake which is 25 miles away. Our being 16 and the girls were 15 the right thing to do was hop in and go for a hayride. This is where I met my high school sweetheart.

She lived at 1067 Linden Avenue and I lived across the river in the other side of town. To see her I had to cross two bridges with my Whizzer. The 6th Street bridge was flat with a drawbridge to let boats pass, but the 5th Street bridge was one tall hump from one side to the other to let boats pass under it. This hump was quite a chore for my Whizzer; sometimes I had to ride in a zigzag pattern to make it, but my girlfriend was waiting on the other side and I just had to make it to the top of that bridge.

She and I took many rides on that old Whizzer with me setting forward on the gas tank and her setting on the bicycle seat. One trip we remember the most is going up the North River Road as far as the old Bell Farm and having a little picnic

She was a wonderful girlfriend; we went to three Junior-Senior proms together and we went to all the Teen-Time Dances at the local YMCA every Friday and Saturday night. We are still close friends today and when we have special gatherings such as New Years Eve, many of the people there are ones that were on that long ago hay wagon ride...Joe.

Cute and Cuddly Baby Skunks

by Richard Metheney of Quaker City, Ohio
born 1942

In the early 1950's, my grandparents lived outside of Coolville, Ohio, in Athens County. Nine of their eleven children were married and had children of their own. Eventually there were thirty of us grandchildren, but at that time there were only about six or eight of us old enough to spend two weeks away from home. During the summer each of the grandchildren were allotted a two week visit with Grandpa and Grandma Metheney. We would have to share this week with another cousin in order for everyone to get their two weeks in before school resumed in the fall. Among the grandkids, this was a coveted time away from siblings, chores and parental control.

My sister Mary, five or six at the time, got her first opportunity to stay for the whole two weeks. She drew the same weeks as our oldest cousin, Fred Bailey. Fred's dad was in the navy and he had lived on navy bases all of his life. When he came to visit he always had some tall tales to tell the rest of us kids. During their two week sojourn, Fred and Mary spent their mornings helping with chores. After lunch, they usually went off to play along the little trickle of water that wandered across the neighbor's pasture and around the end of Grandpa's garden. This was an ideal place to keep cool in the heat of the day; the brook was only ankle deep at the most.

There were always tadpoles to catch, frogs to chase, a water snake to throw rocks at or crawdads to capture. One sultry afternoon, they found three baby skunks playing along the shady brook. Now, Fred had never lived in a rural area and Mary was a momma's girl. Neither of them knew anything about baby skunks, except they looked cute and cuddly.

When the two of them tired of playing with their new pets, they headed back to the house to try and beg a cookie or two from Grandma. Their entry into Grandma's kitchen was brief and dramatic. Grandma was not about to allow grandkids or anyone else in her kitchen smelling like a skunk. The two culprits were sent to the woodshed, but not for the usual reason. That was as close to the house as they were allowed to come until after they had taken several baths with lye soap in one of those galvanized double washtubs.

That it was an educational experience was putting it mildly. At the end of the two week vacation, Cousin Fred was returned to wherever his parents were living at the time and my sister came home just a little wiser in the ways of the rural world.

For years afterwards, all I had to do was hold my nose and loudly say, "I smell a skunk," And Mary would break into tears and run to tell our mother on me.

Hoeing Corn, Milking Cows...and Hoeing Corn

by Faye Wines of Bethesda, Ohio
born in 1937

I was born in 1937, about three miles east of Somerton, Ohio. Back then, women had their babies at home. The doctor came to the house. I was the second child born to my parents. We lived on a farm with my grandparents. Dad and Grandpa worked the farm. I didn't know we were poor. We had plenty to eat.

Grandma made all our clothes usually from printed feed sacks. We got one pair of shoes each year. Of course, we went barefoot in the summertime. We raised our own meat (hogs and chickens). We had no telephone or electricity until around 1950. When I got about eight, I hoed corn with Grandpa while my older brother worked with Dad in the hay field.

My brother and I walked two miles to catch the school bus. We went to a one-room school. What I liked about this school, you could learn from the older children. We had very dedicated teachers. When the snow came, we had to walk an extra mile to catch the bus, because the bus could not get to us, so we had to walk to the main county road. The school was never closed because of snow. We always had school.

House where Faye Wines grew up. Front: Frank Farrabee (dad) on right, Carl Saunders. Back: Sarah Saunders, Hazel Farrabee, Edith Saunders.

When I got older, I had to help milk the cows, put in hay, feed the hogs, and hoe corn. My job when I was in the house was to churn the butter. We had chickens. Sometimes Grandma would kill a chicken for Sunday dinner. You don't get such good tasting chickens from the grocery stores. We also had homemade noodles.

One time Dad, Dad and Grandpa were threshing barley and Grandpa threw his empty chewing tobacco packs on the ground and I picked it up and ate the small scraps. I got so sick, Grandpa had to wheel me to the house in the wheelbarrow and gave me milk to drink. Then I was okay.

One day, I was walking in front of the horse stalls. There was a big snake laying on the barn log. It scared me so bad, I jumped over a cow manger. I have been knocked down by a steer, but wasn't hurt.

Grandpa and I picked strawberries, black raspberries, and blackberries from along the roads and in the woods. When Dad and Grandpa cut trees down for mine posts to sell, my brother and I would swing on big grapevines.

We had our own coal mine. It was small but enough to keep our home warm. Grandpa cut small sticks of wood to use in our cook stove.

We grew hay, corn, wheat, oats, and barley. One year we had sugar cane and made our own molasses. Also, we had a neighbor make us brooms.

A man from Barnesville had a threshing machine. He went from neighbor to neighbor threshing grains. Neighbors helped neighbors from one farm to another. At noon, we had a big lunch for all of them.

Sunday was church day. We went to church every Sunday. Then, in the afternoon we visited with the relatives going to their home or they came to ours. Lots of times they came for Sunday dinner.

Grandpa had a battery operated radio. He turned it on in the morning to listen to a church program which was broadcast for 15 minutes. Then, he turned it off and we were not allowed to turn it back on, as he wanted to save his battery.

The big snow of 1950 came. We were snowed in for over a week. A bulldozer came and cleared our road. In the meantime, Dad rode one of our horses to Somerton to get flour, sugar, etc we were out of.

Sometimes we walked to church, which was about four miles away, for evening prayer services. I wouldn't do that today.

My grandmother and aunt made quilts. We never had blankets. We slept on straw ticks and when it got real cold at night, Grandma would heat old fashioned irons in the oven, then wrap them with heavy towels to put in our beds to keep us warm.

My brothers and I went skinny dipping in the creek in the summertime. We would try to catch fish with our hands. We were always barefooted except for church.

Lots of times after a big thunderstorm, the creek would flood out of its banks and would come almost to our house, which sat on a bank. Our house was at least 500 feet from the creek. We loved running through the mud in our bare feet. Those were the good old days. I sure miss them.

We never had a Christmas tree or got gifts, but we had a nice dinner and Grandma and my Aunt Mae made candy. They also cracked black walnuts and hickory nuts.

I wore my shoes out so fast, one year Dad bought me boys hi-top shoes. He thought they would last longer.

I barely remember Grandpa and Dad growing tobacco. When it was ready, they strung it on tobacco sticks to dry. Then they sold it. They both chewed tobacco, so I am sure they saved some for themselves.

I never played hooky from school. Some of the mischief my brother and I got into: We would get an egg from the chicken house and mix it with milk we got from one of our cows. Then we mixed it with dirt and made mud pies.

We took baths in a wash tub close to the cook stove so we could keep warm.

Of course, we had a gasoline-powered washing machine. We washed clothes twice a week. In the winter, there were lines strung up behind the kitchen stove so they would dry. We heated our old-fashioned irons on the kitchen stove.

We had a Victrola that played records, but only the grown-ups were allowed to use it. We used tobacco sticks for a ball bat when we wanted to play ball.

The Long Walk Home and the Pounded Peeps

by Peggy Milhoan Treat of Coshocton, Ohio
born in 1945

My name is Peggy (Milhoan) Treat of Coshocton, Ohio. I'm the youngest of nine. I have three older brothers and five older sisters.

My father was a farmer, worked and repaired typewriters and adding machines. We had a sawmill and a coal mine on our property. He also worked on the WPA. We were extremely poor with many mouths to feed. My mother had her hands full with nine children to care for in such meager conditions.

We were very poor in material possessions but extremely wealthy in love and integrity and family values.

My mother had a stroke which left her right hand paralyzed; even though she was right handed she had to learn to use her left hand. She couldn't talk for about one year during which time she was pregnant with her third son. This had to be quite a handicap to overcome with all the cooking, cleaning, canning and washing clothes for a family of eleven on a scrub board.

Being the youngest I wasn't as privileged to know my mother as well as my other siblings. I was born in 1945 and my mother died of congestive heart failure in 1950 when I was five. This left my older two sisters, Bonnie and Crystal, with much responsibility.

My dad and brother were trying to support the family. My other two brothers were both married and starting families of their own.

My dad and three brothers all worked for Nelson Tree Service. This company was to play a very important role in my family's life. My dad was a foreman for Nelson's. All of my brothers were tree trimmers at that time. My brother Vernie later became the president of the company with offices in Dayton, Ohio.

My oldest brother Jimmy was run over by a caterpillar (bulldozer) that had pulled a wagon into the woods so they could remove logs from the area. As the men were trying to load a heavy log, the wagon began to coast backward. They all jumped out of the way except for Jimmy who tried one more time to shove the log onto the wagon. The wagon knocked him down and the whole caterpillar ran over his body crushing him very badly. He was in the hospital for some time. That accident affected the rest of his life. The last 15 or 20 years of his life was spent in a nursing home.

In 1959 my father was killed by a tree that just uprooted and fell because of a heavy rain the night before. This also happened at Nelson Tree Service. This was by no means the fault of the company; they were purely accidents.

My youngest brother Gene started his own tree service after leaving Nelson's. He later built a very large chipper which he gave to Nelson's. Since then he has built several of his own stumpers which he has sold. However he still has one that he uses at will for pleasure and income even though he is in his eighties. He enjoys his hobby. Not bad for someone with an 8th grade education from the one room schoolhouse on Rt. 21 in Guernsey County called Prohibition.

Speaking of Prohibition there were five ornery boys who went to school there in the 1930s.Three of them were my brothers; the other two were our first cousins who lived on an adjoining property. Our family had 105 acres and I'm not sure how many my uncle had. One day after school the boys were playing with ants. The teacher told them they needed to be headed toward home.

They ignored him and continued playing. After he had made several requests the teacher said, "Boys, if you don't go home on your own I'm going to walk you home. It's going to be getting dark and your parents will be worried."

Unbeknownst to him they decided on a new path that day. They walked him up and down, hill after hill, taking him all through the woods the LONG way around. They just kept wandering around until the poor old man was totally worn out and finally the house came in view. The teacher asked their mother if that was the way the boys had to come to school every day and she answered, "Yes," not realizing the trick they had played on their teacher by not walking him there by the way of the lane that led to the house. The teacher said he wouldn't blame the poor boys if they never came to school again! '"No wonder these poor little boys didn't want to walk that long road home," he said.

There was a game that was played at recess. It was called Leap Frog. We had no playground equipment so we played games like Jump Rope, Red Rover, Fox and Geese, and Annie Over—group games like that. Well, one day the kids were playing Leap Frog. I heard how one little girl stood there alone longing to join in but there was only one thing holding her back. It wasn't exactly that she was shy and usually she could be quite the tomboy. What held her back from playing was that that day she was wearing a dress. She stood there longing to join the others, oh, and there was one more thing that was holding her back that I forgot to mention. She (because she was so poor) had no underwear on. Oh, how the little girl longed to join the fun. Her desire to join the game could be fought off no longer. She jumped in line. She jumped over the stooped boy in front of her and as she leaped over him her little dress flipped up and exposed her, much to the little girl's embarrassment.

I remember cold winter mornings having to walk through waist high snow drifts to get to school which was almost a mile away straight up hill. My having asthma and bundled in a heavy woolen snow suit was quite exerting on the lungs of a small child. To this day I don't like the winter season.

Another memory I have of our one room school house was that of our morning devotions from God's Word. Teachers realized the importance of making that part of our daily routine. I'm grateful to have had that experience in a public school. Hard to believe that it actually happened.

When I was a small child I wondered why our summer vacations from school seemed so long. After we were grown, we had a Prohibition Reunion. One of our teachers was there and informed us that our summers were extra long because we got out of school in April for planting season and didn't return back to school until after Labor Day.

My two sisters, Crystal and Shirlee, were janitors at the school. They were paid $8 a month. After nine months of janitor work they had enough money to buy a bicycle.

Here's another story about an ornery boy, my brother He took our little baby peeps, coaxed them under our porch where the dirt was damp and soft and put their little beaks into the ground and pounded them on the head with a ball peen hammer.

One day my youngest brother who was a teenager was going up to get oil from our oil well that was on our property. Now we all know how inquisitive boys are. On the way to the oil well he scooped up a small pile of leaves and lit them. He wanted to see how big the fire would be before he got back from getting the oil. Well, it wasn't long before nature satisfied his curiosity because by the time he got back the woods was on fire and the fire was out of control. My parents and siblings began to try to fight the fire. My sisters were sent up to the highway Rt. 21 which was about one mile away from our farm to flag down cars to see if they would help to put out the fire. Several came. Our property was surrounded on all four sides by woods so this was a very serious situation. It took several hours to get the fire extinguished. This was approximately 1944.

Another story in the 1950s. Stanley Home Product Parties were becoming popular. We somehow came up with the money to purchase one of their new UNBREAKABLE hair brushes. We were excited to have this new brush. Our mother had passed away, our dad and brother worked away through the week so us six girls were left alone. My oldest sister was about 21. Now remember, the hair brush was advertised UNBREAKABLE, something like the Titanic (unsinkable). I had very long, poker straight hair which usually adorned my head in a ponytail, braids or just pulled back on the sides. However, one of my sisters took the time and patience to roll it up for me in rags to give me a brand new look. I was so excited when all the strips of cloth were removed to see actual curls and waves in my hair. I quickly pulled up a little stool so I could see into (to my knowledge) the only small mirror we owned hanging on the wall.

I began to brush my hair with the new UNBREAKABLE hair brush. I was admiring the beauty I beheld in the mirror when another sister came from behind also admiring the beautiful hair in the mirror. She began to run her fingers through my hair and asked if she could brush it. I told her no, as I continued to stroke my golden curls and watch them spring back up, again and again. She begged me to let her brush it but, to a little girl who had waited for soooo long to experience this moment, I just couldn't concede to her. I was six or seven. She became very angry, grabbed the hair brush from me and began spanking me with it. Needless to say, Stanley had some false advertising because the handle snapped in two. My oldest sister immediately came to my defense and the quarrel was ended. I am now 63 and so, I survived. Ha, ha.

We have all had many happy years together. We are a very close family and these are childhood things we laugh about together now.

I remember riding in the back of our pick-up truck to Shady Bend outside of Newcomerstown to get a big block of ice for our ice box. Thank God for the invention of refrigerators.

My last story I'll share is about my oldest sister. As I said before, our mother had a serious heart condition so this put a lot of responsibility on my sister. Our aunt and uncle had come to spend the night. Beds were scarce. We had, to my knowledge, three. My parents' bed, the bed for my three older brothers, and the last one for us six girls. I remember bare mattresses, no sheets, pillow cases, and very little amount of blankets for cold nights.

Well, with our relatives spending the night, either the boys or girls gave up their bed for our welcomed company. As my sister Bonnie was preparing the bed for their stay she was quite embarrassed at our meager conditions. My aunt and uncle weren't rich by any means but were a little better off than we. She had just a piece of a bed sheet which she had managed to keep tucked away in a safe place. She placed the treasured piece on the bed, not to deceive but to share of her very best. She placed it across the corner of the bed and turned down the covers slightly to expose the clean piece of sheet in the neatly made bed that would invite the weary travelers for a restful night's sleep.

To this day she is the most hospitable person I know. She has lived her lifetime willingly sharing her possessions but more than that, her time. She will drop anything at anytime to help anyone in need.

We are the children of Dewey and Peg Milhoan. My siblings are Jimmy, Vernie, Gene, Bonnie, Crystal, Shirlee, Juney, Sharon, and last but I hope not least me, Peggy (wife of Richard Treat). Our family journey together has been an exciting, scary, funny and treasured one. Our group of nine children turned into a huge family of over 200. One subject we all learned in our one room school house was math. We all learned how to "multiply" but I hope none of us ever learn to divide.

Party Lines, Picnics and First Kisses

by Wanda F. Mizer of North Myrtle Beach, S.C.
born 1935

I was born in 1935 during a recession like we are now in. Being so young I didn't understand just what it meant, but now at age 74 I well understand.

I well remember going to Sunday school with my two older sisters. The Methodist Church was above us with a garden between. The Church of Christ was in walking distance from us. The Methodist Church had a piano but The Church of Christ didn't. Both, as I recall, rang out with beautiful, meaningful music. When we got old enough, we wore dresses and hats much different from now when women can wear casual clothes.

As a child I recall bath time every Saturday. We carried a tub upstairs, then back down to get the extra warm water and soap needed. In the winter time it didn't take too long as we only had a small stove for heating our room. We did get to wash our hair in the kitchen sink. Our dad always banked our fireplace at night so it was started and quite warm the next morning when we got up. On real cold nights our mother would heat a brick and wrap it and put it on the bottom of the bed to make it warmer.

We definitely had bad winters. The one I remember most was in 1949 and 1950. It started in 1949 on Thanksgiving and continued through Christmas followed with an ice storm. As I recall, we didn't have school for six weeks. We would get together and play games at night. There was no traffic to worry about. We lit candles and had oil lamps to play at night.

My dad put a bathroom in when I was 15 years old. Up to that time we had a chamber pot when weather was bad and we couldn't get to the outhouse. During Halloween the older boys had their fun knocking over the outhouses all through our little town. My dad didn't want ours ruined so he sat on the porch and when he would see the boys coming he would call out and say "Boys, let me help you so it won't be so hard to set back." The boys liked Dad and they let him and then came back the next day and helped him set it back up. We younger kids just soaped windows and knocked on doors and when the folks opened the doors we'd dump baskets of leaves in their house.

One night Mom and I went to use the outhouse and I always stomped on the floor and hit the door to scare snakes or whatever might be in there. One night, as little as I was, I stomped on the floor and I went through it. My leg clear up to my knee went through the floor. I ran to the house and scrubbed my leg with soap and water for half an hour. Still I was afraid it was stinky.

Mom always had daily routine. Monday was wash day, Tuesday we ironed, Wednesday we finished our ironing and odd jobs, on Thursday was a day to do what we wanted, Friday she baked cookies, pie and cake for the weekend, Saturday we cleaned house and Sunday was rest day, had visitors or Dad would take us to visit people at the nursing home and he and Mom would go to the movie in our theater in McConnelsville, the county seat. We kids usually went to the movies on Saturday nights.

We had party phones. Our ring was three. Four people on one line. When it rang four rings I would eavesdrop as we knew it was the man at the grocery calling our neighbor to tell her his wife had gone home to fix lunch and then I'd watch to see her hurrying up to the store and, nosey here, would go up and get candy and listen to see what I could hear coming from the adjoining room. Soon the lady was pregnant and baby looked exactly like the grocerer's daughter.

Now school days. My sister cried the first year every night before bedtime because she had to go the next day and weekends because she had to go on Monday. But crying must have done good as she was the smartest one of us kids. I told Mom, I wasn't going to cry when I was old enough to go. We didn't have kindergarten in my day. In first grade they couldn't have found a worse teacher for such young children. She didn't know what a smile was.

Wanda Mizer and friends playing in the snow.

My favorite teacher was in third grade; Mrs. Hilaman. She was so nice and treated us all the same. I liked about all of the rest of my teachers. We had a variety of teachers the rest of my school years. I aimed to be a good student. One day in high school one of the boys had to drive a big truck out of town so me and my friend decided to pretend to be sick so we could go with him. We had fun, but it took little to make us happy. One of my favorite times was cheerleading. I met lots of nice girls and boys.

I only got in trouble one time. We were in study hall and one of the boys didn't have his book and got permission to sit with me and use mine. Naturally, I asked him what he was doing and during that period we talked three times. Here the teacher was watching us and he put our names on the board and we had to stay in for recess three days.

My girlfriend and I used to clear our throats when we wanted to pass a note to each other. I'm sure the teacher knew what we were doing but we were good students and never caused trouble. One of my class member's dad was on the school board and she made sure that "Daddy" knew everything that went on. We had a beauty contest one year and she didn't win so she cried and ran home to Daddy and the next morning we came to school and we were told there would be no contest.

When we graduated, this girl and another had the same grades, but again she got to be valedictorian. I was third in class, but I didn't care. I had a speech, but I was a nervous wreck and left out half of my speech.

After graduation I didn't further my schooling. I worked in two clothing stores and was the secretary in all. Then worked in a hair salon for a year in the county seat. We had two men (brothers) that lived in our small Quaker village. They fixed up a large park for all the kids to play in. A large fence was around it. There were bathrooms on each end and beside the women's bathroom was a nice church. Lots of seating and outside were lots of benches and chairs for people to sit and gab and watch their little ones play. We had a merry-go-round, four swings, two sliding boards and teeter totters. At the end of the park there was a nice cemetery. One thing was special about it, a Negro, Steven Potty. He had no family and the park committee voted to let him be buried in our cemetery. We kids would visit his grave whenever we went to play.

We had a nice well for cool water to drink. Also, a covered building where we could take our food to eat in case of rain. Every year in August we had what was called The Embree Picnic for all Penn Township folks. Again, all furnished by the Embree brothers. We stopped at the gate as we entered and was given a ticket. This allowed us two ice cream bars, two cracker jacks and peanuts. The party of men made large tubs of lemonade and we could have as much as we wanted of it. In the afternoon we had races of all kinds. Winners got the prizes. This was the main event. The elderly people that wasn't able to go was taken their ice cream.

Then in June, they had what they called "The Colored Reunion." They came from all over the United States. This was a special day and even we were welcome to go and listen to their church service and singing.

One of the Pennsville residents had a special place fixed with seats so people who wanted to meditate could go there and could be isolated from everyone. There was a road clear around it with parking area inside. It was the most exciting place for all ages to go.

We had a station at each end of town. Two stores what we called the upper and lower stores and the upper store had the post office.

We had two paper routes. The Times Recorder and Athens Messenger and as far back as I can remember my family delivered both papers. The Times Recorder came in the morning and Athens Messenger in the evening. We had to deliver the morning paper before going to school. We had to walk as we weren't two car families like today. We delivered them in all kinds of weather.

My dad made most of our toys, table and chairs, sleds, etc. We kids used to take hikes and go in old buildings and look for books, etc. My grandmother Wagoner was my very favorite person. I learned a lot from her (baking. cooking, etc.) She gave me a black shawl to keep and I still have it.

We girls didn't wear shorts and we had water spots we'd play in in hot weather. My friend and I just got in, pulled our dresses up and were splashing around and giggling and looked up and saw a car coming. It didn't take us long to get our dresses down and out of the water.

When I was a senior in high school and I would be excused to go to the bathroom, this one boy would get excused too. When I was on my way back to my room he'd grab me and kiss me. I was shy at that time. I'd say that was my first real kiss. I was very shy, but I remember I was in a class play and I had to kiss a boy in the role I was playing. I was really embarrassed, but lived through it.

I was married in 1957 and had two children. We lived in Morgan County. Then in 1982 we all moved to South Carolina. I quit office work and started babysitting. I have taken care of 50 babies and loved every minute of it.

The Flattened Egg and the Big Win

by Doris George of Birmingham, Ohio
born in 1933

In the late 40s I was a member of our local 4-H club. My project for the year was care of chickens at home. I fed and watered them daily. When it came time for the Guernsey County Fair, I chose three nice looking chickens from the flock to take to the fair.

My parents drove the 15 miles to the fair each day so I could make sure the animals had feed and water. One morning when I checked on them, I found one had laid an egg in the pen. I took the egg to the car and just laid it on the back seat. Later in the day when we started for home, I forgot about the egg and accidentally sat on it. It was a real squishy mess. After we got home, I had the job of cleaning the back seat of our car.

I continued in 4-H for several years but never took a poultry project again.

My dad was a farmer. His usual clothing consisted of a flannel or denim shirt and bib overalls. On Sundays he did like to dress up for church. There was a special need coming up for a new suit of clothes. Mother and Dad went to the Fred Raymond store in downtown Cambridge. While there, they chose a new suit and also a new overcoat. The store was giving out tickets for a give away in the near future. My father signed the ticket.

Early in the spring the give away was held and a winning ticket was drawn. The winner would receive a new 1938 Chevy Car. My dad's name was drawn. We had no telephone to get word of the drawing. Somehow word came through to the local country store that Dad had the lucky ticket. The store owner was a happy-go-lucky person and one that joked a lot. He drove up to our farm to try to tell my dad about the winning ticket.

Dad was working in the field with his team of horses either spring plowing or planting corn. Of course, he did not believe the store owner.

After much persuasion, my dad unhitched the horses and put them in the barn. He and my mother decided to drive the 20 miles into Cambridge. Sure enough, he had the winning ticket. The second ticket had been drawn and that person was there to claim the car if my dad did not show up by the set time. Yes, my dad won the 1938 Chevy car and drove it for 12 years. It was his first and only big win during his lifetime.

Learning to Drive in Reverse

By Esther L. Pitts of Zanesville, Ohio
Born 1941

When I was 12, my sister Virginia and Roy Pitts were married. That first summer I went to their house in Zanesville to visit. They were starting to build a home in Stovertown, Ohio located on Route 555. Back then the address was Philo Route # 1. They had a four party telephone line and were still utilizing an outhouse.

Roy worked at Armco Steel and worked on the house as time and money afforded. But in the meantime, he spent time with this young girl teaching me things that have lasted for a lifetime.

One morning he decided that I should know how to drive a car. At 13, I was really happy. As I got in this old junker, a 1949 Ford, I was really excited and thrilled with the anticipation of driving. However, that came to a halt. His first instruction was to back the car up and go around the basement. I backed the car around the basement until I had grooves worn in the ground. Then he took me down the old abandoned township road (our driveway) and had me back up there. As I got more skillful, he got out of the car and let me continue. I could only back up.

One day, after about two weeks, I said, "Don't I ever get to go forward?" His answer was when you learn backward, you will never have a problem with forward.

Finally the big day came. I got to drive forward. For that opportunity I had to learn to change a tire and do ordinary maintenance on the junker. This included changing the oil and greasing certain fittings.

Many years have passed since those lessons were learned. But they have stood me in good stead. Not only am I thankful for the chance to learn to drive, but the chance to learn about auto maintenance. Of course, now 54 years later, I see a lot of humor in the fact I learned to drive in reverse. Maybe this should be a lesson in driver's education for those who do not know how to or care to back up a car.

Years ago 5th and Main Street was a busy, traffic area. SS Kresge Company, Newberry's 5 & 10 and many other stores and shops were there. Two banks and a Savings and Loan were across the street from Kresge's. This was a high traffic area with lots of pedestrians and auto traffic.

A man driving a 1950 Chevy Powerglide needed a push to get his car started. He asked my brother-in-law if he would push him. The car needed to be doing 35 mph to start. Roy said no: "My car won't even do 35 let alone push yours." A woman stepped up and said, "I'll push you." He told her he needed to be doing 35 and she said no problem. As he was getting in his vehicle she backed way up the street. Her thought being *she* needed to be doing 35. He tried to wave her off, but to no avail.

We were all standing there laughing knowing what was coming. When she hit his old car, all you could see was dust and two destroyed cars. As the Zanesville police were coming, we scooted out the side door of Kresge's and went up 5th street. There were lots of witnesses besides us to give the story of what happened. Roy needed to be at work and we needed to get on home.

However, this was one of the things you would think would have happened in a movie, but in real life it happened and there were many witnesses to that event.

Remembering Zanesville

by William Dicks of Zanesville, Ohio
born in 1940

I spent a lot of time in my youth in downtown Zanesville. I lived only three blocks from Main Street, yet, I might add, we lacked indoor toilet until about 1955. My dad, brother-in-law, and myself dug a hole in our back yard and installed a septic tank. We had the first indoor bathroom on the hill.

The road we lived on was on the south side of Pioneer Park. It was known as "Harvey Hill." It was a dirt road only wide enough for one car at a time on the hill. It went from Ninth Street to Thirteenth Street. Even today, most people don't know Zanesville has Tenth, Eleventh, Twelfth, and Thirteenth Streets! I can recall about fifteen homes on Harvey Hill back then. Now, only six or seven are left.

I was somewhat of a street urchin. I started at nine years old selling newspapers on street corners downtown after school. In the summer, I would also shine shoes and sell paper flowers (made by my mother) in the downtown bars.

Some of the bars were not safe for a youngster. My brother made the mistake of selling flowers on lower Main Street and was robbed and beat up. I only went to the places where men took dates to dance. I remember the Wonder Bar, La Salle Bar, and the Presto Bar. All had dancing and bands playing. It was a gold mine to me, as most men trying to impress their dates wouldn't refuse me if I asked if they wanted to buy a flower for their girl!

Bob Jones, Bill's best friend growing up, Bill Dicks, and Snoopy the dog.

At fourteen, I set pins at Pringle's Bowling Alley on south Sixth Street (above what is now Christ's Pantry). Pin setters had to be careful not to jump into the pit to retrieve pins while someone was bowling on that alley. I got quite a lot of bruises and stoved fingers, but never broke a bone as some pin-boys did.

I also worked at one of Zanesville's first supermarkets, the Big Bear on Fourth Street across from the Shinnick Auditorium, later called the Municipal Auditorium, and now called Secrest Auditorium after Representative Bob Secrest, a much loved local "tobacco chewing" politician.

Most of my earnings bought school clothes. I mostly shopped at Fred's Men Shop at Seventh and Main because they made me feel important. They always took your measurements with a tape measure they carried around their necks. They even measured you when you knew your size. It was all part of the process.

I liked buying my shoes at Kenney's Shoe Store on Main because they had a big treasure chest, and you could take a toy when you bought shoes.

A lot of people shopped at the big department stores. I can remember three of them, A.E. Starr, Bintz Brothers, and Habibs. They were too expensive for me, but I used to go in and ride the elevators.

My main entertainment was the movies! We had five theaters downtown, and I went at least three times a week! We had the Liberty and the Weller, they both showed first-run movies but cost seventeen cents to get in. The Variety and the Quimby (later named State) showed older movies but only cost ten cents. Then, we had the Grand (which was not grand). It showed black and white movies and also had bats and rats in the place, but it only cost five cents!

Other entertainment was a free movie every Saturday at YMCA and sock-hop dances at YWCA. Great way to meet girls. Also, there was roller skating at the Lind Arena on Linden Avenue and swimming at the Municipal Pool on west Main, but I never went there. My best friend was black and was not allowed to swim or skate with white people. They had Mondays at the skating rink and Tuesdays at the pool. And that was the only part of growing up in Zanesville that was bad.

Snakes Don't Die Until Sundown

by Pamela Diana Yakupcak of Cumberland, Ohio
born in 1954

I remember living by the new Interstate 70 while it was being built. We went out to our grandparents in Old Washington and played in the mud puddles where they were making the road. I remember growing up on the County Home Road.

My dad and mom built a new house for our family. We lived on a farm and were very happy. We had a big barn with lots of things in it. I especially remember the snakes. Boy, did they scare us. Once when we got off the bus at the end of our lane, there laid a snake across the road. We had to have the neighbors (older boy) get the snake off the road so we could go home.

We had a creek down in front of the house. I remember wading, fishing, finding leeches between our toes. Once I was fishing at a very young age, and I caught a huge turtle. My dad was so excited he made turtle soup. I would not eat it as the heart was beating for a very long time. But he sure did enjoy it.

We had a very large family. Six girls and one boy. But even though he was outnumbered, he was treated with lots of love. He was always getting fishing hooks in his fingers.

We had a very big hill the old barn was on. In the winter when it snowed, we would take our sleighs (the old runner type) and would ride down the hill really fast and then hit a huge pile of dirt and ramp the sleigh off of it. I don't remember anyone getting hurt. But we sure had a lot of fun.

Life was so different back then. We had our own cow for our milk. I remember my mom always eating the cream on her cereal.

My Aunt Ellie she made everything from scratch. I stayed with her almost every summer and whenever a new baby arrived. She taught me how to cook, clean, sew, and most of all she gave all the love from her heart to me and my family.

She had a very large porch on her house. We loved to play on it and inside in her flower room. I remember sleeping with her in her big bed. I can see in my mind every room as it was and even the basement. She was my second MOM.

Today, I have so many memories of those old days. No school was missed as we had chains on tires, even though snow drifted higher than the bus at times. I remember we were only allowed to wear dresses. We had rubber boots and knee socks. Hats were across our heads with ties under our chins. Our hair was long and pulled back into ponytails. Sometimes our mom would put these rubber curlers that you wrapped your hair up and then fastened them. My sister still has some of those.

I have the original aerial photograph that someone took of the farm back then. It is of my Aunt Ellie's house with all the barns and sheds. We played in those sheds and made a house in one of them. We found these eggs and put them in a jar. When we got to the house with them my dad came to get us and said those are snake eggs. Well, of course we did not wait to see if they hatched. He took them out and took care of those for us.

We always had a very large garden. I can still see all the rows of vegetables. My mom and Ellie canned everything they could so we would have plenty to eat all winter. My dad and mom butchered their own beef and pork. My mom butchered chickens. That was awful as she had to hang them on the clothesline and chop their heads off. Then she had to dip them in hot water to pluck the feathers. No buying eggs at the store or any kind of meats.

Of course, Ellie had a spring across the road. The water was like heaven. How I would love to have some of that water today.

Life was so easy back then. No worries except if someone got hurt.

My sister was outside playing and my family was burning the trash. Her dress caught fire from one of the ashes and she ran, scared. Well, she had third degree burns. So that was quite an ordeal as she spent many days in Riverside Hospital for skin grafting.

My brother was born with a hole in his heart and my parents spent many days with him in Children's Hospital.

I remember climbing over a fence on Ellie's farm to an old junk pile. I fell over the fence and landed on a Sanka Coffee jar. My mom had to have the mailman take me to hospital to have my leg sewn up with 36 stitches.

One of my younger sisters was at a family picnic at Seneca Lake Secrest Park. She must have been three years old. She wandered off down over the hill and fell in the lake. By the grace of God, she did not drown.

All this was our life in the '60s.

We lost our dad to kidney failure at the young age of 34. He was the most loving father anyone could have ever had. I have to tell my younger sisters about his love for us as they don't remember him very well.

He was a farmer, milk truck driver, and then he worked for the State Highway Department. He was a Korean War veteran with many medals including the Purple Heart.

My mom raised us until we were almost all out on our own then she remarried a great man. They have had over 30 years together and are still going strong.

We all still live in this county. Each daughter married and have children and almost all have grandchildren. We lost my brother at age 42 to heart failure. He has a family that continues to grow also with a new grandchild this year. We miss all our family that have gone on before us. BUT our memories are embedded forever in our hearts and minds.

Just to go back and see all them and live the simple farm life without a care, what a wonderful thing we could give to our grandchildren if we could. But we can tell them about the life we had and the things we experienced. That is our legacy to them.

School was the biggest transition in the '50s and '60s. Reading, writing and arithmetic were the main courses to learn. We also had art and music. I remember growing a bean in third grade. Whoever grew the largest won a camera. I won because I used real cow manure with my dirt. I still own the camera.

Back then we had to prime the outside pump to have water.

On Saturday, we got to watch "American Bandstand" and "Sing Along With Mitch." On Sunday night it was "Walt Disney" and "Bonanza." Only black and white TV with only one or two channels with an outdoor antenna. Most of the time we had to take turns going out to adjust the antenna until the channel came in clear, yelling in, "Is it okay yet?"

Bicycles were our mode of transportation. Any fortunate to have one got to learn to ride, bumps, lumps and falls. We also learned to siphon gas with a hose to put in the mower or the car if we were running on empty. What a horrible taste to get in your mouth so you hurried and put it in as soon as you could smell it. Summers were spent making mud pies and playing house.

We grew up fearing and respecting our parents. We knew that was the way to be. Otherwise, we got a whopping with the belt. (Which was not often.)

We walked a lot to visit our family down the other way. My aunt owned a very large farm, over 400 acres. She had a really big pond behind the barn. One day they filled it in and I don't know why.

We went berry picking up on her hill. We picked buckets full of black raspberries but forgot where we put them. So we went home empty handed. She had elderberries and we ate those. She also had a sassafras tree. We made tea and chewed on the roots. In her fields, we walked to the creek and fished. On the way back to the house we would find spearmint and chew on it. Once we made a raft out of an old door. We tried to float it in the small creek behind the house. It sunk to the bottom. Thank God it was not really deep. She had a garden behind the house also.

I remember once my cousin came and found a snake and wrapped it around her neck. We ran from her as we were scared of snakes. Most of the ones we had seen were water snakes and copperheads, which we were taught to be scared of as they are very poisonous. I remember my aunt killing one right outside the back door with her shovel. She told us not to bother one that had been killed as they really aren't dead until sundown.
She had some distant relatives come to stay once with a camper. They were Cherokee Indians, as we have them in our bloodlines. I remember he had a huge amount of knives. But he was kind to us as his wife was also.

I remember homemade canned peaches, homemade bread from scratch, homemade jelly rolls, pies, cookies, soups. I remember eating bread in a bowl with milk and sugar. That was a treat back then.

She had chickens in the coop. We had to watch out for the rooster as he was mean and would chase you and try to flop you.

The big garden was full of tomatoes, green beans, corn by the rows and potatoes. We never had store bought vegetables as everything was hand grown.

I remember in school Dick and Jane books were how we learned to read. Bedtime was at 9:00 because another day would soon start.

Neighbors were neighbors. Everyone knew all the neighbors and helped in any way they could.

When my aunt got sick and was ready to pass from this life she wanted to leave the farmhouse to my mom and us as my father had passed away a year earlier. But her family on the other side decided she was not sane and they got the farm. After she passed away, the one man was in her front yard mowing and the lawn mower picked up a bullet and it struck his leg. He was not supposed to have her home. She wanted us to have it. His family lived in misery from then on. Lots of strife and illness struck them. But we were not bitter, just scared, as we had lost our two strongest loves in our lives. Our mom had the task of raising seven children by herself then.

We moved into a rented house and continued in school. Each year another went to school until we all were ready to move on with our own lives. I had a son after I graduated and stayed home with my family until he was two months old. I had to let him sleep in a drawer as I had no bed or crib for him. He grew up to be a great son and an upstanding citizen.

We all went on our own never leaving Guernsey County. We all worked at a local factory except my brother. He worked various jobs even though he was disabled from a birth defect. Love was truly in our home and still in our lives as we all share memories of our youth with each other.

The Snow Lamp

By Martin R. Baumgardner of Warsaw, Ohio
Born 1942

The story of the snow lamp begins with a part time job that I had when I was a sophomore at Roscoe High School in Coshocton County. After school and on Saturdays, I was a "brush out" worker at Davis Dry Cleaners on Sixth Street in Coshocton. The job was to pull out the pockets of pants brought in to remove crumbs and other objects so that they may be dry cleaned. Can you believe that one day I found $300 dollars in a pair of pants that had been brought in by a local doctor! I did receive a small reward for my honesty in turning the money in to the manager.

The snow lamp.

However, another part of my job was to get the flavored soft drink orders of the other employees and then go to the Brungart Drug store soda fountain to bring them back to the cleaners. Remember, there was no flavored cokes and of course no pop cans in 1958. One December day in 1958, while waiting on the flavored coke order to be filled, I noticed a lamp on a shelf that I will refer to as a snow lamp. I have always loved snow and winter weather and especially Christmas time. At the time I lived at the top of Roscoe Hill which was super for sledding! Now, I need to describe this special lamp. It was a cylinder with a painted snow scene on the outside. Inside the cylinder was a second cylinder with perforated lines that surrounds a clear light bulb. When the heat from the bulb caused the inner cylinder to rotate, it gives the appearance of snow falling. Little did I know on that day while waiting for the flavored coke order to be filled, that the lamp would be a special part of my life to this very day at age 67. That night I told my mom about the lamp I had seen and how unique it was.

It was Christmas morning 1958 atop Roscoe Hill that I descended the stairs and there under the real Christmas tree was the Snow Lamp! I had no idea that the lamp would be mine. My mom knew that snow was special to me and it is still the best Christmas gift ever! The lamp with the fragile inner and outer cylinder, though held together with tape from the scars of the years of use, still graces my living room from the first of November till the first of March. No amount of money would I ever take for the special Snow Lamp gift of 1958.

Coming Home for Christmas Vacation from College. It was Christmas vacation my freshman year at Ohio University and I took the Greyhound Bus home from Athens, Ohio. Arriving at the bus station on Second Street, I was in awe of my hometown's decorated Main Street for the Christmas season. It was December of 1960 and my hometown was Coshocton. Actually, I lived atop Roscoe Hill, but Coshocton is also considered my hometown.

Carrying my suitcase, I began walking up Main Street to the M'Oneil store where my dad worked. Coshocton had for as long as I could remember strung multi-colored lights entwined in artificial pine across the width of Main Street. It had always been special riding home with my parents from Grandma and Grandpa's on Thanksgiving night to see the lights lit for the first time of the season. The strings of lights were at intervals the entire length of Main Street. In those days the street lights were not very bright and the multi-colored Christmas lights were a beautiful contrast to the dark winter sky.

Now there is one other humorous note about these special Christmas lights of Coshocton that I want to mention. I cannot recall the year but for the Christmas parade, it was decided to have floating balloon characters. It was to be a Macy's type parade in Coshocton! It seems that the balloons had to be somewhat deflated to be paraded down Main Street. Dumbo and other characters had a few wrinkles, but it was Christmas time in Coshocton. Today our town is still one of beauty at holiday time. Today, it is "Miracle on Main Street." The lights no longer are strung across the width of the street. Instead, the buildings are outlined with white lights and scores of miniature white lighted trees grace our sidewalks.

Family Farming

By William K. Fulton of West Milford, New Jersey
Born 1925

Family farming was a business, but more than that, it was a way of life and a good way. Everyone worked on the farm: men, women and children. And the work lasted from dawn until dusk. In wintertime, it was before dawn and after dusk. Work was hard, but not onerous, because everyone was used to it and was in good physical shape. In truth, they loved the life. After a long day's work, a good night's sleep was essential to rest the body and to restore energy for the next day. The workweek was Monday through Saturday with Sunday being a day of rest and religious observances. However, even on Sundays, the cows had to be milked morning and night, all the animals had to be fed and watered and meals had to be prepared.

On Saturday, Mother usually went to town, Bellaire most often, to shop for "necessities." Dad or one of the older brothers knocked off working to drive her to town. Often, one or more of the younger brothers or sisters went along.

Going to town was a real treat and a nice break in the week's routine. We children did not do much in town. It was more a variation from the usual. After a glimpse of the Ohio River, it was a visit to the Woolworth's Five and Ten-Cent Store to see what could be purchased for a dime, which was usually all I was allotted to spend. If Woolworth's had nothing of interest, then my wealth was usually spent on a five-cent bottle of orange Nehi and a five-cent Powerhouse candy bar. After a day in the "big city" it was always good to get home to the farm.

As we got older, into the teenage bracket, we would go into St. Clairsville for a haircut, a movie or a date and a movie, followed by sundaes at Corbin's Grill on Main Street.

On Sundays, no heavy work was done. Mother especially would not let us do any work other than basic housework related to getting meals and to care for the animals. Mother often said if we tried to put up hay or cut grain on Sundays, it would spoil. Who were we not to take these admonitions as certainties comparable to the Bible's depiction in Genesis of God's creating heaven and earth in six days and resting on the seventh. So Sunday was a day of rest.

After breakfast, we fed and milked the cows, fed the chickens, hogs and horses, then turned the cows and horses out to pasture. Then we all went to Church in Warnock. In earlier days it was by horse and buggy or sleigh in the winter, and later by car.

Sunday school started promptly at 10 o'clock and lasted for an hour. Regular services started at 11 o'clock and lasted for another hour. Those Presbyterian ministers could be long-winded and the pendulum clock on the wall was like a metronome that acted to lull a less than pious kid to sleep.

Just prior to leaving for church, Mother would have put either a pot roast or a stuffed chicken, surrounded by a variety of vegetables with a little water, in a Dutch oven, which she put into the oven of her old coal-fired cook stove. When we got home, the Sunday meal was ready and promptly devoured.

After dinner, in the summer, the boys headed out to play baseball, much to Mother's disapproval. She was not against baseball, per se, but for playing on the Sabbath. Of course, as the brothers and sisters got older Sunday afternoon was also the time for dating. Older family members visited or were visited by friends and relatives. So Sunday afternoon was a time for relaxation and socializing.

This description of games we played is primarily from the boy's standpoint. I will leave it to sister Laura Belle to describe games played primarily by the girls such as Red Rover, Ring Around the Rosy and "Community Store." Our games were mostly at school. We played softball, marbles, mumbly-peg, tag, king of the hill, skating and sledding in the winter and fishing. We had a rule: whoever caught the largest fish took the whole catch home. That way one family would have a nice mess of fish and no one would be taking home just one smaller fish.

In the fall, during hunting season, we played a game we called "Rabbit" with spent shotgun shells. The "hunter" would try to hit one of the "rabbits" by throwing the shotgun shell at him as he ran from tree to tree that were predetermined to be "safe holes." A whack on the back of the head by the brass part of the shell is still remembered.

At home we had swings hung on branches of apple trees in the orchard. However, we also had natural swings. These were vines located in trees in the virgin forest that were part of the pasture on "31." The vines had grown with the trees and the leafy parts were entangled in the tree canopy and were a hundred feet or more high. The trunks of the vines, usually two or three inches in diameter, hung down detached from the tree trunk. We would cut the vine at ground level and would swing on it out over the valley below. It was quite a ride. The vine died and eventually became unsafe and the dead vine fell down from where its branches were entangled in the canopy. Then we would have to locate another vine to cut and use as a swing.

In winter we had sleds and plenty of hillsides to sled down. Dad made a "bobsled" consisting of a front steerable part and a rear part with a long two-inch plank attached between them. The plank was eight or ten feet long and six or eight of us could sit on it, one behind the other, with the person in front holding the legs of the person behind off the ground. The person in front did the steering.

We did some swimming, but it was a couple miles walk to "Rock Hole," located on Harry Warnock's farm at a bend of McMahon's Creek, where a rock ledge gave the place its name. It was the only place for miles around where the water was over our heads and deep enough so we could swim properly.

We also played Cowboys and Indians plus our version of Cops and Robbers, which we called "John Dillinger" because he was a notorious bank robber and killer of that era. Of course each one wanted to be "John Dillinger."

Playing "Indians," I recall building a teepee in the second yard out of tall bean poles covered by a couple of old Indian blankets. I once built a small fire outside the teepee, borrowed one of Mother's frying pans, cut a chunk of ham hung to cure in the smokehouse and proceeded to fry the ham. Being too impatient, the ham was not cooked long enough and I got sick as a dog.

Finding Indian arrowheads was a preoccupation. As a little kid, I followed along in the furrow behind the plow looking in the freshly turned earth for arrowheads. However, I never found any.

In the fall, hunting was a popular pastime for we boys. We hunted squirrels and rabbits mostly. There were no deer, turkeys or pheasants in those days. They had been pretty well hunted out for hungry miners' tables in those lean days. We had shotguns and rifle, and were taught by Dad and the older brothers how to respect and handle firearms safely. I recall, at age six, I inherited a single shot Stevens .22 caliber rifle that was handed down through four older brothers. Even though I had my own .22 rifle, I recall that about ten years of age, I wanted, and got, a Red Ryder BB gun for Christmas. (Shades of Ralphie in "A Christmas Story.")

We played some team sports. Brothers James, George and Albert did not play high school sports because they took the train to and from Bellaire and therefore could not practice or play sports. George and Albert played baseball on the local Warnock team. George was a very good baseball player. Chuck played junior high school and high school baseball. He was a catcher, fast, and a good hitter with the quickest and fastest swing I have ever seen. Several times I heard the umpire call strike and Chuck would snap his quick wrists around, slapping the ball into right field. Chuck and I also played football on the St. Clairsville High School football team.

As a kid I played baseball with neighbor kids, like Bill Fox, on Sunday afternoons. We made our own ball field out from the Hill Sheep House and used bales of hay piled up as a backstop. I would mow the field on Saturday with a horse-pulled mower. With only a handful of players, our baseball "diamond" became a three-base "triangle," not four bases. Once we played an "away" game on a leveled-off slate dump in Stewartsville. That was one tough ball field, where sliding was avoided. Chuck and I also played some baseball with the St. Clairsville Merchants in the United Mine Workers League.

Occasionally, on Saturdays or Sundays, we would have what we called "Ridge Parties." These were get-togethers at our home, Uncle George's, Uncle Bert's, Aunt Minnie's (later Ralph and Della Aults,) Fox's and Kettlewell's. All were residents on the Ridge between our home and Glencoe. These parties varied between wiener roasts, barn picnics or just plain parlor visits.

I recall one evening party at Uncle George's when Dad hooked up a team of horses to the big sled in which he spread some hay. He hung bells on the horse's harness, and we had "Jingle Bells" all the way there and back. I was probably three years old at the time, but I have a vivid memory of that ride. We sat in the hay with me in Mother's lap and we were covered by an old buffalo robe. It was wintertime, with lots of snow on the ground, and the night was cold and crystal clear. The heavens were bright with stars that can't be seen in today's perpetual haze and smog.

During the afternoon of Christmas day, the families of Uncle George and Uncle Bert, as well as Aunt Mary, always visited us. This was a kind of tradition because our farm was where they were born and raised and our house was where they grew up as children. So it was a way for them to maintain sentimental contact with their roots on the Fulton Family farm.

Dad was a charter member of the Ohio Farm Bureau, which was a cooperative of farmers that operated retail outlets for feed, seed and fertilizer at locations such as in St. Clairsville. Farm Bureau members were prominent farmers throughout the county. Once a month, on Saturday evenings, there would be a gathering hosted by a different farm family on a rotation basis. The meetings were opportunities for good conversation, exchange of ideas and general good fellowship.

Of course there was lots of good food, which was a special delight for the children. Each meeting had a food theme that varied according to the season. In the spring, pies were featured: strawberry, rhubarb, cherry, peach, blackberry and raspberry. In the summer the features were ice cream and watermelons, plus wiener and corn roasts. In the fall, we enjoyed pumpkin pies of all kinds. I recall seeing a black pumpkin pie for the first time and was hesitant to try it, but it was delicious.

There was one meeting at our farm where the theme was Halloween. Sister Laura Belle should give us the details of that one. Meetings were suspended in winter because of the difficulties of travel on country roads.

Concerning the Grange, I am not knowledgeable about the Grange organization. I know that the ladies were very active in its doings.

Church Socials. The churches in Warnock occasionally had festivals, often in the basement of the grade school. The themes again, depended on the season: strawberry, watermelon, ice cream and pumpkin.

Cakewalks. This was a social event of a type that seems to be unknown today and was unknown outside our community. The cakewalk was organized by the Pythian Sisters, which I believe was an adjunct of the Masonic Order. The cakewalk was held in the Pythian Hall in Warnock and was a combination social gathering and fundraiser. Cakes were baked and brought to the event by the ladies who donated them for the event. Attendees would purchase a ticket, pick a partner and the couple would walk in a circle around the room to Victrola music. When the music stopped, the walking couples stopped. The couple that stopped on a predetermined spot won the cake for that round. Cakewalks were a good way to visit, talk and share some good desserts.

House Parties. Each farm family would occasionally hold a house party for friends and neighbors. Depending on the season and weather, these parties could be in the house or outside and featured a wiener or corn roast.

Family Picnics. Once in a great while, we would have a picnic outside under the trees. This was an efficient method of handling a get together of a large number of family, extended family members and friends. Remember, we had a large family.

Belmont County Fair. The County Fair was held once a year for a week, in early September, at the fairgrounds in St. Clairsville. Farmers brought their animals, cattle, sheep, hogs, chickens, etc., which were kept in pens in barns. The animals would be judged by categories and ribbons awarded. Farm wives and daughters brought canned and baked goods, sewing, quilting and a variety of other craftwork, which were exhibited in buildings for that purpose. Prize ribbons were also awarded.

A feature of the Fair was the grandstand and quarter-mile racetrack, where sulky races were run during the day, along with horse pulling and tractor pulling contests. At night, shows were conducted on a stage in front of the grandstand. These included acts such as acrobats and clowns. The grandstand and racetrack have disappeared, replaced by a stadium, and the infield now consists of the St. Clairsville High School football playing and practice fields.

The part of the Fair that was most enjoyed by the kids was the Midway, where the Merry-Go-Round, Ferris Wheel and a variety of other rides and games of "skill" were featured. There were plenty of tents selling hot dogs, hamburgers, ice cream, soda pop, popcorn and candy. I remember the cotton candy spun onto a paper stick. Dad said that it was a waste of money to buy cotton candy because it consisted of a just a little sugar and a lot of air.

4-H Clubs were/are a wholesome, educational, spiritual and social experience for children and teens. Under the guidance of the County Extension Agent, 4-H'ers learn sewing, cooking, electrical, caring for animals, photography and many skills that will benefit them throughout their life. Projects were displayed at the Belmont County Fair, and a few were selected to participate in the Ohio State Fair. Some gave educational demonstrations; some modeled outfits the 4-H'ers had sewn and some had other projects on display at the State Fair.

To make a well-rounded young person, emphasis is placed on the 4-H's head, heart, hands and health.

Older teens could join the Junior Leaders, which gave them the benefit of many enjoyable social events such as square dancing or being a counselor at the Piedmont 4-H camp. This camp was a special time, whether you were one of the campers or helping to teach younger members and set a good example for the younger members.
(Since my recollection of 4-H Club activities is dim and distant, I asked Sue Lane to explain because she was active in 4-H.)

As I am always interested in the origins of expressions in the American lexicon, I was intrigued at where the origin of the expression "It is a cakewalk," meaning it is very easy. Here is the origin: The cakewalk was originally a 19th century dance, invented by African-Americans in the antebellum South. It was intended to satirize the stiff ballroom promenades of white plantation owners, who favored the rigidly formal dances of European high society. Cakewalking slaves lampooned these stuffy moves by over-accentuating their high kicks, bows and imaginary hat doffings, mixing the cartoonish gestures together with traditional African steps. Likely unaware of the dance's derisive roots, the whites often invited their slaves to participate in Sunday contests, to determine which dancers were most elegant and inventive. The winners would receive cake slices, a prize which gave birth to the dance's familiar name.

After the Emancipation, the contest tradition continued in black communities; the Oxford English Dictionary dates the widespread adoption of "cakewalk" to the late 1870's. It was around this time that the cakewalk came to mean "easy" not because the dance was particularly simple to do, but rather because of its languid pace and association with weekend leisure.

A Skunk Named Aroma

by James L. Winkler of Stonecreek, Ohio
born 1928

I was born in New Philadelphia, Ohio on March 27, 1928 and lived there until I was in my early 50's.

On December 6, 1941 my Dad decided to get me a .22 caliber rifle, as I had wanted one for some time. He took me to the Montgomery Ward store, which was located where the Tuscarawas County courthouse annex is now located. With his advice I picked a Remington

Target Master. The cost was $6.25, which was a considerable outlay of money at that time.

The next day my mother, dad, a neighborhood pal, Al Maloney, and myself got in Dad's 1928 Pontiac—with yellow spoke wheels—and drove to the farm of family friends, Floyd and Myrtle Parson, just south of New Philadelphia. We had put up a target and were taking turns shooting at it, when the lady of the house came out of the kitchen door and shouted to us that it had just came over the radio that the Japs had attacked Pearl Harbor.

In the spring when I was fourteen I was allowed to take my rifle to the Tuscarawas River. Near the Puritan Laundry was a slaughterhouse and even though it was in the corporation and within two hundred yards of quite a few houses - I often shot rats at the rear of the building. No one ever objected, nor did anyone call the police department. About that time I decided to go groundhog hunting, and walked to the Southside of New Philadelphia and on out of town. While hunting, I saw a very young skunk. It reminded me of a cute kitten, so I picked it up and of course, got sprayed. I carried it by the tail until I passed a farmhouse and the farmer, Frank Kurtz, was kind enough to give me burlap, or a gunny, sack to carry it in. When I got home, I put it in an empty rabbit pen Dad had made for me. I named her Aroma. I was able to handle Aroma as long as I was careful not to scare her.

Jim Winkler in 1940.

One evening a friend, Darold Dennis, came over and wanted me to go to a movie with him. I said I would but I would have to put Aroma away. She had gone under the back porch. I placed a container of bread and milk, which was her favorite, just off the porch and I waited. She came out and was just finishing it when my friend said, "you had better grab her, she's got it nearly finished." I had been putting it off because I thought that grabbing her might excite her too much. It did! I had to change my clothes and we went to the Quaker Theatre.

The Quaker Theatre opened in 1940. We sat near the front, as kids do. No one was near us, but shortly I began to hear people several rows behind us saying, "I smell skunk." Then, "There's a skunk in here!" Then I remembered that I hadn't changed my shoes. They were slip-ons and I believe they were called "Penny Loafers." Anyway, I kicked them off and crawled maybe 30-feet on my hands and knees, and deposited them under an empty seat. I then crawled back and we finished watching the movie.

I took Aroma to a local vet to have the scent gland removed. He told me that, "She's too small." I waited several weeks, I guess, and took her back. The vet said, "She's now too big." So I decided he didn't want to perform the operation.

Not long after that, the area game warden paid me a visit. His name was James Holleyoak, a fine, well-respected man. He asked me if I was keeping a pet skunk. I said yes. He told me I would have to release it and advised me to do it across the river or it would come back. That evening I released it in the backyard, and never saw Aroma again, nor had any reason to think that she might still be around.

Incidentally, I still have that rifle, after more than sixty-seven years. I have never had to replace a firing pin, a screw or a spring. As near as I can tell, it's as accurate as it was on December 7, 1941.

Goosefeathers and Amish Friends

By Patricia Wilson of Newcomerstown, Ohio
Born1933

In 1961 my husband and I moved our family of five girls to Peoli, Ohio, the hometown of Cy Young, a professional baseball player. He grew up here and is buried in the Methodist Cemetery. We felt like this would be the ideal place to grow and live and raise a family. I have so many memories that it is hard to put them all down on paper; so here are a few.

Across the street from the house was a hog pen. Inside the hog pen was a huge sycamore tree. Our first task was to clean up around the tree. The tree is now over 400 years old, 80 feet tall, 165 feet across and 20 feet around. We hung a tire swing from a branch for the children to play with. There were also steps up the side of the tree for them to climb the tree.

The first animals to move onto our farm were cows, pigs and sheep. One of the cows we purchased had the unique ability to lift the fence up and get out of the field. No one thought a cow could do this and we had a hard time believing it ourselves until we actually witnessed her doing it. We also had a cow that the children could ride. They would get on her back and away they would go. They were not pleased when we had to get rid of the cow.

One fine summer day, the children had one of their city cousins down to visit. They had the pony out and were having fun riding her in the yard around the house. I was busy hand scrubbing and waxing the linoleum dining room floor. The children all knew to stay outside and play until the floor dried. For whatever reason, they decided to be cute and try a new trick. They actually got the pony to climb up the three steps that led into the dining room. Then they led her into the dining room, where she slid all over the floor. Needless to say, I was not very pleased with any of them.

Our children were not all blessed with great eyesight. Becky had glasses when she was in second grade. Eyeglasses were not as stylish as they are now. They were black, plastic framed glasses. We had just gotten her a new pair. One day, she went down to the barn to feed the hogs. A few hours later, it was homework time and Becky did not have her glasses. I asked her where they were and she replied that she did not remember where she put them when she got home from school. We tore the house apart looking for these glasses. We never did find them, so had to go get her another pair. It was not until years later that she admitted that she had fed them to the hogs when she was feeding them.

One of our summer tasks was to put up hay. This was a family project. Bob would cut the hay one day and leave it to dry out. The next day, it was my job to rake it into rows. The children were to sit on a blanket and play nicely with their toys until I was finished. They quickly learned how far they could venture off the blanket and return to safety before I made it back around to check on them. When Bob came home, he baled the hay and we loaded it onto the wagon. To speed the process up, some of the children would roll the bales into a single row so it could easily be picked up. One or two of the girls would be on the wagon, stacking the hay as it was thrown up to them.

If the hay was not stacked securely, it would all fall off as we rounded a turn. One time, we were in a hurry to get done because we were going away that evening. The girls were all on top of the wagon and when we were leaving the field and going onto the road to put the hay in the barn, the hay fell off the wagon. Kay fell off the load onto a barbed wire fence. She gashed her arm open, thus putting an end to our plans of going away that evening. She still bears the scars on her arm from that incident.

Another time, we were in a back field, getting our last load of hay in before the rain came. As we went out of the field onto the dirt lane, the load of hay overturned with some of the children being dumped off. This wouldn't have been so bad had the electric fence they fell on been turned off. The children learned from this mishap that they would not be killed from a little shock by an electric fence.

It was getting late in the evening one day of hay making, and everyone was getting hungry. I sent Anne, the oldest, up to the local store to get a package of macaroni; with the instructions that she was to purchase the macaroni, bring it home and make some macaroni salad. I was in for a big surprise when I went in to check on the progress. I was thinking a one pound package of macaroni, but she purchased a three pound package. She ran out of pans in her attempt to get it all cooked and made. We ate macaroni salad for a solid week.

The Methodist parsonage was across the street from our house. One of the preachers was very willing to help out with the hay making whenever he had the time. It seemed like every time he offered to help out it rained. We had many laughs with him over his bad luck. The hay was brought in and sent up a hay elevator into the haymow, the upper part of the barn. The children took great pleasure in going up in the haymow to play and hide out.

The children all anxiously looked forward to the last day of school. They attended a four room elementary school about three miles from the house. They knew as they got older that they could walk home from school on the last day if they so desired. This was a great adventure for them and it gave me a couple more hours of time without them. One year, they walked home from school, excited to be out of school for the year. I am sure they were busy making plans for the summer. They surely were upset when they came down with chicken pox the first day of summer vacation. The great thing about living in a small community is that they were still able to get outside and play despite the itchy, itchy chicken pox.

There were many hot nights that the children were able to take their blankets and pillows outside and "camp out" under the stars. We did not have to worry about safety then. We knew we would find them safe and sound the next morning.

Another activity the children enjoyed in the summer was hiking and picnicking in the woods. There was a creek running through the woods that the children could wade in. Several places were deep enough that they actually thought they were swimming. A peanut butter sandwich and a fresh apple off the tree was enough of a lunch that they could be gone for hours.

We had two ponds on the farm; one of which was only about 4½ feet deep. The children enjoyed swimming in this pond. The pond was stocked with bass and bluegills. Some of the children enjoyed fishing for dinner.

My parents came out from Iowa every summer to visit us. One memorable summer, Dad decided to go fishing in the pond. He had caught a nice sized bass and had it in his bucket of water to bring up for dinner. He happened to look over in time to see a big blacksnake slithering away from the bucket with his fish in his mouth.

During the winter, the children would get their sleds out, and starting at the top of the hill, they would frequently make it down the hill and across the pond. The girls also enjoyed ice skating on the frozen pond. A great aunt and uncle who lived in the Washington DC area sent us ice skates every winter. If there were not enough pairs of skates to go around, a pair of boots would work almost as well.

Shortly after we got married and made our move to the country, Bob said he would sure like chicken for supper. Being a good newlywed, I told his mother his request. She pointed to the chicken pen and said, "There they are." Now, I grew up in the city and I knew that you bought chicken at a grocery store. I had never killed a chicken in my life, but I knew it was something I had to do. I saw the stump out in the yard, so I went to the henhouse and got me a chicken. I gathered up my bucket and axe and set about killing the bird. I put the chicken's head on the stump and looked down. It was staring back at me, so I took my bucket, put it over the chicken's head, and swung the axe. The head remained on the stump, under the bucket, but the rest of the chicken was up running around. I finally caught the chicken and ensured that it was dead. I then began cleaning the chicken in preparation for dinner. I remembered that Bob said that he liked the gizzard, so I knew I had to cook it also. I did not realize how badly it would stink. I got my brush and began to scrub that gizzard as clean as I could get it. I cooked it along with the chicken. Dinnertime came, and Bob was certainly excited. "Oh boy, chicken! Did you save the gizzard?" I replied, "Of course I did." Well, try as he might, he could not eat the gizzard. I did not know that you had to remove the lining from the gizzard. But, I knew then where the saying, "Running around like a chicken with your head cut off," come from. I had a hard time eating chicken for the longest time. It was with great pleasure when I had a grandson years later that didn't mind killing and dressing chickens. We even dressed and sold chickens after that.

It was my turn to host Thanksgiving Dinner for the family. My brother-in-law told me he had a goose we could use for Thanksgiving. "Hurray!" I thought, "Meat is taken care of." That excitement lasted until about a week before Thanksgiving when John brought the goose out to me. It was still alive! Well, I had mastered the art to chicken dressing, but this was my first attempt at dressing a goose. One neighbor told me to put paraffin on top of the hot water to remove the feathers from the goose. Another neighbor told me to put vinegar in the water. This will soften the water and make it easier to pluck. So, I tried it all. Every hint I was given was up for a trial. Nothing seemed to be effective. I finally got a decent looking plucked goose. I prepared it for the oven. It was in for about an hour when I decided to check on it. Imagine my dismay when I opened the oven door and was faced with a goose that was full of feathers. I took that goose out of the oven and plucked those stubborn feathers again. I put it back in the oven, got busy preparing other dishes for dinner, and went back to check on the goose one more time. You guessed it. More feathers! Well, by this time, I was getting pretty frustrated, so I got me a good sharp butcher knife and skinned the goose. I finished cooking it and served it for dinner. It was so bad that no one could eat the goose. That was my one and only attempt at butchering and cooking a goose.

The Amish began moving into the area in 1973. The first one was a red-headed, barefoot Amish who lived about a mile away. He and his family moved in. The first time I saw him was in the summer. I was on the porch, peeling peaches. Johnny and his two boys came up to the porch and I offered the children a peach. They did not take the peaches until their Dad spoke to them in their native language. They then reached up and took the peaches. John was the one who did the plans for the new barn when ours burned to the ground. His only price was that I feed them and he also requested a cake made by my son-in-law that had him (John) standing in the door of the barn. It was to be an Amish with flaming red hair. The barn was put up in one day. Even though we were certain that we had plenty of food to feed the crew for the day, we ran out of food at lunch time and had to go to the store to purchase supplies to feed them a supper.

The most memorable event that happened after our barn burned to the ground was when John's wife, Susie, came up the day of the fire and just sat under the sycamore tree. When John was ready to leave, she took my hand and said, "I'm sorry. I will help you cook." She was my friend.

I would go with Bob when he went to see John. I was taken to the front room and sat in one of the rockers and talked to Susie. I could hear popcorn popping. I always teased them about taking their popcorn. One morning, early, we went down and I could hear, pop, pop, pop. Soon a pan of popcorn arrived in the room. It was handed to me. I tried to share, but the girl said, "No. It's for you." So, I ate popcorn at 8:00 in the morning.

One time, after putting up hay with John's help, we were discussing whether to have a wiener roast or make ice cream. John said, "Wait until Monday. You get the ice. Susie will make the mix." She made seven gallons of mix. We scrambled to make ice cream. We took it to John's when it was done. It soon disappeared.

John and Susie's last children were twin boys. Becky and I went down to get shoes for her children. John asked if we wanted to see the babies. We naturally wanted to see them. They were beautiful babies. They each lay in a banana box. Since Becky could never remember their names, we called them Chiquita and Dole.

The Amish have been very good neighbors and friends to have. We know they will be available if we need them and they also know we will be available if they need us.

It was a hot summer day. I was outside with some

of my children and grandchildren. We were cleaning and freezing corn in anticipation of the long winter days ahead of us. I happened to look up and a gentleman was standing in the driveway. He was not very well dressed and carried a pack on his back. He said, "Your neighbors said you would feed me. I'm awfully hungry." I replied, "Of course you can eat with us. I am just about to prepare dinner now." Bob was down over the hill and I was just a bit leery of leaving him outside while I went to the barn to finish the corn. He seemed surprised that I asked him to wait and eat with us. He sat at the picnic table and waited for dinner to be ready. Soon I had dinner on the table. Before we ate, we bowed our heads and prayed. He ate dinner with us, thanked me for the food; and before he left, he asked if he could say a prayer for us. He did a very nice prayer for our family. After he left, I called several neighbors and no one else had seen this gentleman, either entering or departing town.

One time when I was in the hospital my roommate was a lady who was the owner of a tavern. All day and night, she cursed and called for drinks. She was not very quiet about it either, so I was not getting any rest. One morning, she was very quiet. I thought perhaps she had died during the night. She quietly asked me if I believed the Bible. I told her that I did. She then asked me if I had seen Jesus last night. I said, "No." She said she had seen Him. He was at the foot of her bed. About noon she passed away, after spending a very quiet morning. I truly believe that Jesus was there that night and He came to take her home.

My mother was a very beloved person in town. She had rheumatoid arthritis very badly. She walked crippled over and her hands were so bad that they were gnarled up. She knew that if she gave in to this disability she would never walk or use her hands again. Despite this, she always had a smile on her face. When she passed away, there were many people who came to pay their respects. After calling hours were over, several people suggested that we go get something to eat. I asked to stay with her just in case anyone else came. I also felt the need to be alone with her for a little while. No one else came, but as I sat there beside her, I could hear her talking to me. She said, "Don't grieve, Patty. I am fine. I can walk, I can straighten my hands. I have no pain. Remember me like this. I love you and always will."

A Teenager in the Fifties

By Barbara Jane Sponaugle of Mineral City, Ohio
Born 1939

There are special things stored in one's memory that a certain smell or thought will bring to the surface; and we remember a time long ago.

Barbara McCully Sponaugle after prom in 1956.

She sees a metal box filled with ice on the front porch where the milkman will deliver milk and dairy products.

On the kitchen table is a small container with a mixture in it which looked like lard. There is a yellow capsule which will be crushed and mixed with the white to form Oleo.

Clothes were washed using a wringer washer and hung on lines in the basement to dry. In nice weather they blew freely in the breeze outside and smelled fresh as the first flowers of spring. Beds and towels contained the smell of freshness from outdoors. Curtains were washed and placed on stretchers. Many fingers were pricked and bled performing this task.

The neighbors next door had a beautiful blooming cherry tree in their backyard. What fun it was to help pick the cherries, pit them and later eat cherry pie. The neighbor on the other side, boiled tomatoes in her basement and stripped the skin preparing them for canning. It was a joy to help skin the tomatoes.

Sometimes in the evening, my family would take a ride for a sandwich to a drive-in restaurant where the waiters came to your car on roller skates. This was great pleasure to a child and a special treat.

On Memorial Day we bought flowers to decorate the graves of our loved ones. The aroma of "flags" and spring flowers still fill my memory.

The smell of fresh cut grass mowed with a hand mower and powered by one's own feet was a sure sign of spring.

My aunt and uncle had a Model T Ford with a rumble seat in the back. The laughter of a child could be heard riding in this vehicle.

A radio program called "Inner Sanctum" was listened to by adults. The door would screech at the beginning and ending of the program.

On my way to high school in the morning, passing by an office supply store, often times I would stop to get a bottle of colored ink for my fountain pen. Each desk had a round spot cut out for the ink bottle.

Girls would cut off tops of their old Bobby Socks to make layers in the tops of new socks. Sock hops were the rage of the fifties. The fullness of skirts was enhanced by a crinoline underneath. Poodle skirts and saddle shoes were worn to dances. Boys greased their hair back into ducktails and girls wore ponytails. Loafers with a penny in them were popular. An artificial flower placed in a teen-age girl's hair added to an outfit.

It was great fun after school to walk to the nearest diner for a cherry coke. A jukebox would be on the table to play a favorite record.

You could see two movies for 75-cents. This made for a cheap date. After that the custom was to "cruise the drive-in restaurants."

Drive-in movies were very popular. You pulled your car into a space by a speaker, turned off the radio and sat under the stars to watch a movie.

Canton, Ohio, our hometown, had Meyers Lake Amusement Park and Moonlight Ballroom. On a summer evening a couple could dance outside under the stars to big band music. During intermission, a stroll around the amusement park was delightful. The Park and Ballroom are now gone.

I feel so lucky to have been a teenager during the fifties. Who would have thought that it would be a special time remembered through the years and imitated so often?

The Time When Bombers Darkened the Sky

by Fern E. Wentz Stewart Sperduti of Zanesville, Ohio
born 1933

This is a story of some of my life back in the "good ole days," some of the things that I really remember.

I was born during the Depression on February 15, 1933 in a small house in Duncan Falls, second house from Route 60 on Millers Lane at the end of my Grandpa Wentz's farm. My grandfather, Philip Henry Wentz, had a farm on Mound Road. The house and barn still remain there today. My father, Clayton Wentz, told me that my grandpa [illegible] and some neighbors built my grandfather's house that he had ordered from Montgomery Ward for $500.00.

I was born with asthma and sick a lot at that time.

I remember we had a German shepherd dog named Scrap. My brother and I always got to play in the yard when Dad was mowing grass. We would build houses and roadways out of the grass. One day a man came up to my dad and wanted to buy our dog for a Seeing Eye dog. Dad said, "No," and a week later, our dog disappeared. Scrap did not like this man and growled all the time he was there.

The next thing I remember, we moved to Butterbean Ridge, away from the Muskingum River, when I was about four years old, because I was so sick. After we moved I got better.

My dad worked at the Ferro Alloy at that time, until he retired 41 years later. When we lived on Butterbean Ridge, Mom and Dad tapped the maple trees and made maple syrup. It was really good; we also picked berries, raised cows, chickens, ducks, and pigs. Mom canned everything and baked bread. It was so good.

One time, my mother sent my brother to the basement to get a jar of something that she had canned for supper. He didn't come right back up. So she sent me down to get him. My dad was at work.

The basement door was on the outside. I went down the steps to get him. He had a little car playing with it on a table. When I got to the bottom step I seen this snake hanging from the rafter right above his head. I ran back upstairs and hollered for Mom. She came running, picked up the hoe by the back door, and told my brother to back up real slow. She knocked it down and killed it. It was a copperhead. Neither my brother nor I would go back down to the basement after that.

We had a lot of fun on that farm. We got cardboard boxes and made slides out of them. We would put water on a small bank, make it real muddy, and slide down it. It was a lot of fun but we were sure a mess. We had to take a bath outside in a big old round washtub.

There were a lot of things that happened while we lived there, too many to tell.

After a few years we moved to Route 555, to take care of my mother's father, my other grandpa. My grandmother had passed away in a big house with ten rooms.

I remember one time when World War II began, we heard this loud noise, and it started to get dark in the middle of the day. We went outside to see what was going on and the sky was full of bombers going to war. When Dad told me this, I was scared. I thought he meant right here, until he explained it to me. Pearl Harbor had been bombed (1941).

We had an outhouse on this farm. I was afraid to go to it because it was close to a creek and there was always snakes and spiders crawling around. Somebody always had to go up the path and check on it before I would go. My brother thought it was funny; I didn't.

My sister was born that year in the hospital, because my mom had the measles and was very sick. Later, we moved to another farm up the road a little ways on 555. Sometimes, as I got older, I would ride my bike down to check on my grandpa and then he passed away.

On the big farm, we had 200 acres, about 15 head of cattle, eight milk cows, four workhorses, lots of pigs, chickens, cats, and one German shepherd dog. I remember helping Dad milk the cows. We did it by hand, and sometimes they would kick the bucket and spill all the milk. We always had to put their tail under our left knee and hold it there while we milked because they would swing it and hit us in the face causing us to spill the milk. Sometimes while we were milking, we would squirt milk into the farm cats' mouths. That was really something to see; they would sit up on their hind legs and open their mouths. It seemed they got more milk on the outside of their face then in their mouth. My brother and I had to milk these cows some mornings before we went to school, by hand, because my dad would be working at the Ferro Alloy and the cows udder would be too full of milk to go all that long to be milked, about 8:30 or 9:00 a.m.

We did all the milking by hand. Sometimes my hands would cramp. After milking we had to run the milk through a separator. There were a lot of pieces to it. It would separate the cream from the milk, and then Dad would bring the milk and cream to Zanesville to sell it. Sometimes we would keep some cream and make butter with it.

Living on the farm was rough, it seemed like there was always work to be done. If we weren't helping with feeding and milking the cows, we were feeding the chickens and pigs, hoeing in the garden, helping in the hay field or cornfield.

One time, when Dad was at work, the cows got out of the pasture and into the garden. I went to put them back in the pasture; I had a big long heavy stick to scare them, I thought. There was this half-grown bull who decided he wasn't going to be put back. He started to paw the ground. I decided I wasn't going to fool with him and took off running for the house. I looked back and he was right behind me. I made it to the screened in porch just in time. I was glad no one was watching. They would think it was funny. I didn't. He stayed out in the yard till Dad came home from work and put him in the pasture.

We had banty hens and a rooster. This rooster, if he got out of the chicken pen, he would always head for the backyard and if he caught us out, he would chase us. Dad said if he didn't behave, we would have him for Sunday dinner.

We had a lot of good food back then, in the 40's. My mom canned everything, vegetables from the garden, berries that we picked, fruit from the trees, apples, peaches, etc., and meat when Dad butchered, like pork or beef. When Dad butchered there would be two or three men help him. We had lots of pork chops, sausage, headcheese, ugh, I hated that, liver, steak, ribs, etc, it was good eating.

I remember one time I was helping in the hay field. The wagon was pulled by a team of our horses called Charlie and Prince. I was on the wagon stomping the hay down. When my brother and Dad threw it on the wagon there was a blacksnake on one of the bundles. Dad killed it. From then on, I got to drive the horses and my brother stomped the hay.

There was one winter I will never ever forget in 1950. We had a blizzard. I had got married and had my oldest son. At the time he was one year old. My husband and father worked at the Ferro Alloy. We lived in a two-room house on the farm. They had went to work on the night shift. The next morning my husband and Dad couldn't get home from work because the roads were all closed because of the snow. They stayed at my grandpa and grandma's house in Duncan Falls. They had to stay three days because of the roads. I had to shovel my way down a big long sidewalk, cross the road to the barn; I had to carry water by bucket full to each animal because I couldn't get the barn door open for them to go to the trough to drink. Four horses, all of the cattle, the pigs and then milk the cows. By the time I was done, it was about 1:00 p.m., almost time to start all over again. I did this for three days.

I swore I would never live on a farm ever again. I was so tired. Don't get me wrong, the farm is great now because there is a lot of modern machinery to help.

There were good times too. I grew up belonging to the 4H. We had barn dances where everybody would come. We took things to the fair, we would have a good time, we had Halloween parties, and all the neighbor kids would come.

Some of the things I remember, when World War II was going on, we had rations for sugar and canning things, also, gas for the farm machinery.

My mom cooked on a coal stove and the food was great. We also had a coal furnace which kept us warm in the winter. We had a nice floor model radio. My dad always listened to the fights, Joe Lewis. Everybody had to be very quiet. My mom listened to Stella Dallas in the daytime and we also got to listen to Jack Benny, Amos and Andy and The Shadow knows.

Mom and Dad would have company sometimes and play Euchre. Us kids learnt to play at an early age. While they played cards, we would play checkers, tag, hide and seek, jump rope, or who could make the funniest face without making us laugh.

The most memorable people in my life were my grandparents. My Grandpa Wentz was a retired schoolteacher. He had taught school in a one-room schoolhouse. He was quiet, reserved, and we respected him. It was always fun to play checkers with him. We really thought we were smart when we beat him, but always found out later that he let us beat him.

I could go on and on remembering things. When they came to Zanesville on Saturdays, Grandma had eggs, butter, cake, pies and cookies to sell. She had regular customers. Grandpa would wait at the corner of 5th and Main in front of Kresages and talk with neighbors that came to town.

I'm now 76, my birthday being February 15th. Talking about these memories has brought back a lot more than I could write down. My first marriage went bad and I married a second time to a wonderful man, Tom Sperduti. He passed on November 2004. I raised six children by my first marriage and I have passed on some of my memories to them. They are all in the 50's except my youngest who passed at age 30 from cancer.

Broken Teeth and Portable Movies

by Viola Reed of Barnesville, Ohio
Born 1914

My family lived on a farm in Beaver Township, Noble County, in southeastern Ohio, 40 miles west of Wheeling, West Virginia. Families operated their own farm manually and had diversified farming. There was plenty of work to keep family members occupied all day every ay. Never heard kids say they were bored in those days for lack of something to do. We worked all week and looked forward to weekends for activity. Church activities predominated then.

The schoolroom was a good place to exchange cold germs. Kids had impetigo, colds and headaches. We carried lunch boxes each day. There was a water well on the school lot to provide drinking water, but no way to wash hands. If one person had a cold, chances were good everyone in the room would also. There were four grades in each room, a total of 20-25 kids. Castor oil in orange juice was the standard cure. I was probably a high school graduate before I would drink orange juice and enjoy it.

We had a party telephone line with a total of 16 subscribers. To "nib" was a pastime for many of the 16 families. The conversation could last for 45 minutes or an hour, but if an emergency arose it was alright to ask for the line long enough to call a doctor or notify if there was a fire somewhere.

Saturday night baths were quite an occasion. You lowered the blinds and brought your pan of bath water to the living room in front of the grate fire. It was cozy and warm. Body odors were easier to control then than they are now, with all the chemicals in everything that pollutes the human body. And the deodorant we use with the aluminum ingredient compounds the issue today.

We never had a wind up record player until 1938 after my grandfather died. My dad's sister came to help take care of her father in his last years. After his death she gave her record player to my sister and me before she returned to her home in Nebraska. We thoroughly enjoyed that Edison player.

We had a washhouse where we did the laundry in the summer. That operation was moved to the kitchen in winter months. You moved the dasher back and forth manually to rub the clothes clean. A galvanized tub held the garments as they dropped from the wringer into the tub of rinse water. You added indigo blue to whiten the clothes and you used homemade soap to clean the clothes.

My mother baked white bread and it had to be baked about three times a week to keep us supplied. She was a good cook and enjoyed preparing the food her family enjoyed. We were never without cookies in the cookie jar. We had cake on the weekends. She taught my sister and me to bake and cook. My sister was older than me and after she started to school, I was a lonely one, but Mother took me to the kitchen with her. When she baked bread, she would give me a hunk of dough. I would knead it and then put it in a toy-size bread pan to rise. It was baked along with Mother's bread for the rest of the family. Because Mother allowed me to participate in the activities in the kitchen, I thought I should have a little utensil just like hers.

In those days, every family had a Sears Roebuck and or Montgomery and Ward catalogue. In the fall when we received the new issue, we always selected a complete new outfit of clothing. We never received a complete new outfit, but if we needed some garment we would probably receive it for Christmas. Clothing or a book was Christmas, no toys. One year, I found in one of the catalogues a set of aluminum cookware for youths. I announced that was what I wanted for Christmas and they could forget the clothing. On Christmas morning when I came downstairs and looked under the tree, there was a box labeled for me. On top of the box, sat a miniature teakettle. My mother said I jumped 12-inches off the floor with a shriek, "My little teakettle!" We always stopped to see the grandparents for a brief time on Christmas, so I took the little teakettle with me. One grandmother thought I was bringing it to her, I was quick to tell her it was mine.

Mother made all our clothes. She had been a seamstress before she married, so she was skilled in the art and taught us to sew as well as all the other household chores.

I liked all my teachers as I was taught to respect them. After all, they were helping teach me how to live. Their guidance has been very helpful all of my life.

There was much snow during winter months, from November to mid-March, then it would warm up and you could discard your long underwear and that was a welcome event.

One day on the playground, we were playing "prison base." One of the smaller boys and me collided. He was shorter than me and his forehead struck me in the mouth. It knocked out one of my front teeth. They took me to the local doctor's office in the village. He took three stitches in my lip without anesthetic. My lip was numb from the blow and the first stitch was okay, the second, I could feel it, the third, the lip was no longer numb!

When I was in the eighth grade, two men from Summerfield, John Kent and Elwell Moore, had a portable moving picture outfit, which they brought to the village occasionally and we had a movie on Saturday night. They were usually western pictures. The roll of film would break at least once and sometimes two or three times during the evening, but we didn't care, it was something to do and time was not that important in our young lives.

Chevrolet Agency in Batesville in 1925 owned by George and John Atkinson.

When I was a sophomore, one of my classmates showed an interest in me. He wanted to take me home from school one day. He had his father's car and my home was about one and a half miles east of the village. On the way, on a straight stretch of road, he reached over and kissed me. From then on I knew who was foremost in my dreams, but it didn't last long. His folks moved to another town and the girls in that town knew he was a charmer!

High school days were interesting, basketball for both boys and girls. I was on the girl's team. We were winning the game from the number one team in the county. The opponents were frustrated and unhappy with us. In an attempt to overcome us, one member of the opponent's team jumped into the back of one of our team as she shot a basket and injured our teammate. The team effort fell apart and we lost the game.

Many roads in the county were dirt as was the case in Beaver Township. In the summer of 1927, State Route 147 was graded for travel and topped with slag. It started south of Sarahsville and ran across the county through Batesville and on to Barnesville, then to the Ohio River at Bellaire. It was graded well for summer traffic, dust and all, and we enjoyed it. Winter rain, snow, freezing and spring thaw changed it from being a joy. It became impassable: no cars, wagons or buggies, and riding horses was dangerous, fearing the horse might pull a shoe in the deep, stiff mud. There were no berms to walk, they were graded away. My sister and I walked over the hill and through the meadow to the cemetery, just east of the village, where we picked up the road for a few rods on into the Corporation. In the evening when we left school, all the youth living east of the village grouped together to travel together until we came to the first crossroad, when the group would divide. We had much fun and thoroughly enjoyed the members of the group. Everyone wore four buckle galoshes so we were prepared for the mud, but glad when April wind and warm sunshine dried the mud enough that roads could be graded, ruts filled in and travel could resume in its normal way.

I was reared in a conservative home atmosphere with not too many opportunities for pranks. There were always chores to do at home in the evening. One year at Halloween, a cousin came to our home in the evening and we went out with him for a couple hours. We put people's milk buckets on the roof of the chicken house. The next morning we found our milk buckets on the roof of the chicken house. He returned to our home later in the evening to remind us it was Halloween at all farm homes. Some folks were brave enough to tear down a buggy and take it to a rooftop, then reassemble it. The next morning on the way to school, there it was on the roof of the skating rink. What energy youth has.

I neglected to say there were no milking machines in this area at the time.

Our neighbor raised guineas. They are profitable for they lay an egg each day. They are also God's best alarm clock. Every morning at daybreak they begin the day with their song. "Shimmy shack, shimmy shack, potter ack, potter ack," and if they are very close to you, you can't escape the sound of their shrill voices.

Especially memorable people in my life were Mother, Father and Sister (Mary and Forest Reed and Doris). They helped me formulate a foundation for living that has taken me through all the ups and down of ordinary living as well as the crisis times in life. They have all been gone for over 35 years, but the memory lingers with their teaching and guidance. Thank God for his watchful care.

There was no T.V. or radio idols at that time in our area to mimic. There was radio in the 1930's. We had telephone and newspapers in the 1920's and that was the means of communications outside the local community. Today this sounds like living in the dark ages. To me, it was some of the greatest lessons in life. You learned to live with family members, neighbors and friends. I am glad I have lived from the horse and buggy days to the space age.

What it Takes to Be a Real Farmer

By Elizabeth Whited of Cumberland, Ohio
Born 1941

This might not be considered the "old days," but someday it will be. I married a soldier in 1968. We finished up his enlistment in Colorado Springs, Colorado and then moved back to Cumberland, Ohio to join his family on the farm. His mother and father were raising four of their grandchildren and had moved to Cumberland from Barberton, Ohio.

I was a young bride who had a lot to learn about life and southeastern Ohio as well as doing some growing up. Ever since I learned to read, I had read novels that included living on a farm and I thought that this was what I wanted. I was thrilled to get the chance to live this life.

My husband, our son and I arrived at the farm in the fall. The family welcomed us with open arms and we soon settled in. I got to help bring in wood to stockpile for winter. My mother-in--law taught me how to can tomatoes, green beans, corn and peaches and to put up jelly. Everyday was a beehive of activity. We started by going to the barn in the early morning and milking the five head of Guernsey cows and the one Jersey cow by hand. The kids would come over and do their morning chores and then go back to the big house and get ready for the school bus while Mom and I finished the milking and turned the cows out to pasture. There were other cows that we were not milking plus a big whiteface beef cow. Milking was done twice a day; in the early morning and at 4:00 p.m.

When we first came to the farm, my father-in-law gave me a large sow named Porkchops and the Jersey cow named Buttercup. Porkchops was huge and had a clean, dry corner of the barn to stay in. It had been a horse stable, but they converted it to a pig pen when Porkchops arrived at the farm. She was white and when she stood on her hind legs she could hook her front legs over the top plank of the stable and stick her head over to holler and squeal for her breakfast and supper. She was rather terrifying as she was taller than six feet.

Buttercup was a tiny little cow; she had a lovely yellow coat and a sweet "dished in face" and tiny curled horns she wore like a tiara. She had liquid brown eyes and a wide black nose and was beautiful to look at. Unfortunately, she did not like me. Her udder was so small that I could only use two fingers and a thumb to milk her. I should say, *try* to milk her because I would get a couple squirts of milk and then a ridge would pop out on her round udder and no more milk would come forth. She had locked it up and was holding her milk. I would complain to my mother-in-law and she would trade places with me. She would place her stool and sit down with the bucket and soon I would hear the hiss of a steady stream of milk hitting the bucket.

In the meantime, I would go and milk the big, gentle brown and white Guernsey cow that Mom had been milking. The Guernsey's udders and teats were so large that I could use my whole hand to milk with. Milking in the barn was a lovely, quiet time.

Today, 40 odd years later, I can close my eyes and recall those wonderful days. The cool of the morning, the cows noisily chewing on their hay, the hiss, hiss of milk into the bucket, the morning sun creeping through the dusty window, barn cats crossing the beams above us waiting for their portion of the warm milk to be poured into their big flat pan, the earthy smell of the barn and occasional snippets of conversation between my mother-in-law and me. I felt close to the natural world during those moments. As always, there are good times and bad times in each day, this was always one of the good time

I remember once I was pregnant with our first daughter; it was time for the four o'clock afternoon milking and I recall crossing the field to the barn, the sun was warm because it was spring. I had on a dress and knee high rubber boots, the bucket was in my hand and I was happy because I was living my dream on this farm. I felt like a milkmaid in my dress; my hair lifting in the gentle breeze, the sunshine on my face; it was idyllic. The grass was turning from winter brown to bright green and the cows were eating their fill of the fresh bounty that nature was pushing forth. I entered the barn, always dim with dusty motes floating about and started letting the waiting cows in the milking parlor. Mom and I hooked the chains around their necks and started washing their udders before milking. Something happened just outside the gate to the milking parlor, I don't remember now what, but I stepped through the gate to take care of it. When I was done, I turned around and opened the gate, I took one step back through and suddenly everything went black. I could feel a warm wetness on top of my head and down the front of me. I think I mentioned that it was spring. One thing that happens in the spring is that the cows eat the green grass and their bowels get loose. As I stepped through the gate the cow closest to me had cut loose and shot cow manure across the manure ditch and up against the barn wall. In the process, manure had hit my glasses (thank God not my eyes) and splashed on top of my head. When it hit the wall and the floor, splashes caught the front of me and even splashed up under my dress and landed on my legs! I shook off my glasses and thought that I could either be sick, angry or laugh. I stormed over to the farmhouse and hollered for my father-in-law. When he stuck his head out the door I asked him if he was happy because he always said I wouldn't be a true farmer until one of the cows pooped on my head. He found the situation extremely funny. (I did too, but it took awhile.) A quick shower later, I was able to go back and help finish the milking with a true appreciation for caution.

It was quite an adjustment when winter arrived at the big white farm house perched high on a hill. It was heated with a fireplace in the front room and a coal furnace in the basement. The furnace was a big surprise to me because I thought that coal furnaces had been done away with 20 years earlier. I learned a lot in a short time about being cold, dressing properly, heat, soot and dust.

The furnace was located directly under the huge old bathroom and this was the warmest room in the house. We had to be careful about not letting clothing touch the register as they would be ruined from the intense heat. It was a gravity fed furnace meaning that there was no fan to force the heated air throughout the house so the kitchen was pretty warm and during the day the downstairs remained livable. When nighttime fell, it was a different story. Grandpa didn't believe in television so even though we had one, it was not turned on. We either gathered in the kitchen around the large table or in the front room around the fireplace. We read, put together puzzles, talked, worked on crafts and passed the time until bedtime in front of the big old fireplace. It didn't seem to throw heat out into the room very far and it had no draft control and when they banked the fire before going to bed, the heat from the furnace was drawn up the chimney all night long so that by daytime the temperature in the house was dramatically cold.

When we had arrived from Colorado they were expecting us, as my husband had promised to come live on the farm and help to raise his niece and nephews. We were ushered in and that evening they showed us our room. It was long and seemed narrow because of the huge old wooden wardrobe that took up one part of the room. A huge dresser sat across from our double bed. I had never seen a wardrobe before and quickly learned that it was basically a freestanding closet and was in place because the room had none. The room had no heat register and the bed was piled high with quilts. After the first cold night, I started to wear my husband's extra cold-weather long underwear that the Army had provided him with. We were a matched pair: even though he was very warm blooded, he wore a set also.

My next culture shock was not having everything within a 15 minute drive. I was spoiled by the big cities of Cuyahoga Falls and Akron. You could go to any type store or restaurant within just a few miles. Not so in Cumberland! You had to travel 25 to 35 miles to get to Cambridge or Zanesville. This was really hard on me. It took me about a year to get used to travel time. Speaking of travel, when driving in the city; staying in the lines on the pavement was an absolute. If you didn't, you were pretty much guaranteed to be in a fender bender. Everyone in the Cumberland area was so much more casual about where they drove! They would cross the center line, pass on a double yellow and wander up the middle of dirt roads. And there was no white line up the side of the road, let alone curbs! I had grown up and driven all my life on curbed streets and had a terrible time adjusting to those wide open spaces. I was so glad when the Governor had lines put on the right side of the road. They are a life saver.

We had so many adventures on the farm. We were not rich, but we had good times and hard work that fulfilled us. Eventually, my husband and I bought a trailer that we set up in the pasture next to his mom and dad's house. Until we got it fenced off the cattle used to stand around and peek through the windows to watch us and our TV when we had it on. Once, my husband had a western on and there was a cattle stampede. The cows outside the trailer heard them bawling and mooing and ended up answering them with their own moos.

Another time, quite a while later, I had my son, a daughter that was walking and her sister, who was still crawling, when my mother-in-law informed me that the grandkids had been out to bring the cows in to milk and found the Herford's new born calf dead in the field. It looked like a hunter had shot it between the eyes and she was going to check it out. I said that I would go too and gathered up my girls. I put the youngest on my back and tied her into place with a piece of an old chenille bedspread. We started out and my mother-in-law kept pointing out to me that our housedog, a small black part cocker spaniel mutt, Mitty, was following us. I kept telling her that it was okay, that I wouldn't let Mitty eat the dead calf. Oh boy, was I ever being ignorant. The baby on my back was asleep after I had taken five steps. She is still like that to this day; put her in a car and she is out within 15 minutes. Anyhow, we walked behind the barn, down the path to the creek, crossed the creek, climbed the bank and took the long curving path through the upper pasture until we got to a wooded ravine. I took four steps into the woods and I heard the Herford beef cow snorting. I saw her put her head down, (she had an awesome set of horns) and take after Mitty. In a blinding flash I realized why Mom didn't want the dog to come. No cow would let a dog near her newborn calf. Mitty ran in a large circle with the cow hot on her heels and then she turned and ran towards me for help. When I realized what was going on, I turned and started to run with my baby on my back. I heard the cow thundering behind me and saw Mitty run through my churning legs and then – Wham! The cow hit me between her horns with her head. She made contact just below my buttocks and threw me into the air. I remember thinking, I have to stay upright and land on my feet so I don't land on my little girl and so that I can keep running. That was just what I did. I landed and like a cat I kept on going. By then Mitty was out of sight and well on her way back home so the Herford was satisfied and backed off to return to her calf. I made a quick return to the trailer, this time in a direct line, by hiking down the ravine, crossing the creek and climbing up the other side and cutting through woods and pasture. The baby on my back slept through it all. My other daughter had her adventure when we crossed the creek. It was wider than she could jump and too deep to wade so my mother-in-law had one of the grandsons go over to the other side. The plan was to take my daughter by the arms and swing her across so that he could grab her and set her down. Unfortunately he caught her legs by her calves and of course she bent at the knees and swung backwards down over the creek. He raised her up, but her hair trailed down into the water and scared her pretty good.

The elementary school was in town, it had classes Kindergarten through six. The first Booster Club we attended had very few people and they tried to talk my husband into being president. He refused and never attended another meeting. I must say, despite that inauspicious beginning, the school was the core of the town. I was surprised when I saw that everybody in town and from the township around Cumberland came to the functions. The auditorium was always full to bursting with standing room only. It would give me a thrill of pride to see all those people supporting the school and the children. Today, all of that is gone. The schools consolidated and the kids are all bussed away. The school is closed and with it, the heartbeat of the village. This is just one story about how the village of Cumberland is trying to survive loss.

The village became official the same year that Chicago was established. At that time, there were hundreds of farms in the surrounding area. The village had grocery stores, hotels, jewelry stores, drug stores, a blacksmith, a lumber mill, a creamery, a bank, a post office, a hardware store and more.

The coal company moved in and bought out the farms and Cumberland lost a population base. Still struggling to survive, it downsized. Eventually, the population base was established at lower numbers as the strip mine hired laborers who lived in the area. They also brought in people from their home mine in Kansas. A lively business continued and supported two gas stations, a funeral home, two groceries, a post office and a bank.

The bank got robbed and closed down. Eventually the mine was sold and most of the workers were laid off. Cumberland struggled on and currently has one grocery store. The gas stations are all gone; victims of more stringent EP A rules.

When we first moved to town, there were no house numbers. Mail was sent to either Route 1 - in the village, or Route 2 - out of the village. It worked quite well as everybody knew everybody. UPS delivery would go to the local grocery store and get directions. The phone company finally put its foot down and said it would not install one more phone unless house numbers were assigned. A few years later we got 911 services and had to be sure that the village and township numbers were in place.

My time on the farm was a learning experience. When we canned, the kitchen would get so hot and steamy; it made it miserable for everyone. Many of the houses in Cumberland had a small out-building that used to be a summer kitchen. All the cooking was done there so that the main house would stay cool. Our farm did not have that luxury. One year my mother-in-law had more than usual to "put by" and she decided that she would not do it in the house because of the heat it generated. Therefore, she went out in the back garden behind the house to a spot that had been cleared, and set up an old stovetop on bricks. She had the grandkids gather up a lot of wood, branches and such and stockpile them nearby. She got two oval canners ready and after a good hot fire was going she put them on the stovetop and started the canning process. I know there was a temperature gauge involved somehow, but memory fails me when I try to remember the details. Anyhow she spent hours out in the garden, feeding the fire and keeping the canners going. Shortly after she started, a brisk breeze built up making her task even harder but she kept at it.

I used to call winter the long quiet time because chores were at a minimum and there was a hush as the snow muffled the noises. As I said, we lived towards the top of a hill. There were days when we never saw a car come down the road in front of the house. It was considered a busy day if two cars went by. We could sit on the front porch swing and hear a car turning off the main highway onto our dirt lane. If the kids were playing out in the road, we would holler "car" and warn them out of the way. The mail box was at the end of the lane, on the highway.

In the winter, we would take a sled and slide down our lane to the flat and then walk to the highway to get the mail. Once, in the summer, the oldest grandkid walked down to get the mail and a long time later he still was not back. Finally, Pappy got in the car and went to find him. He was sitting on a large rock reading a magazine and had lost track of time.

We had lots of adventures on the farm. Once as we (me, Mom and the grandkids) left the barn after the afternoon milking, dusk was falling and we could hear a car coasting slowly down the hill, its door opened and closed and we realized that someone was trying to sneak over to our fuel tank area to steal our gas. The boys charged over to the big house and ran through the back door alerting their Grandpa and ran out the front to go down the sidewalk to the fuel tank. There was shouting, whooping and hollering going on from the barn and the house. You never heard such a commotion. Suddenly there was the report of a gun going off as Pappy shot straight up in the air to warn the thief off. The coasting car picked up speed and cruised up to the walking thief who jumped in probably in fear for his life. The motor turned over and they sped on down the hill. Word must have gotten around because we were never bothered again.

One Christmas Eve, we were in the barn milking and I realized that this is what Mary and Joseph had done so many years ago. I tried to teach the children about what a special night it was. We walked out when we were done and the cold wind was blowing and the bright moon lit the night up. There were clouds swirling around. We stopped for a moment and just felt the closeness to the earth and the peace of the night marking that special time so many Christmases ago.

Then there was the time one of mom and dad's daughters and her husband were visiting them. We were living in the trailer in the pasture next to the house and that evening they came over to the trailer to visit. They called us outside and there in the field and trees and the hay field across the road were thousands and thousands of fire flies. They were a flashing on and off in the dark. We didn't have security lights because we preferred the darkness at night. I have not got the words to describe that special night. It was warm, with a soft gentle breeze, the normal night noises were present and this extraordinary display from all those fireflies took our breath away. We sat on the porch and marveled at the performance. It touched us all.

If you live in the city, you know that all of the night sky cannot be seen because of the glow from the street lights. When I moved to the Cumberland farm, I was thrilled when one dark night I looked up and saw the Milky Way. I had thought that I would never see that sight and I never ceased to marvel whenever I got to see it.

When I lived in Cuyahoga Falls, my parents let me have a small patch of yard to grow flowers and vegetables. It was never that much, but I enjoyed working in the dirt and bringing onions and radishes to the table. When I moved to Cumberland, my mom-in-law taught me how to plant a real garden. We would unravel string from where it was wrapped around a stick and make long straight rows to plant in. The seeds would be "dropped" into place and covered. I remember one year we had a huge plot for sweet corn. We trekked out to the field and laid out the rows in the plowed ground. It was like hoeing and moving around dusty chunks of soil because the ground was so dry. The sun was beating down and it was so hot that you could feel your heart thumping each time it beat. There was dust and dryness everywhere. Personally, I thought it was a waste of time to plant. When we were done we put our tools away and cleaned up. A few days later it rained and the dry clumps in the field turned to moist soil and the corn began to sprout. In a few months we began to walk down the rows of green corn, taller than my head, and harvest the sweet corn. I couldn't help but wonder at the miracle that had occurred. We enjoyed roasting ears and then I learned how to can and freeze sweet corn.

Time went by. By now, we had three children and the trailer was too small. It was time to get a house. We ended up leaving the farm and living in Cumberland Village. When I look back at our life on the farm, it was a good time. We all did a lot of growing up and I learned so much about self sufficiency and gardening and life. His mom and dad had survived the Great Depression and WWII. They knew about times harder that we have ever experienced. They are gone now, but their life lessons were passed to us. If hard times come again, we will be able to draw on what they taught us to make it until good times come again.

The Booming Maytag and Chickie Brownie

by Lillian Elaine Touvell Tucker of Lore City, Ohio
born in 1932

Years ago, when we lived on Finley Avenue in Cambridge, the gang (we called ourselves) used to all play together, and our neighbors had a shed. We would catch lightning bugs, put them in a jar, and sit around them telling ghost stories.

Also, on Saturday, we would all go up to the Strand Movie Theater and sit all day watching the westerns. We would either take a big peck sack of popcorn or stop at the ten cents store and get a nickel's worth of kisses. Back then, five cents bought a big sack of candy.

We walked everywhere. To school every day, to Garfield, which was many blocks away. No one ever thought of being driven anywhere, like today's kids. On the last day of school, we would meet at school, go as a group to march in the Memorial Day (Declaration Day, it was called) parade. We walked to the courthouse, and there was no parkway then, and sometimes out to the Northwood Cemetery. Believe me, it was a long walk, but we never thought a thing of it.

Lore City Airport in the 1940s.

When my grandfather and his wife (second one) separated, we went out on the farm to live with him to help take care of him. He had no electricity. Water was out of a pitcher pump. Not what we were used to. So we went by bus to Old Washington School. I was eighth grade, my brother in grade school. We studied by oil lamps. No inside plumbing. An outhouse sit on a hill. I was always afraid it would fall over.

Grampa had an old Maytag washer, gas powered. When it was washing, it was boom, boom, boom all over the hills. You could hear it for miles. My mom was scared to death of it and wouldn't use it unless Dad or Grampa was around to start it for her. I can still hear it.

Grampa didn't like us to make pets of his animals, but my brother and I had a pet chicken each. His was Chickie Billy, and mine was Chickie Brownie. We would call those chickens way out in the woods, and they would come running. 'Course, we had a dog since a baby, and Dad had airplanes out at Cambridge Airport (the old one). Pal would greet the people coming in on planes with a leg on their suitcases. We did get embarrassed over that.

We did lots of camping. Dad loved it. We were camping at Wills Creek Dam in the '40s. My uncle was with us. On the way home, we saw three little skunks. I said, "Oh, I've always wanted a pet skunk." Uncle Wayne jumped out. We didn't see the mother, but she sprayed Uncle Wayne. We didn't get a skunk, and we had to smell this all way home, and us with our heads out the window.

Uncle had been hurt in the Army and had no sense of smell. So he was mad at us 'cause we were trying to keep away from him all way home. Mom had lots of tomato juice she had canned, and she soaked his shirt. That shirt was on the line for days. I don't know if it was ever out of it.

I remember a big snow in 1950 or thereabouts. Two of my school friends had to stay, as couldn't get home. My mother first had to go down and open the restaurant she thought. She got stuck in the snow and had to have one of the guys pull her out. She would always get panicky.

This was after we moved from farm to Lore City. Dad had built the airport there. Dad and a man in Cambridge, that was also a pilot. He later was killed in a plane crash in Cambridge, several years later, after they built the Lore City Flying Service.

My favorite teacher was Mrs. Morgan in the third grade at Garfield. She was always so nice. But she was also the only teacher to paddle me. Three of us kids were giggling, and we all three had to get in front of class, over her knee, one by one, and get a really hard paddling. I didn't cry, but one other one did. The boy was always getting us in trouble, causing us to laugh.

My grandson is always wanting to know about the "good old days." He's twenty and loves to hear about my olden day stories. Of course, there are more, but I hope you enjoy the ones I've wrote about. I'm sorry I went over six pages.

My mother died a year ago, but she always loved to tell the tales of old. She was ninety-six.

Salt on a Bird's Tail

by Jean Overman of Zanesville, Ohio
born in 1917

My grandfather, George W. Richards, owned a thriving grocery and feed store, located on West Main, in the middle of the block, between Pine street and the Y Bridge in Zanesville, Ohio. It was a typical store of that era, complete with a pot-bellied stove; wall-phone you had to ring in; a roll of paper and a ball of old-fashion scales with various weights to balance; a cash register with a loud, PING; plus a rolltop desk in his office.

Some of my favorite memories are connected to my grandfather and his store. On Pine Street, between West Main and Dug Road, was an alley leading behind the buildings fronting West Main, where farmers would drive their wagons into a courtyard space between the store proper and a small barn that housed the feed store. In the process of loading the wagons, some seeds were usually scattered over the ground. Consequently, there were always a lot of birds skittering around, pecking away.

My grandmother had a canary in a cage. I loved that canary and I wanted a canary in a cage. I probably was only two or three years old at that time. My grandfather very solemnly told me, if I could manage to sprinkle salt on one of those birds' tails, I would catch him and have my own bird in a cage. He even furnished the salt. I had my eye on one particular big, fat robin. So I spent many happy, busy summer hours stalking those birds, sneaking up on them, trying to get close enough to sprinkle salt on their tails. Needless to say, the birds were faster than I. I was never fortunate enough to have a canary in a cage.

One connection to the store includes my grandfather and father. When I was six years old, we moved from West Muskingum Avenue to Brown Street, at Terrace Point. My grandfather lived next door, but facing what was called, "Frazeysburg Road." For several years, on one summer night, my father would waken me with a whisper, "Shhh, don't wake the others." I would dress quickly and we'd hurry out to join my grandfather, who was awaiting for us in his Model T Ford. We'd drive into town, down to the bottom of Market Street. All was quiet, with only a few streetlights glowing and then suddenly, puffing and chugging loudly, noise and lights erupting, the circus had come to town!

Roust-a-bouts were shouting orders. Some wakened animals were roaring, the elephants trumpeting! What excitement and fun! The elephants were off first and were put to work getting the various wagons off. One by one, they were hitched up to the elephants to be pulled up to Main Street, over the Y Bridge, and out to Gant Park, where they immediately started to set up the tents. For many years, especially when the circus was held at Gant Park, The circus would have a parade and I would sit on the steps of my grandfather's store and watch as the elephants lumbered by with their trunks holding the tails of those ahead of them. There were pretty ladies wearing sparkling outfits on dancing horses and sometimes a wagon cage with lions or tigers. Quite a few clowns scampering about and, of course, a calliope.

My grandfather's store was two or three steps up from the pavement. On either side of the door were large plate glass windows. Prior to the circus, an advance man would be in town, setting up advertisement. My grandfather always allowed them to put their posters in his windows. For this privilege, he received several free tickets to the show. For quite a few years, I never missed a circus!

My grandfather liked to build things. He liked to work with wood. And over the years, he made me several articles and toys. The first was a toy box, a rectangular wooden chest with a hinged lid. He lined it; he actually papered it with wallpaper. He padded the lid and covered it all with what was called cretonne.

He also made me a desk, similar to his rolltop desk, but smaller, of course, and without the rolltop. It was higher with longer legs, so he made me a stool to sit on rather then a chair. It also had all the little shelves and pigeonholes.

My grandfather's store was strictly a grocery store. He didn't handle meat or dairy products. For meat, you went to a butcher shop. There was one in the next block, called John's sometimes. When I was there with my mother, John would give me a raw wiener. To this day I still like raw wieners.

In his store, my grandfather carried primarily what we call staples: sugar, flour, salt, potatoes, onions, spices, and of course, fresh vegetables in season.

Oranges came in a sturdy wooden crate, rectangular with a wooden divider across the middle, making two square spaces. He took one square space from another crate and added it to the first two. Laying the three squares on its side he cut holes in the sides and back for windows, and in the dividers, for doors between rooms. He then painted the outside white and papered the inside. I had the nicest dollhouse that a child could ever have.

Up until and during the first year of the Depression, my mother, Ruth (Richards) Bowers, made most of my clothes, especially dresses and black sateen bloomers. (Now I wonder, why black? Why not white? Or even pink?) I don't remember how I came to do it: I was eight years old and should have known better, but I had a pair of scissors in my hand and was cutting away. Only what I was cutting on was the bodice of a dress my mother was in the process of making for me. I think my ears are still ringing from the scolding I received!

In Depression days, there wasn't much choice in fabrics. If people couldn't afford new material, many items would be made from flour and feed sacks, or used material. I believe my dress was made from one of my mother's old black, long skirts. But Mother didn't despair. She put a patch in the hole I had cut in the dress and took bright colored floss and embroidered a bouquet of flowers, completely covering the patch. So no one knew but my mother and me that there had been a hole in my new dress.

Moxahala Park was an important part of my childhood. It was located approximately five miles south of Zanesville. It was a vibrant, bustling place in its day. It had a midway with food and game booths, and an arcade. There was a merry-go-round and a little later, a tilt-a-whirl and a swimming pool. There was also a wooden roller coaster which fascinated me, but I had no desire to ride it. There were several roofed, large pavilions that were great for family reunions. And, of course, an open-air dance hall. Years later, an enclosed dance hall was built. And the old one became, I believe, a skating rink. For a good many years, the Richards family reunion was held at Moxahala Park. I started looking forward to it as soon as school was out. I nearly always got a new dress, homemade of course, and a quarter, which had to last me all day. But, hey, it only cost a nickel to ride the merry-go-round then. However, there were still lots of free things for a group of young cousins to get into.

My mother, Ruth (Richards) Bowers, was a schoolteacher. As a teacher, she had the summer off. My grandfather, George W. Richards, owned a cottage on the hillside across the road from the park. The family spent a good many days there during the summer. Since it was available, my mother took a job selling tickets for the merry-go-round. On the corner of the path, leading from the midway to the dance hall, there was an ice cream stand, One summer, a tall, handsome young man by the name of Ben Bowers came to work, dipping ice cream cones. He soon met the young lady selling tickets for the merry-go-round. It was love at first sight and they became my parents.

My grandfather's cottage was very primitive, but did have one of the first telephones which was fastened to one of the studs in the wall. There were no wallboards, but the walls were draped from ceiling to the floor with cheap gray material.

One summer night as my grandparents lay in bed, my grandmother began to dream that there was a snake in bed with them and it had crawled over her as it slithered out of the bed. She woke up feeling that the dream felt like it was so real. She was certain there was a snake in the cottage. Almost hysterically, she woke my grandfather, insisting that he get up immediately and search the entire cottage. He demurred, thinking she just was dreaming. Nevertheless, he began to look around. To his surprise, he did find a big blacksnake curled up on the floor between two studs behind the gray drapery. With the help of a broom, he managed to toss the snake outside, and prepared to go back to bed...only to hear my grandmother say she had heard that snakes traveled in pairs, and insisted he continue to search. And sure enough, he found another snake behind the gray drapery and curled around the back of the telephone. I'm not sure, but I believe my grandmother refused to return to that cottage for quite a while. Who could blame her? I've always wondered how the snakes got in there in the first place.

A Lesson in Fiscal Responsibility

By Barbara Hinkle of Wheeling, West Virginia
Born in 1949

Growing up in Barnesville, Ohio in the 1950's was really like scenes out of "Father Knows Best" and "Ozzie and Harriett." Our town had fewer than 5000 people, so everyone knew each other, and many of my teachers had been my mother's teachers. Believe me, a kid couldn't get by with anything. There was always someone to see every misstep a kid made and would promptly report to the parents! By the same token, it was a safe place to live.

Our parents were hard working people who tried to instill their values in us. To that end, my dad did something that made a lasting impression on me.

I was 10 years old and was begging for a 24 inch, two-wheeled bike. My dad finally said, "Come on, we're going up to Western Auto." On our walk up through town, I could hardly contain my excitement! My dad was finally going to buy me a bike!

We arrived at the Western Auto and I raced directly to the bikes. There it was: the girls' blue Murray two-wheeler with a white seat and white handlebar grips. What a beauty! I could conquer the world if I had that bike! Oh, the places I'd go.

Dad eventually appeared and said, "Are you sure that's the one you want?" "Yes, I replied." "Well, come on back to the register." At the cash register, my dad's friend who worked there handed me a payment book. My dad said, "I've worked it out that each week you'll bring your $2.00 allowance up with your payment book, and pay on your bike until it's paid for. It will take you 11 weeks. I've paid the initial payment for you. The bike is $24.95, and you now owe $23.00." I can't tell you the sense of pride I felt! I felt like a grown-up.

My grandmother was recovering from breast cancer and I was paid $2.00 a week to wash her dishes three times a day plus other chores. I couldn't think of a better way to spend my allowance.

Throughout that summer I explored every alley and side street in our town. I became friends with all the department store delivery men because I rode the alleys behind the stores and often stopped to watch various workers unpacking merchandise. It was an idyllic summer.

To this day I thank my dad for not buying my bike, but instead, instilling in me my first lesson in fiscal responsibility. In addition, I am thankful to have grown up in a small town in the 1950's where people trusted each other, and the whole town helped raise its children.

Bits and Pieces

By Donna M. Pirolozzi of Zanesville, Ohio
Born 1927

Loading up a station wagon of four adults and four children and going to an auto-theater (drive-in movie) for a dollar a carload. Stopping at Burger Chef (not King) on the way and picking up 10 burgers and a pitcher of Root Beer for a dollar. Done it many times. I miss the outdoor theaters.

Walking to school in all kinds of weather; summer and winter, rain or snow and never missing a day. From one end of town to the other: no school buses then. Each grade was taught by one teacher. Classes were held in one room. She taught all subjects and there was no study hall, Homework was taken home and completed.

Walking uptown on Sunday afternoon to a movie theater and watching a double feature for ten-cents. Over 12 years of age it was 25-cents.

Bread man bringing the bread and rolls to the door in a large basket for Mom to choose what goodies she wanted to buy. Or if no-one was home leaving the bread in the entranceway. Never had to lock the doors way back then.

Milkman leaving milk on the front porch and by the time the family would go out to get it the cream would have pushed the cap up off the bottle and could be skimmed off for coffee-cream. No Homogenized milk yet. Pasteurized, yes.

Having only two pair of shoes year round. One good pair for Sundays and special occasions, one sturdy pair for school (Buster Browns). They were sturdy, but certainly not very stylish. Broom-stick skirts with peasant blouses. Pleated skirts and sweaters with bobby-socks and saddle shoes.

Having a "cold box" attached to the outside window sill in the winter for storing things that needed to be refrigerated and could be reached by raising the window. Ice-boxes in the kitchen that held a 25 pound block of ice with a pan underneath to catch the water as the ice melted. Ice could be bought at the ice house; or an ice truck would cruise the neighborhoods and carry ice into the home if a resident hailed them down. Some also had a route to deliver and kids would follow the truck and gather pieces of ice off the truck when the driver wasn't looking or was in a home.

Roller-skating on a cement sidewalk with clip-on roller skates. They were fastened to the soles of one's shoes and tightened with a skate key; usually on a string around one's neck.

Anna Drye, Donna Pirolozzi's mother, changing a tire in 1925.

Going to the local woods with a buddy in the spring and picking wildflowers: especially violets.

Playing Hop-scotch, a game of Jacks, Kick-the-can, Fox and Geese, Marbles and Mumbly Peg with the neighborhood kids or a special buddy.

Scooters made from wooden orange crates with skate-wheels. This was a "guy thing."

Swimming with friends in a small creek that had been damned up to make it deeper. These usually ran through a pasture field.

I am sure there are many more that I have overlooked or forgotten. These I do remember.

The first seven years of my life was spent with my grandparents in the rural areas around Coshocton County. At age seven I moved to the big city of Canton, Ohio to enroll in my first year of school. But that is a whole other story.

We moved quite often in those days as the work locations my grandfather had changed fairly often. He was a coal miner with a Mine Foremans Certificate. Many of the well-to-do farmers at that time had small "hole in the wall" mines on their properties. Grandfather was always in demand due to his honest and hard working ways. He usually had anywhere from six to eight men working for/with him at any given time. It was pick and shovel work and anywhere from six to ten cars a day per man was considered a good day's work. The coal was pushed manually in and out of the mine in large carts on a small railroad like track. He walked to and from work as the mines were usually within walking distance of where we were living. The houses we rented were usually, but not always, owned by the owners of the mines. Sort of like a tenant house only it was rented to them for a reasonable amount. It was hard work, but that is the only kind my grandfather knew. He reported the number of cars each man mined a day to my grandmother and she kept a record of the number of cars a day for each man to be turned in for their paychecks. She was a volunteer bookkeeper for the mine owners.

During the summer months the mines would shut down and he went to work helping the same farmers with farm work. Ditching, haying and other odd jobs gave him a paycheck for that period of time. He also put in a large garden and mowed a large yard. His lawn equipment consisted of: a reel push mower, a sickle and a scythe. Those were his main tools. He done all his gardening with a hoe and a rake and maybe a garden plow (similar to a roto-tiller without the motor.) to turn over the soil and make his rows for planting. None of these tools were power operated, only man power. He tells a story that at sometime earlier in their marriage he was offered a job in Michigan working for Ford Motor Company. He and my grandmother loaded their belongings into a horse and buggy and traveled to Michigan. When he arrived there and inquired as to the job offer he was told there was none. They came back to Coshocton County and he swore he would never own a Ford Automobile in his lifetime. And he never did.

Grandmother was just as industrious about her homemaking. She kept a spotless house and was a fantastic cook. At times I often think back on those days with admiration and also amazement at what they both accomplished on any given day of their lives. Her cooking was done on a huge coal burning stove in the kitchen, which had at least two buckets of coal and a woodbin sitting behind or at the end of it. There were ashes to be taken out daily; sometimes twice daily. Fire had to be banked at night to keep it from going out and if it did happen to go out it had to be rebuilt again in the morning before any breakfast could be started. The sitting room had a large parlor furnace (also coal), which kept the sitting room comfortable; and each bedroom had a fireplace for heat. Monday was always washday and Tuesday was for ironing. Sunday, late afternoon, Grandfather would begin carrying water to fill the tubs. There was a big boiler on the stove for boiling white clothes and linens. Hot water was also available from a reservoir built in one end of the stove. There was also a large teakettle on the top of the stove at all times for a quick cup of tea during the day or for a basin of hot water to wash hands, etc.

The water supply usually came from a natural spring that was located approximately half a football field from the house. It was secluded in a shady place and had a cover over it to keep the varmits out. Grandfather would dip his water buckets down and fill them and then carry them to the house for the laundry. When all of the tubs and the boiler were full he brought two full buckets in and sat them on the kitchen cabinet for drinking. A large container was placed under the down-spout to catch rain water which was "soft" water; used for washing hair. None of the homes we lived in at that time had running water or electricity. Lighting was coal-oil (kerosene) lamps and we had a battery run radio.

Grandmother's "washer" was the old fashioned wash-board. She had a wood contraption that opened out with a platform on each side for a tub of water with a hand-wringer in the center. One tub was filled with rinse water and one tub with hot water for washing. Scrub them on the board, wring with the hand-wringer, put through a couple times into the rinse water and repeat the process for two rinses making sure all the soap was out of the clothes. Her "dryer" was a clothes line stretched around the yard from the corner of one building to another and back again, with clothes props to hold up the weight of the clothes and clothes pins to keep the clothes in place on the line. She had a pan of
starch on the stove, "No spray starch" and she starched all her doilies, pillowcases and some of the personal clothing. She generally was out of bed by daybreak and after getting Grandfather's breakfast; packing his bucket and sending him off to work; would have the laundry out on the line before 9:00 A.M. Clothes were washed, dried, some starched and then sprinkled down for ironing on Tuesday.

She took the soapy water in a scrub-bucket and a broom to the outside privy, (half moon and all) and scrubbed it out with a vengeance. She would toss a can full of lime down inside to help control odors and discourage pesky things like flies, etc. Rinse water was used to scrub the porches. Of course with the outside privy came the chamber pots that were cleaned and bleached regularly and were used for night time if needed.

Tuesday was ironing day. Making a hot fire in the coal stove she had two flat-irons that she placed on the stove to get hot. She put up the ironing board and alternated the use of the irons. She would hold it with a potholder and run it across a bread wrapper or anything that may have a waxy surface to make the iron move more smoothly over the article being ironed. When one iron cooled she would switch irons and continue on. I might add that for all the primitive ways of doing her household chores she had a spotless house, beautifully done linens and was a fantastic cook. She would wear a "dust cap" when cleaning. It was shaped like a bonnet and always had a ruffle around the outer edge. This ruffle was ironed as professional as any laundry could have done it.

She was cook, homemaker, janitor, seamstress, wallpaperer and painter. I seem to remember her painting and wallpapering every house we moved into. She canned everything from the garden; saved rags; cut them in strips and braided them together and made throw rugs; she done quilting and made quilts and blankets. She baked bread and made the best biscuits. Our milk came from a neighboring dairy farm. One of my chores was to take an empty Mason jar to the farm and return with a full one. I think they charged a dime; not sure. We bought milk three maybe four times a week. They used part of the milk for separating and then churning for butter. They gave Grandmother a quart of buttermilk, (ugh!) and sometimes a chunk of butter. The butter was a treat since my grandparents bought only Oleo. At that time it came in a white form, looked like lard, with a small packet of coloring to make it look more like butter. They could not afford to buy real butter. They always had a few chickens and a rooster which gave them fresh eggs daily, and a dozen or so extra to sell and a chicken for the pot occasionally. She had "setting hens" usually in the spring which gave her "peeps" to raise.

She would usually take a power-nap in the afternoon. Usually a half hour or less. Then she would start getting things ready to prepare the evening meal. Grandfather usually came home anywhere between four or five o'clock. Supper was always ready to put on the table. There was always a washtub of hot water for him to wash away the coal dust. He wore a couple layers of clothing for work and a miner's hat with a Carbide lamp attached to the front. (No battery powered lamps in those mines.)

Payday was Fridays. Grandfather would bring his pay envelope (cash) home and hand it to Grandmother whose responsibility it was to stretch the money enough to meet the weekly expenses. Saturday was the only day we went to "town." Grandmother had her list for each and everything they would need to purchase. Her shopping list was on-going throughout the week, for each store she intended to shop. There was Bob Stevenson's for groceries, Sanitary Meat Market for meats, Cussin & Ferns for hardware and linoleum rugs. They were the most common in those days. (They were affordable and easy to keep clean.) Newberrys 5 and 10 for sewing supplies, floss for embroidering and small notions she had marked down. She also had a Spiegel Catalog where she occasionally bought a variety of goods. Bob Cartons for footwear, which was not very often. One Sunday go-to-meetin' pair of shoes, 1 everyday pair and possibly a pair of boots. Grandfather wore "Gum Boots" to work and heavy work shoes for outside work, (gardening and mowing, etc.) This made up the number of shoes in the family. No sandals, flip-flops, tennis shoes, high heels, etc. There was also a "Big Little Book" for me. I don't think those are around anymore.

Their gardens contained sweet corn, green beans, yellow wax beans, carrots, leaf lettuce, green onions, radishes, peas, cucumbers, tomatoes, potatoes, turnips, cabbage and depending on the soil maybe strawberries. His garden kept him busy. Needless to say when each vegetable was ready it was canning time for my grandmother. She done a lot of cold packing and canned everything thing that she could get her hands on. Generally apples were forthcoming from a neighbor with an orchard which was turned into apple sauce. When berries were ripe she was up early and out picking black-berries and/ or raspberries for jellies or jams. The pantry was usually bulging at the seams by the end of the gardening season.

As the sun was setting Grandfather would relax in his easy chair; read the paper, which was delivered by the Rural Mail Delivery and was a day late, then he would listen to Amos and Andy, his favorite radio program, maybe some news and then to bed for a well-earned nights rest. We also had an Omar Bread Man who delivered bread twice a week. Once in awhile Grandmother would purchase a package of maple rolls as a special treat for me.

As I look back now I realize their's was a very productive life and a happy life. I never heard any cross words between them. All this from the eyes of a youngster who can look back at those years as the best of my life. It was a happy time, a loving time and an unforgettable time.

From Baby Buggy to Model T

by Jack Baumgardner of Coshocton, Ohio
born in 1917

I can recall as a Coshocton boy of ten or twelve years old, how we used to get our exercise. We would get an old baby buggy with wheels about 8 or 10 inches in diameter. Then we would go over to the Coshocton Lumber Yard, near where we lived, to get a couple of lath that they used to dry lumber with. We would cut one to make a cross piece and nail it to the lath and then run all over town. It was great fun!

Another item was the use of stilts. We would nail blocks of wood onto the uprights and walk all over town. One of my neighbor friends had the tallest stilts around. He had to get on a porch to get onto them.

We also made scooters. We would get old skate wheels and nail upright onto a scrap of wood and run on the sidewalks. I guess it was the first skateboards.

When I was in the first grade, I recall that there was a classmate by the name of Bob Shoemaker, who was the best marble player in school. We would draw a large circle and put marbles in the center. Then, we would use a large shooter to knock them out of the ring. The same boy came up with a creation to make turtles from walnut half shells, using whole cloves for head, tail, and feet. I used this later when I was a cub master for Boy Scouts. My son and his colleague, Cub Scouts thought this was really great.

I also remember when I was younger, of going to Jim Moore's hill along the Wheeling and Lake Erie Rail Line north of Coshocton, to pick blackberries. I would pick about a gallon or more and we would eat some or Mother would bake pies. We also helped her can them for future use.

My first car was a 1923 Model T Ford, which I bought for ten dollars. At the time, I was working as a timekeeper, on a crew that was building gauging stations for the Department of Agriculture just north of Coshocton. This is now known as the North Appalachian Experimental Watershed. This project was part of the National Youth Administration of the New Deal. Carl Barrick, who was working on the crew, was a barnyard mechanic and said he would sell the Ford to me for ten dollars. I told him that payday, I would buy it. I took it home, filled all the grease cups and patched it up. My dad, who had been a mechanic, said it was not in bad shape. I later sold it for $40 to a local Justice of the Peace who was just starting Old Age Pension for the government.

My next car was a 1926 Model T, that I bought for $45.00. It had belonged to an older lady from West Lafayette near Coshocton. The upholstery was like new as the car had been stored in a garage for a long time. It had some dry rot above the windshield on its top. I patched it up with pitch.

These were the good old days when kids found ways to get their exercise and entertainment. These, along with memories of my first automobiles, are a few of fond recollections of a ninety-year-old.

Our Lake Park Drunks

by Cinda Watson of Coshocton, Ohio
born 1946

Growing up at Lake Park in the 50's and 60's was a great adventure, to say the least. There was a multitude of wonderful people living in the 25 cottages along the lake. It was like one big happy family with all kinds of different personalities, experiences, joys, trials, tribulations, and mysteries of daily living.

There was also a huge variety of ways to be entertained, both in summer and winter. We always had a fishing pole in the water and at night we went frog gigging. We sunbathed, swam, rowed boats, skated, rode horses and bikes, camped, explored, golfed, played cards, baseball, basketball, hockey and tag. There was a dance hall that boasted such entertainers as Tommy and Jimmy Dorsey Band, Les Brown and His Band of Renown, Duke Ellington Band, and we could "Swing and Sway with Sammy Kaye."

We were a tight-knit, fun-loving bunch and no one ever locked a door. We ran in and out of each other's houses on a regular basis and it seemed to work in our special little community.

There were several (how do I say it?) "DRUNKS." Yep, drunks. Well, that may sound a little harsh, but we did have a few neighbors that could really tie one on. There were nights when one fella would come home so drunk he could barely walk and other nights he couldn't even get out of the car. He had a teen-aged daughter that was embarrassed by his antics.

One night he came home loaded to the gills. Not only was he unable to get out of the car, but he kept falling asleep with his head falling forward and hitting the horn. The blasting horn woke everyone in the neighborhood, except him. His daughter would get out of bed and yell out the window, "Dad! DAD! Wake up, WAKE UP!" Now and then that worked but other times before he could get himself reoriented and out of the car, he would fall asleep again, his head would hit the horn and once again blast the sleeping neighborhood. Then his daughter would go down, grab him, yank him out of the car and physically direct him to his bed. She was not nearly as big as her father, but she was plenty hopped up on adrenaline by that time. She had no trouble manhandling him, and size had little to do with it.

This happened once or twice a month but the next morning nothing was ever mentioned. We were neighbors and friends and we dealt with our problems in the easiest method available: silence.

Another of our "DRUNKS" came home one night totally wasted. His wife had locked him out of the house. She also threw his clothes and most of his belonging out the door. It was winter and the lake was frozen or his belongings would have been in the water.

He started picking up the clothes, stumbling and fumbling, but there were more then he could manage, so he started putting everything on. He banged on the door, yelled, pleaded, cussed and cried, but she continued to ignore him.

Finally he got on her last nerve. She opened the door and with a grand gesture, she threw his beloved bowling ball out the door. Everyone knew that bowling ball was his pride and joy. It landed on the ice and rolled nearly to the other side of the lake before coming to a stop.

He was plastered but not so far gone that he didn't recognize that bowling ball and it was rolling away. In typical drunk fashion, he took off after it, fully dressed in ALL of his clothes. His increased bulky size, due to all the extra clothing and his inebriated swagger across the ice, was about the funniest thing I ever saw.

This same man came home toasted one night and decided to go for a late night swim. He took his clothes off, except for his tighty-whities, and dove straight into his rowboat. It was berthed in its usual place beside the dock. Why his intoxicated stupor caused him to forget where his rowboat was tethered is beyond me. It didn't affect his ability to find his car and drive himself home or to take his clothes off before he went in the water!

Our family has suspicions that the mysterious late night visitor to our home could possibly have been one of our bombed, boozer buddies. We were all in bed sleeping, my parents, two sisters and I, when someone walked in our back door. Our cottage had three floors, four bedrooms on top, living rooms and kitchens on the main floor and the two bathrooms were in the basement. The cottage was a duplex at one time, so there was two of everything. The bedrooms were an open balcony style with latticework and curtains for a little bit of privacy, but we could hear everything going on in the main living area.

Our visitor was not very quiet but must have known his way around our house. He knew exactly where the basement door was and found the light switch without a problem.

Mother and I were the first to come awake and were startled by the intrusion. We first lay in our beds and listened. We knew the rest of the family was each in their respective beds, so who was the person downstairs and what was he doing? Someone had just walked in and made his way down the stairs. He must have used the bathroom, flushed and washed his hands. He came back up the stairs and out the same door he had entered and didn't make any stops along the way.

Mother and I met in the hallway of our balcony bedrooms. We were both curious and I noticed Mother's expression mirrored mine. It registered a little shock and fear along with curiosity. We knew there had been an anonymous visitor, it was male and whoever he was, he did not live in this house!

A few nights later the "late night visitor" returned and this time I was able to catch a glimpse of him leaving. I only knew it was a man in the distant shadows.

The following week he made another visit and periodically over the years would show up every now and then. He never bothered anything or caused any trouble. We were never quick enough to be able to identify him although we tried to sort it out for years. To this day it remains one of those unsolved mysteries.

The Link Belt Landmark and the First Buckeye

By Arthur Sam Bennett, Jr. of Coshocton, Ohio
Born 1957

In the summer and fall of 1962, a few miners from Eastern Kentucky were brought up to Coshocton by the Peabody Coal Company to start work on opening up an underground coal mine. Union construction workers were at work erecting the mine conveyor belts that traveled from the mine on S.R. 83 South, two and one half miles to the Conesville Generating Station, Columbus & Southern Power. The conveyor belt crossed over S.R. 83 South and a sign on both sides read "Link Belt." This became a popular landmark around Coshocton during this time.

Simco-Peabody Coal Company entrance to #4 U.G. Coal Mine in 1972. Belt line and track entry are in the same opening. The pipe above the tracks pumped water out of the mine.

Operations of the new underground coal mine started in November 1962 by the Simco-Peabody Coal Company known as Simco #1 U.G.

Peabody had already entered into an agreement with Cols & Southern to mine the coal and supply the men and know how. Columbus & Southern would purchase all the equipment and pay for all costs associated with the mining operation including supplies, electric, etc. This was the subsidiary that was formed between the two: Simco Inc., owned solely by Columbus & Southern power. All of the coal that the mines produced would go directly to the power plant via conveyor belt to fuel the coal fired boilers.

As each year passed by, the power plant increased the amount of coal they would need to operate the plant.

The Simco #1 U.G. mine opened up in 1962 and only operated six months due to bad conditions. During this time, the mine produced coal on first and second shifts and did routine repair on third shift.

There were only nine miners on each crew on first and second shift for a total of eighteen men plus a few on third and a few bosses. Up until this point, most of these men came to Coshocton via the coal fields of Eastern Kentucky where Peabody had operated a mine at Alva, Kentucky. Black Star Coal Company had closed that mine in 1959.

Now that Simco #2 U.G. mine was operating, the mine became very profitable and Peabody hired on another coal crew of miners for first and second shifts. To get these extra miners, the company men would ask the current miners if they had any kin or friends back home that needed a job. When the miners said yes, the boss would literally go out of the mine and call the miner on the phone and offer them a job.

Somewhere about this time, a man from Coshocton got out of the service and applied for a job. Up until now, all miners were Kentuckians. As soon as he was hired in, he received the nickname "Buckeye," and is still referred to by this name today (Tom Stoker). He was the first "Buckeye" hired there.

Each mine had a basic life span of two to three years. Simco #4 Mine opened in 1971, Simco #5 Mine opened in 1972, and Simco #7 Mine opened in 1973. Simco #4 & #5 Mines, by this time, had all of the economical coal mined out of them by 1978.

Simco #7 Mine was being developed when it closed in 1978. This mine was billed as the "super mine" by Peabody officials, meaning it still had at least twenty years of coal to be mined. This mine was going to be the future home of coal miners from Simco #4 & #5 Mines when they closed.

The total number of miners employed at the three mines upon closure, including company personnel, was between two hundred fifty and three hundred. There were three women miners employed upon closure in 1978.

The coal seam we mined was the #9 seam which "outcropped" badly, meaning it had a lot of hills and curves in it. The coal seam height averaged thirty two inches, accompanied by soft flooring and lots of water and mud. The roof was not the best, either. Just imagine, for a moment, what it was like underground to work daily in these kinds of conditions: the ceiling height averaged thirty-two inches, plenty of water, pitch black dark, and the air temperature a constant fifty-nine degrees. Wow, what a way to make a living each day!

I worked in the mines for only five years and found a camaraderie there that I have not found since. We depended upon each other to work safe.

The mines were closed in 1978 for so-called "economic reasons." This is what Peabody officials told us, even though there still remains at least forty years of black gold in them hills.

Upon closure, it took some miners at each mine about six months to pull all equipment outside and then seal each mine per State and Federal regulations.

Simco #4 Mine was located off of S.R. 83 South where the old Link Belt crossed the highway. Simco #5 Mine was located about fifteen hundred feet past the little church on the left side of the highway (Royer Chapel). The mine was located on the right side of the highway. Simco #7 Mine was located on a haul road about five hundred feet past the current Conesville Coal Wash Plant (opposite side of the Wash Plant).

Simco-Peabody Coal Company had a total of six different underground coal mines that operated from 1962 to 1978. These include the following: Simco #1, #2, #3, #4, #5 and #7 underground mines.

Slingshots and Runaway Mules

by Joseph E. Sayre of Dover, Ohio
born in 1928

Yes, I do remember some of the things that we did in the good old days. Here are a few. Hope you enjoy.

Bill Daley, Bob McMillen, Bill Glowins, Gene Martin and Eagar Martin, also Dwhite Martin. I lived on the south side of New Philadelphia on Commercial Avenue.

We boys would stomp on small milk cans so that they would bend up around our shoes. Then would run up and down the street to make it sound like a horse.

We also had some old automobile tires, so we made a handle and nailed another piece of wood across the other end of the handle. We would push and guide the tires down the street. Sometimes, we would choose up sides so we could roll these tires toward each other to make them crash. If a tire got away from us and go over into a garden, we would have to get it back soon as possible so my dad or Mr. Richmond did not have to give us *heck.*

There was a path beside our house that went over to Bob, Sterling, Floyd and Junior Lane's house. There was a canal between their house and ours that we traveled looking for snakes and birds to shoot with our slingshots. One day, the chief of police, Emery Gintz, came over to the south side looking for some boys with slingshots. All of us boys had gone berry picking and took our slingshots with us. The only one he got that day was Mr. George Martin's. He would use it to shoot knotholes out of a fence. The little Martin girl was playing with it out on the porch.

The house that I lived in was located at 219 Commercial Avenue next to Johnny Carisle's gas station. Johnny and his sons, Jim and Glenn, worked on Ford tractors next door. Later on, this building was a Goshon Dairy Store.

Walt Graff had a big barn and a cow pasture where the New Town Mall now stands. The slaughterhouse was down in that area also. A couple times, Mr. Graff's mules would get away and come running over to our house right through the garden. My dad would catch them and hold them 'til someone come to get them. I remember being very proud of my dad, Ellis Sayre, standing there holding onto those two big animals.

My school principal was C.D. Stiffler and one of my teachers was Miss Cline.

That's all for now. Oh for the "Good Old Days."

At That Time...

by Moses A. Kaufman of Sugar Creek, Ohio
born in 1916

I still remember my Grandpa Moses Gingerich of the maternal side of my family. He was born January 25th, 1860 and was four years old when his father died in 1864. His father was Jakob Gingerich and immigrated to America in the early 1830s. At the time of his death, the Civil War was just about over with. Abe Lincoln was President at the time.

Nationally, it was a time of problems and also locally, it was the time of division among the Amish in Holmes and Wayne Counties. At this time, it was over with. The result was a large percent formed a new church and called them Mennonites and had church in church houses while the Amish retained the old style of meeting in their homes.

Jakob immigrated to America soon after the Napoleonic times in Europe. Those were hard times for people in Germany. He landed in Germantown, Pennsylvania in the early 1830s. By this time, the tide of immigrants had reached Somerset County, closer to Pittsburgh, and that is where he stayed for a while before coming to this area.

This area had its first settlers from Somerset in 1810, a covered wagon with four families. There were four families: Yoder, Masts, Miller, and Troyer. They settled along the Walnut Creek. This creek and the Goose Bottom Creek join on the farm that I live. This is about one mile east of the town of Walnut Creek. In the start, this town was called New Carlisle. Carlisle had been the name of the town in Pennsylvania where they came from. But when the town people wanted a post office, they had to change it. In my youth, I still remember still calling it Carlisle with a silent "s."

At the time of the first immigration here, the people

had to go down to Zanesville to file their claims for their land. This was military land that George Washington had reserved for his soldiers after the War of Independence. But evidently, the land was also sold to the settlers. The price was usually around two dollars per acre. Holmes County was formed in 1823, and then they could file their claims there in Millersburg, the county seat.

I was born on October 23, 1916 in the vicinity of Millersburg in a farmhouse. I was the fourth child of a family of ten children, five boys and five girls. This was at the time when the first World War was starting in Europe, and we had Woodrow Wilson for our president.

It was also the time when the power of steam for power was very much in use for train locomotives and also for steam engines for threshing and stationary power plants, like cheese houses. The internal combustion gas engine was just coming into use.

At that time, we still had a livery stable in Millersburg, where they had horses and buggies that they would rent out to traveling salesmen that would come into Millersburg by passenger train and then hire a horse and buggy to sell their wares.

At that time, State Route 39 was being improved, and I still remember the old trucks that hauled the gravel and material. They had no cab and were still roller chain drive from the gearbox to each of the two back wheels. At that time, we could still drive a herd of ten to twelve cows down 39 to a field on the other side of the road.

This was at a time when most farmers were milking from ten to twelve cows for the cheese houses that made mostly Swiss cheese.

At that time, there was a small cheese house a little north of Route 39, where we hauled our milk to. At that time, they only made cheese in the summer months, and most cows were dry during the winter months, like January, February, March. At the start, we each had to haul his own milk to the cheese house, but by the 1930s, we had a truck that picked the milk up and took it to the cheese house, and soon, we made cheese the year round.

In wintertime, they only made cheese every other day. But later on, they made cheese every day. At the start, we had big milk cans that probably held fifteen gallons or maybe twenty, and they had a winch at the cheese house, with a cable and a crank, that would swing out, hook to ring on each side of the milk can, and then you could lift it off with winch and swing it around and empty it into an open tank on a scales, that would weigh it, so every farmer knew how much milk he had. Later on, it was all sold in ten-gallon cans, and now it is mostly bulk tanks.

At that time, most farmers also raised hogs. Then these hogs ate and drank the whey, but then the farmer had to wash his own cans. So that meant that if you want the whey for your hogs, you will have to wash your own cans, and if you did not use the whey, the can would be washed at the cheese house with hot steam and water. And the whey was sold to a whey company that processed it for animal feed.

At that time, they stopped making cheese in the wintertime from November or maybe Thanksgiving to spring. The cheese maker tried to get a job in the brickyard or maybe in a coal mine 'til spring came again. But then in the 1930s, they started to make cheese the year round, but some cheese houses only made cheese every other day in wintertime.

Normally, the cheese houses had plenty of hot water and steam. They used steam to power the agitators to stir the milk in the big kettles and also to heat the big bottles. Then the milk began to curdle, and at a certain point, they stopped the agitator and took a big coarse cheesecloth and screened the curds out of the bottles and put them in a round press at that time.

Then they put a lid on top of the curds and put pressure on the lid to press out the liquid whey and just leave the curds in the round cheese press. A Swiss cheese of the round wheel type was probably around a hundred pounds, a little more or less. At the present time, I do not see any of those big round wheels anymore. They have different forms for their presses. Now it forms a block of cheese instead of a wheel.

In the days of my youth, I grew up on a farm that still had an old cheese cellar, that was built into the hillside, beside the road, with a rounded top of cement, and was covered with earth and blending into the hillside, with the front door opening toward the road. The small cheese house was on the opposite side of the road. There was still some evidence of a building there at one time. I think this would have been in the late 1800s and early 1900s.

In the early times of cheese making, it was always done by immigrant cheese makers from Switzerland in German. It would be by (the surnames for some of them) Schuliz, Steury, Dauwalder, Steckly, Pauli, Lanz. But in the 1930s, we began to have local men that learned the cheese making trade.

After World War II, the farm began to get bigger with more cows—sixty to seventy—which was very big at that time. And now you hear of places where they have as many as five hundred to a thousand and are milking around the clock. The milk supply is a lot more fluid than it used to be. With refrigerated trucks and storage, they can shift the supply of milk from one state to the other, and a lot of the small cheese houses are gone. I do not know how many are left, but I don't think that we have half a dozen anymore, and the ones that are left are a lot bigger than they used to be. Now days, more milk is going to condenseries and bigger companies.

This is what we call progress, and I think progress is taking one step forward and a half step backward. I think we always lose something in a change like this. I think that all true wealth comes from the soil, and we do not have very many tilling the soil anymore.

At the time, about everybody knew who the Secretary of Agriculture was. It was Henry Wallace. He received about as much recognition as the President did. But now, nobody hears of that position anymore. But we do hear of our military exploits and our economic crunch at the present time. We would better get back to basics and learn to live within our means. The law of sowing and reaping is still in effect.

I have enclosed a brief history of Swiss cheese making if you can use it. I could write you an article a little like that about the poultry and chicken broiler industry if you could use it.

The Best Place to be Raised

by Richard Meese of Centennial, Colorado
born 1941

I was raised in Dover, Ohio and I left when I entered the Air Force in October 1959. I was seventeen. My brother Jim, 65, and my mother Virginia, age 93, still live in Dover and are still vital active residents of the community. I visit regularly and still love this wonderful town. I currently live in Centennial Colorado. I had fun reminiscing with my family as we laughed at our memories.

I was born into this world in 1941. I was raised in the small town of Dover, Ohio a town of 10,000 people in Tuscarawas County. Dover is about 90 miles south of Cleveland, Ohio.

I remember the home services that were offered to the public in the forties and the fifties and how and why they were done in the way they were. Under certain circumstances I find it hard to say that those were the good old days, compared to the way things are done now.

The story of what life was like during that period in time is as follows:

Most of the services that were offered were services that were of necessity. For example, most people in my small town had coal furnaces. Most, if not all, have been converted now to natural gas, a much cleaner and a more environmentally friendly method of heating our homes. The home I was reared in was built in 1903 and still had the original coal furnace.

The coal was delivered to us by dump truck through a manhole lid into a coal room underground next to the coal furnace. They would deliver about two dump truck loads a winter. The furnace had a shaker grate that had to be moved back and forth to drop the ashes through to the bottom. Then, with a wide coal shovel, the ashes were dug out and put into trash cans. We then had to carry out the ashes from the basement up the steps and out to the curb where the city would come and pick up the ashes. This job was assigned to my brother Jim and I when we got big and strong enough to carry them out of the basement. I think back on this method of heating and marvel that our two story house was always cozy and warm.

Some of the hazards of coal fired heat was that if the fire was not started properly, a mild explosion would occur in the furnace. People called it puffing. What happened was, if there was not a flame you could see after the furnace was stoked, then you closed the door to the furnace. It was just a matter of time when the gases from the smoldering coal would ignite when the coal started to burn or ignited. There was a low muffled boom in the furnace. The next thing that would happen was our mother being very upset. She would not be happy, for the fine dust that had accumulated in the duct work would be sent throughout the house. You could see this fine dust that settled over time all over the inside of the house. We all had to dust and vacuum to rid the house of dust.

The way they cleaned the ductwork out was to bring a huge vacuum truck that they used to clean the ductwork. This was a big deal to us kids for the vacuum bag was huge to us. It was about seven feet in diameter and about twenty feet long.

The last and, probably the most problematic of coal fired heating, was a situation called a chimney fire. This would occur from the accumulation of soot that had built up over time on the walls of the chimney. To help prevent this from happening homeowners hired a chimneysweep to clean out the soot from the chimney. He would use 12 foot long bristled brushes that he could add extensions to the handle and swab the inside of the chimney wall to remove the buildup of soot. They would then use a round mirror attached to the extended handle at about 45 degrees. Using a flashlight they could reflect light on the walls of the chimney and inspect the chimney for cracks etc. to check for its structural integrity. The chimney sweep had to know how to do this job, for it could be quite messy and the rooftops on those old second story homes were quite steep. One mistake and it was a long way down to that sudden stop. They always said back then, just as they do now, that stop is what ruins your day.

I think of the amount of pollutants that was put into the air back then it was an awful lot. When people raked their leaves up in the fall everyone burned their leaves in the gutters of the streets. The burning leaves always smelled so good in the cold fall air, it made your appetite soar. When you think about all the leaves that were burned it was like having a forest fire every fall.

The coal smoke from the chimneys emitted from every home was also quite strong at times in the winter.

Almost everyone had a wire type incinerator in their backyard where they burned their trash. The smell from this type of burning had an acrid aroma that wasn't pleasant at all. The smell made you think of burning trash at the city dump.

We never had a thing known as a garbage disposal. So anything that you might put down a garbage disposal now was put in a garbage can out back. The garbage man would come and pick the garbage up and haul it away.

Monday was wash day and that was quite a job for Mom. Our washing machine was in the basement. It was an old wringer type washer. This was what was required for our mother to wash our clothes. She first had to put up the clotheslines in the backyard. She ran a line from the house to the garage. She always had to hope that Monday was sunny with a mild breeze. Using clothespins, she would hang the wash on the lines to dry. She used clothes poles to support the weight of the clothes on the line to keep them of the ground.

Mom would then sort the clothes just like we do now, separating the colored clothes from the whites. She would fill the washer with a hose and adjust the temperature of the water at the valves. She would run the washer and, when they were washed, she would have to manually rinse each item of clothes. Then she would wring them out through two powered rollers to squeeze the water out. She had to be extremely careful not to get her fingers caught in between the rollers.

After she had a basket full of damp clothes she would carry them up the stairs and out to the backyard and hang them out to dry. When they were dry she would take them down and fold them real careful and carry them back in the house.

The work was not over yet, for the next day she would have to iron them. Back in the 50's, when we were teenagers and we were going out, I remember many times ironing my clothes so they looked nice when we went out. Our shoes were polished as were we, for it was important to look our best.

Washing clothes back then was a two day ordeal. I never heard my mother complain. We finally got a washer and dryer I think around 1958.

Standing, left to right: Norm Singleton, Bill Bodine, Fred Singleton, Bill Fieger, Ronny Tschudy, Jim Lanzer, Tom Anderson, Jeff Secrest. Kneeling: Leland Knepplet, Bill Levengood, Jerry Bigler, Richard Meese in 1959.

Back in the 1940s, up till about 1952, we had an icebox for a refrigerator. The iceman would bring ice in a horse drawn wagon and deliver it to our house. That is how we kept our food from spoiling.

When the iceman came in the summer it was a big deal for us kids. We always met him and he would give us a small piece to eat.

I think it was 1952 when we finally got a Philco refrigerator. It sure has served us well. My mother took this fridge with her when she moved into her new home. She still uses it as a backup refrigerator. She puts her soft drinks and miscellaneous food products that she needs to keep chilled in her garage. It works as good now as it did when it was new. That refrigerator is now 57 years old. My mother is 92 and besides keeping it clean has never been serviced or failed.

The milkman was an important member of the family. My brother and I felt that he brought the most important necessity for our survival.

You might laugh at the fact that we called him a member of the family, but that is how important he was to us. Mr. Steele owned Steele's dairy. They had a dairy farm about a mile out of town. Mr. Steele would deliver to our house, when my brother and I were teens, 21 quarts of milk a day, six days a week in those old glass milk bottles with the press in caps. Yes, I said 21 quarts a day.

The advantage of having milk delivered was it was so fresh and tasted fabulous. The downside of it was that in the summer you had to get it in the cooler so it would not start to spoil and in the winter, you had to get it inside because it would start to freeze.

We both played all the competitive sports, lifted weights and swam in competition. Milk was our rocket fuel. Mom paid, I think, 22 cents a quart back then because we drank so much. Our mother never said a word about how much milk we drank. She always has introduced Mr. Steele as the man who helped her raise her boys.

For spending money I had a few mowing jobs that were, to say the least for what I earned, demanding. I must say, however, these jobs taught me discipline to do a good job and take pride in my work.

My mother, one summer day, said to me, "Dick, I want you to go down to Mrs. Kirk's house on Saturday. She has a little work for you to do." I was there at 8:00 AM just as ordered. Mrs. Kirk came out and said, "As you can see, our property is quite large. I'm going to show you how I want you to mow it. I want you to start by policing up all the debris and litter first. Next I want you to power trim all the edges of the walks, then trim the areas around the flower beds and such, then follow up by mowing the lawn in a different direction every time you mow. I want you to take these stakes and put them in the ground, then take the cord and stretch it tight between them. Your first cut with the mower, follow beside that cord, I want your mow lines to be perfectly straight. Dump all your clippings in the compost pile. After you have mowed, I want you to take the push sweeper and do the same thing. When you are finished with that, wash all the equipment off and put it away, then hose off the sidewalks. Then you are finished."

I worked from 8:00 AM to 4:00 PM. I was paid 62.5 cents per hour or $ 5.00 for the day.

Now I will address the good old days. Our neighbors that lived across the street from us got the first TV in the neighborhood. I think every kid on 13th Street arrived at their house at 5:00 PM to watch Howdy Doody, the cowboy shows called Roy Rogers, Gene Autry, The Cisco Kid and The Range Rider, just to name a few. We finally got a TV around 1955, a GE black and white. Color had not been invented yet.

I could not continue with this story without mentioning the gasoline for our car sold back then for 28 to 32 cents a gallon. To take your girl out on a date, it would cost you about $5.50. This would cover the gas for the evening, about three gallons for $1.00 was enough to drive about 40-some miles. The cost to get both of us into the dance, 50 cents; to buy a pack of gum, 10; to buy a couple of soft drinks, 50; and after the dance, go to Mary Zifer's pizza place and pick up a large pizza for $1.75 and two soft drinks for 50 cents and still have some change left in your pocket.

Dover, Ohio was the place to be raised if you were a kid. This little town had it all.

The following is a list of the things a kid could do during the week in the summer and the winter in Dover. Our town had four tennis courts, nine baseball diamonds, you could go swimming at the YMCA, Gibb's Lake, Atwood Lake or New Philly Park. You could go fishing in five different lakes: Tappen, Atwood, Clendening, Piedmont, Camp Kane and also the Tuscarawas River and the Sugarcreek River as well as Philly Park. I caught my first big fish there—a 21 inch carp on a cane pole.

We could ride our bikes just about anywhere. We used to roller skate with the old style clamp on metal outdoor skates on the sidewalk. We played games like marbles, kick the can, Andy Over and Hide and Seek. The city provided an ice skating pond that was safe for kids to use, as it was only about four feet deep.

They also had a park overlooking our town that had a sledding hill for the kids to use. This baby was steep and had a long run.

We could, as teens, go to the park for a place to dance outdoors in the summer on Monday, Wednesday, Friday and Saturday. We could also go to the YMCA to dance on Friday and Saturday night, as well as the Youth Center in New Philly. They also had a place they called the Spanish Ballroom that was about the size of a basketball court that had dances and Jitterbug Dance contests on Friday and Saturday nights.

We could go on a hike out in the country by just walking about four blocks and we were in farm country. We trapped muskrat and hunted rabbits with bow and arrow. We camped all over this area and our favorite place to camp in the summer was the Boy Scout Camp Tuscazoar. I went to this camp for a week each summer. The cost was $14.00 from age 11 to 17 and I served on its camp staff for two summers.

Our town was a safe town; there were no fences around properties like you see in cities out west. We slept, as kids, in tents in our backyards.

Almost everyone had a garden and we kids helped ourselves to many a vegetable. We ate apples, plums, peaches and cherries off our neighbors' trees. Many of the fields or vacant lots had blackberries and red raspberries. We ate them also.

Even though we had groomed little league baseball fields to play our baseball games, we still played on the open lots that were in our neighborhood by mowing them with our families' lawn mowers. We played baseball and football on these lots. There were two separate fields that covered about a quarter of a block total in area.

We didn't know it at the time but we were assisting the city with their weed abatement program as well as making our neighborhood look nicer. I wonder if the kids of today would have that kind of initiative just to play a game? We had in our neighborhood, just to play basketball outside, about six hoops within a two block area.

Cub and Boy Scouts for us boys was a really big deal. The girls had Brownies and Girl Scouts to fill their lives with fun.

Camping out for kids in our neighborhood was always a big event. We slept out especially in the summer in everyone's backyard. The neighbors across the street had a huge army tent, about 20 x 15 feet, that they put up for us kids to sleep in. My brother and I had a tent that was about 10 x 15 feet in size. After summer was over and we took down the tents, both yards had a spot where no grass could grow.

Our yard was big enough to play corkball. So in the summer, we had baseball paths worn in the grass. During football season we had a worn out yard. The grass looked pretty tired from us kids playing football. When spring arrived we had an area around the basketball hoop that was void of any grass.

Some of the adventures that happened to us kids, and some of the things we did are as follows: One Christmas the neighborhood boys gathered up all the Christmas trees we could find; as I recall we had about 60 trees piled up in our backyard. We played in those trees through the month of January 'til Mom, afraid they would catch fire, called the city and had them hauled away.

The Boy Scouts had a paper drive and we used our garage to store the paper. In just a few short weeks we had the single car garage filled to the rafters. I think the paper drive was to help support the government fight the Korean War.

There were so many camping trips I can't even begin to count. My mother, after I got to the age of fourteen, hardly ever saw me in the summer for I was always camping out somewhere. One year, the Boy Scouts took a trip 600 miles north into Canada for ten days. We had a ball. The cost per boy was $40.00.

Some of the accidents that we neighborhood kids did have and the causes of the injuries are as follows: I don't ever recall anyone ever breaking a bone, but we had lots of serious cuts, etc. Marvin tore his calf open with a six inch slash when his foot slipped off of his bike pedal. He just had the post for a pedal for the rest of his pedal was gone. He also got shot in the lobe of his ear when a BB shot ricocheted off a mailbox flag I had shot at during a hike. It lodged in his earlobe and his mother squeezed it out when he got home. I lost my BB gun privileges for a month.

My brother and I tried to catch a red squirrel one day. We cornered it in a garage. To make a long story short, it jumped off a shelf and onto my head and spun around about what seemed like four thousand times before leaping off my head. My brother caught his throat on a clothesline as he was in hot pursuit. It flipped him up and he landed on his back, knocking the wind out of him. He had a rope burn across his neck and I, from the head wounds, was bleeding like I had been scalped. I could not comb my hair for a week because of the scabs.

My brother and I were in the backyard with our archery equipment. We were shooting the arrows straight up into the air to see how close we could come to each other. The next thing I saw was my arrow striking him on top of his head point first. It bounced right out as he fell grabbing his head. He was yelling, "You shot me! I'm going to tell Mom!" I ran over and said to him, "Please, Jim, tell her you fell or something." Well, he never told her how he got injured. I think he said he fell. I remember my mother saying to him, "Jim I don't understand. It's a perfectly round hole." He bled a lot, but we already knew that because of the way I bled from the squirrel attack on my head. I think our mother was in her seventies when we finally told her what really happened that day.

Then there was the time when the swing tipped over, the times we jumped off the roof of the garage and the time I fell out of the tree dropping a good ten feet to the ground, right on my back...or the time at the Sugarcreek River when I had the fishhook caught in my thigh. Boy, did that hurt.

I'd be remiss if I didn't include that bicycle nemesis when, as a boy racing real hard, your foot slipped of the pedal. Need I say anymore?

There are a hundred other stories to tell; these are just a few of what it was like in my life, to live back in the days that you hear us old folks call the good old days.

I Used to Have One of Those

by Billie Borland of Freeport, Ohio
born in 1941

This is being done at the suggestion of my sister, Mary Lou. I am the oldest of three. We have a brother who is now 65. I will not mention my age, but you can guess. I have diabetes, and my eyes are shot. I used to be a rural carrier, and believe me, there are stories out there about my patrons on the route, as the years added up. I have been retired for seven years. That hardly seems possible.

People talk about down-sizing when they get older. We really tried to do that when we moved to a small community to be closer to our daughter. My husband didn't want to take any of his collection that he had over the years in our somewhat shoddy garage. One toolbox. He didn't need that junk, and didn't want to clean it out either. Needless to say, all I hear is, "I used to have one of those," and I say, "Yes you did, but not now…" The kids toted things up to Goodwill and some went in the dumpster.

Our daughter and son-in-law found a cute little house right in the middle of town. They are only a quarter mile away. We have everything here: A bank which really does have banker's hours, open nine a.m. to two p.m. every day except Friday, which is payday, open until six p.m. Open Saturday nine to twelve. Across the street is the grocery and library, and on up the street is a clinic. Nice people up there. We have a funeral home, insurance company, a restaurant, fire station, barber shop, and antique and junk store which opens in the spring until fall—not much business in the winter. Down the street is a Gas & Go Garage, which really smells good, as they sell sandwiches, pizza, and coffee. There is a greenhouse on the edge of town and an apartment complex with a senior center where we meet with friends monthly.

We have several people who are walkers. Our daughter bought both of us rocking chairs for our porch. My husband really enjoys being outside where he can visit and talk to people. He had lived in Carroll County all his life until coming here. He is on oxygen, so he can't get too far.

The town we used to live in, he had a friend who he used to spend a lot of time with discussing about old cars and old jobs and people they knew.

Our new place is really friendly. One lady, who writes for the newspaper, stops by to visit, and her husband uses our porch to be close if an alarm comes in for the fire department or emergency. We now have 9-1-1. One man goes by every day. He walks five miles and is 80 years old. A lady, who lives on the next street over, walks by a couple of times a day. Another girl, who does not drive, walks by several times a day. She fills us in on the news.

Our grandchildren like to ride their bicycles on the sidewalk, and the neighbor girls ride their bikes and play hopscotch in the sunshine.

A lot of motorcycles, fishing boats, and horse trailers go by, as we live on the state route. Any time you see us out, stop by. Jim would enjoy a visit.

Our kids take us shopping and to family functions and doctor appointments, but we pay a neighbor, who is out of work, to take us places we want to go. We can't drive, since we have medical problems. Where we lived before, our daughter had to drive 38 miles to come get us, then take us places, so we really moved here for convenience.

We tell people we live in the boonies, as it is 20-30 miles in any direction to shop. Many people are out of work, and we are noticing it here. We get a daily paper and Meals on Wheels. What else could you ask for? Good food, family and friends, just the right spice for life.

I forget to say we have four churches and a grade school near. The kids are always busy with Scouts and library and choir. Plus, they have Nintendo to keep them occupied. I write little stories in a book for my grandchildren for when they get older. My daughter says she is glad she had her babies when she was young. I was 37 and he was 40 when she came along.

Follow in my steps. When we were young, my parents worked at a factory which made dishes and cups. We had a cousin, Bill, who stayed with us and took care of the three of us when my parents were working. It was in the early 50s and a big snow came. Bill also helped a neighbor man, who was old, milk cows. He lived over a half mile away. Our parents couldn't make it home, and my cousin had to help milk, so he got us dressed in the warm clothes, gloves, and boots. The snow was really deep, as there weren't snow plows like there are today, and since we were the only ones up our way, we went with him to milk. He carried my sister, and my brother held on his back. I followed in Bill's footsteps down the road, clumping and trudging to stay in his tracks.

We made it down to the barn. He made a place for us to wait, while he did the milking. There were no milkers like they have today. It was done by hand, and it took a while, as they had to feed the cows and give them hay. It wasn't the nicest smell, but when he was done, we got ready to follow him back to our house, and he fed us and fired the furnace to make us nice and warm.

They say that was the year the big snow came. People still talk about that time to this day. We didn't have school, because no one could get around.

Billie and her dancing man. We went to a two-room school in a small town. Eight grades of about 50 to 60 kids. Our teacher taught all our classes, even exercise. She was a little on the round side, but we loved her, and she liked us.

If you had a talent, she would let you entertain. We had one girl who went to our school. She could do everything. She took acrobatics, did rollovers, backbends, and could roll up like a pretzel and drink a glass of water. She also played the steel guitar.

Another boy played the accordion. His mother taught lessons at their home.

My dad had carved out a wooden man. He had rivets in his arms and legs and was anchored on a coat hanger so you could hold him. He made a special board, which was flexible, and I sat on the edge of the board and tapped the board so the man could dance to music.

Sew and So 4-H Club. My first year in 4-H was exciting. I had never belonged to a club before, so everything was new. I think we had dues to pay, maybe ten cents every meeting, which was once a month.

It started in the spring, and in the late summer, we went to the County Fair with our projects. I made a tea towel, an apron and a pin cushion. I was proud of my stitches, as we were taught to be neat. Our advisor was a nice farm lady.

We had a picnic in the summer at a state park in our town. I think we brought sack lunches and played games. We always opened our meeting with the 4-H pledge still used today, and we had officers. I was the newspaper reporter.

Proud of my parents. I want to write a story about my mom, Helen Gatts. Her mother passed away when she was nine years old of tuberculosis. They wanted her to go to Arizona for warmer weather, but she couldn't afford it, and didn't want to leave her family.

Growing up, my mother taught me early on where she kept the bills that needed paid and what to do if we ever needed help.

My mom and her sister married my dad and his brother, so our family was really close knit.

My mom has passed away at 82 years of age, and I miss her every day. I could always count on her to feed me and always be there when I needed her.

My parents were married 61 years before my dad died in his sleep. When he was tired, he would lie down and take a nap. I told Mom that Dad would be happy, as he died like a cowboy, with his boots on. He was 82.

Childhood Freedom in a Small Town

by Shirley Smalley of Canton, Ohio
born in 1933

These are my childhood memories of a small town, South Olive, Ohio. I was raised in, a place of fond memories of family, uncles and aunts, cousins and friends.

My family consisted of two brothers, a sister and my mother and dad. We lived on a small farm of seven acres of land. We had a large garden which we were involved in planting, tending, and harvesting. We raised pigs for meat, chickens for meat and eggs, we had a Jersey cow for milk and butter, and two work horses. We also helped raise grain, corn, and hay to feed the animals.

Most of all, I remember the freedom we had to be kids. We all got together to swim on hot summer days in Duck Creek, a special spot we called the twenty-foot-hole. It was very deep there and there was a large tree trunk floating in the water for us to dive off of. Sometimes, we dammed up a small stream to make a smaller swimming hole. We spent many hours there. We played in nearby wooded areas, went hiking and climbing rocks. And no one complained. We picked wild blackberries and raspberries, walnuts, and hickory nuts. We went fishing anytime we wanted, with a cane pole and garden worms. We also caught minnows from a small stream that we swam in. We caught all kinds and all sizes.

There was a very special couple, Frank and Goldie Baker, that owned a gas station and grocery store on Route 21. They were friends to all that stopped there. Also, there was a general store in town, a post office, and two churches which we attended. There was a large boardwalk that spanned from a large iron bridge that crossed Duck Creek into town. The only means of crossing that road into town was that boardwalk because it flooded there very often. Everyone gathered there to see the high water and discuss the latest news.

The town has changed quite a bit since then. The course of the creek has been changed, to stop the flooding, the boardwalk is gone and the bridge. Some of the people have moved since the big flood a few years ago in southern Ohio, which affected South Olive terribly. Most of my family, relatives and ancestors and friends are laid to rest in the old, well kept cemetery, high on a hill in South Olive, Ohio.

We still have fond memories when we were young and how much the wonderful people influenced our lives and the peace and security we had knowing they cared for us.

In the spring, when the wild violets bloom, they cover the entire cemetery. They are a beautiful sight for anyone who cares to visit.

Grandma Riesbeck's Little Store

by Phyllis A. Shreve of Woodsfield, Ohio
born in 1923

I was born in November, 1923 and during the following years I remember my mother taking me to Grandma Riesbeck's little store which was located near our home. I will list a few of the items and their price at the time. Bread was nine cents a loaf and milk was fifty-four cents a gallon, a new car was $285. Gas was twenty-two cents a gallon, a house was $7400, a stamp was two cents each, average income was $1176 a year.

Woodsfield "Corner Store" circa 1920. Margaret "Grandma" Reisbeck with Paul M., Sr. and Mary Riesbeck.

I remember Sad Sam Jones living a short distance from our house. We all thought he was a big hero. He played professional baseball with the New York Yankees, for a yearly income of around $25,000. How times have changed!

Two of the old radio programs were Fibber McGee and Molly and Amos and Andy. Kate Smith was a great singer, and sang When the Moon Comes Over the Mountains. There was, of course, no TV so we had to listen to the radio for entertainment.

My grandparents had a telephone which hung on the wall. When it rang everyone ran to answer it to hear the latest gossip.

Every Saturday night my dad gave me ten cents for

the movie and ten cents to spend for candy or popcorn. I was happy because I thought I had a lot of money.

My doctor, O.C. Jackson, delivered my first baby at home for $25.00. This was in 1946. When he delivered my fourth one in 1958, he said he would have to charge $30.00 because of the times. When my fifth baby was born by Caesarian section at the hospital, we were charged around $600. This was nothing compared to what it would cost today.

By the way, Grandma Risbeck's little store has grown to a chain of Risbeck's Food Markets located in Woodsfield, Barnesville, Cambridge and St. Clairsville. Grandma would be truly honored if she knew this.

The Cold Nose

by Joan C. Hibbitts of East Sparta, Ohio
born in 1934

I was living in the country while I was in school. No bathroom in the house. Every night, my mother and I went to the outhouse before bed. Part of the outhouse was some open in the back. My mom always flashed the flashlight all around for snakes. Well, we were talking, and I screamed. Our dog had gotten loose, and he touched me with his cold nose on my "butt." All I could think of was a snake.

Cats and Dogs in a Chicken Coop

by Donna McFee of Byesville, Ohio
born in 1947

I come from a family of four siblings, one sister, and two brothers. I am six years younger than my sister, two years older than my brother Bobby Jr. and four years older than my brother Butch.

I was like the older sister with Butch; he was rather quiet and he listened to me, but as far back as I can remember Bobby Jr. and I fought worse than a cat and dog locked in a chicken coop.

We fought from the time we got out of bed 'til the time we went back to bed and all day long in between. I don't know how our mother put up with us fighting, arguing, and bickering all the time. We never gave her a moment's peace. If I had children like us I would have shipped them off to the gypsies.

She tried to settle our little disagreements, which was really trivial things, but you would have thought that they were major problems with all the screaming and yelling we did. Momma took us to church and quoted the Bible to us every time we fought; you would have thought that we should have known the Good Book word for word front and back. Bobby Jr. was more than a mischief maker, he was a troublemaker, and he did everything he could think of to keep me in an uproar.

One summer day when I was five, I put some dirt in a bucket, added a little water and mixed it 'til it was nice and thick; I put it between two big maple leaves and made mud sandwiches. I laid them in the back of my three-wheel wagon bike and rode up and down the sidewalk in front of my house yelling, "Choc pies for sale, choc pies for sale! Get 'em while they are fresh!"

All that yelling sure did make me thirsty and while I was in the house getting a drink Bobby Jr. scraped all of the mud out from the leaves and smeared it all over my wagon bike. When I saw it I screamed, "I hate you! I wish you were not my brother! Mom, come and get Bobby Jr." Butch came over and said, "Can I help you wash your bike?"

Dancing was my favorite thing to do. I dreamed about being on "American Bandstand." I loved to dance; it seemed like my feet were made to dance. I was dancing around the front room when Bobby Jr. came in holding Dad's hatchet. He started dancing around like a wild Indian, swinging the hatchet around and around, and he said, "I'm gonna chop your feet off," and he chased me around the living room. I tried to stay away from him and that hatchet but it was too late. I looked down at my foot and all I saw was blood seeping from my white sock; he had chopped my foot with that hatchet. I screamed, "I hate you! I don't want you for my brother! Mom come and get Bobby Jr."

Butch came over and offered to help me clean my foot.

After school every day I would run home and play my Victrola and listen and dance to my forty-fives. Bobby Jr. would come in and turn the TV up as loud as it would go just so I couldn't hear my music. I turned the Victrola up as loud as it would go; you would have thought that every window in the house would shatter.

I screamed, "I hate you! I don't want you for my brother! Mom come and get Bobby Jr." Butch said, "Why don't you leave her alone?"

Bobby Jr. loved to throw rocks. He was pretty good at hitting what he aimed at, and after our neighbors moved, he threw rocks and broke every window in that house. Unfortunately, I was standing in the neighbors' yard at that time and one of those rocks hit me right in the face above my lip, and to this day I carry that scar. I screamed, "I hate you Bobby Jr.! I don't you for my brother!" Butch went and got our mother, and boy did Bobby Jr. get into trouble for breaking all those windows; he had to mow the neighbors' grass and pull weeds all summer. "Yeah, yeah, that's what he gets," I said.

Thirteen was a magical age for me because I was allowed to have friends over and I had a very special boyfriend, and Mom said he could come for dinner this one evening. After dinner, him and I went out in the back yard to swing, and wouldn't you know it, Bobby Jr. started throwing rocks at him. He climbed up into the apple tree to avoid being hit. I screamed, "Bobby Jr., I don't want you for my brother!" Butch ran into the house and told Mom that Bobby Jr. wouldn't let Larry out of the tree.

At age seventeen I was allowed to date and go for rides with my friends. We went to Winsor's Drive-in Restaurant, pulled up and when the waitress came over to the car to take our order, Bobby Jr. popped up from the backseat and said, "I'll have a burger and fries." I should have made him walk home, but I just said "Bobby Jr., I hate you and I don't want you for my brother."

Nevertheless I married at age seventeen. Bobby Jr. was fifteen and as I was walking out the door to go to the church he said, "I know you hate me so I'm not coming to your wedding," and he didn't.

I matured at age seventeen, married, had a husband and a baby on the way. I learned that family was very important and that included Bobby Jr.

Bobby Jr. enlisted in the Navy and just before he left I said, "Bobby Jr., I don't hate you. I love you; you're my brother. Mom, I don't want him to leave, please make him stay!" But he left.

We wrote many letters to each other; we talked about our silly arguments and we forgave one another, and upon our mother's dying day she looked at us, Butch, Bobby Jr., my older sister Dee, and I, and she said, "Take care of one another, especially Bobby Jr." Today my brother Bobby Jr. is very sick and when he needed a kidney transplant, I was a perfect match for him so I wanted to give him one of mine, but his daughter gave him one instead.

He has cancer of the brain but he is a fighter and is doing well. I call him often and see him when I can. I still tell him, "Bobby Jr., I love you, and I'm so glad God picked you to be my brother."

I would not trade my brothers for anyone else in the world because I need them.

Hard Times and Good Times

by Mary Esther Vroom Vensil

Born 1915

I have lived a long time and I have seen hard times and good times. I lived at this address since 1917; the road didn't have a name at that time and you knew everyone that went by your home.

The mailman was a great treat; I always met him or her, the one person that you seen that day.

Mary Esther Vensil's birth place.

Before I was ten-years-old my mother died on Mother's Day. I had a little sister not yet two years old. I became a mother to her. My father remarried after a few years and I had a great stepmother; always good to me.

I have always worked; I liked to work and still do inside and outside work everyday. I have great health; no aches or pains. I still have my right mind and I get the *Times Recorder*. All my life I have never been without the daily news.

I remember the chamber pots. Here is an example. My mother was sick and they thought I should go and stay with my grandmother. I said no, because I wanted to help take care of her. "What can you do?" they said. "Well, I can dump her pot." So I got to stay home.

About the radio. I remember listening to it, but my school teacher, Mr. William Fletcher, said, "If any of you live long enough, you'll find out that it will be the ruin of our country." Now I think he was about right, because now, nothing can happen on this earth that everyone the world over knows about it.

I never got a spanking in school, but two boys were so bad that one day the teacher took them in the cloakroom and whipped them oh so bad with a strap. Now you can't even touch a child, but after he gave them a whipping, they behaved; never had to do it again.

Wringer washers. I go back to when you used a washboard and wrang them out with your hands. I still have my Maytag washer; don't use it now. When we bought it, it had a gasoline engine. Later we got one with an electric motor in it, and by this time we had electricity.

The Depression. I sure do remember it, but I never was hungry. We had our milk, eggs and our own meat. We canned the meat.

About the snowstorms. Sure I remember them; we shoveled the road open. There were no snowplows to clear the roads.

I live on a hill so I never was in danger of floods, but our road got flooded and we could not go down the hill, but we could go out the other way and get to what is now Route 146.

The house that I was born in is still lived in. My father built it in 1900 and when the Dillon Dam was built, it was moved to New Nashport and it still looks real good.

I was married on July 12, 1939 to Austin Vensil. We celebrated our 50th wedding anniversary in July, and the following September my husband died. We raised six children: three boys and three girl; all are still living. I have many grandchildren and great grandchildren. Last Christmas, 87 people were here sometime during the day; a house full and all relatives.

I almost forgot castor oil, do I ever remember it! My father would pick up the bottle of it and drink it and tell us kids how good it was. None of us ever believed him and made sure we didn't need it.

Homemade clothes, sure I do remember them, also feed sack clothes. We were sure to get two alike when we went to the feed store so we could make something for the girls to wear.

I better bring this to a close; give me a call if you want to know more.

Disqualified by Tears

by Catherine A. Salrin of Uhrichsville, Ohio
born in 1924

When I was 35 years old, I started to work for the United States Department of Agriculture at the research station near Coshocton, Ohio. I met an employee that said he and his wife were at a baby contest and he remembered me winning the contest when I was about one -year-old. It was a complete surprise to me.

When I went home and asked my mother about the contest, she said I had won a set of silverware that we were still using. Since Mary and I were entered together, I asked why we both didn't win, since we were identical twins. She said, "Your sister cried." That was the reason we both didn't win.

Ask Your Grandparents

By Emma Carolyn Wolf of Farmington, Michigan
Born 1923

I am Emma Carolyn Wolf. I was born October 4, 1923, on a farm near Baltic, Ohio. I was number five in a family of six children. As I write this, there are only two of us left; my sister Helen and myself. We were always close and still keep in touch even though we are 240 miles apart. We have always found humor in nearly everything. We even had to laugh in church and at funerals; it was the way we were wired.

Farm life was very different. We had a path instead of a bath, as they say. Catalogues were used for toilet paper. There were some rare occasions when an old dress pattern was discarded and we got to use those soft wonderful sheets. Some pieces even had directions on them like "left side" or "right side." How helpful. What luxury!

Also, we did not have running water, but an outside pump nearby gave us clean, fresh water. We had a coal stove with a reservoir on one side that we kept filled with water. That way hot water was always available for washing dishes or bathing. The bathing was done in a galvanized tub and the water was used by several people before it was thrown out. I also remember the homemade soap that was made out of lard and grease and lye. It was strong enough to drive away any germs.

We attended a one room country school. It had its advantages. We heard all the grades being taught, so going to the next grade was not frightening or a big deal. The teacher usually played baseball or "shinny" with us on the playground at recess and noon. My brother Don spent part of his Saturdays looking for small trees with a hook by the root that could be used for a hockey stick or "shinney" as we called it. I still have a scar on my forehead where I got hit with a puck (an old tin can). We used what was available and sometimes played other schools; so we learned a little about competition.

About twice a year we would put on a program. We read plays and learned parts to entertain the parents and the community. That usually ended up with a "cake walk." If you don't know what a cake walk is, ask your grandparents. We also had a small library. My sister Helen was the reader in our family and read every book in that little library. We teased her when she read Helen's Babies.

We also had the usual farm chores and animals. We had horses, cows, chickens and pigs. We were up early to milk the cows and take milk to the cheese factory. There, Ed Steiner, a good-natured, fat-bellied guy, would frequently give us samples of cheese. Cheese was also a regular dish on our table.

I remember that we had a silo that had to be filled each fall to store food for the cows. Haymaking was another big job summer and fall. We had one mow for the horses and another mow for the cows. During the winter months we fed the animals with what we had stored during the summer. We had to store food for the family too. We had Mother and Daddy, six children and usually two hired men to feed.

One hired man I remember was Raymond. Raymond played a guitar and entertained us at night with classics like "There's a Light Shining in the Window," "I Was Born about 10,000 Years Ago," and "I Wish I Was Single Again." Seventy some years later I still remember the words to those songs Raymond used to sing.

What a lot of cooking and washing clothes there was! We had no dryer, so Mother hung the clothes on long lines going from the house to the barn. In winter months clothes would actually freeze. We would have to bring them into the basement to finish drying. They sure smelled good!

The basement had two parts; one was for coal and furnaces, the other side was where we stored canned goods and potatoes. We canned all summer and put everything we could into jars. We had hundreds of cans of peaches, cherries, blackberries and every vegetable from our big garden and truck patch. Most vegetables had to be boiled three hours to be safe to can and store, so the stove and the double-boiler, which held 14 quarts, was going all day for days at a time. The glass jars were closed with a rubber ring and a zinc lid that had to be put on tightly or the food would spoil.

My mother baked all of our bread. She made lots of it and usually made coffee cakes too on her "baking day." Since we had a wood and coal stove, the temperature had to be regulated by the amount of fuel fed into it. We often had more than slightly burned loaves and cookies. In fact, if our baked goods were not dark, we felt they weren't done.

Paper products were hard to come by. I remember that some of our "city relatives" would save their store-bought bread wrappers for us to use. I don't remember having paper towels or Kleenex tissues either. To this day, when I see a waste of paper, I cringe! To me it is as bad as a forest fire. Having been brought up so frugally, I still can't stand waste of anything. I always think that everything probably still has one more use before being discarded.

Daddy particularly was a very religious man. Often at night he gathered us for prayer. We would not miss church or Sunday school for any reason. He usually gave us each a nickel for our offering. We had clothes that were just for Sunday and we had better not lose a "Sunday sock!" We changed clothes as soon as we got home from church.

The man and his wife who owned the town drug store were an important part of our life as children. They belonged to our church and each Christmas they gave each child a brown bag with candy and an orange in it. I remember that the candy was hard tact and chocolate-covered cone-shaped creams. Yum! How we looked forward to that treat. Bless their pea pickin' hearts!

We were not allowed to dance, play cards or wear nail polish. Eventually, we did go to square dances at the Grange meetings. (Ask you grandparents.) Now, I like to play cards. I like to play euchre and Shanghai Rummy; and God gave me such beautiful nails, that it would be a shame to spoil their good looks by putting polish on them. (If you believe that....)

In the fall we also took a large two-horse-drawn wagon to the orchard to pick apples. We would fill the wagon with apples and head to the cider mill, where we got gallons of cider. Then it was our "apple butter day." At home, cider was put into a very large copper kettle and brought to a boil. Peeled apple slices, sugar and spices were added, and we stirred it most of the day until it was the right consistency. It made gallons of apple butter, which lasted us all winter. It was used for lunch sandwiches. I never cared for apple butter much, but it was better than Smuckers today!

We had "butchering days." Pigs were shot and processed. The ham and bacon were smoked in our smoke house, and sausage and chops were preserved in the way country folks did in those years.

I married, moved to Michigan, have seven children, 25 grandchildren and 22 great grands. I still consider myself a country bumpkin.

Well that's about it. I would not want to go back to "the good ole days." But, I would not trade the experience and memories for a gold mine.

Frank Roland's Picnic at Armco Park

by Beverly Huey of Zanesville, Ohio
born in 1932

I grew up in Zanesville, Ohio in the 1930s and '40s. Zanesville is located fifty miles east of Columbus, which is Ohio's capital.

Zanesville was once the pottery capital of the world, being the home of Roseville, Weller, and Shawnee pottery. They are now valuable collectors' items. Also, Zanesville has the only Y bridge in the country.

Frank Roland's picnic at Armco Park in 1945.

I lived on Linden Avenue. It was a brick street with maple trees lining the street. I can still hear the horses pulling the milk delivery wagons during the war.

I have so many great memories growing up on Linden Avenue, but one of my fondest is "Frank Roland's Picnic." Frank was my neighbor and worked at Armco Steel. Armco owned a park for their employees and their families. It was a beautiful park with flower gardens, a swimming pool, all kinds of playground equipment, tennis courts, horseshoes and shuffleboard.

Every summer, Frank would rent city buses and take all the neighborhood kids to Armco Park for the day and furnished our lunch. There would be at least fifty or sixty kids. That was the "highlight" of our summer.

After I grew up and looked back on those days, I realized what a kind, generous man Frank Roland was. No doubt for many of those kids, it would be the only time they could go to "Armco Park." What a fun day.

The Irreplaceable Black Kettle

by Dorothy G. Frie of Tahlequah, Oklahoma
born in 1923

My grandmother and grandfather Lichti lived on a small farm, outside Urbana, Ohio. Summertimes, my family and I would travel from Toledo, Ohio to visit. We knew, with great anticipation, the fun things that were in store for us: going through the barn where two or three mean Plymouth Rock roosters were housed; playing in the hay mound on the second floor; swinging in a long, high swing which my grandfather had thoughtfully installed for us in the pear tree, beside the house; and even getting to ride on their horse, "Old Bonnie."

But this time was different. We got to watch how lye soap was made as well as do all those other things. Grandmother Lichti brought out the big, heavy black kettle and put it out in the backyard, where my grandfather was building a great open fire. Then, I remember my grandmother stirring the concoction for a long time and finally stopping to let the mix harden. Later, she would dump out a hard, round cake of lye soap and cut it up in smaller sizes to use for bath soap and laundry. What would we all have done without that big, heavy, black kettle?

Remembering From Last Year

by Donna Niceswanger of Zephyrhills, Florida
born in 1939

I was raised on a farm outside a small town in Ohio, Malta.

Yes, we heated with a wood stove, but the fun was cutting the wood for the stove and hauling the wood home through the snow on a sled with horses pulling it. Sometimes we started a fire and cooked hot dogs while we were in the woods.

I remember Mom chasing me around the house trying to get me to take my spring dose of castor oil. She would tell me it was peach juice (the kind from home canned peaches). She thought I wouldn't remember the taste from last year, but I did.

The outhouse—ours was on a path that went down hill. We never had to worry abut getting there in time, because we usually fell down and slid on our backside.

Old radio shows—The Lone Ranger and Tonto, Amos and Andy, Twilight Zone, Dragnet, What's My Line, Dick Clark, Ed Sullivan, and Grand Old Opry.

Party line phone—our number was two longs and one short. The phone box was wall hanging and made of beautiful oak. When we got the new black plastic phones, we thought we had really moved up and they threw the oak phones in the dump on our farm. Wish I had them now.

Special holidays—At Christmas we always got together with all the extended family; aunts, uncles, and cousins. Us kids always had to wait in another room for Santa Claus to come. We always heard the sleigh bells and we would get so excited. My dad was always Santa and it took me a few years to catch on. There was always a gift or two for everyone. Mostly homemade things, not like today. We knew the real meaning of Christmas and always went to the candlelight service at church. Back then Christmas was Christ's birthday.

Tin tub baths—We always took our baths by the wood stove and shared the water with everyone.

Drive-in movie—We went to lots of drive-in movies. Sometimes we had friends in the trunk and I remember the time we went to the drive-in in my dad's flat bed ton truck. We pulled in backward and had lawn chairs sitting on the back. We had all kinds of food and a big watermelon. We ate it and spit the seeds on the top of a convertible sitting next to us. I wonder if they thought it was raining or birds had gone over. It was fun then, but now I know that was not very nice. It cost one dollar for two movies. Good old days.

Feed sack dresses—We lived on a farm and had pigs, cows, and chickens we had to buy feed for. We had a mill called Holbien Feed Store. The feed was in all kinds of prints. We were poor and my mom made all my clothes including my underwear. I remember how embarrassed I was to have homemade panties with umbrellas on them. She made her aprons and kitchen towels and curtains. It helped save money and was a blessing, even though I didn't feel blessed at the time.

Saturday movies—We went to the movies at the opera house on Saturdays; 14 cents for two movies and a weekly serial. It always left the movie at a time when you didn't think the actors would live through it. There was no way you would miss next week. Popcorn was five cents.

Farm animals—I've always loved animals and felt their unconditional love. They loved me when I felt so fat and ugly. My dog was my best friend. Fido went wherever I went. I love the cows and calves. I had a special cow (a jersey cow). She had the most beautiful eyes. She was a good milker and had a really big udder. I would put the horse's harness on her and hook her to my red wagon. One time she pulled me up the road to my friend's house. Got along great. Her udder bounced back and forth. But I forgot about coming back down the hill. The handle of the wagon went between her legs and I went far enough forward that I looked up and hoped she wouldn't poop. She didn't, but I caught heck from my dad for having her out on a main road. I guess I was lucky; no cars and no poop. I spent a lot of time pretending to be a rodeo rider and rode the calves around and around the barn.

I met my husband on the school bus we rode to school. My friend kept egging me on and him too. So now we have been married 53 years and still remember all the good times then, but this is the best time of our lives. We're above ground. Praise God.

Frog Leg Breakfasts and Listening Pets

by Brenda "Todd" Pressdee of Cambridge, Ohio
born in 1947

My childhood memories of the good old days was going camping and fishing with my family on weekends. We would start fishing 7:00 AM, catch bass, bluegill, catfish, even frog legs and a turtle, go back to camp, Dad would clean them and Mom would cook them for supper, then save the turtle for soup. And frog legs for breakfast. My brother and I loved them, even Brother Butch, more than chicken. The kids today don't know what they're missing.

Our family raised a big garden. We canned and cool packed from vegetables to meat to fruits. Picked all kinds of berries for pies, jellies, jams, homemade wines and cough syrup. Picked walnuts, hickory nuts to put away for the winter months.

Our town of Buffalo, Ohio was probably five-hundred families. Where everyone was like family helping each other when needed. Our post office was small and we also had one barbershop and a food market.

I had two ducks I got at Easter, named them Ronald and Donald. Sometimes they would follow me to the post office where I picked up mail for some of the old timers and our family, earning fifty cents a day. I would use it shopping at our country store, where you could get an ice cream cone for ten cents and a bottle of pop for five cents and a brown bag of one cent candy which would last all week. Also a loaf of bread for ten cents. That's in the late fifties and early sixties.

At Easter our family would get together for dinner and a Easter egg hunt. Our mother had to work second shift, leaving Dad to cook for us. I'll never forget coming home from school, and Dad would have a big pot cooking on the stove. You never knew what was in it maybe a rabbit, or a squirrel or quails. We were raised on wild meat from the land and my dad and Brother Butch [?] would go hunting for venison and wild turkeys, rabbits, squirrel, and quails. We also raised chickens and gathered eggs but you had to look out for our old mean rooster named Jack. Sometimes he would chase you.

Our cow's name was Buttercup one of a kind, you could even ride her but Grandpa [Salladay with work horses Ted and Fred?] and Dad never knew it. When I milked her, our cat Wiskers would come around and I would squirt her in the face. Then she would lick her face and paws. I think she liked it 'cause she always came back.

We had two large work horses, Ted and Fred, both black and beautiful. They worked the plow for our garden and hayfield. Dad brought me home a puppy German shepherd, white all over. I called him Whitey, I took him everywhere I went. For Christmas I got a little pony named Peanuts, he even liked candy and ice cream. All my friends loved Peanuts. And I loved talking to all my animals because they always listened to me and I could tell them anything.

Going to school was about six blocks from our house, but our grandpa and grandma, Todd, lived in between. I could go to Grandma's at 7:00 AM and she would be up making homemade cookies, peanut butter, oatmeal, chocolate chip, cut outs, no bakes and raisin filled one of my favorite and still is today. Sometimes I'd have two cookies and a cup of hot tea, then go on to school. My dog Whitey would go to school with me, waiting for school to get over so he could go home too. All my school friends loved my dog. Sometimes Grandma Todd made homemade vegetable soup and I would come home from school at noon, eat soup, and go back to school.

On weekends, Mom would wash clothes with her wringer washer. Then hang them on the clothesline in the fresh air and sunshine. I loved that smell especially on my bed linen.

Brenda Pressdee's mother, Lorene Salladay Todd, on her horse.

I'll never forget the old family outhouse. Sometimes you could see cobwebs starting to grow with little spiders. I'd leave the door open for fresh air and the smell of roses growing beside the outhouse.

We also had several apple trees, pears and plums a big cherry tree the birds would get into and the wild deer would eat beans in our garden and some of my flowers.

Today I got up planning to go

to school, but the sun was shinning and all I could think of was going fishing in an old farm pond called Blacky's. So I played hooky and went fishing. I caught ten bluegill, two bass, one big catfish. I thought it was all okay when I woke up with poison ivy all over me, from my face to my legs and arms.

Well, it won't be long until Halloween and our school was having a party. We had to make our own costumes. But in our small town, they gave out cookies, candy, homemade caramel apples and sometimes a nickel or a dime.

Fall would be here soon, we would rake all the leaves and pile them up and jump in. Then up and down just having fun. Soon winter would be here, and everyone's talking about the big snow we're supposed to get. The last time it was snow up to my knees. I would go out and build a big snowman, maybe two more, but what I really liked was making an angel in the snow. I would look up to the sky and talk to my family who's passed away and let them know how much they are missed and loved every day.

Our school busses ran because of Christmas coming and back then they put chains on. When I'd walk to school with snowflakes on my face. By the time I got to school my feet and hands were frozen but I'd stand on the registers to keep warm. While the other children rode the school bus.

When spring was here, we played softball, football, and hide and seek, chalk games and sometimes I'd put on a pair of roller skates and skate until I can reach home.

This old memory was about an old wooden boat tied to a tree down by an old creek in Buffalo, Ohio. It was a beautiful day, so four friends and me took the boat to a little town called Pleasant City, Ohio, about three quarters of a mile. Where there was a country restaurant called Vic's. He was famous for his homemade pies, but we went for chocolate shakes and ice cream. Rowing the old boat, we never thought of any danger, wearing no life jackets, I couldn't even swim and I don't know if any of them could swim either. At age eleven to thirteen you just wanted to have fun.

At fifteen years old I got asked to the freshman prom. Mom let me go because she knew the family and we were going with another couple. Mom got me a beautiful blue dress and I wore my hair in a ponytail with a blue ribbon and shoes to match. Mom took my picture so I could remember the first prom date for me.

Soon it was Thanksgiving and we would be eating Tom the Turkey with all the trimmings. Mom and I would bake for two days, pies, cupcakes, nut rolls, homemade bread. Next was Christmas and I always enjoyed going with Dad to get a tree. I loved Christmas. We would pop lots of popcorn to string up for our tree, most all our decorations was homemade.

One Christmas, my brother [Butch?] wanted to peek at our Christmas gifts. I said, "Okay, let's do it." Well that was the year Mom wasn't working good and we only had one gift each. Now a week before Christmas and we knew what our gifts was, so at Christmas my brother [Butch?] and I acted so surprised to fool Dad and Mom. But I told my brother I'd never peek at any gifts again, but I realize it's not the size of a gift or cost a gift has to come from the heart and feel special.

On Sundays we all go to church together and then come home for a big chicken dinner, homemade noodles, green beans from our garden and homemade loaf of bread still warm with homemade jelly. Cream pie and ice cream for dessert, fresh coffee, and sit around and visit with family, talking about fun times with all our school friends.

Grandma and Grandpa Todd would come over and visit, talk to our family about Grandma's quilts, and wood things Grandpa made like flower boxes and wheel barrels for flowers. Also he made Grandma wood end tables and wood shelves. Grandpa would sell them for two dollars each, and today shelves would cost ten to twenty dollars, and end tables sixty to a hundred fifty dollars today.

My dad was a mechanic and worked for Schicks Chevy Garage. On weekends he enjoyed taking me and my brother and half the neighbors' kids to go fishing and swimming. If a car broke down on the highway, the state patrol would bring them to Dad's garage to be fixed and back on the highway. Sometimes Dad never charged the families for fixing their cars. Dad was good to everyone and everyone loved him.

Mom baked things for all the church bazaars, she always sold out of everything. Mom also had two horses, she showed them in horse shows and trail rides. She drove a school bus for Meadowbrook and carried the American[?] Flag in the Rose Bowl Parade.

I remember sitting on the front porch swing and smelling the fresh spring flowers, talking with Grandpa and Grandma about the "good old days." God bless everyone in our family. Grandpa and Grandma Todd.

Penny Candy Days

by Sherry Thornton of Zanesville, Ohio
Born 1947

In the good ole days, and as a child growing up, a nickel and dime went a long way. I remember going to the neighborhood grocery store with my cousin to buy penny candy. My aunt would give us a nickel for washing dishes or just for a treat and we would head to the grocery to buy candy. There was a variety to choose from and we usually got the large, sour grape bubble gum balls.

Sometimes, we would get Dixie cups of vanilla or chocolate ice cream, with a little wooden spoon.

The grocery in my neighborhood had a wonderful selection of penny candy and nickel candy bars. Some of my favorites were Bazooka bubble gum, jawbreakers, rod licorice and buying Cracker Jacks just for the prize.

Once, my sister and I collected states and capitals inside the wrapper of the Mallo candy bars. When we collected all 50, we would receive ten free in the mail. We must have eaten quite a few to have collected all fifty!

We have now exchanged the traditional mom and pop groceries and five and dime stores with Super Wal-Mart, pizza deliveries and McDonalds with happy meals for the kids.

Other treats we enjoyed was making brown cows, made with vanilla ice cream and 3V Cola. Popcorn was even special, that we popped it the old-fashioned way and drizzled it with butter or margarine. Mom used a large pan with an uneven lid. Later, with modern times, we used the automatic popper.

Today we have few neighborhood grocery stores left. They have been replaced by stores such as Super Wal-Mart, K-Mart, the "Dollar" stores and others.

Times have changed and life is easier with modern day conveniences, but I'll always remember the good old penny candy days.

The Bed of Many Colors

by Nancy L. Marshall of Sugarcreek, Ohio
born 1947

When I was growing up my father, Clifford Titus, was an upholsterer. We had an upholstery shop right behind our house. I remember looking through the many sample books that hung from the wall so that customers could look through them and choose the fabrics, patterns, and colors to refurbish their chairs and sofas, etc. I particularly liked the tapestry fabrics and their tight weave, and I still do today.

When a particular fabric, pattern, or color was discontinued, Dad would take those samples out of the display books. You've read in the Bible of Joseph and his coat of many colors, and heard Dolly Parton sing of "the coat of many colors her mama made for her"? Well, my "mama," Marie, couldn't stand the thought of just tossing those fabric swatches away—they were too pretty. So, she would take those swatches of various sizes and fabrics, patterns, and colors and make us kids "bedspreads of many colors." Being made out of upholstery fabric they weren't exactly soft to the touch, but they were colorful, and served their purpose.

My bedroom had no heat. The house was heated with an in-floor fuel oil furnace topped with a floor register. I remember watching Mom lift the register and use a match to light the furnace, and then lower the register again. There was a register right above it to let heat from it go upstairs, but that register was in my sisters' room. So in the wintertime, sometimes I'd stick my feet on the wall where the chimney went up through in my bedroom to get some warmth. I'd snuggle down under my blankets, and cover even my head to get warm. So I appreciated the weight of my "many colored bedspread."

Mom also made throw rugs and baby blankets for my dollies out of fabric samples. I still have a couple of those little blankets. As a little girl, I made doll clothes out of some of the lighter weight fabrics that Dad discarded. I still have most of those doll clothes. When I look at them, it amazes me that I actually hand-sewed them myself—believe me, I'm no sewer. Shows what a little girl's imagination would let her do.

I am one of five children. So to feed their family, Mom and Dad always had a garden. Dad enjoyed fishing and hunting, and that also helped feed his growing brood. I remember watching Dad "skin" rabbits, and squirrels, and "fillet" fish he'd caught, and Mom cooking them all up for us. We also had venison, and pheasant he hunted, and mushrooms that he'd gone out and gathered. I remember Mom's huckleberry pies—the huckleberries gone out and searched for in the woods and hand-picked by Mom and Dad. Not to mention the rhubarb pies made from the rhubarb plants growing in our backyard and the gooseberry pies made from the gooseberries growing on the bush beside our house. We also had a grape arbor—nothing better to drink than Mom's homemade grape juice.

The garden also had red and black raspberries, and blueberries, and I remember Mom had strawberry plants in the side yard and apple and cherry trees, and her giving the birds heck for eating her cherries. They put netting over what they could so the birds didn't get all the fruit.

Dad also kept beehives. He'd don his netted hat and heavy gloves and go out and "smoke" the bees to stun them so he could gather the honey. (Me, I was afraid of those bees, and I stayed as far away from those hives as possible-believe me!) I've watched Mom and Dad put the honeycombs into a big galvanized steel tub, and separate the honey from the comb. We used the separated honey to make honey butter to spread on our toast, by itself as syrup, and I'm sure Mom used it in her baking. We also took honeycombs with the honey still in them and "sliced" a bit off and ate comb and all.

We didn't go to "fast food" restaurants—or, for that matter, restaurants in general. I'm sure the cost of feeding seven people was a factor in that. (I remember the first time I ever saw a "drive-through window" at a restaurant,

I thought it was odd.) Our treats Mom usually made—frozen grape juice popsicles (made from the grapes in our arbor), cookies, apple crisp, and apple pies, the apples grown on the tree that grew between the house and the shop, and that Mom sat and peeled and sliced herself. How she ever got enough apples to cook with I'll never know, for I remember us kids sitting at the kitchen table eating apples slices she'd give us as she peeled and sliced them. Sometimes, as a special treat, she'd take us and buy us ice cream cones—that was our "fast food" outing-and we looked forward to that.

We did have a TV, black and white of course. (We did get a color TV later on, but I remember some of those color TVs weren't very good.) I can remember watching Roy Rogers, and Dale Evans and singing along with them to "Happy Trails To You," the Lone Ranger and Tonto, Gene Autry, and Hopalong Cassidy. I can remember Buffalo Bob asking,-"Say, kids, what time is it?-It's Howdy Doody Time," and Clarabelle the Clown, and, of course, Howdy Doody. I watched the original Mickey Mouse Club in black and white-with such populars as Annette, Bobby, Cubby, Karen, and I don't remember who else at this minute. I remember Kukla, Fran and Ollie, and ventriloquist Paul Winchell and his puppet, Jerry Mahoney. Lastly, I'll mention ventriloquist Jimmy Nelson, and his puppets Danny O'Day and Farfel. Farfel was a floppy-eared dog that sang: "N-E-S-T-L-E-S...Nestles makes The very best...chaaawwwwclate."

I played with hula hoops, and roller skated out in the garage. Our roller skates were metal and had to be attached to the soles of our shoes. We had to use a "key" to tighten them so they would stay on our shoes. Sometimes they'd come loose-and, if you lost the key, well, forget skating for the day.

I learned to ride a bike on a hand-me-down bicycle that had been my older sister's. My younger brother and I had little red wagons that we'd pull around the yard, or get in and steer and ride down a hill in the side yard. We'd lay down on the grass and roll down the little slope beside the house, and laugh and get up and do it again and again. Of course, in the winter we'd sled down those same slopes on our wooden sled with red metal runners on it.

I remember some of the other kids thinking we were "rich" but, you know, that wasn't true. Mom and Dad were from the "Depression era" and had learned how to do the best with what they had, and take care of it, and stretch what they had as far as possible. Mom was a housewife who took care of the house and her kids. She was always busy, and Dad, he was the provider for his family, and he worked hard to keep afloat. Their love for us wasn't often spoken out loud, but they showed that love in providing for us the best they knew how, and in their demeanors, and in how they treated us, and the friends we brought home—I think that's what made us seem rich to the other kids...and in that sense, I guess we were "rich"—not with fortune, but with the type of riches that really matter. It strikes me now that this is a fact that as a child I didn't realize and appreciate or understand but looking back as an adult, I do.

Shaking the Corn Stalks

by Leslie M. Smith of Cambridge, Ohio
born in 1912

Summer vacation, all four Smith boys, my dad, George, and my uncles, Clyde, Herman and Clarence's, job was to hoe the corn that was planted in the big valley near a creek on the way to Quaker City. They loved to swim in their favorite swimming hole, so they worked out a foolproof plan. Two of the boys at a time got to skinny dip while the other two would shake the corn stalks to look as if they were working when viewed from the house. They all stated they were not going to spend their lives hoeing corn and they didn't. Dad had his own car dealership; one an engineer for the railroad; one a conductor and one a Teletype writer at the depot.

Came from school, had no drinking fountain, stopped at grocery by school to get a 5 cent pop, and saw a truck getting ready to leave and I said, "How about a ride?" When we came to the path close to home, I jumped off the Model T flat bed, solid-rubber-tire truck and it ran over my right foot. I whooped and hollered as they carried me all the way home. Doctor came to the house and wrapped it up 'til it would be all right. No bones broke; spread my big toe and my little toe is laid back. Looks like I have only four toes. Still that way today, at age 96, and to this age, have never broken a bone.

There were four or five theaters in town: Strand, Colonial, State and Lyric, down on seventh Street. Once a week, if good show on, went to Colonial across from Berwick Hotel with cousin Bill Kennedy and sat in peanut heaven for 10 cents. Up at Oakland Garage (my dad built) next to Kennedy's Bakery, they would have place cards in windows, showing what shows were on.

Around 1920, my brother, Paul, and I rode our flexible flyer sleds in a very fun and unique way. We lived out at Four-Mile Hill and there wasn't much traffic at that time. We would wait and watch for a car heading west on Route 40, National Road to Cambridge, catch up with it and grab hold of the back bumper, each on one side (Never tie a rope on...you could really get in trouble) and ride to Cambridge. The sparks would really fly, going through the flat area where Memory Gardens is located today. It always flooded there and had a lot of deep ruts. We would let go at the top of the hill by Ford Motor Company and Park School. After sledding, we would watch and wait, sometimes a good while, for a car going east and hang on to get back home.

When I was in the eighth grade, I was the only one that knew how to drive. I used to drive the principal's car, a Chrysler, to go on errands for her. Was called to the principal's office for this. Her name was Grace Tribbee.

When building Seneca Lake, they were paid in silver dollars to show where the money was going in the area.

Harry Totten's, in center, shaving parlor before he became sheriff of Cambridge.

When the snow starts flying, we started hauling black ammy from down at the end of Wheeling Avenue. It melts. Pavements supposed to be warm, but that's politics. Now and then I had a load of coal. Down below Caldwell, I'd pick up load of coal and bring it home to Four-Mile Hill. That's when I slipped off the truck and dislocated my right elbow. I was driving a 4-speed, floor-shift and had to drive it with my left hand down the real steep hill at about dark. I pulled in the square at Caldwell. The dentist's lights were still on, so he called his buddy and between the two of them, they reset it and put it in a sling. Dad came and took the load and me home.

My brother, Paul, born 1906, graduated from high school in 1925. He had an Oakland Coupe that had a V8 engine. Had to pay $85.00 because of high horse power, for the state of Ohio license. He switched motors to a V6 to save on tax again. Just had to pay $18 to $20 instead.

In early 1930's, I had a black roadster with wood spokes, with rumble seats, with cloth top and side curtains.

1933-1934, Dad got my brother, Paul, and I a job hauling batch when rebuilding Route 40 past Casa Loma. When that finished, we started hauling brick for the job from Ava to make the brick road.

I married Margaret Totten, daughter of Sheriff Harry and Nora Totten, on November 27, 1935. My brother, Paul, and his wife, Viola, were our witnesses. Special night in Cadiz at General Custer Hotel. Next night, we went on to Pittsburgh and next day we came home.

Before we got married, Margie called me at the garage to come down to the beauty supply shop her dad owned and she plucked my one long eyebrow and it never did come back.

I was a special Deputy at times for my father-in-law, Sheriff Harry Totten. One time, he gave me papers to serve on my former boss. Tom Gracy, the Sheriff before my father-in-law, Harry Totten, kept a machine gun in his cruiser. Took two men to run it. Harry didn't want it. When Jury Duty was held over, they were taken to the Berwick Hotel to eat. The Sheriff and Deputy went along to make sure they didn't talk to anybody.

Home from Military Service in Texas in 1942. Had no car. Worked at Continental Can, down where the RCA, NCR was later in Cambridge. Red Sweet had junk cars across from Viaduct. Bought a wrecked 4-door Chevy for a couple hundred dollars and fixed it up; probably a 1940 model. Drove it to work at Continental Can 'til it shut down in 1953. I got $750.00 severance pay and got a new 1953 yellow and white Chevy from Kenny Hammond Chevy dealer in New Concord.

I am a woodworker and have built many things. Sophomore in high school year I built a cedar chest. Junior year, a poster bed and built Mom an octagon table with an inlaid top. The table won a prize at the State Fair. Dad and Paul drove me to the State Fair.

After Continental Can shut down in 1953, my brother, Paul, told me to come and work for him at his Cambridge Tool & Die that he began in 1947. It started out on Marietta Avenue then he moved it to East Wheeling Avenue. I learned to be a toolmaker. Depression came along and caused a slow down and I got laid off. Worked in Shadyside, Ohio, at Henry Keiser Plant. Then word getting around, they were hiring up at Chrysler, in Twinsburg, Ohio. I got hired in 1959. I drove back and forth to Twinsburg every couple of days, working the 3-11 shift. I even bought an airplane, but after hitting the telephone pole located too close to the Airport Inn, I decided to go back to driving. Never had a car accident, but had lots of different vehicles. I retired from Chrysler on May 31,1978. Then, I drove for Cambridge Tool & Die, which had moved to Route 40 West of Cambridge, driving many miles, delivering molds.

Walter Smith, Public Servant

by John Hardwick of Silver Spring, Maryland
born 1915

When I returned from service in World War II, my good friend, Walter Smith, a World War I veteran, was serving his second term as mayor of Barnesville, Ohio.

I was encouraged to run against him in the next 1947 primary election. The *Barnesville Enterprise* described it as a World War II veteran vying against a World War I veteran. I was fortunate to win by a vote of 458 to 154. This ensured me of success in the following general election.

Toward the end of my term as mayor, my law practice was taking so much of my time that I decided not to run again. I conveyed this information to Walter. He ran and got his old job back and served another term after that.

I would commend him, if he were still alive, for the many years of faithful, dedicated, public service that he rendered to the citizens of Barnesville—as he loved to do—and made history in doing so.

Yellow Jackets, Bats and Sally's Snuff

by Ray Howard of New Lexington, Ohio
born in 1922

I was born in Insull, Kentucky in Bell County in 1922. My sister was two years older than me and I sure was glad, because on my first day of school I got in trouble.

It was 1928. Our one-room school house had a yellow jacket nest at the end of the school room under some slate rock. Me and three other boys decided we would whip the yellow jackets out. We got us some brushes with leaves on 'em and we took turns runnin' in and killin' as many as we could.

But me, I stayed longer and that's when I noticed I had a lot of yellow jackets on me, and they began to sting. I don't know how many stings I had, but that's when my sister came to me and tried to get them off me. She took rocks and started beating them together, and she took my clothes off, all but my pants. I ran to the outhouse and got what was in my hair. Just then, the school bell rang for everybody to come in.

I was getting sick, so our teacher, who had a car, took me home. You can bet I never tried to whip out yellow jackets no more.

The name of the school was Burnt Holler School House in Bell County. I went there through the fifth grade.

My parents, Byrd and Nora Howard, moved to Harlan, Kentucky and I started school at Pathfork, Kentucky in the sixth grade. We had a two-room school house there, which served through the eighth grade. It was nine miles from home up to Black Star High School.

My dad rented a house three miles up a hollow they called Mill Creek. Me and one buddy of mine got away with things we thought, at the time, were fun. One day we went to school early to clean everything up for school. After we got through, we went looking for something to get into.

We climbed the ladder going up to the bell tower in the attic. This had a tin roof on it. My buddy was looking around and found bats. We spied a five gallon bucket but no lid, so my buddy took his shirt off and put it over the top to hold the bats in as we caught them. I don't know how many, but a bunch!

We waited until school started and then dumped all those bats into the school room. The kids started screamin' and swattin' and runnin' for the doors and windows to get out. So we scooted down that ladder as fast as we could, because no one knew we were up there, and ran for the door too. We sure had a lot of laughs over that one. Especially after we knew we got away with it.

Well, I survived the eighth grade at Pathfork in Harlan County, and then went on to Black Star High School. My home room teacher was Miss Ketchum, and she was very nice. Things didn't go so bad for me, but my buddy, Snip, was known for doing things for fun. Some good and some bad, like shootin' our teacher with paper wads.

I had made him a slingshot out of paper clips and never thought that he would shoot Miss Ketchum. Everybody was laughing but Snip and me, and he had an ornery smile on his face, and he pretended to be reading a book when Miss Ketchum walked back to where he was sitting and she started to pass him. Well, he let his book down and she looked back at him, and he gave himself away. He looked up the other way, and she open handedly smacked him. He started to get up and she smacked him again. Then she looked back at me and said, "Ray Howard." I said, "Yes Ma'am." She was mad and asked me if I had anything to do with Snip shootin' that slingshot.

I said, "No, Miss Ketchum. You don't think I'd do a think like that, do you?" And she said, "Yes I do." Then all the kids just roared.

Well, I guess I got started out right at Black Star High School. There are a lot more things, but I'm ashamed to write them. So, I'll tell you about my first date.

Our principal at Black Star and another man put in a movie theater at Pathfork and Boy, did everybody enjoy that. Some people came five miles or more. Anyways, this girl and her parents lived up Pathfork Holler about three miles to the foot of the mountain. I was going to the show with Snip and was waiting for him. When the people came up to buy a ticket, I was talking to this girl's dad and he told her, "You can't have any popcorn tonight because I don't have enough money." I told him, "I have an extra ticket," so there went Snip's show! The girl said, "Can I sit with you?" and I said, "I don't care."

So we went in and sat down and I asked her dad if they wanted something to drink and some popcorn. He said yes, so his daughter (I'll call her Sally) went with me, and I bought all of us a bag of popcorn and an R. C. Cola. We talked a lot and I ended up walking Sally up that holler home. Her parents went ahead of us about 50 yards all the way.

When they stopped and we caught up with them, her dad told her not to stay out too long, and she said okay, so they went in and we got a little closer and talked some more. The moon was shining real bright and I was bout to ask her to go to the movies with me again. She turned away a little and I didn't know what to say or do. She had her hand in her bosom and when she turned back around—lo and behold, she was getting her box of snuff out!

Then she pulled out her lower lip and was filling it up with snuff. I didn't know what to say or do, so she said she had to go in. Then she said, "When will I see you again?" I just said, "I don't know," and thanked her for going to the movie with me. All the time I was backing up (I sure didn't try to kiss her) and was saying good night.

The next day, my buddy, Snip, wanted to know "everything." So I told him everything I wanted him to know about my first date. It was quite an experience.

So I just let everything go and remember my first date. But after that, I sure was careful where I went and who I went with. Amen.

I went to school through the 11th grade and then quit to go to work. Eventually I got a job with Peabody's Black Star Coal Mine and worked there until 1942 when I went into the Army. Then I went back to the mine and worked there until they closed the mine down.

Later, Peabody called for some men to open the deep mines in New Lexington, Ohio. I was the first man to sign up in 1962 and worked 42 years altogether for Peabody. I never worked in a non-union mine and I'm 87 years old and still am, and always will be, a member of the United Mine Workers of America.

Three Fences and Crossing the Run in Spook Holler

by Charles R. Augenstein of Shelby, Ohio
born in 1925

Well, here's my story. It's Thursday, January 22, 2009, and I have had another birthday. I am 84, born January 18, 1925. I am looking out the window, and we have eight inches of snow on the ground. Reminds me of when I was a kid. Seems like winter came early this year, like it did when I was a kid. Came in November and stayed until March, and it seemed like winter was about over in March, cause I can remember my dad plowing in March.

I can remember my dad and mom and sister talking about when I was born there was a lot of snow on the ground, and Dad had to take the horses and sled up the main road to get the doctor, for he didn't want to come down in the holler with his car, but I guess I was born okay, for I'm still here. There was nine of us kids, and we were all born at home by the same Dr. Turner from Beverly, Ohio.

We lived down in Spook Holler about seven mile from Beverly, Ohio and about the same from Coal Run. Coal Run was the post office at that time, but we had to go to the store at Dunganon. To get our mail, it was about two mile to the store around the road, but if we would walk up the holler back of our house, it was closer that way, and that's the way we would usually walk to school. School was a little farther out on the road.

When we went for home down the holler back of the store, we would have to go over, under, or through three fences and cross the same little run four times before we got to our house. There was always water in the run, but not deep. It was called a run, because it wasn't big enough to be a creek. When it got to our house, it run alongside our house and garden and then across the road and emptied in to the creek coming down the other holler.

There was a place down below the store that, at one time, they had muzzle loading rifle shoots and on our way to our house, we had to walk down over the bank and after a rain, we would find lead bullets there. We would take and make fishing sinkers out of them.

Dunganon is not a very big place. The store, a church, and four houses, and that's about all. A lot of the time on Friday nights, there would be music there. Just people from around the area would play a fiddle, guitar, and a banjo and a harp. That is about all the music we had around there, 'cause we didn't have any electric around there until 1945.

When I got back from the army, one neighbor had radio, and I remember walking up there and listening to the Jack Dempsey Fight. So us three boys and Dad would walk up to the store on Friday nights and listen to the music, and if we had any money, we might buy a nickel's worth of candy. When we went home, we would go out and down the old road to home, 'cause we didn't want to go down the holler after dark. I still remember walking down that old road, just a narrow road with weeds and grass growing up the middle. I still remember the smell of sweet clover that grew along the road and the sound of the katydids that would stop when you were along side of them and then start up behind you. Sometimes we would smell cucumber and Dad would say that a copperhead snake had crossed the road.

One night we were walking home down the road, and there was an old log lying along side of the road, and it looked like there was a fire in it. Dad kicked it apart, and it glowed just like fire. That's the first and last time I every saw foxfire.

When you went down the road, you would cross the creek, and then on down you would cross it again over a plank bridge, and then just past our house you would cross the one from the back of the store. They came together there and made a half circle around our barn, then crossed the road again. There was always water in the creeks back then.

We had an organ in the house and my older sister played it in the evenings, and we would sing the old songs that you never hear anymore. I remember my mom sitting in a rocker holding one of the girls after me and singing about Red Wing and Indian Maid. I don't remember the words.

We were always singing. There wasn't much else to do. We walked to one of the neighbors' sometimes and sang. It was about three mile to there. One of their sons married one of my sisters. But there must have been something in that old holler to make us sing, because sometime after we moved from there Connie Smith and her folks lived there. I don't know when that was, but she went to Dexter City School and eventually went to Nashville.

We moved out of the holler when I was in the seventh grade. Then right after that, they closed the one-room school at Donganon, and I went to Jackson School for the eighth grade, then to Dexter City. I don't know why we moved. Maybe it was on account of the Depression and Dad had to sell the farm. I don't know, but he got a job just over the hill from where we moved to. Dad just had to go over the hill to Bocatcher Holler where he ran the limestone crusher. They were starting to put stone on the old dirt roads.

Down below our house about half a mile our land ended and a neighbor's started, but he didn't live there. He lived down at the end of the holler. There was only three houses in the holler, well four, but the one at the end of our land was haunted, or so we thought. No one had lived there for years. It was just a shell of a house. No windows or doors. Our house, then the haunted house and a log house that people lived in sometimes, and then the farmer that owned the land next to ours. It was mostly just hillside, but the creek that ran down the holler went through there right along the road and the fence. The fence wasn't much, just rails and barbwire. Sometimes he kept cattle in there, and it mostly kept them in. There was a fence across the creek, and when the creek got high from the rain, it would wash the fence out 'cause brush and logs would come down the holler.

Anyhow, Dad and the farmer put in a flood gate. I was there with Dad and my two older brothers on each side of the creek. They dug holes with a posthole digger and put in good sized posts, a fork at the top, and then back of the posts a ways they dug square holes down in the ground. They was pretty deep. Then they made what was called a dead man in them. It was made like an X then a steel cable was fastened in there, and it run up over the posts and across the creek from bank to bank. It was about 30 feet. Then the gates hung on the cable. They were made out of planks and would swing when the water got high. They worked pretty good.

When we would visit the neighbors on down the holler, we would go in the evening when it was still light and when we passed that old house, there was not any noises, but when we came back up the road after dark, there seemed to be moans and groans and all kinds of noises. I remember my brother telling about one time when they were going past the old house, there was some kind of a weird noise, and everyone took off running and left him. He wasn't very old at that time and took off trying to catch them, and he run and run till he could hardly run anymore. Anyway, it was really spooky down that holler. The trees over hung the road and it was always darker in there. I often thought about them noises. Maybe it was those flood gates swinging on that cable or the wind blowing through that old house, but there was noises there.

Snakes, snakes and more snakes. We had a lot of snakes. All kinds: blacksnakes, copperheads, garter snakes, adders, and there was always someone saying they had seen a hoop snake, and it would but its tail in its mouth and roll up in a hoop and chase you. I think that was a bunch of hooey.

Anyhow, we mostly killed every snake we come across. I had a few encounters with copperheads. One was I heard the dog barking down the road an up on a bank.

First I have to tell you about the dog. He was death on snakes. We had other dogs, but he was the only one that run loose all the time.

Anyway, I run down there. He was barking on the other side of a good sized rock. I climbed up on the rock and peeked over and a copperhead was staring me right in the face, and right then the dog grabbed it and shook the stuff right out of it.

Another time, my older brother and me was up on the hill at the sheep barn fixing a fence. It was summertime, and I was barefooted. There was running briers on the ground, and I was standing in them. My feet was pretty well toughened up. All at once he said, "Stand still." I thought he was going to cut my toes off. He swung the axe down and cut the head off a copperhead.

Another time, there was about a ten or 12-foot space between the side of the house, and there was a copperhead stretched out across the way. I couldn't stop so I jumped over it and kept on going. Someone killed it with a hoe.

We kept a rain barrel at one edge of the house, and I would reach up and grab the rim of the barrel and pull myself up and lean down in, and yell. It sounded funny. I was not very big at that time. One day I did that, and it was about three quarters full of water, and I slipped and fell in. I don't know how I got turned around in there, but they found me in there with water up to my neck.

Another time I swallowed a penny and it stuck in my throat, and I kind of remember this. I don't remember how we got to Beverly, just Dad and me, but I remember on the street car from Beverly to Maretta. That is all I remember, just the ride. The doctor just poked it on down, my older brother told me. When we got home, my dad went hunting that night and caught enough fur to pay for the doctor and the trip, which was around eight dollars. That was a lot of money then.

We always hunted and trapped a lot, and we ate rabbits, squirrels, and there was quail around back. Then we would walk down to a bigger stream and catch bluegill, sunfish, and bass, sometimes a turtle, but mostly we ate hog meat and beef.

I got my first rifle when I was ten. It cost 12 dollars. We had ordered it out of a catalog, and it came in the mail up at the store, a Remington bolt action single shot. Back then there was a lot of rabbits around, and you could get a quarter apiece for them. A box of shells was only a quarter. Well I used up a lot of ammo on them groundhogs, and I would get the rabbits sitting in their squat. My oldest brother was a good shot. He could hit a rabbit running with his .22. His name was Paul, but everyone called him Lew, cause way back in our ancestors, one of them married Lew Wetsel's sister. Wetsel was around when they settled Maretta. My great, great, great grandpaw came from Austria and came to Pittsburg down the Ohio River and up the Muskingum River and had a cabin somewhere around Coal Run, Ohio.

Dunganon one room school in 1937. Charles Augenstein is on the back row, third from right.

The old school house was one room with a round stove in the middle with things on the sides down where the ashes was, maybe foot rests. I don't know. In the wintertime, we would put our wet gloves on them to dry. If the stove was hot, the gloves would get to smelling a little.

There was never more than 15 or 20 kids in the whole school. We would walk up the holler or around the road to school. It was about a half mile on out the road past the store. There was four or five of us kids in school from our family, and about all the time we were the first ones there, and the last ones to leave. For when it was cold, we would get the fire going and carry in wood and coal and in the evening, we would take out ashes and sweep up.

There was two outhouses. One for girls, and one for boys. Privies, we called them. There was no well at the school, and we carried water from a farm that was nearby. If we run out of water during school hours, sometimes the teacher would send a couple of us to get water in a bucket, and we would dawdle along. We would pour it in a big jug with a spigot on the bottom. I don't remember if we drank out of the same cup or not. If we did, no wonder we got what everyone else had.

I don't remember ever getting a whipping at school or no one else.

We would play games at school, ante over the school roof and the kids on the other was supposed to catch the ball and throw it back. Sometimes the ball would get stuck behind the chimney, and we would have to wait till the wind blew it down or get another ball.

When the snow was on, we would play fox and geese, make a big circle in the snow and a spot in the middle where you was safe. We played crack the whip; make a long line holding hands and start running in a circle. The ones on the end going real fast then the ones in the middle would turn the other way when it came to the end of the line, you had to hang on, or off you would go.

We would play red rover, two lines across from each other holding hands. Then someone would call out, "Red rover, red rover send her or him over," and they was supposed to break through the line. The girls played right along with the boys.

At Easter time, all the kids brought eggs and the teacher and us kids would take a kettle and the eggs down back of the school a ways to a creek where there was a big flat limestone rock. We gathered sticks and wood and made a fire and boiled the eggs. Then before the eggs were done, us older ones would wander around in the woods. You can imagine the girls and boys in the woods. That is all I have to say about that.

Back then when someone got something, all of us kids got it; chicken pox, measles, mumps, whooping cough. One time we was butchering hogs, and I was out there watching or helping, mostly in the way, and someone said, "You're all broke out with rash," and I had to go in the house and stay. I don't remember what I had, measles or chicken pox.

I always liked butchering time. Two big iron kettles

of water with a fire under them, and you could warm yourself and poke sticks in the fire. We would butcher two hogs and two later on. Dad would say, "We eat everything but the squeal."

One time we were sleigh riding down a pretty steep hill. We had two or three old wood sleds that would go purty good, but Paul and Robert got an old piece of roofing tin and curved it up in the front. I wasn't very big, but I wanted to go on it with them. They kept telling me I was too little to go on it, but they finally let me on. The hill was long and steep with a flat place at the bottom where the wooden sleds would stop. Then there was the creek. Well, down the hill we came on that tin, and it did not stop. They rolled off, but I didn't. The tin went into the creek, and there I set in water up to my waist. I went to the house crying, my brothers saying, "We told you, we told you."

For washing clothes we had another building away from the house that had a flat-topped stove in it that Mom heated water in. Then there was two tubs and a wringer that you turned by hand and she did the clothes on a wash board with old yellow soap that she made in them iron kettles in that same building. We had a cream separator and what we didn't use for butter, we took up to the store and sold. We took extra eggs to the store and sold, for we had chickens everywhere, big speckled ones and red ones.

We had lots of fried chicken to eat. We also had young beef to eat and Mom could pack that in jars. That was the best beef I ever ate.

I said something about those old iron kettles. We used them for butchering, soap making, and we made apple butter in them. I remember going up to the store and getting a sack of red drops to put in the apple butter. They was cinnamon drops.

I always liked when the threshing machine came to do our wheat and oats. We would catch the grain in sacks and carry it to the granary and pour it in the wooden bins. Dad always made a big straw stack beside the barn. I remember one time my mom filled my straw tick with new straw, and I had to make a running leap to get in bed.

Bathing: Yes, we took our baths in a wash tub out in the building. I don't know why we called it the building, but it was a better name than a shed. Sometimes in the summertime, we would go down to the stream where we went fishing and there was a long, deep pool of water us boys and a couple of neighbor boys, and no, we did not have bathing suits. There was a nice sand bar at one end, but the water got deep right off of it, and sometimes they had baptisms there. We always went down and watched but never took part. I guess we were a bunch of heathens.

We didn't have a well at the house. We had a cistern, but no well. We had to go across the road through the gate across the creek to get water to drink in a spring. It was at the bottom of a hill, but it was all walled up with stone and a big flat stone on top. The water was cold even in the summertime. I always thought it was the best water I ever drank.

There was a place I could always remember up a little holler past the spring and over a rail fence. There was a little hill or knoll that had the thickest moss that I had ever seen. It was just fun to walk on it in your bare feet. But one day I was up there fooling around and a chunk of moss came loose and a big old centipede with a million legs come up out of there. I don't think I ever walked on there in my bare feet again.

We never had a car till after we moved from out of the holler. Then my oldest brother got one. We had a two-seated Surrey, and I remember going to Beverly with Mom and Dad in it and Mom going to the hardware store and getting a grate for the cook stove that had burnt out. Then we went to Waterford, just across the river to the mill, and got flour and some cornmeal and Dad stopped at the ice plant and got a big chunk of ice. That evening we made ice cream.

At Halloween we always went out messing around. There was this old man that lived up on the main road. He lived mostly by himself. I don't know why we pestered the poor old man. One time we went there and caught one of his geese and raised a window and put the goose in the house. That was probably a mess. Another time we switched wheels on his wagon, put the rear wheels in front. The wheels were different sizes. The front wheels were always smaller than the back ones so you could turn the wagon better. Right after that we were up at the store when he come out the road with the horses and wagon, and he stopped at the store and come in and was sitting there talking to Dad. Then he said to Dad, "There's something the matter with my wagon, would you look at it?" Dad went out and looked. "Well," he said, "your wheels are on wrong." Dad looked at us and said, "I know you boys were in on that, so get to work." We had an awful time changing them wheels back around. Dad said, "You might as well grease them, since you got them off."

I don't know when this was, but they started having picture shows at Beverly. I think it was on Friday nights. They had them in the street, and they were free. They didn't start till dark, but us kids would start walking right after supper. It was about seven mile. We would pick up kids along the way. Sometimes there would be 12 or more. You had to stand to watch the movie or bring a chair. We sure didn't want to carry a chair along. Us smaller kids would sit down on the street in front if there was room, then we would walk home after dark.

We walked everywhere. I remember walking to Coal

Run with Mom to see her mom. We stayed all night, then walked back home the next day.

We played hooky some. One day we were going to school, and my brothers kept saying stay back a little so when the girls was out of sight, we went over the hill in another holler where we had built a log cabin and stayed all day. I don't remember that punishment. We got just some more chores maybe. Sometimes we would say we just didn't feel good and stay home, cause with nine kids there was always someone sick.

When we had time, us boys was out in the woods hunting or digging roots. Yellow root, ginseng, sometimes May apple and ginger root. Sometimes we dug up sweet anise to chew on. It tasted like licorice.

Sometimes we would find a bee tree and cut it down. We had a smoker, but we would still get stung. But it was worth it when you would get a tub full of honey.

Skating in the Attic to Edison

by Sharon L. Work of Urichsville, Ohio
born in 1947

The year was 1957, and in the small town of New Cumberland there were at least three to four families on the ole party line. When you picked up the receiver you listened a few seconds to see if anyone else was using the line. If so, you just hung up and waited a good 15 to 30 minutes until the line was clear. Then came the time I wanted to make a call. The phone line seemed clear, but then after listening closer, we could hear people talking and the occasional bark of a dog. We determined which neighbor it was and took turns whistling loudly, which we hoped would cause the neighbor to find that their phone was off the hook. But all it did was cause the dog to bark more and the neighbor to yell at the dog, due to its excessive barking. This went on a good half hour. Finally, my mother got in the car and went to the neighbor with the phone off. An apology was made and shortly after that, the phone line was back in use.

Must say, I do miss that ole party phone line, for that was a time you could depend on a neighbor. You did know your neighbors and folks didn't seem to be in such a hurry.

* * * *

The year was 1956. We lived in a two-story wooden frame house in the New Cumberland area. In the upstairs was two bedrooms, a long hallway with a small closet door to the left, then the attic door and last the bathroom with the huge tub with the claw feet. Inside the attic, which was a good 30 feet square, sat the Edison Record Player. You would crank it by hand a good four to six turns, put on a cylinder record, and skate around the floor at least twice, stop record, put on another, and do it all over again. As for the skates, they were the clamp-on type with the huge key to adjust shoe size.

The Edison sat in the attic until 1969 when the farm was sold to a coal company. The Edison was moved to my Grandma Strawn's house in New Cumberland, which remained Mom and Dad's home. The Edison sat in a back bedroom until about the year of 1982, and my sister moved the Edison to New Philadelphia to an upstairs bedroom. For my younger son was hyper, so that was how Monna came to get the Edison. Then I began to question as to why she wasn't playing the Edison, but found out it didn't work. Several years had passed; I had married my second husband and moved to Uhrichsville. So, since I was the oldest of us two girls, I felt the Edison should be mine. So, my sister finally agreed that I could have it.

My neighbor lady helped me to get it inside the house, and she remarked that I had one fine antique there. So, I brought it inside and began to tinker at getting it to work.

There is three sets of screws along the piece holding the needle, so I screwed each on just a bit and finally got the needle balanced. Yes, it works. So then I began to search for more records. And one day, while in Bysville at a flea market, I asked the guy if he ever got records for the Edison players. He informed me that he had gotten in a box of nearly 50, so I could have fun selecting which ones I wanted. I came home with 30 to add to the ones I already had.

In my Edison there is three shelves. I have the records as "music alone" on top, "comedy or story telling" on second shelf, and "music and singing" on bottom shelf. I even have three Christmas records and several gospel. All total, I have 85 records and there isn't enough money in the world for me to part with this great antique.

* * * *

The years of 1956 to 1960 were the ones associated with our fishing in the small creek on our 150-acre farm in the New Cumberland area. The creek wasn't that deep, it was mostly there to serve the sheep and Holstine cows their water supply.

So my sister, Monna, and I got the bright idea we could make this one spot into a really nice fishing hole. We made it deeper and also widened the sides and in several days we noticed "chubs" (which were oversized minnows) had made their way to our "fishing hole." We didn't have the modern fishing poles; instead it was a straight stick, string line and a bent straight pin for a hook. I still don't know how those fish actually stayed on that pin. As for bait, it came from the pigpen, and all you needed was at least three good turns of the shovel and you had all the bait you needed. Then one day Dad surprised us girls with tiny fishhooks and several size corks. Now we were true fishermen and could wait till we tried our new supplies. After each fishing adventure we'd dump the fish back into the creek so as to have fish on the next trip.

* * * *

I started first grade in 1954 and went to New Cumberland Elementary School. My teacher was Mrs. Threesa Moore. Then came second grade and came to find that I was to have Mrs. Moore again. In third grade we seemed to have a substitute teacher the most of the year, and I can't even recall what her name was. Then came fourth grade, and wow, here is Mrs. Moore and the classroom is upstairs next to the cafeteria. Next I am in the fifth grade and find that I have Mrs. Moore again for my teacher and this classroom is also upstairs.

For sixth grade I had my first man teacher, Howard Mizer. He was kinda strict and math was one of my worst subjects, but I recall this one time that I was to tell the three steps of a division problem, to which I had to write all three steps over and over, which I missed lunch. Needless to say the main cook came to my rescue and came to Mr. Mizer to see why I wasn't at lunch. To this very day I can still recall those three steps: The divider—dividend—and quotation.

Along with the teachers was the several field trips. In second grade our class went to our farm one day with a sack lunch. Several took turns at feeding baby lambs by bottles, then we spread a blanket on the lawn and everyone ate their sack lunch and we returned back to school.

In fifth grade we went to the Schoenbrunn Village which began in 1772. Historical Society took over site in 1923 and reconstructed village between 1930 and 1939. Today there's 17 log buildings, original mission cemetery, museum, and visitor center and gift shop. How well I remember the gift shop, for quite a few of the classmates bought Indian articles.

* * * *

It was the Christmas of 1953. Ole Santa brought my sister and I a reddish buff colored cocker spaniel which we named "Blondie." At the same time, my first cousin got Blondie's brother, which was black, so he was named "Blackie." My Aunt Lois was to move to Dover and for some reason could not take her cocker spaniel, so we kept "Susie" at the farm.

One favorite adventure I recall with the two dogs was getting the live Christmas tree, and we took the sled and walked a good quarter mile with these dogs jumping in the snow. That tree looked lovely on the ground, but in looking back at some of those pictures, I can't believe we actually picked out such a misshapen tree. That was truly pitiful.

On the farm, there were numerous cats at the barn, but this one Angora cat named Fluffy had quite a many kittens, which always got homes, but this one kitten "Spooky" an all black kitten also made his way to the house. The farm was sold to a coal company in 1969 and Fluffy and Spooky both moved to Grandpa Strawn's home which remained Mom and Dad's home, then one day Mom couldn't find Fluffy, but we found her body at the edge of their property, so Dad buried her out near the pine tree. Spooky lived out his life and had been quite a healthy cat, but in his older years, he began to just look like fur, skin and bones, so we decided it was time to put him down.

My dad and I took this cat to the vet. Both of us were crying all the way. Dad kept saying, "Ole Spooky, why couldn't you have died on your own?" The cat was put to sleep and we brought his body home where he too was buried under the pine tree. Mom got other cats, but none took the place of Spooky, who was a cat that was definitely one of a kind.

Yes, we were farm girls and we had an assortment of animals in our childhood years. There were goldfish, parakeets, baby lambs, cats, dogs, and some lizards.

Every child gets to learn of death. It's a bit rough when you're close to a certain animal, but my sister and I had our own animal graveyard about a quarter mile beyond the barn. Since we were raised in a Christian family, this meant that most of the smaller animals were the ones that got a burial. One of us would dig a grave, the other would take the songbook from church and we read several verses and sang "In the Garden" or "Jesus Loves Me." But there was more, for our animals also got a state tombstone. It told of the animal's name, date of birth, date of death and its age. There must have been at least over 20 or more animals buried in our little graveyard.

The coal company bought that farm in 1969 and I bet no one even realized the many tears shed, the kind words spoken about the animal or that this really meant something to two little girls who grew into adults.

* * * *

As a youngster I enjoyed being around older folks and listening to the many tales being told. So I'd have to say my most memorable person was the late Mooney Warther, the Master Carver of Dover, Ohio, and his wife, Frieda.

My friend, Margaret Gibbs, and I would go to the Garden Clubs at the Warther Home. Mrs. Warther was quite soft spoken, while Mooney could be heard several feet away, but yet this "gentle giant" had a way for the children and delighted in making the wooden pliars for them.

Mrs. Warther started her button collection at the age of 10. She hand-sewed the most of her 73,000 collection in quilt patterns, and I've visited the button shop quite often.

But the greatest thing at Warther's in this era was the "Great Swing." It was the thrill of all thrills to walk out that wall and a bit scary that first time, but after that 40-minute sawing, you couldn't wait to get back in line to do it all over again. Then in 1968 the swing had to be dismantled and the great elm chopped down because Dutch Elm had destroyed the tree. Calico ditch would soon be forgotten with the tree gone.

Mooney and Frieda raised five children. Mooney passed away June 8, 1973 at the age of 87. Mrs. Warther passed away June of 1988 at the age of 97. Both of these fine folks are still greatly missed at the Warther Museum.

* * * *

Being farm girls, there wasn't that many times that we could actually get away to take in a movie. But I do recall that Dad took my sister, Monna, and I to see "Shaggy Dog" at the New Philadelphia, Ohio movie theater. And we also got to see "Darby O'Gill and the Little People" along with "Babes in Toyland." In 1961 our eighth grade took a trip to Canton, Ohio to see the movie "The Sound of Music." I got to see this movie another four times before it did come to television. Course, we can't forget all those "Benji" movies that usually left most of the people wiping their eyes as they would exit the theater.

* * * *

It was the winter of '55 and I was in second grade. We awoke that January day to a covering of over four feet of snow. Mom fixed my sister, Monna, and I a breakfast of hot oatmeal. We bundled up with coats, scarf, mitten, and snow pants. Now, we knew that girls were not allowed to wear pants at school, so they were to be taken off after we got to school. And school wasn't cancelled that often back then. Dad fired up the Massey Ferguson tractor, hooked up the railroad drag, and we girls rode the tractor out the lane to catch the bus.

This was picture day. Several weeks passed, then the group picture was sent home. In the front row is Sharon Strawn wearing her corduroy snow pants. No! I've not lived this down yet, for it seems to somehow surface at family gatherings.

* * * *

The year was 1965 and it was summer on the farm. Dad did the evening walking of our 22 Holstines, but discovered that Bessie didn't make it to the barn. My sister, Monna, and I got our Shetland ponies and we rode down along the fence line of the pasture that the cows had been in. We came back to the barn and about that time friends from Canton had arrived, so Dad, his friend, George, my sister, and I went back out for the search. This time we went along the creek line. Monna and I took the lower end; while Dad and his friend took the upper, but within minute we heard Dad say, "Hear she is." I just knew it wasn't good, for Bessie had gone in at the one point where a spring ran into the creek. It was quite soft, and yet the opening just wide enough for the cow. We figure she went to get a drink, slid forward, and went nose first into the water. Her body was wedged and there was no way she could back out.

Dad came back to the house and called our one neighbor who had a larger tractor. He put chains on the cow's legs and pulled her out. Dad then called this one company that came to haul away the larger animals.

It was a sad time for everyone, yet Dad tried to hide it from us girls. My sister and I had given names to every cow in the barn. In fact, we even made name cards and when a new heifer would take the place of another previous cow, we girls would draw straws and a new name card was made.

For most of my childhood I had dreams of having a horse on our farm, but I also knew that you could not have the cows and horses in the same barn. Then, in May of '65, I came to learn that my one friend's cousin was selling their farm. Now, they had boarded these two Shetland ponies and so this meant the ponies would need a place to go. So my sister and I began to check out some of the buildings on our farm and decided this one chicken coop would work. So we gutted it, cleaned it out, and got Dad's approval of the ponies. We contacted the owner and they brought the ponies to our farm.

Now, "Flicka" was 25 years of age and a brown and white pony, where her daughter, "Friskie," was 14 years of age and was black and white. But there was a wee problem with Friskie, as she had been foundered at a younger age, which meant her feet would split and bleed. So most of the time, she couldn't be ridden. Our vet gave me information as to how to trim her feet and how to care for them.

I was not skilled at getting the saddle on, so I finally learned to ride bare-backed most of the time. It was the catching the pony that would get under my skin. For this critter was quite ornery. She would come just to my finger tips where she would get the corn or oats and then turn sideways and run away. My dad would get such a kick out of these deals. But for most of the time I would grab her halter and then lead her to the shed where I'd get her bridle and off we'd go.

Then came the summer. There was two plum trees in the pasture field where the ponies were. So we girls would have to pen up the ponies each night. Then the next morning we would have to take buckets and gather those plums and also the low hanging ones on the tree. There was also this huge mulberry tree in the same pasture and we tried to prop it up higher, but still the ponies would suck the berries from the branches. Finally, Dad came to our rescue and put a small fence around the tree.

We had a quarter mile lane, so I would ride the pony out to get the mail. At the mailbox you had to secure the mail, for the minute that pony made the turn, she would be coming full speed, and I rode her in this one field along the driveway, but there was a path made, and when she reached this point, she would jump back on the driveway. Well this one time, the pony fell. I got a skinned elbow and knee. The pony's nose was skinned and she was limping. I lead her into the spring trough and was washing off the pony's nose when once more Dad came to check on us. I was so sure that she was going to be put down, but Dad assured me that she was fine, that I should go take care of my own scrapes.

Summer was always dreaded, for these ponies would get a very thick coat for winter, so this meant quite a bit of brushing both of them, and if you rode, you most likely would be covered in hair.

I enjoyed that pony quite a many hours, but then in the summer of "67 the ponies' health was really going downhill. We contacted the owner and she decided that it was best to have the ponies put down. So a guy was called. He brought a truck. The ponies were loaded, and as they drove out the lane, there wasn't a dry eye on any of our family.

* * * *

It was the summer of '53. I was six years of age. Dad had gotten this buck sheep from a neighbor to use for breeding. We girls were highly warned that he was quite nasty and this meant we were to stay clear of him. But "Miss Daring" decided to check it out for herself.

I got several ears of corn, took them to the barn to shell. Then I put the corn in a can and made my way to the buck sheep's pen. The front of the pen was stacked railroad ties which numbered at least five, so I crawled over them, poured the corn in the pan for the sheep, and noticed he was eating. Now, it was a good 20 feet back to the ties and I proceeded to crawl back over in a period of 10 minutes at the most, when all of a sudden I was pushed over the ties. My belly was scratched and skinned and it felt as though I had been hit by a fast moving truck. I made my way to the house crying and saying, "Monna hit me with a board."

Now, my sister was slow in talking, but she came through loud and clear by saying, "But sheep hit Saron." Dad turned away to hide the laughter, then in a calm voice said, "I believe the buck sheep gave you all the punishment you need." Yes, I did learn one great lesson the HARD way, in more ways than one.

It was the fall of '53. I was six and sister Monna was three. Mom and Dad were doing evening milking at the barn, when we girls decided to make some cornbread. We had watched Mom, so we got out corn meal, flour, sugar, eggs and milk. The bad part—we didn't have any idea as to how much of things went into this corn bread. We put our ingredients in the mixing bowl, turned on the mixer and the stuff hung from the cupboard like stalactites, and we girls were covered along with the flour. About that time, Mom came in the door. She exclaimed, "Girls! What on earth are you doing?" And in a voice of innocence, I replied, "Mom, we watched you make cornbread, so we decided to make one for you." Mom was quite glad that we hadn't gotten our fingers in the mixer blades, and we were given a quick bath. The kitchen was cleaned, and our mess mostly dumped because of no proper measurements. Shortly after that, we were taught the correct items and measures in making cornbread.

It was mid March of '55. A day that had warmed up with sun shining, but there was still snow in the valleys along the edges of the springs on our farm. But sister Monna and I had been inside long enough, so we decided to take a walk out across the fields. We girls had been warned about a certain wash out on this one hill, and with the slight thaw, it was definitely off limits for sure. We walked down through the valley, taking care not to get wet feet and decided to check out the wash out. Sister Monna, at age five decided to walk across it and immediately her boots sink. She cried and claimed that I should come in to get her out. Yes! My boots sank also, and we're standing there side by side.

I knew we had to get back to the house, so we both pulled our feet from our boots and made our way back. I, the smart one, went around the barn through the one field, while Monna walked on through the barnyard. All the while we were in stocking feet and it was way too cold to enjoy it. Mom heated up water, and we warmed up our feet, while Dad was on the hunt for our boots. He came back to the house, I got another pair of shoes and boots and he informed me that I best know where the boots were. He dug down in the mud and both pairs were completely covered. Mom was so thankful we didn't have frostbite, and we didn't catch our death of pneumonia, that punishment was kinda forgotten. But we never walked across the wash out until it had dried up quite a bit.

Old Man Ezra Wants His Land Back

by Linda Hudson Hoagland of North Tazewell, Virginia

I spent my elementary and junior high school years in the small town in Ohio called Twin Valley. The next bigger town was New Boston and then Portsmouth. We lived in a rural area where the houses were built in clusters and that became our neighborhood.

Halloween was a memorable part of the year each year because you just never knew what was going to happen.

"I'm not moving from this place," Ellen Hudson mumbled as she tried to convince herself that she should stay until the bitter end. It was dark and cold under the church steps and she was crunched up and uncomfortable.

"How much longer?" she whispered to no one because she was alone thinking about why she was there.

"You can see him walking up the church steps just before Halloween," said Terry, Ellen's brother, in a conspiratorial whisper.

"Who?"

"Old man Ezra Hudson."

"Who was he? I've never heard of an Ezra Hudson."

"He is my great-great grandfather, I think. He used to own the land that the church is built on. They say he wants it back - the land, I mean."

The Hudson House in Twin Valley. You could see the church across the street from the front porch.

"Who is they?" asked a skeptical Bobby.

"I don't know. People who live around here; old people. It's just an old story I heard."

"Why is he still hanging around? How old is this guy?"

"The original Ezra Hudson is dead, Bobby. He's been dead for over a hundred years."

"Have you ever seen him?"

"No, I've never really wanted to see a ghost, especially a mean son-of-a-gun like Ezra Hudson was supposed to be."

The conversation stopped suddenly when Ellen bumped into them. "Back off, Ellen. Me and Bobby are having a private talk."

"Sure, Terry. I didn't hear anything anyway."

"Do you think she believed me?" asked Terry.

"Every bit of it. You could see it in her eyes," answered Bobby as they both smiled about what they had done.

Now Ellen was sitting under some nasty, dirty steps, freezing cold, waiting for a ghost to appear.

"Am I stupid, or what?" she asked herself as she moved forward a little so she could change positions and get a better look down the road. She looked through the step treads towards the area where the one and only street light was located.

She heard a dragging sound, like something heavy being pulled across the pavement up near the street light. She inched forward trying to force her eyes to see what obviously couldn't be seen. She had to move out from under the steps.

"Throw it up over the limb," said a masculine sounding voice in a harsh whisper.

"I'm trying to. Shut up already."

Ellen didn't move away from the steps. She didn't want to be seen by those who were out in the dark of night.

"The rope is long enough so I'm going to drop it all the way to the ground. I'll tie it off on the bridge railing over here and then we can finish the job. Grab that noose."

"Okay, okay, I've got it."

"Wrap it around that tree over there. I think I hear a car coming. Get out of sight,

"I don't see a car."

"It must have turned off on one of the side roads. Let's get this finished."

Ellen's eyes widened with fear.

"Get the body."

"I need some help. He's awfully heavy."

"Okay, okay, quit your whining."

"I'll hold him up so you can put the noose around his neck." They were hanging somebody.

"It's going to take both of us pulling to get the body in the air. I want it all the way up swinging in the breeze directly under the street light for all the world to see, especially Ellen."

Suddenly Ellen knew the voices. Payback was going to be had. Ellen knew about the broken lock on the window that opened into the basement of the church. She got down on her hands and knees, gently pushed against the window, and crawled inside the basement of the church. She found the candle and matches that were always left in the basement for emergencies when the lights went out. She lit the candle and made her way to the first floor of the church.

Ellen ran to the church organ and played a really loud chord that could be heard all the way down the street. Then she ran back to the front door of the church where the bell pull for the church bell was located and quickly yanked the bell into life.

She snapped the front door lock and pulled it closed behind her as she left the church leaving a flickering candle in the window. Again, she ran to the steps where she would hide just in case someone wanted to do any investigating.

"What was that? There's someone over at the church. Look, Bobby, there's some kind of light over there. See!" said Terry as he pointed towards the church.

"Don't lie to me, Terry, there's no one over there," said Bobby as he worked with the rope he was trying to tie down so the body wouldn't come crashing to the ground scattering the straw stuffing all over kingdom come.

"Look, Bobby. Look!"

Bobby turned his head towards the church just as

the church organ sounded. "Who did that?"

"Nobody. There are no cars parked in front or lights on in the church except that one over there flickering. It must be candle."

"Somebody has to be in there. Somebody is just trying to scare us."

"Well, they're doing a pretty good job of it," whined Terry.

A strange masculine but wavy voice shouted out from the sparkling white floating form above the candle, "I want my land back. Give me my land."

Bobby and Terry took off running while Ellen laughed until tears streamed down her cheeks.

At school the next day, Ellen smiled at Bobby and Terry each time she passed them in the halls.

"Hey, Ellen," shouted Bobby, "were you out by the church last night?"

"Why would you ask that?"

"Just wondering. You heard about the commotion didn't you?"

"You mean the bells ringing? Must have been somebody pulling a Halloween prank."

"Terry said he heard old man Ezra Hudson shouting about wanting his land back."

"Oh, really?" Ellen said as she puzzled over what he was saying. She hadn't heard or seen old man Ezra Hudson and she had been standing right there.

Ellen is me. My name was Linda Ellen Hudson it is now Linda Hudson Hoagland.

The Little Roof Tar Indians

by Carl Gardiner of Quaker, Ohio
born in 1923

When I was 11 years old, my brother Bill was near ten. He was small in stature but big enough to poke me in the stomach and run to the other room, lock the door and scream like a wild Indian. I heard my grandmother tell my mother, "You had better get in there. Big Carl is going to kill little Billie some day," amen.

My brother Bill and I went to Fairview Pennyroyal Opera House to watch a show. We thought it was very comical. The following morning, we searched to find something to blacken our faces with. We were both laughing at each other until Mother appeared and said, "Oh my God, have you lost your minds? You will have a very hard time getting the roofing tar off your faces."

Mother found a half gallon of kerosene and rags and started wiping our faces. We were two little white boys who were pretending to be colored. After Mother got done cleaning our faces, we looked like two little Indians

Saved by Prayers and Laughing at Recipes

By Diana Bowers Short of Cambridge, Ohio
Born in 1939

When I was a sophomore, my sister Jean (Bowers) Cain and I were in the house, and my two brothers Ralph and Floyd were with my dad (Hubert Bowers) in the hay field putting up hay. Floyd came in to get something, and I had the thought my sister and I should pray for him before he went back out. I hesitated to ask him because I thought he would think it was dumb or something, but the thought was so strong and kept getting stronger. Just as he was about to go out the door, I asked him if we could pray for him. He said yes, that he would always accept prayer. We prayed for him.

A little while later, he came in and gave this account of what happened. When they put up hay, they liked to make a little game of it to break the monotony, so the one on the ground would throw the shock of hay onto the one on the wagon. Floyd was on the wagon, and Ralph threw the shock of hay on him, and a big snake was stuck on the tines of the pitchfork. I believe that if we had not prayed for him, that snake would have been thrown on my brother.

When I was a junior in high school, my dad, Hubert Bowers, took a neighbor girl and I with him to the general store across Route 21 from Derwent. While Dad shopped, the girl and I looked around. She picked up a squirrel tail and rubbed it in my face and laid it down. I picked it up and rubbed it in her face; she grabbed it and it broke in half. She put it back in the pile under others so it would not be seen. I knew I had to tell my dad, so when we got outside the store, I told him. He said that I would have to go back inside and tell the man what I did, and he would have to pay for the tail. The other girl refused to go, but I had no choice.

I got the tail and told what happened, and Dad paid for it. The man said that no one wants to buy a broken squirrel tail so he told me to pick out a fox tail. He had long fluffy brown ones and silver ones. The silver was more expensive. I felt I should not pick the expensive silver one because he was giving it to me free. I chose the brown one. He said that no teenage girl wants a brown fox tail, and he gave me a silver one and told me to keep all three of them.

I kept them and sewed the squirrel tail back together. When I married and had three children, I gave each of them a tail. My oldest, a daughter, Rhonda (high) Firnhaber, got the silver one. My second, a son Terry, got the brown tail, and alas, my youngest, Diane (High) Johnson, got the squirrel tail.

All our lives, my sister Jean (Bowers) Cain and I have enjoyed just being together. We could laugh at anything. We would read titles of recipes in a cookbook and laugh.

In 1974, our parents, Hubert and Evelena Bowers, lived at West Milton, Ohio. My dad passed away that year. My three brothers, Carl, Ralph, and Floyd, and my sister Jean and I, all met at Mom's house. We had not seen each other for two or three years. I guess the sorrow of Dad's passing, and the joy of Jean and I being together, collided.

That night she and I slept on the studio couch in the living room and my three brothers were on the floor. Our mother was in her bedroom at the back of the house. Jean and I started giggling and could not stop; we even put our hands over our mouths but could not stop. We felt so ashamed to laugh when Mom had just lost her husband, and we, our dad.

The next morning we apologized to Mom and she said, "Oh no, your laughing is what got me through the night. As I listened to your laughter I thought, in the midst of all this sorrow, my daughters can still laugh. I know there is hope; I know life will go on."

Since then, my mother has criss-crossed this United States, and traveled into Canada and Mexico. Her prayers have circled the globe, even praying in 1994 or '95 that a hurricane would not hit Saint Lucia Island because her eldest son was there, and it turned fifty miles before the island, and went around it. Mom will be 95 years old on July 24, 2009. Today, many say Mom is a blessing to them.

The Journal and the Banjo

by Linda Lahmon of Glenford, Ohio
born in 1940

I have a journal that was written by my dad, Rexford D. Nay, and begins Saturday, June 13, 1931. Rex Nay was 16 at the time; he was born August 12, 1914.

Dad and his sister (my aunt, Dorotha Louise Nay), his mother, Lu Lu Pearl Summers Nay, and father, Creed Burton Nay, lived in Logan, Ohio when this was written.

I have many mental memories my dad mentioned over the years, but when I came across this journal that I received after his death I now have, in his own words, what he did daily as a teenager for four years during the Depression. I have to admit I cried, laughed, and also was truly amazed at his skills.

Over the span of the four years I have in front of me, my dad bummed many, many, many times to Hollister, New Straitsville, Corning, Shawnee, New Lexington. Then there were places to Gore, New Pittsburg, Ohio, Murray City, Athens, Bremen, and McConnelsville.

The Wonder Bar in 1934. Rexford Nay, banjo player, is second from left by piano.

In the four years I read of his teenage period, he had many boils on different parts of his body, worked in the mines, stoked fires at Gore schoolhouse, rabbit hunted, picked berries. He got chiggers bad and gave banjo lessons. My dad's "love" was music, as he taught himself the banjo and later he owned a guitar. He wrote his own music.

Since I am not a writer and have no idea of how to let you know in my words about this journal, I thought I'd let you know some highlights.

Thursday, October 16, 1932—Rex Nay met Elizabeth Rose Jennings of Hollister, who was playing a piano at a dance in Murray City.

He begins June 13, played for an old farm dance at Dick Lang house, Heather Ridge. He joined the Ned's String Band and writes about the following people: Ralph McDaniel, Wendell Enricks, Ned Barthlow, George Langley, and Ray McMullen. George Langley played a sax and a Carl Little John was a drummer. Dad would get to Columbus and the band would play on station WSEN. He made three phonograph records at the Pythian Theatre in Logan.

There were many basketball games/leagues. One league was "Mike Mullens Street Cleaners," from Logan. The "Cleaners" played Dave Miline's Smokehouses—Cleaners won 21-3. Then against Don Spencer's Stenographers—Cleaners won 7-1.

July 3, 1930, he listened to the Stribling-Schmelling fight at Cleveland. Schmelling won by a technical knockout.

Dad's banjo would become broken in need of repairs. He also gave banjo lessons. He writes about a Fox Hunter's Association in the Junior Mechanics Lodge Room and the Franklin County Democrat Convention at the Southern Hotel, Columbus, Ohio.

He talked about picking dewberries at the Kehota Dumps and at Lost Hollow.

More of his love, music. He writes of Virgil Bright and a "Bobo," then a Dick Lange and Mt. Zion, Sam Hartman from New Straitsville.

When he turned 17, he played at Ash Cave, a theatre in McConnelsville and the Grand Theatre in Circleville. Then he writes about the "Doodle Sockers" —played music with them in Logan. Also he played at the Majestic Theatre in Athens and Palace Theatre in Lancaster.

He loved to listen to OSU football and local football teams. October 8, 1931 Logan vs Lancaster—Logan lost 25-0

He writes about more people: Virgil Spencer, Duke Canton from Shawnee, Roy Palmer, Jake Blankenship, Pappy Stewart—all of these were someway musicians.

Dad has more sport scores. Baseball with Greendale and Gore—Gore won 6-5.

There was the K.P. Hall at Shawnee, Eddie Kremer's orchestra at New Straitsville, Nutter's Store, Hocking County Fair; a place he also wrote about was "Twicherville."

Dad and his father Creed Burton Nay worked at the coal mines and for the township on some roads.

Labor Day, 1933, United Mine Workers Celebration—lots of fights between scabs and union men.

He talks about playing banjo in New Pittsburg, Ohio and Buchtel, Ohio, also at a Moore's Restaurant in Logan.

He graduated Logan High, 1932. Then writes about Dowlers Filling Station in Lancaster, Cable's Hall near McCunesville, Lido Venues Hall, "three miles north of Athens on 31."

On October 6, 1932, he met who would be my mother: Elizabeth Rose Jennings. Her dad, Alphonso "Peck" Jennings, and mother, Eunice. "Peck" ran moonshine during the Depression and drank it too, I hear.

There was a Bill Lawson orchestra in Glouster and a Lamberms Pavillion had a Charlie Wolfe Orchestra.

Dad writes about a John Pelsk, a noted wrestler/boxer. He saw him at a Dispatch Charity Show in Columbus. Dad also played on a station, WSEN in Columbus.

The Eyelevel Outhouse Snake

by Virgil Founds of Chandlersville, Ohio
born in 1938

I am now in what they call the golden age years of my life and I do appreciate the modern conveniences that we now have—especially the indoor plumbing and the modern bathrooms. As I think back to my childhood days, like most other farmhouses of that era, we had a path that led to a little building out back of our house. That was known as a back house or toilet and some folks had other names for it. Ours was about one hundred fifty feet from our back door.

One particularly hot evening in the middle of the summer, I decided I needed to visit this little building before starting my evening chores. My dad and mother had already gone to the barn, which was about three hundred feet on the other side of the house, to start milking. I entered this little building, slipped my bib overhauls down to my knees and sat down on the hole. Now, facing the door, I had the surprise of my life: a blacksnake was right in front of me about eye level. It was on the two by four framework of the building and ready to crawl across the door and block my escape.

I immediately forgot I had to use the toilet. Bursting out the door with my bibs still down around my knees, I'm sure the snake was as surprised as I was by all of this. When I now think about this, wouldn't it have been hilarious if somebody would have caught all this on tape?

At that time, I didn't tell anyone about this event. I just went about feeding the chickens and hogs their evening meal.

To this day, I don't particularly care for snakes, although, if they are not invading my space, I just leave them alone and that works out fine for both of us.

The Farmhouse Porch

by Marie Wells of Corning, Ohio
born in 1943

To begin, Dad (John Reed) only went to the eighth grade. He started working in the local coal mines at age thirteen. Him and Mom had thirteen kids, nine still living. Mom had already lost a baby at two years old with summer complaint. Then a second baby at about eighteen months on August 27th, then on August 28th, this brother, Bob, was born. I can't imagine the heartache.

They lived in the New Lexington area. They went to Michigan for a few years, and I was born up there. Then in 1946, we came back to Ohio. I was told we looked like the Beverly Hillbillies. We had three trucks loaded up with horses, rabbits, chickens, my lamb and anything else you could think of, six kids at the time. Mom had already lost four—one, fourteen days, one stillborn. I was born with a bad lung. They had to keep me crying for about three weeks.

Dad had bought a hundred acre farm. When we was little, Mom used to tell us to go catch tadpoles in the creek or swing on the grapevines in the woods, and our only games were checkers, Chinese checkers and later on, Carrom. I remember our first TV was black and white, and we had a piece of red, green, and blue plastic to put over the screen to make it colored.

One day, my sister Gloria and I were washing diapers on the washboard on the porch. I was about eight. My brother, John, was about five. He had a little red wagon. It set about a foot off the ground, and he wanted me to give him a push. Well I didn't think, but I pushed him down a small hill in the yard, but he was going so fast, he couldn't get stopped, so he went under the cow field fence, laying down screaming. We ran over, and the wheels on the wagon were flying everywhere. He went straight down a big hill and landed at the creek. It's funny now, but Mom didn't think it was very funny.

We did a lot of things on that porch. We always did a lot of berry picking and canning. I bet we washed hundreds of jars in the washtub on that back porch. Dad would give all the boys their haircuts on that porch, and on Saturday, we'd put an electric heater in the washtub of water, and everyone would get their baths. Then on Monday, the old wringer washer and washboard would get their turn on the porch. Everything had to be starched and ironed.

Dad had two work horses, Tom and Prince. Back then, there was a big hay fork in the barn. You would put a wagonload of hay in the barn, then you'd put that big fork in the hay, then Dad would put me on one of the horses, and they would pull until the fork took the hay up in the hay mow, and one of the boys would be up there to release the fork and drop the hay.

Marie Reed Wells and Johnny Reed in front of Gloria's '56 Chevy.

We also had a riding horse named Prince. He was my best friend. Whenever I had a problem, I would go talk to him. He would nuzzle me and whinny, and he always made me feel better.

One day, me, John, Kay and Ken decided to ride to my brother's house. I was probably twelve. They were all younger. We made it there fine, but when we started home, it started to rain, and Prince decided he wanted to run. Well, we were riding bareback, so one by one, we went sliding off.

We weren't very far from home, so Dad could hear us yelling and hollering, so when we came walking in and leading the horse, he said, "What happened?" and we said, "Oh, we just decided to walk." He just laughed and said, "Yeah, I heard you's."

In Sayre, Ohio, where we went to school, there was two stores. One was George Street's Store, and one was Vernie Hammond's Store. If you got a penny or a nickel extra, everyone went to Street's Store. It was kind of the hangout then to get a soda or a piece of candy. I loved going there.

But Vernie Hammond's Store was scary. I don't know why, but it was big and dark, and she had a lot of household items. Sometimes Mom would have me go in there and get needles and thread or something, and I was so scared, but I'd go because Mom told me to.

I don't want to forget Halcey Appleman's Store in Portersville. Dad would drop us off at Sunday school, and if he had extra money, we could go to Halcey's and get some candy while we waited for Dad. Halcey was always so good to us kids. Sometimes he would give us extra candy.

Sometimes we would get to go to the movies on Saturday night. I don't remember what the occasions were, if it was Christmas or what, but there was a five cents and ten cents store in New Lexington called Walters, and I can remember Dad giving us money to buy Mom something, and we would go in by ourselves, and it seems like we were in there for hours looking. Should we buy a handkerchief or a broach? I'll never forget the big candy counter. We never saw so much candy, and inside was a carousel pony that you could put money in and ride. Oh how I wanted to ride that pony, but we never got to.

There was a lot of work with that many kids, but a lot of good times too. My older sister Gloria and I had to dust and mop and wax every Saturday, nine rooms. I hated housework, so I would sneak off as much as I could. I would rather milk the cows and squirt milk in the cats' mouth as they sat in the window of the barn. Many a times I've carried two five-gallon buckets of water or slop to the hogs, and I weighed about ninety pounds, and boy does that manure get heavy when you have to pitchfork it out the door to the manure pile.

Then there was the cooking. We had most of our own meat. Back then, we had a threshing day or days. It depended on how much wheat you had. We had neighbors and some family come. We would set up big tables out in the yard so all the men could sit and eat. We also had a smokehouse where Dad smoked his own meat. It seemed like Mom and them cooked for days. When Mom made pies, even on Sunday, she would bake ten or twelve pies.

When I was about twelve or thirteen, my brother, John, and I got the job of killing the chickens for Sunday dinner and scalding and picking the feathers off. *Yuck*!

About that time, my big sister, Gloria, went to work, and I got the job part of the time of fixing breakfast and packing lunches, and breakfast at our house was bacon, eggs, gravy, pancakes, biscuits, etc. It was go to the smokehouse, get the meat, go to the chicken house, get the eggs, etc. It wasn't pour a bowl of cereal.

Dad taught us to husk and shuck corn at an early age, but he also took us to the square dances on Saturday night and played ball with us on Sundays. As we got older, we joined 4-H. Of course, I was a tomboy, so I wanted to take a calf to the fair like my older brother, Raymond. He had won the championship with his steer the year before.

So you have to learn these calves to lead. Well, I was teaching my calf to lead and not knowing any better, I had the chain wrapped around my hand. Well, the six-hundred pound calf decided he didn't want to be led, so he took off running, and since I couldn't keep up with him, he proceeded to drag me down the gravel driveway. Needless to say, I was sore for awhile, but he did learn to lead, and he got a blue ribbon at the fair.

My dad's sister Marge lived in Michigan. Every Thanksgiving, they would come to our house to go rabbit hunting. Her and her husband would always have hunting clothes, which my dad didn't have. They didn't have any kids, so they would bring nuts, apples and oranges and bag after bag of candy, and I used to think, Wow, they must really be rich, which I guess they were compared to us. But they loved coming to our house.

And also, my mom's sister, Elizabeth, who lived in New York, would send us boxes of clothes that her girls had outgrown. To us it was like Christmas, but some of the New York styles didn't go too well on the farm.

Talking about Christmas, one night, Mom sent Johnny and I out to the meat house to get some meat, but we weren't to look in the smoking part. Well, we looked, and there were Christmas presents. We saw these wonderful airplanes. Well, being the tomboy I was (I think I was only about eight), I just knew I was going to get one of those.

So Christmas morning, Johnny and Kenny opened their airplanes. Oh they were beautiful. The smoke rolled out of them when you ran them on the floor, they sparked and the lights flashed. I could hardly wait to open my present. It was the most beautiful Bonnie Braids doll you ever saw. I never played with it one time. I hated dolls.

Dad and Mom always made us feel so proud when we got good grades in school, so we were all good students. One of my favorite memories of school was my fourth grade teacher. Bertha Penrod taught us the Scripture, "For God so loved the world that he gave his only begotten son that whosoever believes in him shall not perish but have everlasting life."

And then Mr. Kermit Weaver, he always played Carrom with us, played ball with us at recess and ice skated on the creek.

One of my worst memories was the first time I saw my best friend, Arlene, have a seizure. She was legally blind, so she didn't have very many friends. The other kids would make fun of her, but my sister and I used to walk about two miles through the fields to go to her house to play. Her mom cut her sandwiches corner to corner, and they prayed before they ate, so we thought they were really neat people.

I'm going to end this the same way I started it, with my dad. I don't know when, but I remember my dad being in bed for weeks, vomiting pans of blood. He had bleeding ulcers. I was so scared he was going to die. Dad became a prison guard and a state meat inspector and bought a grocery and gas station at Six Mile Turn and still owned the farm when he died at age sixty-one.

The Memorable Spanking I Never Got

by Jerry L. Klingler of New Lexington, Ohio
born 1941

Played some hooky while in high school at the New Lexington High where I graduated in 1959. I lived in a little area called Redfield, about eight miles away. So we had to be bussed to school. We usually arrived just as the bell that signaled the start of school was ringing. I remember several times just exiting the bus; ducking down and sneaking around to the other side of the bus, going up over the bank and sneaking away for the whole day. Sometimes I came back to catch the bus ride home and sometimes just hitched a ride. Usually had to get out of town or someone would call the school and report you truant.

Our chamber pot was a galvanized 10-quart bucket. My parents slept on the ground floor and the rest of us slept upstairs. Of course we didn't empty the thing until it got so full you could hardly carry it without slopping it everywhere. We had to take it to the outside toilet (called a two-holer) about 30 yards from the back door. We had no indoor plumbing until I was almost in high school as I recall.

I remember my grandmother on Mom's side died of a stroke. Then in 1952, when I was 10, my dad died in a work related accident at Sidwell's stone quarry in White Cottage. Shortly after that, Grandpa Nutter and the twins moved in with Mom and me. The twins were my uncles who were just 10 months older than I.

Grandpa was handy with wood, so I remember him building a bathroom onto the old house. By this time Mom had remarried, and it was my stepdad's idea, as I remember. Since no house can hold two families, Grandpa eventually bought a house in the White Cottage area and he and the twins moved out.

I do remember Mom making me take castor oil. I think because I was a child that had a problem stopping playing to go to the outhouse and seemed to get "bound up" as she called it.

I remember having to knock down the wasp nests at the outhouse. They didn't build them inside, but under the roof overhang on the back side. So you would be inside sitting down with your pants around your ankles before you realized they were there. Then they would crawl in the crack up there and start buzzing around your head. Sometimes causing the cutoff of your business before it was finished. Like everyone else at the time, we had newspapers, old catalogs and phone books to wipe with. Never any rolls of actual paper. Guess that would explain the "racing stripes" in my underwear in those days. At least it was easy to tell the front from the back.

Of course, we had no television until a few years after my father died in 1952. He had seen some, but never owned one. I remember hearing him tell his dad that he planned to get one "for the kids" as he called me and Mom. I think we finally got one about a year after Dad died.

I think Dad would be amazed at what people take for granted today. I do remember listening to programs on the radio: Strait Arrow, Red Ryder, Sky King and Gildersleeve just to name a few. Oh, can't forget Henry Aldrich. It always started with Henry's mom calling his name several times. Also: Amos and Andy, Roy Rogers, Gene Autry and others. Used to sit down by the radio with my cap guns and cowboy hat on to listen.

We had a party line phone for years. No dial, no buttons to push. You picked up the receiver, put it to your ear and if it wasn't in use by someone else on your line, the operator would come on and say, "Number please." If you were calling someone on your party line, you could just give the last number, like ours was 724R2, I think. So all you had to say was R1 to call the person on our line whose number was 724Rl. But if you were calling someone out of your "party line" you had to recite the whole number.

I never used the phone much; not very many of my friends even had a phone in those days. Plus we had a party line where a couple of women tied the thing up for hours at a time. They would not hang up even to change a diaper or answer the door. They would just lay the phone down so no one else could get on and they'd have to wait their turn to get back on.

One spanking I remember the most was the one I never got. Don't remember what started it now, but my dad happened to still be home when I was getting ready to leave for school. I was still in grade school below the 6th grade. He had said something to me and I was in a bad mood and smarted off. He was going to spank me then, but Mom said not to send me to school crying. So he promised to see me when I came home.

After one of the longest days of my life, on the walk home from school, a bunch of the kids were going to play badminton at a house a couple of houses from ours. They asked me to stop and play and I said I couldn't. "Why not?" They asked. "I got to go home and get a beating." I replied. "Can we come and watch?" They said. "No," says I. "Don't want to make him any madder."

I went on home and waited for Dad to come home. After what seemed like hours, he finally came home from work. I kept waiting, but finally I couldn't stand it any more so I asked for his knife. "What for?" He asked. "Got to cut a 'gad,'" says I. "You been thinkin' about that all day?" "Yes," I said. "Well, I think you already had more pain than I want you to. Let's just let it go, okay?" "OK," I say with a great load suddenly lifted from my shoulders, "Can I go play badminton over to....?" Before I could get it out, he said, "Let's not push it now."

I knew better than to keep talking, and started on my chores right then feeling like one lucky boy.

By the way, a "gad" was what he called a switch, which is a piece of a small branch off a tree or a willow bush. He made me go cut my own and if it was too small he would go and cut one. I never wanted to let that happen so I tried to get one big enough to satisfy him not to have to go; yet smaller than he would cut.

We usually took our baths on Saturday morning. That was the day we went to town when I was a kid. We took our baths in a laundry tub. We had no plumbing, so we sat the tub in the kitchen and carried the water with buckets from the well outside. When it was full enough we had an electric heater that you just put in the tub and plugged in. You never touched the tub or water with it plugged in, let alone get in the water. People had been known to get electrocuted when one of those things malfunctioned.

The rule was, whoever carried the water got to bathe first in the water while it was clean. I remember one time while my twin uncles were living with us. I had carried the water and waited for it to get warm. As I unplugged the heater and checked it and found it was warm, I removed the heater and was letting the water drain out of it and one of my uncles was standing there and just slipped his shorts off and jumped in. I threw the heater back in the water and started reaching toward the outlet with the plug. I never saw anyone jump out and pull their pants back on so fast. Guess who got the clean bath water that time?

Never actually did a lot of fishing. The places available to us were sulfur creeks and strip mine water holes. Did some hunting in my teenage years; mostly rabbit and squirrel. We did get to go hunting for pheasants a time or two, but never even shot at one. Never saw any as I remember. Same with deer, there just weren't any around with all the mining going on at the time.

Once I came home from school during squirrel season and after my chores got my gun and went to hunt. I went into the woods and sat down under a tree to see if I could see any squirrels. I sort of dozed off and was awakened by some noise overhead and in front of me. It was a couple of squirrels playing on a high branch and the branch ran across a spot where it shone against the sky. I very slowly raised my gun so as not to scare them away. Just as I was about to shoot, a third squirrel joined in the fun and they were all running back and forth on the limb. I waited for a good shot and then another joined in. That was four all there together. Finally got the perfect shot and took it. They all fell, but I don't know if I hit all four or not as I could only find three in the thicket below. I went home to clean them and my stepdad asked if I got one. I said I had three and he said he only heard me shoot one time, I said, "Yep, should have four, but couldn't find the other one." Don't think he believed the fourth one, but he had to believe the three because we ate them for supper the next night.

Mom did laundry with a wringer washer for many years. For a long time we had to carry the water from the well in buckets to fill the washer with water to heat, and the wash tub to rinse them in. They would be set up in the kitchen for about two days to do the job. It would take overnight to heat the water in the washer to hot enough to get clothes clean. All the cold water detergents and liquid stuff that's around today wasn't even thought of then. She never had an automatic washer until long after I had left home although we had gotten some indoor plumbing while I was in high school. But even then we never had a shower. Just a bathtub, which was a great improvement. I never used it that much because I took showers at school in the gym and liked it a lot better than sitting in the tub.

My best friend lived across the hollow in the edge of the woods. They didn't have electricity for several years after we moved to the area. His mother cooked on a coal cook stove. She did laundry with a gasoline powered wringer washer on the back porch of their house. The water had to be carried in buckets for that too. They also had coal oil lamps, no TV, but did have a battery radio they were never allowed to play because the batteries were so expensive. Finally they did get electricity, but she still would get up in the morning and bake biscuits in the coal cook stove oven. One morning it overheated, and burned the house down. Luckily they all got out without injury. They then moved into town: New Lexington. After that I would hitchhike over there on Saturday and we would go to the local picture show for the afternoon matinee. It was a whopping nine-cents to get in for the double feature. Then I would spend the night and hitch a ride home the next day.

Guess I missed the Depression. I do remember my dad being in the army in the Philippines during WWII. Mom and I lived in a two room apartment behind a house next door to my grandparents. I remember having a wooden wagon with wood wheels. Because of the war, there was rationing of rubber, metal, gas, oil, sugar and a lot of other stuff, so a lot of things were made of wood. I left the wagon outside one night, and the wheels, being made of wood like plywood, fell apart because it rained during the night.

We had a big snowfall in 1950 (I think). No one could get out to go anywhere. The men in the area shoveled the road out to the main road. We lived on a slight grade, so when they got it done, us kids started sleigh riding down the little hill. Made it so slick they still couldn't get out. Didn't really matter, the main road wasn't cleared for several days anyway.

For as long as I can remember, we always had a dog or two around. They never got store bought dog food. I don't remember any of them going to the vet for shots or anything else. They got fed the table scraps, which were not that plentiful, and anything they could hunt for themselves. I believe they were healthier than our spoiled dogs of today. Of course they can't run loose as they did then. Once in a great while they would get a bone from the butcher shop as they were practically free then.

Homemade toys were a lot of growing up around here. All one needed was an old inner tube and pocket knife. We made slingshots with just some pieces of rubber, a "y" tree branch and usually the tongue from an old boot or shoe. A little more work would make a rubber gun from an old board, a couple of sticks and three or four rubber bands cut from the old inner tube. Then if you got lucky and found some old wheels of some sort, we would make a very unsafe cart that we rode down a big hill in the woods nearby. It's a wonder some of us didn't get killed. We did have more than our share of broken arms, legs and ribs. But everyone survived. We also made our own bow and arrows. They weren't good enough to hunt with, but we had fun with them anyway.

Skinny dipping was a regular part of our lives before the teens when we got conscience of ourselves. We were surrounded by old strip pits with really awful water, but we jumped in anyway. At least we knew there were no snakes or any other living thing in there.

My chores mainly consisted of cutting about an acre of old wiry crabgrass with a push type reel mower. The reel was driven by the wheels as you pushed the mower. I usually had to run at the grass and the mower would stop after about a foot and back up and do it again. Used a sickle to cut the high grass and usually it went faster than the mower did. In high school years we finally did get a power rotary mower. I thought it was the best thing I ever saw.

In the winter it was my job to make sure that there was enough coal on the back porch to get Mom through the day while I was at school and step-dad was at work. We had about eight or nine buckets all together. Two or three of them were regular coal buckets and the rest were five-gallon buckets. We kept the coal in an old corn crib so it wouldn't get all covered with ice and snow. I also had to take the ashes out. We heated with two coal stoves at the time and just spread the ashes in the driveway. We didn't use limestone as everyone does now; and concrete was out of the question for us.

At night, we banked the fires. This means we loaded the stove with coal and then turned the damper and closed the draft. The stove would then just lay there and smolder until morning when someone got up and shook the grate, opened the damper and draft and let the fire get hotter. The house really got cold during the night. In the morning we would pull our jeans into bed with us to warm them some before putting them on. I'll never forget how great it was when I moved to the city where you could get up in the night and use the bathroom without dressing and putting on a coat first.

My grandchildren think I make this up, but if you are old enough, you know all about it.

A Hearty Set of Lungs and Telephone Pole Math

by Larry Sarbaugh of Ann Arbor, Michigan
born in 1921

I was born in a house in Adamsville, Ohio which my maternal grandparents bought in 1897. My mother was two years old when they moved there, and she lived there until the mid 1960s. It was an old brick house. My grandfather took out the crumbling bricks and replaced them, and the mortar between the bricks.

The first year my grandparents lived there they kept chickens in an L-shaped wing, which later became the kitchen. By the time I was born, the house was in quite good condition, having been stuccoed over the bricks. Brick dust would still filter into some rooms around the door casings.

Picture submitted by Larry Sarbaugh.

I was born there May 17, 1921. Dr. Hunt came two and-a-half miles from Adamsville to the farmhouse to deliver me. I was told I had a hearty set of lungs from the moment I emerged, and continued to have them through my early childhood. My arrival made four generations in the household—my parents, my mother's parents, my mother, maternal grandmother and me.

As a child, I remember Great-Grandmother sitting in a platform rocker beside the window and slowly rocking back and forth. If I started to do something I was not supposed to do, I would hear her, "Tut, tut, tut," and that gave me pause. I remember how nice it was to be held and rocked by one of the adults.

Growing up on a farm in the hills and near a creek (or crick) was a blessing for a small boy. They were all kinds of exciting things to explore. In winter it was sleigh riding on the hill beside the house, or as I got older, in the pasture field across the road from the house. There were various degrees of steepness and as confidence grew, I and my neighborhood friends went to steeper and steeper hills. Sometimes when the creek was frozen we would go sliding on the ice. We could go nearly a mile up and down the creek on our sleds.

In summer it was wading in the shallow places in the creek. One spot had slippery rocks which we would struggle to walk on and often our feet would slip and we would come up soaked clear through, but we would try again and sometimes we could get all the way up the rock ledge.

Another spot that was lots of fun was to take the car to a place by Mollies Rock. This was a high rock ledge along the creek, and there was a driveway down in to the shallow water. The name came from a myth that a girl jumped off the rock to escape from Indians. With pails and rags we would throw water on the car and rub it with rags until it was nice and clean. This would get the dust off from the dirt roads.

The car was a 1922 Dodge four-door sedan with black covers like the roof of the car that could be added when it rained. There was an iron pole that fit down in a hole in the doors, and then the cover would slide over the pole and snap onto the roof and the door. In winter, these covers helped keep out the cold air too. Although in winter the roads often required going to the horses and a farm sled, which my grandfather made of three inch by three inch pieces of lumber. With the sled there was always a thick layer of straw and blankets to snuggle into to help keep warm. This was how we would go to church or to town to shop at the country store.

At the store there were hard stick candies and cookies with marshmallow and coconut topping, my favorite. In winter there also would be salt fish and oysters. I never liked the oysters, but the broth in which they cooked the oysters was good. The fish came in wooden pails with a wooden top. The store keeper would take out as many fish as you wanted and put the wooden top back on the pail. He usually kept this in the coldest part of the store. Most of the things we would buy came in barrels from which the storekeeper would scoop out the amount a person wanted, weigh it, and put it in a paper bag.

Our basement was always full of canned fruit and salted pork stored for winter. And there was a barrel of cider from the apples we had hauled to the cider mill in the farm wagon. A slippery blob called "mother" was added to the cider to produce vinegar. The hams, sides of bacon and shoulders of pork covered with brown sugar, salt, and spices hung from nails in the floor joists in the coldest part of the basement storage room.

Our house was one of the few in the community with a furnace which provided central heat. In the evenings everyone would gather around the register in the floor and toast their feet over the warm air from the furnace. Another favorite gathering spot was the kitchen around the coal and wood burning range. My father was always the first to get up in the morning, slip into his clothes and get the fires burning nicely so that the house was warm when the rest of the family got out of bed.

When I was about three or four years old, I would go to the barn when my parents milked the 12 cows in the stanchions (metal bars that clamped around their necks to hold them in the stalls). I would stand on a ledge along the barn wall behind the cows and watch while my parents sat on a stool with a little shelf that stuck out front of the part they sat on. The pail for the milk was put on the board that stuck out front. When they finished the milking, my father would put me on his back with my feet in the hip pockets of his bib overalls and my arms about his neck. Then he would pick up two three-gallon pails of milk and carry me the 100 yards to the summer kitchen where the milk was strained into the cream separator. Sometimes the barn was muddy, which made walking more difficult. I'm not sure how he did this. He was about five foot six inches and weight about 150 pounds.

The cream separator had a big tank on top to hold the milk, and then it would go down through a device called a bowl that had a series of disks. One of my parents would turn a crank which would spin the disks and that would separate the cream from the skim milk. The cream came out the top spout since it was lighter in weight and the skim milk came out a lower spout in the milk pails. The skim milk was used to feed the pigs and baby calves. I always had one or two cups of the warm milk from the tank. It was great!

When I was five years old, most of my playmates were old enough to go to the one-room school. I would stand on the board fence at the end of our driveway and watch them walk by with the school teacher who lived about a mile from the school and walked to the school, picking up a trail of children on the way. To help deal with my regret at being left out, my parents bought the first grade reading book and read it with me. When I entered first grade the next year, I had read all of the stories and had memorized some of them.

When I was older and was having some difficulty with addition, my father and I would add the numbers on all the telephone poles as we rode to town or wherever else we were going. I soon got my number facts learned with this supplement to the classroom work.

Spelling was always enjoyable. At least once a week we would choose up sides with one row of students on each side of the school room and we would have a spell down. The teacher would pick easier words for the younger children. When you missed a word you would go to your seat. It was always a great treat to be the last one standing.

When I was in the fifth grade, we walked a mile and-a-half to a neighboring school for a spelling contest. The winner would go to the county contest. I was supposed to do very well, but I missed the first word. It was "meant." I froze and couldn't remember it, what an embarrassment. The next year we again went to the neighboring school, and this time I won the contest. Then came the county contest. It was a written test, 20 words at a time. Finally, it was down to me and another boy who was from Adamsville. On the last 20 words he missed three and I had them all right. One word I remember in the list was license. I spelled it different ways and finally decided that license looked right and it was.

At recess, we played lots of running games. And in winter there was a hill beside the school ground where we could sleigh ride. When I was in second grade, there were only two boys in third grade and the teacher decided to put me in with them for recitations. This teacher didn't pay much attention to grade level. He had all grades doing the same spelling and arithmetic; sometimes he would even have us work through recess time.

The school room had a pot bellied stove in the center for heat and a bucket with a dipper in the back corner for water. Students would take turns going to a farm spring about 100 yards away to get water for drinking and washing hands. The shelf for the water bucket also had a wash pan for washing hands and a towel hung on a nail. The seats had slanting desk tops with a shelf under them to store paper, pencils and books. Each class would take turns going to a long bench in the front of the class room for recitation of the day's lessons. The teacher would ask questions about the assignments to be sure we had learned the material and understood it.

The desks were different sizes, so the first graders had small desks, sometimes single, and sometimes double, with two to a desk. As you got older, you got a bigger desk and moved to the back of the room. As you came in the door, there was a shelf on which to put lunch boxes and hooks on the wall to hang coats and caps.

Every boy had two pairs of bib overalls and denim shirts. We would wear one while the other was being washed. There were sweaters, usually home woven, and denim jackets to keep warm in winter. Also, there were crocheted toboggans to keep one's head warm. In spring and summer it changed to straw hats.

After school there were always chores to do on the farm. At first it was giving grain to the chickens, then it was feeding hay and silage to the cattle, then cleaning the animal stalls and putting straw for the animals' beds, and finally helping with the hand milking of the cows.

The sheep barn was about 300 yards west of the main farm buildings. I guess it was built there because it was in a protected area near a small stream that was safe for sheep to drink. The big task was to carry about a bushel of grain from the main buildings to the sheep barn on one's back or shoulder to feed the sheep. Hay for the sheep was in a loft above the sheep. This helped keep the building warm in winter. Sometimes a mother would not have enough milk for her lamb, and we would have a bottle of warm milk with a long nipple to feed the lamb. I usually got that job. The walk to the sheep barn on a cold, windy day was not a pleasant trip.

In summer there was field work. I felt real grown up when I finally was trusted to drive the horses to mow hay or plow corn by myself. Some field work became a neighborhood project: hay stacking, or threshing wheat or filling silos with corn silage.

Hay making was a fun time. The hay was put in small shocks about three feet high and the same size around. Then a long pole was pushed under these shocks and a rope pulled over the top. A ring on the end of the rope was slipped over the end of the pole sticking out of the shock away from a horse, and the other end was hooked to a single tree fastened to the horse's harness. The boys would ride the horses to pull the shocks to the stack where the men would pitch it up to the top of the stack. A person there would arrange it so that it would shed the rain and be dry for winter feeding. The stack was built out to a bulge about a third of the way to the top, and then tapered into a cone shape. There were races to see who could haul the most shocks to the stack. The men would take turns hitching the horses to the shocks and pitching the hay up on the stack.

Work on the farm became a social event with a big community meal at noon. And the boys had good role models for doing good work and enjoying it. There was great pride in the quality and amount of work one could do. Children today miss that opportunity, nor do many of them have any opportunity to see or work with animals.

On Sunday we always went to church. In summer we drove the car. In winter we would sometimes take the horses and a sled if there was snow on the ground. Then once in a while my father and I would walk about a mile and-a-half through the fields, climbing over fences. This gave us a shorter distance to walk.

Ice cream socials were always a treat. All the families would gather at church. The men and boys would turn the ice cream freezers after the women had prepared the mixture of milk, cream, sugar, and flavoring. The women also would have baked cakes and pies, so you could put the ice cream on them, or eat it without the cake or pie.

Periodically the youth would have group meetings, sometimes for bible study, and sometimes for wiener roasts and games of various types. The games usually involved chasing and trying to catch another person before they could stop in front of another couple and the one behind would have to run to avoid being tagged.

One treat was to go to Adamsville to visit my mother's parents—Grandpa and Grandma Thomas. My Great Grandfather Thomas was the first cabinet maker in Adamsville. My grandfather and all of his brothers were good carpenters, and I learned to drive nails and saw a straight line while helping my grandfather repair fences and barn doors.

As I reflect on the early years, they were great for my personal growth and lots of fun.

Snows, Floods and Higher Prices

By Floyd F. Busche of New Matamoras, Ohio
Born in 1937

I went to Brownsville School. Eight years grade school and went to Antioch High School.

Went to Army for two years and four years with the Reserves. I worked at Hannibal Aluminum plant for 35 years and retired in 1999.

I saw the big snow in 1950—about 36 to 40 inches fell overnight. A lot of it was removed by hand or horses.

The flood of 1964, 45.2 feet. We rowed a rowboat up Route 7 in Fly, Ohio. I also remember the one in 2004-2005. 43 feet to 44 feet.

Work at several different jobs. Sawmill drive- in theater and a lot of farms. In summer, gas station. I was township trustee for eight years. Belong to American Legion for 20 years. Post 760 Hannibal, Ohio. I live near Brownsville all my life outside of service time. Married for 38 years. Wife passed in 2001.

Bought a little farm in 1973. Had four children. Still live on farm near Brownsville Monroe County.

Mother had wringer washer for years. Old pitcher pump in kitchen for water. We had collie dogs for years—they were good with children. Heard Amos and Andy on radio. Favored teacher Helen McHugh Dye. Glen Dye at Brownsville at Antioch Ervin Straight Clyde Hawkins.

We always went to town on Saturday night for groceries and stuff for week. We went down to Tailor Place on Sunday afternoon and played softball and went swimming. All the old country stores are closed up now. Have to drive farther for supplies or anything you need. Everything's higher now. Gas, diesel, cars, trucks, fertilizer, seeds, tractors, machines.

Chasing the Bad Guys

by Elaine Triplett of Cape Porpoise, Maine
born in 1943

I was raised in Summerfield, Noble County, Ohio. When my dad, Frank C. Triplett, returned from WWII, we lived in four rental properties in Summerfield before moving to a 120-acre farm on Glady Valley Road, one and one half miles outside of Summerfield.

While living in the four houses in Summerfield before moving to the farm, we had "outhouses." After moving to the farm we had a large bathroom and running water. We also had a gas well on the farm which was 40 years old when we purchased the property, and it is still furnishing five families with free gas in 2009.

Life on the farm was magical for me. My mother had never lived on a farm and my two older sisters, Carol and Ruth, were not farm material either.

I loved being able to ride the school bus and torment our bus driver, Elmer Moore. He put up with a lot of tormenting from us.

In the spring and fall, we (Beverly Dodds and I) would walk home from school and stop off at Dick Weavers and drink from his water pipe. Then we would tease his Hereford bull and try to get him to charge us.

The summer was the best time of the year. I had to help pick peas and berries, usually early in the morning before the sun got too hot. Then I would call Beverly or Norma (Bates) Hannahs, and we would line up something to get into. Norma had a larger swimming hole than me, so I liked to go to her house to swim. I was not allowed to go swimming on Sunday because that meant my hair would get wet and dirty and I had to go to church that evening. I usually went ahead and jumped in knowing that Mother would be upset. However, it was worth it.

Most Sundays it went like this: first we went to Sunday school and church. Then we had a large Sunday dinner followed by Mother and Dad taking a nap. Tim Reed usually came down to my house, and we played in the woods cutting down trees and building forts. We ran our legs ragged chasing the bad guy. If Beverly Dodds played with us, she wore her guns, cowboy boots, and cowboy hat. I didn't have any of those items since Mother didn't like guns, not even toy ones.

My dad was a coon hunter, and he took me with him most nights. No one else liked to hunt, but I liked to hear Dad talk about the good ole days and how he made a lot of money by hunting and selling the hides. I hunted with Dad since I was three years old. Mom would make me an egg sandwich in case I got hungry so Dad and I would share the sandwich and sometimes the hound would get a bite too. He had one dog named Ole Nick which was his prize dog. He would hunt all night and show up the next morning tired out.

We had a 14-foot boat that was docked over at the Thompson's boat dock on Seneca Lake. We would make a picnic and go over to one of the islands and tie up. We'd have a good swim and then eat our picnic and sing.

Watching the sun go down and then catching lightning bugs was an every day event in the summer. Once in a while we would go to the beach over at the lake. We could tie up at the beach and we wouldn't have to pay admission to get in.

When I was a freshman in high school, my dad bought a larger farm on Route 513 (the mile stretch). Things changed for me then. I had to put up hay and milk cows, which I was not thrilled to do. However, we had an underground gasoline tank which the guys that I dated were free to use. I'm not certain if they dated me for the gasoline or not. Oh well, most of them are still my friends after all these years.

My high school years were great. We only had one sport and that was basketball. I never missed a game unless I was sick. The competition was terrific between Batesville, Sarahsville, Dexter City, and Harrietsville.

I remember one time, Jerry Craig had this old, old car and he agreed to take Vivian Moore, Gene West, and me to Columbus to buy cheerleading sweaters. We stopped on our way home to see my sister, Carol, and sponge a dinner off of her. We didn't have money to buy dinner, so she obliged.

Our junior/senior banquet was a big happening. You couldn't beat the Baker's Motel dining room for our banquet. We never had such a thing as a "prom" or a "yearbook." When I went to business school, my friends in the dorm couldn't believe that our school didn't have a prom or a yearbook.

Our principal wouldn't allow us to dance. However, we used to go to Harry Moore's garage and put a nickel in the jukebox and dance to Elvis and Ricky Nelson. We tried to mimic American Bandstand, but it was a bit different since none of the boys would dance. So we girls danced with each other and had a great time.

Girls in our school wore their boyfriends' ring not around their necks but on their finger. We would take angora yarn and wrap the ring, then we put it in the freezer and it would puff up and it would fit and look snazzy.

We didn't have any foreign language courses in school when I attended. My sister had Latin but by the time I was in high school, Otis King had retired.

One of the things that we did have at Summerfield High School was a music program. I sang in the choir and played clarinet. Mrs. Day was our teacher and I truly learned a lot from her. We had fun singing at the Spring Festival and playing in the orchestra.

I graduated from Summerfield High School when I was 17 in 1961 and went off to Columbus. I went to business school and then worked. I later went to Ohio State University and graduated in International Relations.

Over the years, Noble County can be proud of the students who have went on to further their education. We did not have the best education curriculum, but we did have the determination and brains to complete our mission.

Snookie and the Easter Chickens

by Shirley Ann Gardner of Zanesville, Ohio
born 1931

I am a lady born into many time frames. This includes many wars such as Vietnam, Korean, World War II and the present ones.

I was born on Christmas Day during the Depression times. Then, only strictly allotted food was given to families such as soup bones, rice and flour that required good old home town cooking.

My father took any job available, including the WPA that built roads, bridges or any physical, daily jobs sometimes paying less than ten dollars.

My mother was one of the first usherettes in then a

new movie theater. She must have seen too many Shirley Temple movies, as she gave me a curly top hairdo and dressed me in tafetta ribbons and patent leather shoes.

In one of our then five theaters, a "kiddie hour" was on stage with emcee "Uncle Nate" each Saturday. I was privileged to sing "Mickey Mouse's birthday party" and tap danced. I truly can brag that I tap danced on radio as the mic was put at my feet.

Shirley Gardner, age five, dancing on the radio.

I grew up with grates on fireplaces fueled with coal for heat, castor oil and orange juice as a medicinal remedy and Vicks for everything!

The wringer washer was a must with two rinse tubs. You must not get too close to the wringer as your own clothing could get caught. Hit the release!

Even everyday functions such as using the telephone was the dialing of four digit numbers and actually talking to a real operator. Pay phones were five cents.

I also had a cat that was named Snookie and he intimidated my two Easter chickens. Later they grew up together peacefully (two big white Leghorns).

In grade school, we wore leggings in the winter and boots. The coat room was called cloak room.

Our *Weekly Reader* school newspaper predicted in the '40s that someday people could watch movies in their homes as big as a newspaper. Also in the future, men would, at a young age, become bald.

In the sixth grade I was lucky to produce "Snow White and the Seven Dwarfs." We made the dwarfs' noses out of paraffin. We performed in each school room in the building separately as we had no gym.

Something unlikely to happen today was knocking on doors and trading funny books with strangers, having pop in glass bottles only once a week. Perhaps eating out once a week. Likely was home cooked meals including fudge cake, homemade maraschino cherries, nut ice cream, coconut cream pie and the roasts and potatoes. Why would you want to eat out?

During World War II, I was in grade school. I remember the ration stamps that were used when my mother sent me to the store. Dark, bitter cocoa was put in a brown bag. Coffee was very minute and the white block of margarine had an orange capsule used to mix for color.

Gasoline was rationed with stamps, aluminum and rubber was saved. Many soles of shoes were patched and many people just put cardboard cut to fit inside shoes.

At school we could buy war savings bonds for eighteen dollars and seventy-five cents which matured into twenty-five dollars. We also learned to line up quickly in case of a wartime disaster.

In the evenings, families could practice in special huts for a sudden hit by foreign planes. Inside we felt safe as recordings were played of overhead planes (a little scary for children).

Movies were a must, as each Saturday movies were attended by my friends and myself. We enjoyed Abbot and Costello, The Mummy, and musicals. Afterward we went to a shop and had big, hot fudge sundaes with real whipped cream and cherry phosphates (movies were twenty-five cents).

Out of high school I started to participate in beauty pageants. Ms. Central Ohio was at the Buckeye Lake, Ohio. We walked on platforms across the swimming pool to be judged. Many famous bands performed there such as Xavier Cugat, Tommy Dorsey, Jerry Lee Lewis etc.

After having three children I participated and won the citizen's award the "Delores and Bob Hope good Samaritan award," Beauties of America national pageant in Orlando, Florida, Ms. Radiance in Akron, Ohio, Ms. Senior Ohio of America in 2002 and was sent to Biloxi, Mississippi for the nationals.

I was chairperson of a twenty-five year three-day yearly festival, founder and chairman of a "Ton of Talent" talent show for singers, dancers and musicians in eleven schools (money was given to a high school student for college).

Presently I am a appearing in the twenty-one-year-old "Follies" which gives to hospice all the proceeds.

I am also in the Pilot Club which gives monies to all brain related diseases and Alzheimer's.

Many things bring humor such as swatting my eye as I went on stage and finding that it was only a false eyelash. Another time spraying my mouth with a little bottle of not mouth spray, but perfume. My breath was wonderful!

I love to write and I wrote about the trip from my grandfather's that ended up in a snowstorm and plowing into a snow drift. My father walked five of us individually to a farmhouse where we were given hot drinks and eventually taken to a hotel.

Did I mention that I retired after thirty-one years as a manager of four different school cafeterias? I still retain a job at a store after thirteen years.

Life can be great, wonderful, terrible, monotonous, intimidating, hurtful, both physically and mentally but it takes a strong person to continue to smile.

I have experienced most of these emotions as of late. You see, my husband, Glenn, died in October 2008. We were married fifty-five years. He was the greatest piece of my life.

The Comfort of a Pump Inside

By Carol A. Conrad Moore of New Matamoras, Ohio
Born 1943

The annoying sound of the alarm clock that also gives the morning's weather of additional snow and the January's cold of minus eight degrees seemed to lull me back down into the comfort of the warm and cozy bed. Somehow, my thoughts went back to being a young girl awakening on a bitter morning much like today's weather report. How thankful I am to have a warm and cozy bed. How I could still hear my dear mother awakening me, saying, "Time to get up now, it's a school day and a cold day." How I hated to leave the piled high covers of warmth and hear the wind whistling around the blanket covered iced over windows to shield the cold air.

As I reluctantly struggled out of bed, I could hear Mother fixing breakfast and smell the bacon and sausage that came from the fattened two hogs that had been butchered early that winter. Sometimes I hated that smell because it clung to the clothing that I would so proudly wear to school. Some of our "poorer" kids smelled like that.

Mother had the tea kettle whistling with hot water and we had a pitcher pump on a makeshift sink with an enamel wash pan to wash up for whatever the occasion might be. Mother said we were blessed to have the pump inside the house instead of going outside and lowering a bucket into the water well.

Dad wasn't at home this weekday because he worked "away" from home in the oil fields of central Ohio. My two older brothers were up and had the morning milking done and were quite anxious to wash up and have that hearty breakfast; all the while teasing me, their much younger, silly sister, who didn't care to eat anything but the sausage gravy and some homemade bread.

"I know what you want to be when you grow up," my elder brother, Max, teased, trying to anger me to add more fuel to the fire of orneriest. "How do you know?" I coyly replied. All the while Mother was busy adjusting the flame on the old kitchen range which had no thermostat; continuing on with her duties of the fresh milk. Perhaps I would be cranking the old butter churn this evening. Mother seemed to glow with her remaining three of her eight children being fed and hearing their voices innocently tormenting one another.

Max yelled to me, "You want to be a singer; I know because you have bird legs!"

I hurried to find a warm place to dress while the boys went upstairs in their bedroom to dress by the warmth of the chimney pipe that went up through their room from the downstairs large lease gas heating stove.

I also went into the summer kitchen to use the chamber pot that we girls were allowed to use in wintertime. We arranged our clothing the night before while it was daylight because the old gas lights didn't give off much light for studying and matching clothing.

Mother said, "You may not have any school today with the cold temperatures and more snow on the way." She tried to tune in the old radio with a huge battery, but it was a bit "scratchy" this morning and no local news. Our telephone, which worked part of the time; with our phone number being a long and two shorts hadn't buzzed this morning. Nor did any others on our party line of many. Sometimes when a call would come in many would eavesdrop trying to hear any news. Also it would be too noisy to hear, so one would have to say, "You can all hang up now, we don't know any more news."

Mother was still adjusting the seemingly weaker flames trying to get more heat while advising us to dress warmly and not to get wet snow balling one another. As certain as she advised, the certainty was that we would do the opposite all in the name of fun.

"What's wrong, Mother? I see your concern about the gas this morning." my brother, George asked.

"I'm sorely afraid that the gas lines may be freezing. You boys get your four buckle artic boots on and I'll get the kitchen matches and newspapers; we must thaw the gas line even if it means missing school!"

It was nearing eight a.m. and no school bus in sight, which is how we knew when to start down over the steep hill to get on the bus. There was no hesitation nor complaining about the forthcoming job; just the antics of two happy carefree young men. They were used to hard work and needed no advice. Our dad had instilled in each of us the benefits of hard work.

Winter weekends meant that Dad was home and there was lots of work to be done on a two hundred acre farm. Barn stalls to be cleaned, fresh hay moved closer for easier access, ice to be broken on the nearby creek for fresh water for the cattle and horse. Baby calves being born and sometimes having to be carried back to the barn to keep from freezing. Dad would go to town, which was New Matamoras, Ohio for essentials and to take the freshly washed and crated dozens of eggs to be sold to help buy grain, chicken's feed and our minimum staples. Mother would remind Dad to look for the feed sacks like he got the last time to match the others because Carol would be needing some new spring dresses and to perhaps get some Vicks or Musterole salve in case one of us caught a chest cold.

While Dad was in town sometimes my older sister Mary would bring her two girls close to my age to play for the day. We headed straight for the barn to jump into the "doodled" up hay mow; giggling and just creating a mess with the fresh hay that our cattle and horse would need this winter. Dad would surely scold us if he thought we had bothered his pristine haymows. Dad would sometimes come home with whiskey on his breath; a foul mood and a pint of moonshine that he had gotten fresh from a nearby still.

Weekends for the brothers meant they would like to go *somewhere*. Even if they rode their bikes to a neighbor for a long game of gin rummy playing cards. If they were lucky, they could catch a ride with a neighbor and go to Beavertown, Ohio to the dance hall. There they would meet their older siblings, who were living with their maternal grandmother so that they could go on to high school, have class rings and senior pictures that Grandma could afford. The older siblings had gone to a one room school house on Sheet's Run and it stopped at grade eight. Grandma lived in Beavertown on Route 7 and they could board the bus there. Besides that, Grandma had electricity! They had gone to live with Grandma during the Great Depression. Sometimes Mother and Dad would listen for awhile to WWVA jamboree or listen to the Grand Old Opry on the battery radio if they had a battery. Dad would not allow the boys to leave the house for any "fun," so they waited until he was tired and drunk. Dad seemed to have forgotten that the boys needed excitement along with the hard work.

Sunday was my favorite day. It meant Sunday school and church that I would go to with neighbors. It also meant a different menu from the pork. Most of all; I loved the company. The older siblings would come to eat and visit and talk about such interesting things to a seven-year-old. If my two nieces came, we would play with whatever we had and in summer months we played ball in our pasture fields; get hot and sweaty and head for the nearest swimming hole, which we had been warned about time and time again. One time we ventured too far and took off all of our clothes so not to get them wet and placed them far enough away from the splashing of water. When we tired of that we sought out our piles of clothing. They had vanished, we thought. We searched and couldn't locate them, so we walked stark naked up the main road towards home feeling half scared of a "switching" and afraid a car would come by and see us. There was a problem, we tried to explain. With that, my sister walked us back to the spot where we were sure our clothes would never be found, but there they were, and dry as a bone. Mary said, "Before you put your underwear on, just bend over, you are going to get a whipping!" And that we did; with a willow stick! We didn't try that again.

Winter is waning; spring is approaching and with it begins a different kind of labor and life in southeastern Ohio. Dad tells Mother to order by mail at least fifty baby chicks; "biddies" we call them. They soon arrive by mail all yellow and fuzzy and were placed in a large box with the bottle of water with the purple dissolved pill for nourishment and were kept by the gas stove for warmth until they could be turned into a larger space when the nights became warmer. Also, Mother had my eldest sister to make the feed sack bright dresses for me. They were lovely and had embellishments of lace and fancy buttons. If only Dad would allow me to have a pair of lovely white shoes instead of the drab black or brown lace-ups that I had worn for a long time. Dad always chose my shoes, saying that the lace-ups were good for my feet and ankles. No shoes for summer; we went barefoot. My feet would become so calloused that I thought I could step on a nail and never know it! When my eldest brother married, his wife's niece started giving me her good as new hand-me-downs. And, there was my white shoes. HAPPY DAY! My drab brown lace-ups came in handy one day as Mother asked to gather some eggs that she needed promptly. I slipped on the shoes and had stretched up into the nest, and grabbed a few eggs when I saw a large blacksnake on the floor of the hen house. I literally ran out of my shoes headed for the house with the unbroken eggs. I told Mother about the snake and she promptly grabbed a nearby hoe and started toward the hen house intending to take care of that pesky snake, but nothing was found but the lace-up shoes that were strewn about close to the hen house.

A treat was to be had usually on Sunday afternoons when Dad would pull the long rope out of the dug water well with a large watermelon in a white feed sack that had been chilled overnight in the cold water.

When I had no playmates on Sunday, I would listen intently to my older siblings talk about the Great Depression. I sometimes would see Mother wipe tears as they remembered together the hardships and separation of that era.

During the Great Depression we didn't have a home of our own. Mother, Dad and the five siblings who were born before and during that time were forced to move into a one room, with a loft; drafty and cramped log cabin that was part of the original Hutchison settlement of early 1800's in what was and is still historically named Hutchison Hollow. It was located on Sheet's Run Road and up a long, steep hill. There was no road, just a path for a horse and wagons and cut off virtually from the outside world. The only folks living there were my Dad's older relatives which amounted to several log cabins. They were self sufficient in that they raised their own crops, had an established orchard, had chickens and cattle and teams of work horses. The chicken eggs were usually saved to trade for staples such as flour, sugar, yeast and very meager necessities. Cattle were sold or traded for whatever the need was. Their main meat was venison, rabbit, squirrels and sometimes a wild turkey. Their source of cooking was large kettles hung over hooks in the fireplace which was the only heat source as well. Mother would grind the corn for cornbread and mush and she sometimes didn't have any yeast; so it was unleavened bread. Sugar and gasoline were paid for by rationing stamps, Mother recalls.

The older siblings walked down that steep hill in the winter and then another mile to go to the one room schoolhouse. They would be wet and nearly frozen due to lack of rubber boots or leather boots. They would dry off at school near the wood burner stove. Lunch time was usually spent talking because very few had much food to bring. Sometimes they would have homemade bread and some lard spread on it or a hard boiled egg.

All the children of that era were malnourished and underweight and labored right beside whomever needed them that day.

There was no electric power and everyone who lived there shared a spring for their water supply. They stored their potatoes, beets, squash, turnips, apples and pears in a hand dug hole in the garden where they wouldn't freeze and stayed preserved. There were no canning jars, but they did have different sizes of heavy crocks that sauerkraut and pickles were made in and later stored there. The hand churned butter was kept in a cellar if you were fortunate to have one. They exchanged recipes and food and helped one another including being a midwife who would help deliver babies if a doctor couldn't get there in time.

Bessie, the eldest sibling, had learned wisdom and survival instinct; she would heat rocks in the fireplace and place them in their heavy pile of covers to keep however many that slept in a bed warm. She served as a second Mother who settled many arguments and tried to solve problems such as when younger brother, George, who started first grade at age five, told of a classmate calling him "a big black chicken turd, and I told the teacher!" Bessie inquired as to how the teacher handled that remark. George confidently said, "He had to stay inside for recess and I went out to play!" as he skipped across the floor towards the outdoors.

Mother was never happy there in the wilderness of the hollow and longed to see her own mother, but it would be two years until she would see her since Mother would have to walk through the woods pregnant and was busy with other siblings. The older siblings found a short cut through the woods to get to Grandma's house where she would await their arrival each week. Mother would send letters, some fresh fruit or milk with the kids to Grandma's and she would in turn send necessities that was needed along with letters, newspapers and books which was the only contact with the outside world. Mother sent buttermilk in a jar with the kids and they ran so fast that it was churned into butter when they got to Grandma's. Grandma lived on Route 7 in Beavertown where she had the privilege to ride the Greyhound bus to Marietta to purchase what she could afford. She was widowed young and her only son left for the Oklahoma oil boom where he lived out his life. She raised a large garden and contributed to less fortunate folks, as well as the many hobo's that walked the unpaved road every day; stopping at homes to ask for food, water and sometimes shelter outside where it was safe for the night's rest.

Laundry day meant fetching the rain water collected in rain barrels into the house or outside wood fire pit to heat. Then a washboard and home-made lye soap was placed in a galvanized round tub and lots of rubbing with the heavily soiled clothing resulted in sore knuckles and shoulders. It was an all day job to hang them on a clothes line to dry. In winter months they were hung about the house to dry and later iron. The heavy irons were heated by fire and wiped off with rags to keep the soot off the clothing.

Once Bessie was visiting an aunt and was taking her wash pan bath and got so chilled that she backed up to the Hazelwood wood burner too far and "branded" herself "Haze" on the buttocks. Sister Norma, bathing there also, set her kerosene lantern too close to the dresser mirror and shattered the glass.

Dad and many other men were without paying jobs a lot of the time, but Dad did get work with the WPA and helped build a bridge at Jericho, Ohio, which still stands today. The men also would congregate at the many historical moonshine stills in Beavertown, Ohio. Men of that era was the boss of his wife and siblings; body, mind and soul. Moonshine caused many wife beatings and child abuse, which usually went unseen or unheard of except to the innocent victims.

With true grit and determination; all four sons served their country in war time and in peace and all but one of the eight graduated high school with high achievements in life.

Finally World War II was over and slowly the factories began to build and blessed peace returned to the ones who sacrificed so much and loved so deeply. Perhaps the best was yet to come in hills of southeastern Ohio.

A Time of Love and Laughter

by Margaret Joan Shepherd of Bethesda, Ohio
born in 1929

I remember when I was a little girl how our days were spent so slowly—no one seemed to be in a hurry—of course we didn't own a car, so we didn't do much traveling. Back then, not very many did have a car. We traveled like the Amish do today!

My family was always up early, baking bread, taking care of the milk and cream and carrying it to the spring house to keep it fresh. Then later taking the cream for butter and the sour milk for cottage cheese. The women were always kept so busy, they would feed the chickens and gather the eggs and even kill the chickens and cook them. Then they would make the best homemade noodles and cook in the broth.

When spring house-cleaning time came they scrubbed everything; windows, floors, beds, the furniture, then took the rugs up off of the floor and hung them over the clothesline. Then they would beat the dirt out of them with a metal rug beater.

Main Street of Bethesda, Ohio in the 1920s. Shepherd Chevrolet Company, John Shepherd, dealer.

My grandfather always planted the gardens and the corn and wheat fields that fed the cows and other farm animals. He did the harvesting and milking and butchering. He was the only man in our home and always worked so hard keeping everything cleaned up around the home and the barn.

I can remember there always was a quilt in the quilting frames in our living room, and when the women would find a time to rest, they would sit at the quilting frames and quilt.

Mondays were always wash days. They had big wash tubs and washboards to scrub their clothes on. They also had wringers you turned by hand to run the clothes through, which did get most of the water out. Then they were hung on a clothesline to dry. In the winter, the clothes would freeze dry—and everything had to be ironed. The sheets, pillowcases, towels, of course all the clothes and even the underwear.

Saturday night was bath night. We always got to sit down in a big tub of water to soak. Through the week, we washed off in a little wash basin, but we were always clean and just as healthy as kids are today, maybe even healthier.

Nothing was ever very easy for the wife or the husband, and yet, they were mostly wonderful parents and had time to read us stories and make sure we said our prayers at bedtime.

At Christmastime we always had a live tree decorated with some glass bulbs, paper chains, and popcorn garlands. We girls always got a doll and a new feed sack dress, a nightgown, and books and homemade candy. Most everything was homemade, but we were so happy on Christmas morning to have so much. Then, we always had such a happy time, and I'm sure that is why Christmas is still my favorite holiday—a good memory!

Our feed sack dresses always had panties to match—actually, some were very pretty, with flowers of all colors on the feed sack material. All of the women could sew, knit, and crochet, so we had beautiful collars and cuffs for our dresses.

We had outside toilets for the day time called two holers (our bathrooms), and I don't think I ever visited that outside toilet that I wasn't greeted with a spider, bee, frog, or snake. Who would have thought that someday these would be good memories? At nighttime we had chamber pots that would go upstairs with us for those who needed the bathroom in the middle of the night. Then they were emptied in the morning.

We always slept two to a bed, and the upstairs was so cold in the winter and so hot in the summer. We always had feather–tick mattresses to sink into. They were homemade too!

Sundays were always quiet days. The Sabbath had to be kept quiet—we could ride bikes, swing in the tree swing, play card games, and play jacks because these things didn't make noise.

Every mealtime was a family time as everyone sat down at the table together for breakfast, dinner, and supper—of course, we had no television to sit in front of.

My mother and I lived with my grandfather and grandmother, as my parents had divorced. My aunt and her three children lived there also as her husband had died at age 29 and there was no widow benefits back then. We were very lucky that our grandparents took us all in to live with them. People used to take care of their own without ever complaining of it.

We were poor, but we didn't know we were. We always had everything we needed. We were so fortunate to have the loving family we had. Most families pulled together in this way, maybe to survive, but I like to think it was because of love!

It was a time of love and laughter, and taking the time to drink tea and coffee and talk together as a family. Wouldn't it be nice if we still did that, instead of making televisions, computers, and cell phones the center of our existence?

Oh, Gee!

by Ruth E. Chappelear of McConnelsville, Ohio
born in 1923

Born July 12 in Joy, Ohio to Warieux Deesie Duncan Vniller [or Miller?]. I was five and-a-half years young, and my daddy was pretty easy when I asked for some things. So, I talked him in to letting me invite four more. All of us were close to the same age, boys and girls. We all lived in this wonderful little burg named Joy, Ohio. There was 19 families, but some of them were elderly folks, and their children were all married and gone. They had great grandchildren who came to visit often and all of us were very close friends.

Back then, we didn't have many toys. We didn't know what toys were, but gee we did have lots of fun.

Back to our trip to cut Christmas trees: I talked my daddy into letting me lead the way, as I had went with him the past two years and talked and talked until I was let to go get our Christmas tree. So after church and Sunday school and our dinner was over, everyone went all bundled up, as it was pretty cold with a lot of snow on the ground, with our little hatchets to cut a nice Christmas tree. It was around two o'clock. We told our parents we would be back before dark, and in time to do our chores, as we all had to do: feed calves, chickens, and carry in coal and wood for to keep us warm. And, oh yes, we all said we knew the way.

It wasn't too far away from home, but we somehow got turned the wrong way. We walked and walked but did see the place we thought we all knew because we had all went with our daddy times before. We didn't have a watch, but it wasn't long before it began to get sorta dark, as we all said but could make it.

Becoming all sorta afraid we really didn't know for sure where we was, and then was never a house in sight, but we kept on walking and talking and sometimes we would sing Christmas songs we all knew. We walked and walked but just got the wrong way more, but we were not too afraid yet but beginning to really own up to we were just lost and didn't know which way should we go. But every way we went was not the right way, only farther and father away from our home. But we really didn't want to get scared as yet. We just knew we were going to find them trees. It surely had to be the ones the next hill. But it just wasn't.

Pretty soon it was really dark and we were cold and scared now. But none of us cried. We just kept walking and talking and singing. We were oh so cold and hungry and wanted something hot to drink. But we just kept going the way we was sure had to be right.

Oh gee, pretty soon we saw lights in a big house's windows. We all were so happy and we guessed who lived in the big house was friendly. We thought for sure we knew who lived in the big house with lights. Some of us knew who lived there. We knocked on the door and the lady came to the door. Right away she knew some of us, called us by name, and asked why we were so far away from home at this hour of night. I spoke and said, "Ms. Kasler, call my Grandpa Duncan and tell him to get my dad and come get us as we were all so cold and hungry." She called my Grandpa Duncan and he told her that everyone was so worried and would be to get us very soon. We were about 17 miles from our home over the hills the way we came, but only 5 miles around the road the right way.

Ms. Kasler gave us something to eat and, oh gee, what we was wanting so bad hot chocolate. We never forgot Mrs. Kasler for being so kind.

We all got a good talking to and was told that the next time our dads would go with us, which made us oh so happy.

So the next week we all went to get the trees for all our families, but with our dads with us, and we were back home in about two hours and had five very nice trees.

We was always reminded about this each year when Thanksgiving came, but we did all have a great time the second trip with our daddies, and all got nice trees for some of our friends who didn't have kids to go get them.

Joy was a wonderful little burg to grow up in. Everyone loved each other and we all had good times. Our mothers took turns in having a party for all of us on Friday night in the wintertime. We popped popcorn, played games, and once in a while our mothers put their sugar together and made us candy and sometimes we took good old sorghum molasses and made taffy. Oh gee, that was fun.

Oh for the memories of our good old days in Joy growing up. I don't think there is many of us kids left anymore, as when the WWII came, families moved out to far away to find work and didn't move back. That was an unhappy time for us kids. We kept up with each other for a few years, but finally we lost track of each other. But we all had good memories.

I never had any brother or sister, so I really missed my friends. I spent the first 21 years of my life in Joy with Mother and Dad, Warren and Dessie (Duncan) Miller. They both have been gone a long time, as I am past 85 years young, but I surely do love to sit all alone at night, as my husband has been gone over seven years now. So I have lots of time to think about the good old days. My parents have been gone a long time. My mother passed away in 1991 and my father in 1956, but they sure were great parents.

* * * *

Our big hill behind our barn. The big hill is all the kids in our little village, Joy, Ohio, what at the time I was thinking about there was 19 families. Not all had children now at home, but they all did have grandchildren who came once in a while to go sleigh riding. This big hill was pretty long then went on to a place that was flat, which was our field we put our cuttle in the summertime over night after milking was finished to eat and sleep till morning.

Now back then, we didn't have milking machines. We did it all by hand, so we only had seven cows we milked and the milkman came each morning and picked up our milk. My dad and I milked. We have to tell you about then a little later. But my dad was really a kid of heart always he loved kids. He was from a big family of

13, so he enjoyed having lots around and always I had lots of cousins like to come to our house real often, like every day. We liked them to be there also back to our place to sleigh ride and after the flat place we had a smaller hill we went down into the creek, frozen early in October or November until April. We went down the big hill then the flat place on to the smaller hill and then on the frozen creek. It sure was fun. It was a long ride, and then a longer time to walk and pull our sled up to the top but oh gee, we sure did enjoy it lots.

Then about the milking. I was after my dad from the time I was three years old to let me milk. I followed him to the barn real often, but until I was past four and-a-half did he make me a wooden milk stool and gave me a bucket one night. He said, "Come on honey, you try your hand at milking the oldest cow we have." I don't remember how old, but she was real tame and I loved her.

So, Dad set me down beside Betty, as what her name was, and started her milk coming, but I milked for a short time until she started to hold her milk, as my hands were not as strong as my dad. I didn't pull as hard, so she held her milk. I started to calling my daddy, "She won't let me have her milk." So he came over several times and started again for quite a few times before I could milk her dry.

I only milked at night for quite a while then had to get up and do both morning and night, but I loved it. When I started to school at six years old I was getting up quite early to milk before school time.

The first two years, I went to school was to a one room school with eight grades and one teacher. The teacher roomed at our house so I walked to school with him, but when I started third grade they closed our one room school and I rode the bus that picked me up at 7:15. So I had to get up at five and milk so I could clean up and eat breakfast before the bus picked me up, but oh gee, did I love to milk and be with my dad all the time.

Children now days has no idea what a wonderful time that we used to have back in the 20s, 30s, even 40s wasn't too bad. I loved every day of it and I still love being in the country.

There is nothing like living on a farm. Back then I sure had lots of wonderful times. No radio, no TV. We played games with our parents or neighbor kids and we had the most wonderful time. Now children get in a car and go to some other kind of fun. It will never be what good times back when we were very poor, never knew what it was to do the good times they call it.

I never went to a movie until I was 15 years old, but looking back now I thank God for those good old days. I have something to really remember when children don't have now days. The good old days are really something to remember. I love oh so many memories that I have.

Riding Bikes and Skinny Dipping

by Paul Joseph of Zanesville, Ohio
born 1938

Back in the late 40's and early 50's there were many farm families in the area and we were all related one way or another. We shared bicycles in the summer and sleighs in the winter.

Our bikes were old hand me downs and always needed repair. Often we had flat tires and if we were lucky, could afford a new inner tube. Sometimes we would have a repair kit with us. Mostly we put in two inner tubes and even one old tire inside another and off we went. There were many times when we lost our chain and went down the gravel hills and hoped there was not a car coming up.

Staying out all day we could always find apple, pear or peach trees and had plenty of fruit to keep from starving until supper time.

Summer of 1950. Row one: Bobbie Miller, Mary Joseph, Dorothy Durant, Rosie Durant, Fred Barker, Dick Emmertt, Paul Joseph, Ruth Soller, Becky Smith. Row two: Sid Barker, Patty Barker, Bob Emmertt.

We boys also would go skinny dipping and if the girls found us, they would steal our clothes and we would have to run through the woods home. We never were able to catch the girls skinny dipping. They just did not make the noise we boys did.

Tom, Huck and the Truant Officer

by Larry E. Kirk of Chandlersville, Ohio
born in 1941

Living in a somewhat small midwestern town (Zanesville, Ohio) during my early youth was an exciting time for me. Although we didn't have much money, it was, nevertheless, a fun time.

My cousin and I were like the Tom Sawyer and Huck Finn of our neighborhood. We both loved to fish and be mischievous. During the spring when the fish were "hitting" we would take off and go fishing at the dam. Of course, this was while school was in session. If we were at school in the morning then we took off in the afternoon. Sometimes it was the other way. After several times of doing this, the school would call the "truant officer" to locate us. Knowing that we loved to fish, it didn't take much to locate us. After being caught several times and talked to, I think the officer finally gave up. Before we knew it, he was bringing a fishing pole with him and sitting down with us and fishing also. Our parents never did find out, and we still passed our grade.

Another favorite pastime was running through the big grain mill that set on the west end of the dam. It was a big place and after it closed at noon on Saturdays and all day Sunday we sometimes would play hide and seek. At the base of the dam where the mill stood were a couple of windows with bars in them. This was to keep out driftwood. The water current would go through the openings and turn a big paddlewheel that turned the shaft upstairs to grind the grain. Being small and skinny, we were able to slide between the bars and grab onto the wheel and ride up to a landing. From there we could go any place in the mill. I don't think anyone knew we were there. Sometime later, my cousin's dad found out and really thumped us. We never done it again.

Other times we would hitch a ride from a passing car and go fishing up the river for several miles. All we had was an inner tube, fish stringer, and a pole. We carried our bait under a hat on our head. Mostly it would be worms, but once in a while we were lucky enough to get a couple hellgrammites. Floating down the river we saw all kinds of birds and animals, and we also sometimes went ashore and done some swinging from vines that overhang the banks. Our down river fishing trip could take up to five or six hours to complete. We always told someone that we were going to the river, just not out of town.

Once several of us went on a camping trip and we had a couple wooden canoes. During the return trip home we had to carry the canoes down over a stone earthen dam. About half way down, two of the other kids stirred up a hornets nest. Instead of just dropping the canoes, we tried to outrun the hornets while dragging the canoes over the rocks. Needless to say, the canoes got busted up and we all had stings from the hornets.

Turtle hunting with my uncle was interesting to say the least. Most turtles go in head first along creek banks and when you reach in the hole in the bank you can feel their tail or shell. One time my uncle reached into a hole and a snapper bit him on the left thumb. Now, a snapping turtle doesn't let go after he bites. The turtle was about six pounds, and I had about four others in a burlap bag. My uncle said we were going home, and off we went to the pickup truck. Now, this snapper is still on my uncle's thumb, and we drove about eight miles to get home. Once there, he tied the turtle up by the tail on a clothesline, cut the head off, and then went in the workshop and put the still clamped on turtle's head in a vise and started to crush it. Pretty soon the jaws of the turtle snapped open and my uncle was free. His thumb was sore for several days afterwards.

Train rides were another adventure for us. We lived not far from a roundhouse and every once in a while the engineers would give us a ride on the engines. After learning how to get up and down off the ladders, we graduated to the box cars and used to "hop" a ride on a west bound to a town about 27 miles away. Now, when you're young, certain things stick in your mind, like, from overhearing the fellows talking, we knew when the early morning freight was going to leave and when the east bound from the other town was coming back.

We even learned to walk on top of the box cars. We probably did this for about two years before someone spotted us and the police came to our house. It was enough to scare us from doing it again.

One year, the big circus came to town (Ringling Brothers). It had about three different trains loaded with all kinds of wagons and animal cages. Being we didn't have enough money to go see the circus, we did the next best thing. We went down to the yard where they were and set on the dock of the railway express agency. It was a ringside seat. They used small "cats" and elephants to pull the wagons off the train trailers. There was action everywhere and even the performers were working too. As the wagons were unloaded, a team of horses were hitched up and before long we were watching a parade. All the elephants were lined up trunk-to-tail and started for their trip to the fairgrounds. At the fairgrounds we watched the big top go up with elephant power. It was the biggest blue tent we had ever seen. Back in those days, the circus just stayed one night and then it moved on. The next day we were back at the dock and watched it get loaded up. It was exciting to see something you never forget.

When my parents moved out into the country, I walked to my cousin's house. About 4 miles. Now I went to a four grades in one room school. When it snowed, we wouldn't have school, but my cousin did, as he just lived across the street from his school. I would go to his house and he would skip school, and we used to clear snow from the walks of the neighbors and earn some money. Then on Saturday and Sunday we would go to the movies. We would see all of the ones on Saturday and then see the new ones on Sunday.

Our town was hit by a flood that covered a big part of the area just where my cousin lived. Although his home wasn't involved, it was very close. We got the big idea to get out the johnboat and explore the area. As we rowed past stores and shops we could look into the windows and see all kinds of stuff floating around. At one intersection the street goes up over a small arched bridge. Now, there was a pretty strong current, and all at once we see a guy coming past us rowing like mad. He was in a kayak. All of a sudden he got caught in the current and ended up getting wrapped around a telephone pole. The kayak broke in half and the guy vanished and then surfaced. We pulled him out and rowed as fast as we could to my cousin's house. This guy was shivering really bad by the time we got there. By the time we got to the porch he was walking stiff legged because his pants turned to ice. My aunt made him strip right there in the kitchen and stand in front of the oven. He was so cold he could hardly talk. After he warmed up he said he was just trying out his homemade kayak and got caught in the rapid current. He said it wasn't the smartest thing that he ever done (really). Everything turned out okay, and my uncle took him home later.

I can remember the first TV my grandparents got. My grandpa always enjoyed "Queen for a Day," and every once in a while, you could see a tear form in his eyes. Another favorite was "Championship Bowling." He just didn't understand that these fellows couldn't throw a strike all the time. Favorite radio programs for my grandma was Amos 'n' Andy and Fibber McGee and Molly.

After my grandpa passed on, my grandma went to live with one of her daughters. Now, I didn't know this, and one day I walked into her house and headed straight out to the fridge to get a glass of milk. Now, when I walked in there was a man and lady setting there watching TV. I said, "Hi," and kept right on walking. After I got my glass of milk I went back into the living room and asked them if they knew where grandma was. They told me, and I drank my milk and left. Upon arriving at my aunt's house, I told Grandma that there was some people at her house. That's when I found out that she had sold it, and they were the new owners. Boy was I embarrassed.

These are just some of the moments that I cherished as a boy growing up. There are other stories, but these I remember the most.

The Caldwell Football Legacy

by Dale Caldwell of Beallsville, Ohio
born 1930

My name is Dale Caldwell. I played on the first football team at Beallsville High School. I was co-captain with Jack Whitchey. It was a very fast game. You had two ends, two halfbacks, a quarterback and the center. You had to make fifteen yards for a first down. We had no facemasks on our helmets. The quarterback could not run with the ball. The center was eligible for a pass. We were coached by the Henry Prichard and Fred Abel. We played a seven or eight game schedule.

Back row, left to right: Don Powell, Co-captain Jack Witchey, John Howell. Front row: Raymond Gates, Co-captain Dale Caldwell, Nelson Baker.

It will be sixty years of football this year at Beallsville High School. There are four of the starting six still living. I have pictures of this team.

This football team started in the fall of 1949. The Caldwell family has three generations of varsity football at Beallsville High School. Their names are Dale Caldwell (father), Randy Caldwell (son), and Luke Caldwell (grandson).

Around and Around the Somerset Square

by Dorothy J. Snider of Somerset, Ohio
born 1923

Twelve years in school and one and a half years in business school. Never played hooky one day, honest.

Lived on a farm in Perry County and had a two hole outhouse and a chamber pot for nights.

Never took castor oil, but that was all there was back then. We ate apples.

We had a re-chargeable battery radio and I do remember Amos and Andy.

We had a three party line phone and all the news you ever needed to have.

We had a wind up Victrola that took cylinder rolls and the Old Gray Mare was a favorite song.

Never ever got a spanking at school or at home. I was one good girl.

Saturday night baths were required behind the kitchen coal stove in a wash tub. Taking turns.

We had a wringer washer that you turned the handle to run the clothes through and sometimes your fingers.

We had a movie theater in town open Saturday nights only. Full house for sure. Black and white.

All our clothes were home made by Grandma, and we passed them down to the next younger sister. I think my first dress bought in a store was Junior-Senior Prom dress…all mine and then graduation. One dress for both occasions.

Every teacher was a favorite. Walking a mile to a one room schoolhouse for three years before consolidation. Twelve grades in one room, you learned a lot and quickly if you wanted to learn and get all A's.

We had many pets to choose from. On a farm, you can have them all. Chickens, ducks, geese, lambs, pigs and goats. We had them all.

We never missed church on Sunday and I believe my favorite teachers were Sunday school teachers. I loved hearing about God, and the only book we had in our house was the Bible…except for school books which we sometimes left at school, because they weren't ours.

We got one toy every Christmas and with five sisters to share, we were just fine; we had a jump rope, one pair of roller skates to share, a ball to play "Andy Over," and a rope from the barn to jump rope. We played "house" a lot. Mom, dad, children, babies—we always had a pet puppy or two.

Our summertime fun was visiting your neighbors on the next farm if they had children.

Saturday evenings we always went to town to get groceries for the following week. Of course we had milk, cream, eggs, meat and garden supplies. So you only had to buy flour, sugar, spices, fruits and vegetables you couldn't grow. We always each got a nickel to spend on candy at the candy store. Believe me, for a nickel you could get a bag full to take home and last all through Sunday.

Our jobs as children was to feed chickens, gather the eggs, milk cows, separate milk from the cream, keep things cold in the cellar under the house with a continued stream of water from the well or the cistern.

When a boy liked you he would ask to walk you around and around the square of Somerset and eventually take you home when he could drive. My first kiss was on Lover's Lane in Somerset after many dates, maybe six months. That was special. When you grow up in a family of girls you learn slowly and cautiously and definitely a lady at all times.

This is enough of the past and me. Hope you can use some of it and enjoy doing it. I enjoyed writing it, and definitely want to buy a book, if you don't take too long. Thank you.

I am now a mother, grandmother, great-grandmother and a great-great grandmother, and I love every minute of it.

I have had many, many hobbies through the years, and now rely on reading.

Best childhood ever and we had nothing, but back then there wasn't much to have, but neither did anyone else and we didn't know it. Now everything is so modern, so perfected and so easily obtained and I love it, and I feel I have earned the right to have it all.

I drive by the home where I was raised and the new one built beside it. It was a good life and we all still love to get together and talk about the old times.

The Singing Mayhughs and the Snow of 1950

by James Mayhugh of Bethesda, Ohio
born 1935

It's really hard to find a place to start when you have memories that go back 70 plus years. I guess I could begin by telling you that I was born January 16th, 1935, about six miles south of Bethesda, Ohio, on County Road 92. My dad, mother and sister lived on a little hillside farm that Dad rented when I came along. Things were very hard at that time, just coming out the Great Depression. We never had any money, but being farmers, we always had plenty to eat. Our family raised a big garden and Mom canned everything that she could get her hands on. We also had our own meat, eggs and milk.

By 1941 Dad thought that he should buy a farm and we did, just up the road about two miles. Dad got a government loan and at that time they sent someone out around two to three times a year to see that everything was up to snuff. Mom had to can a certain amount of fruits and vegetables to take care of the family. To be sure that this was being done an agent checked the cellar to make sure that we had what we needed. If you didn't do what they expected, well then, they read you the riot act.

I started to school about 1942. We lived down a township road about one fourth mile from the paved road. My sister and I had to walk up the hill to catch the bus in all kinds of weather. At that time the school bus was owned by an individual instead of the school district. Our bus was an old Ford, probably about a 1939, and we kids named her Josephine. Well the guy that owned the bus had to maintain it and it always seemed to have lots of problems. Many times it broke down either coming or going. If the driver couldn't get her fixed then we had to walk. Another thing was the roads. In the winter time we quite often got stuck in the mud or snow and some farmer would have to come and pull us out with his horses since at that time there wasn't many farmers with tractors. We went to school anyway, the best way that we could get there.

I always loved to sing and it wasn't long before some of the older guys found out that I could sing pretty well for a little kid. They would pester me to sing on the bus and since I loved to do it, it didn't take a lot of coaxing to get me going. After a while I decided that if I was going to sing then I should get paid, so I wouldn't sing unless they took up a collection and paid me. Mostly it was only a few pennies that they could get together, but that was enough to make me sing like a bird. In those years we didn't have TV sets and a lot of times we didn't even have a radio. Dad finally got an old battery operated radio, and sometimes when it worked we could even tune into W.S.M Grand Ole Opry on Saturday night. I learned a lot of songs from listening to the Opry and WWVA in Wheeling, West Virginia. I still can remember the guys singing on the radio such as Big Slim, Doc Williams and others. When I heard a song that I liked, I'd run down to the henhouse and crawl through the hole that the chickens came in and out of. I'd take an ear of corn with me and as I shelled the corn the hens would gather round me and I'd turn loose with my latest song. A more attentive audience you never have seen - as long as the corn held out.

About this time we began spending a lot of time in the evenings, after the chores were done, singing and entertaining ourselves. Mom had an old pump organ and she would play and sing alto. My sister Ramona would sing tenor and I would sing the melody. After a few years we started singing at different functions going on and at church. We had a really good time, but the problem was that we didn't have any transportable instruments. As long as we performed where there was an organ or a piano, we were fine. If an organ or a piano weren't available then we sang acapella. Finally someone gave Mom an old push and pull accordion, and someone else gave Ramona an old tater bug mandolin. That was fine, but I really wanted a guitar in the worst kind of way. This was about 1948 and still no extra money in sight to buy a guitar.

As fate would have it, someone gave me a buck rabbit and a couple of does. Well, you how that goes. In no time at all, I had all kinds of rabbits and also a market for them at Barrett Poultry Farm. They would buy them when they weighed about four pounds at about 25-cents per pound. I started selling rabbits and saving money and soon I had enough to send in the Chicago Mail Order catalogue for my first guitar. Boy, were we in the big time now. After a few months, a Doc Williams guitar course book and some sore fingers I learned a few chords. We got it all together and started singing and playing for anyone that would listen. At that time there were lots of social gatherings in the community; like cake walks, pie socials, Farmer's Institutes and church revivals, so we stayed real busy.

About this time also, Dad went to work for a construction company so that we could keep up with the farm expenses. That brought about another change. Dad had to have a decent car to get back and forth to work and that's something that we never had before. Now we could go farther to do our pickin and grinnin. Things were really looking up and about that time we were joined by my younger sister and brother. We now had five in the group and Mom made our outfits to wear to our show. I mean fancy outfits with all kinds of glitter and embroidery. What we couldn't do with our picking and singing, we made up for by looking good. We spent many years doing our music and my wife and I still maintain a group. We have been known as the Singing Mayhughs for over 60 years.

After Dad went to work on construction, it kind of gave us a lift financially. In 1952 Dad bought a new Allis Chalmers C. A. tractor with plows and a disc. We like to near ploughed up the whole farm. It certainly made things faster and easier with him working away and my brother and I farming in the evenings after school.

One thing I remember very vividly was, as soon as we got home from school, we changed our clothes. We had old clothes and school clothes. Every year right before school started, Mom would send in the Sears catalog and get our school clothes. Us boys would get two pair of bib overhauls, two shirts and a pair of shoes. If there weren't any hand me downs, we sometimes got a new coat - if we needed it. This happened clear through grade school. When we got into high school, we graduated from bibs to jeans.

Of course the girls only wore dresses, bobby socks, and mostly saddle shoes. When we got home from school and changed our clothes, we mostly listened to the radio for an hour or so before we started our chores. At this time of day we listened to radio shows such as: Terry and the Pirates, Jack Armstrong and of course the Lone Ranger. That was the highlight of the day.

After the chores and supper was over came milking time. We milked 12 to 18 cows by hand; Dad, my older sister and I. Then in the morning before going to school we milked again. I can't remember anything much worse than getting up at 5:00 AM on a cold winter morning, going to an icy cold barn and sitting down to an old cow with those icy cold teats. It still sends a shiver down my spine just to think about it. Well, there might be one thing worse, and that was going to the outhouse in the winter. Down to 0 degrees with the wind blowing snow through the cracks in the weather boarding. Let me tell you, you didn't spend much timc looking through that old Sears Catalog.

Then there was Mom's old Maytag wringer washer. The washer was powered with a gasoline motor due to not having electricity on the farm at that time. She washed in a room off the kitchen and hung the exhaust tube out of the window. We called this room the pantry, and it also served as a cold storage room in the winter, where she kept head cheese in a crock bowl and also a large crock of sauerkraut. The old wringer washer also served as a pea sheller in the summer time. We raised bushels of peas, and Mom would feed the peas through the wringer to shell the peas.

Earlier I mentioned that we had a lot of cake walks back when I was a kid. Well, just down the road from our farm was the old Hunter school building. On Saturday nights there were often cake walks at the old school building and it was also used for farm bureau meetings. The line between Goshen and Wayne townships was near our farm. We lived in Goshen Township and went to Bethesda to school and the kids that lived over the township line went to Hunter to school through 8th grade and went to high school at Bethesda. Another social event at the Hunter school were Saturday night movies. Admission to the movies was 25-cents. We saw Randolph Scott, Gene Autry, Roy Rodgers and all of the big cowboy stars of the day. Then when we went home, my brothers and I (and my sister when we could talk her into it) would reenact the movie with wooden guns and stick horses. It didn't take a lot to entertain us in those days.

Mom was also famous for her home baked bread. I got into coon hunting a pretty early age and often had buddies that hunted with me. When we came in late at night; tired and nearly starved, as only young boys can get, Mom would have home baked bread, butter and jam or jelly waiting on the table for us. One buddy told me years later that he thought that home baked bread was the best thing about coon hunting. No doubt, it was a big asset.

In 1950, when I was 15 years old, came one of the most memorable occurrences of my youth, the big snow of 1950! It started, I believe, the day after Thanksgiving and snowed like it had to. It snowed all day and that night and I don't know how much longer, but we ended up with 36 inches of snow. Then the wind started to blow. Snowed in, yes, for about a week. The county didn't have the equipment big enough to open the roads and had to recruit help. They brought in the big dozers and end loaders, and moved the snow along with the farmer's fences that were near the road. After the snow stopped we had to shovel paths to the barn, chicken house and outhouse. Then, we started to shovel out the lane. The lane sat down in, with banks high on each side, and made a real nice trap for snow. We had to shovel a path just wide enough for Dad's old car. The bad part was throwing the snow high enough to get up over the bank and then sometimes over six-foot high snow drifts. It took us a whole week to see daylight, but we finally made it through.

During that week, Will Kemp, one of our closest neighbors, made a couple of trips to Bethesda on a horse to get things that people really needed. When we finally got shoveled out it was kind of like going through a tunnel. We then put chains on the old Model B Ford and away we went. Of course, we had no school for over a week, which us boys really enjoyed. We built all kinds of snowmen, forts and such things. Well, so much for the snow of 1950.

Through the years we always had dogs and other pets and I have to say my life hasn't changed much in that respect. My wife and I still have assorted animals and I would hate to think about living without them. They are a constant source of entertainment to us. The first dog that I really called mine was a hound dog given to me by Woody Kemp. Woody was an avid coon hunter and close friend. He was the one that got me started on a lifetime of coon hunting. Now coon hunting is not a sport that appeals to everyone. An awful lot of people can't imagine why anyone in his right mind would want to go out in the middle of the night, in the wet and cold, and stumble around in the dark. I will be the first to admit that there have been times that I swore that if I ever made it home, that I would never go again. But, then by the next night, I would be raring to go again. At that time, we would start out at dark and many times didn't come in until the sky was starting to lighten up at daybreak. Needless to say, it doesn't take nearly that much to do me now. After about 60 years of following the hound, about two to three hours seems like plenty.

About 1954 I met a young fellow, where I worked at Campus shirt factory in Barnesville, Ohio. I talked him into some coon hunts and with a little persuasion had him going pretty good. His name is Bill Crawford and he stayed with me through all of these years. We came to be real close friends and still are. He has kind of slowed down on the coon hunting over the years, but will still go now and then. We had experiences out in those woods that would fill a book on their own, if I were to tell all of them.

We've been shot at, fell in icy creeks and everything in between. I remember one night we were out hunting after a long cold spell had kept us out of the woods. It had warmed up and we thought we should take a little hunt. We started down a creek called Blood Run just below the old home place. We had followed along the creek for three to four miles, when the dogs treed on the other side of the creek, up on a steep hill. The problem was, the creek was high, with the ice starting to break up and the dogs were on the other side. We looked up and down for a crossing, but there wasn't a good place to cross. Bill finally told me that he had heard that if you crossed on a riffle, that it wasn't very deep. Well, he started across and the next thing that I knew all I could see was his hat floating on top of the water. He came up out of the water, trying to get his breath, with water pouring out of both sides of his hunting coat. I finally got him over to the shore and on the dry land. The cold water had taken his breath and he couldn't talk, but his teeth chattered about 90 times a minute. He finally was able to ask me what we were going to do. I told him that I had two of about everything on, to strip down and I would give him half of what I had on. It was a cold night and I had on two pairs of pants, two shirts and two pairs of socks. He stripped down, put on a dry shirt, pants and socks, and stuffed the wet clothes into his hunting coat and we headed for home. We never stopped until we hit the porch of the old home place. We left the dogs treed, but they came in the next morning. You know, it never made him sick or anything and we were ready to go again the next night. We were more careful from than on about crossing on riffles. We figured out the next night that what had happened, the creek was up and running on top of the ice. He took about two steps; hit the wet ice under the water and that was all she wrote.

When I first started hunting, back in the late forties, we used an oil lantern for light to walk by. Of course, we had a five or six cell flashlight for shining the tree to spot a coon after the dogs had treed. It was probably in the middle fifties when we graduated to carbide lights, which was a big improvement over oil lanterns, as long as the wind wasn't blowing too hard. If it was really windy you had trouble keeping the lights burning. We would keep turning up more water to make the flame bigger and if you weren't real careful you drowned it clear out. Then you had to start all over with a refill of carbide. After a few years of that we went real big time, with electric mine lights and 200,000 candle power spotting lights, insulated boots, and clothing, etc.

Coon hides ready to sell in 1950. We were still carrying lanterns instead of flashlights.

Probably the worst thing about the sport, to me, was carrying all of the equipment that you had to have. To start with, you had a big hunting coat and hunting pants, then the battery for the light, along with the spotting light, hunting knives and mostly a pistol or a rifle, with a couple of boxes of ammunition. If you are hunting by yourself you carry about 40 pounds of equipment before you put any coons in your coat. On top of that, part of the time, you are leading a hound or two. Talk about fun. Well, I could go on and on about all of the things that have happened to me out in the woods; like the time I broke my ankle and walked home on it or the times that we were shot at and run off by unappreciative land owners, but I will save all of that for another time. So much for coon hunting.

When we were growing up hunting and fishing were two things that we did every time that we had a spare minute. I can remember when I was probably eight or nine-years-old, every once and awhile, usually when it was too wet to work in the fields, Dad would take me fishing. We'd get our worms dug, our fishing tackle (consisting of some hooks and sinkers with maybe a cork for a bobber) together, load up in the old 32 Model B Ford and head out. We mostly went to a creek like Captina or Bendfork. Dad would stop in Belmont at Palmer's IGA store and get us some crackers and a couple of cans of sardines and we were ready. There were a couple of pretty good holes washed out in the creek in the spring of the year. White suckers would come up Captina from the river and sometimes some nice horny chubs. I couldn't wait for my Dad to cut a couple of limber saplings and tie on our strings, hooks and sinkers. You could hook on a big juicy fishing worm and he wouldn't any more than hit the water before one of those horny chubs would hit. You would think that it weighed at least five pounds. If you were lucky enough to land one, sometimes they might be eight or ten inches long, and I would be so excited that I literally jumped up and down. I couldn't have been happier if I had caught something two feet long.

After we fished for awhile Dad would set our poles and bring out the crackers and sardines. Talk about a feast, things just couldn't get much better than that. We'd fish awhile longer and then pack up and head home where we would mostly have fried fish for supper. This probably doesn't sound very exciting by today's standards, but things like this are among my fondest memories. When I was old enough to go out with a gun by myself, I also got into groundhog hunting. At that time, after we had mowed off the hay, you could slip over in the meadow and see a half dozen or more groundhogs out in the field. Now it seems that groundhogs are about extinct, unless you see one around your house or out buildings. They tell me that the coyotes have about cleaned the groundhogs out and I really hate to see that. A groundhog makes a hole that furnishes a home for a lot of wild animals; coons, rabbits, foxes, etc. Anyway, at that time, they were still thick, and a lot of fun to hunt with a 22-caliber rifle. You had to get within 40 to 50 yards from them to make a good shot. I started hunting them with an old 22 Stevens Favorite model 1915 that Dad had got in trade for a double barreled shot gun when he was a boy. We also used that old gun for years for coon hunting. Sometimes before coon season came in, it would come apart where the barrel fastened on and you could put it into your hunting coat, where it couldn't be seen.

Once we were in the woods, if we happened to have a young dog that we were trying to train, then we might knock one out to them. Now, we didn't do that a lot, but now and then we would, just to get a dog started. Bill Crawford and I probably carried that old gun 500 miles when we were coon hunting. Back when I groundhog hunted quite a lot, I had an old dog named Buglar that just loved to go with me. We would sneak into a mown hay field and check for hogs. If we saw one, I would lay down on my belly and crawl up for a shot. Buglar would lay down on his belly and crawl right along with me. When we got close enough for a shot he would wait until I pulled the trigger and away he would go. He seemed to know right where I had shot. If the hog wasn't dead, he would finish it off and we would hunt for more.

After Dad had been working at a construction job for awhile, he came home one day with a Remington Model 510 Target Master. He bought the gun over at Belmont, Ohio at a store owned by Tom Johnson. My brother Bill and I thought that it was a high powered rifle and had a few scraps over who was going to use it. It was an improvement over the old Stevens and we shot a bunch of ground hogs with it. We also ate quite a few young ones in the early summer. Mom really knew how to fix them so that they were fit for a king. I can just taste one now, all fried to a golden brown. Yum, Yum. Well, so much for hog hunting.

One of the most memorable people that I remember was an old fellow by the name of Dallas White. Dallas was probably about the age of my Dad and lived on a farm off of County Road 86. He lived by himself and loved to hunt. What a combination. He raised a garden, kept a bunch of hounds (coon, fox and beagle) and never owned a car or a tractor. He did all of his work with horses, right up until he passed away, a few years ago. When you went to his house it was like going back in time. He always had a pot of some kind of wild game on the back of the stove and the first thing that he did was when you came to his house was to ask you if you were hungry. If you went down during coon season he was always ready to go on a hunt.

He had an old pot bellied stove in the middle of the living room, along with a cot where he slept. Dallas didn't spend a lot of time housekeeping and before taking off on a hunt he would grab the coal bucket and throw a dash of coal into the stove. Sometimes the coal didn't all go in the stove, but that didn't bother Dalley. He just kicked what missed the stove underneath and hunting we would go. In later years, I started taking Bill Crawford with me when I went down to hunt. Bill was a little squeamish when it came to eating and never wanted to try any coon, groundhog or whatever Dalley had on the stove. Dallas also trapped for a little money. He lived off his little farm, except for a few staples that he bought with trapping money, and money that he made hiring out to farmers during the summer months. He passed away at a pretty young age about 20 years ago. I still really miss him and the way he lived. He was beholden to no one and pretty much lived as he wanted to. After he passed away I wrote a song about him and his way of life. He was really linked to the past and you just can't hardly find anyone like him anymore.

Another person that I would like to mention before I quit all of this rambling is my Granddad, Allie Mayhugh. Back in the 1940's he lived over on route 145 toward Beallsville, Ohio. He had a little hillside farm where my Dad grew up. I don't know what all that they had on their farm back then, but one thing that they did have was copperhead snakes. I remember my Dad telling about putting up hay with the copperheads in the fields. He said that one time his Dad was pitching hay onto the wagon and he was loading it when his Dad pitched on seven copperheads in one load.

I don't know about you, but that would have been enough to make me leave the farm. Dad also told that he had an old dog named Bob who got bit by copperheads every summer. The first time that he was bit he swelled up all over and got pretty sick. They thought for sure that he would die. But, he pulled through and every time that he was bit after that it affected him less and less, until all he got was a little swelled place at the bite.

I used to go to Granddad's farm two or three times a year and help him clean his chicken house. He had this huge chicken house, around 30-feet wide and 100-feet long. He raised lots of chickens and sold eggs all over the area. One time he told me that he had started to lose hens, just one at a time, but over a period of time it was starting to count up. One night he decided to camp out in the chicken house. He took his shotgun and went down about dark. At that time he kept lanterns burning throughout the chicken house at night to keep the old hens working as much as possible. He said that he hadn't been there very long when he saw something moving over toward the roosts where the old hens were sleeping. He said that it was a big possum. He watched that old possum and it walked over to a roost, backed up to one of the hens and wrapped his tail around her neck. He said that he started to drag her across the floor just like a caterpillar tractor when he blew that tractor up and stopped the hen stealing.

We never had any money growing up, but we were just as happy as if we did. We made most of our toys, like wooden guns or stick horses for me and my brothers and cloth dolls and doll clothes for the girls. We didn't have a lot of material things, but we had a lot of love and our music. I don't think that I would want to live through the good old days again, but I'm kind of glad that I did. Sometimes I really worry about what so many of our youth are missing today and what will really happen on down the road. It seems that so many of our young people (and older ones for that matter) are straying so far from God and the simple life. It makes you really wonder where it all will end.

The Wooden Pig and the Persistent Tomcat

by Don Bryan of Palm Harbor, Florida
born 1937

We had decided to take my parents to a small, rural Ohio village for Thanksgiving dinner. Having been to the village many times before, we anticipated Mother and Dad enjoying the New England setting of steepled churches and quaint shops. The down home cooking restaurant was next door to a butcher shop, complete with plank floors and barrels of crackers.

It was a typical November day. The temperature was comfortable for walking, so we decided to walk around the village square to stretch our legs before dinner. The village was right out of a Norman Rockwell painting, Small Town U. S.A. Glad to be an American was the feeling of the day.

As we approached the restaurant, a large dog was barking at a wooden baby pig statue put out by the butcher shop to attract customers. The barking dog seemed as though he expected the pig to run off at any moment. Everyone was smiling and laughing at the dog's honest antic. It was good humor and good fun. The motionless pig finally lost the interest of the harasser and the dog wandered off.

This unplanned event added our entertainment for the day. It provided us all with a good laugh before dinner. Little did we know the entertainment was not over yet. We had no idea what was to happen next.

The restaurant had a flower box beneath a large French window. As we were walking by to enter the restaurant, I saw a fuzzy leg stick up out of the flower box. A big tom cat was napping on his back in the box, under the window. He wasn't the least concerned with our looking in. He reeked with aloofness, and hardly gave us a glance.

We went inside, and settled into a booth much too small for four people. The waitress came to take our order. We were not halfway through our ordering when the waitress turned toward the door and grunted with disgust. The tom cat had entered the restaurant, and was walking with his tail proudly raised high, right down the aisle way. The waitress did what any waitress would do to protect the reputation of the restaurant: she quickly picked up ole Tom and carried his bushy body to the doorstep. The screen door slammed shut, and that was that. She was back in a jiffy to finish our order.

Well, as you know, ole toms are pretty much rejection free. The next customer through the door was accompanied by you know who. Ole Tom was in again, and walking down the aisle like a general surveying his troops. The waitress, while of slight build, did an incredible athletic move to retrieve ole Tom, and this time, tossed him out the door.

By this time, ole Tom was the main event. Customers were laughing and talking about him. After all, even in a down home restaurant, Thanksgiving dinner was special...and there is a contrived effort on the restaurant owner's part to achieve a certain amount of formality. But ole Tom would have none of this. He was going to do his part to dispute any formal atmosphere.

This time, he appeared as if with the confidence one has when knowing the chef. The waitress, by this time, had had enough. She worried not about formality or expressing any kindness toward animals. She followed ole Tom's tail, which was gliding between the tables like a cruising submarine. She latched onto his tail with the grip of a hand wrestler, and went to the door, flinging ole Tom further than he could ever fall from a tree.

Tom did make a shrieking sound, kind of like a seagull imitation. He was out the door so fast the sound really couldn't be identified as that of a cat.

Mother and Dad laughed and laughed. Mother always had a hearty laugh. She trembled with laughter and the tears came rolling down her cheeks.

We finally got our dinner, but the food was not like Mother would make; nor did it compare to a fine restaurant...but we had a special day indeed. This Thanksgiving Day will be remembered for many years to come.

Educational Chronicles of a Sardis School Girl

by Virginia Stewart Goergi of Paramount, California
born 1935

I was born January 25, 1935 on a snowy Friday morning at 7:00 a.m. in Sardis, Ohio. My neighbor, and life long friend, Thelma Merckle, was born eight days earlier. I shared my birthday with classmate, Bill Gano, and Marlene Richie, who was born a year later. If there were others in our school with the same birth date I was not aware of them.

In grades first through third I had Miss Gladys Barker. She would have us color flags and pictures of Uncle Sam. I credit her with instilling patriotism in me that lingers to this day. Fourth grade I had Mr. Roy Barker, who gave me a love of music. I still remember singing "I Dream of Jeannie with the Light Brown Hair."

These teachers did not specialize in one subject; they taught us all we were supposed to be learning at that particular age.

Part way through the fourth grade my family moved

to Columbus, Ohio. The summer following the sixth grade, I came back to Sardis and started the seventh grade with Mr. Leonard Mobberly. He seemed gruff, but had a good heart. I learned from him how to look below the surface to find the good in people. Again, back to Columbus for eighth and part of the ninth grade, when we moved back to Sardis.

In ninth grade, I had Mrs. Golda Straight for homeroom teacher. Of the many things she taught me, I loved poetry best. Grades tenth, eleventh, and twelfth, I had Mr. Harry Ullman and Mr. Urban Mallett as teachers also.

Sardis School, grades one to twelve. Painting by Mace.

In the middle of 12th grade, I left Sardis High to get married. I moved to Cleveland, Ohio where I graduated from John Hay High School.

After moving to California in 1961, I attended two years of college. I was able to get a job as merchandiser for 28 stores for Sperry and Hutchinson Company and after five years, was lucky to be hired by Downey Police Department, where I worked for twenty-four years, until I retired in 1998.

I give credit to my teachers at Sardis for giving me a good basic education, and instilling in me the knowledge to be able to go out into the world and make the best life you can. I tell myself, "For a little country girl from a small town in Ohio, You've come a long way baby!"

Now, I'm living the good life, and enjoying my retirement years. Life is good.

I would like to add one thought: the friends I had made in Sardis are still my friends and for this I am thankful and blessed.

Depression Roller Skates

by Jane A. Price of Zanesville, Ohio
born in 1920

My father died when I was nine, and just a few months before the start of the Great Depression (September 1929). He had been a doctor and there were many outstanding fees on the books. My mother began to teach piano for 25 cents a lesson to support my sister and me with food, heat and clothing.

We knew that money was "tight,'" but my sister and I wanted skates for Christmas in 1930. These were metal, adjustable skates, with clamps and bolts, as well as ankle straps which could be fitted to each person's shoes. Five-year-olds, eighteen-year-olds, moms and dads all could have the skates adjusted to their feet! Although the indoor skating rink was newly opened, most people skated on the sidewalks or the streets.

So Pat and I really wanted skates! We spent Christmas with my grandma and Auntie Mary. There were two shoe-sized boxes under the tree marked for us. However, when they were handed to us, we realized the boxes were not heavy enough to contain our longed-for skates! Whew!

We found they contained baby dolls, complete with handmade layettes. Grandma told us that "every little girl needs a baby doll." We tried to be appreciative and thankful. Inside our hearts we still yearned for skates and, after all, we were eight and ten and almost through playing with dolls.

Somehow, later toward spring, my mother managed one pair of skates. It turned out that Pat was a much better skater than I, so she used them more than I. However, we were so thrilled to possess skates!

I was a nine-year-old just before the beginning of the Depression.

I remember making biscuits after I came home from school, because flour needed for six biscuits was much less expensive than flour needed to bake bread. We rented our front bedroom to two young women who worked in Zanesville, but who lived far away—15 miles away in Dresden.

Because the U.S. government had not supported any public works since the pioneer days or during wartime, everyone was surprised by President Roosevelt's plans to have a public works administration (WPA) under the National Recovery Act to provide jobs for the many unemployed men.

Building roads and paving streets were among the many projects arranged for cities throughout the country. In Zanesville, Brighton Boulevard and Lexington Avenue were paved with what we call today "black top" and in those days "macadam." Oh, those smooth black streets! Those who had autos, and could afford to drive them, drove back and forth, enjoying the unrutted surfaces.

Families were looking for no-cost or inexpensive entertainment. Roller skating was the popular way of fun (and also exercise) for both children and adults. The indoor skating rink had opened, but most people used the sidewalks, because of metal wheels. Skates were made with adjustable clamps, which allowed for altering to fit many shoe lengths and widths. The skates also had ankle straps. In fact, five-year-old Bobby and eighteen-year-old Geraldine, as well as Mother and Dad, could all have the skates adjusted to fit them. Many families indulged in several pairs of skates, but with even one pair, everyone could skate by taking turns. By the way, the skate key, which adjusted the screws, was always hung on a string and consigned to be worn around the neck of the most reliable person!

After the macadam dried, many families spent innumerable summer evenings on Brighton Boulevard or Lexington Avenue, and later on one connecting block on Ohio Street, using the smooth thoroughfares as an outdoor rink. They'd bring suppers in their picnic baskets. Families sat on the steps along the sidewalk, ate a picnic supper, took turns skating and would leave before dark. The trouble was that many times they would also leave trash. Careful homeowners sometimes put out trash cans.

I don't remember youngsters or teenagers frequenting the area to skate on the summer vacation afternoons. Perhaps most skaters did not live near enough to go by themselves.

What a wonderful way to spend a family-oriented, congenial summer evening! Families met, romances were fostered, bodies were limbered and, best of all, it was inexpensive. Some good did come out of the Great Depression!

Rabies, Mud Pies and Blowing Smoke in My Ear

by Helen Weiss of Woodsfield, Ohio
born 1929

I was born during the Depression in 1929 at Calais, Ohio in our home. As I recall things weren't that bad growing up; our family didn't seem to lack for anything. My granddad, John S. Goodhart, owned the Country Store in Calais. I remember being given a dime by my mother to go about 100-feet or more through the yard, across the road, on the little foot bridge over the creek, to the store to buy a loaf of bread. The bread cost eight-cents and I was told I could use the change to buy candy. For two-cents I got a little brown paper bag full, which was a lot. Granddad would always say I didn't need it because it was not good for me. But I probably had to share with my sister and brothers.

We didn't have bathrooms just outhouses. During the day we had to trot out to the outhouse. No toilet paper then, we used the old Sears and Roebuck Catalogs or old newspapers. Sometimes we had to hurry or the wasps would run you out. The spiders never bothered me for they would get swatted with a newspaper; the same with the flies. I liked to see how many I could kill. In the winter you never stayed very long if it was cold. When it was too cold we would use the chamber pot with a lid on that was kept near the beds. They were always carried to the outhouse everyday and cleaned.

Of course we didn't have electricity then. We used oil lamps and stoves that used coal or wood. In the winter we would take a bath once a week behind the big coal stove in a big galvanized tub; the same one that clothes were washed. Or take a sponge bath, which was a small wash pan full of water, a washcloth and soap. We all used the same water. There was no running water in the home. We had to carry our water from the well a few feet outside of the dining room door and fill the reservoir on the kitchen coal stove. A bucket was on the end of a rope and let down and we cranked the bucket back up and the water was carried in the home.

It seemed I had a lot of earaches. One time I remember that my uncle Frankie Brown, Mom's brother, and his family was visiting and he smoked. He told me that he could make me feel better. He took a big drag on his cigarette and slowly blew the smoke in my ear. I guess the heat from his mouth made me think it felt better. I also remember having to take castor oil when I was sick. The castor oil was stirred into orange juice or lemonade and it was still horrible tasting. If you needed to throw-up, that castor oil would do it for me. It sure turned me against lemonade and orange juice for awhile. When I was about 14-years old I had rheumatic fever. I could not go upstairs to bed because of the pain climbing stairs. The right side of my body was the worst. I missed over two months of school. Barbara Rubel was my teacher at the time. My parents made arrangements with her to stop after school and give me homework.

I don't remember being bored. We had lots of games to play like: checkers, dominoes, old maid, jacks, tag, hide-in-seek, Red Rover, my doll and play under the porch in the summer in the dirt and make mud pies. If it was okay we would play in the creek with the other kids in town, but mom, Mary Lillian Brown Goodhart, could watch us from the porch.

We had a Victrola that my sister and I loved. We would put a record on, wind it up and try to sing along. The radio was battery operated, but we as kids never paid much attention to it till we were older or maybe weren't allowed to for fear of running the battery down. I remember being older and listening in the evening on the radio to The Lone Ranger, Screeching Doors, Fibber McGee and Molly and country music from Grand Ole Opry in Nashville, Tennessee. It was hard to hear at times. When visiting my grandparents, my granddads always like to listen to Ed Morrow with the news and they always had their ear up against the radio to hear

Mom's parents, John D. and Lillian A. Carpenter Brown, lived on a farm and sold cream and eggs. Granddad had several Jersey and Guernsey cows and their milk was richer with cream. Grandma always had a lot of chickens. In the spring it was fun to go to their home and help feed the baby chicks. As I remember there was a couple of big buildings that was round and she had about 200 or more little chicks in them. When the chicks got bigger they was moved to the big chicken house. The chickens were left run outside all over the farm, but they laid their eggs in the nest inside or we would have to check the hay mow in the barn if the big door was left open to see if they laid in the hay. If there were too many roosters they and the older chickens were sold or butchered and cold packed in jars to be eaten later. Everyday was a busy day on their farm. The milk from the cows was taken to the spring house and put through a separator which separated the milk to get the cream from the whole milk. A skim milk was kept back and some cream was kept to make butter for the home. The skim milk left over after separating was for the chickens and pigs

My dad, Ward S. Goodhart, made a living hauling cream, coal, cattle and sheep to Pittsburg, Pennsylvania and moving anything that could be put on the truck. I'm not sure when the cream stopped being hauled and he started to haul milk to Barnesville, Ohio. He hauled away the tobacco from the old tobacco barn in Calais. One time I was watching them load the big barrels of dried tobacco. The barrels were very, very large and took several men to load them. The flat bed truck would only hold about 4 barrels. As I remember the barrels were called Hodges. And the tobacco was pressed tight in the barrels.

Calais tobacco barn in about 1940.

In 1938 my parents bought the Dick Wehr farm on the edge of town. We could stand on the front porch and see the tobacco barn and watch people working outside. Before we moved a bathroom was installed (which a lot of people didn't have) with running water inside. Dad had built a holding tank to hold water from the spring, but we still only took a bath on Saturday evening. All other times we used the sink and took a sponge bath. Sometimes the tank had to be cleaned. The hole to get inside the tank, made of cement blocks, was too small for dad to get into so he put me inside to do the cleaning. The water was very low at the time. It was a mess with mud and tiny transparent crawdads, etc. It got a good cleaning and I ended up a mess.

It was a lot of work on washday; a fire was built in the washhouse stove and water was carried from the springhouse to be heated and put in the wringer washer which had a gasoline engine (used only when the door could be opened because of the fumes) that had to be started by using a foot to pump to start. When I got older and did the washing it sure made me angry when it was hard to start. Looking back now, washday for seven of us wasn't easy. We always hung the clothes outside even in cold to freeze dry. If it was raining we hung them in the washhouse on the clothesline. We finally got electricity in the home about 1940 and Mom and Dad bought an electric washing machine. It was wonderful. Before the electricity was put in we had gas lights that hung from the ceiling and had to be lighted very carefully.

We had an old telephone that hung on the wall in the living room. At the time it must have been the only one in town because people came to our home to call a doctor or important business. There was a metal box beside the phone to pay for a long distance call. It had three slots for quarters, dimes and nickels. The operator would ask for a certain amount of money to be deposited before being connected. Each coin would make a different sound that she could hear. The box was locked and someone would come to collect the money. It was a party-line with 10 to 15 people on. We always knew when someone was listening; you could hear them breathing or the line would get weak when they picked up the receiver. There was always certain ones that would pick up and listen. The ring would go into everybody's home on the line when we called. Sometimes we would get angry with them or if it was important we asked them by name to hang up. Then you would hear a bang of the receiver. The Central office was in Batesville, Ohio

My grandma Brown taught me to sew on the old treadle machine. It was good exercise for the legs. I made a few clothes. She made all of her clothes, even her underwear and bonnets out of feed sacks. When we would buy feed for the cows, chickens and hogs, the bags that the feed came in was always beautiful prints or muslin bags. They were always washed, the muslin bleached white, ironed to use for clothes and to piece quilt tops. I still have a "Feed Sack" quilt that my grandma Brown pieced and I quilted.

In the summer I sometimes went with grandma Rachel Carpenter Goodhart to pick wild berries for canning or jelly. I had to wear long sleeves and gloves with the fingers cut out. It was really hot. We always wore longer dresses then. Also, took our little beagle dog, Peggy, to scare anything away and she didn't like copperheads or any snakes. She would shake them really hard to kill them. Between Peggy, Grandma and the hoe the snakes got killed. It seemed we always saw a snake in all that shrubbery. Peggy was bitten a few times and the poor soul would swell up. Everyone took good care of her and she always got better. I really liked Peggy, she always followed us when we went to the store and met us when we came home from school.

There was always big floods in Calais and the covered bridge was at the end of our lane. It sometimes looked like it might take the bridge down the creek it was so high, but it never did. It was always fun to play under the bridge in the mud and water. We would get all muddy, then go in the shallow water to wash off. A lot of mud-pies was made then

When I started to school a new school had been built and the old one torn down. I enjoyed going to the school. I liked all my teachers and I liked arithmetic best - that is what it was called back then. We always walked since we lived only about a mile from the school. When noon came a lot of kids headed for granddad Goodhart's store for candy and pop. The pop was in glass bottles. The store was only about a half-mile or less from the school. And he was bombed with kids. Some of the boys would cut through granddad's field to get there before the girls. Sometimes there was a big race to see who got there first and at times the boys would get caught in the barb-wire fence which slowed them down a little.

Some of the men around town would get together on weekends when dad wasn't working and go fishing in the creek with a big net that would stretch across the creek. This was not allowed so someone would always be on the lookout for the game warden. They always got a lot of big catfish. Sometimes reaching back in those big holes on the sides of the bank they got scraped with the catfish and it brought blood.

One summer there was a big scare of the rabies in dogs. A lot of people always walked to granddad's store. Martha Lou Mercer was on her way to the store and a dog chased her, so she ran to the covered bridge and climbed up on the large beams inside the bridge and someone at our home heard her screaming, since the bridge was so close to our home. Mom could whistle very loud on her fingers. Most everyone in town knew when she did that certain whistle that something was wrong. When she knew what was going on everyone was told to get inside and she let out that whistle and dad heard it from his garage in town and came on the run. He knew something was wrong. The dog was then headed down along the creek when he couldn't climb up the beams. Mom went to get Martha Lou and dad and a few men with guns went after the dog and killed it. The game warden was called and the dog had rabies. Mom said, "That girl was really scared to have climbed those beams," which was hard to do.

Dad and Mom would take us to the movies in Barnesville or Woodsfield almost every Saturday night. It was always movies of Roy Rogers and Dale Evans, Gene Autry, and Clark Gable. On the way home we all feel asleep in the back seat.

During WWII sugar and gasoline was rationed and each family was given coupons for the amount that could be used for a certain length of time. I remember we really had to be careful or you would run out of coupons before the next ones would come. If some relatives didn't use all of their coupons we could buy the coupons from them if we had the money.

Being a teen was fun. We did a lot of walking in groups going to friends' home to play card games, softball, baseball, singing, getting in a car and going to Seneca Lake in the summer to swim, square dancing and movies. Most of us on the farm had to milk the cows and feed the animals before we went to school. We probably all smelled alike. No one seemed to notice as I remember. Life was sometimes hard back then, but it was a good life.

The Anonymous Twin Cities

by Donna J. Work of McConnelsville, Ohio
born 1947

There wasn't much to do in our two small villages. When I was in my preteen years, most of our activities were bike riding, swimming and the always crowded town pool. If we were lucky enough to catch a ride four miles up the state highway, we would go roller skating. The thing that was my favorite to do was to hike up to the tops of one of the hills that crested our villages in the valley and just sit and talk and watch the villages below. I love the smell of the forest.

We were lucky enough to have the old pharmacy with a real soda fountain, where one could go to enjoy a five cent Coke and a five cent bag of Conn's potato chips. Sometimes we would have the soda jerk add either chocolate or cherry syrup to our Coke. Oh, how good that was.

I enjoyed my small town [name of town not given] where I was born and grew up until I became restless in my teen years. I met this three years older than I boy that thought he fell in love with me at first sight. We later married and moved to a bigger town for a while, After having three children we settled back in to raise them in our small twin cities, as folks call it. They are all grown up now and have families of their own, which they raise their children here also. I feel sad that they didn't have the opportunities to enjoy the same things that I had to enjoy.

One of the things I miss the most that is no longer here is the big steam engine train that used to run right through the center of the village. We would put pennies on the track to collect after the train rolled over it.

They're also used to be a small restaurant right by the tracks where one could go to have the best homemade noodles and pies, which one of my friends' mother would make when working in the restaurant.

I believe everyone should have the chance to go back in time to enjoy the calm, slow, and quiet days that I remember growing up in such a close and great little village as the one I hold so dear. I now refer to it as being my Malta whenever I see old photos and hear the stories from some of the residents.

I now take care of in the nursing home and assisted living home while I work. I love to hear the stories they tell about the days gone by as they lived them. History is amazing, especially when one can take time to listen to stories that can be told, and take time to search out some of the happenings in places that one can learn about in your own backyard.

I will turn 62 this year. I'm only sorry I didn't take time sooner to really learn about my own surroundings. For you see, even the smallest of towns and villages holds many untold stories.

I wish I could have been living at the time of the beautiful riverboat that used to travel up and down our river (Muskingum). What a sight that must have been. By studying my family tree, I discovered that my great-great granddad was a riverboat navigator. Oh, how great it would have been to ride beside him and hear his stories.

History goes on forever, take time to enjoy it in any way you can get a chance to.

Going to Sunday school and church, youth meetings, and vacation Bible school, walking to and from church, running when it rains, trying to keep as dry as possible under my umbrella, enjoying the beautiful stained glass windows and singing of the choir during church and how great were the Sundays after church potluck. What great food and fun we had in our plain, small, quaint town church.

The old grade school, with the creaking old board floors. I liked the top floor the best, where one could gaze out the windows and view the lovely old homes and Muskingum River that flows between our Twin Cities [name of cities not given].

We really like to watch the snow falling with thoughts of sleigh rides after school or on weekends. Sometimes we got lucky and had a snow day, in which we could have more time for building snowmen, sleigh riding, and not to mention, the snowball fights. Although I was a girl, I still enjoyed joining in on the winter fun with my older brother. In those days it was a bit tomboyish for young girl to join in some activities. It wasn't ladylike, the older folks would say.

Sundays, during summer vacation, my best friend and I would ride bicycles hours on end. We loved riding along the River Road. Some days we would be brave and ride our bikes down First Street, which was very steep. Halfway down the street was the old railroad track. After safely crossing the tracks, straight ahead of us lay the river. What a thrill was just thinking of having brake trouble. We always stopped for a chat and a laugh at the foot of the hill.

I could go on forever telling about our lovely small towns. We even have a haunted opera house and other ghostly places. The more I read and learn about our Twin Cities, the more interesting and entertaining they become. I urge anyone that grew up in a small area to read and research about their surroundings. When we are young we don't realize what treasure we have.

Summertime Scent, and a Farmer's Tan, and Paperwork

by Lizabeth Braskey of Parma, Ohio
born in 1935

When we kids were growing up, Mom had a weekly schedule that was followed religiously, most of the time. Mondays meant doing the laundry. During winter, I hurried home after school to help my mother hang the wet stuff in the basement and leave it to dry with the heat from the coal furnace. But in summer, my younger sister and I were in charge of the wringer on the washing machine, switching its position from one tub of rinse water to the other. Mom usually put the items into the moving rollers because we girls had a few close calls already. But the real work happened outside.

Our older brother, Jerry, was taller and could stretch the rope clothesline from the house to the garage several times over so Mom and I could secure each item with clothespins. We filled up every inch of those ropes while Jerry followed us with clothesprops to hoist the heavy load and keep the laundry from dragging on the ground. There was always a sigh of relief when everything was on the line and we could rest for a while.

This is when we kids could play outside until lunch. Usually, we skated on the front sidewalk until we felt brave enough to start at the top of the driveway hill, then coast down, turning right or left on the concrete to see how far we could roll. We looked forward to this contest every week, keeping a mental note of our best distance. Even though this was reckless and dangerous for the three of us kids, we rarely fell on the hard surface leaving evidence for Mom to see. Grass was softer and cushioned our courage.

Being in the front yard for awhile prompted our mother to have us watch for the weekly hucksters that came down our street with their horse drawn wagons full of fresh produce. Our small garden provided us with some of our veggies, but Mom and Dad believed we could never have too many healthy foods. We got to know the regulars and waited patiently, hoping they would give us a few cherries while Mom selected some of the season's best. Our favorites were peaches, sweet corn and melons.

Sometimes, we'd see the iceman come through our neighborhood, looking for the sign in a customer's window, telling how large a block they wanted. Kids would follow his wagon, watching for falling chunks of ice they could lick like a Popsicle. But not the three of us! We were waiting for the driver of the bakery truck. The goodies Mom baked the previous week were already devoured. So once in a while, she would put the "star" sign in the front window, signaling the driver to stop. What a selection he had! Our mouths drooled over what she would pick. Always, he would give us kids a cookie.

We would eat that cookie for our dessert at lunch. This would give us the extra push we needed to take down the dried laundry. There was a time-saving method that our mother had perfected. We sorted our socks and put things to get ironed in a separate basket. We folded our shirts and shorts, sniffing the fresh fragrance that would cling to the clean laundry for days. It took two of us to fold the bedsheets right off the line, knowing the summertime scent was worth the time it took to do this task.

As soon as we got everything into the house, we immediately put the clean sheets back on the bed. After inhaling deeply, then admiring our handiwork, we felt the satisfaction of a job well done. Going to sleep at night was always a nocturnal delight. There was a comfort level that wrapped around us, and made us feel loved and secure. The aroma of the clean sheets contributed to our peaceful night's rest and allowed for kid-time dreams while remembering the events of the day. And that was a good thing. We had another Monday memory.

Jerry, Mary Jane and Lizabeth.

* * * *

When we were growing up in the 1940's, Victory Gardens were a patriotic answer to the terrible war that was affecting our country. We kids were just beginning to understand the meaning of it all, the year that my older brother, Jerry, was 9; my younger sister, Mary Jane, was 5; and I was 8. Up to this time, summers were our days of glorious freedom. Of course we had small chores to do, but school was out and we looked forward to three months of fantasies in the great outdoors...lazy days of challenging our creativity, playing board games, baking with Mom, or listening to her radio.

Our small city yard had lots of concrete and trees, but Dad dug up a small corner next to the garage for our part of the war effort. This was the beginning of our very own garden, and to us kids, the end of our summertime fun. The first year we planted about eight tomato plants, two rows of beans and a patch of carrots. We kids hoped we were done with the work, until we were told this was our job for the summer. We were taught what weeds looked like and how to cultivate tomato plants.

The watering was another story. Since our hose didn't reach that far, we had to put two full pails and a sprinkling can in our wagon and pull it to the back of our yard. This was work, until we found out that if we were clumsy, we could splash each other and cool off.

By the time we accepted this reality and saw our efforts result in healthy plants, we again thought our work might be over and we could now be free to enjoy what was left of our summer vacation. Not so. We were shown how to pick the beans, being careful not to disrupt any blossoms that would produce more of this "dreaded" vegetable.

The tomatoes were easy to harvest. They were our reward when we selected a warm one to enjoy while picking some for supper. Luckily, Dad took care of digging up the carrots.

Eventually, we kids became accustomed to planting, weeding and picking the crop, and thought we were finally nearing the end of our duty. Oh, no. Mom had a wonderful surprise for us. Now, was canning season and we would be helping her cut beans, scrub carrots and peel tomatoes. She had supplemented our harvest by ordering more of the same from a farmer. This can't be happening! Where are the plans we had for our lazy summer? Someone just let the air out of our balloons and stole our pot of gold!

After a few years, we moved to the country where we found out what a real garden was. Mom and Dad purchased property that contained a huge area where the previous owners had grown their annual supply of veggies. Since the hard work was already done, we had our summer vacations all planned out. You guessed it: every square foot of that tilled land was sprouting one variety of vegetable or another. Dad cultivated the many rows with a gas powered rototiller.

Weeding was an endless task we all had to do by hand. Watering was another issue. If rain was not in the forecast, we had to fill pails from a nearby pond and give every plant a drink. The bean crop was especially plentiful and I still hated to pick them.

As we grew older, we became more understanding and accepting of family responsibilities. We adjusted our attitudes and accepted our summertimes, getting a farmer's tan while working toward our harvest.

Sure, we were rewarded with days of fun and time

with friends. But, the only benefit we kids could agree on was the wintertime wealth of delicious canned or frozen vegetables that graced our table. Then, and only then, would we admit there was a victory in having a garden.

*****

Since our older brother, Jerry, was the only boy in the family, he recruited our younger sister, Mary Jane, and me to help him with his paper deliveries. In the mid-1940's, the best way for our downtown merchants to advertise their sales was in a newspaper called the Shopping News. This free, thick paper came out twice a week, with delivery on Wednesdays and Saturdays in our Cleveland, Ohio neighborhood.

Jerry's route took us down one side of our street, around a busy intersection that housed the various grocery, hardware and drugstore merchants and back to finish the homes on our side of the road. There must have been at least 150 thick papers that had to be folded to fit on everyone's doorknobs or put in between the spokes of their front porch railings.

Mary Jane and I took turns, but sometimes, both of us were drafted to help with the twice-weekly distribution of these welcomed notices of downtown bargains. Come rain, sleet, humidity or snow, we helped Jerry and were rewarded with a chocolate phosphate while delivering to the drugstore, when half the route was completed. Our brother earned some money from this endeavor, so the pay for us was this delicious concoction, plus a tip.

After a year or two, the lessons learned from being a conscientious, trustworthy paperboy, led Jerry to trade this smaller job into delivering a daily, morning paper. Now we're talking sleepy eyed; never having a day off; helping with delivering two streets away; to toss papers by people's front door; so they could read them with their morning coffee. Our brother touched our sibling sentiment and with a few bribes, received our customary help for this daily adventure. Once I was awake, the task wasn't so bad . Soon, Jerry taught me how to fold the paper to throw on some upstairs porches. It took a few mishaps that ended up in the bushes or the gutter, but occasionally, my aim hit the mark. And all this took place before we went to school each morning.

That was during the week. On Sundays, the whole family got involved. Some parts of the Sunday Plain Dealer arrived on Friday or Saturday, giving us time to put the sections together and adding it to the front part of the paper that arrived early Sunday morning. Mom and Dad piled us three kids and the bundles of paper into the car and drove the route, with Mom reading the list of customers and us kids folding or delivering to the houses. That early morning exercise really gave us an appetite that was fed right before we had to go to church.

One of the perks of this paper route was the weekly Saturday afternoon spent collecting what was owed from the customers. My brother took one side of each street and I took the other. In those days, we could safely step into people's parlor or side door kitchen. Some of the homemakers on my section of the route, were just pulling cookies out of their ovens and treated me to a sample. Not only was this a bonus, but I was usually given a tip. My "boss" also paid me a dollar. My piggy bank was getting fat.

The route lasted until Jerry started high school. This early occupation provided us kids with a sense of responsibility that helped build our character. Not only was my brother the CEO of our small business, but being dependable and ambitous helped me with multi-tasking and organization. I later became the mother of eight and assumed the role of parenting the delivery kids in my house. They passed the weekly duty down the line, also recruiting their younger siblings. This brought back a load of memories for me and left me with the parental compassion, pride and empathy for my own rookies in training.

Bologna, Baked Beans and Bingo

by Genevieve Armstrong of Barnesville, Ohio
born in 1918

I was born April 15, 1918 in a small village east of Barnesville, in Bethesda, Ohio, the sixth child in a family of 13. My mother and father, Edna and Delbert Lucas, lived in this small little house, working at odd jobs to support the family. My dad raised tobacco; the job of my siblings and I were to go through the rows of tobacco and pick the worms off the plants for the plants to grow. I hated that job and the worms were so gross. We would then have to cut the plants and string them up to dry for harvest. He sold to various places.

My second worst job as a young girl was riding the ole horse while my father planted the corn and cultivated it. Those were some long hot days to put in. My dad grew grapes only for winemaking of course. He would never let any of us eat them making sure he had a good crop for his wine. He also made beer but I don't recall how or what he used to make it with.

I can still remember how my dad would load up the family in the ole Ford car and head to Cambridge, Ohio to visit my uncle. After a 30 mile trip we would enjoy the day fishing, picnicking, playing games and mostly playing a card game called Cinch which we still play today. Those were some fun times.

I went to school until I was in the 8th grade quitting to go to work to support myself. While in school our school was about a mile from home, at lunchtime we would have to run all the way home for lunch then run back so we would not be late. I did get to play basketball when I was in the 7th and 8th grades. We all had to wear these big bloomers and one day mine fell down. All the teammates huddled around while I pulled them up and pinned them so we could finish our game. I was so embarrassed.

When I started work, I would clean houses and do laundry on the wash boards and wringer washers for people so I could buy my own clothes and shoes. Dresses would cost 49 cents and shoes 99 cents. But that was a lot of money when you only made 25 cents an hour or $1.00 to $2.00 a day.

Finally I moved to Barnesville to live with my sister in my twenties and got a job at the shirt sewing factory. While living with my sister, I met the love of my life, sharing 61 years together. His name was Lefty Armstrong, and he would take me to work when he would go to work. He lived with his dad and was very bashful until one day he got up enough nerve to ask me to go to the square dance with them, starting our relationship. Oh what fun we had!

We got married and I moved in with him and his dad. We had no electric or indoor plumbing. They used oil lamps to see by and used an ole wood cook stove to cook on. I had to learn to cook and bake on that ole stove, making lots of bread and pies. The only thing Lefty and his dad ever ate before we got married was bologna and baked beans.

We never had a vacation. The only fun things we got to do was go fishing at Piedmont Lake catching lots of fish to take home to clean and eat, and playing cards, and making home made ice cream.

We soon started to raise our family which consisted of three boys and three girls. Our oldest son lived until he was six months old getting sick with pneumonia. We then had another son, a daughter, and another son who was born with kidney problems living until he was eight years old. After that we had two more daughters.

Life got a little better then. Lefty got a better job and we were able to move into a house that had indoor plumbing, consisting of cold water and a flushable toilet.

I have been an avid Bingo player since the late 50's still going two to three times a week.

The Elephant's Hump

By Robert C. Taylor of Crestline, Ohio
born in 1919

To remember my boyhood is to pleasure my soul. I grew up in a small town nestled in the Tuscarawas River valley. Newcomerstown, Ohio was home between 1919 and 1938. The haunting sound of train whistles echoing through the valley is a fond memory. The train tracks ran through the center of Newcomerstown and you could actually feel the beds shake at night as the trains rumbled through the valley.

My parents owned the town hardware store, Taylor Hardware, and worked long hours giving my two older brothers, two older sisters and me plenty of free time to roam and play in the safety of a small community. Neighbors knew neighbors, and the front porch swings of many homes served as the networking for the community.

Kids did not have I pods, cell phones, TVs or video games to entertain them. This was the age of creative play. We listened to "Amos and Andy" on the radio, we skinny dipped in the Tuscarawas River and the quarry outside of town. A scary memory I have of swimming in the quarry was a time I dove into the water and swam a ways only to come up to a cover of dirt over my head. I was in a cave under the water. Fortunately, I was able to reverse my path and swim to safety.

In the winter, when it snowed, we would build a fire for warmth and spend hours sledding down Park Street hill.

One summer, I built a boat in the back of my dad's hardware store. I'm sure it would have won the "junk boat derby" of the year award, but there was no contest to enter. I just spent many hours of pleasure playing on the river.

Lovely two story homes lined Canal Street where I lived. The W.B. Hayes family lived a few doors away. They had three children: Ike, Mary, and "Woody." Ike became a veterinarian and moved to Iowa. Mary was a close friend of my sister, Etta Taylor Barnett. Mary later wrote for the radio series "Mr. & Mrs. North." She and my sister, Etta, remained good friends throughout life. Woody was in my other sister May's class and they too remained good friends over the years. Of course, Woody became the famous Ohio State University football coach. Needless to say the Taylor clan and their kin have remained staunch O.S.U. fans!

During the summer of the polio epidemic, my mother sent us to her parent's farm outside of Port Washington. She thought we would be safer in the open, fresh air of the country. The Hill farm sat at the top of Centenary Hill. One side of the hill had a decent road leading up to the farm. The other side of the hill had a road leading down that we called the "winding stairs." It was a gravel road with horseshoe curves and ruts. Often, rain washed out the road. We called the top of Centenary Hill the "Elephant's Hump".

Although the farm house is long gone, we continue to have family reunions there and entertain children, grandchildren, and great grandchildren with stories of the past.

Today's cleaned-up version of the "good old days" of life on the farm cannot begin to convey the hardships of that rocky, hilly area that my grandparents homesteaded with horse and plow.

Today, we climb to the highest point of the Elephant's

Hump, walking through wavy fields of grass and look out over a vista of forest that goes as far as the eye can see. This view has changed little since my childhood. Grandchildren beg to drive down the "winding stairs" when we leave.

Over the years, I have taken my children and grandchildren back to the top of the Elephant's Hump for picnics and the search for arrowheads. My nephews still hunt the area every year for deer. They spend a week of macho-togetherness in the expanded, mobile home my nephew built as a tribute to the Hill family farm. It is a place for all of us to gather every Labor Day to reacquaint and reminisce.

Tuscarawas River below the winding stairs.

I was in high school between 1933 and 1937. W.B. Hayes was the superintendent. We watched movies at the Ritz Theater for 10 cents. We bought ice-cream cones for 2 for 5 cents, and a quart of milk cost 10 cents. Cy Young would come into my dad's hardware store every week. We danced to the juke box at Stoffer's Restaurant, and our parents bought their Chevrolets at Barnett's Garage on Canal Street. Heller Brothers Factory was a major employer. Davies Drug Store and Curtis Jewelry were a few of the downtown businesses.

I married the daughter of the family who owned Morton's Dairy in Newcomerstown. We have had 69 years of wedded bliss. What great memories we have of piling into a borrowed car and riding in the rumble seat for a trip to Coshocton Lake Ballroom for a night of dancing. Shively Yates from Dover and Port Washington was a popular band at that time. The Blue Baron Band was another well known group. We danced to "Harbor Lights," "Red Sails in the Sunset," "Sleepy Time Gal," "Stars Fell on Alabama" and "It's a Sin to Tell a Lie." Some of the big band sounds were just beginning to become popular.

Although by today's monetary standards, we were far from wealthy, we nevertheless had a wealth of experiences in an era of honesty, integrity, and clean living. The beautiful Tuscarawas Valley that I called home still holds a special place in my heart.

The "Switzerland" of Ohio

By Jennifer Burkhart London of McLean, Virginia
Born 1955

As many times as I have traveled all over the world I find there is a fondness and familiarity about Southeastern Ohio that pulls my heart and mind back to a place called "home." When I think of home it is our farm where I grew up with my mother and father and ten brothers and sisters that evokes the sentimental journey of past memories of childhood. There I always see a warm sunny day, blue skies, green fields and the sound of laughter in the distance, most likely one of my siblings playing a joke on another. I can feel the grass between my toes because in summer we would never consider shoes, unless by necessity. Sometimes I hear my mother singing because she loved to sing and her beautiful voice often floated above whatever task she had at hand.

I was taken back to those memories a few years ago when I figuratively almost "bought the farm." My husband and I were riding in a helicopter over the Golan Heights in Israel after taking off from a military base. It was getting toward dusk and a bit foggy. As we gained altitude I was looking at the sheep perched on the steep hills grazing serenely among the jutting rocks of jagged cliffs. Suddenly, we were in a "white out" with no visibility, heading for the mountain. My husband, a former Navy pilot, stiffened as he mumbled "This is not good. This is not good." I was gripped with a paralyzing fear, but also an incongruent parallel calm acceptance that this is where and how it would all end for us. Yet as I contemplated our demise I also thought it strangely comforting that we might go down in a beautiful green pasture among the animals much like home; the farm and Monroe County. Fortunately, our skilled pilot veered quickly out of danger with an apology and headed back to our destination along the coast following a lovely pink sunset, not even stopping for the originally planned refuel (at a place called Armageddon as fate would have it.)

There are rolling hills everywhere, but not as lovely as Southeastern Ohio which has deservedly earned the name "Switzerland of Ohio." And although I have seen many lovely sunsets in many exotic places, my favorite is right there from our front yard. Often at night after a long day of hard work my father would relax on our front porch swing (one of many porch swings that are the focal point of the various farm homes dotting the winding roads of Monroe County) as the sun set in the pink and orange sky with a blue backdrop. His eyes reflected the same blue as the sky, which he would sit quietly gazing into. It was there that he taught us the wisdom of "Red sky at night, sailor's delight. Red sky in the morning, sailor's warning." When it got dark he would sometimes point out for us children the big and little dipper in the stars. Occasionally we would catch lightning bugs running through the dewy grass to see how many we could retrieve (and leaving them on our nightstand when we went to bed to create our own nightlight.)

My father read the sky all the time, day or night, often looking up from what he was doing (as I am sure all the farmers there did and still do) in order to predict the weather so he could plan his crops and chores. He died peacefully there on that farm right around Easter of 1995; exactly where he wanted to be. It was overcast on the day of his funeral, but the sun made one brief appearance as the funeral procession passed our farm. I couldn't help but see my father in that little bit of sunshine giving us a nod to let us know he was still with us and that is where we could find him.

There is a hill in the road next to our house comprised of two slopes which we called the "big hill" and the "little hill." These "hills" provided the defining moments in the lives of most of us children. They were there to be mastered; on a bicycle of course. We would start our adventure on the "little hill" (the lower slope) and as we became more skilled and adventurous, we moved up to the "big hill" (comprised of both slopes.) When we really got going fast we would take our feet off the pedals and fly down the hills. Each of us took our turn wiping out at some point in our young biking careers and I am sure we all have the scars to prove it. But living on a narrow dirt road (which are common around Southeastern Ohio), we also had to be alert to and avoid oncoming cars which added another dimension of danger. In those instances we headed straight for the ditch no matter how fast we were going. Ouch.

The berries and cherries, apples and pears, plums and grapes that grew on our farm provided the best outdoor cafeteria that I have ever experienced. Depending on the time of the year we could find something delectable to munch on. Unfortunately (or fortunately), our mother was savvy enough to know that if it was ready to eat it was ready to pick and can. She had a knack for corralling us into such jobs. Just when we thought we had found a nice berry bush to enjoy all to ourselves, our mother would appear with buckets in her hands.

We had a large vegetable garden back toward our woods, which had a wide assortment depending on what we planted in any given year: potatoes, onions, cabbage, beets, green peppers, cucumbers, melons, sweet corn, tomatoes, radishes, carrots, celery and much more. There seemed to be no end to the variety and no end to the hoeing. But we would often pick a row to hoe and race to see who finished first.

We picked and canned hundreds of gallons of fruits and vegetables over the years. But somehow that was not ever enough. My parents would occasionally decide to buy something else, like pineapple in bulk, and there we were coring 40 pineapples for jelly, freezing and canning. Once we made a lot of hominy, putting a sack of hard wood ashes in a kettle to tease the hulls off the corn. After hours of boiling and soaking the corn was put into a large tub. Then my father got in with rubber boots that had been scrubbed and disinfected to stomp on the kernels bringing the last stubborn hulls off the corn. We canned 90 quarts and I think we had hominy every way it could be prepared. I haven't touched it since.

For many years we had a strawberry patch. It was more pleasant to work there because the sweet aroma of strawberries wafted through the air. I was smaller then and I remember the tall grass on the way to the strawberry patch always scratched my legs. So once I got there my legs itched as I worked and, adding insult to injury, I could never keep up with my older siblings who always moved along their rows more quickly. But picking was better than hoeing because we could follow the rule "one for me, one for the bucket" (at least until my mother caught our eye.)

Sometimes as a preschooler I would accompany my mother as she went door to door around the county to sell strawberries and vegetables from our garden. The little extra money she got went a long way in helping with household expenses for our large family.

My mother was very resourceful and could make pretty much anything out of virtually nothing. Although we made ample use of local flea markets and rummage sales to put together our wardrobes, she made us the most special clothes. When we were very little we had several matching outfits among the girls complete with coordinated hats and gloves. She also made almost everything in our house including curtains, covering for the furniture, quilts, etc. Her resourcefulness came in very handy since we did not have a lot of money to buy things. One Christmas my parents did not have a gift to give one of my brothers who was just a toddler. So on Christmas Eve my imaginative mother crept into the room where my brothers slept and pulled his favorite tattered teddy bear out of his sleeping arms. Then she stayed up all night to sew a new covering for the teddy bear as his gift the next morning.

We raised various crops that were rotated in the fields from year to year. And we had lots of livestock on our farm: cattle, pigs, ducks, chickens, dogs, cats and occasionally a pony. As I grew older, my primary job on the farm was taking care of the pigs. We had a large furrowing building with twenty stalls for our sows to give birth and raise their litters. I enjoyed taking care of the pigs over the cows because pigs are more interesting and smarter. But I could never figure out why the sows would often lie on their young and, despite the desperate squealing, did not connect that they were squashing their own babies to death. We lost a lot of little ones that way. But we would often keep an ear out for those squeals at that stage of development and when we heard them we would run to the pen and pull the sow up by the tail thus releasing the bewildered piglet. I would also clip their teeth and notch their ears when they were very little too. This on the other hand did not evoke much response perhaps because the nerve endings were not so developed. Pigs get a lot of nourishment from mud and I would dig up nice "clean" mud for them which I put in the pens once a week until they were old enough to be let out into the field. Of course lying in mud is important to pigs because they do not sweat so they need the mud to hydrate their bodies.

We had dairy cattle for a time, but then we converted to beef cattle although we always kept a milking cow around for fresh milk and butter. Each of us had our turn at the butter churn. For me it was when I was about 5 years old during the "Captain Kangaroo" TV program. As my youngest sister later described, when we were about that age my mother would offer to have us sit on the floor to watch TV and just as we were thinking this was a real treat, the butter churn would appear in front of us. But my mother always had homemade bread on hand and the taste of warm bread with fresh butter is divine. We also made homemade ice cream, but taking turns at that crank took on a whole different level of anticipation.

My father, who went to Ohio State on a full scholarship, got his degree in Agriculture in 1940. He was always pursuing new and interesting endeavors on the farm. Often he was the first or only person in the area to try something new like breeding Beefalo (a cross between cattle and buffalo which produces leaner meat). He also grafted trees and planted unusual and varied trees on our farm including, at one point, Redwoods and pecan trees. He was an inventor who was ahead of his time. In the 1980's he came up with a formula to replace gasoline using sugar cane which he tested many times to show that it actually worked. But he was unsuccessful in getting a patent on his formula and eventually abandoned that project. Seeing the success of Brazil in using a similar formula today makes me wonder if he had just found the right avenues back then things would be different here too. One thing that he made with great success was homemade wine using a number of sources over the years including dandelions. Once the wine was corked too early and my parents, who slept over the portion of the basement that housed the wine bottles, were awakened at night on several occasions to the sound of corks popping.

We also had sheep at one point and sometimes there would be several lambs in a cardboard box in our house. The window for imprinting between the ewe and the lamb is very narrow and immediate after birth so if this does not happen right away the mother will permanently disown the baby. So, on occasion, we would have a few orphaned lambs in our house that required bottle feeding using an old glass root beer bottle and a large rubber nipple. We had to hold the nipple on though so the lambs would not suck it off and swallow it. But their little mouths would tickle my hands and it was hard to hold on without laughing a lot. Once a flock of our sheep was struck by lightning, having sought shelter under a large oak tree during a thunderstorm. I will never forget seeing from the wagon as my father went to retrieve them, the sight of a dozen dead sheep huddled together under that tree split open from the lightning.

My parents and visiting relatives often sat around our kitchen table telling the most interesting of stories of by gone days. One story was of my mother's distant cousin, Chris Brownfield, who was so obsessed with flying that he built and flew his own airplane in March 1915. He had bought his first plane in 1913, but after months of labor was unable to get it off the ground. His homemade Curtis type bi-plane made his first and successive flights from an air field at Military and Frazeysburg Road near Zanesville, Ohio successful enough that he was featured in the local newspaper.

Living on the farm did not deprive us of the benefits of the "city" which to us was Woodsfield. Barnesville was the "big" city (similar to the distinction between Mayberry and Mount Pilot.) We went to school at St. Sylvester's where there was never a shortage of nuns to keep us in line. I grew up often feeling there was a nun behind me watching. The benefits of Catholic school are plentiful, not the least of which are the statistics that show greater academic success later on in students who attend Catholic schools. But it also instills a foundation of principles that can serve throughout life; the concept of "doing the right thing" even when no one is watching. Going to a Catholic school didn't mean much at the time, but I realize today how fortunate we were to have that rich experience.

High school was a much different experience. We did not sit in the same room all day as we did in elementary school, but got to move from room to room. This is where a lot of memories were built for many of us who attended Woodsfield High School. I remember my lab partner passing out during frog dissection in biology class. I remember having to repeatedly type the same sentence in typing class (does anyone remember what a typewriter is?) I remember trying to comprehend the admonitions in French from the French teacher. I remember trying to comprehend anything in Algebra class. I remember an English teacher once chose the unlikely word "assassin" to demonstrate how to hyphenate words. And amazingly, the class all kept a straight face as she broke the word apart on the black board. I remember how the history class just after lunch often smelled like pot. And I remember counting the days until I could get out into the "real world."

I love the Woodsfield High School building with its large lettering on the front and long wooden halls. It is a real architectural gem that is hard to see fall into disuse.

My parents and each of my siblings went to school there as I am sure is the case with many families around Monroe County. Every year Woodsfield offers a celebration for all its graduating classes with a parade and party which provides the opportunity for classmates to reunite and reminisce. Maybe one year all the classes will come together to do a fundraiser to help revive the high school building itself. I think there could be so many uses for the building while preserving a place that was a big part of our lives. If only those walls could talk...

Another little "diamond in the rough" of Woodsfield in days gone by was a most unlikely place, the city dump. Yes, the dump could be quite the archeological wonder for the occasional adventurous scavenger hunt. The person who said "One man's trash is another's treasure" must have been referring to the Woodsfield dump. Being antique collectors, our family would go in search of old bottles, crocks etc. that someone might have thrown out not knowing the value. But we came away with some other great finds too. We once got some nice dolls there that looked great after a thorough washing and they brought a lot of joy to our play time for years thereafter. We found other items that someone else no longer found useful, but once recycled, got a second life in our house. My mother even found plastic flowers that she took to decorate the tombstones at our church cemetery. But there was an industrious "entrepreneur" who lived next to the dump who made the most of his unfortunate location by picking out the nicer items from the dump and selling them to passersby. My father once bought a wool camouflage Army coat for 25-cents there which kept him warm for years to come.

During my summer job at Morris' Market I encountered some interesting town "characters." One, known as "Grant," always took on a different persona every time I saw him. One day he was a "minister" dressed in black and claiming he had worked in the South Pacific. Another day he appeared to be a handyman wearing a belt of tools and a hard hat. Then there was the day he was a "cowboy" complete with the ten gallon hat and gun in holster (I never did know whether the gun was real or not). As he approached the cash register I managed to maintain a straight face until the stock boy who was behind Grant pretended, using his hand and index finger, to pull a gun out of his pocket. Even so Grant remained serious about his roles and I treated him with equal seriousness. The last time I heard about Grant was the day folks stopping in the store seemed unusually exasperated and there appeared to be a greater buzz on the streets outside. When I asked someone what was going on, I was told, "Grant thinks he is a policeman today and he is down on the square directing traffic. It is a mess down there." Perhaps he is one reason I ended up with a Ph.D. in psychology.

I moved away from Monroe County when I went off to college. But I enjoy visiting my mother there whenever I can. A few years ago I got out of my car on the town square and pulled out a quarter for the meter only to find that the meters there still only took a nickel. It must be the last place on earth to continue to take only nickels in the parking meters (hence the feeling that you are in Mayberry). The Court House in Woodsfield is another beautiful architectural jewel. It stands tall and regal; an appropriate symbol that one is entering the county seat. The unique circle on the square in the center of town put Woodsfield among the ranks of such distinguished cities as London and Washington, DC that have similar "round-abouts." Sadly that special, defining landmark is now gone.

These are just a few of my treasured memories of Southeastern Ohio. My primary reason for writing this was my mother, Bertha Burkhart. She felt this was such an important and worthwhile publication that she spent a lot of her personal time calling people to get them to write about their own memories. She has a deep rooted commitment to Southeastern Ohio and wants to help retain its history and culture. She is still there on our farm and won't leave it. She still sings around the house; in latter years mostly hymns, but I remember a time when she could belt out "Pistol Packin' Mamma" and "Frankie and Johnny were Lovers." Even though she could live a comfortable and relaxed life elsewhere, by visiting each of her children as our houseguest for a month or so (that could be year round given there are 11 of us) she is firm in staying right there in Southeastern Ohio. That is where she is rooted; in her home, in her heart and in her memories.

Raising Cane

By Myron C. Cline of Findlay, Ohio
Born 1934

It's an early March evening in 1943, in the little Appalachian hill village of Lewisville, Ohio. I am eight years old. I was still considered too young to do the milking, so my time is my own until supper. It is over a half hour until my radio programs begin, so I read and play with my flip-top tank and airplane books. When you learned to flip the corner pages at just the right speed, you had a perfect battlefield action movie. I managed to massacre a couple battalions of Japs and bombed and strafed several machine gun nests of Germans that way every evening.

Finally it was time for the radio shows. They are 15 minute long weekday serials. Like Cato, I zoom around the streets of New York in Green Hornets Black Beauty, fly high and even develop a crush on Sky Kings Niece

Penny and ride the western range with Tom Mix, without straying from the old Philco in our living room. When I hear Tom Mix say, "Take a tip from Tom, go and tell your Mom, Shredded Ralston can't be beat" it was the end of the most exciting part of my day.

Now it was on to Lowell Thomas or H. V. Kaltembom and the news of the day. The news was nearly always about the war. The war was a very scary thing to us all. It was what my parents and grandparents talked about over supper every evening. Everyone was afraid we would be defeated and have to pledge allegiance to the Japs or Germans. Also, my Uncle Mansel was in Seattle in the army and they worried that he would be shipping out soon. They didn't talk about this much around me, but sometimes I could hear them discuss it by listening down the register in my upstairs bedroom when I was supposed to be asleep.

We had another smaller crisis on our hands this evening. We were out of sugar. Many commodities were rationed doing the war. This caused us little difficulty as we produced our own vegetables, fruits, meats, milk and butter. Since we rarely went anywhere, the tire and gasoline rationing was no problem, but we now needed to take our ration books to the store to buy sugar. The books were filled with stamps, which would be torn out each time you made a sugar purchase. My Grandmother Young had an all world sweet tooth. Almost every evening in those days before calories and cholesterol were household words; she or my mother would make a batch of fudge, caramel corn or taffy. This was in addition to the supply of cookies, pies and coffee cakes always on hand. Nothing was spared to make these treats first class. We had virtually unlimited supplies of sweet cream, butter and lard, but we finally had exhausted our entire sugar ration.

Molasses!" my grandmother said. "It's hard to tell how long this war is going to go on and I don't want to have to go through this ever again." Her proposal was that we should literally raise cane. It got my grandfather's half-hearted approval, as he said it was a lot of hard work. By that time I had developed a pretty strong nighttime habit myself, so I was all for it.

I watched my dad plow the field in May with our black mare Molly. The old girl had very little work to do on our 20-acre farm, but seriously resented having to do anything at all. She would refuse to take the bit in her mouth and be generally cantankerous in the harnessing process. When finally in harness, she would whinny pitifully, stamp her feet and break wind loudly before finally committing to the job. My dad was an even-tempered Christian man and about the only times I can recall hearing him use profanity was getting old Molly into the harness. Once she bit him on the shoulder, where upon he swore punched her hard in the forehead. She didn't even blink but he broke a couple of bones in his right hand. "Not a smart thing to do," he confided to me later. Anyway, it made for an entertaining Saturday to watch the plowing of the cane field.

Dad continued to work it down, first with a harrow, then with a drag. After all the soil had been broken into fine pieces, he hitched Molly to a different plow to mark out the rows. When that was done, a relieved Molly was through for the day, but Dad was just beginning. He then took a hand corn planter and planted each seed. He would take a short step, plunge the toe of the planter into the ground, then pull the handles apart, which released the seeds, pull it up and repeat the process. Slow, laborious, boring work and I quickly found something else to do.

When summer vacation began the cane was already up pretty and green. I kept a fairly close watch on it, but my buddies and I were pretty wrapped up in the home front war effort. We scavenged for scrap iron and old rubber tires. We would take them to the county seat where they would be weighed and actually pay you money for what you brought.

By late June the plants were 12-inches to 18-inches high. Then Dad cultivated through the middle of the rows to break up the soil and get rid of the weeds. He and I then hoed the cane. I expect this was a case of "Pap and I shot the bear," as I probably played around more than I hoed. It was a really big deal for me because I was actually being a part of the process, instead of just a spectator. You would carefully hoe out all the weeds, and then pull the soil up around the base of each cane stalk. We made sure our hoes were kept sharp by frequently stopping to file the edge on them. "You never lose time by stopping to sharpen your tool" was a quote of my dad's that I have since found is a pretty good principle no matter what you are doing.

It seemed the summer lasted nearly three years. In between playing war games with friends and listening to the Cincinnati Reds on the radio, I watched the cane as it grew and grew, until it looked like a field of mature corn, only instead of ears; it had this red bushy head at the top of the stalk. I believed that we were going to get molasses out of those green stalks, but I'd be darned if I could figure out how.

I started back to school, beginning the 4th grade. Early in the fall we had a man come to our school who said that we students could do a vital job to save our soldiers' lives and help win the war by collecting milkweed pods. To top it off for every large mesh bag filled with the pods we would receive 50 cents. It doesn't get any better than that. Be a hero in the war effort while at the same time getting a shiny half dollar when a nickel will buy a 16 oz. Pepsi.

Monroe County, Ohio has always been one of the very poorest counties in our state. The unglaciated steep hills make most of the land unsuitable for cultivation, but we stood second to no one in nature's production of blackberry brambles and milkweeds. The 4th grade boys were quickly into a spirited competition over who could fill the most bags. My hands were always sticky from the milky sap that fall. When we had wiped out every milkweed pod within a two mile radius of town, I convinced my dad to take Sunday afternoon drives to more isolated areas where there were still milkweeds in abundance. Both my mom and dad got into the collecting as well so that's the way we spent several happy Sunday afternoons that fall of '43. I can't recall exactly how many bags I turned in or if I won the competition, but I know it had to be an impressive number as my bronze Charles Lindbergh bank had a new heft to it.

Myron Clines's family. Front row: Grandmother, Lorena Young; Myron Cline. Back row: Grandfather Wes Young; mother, Vivian Cline; father, George Cline.

Finally it was time to harvest the cane. My dad cut the cane with a sharp machete-like corn cutter. I wasn't permitted to help as it was feared I would hack of a chunk of my leg with the sharp cutter, which would have been easy enough to do. After it was cut, it was topped, had the leaves stripped and was bound into bundles with binder twine. We then loaded it into our hay wagon and hauled it out to the road. My dad had borrowed a truck from a friend and when we had all the cane stalks loaded into it, my mother, dad and I headed to get it milled.

The molasses mill was located about ten miles away between Stafford and Harrietsville. It was already in full operation when we arrived. Wood smoke filled the air. It looked like an exciting operation. (Actually it was a several step procedure.) First, the cane stalks were thrown into sort of a pit that had a stone turning around in the middle that crushed and ground the stalks. The stone was turned by a donkey, which was harnessed to a big wooden pole that was attached to the grindstone. As the stone turned, the juice came out a spout and ran into the first of a series of long shallow pans. As I remember, there were four different pans like this, each one setting lower than the one in front of it. When the sap flowed into the first container it was mostly clear and looked nearly like water, but it became progressively darker and thicker in each succeeding pan. Under each pan were red-hot wood coals.

As I watched the man tending the fires, he tested the batch by dipping a stick in it, then opening a valve in the final pan and filling gallon jugs with the thick brown-black mixture. When the pan was empty, he closed that valve, then opened the valve in pan three and let it gravity into the final pan. He then repeated the procedure in pan one and two. All the while the donkey is plodding round and round grinding up more cane stalks. It was fun to watch, but as the Saturday went on it began to grow a bit old. I had hoped to be home in time to hear the Ohio State football game, but it soon became clear that wasn't to be. The mill was operated strictly on a first come first serve basis and we were well down the line. The sun became low in the sky and still we were waiting. Mom had packed a large lunch and we downed the leftovers for supper. It got pitch dark and began to turn cold. Dad and a man from another waiting family gathered firewood from the nearby woods. We moved close in around the flames getting acquainted while toasting on one side and chilling on the other. It was 9:00 P.M. From being bored, I was now getting excited. I was about to set my all time stay-up late record. The hours slowly slipped by. It was close to midnight when our cane stalks were processed. I would have really been excited earlier, but now I was too tired to care. I had nodded off on the ground by the fire when they came to tell me we were going. Both were pleased by the number of gallons of molasses we had in the truck after the mill had taken its share.

The heater was warm and I felt wonderfully secure sitting between my parents. I thought about molasses on corn cakes and sugar cookies and taffy and fudge and caramel corn. The winter of '43 - '44 was looking pretty good. I vowed I'd stay awake to see what time it was when we got back home, but I never did.

Hoppy's Newspaper Trail

By Patricia Johnson of Dennison, Ohio
Born 1948

We knew him as "Hoppy." His mom and dad knew him as Gerald Crafton Burnside III. He came from Meigs County and he was our bum.

When Aunt Marg was a young schoolgirl walking along the street on her way to school one day, she saw what appeared to be a homeless man possibly around the age of 20 years. She watched him as he went from door to door, coming down from each porch after talking with the homeowner, looking rejected and miserable.

Aunt Marg approached him, asking point blank, "You look hungry, Mister, have you had anything to eat?" and when he said he hadn't, she told him, "Go up to the house on the corner of North and 5th Street and tell Mom that Marg sent ya." He did and that was the beginning of a relationship that would last for the next 30 to 35 years.

The man was family. He came to our home to eat at our kitchen table on a regular basis, every other day through four generations of Putnams. So much so that on one occasion at the local hospital when a man was brought into the emergency room by ambulance, unconscious with no identification, our neighbor and friend nurse Margie Collins walked into the situation and recognized him immediately stating with certainty, "Well, that fellow is the Putnam's bum." Grandma was called for identification and treatment agreements.

Upon arrival at the hospital, Grandma was taken to his room. What she saw unnerved her and she yelled at him, "Hoppy, what in the world are you doing here? What's the matter with you? Wake up and talk to these people so that they can take care of you!" From the evidence of the witnesses, Hoppy sat straight up in the bed IMMEDIATELY upon hearing Grandma's voice. He was treated with excellent care, cured of what had been ailing him and was released.

His main feature was a bad leg and he walked with a limp. He didn't talk much; just made kind of low grunting noises and always "sniffed" as if he had a cold. "Dirty as a pig in the pen," Grandma used to say, but after a few years of trying to get him to take a bath she just wrapped a bar of soap up in a newspaper along with sandwiches to tide him over for the night.

I only saw Grandma in a huff a couple of times with Hoppy. Actually, Grandma and Hoppy got along better than Grandma and Grandpa. He knew she was the boss and he didn't argue with her, except one morning. Hoppy decided to tell Grandma that he would prefer not to have "the usual" for his meal. He mentioned that he might care for "something different" than the usual coffee, Mother's Oats and toast and eggs and whatever was left over from supper the night before.

Silence lasted for a minute or two. You could have heard a pin drop as Grandma threw a dish towel over her right shoulder; whipped the butter into the skillet to make him potato cakes, looked to the end of the table where Hoppy sat and announced for all to hear that, "YOU WILL EAT WHAT I FIX and YOU WILL LIKE IT!" And that was the end of that discussion.

There was the "ritual" every time he stopped by to eat. He'd rap on the side door and Grandma would get old newspapers and line the floor from the door to the kitchen. Hoppy dutifully followed the trail while saying, "Good morning, Missus." Grandma placed newspapers on the chair for him to sit on and he'd sit. He was served a cup of coffee while Grandma cooked up the meal. After he'd eat, he'd follow the trail of papers back to the door as he said, "Thank you, Ma'am, that was right nice of ya to feed me such a good meal. I'll be on my way now." And off he went.

As children we'd watch him go yelling, "Goodbye, Hoppy" and "See you in a couple days."

Grandma picked up the newspapers and threw them in the trash, Mom washed up the dishes and the pots and pans and that was that.

When Hoppy died, Lindsey's Funeral Home called Grandma to tell her that they had been called to collect the remains of "Our bum" from the hospital and would she like to help defray the cost of burying him. Of course she did. He was laid out in a clean shirt and suit (Grandma found them in an upstairs closet) and a warm pair of white socks in an inexpensive, but yet nice, coffin with a bouquet of flowers. He had nice music and a minister to say a prayer over him and there were people who cared that he had lived attending the service and shedding a tear at his passing.

If she knew the reason (and I'm sure that she did), Grandma never told us why Gerald Crafton Burnside III from Meigs County became a bum. It didn't seem important why, it was just important that he was in our lives.

Ours was a simple life. As a child I don't remember my family ever sitting around the kitchen table talking about going on a "vacation" to anywhere. The subject never came up. There was no place my mother and dad wanted to be except in Ohio.

We used to just take a couple of lazy days: get in the car and drive out by Tappan Lake, Leesville Lake or Piedmont Dam and on the way we'd take some buckets and go berry picking, blackberry or raspberry, or nut gathering out in the countryside, walnuts or hazelnuts. Or we'd pick wildflowers that grew along the road: Indian pinks, day lilies, wild wheat, pussy willows, corn flowers...or pick up pine cones underneath the pine trees or fallen buckeyes from the buckeye trees. Then we'd top the day off with a scumpdillyishush homemade ice cream cone from Coultrap's Store before we went home.

I have always resided in Ohio. For all I knew, the only reason for the other states of America even existing was because Ohio was full up and the people had to go elsewhere.

I mean, I figured in my own naive way that no one would choose to live anywhere else. Ohio has everything. It is, as we proclaim, "The heart of it all!" For instance, Ohio in the autumn, my oh my, what a treasure my eyes behold as they gaze around at the kaleidoscope of colors in the heights of the hills and the depths of the valleys, during the season of the Harvest Moon.

The grandeur and geography of Ohio have been choreographed so wonderfully by the tag team of God and Mother Nature, that truly, I do not believe there is any comparison to its beauty anywhere in the world.

As a child I can vividly remember that I had to be very quiet and allow my father to get a restful nap before we started on our journey to Indiana: it was a long way. Mother and Grandmother packed a big thermos carrier full of food and a jug of water and a thermos of coffee for us to take on the trip.

There were pillows and blankets in case someone needed to rest a bit. In fact it was so crowded in the backseat, that there wasn't much room for the people. By the time our car had reached the county line, Mom was getting the food out of the carrier and after filling my belly with sandwiches, chips and cookies, I would fall sound asleep and go off into dreamland until I'd hear Grandma hollering, "We've made it, we're here! Wake up!" The first time I actually stayed awake for the trip I believe I was in high school. (By then I had learned not to eat so much.)

Our destination was always Richmond. A friendly town, right off of Old Route 40, just across the border from Ohio. There are all kinds of things to do and attractions to visit: Glenn Miller Park, Earlham College, the Pioneer Trail and Webb's Antiques. But, "THE" place to be in Richmond is on 10th Street: the family home. There you will find hospitality (comparable to the Ritz) and kitchen table conversation, where problems of the day are discussed at length (and solved) over coffee, Coca Cola and cookies.

The only problem: as long as it took to get there, it took on the return trip also. So our time to visit was short. But it sure was worth the trip.

Threshers, Fox School and Insurance

by Ray W. Straub of Sardis, Ohio
born in 1929

Growing up on a 186-acre farm, there was always much work to be done. I believe we had 8 milk cows, and 20 head of beef cattle. We did custom work for other farmers, such as threshing grain, bailing hay and straw, grinding feed, hulling clover and cutting fodder. This kind of work was done before combines and other modern farm equipment came on scene. During the wintertime, we also had a sawmill that we used to saw lumber for different farmers.

For power to run this equipment in the mid 1930's, we bought a John Deere model D, with rubber tires and a Red River special threshing machine with a self-feeder and a blower. In 1940, we also bought a LA Case tractor. These two tractors had the most power in the years that they were built. The John Deere D was 45 horsepower, and the LA case was 75 horsepower.

In January of 1945, my oldest brother went into the army. At the time, I was 15 years old and my father did very little operating of the tractors. I assumed the responsibility of operating these big tractors at a young age. Our L. A. Case tractor had no power steering. You had to move the tractor in order to steer it. I was the main operator until my brother got back from the service in October 1946.

During the war years, there was more grain raised, so it required more threshing.

In the spring of 1947, we bought a Case threshing machine, which would take two sheaves of grain side by side. With the Case 75 horsepower tractor, we could thresh more grain in less time.

My brother and I would start threshing wheat from the fields around July 5th. This usually took about 15 days. Then the farmers would haul the grain into the barn and allow it to go through a sweat. The last part of July, we would begin threshing grain, which consisted of wheat, oats, rye, and buckwheat (in the late 1940's). We would finish up in the middle of September. Our biggest threshing set was at the Monroe County Home, just outside of Woodsfield, Ohio. We threshed around 1300 bushel of oats and 900 bushels of wheat every year at the County Home.

My brother and I threshed in Monroe and Noble Counties in Ohio and also Tyler and Wetzel Counties in West Virginia. A threshing crew usually required 15 to 25 workers. We were always fed lunch at noontime and dinner in the evening. My brother would do what was necessary to level the thresher, set the riddles and adjust the wind so the thresher could produce clean grain. I would unhook the tractor from the thresher, unlatch the self feeder extending it out, and unwind a 95 foot rubber belt, and took it with me when I drove the tractor away from the thresher. I would then turn the tractor around so it was facing the thresher and line the tractor pulley up to the pulley on the thresher and attach the belt to the tractor pulley. I would look at my brother and he would give me the motion to start power to the thresher. This would all occur in a matter of 5 minutes. Sadly, I lost my brother 13 years ago. I will never forget all the time that he and I spent working together.

* * * *

Fox schoolhouse was built around 1880. It was located in Green township on road state route 536, 7 miles northwest of Hannibal, Ohio in Monroe county.

Fox was a one-room building in which the first eight grades were taught. Two outhouses were located behind the schoolhouse about one hundred feet apart. The coalhouse was downhill from the schoolhouse, and was rebuilt in 1925 by a neighbor for $45.75.

A potbellied stove was used to heat the schoolhouse during the cold days, of which we had a plenty back then.

In my first year of school, in 1936, there were around fifty students in grades. One through eight of which one teacher had the sole job of teaching and responsibility for.

Girls were seated on the right side; boys were on the left side of the schoolhouse. The teacher's desk was approximately six inches rise above the rest of the floor in the middle of the building. The raised stage allowed teachers to observe the students better. The blackboard went all the way across the front of the room behind the teacher's desk.

Threshing at the barn.

The girls all wore dresses and the boys wore bib overalls. School took up at 9:00am with one fifteen minute recess in the morning, lunch at 12: 00-1:00pm, and one fifteen minute recess in the afternoon. School let out at 4:00pm. The teacher always rang the schoolhouse bell to take up school after each break.

Following are some items found on records: Teachers were not to be janitors if there were students available to clean the building, carry drinking water from a nearby farm, carry in coal and fire the stove. In 1920, janitors received $2.00 per month for his work. I was told by a teacher who taught at Fox, that the school excelled in penmanship through the years, for the school had teachers that took pride in writing.

Schoolhouses during this period were located about three miles apart, which allowed usually about 1.5 miles to walk either way. I remember during the winter months, very few cars traveled the roads that we had back then. During the winters, teachers would stay with some students' parents so that they would be within walking distance of school. Several parents would bring their children to school when weather was bad with horses and sled or buggies. It would start snowing in November and there would be snow through into February, which gave us good sled riding. We built our own sleds out of mostly white oak wood, which made faster sleds. My eight years spent in a one-room schoolhouse will never be forgotten.

Also there were Sunday school services at Fox school every Sunday. It was known as "Fox Sunday School" which started in the early 1900's and continued through the late 1930's. Mother, sister, brother and I had to go to Sunday school every Sunday at Fox schoolhouse. My aunt and cousin went too. We three boys were all under ten years old.

One Sunday, my cousin, brother and I were singing and maybe not quite in tune with the rest of the congregation. My mother and aunt shook their heads at us three boys while we were singing. The next time to go to Sunday school, My mother told us to get ready, and we said we weren't going. Dad said, "Why are you not going?" We told him what happened. He said if that was the case, we wouldn't have to go anymore. So my brother and I both graduated from Sunday school, but our cousin had to continue to go. When the weather warmed up and the roads were better, we had to go to our church and Sunday school, which was Methodist.

* * * *

In 1872, Mr. John Ruby, Ohio Township of Monroe County, [from?] Ohio had built a three-story barn. He decided to get some local farmers together for the purpose of insuring each other against fire and lightning losses. They decided to call their company Mutual Aid Association of Ohio Township. They would operate one year at that time and then figure their losses. Then each member would pay toward the losses. They spoke their dialect, which was spoken in Switzerland. Their study in school was German, and they also wrote in German.

In November of 1879, they became incorporated according to the Ohio Law of March 30, 1877. They became known as German Farmers Mutual Insurance Association; address Morton, Monroe County, Ohio. They held their annual meetings at the Morton Schoolhouse. The board meetings were usually held in the home of the secretary. The first policies were written under the incorporation in March of 1880. Pointing to the area's heritage, all policies and minutes were recorded in German until 1897 when by a motion was agreed all business thereafter would be in English.

Ruby, Luedy, Fankhauser, Reithmiller, Thonen, Berger, Ischy, Schindler, Fraley, Zeh, Bruney, Bertschy, Marty, Bauman, Tisher and Winkler are among names in early records, ancestors of many people still within the county. They operated with six members as board president, secretary, treasurer, and three directors. They met quarterly to conduct business. In January of every year, an annual meeting is held open to all members of the association to attend, which is still the practice today.

The organization grew rapidly, and peaked to 2400 policyholders in 1959. The association operated this way, offering fire-lightning insurance, until 1975. In 1974, the board held many lengthy articles of incorporation for German Farmers' Mutual of Sardis Insurance Association, offering fire, lightning, wind, tornado, and extended coverage in one policy to its members giving the association a new look. The new articles of incorporation were adopted at the annual meeting on

January 5th, 1975.

German Farmers' Mutual of Sardis Insurance Association celebrated its 100th anniversary at the annual meeting in January of 1979. The board had Mathilda Liechti (a member) translate the minutes of the association prior to 1897, which was written in German. The association was very grateful for her translation which gave the company much insight to the people involved in starting the insurance company over a century ago. The company is still in business today.

The Bean and Potato Depression

by Juanita Adkins of Stockport, Ohio
born in 1924

I'm just an old woman who lives in southeast Ohio, but not always. My husband of 63 years passed away December 20, 2008. We were married at Columbus, Ohio in 1945 soon after he got out of the Army. We have one son and two grandchildren, small family. We live on a small farm in Stockport, Ohio. My husband was raised on this farm.

I was born in East Liverpool, Ohio in a small house on Eire Street on the east end of Liverpool. My father was Bert Willard and mother Mary. They had six children. I was the fourth child of the six; three girls, three boys—a family of eight.

My father was a hard working person. My mum was a good housekeeper. My father worked at a pottery in Newell, West Virginia. He was a foreman at a pottery called T.S.T. My mum stayed at home. Took care of kids and kept the house. Then the big depression hit the whole country and that is what I want to write about.

My pop, or father, lost his job at T.S.T. Pottery. The pottery shut down. We had a hard time, but we made it. My pop found a job working on a farm for one dollar a day. The man that hired my pop owned a store, and we bought all our food from him. We never had much.

Mum bought her flour and salt, lard, potatoes from the store. We never had milk, sugar, meat. In other words, we ate beans and potatoes. We had a little garden in our yard, but our yard was small. Mum—mother—would bake homemade bread every other day.

In the summer we all picked blackberries and Mum would can them without sugar, for we could not afford it. When we went to school, Mum would put a slice of bread on a dish and put blackberries on top of it. That was our breakfast, no butter. The rest of the meals were beans and potatoes, but when the soup kitchen was open, we would have soup of whatever kind they had. My pop would take me by the hand and we would walk down to the soup kitchen, about two blocks away. Pop carried a bucket with a lid, and they would give us soup when they could open the kitchen. They did not always have vegetables to cook. No cookies, milk, candy. We drank water.

My pop and my older brother, he was about nine years old, went down to the railroad every night and picked up coal that had dropped off the train. Pop had a sack. He and brother picked up coal and put it in the sack. Pop carried it home on his back every night. That is how we cooked our food and kept the house warm. You know, I don't remember being hungry. Wonder why?

My aunt Bess lived on a small place where she could have a goat and two apple trees, so when she came to town (she walked), she would bring us some apples and popcorn she raised in her garden. So we had apples and popcorn now and then. Mum and Pop picked greens in spring. We ate lots of them.

At Christmastime we had a good time. We kids got a sack with apples, oranges, and a few nuts in them. We thought it was great. I don't remember anything about Thanksgiving.

My mother would pop a large pan full of popcorn and we would have an apple. In the evening Mum would tell us ghost stories and keep us on pins and needles all evening. She was a great storyteller. We did not have TV or radio, so Mum and Pop did a lot of entertaining. Pop played cards with us, a game called rum. In summer we played outside—hide and seek, and ball. Lots of fun. We went in our bare feet in the summer and in winter we had to save our shoes for school. When we came home, we took our shoes off and we wore socks Mum had quilted old material on the soles so they would be heavy and warm.

Mum washed our clothes on a washboard, used lye soap made from wood ashes. My two sisters had to help with the wash. Mum could not wring out the clothes, sheets, and blankets by herself, so my sister would hold one end and she would wring the other end to get the water out. In summer we would hang them outside to dry and in winter we would hang them in the kitchen on a rack near the stove. We kids were taught to work.

Schools did not have buses or free lunch at school. We walked to school about a half mile from our house. We walked home for our lunch, ate our bread and beans and walked back to school. No complaining. We never had boots. We were lucky to have shoes.

We went sledding a lot in winter, but we were not allowed to stay out very long. I don't remember ever going to a doctor when growing up, nor my brothers or sisters.

One thing my pop did for us that we all loved was going swimming in the summer, and he took us down to the river (the Ohio). Fact is, he taught us all to swim. We were all good swimmers. I have never got over swimming. Still love to do it.

Our family was very poor, but happy and we were all taught to work hard. We lived this way for several years, but we never did get rich.

My father was the head at our family. We did what we were told to do.

After some time, about five or six years, things started up a little better. My pop got a job at Homer Laughlin Potter. Things went better. My pop worked at Homer Laughlin Company for 42 years. He quit work at 72 years old. He never took a vacation, and I don't think he took off for being sick.

We never had a car, but you could ride the street car for four cents.

When things got better, Mum would make candy and my sisters would sell it for five cents a bag at the potteries. That is, when we could buy milk and sugar. They could make 35 to 50 cents a day.

This is the way most people lived through the big Depression, but my husband lived on a small farm. He did not remember very much about the Depression. On a farm you had milk cows, chickens, a big garden, and you butchered a hog every fall. Having food made a big difference. No one had any money, but there is lot of way to preserve food. I wish I could tell the young folks now.

After we were married, my husband worked on the farm. He built our house and my son's house. He learned to fly just because he liked to. He was a very good carpenter.

After all the bad times we had some good times. We all worked hard, but we played hard too. I have worked all my life, but that is another story.

I am 85 years old. I'm a good cook. I keep my house clean. I burn wood for heat; get all my wood carried in to burn. And in summer, help do all the seeding and transplanting to run the greenhouses.

I retired from a place called Malta Manufacturing in 1988. I worked there 25 years and liked it fine.

I could go on and on, but my hands are tired. I'm still going and not planning to sit down yet.

Children's Stories

by Helen Ray of Canton, Ohio
Born 1932

The Christmas of 1944 was over and the New Year was here. It was a time of happiness for us, as in the month of January of 1945 we planned to move back to our farm home on Ozark Ridge. Our tenants were moving to their own home and the house would be unoccupied. We were getting anxious to be back in our own home and didn't realize how much we missed it until we were settled in it again.

And we got to ride the big yellow school bus until May when school was out for the year. Several of our young neighbor kids from Ozark who rode the school bus planned a sledding party. Snow was on and the weather was just right, not too cold but just comfortable. "Oh boy!" I smiled with glee. "I'll get to ride my new sled. Richard has his own sled so we can have a lot of fun."

Mother was a little concerned about us. She said we could have an accident if we ran into another with our sleds, but she told us, "Be careful, don't stay out too late even though it is Friday and no school tomorrow."

We left early and were to meet at the Church of Christ building on Eddy Ridge in Ozark. Bobby, Paulina, Richard, and I started walking; pulling our sleds behind us.

Along the way, we stopped at Speece's. Bobby Speece and his sister, Teddy, were walking with us. Next, we stopped in Ozark at Bilyeus' where Harold and his brother, Lewis, joined us. What a crowd of kids and sleds as we went on to the Eddy Ridge Road where we were to meet Helen Yerian and Wilda and Thelma Jean Eberle.

The full moon made it easy for us to guide our sleds down the icy slope. The laughter was joyous as we took turns sharing our sleds with one another.

My, I was a little selfish. I remembered when the weight of Bobby broke our old sled and I didn't want my new sled broken. I had worked for Wilma Hudson babysitting her son, Charlie Bill, when she had to go on a short errand. I was proud to receive a dollar and I wondered what I could get with it. Sleds were still on sale from Christmas and this small sled was just a dollar. So I proudly held onto my sled.

Paul Stine came along and joined the crowd. My brother, Bobby, Harold Bilyeu and he were seniors in high school. Wilda was a classmate of Paulina's. Helen Yerian was a year or two older. Thelma Jean and I were in grade school together. I don't remember what grades the others were in, but we really had a lot of fun sledding.

Quite a while later, one of the fellows said, "We had better start for home." It didn't seem late as the full moon was so clear. We started then in our own directions towards home. When we got to Harold and Lewis Bilyeu's home, they invited us in to get warm. We had a short walk then to get home.

Mother was waiting for us. She was glad to see our happy vibrant faces. "Didn't you know it was getting late?" She asked us, "You must be tired." "Oh, Mother," I said, "We all had such a good time. I'm so glad we moved back to the farm." Then we all had a cup of hot cocoa before we climbed the stairs to our bedrooms.

As the snow falls each winter evening, my fondest memories return to the happy and joyous sled riding with the Ozark gang.

* * * *

The last Tuesday of August was here and no matter what the year, that was when the Belmont-Monroe County reunion was held on a large acre or two of the Peterman's farm in Jerusalem, Ohio in Monroe County. The two counties sponsored an entertainment of food, politics, and children's rides: merry go round with small wooden horses, Ferris wheel, and swings held together on long chains which circled around several feet above the ground. Rides and amusements for young and old.

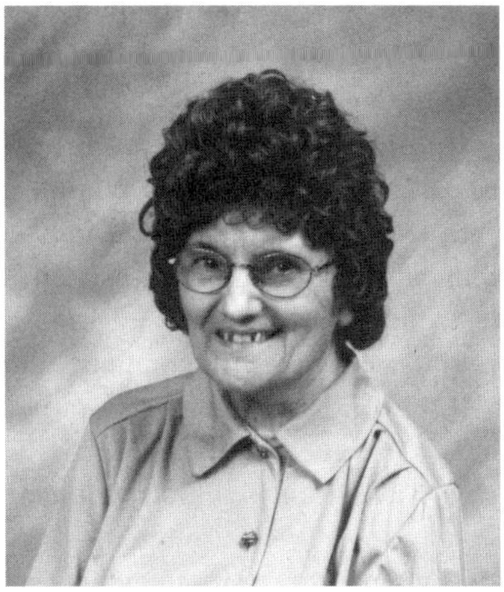

Helen Ray.

The grounds had several large trees along with a large parcel of land covered with soft smooth grass. One part of the lower level was for the different rides and concessions.

A wooden shelter which had several rows of long benches was used to have a school band hold a concert of popular music or a group of country music musicians with their fiddles, banjos and guitars, and a long-winded politician or two wanting a vote for a political office. Honorable Robert Secrest was the most popular.

One thing it was not to do that day: rain! Usually there was not a cloud in the sky. People from miles around started arriving at daybreak to visit and renew old acquaintances and make new ones.

First thing our mother did on that bright Tuesday morning was to fill a large basket with the tempting homemade food from the kitchen along with a large tablecloth and eating utensils and plates.

A quick breakfast and we would be ready to go the mile or two in our fresh-air car, a Ford, which twenty or twenty-five miles an hour was all it could do.

This was a treat every year for the Elmer and Martha Adair Thomas family. Along with friends, relatives and cousins. One who we saw once or twice a year was Mother's cousin, Jim Adair, from Beechbottom, West Virginia. Jim Adair always arrived at our farm very early Tuesday morning and we watched out the window until someone spied his truck. He was a man who, along with his son, Cecil, had a large acreage of apple trees so he used the truck to haul bushels of apples to the market.

I was the first one to see him and ran out the door to greet him, but after greeting me with a big hug, he held his arm behind him. "Hi, Helen Gertrude. Now, what do you suppose I have here in this large white paper sack that smells um um good?" teased Jim Adair. We were told to call him Uncle Jim instead of Jim, cousin or Mr. Adair, showing respect for his age. Paulina and Richard came closer, but Bob held back. Paulina smiled and said, "I know, it's peppermint candy, that's what you brought us last year." "You're right," he chuckled and each of us picked a couple of delicious peppermint candies and then we all went into the house. After a short visit, it was time to get started to the picnic.

Daddy and Mother, along with Richard who had just turned four years old, went in the car. Ten-year-old Bob, seven-year-old Paulina, and I, a five-year-old, would ride in the truck, talking and eating peppermint candy with Uncle Jim.

Upon our arrival, we entered a pathway with a tall white arch sign reading Belmont-Monroe County Reunion, the last Tuesday in August.

Daddy tried to find a parking place which was not too far from the building, which now we would call the rest area.

At our age, four of us kids needed to go every so often during the all day affair.

Uncle Jim followed Daddy's car to a spot near a large tree, which shaded the car and food when we ate around noontime.

In the meantime, Mother had the small dime bank, which held the ten dollars worth of dimes she had saved for this occasion to see that the family had a good time on the rides and maybe a little ice cream later.

Bob, being the oldest, was given a few dimes and was told to report to the car around noon. "Yes Mother, I will," he said as he ventured off. "Maybe I'll find someone I haven't seen for a while."

Daddy and Uncle Jim decided to find some old friends and reminisce, while Mother took Richard by the hand and Paulina held onto mine.

"Mother, please let's ride the merry go round. I love the horses and music," I said as I ran over to where the man was selling tickets.

"Let's sit down on this bench a few minutes and wait until it stops. Paulina, you find a horse close to Helen Gertrude's and I will hold Richard on one. And don't forget, make sure it completely stops before you try to get on or off," Mother reprimanded.

Finally, after getting tickets and settling on the horses, the music started and the horses slowly turned on the carousel. A man walked through taking tickets.

Mother was helping Richard hold onto a horse and I looked beside me and saw Paulina smiling and saying, "See, this is fun. Hold tight now." "Oh, yes, I wish we could ride all day," I said happily.

All too soon the music slowed down and stopped. We carefully got off our horses. "That's all for now," Mother said.

Next, we walked around the grounds and Mother would speak to some of her friends. Soon it was time to go to the car. Mother put the tablecloth on the flat ground and told Paulina to get the damp washcloth and wipe our hands. The men folks came along with Bob trailing after. "I saw Bert and Bessie, and Eileen, too," he said. "Eileen said school starts soon."

After a delicious dinner of friend chicken, biscuits and a dessert, Mother put a blanket on the ground so we children could take a short rest. "Mother, you promised to let me ride the Ferris wheel this year. I won't be scared. Paulina can watch Richard, please?" I begged. Mother gave Paulina some coins to get Richard a balloon while she and I got tickets for the ride.

As we sat in the seat, the attendant made sure the bar in front was secure and when the last seat was filled, the wheel slowly started up, up and away we went. "Don't look down," Mother suggested. "It may scare you at first." But, as I looked over the crowd from the top of the wheel, I saw Daddy talking to his sister, Aunt Ethel. Sam and also their cousin, Blanche Seal, was with them.

Soon the Ferris wheel stopped and Mother and I got off, while Paulina and Richard came to us. May Eileen Winland was with them.

"Were you scared, Helen Gertrude? I want to go next," said Paulina. "May Eileen said she would ride with me."

"It was fun, but don't look down and don't shake the seat. Mother and I liked it," I smiled.

Daddy came to us and said he was leaving to attend some farm chores and would be back later in the evening in time to hear the music and the speakers. We also said goodbye to Jim Adair as he wanted to get an early start home to West Virginia.

Later, we found seats in front of the building while the band was preparing their instruments. Little did I know I would be playing my clarinet in the Beallsville High School band several years later, in that same building.

"Mother, could we have our ice cream sandwiches now? My head aches and ice cream would make me feel better, I pleaded.

"Paulina, you hold to Helen Gertrude's hand and get yourselves ice cream sandwiches. I'll wait here with Richard and Bob," Mother said.

While we girls waited in line, with so many ahead of us I managed to lose sight of Paulina so I started looking around. I saw Aunt Ethel among the crowd, but couldn't find Paulina. No other faces looked familiar. I waited and waited, little frightened. Fortunately Mother grabbed me by the arm. "Are you lost, Helen Gertrude? Paulina said you got lost from her." "No Mother, I wasn't lost. I saw Aunt Ethel over there, but I couldn't see you. May I have my ice cream now? My head still hurts."

Mother got me strawberry ice cream, which was between two squares of vanilla wafers, but I felt so sick, that to this day I don't care for strawberry ice cream.

"Mother, what would you have done if you couldn't have found me?" I sheepishly asked. "I would have your name announced on that microphone over there. Then someone would bring you to me," she smiled. Then I felt better.

Soon Daddy was back with us and the two of us smaller children were ready to leave the picnic grounds and go home. Naturally we wanted a toy of some kind, so Mother let us choose a pretty yellow bird on a stick, which would make a whistling sound as it was swung around in the air. I was different. I liked the little brown monkey on a stick. It was cute with its bright hat, gloves and slippers. Later in the car, and almost home, Bobby said, "Mother, Helen Gertrude is asleep." "Don't wake her," Daddy said. "I'll carry her into the house. After being lost and not knowing it, she is tired."

Bob turned the lights on in the house while Mother carried Richard. The bright lights blurred my eyes and I pretended to wake, but I really wasn't asleep. I wanted Daddy to carry me in his strong arms.

It's been a little over 50 years, but the Jerusalem Picnic of 1937 was one of my best memories of the past. My parents and most of my relatives of that time are gone now, but happy memories will remain forever.

Flaming Flares and Forgiveness

by Wilma Meek of Coshocton, Ohio
born in 1924

I graduated from high school May 26, 1943. Soon after graduation, I started to work at a small grocery store in Conesville, Ohio.

The village of Conesville is an old village. The Pennsylvania Railroad tracks ran through the middle of the village. History tells me in the year 1897 a train ran over a mail pouch. I am not sure why the tracks ran through the center of the village. Possibly the south side was built at a later date. We people who lived below the tracks were considered as good as those living above the tracks.

I am saying this to explain, the little store sat just opposite the Pennsylvania Railroad tracks.

As the trains passed by, we could see the passengers on the trains. I worked the afternoon shift. A twenty-four-year-old friend, Betty, worked with me.

One afternoon a train having trouble had to be side-tracked for several hours. Betty and I noticed men in uniform sitting on the train. We wondered why they had not flagged down some child to go into the store and buy candy bars for them. This sometime had happened before.

Finally, a local man told us, those coaches, sitting outside our window, were filled with German prisoners of war. This frightened us, we thought some of them might escape. We had to work until nine o'clock. At that time Conesville did not have streetlights.

A brakeman from another train came in the store. He learned of our fright and gave us a handful of flares. He used the flares to warn other trains that there was a train in distress.

Finally, repairs were made and the train went on to Columbus.

At closing time we had to go outside the building and close the wooden doors that protected the two windows at night. We had also to hook up the burglar alarm systems.

We ask the Good Lord to protect us, went out and closed the windows and hooked up the burglar alarms. Then locked the store door, lit our flares and ran the two blocks home as fast as we could run.

The next day customers came into the store and told us about the strange sight they saw the night before. They had seen a flashing light. Then they noticed two people running carrying flaming fire.

At this same time back in Germany, there lived two little girls. Alfredia lived in Berlin. She lost her home in a bombing raid. Renate lived in Augsburg. Her home was also lost in a bombing raid.

Both little girls grew up and married American soldiers and have lived happily in America for many years. Alfredia helps me with my grocery shopping, brings the church bulletin to me each month, and does other nice things for me.

Renate checks on me every Thursday, and we usually eat lunch together. Renate's mother is now deceased. She says she can't do nice things for her mother, so she will do nice things for me, and she certainly has. What a difference time and forgiveness makes!

I am eighty-four years old now. I can't run as fast as I did that miserable night, carrying a flaming flare.

Summer Tanning

by Ronald Behman of North Royalton, Ohio
born in 1935

To the best of my recollection, the year was probably 1947. I was a 12 year old boy who lived in the suburbs of Parma Heights, Ohio. Back then, my parents had a home on ole Green Road. In those days, there were only seven houses on that street, leaving a lot of open country for a young boy to explore. Being 12 and full of energy, I can remember running through the woods over logs, never stumbling, feeling like my feet never touched the ground.

Sometimes, this boy I once was, would take his ole Daisy BB-gun out for some serious hunting, just looking for some likely targets to shoot at. Back in the woods, adjacent to my parents' property, I came across some bee hives which were adorned with glass jars. These ornaments were just what I was looking for. Being an expert marksman, they had no chance to survive.

Ron Behman in 1947.

Putting the day behind me, I took off to the movies at the Parma show. Coming home, I was walking down ole Green Road and saw my father standing at the mail box with his arms folded. It didn't take long for me to find out why he was waiting for me. That's when I got my last "summer tanning" and a good reason to behave...or should I say, "bee hive?"

The Only Girl in the Fifth Grade

by Martha King of Carrollton, Ohio
born in 1926

"You mean it's my turn again?" I asked my sister. We took turns taking my grandmother's "slop jar" to the little house out back.

Our paternal grandma lived with us until she died. Nursing homes, visiting nurses or hospice were unheard of in the late 1930s. There was the old folks' home, but that was for only the really poor or those with no family to care for them.

We lived on an old farm with our cows, pigs, chickens, sheep, and the garden. So we were well cared for food-wise.

The house had no running water. We carried it from a spring house (an enclosed building over a natural spring) that kept things cold. Think a refrigerator away from the house.

On laundry day, the water was heated on the coal kitchen stove in a "wash boiler." Dad worked some at a coal mine in addition to farming, so we got coal as needed.

He plowed using a two-horse team with a walk behind plow.

Threshing grain was a big neighborhood event, with all helping each other and a bounteous noon meal.

Our one-room school had water carried from an outside neighbor's hand pump, and also that outhouse outside. There were five of us in the fifth grade. I was the only girl. Neat!

Before I left home, we had an inside hand pump for water and rural electricity wired in.

Our parents worked hard, but led a full and satisfying life that was considered normal at that time.

Confessions of the Fourth Street Gang

by Naomi Baab Harper of Dover, Ohio
born in 1944

We were five little girls, growing up in the town of Dover, Ohio. The first two girls meant when they were going on three years old, followed by another of about five and the two sisters. We lived about four blocks from the sisters.

At that time it was all field, which we would cut across to get to their house. We would have to jump the creek, but for five little girls, this was a perfect play area. We'd be all wet and muddy half the time from playing in the creek. One time, one of us got stuck in mud in the creek. The others went for shovels and we dug her out from the mud.

As we got older, things around us started changing. Our field became a new school building, with new houses close by. We no longer could go through the field to our friends' house. That didn't stop us.

This led to our hikes through the pines of the back of their house, then the cornfield, and next was the Weaver Barn. We spent lots a time there. Going in with the cows or pigs was a simple thing for us. That soon stopped, when the cows chased us down over the hill, and an angry pig jumped the fence to come after us.

Fourth Street Gang. Left to right: Sarah, Patti, Diana, Naomi, Margie, and dog, Toby, with pups.

At Halloween, we would go in the cornfield and get our corn to throw. We'd fill big boxes full of corn and our Halloween would start very early in October. The neighbors soon got to know for our corn throwing. One neighbor would spray us with his hose, getting us all wet, which would just bring us back for more.

The new school was being built, and us five had the look see. We would walk across the steel beams, and as the school was being completed, four of us got locked in the school. Well, the police came, and there was an article in the next day's paper about some girls getting locked in the school. One of the fathers saw the article and made the remark, "What parents would let their children play there?" With a response from his wife, "Honey, those children are our girls."

Winter was always fun for us girls. We liked sledding, and would go up above Weaver's Barn. I was going down on my sled when my gloves got caught and I could not remove my hands from the gloves. I headed right for the barn where there were two big sewer pipes sitting. I hit head on. I remember my friends crying and saying, "I think she is dead." They loaded me on the sled and went to the closest house, which was the two sisters. By that time, I had come to and seemed to be fine.

They called my dad to come after me. He tied my sled to the back of the car, but when we got home, my sled was gone. I was so upset that my brother went looking for it. He found my sled about a block away in the middle of the street.

As us five growing up, more and more adventures we had. We set the pines on fire one time. One of us fell down in a big hole which was being dug for a pipeline. One other was with her at the time and went and got a ladder to get her out.

We all had bicycles and as we got older, rode our bikes to a neighboring town three miles away. One of us girls was only to ride her bike as far as the police station, and parked it there. She and I were going to Bible school and rode our bicycles. She decided to walk her bike across the street to the church. As she was crossing, a car hit her. It knocked her down but did not harm her or the bicycle. Oh, did we do some praying that morning. No one ever found out.

The town of Dover has sure changed in sixty years, and so have us five. The Fourth Street Gang we called ourselves. We still get together and talk about our times together. Our parents are gone now, but we can still hear them say, "You did what? We never knew that!" Through joy and sorrow, the five of us have remained friends. We still get together and talk about our wonderful times growing up in the town of Dover.

Remembering My Schools

by Mildred Kessler of Zanesville, Ohio
born 1918

My first year of school was 1923 in the "old school."

There was no running water and the outhouses for the boys and girls were at opposite ends of the playground. This school was in downtown Zanesville. My second grade was in the new "Pioneer" school at the head of Main St. We had to walk up about 100 steps, or maybe it was 1000 steps. I know it wasn't that bad, but some days it sure felt like it. It had a place for us to eat and inside bathrooms.

I went home every day for lunch all through school. I later went to Grover Cleveland Junior High. It was over a mile and I also walked to school and home for lunch every day. I was the only one of four children to graduate from high school. My last year of school I started to work at the local 5 and 10.

I went to school in the morning and worked eight hours every day. I got 12-cents an hour and felt very rich. I worked there for ten years.

Potty Adventures and Prell Toothpaste

by Sharon Milhoan Lawver of Coshocton, Ohio
born in 1941

When I was in the first grade, I attended a one-room school, grades one through eight. We raised our hands if we needed to go to the potty; it was outside. The teacher said, "Yes, you may go." So I went outside to the restroom.

I was sitting in the restroom and thought, "I think I'll just go home," so I did. It was about one mile. We walked it every day. My older sisters had no idea where I was, and neither did the teacher. There were no phones in those days. So when I got home, my mother couldn't call, but I did get in trouble.

I'm not sure just how old I was, but it was when Prell Shampoo first came in a tube. I was brushing my teeth, and I picked up the wrong tube. It sure was nasty.

I remember the two-holers, and we had three holes, a baby pot. When I had to go out at night to the outside toilet, I would shine the light down the hole and on the seat to make sure there was no snake or spiders. Then I would sit down and shine the light in the cracks to see if there were any roaches. The paper magazines were rough. We had to crunch them in our hands to soften them some.

I remember when I was six years old, we lived twenty miles north of Cambridge in the country. My parents had to drive me to the hospital at night. I was very, very sick. I vomited a lot. The doctor wanted to know what I had eaten. I told him my older sister (Juney was her name) told me to eat a potato root, so I did. I guess it was a poison root. I always did everything she told me to do, 'cause she always said she would never play with me again, and that's a long time. We were good buddies.

Chamber pots—I had one of those. I was only seven years old when this happened to me. We had Delco lights when I was a child. That's when your lights are hooked up to a lot of batteries. The batteries sat outside the house in big glass containers about one foot by one foot and as high as the batteries. Well, that's what we used for a pot or thunder mug.

Sharon Milhoan Lawver.

For some strange reason, it was my job to empty it. We lived in a big two-story house with a long stairway. I picked up the pot and started downstairs, dropped it, and it spilled all the way down the steps. What a mess!

I remember I had to drink kerosene and sugar for the croup.

Something my sister thot [thought?] was a lot of fun when we were little was to play horse. She would find four tin cans, stomp on two of them to mash in the center so they would stay on her feet. Then she would hold two on her hands and walk on all fours. My sister, Juney, was the house. My job was to hold my dress to make a pocket. The pocket was for her food, like cornflakes or oats. I liked her very much.

Another thing I'll never forget. I was a very young age, maybe five years old. I tried to lick the frost off of a metal tracker tire. The skin of my lips and tongue stuck fast. I don't remember who, but someone blew hot air to get them off. It took a lot of skin off—OUCH! That hurt. Never tried that again.

A Rest Room and Nothing Else

by Ralph Raymond Gibson of Cambridge, Ohio
born 1935

There were two businessmen in town, one being Mark Snyaler, a bank officer, and had a construction company. He also had a real estate business. He had a filling station for sale.

The other businessman was Gail Marks. "Real names," he was into trucking and storage and that sort of thing. He was interested in the station. So he looked it over, but not too close apparently, because he asked Mark if it had a restroom. Mark said, "Yes." But the bottom line was it didn't have fixtures, ha-ha! True story.

An Outhouse Companion and a Smoking Washer

By Ellie Behman of North Royalton, Ohio
Born 1937

A smoky wringer washer. When I was just a new naive bride, I wanted to please my husband's parents desperately. The harder I tried, the more I failed. We lived in the same apartment complex so I was to use their wringer washer. My first time was a complete disaster.

I had never used this kind of washer before, but had seen others doing the laundry so I didn't feel it was too difficult. Item after item went through the wringer beautifully and I was beginning to feel successful, until I washed some braided rugs. They were heavy and became heavier when logged with water. Each one had a fringe completely across the ends and as I slipped the first one up to the rollers on the wringer I knew immediately I had made a mistake.

The fringe got tangled in the roller and instead of the rug sliding out in an orderly fashion, the rug started to roll round and round on the rollers until they both popped up and began to smoke. I panicked and reached for the first thing I could find and, sadly, it was a saw. I began to saw away at the rug, failing miserably to cut it away from the rollers.

I ran upstairs in tears to my young husband and babbled about how I had ruined his parents' washer. He came to my rescue, retrieved the tangled up rug and gave me a kiss that brought me comfort. Comfort, that is, until I saw his parents standing in the doorway observing the entire fiasco.

A day at the movies with my dad. My father was a movie buff. He loved westerns and passed that love down to me. Most every Saturday he would hustle us kids into the car and take us to the local show. In the forties the movie theaters would offer serials that continued week after week. We couldn't wait to find out the ending of a story and loved spending that time with our dad.

We would laugh at the antics of the Three Stooges or watch with awe at how Red Rider and Little Beaver braved the frontier. I remember the famous line uttered by Little Beaver (played by Robert Blake) "You betchum Red Rider!" Funny how some things just stick in your mind.

Those times with dad were some of the most special moments of my life. He filled us with the love of the arts and to this day, when I watch a Western, I think about my dad and how much he would have enjoyed sharing a bag of popcorn with me and watching the movie.

A "friendly outhouse." Back in the late forties my parents decided to move us to the country. While that had been their dream for many years, it was more of a nightmare for me. I loved where we lived and the thought of moving to a strange area didn't sound appealing to me at all.

A day at the movies with Ellie Behman's dad, Sam Jakabcic.

When our home was nearly built we were able to move in and remain fairly comfortable. There was one awful drawback and that was the dreaded outhouse. Oh, mom put curtains on the window and a colorful rug on the floor. She even wallpapered the entire inside, finishing off the decorations with many Sears catalogs. That should have been tempting to even the most unappreciative occupant, but there was one little drawback. Our outhouse had two seats! I have absolutely no idea who came up with that decision, but I often wondered: who on earth would you want to be seated next to, no matter how friendly you were with them?

The most memorable person in my life—my dad, Sam Jakabcic. With gas grills and pre-packaged meats, a barbecue can be under way in minutes. Ah, but the memorable extravaganza that my dad prepared over half a century ago took days to create. It was an art form that doesn't seem to be present in today's fast paced culture.

The meat was sliced and seasoned to perfection days ahead. The ingredients then had ample time to acquaint themselves with one another, resulting in an interesting blend of flavors. Up at dawn on the day of our picnic, dad would burn large stacks of kindling until the coals were hot and smoldering. He was a master at his craft and knew the precise moment to begin. Ceremoniously the meat was slid onto the skewer as delicately as an artist sweeps his brush over the canvas.

The family gathered around him as he patiently turned the barbecue rod over the crackling fire. He was the lead player in this performance and we were the extras. Looking up with a mischievous grin he would pour his homemade wine over the sizzling entree. Then, with a wink, he would sample a sip or two along the way.

Smoke billowed toward the sky as the cool wine dripped onto the glowing embers. The aroma wafted through the air and teased our nostrils while our mouths watered in hungry anticipation.

Dad's blue eyes mirrored his inner soul as they sparkled with child-like happiness. Pure white hair lay in matted ringlets beneath his favorite cap.

Now, so many years later, I realize that it wasn't the food or wine that made those picnics so special. It was the man himself that drew us back time and time again, the nucleus that bonded one to the other with a ready smile and loving heart.

Now when we take time to prepare the traditional family recipe, we capture a small corner of the past and hold it close, if only for a little while. Although our lead player has changed and some would say that our memories have gone up in smoke, I know in my heart this is not to be. As we all stand around the fire pit and smell the familiar tantalizing aromas, I can close my eyes and picture dad smiling down at us as if to say, *"Carry on, you're doing fine."*

Raw Squirrel, Green Peaches and Overripe Corn

By Franklin S. Dye of New Matamoras, Ohio
Born 1916

My brother, a neighbor boy and I enjoyed several hunting trips together. I will tell you about a special one.

One Sunday morning, armed with our guns, kettle, silverware and a bowl apiece; we went to a set of high rocks with a cave under them. There we left our picnic utensils and water and went squirrel hunting. We only got one. We dressed it and put it over a fire to cook. We got field corn roasting ears from a field nearby. While I watched the squirrel cook, my brother and the neighbor boy went out the ridge to a peach orchard. Well, we had a great dinner of partly cooked squirrel, unripe peaches and over ripe roasting ears. You might say squirrel season and roasting ears of field corn do not match. No problem, we just moved the seasons forward.

This neighbor boy knew who had watermelon patches. Each fall we would visit one. One fall he had one spotted on a neighbor's farm. One fall night we went; parked our car some distance away, found the patch, felt around, found some small ones and finally we found a big one; took it a safe distance from the house and enjoyed a watermelon feast. Now this neighbor was a cousin to my mother. On her way to the general store she would stop in and visit. She told Mom about someone taking a melon; said she wouldn't care, but it was the only big one there was. She thought it was a neighbor's boys. My brother was sitting there reading the paper. He didn't correct her. Many years later I told them who got the melon.

This incident occurred after I was grown and had my own farm. There was a steep bank between the road and the garden. On this bank was a groundhog den. The groundhogs were eating my vegetables so I set a steel trap in the hole. When I went back I had caught one, but he had gone back in the den. I pulled, but couldn't get him out. I didn't want to pull the trap off his leg so I laid the rifle in the hole and shot. When I pulled Mister Groundhog out I saw he wasn't caught by a leg!

Kennard's Magnificent Bobsled

by Betty White of Malta, Ohio

In the year of 1959, my multitalented husband, Kennard White, decided to build a bobsled...not just an ordinary bobsled, but one with distinct features. We lived at the top of Poplar Ridge hill so I believe that he had notions of high adventure.

To describe the sled, I recall that it was probably over 8 feet long and stood about 16 inches off the ground. It had foot pegs and hand holds for six riders. The steering mechanism was devised from the steering box and wheel from a Model A Ford (a real classic old timer). This worked extremely well.

The magnificent bob sled with Tracy, Kermit and Howard White in 1965.

The wooden sled was a real beauty with a red paint job. The dual set of runners were plated with steel which provided beautiful sparks if the sled dug through the snow to the road surface. The floating runners were also designed to accommodate bumps in the road or whatever the surface.

On completion of the sled, we were anxious for the test ride. Finally, we got the big one. So the race was on to get the party going before the county road crews took over.

As luck would have it, my brother, Ben Almendinger, provided the jeep that pulled the sled back up the hill after each trip down. As a safety precaution, the jeep would park under the railroad trestle at the bottom of the hill to prevent any traffic from starting up the hill while the sled was coming down. We even enjoyed being towed throughout the villages and riding back up the hill for another thrilling ride down and believe me, it was thrilling. The speed increased with each trip as the snow packed.

First order of business was to build a big bonfire at the top of the hill, to warm ourselves between rides. All the neighbors were invited to join in if they were brave enough. Many were. Some were not. We had a diversified age group participating. There were so many turned out that we had to take turns, so everyone had a chance to enjoy the "thrill of the hill." We also took turns as jeep driver, so Ben could also participate in the sledding fun.

We had many winters that the sled was used and several that the weatherman did not cooperate. I don't recall the last year the sled was used, but I do recall that this time, the old folks did not go. But the thrills were provided to several teenagers. Some were our own sons and some were not. We provided the tow vehicle (an International Scout). Apparently, their joy got out of hand. The sled was wrecked and two went to the hospital for stitches. The sled was not heavily damaged, but set in the barn for several years until Kennard decided that it needed to be moved. As it was too large and too heavy for one man to move, he applied the chain saw and burned it. We never forgave him for destroying his magnificent creation.

Putting Up the Stoves

by Denny Easterling of Lewisville, Ohio
born in 1925

When I was a kid, the stoves weren't put until the weather got cold; it was put on a jacket or go to bed.

We had three stoves. One stayed up all year in Mom and Dad's bedroom. I'm not sure where we stored the living room stove, but the dining room stove was stored in a closet underneath a set of stairs in the dining room.

After the stoves were in place, it meant keeping a fire going, carrying out ashes and filling the coal buckets with coal we dug from our own mine during the summer.

Thick Water for the Youngest

by Bob Stauffer of Leesville, Ohio
born in 1942

Born and raised in southeastern Ohio. It was a joyable event that most people never experienced or will in the future.

I was the youngest of seven children. We were a close family. My brother, Charlie, and myself was real close. We sawed wood together, split it, and carried it to help heat a 200-year-old, eight-room house. We also picked up coal and hauled it to help heat it.

We had a two-hole outhouse that was hard to go to in the winter weather when all snuggled up under a couple of quilts and a down comforter at night in bed.

We enjoyed playing cowboys and Indians in the woods on fifteen acres, shooting our .22 rifles, playing baseball in the school yard, skating on the ice on the Conotton Creek backwaters, sled riding on homemade toboggans in the snow storm of 1950. Also, sliding on coal shovels and metal roofing.

Bob Stauffer with a pair of twin goats in 1944.

Saturday night bath was a real good time for my brother and sisters. My mother would heat the water on the wood coal stove in the kitchen. When hot, the oldest would get in. When done, more water was heated and the next would get in. No water was left out. Being the youngest, the water was quite thick when it got to me. To this day, I will take a shower and not a bath.

We had no boughten toys. As a young man, my rocking horse was a saw horse with wooden nail keg between it, and one old stirrup. But me, Roy Rogers, Gene Autry, and The Lone Ranger rode many, many miles together.

We had the first big wheel in the country as far as I know. It was a tricycle turned upside down. The pedals was removed and brackets were put there to put your feet on. You would stand up and push it, then jump on and go rather fast down the hill that we lived on.

Our chores consisted of many. As mentioned, sawing wood, carrying water, making hay for the goats, which my father cut by hand with a scythe, picking potato bugs in a coffee can. Another job was cleaning the wallpaper with wallpaper cleaner after the coal furnace would blow soot all over.

Another chore of mine was carrying coal for the local hardware store; an average of four to seven buckets a day for a dollar a week.

On of the fondest memories was sitting by the coal stove in the kitchen in the winter and carving monkeys out of peach pits with my father. We also carved wooden chains out of one piece of wood. I still carve today.

I left southeastern Ohio in 1960 to join the Air Force, so naïve that I did not know how to use a pay telephone, and returned 40 years later to the old home place I enjoyed as a child.

The Bountiful River

by Norman D. Zimmerman of Cambridge, Ohio
born 1927

Southeastern Ohio is known as Appalachia by some. To all who are lucky enough to live here, it is called "home"; is now and always has been.

The rivers, too, are important and always have been. In the 1930's the rivers were a source of food and income. The Depression pretty much did away with any work for most folks.

I had an uncle who would say, "Boy, get that burlap feed sack seine and you and me are going to put in a trot line and catch us some fish."

He and I had built a "john boat." Now, a john boat is made out of rough sawed lumber right from the sawmill. Ours was about 14 feet long by four feet wide. It had a seat on each end and one in the middle where you sat and rowed. The oarlocks were two short posts set on the side gunnels. It floated good and rowed good, but it was so heavy we just kept it tied to a tree.

To set our trot line, we would tie one side to a tree, then row the rest of the line across the river and tie it to a tree on the other side. This line was a heavy staging type line. To this we tied drop lines about every ten or fifteen feet, and then added some weight to make it sink. Now, we baited up with the minnows I had seined up.

Next morning, and every morning for a week or so, we would run our line, take off any fish and re-bait.

Any fish we didn't eat right away was kept in a fish pen. A fish pen is a wire box made out of chicken wire.

The open end was nailed to a wooden top with a hinged door. This was left to float in the river tied to a tree. Just put your excess fish in the box, and any time we needed a good meal go down to the fish pen and take out enough for everyone. Some mighty great meals were had this way, and some mighty good conversations, too!

The river was also a source of income. About the only work around was helping someone at planting or harvesting time, and the pay was 50 cents or $1.00 per day. To supplement our income, we decided to trap some muskrats. We got about 50 leg hold traps and set them along the riverbank. You set your traps close to deep water, so when you catch a muskrat, he jumps in and the trap will hold him down. This way he don't have to suffer very long. I know this doesn't sound good, but these were tough times, and the ladies liked them soft muskrat coats.

The river floods once in awhile, and the muskrats learned to adjust to it; they would have their babies after the flood season was past. Oh, once in a while a late flood would wash them out and drown all the babies, but most years they all survived.

It seems that muskrats are smarter than some people. Some folks build their homes in river bottoms, so every year or so, they would get their basements wet.

The State of Ohio wanted to keep all these folks coming to the polls and decided to build five flood control dams. These dams were started about 1937, and when completed were used to impound the water till after flood season had passed. Then, about May or June, the water was let out, clear up to the top of the riverbanks.

Too bad for the muskrats. The babies drowned in their nests that was supposed to be dry. It wasn't long until they pretty much disappeared. Seems like a shame; their fur was so soft, and they were pretty good to eat. Some folks called them "marsh rabbits."

Things were different then, but better than you think.

Teachers' Hugs at Nashport School

by Trudi E. Joseph of Zaneville, Ohio
born in 1947

One of my fondest memories is of my first two years of school at Nashport School. Nashport School was an old school in Nashport, Ohio. A few years before I started attending, it was grades 1-12. There was no kindergarten class. There are not many people who graduated from Nashport High School around anymore. When I attended, it was grade 1- 8. The 5th and 6th grade and the 7th and 8th grade were in one room. I went there in the 1st and 2nd grade.

I can remember it took an hour on the bus to get to and from school. We went in all kinds of weather. In bad, snowy weather, the bus would have chains on and they sure made a rattling noise on the main roads. We never got stuck and I don't remember ever being late, going or coming from school. On the really bad snow days, the bus driver would stop at the teacher's house and they would ride to school with us. Grades 1 -12 rode the bus. They would let us little kids out at Nashport and then take the high school kids on to Frazeysburg. We sat and behaved ourselves on the bus.

Girls wore dresses to school. In the cold winter, we were allowed to wear snowsuit pants to school. But we better have had a dress under the pants or our parents were called, and we had to go home to change. If we disrupted class or misbehaved, we were spanked. Parents usually gave us a spanking or a good lecture when we got home.

My most cherished memories are of my first grade teacher, Miss Farrell and second grade, Miss Nethers. I had many hugs from those teachers. I can remember a drinking fountain in the hall, by the lunchroom.

There were two cooks working every day, but I always carried my lunch. I had a black and red plaid tin square lunch box with a matching thermos. The thermos being glass inside, I broke it once and couldn't take any milk to drink.

Nashport School 2nd Grade Class 1954-1955. Miss Nethers was teacher.

Although there was running water in the school, we did not have bathrooms in it. They were two outhouses on the far side of the playground. One side of the playground was the girls and the other side was the boys. The teachers had to use them also.

I remember one time when I was picked up for school, my dog, Goldie, got loose and chased the bus tires. I heard a bump. The kids in the back of the bus said my dog got run over. The bus driver would not stop and I cried all the way to school. She was a golden cocker spaniel. I loved that dog, and to this day, I have never had another dog to match her.

The Red Coat and the Frozen Dentures

by Ida Labaki of Zanesville, Ohio
born 1936

My story begins around 1943-44 when we moved

to the Bauserman House. I was in the third grade and my sister was in the first grade. We also later lived in the Orr House. That is another story. It seems every house we lived in back then had a name.

The Bauserman House set way back a lane in Chandlersville, Ohio. Mother, Dad, my younger sister Roberta and I lived there. Dad worked in Zanesville at the Cussins and Fearn store. I'm not sure of this spelling, and I don't remember what they sold.

During the long, bad winters we had back then, Dad stayed in town with relatives and only came home on weekends when he could get through the lane to the house. When he did come home, he would bring groceries for us to live on until he got back again.

One Sunday we came home from church and there was a large bag of clothing for us someone had dropped off. Mother was so excited. She knew someone from church had left those clothes for us. The only thing I remember being in that bag was a lady's red coat. Mother took it and got busy cutting it down to fit me.

I thought it was a beautiful coat but what would I do? Someone had told me that bulls hated red and would come after any red thing they saw.

It just so happened that the Coffey farm was on one side of our lane and their pasture was right along the lane. There were several cows and one bull in that pasture. Every morning my sister and I had to walk down the lane to the main road to catch the school bus. I was scared to walk past that bull, so I would walk on the other side of the lane with my little sister on the side next to the bull. I thought he couldn't see my red coat if I hid beside my sister and walked fast. Somehow I made it through the winter and didn't get attacked by that bull.

We had a collie dog named Brownie, and Brownie always came to the end of the lane to meet us when we got off the school bus. This day we had a bad snowstorm, and snow had drifted into the lane almost over the top of our heads. Brownie went back to the house without us. Mother said something is wrong. It happened that our Uncle Sam was there, so they came down the lane to find us. They each put one of us on their shoulders and we walked back to the house that way.

At night, Mother would "bank" the fireplace to keep the ashes alive until morning, so this made the house very cold at night. Dad had put his dentures in a glass of water. The next morning when we got up we saw his teeth frozen solid in that glass of water. We had a big laugh over that.

We made it through that terrible winter and spring finally came. One day we came home from school, and I couldn't wait to tell her the news that President Franklin D Roosevelt had died. We had learned this in school that day. Mother said she knew something bad had happened because Brownie had run around and around the house all day. Mother had always been a superstitious person.

Times were bad back then, it was hard, but it sure makes one appreciate the things we have today.

A Treasure From My Childhood

by Mary Power-Dixon of Zanesville, Ohio
born 1928

Gold, silver or diamonds could never be as precious to me as my many, magnificent and cherished childhood memories. Time cannot lessen their value, nor can they ever be stolen from me, as might costly gems.

Sometimes it seems (I am now in my eightieth year) that I can recall events or places, in my mind's eye, that took place before I could even speak. Then there are moments a faint glow will come upon me as I drift back in time to those young, wonderful years.

I was the first child, and I owe much to my loving parents, F.L and H.P. Power (who were only twenty year old youngsters themselves), and a neighborhood of caring, older people who watched over us all.

From my sixth month to my twelfth year of life, we three lived on a quiet street in a big, old double-house tended by a kind, stately landlady who lived in the other half. I can recall many a summer's day standing on tiptoe with my small, pugged nose pushed against her back screen door as the pungent aroma of fresh, fried cabbage and onions floated out on the clear, warm air of the day. Now, the times I was invited in to share her meager lunch were of supreme joy to me, for afterwards I was carried into the front parlor, lifted up to the piano bench, and my little fingers gingerly placed upon the keys. Oh, what delight! What a glorious sound came out of that big, black box.

Now, most every Sunday would find me dressed in tiny, shiny, black shoes, white anklets and a crisp, starched, best dress so that I might accompany our dear landlady to Sunday school and church. Although I was no more than three years old at the time, I enjoyed marching around the "collection box" with other toddlers to deposit the scarce few pennies my mama had tightly tied in my nice, clean hanky.

At all the Christmas programs, a very pretty, very patient mother had already taught me, even at this tender age, to recite the entire "T'was the Night Before Saga," to be performed before every audience, so perform I would (this included all the well known Bible verses read to us by our Sunday school teacher).

I can still envision a picture of our tiny backyard (which was my big, wide world). It had a high brick wall with a locked gate on the right side with a terraced wall that had a large, wooden step down on the left. A lovely bush of pale and pink bleeding hearts, big stalks of hollyhocks and giant yellow and brown sunflowers would all catch my eye when in full bloom. So too did the small, cherry tomato bush belonging to our neighbors below the terrace, but over there lay many a fantastic adventure to remember.

Their home was a quaint, old one complete with everything from homemade, carved cornices to a dark and damp outside "root cellar." Being a child of the Depression, a house too hot and stuffy in summer (no air conditioners back then) or too cold and drafty in the winter were just commonplace. So it was sheer heaven to visit with them on a bitter cold evening to bask in front of their cozy grate fire and poke up the coals when I thought no one was watching (but I always got caught).

Then I think of all the Monday mornings way back then, when I watched those two prudent German ladies of the house do the laundry in the backyard. They would rub by hand, on a washboard, using two very large wooden tubs. Scrubbing the clothes in one (with pieces of soap I helped to chip from a large cake), then rinsing them out in the other tub. I always insisted on doing my part, but had to stand on a tall box to reach into the water. Later on I would hand out the straight little wooden clothespins with which to hang the wash on the line so it might dry in the sun and blow gently in the breeze (but sometimes it rained).

If I was not too tired after all my arduous labors, my friends sent me out to their tiny, fenced in front yard to play. While there, I would gather up seed from the little back caps of the beautiful Rose Moss that completely covered their lawn on one side of the yard. It was a chore I truly enjoyed, for the small, thick flowers were of vivid colors, like a rainbow of red, yellow, pink and white.

I would never go home until I was allowed to sneak a few of those cherry tomatoes (which really were left for my fingers alone) planted along the side of the house. These fine folk made me feel big and important for they treated me as one of their own. However, when I became too much of a nuisance (as I often did), I was handed back up to my own yard, and that big, wooden step was removed from our wall.

As I ponder back over fifty years, my marvelous memories fill me with warmth and nostalgia. Like our smooth, dirt street and the crooked, red brick sidewalks that had little clumps of green grass peeking through the cracks, the ice wagon bringing large blocks of ice for our little brown icebox in the pantry. On a hot summer's day, a chip off that block was a piece of cooling relief (replacing ice cubes).

Mary Power-Dixon on the red brick sidewalk.

Then there was a large maple shade tree in our back yard where I sat with my "Dollie" to watch fleecy, white clouds sail by in a bright, blue sky and wished to have wings like the birds so I too might fly away and see the world. Some days, I took extra delight in fixing sand pies from my tin pail and shovel to give to my handsome, jolly daddy when he arrived home, tired from a long day at the "filling station" where he worked.

I still see a rough, wooden rain barrel which, placed beneath the drain, would gather soft rainwater with which to wash my childish head, and the tall red and white, striped barber pole that meant a frightening experience for me with giant scissors to clip off my unruly locks, and let me look like a lady again.

Several times a week in summer, besides the ice wagon, a horse-drawn cart of fresh fruits and veggies would slowly drive down our quiet street. An old man hawked his wares as "the ladies" in calico sunbonnets came running. They would feel, sniff, deliberate then fold up their gingham aprons into pockets and fill them with a few, well chosen green beans, ears of corn and, naturally, the best tomatoes, melons and strawberries they could find.

I think it was a time of life that was a bit richer. They moved a bit slower, but still things were accomplished. For example, if you needed eggs you waited for the butter and egg man to come in from the farm once a week (of course I lived in a small town).

Let's not forget to mention that every morning, while it was still dark out and I lay in my soft, cozy bed, one could hear the tinkle of glass as our milkman made his early rounds through the neighborhood. Often in the winter we would wake to find the cream at the top was frozen and pushing its way right out of the bottle, the paper cap sitting atop like a comical hat.

In closing I must mention one terrific remembrance from which I still can get a slight tinge of happiness and a picture (at least to a child's eye) of beauty. On the rare times at week's end when Mama would find a few extra pennies in her purse, she would dress me up on Saturday night and my parents and I would walk, hand-in-hand, to Meyer's Grand Ice Cream Parlor. Oh, the sights to behold! There were large bladed fans swaying 'round and around from their ceiling. Pretty, black wire heart-shaped chairs nestled under tiny, circular, marble-topped tables upon which they would serve dainty, but tasty, scoops of delicious, homemade vanilla ice cream. Always in small, silver cups under which they placed a lacy, paper doily. That was happiness!

Could any child ask for more? Truly I think not. For even now I count among my precious treasures the closeness of our family unity. How can I ever repay for all those "magic moments" more valued to me than mere rubies, emeralds or pearls?

Now to you, these recollections may seem only the ramblings of a young child, while to me, my memorabilia represents the joys and freedoms in my life (as at no other time since). Back in those days, a child was allowed to be just a child; nothing more than simple courtesy and obedience to elders was ever expected from you. Minding your P's and Q's they called it then.

So, such are my earliest, treasured memories that shall remain with me forever. Just as the nighttime prayers, "Now I lay me down to sleep," taught and listened to by Mama as soon as I was old enough to talk (I still repeat them at bedtime).

There is no doubt it was a wonderful time of my life, though mostly occupied by grownups.

I have much more I could tell, for when I grew a few years older they gave me a baby sister and brother to share in my life.

I guess I could go on and on of my childhood blest, because, for me, it was nurtured with such love and caring. Thank you, Mama! Thank you, Daddy!

Dressing Up For Saturday Night Downtown

by William N. Arbaugh Sr. of Zanesville, Ohio
born in 1920

Things were much different back in the 20s, 30s, and 40s. When I was a kid, we would listen to the radio, as TV was unheard of back then. We would listen to Jack Armstrong, Fibber McGee and Molly, Jack Benny, etc.

The winters were really bad, as it would start snowing by the end of October, and we had snow knee-deep till the end of April. We still went to school, as there was no such thing as snow days. I walked to Grover Cleveland from Putnum Avenue every day. The river even froze over solid.

Before you got up in the morning, you had to wait till your dad fired up the stove in the dining room. It would get so hot the stove would be red and crackled. We stood in front of it till we got warmed up.

The coal heat was very dirty, and your walls would be covered with grime. Your mother would buy wallpaper cleaner and go over all the walls in the spring. She would also take the rugs off the floor and put them on the clothesline in the backyard to beat them with a rug beater. Today is much better with clean electric heat and carpet cleaners that come to your home and clean everything.

I remember the old wall telephone. Everyone was on a party line. You would go to make a call, and someone else would be on the phone talking. If our phone would ring, someone else could pick it up and listen in.

You could ride the bus anywhere in Zanesville. Tickets were five for $1.00. Most everyone rode the bus, as not too many people could afford a car. Some of the old cars back then were Desotos, Packards, Hudson, and Terraplanes.

It was a big thing to go downtown on Saturday night. There was no malls or shopping centers. Every store on Main Street was filled up. Some of the bigger stores was Starr's, Bintz's, Weber's. Dress stores and shoe stores line both sides of the street. A few were French Shop Artwell, Samilsons, Beverly, Jane Lee Cotton Shop, Combs Brothers, Nobils, and Dan Coehen. There was jewelry stores; Roberts, Best, Pugh's also. Furniture stores; Quality, Roses, Plus, SS Kresge, Five and Dime, and Dollar store, Woolworth's, and Newberry's. People dressed up back then to go downtown. Some even wore white gloves and hats.

Zanesville had a few local characters you always ran into like Nell Shrack and Railroad Jack. They were harmless, and everyone treated them with respect.

What a difference about 60 years can make. Wonder what the next 50 or 60 will be like.

The Roller Skating Mom and the Pig Rider

by Carol McIntire of Clarington, Ohio
born 1946

Spanking at school: my first grade teacher was Mrs. Little. She had cleaned the blackboard and I decided I would go to board and mark on it with chalk. She whipped me with a yardstick. I never forgot her yardstick and I never marked on her cleaned board after that.

Favorite teacher: I had two teachers that was my favorite. Their names Garnet and Mary Garnet was my eighth grade English. She made me feel special. She always complimented me on my writing. She told me I was a beautiful writer. Mary was my eighth grade Home Ec teacher. I had to take material to school to make an apron. She didn't like my material, so Mary used her own money to buy me new material. I felt special when she gave me my material that day for my apron.

The games I played: I remember drawing a ring in the dirt to shoot a game of marbles. The marbles was always put in the middle of the ring. We would take turns shooting. I tried to keep my Catseye and Aggie, but would lose them sometimes. It was fun to see who got the most marbles when the game was over.

I liked to go sled riding. We never had a sled. Used cardboard inner tubes, or old car hoods. Then I would get in a snowball fight with the others, or make a snowman.

Hunting: Dad wouldn't take his dogs when he went rabbit hunting. Dad took me instead. I had to get in the brush and get the rabbits out for Dad.

Saturday night baths: Mom would put a tin tub behind the coal stove in the living room. The cleanest one would get their bath first. And the dirtiest one went last. I always tried to stay cleaner so I could get in there first. I always felt scummy with the Ivory soap Mom used. I still don't like Ivory.

Snowstorms: the bad snowstorm I remember, I was fourteen and in eighth grade. The snow started about 1:00 PM. Kids that rode the bus got to go home early. I didn't like riding the bus, so I stayed in school. Mom called the school looking for me.

Floods: the last flood I remember in our town was the spring of 1964. I was seventeen at the time. Our town was hit real hard. We had to go the back road to get to town.

Mischief I got in: I went sled riding one day, and this boy spit on me. I waited till we got back in the house, then wailed a half-gallon of milk at his head. He never spit on me after that.

I broke the lock on my mom's freezer. My sister was always into things, so she got blamed for it. Just kept my mouth shut and let her take the blame for it.

My younger brother and I had an all day sucker. I don't remember where we got it. Mom didn't know we had it. We heard her coming, Went to the outhouse and threw it down the hole.

I burnt my mom's kettles and I would hide under the porch. She asked Dad about the kettles. He didn't know what happened to them. Mom got to looking and found them under the porch.

I got my cousin in trouble for sneaking my mom's homemade buns off the dryer. She blamed Dad's dog for taking them. He went back to get more. Mom told him, "That's the dog that's been in my bread." We all got in trouble that day.

We decided to throw green apples at each other one day. Mom lined us up and got us all with the switch.

Mom grew up during the Depression. She was thrifty, and a hard worker. Always working for what she had and saving what she could, Mom always taught me a penny saved is a penny earned and to waste not want not. If I wanted a friend I had to be a friend. I remember the things Mom taught me and I still go by those things today. I am glad she raised me the way she did. It made me appreciate the things I had and to be a good person. I owe it all to one special lady, my mom.

Dad grew up during the Depression also. He worked on WPA, like my granddad. Dad was quiet and easy-going. Didn't have temper Grandma had. Dad taught me different things, like how to tie my shoe, to tell time on the clock and how to cook his beans. Once I forgot about them, and yes, they burnt. I poured water in the kettle and stirred them up. Dad told me I ruined a good kettle of beans.

Carol Stewart McIntire on right, Helen Ullom Stewart and Delbert Stewart.

My husband was young during the Depression also, but he remembered the ration stamps and the commodities they got. Like myself, he was poor and had to work for what he got. Also had to wear hand-me-downs and didn't get much at Christmas. My husband was a hard worker and a good provider for us. I married to him for forty-one years. He passed away in November '08. I still miss him.

My two grandmas was as different as night and day. Mom's mother was Dutch, quiet and easy-going. If I got into things around her, she would tell Mom and I got a switch used on me. Dad's mother, on the other hand, was Cherokee Indian, and she had a temper. What she said, went. It was old-school with her. Kids was seen and not heard. Grandma was goodhearted and would help anyone she liked, but someone that she didn't like best stay out of her way.

One night, Mom went roller skating with us. Some one tripped her and she was gonna fall. This guy was in the front of her. Mom grabbed the back of his pants so she wouldn't go down. He looked at her like she was gonna strip him. Mom finally got her balance. It was fun to watch Mom that night.

This boy came to our house and he was gonna ride one of Dad's pigs like a bull. The pig slung him off. He was covered from head to toe. His mom wouldn't let him in the house. Made him take his clothes off on the porch in winter, then she turned the water hose on him. He never got on another pig's back after that.

Holidays in the 50s and 60s for me was different. I never got an Easter basket, just a cottage cheese container that was filled with grass, duck eggs, marshmallow chicks, jelly beans and colored eggs. Never got new clothes. Thanksgiving, I got a kettle of soup beans and cornbread. I was thankful to have that. Didn't have a turkey.

Christmas was special to Mom. I always got a good meal that day, one present under the tree for me. That was the only time I got oranges and chocolate candy. A fresh pine tree was cut in the woods. All of us had to be home that day to be together. I looked forward to Christmas when I was a kid.

One year at Easter, my grandma was with one of her male friends and she didn't want the rest to know she was with him. Grandma got me a doll with jelly beans around her so I wouldn't tell on her. That was the only thing Mom's mother ever got me.

Hooky for Billy Mitchell

by Linda O. Ross of South Zanesville, Ohio
born in 1941

I was a freshman in high school in December 1956. Several classmates and I decided to "play hooky" at noontime so we could catch a public transit bus to Main Street in downtown Zanesville, to see a movie premiere parade.

The movie to be shown at the Liberty Theater on South Fifth Street was "The Court Martial of Billie Mitchell," staring Natalie Wood and Tab Hunter.

Needless to say, we got "busted" and our penalty was one hour detention after school for the next five school days.

Words of advice come from my mother saying, "Don't spend your lunch money for a bus ticket again."

Taking Mary Home Too Soon

by Bertha Burkhart of Woodsfield, Ohio
born in 1921

On May 28, 1921 my mother was experiencing labor pains. Dad, driving horse and buggy, brought their friend, Mary, to midwife the delivery, but the labor pains stopped. After a discussion, Dad returned Mary to her home only to return home finding Mom in advanced labor. Dad experienced midwifery, as I, Bertha Louella Christman, was born.

My earliest memory was of my sisters laughing, carrying me on their arms between them.

When I was three years old, we moved to a nearby farm my parents bought. My invalid grandmother, in her bed, was placed on a horse-drawn sled to be transported to our new home. I rode on Uncle Alex's lap on his horse's saddle.

Our house was of sturdy oak, but in need of plaster and paint repair. As they removed old plaster, I was warned to avoid plaster dust in my eyes. Our 220-acre farm seemed a refuge for blacksnakes. The old couple who had lived there protected them.

Summertime was barefoot time and a time when someone would be limping because of stepping on a nail protruding from boards lying where they had fallen from old buildings.

My brother and sisters helped Dad remove the old clapboard barn roof. They thought it funny when they took me, a three-year-old, to the top and called Mom to see. Mom saw nothing funny and ordered me safely brought down. A new galvanized standing seam roof was placed on the barn.

Being a nosey three-year-old, I found Grandma's heart pills and discovered I didn't need water to swallow them. Very shortly, Dad asked me to hand him an oil can. I said, "I can't Daddy," as I went into convulsions. My sister held me as Mom called our old doctor on the oak wall phone. I wondered why my body was stiffening and my eyes rolling. The cause of my attack was the pretty pink pills which fell from my apron pocket when Mom put me in bed. Dear old Dr. Steward came five miles by horseback. He pumped my stomach. My mind still pictures the tear-stained faces of my family round my bed when I awakened.

A broken floorboard along one side our buggy shed seemed, to me, an ideal base for a commode. A wooden box, less top and bottom, was placed over the floor opening. A horse collar, soft-side-up placed over the top opening for comfortable relief for a four-year-old. Strips of shoebox tissue wrapped on a corncob hung by bailing wire nearby for a soft wipe. I, the inventor.

The outhouse was my favorite place to play. The seat, an imaginary cook stove. A large kettle covered the large hole. An old coffee pot fitted the small hole, with my parents' disapproval.

Making wallpaper paste, we girls papered the walls with pages from wallpaper catalogues and placed Sears or Montgomery Ward catalogue wiping supply and shining pictures to enjoy wishing for items pictured near the seat.

Wasps built nests in the roof of the outhouse. Our brother laughed as he threw green apples against the roof, a sister inside. Sometimes he hooked the mattock under a corner of the outhouse and rocked it back and forth. My brother was well practiced in avoiding the hail of clods and stones as a sister burst out the door to retaliate with her weapons.

Accidentally, my doll fell into the toilet. I retrieved the doll and cleaned it. Grandma's nurse refused to clean it for me.

My sister and I walked two miles to Miltonburg School. My sister rode on to Woodsfield High School with classmates. On rainy mornings, our dad and two blanked horses took us to school. When walking, we walked through fields, woods, and Andy Wagner's yard to avoid mud, snow, and ice on unimproved roads. Our path led us between Andy's garden and bedroom window, where many mornings Johnny and Frankie, in their little white gowns, waved to us. On hot evenings, Andy gave us a cool drink on our way home.

The path ended at Main Street, Miltonsburg, by the home of elder brother and sister Seif and Emaline Schell. They sometimes invited us to stop by on our way home, once to see their black and orange painted stair banister. Another time, she showed us a cigar box containing gold coins. Neighbors found him with pick and shovel digging a grave in the family plot to bury Emaline, who had fallen down the cellar steps and died. He was told about necessary burial laws. I remember attending her wake at five years old.

Family of Bertha and Michael Burkhart in 1984.

Living three quarters of a mile from our neighbors, our family, and walking to visit them. About halfway we met our neighbors walking to visit us on a beautiful sunny day.

A neighbor, seeming to draw the future to himself, owned the first radio in our area during The Depression. Placing the earphone on my head, he held me on his lap to hear KDKA. He planned Midland Park. Charlie used the first steam tractor to farm in our area. He hired neighboring farmers with their horses and dump scrapers to build a 1500-foot by 200-foot pond, 33 feet at deepest end and 50-acre golf course. My dad, George M. Christman, helped build both.

A beautiful large dance hall where dances were held each Saturday night, a specially housed generator provided electricity for lights and preserving food for a refreshment stand. I was nine years old when Dad asked me to be his square dance partner. Dancing filled my heart forever.

Dad, with neighbor farmers, their horses, and dump scrapers, built another pond a few miles away, Shadow Lake, for a "well to do" insurance executive of Conservative Life Insurance Company in Wheeling West Virginia. His hobby was raising buffalo, deer, elk, moose, and peafowl. The caretaker was a family friend. I spent much time there when I was a small child. The farm was surrounded by an 18-foot high woven wire fence.

It was said that Mr. Peters, a large man, ate a whole chicken at one meal. I remember him coming in his chauffeur-driven limousine wearing a black suit and red bandana around his neck to remind him of his humble beginning. He bought chickens, which he dressed and prepared himself. He would pat my head and asked me to dance a jig, then gave me a quarter. My daddy was very proud of me and had me dance for friends to see. They rewarded with their pocket change that usually added up to a $1.98 pair of shoes at year's end.

Each fall, a farmers' institute was held in Miltonsburg for three days. Each morning opened by singing *America*. Close by schools were also in attendance. Students displayed farm and health-related posters. Farmers showed their superior products. Awards were given. Speakers spoke about health, crops, and improving ways of farming.

My first love came from a nearby school. There he was, wearing a sailor suit, sailor hat perched on blonde curls, blue eyes twinkling. In our teen years, we were square dancing. Sometimes he brought his guitar and sang to me. Ironically, his favorite song was, "I Only Want a Buddy, Not a Sweetheart." Sometimes he helped me feed chickens and collect eggs and ate with us. His family moved away.

I attended high school and was pursued by a handsome senior who earned a four-year agriculture scholarship to Ohio State University. After his graduation, we were married. Meanwhile, I worked at a sewing factory. One day after work, while napping on my bed, I dreamed my first love was passing on the street. I jumped up, rushed to the window, and as I brushed back the curtain, I passed out. My head hit the door. Cold air from under the door revived me. My roommates coming in asked why I was green. We realized I was overcome by gas. I will always believe my first love saved my life, by causing me to awaken!

We had no contact for several years. I attended his mother's funeral, and his wife's funeral, also his brother's wedding anniversary. I heard he had been jilted by a woman he had planned to marry and moved to assisted care. I decided to be his faithful friend, to bring him cheer by visiting him when in Barnesville. I explained I was not looking for another man after my husband's death. Our joy grew as we recalled our happy young years of caring for each other, holding hands, laughing. The call came; my first love had passed to his reward.

My beloved husband and I contributed 12 wonderful human beings to God, USA, Ohio, Monroe County, and Southeast Ohio. Our first daughter, taken by meningitis, Rebecca, was laid to rest on her fifth birthday in St. John the Baptist Catholic Cemetery, Miltonsburg, 1944-1949. When I look into the eyes of our 11 living children, I see a part of my beloved husband, Michael. Eleven professionals: Dental hygienist, computer copier repair man, two registered nurses, two teachers, masseuse, road machinery maintenance foreman, air quality mechanic, doctor of psychology, computer operator, farmer, CEO of Marion Rural Electric and later CEO of Mid-Ohio Energy Corporation, certified welder who bought, cut, and welded an 8-foot cross to replace the storm-destroyed cross topping St. John the Baptist Catholic Church in Miltonsburg. It stands straight and strong where Steve and neighbor parishioner, Paul Crum, placed it 26 years ago.

The customer-owned Telephone Central was first located in Vance Shlusher's Store, later in Henry Zwick home.

The bellowing of our bull at 2:30 a.m. awakened Dad (and all of us), not stopping to put on his pants. The bull ran through the swamp grass, Dad behind him. The bull ignored the open gate to the field where he belonged. He ran into the open barn, fell through a trap door. Dad, in hot pursuit, fell behind him. Dad's legs and thighs lacerated and bleeding allowed him no more sleep and prevented several days of rest.

I remember the pleasure of lying on my belly sipping cold water from the spring at the end of our cornfield. Hoeing corn was hot work causing thirst.

One school morning, my sister and I arose early to help Dad drive five hogs to Miltonsburg to be weighed on August Landefeld's scales. We were instructed to not allow the hogs to lie down in the muddy swamp around the overflowing watering trough by the roadside. Water from a hillside spring supplied the trough. Nature did not give hogs the ability to sweat. They need cold air or water to lie in to cool.

In 1943 I was plowing with a tractor. Looking ahead, I saw a shining object in the furrow. It was an 1882 silver dollar lying flat. The plow had skimmed over it.

Mom and Dad talked about their first car in the early 1900s. It always had to be pulled by horses to start it, a Maxwell.

We girls, afraid of hobos and tramps, didn't answer the knock on our door, but peeping out the window, saw the Zanol Products salesman drink hair tonic from a bottle in his bag. He napped in the shade before going on.

I loved Halloween. My high school girlfriend, Ruth Neuhart, sister Leora, and I masked, and Leora's husband drove us to Miltonsburg. We got out of the car at the upper end of town and walked in the middle of the street. The storekeeper's wife, standing in her doorway, yelled for us to bring back her steps. We walked on. Suddenly, three young men appeared, saying they were going to unmask us. My sister and I were strong farm girls. We fisted our attackers as we rolled in the ditch. My attacker called to his buddies, "This is a man! I know by how he fights!" My classmate remembered she was a lady, giving little resistance. They removed her mask but did not know her. They took her inside the store. Leora and I decided we needed to rescue her, risking another fight for our privacy. We walked into the store and lead her out with us. Several years later we revealed to the guys who we were.

Serenading a new married couple with many noisemakers. My favorite was an iron griddle I pounded with an iron bolt. Horsefiddles with a board on tension struck another board when the handle was turned. A serenader, shooting into the air, accidently shot the eaves of the house. Having the couple ride in a small trailer pulled through and around the nearest town, Woodsfield.

Sometimes our farm horse was in field with cows. I coaxed him to a stump and rode him bareback to bring cows to milk.

Hundreds of apple trees on our farm. Each fall, we kids picked up many burlap bags of fallen apples. With horses and wagon, Dad hauled the apples, and several cider barrels, to the cider mill. Dad sold barrels of sweet cider and kept one or two for sweet cider and hard cider to share with friends, and eventually, vinegar.

Little me sitting on cellar steps watched Dad place a spigot in the end of a barrel of cider. The spigot increased pressure in the barrel and caused the bung to hit the ceiling, followed by a stream of cider. I ran up the steps yelling, "Mom, bring the shotgun and shot it!"

A calf strayed to my clothesline and sucked on the sleeve of our son's surplice he wore to serve mass. It was ruined. I had a friend buy white nylon in the city. I sewed a new one in 1962.

For 20 years I bought junky antiques, repaired, retied springs, upholstered, caned furniture, dressers, washstands, beds, tables, secretary bookcases, chairs, pump organs, fainting couches, stands—251 pieces!

I had 76 first cousins. I made 20 370-page genealogy Cristman-Pfalzgraf 1748—books; Burkhart-Weisend 1528—Burkhart-Zwick-Wahl-Letzelter 1760-.

In the early 30s, Mom and Dad moved furniture, rolled up carpets. With music by our live-in violinist and chording on our Beckwith organ by Mom or older sister, resulted in square dance joy for neighbors and friends.

I recall a warm breeze streaming through the screened kitchen door in 1952. Dan, four, and Steve, two-and-a-half, playing on the floor. Suddenly our pet lamb ran to the top step outside and pressed its body against the screen. Opening the screen door, I heard dogs barking in the sheep field. Quickly I gave the boys extra toys, asking them to be good while I was away.

With our wonderful dog, Nick, I hurried to the barking. The sheep, huddled and shaking, were in a corner. Two dogs were killing a sheep nearby. I knew I needed to get the killers. With a soothing voice, I called the dogs. One ran away. One came slowly to me. I needed to lead it to be penned. I tore a strip of cloth from the bottom of my petticoat, placed it around his neck, and led him to the empty corn crib to be penned. The dog warden took the dog and found the one that ran away. Nick stayed by my side. Later, a dog we failed to catch was chasing our sheep. My husband and I took turns guarding the sheep nightly. We finally sold the sheep, tired of being vigilantes. We can still feel cozy and happy under the pink and white plaid, 40-year-old blanket made of our own sheep wool.

The mighty Shenandoah flew very low over my childhood home before crashing a few miles away. Seemed I could touch it.

In the 30s I saw the stored horse-drawn hearses replaced by motor hearses. Dad told of him and his horses pulling horse hearses in the Miltonsburg area taking deceased to cemeteries.

Grandson, Mark Burkhart, won World Champion Motorcycle Racer in 2008.

I live in underground home we built in 1980.

The Wringer Washer

by Jean Page of Strasburg, Ohio
born in 1930

As I was finishing the washing I left my six-year-old to mop up the basement floor while I went out to hang the last of the clothes. Rebecca had watched me put the clothes through the wringer. Then she put the mop through the wringer and burned up the washing machine motor.

That was in 1961. Today in 2009 I still do my laundry with a wringer washer but I have a little spinner washer to get the water out of the clothes. An hour or so in the basement and I'm done with the laundry for a week.

Clicking Mary Janes on the Road

by Mary J. Barrett of New Philadelphia, Ohio
born in 1930

Everyone called it camp, although later I knew it was called Duncanwood, Ohio. My father worked at the coal mine for many years until it was shut down in 1939. My mother used to say coal miners never lived very long, and I would pray every night for my father, that he would live a long life.

I was born in Duncanwood, Ohio in 1930 and spent the first seven years of my life there until we later moved to the country. This is some of my recollections of my first seven years of life in the camp.

The houses were all built on the side of the hill in a straight row, several rows, in fact. Each house had four rooms, not much of a cellar, and an outhouse. Water was brought in from the pump outside. There was one pump to every four or five houses.

We were a family of eight; Mother, Father, three girls, and three boys. My grandfather lived with us too, most of the time. When my oldest brother became of age, he joined the C. C. C. Camp.

We heated the house with a potbellied stove. That's irrelevant, I know, but I can remember my father using the soot to make me up for Halloween. We never had money for costumes.

Sometimes my brothers would go "serenading" newlyweds, and Mother would insist they take me. The bride and groom always treated us with lots of candy. We banged pots and pans for hours.

Food was always scarce at our house. I can remember Mother sending us to the Company Store, and when the miners were on strike, we could only get a dollar's worth of food, which was usually milk and eggs. The man at the meat counter always had a big bone for our dog, "Cubbie." We would take it home, and Mother would cook beans with it, and then Cubbie got it.

My mother could always bake the most fabulous bread, and she would set it on the windowsill to cool. It never failed that one of the neighbors below would come up to borrow a slice of bread.

There wasn't much in the way of entertainment for us, but sometimes we would go to the movies in Cadiz, Ohio. It was always on a Wednesday, because they would have a drawing for $100, and once my father actually won it. I should tell you, my siblings and I always got in free by lying about our age.

Once a year in Duncanwood, a large sewage truck came through. We called them the "Honeydippers," and you could smell the results of cleaning the outhouses all over camp. Doors and windows were closed for days. Also, we always could smell the sulfur from the shale dumps. They burned night and day.

There was a milk truck that came through the camp for those that could afford to buy milk. The kids at the camp would hop on the truck and steal ice when it stopped. My brother, Will, did this and ended up with a broken leg. The truck was still moving. At five years of age, it scared me silly. I thought for sure he was

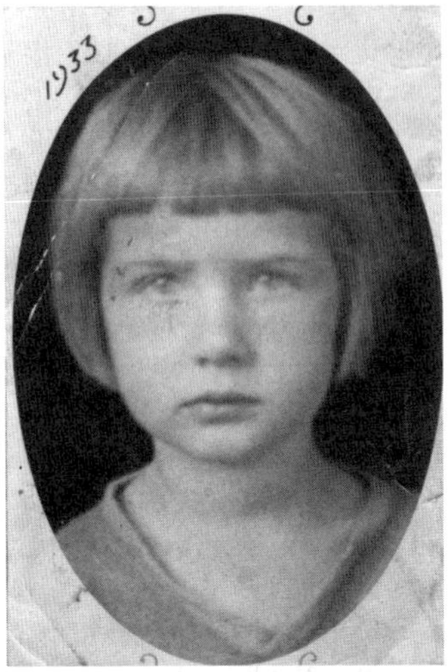

Mary Jane Howes Barrett in 1933.

dying.

Will was the one always trying something out, always inquisitive. He took an umbrella up on the coal shed and jumped to see if it would help him fly. He just got bruised a little. Also, the first radio I ever heard, Will put together with cans and wires and batteries. You could actually hear the WWVA station.

I had a best friend, "Margie." She lived down below us on the row, and we walked together to school. In the first grade, Mother had bought me a new pair of shoes, "Mary Janes," and I loved to click them on the road we traveled to school. Margie and I would take shortcuts up a hill and to a garbage dump. We never failed to find a dead cat or something we could bury and have a ritual or ceremony for, which often left us being late for school. We were such good friends; we would take turns chewing gum from recess to recess until school was out.

I can recall Mother taking a basket when the field corn was young, and Dad would drive us to the country, and she would fill up the basket for our supper. I am sure the farmers would not have objected, but I guess it was stealing.

There was a large house in the middle of camp where meetings of officials met with the miners. Sometimes they even had church there. On Christmas it was where the candy and fruit and toys were handed out to the miners' children. This came from the mine officials. The line was always very long. We tried to be the first ones there, and my brothers would pick out a toy and get our goodies, then take them home and go back through the line. Evidently, they never kept a record, because the overseer would say, "Kid, wasn't you here before?" It made our Christmas extra special.

My mother was never real well. She worked hard to keep the family going, clean, and healthy. Dad said she had something called a goiter. I remember her having a set of triplets that were stillborn because of it. Dad called me to see them, and I remember tears running down his face, and I could feel his grief.

Down over the hill from us was the deadly railroad tracks. We were told every day to stay away from them. Engines carrying the box cars with the shining black coal went up and down several times a day. When the trains weren't running, all the campers would take buckets and pitch coal that had fallen from the cars off the tracks. It sure helped keep us warm in the winter.

There was a little girl I knew, but had never got to play with that lived above us. One day, Mother said we were never to go up there. Later, she died with spinal meningitis.

I guess life was not as bad to me as it was to my parents. We finally moved to the country when I was seven. The mines closed down, and eventually Duncanwood was torn down. As for being a coal miner, my dad worked so hard and eventually died from black lung.

Model T Laundry

by F.R. Magness of Plainfield, Ohio
born in 1925

Growing up in rural Coshocton County on a farm before electricity. On Monday my mother would do the washing. The washer was a hand operated by a lever that was moved back and forth driving a flywheel that drove the inside parts.

My mother's dad, Charles Remick Randles, was an inventive sort, always working for things that made life easier. He decided to power the washer with my dad's Model T Ford. He fashioned two wooden pulleys, one for the washer, the other fixed to a rear wheel. The Model T was backed up to the wash house, rear wheel jacked up with a belt on the two pulleys.

And don't you know it worked! I don't believe my mother used it much.

Later we got a Maytag with a gas engine. That was real progress at our house.

Clayton's Smokes and Lauribel's Dimples

by Bernie Porter of Laurens, South Carolina
Born 1933

The Cardboard Box. Everyone has probably heard the phrase, "He couldn't punch his way out of a paper bag." I had a similar, very traumatic experience when I was about five or six-years-old, that really proved this point.

On warm summer days in Stockport, Ohio in the late 30's, we played outside all day unless it was raining. We had very few real toys, so we made do with what we had. One of my favorites was a big cardboard carton that breakfast cereal had been shipped in. With that box I could escape from the world. When I got in and pulled the four flaps over me, I was safe from anything. If the Indians would attack me it didn't matter how many arrows they shot; I was safe. If I would sit real still when the "bad guys" in the black hats came past chasing the "good guys" in the white hats, they would never see me. There was no limit to what that box could protect me from; even wild animal attacks.

One day I was inside, all closed up, when I heard my dad come into the driveway and get out of the car. I sat real quiet and still, intending to jump out and yell, "Boo!" after he got past. All at once, without a sound, my world turned upside down. Dad turned the box over, which left me sitting on the flaps. I didn't move for a little while and then I thought, "I'll still sneak up behind him and scare him." The only problem was, try as I may, I couldn't get out. I tried to stand up, but couldn't get my legs straight enough. Every way I moved trying to turn the box over wouldn't work. All I could do was to start yelling for help. Dad had gone on into the house and was talking to Mom so they couldn't hear me for a while. After a lot of yelling and crying they finally came and rescued me. By that time I was scared to death.

I don't remember the exact words Mom said, but it was something like, "The very idea leaving that boy trapped like that," and Dad was saying, "How did I know he couldn't get out?" Poor Dad, he only meant it in fun, but he ended up in the doghouse himself.

I never was claustrophobic up until then, but for a long time afterwards I had a little trouble with it and remember having some bad dreams. If you think this story is purely fiction, try it yourself sometime, or try to punch your way out of a paper bag.

Funny the things we remember from our very young years and how they affect out later life.

Secrets of the Stockport Bridge. Clayton Williams lived across the street from us in Stockport and although he was a couple years older than me, we hung around together. I sort of looked up to him as an older brother. One day about 1940 when we were trying to find something to do, he said, "Let's go down to the mill." Even though I was forbidden to go near the river, I said okay and we were off.

We messed around the mill a while, climbed down the steep bank below the mill and went out on the sand bar. After a while, Clayton said, "Come on, I will show you where I hide my cigarettes." This came as a real revelation to me. Talk about "hero worship." Here was one of my friends that really smoked.

We went over to the bridge and walked out on it about 30 feet. He said, "Now, you wait here and watch to make sure nobody comes along." I never was too sure what I was supposed to do if someone did come, but I waited and watched. He climbed over the railing, down the outside and disappeared under the bridge. After what seemed a long time, he came back up with a pack of cigarettes and lit one up. He puffed away for a while and flipped it over the rail into the river.

Then he said, "Since you were the lookout, I'll give you a couple puffs." Then I was really in heaven. After a few puffs he said, "I got to put 'em back now," and disappeared under the bridge again. When he came back up he told me never to tell anyone where they were, but if I wanted to get one I could. I remember thinking, fat chance of that.

I have thought of this a few times over the years and I have wondered which was the most dangerous; climbing under the bridge, or smoking the cigarette. I don't know about Clayton, but I never started smoking.

School Days: The Three R's. When I hear it is time for school to start again it makes me remember my first day of school at Windsor Rural School in Stockport in 1939. By the third grade, in 1942, they called it Stockport Elementary School. Even though that was nearly 70 years ago, it is something I will never forget. I could not figure why going to school was such a big deal, but I learned quickly that I didn't like it. I always did like "readin, but never really did catch on to the "riten" and "rithmetic" stuff.

My first grade teacher was Miss Mary Simpson. I don't remember how many years she taught school before she finally retired, but it was a long, long time. And I also don't know how long I endured school that first year before deciding to go home, but one day I walked out and went home to see my little sister. My mom was a bit surprised to see me home and did her best to convince me that school was mandatory, not optional. When she took me back to school, Miss Mary was a bit upset as well; I think because she didn't know I escaped!

One day when we were at recess, a classmate came to me and said, "We need another guy for our softball team, come on." I didn't have any idea what he was talking about. The only thing I had ever done with a ball was play catch. They said all I had to do was hit the ball with the bat and then run to first base. I watched a while and said, "Okay."

I took the bat, swung three times and everyone yelled, "Yer out!" So I left. After school that day he asked me why I quit and I said, "You said I was out."

So much for my ball playing career. I never played much ball after that.

The second grade went a little better. I was in a mixed first and second grade class with Miss Mary and my sister Marie was in the first grade on the other side of the room. The real trouble started the next year. For the third grade I had Miss Lauribel McCoy. She had dimples in both cheeks, was a little easier going and I liked her right away.

One day my mom made me wear short pants to school, which I never liked to do. At recess that day, while I was sort of leaning against the building, two older girls came by and started laughing at me. They said, "Look at the little girl with a skirt on." That had such an impact on me, that to this day I will not wear shorts. I do own one pair that I have worn to walk on the beach a couple times. I told Mom never to send me to school with shorts again, and she never did.

For a long time I thought if I ever found out who those girls were, I would give them one up along side the head, just for kicks, but the more I think about it, after years of seeing all the hairy bow-legged men all over the place wearing baggy shorts, golf shirts and running shoes with white socks, in public, I consider myself lucky that I will not even wear them in my own backyard. If I were to find those girls now, I would probably shake their hands.

I think that was the same year we were to put on the play, "The Three Little Pigs" and I was to be one of the pigs that got away. I was supposed to be picking apples when the big bad wolf came by and then jump into a barrel and escape by rolling down the hill. We used a stepladder with an apple on top for the tree and a wastebasket for the barrel. I climbed the ladder, grabbed the apple, jumped into the wastebasket and rolled right off the stage. The wastebasket was bigger at the top than the bottom, so it wouldn't roll straight. I remember the teacher saying, "Oh my!" But I don't remember what we did on opening night; I think I just rolled across the floor.

Needless to say, I never became an actor either.

Funny, the things one remembers from school days and how many of those things can control one's life later on.

The Stockport Dam Adventure. In 1937 we moved in with my Grandpa Porter in Stockport after my brother, Phil, was born. There wasn't much to do in Stockport, but we pretty much covered the whole area from the river and railroad track to the Big Spring Inn, and from Bald Eagle Creek to as far down the tracks as we cared to go. Of course Mom and Dad always told us to stay away from the river, which we ignored. For some reason I never had any fear of the water even though I couldn't swim. I guess it was because the "Old Elk Eye" flows so smoothly past the town. Dad always said he was really going to throw us in the river to make us learn to swim. That was always in the back of my mind, but I never really thought he would do it; he couldn't swim either.

One fall day in 1940 or 41, Phil and I decided to go over to Bald Eagle Creek to watch the fish. There were several pools where you could always see them. Of course it was a lot of fun to throw rocks at them and watch them scatter. Phil was only three and of course Mom said, "Now you hold his hand and don't let him get in the mud; he has his new sandals on." And of course I promptly forgot both.

After we got tired of watching the fish, I decided to walk across Bald Eagle trestle. Phil's legs were too short so I made him wait by the tracks. As I came back across, my classmate, Gene Maynard, was walking up the tracks from the other way. He said, "I'm just going over to check my dad's boat, come on." There were a couple of boats chained up there on the riverbank and one of them belonged to them. He started telling me how he helped run the trotline with his dad. He said, "I know how to row it, want to go for a ride?" Of course I said sure, but not my little brother. So I told Phil to stay put and not move from that spot until I got back.

When we got out from the bank of course we started downstream. I heard Phil crying and when I looked back, to my horror, there he was trying to follow us. He was stuck in the mud right at the water's edge. I told Gene we had to get back to him, but that wasn't so easy. With one on each oar, we did get back to the bank, but I couldn't get him out of the mud. We finally dragged the boat back to where he was and I sat in the bow, reached over and pulled him into the boat. Then the trouble really started: that action launched the boat back into the river.

There was mud all over everything: so much for the new shoes. Gene started yelling about all the mud and while we were talking about that, the boat got farther and farther out into the current and downstream. We were already passing the warehouses that hung out over the water and getting closer to the bridge all the time. Someone in one of the buildings was yelling about a bunch of kids in a boat. We really worked at it and finally got back to the bank. We left Phil in the boat and both got out and pulled it part way back to where it had been.

Gene was all worried about all the mud in the boat and figured he was going to catch it. I knew I had to get the mud off Phil. His feet looked like two Tootsie Roll pops. I scrubbed him up best I could and we headed for home. I knew there was a yardstick waiting for us at home so I stopped and filled my back pockets with gravel. Mom never did figure out why she broke the yardstick on me and I didn't even yell. Of course, I watched Phil get paddled and sort of gloated I guess. I told Mom he fell in the creek and she said, "At least you didn't go near the river."

It was many, many years before I ever told her the truth and she nearly had a heart attack then. Over the years I've thought about this many times and wondered how two eight-year-old boys ever got that boat back to the bank. The Lord had His hand on us that day for certain. If we would have gotten to the bridge, it would have been all over for sure: over the dam that is.

I never found out how Gene made out. Brother Phil passed away last year from cancer at age 67 and I don't think I ever talked to him about how much he remembered about it. One thing for sure, as long as my "rememberer" works, I won't forget it.

My Most Memorable Christmas. Way back in the 30's in Stockport, Christmas was a big deal, even though we usually only got one gift and some clothing that we really needed. One year, about a week before Christmas, my sister Marie and I decided to do a little snooping. We had seen Mom going into the back bedroom that wasn't used with a big sack. She didn't think we saw her, but you know how kids are.

One day, she went over to the neighbor's and we saw our chance. Behind the dresser, way back in the corner, were two packages, one with Marie's name and one with mine. We pulled them out and after shaking them a few times, we ripped the paper just enough that we could see what they were. I'm not sure what mine was, some board game I think, probably Chinese checkers.

Boy, were we happy, but it took a while to "soak in." All of a sudden it hit us! What were we going to do Christmas morning, since we already knew what we were getting? We agreed that we would do our best to act surprised. I think we pulled it off okay and I don't think Mom ever found out, at least I never told her.

Stockport Ohio Bridge (no longer standing), dam and old mill.

But I learned a great lesson from that. There are a lot of things you are better off not to know in this world. That was over 65 years ago, but never again was I even a little tempted to try to find my Christmas gifts. They could have been on the table covered with a sheet and I wouldn't have looked.

The real meaning of Christmas has been so completely covered up and forgotten that it has been many years since any gifts that the world has to offer is of any interest to me. We are much better off spending some quiet time remembering what Christmas really is: a celebration of Christ's birth and reflecting on the gift He gave to us. That will take away any chance of having a miserable Christmas.

Another Christmas I remember in Stockport was the time my Sunday school teacher at the United Methodist Church chose me to say a poem at the annual Christmas play. I was a little, skinny, bashful kid and there was no way I was going to do it. After many threats and "You can do its" by her and my mother, I finally agreed—if Mom would sit in the front row with me.

The funny thing is I still remember the poem: "Christmas comes but once a year, and I tell you its mighty handy. Now that I've said my little piece, give me a sack of candy."

If I just would have been able to remember my studies in school and other things that really mattered the way I've remembered that, I could have been a rocket scientist instead of a machinist. Oh well, I did work over 40 years before retiring.

Merry Christmas to all and to all a good night.

Grandpa's Mantel Clock. One of my most cherished family heirlooms is my Grandpa Porter's mantel clock. He didn't even have a mantel, just a wooden shelf beside the chimney for the pot-bellied stove. We got our Saturday night bath in a big washtub in front of that stove. Water from the pump out front was heated on the gas range in the kitchen and Mom added it as it was needed.

The clock always fascinated me from the time we moved into Grandpa's small stucco house on Main Street in Stockport. I loved to watch the steel striker hit the big spring and always counted the number of times it struck. Grandpa not only taught my sister Marie, and me to count that way, he also taught us the Roman numerals from the face.

The Seth Thomas clock was made in the late 1800's and I think it probably was a wedding present to Grandpa and Grandma when they were married in 1896. My father, Walter Porter, was born in 1907 and his story of the history of the clock is this: he said when they moved to another farm in 1908 or 1909, in a farm wagon, they put their two most prized possessions, him and the clock, on top of the furniture, wrapped in blankets. Somewhere along the rutted dirt road, the wagon hit a big bump and they both fell off and rolled down a bank. He said neither one was hurt, so they were gathered up and resumed the trip.

The clock was passed on to Dad when Grandpa died. Dad gave it to me before he died and said he wanted it to go down to the eldest son. I used it for a while, but it was in sad shape. Somewhere along the line, Grandpa must have decided it should be brightened up, so he gave it a coat of varnish, right over the brass trim and everything. After it sat in the attic for a while, I decided to restore it. The brass trim was cleaned up, but as I started taking it apart, I noticed how the walnut veneer was peeling and missing in several places and quickly lost interest. I put it back in the attic where it stayed for about 35 more years.

A couple of years ago I got to thinking about it and decided if I was ever to finish it, I'd better get moving, so I started again. I was able to remove some veneer from the back where it wouldn't show and replaced the missing pieces. The old finish was carefully removed, then sanded, and refinished. The project is now complete, right down to the original "salt cellar" inside the clock that Grandpa kept filled with coal oil. He said the vapor from it kept the clock mechanism lubricated. He must have had something there since when I cleaned it up and put it back together it ran.

The ends of the shafts are worn enough that it doesn't keep real good time, but it works. My oldest son, Jeff, now has it and will save it for my grandson, Mark. It looks like new again and with a little TLC it may last three or four more generations.

First Born, First Bathed

By Jeanette Rubens of Murrieta, California
Born 1921

When I see a woman with six or more children and they all look clean and well groomed; I know they didn't take their baths on Saturday morning in a tin wash tub like I did.

Every Saturday morning my mother would fill up the wash tub with warm water and all the younger children bathed first. I was the last and by that time the water was cold and dirty, I hated it, but that was the way it was when you lived in the country and had no bathtub.

I hated being the oldest; like the time it was Christmas. My parents couldn't afford to buy us toys; so Christmas Eve we went to the community Christmas tree where all the poor children got donated toys. All the younger ones went first. When it was my turn I saw a beautiful blond doll I was sure I would get, but the girl in front of me took it and I got one with one arm missing. I remember I cried a river. I kept the doll as a reminder if I ever got married and had children, they would never have to go to a place for second hand toys.

Later in the evening they gave out tickets for a drawing. The winner would get a basket of food for the holidays. Well you guessed it, my number was called. I was so shocked I couldn't respond and a lady called out for me. When they gave me the basket they asked me my name and I couldn't remember my own name! How's that for being embarrassed?

All my life I thank God I have been able to care for my own, but I'll always remember my parents did the very best they could for their family and I'll always love them for it. I thank God for giving me to them.

Indeed the Old Days Were Good

By Sue Todd Edwards of Zanesville, Ohio
Born 1947

Growing up in Zanesville in the 50's and 60's was great, at least for me. I know it was a time of racial turmoil, but I was never aware of it. There were children of different races in the schools I attended. Our doctor, Dr. J.D. Mitchell, was African-American (at that time he was considered "colored") as was a local policeman, Bobby Martin, who was a good friend of our family. They were always a part of our lives and I never even thought about their race. If there were community problems my parents kept them from me.

I remember so many things about those good old days and indeed, they were good. I remember always looking forward to the church picnic. Trinity Lutheran Church and its members were a large part of our family life. My parents, Chuck and Dola Todd, grandparents, aunts, uncles and cousins all attended there. Our church picnic was held at Rehl's Grove off of West Main St. in Zanesville. The service was held outside with a picnic lunch followed by games and prizes. Water balloons were considered the ultimate weapon at the Grove, the enemy of most parents and the cause of grief for a lot of kids. We spent the entire day there and ended it with the adult's softball games. Our Sunday school superintendent, Walter Mees, always had "Blackjack" gum in his pockets and he never passed a child without giving them a piece. To this very day I enjoy finding that gum (or Teaberry) in a store.

TVs were new. Our neighbors, the Merriams, had one because the father sold them along with radios, both the regular ones and "HAM" ones. We were invited to their home on Saturday mornings to watch Howdy Doody. Later we got a TV. It was small, black and white and received only one channel. You had to turn it on five minutes before you wanted to watch it so it could "warm up." Later, when TVs became more accessible, there were more shows to watch. Saturday morning cartoon shows consisted mostly of Mickey Mouse, Tom and Jerry and Underdog. Afternoons and evenings we would watch things like Laurel and Hardy, Roy Rogers with his horse, Trigger and Bullet, the German Shepard, The Lone Ranger, Zorro and The Cisco Kid.

Summers were fun. They were full of baseball games, (which didn't have to be supervised by an adult) swimming, running through the sprinkler, walking or jumping in mud puddles after a rain, catching lightening bugs, jumping rope, doing the hula hoop and riding bikes. Playing cards were put in the spokes of the bike so everyone would think you had a motorcycle! The neighborhood kids would gather for games of Hide-n-seek and Red Rover. "Red rover, red rover, send "Linda" right over!" What fun! In the quiet times we loved to read. I shared many adventures with The Bobbsey Twins, Nancy Drew, the Hardy Boys and Lassie. Speaking of Lassie, I was lucky enough to have a purebred Collie named Lady. I remember well my dad's hesitancy at having to spend $20.00 for a dog. There were other dogs available, but with the TV shows and the books, my heart was set on a Collie. She was one of my, several, best friends.

A Sunday afternoon was spent doing your homework, listening to the record player and the 78 RPM records, visiting friends and going out to buy ice cream with the

50-cent piece your grandpa gave you for being quiet during church. That one coin bought five ice cream cones. One for each of my siblings and one for me! When we got back home we would lick the Green Stamps that came with the weeks groceries, and put them in books. When there were enough books filled we would take them to the redemption store and trade them for really great things - like toasters or silverware!

Dinner was ready and on the table every night at 4:00. After dinner everyone had their assigned jobs to do. Some would rid the table. Others washed, dried or put away the dishes. No one left the kitchen until that was done. There was no "I'll do it later!" On Saturdays we went to my aunt's and uncle's—the Appleman's—farm and brought back a chicken. Dad killed it in the backyard, soaked and plucked it. Mom fixed it for Sunday's lunch. I also remember my grandparents going turtle hunting. Grandpa would cut the turtle's heads off and throw them in the alley. Their mouths continued to snap after their heads were severed. To this day I refuse to eat turtle soup and I'm not too big on chicken! About once a year we had a treat. My mom would call on the phone (all phone numbers in our area started with "Gladstone") and order something from "Chicken-On-Wheels." We'd stand in the yard anxiously awaiting the delivery. It certainly was more exciting than today's 30 minute pizza deliveries! Perhaps it was because it was a really rare occasion!

Sue Edward's father, Chuck Todd, and uncles, Bill and Bob Todd.

When I was in 7th grade I was allowed to baby-sit. I was certainly proud of those 25-cents an hour I earned, but then it went a long way. I could go to the store and buy movie magazines for, you guessed it, 25-cents. If I wanted I could get two 45 RPM records for $1.00. I could buy lunch at "The Hut" on McIntire Avenue during lunch break from Roosevelt Jr. High School. Then the teachers preferred you NOT eat at school. They wanted you to leave for those 45 minutes. The "Westview Grill" on Dresden Road served a bologna sandwich, chips and a drink for a quarter. You could always go there after school, if you had a nickel, and buy candy cigarettes or wax bottle shaped candies with different colored sugar water in them. There were several in a package so you and your friends could enjoy them on the walk home.

There were so very many good things about the old days that I could list but it would take forever. So I will mention just a few. The weather in southeast Ohio was always changing. My little sister, Sherry, was born in April of 1953. When mom went to the hospital there was three-inches of snow on the ground. When she brought the baby home, 3 days later (yes, hospital visits were allowed for 3 days!) I was outside picking violets to welcome her with.

There were two outdoor movie theatres and two or three indoor ones down town. The 1st movie I ever saw was "The Ten Commandments." I remember going to the downtown theatres with friends when I was older. It cost us 25-cents to get in. Also when I was seven I would walk two blocks to catch the bus every Saturday morning and ride to downtown. I would then walk from the bus stop in front of the 5&10 at the corner of 5th and Main Street to our church on South Seventh St. for Confirmation classes. After two and a half hours there I would walk to The Tasty Burger on Market St (I think) and get lunch. From there I would walk across the 5th St. Bridge (it came out beside the Lind Arena, a skating facility, on Linden Ave.) up to the Zanesville Art Institute at the corner of Maple and Adair Avenues. After art classes I would walk home to Leonard Avenue. A seven- year-old could do that then because Maple was only two lanes and no one wanted anyone else's children - for any reason!

I remember Hall's Brown Cow, a restaurant, on Maple at Princeton, although then it was called Livingston Ave. Later McDonalds built the 1st fast food restaurant a few doors north of there. My father purchased the house that sat where McDonalds is today and moved it to Leonard Avenue for a rental property. The entire neighborhood and some of the townspeople gathered to watch that house come riding up the street on the back of a flatbed truck owned by Dingy Movers.

This will be my last memory of the good old days. I feel I've saved the best for last. In the winter, when it snowed, my dad would contact the city and arrange to have Bell Street blocked at Wabash and Princeton. Bell Street didn't go all the way through from Taylor to Maple like it does today. The entire neighborhood kids: Todds, Thomes, Waltermires. Merriams, Hueys, Kinneers, Clarks, Colleys, Huffmans, McGees etc. would gather at the top of Leonard Avenue. A bonfire in my Grandparent Paynter's yard was built to keep us warm, (adults always stood guard) and we would sled ride for hours. What a thrill to race with our friends to see who could go the farthest. It was nothing to pass over Bell Street and continue on down the street. Snowball fights (friendly ones) would take place on the walk back up the hill. After building snowmen and snow forts we'd stand by the fire to warm up so we could go sledding again. A neighbor, George Eppley, and my dad built a wooden bobsled. It held six people and wow, could it go. We had to take turns, but each kid got theirs. Sometimes we would attach individual sleds to the bobsled and many of us would go down the hill at once. It was great fun until the bobsled stopped and the attached individual sleds didn't. I don't recall anyone getting hurt or anyone complaining about things. It was just a fun time for the entire neighborhood and their friends.

Growing up in Zanesville was great. Things were simple and safe then. Progress happened but it didn't seem to happen as fast here. It was a nice time when you could enjoy the simpler things and the slower pace. Writing this article has made me very nostalgic. It makes me appreciate the family I had then, and the friends and the good times. A lot of those people and things are gone now but the memories will always last. I am soooo glad I got to grow up in the 'Good old Days' in southeastern Ohio.

Farm Life and Earl's Medical History

by Clara Mae Bean Law of Lore City, Ohio
born in 1927

I, Clara Mae Bean, now Mrs. John Law, born March 24, 1927, can remember the depression in the 1930s. Farmers grew their food. My dad, Carl Bean, grew wheat and corn and took both to be ground into flour and cornmeal. Mother made homemade bread from the flour and cornmeal into corn bread, mush, and pancakes. Pancakes were fried on the coal stove heated with wood and coal with a reservoir on right side of the stove and a warming closet on top. We'd eat mush while it was warm with milk on it. When the mush was cold, Mother would fry it light brown with meat fryings or lard.

Milked cows by hand—no refrigerator. Saved milk morning and night in a pan.

As there was six in the family, two brothers, two sisters, the farmhouse was two stories. We slept upstairs with no heat.

Raised our meat—hogs, beef, and chickens and turkeys. Grew a garden—canned and cold packed all vegetables in quarts and half gallons and stored in a cellar under the house. That was where milk was stored for daily use.

Used a hand pump from a water well for water to use and to fill the reservoir on the stove. Had warm or hot water to wash hands or wash dishes. Always had a ten-quart bucket of water setting in the sink to drink and when real cold, it would freeze in the kitchen.

We all got up of a morning and ate breakfast together, mostly rolled oats until we could afford to purchase Corn Flakes and that was a treat. We were poor like everyone else, but we never went hungry.

Could purchase 25 pounds of flour 95 cents and sugar, 25 pounds $1.95. Sold eggs, 12 cents a dozen, sold milk $1.25—100 pounds. Could buy two weaning pigs for $5.00, and sell cattle two to three a pound.

We grew cane and had it made into molasses and used that on pancakes and did baking. Also tapped maple trees and boiled the sap down to syrup to use instead of sugar.

My first four grades of school, I always had to walk one to two miles to the school. Then the last eight grades I had to walk one-and-a-half miles to meet a school bus.

At grade school, I took my turn carrying drinking water in a ten-quart bucket for students to drink. All drank from same dipper, unless a student was fortunate enough to have its own cup.

Had no electric in grade school. When we had entertainment at night, we used oil lamps or lanterns. At our home, we used oil lamps. I never had electric to use till after I married my dear husband, John Law, June 19, 1946. We had access to electric in December, 1946 in our farmhouse.

Before this time, my mother washed clothes on a washboard, then used a gasoline engine to run a washing machine that had a wringer to wring out the clothes through round rollers. Then hung clothes on a line to dry. When cold, they'd freeze.

Back then, most everything had to be ironed. Irons would be heated on coal cook stove. Didn't have soap powder or liquid. We made lye soap from lard, lye, borax, etc.

Most every farmer had an orchard and had kinds of fruit: apple, peaches, pears, plums, and etc. Also grapevines. My mother would make apple butter by the gallon and seal it with sealing wax. She'd dry apples, peaches and sweet corn and store in gallon jugs to be used in winter.

We had a "separator" to use to separate cream from milk. Used a "churn" to make butter from cream and sold cream 50 cents a pound.

I had two teachers that taught all eight grades in a one-room schoolhouse. The other six grades I was taught in a two room schoolhouse and all had an outdoor "privy." No tissue paper, catalog! We all carried metal lunch buckets.

All of our clothes were made by our mothers. Our schoolbooks were "hand me downs" used by other former students. Reading, writing, arithmetic, and geography and spelling.

I can remember the "gypsies"—bums and hobos. Bums were looking for work. Hobos wanted to work but was none, as no one had any money to pay. A dime was precious.

By not having electric, the way we listened to a radio, had a "wind mill" to charge batteries. We'd pray for the wind to blow, so we would listen to Lum and Abner, Amos and Andy, Fibber McGee and Molly and others.

My brother Earl has had a very stressful life with several tragedies. He was born October 19, 1921 to Carl and Grace (Casterline) Bean in Washington Township north of Antrim. The first school he attended was MaryAnn Valley, located below Middlebourne.

When he was seven years old, it was on a Saturday and Everett Mack was with him. He stepped on a broken glass bottle and cut his foot clear across. We lived at the S Bridge, west of Middlebourne, and Mother put brown sugar on it to stop the bleeding and Dad had gone to a funeral. Dad made him a pair of crutches.

When he was nine years old, Earl fell on an ax and cut his right hand. We lived at the Gray Farm, north of Antrim. A neighbor, Will Harding, took him to Antrim to Dr. Paul Fairchild and put two clamps in his hand.

When he was 16 years old on January 5, 1938 and a student at Madison High School, he was helping his dad husk corn for Uncle Melvin Casterline using a corn husker machine which was powered with a tractor and got his left hand in the rollers. He had to have it amputated five inches above the wrist. He was in the hospital five weeks and five days. He learned to do everything with one hand and the use of an artificial hook except tie shoes or a necktie. He had an artificial hand for when he dressed up.

He was also a very popular boy with schoolmates and friends. It was in the late 1930s he learned to play the guitar and I would sing "Oh My Darling." When he was dating, he would ask for to'd-me-do'd (perfume $.10 Sweet Pea).

He married Pauline Moffett July 21, 1943 and had two sons, Dale Delbert, born June 24, 1944 and Paul Earl born November 27, 1946.

At one time, Earl owned 342 acres, milked cows, and farmed. They purchased the former Bob and Ella Ogg farm. On April 18, 1947 at 12:14 a.m., an oil light that was keeping baby chicks warm got knocked over and the house caught fire. It burned completely down along with his truck. He purchased an older house in Antrim, tore it down and with help from his dad and others, dug a basement and built a new house.

In the 1950s Earl went to the hospital with phlebitis, blood clots in the leg. February 7, 1966 a shed roof collapsed from a large amount of snow and came down on his son, Dale, and broke his pelvis in two places.

November 6, 1969 Earl had a heart attack and another one on December 26, 1969. Due to health problems, he was forced to sell the farm and had a public auction January 4, 1969. Temperature was below zero.

They purchased property at 1423 Woodlawn Avenue, Cambridge, Ohio in December of 1968.

In May of 1974, he was using a push lawn mower on a slope and slipped and got his right foot cut, resulting in four toes being amputated. August 1975 Pauline had a stroke.

In 1979, he had the house lifted and put a basement under it. During a strong wind, the house was blown off the supports and into the basement. They tore the house down and had a new one built. They lived in a camper while the house was being built and moved into the new house September 9, 1979.

May 19, 1994 he had a diabetes attack and was hospitalized in Columbus.

On April 3, 2000, he and Pauline were in an accident with their truck. They were taken to Guernsey Memorial Hospital and at midnight he had a heart attack and put in the ICU. Then on April fifth he was taken by ambulance to Riverside Hospital in Columbus. A catheterization was performed and four blockages were found. On April sixth, Thursday, he had bypass heart surgery for the blockages. They took a vein out of the left leg and he was dismissed to his home April 11. May first he went back to Columbus and again May eighth. Infection had formed in his left leg where the vein had been removed. A nurse came twice a day for a week and then once a day afterwards. In November, 2000 the skin had grown back.

November 2, 2001 he was taken to the hospital and was very nauseated, resulting in gallbladder surgery. He was dismissed on November 5, 2001.

January 2002 had a bout of diarrhea and went to the doctor February fourth.

August 7, 2002 had much concern for Dale, as he had double pneumonia and not able to drive the semi.

In December 2003, a doctor found he had an eye problem. He went to Canton to a specialist on December 15th.

February 4, 2003, Wednesday, Earl fell outside feeding his dog. It took three guys to carry him into the house. An ambulance was called and took him to the Medical Center. On Friday February sixth, they did surgery on top of the foot at little toe. On March 14th, his grandson, Kevin Bean, took his own life. The day of his burial services, March 18th, Earl was readmitted to the hospital. Then April second he was transferred to Grant Hospital in Columbus and Monday April fifth had leg surgery from knee to foot to repair the vein. On April seventh he was brought back to Cambridge Medical Center. On April 19th went back to Columbus for check-up and doctor took out the staples and back to the Medical Center. He was then dismissed to his home April 21st.

However, he could not keep the foot healed throughout the summer until Pauline was admitted to the hospital on October 12th on her 81st birthday. Her death was November second at 12:30 a.m. with burial Friday,

November 5, 2004.

With health nurses, Paul and Sharon's assistance, he was able to stay in his home until June 9, 2004. His foot problem was back and again had to go to the hospital on July seventh. He had nose bleeds and back home July 15th, then back to the hospital July 18th with a foot bleed and to extended care July 25th. He was there until he was transferred to rehab at Health Care Center in August 11, 2005.

November 21, 2006: to the hospital with two kinds of infection in leg and in blood. Back to Care Center and back to hospital December third and in ICU. Back to Care Center and Hospital, three trips and Sunday, December 10th back to hospital and in room 218. Back to Care Center December 19, 2006.

Johnny and I went to see him Thursday, December 20th and he was setting in his wheelchair. He took worse that eve with blood pressure and oxygen low. The nurse called for Paul to come.

Then we were back to see him Friday forenoon and he was very short of breath and very restless. He knew us and asked questions rationally. He cried and spoke about his dad and shouted when he was so uncomfortable. That eve around 5:20, the nurse called Paul and said his blood pressure had dropped to 60 and deteriorating fast.

December 4, 2006, day before Christmas, all of the family members stayed a time by his bed all day. Deceased December 25, 2006 at 5:17 p.m.

Grandparents Along the River

By Norma Jean Dye Antill of Rinard Mills, Ohio
Born 1937

The author of this story is the grandmother of six: Jennifer, Tiffany, Lauren, Amy, Nicodemus and Anna and great grandmother of one: Leigha. I, Norma Jean Antill, wife of L. Dale Antill, plan to tell them of my brother, Roger Dye, and I growing up in Rinard Mills, Newport, Brownsville area of Ohio.

Living along the Little Muskingum at Rinard Mills, we did have a riffle for wading and a hill for sleigh riding—so slick that Roger slid under the feed storage building and had to have stitches in his head. Kite flying was also a fun afternoon. Our parents owned the general store in 1943 that was built in 1886 where people brought eggs and chickens to sell or barter for their groceries. Coca Cola sold six bottles for twenty-five cents. There was a feed store and grinding machine and a corn sheller. There was a loafing bench along the front porch and also a bench around the store inside so loafing and telling stories went on the year round.

Rinard Mills General Store.

Norma Jean attended her first grade in a two-room schoolhouse, which later became her home and at the present is a United Methodist Church. We knew all our neighbors by name and had a concern for each one.

We lived a short time at Newport along the Ohio River, a beautiful river town in 1949. Then we moved to Brownsville (Jolly) and my parents built a country store. This town had a two-room school with two teachers for grades one through eight.

We rode bicycles with our friends and delivered Grit paper with a friend old enough to drive. We attended church and enjoyed the Grange Hall with its meetings and square dances.

Grandparents were also an important part of my growing up years. Cora Fox Dye, Wynona Edwards Barnhouse and Sarah Edwards Barnhouse, my grandmothers for an average of forty years. Oh, the wonderful memories.

Cora, the farmwife, mother of six, didn't have a clock in 1903 so she used a rock in her yard with the sun for the time. When they moved to their Rinard Mills' farm from Dye Ridge and the men would be in the fields she would blow a conch shell and they would know it was meal time. My dad has said that sound was really welcome at the end of a long row of hoeing corn in the 1930s. At meal times, the men ate first, then maybe the plates would have to be washed before the children and women could eat. One uncle would not eat at a table with 13 seated.

Each grandchild upon high school graduation received a quilt that she had cut, sewed the top and quilted. She helped many families with the birth of their children; several people still speak of her helpfulness and kindness.

The dog would get into the hen house and eat eggs. A remedy was to open an egg and sprinkle pepper into it, put the egg into the dog's mouth and hold it shut until the pepper took effect. This taught the dog not to suck eggs.

She always had a glass covered candy dish with the candy called lozenge; pink or white. Cora now lies buried beside her husband of sixty-one years in a lonely country cemetery at Jericho.

Wynona, the wife of a public laborer, mother of five, was motherless at age twelve making for a lonesome little gal. She was a great homemaker, canning all summer; jars of vegetables and fruits, some with sugar and some without because a son developed sugar diabetes at an early age. This she seemed to accept without any self-pity.

Doing laundry on the washboard, my mother remembered going to school in the morning and her mother scrubbing clothes and still being busy at it when the children returned home in the afternoon. In later years, the washing machine would have a wringer and was powered with a gasoline motor. Then in 1942, Rural Electric came into the country and helped with lights, motors, toasters, etc.

She owned a rug loom in later years and spent many hours tearing and sewing strips of clothes into balls to be made into beautiful rag rugs. Then she sold them for a small amount of money. Mom B., as I called her, used to make me the circle skirts of the fifties out of printed feed sacks - very pretty. She made the most delicious potato salad dressing. Her quilts were more than beautiful and she gave me one as a wedding gift. She made soap from lye and hog fat. It made lots of suds. I always was invited to spend some summer vacation time with my grandparents in Newport and they had a bathroom which we didn't. There was always a thoughtful gift of bath salts for me.

Seeing three sons die had to be so hard on a mother. Her husband worked on the river barges on the Ohio River and I remember meeting at the river's edge to get him home for his days off work. Wynona now lies buried beside her husband of fifty-four years in the family plot at Newport Cemetery.

Sarah, mother of six, was my great grandmother and I only knew her for the first ten years of my life. She and her husband lived and farmed on Middle Island in the Ohio River. A grandchild, Mildred, was born on this island. Sarah now lies buried beside her husband of forty-eight years at the Newport Cemetery.

Ary Ridgeway Dye, a mother who gave five of her seven sons to serve in the Civil War, was my great-great grandmother. Benjamin Franklin, Bazil Riggs and Isaac served from Monroe County, Ohio and returned home; Joshua died at Morris Island, South Carolina and Elam died at Carthage, Tennessee. These men are descendants of their great grandfather, James Riggs, a Revolutionary War soldier. Riggs settled and built a log cabin 1797 at New Matamoras. Ary was given a pension, so she is remembered by Norma Jean's grandfather, Forest Hunter Dye, as having sugar on the table. Benjamin Franklin came home to Monroe County and raised a family giving them the names of Civil War officials - Benjamin Franklin, Jr., Forest Hunter, Marcellus Sheridan, Sherman, James Willard and Virginia.

The Occupied Outhouse and Insecure Undies

by Mrs. Frank Sayre of Senecaville, Ohio
born in 1933

When I was a kid, we lived on a farm and had cows. Grandpa milked them and then would let the milk set for a couple days and skim the cream off. Then he would put it in this big wooden churn and would churn it until it made butter.

Grandma made the cottage cheese from the milk, cooked it until it thickened to curds, then put in a cloth bag that we had gotten sugar in, and hung the bag on the clothesline to drain. Had to keep the birds from landing on it.

When Frank and I were first married, we had cattle, and when we went to the feed store, we always got printed feed sacks. So when the two kids were born (girl and boy), I made their clothes. Shirts for him and jumpers for her and made them "look alike."

I still made David's when he went to school, but when LaRose started, that was different. He came home and said not to make his shirts like his sister's jumpers. I didn't make his, but made hers for a long time.

All of us in the neighborhood had an outhouse with two holes (seats) in it. Every Halloween, we kids went Halloween! We got a heavy rope, and off we went. The first outhouse we saw, we decided to "dump" it. We put the rope around (quietly as we could) and started to pull it over, and all at once, we heard this man holler, "Wait until I get out." Nevertheless, we ran like the dickens and left, rope and all.

During World War II, buttons were in place of elastic in the women's panties. My friends and I were walking down Main Street in Byesville, Ohio when we saw this girl and soldier walking down the sidewalk, when at once, we saw this pair of panties fall down the legs of the girl and hit the sidewalk. She stepped out of them, handed them to the soldier, and he put them in his pants pocket, and they went on, just laughing like nothing happened.

A Wee Village, Nicely Nestled

by Linda Laughlin of Scio, Ohio
born in 1943

Oh, where shall I begin? Not "A Tale of Two Cities," but the story of a wee village nicely nestled between two lovely hills dissected by railroad tracks. In years past, it was known as New Market. Later its name became Scio. Scio, in Latin, means, "I know." All I know, is I loved my little town from the moment God gave me the honor of inhaling that first breath of air in it.

I was not even a twinkle in my parents' eyes when it was called New Market. I do remember most of the stories which were heard during my life there. Most were heard when the families would come together on holidays or special times in our lives.

Here we go on a tour of memories filled with funny and happy times as well as historic and sad moments. Some moments had the sad and happy entwined.

Moving forward; Scio was an oil boom town in the 1800s. There were oil wells scattered throughout Scio and the area. I think there was one on my Grandparent Wood's property. Pap turned it into a beautiful flowerbed when the well ran dry. The border was made of willow sticks which Pap and I collected from the swamp area along Connotton Creek. They were easy to bend; flexible is the word. We'd scallop them around to give the flowerbed a fenced-in affect. We did this especially for Grandma and Aunt Virginia who lived with them.

Just know, Pap taught me all kinds of things while growing up. He taught me to carve items from wood, make a whistle out of an apple tree branch, to play the juice harp, sweet potato, tambourine, drums, and mouth organ. The list could go on for miles.

He even taught me the art of throwing a knuckle ball, slider, and curve ball. I was really bad at throwing a fast ball.

Being born in 1876, he was filled with stories of old days. In the 1900s he told Scio was a true college town. Scio College was moved to Alliance, Ohio and is yet in the higher education business. It is now named Mount Union College, but the street is still known as College Street in Scio where all the brick buildings stood in the 1900s.

Silos at Old Scio Pottery where they now make cement.

I suppose I became a teacher partly because of his many stories about college life and the importance of a higher education. Only God really knows.

Not only did Pap teach me fun things, but a good work ethic, love of people, town, state, and country; and to love God first and foremost.

Thus, being blessed with wonderful parents, grandparents, and relatives in my formative years, I was also blessed with a deep caring for knowledge of past, present, and even future events. I truly enjoyed history.

I was born in 1943, who some would call a wartime baby; Dotty (Mom) never named me for a week, as my birth caused her to have a mild heart attack. I weighed seven pounds, 11 ounces and was 21 inches long. Those are my lucky numbers yet today.

Mom named me Linda Lee Laughlin. That's where, in later life, my CB handle, "Triple L," was spawned. That was just one of many nicknames.

Dotty was a nickname, even though Mom's real name was Florence Mae. I guess nicknames ran in our families. Dad's name was Albert Ward, and many called him Red for his brilliant thick red hair.

I recall the neighbor lady, when Mom was with child, so the story goes; she yelled across the street saying, "You are either going to have a string bean or a bottle of Coke." Mom's most favorite food and drink were green beans and Coca Cola. I still think of dear Mom when I have a Coke or a serving of green beans. As previously stated, I was born in '43. So commences the first laughable memory. While surrounded by family one warm summer evening, I told them I really remembered the trip to the hospital to be born. Mom told me in later years that the neighbors all over town could hear the laughter from what I said that evening. A few years later I told my family at the dinner table I actually didn't remember the trip to the hospital, but the bumpy ride home while Mom held me. Vague chance, but I still think I really do remember something. Funny even now!

Next, at two years old, was the most painful of events. Tripped on a rug and fell, hands first, onto Pap's large cylinder-shaped heating stove. Grandma rushed, grabbed a medium-sized glass brown bottle from the shelf above the stairway and rapidly poured the liquid all over little hands. It stopped the blistering and reduced the severe pain. Thanks to the quick thinking of Grams, have no scars from it.

Continuing, got another nickname and funnny memory. Iodine became nickname to stick for at least a year or so. They called that from the name of a comic strip. Iodine was mischievous, as was [requested deletion of personal pronouns]. Would sneak bottles from the medicine cabinet and mix them in the sink. The sink turned all colors, and the stain was difficult to clean. Excuse to Mom was wanted to be Einstein. She made sit on a chair for an hour for punishment.

Also, funny yet not too, was when awaited Pap to move into a trapped area. Would sit atop Pap's old grape arbor with a squirt gun and lasso in hand. It so happened, Pap walked below the grape arbor. Threw my lasso around him and squirted him with gun. Got used to that old hard chair. Ha ha! Punished again!

Last funny episode was at 12, believe it or not. Took a suction dart from dart gun, licked it really good, spit on it again for good measure and then stuck it onto the middle of forehead. It really stuck well. Pulled and pulled, but no dice. After one more giant tug it came off. Flew through the air and landed on rump. With pride wounded, walked slowly into the kitchen for lunchtime special, a peanut butter sandwich. Wondered what Mom was laughing about so loudly with tears rolling down her cheeks. was told to look into the mirror. Shock time! All kinds of emotions exited body. Fear—what would peers say and do; crying—how stupid; anger—how mad at Mom for laughing at her own flesh and blood. Yes, the mirror reflected a perfectly positioned purple ring on forehead. Pulling had caused tiny blood vessels to break where the dart was attached. Why do this? Was an intelligent sixth grade girl. Wanted to pretend was that unicorn in the book, and thought the dart would make a nice horn also.

It took at least three weeks for the bruised purple, then green, then brown ring to fade. Attempted everything under the sun to hide it. The peers' jokes and laughing faded, as did the perfect positioned ring on forehead. Still, this act of stupidity lingers on through the years.

At 17 acquired a position at the Scio Pottery Company while attending night school at Kent State Branch. There are lots of teachers in family, so became a second grade teacher (teaching 34 years). Knew both mental and physical labor.

Ironically, June 6, 1961 was exactly 10 years after L. P. Reese's demise. He came to Scio with only 35 cents and built the largest white ware pottery on the globe. Truly loved this man. He was admired and loved by all in Scio and surrounding areas. When was but a mere child, he'd sit on his over-stuffed office chair to watch a nine-inch black and white TV that whisked to the Old West to live the story of Hopalong Cassidy and his horse, Topper, provided.

Regressing, he gave me a book Shall always cherish. It was Charles Dickens' *A Christmas Carol*. On the inside he wrote as follows, "To my dear little Hopalong Cassidy pal. Love, L.P. Reese." It is still on bookcase shelf.

Back to fond memories of L.P, which are still painful. Sadly, hundreds of people leaning against trees, houses, stop signs, and poles lined the street where L.P.'s home was located. There was only room for those close friends and family members during the biggest and still largest funeral in Scio's history. Was only around seven and-a-half, but Mom and Dad wanted to view him. Never saw a real dead person. Was the saddest moment and most frightening. The casket was like King George IV's of England. Braces were under floor due to its heaviness. His face was as if put into a barrel of flour, as was its lining. Rectangular shaped, as was bathtub at home. For many weeks wouldn't go into the bathroom unattended, thinking he was there, and a ghost.

Never to this day forgot him, a fine man who made Scio a home for more to enjoy and work. Scio Pottery is another industry now.

Time for bed! Memories of "The Way We Were" are now drifting into dreams of yesterday. Am waiting to see L.P. Reese, my folks and friends, and all the loved ones who have passed through God's Pearly Gates into eternity. Please, God bless, and cherish your memories.

School Days in Monroe County

By Denzel Rinard of Rinard Mills, Ohio
Born 1915

A young six year-old-boy goes to the first grade of school. I attended Bells School with students' grades one to eight all in one room in Monroe County, Ohio. I walked with friends. We carried our lunch pails. Our drinking water came from a spring.

There was one teacher for all the grades, Zinna Cline Graham. When this school was discontinued, we walked to Rinard Mills. We attended school in the town house until the new two room school was built in Rinard Mills in 1922, consolidating Bells School and Summit Hall School and later Low Gap School.

There was a large lawn and on Arbor Day many Catalpa trees were planted. Schools were built so that children had to walk no more than two miles. The water was carried from a neighbor's home and later a state well was drilled along #26. We had our own folding cups to drink out of.

There were two teachers, each having four grades. One year there was a two-year high school.

The Rinard Mills School was discontinued in 1943 when the students were bused to Graysville or into Washington County to Ludlow School. I attended Ludlow as a freshman in the new building in the town of Bloomfield. I graduated 1934 from Ludlow High School.

Seventy Years of Stories

By Ronnie E. Myers of Caldwell, Ohio
Born 1939

As I sit here looking out my window and watching the snow come down my mind goes back to childhood days which are no more. I was born in 1939 in a coal mining camp in Pennsylvania just before the war. Things were hard back then and even harder times were to come.

Along about the time I was three or four-years-old I can remember my mom taking my older brother and I to our grandparents whom I knew only as Mom and Pop Stitt. They lived on a small farm outside of Racine, Ohio. I didn't understand at the time why, but Pop always found something for me to help him with while Mom slipped away. How I hated that. It took years for me to understand that she wasn't doing it because she didn't want me, it turns out she and Dad worked at the TNT plant outside of Point Pleasant, West Virginia and there was a war going on. Little did I know at the time that these would be some of the best memories of my life. The time Pop spent with me, I would not take anything for.

Now Mom Stitt was a great lady as I came to find out later in life, but back then I felt she didn't like me much and really didn't want me there. Later I found out it was because they had barely enough food to feed themselves. Pop had been a miner and had what they called black lung and no longer could work the mines, but he always kept going. It was hard at times for him. But I can remember no matter how hard things got, he always thanked God for what he had.

Ronnie Myers, the boy who felt he wasn't wanted.

Now they lived in an old farmhouse with no inside water, no electricity and I can remember him sitting in a rocking chair reading his Bible by the light of a coal oil lamp. Somehow I still have that lamp, old chair and small table the lamp set on.

Some of the things I remember was Pop letting me walk behind him while he plowed with an old horse and the reins over one shoulder and the other under his arm. I remember some of the arguments he had with that old horse and about the time he was ready to just give up, well here would come Mom Stitt with our lunch, which most always was a ham sandwich with homemade bread and a jug of sassafras tea. The tea was made from roots which Pop and I had dug some time earlier in the year.

One of the memories I have is Pop hitching up that old horse to the farm wagon and putting boxes of eggs and a can or two of cream in it and heading off to town, maybe some five miles away. But it could just as well have been across country as far as I was concerned. We first dropped off the cream at what he called the creamery, then went on to the general store to sell his eggs and get a few things and then it was off to the feed store. He always had a small patch of material he would pull out of his pocket and would match it up with whatever sack of feed he needed. When they got enough feed sacks Mom Stitt made a dress or new apron and a sun bonnet.

Another big thing I remember was going to church. It was about a mile and half or so down the dirt road. I can remember how glad I was when he hitched up the horse and wagon because that meant they were having a church dinner. Wow, what food! All the kids played games and all the men stood or set around and talked about the crops or the new horse someone had just got. I liked hearing about the old days and them telling how better it had been when they were all younger.

But the times I didn't care that much for was those Sunday night services. In the winter when there was snow on the ground; I still can hear the snow crunch under our feet. Also, I can still hear Pop humming an old church song. My, what I would give to hear that again.

Oh there are so many things I remember about the time I spent there on the farm with them; like the time I was going to help gather eggs. Problem is I couldn't carry them all so I put some in my pockets. Everything was going just fine, that is 'til I tried to get through the fence. It was then that I heard this noise coming from inside my jeans. Then there was this awful feeling of something going down my leg and my chest. You see I had also put an egg or two in my shirt pocket. Then the real problem came when Mom Stitt found out what I had done. Now Pop just kind of smiled and walked off and left me to face her on my own. Would you believe she would not let me change clothes, but made me wear them the rest of the day? I bet there is no need to tell you I never helped gather eggs again!

The only time I remember Pop having a cross word for me was when I got hungry and tried to boil an egg in a tin can. Problem is; I built the fire right next to the barn. Thank God there was smoke. Pop dusted my jeans that day, but I did hear him tell Mom Stitt later, "The boy was just trying to fix himself a bite to eat." I don't think she was buying any of it, but never said anything about it to me. I think now that she and Pop might have had an understanding that he would take care of it. Later that day he and I took a long walk together and talked a lot, but never another word about eggs, water and a tin can. But I had a pretty good idea it would not be wise to try that again.

Another great memory I have of those days was Pop's father lived with them. As I look back it is no wonder Mom Stitt was always in a bad mood. Now we called him Grandpa Stitt, but he was really my great-grandpa. Now the story goes he was born on an Indian reservation somewhere in Indiana and spent his first six years there. He was a story in himself: about once a month he had these spells and could not get back up the hill after walking into town. Pop would have to go out in the night to help him home. I couldn't understand at the time why Pop wouldn't let me come along to help; I always tagged along with him. Well anyway, then as I got older I found that those spells that Grandpa had were caused by a bottle of something which I guess he would hide out in the woods and would walk out every now and then just to check on it. And there was Grandpa's brother-in-law who lived in town who had gone out west by covered wagon to work the oil fields, but that's another story for another time.

After setting here thinking back on just a few of the times gone by the wayside I get kind of sad. You see, we have five children and fourteen grandchildren and now I find myself with 70 years of stories to tell and no one to tell them to. Everybody is either too busy or just don't care to hear them. It breaks my heart to think the people who have gone on before will somehow die with me. They all had a story of their own and deserve to have it told. These were hard people, living in hard times, for it is the true history of the people who made this great land, not just the way someone wants it to read in the school books, but the way it really was; or as Paul Harvey would say, "Now you know the rest of the story."

Granny Jones and the Skunks

by Kenny Johnson of Zanesville, Ohio
born 1930

I was born in 1930. I've lived on the same farm outside of Zanesville most of my life. I'm now seventy-eight years old. I could tell you a lot of stories about the good old days but this one is in memory of our neighbor. We called him Old Granny Jones.

I was a teenager, I'd say around the age of fifteen or so. Old Granny Jones was probably in his early fifties or late forties but, to us, that was old. He was always playing pranks on us boys but this one I recall the most.

My younger brother Norman, my older brother Dean and I were always looking for ways to make money. One way was through selling raccoon hides. We would get around five dollars a hide, and back then, that was a lot of money. We would save our money all year in order to get enough to go to the fair.

So, when Old Granny Jones told us he'd seen a huge raccoon go down in a hole on his property, and we were welcome to dig it out, we were all for it. Norman, Dean and I ran to the barn to grab Dad's tools, me with a mattock in hand and Norman and Dean with shovels. We ran for the hole. We dug for a long time, I'd say we dug for a good twenty feet finally reaching the end of the hole. Norman, along with Dean, held their shovels high ready to clobber that coon. I swung, the mattock slammed into the hole for the last time.

To our surprise, we were engulfed with the worse smell I had ever smelt in my life. My brothers and I, wide eyed and choking from the stench, watched as two skunks made there way to the woods. That Old Granny Jones got us again. We smelled like skunk for days.

The good thing was that we did earn enough money for the fair by selling berries along with hulling hickory nuts and walnuts. I wish that I was as wise as I am now; I would have got that Old Granny Jones back!

Fond Memories

By Helen M. Frye Clements of New Philadelphia, Ohio
Born 1921

I was born in 1921 at Uhrichsville,Ohio, the oldest of five children. My dad was lucky to have a job as a fireman. However, he never had enough money to pay the bills. Even so, he always helped our relatives. I remember my mom and me pulling a wagon full of groceries to my aunt's house across town.

"Fond Memories" of my brother and I going to silent movies in the afternoon to see cowboys, such as Hoot Gibson, Hop Along Cassidy, Gene Autry, Roy Rogers and Dale Evans.

"Fond Memories" of going to my Grandma Laughlin's house about two blocks away to hear her play the organ. We would sing hymns. Two of our favorite ones were "In the Garden" and "The Old Rugged Cross".

"Fond Memories" of going to an aunt's house next door to play records on her wind up Victrola. There was one song that I would play over and over until I memorized it. I think it was "In Old Shanty Town". The first line is "It's only a shanty in old shanty town; the roof is so slanting it touches the ground." I think there was a talking part in the middle of the song. When I went to the fire station, my dad would have me to sing it for the men there.

Fire Chief Clyde Frye, Helen Frye Clement's father, with daughters Velma and Juanita.

"Fond Memories" of going for a ride in my dad's old car. When going down a hill my dad would turn off the ignition. I guess it was to save on gas. Also while in the car we kids would shout, "You scream, I scream, we all scream for ice cream." Usually we got a cone.

"Fond Memories" of when I was in the 3rd or 4th grade, I had a friend who had a large playhouse with furniture and people in it. That was really neat. She lived on top of a hill that had a steep bank in back with the Stillwater Creek at the bottom. My mom would remind me not to play back there. However, we did it anyway. One time a third friend came to play. We climbed down the bank and back up. He fell down from halfway up. He never said a word but took off for home. We never climbed that bank again.

"Depression Memories" of wearing shoes that my big toes had worn a hole through the top. I was so embarrassed I made a vow that when I was old enough to get a job; I would buy all the shoes I wanted. At one time, I had a closet full. Due to aging, I had to give away the ones with heels. Now it's a matter of finding a comfortable pair.

In seventh grade I learned to sew so I made clothes for my sisters and me. My grandpa Frye's wife was a large woman who gave me two wool coats; one navy, one black. I made my sister a navy skirt and me a black one. At the time, I was babysitting two cute girls for 25 cents a night. I saved enough to buy material for two blouses. One night a funny thing - well not funny, but irritating thing, happened while babysitting. They had a cat. I'm not a cat person so I always closed the bedroom door. However, the door must not have been closed tightly. I woke up with this awful smell in the room. The cat must have vomited! I cleaned it up the best I could but the smell was still there. So I went to the parent's room and took a bottle of perfume, sprayed it on the floor and into the room. What a night!

"Bad Luck Memories." I was always getting hurt. Mom sent me to the store and I walked across an iron cover that laid over a hole in the sidewalk next to the building. It slipped and scrapped my leg to the bone. I complained to my mom about it hurting so badly, but she said it was only a scrape! Well I got infection in it. I would sit near a pot belly small stove in my room and cry. I still have a scare about two inches long and one inch wide.

Another time I went sled riding on top of a kid going down a steep hill and we wrecked about half way down. Who got hurt? Me!

On my way home from school, I fell on the ice skinning my knee through my stocking and long underwear.

Even after I was married, accidents still happened. While taking off a dress that had a long zipper in the back, I couldn't get it off so I reached in to unzip it more but the zipper got caught in my eyelid. It took a long time to work it loose. Needless to say, I had a sore red eyelid.

Later, we moved to New Philadelphia to my mother-in-law's house. My automatic washer stopped running while washing sheets so I used an old Maytag washer that was in the basement. Guess what? I ran my hand through the wringer with a sheet. I didn't think about it having a release so I put the wringer in reverse and ran my hand back out. I went next door and the lady took me to the emergency room for x-rays. No broken bones but it was bruised and swelled so high, the skin broke. That took a long time to heal.

I still do dumb things like hiding money and not remembering where, going into a room for something but don't remember what it was so I stand awhile and it comes to me, and coming in from outside and locking the door with the keys on the outside all night. Luckily I have a sun porch. Now I attribute these dumb things to old age.

So much for the "Golden Years" with all its aches, pains and pills.

However, I have much to be thankful for. I can still walk with a walker at home and a cane when I go out. I live alone in a nice apartment and have Mobile Meals and Senior Center help to do my laundry, etc. I also use the senior bus to go to doctor appointments and the church bus to attend Sunday school and church. And I am blessed with a loving family: daughter, son, five grandsons and a great-granddaughter.

Washday, Bicycles and a Sack of Cats

By Frances Clawson of Bairoil, Wyoming
Born 1946

Washday came once a week on Saturday at our house whether there were plans for anything else or not. Since I was the oldest of what was to become a family of ten children plus Mother and Dad, the lot fell on me from nine years old and on to do the family's wash.

Washday really began on Friday night after supper dishes when all of the baskets and buckets of laundry, including diapers, were carried down the steep steps to the damp basement.

The diapers, sad to say were usually still in the condition they had been when they were taken off of the baby. Thus they had to be dumped of their contents which sometimes included fly maggots, into the floor sewer drain. The diapers were then shook out and put to soak in an old boiler tub containing hot water with Clorox bleach added. A time or two I didn't get them rinsed and soaked the night before and tried just dumping the diapers as they were into the washer. This act resulted in having to drain, clean and refill the washer. Our water supply was a cistern with a limited capacity so my action did not set well with the parental authorities.

The handkerchiefs were next to be taken care of; no paper tissues then. They were put to soak in another enamel pan to which had been added Borax to the hot water. The sorting of the other dirty clothes was next.

Whites, underwear, light-colored clothes, sheets pillow cases, towels and wash cloths, dark-colored clothes, jeans and heavy work clothes all had their separate piles on the concrete floor.

Saturday morning as bright and early as I could be motivated to descend to the basement the washday began. The diapers were taken out of their boiler, put through the wringer into the washer where the tub had already been filled with hot water and the soap granules. They would wash for twenty or thirty minutes while the two rinse tubs were filled with cold water. The second rinse tub had liquid fabric softener added. In with the diapers were usually several pairs of plastic pants. Mother had cautioned me not to put them through the wringer as they would form a water bubble and pop a hole in them. Sometimes though a pair would "accidentally" get put through and ruined.

We would not want to forget the faithful "wash stick". It was a piece of wood about 24 to 30 inches long and usually flat about one inch wide. It was used to push the clothes down into the hot, sudsy water and to "fish" them back out as I was too short to reach to the bottom of the washer. It helped to keep my sleeves from getting soaked too.

After the diapers, the whitest clothes were washed; then the sheets, underwear with the handkerchiefs added, and on down the line to the dark-est and dirtiest clothes until the washing was all done. When the clothes were put through the wringer and two rinses, they were taken outside in wooden bushel baskets with oil cloth liners to be penned on the metal clothes lines. There were clothes lines strung up in the basement for winter or inclement weather. I was probably 14 before we were able to buy an electric clothes dryer. Even then we did not try to dry all of the clothes in it.

I also learned to use that first dryer to dry my hair as we did not own a hair dryer. It could be turned on to run with the door open, and I would kneel down in front of it and put my head in the middle. It did work, but the dryers I have seen since then won't run with the door open.

One other special step in washing the clothes was to take the pan the handkerchiefs had been soaked in and clean it and add very hot water into which starch cubes were added to be dissolved. The clothes that were to be ironed were starched in this solution before they were penned up to dry. They could never be dried in the dryer. I was in trouble a few times for starching Dad's handkerchiefs or some other garment that should not have been. I was glad when liquid starch came on the market and could just be added to the water as it was.

It is evident that this washing chore usually took most of Saturday by the time the clothes on the lines were dry and ready to be brought in to fold and put away. The ironing was saved for other days, thankfully. As my siblings grew older, they were included in the hanging and folding detail. But the wash was mostly my responsibility until I graduated from high school and left home.

I have never washed with a wringer washer since then. Not many years after I had gone from home, the folks purchased an automatic washer. So most of my younger sisters were left out of the "wringer washer" wash day.

The desire I had to have my very own bicycle began when I was about ten years old in the fourth grade. The neighbor boy who was a year younger than I had acquired his very own used bike, and he would ride the quarter mile down to our house and share it with me. He patiently tried to help me to learn to ride. The biggest obstacle being that I was a very short girl and his bicycle was a big 26-inch man's with the bar between the seat and the handle bars. However, I did learn to an extent and was able to ride a little way with a "push off" and he holding the bike up on one side and running along to help me keep balance.

My allowance was twenty-five cents a week, as I did the family's wash every Saturday, the dishes after supper each night and many other household chores in our big family. I held on to that allowance and added to it whenever my grandmothers would send me birthday money or any other money that would come my direction. By fifth grade I finally had saved around twenty dollars.

In the weekly hometown paper there was the advertisement that I had been watching for; a lady's bicycle! I pleaded, begged and talked my dad into going and looking at it. A girl older than I had grown to the age to drive a car and was selling her bicycle. (I still remember her name and knew who she was.) Wow! It was a beauty; a blue Schwinn 26-inch lady's bicycle with a luggage carrier on the back where a second person could ride, a light on the front and a basket mounted to the handle bars over the front fender.

If I recall correctly, I did not have the amount she was asking, but my folks made up the difference, and I was the proud owner of that beautiful bicycle. I rode and rode that bike any time I could get my work done and have permission to do so.

I decided to carry my three-year-old sister in the basket; the other younger siblings had ridden on the luggage carrier. The basket worked just fine for her several times until one time riding on our gravel road going down hill we hit a patch of gravel and I had my first wreck. She mentioned recently (41 years later) about a scar on her chin. I had to admit that I was the one who caused it, and I then showed her the one on my elbow from the same incident.

That bicycle was still there giving my brothers and

sisters many riding miles of pleasure when I was graduated and married.

We did not go to the dentist in my childhood for "wellness" checks. When the pain was severe enough and/or the tooth was nearly rotted off, then we called the local dentist and got in to see him as soon as possible.

I was about nine years old on that first climb up the long flight of stairs to the little room with the unusual medicinal odor to have my aching tooth extracted. I had imagined all kinds of horrors that awaited me there. I was seated in a special chair that was pumped up higher. When the dentist told me to open my mouth so he could check the bad tooth, I began screaming in terror. He did finally get the examination finished, lit the Bunsen burner with a match, and sterilized a needle to numb my mouth amidst more crying of protest from yours truly. I do remember being able to spit the nasty-tasting Novocain into the little chair-side porcelain basin. My dad finally had to hold me down while the dentist pulled the tooth, which amazed me that it was out so quickly and painlessly. I have had many trips to the dentist since then and never have found any enjoyment there, though the modern techniques and equipment that are available today are far beyond that little Bunsen burner and chair-side spit bowl. I am thankful now that such a patient and kind elderly dentist was willing to tolerate this scared girl.

My mother found a nest of baby mice in an aluminum canning strainer she had under the kitchen sink. Of course I being four years old ran to look when she gave a cry of alarm. Mother had been canning tomatoes that day and had a "slop bucket" full of peelings and whatever else had been pitched in to go to the pigs. From birth almost I had been covered head to toe with eczema, and it didn't take much to irritate my tender skin. I can still hear Mother saying "Get back!", and I did as I sat down right into the slop bucket!

My parents were raising chickens and selling eggs to make ends meet. I can still remember at about five-years old being afraid of the big ole rooster. "He won't hurt you. Just run on by him." is what I was told. The day came that it didn't work for me to "run on by him", and he landed on my back. Thus, I remember a few days later when Mother opened the little freezer door at the top of our refrigerator and showed me that I didn't need to be afraid to go out to play any longer.

The neighbor children were taunting me; "You told a lie. The devil's going to get you!" They were all older than I and didn't want me along to tattle on them. After I had gone to bed one evening, I came up out of my bed screaming, "The devil's going to get me! The devil's going to get me!" It seems my dad was outside doing chores and walked by my window with a red handkerchief over his face as he suffered from hay fever. I don't remember whether he looked in through the window, but I knew I had seen him and the red handkerchief.

It was my sixth birthday in mid-January, and I was able to attend my very first day of school. But, it was only for a visit; no kindergartens then in our area. It was a very exciting day for me, and parts of it I remember well.

After school my mother was going to the neighbors to borrow something, and the neighborhood children kept asking her what time they were to come for my birthday party. I had invited all of them to my birthday party which was a surprise—to my parents!

Even though we lived 10 miles from town, some way Mother was able to get a pint of ice cream and bake a cake. One neighbor lady made me a green and white checked apron which I kept for many years. I was reminded many times afterward not to plan my own party again.

When my parents, my sister, two brothers and I moved to south eastern Ohio from West Virginia, a neighbor man from West Virginia helped us move with his cattle truck. He went back to West Virginia and brought another load a few days later. When he came to the door, he held a burlap sack in his hands which he opened and dumped the contents out in front of my mother and us siblings. He said he couldn't tell which cats were ours, so he just brought us all of them that he could catch. Cats went in all directions. We talked about that sack of cats many times over the years.

We had just moved to southeast Ohio, and I was seven and in the first grade of a two-room eight-grade school. My walk to school was over one-fourth mile downhill and around a thick, wooded turn where there were no other houses. It was called "Tunnel Hill," and neighbors told tales of bears being in the woods and the abandoned tunnel. We never did see or find evidence of any at that time, but this is one first-grader who walked scared all the way to school and back home. I think the bus driver got word of my fears and took pity on me, as he began picking me up and letting me off as part of his route.

My first day to attend school there a big boy in my grade who began teasing me, and I began to cry. When Mrs. Richardson, the teacher, asked my trouble, I told her I had a toothache. She put cinnamon oil on the one I indicated. I guess cinnamon oil is good for calming nerves too.

The Vanished Store in the Lost Village

by Ruth Liggett of Dennison, Ohio
born in 1926

About 80 years ago, Tappan was a small village, nestled in a beautiful, hilly valley in Harrison County, Ohio.

It was a typical small town of the time, with tree-lined streets, frame houses and as many as one hundred people. Green hills surrounded the town with flocks of sheep grazing on the lush grass, watered by a creek, which ran throughout the valley.

Today, there is little left to show that people once lived there. Instead, there is a beautiful body of water, Tappan Lake. The hills are covered with trees that were planted in the late forties and in the fifties. It is a Mecca for fishermen and boaters. In 1936, the Tappan Dam was built to help control the waters that once flooded areas as far away as Dayton, Columbus, Zanesville, and the Mississippi River Valley. As the water was held back, the creek water began to fill the valley. People moved, homes were torn down, and water covered what was left. The village of Tappan was gone. Today, when the water is low, you can see portions of the old road. The site of the village is under the water.

In Tappan, there was a two-story, 40x100 foot general store, owned by our father, Earl Reed, in partnership with his father-in-law since 1923. In 1938, Grandpa moved to Cadiz and Dad was left to take care of the store. Our memories and experiences stem from this store. The Tappan Store, known as Cramblett and Reed, was beside old Route 250 that was about 16 feet wide at that time. Dad built a house across the road from the store beside Grandpa and Grandma's house.

Granddad Cramblett in front of store in 1920s or 30s. The road in front is old Rt. 250.

Walking into the store, one could buy anything they needed. On one side of the building was aspirin, cold medicine, Pepto Bismol and laxatives. These were on the shelf, but in a glass case were handkerchiefs, penknives, billfolds, and other fancy items. Cotton hose were there. Long-johns, shoes, hats, material, needles, thread, thimbles and many other items were called for.

At the back of the store was Grandpa's roll-top desk and steps leading upstairs. Upstairs, we found bustles and high-buttoned shoes which had been stored when they were no longer in style. Downstairs again, we found a meat and cheese case. A large knife was ready to cut a sliver of cheese for a cracker or a pound of meat to take home. Many men would stop by for cheese and crackers for lunch.

The store had a candy counter with mostly penny candy. Candy bars, such as Clark bar, was a nickel. Cracker Jack was popular because of the prize in the box. Behind the candy case was an ice cream cooler. Five cents bought a large cone...chocolate, vanilla, and strawberry were the most popular. Then, there were the dried beans, peas, macaroni, sugar, flour, lima beans etc. Very few canned foods were available. Tobacco was plentiful, such as Redman, Redhorse chewing tobacco, as well as Prince Albert smoking tobacco and snuff, which was used by women as well. Cigars and cigarettes were plentiful.

Near the counter was a large barrel of salted fish. And of course, there was a large jar of dill pickles. Bread was eight cents a loaf and many women were starting to buy it. Yeast, in cake form, was still in demand. A local bakery delivered bread around 4:00 AM, leaving it in a bread box on the porch. Standard Oil gasoline pumps were at the front of the building with motor oil and a watering can. An adjacent building had feed and farming supplies. The floor was wooden, treated periodically with oil. The store had to be swept every day.

Looking for new ways to earn money, Dad started what he called "the routes." In those days, the late twenties and thirties and forties, county roads in our area were dirt. Very few had gravel and certainly none were paved. Getting to town to buy and sell goods was difficult. Dad would load his truck with candy, cookies, sliced bread, oranges, cake yeast and other things you might find at a convenience store today. As he sold his goods, he bought sweet cream, eggs and poultry. He would take the cream (used to make butter and ice cream mix) eggs and poultry to Canton, Ohio where he sold them. If he made more profit in the eggs than he expected, he would share it with the people who had sold him the eggs. Dad didn't mind dickering about the price of eggs, but one fellow told me if Dad's neck started to turn red, he knew it was time to stop. Sometimes, the cream that he was carrying would get too hot and the lid would blow off of the five gallon can, spewing cream all over everything. Dad would have to stop and spend valuable time mopping up.

Children, especially, looked forward to Dad's arrival. He said they would run to the truck to check things out. One popular item was cake yeast. For some reason, the children thought if they ate the yeast, the mosquitoes, which were plentiful in the summer, wouldn't bite.

Dad extended credit to many of his customers. Several years ago, a stranger approached me and told me he came from a large family and if Dad hadn't given them credit from time to time, they would have gone hungry. Dad remembered the family and said that, eventually, they always paid their bill.

The roads, in winter especially, were awful. Dad went on the route in all kinds of weather, rain, snow, sleet, and ice. Many times he would have to lie on his back in the snow and mud to put chains on the truck tires. Lanes leading to farmhouses were even worse. In later years, he delivered feed to the farms. The cow, pig, chicken, and horse feed came in 100-pound bags. Dad would hoist the 100-pound bag on his shoulder and put it anywhere the farmer wanted it. One farm had a steep downward path to the barn. When it was icy, Dad would shoulder the bag of feed, set his feet and slide down the path balancing the feed sack. (When I was 25 and Dad was nearing 60, I would tease him that he couldn't pick me up any more. He swept me up in his arms, all 125 pounds of me, and tossed me in the air. Not once, but several times. He was still strong at 90.)

Sometimes, he would slide into the ditch due to the bad roads. He would have to hike to the nearest farm to ask the farmer to pull him out with horses or a tractor. Many times he would make it out on his own.

In bad weather, when Dad was late, Mother would worry and pace the floor (no cell phones in those days). She would fuss and fuss and supper would wait on the back of the stove or in the oven. But when he came in tired and hungry, she would smile, give him a kiss and say, "Honey, supper is ready." I never heard her fuss at him because he was late.

Holidays were a big time for poultry. Dad had chicken and turkey crates. They were low boxes made of wooden spindles with a small door in the top. The turkey crates were taller than the chicken crates for obvious reasons. He would buy the chickens and turkeys, put them in the crates and haul them live to Canton. Arrangements with the farmer would be made the week before Dad needed the poultry. The farmer would pen up the poultry the day Dad was expected and Dad would easily put them in the crates and be on his way. Running a little late one evening, he headed to a farmer's henhouse for a load of turkeys. There were no turkeys in the henhouse. Dad had promised these turkeys to a store in Canton the next day. He had to have them. Knocking on the farmer's door he asked where the turkeys were. "Sorry," the farmer said, "we didn't think you were coming so we let them out." "Well, where are they?" asked Dad. The farmer pointed to the surrounding trees. They had gone to roost. Dad spent quite a while climbing trees and catching turkeys. That was one of the nights he was late.

As time passed, Dad sold more and more feed. Feed companies began printing sacks in cotton patterns suitable for dressmaking. They became very popular with farm wives. They could outfit their daughters and themselves for a very reasonable price. But it was a bit of a headache for Dad. He would have to do some real juggling to get the special sacks the ladies wanted. Later, the feed companies made the sacks out of really nice pillowslip material with printed borders of pink, blue, green, and yellow. Of course each bed had two pillows and needed two matching pillow slips. Dad always tried to find the appropriate one.

From time to time, Gypsies would come to town. They were dark-skinned and traveled in groups in old touring cars. The women wore large skirts with many pockets inside. The whole town would become alert because the Gypsies had a reputation of taking anything that wasn't "nailed down." With their crafty, well practiced hands, they took many things out of the store. Once, a Gypsy girl ran across the street, taking my baby doll.

The store was heated by a pot-bellied coal stove, sitting in the middle of the room. This stove had many purposes besides giving heat. In the evenings or afternoons, the local men would come to hash over worldly news and spin yarns far from the truth, while spitting tobacco juice at the red-hot stove. I can still hear the sizzle as the moisture hit the metal. Still on denial that their town would soon be gone, the men would declare "That little creek will never fill up this valley," but they were wrong. It took several years, but the valley did fill with water.

Fels Naptha Soap Co. introduced soap flakes. They were medium brown flakes and delivered in barrels like everything else. One of the local ladies came in, admired the recent shipment and asked if it was something new. Dad said, "Yes, they had just arrived." "Well," the lady said, "I'll give them a try. Give me a pound." She carried the soap chips home. The next morning she proudly served them to her husband with milk and sugar. He took one big bite, sputtered, coughed, spit it out and demanded to know what "that stuff" was. Surprised by his reaction, she quickly told him it was those new cereal flakes from Earl Reed's store. After tasting them she realized her mistake and, with good humor, told Dad the story the next time she came into the store.

On Saturday night, the young men of the town and area would dress up and "step out" for the evening. Often they would stop by the store for a Coke or a chat with the guys sitting around the store. Usually, the guys would ask each young man where he was going. If he told them, then everything would be fine. If he resented them asking and wouldn't tell them, the guys would pick him up, lay him on the counter and remove his tie. The more he fought back, the more fun it was. Dad said some of them left looking pretty messed up, but they would be back the next Saturday.

A young lad was sent by his mother to ask Dad if he would buy her chickens. "Well," he said with a twinkle in his eye, "it depends on the age, and how many teeth they have." Before Dad could stop him, the boy ran home to ask how many teeth their chickens had. The mother understood the joke, but gently told her son, "Chickens don't have teeth."

The store had a burglar alarm. One night, late, it went off. We lived across the road, but by the time Dad got there, the culprits had gone. There was evidence (a ladder) that someone had entered an upstairs window. Nothing much was missing except several pairs of old shoes. The sheriff was called, but the trespassers were never found. Fifty years later, Dad was shopping for groceries. When he returned to his car, a man was sitting in a car next to Dad's. Dad loved talking to people so it was not unusual that Dad and the man fell into a conversation. During the course of their exchange, Dad mentioned he had been one of the owners of the store in Tappan. A strange look crossed the man's face and he became silent for a moment. Then he told Dad that years ago he had broken into that store. "We didn't get much," he said, "just some old shoes." With that statement, Dad knew the stranger was telling the truth. The man went on to say that, after that incident, he had gone from bad to worse, even spending time in jail. With tears in his eyes, he asked Dad to forgive him. Dad expressed regret that the man's life had been so difficult and immediately forgave him. The conversation ended and Dad never saw him again. God does work in mysterious ways.

Dad continued in the store business until he was nearly 90. Often, people would stop by just to talk to him and he always loved their company. He had a couple of ice cream parlor chairs that came from the old store in Tappan and his visitors would often sit on them. In fact, when one of them finally gave out, the fellow who sat on it the most took it home, repaired it, brought it back and continued to sit on it.

The Bonfires on McGrath Hill

by Jeanette McGrath Kirkbride of Malta, Ohio
born 1938

I was born in 1938, the only girl in a family of four older brothers. We lived in a house at the top of the hill, behind the old Malta Grade School. As early as I can remember, my brothers had me out on roller skates, bicycles, or sleds. The most memorable was sledding on the hill in winter.

At school, the kids, first through eighth grade, got out the same time at recess and lunch time. So, we all headed up McGrath hill to sled. The town workers closed the road so no cars could come through and hit a kid. There would be between 50 and 100 kids on the hill. After school, some of the town kids would come back and stay till ten or eleven o'clock to sled. Sometimes their parents would come too.

After dark we would build a bonfire with wood, furnished by the old Malta Sash and Door factory. At the bottom of the hill we would build a jump-up over the curb so we could go across the schoolyard. Some of the older boys and parents would keep the fire burning so when we got cold we could sit around the fire on your sled and get warm.

My dad, Watt, as he was called, fixed a floodlight on our front porch that would light up the hill like it was afternoon. All the years we played on that hill there was never no fighting, smoking, or drinking.

The only serious injury was when one of the older boys thought to be smart, so they tried to dump one lady off her sled into the snow, but she beat them to the bottom before they got there. She went over the jump and the boy went into the telephone pole and broke his collarbone. Needless to say, that was the end of his trick that year.

The old school is now gone and we don't have that kind of snow anymore, but I will never forget the fun we had sledding on McGrath Hill.

Orange Juice, Castor Oil and Player Pianos

by Jack E. Wallace of Zanesville, Ohio
born 1926

I went to Grover Cleveland Jr. High until the ninth grade, then I went to Lash High School for tenth, eleventh and twelfth grades. J.R. Richards was principal at Grover Cleveland. He called me into the office and told me I had skipped half a day over the past ten days. He said, "I should fail you, but I'm giving you a D- to get rid of you."

It really didn't matter too much as I ended up in the U.S. Navy. I was at the Great Lakes Training Center on my seventeenth birthday for World War II.

Castor oil was used for every ailment. My mother used to try to hide it in orange juice and soda. I'm eighty-two and I can't drink orange juice to this day. I can still taste the castor oil.

The radio programs, if you were lucky enough to have a radio, were Major Bowes Amateur Hour, Amos and Andy and Fred Allen. The only stations you could get were KDKA Pittsburg, whenever and WALR, Zanesville on a clear day.

Saturday nights were bath nights, cleaning you up for Sunday school and church.

Saturday movies always included several movies at the Imperial Theatre: Flash Gordon, Buck Rodgers and Tom Mix were a few, along with a full length western movie.

I went to Munson Grade School and every year we had a flood on West Main and covered most of the State Street. Dillon Lake cured this problem. We could see the high water from school.

I grew up on Schaum Avenue. I remember Moores and Ross Dairy delivered with a horse-pulled wagon. Also any ice. Very few had fridges. Ninety-five percent of people had coal fired furnaces. You could cut the air with a knife in the morning with all the smoke and soot from everyone firing up their furnaces.

There used to be a man named Harry Waterman that pushed a push-cart to collect trash of any kind. As kids we used to tease him. The funny thing is the war came along and he opened a large junkyard in Zanesville, Ohio and ended up a wealthy man owning a lot of property in Zanesville.

After I was hired at Zanesville Mould Company making cast iron moulds to produce glass bottles. We had a four year apprenticeship and for the first year I made 69 cents an hour and took home twenty dollars a month.

I got married to my wife who worked for Dr. Renner, an eye doctor. She made a dollar per hour. We had it made. In 1947 we had a daughter.

We used to skinny dip in Timber Run Creek, and Edge Water Beach used to be pretty crowded on a warm summer night.

When I was growing up, the highlight for me was the weekends and visiting my grandparents. They had an old player piano and it was a ball playing the rolls and singing Barney Google with these Goo-Goo Google Eyes. Never will forget it or getting into the cookie jar, or the dill pickle jar in the basement.

Saturday nights were big in Zanesville when I was young. The sidewalks would be filled with people. There were no shopping malls, as the shopping was downtown. There was a Sears, Montgomery Wards, Kresges Five and Ten, and Woolworth Five and Ten stores.

Those were the good old days. People would go park on Main Street just to sit and watch the cars go by. People came from miles around just to stop in Zanesville.

The Mast Family Entertainers

By Bertie Showers of Sugarcreek, Ohio
Born 1928

Little did I know that as a small child, I would be a member of the famous Mast Family Entertainers who grew up in the small town of Sugarcreek and had the opportunity to perform on a large stage in the heart of New York City. This is my story of me and my family in our "good old days" of growing up.

There were five children in all: Kenneth Eugene, Marilyn, myself (Bertie Lou), Wanda and baby; Abie Lee; eight years younger than Wanda. My dad, Abe Mast, was a wonderful dad who was superintendent of The Clay Craft Brickyard, now called Belden Brick. My mom, Esther, was just a housewife who took good care of us all, but did most of the disciplining to keep us well mannered children. She didn't hesitate to use a switch from the old mulberry tree if needed. We children grew up as normal kids do; playing basketball in the barn, crawling through bales of straw tunnels, playing cowboy in the pits of the brickyard, riding bikes and roller skating in the brick shed and lots of sled ridding down Main Street (which was closed for all the town kids to enjoy when we had a big snow) and swimming in the old Richardson pool, "at your own risk," down by the golf course.

There was just one thing different about our family that other kids didn't do. Mother, being an accomplished piano player, and skilled in music, had other ideas added to our kid's activities. Besides having schoolwork to do and school activities such as operettas and sports, we were taught to sing and dance; and that took practice, practice, practice.

At a very young age we learned to harmonize with each other and made up trios, duets and solos. Each one of us also took up dancing; mostly using our natural talent. I remember how we three girls had to practice dancing on a tap board hardly big enough for us. Dad was good at singing, and Mom was good at dancing. We had a few lessons and took it from there. So my parents decided to use us to entertain others. We became the Mast Family.

In the early 1930's in Baltic, Ohio, a minstrel show was being planned and Dad was asked if my brother, Eugene, the oldest at five years old, could blacken-up and do a skit. Mom taught him some dance steps she did when she was young and Eugene sang and danced his way into the hearts of many people. The next year, when asked to perform again, Eugene's own natural talent took over and his clog dancing became quite spectacular. My parents entered him in dance contests at Garver Brothers Store in Strasburg and he won every time. When asked to participate in an amateur show at the New Phila Opera House where they needed to be an act, mother taught Marilyn, age five, to harmonize with Eugene, age six, and the two kids won that show and went on to win first place in Burt's Amateur Show in Cleveland, Ohio in 1934. Later on, at age six, I joined the family act and Mom, who played piano by ear to fit the children's voices, added Wanda to the family act by the age of five. Our family of four children sang and danced and became in demand all around the area as the Mast Family Entertainers. We children's talents came natural and was God-given.

In 1939 Sugarcreek Merchants held a series of amateur shows right in front of the old Blue Bird Restaurant on Main Street in Sugarcreek. With ten amateur shows in all, each Saturday night, all the winners came together for a final performance with the winner winning $50 and a trip to New York City to audition for the famous Major Bowes Amateur Hour Program on the radio. Dad wasn't too keen on us for the final night because we always won everything we were in. Mayor Odenkirk urged us to enter, so after much debate, Dad finally consented and our family won this all expense paid trip to New York. So our family of seven went (Abie was a year old) and Dad's sister-in-law, Eva Mast, went with us to care for the baby. We all piled into our 1936 Ford and made the trip.

Mast Family Entertainers in 1939, left to right: Wanda, Bertie Lou, Abe (father), Marilyn, Eugene, Esther (mother) at the piano.

The family succeeded in getting a five minute spot on Major Bowes program Thursday night of that week after many auditions took place. Major Bowes interviewed my mother and even let her play for us as we went from one song, to dancing, to ending the program with Dad joining in and singing with us children; standing right in the middle of us four kids. You should have heard all the yelling and clapping when we finished. It was overwhelming and we were voted by telephone calls and received second place to three local hometown trumpeters from Jamestown, New York. The Mast Family won the hearts of the audience present, as well as the listeners on radio and we were the only act to get our picture taken with Major Bowes.

In spite of an offer to join one of Major Bowes national traveling troops; dad decided to entertain only locally so the children could get their education and live normal lives. We left New York on a Friday and made it home for Eugene's Saturday night basketball game where Marilyn was a cheerleader. Getting home meant more to us kids than staying in New York City. Our programs continued until Eugene joined the Navy at the age of 18 and while in the Navy he changed his name to Kenneth. His natural talent was displayed while in the Navy and he danced in many shows.

In the meantime; we girls back home sang trios in churches and for special occasions. When Kenny returned from the Navy, the family act was still broken up as he entered Heidelberg College, Tiffin, Ohio, after marrying his childhood sweetheart, Patricia Zimmerman. When he was in high school Kenny was a star basketball player and had the best golf record at Sugarcreek Golf Course. Not only a dancer, but a natural in sports! Today, after building Bluffton Golf Course, Kenny still teaches golf as a pro.

In a few years all us children were married and raising our own children. There were 22 grandchildren for my mom and dad to enjoy. Our children were also very talented and learned to sing all our childhood songs just like we did. We are very proud of them and blessed because everyone of them are wonderful Christians and today I make sure our families still get together for gatherings and we have such good times and many good memories that we will treasure in our hearts forever. God has been good to our Mast Family! Our parents are deceased; Kenny lives in Florida, Marilyn is deceased, Wanda lives in Wauseon, Ohio, the youngest, Abe, lives in Trail, Ohio and I still live in the town of Sugarcreek where I was born and raised in a wonderful Christian family.

If anyone would like to hear our Major Bowes performance, stop by anytime as I have a recorded cassette of the program which still puts a tear in my eye when I play it. Now my life is filled with seven grandchildren, I'm very active playing golf, quilt for others with other Mennonite ladies in First Mennonite Church of Sugarcreek, making quilts for grandchildren, sing in the choir, sing solos, and work part time for my brother, Abe's, Kids Collection Toy Store in Berlin and Kids Furniture Store in Walnut Creek, Ohio. At home, flower beds, trimming and lawn keep me busy. My greatest asset is "hospitality" and getting along with people, even strangers, and I will try as long as I live to keep our family together. God has been good to me and has given me good health, a young spirit and young at heart. One of my favorite scriptures is Hebrew 13: 1-2: "Always love as brothers, and don't forget to entertain strangers, for by doing so, you never know when you might be entertaining an angel."

Eighty Years and Still Hanging

by Dorothy Browning of Zanesville, Ohio
born in 1924

My school days started in September 1929 at the old George Ridge School on Coopermill Road, halfway between Zanesville, Ohio (Hopewell Township, Muskingum County) and Mount Perry (Perry County). George Ridge was a one-room school, all eight grades with one teacher, Miss Margorie (George). I was already acquainted with the school, as I had two older brothers, LaVerne, ten, and Johnnie, eight.

As a family, we attended many school activities—pie socials, musical programs, holiday celebrations, and most especially the last day of school picnic for all students and families. Local musicians in our neighborhood were Ray Blackstone (banjo) and brothers Earl and Ralph Westcott (accordion and guitar). Earl and Ralph were older brothers of my best friend, Mazie Westcott. We are like "two peas in a pod" and have been "hanging around together" for over 80 years—and still hanging. We graduated together in May, 1942 in a class of 28, nine of whom are still living.

Hopewell Rural School was built in 1933, and opened for classes in January 1934. Mazie and I were in the fourth grade with Miss Marjorie as our third and fourth grade homeroom.

Mazie Taylor is a widow, as I am also, and mother of five children, two of whom are the same age as my two eldest of four. We both are blessed with a lot of grandchildren and great grandchildren.

Mazie and brothers and I and my brothers all walked to school a distance of approximately one mile from George Ridge. Mazie, north of Coopermill Road, and I south of Coopermill Road. "As a crow flies," we walked across roads and through fields.

George Ridge School was heated with a Round Oak heater, cast iron, not oak. It burned coal and wood. Drinking water was carried by bucket from the nearest residence and poured into a stoneware jug with a spigot. That was the home of Edgar and Jenny Hill, who were our custodians, and their son Benton was also a student. In addition to the school building, we also had a coal house and two toilets, one on each back corner of the school.

Our early school years were Depression years. We never had more than we needed and sometimes not enough. We were not in this boat alone, as everyone was affected. We appear to be going the same direction today, sadly. The good part about it was we never missed what we never had.

The few clothes we had worn and worn and worn. Little girls wore dresses to or just below the knees (never slacks), and boys wore knickers just below the knee and high top laced boots with a side penknife pocket, something that is not allowed today. My dresses were hand made or hand-me-downs made over by my Aunt Anna, who was a seamstress. She worked in a coffin factory lining caskets. I was one of her three nieces, and she helped keep us well-dressed with her clothes or feed sack dresses of pretty patterns, wash and wear.

I wore dark bloomers to the hem line or below. One day when I was in the first grade at the blackboard, my bloomers fell to the floor, the result of worn-out elastic. I was embarrassed, but I didn't cry. I simply reached down and pulled them up. I'm sure others were amused more than I was.

We always enjoyed our play times at school, just before the first bell, recess, and lunchtime. Some games I remember especially were outside games: Anthony Over—I could not throw the ball over the school house, but I could run from one side to the other without getting caught. One day, I stumbled and fell and struck my head into the corner foundation. I had a blue angora tam. By the time they carried me into the schoolhouse, blood was coming through my tam. LaVerne was sent to Hills to call our parents. They came and took me to Dr. Harry A. Martins in Gratiot (about three miles north on Morgan Road, Ridge Road to Old US Route 40, west another mile). Dr. Martins stopped the bleeding of an artery. I was taken home. I felt good and asked to return to school for the remainder of the day, which I walked again and felt proud to do it. I still have the scar in my hairline.

Dr. Martin, our hometown doctor, delivered me and brothers at home, John in 1922, me in 1924, and Carroll in 1928.

I'm sure we played inside games, but we were all used to the cold winters and enjoyed our outside games. Another game we played was Fox and Geese. There was a well-worn track in the snow and grass, as we played through the end of the school year in late spring.

When was school was out, that was always a problem for me, as I would say to my mother, "What can I do? There is nothing to do." I really liked school, and I missed it.

Mazie's brother, Ralph, and my cousin, Glen Riggle, made six-foot-high stilts, climbed to the top of the coal house to mount, and walked around the school house and in the yard. We thought that was amazing. When they were ready to get down, they just jumped down and didn't have to return to the coal house to get down.

In January 1934 we were bussed to the new Hopewell Rural School, which was comprised of nine "one-room" schools, to consolidate and form the new Hopewell Rural School. They were Gratiot, Brownsville, Humphry, Burrier, Pleasant Valley, Poverty Run, Wise, George Ridge, and a school called No. 4 on Burkart and Sandy Ridge Road. The students at Brownsville were given the option to go to Glendford (Perry County or Hopewell in Muskingum County). As I remember, our first bus driver was Clayton Mason of Gratiot, Ohio.

Before 1940, Route 40 (the Old Nations Trail from Zanesville west to Brownsville and Jacksontown, Ohio) ran through the middle of Mount Sterling (Hopewell Post Office) and Gratiot, Ohio. When New Route 40 was built in 1940, it outskirted Mount Sterling, Hibb's Hill, and Gratiot, and then continued on through Brownsville. It was feared to be a real problem to local residents and businesses. Even Edwin Gillogly, original owner of The Red and White Store in Gratiot, was so affected that he had a heart attack and died.

Mazie and I were in a third and fourth grade home room with Miss Marjorie as our teacher. We were promoted to the fifth and sixth grade homeroom with Ms. Opal as our teacher. Many years later, Ms. Opal married Edgar Hartness of Gratiot. Miss Opal was well liked and one of our favorite teachers. Miss Opal died April 2, 2008 at the age of 95 in Cape Coral, Florida.

When I was in the fifth grade, I was challenged to race a sixth grader, Kenny Aggas, and I beat him. Kenny really didn't mind, but it was hard on his ego. Many years later, I saw him in Gratiot. We talked about it and laughed. As I was in the fifth grade, Johnnie was in the sixth grade, as he had failed his first grade (Miss Wilson, his teacher at George Ridge). Then he failed the sixth grade, not because he was dumb, but lazy. He never let me get ahead of him, and we graduated together in 1942. I was a good average student, but it seemed I had to cram to get my lessons, and it also seemed that brother John never had to open a book. He was kind, jolly, and well liked by everyone and graduated as our senior class president. Johnnie and I were very close, and he was also very protective of his only sister.

In 36-37 and 37-38 we were in junior high with George Watson and Miss Edna Maxwell as our teachers respectively. This was a new way for us, as we changed classes for different subjects. We became more acquainted with our upper classmen. We looked up to them as role models. Namely, Bessie Bissett, Clyde Gard, Helen Holmes, Mary Kreager, Eleanor Morhead, Loraine Boyer, Gerald Fisher, Marjorie Francis, Jack German, Opal Gutridge, Ada Harkness, Geraldine Hursey, Daryl Porter, Bess Read (her brother, Billy was one of my first boyfriends), Rose Zandlo, Dorothy Shiplett, Stella Wiseman, Ward Aggas, Verna Burrier, Roy Colin, Dorothy Dick, Lucille Felton, Juanita Fennegen, Herbert Gard, Pearl Hursey, Doris Irvin, Charles Maston (whose father was Hopewell Superintendent), Margaret Snider, Franklin Vanderbank, Ruth Williams, Laird Ankrum, Opal Gard, Paul Linn, Marion McPherson, Emma Parr, Doris Porter, Ted Porter, Jane Smith, and Ernestine Zwahlen (all of the above were graduates of 34, 35, 36, 37). My brother, LaVerne Ardrey, graduated in 1938, 38 members. LaVerne died this past March 28, 2008, then his widow, Doris (Solenbarger) died August 30, 2008.

In high school I took home economics (cooking and sewing). I always wished I could take manual training, but it was not permitted My cousin, Carlow Riggle, wanted to take home economics. Later, he learned to crochet and macramé.

I loved school and most of my teachers. My physical education teacher was Miss Gertrude Williams. We played basketball (only half the team on half the floor) where you could only dribble once, shoot, pass the ball, or get rid of it—not very exciting. That has been changed. We played volleyball as well.

Dancing was not allowed in school, but Miss Williams got permission to teach us the Virginia Reel. Miss Williams was a tiny little lady, and I was able to pin her in wrestling—or she let me. She was called "Sprig" by her family and friends. In our senior year, she gave Mazie and me permission to call her "Sprig" in private, but never in public.

During our early years at Hopewell, Mazie and I could get permission to walk to Gratiot, less than a quarter mile, to Gillogly's Red and White Store to buy a tablet or pencil. If we were lucky, we might have enough to buy a penny sucker or five cent candy bar. Also, on one occasion, we got permission to walk home. Our home bus was the second bus after delivery to Gratiot. We enjoyed the walk as friends, and it was good exercise, about three miles.

During the summer months, we tried to visit each other every Wednesday over night, alternating homes, and returned, walking each other half the distance on Thursday. Mazie lived about one mile north of Coopermill Road, and I lived about the same distance south of Coopermill Road.

When I was about 12 years old, I learned to drive out in the field on our farm. My dad made a homemade tractor out of a truck. Upon graduation, Mazie was always quick to tell everyone that I was the only girl who knew how to drive. I loved to drive. As a family, we moved to Gratiot in 1955. In 1960 I was hired as a Hopewell School bus driver, and during my ten years, I also trained other bus drivers.

Mazie's uncle, Charlie Westcott, was our history teacher. He had been in WWI and told us many stories. He and my dad, Ralph Ardrey, were very good friends, but Dad was too young to get into WWI and too old to get into WWII; however, my three brothers served WWII: LaVerne in the Air Force, John in Army Infantry, and Carroll, late 40s, Korean War.

Pearl Harbor was hit December 7, 1941. My boyfriend, Archie Browning, knew he would be drafted, so he elected to join the US Marine Corps Reserves on January 12,1942. I was a senior in high school. Boot camp training was in San Diego, California, then to the South Pacific. He was wounded the first day of battle, as tank battalion beach Eniwetok Atoll, Marshall Islands. Hospital ship to Honolulu, Hawaii. That was February 22, 1944. In August, 1944 a 30-day furlough to Newport Rhode Island, stopped in Zanesville. I quit my job at Firestone Tire and Rubber Company where we made gas tanks for planes. We got married at Coburn United Methodist Church in Zanesville, Ohio. In November, Archie found an apartment we shared with another Marine and wife, and I worked (civil service) at the US Naval Torpedo Station, ferry to Goat Island. We lived at the Ankorage. Archie was discharged April 12, 1945. On our way home by train, we learned that Franklin Delano

Roosevelt died (that's a bit of history).

Back to my subject, school. My junior and senior years, I worked in the school office as Mr. O.F. Leckrone's secretary for experience and credit. Mazie and I (and brother John) graduated May, 1942. A class of 28, only nine of us still living. Our 1942 class was the first graduating class NOT to go Washington, DC for a class trip, and my brother, Carroll, graduated in 1946. His class was the first to go to Washington DC after WWII. We did, however, have a one-day picnic to Ohio Caverns, with Bob Frampton as our bus driver.

May God bless America Always.

House Fires and the Moon Rock

by Crystal (Milhoan) Welch of Fresno, Ohio
born in 1933

Being born in the early thirties (1933), I lived through the last part of the Great Depression. I remember very well sugar, gasoline, and I believe flour was rationed. I remember we had to use stamps and little red tokens. I grew up in a large family, three boys and six girls. The three boys were the oldest, then us six girls. We grew up very poor but very close.

My parents were great; they worked very hard to provide not only food and clothing but integrity for us kids. We had no electricity or running water except the little creek that ran down beside the house.

Speaking of the creek, it served as a place to bathe all summer long. Us kids would grab a bar of soap and head for the creek. It sure beat carrying water from the creek to fill the old galvanized tub.

Winter was a little different story. I know what it was like to chop and carry wood and carry water for all our household needs. I also knew what it was like to iron clothes with the old irons that you set on top of the stove to heat them.

We had two houses burn when I was a kid, one when I was seven and the other when I was fifteen. We lost everything we had both times.

All nine of us attended a one-room school. The name of it was Prohibition, located on Old Route Twenty-One, about halfway between Newcomerstown and Cambridge. It still stands today as a beautiful home with a large wrap-around porch.

Speaking of the old schoolhouse, my sister, Shirlee, and I had the janitor job. We never owned a sled, so we had an old piece of tin, and we tied an old piece of rope on the front to pull it with. We would lay small pieces of wood on it and start out before daylight on the long trip up the hill to the old schoolhouse, where we would unlock the door, go in and build a fire in the old potbellied stove that sat in the middle of the floor. Then at night, when everyone went home, we had to sweep the floor, clean the blackboard, dust the erasers, then fix the fire before we went home.

Marge, Crystal and Bonnie hauling a load of coal in 1951.

I wore hand-me-down clothes. My mother made our dresses out of feed sacks. I remember cutting the sleeves off of old sweaters and put them on my feet like socks. No one knew but me that they didn't cover my toes. One time, in the hot summer, someone about four miles out the road from us gave us a box of clothes. My sister, Shirlee, and I carried it all the way home in the hot sun, sitting down every little bit to rest.

We were pretty much raised on soup beans, fried potatoes, and bread and gravy, although we sometimes had chickens and pigs. I remember on one particular day, having nothing but a biscuit with a little bit of oleo on it to take in my lunch. It was in the winter. I didn't want to eat it in front of the other kids at lunch, 'cause I knew they would make fun of me, so I hid it outside. When lunchtime came, I went outside to eat it, but it was frozen, so I just pulled my little coat around me and sat behind the schoolhouse and ate it.

We had little money for anything except necessities. I was always trying to make our house look better, so me and my sister, Bonnie, papered our bedroom with magazines. Not too bad. We could read and look at pictures at the same time.

I remember the old chamber pots. We had a register right above our old potbellied stove in the living room. Some of the younger kids were playing upstairs, and the pot was about a third full. Yep! You guessed it! Right down on top of the stove.

About snakes. My sister, Shirlee, and I used to catch little water snakes, put them in old cans, build a little fire out of sticks—set the can on them and boil the little snakes. I guess we just wanted to see them squirm.

There are so many things I remember as a child, it's hard to sort them out. Like a little rock in the woods that we called the Moon Rock. We always pretended there was a little girl who lived there that we called Moonie.

There were countless kids over the years that played on that little rock. When they come down today, they always want to go see that big rock called the Moon Rock. They are so surprised to find out it's so small. They forget, when they played there, they were kids. Now some of them are grandparents.

The place where we lived is called Frog Holler, because when summer comes or springtime, you can hear the frogs singing all night long. As a matter of fact, I was just talking to someone today about the Moon Rock. She said she remembered playing on it when she was a kid. My oldest sister still lives there.

For entertainment growing up, we spent most of our time playing in the creek. Every year, we have Cousins' Day in the month of July. That's when we get all the little cousins together for a day of fun and playing in the creek. I guess it's sort of a tradition. We all love it.

I realize this is not in story form, but I'm just trying to hit some highlights.

My sister, Shirlee, couldn't wait to get home from school and sit in front of the old radio and listen to Jack Armstrong and Tennessee Jed. I guess I can relate to just about every one of the subjects you mentioned.

I remember when our first house burned down, we had to move in with my aunt and uncle. They had four kids at the time, and we had seven. There were nine of us, including our parents, and six of them, fifteen altogether. We probably lived together for about a year, then my aunt and uncle moved to Buffalo, Ohio, and we bought the house we were in for I believe $3,500. It had an old house and barn and 105 acres. Later on, that was the second house that burned.

We lived in a little one-room building until we built the house my sister is still living in today. We still have a get-together every year on Memorial Day. There is probably close to three hundred of us altogether, although some of us are in different states, and everyone can't get there.

We've lost both parents, two brothers, and a sister. We miss them terribly, and we still get together every two or three weeks for breakfast or lunch. We are still very close. I thank God for my heritage. I wouldn't change the way I grew up. God is good.

Washing, Baths and Cows

By H. and E. Hershberger of Millersburg, Ohio

When we were little children we didn't have built-in cupboards in the kitchen or a bathroom in the house. We had a granite table for our dirty dishes and an old-fashioned sink and a cabinet for our clean dishes. We also bathed in the living room beside our coal and wood stove in an aluminum washtub. Also, when we washed in the winter we dried our clothes in the living room on a wash line we put up on Mondays and had a drying wash rack for our smaller things. We also had to go in the outhouse in the winter and summer, which wasn't at all fun when it was really cold.

We milked around eight cows when we children were small. We butchered our own pigs and beef for our meat, which we did at home.

Stamps were three-cents each and bread was 39 cents or less a loaf.

Parking at Maggies and Time to Stop

by Max A. Williams of Coshocton, Ohio
born 1920

Dad's Justice. My father was employed by the Coshocton, Ohio Post Office and served for about 30 years before retiring to Florida with my mother during the 1960's. One day during the mid 30's he told me that the boys working with him, putting up mail, were teasing him about his car being parked in front of Maggie's (a local beer parlor) on a Saturday night.

Jean and Max Williams, Captain U.S. Army 83 Infantry Division in 1943.

My father, who did not smoke or drink beer, asked me if I had been drinking beer. He had me cold, so I said yes, that I had taken my buddy to the tavern to meet with some friends.

I was 16 years old, a senior in high school. He had taught me to drive when I was 13.

As I recall, my buddy and I had some wine as we did not like beer.

I could see me having the law laid before me with restrictions...no car, no dates, etc. But to my surprise he said, "Next time, please park the car in the rear of the building."

WHEW!

* * * *

At a church supper, our family, Mom and Dad and six of us kids, had enjoyed our meal and settled down for some entertainment. It was around 1930. I was born in 1920, had four brothers and a sister, one year older.

The program of the evening started with an inquiry as to the largest family in attendance. The Williams won the applause of the crowd. Of course, the minister had to have something to say to us. He said that he knew that the first born of the family made the parents so happy that they purchased a nice big perambulator to show off the newborn. The second born (that's me) also rode around so much, that a new pair of tires was needed. Then, according to the preacher, when the third child came along, a paint job was needed. With the fourth child, also a boy, a new set of handlebars was installed. For number five, a set of modern headlights were attached. And for the last, and sixth, a stoplight was added.

A Room Full of Herns

by Roberta J. Gee of Zanesville, Ohio
born in 1939

I was born on April 11, 1939 in a log cabin my dad, Morgan Hern, built. I had an older sister, Ida, two and-a-half years old. I don't remember much about my life until I was six years old. We had moved to Chandlersville, Ohio. My sister was in the third grade and I was in the first. Our teacher, Mrs. Graham, taught first, second, and third grades all in one room, so I got to be in with my older sister. That made me happy until we moved back to Zanesville, and I was in the second grade and no longer with my sister. I didn't like that very much and every morning I would complain of a stomachache so I wouldn't have to go to school. I was scared to death to be by myself. After a checkup with my doctor, my mother, Anna, decided there was nothing wrong with me, so my complaining didn't do any good. I went to school and made the best of a bad situation.

We moved again and this time I loved school. I was eight years old and in the third grade. My teachers all liked me and my fourth grad teacher remarked about how she "would like to have a room full of little Herns." That made me proud.

Life in this house from age eight to 16 was a story in and of itself. We didn't have a water heater, but didn't know we were supposed to have one, so my mother heated all the water for baths, dishes, etcetera on top of the gas range in the kitchen. Also, we didn't have any central heat, just a pot-bellied stove in the center room of the house. Every night we would heat our bath water on the stove. All during the week, we only took sponge baths. Like Dolly Parton said one time, "I washed up as far as possible and down as far as possible and when my brothers left the room, I washed ole possible." I didn't have any brothers but I did have four sisters.

My baby sister, Patty, was born when I was ten years old. I remember washing her diapers in the old wringer washer. I loved that. Of course there were no clothes dryers then, at least we hadn't heard of them yet, so in the winter, my dad would put clotheslines in the kitchen—that's where we dried our laundry.

Instead of Saturday night baths, we took Sunday night baths. That's when we got to get in the big galvanized wash tub, one after the other. My mother would add some hot water to it before the next one got in for her bath.

We got our first telephone in 1949. That's when the operator would say, "Number please," and you gave her the number you were trying to call. Well, I rushed home every day from school to play on that telephone. My older sister said to me one day, "If you don't stop playing on that phone, the operator is going to get after you." To me the "operator" meant a doctor or some medical person, so I quit playing on the phone.

My Grandmother Lovejoy was living with us for a while and was bedfast. I remember her listening to a soap opera every day called "Young Widow Brown." I got interested in it too, during the summer, and I listened to it with her. I was probably 12 by this time and didn't understand a lot about what was going on.

On Saturday nights I would climb into bed with her and we would listen to the Grand Ole Opry together I grew up loving country music. I remember there was an ad on that show for a bible in pictures. She sent and got it for me and after 60 years I still have it.

I remember going to church in a little country church in Chandlersville, Ohio. Our dad would give us each a dime for the collection, and my younger sister, Janet, would put her dime in, but she wanted to take out a nickel—I guess because it was bigger.

At the age of 16, we moved into a house with a bathroom and a furnace. I thought I had died and gone to heaven. A bath every night in a normal bathtub and we didn't have to heat the water on the stove. Boy, was this living or what? I think the best thing though was no more going out to that ole two-holer and brushing the snow off the seat in the winter before we sat down.

Our mother made most of our toys in the "good ole days." She made us dolls out of our dad's long white work socks and little baby cradles out of oatmeal boxes. She even upholstered the furniture for the dollhouse she made for us. She was good at that kind of thing and of course she made all of our dresses until we went to junior high. That's when we were allowed to have "store bought" dresses and permanents in our hair. Up until then we had long braided hair. We didn't wear shorts or pants until we were married. Our parents were very strict on a lot of things.

At age 19, in 1958, I married my high school sweetheart, Jim Gee.

Our boys, Danny, Jeff and Jimmie, still laugh at me when we talk about the 40s, especially when I tell them I walked ten miles to school every day in five feet of snow. I think the miles and the amount of snow get larger with every generation. We did have long, hard winters back then, but I'm pretty sure it was only about one to one and-a-half miles I walked and the snow was only a couple feet deep.

Now that I'm 70 years old, would I go back to "the good ole days?" In a heartbeat! If I could have everyone with me again who was with me in the good ole days, yeah, I'd go back.

Her Kids in the Isolated Schoolroom
by La Joy Green of Zanesville, Ohio
born in 1940

Back in "The Good Ole Days" in 1948, I was in the third grade at Adamsville. There was no room for us in the big old white wood school building, so we were assigned to have our class in a shed. There were around 20 of us students. The old shed was a mite airy, to say the least, so our teacher (a bit on the masculine side) had the boys help her tear up cardboard boxes and nail them to the walls to keep the snow out.

Our teacher did not allow us to go to the main building for anything. At recess time we played with each other. The boys had a bat, ball and glove, and the girls a long rope to jump. We dug our own spring out back behind the shed, and the boys took turns carrying in buckets of water. We all drank out of the same dipper.

Adamsville's frame grade school - grades one through six.

Our room was so cold in the winter we wore our coats, hats, and gloves. The girls wore leggings. They were made thick like layers of a coat and you could not run in them.

We had a coal stove and above it was an open stairway. When it was real cold, the teacher had us sit on the steps above the stove with our coats and gloves on for our classes. Our drinking water froze in the bucket.

Mrs. Smith was so strict; she put the fear of God in us. Her paddle lay on the top of her desk and she often used it. Another one of her punishments was The Dungeon, if you were caught whispering or disobeying. It was a small room around nine by twelve with black curtains and spiders and webs and mice.

One day, the boy in front of me turned around to ask if he could borrow my pencil and the teacher caught us. Off to The Dungeon we went. It seemed like we were in there hours. You could only stand up still because it was cold and so dark and scary. Everyone came out teary eyed.

All twenty of us sat in alphabetical order. Our ole school room was very clean and we all had our jobs: Sweeping floor and mopping, taking out the stove ashes, erasing and washing the blackboards, dusting the erasers, straightening the lunch buckets, coats and boots and washing the desks.

Our third grade teacher was different in many ways. We never saw her in a dress, always a shirt and slacks. Her hair was cut like a man's and there was nothing feminine about her, when all of our other teachers in the 40s were wearing dresses and skirts. My first meeting with her, I was trying to figure out if she was a she or a he. But we all respected her, and she did her best to keep us warm and keep us her kids!

A girlfriend of mine had worked for an award for perfect attendance, and she never missed a day until both her grandpas died and she missed two days. Someone else got the award, but our teacher gave her a Bible, and my friend still has the Bible.

One day, Mother didn't have time to pack my lunch (there was no cafeteria in those days), so we walked up town Adamsville to the confectionary for lunch. With a bunch of students to wait on, I was last to be served, and the lady who owned the store told me to hurry because I would be late getting back to class. I ran down the street as fast as my legs would carry me, and sure enough, I was late. Mrs. Smith said, "Where have you been?" and I told her as best as I could, scared to death and out of breath, and she did not punish me.

When the old schoolroom was too hot to have class in, she let us go out back where there was a tree and a log for us to sit on and a tiny stream of water, and we sat there and had our classes.

Sometimes we were allowed to take our lunch buckets out and eat on the log under the old tree. Never did any other students come around us, because she had let everyone know this was third grade territory, and she was in control.

On Monday morning, we said Pledge to the American Flag and The Lord's Prayer. Then we were each to say our memorized Bible verse and no two were to be alike. I'll never know how we did it, but we did.

At recess time, we were not to play with kids from other grades. "We were her kids."

She drove an ole big car that needed to be pushed to get it started more often than not. So before time for us to get to our school buses, at last recess, we would all go out and push her car, and then it would start. We were happy to get a break and make her happy.

At the beginning of the school year, our teacher warned us not to have our parents come to school to visit. I obediently went home and told my mother not to come to school to visit us. The teacher said so! Mother didn't always believe me, because I had quite an imagination, so one day while we were having class, there was a knock on our door. It was so quiet you could hair a pin drop. It was my mother! I thought I would die; my heart was beating so fast! Our class was in shock. How would the teacher punish me? Mother introduced herself, and she and our teacher got along fine. To God be the glory! My life was spared!

Nothing Sold on Sunday

by Bonnie Hensley of Byesville, Ohio
born in 1927

Going to the outhouse on a cold winter night. Hand crank to start the car, quite a kick to it. Gas lights with fragile mantles easily broken then on to coal oil lamps. Washed clothes with a washboard, hard on knuckles. Coal stove in kitchen with oven, water tank on side and warming oven on top. Many uses, heat, cook, bake, hot water. Heat flat iron on kitchen stove for ironing. Heat water on stove for baths in wash tub. Get in line.

Dresses made from feed sacks. Trade different color and patterns.

Ice man brought blocks of ice on his shoulder for the top of the ice box. A card was put in the window for the amount wanted. Kids would follow the truck for chips of ice left.

Nothing was sold on Sunday.

Exactly What Happened

by Tom Harmon of Zanesville, Ohio
born 1933

I was raised in a town in Ohio, but my mother's parents lived on a farm south of Duncan Falls, Ohio.

Every summer as I was growing up, I went to my grandparents' for about a month to help on the farm.

We slept on feather tick beds and got up about six AM. Grandma would have a big breakfast ready: ham, sop gravy, fried potatoes and fried eggs, toast and apple butter or homemade jam or jelly. Everything was served on a big meat platter except the gravy, butter apple butter or homemade jam or jelly.

We had no electric and everything was cooked on an old coal stove. We used oil lamps mornings and nights.

Grandpa would have the cows in the stanchions ready to be milked. We helped with the milking, then went back to the house to separate the milk. Grandma would do the pouring of the milk into the separator and turn the handle. This separated the cream from the rest of the milk. This was put in the spring house, which was a wood building with a spring running through the bottom of it. We drank the milk with our meals and churned the cream into butter.

Finally, we were ready to go to the field. If it was the corn field, Grandpa would plow the corn using Buck, one of the horses, and the corn plow. The boys would hoe the corn which was cutting all the weeds and pulling them up around the hill of corn.

Grandpa would get the hayfork, which was a U shaped iron piece of metal with little pieces of metal attached to the bottom or open end that worked like scissors and kept the hay from sliding off the hayfork. Grandpa would then loosen Buck from the wagon and use him to pull the fork and hay by pulley, up to the hayloft where we boys were waiting to mow back the hay.

After we had put up a wagon of hay, it was time for lunch. We took the two horses, Buck and Maude, to the creek for a drink of water. We had a jug of water keeping cool in the creek. We ate the sandwiches Grandma had packed for us. Then we went back to the field to collect more hay.

We worked until we heard the dinner bell when it was time to come in. We took the horses to the creek to get a drink and then to the barn where they were put in stalls and fed. We ate supper which was a big meal of meat, potatoes, vegetables, tomatoes , salad, homemade bread and homemade apple butter or jam and milk to drink. Grandpa said grace at every meal.

After supper, we milked, separated the milk, slopped the hogs and fed the chickens. Grandpa gathered the eggs of which part of them were sold at Krogers and the rest were kept to be used on the farm.

In our spare time we picked berries for jam or jelly. Sometimes we would go help the man case oil wells.

When it was time to go back home, Grandpa would give each of us ten dollars to give to our mother for school clothes.

A Chronology

by Edison W. Lucas of Enon, Ohio
Born 1930

Background (1930–1938): I was born in Wayne Township, Belmont County, in the same log house that my mother was born. My grandmother delivered me since she was a well-known midwife that delivered many babies in the area. She would deliver the baby, cook all meals, wash clothes by hand, take care of the mother and any other chores the mother would normally do for seven days for a total payment of $5.00. Having no automobile and no phone, my father rode a horse eight miles each way to Somerton, Ohio to have Dr. MacMillan prepare and sign my birth certificate.

The log house that I lived in for 18 years had two bedrooms upstairs and a living room and kitchen down stairs. It had a fireplace and a wood burning stove for heating and cooking.

First grade Lane's School in 1936.

During those 18 years, we never had electricity, phone or running water. Water was available from a drilled well by a bucket, rope and handed cranked reel.

We did have a radio that required three different batteries (most of the time; at least one was dead). I always listened to The Lone Ranger, Captain Midnight, Tom Mix, Inner Sanctum Mystery, Lum and Abner and Amos and Andy.

Between my fourth and eighth birthday, I had two kinds of measles, chicken pox, whooping cough, mumps, diphtheria and a ruptured appendix. The ruptured appendix occurred when I was five years old (July, 1936) and almost did me in. I had been complaining of stomach pain for a couple of weeks and the doctor decided it was probably from green apples I had eaten. When my mother found me unconscious, laying in a coal ash pile, she carried me about a half mile to a neighbor's house since my father wasn't home, plus they had a car. While taking me to the Barnesville, Ohio hospital on a very hot July day, the Model A Ford had two flat tires that had to be patched and pumped up by hand along the side of the road. The surgeon that performed the operation had to travel from Pittsburgh, Pennsylvania. During the operation, my father was allowed to watch the surgery through a window. In the middle of surgery, the surgeon came out and told my father and the family doctor that to finish the surgery was hopeless because my bowels and intestines had holes from the rupture and infection. The family doctor directed the surgeon to finish the surgery and let God determine the outcome.

I was unconscious for two and half weeks of the four weeks in the hospital, which would be considered intensive care now.

Since we didn't have health insurance, my parents had to come up with the money to pay for a total hospital payment of $450.00 (that included the hospital care, family doctor and the surgeon from Pittsburgh). My parents sold milk cows for $5.00 each, hogs for $2.00 each and borrowed the remainder from a neighbor lady that, during the Great Depression, had her money stored in a sock, not in a bank. To pay off the neighbor lady's loan, my mother hoed out weeds in tobacco plants for 50 cents a day. In addition, my father moved oil well drilling equipment with a team of his horses for $2.00 a day, which amounted to a 14-hour day when including the travel time to and from our home.

When I had membrane diphtheria, the county nurse quarantined my mother and I for six weeks. Since my father drove a school bus, he had to stay in the barn, in the wintertime, for six weeks, and my mother carried him his meals to the barn.

Grade School Years (1936-1944): My first eight years of school attendance was a one room school; one teacher for all eight grades, one coal burning potbelly stove, no electricity, no phone, two outside toilets and a hand pump water well (when it didn't go dry) by the name of Lanes School. The school library consisted of approximately six Zane Grey books, which I read numerous times.

We didn't have any school athletic equipment, but at recess we would play anti-over, Red Rover Red Rover come over, sled ride, fox and hound, cowboy and Indian and sometimes lock the teacher in the girls' toilet.

The wood floor of the school had many holes, burnt with a hot stove poker, that kids would stuff notes to other kids in before the teacher could get hold of them. During school hours we would fish these notes out by fishhooks, string, glue and other techniques that were successful. Many of the notes retrieved were between boys and girls that were written many years earlier who were then married and had children in the school at that time.

During my eight years in grade school, we had two tongues frozen to the well pump handle and one fifth grader was upset because he wasn't chosen on a ball team, so he decided to smash some dynamite caps with a rock, losing several fingers.

Behind our grade school was a well-known lover's hideaway. Several times the teacher was seen taking little white water balloons from the first and second grade boys chasing the little girls with the balloons they had filled at the hand pump well. In addition to locking the teacher in the girls' outside toilet about twice a year, someone shoved potatoes into the tailpipe of her 1930's Chevrolet Coupe. When she tried to start it, the muffler and tailpipe blew up and she thought someone had put a bomb in it.

High School Years (1944-1948): My high school years started during World War II therefore extra curricular activities were limited. Our sports consisted of boy's basketball, baseball and field/track meets. The girls only had inter-class sports activities.

To help the war effort the school FFA had students collect milkweed pods to be used in the making of life jackets, and collect iron, aluminum, copper, lead and other metals to support the war.

Another program was to collect the two front feet of foxes, tails of mice and rats, and the feet of crows because these animals destroyed crops and poultry. For each pest destroyed, the student would receive war saving stamps that when saved they would eventually be able to receive a war bond.

Farm Chore Years (1938–1948): From eight years old to eighteen years old, I was required to hand milk one to five cows every morning and evening, year round. In addition, on non-school days, I would bring the cows in from the pasture every morning and evening for milking.

Since I was only able to have one pair of new shoes a year, I went bare footed when I was at home from April to October. Some mornings in the spring and fall, the grass would have frost so you tried not to walk where there was a frost, but that wasn't always possible. Cows in the morning were generally laying down, so when they got up you would stand where they had been laying to warm up your feet. Numerous times I have stood in very fresh, steaming cow manure to get my feet warm. During the summer your feet would become fairly tough, but I always hated hay and wheat harvest time because the shin briars and stubbles are rough on bare feet.

By the time I was 15 I was able to have more than one pair of shoes a year. To earn some money in the summer I sometimes worked for an oil well drilling company where they run or pulled well casing for 12 hours at 50 cents an hour.

I also hand cut and shocked field corn for neighbors for 10 cents per shock. These were enormous shocks because the farmer would plant wheat in the fall and wanted as few shocks as possible. Each shock would take 30-45 minutes and if you worked real hard from 7:00 a.m. to 6:00 p.m. you might make $2.00, and a few times I never received pay.

When it was wheat and oats threshing and silo filling time, farmers would exchange help. Being a teenager, 15 to 18, and not having a tractor, the choice of which jobs you were told to do were few. I always ended up as a field hand loading corn or wheat wagons with wheat/oat shocks or heavy corn stock bundles tied up with enormous ragweeds still rooted in the ground. I remember one instance we started filling a large silo at 7:00 a.m. I was in the field loading the wagons with corn bundles when they said it was dinner time, 11:30 a.m. It was hot and I was thirsty and hungry and the farmer said the women didn't have dinner ready, but we could help ourselves to some cold watermelons he had in the milk cooler. We had about an hour delay before dinner was ready and during that time I must have eaten ten pounds of watermelon. When I got to some real food, I ate so much watermelon I didn't have room for it. Going back out in the field to load more corn bundles, I was again hungry in 20 minutes. About 6:00 p.m., the tractor drivers seemed to think the next load would be the final load and this optimism continued for the next seven to eight loads, or until dark. That was the hardest day of work of my life and I must have lost ten pounds. I later learned that the delay of dinner and bringing the watermelons was planned by this farmer to reduce the amount of food that would normally be eaten.

Hunting and Fishing Years (1939-1948): I started hunting rabbits and squirrels when I was nine years old. Two neighbor boys and I would hunt rabbits with a little rat terrier dog and a cat. The dog would chase the rabbit into a hole or under a rock and the cat would sometimes chase the rabbit out. My parents wouldn't buy me a gun when I was ten years old, but a neighbor, who was the most successful hunter in Wayne Township, gave me a bolt action, single shot, .22 rifle and a box of shells. I never hunted with the rifle with other kids, except for coon hunting, and then it was always empty of shells.

Many times I'd find squirrels in holes in trees, raccoons in holes in trees or under rocks, and groundhogs and opossums in holes in the ground. To remove these critters I would find a long skinny live tree, no larger than an inch and a half at the big end and ten to 12 feet long. I would remove the limbs and hammer the small end between a couple of rocks to splinter the end. I would push the stick into the hole until I could feel the animal on the splintered end of the stick. When you could feel the critter moving, you would start twisting the stick and the splintered end would twist and tangle in the fur of the animal and then you could pull it out. When you twisted out a raccoon, fox or groundhog, you better have a plan ready when it comes out of its hole.

When I got older I bought some leg hold steel traps and would set a 20-30 trap line. In the summertime I stored the traps in a horse manure pile to remove human scent. My neighbor taught me many ways to trap animals and with a couple I had some success. Foxes normally mark their territory by dumping on the top of anthills, so I would bury a double spring steel trap in the loose dirt of an anthill. Another technique I used was to put a chicken in a wire cage and hide several steel traps in the grass or dirt.

The Outhouse Rooster and Fried Bean Sandwiches

by Margie Auker of New Lexington, Ohio
Born 1924

My name is Margie Auker of New Lexington, Ohio.

I am writing my experience of the Depression in the 30's. I am 84 years of age and a cancer patient since March of 1991. I am a survivor. I had cancer in my bladder, a breast removed and now I may have it in my thyroid. I'm going through tests at the time. I've also had a hysterectomy and radiation on my lung last year: 34 treatments.

My family lived in the country on Route 93 in Crooksville. We was poor folks like everybody else who lived in the area. My father worked on WPA and the coal mines for $2.00 a day to provide food for the family.

We had a combinet we used at night, and Dad would carry it out in a paper bag, so the cars going by wouldn't know what he was carrying. So he thought!

We also had an outside privy and one night my sister had to go and my mother said, "You go, I will watch you, you will be okay." As she entered the door, a rooster flew out. He was there roosting for the night. It scared her half to death.

My dad raised a little corn. My brother went to the outhouse after dark before going to bed. I found some fodder shocks and when he came around the garage I started beating on the garage. He said he wasn't scared. He wouldn't admit it.

My mother sewed some. She made two new dresses for my sister and I. One was brown print and the other green print. The next day we wore the opposite cause we didn't have anymore.

At school we took fried bean sandwiches to lunch. The other kids traded their lunchmeat sandwiches for our fried bean.

Saturday night was bath night. Dad fired up the old coal stove to heat the water for the No. 3 tub. There was four kids and Mom and Dad. The cleanest ones went first, and so on until we all had our bath. There was extra hot water on the stove heating up when that got cold.

There was hard times, a house full of love and we got by in them good old days.

The Dining Room Tonsillectomy

by Rita Marie Christ of South Zanesville, Ohio
born 1924

One of my favorite memories is when my mother, my grandmother, my sister, and I went to the movies on Sunday afternoon.

First we stopped at Scotly's nut shop on Main Street between 4th and 5th Streets for a box of popcorn. Afterwards, we went to Kalsampe's Ice Cream Parlor on North First Street for a soda. The theater we went to was Liberty Theatre. Unfortunately none of those places are in existence today.

In 1937 there was the big flood that engulfed lower Main Street and came up to Muskingum Avenue on Pine Street. It was so amazing to see the water lapping at the intersection.

When I was 19 years old I got diphtheria. I had gone to a Cleveland Browns game and had to stand in drizzling rain the whole time. This was a bus full of people from Line Material, which also no longer exists.

Unfortunately, our house was quarantined and my father had to stay with his parents so he could go to work. Dr. Martin was in attendance to me and kept running tests. First it was positive, and then negative, and then positive again. To be sure I was cured he decided to remove my tonsils.

This was done on a long dining room table. They covered it with blankets, lots of newspapers, and a sheet. My sister wanted to watch, but she got scared and hid behind a chair in the living room. My boyfriend, Bob, sent me flowers.

This was just before Thanksgiving and I couldn't eat solid food, so my mom gave me mashed potatoes and gravy and applesauce. By the first of December, we were out of quarantine.

Another memory I have, when I was a teenager, was about my grandmother. She lived with us and when she got sick and went into the hospital, children weren't allowed to know what was wrong or visit in the hospital. When she died, her body laid in state in our living room, and someone needed to stay with her all the time. The first night I was elected and slept on the couch.

The Mysterious Separator and Grandpa Zwick

by Francis Blackstone of Lewisville, Ohio
born 1946

I was born June 26, 1946 in Lewisville, Ohio. Other than two and half years I spent in Orrville, Ohio, I have lived my entire life in Monroe County, Ohio.

Myself and all my siblings had to work around the farm from a very young age. We fed the chickens, hogs and cattle. We had to milk cows and sold cream. Cranking the cream separator was one of my least favorite jobs. I never did understand how it separated the cream from the milk.

Two of my most memorable childhood memories took place at my Grandpa Joseph Zwick's house. On a Sunday afternoon in October, we would go to my grandpa's place and spend the afternoon gathering hickory nuts from two trees on a steep creek bank. The nuts would later be cracked to use in Mom's homemade candy or just to be ate.

In late November, Grandpa would have the annual

Grandpa Zwick's separator.

butchering. Grandpa and my Uncle Leander Zwick would spend two or three days getting everything ready. My dad, mom, brothers, sisters and I would get there before daylight. Grandpa and Uncle Leander would already have the fire going to heat three big cast iron kettles of water for scalding the hogs. This was an all day job involving cutting up the hogs, cooking the head meat, rendering the lard (which was my job), grinding the sausage, stuffing the sausage, and salting the hams and shoulders.

To this day, every year at that time, I think back to the good times I had at my Grandpa Zwick's.

Working for What You Want

By Gerald C. Bowman of Lancaster, Ohio
Born 1929

I grew up in Cambridge, Ohio and the surrounding area.

My childhood was a lot different than the childhood of today (thank goodness). My first five years was pretty normal; they were also the first five years of The Great Depression. Then as I got a little older and a little bigger, my family realized I could use a shovel, hammer, saw and so forth. I was taught how to milk cows, weed the garden, drive horses and clean the barn. Yuck!

I had to go back over the hill to bring in the cows at five in the morning, winter and summer. Then I fed them corn that I shelled on a hand operated sheller, one ear at a time. I then carried water for seven cows and two horses and fed them hay while my uncle milked six of them. I was only able to milk one, but the cats liked me because I would squirt them with milk.

I was soon able to drive a hay rake. I drove one horse pulling a rake that had to be dumped every 50 feet by jumping up and down on a foot pedal while pulling on a lever at the same time and still keep the horse going in a straight line. When I was about ten-years-old I drove two horses pulling a side bar mowing machine to mow hay. It was a very difficult and dangerous job while handling two horses at the same time. Fortunately, Child Labor Laws would prohibit this today.

Another time we moved and I went to a one room schoolhouse with a pot bellied stove in the center for heat. My father pulled up in front of the school and handed me my grade card and told me to go in and give it to the teacher. He did not even go in to introduce me to the teacher (quite a difference from the way things are done today). I went to country schools until 5th grade when we moved to town.

In moving to town, we now had a bathroom inside our house. We could take a bath any day of the week, not just on Saturday night and we did not have to carry water from a well pump or walk down a path to the outhouse. We now had a telephone we did not have to crank to call someone and your neighbors were not able to listen to your conversation. Electric lights now replaced our kerosene lamps. I also found out that bib overhauls were not the proper attire to be wearing in city schools. I asked my mother for different clothes and she advised me that they didn't have the money and now that I'm eleven years old I should get a job.

I got a job that night selling the Columbus Star, a weekly paper that sold for ten cents each. I got one cent per paper and made eleven cents the first night. I got another paper route and made 35 cents a week delivering 103 papers six days a week. I delivered papers for a neighboring city at 4:00 o'clock in the morning to about eight customers all over town. I mowed yards for 25 and 35 cents. When I was 14-years-old I got a job at Woolworth Company 5 and 10 Cent Store. I worked one hour before school, one and a half hours at lunchtime, two hours after school and 13 hours on Saturday. My take home pay for the week was $3.57. From that time on I was never without a job.

I had to retire at the age of 71 years because of my health. I am now almost 80 and have had a good life because I learned at an early age that if you want something you work hard for it. I was fortunate in my later career to have made a six figure salary by using the work ethic I learned early on. I complained to a doctor once that I was working too hard. He advised me that he had never lost a patient because they worked too hard. I never complained again.

Gabby, the Popsicle Girl

by Joan Coury Mohler of Zanesville, Ohio
born 1945

As a child growing up in the 40s, my father passed away when I was five years old. But I can remember a lot of things about him. He was a wonderful man whom everyone liked.

My grandpa owned a grocery store on 6th Street called the Imperial Market. That is where Dad worked.

My dad brought Popsicles home after work for me every day. My family called me the Popsicle girl. They also called me Gabby, because I talked a lot.

I spent a lot of time with my grandparents after my dad died. On Fridays my mom would take me to Grandpa's store. While I waited I read comic books and get bubblegum and trinkets from those little machines. Of course you don't see those kind of machines now days. Once I got an Elsie the Cow stuffed animal. Can you even imagine what that would be worth now days? I'll never know because it's gone. It was brought in by the Borden man.

There was one day when I was at the store and the stagecoach with the Budweiser horses came to town. Boy was that exciting. I got my picture taken with them along with my two uncles.

No one knew what happened to that picture. It came up missing. Well, I got a phone call in November of 2008 from my aunt. She wanted me to come to her house. When I got there, she said, "Is this the picture you have been looking for?" Oh my gosh, there it was. I took the picture to our corner shop and had a 11x14 and made to put in a frame. It is a great photo. One of our local restaurants has a print of the picture hanging in their restaurant. It's quite a conversation piece.

I have the memories of our downtown. I can remember when it was so busy. Cars and people and buses and businesses such as 5&10 stores. Woolworth's, Kroger's and many more. Everyone hung out on Main Street. It's hard trying to tell kids now days how it used to be. All they know is the mall! Ugh! I hate it. I would rather go in and out of stores.

Christmas was fun downtown. With the snow, Christmas carols playing, all the people, the running all over town in the snow, I loved it! I miss it!

I forgot to tell you my grandpa took me to the movies downtown every Sunday and my grandma took me shopping every Saturday and bought me paper dolls. Now days those dolls would probably cost a fortune. I had Blondie and Dagwood, Annie Oakley, Janet Page, Roy Rogers and many more. They came in a folder that, when you opened it, you could put your paper dolls in after you cut them out. I had so many, I would sit in the middle of all of them and build a house around me. A lot, huh?

I remember my first dance was with the boy across the hill. On his way over to my house, he was bringing my flowers and fell and broke his arm.

Oh, do you remember Howdy Doody? I was at Cracker Barrel restaurant and they had a copy of a tape they were selling. I did everything but roll on the floor with excitement. Well I bought it. I thought my granddaughter would like it. It was in black and white. I put it in the VCR, and oh my goodness, how in the world did I ever watch that? I asked my husband, "How did we watch that? My mother let me watch that?" My granddaughter looked at it and went on to play with something else. That was awful. I also bought a Annie Oakley tape. Not tape, but DVD. It was fun watching that.

Well this is some of my memories for you. So if you want a picture of the horses and the grocery store, let me know. I also have a picture of the Liberty Theater if you're interested.

By the way, I never skipped school. We had black and white TV, some with a halo. The snowstorms we had back then would have been really bad now days. We walked to school in them. If kids now days had snows like we did, they wouldn't survive. Haha.

Dark Coal Mines and Newberry Popcorn

by Beverly Bookless of Coshocton, Ohio
born 1936

My father is gone now, but he would be proud of this. This story is about my father, Eldred Young. He worked in the old coal mines. He worked very hard and it was a dangerous place to be. He took some schooling and learned to read blueprints. He became a mine foreman, but he had to be in the mines with the other men every day.

When I was about 11 years old, I begged him to let me go into the mine. Every Sunday he had to go there and turn on this huge fan that circulated the air. So, he finally said that he would take me.

He went up to the mouth of the mine and away we went. I couldn't even stand up straight in there. I bumped my head about three times, and then I was stepping in wet mud and clay. Water was dripping down on my head. It didn't take me long to get out of that dark, wet, scary place and I never wanted to do it again.

They wore carbide lights on their hats. Their dinner pails had a handle. You put drinking water in the bottom and the top tray you put your lunch in.

Eldred Young, dad, and Gene Lohna, old freind in an old mine work shed.

Mines were hard work and no one would want to do it today.

Friday night on Main Street in Coshocton was fun. My parents would park and visit with people, and us kids would go into Newberry's to get a big bag of popcorn for 10 cents, and sit in the car and watch the people go by. Sometimes we would go to the movie matinee on Saturday for twenty cents. We would have cartoon movies all day at the old Sixth Street Theater.

We would also go out in the country in the summer and have picnics with fried chicken, potato salad and more. Our dads would fish for awhile.

Every summer, our family had a big birthday party for me and my uncle on the same day. My dad had a big fire going in the barnyard. We would all roast hotdogs, and then my uncle Chub would make homemade ice cream. Then we would have homemade birthday cake.

The kids and adults would play a game called red rover, red rover, let Tene come over. Then they would run across the yards and try to break through their arms. Of course, us kids would end up just swinging on their arms. It was so much fun for adults and kids.

When we were done with all of this, the adults would sit and talk. My aunt Esther would play the piano. It was so much fun. The things of the past, it's fun to remember.

Call Boys

by John Croft of Cambridge, Ohio
born in 1931

In the days before very many people had telephones, and you had to send a quick message on a regular basis, teenage boys were often employed for this purpose.

In cities that were dispatch centers for train service, the dispatch office had a call board. The call board listed the crew assignments as well as a list of substitutes that were "on call" if someone called in sick. Teenage boys were hired to wait in the office until needed. These boys were called "call boys," and often were sent out to contact a substitute in the middle of the night. They were made familiar with the inside of the home, even to the location of the bedroom of the individual they were seeking, and given a key to enter the house.

This was the setting for one of the visits to my aunt and uncle in Lima in the early 30s.

When we arrived, my aunt told us they had a boarder, and he was "on call" the weekend we were there. This meant my younger sister and I, along with our cousin, who was a couple of years older than me, would have to sleep on the floor in the living room. My aunt told us not to be alarmed if, in the middle of the night, a "call boy" came to get her boarder.

Sure enough, in the middle of the night he came. Because he thought he could see well enough without using his flashlight, he didn't turn it on. He hadn't considered the possibility of kids sleeping on the floor in his path.

My little sister screamed when he fell over her. I don't know who was scared the most, my sister or the call boy. He blurted out, "Oh my gosh, oh my gosh! It's okay. Call boy! Call boy!"

My cousin, who had encountered call boys before, shouted out, "It's alright, we know who you are, stop shouting. You're going to wake the whole house."

He quieted down, gathered himself, and went up the stairs to complete his mission. We spent several minutes giggling amongst ourselves before we were able to get back to sleep.

Spankings for Talking (and Not)

by Martha Ellen Haislet of Dexter City, Ohio
born 1928

I was born Martha Ellen Tidd, January 7, 1928 in Noble County, Jackson Township, near Dungannon, Ohio on State Route 339. I lived on a 96 acre farm with three brothers and one sister and Mother and Dad. I lived during the 1930 Depression. I attended a one room schoolhouse and east on 339, just one mile, was a two room schoolhouse that was a high school. My older sister and brother graduated from it. My other brothers went two years and the last two years rode a bus to Dexter City to a high school.

Back to my life on the farm, we had no electricity, gas, or water. To see with, we had kerosene lamps to study with. We got our electric in the year of 1945 in August. And the first thing my dad bought was a fan and a refrigerator.

We had a big black cook stove that had a reservoir on the side that we kept full of water so we always had hot water when we needed it. We burned wood and coal in the stove to cook and keep the house warm in the winter, when it was cold.

The winters were much colder back when I was young and we got lots more snow back then too.

I started school in 1933. I had to walk to and from school. I was very bashful and didn't want to talk, so the teacher had to spank me to get me to talk. I had the same teacher in the eighth grade and she said to me, "Do you remember what you got when you were in the first grade for not talking? Well, I'm going to give you another spanking now for talking."

In 1936, when I was in the third grade, on April First, I fell and broke my right arm and had to miss a half a day of school, and that half day was the only school I missed out of 12 years of school. My youngest brother went to all 12 years of school without missing a day.

In 1939, it was the last of the one room school for me, the seventh and eighth grade was sent to the Jackson High School building and the high school were sent to

Dexter City School; they got to ride the bus. I rode the bus the one mile to the Jackson School.

There were but very few cars back then. If I remember right, there were but two cars around our neighborhood. The ones that owned the Dungannon Store, and one down the road, about a mile from where I lived. My dad got his first car, a Model A Ford, back in 1938. He always drove horses and wagons everywhere he went. He used horses to do the farming, and to go to Beverly, Ohio, eight miles south on 339, to get groceries. My mom baked all our bread, so Dad would buy flour in 25 pound bags, eight to ten bags at a time. Also, sugar in 25 pound bags and 25 pounds of salt that would last about three or four months. We had a cellar full of canned fruit, vegetables, and all kinds of meat. We had lots of chicken, so we got lots of eggs every day. Dad would take the eggs to town and sell them to pay for what he got.

I sometimes would ride with Dad to Beverly. It would take all day to make the trip. The road was dirt and some places it was hard for the horses to make it through. The ruts were so deep, especially if it had rained.

We had a steer calf we were fattening to butcher 1931 that winter and my mom was using an axe to cut up small ears of corn for the calf. I was putting the cut up pieces in a bucket when I accidentally put my hand under her axe and she cut my finger off. I was so lucky she only got the end of my longest finger. It could have been my whole hand. So, to this day, I have one short finger.

On January 25, 1932 My youngest brother was born and the doctor wanted to see my finger to see how it was healing and I ran and hid it under the kitchen table.

Back in those days we had a lot of hobos that walked the roads and they would always stop by our school. They would usually stop by our home and my mom would give them a meal. They would stay nights and sleep on the hay in our barn.

My grade school teachers are all gone now and I am the oldest one of the school kids left in these parts. I still live within one mile of where I was born and went to school. Things has really changed since I can remember 1931.

The last of November, in 1949, we got a big snow, better than eight feet of snow. I was working at the Dungannon Store and couldn't even get home, the snow was that deep. The owner of the store worked for a coal company and he managed to get there and brought a bulldozer back and opened the roads. There was no one going anywhere except on horses and it was hard for them.

There was a gas pump at the store and gas was 19 cents a gallon. Quite a bit different than it is today. Sugar was four cents a pound, cereal was 23 cents a box, soup beans were eight cents a pound, salt was three cents a pound, soda pop all was five cents a bottle, and candy bars all five cents and had all kinds of one cent candy.

There was lots of things I didn't write about my years in school, but I'm going to quit with this.

Poor Country Folks and Didn't Know It

by Marlene A. Welsh Gentry of Zanesville, Ohio
born in 1940

As I remember my childhood days, I have to laugh and shed a few tears at the same time. So many memories.

We were poor country folks, but we didn't know it. My mom would make us clothes made out of printed feed sacks, or if she could buy material on sale.

She canned a lot of vegetables from our huge garden and fruit from the neighbor's peach orchard up the lane. We got milk and eggs from the same neighbor who had a big farm. He used to give us 11 eggs in a dozen, and my mom asked him why, and he said because there was a double yolk egg in the dozen. One time, our car broke down, and he gave us a ride into town so my mom could do her weekly shopping. My mom asked him how much she owed him and he said, "Just give me 50 cents." You could say he was very frugal, but my dad would call it something else.

My dad was a great outdoorsman. He hunted, trapped, and fished and even loaded his own shells for his guns. Hunters came from all over to get their gun scopes sighted in. He made his own fishing nets by crocheting them, and he built his fishing boat out of wood. He had many trophies on display in our home. He coon hunted a lot and in December he would take the furs to town to sell, so my mom could do Christmas shopping.

The Welsh sisters with stinky fox hides in the 1940s: Marcie and Marlene (twins), Donna.

We might have been poor, but we never went hungry. We ate squirrel, rabbit, deer, quail, duck, catfish, and of course, vegetables from the garden. He would go out in the spring and pick wild mushrooms. He had deer hides tanned and made into jackets and gloves.

He would borrow a team of horses to plow our garden in the spring, and his father, whom we called Grandpa Shortie, would come out and help plant. He would do the plant part, and I would carry the water bucket. We would get right down in the dirt, and I loved the way he would work the dirt with his hands like he was molding something for an exhibit.

We had chickens and pigs, and of course the usual cats and dogs. My dad drove an old '35 Ford truck, and if he took me anywhere, I would duck down so no one would see me riding in it. He would read us stories from Zane Grey and tell us stories of his days in school. He only had an 8th grade education. He was a pretty good carpenter, and he worked at the state highway department, eventually becoming foreman until retirement. He always said any man that doesn't like hunting, trapping, or fishing isn't worth a damn.

Dale Outlaws and Mac's Moonshine

by Richard A. Green of Stockport, Ohio
born in 1946

Dale, Ohio, State Route 676, just a crossroads, a small store with a gas pump, but a big place for all who lived there. Then there were five boys who lived in Dale. Mark, Dan, Spank, Larry, and Dick. Mark, Dan and Spank were brothers, Larry and Dick were cousins, but we were all related.

Dale Outlaws got their name from R.L. Green. He loved all of us. If R.L. had money we all had money, Mark would say. We never broke the law, just bent it a little.

We loved the woods and creeks. A good place to play cowboy and Indians. Also we loved baseball, football and basketball. Each of us had baseball gloves and bats but no football equipment, except for Larry, he had shoulder pads and a helmet. Not being too jealous we tried to kill him.

One of our best times of the year was Halloween, we would throw corn and turn TV antennas, messing up the programs they were watching. That's not too bad, but we would do it October, November, skip December, start again in January.

School is out: let's go swimming. If we found a creek deep enough we were there. A pond was a lot better. One day we were over at Mac Mouser's place. He had a pond near the road and we were in it skinny dipping. Some man came up asked what we were doing. We said, "Mac said we could swim." The man said, "I don't know about that, because I am Mac Mouser. Go ahead have fun and be careful." Hey Mac do you want to see a moonshine? (I hope you know what that is.)

Just a few days in the lives of some good old boys from Dale. I know we still love each other and we all turned out just fine.

Retired and back at the crossroads.

The Young Hitchhiker and the Trustworthy Turk

by Ken E. Richardson of Zanesville, Ohio
born 1948

At the age of 12, it was common practice on Saturday mornings for me to walk to the south side of town (about three miles) and hitchhike to my grandparents' farm for the weekend. The farm was about 25 miles from home. After church on Sunday afternoon, my parents and siblings would drive to the farm to join me for a family picnic. All the aunts, uncles and cousins would converge on the quiet front lawn, bringing blankets, lawn chairs and homemade goodies.

If you got past the first sentence without raising an eyebrow, I would be surprised. Yes, I hitchhiked 25 miles at the age of 12 with my parents' blessings.

When I arrived on the farm, a person-to-person call would be made to my parents' house asking for me. Naturally I wasn't there, and no one was billed for a long distance call. The call was my way of telling my parents that I made it safely.

Getting a ride to the farm was incredibly easy. Elderly couples, no doubt curious about a young boy hitchhiking, usually picked me up. The world was much smaller then. Everybody knew somebody who knew somebody. During my journey to the farm, our discussions would center on the people we knew. It was not uncommon for me to catch a ride with people who not only knew my grandparents, but who dropped me off at their door. In those days, we didn't have the fears of being abducted or abused. "Sexual predator" was an unknown term.

Still, I wasn't careless. I wouldn't accept a ride in a car with out-of-state plates or a single occupant. I watched license plates carefully. Even before the county sticker was required on license plates I could tell generally where the vehicle was from. At that time, the Bureau of Motor Vehicles distributed plates to counties in batches starting with a letter. If the first letter on the plate was "V," such as V-265-E, I knew it was from Zanesville. If it was W-265-E, it was from Morgan County (location of the farm). C-265-E was Columbus/Franklin County. I tried to get rides with Ohio plates beginning with "W." That would almost always get me within walking distance of the farm. If not, a second ride would get me there.

I met a lot of nice people while hitchhiking. Back then; hitchhiking was very common, especially for military personnel. To refuse a ride to a soldier was nothing short of unpatriotic. It was a common sight to see members of the armed forces hitchhiking home on leave.

Today, hitchhiking is illegal. Although I understand why, I will always recall the kindness of the travelers who allowed me to join them in their journey. They weren't aware of it at the time, nor was I, but they were teaching me the value of compassion and caring for others.

While serving a tour of duty in Turkey in 1967, I bought a large, heavy, Sony reel-to-reel tape recorder from one of the guys. I had tried to buy the recorder from him earlier in my tour, but he held out for more money until the last minute. It was too late to crate it up for shipment, so I was forced to carry the recorder and my duffel bag to the airport. Once at the terminal, I was advised that my baggage exceeded the weight limitation. The cost for the extra weight was more than I could afford.

My Turkish driver, Atilla, saw my frustration and offered to help. He said, "You give me fifteen dollars. I send to you in America, later." At that moment, the Pan Am flight for New York was on last call for boarding. In desperation, I forked over $15 and scribbled out my address on a piece of scrap paper, figuring I'd never see the tape recorder again. I ran down the boarding ramp to the plane and never looked back.

As the plane taxied to the runway for takeoff, I imagined the Turkish driver returning to his family that afternoon with my tape recorder and fifteen dollars. Frustration was an understatement. I was sick.

In a few hours, I had accepted that the tape recorder and the $15 were but one of the many costly lessons in my life. By the time I reached New York, I was thinking about the 30 days I would be spending at home before flying to California, then on to Japan. It was early February, and I had just missed my first Christmas away from my family. My mother assured me in a letter that the tree would still be up, and that my presents would still be there. I missed my family and friends, and was anxious to see them again.

My parents met me at the Columbus airport and I talked non-stop during the hour-long ride home. I know I talked too much, because at one point, Dad sighed as if, "Does he ever shut up!" Fortunately, he had served in the Navy for several years and knew I was just getting it out of my system.

When we arrived at home, true to Mother's word, the Christmas tree still stood and twinkled in the window next to the porch swing. She never knew how much that meant to me.

One evening about two weeks later, while we sat at the dinner table, there was a knock on the door. A voice yelled out, "Delivery for Ken Richardson!" I put my fork down and walked to the door to find an amazing sight. There on the porch sat a packing crate, which appeared to have been made by a cabinetmaker. The wood was sanded smooth and heavily varnished. The deliveryman had used a handcart to wheel the crate to the house because of its weight. I signed the shipping paper and thanked the deliveryman, puzzled at what it might be. When I looked at the label to see what it said, I nearly cried. The return address was Ayhan's Boat Shop, Sinop, Turkey. A note in the packing list envelope read, "Ken, my friend Ayhan, he makes boats. He helped me make a box for your tape machine. I hope it is ok. Bye, Atilla."

This happened 38 years ago. I still have a lump in my throat when I think about it. I wish I could tell him how much that meant to me. I am sorry for ever doubting his sincerity.

By the way, the tape recorder arrived in perfect condition.

Dangers of Skinny Dipping

by Donald Paxton of Junction City Ohio
born 1929

I was around ten years old when one hot, summer day I decided to ride my bicycle to a Baltimore and Ohio water tower for a quick swim. This tower was located just north of the Junction City State Penitentiary. This tower was used to furnish water to the steam engines that traveled from Newark to Shawnee, Ohio.

Railroad water tower.

When I arrived, I saw a ladder that went from ground level to the top of the water tower and off came my clothes, and I climbed to the top. Looking down, I saw clear, cool water. I jumped in, and swam around for a few minutes and then decided it was time to climb out. The top of the water was about three feet down from the top of the tower. After several tries, I was finally able to grab the top and lower myself to the ground. For many years, I realized how close I came to drowning. What an adventure.

Apple Butter Tradition

by Jo George of Thornville, Ohio
born in 1942

The George family brought their tradition of making apple butter with them to Perry County from Morgan County in the mid 1920s. My husband, Henry, has early memories of making apple butter with his grandparents, Henry and Jane George and Mabel Cotterman, his parents,

Charley and Annabelle George, his Aunt Laura, Uncle Jim and Aunt Phenie Cotterman, and his sisters, Mabel and Ethel. This event took place every five or six years either indoors, using the stove and oven, or outdoors in a copper kettle over a fire.

This practice continued over a few decades and grew as the family expanded and friends and neighbors were included in the process.

Following the Cotterman recipe, we make apple butter as it was made at the turn of the last century. We cook down 30 gallons of apple cider in a huge copper kettle over a fire until it has thickened or reduced to three gallons. This is done the previous evening. Around seven the next morning, we peel the apples with old-fashioned apple peelers, core and cut the apples with a new fangled corer, snit the apples (cut out dark spots and seed pods) and put them in covered five gallon buckets. Around noon, we start dumping the apples into the cooked down cider, stirring all of the time. The apples have to be put in slowly because they will foam over the edge of the kettle. We cheat and put a little butter in the kettle to keep it from foaming over.

After the seven bushels of apples are in the kettle, we continue to stir until the mixture is of the consistency we like and then we add sugar and cinnamon (if needed) and cook and stir until done. The apple butter is canned and will keep indefinitely.

Apple butter making was and is a neighborhood social event. We, including our children and grandchildren, are trying to continue this by making apple butter on the Henry George Farm every fall. We have over 200 guests each year.

What Were Those Things For?

by Mary V. Cole of Cadiz, Ohio
Born 1918

Let me tell you a little of what the Depression of the late 1920's and 1930's and 1940's was like.

I was born during World War I (1918). It was a home delivery and the doctor charged $5.00. People in those days scarcely went to a doctor. I never remember my parents ever seeing a doctor for an illness. When I went to college it was necessary to have a physical and when they gave me a thermometer to take my temperature I didn't know that it went under your tongue.

I remember going to a larger town when I was about five years old. No one had explained to me what an elevator was for. There was a high stool in the elevator and I thought I was supposed to sit on it and I didn't know what they were going to do to me. I thought maybe pull my teeth.

When I started school there were no yellow school buses. We walked to a one-room school for eight years. The teacher had about 25 pupils and she taught all the subjects in all eight grade levels. She received $800.00 for eight months of teaching, plus five dollars a month for being her own janitor. We would go to a neighbor's house near school and get a bucket of water each day. We all used a communal dipper for a drink.

When you went to high school you either rode the train or later we got a Model T Ford to drive. It had to be cranked to start it. When we got to school we had to drain out the water so it wouldn't freeze and when we were ready to go home, we filled it with water again, cranked it, and we were on our way home. Gasoline was 11-cents a gallon. If you were low on gas and you came to a big hill you turned the car around and backed up the hill so that the gas would run forward and keep the motor running.

We were poor, but we didn't know it. Everyone else was in the same boat. Banks closed and people panicked. We lived on a farm and had an abundance of food. We had; beef, pork, chickens, milk, eggs and we churned butter and baked our bread. We raised a large vegetable garden and canned fruits and vegetables. We had a cave for storing potatoes, apples, squash, pumpkins and cabbages. We picked gooseberries and canned blackberries, raspberries, and carrots. We made many jams and jellies also. We had plenty to eat, but very little money. Just enough to pay the property tax each year. We walked to Sunday school and church about two miles each way. A popular song of the day was, "Brother, can you spare a dime?"

For recreation in the winter we played card games and checkers, and people had parties in their homes. We would roll up the rug and square dance the night away. In the summer we played softball in the roadway or went swimming in the "old swimming hole," which was dammed up creek and sometimes muddy. There were no super highways. The roads were often a sea of mud. No roads were paved.

In 1936 Franklin Roosevelt had programs to jump start the economy and unemployment. He started the WPA and CCC where men and boys would plant trees, pave alleys in town and build many dams. He was able to get things going again.

In spite of the hardships, which we were unaware of, we survived and thrived without public assistance. There was no Social Security or Medicare.

We secured a radio battery in 1936.

In 1959 we had a rural electrification and a TV in 1952.

There were very few beauty parlors, restaurants or motels. We never ate out as it cost twice as much to eat out as to cook your own meals. For motels there were little cabins along the highway that you could rent for a night. Automobiles were scarce and a new one could be bought in 1939 for $810.00. Today, people have two or three sitting in their driveways.

There are many millionaires today, but during the Depression one could scarcely be found.

Today, tour agencies can take you to far-flung places that we never dreamed of seeing. We were lucky to get to go to the county fair. There, everyone got all dressed up in their best. Now fairs are smaller and geared mostly to 4H exhibits.

During the Depression people were lucky to have two outfits to wear. Often they were hand-me-downs or made from feed sacks. Everything was put to use. Today, most people have closets packed with clothes. Each season they go out and buy more.

People today take exercise classes for fitness. We got our exercise from the sweat of the brow. We got our tanning from picking berries or making hay. Children were brought up more strictly. There was a great deal of discipline. Today many children are allowed free reign. Back in those days, neighbor helped neighbor; borrowed machinery and the like.

When a new baby was coming people bought white outing flannel and made diapers for the new arrival. They had not made Pampers yet!

On one occasion in the 1940's a neighbor came for me one night as his wife was in labor and they had no money for a doctor or hospital. I went and by the light of a kerosene lamp, with a pair of scissors, a bottle of alcohol and two strings, delivered a big baby boy. He later went on to college and graduated Summa Cum Laude. It didn't cost them a cent for the delivery and now it costs a fortune to get all the things needed for the new baby's arrival.

Today, people would rather buy prepared foods or eat out at restaurants, where many of the patrons are overweight and it is quite costly.

Sports events are big time now. Coaches and players alike are paid millions of dollars and thousands of fans seem to be able to afford seats to the events. During the Depression, baseball games were held in farm fields or on school playgrounds, with little money involved. You just had the price of the ball and bat.

I have lived through World War I, World War II, the Korean War, Vietnam, the "Cold War," Desert Storm and now the Iraqi war, which has raged on for six years with no end in sight.

Today so much is geared to luxury and entertainment that it does not seem as if there is a depression at all.

I have lived a long bountiful life; hard work has made me strong.

The Umbrella in the Car

By Glenna Hart of Lexington, South Carolina
Born 1934

Here are some memories of my childhood: The old home place where I was born, Stumptown Ridge in Belmont County, Ohio, was the home of my grandparents, David and Amza. This was the same house where my parents; Harry and Ila, lived from the day of their marriage, September 26, 1931 until they moved to Canton, Ohio in 1952.

After years of owning a "Homecomfort," a wood and coal range cook stove, they purchased "On Time" an electric range. Then bad luck came and the chickens they had purchased in hopes the egg money would pay for the stove, got coccidiousis, a killer for baby chicks and they all died.

My dad, a long time farmer, went to Canton and got a job in a factory, Republic Steel. I still remember the delicious meals that came off that old Homecomfort stove and delicious homemade bread, pies, cakes and so forth. Coming home from school to those aromas was a delight.

Attending gospel meetings during the summer months was a common event for us and during my teen years two or more of my friends would go along. My dad had an old Model A Ford and one rainy night the roof leaked on my friends, Credella and Liz Clark. But we just happened to have an umbrella in the car. So we opened it up and giggled about the rainy night for then and many years to come.

We also had a party line phone, another form of entertainment and for me it was listening to some of the steamy boy girl talk as well as the neighborhood gossip. Hours of entertainment through the old gramophone with the cylindrical records, which were shaped like toilet paper rolls was entertaining too. But then we got a radio and I listened to the Green Hornet, the Lone Ranger, Lum and Abner and Amos and Andy as well as the soaps; Stella Dallas, Our Gal Sunday and When A Girl Marries, to name a few.

Cousins John and Bill Naylor sitting on Glenna Hart's dad's Model A with the leaky roof.

Bathing and Washing Clothes: The Saturday night bath was taken in an old tin tub with the water heated on the stove. We also heated water on the stove for washday and used a wringer washer. Mother used such products as La France Flakes, and Satina for making the clothes whiter and fresher.

I have other memories of growing up which I will not share at this time. Attending a one room school for instance.

Bergen's Dummies and Counterfeit Oranges

By Dan Stoffel of Lewisville, Ohio.
Born 1933

My mother passed away when I was three years old. She was 28 years old with five young children. My brother Harry and I were put in the Children's Home for two years. We were blessed when our Aunt Lina and Uncle Art adopted us and raised us on their farm. Those were tough times on the farm, but we thought we were in Heaven.

I have many memories of our neighbors. I remember one neighbor, Charlie Burkheimer. We were at his house listening to the war news on the radio and Charlie brought up that they were going to show a movie at Bethel School on Saturday night. They were going to shine a movie on the wall and it would talk. He didn't think they could do that. Uncle Art said, "Why don't we go and see it?" Charlie said, "We'll just do that." A couple of weeks later, Charlie got talking about the movie. He said, "Didn't that Edgar Bergen have the two ugliest young'uns you ever saw? One boy wasn't too bad looking, but that other boy had the biggest mouth I ever did see. It was pathetic." We never told him any different.

We had this neighbor, Jim Antill, who came to our house one day in his horse and buggy. He said, "Miss Simms, do you think your boys would like some oranges?" She told him that would be nice. He came back later with a bushel of grapefruit. He said, "Miss Simms, I have stewed, fried and boiled these oranges, but there is no way I can eat them. Now, if your boys can eat them they are welcome to them." Aunt Lina cut them in half; put sugar on top and they were delicious.

Now Jim lived in a log cabin. He came to our house one evening and was telling what happened after they had butchered that day. He said, "I was sitting in my chair, minding my own business. I reached in my pocket and got some Hill Side tobacco. I lit my pipe and it went POW! POW! I looked up and the pipe was stuck in the ceiling." He said. "The first thing I thought was the Japs had attacked."

Suze Jackson was a very large and very strong Cherokee Indian woman. She wore size 14 overshoes with no shoes. She lived two or three miles from the store where she would go to buy hog feed in 100 pound bags. She would walk to the store; pick up the bag of feed and start back home. She would stop at our place to get a drink of water; lean the feed on a fence post, drink her water and down the road she would go, bare-footed, carrying her sack of feed.

Suze asked Uncle Art if he would come down and plow her garden. He said he would. So one morning, we got up early, put the plow, harrow and drag on a sled because the only way you could get to her place was with a team of horses. Art worked until noon and he told me to get the dinner bucket Aunt Lina had fixed for us. I got the bucket and took it up to a shade tree so we could eat lunch. When I opened it; it was empty. Well, here came Suze; barefooted of course. Uncle Art said to Suze, "You don't know what may have happened to our ham sandwiches and pie, do you?" Suze said, "Art Simms, you know better than to eat those old, cold sandwiches. Now you come down to the house and eat a good warm meal. I threw your lunch out to the hounds. Now you go on down to the creek and wash. There's a cake of lye soap on a rock and dry your hands on that old pair of overalls hanging there." We got washed up and went down for lunch. Instead of ham and pie, we had eggs and corn meal mush. She stirred the mush with her finger and then snapped her finger back in the kettle. I sat and looked at it for awhile. Uncle Art said, "Now you eat that, Dan. Everything has been well cooked." Being a kid, I was hungry, so I ate it. I'm 76 years old now, so it must have been okay.

When I was in high school, Jim and George Cline, Eugene and Gilbert Schneeberger, my brother, Harry and I built a log cabin on the farm. There were only about 30 students in our high school so we invited all the students and teachers for a wiener roast.

We wanted to put a roof on the cabin and needed some money, so we passed the hat for donations. The hat got pretty well around the campfire when someone knocked it into the fire. Our industrial arts teacher thought we did such a good job that he gave us class credit.

Waitresses in the Hobo Restaurant

by Lillian L. Gatten of Tuscarawas, Ohio
born in 1940

When I was young, we had a fair share of hobos knocking on our back door, due to the fact that we lived beside a brickyard and across the road from a coal mine. The railroad ran near our house. This was in Ohio in approximately 1946 or 1947. The hobos were generally only hungry and would ask for something to eat.

My mother would usually tell them to wait on the porch, then she would make them a sandwich and hand it out the back door. One Monday morning, while Mom was in the basement doing the laundry in our old Maytag wringer washer, a hobo knocked on the back door. I looked at my younger sister and said, "We can handle this ourselves. We know how to make a sandwich."

He asked if we had anything for him to eat. We said, "YES, YES, come right on in." Looking rather startled, he replied, "No, I'll wait here on the porch." "No, No," we said, "you come in and sit down at the table." We felt like we were running a restaurant.

"Would you like a peanut butter and jelly sandwich?" we asked, as we led him to the table and pushed him down on the chair. We got everything on the table, peanut butter, butter and about three different kinds of jam. "What kind of jam would you like?" we asked as we were thickly spreading the bread with butter and peanut butter. Then we spread the jam and sat down to watch him eat.

He acted quite nervous as he ate, and even more so when he heard footsteps coming up from the basement. As our mother came into the kitchen, she looked totally shocked to see a strange man eating at her table and seeing what her girls had done. He said, "I thank you for the food. I told them I would wait on the porch, but they pulled me into the kitchen. I'll be leaving now." He picked up the sandwiches and left.

Our mother looked at us sternly and asked, "Why did you do that? Don't ever do that again." After she had collected herself and returned to her washing, we still thought we had a great adventure that day and we felt quite grown up...and thought of ourselves as very good waitresses.

Almost Anything With Nothing

by Joseph E. Surovec of New Athens, Ohio
born in 1933

I was born in 1933 in the last of the coal company houses in Stewartsville, Belmont County. The "Big 5 Coal Company" was still operating, but dwindling. My dad worked in it hand loading coal. The coal went out to a tipple and onto railroad cars.

Wages were low and times were tough. We never went hungry, but mainly because Mom could cook anything that was brought in. We had a coal cook stove and a fireplace, then later a coal heating stove. My two older brothers hunted, fished and trapped, which I took up later as I grew older. (I still hunt, fish, and trap.)

My parents were from Czechoslovakia, coming to the United States in 1920. Both had to learn English and pass tests to become U.S. citizens. I was the last of their six children. We talked Slovak at home and I picked up some English from the other kids. I had a wild time in school at first, talking broken English with Slovak mixed in.

We had no water at home. We carried drinking and cooking water from the coal company hand pump two hundred yards away. We had kerosene lights, a kerosene lantern, and Dad had carbide lights that went on a cap that he wore in the mine.

Ptl. J.E. Surovec.

We carried wash water from the McMahon Creek that flowed by a hundred feet away. Mom heated laundry water over a wood fire in the backyard. She often baked potatoes in that fire. We didn't have aluminum foil so they got blackened, but tasted great.

In late summer, Mom also canned (cold packed jars of beans, tomatoes, etc.) over that fire. There was a metal rack that stood over the fire for tubs to sit on.

Dad's sister and her husband had things a little better and they would occasionally send us used clothes and miscellaneous. The clothes were mostly large and Mom would salvage what she could. She could sew well with her treadle Singer sewing machine. She cut up one big shirt and made me one out of it. I was about five then and small. She re-used the collar and cuffs. My little shirt with that big collar looked a bit like Batman's cape. The cuffs were wrist to elbow.

We children were all born at home. The population of the area was mostly Slovak, Russian, Serbian, and Polish. (I could converse with them.) The ladies served as midwives for one another. The nearest doctor was three miles away. A birth certificate was made out later.

There was no car in our family until my older brother came home after WWII.

I graduated from Bellaire High in 1951. I had various jobs; truck driver, mechanic's helper, etc. I enlisted into the Army in 1954, went through a military welding school and served in Korea. After being discharged I welded for Consol Coal Mine in West Virginia for four years. I quit that and went through the Ohio State Patrol School Academy and worked at that for twelve years chasing speeders, etc. and retired at fifty-five. I've welded most of my adult years and still do.

With my rough start, making do with whatever, I've done so much with so little for so long, I can do almost anything with nothing now.

Baseball the Hard Way

by Carl L. Paulun of New Philadelphia, Ohio
born 1937

When I was growing up on a 72 acre farm, six miles

from Newcomerstown, Ohio, and two miles from Bakersville, we played a unique game of baseball. We played four man (boy) baseball the hard way...two on a team. Because of the size of the team, we had to create our own set of rules.

Before I go any further, let me describe the playing field. We made it in the pasture field behind the barn. It was anything but level because there weren't any level places big enough for a baseball diamond on our farm. The infield and part of left field and center field was relatively level, and the rest of left and center fields dipped down below the level of the infield. Right field was on a hillside.

Now, back to how we played this unique game: The four players were my oldest brother, Lester; my next younger brother, Gary; the next door neighbor, Dale Everhart; and me, Carl Paulun. It was Lester and Gary vs. Dale and I. Lester was the power hitter, and the best player. Dale, who was the same age as me, and I were virtually tied for next to the best player. Gary was the youngest, and the worst player.

Here are the special rules that we went by: There was no pitcher or catcher. The batter threw the ball up and attempted to hit it. If he swung and missed, it was a strike. And if he swung and missed three times during an at bat, it was an out. The two batters could not be stranded on base at the same time, because someone had to bat, so the lead base runner was automatically out. The two players on defense were fielders who covered the whole playing field. In order to get one of the offensive players out, one of the fielders either had to catch the ball in the air, or tag a runner out on the base path.

These obviously were high scoring games. Dale and I won every one of them because Gary struck out a lot and hit a lot of balls a short distance.

Dale and Lester are deceased, but Gary and I are still living. Can anyone else honestly say that they have played a similar baseball game? I seriously doubt it!

The Lost Pigtailed Maggie Rose

by Rosemary Day Masteller of Powell, Ohio
born in 1937

I was born and grew up in Monroe County. The County Seat is Woodsfield, Ohio. Lived in the country on a farm. One of seven children. My dad worked in the oil fields. Mom did some teaching elementary schools.

My grandmother lived with us. She would bake six loaves of bread every day and 12 big buns. As soon as we got off the school bus and home, that was our snack, hot rolls with butter. Yummy.

Attended Bethel School in Marr, Ohio. Our janitor fired the furnace and drove one of three school buses. Our coach drove one school bus, coached basketball and taught classes. The local grocer at Parks Store attended the store with his wife and drove the other school bus. The bus drivers all repaired and attended to the buses. No fancy mechanics with bus garages. Took them home and cleaned and cared for them.

Most of us grew up poor. Had a garden, had chickens and a cow for milk. Picked blackberries, nuts and everything in the woods and meadows.

In the summertime, three families of us would go to the woods, eat berries, apples, pawpaws, nuts, and had spring water in old wooden barrels to drink. Played in the woods and could stay as long as we wanted. At a brook or run, we called back then, we gathered rocks, threw rocks. Woods were safe then.

One time I took my doll baby to the cow field and left her and never found her. I named her Maggie Rose after a high school girl with pigtails. My Maggie Rose had pigtails.

My mother had friends whose daughters were older than me and my two sisters. She would give us her hand me down clothes. Mom made most of our clothes and made coats out of fabric from used coats. Made our dresses with little belts that tied in the back, and used a lot of rickrack for the bodice; sometimes with three little buttons in the front. She was an excellent seamstress. Used an old Singer Treadle sewing machine for many years.

I spent most of my life on a creek. We swam in the creek. Fished for bass, sunfish, and catfish. Ate fish for our late snack. We would set an old tire on fire and it would light up the creek bank. Fun, fun.

On Saturday afternoon, Mom and Dad would go to town. My sisters and I would clean the old linoleum floors and invite the gang up for softball. We would bake a devil's food cake out of scratch. All of us ate it before they returned home. Used a sheet cake pan. Put powdered sugar icing on it. Delicious.

My mother canned everything available.

I had four brothers. They would fuss over who got the car on Saturday night.

My mother washed on an old tub and washboard for many years.

Our only entertainment was going to the basketball games, home and away. This one game at Stockport, Ohio, two of us met two nice-looking boys and they made a date for the following Saturday night. They didn't show up, but sent two of their ugliest friends out. We took one look and said, "No, we can't go out."

Back then, we all rode the bus to school and all activities. There was no more than 80 or 90 in the whole school. All grades were in the same brick school building.

We had outdoor plumbing outhouse for a while. Our first grade teacher said one piece of toilet paper for number one and two pieces of toilet paper for number two. We didn't have kindergarten back then.

My one neighbor who owned a tire shop in Marietta was our wealthiest neighbor. He said when we skipped school he called it Bus-itis. Real clever neighbor with a good sense of humor.

Everyone in school had a nickname. My oldest brother—Sir; second brother—Dunk; third brother—Buzz; I was chip; first sister—Bubby; fourth brother—Boller; second sister—Chummy.

My third brother made all the rules when we played games. He cut our fishing poles, ice hockey sticks, and we used can lids for our hockey, skated on the creek, swam on creek, fished on creek.

I slept with one of my sisters. We slept two to a bed. Good old iron beds with wood slats and a mattress.

All seven of us children got jobs, raised families and have nice homes. I took clerical courses and got my first job in Columbus, Ohio at the State Tax Department in 1956. My second job with Ohio Fuel Gas Company in 1960. Secretary to a supervisor of purchasing, met and married my husband, Louis Masteller, who owned Masons Sand and Gravel Company with his two brothers.

I have one daughter, Kimberly Masteller, who was Assistant Asian Art Curator at Harvard and is now Curator at Nelson Atkins Museum in Kansas City, Missouri. She is married to an attorney, Donovan Dodrill. She kept her maiden name because, "Mom, I'm pretty well known in the art world."

We own our old stone house on Scioto River with two-and-a-half acres. I came a long way from my background. We loved each other. No one was violent back then. People didn't even lock their doors. I loved every minute of my childhood.

The Secret of Great Grandpa's Garden

by Victoria McGrail Rupe of Zanesville, Ohio
born in 1953

Growing up, I grew up in southeastern Ohio, Muskingum County, Zanesville, Ohio. I had the opportunity to live in a home with four generations. My great-grandparents, who lived through the Depression, and also my grandparents, my aunt and uncle, Father and Mother, and eventually siblings.

This was my father's side of the family in the lower Putnam area. It was so wonderful growing up in the fifties and early sixties! Picnics, jobs were plentiful, a child could grow up knowing who you belonged to, who your relatives were, and oh so safe.

The seven "Vs." Violet, Victoria, Valinda (Dobie), Vincent, Veronica, Vivian (Peachie), and Valerie McGrail in 1985.

I don't know. I think the great-grandparents pretty much dictated what went on in the household. There were two houses on the property. The small cottage is where they lived and everyone gathered for talk, meals, games, especially in the kitchen or front porch.

The other large two-story house used to be a grocery store in the 1900s, but Great Grandfather and Great Grandmother then turned it into a home for all of us. Grandparents, aunt and uncle downstairs. Mother, Father, and children upstairs. It worked. Food, home, happiness, love, what else would you need?

Great Grandfather was great at a vegetable garden. We didn't have a back yard to play in because it was all vegetables. Every spring, everyone had to take a shovel to turn over the garden, spade by spade. There were no tillers in the day. If there were, he didn't know of them. But come summer, there were green beans, cabbage, carrots, lima beans, celery, radishes. Later towards fall, there was always potatoes (half the garden). He always had rhubarb. He had a grape arbor.

And he had a shanty. Now that shanty must have been his gold mine, because if a neighbor needed a part, Great Grandpa had it. People always ask us what a shanty is. It must be some secret building?! It wasn't a garage, no room for a car. It looked like a little junk building, but it was grand to him. He knew where everything was. I know all those shovels he would hand us in spring were in there.

Everyone always knew the garden was grand because we knew his secret. He would go out at night and get night crawlers. Go fishing the next day at the Muskingum river, take our cocker spaniel, Blackie, and fish. It usually was catfish and carp. The catfish, he would put in a barrel of rainwater he would save, feed bread for a week, and Little Grandma (Great Grandma) would fry for supper on Friday since us seven kids were Catholic. Man, that was so good.

Oh yes, I forgot the secret, with the fish. The carp and catfish, heads, innards and parts, were put in dug up holes in the garden. His secret, he said, was from the old Indians he knew. I always thought he was part Indian myself. He was from Athens County.

My Grandfather Bobble was from Pennsylvania. He worked at the Steel Treaty Plant by Big John's Café. He was a good grandpa. He always did things with us. Played ball, jump rope, pushed us higher and higher on swings.

Our grandmother (Big Grandma) was a barmaid/ cook at Big John's Café. She could cook but not as good as her mother, Little Grandma. We always had a family picnic in Putnam Hill Park. All the family, relatives came from everywhere, food everywhere.

But growing up in Putnam was great. Once in 1957 or '59, the area near 146 flooded, and the water was in the street of Putnam Avenue. Uncle Tom McGrail and our father, Robert McGrail, took a rowboat out in the street, rowing it up and down the street.

It was a great childhood, lots of memories, Putnam Transfer, Y city buses, Don's Café, P&M Café, Minnick's Grocery, Powell's Market, A&W Rootbeer Rinks, Grant School and Summer School Park, riding bikes, hot fifties and sixties cars. I could go on forever.

Great-grandparents—Will and Minnie McKnight Johnson; grandparents—Robert and Esther Johnson McGrail; parents—Robert and Gloria Kluk McGrail; siblings—Victoria McGrail Rupe with Veronica Hazen, Valerie Miller, Valinda Kirkpatrick, Vivian Dalton, Violet Neal, and Vincent McGrail, Aunt Eleanor McGrail, Uncle Tom McGrail.

Photographed in the Act

by Roger Mautz of Mount Perry, Ohio
born 1927

If memory serves me right, the year was 1939, a really cold year. My friend Eugene and I left McIntire School, which was located on the corner of McIntire and Blue Avenues. We were on our way to the Y.M.C.A., which at that time was located on South Fifth Street between Main and South Streets. We walked down McIntire Avenue to Linden Avenue. At Linden we went to the left to go to the Fifth Street Bridge. It was located across from Commissioner Street.

Instead of going up onto the bridge from Linden, we went along the north side of the bridge where there was a set of steps going up to the bridge sidewalk. The steps were there for access from the riverbank, where quite a few boats were moored.

When we got to the steps, we could see huge chunks of ice pushed up on the riverbank and the river was frozen over for as far as we could see. Being invincible, as most all kids think they are at that age, we decided we would walk across the river on the ice.

When we reached the river edge, a man with a camera asked us if we were going to cross the river on the ice. We affirmed that we were and started to leave. Then, he asked if we would take a few minutes and let him take our picture. We agreed to let him take our picture. When he started talking about different poses, I became a little suspicious. He took the last picture and asked us for our names. That peaked my suspicion, and I asked him what he was going to do with the pictures. Much to our horror, he said they would be in the Zanesville Signal newspaper.

We refused to give our names and begged him to not publish our picture. We knew if our pictures showed up in the newspaper, showing us about to walk across the Muskingum River on the ice and our parents saw it, our lives would be in serious trouble.

Fortunately, for Eugene and I, when the picture appeared on the front page of the Signal a few days later, it was grainy and blurred enough that the two boys sitting on the side of a houseboat could not be identified.

Oh yes, we made it safely across the river and enjoyed our time at the Y.

When I told my parents about it, 20 or 30 years later, their only response was, "It was a good thing we didn't know about it at the time it happened."

The reason for my parents' concern for us being on the river without supervision came from an experience of my father's. In my father's younger days, there were summer cottages along the east bank of the Licking River, upstream from Dillon Falls. My father was visiting a bachelor friend who lived full time in one of those cottages. While he was visiting, a young person drowned a short distance from them. My father was one of the men who helped in finding and recovering the body. He knew, first hand, the danger that lurks at the river.

A Great Turkey and Butchering Day

By Elnora Grant of Sarahsville, Ohio
Born 1935

Now, you should be able to identify one character in my little story. In my pre-school years our family share-cropped on an 86 acre farm in northwestern Ohio near Lima. Those were the years with no indoor plumbing so the "outhouse" was a usual "room" with a bench and one, two or three holes that was visited by everyone, regularly.

Mr. Gobbler King was a sly, keen, big turkey bird. He watched the back door of our house so consistently. He was waiting for the pre-schooler; Elnora. If she forgot to pick up the broom from the back porch on her way to that "outdoor room," he was ecstatic. Once inside for Elnora, he proceeded to march and strut back and forth in front of the outhouse door, gobbling, gobbling, strutting, strutting, keeping his prisoner inside. No matter the weather, he was on the track! Sometimes he would wait, hidden somewhere, quietly until she stepped out the door, off the porch and started down the path. She had to put it in high gear because Mr. Turkey was there! Many were the times she had to be rescued by her mother who would come out swinging the broom, chasing Mr. Gobbler on his way. Elnora lost count of the number of times this happened.

Then Thanksgiving came. She had her revenge in a real way. BUTCHERING DAY!

* * * *

"Rise and shine! It's time to get ready to travel to Grandpa Foust's! HAPPY BIRTHDAY!" Some might say, "What a way to spend your birthday!" Sometime in Foust history New Years Day had become butchering day. The project included three to five hogs a year depending on the individual family needs.

The day started early, probably the day before for Grandpa. He had A-frames erected and big barrels filled with scalding water. The garage was set up with a fire going to render or boil the fat meat into lard, a sausage press to make sausage links and tables where those great hams, shoulders, chops and tenderloin were carved from the pig sides.

The processes were done by the adults and the kids were back and forth messengers between the garage and the house. We were like the "go-fors." Some may frown on the processes that were done on butchering day, but post Depression years of the mid-1930's and early 1940's were not plentiful years. Cash was scarce. If your family was to continue to exist you used every way possible to live. We had pork, beef, chickens, eggs, milk, butter and plenty of garden vegetables and fruits from our own orchards. Many had to eat whatever existed (some have even said they enjoyed roadkill) in order to survive.

By now the animals are scalded, scraped, and brought by halves or quarters to the garage. The sorting, cutting and saving the needed meats continued. Chops and tenderloins were cut, scraps of lean were saved for sausage and cuttings were sorted for homemade pork rinds. Of course the scraping and cleaning of casings were done for the sausage links. Everything was used, no place for any waste.

The fat was cut off and heated or rendered into lard and cracklings. This was put through a lard press and then stored for home use in baking, frying and any other need. The pressed cakes of pig rinds were used in the ever present beans with homemade cornbread or corn pone.

Grandmother had the awesome task of cleaning and salting the casings for the great sausage. They were clean and no one ever got ill from our sausage. The lard press became the sausage stuffer and the long ropes of sausage were wrapped into a large crock. It was transported home and canned for later use. Hams and shoulders were smoked or salted. Chops were canned or salted. The pig's feet were fixed like the hams. The heart, tongue and ears were put into head cheese if you did not want to cook them alone. The liver was kept to fix with onions. All of this was before the freezers were available.

The only thing not used was the pig's tail. But, the fun loving uncles would somehow find a way to sneak up behind a sister and pin the tail on the back of her skirt. Then some one would give out a big "HA! HA! Got you!"

This may not be appealing to some readers, but when you needed food in those days you used what you had along with skills needed to prepare it. The second great advantage of this activity was the family time we experienced. The years of World War II took some people away and families moved to other states. The economy improved and needs changed as families changed. But, my birthday memories are still alive. I may never have had a fancy birthday party, but I had a great family with whom I enjoyed spending my great day.

An Apron, the Priceless Garment

by Julia Mae Roberts of McConnelsville, Ohio
born 1936

I don't think our kids know what an apron is. The principal use of Grandma's apron was to protect the dress underneath because she only had a few. It was easier to wash aprons than dresses and they used less material. But along with that, it served as a potholder for removing hot pans from the oven.

It was wonderful for drying children's tears and on occasion was even used for cleaning out dirty ears. From the chicken coop, the apron was used for carrying eggs, fussy chicks, and sometimes half-hatched eggs to be finished in the warming oven.

When company came, those aprons were ideal hiding places for shy kids. And when the weather was cold, Grandma wrapped it around her arms.

Those big old aprons wiped many a perspiring brow, bent over the hot wood stove. Chips and kindling wood were brought into the kitchen in that apron.

From the garden, it carried all sorts of vegetables. After the peas had been shelled, it carried out the hulls. In the fall, the

Donnie Webb, Vernie Frances Matis, Judy Ann Matis, Anna Vozar Matis, mother.

apron was used to bring in apples that had fallen from the trees.

When unexpected company drove up the road, it was surprising how much furniture that old apron could dust in a matter of seconds.

When dinner was ready, Grandma walked out onto the porch, waved her apron, and the men knew it was time to come in from the fields to dinner.

It will be a long time before someone invents something that will replace that old-time apron that served so many purposes.

REMEMBER: Grandma used to set her hot baked apple pies on the windowsill to cool. Her granddaughters set theirs on the windowsill to thaw.

They would go crazy now trying to figure out how many germs were on that apron. I don't think I ever caught anything from an apron but love.

Peach Juice and the Blacksnake

by Betty L. Bates of Canton, Ohio
born in 1925

I was born in Monroe County January 14, 1925 and then lived in Noble County until I was sixteen years old. I married my sweetheart, April 13, 1946, after he was discharged from the Army. His name was Denver Bates. He also grew up in Noble County. We raised three children, Terry, Patty, and Danny Bates, but I lost Denver December 23, 2008. I miss him so much. He was eighty-four years old.

My mom used to give us castor oil I think for just about everything. She gave it to us in peach juice, and I cannot drink peach juice to this day. I am now eighty-four years old.

We lived on a farm, and I used to gather the eggs. I was too short to look in this old stove in the barn, so I reached up and down in the nest and put my hand around this blacksnake. I ran to the house, screaming all the way. I never forgot the feeling of this snake.

My grandma was the only one with a radio. It had a bunch of batteries to run it with because we had no electric. We would go to her house and gather around the radio to hear the Grand Ole Opry on Saturday night. We had a wind-up Victrola, as they call them, and we still have it today, and it still plays.

My grandma made my clothes. There was no money to buy new ones. She would take old coats and take them apart and turn inside out so they did not look faded. She made jumpers from the material. She sewed on an old treadle machine and also made us dolls and doll clothes. My aunt was a year younger than me. She sewed for both of us.

There was eight of us, and Mom never had time for me. I was the oldest. So I went every place with my dad. One night, he was going to the house from the barn, carrying his lantern. I was skipping stones; we had a walkway filled with gravel, and he said, "Don't do that. You will break my lantern globe." Of course, I threw another stone. It hit his lantern globe and broke it. Of course, I got paddled, the only one he ever gave me, and I never wanted another one. It hurt my feelings so bad. I was almost eight years old.

My dad took me to school in a buggy. I had no one to walk with. We did not have school buses. This was when I was in the first grade. Then he would come get me. School was from nine to four o'clock. My favorite teacher was Miss Beymer. Of course, I was teacher's pet.

These stories are all true, and I have a lot more if you need them. Just part of my growing up.

Shep and the Barned Elephant

by Edgar St. Clair of Salesville, Ohio
born 1896
submitted by Beth Linton of Salesville, Ohio
born in 1956

[Editor's note: in an addendum to this story, Beth Linton stated that its author is her late grandfather.]

As I look west, down a beautiful little valley in the hills of Southeastern Ohio, I see the home of my grandfather. A two story, stately red brick house standing among the pines on a knoll, built in the late 1850's from brick made in a kiln close by. Also, we find, winding its way through the valley, the B & O Railroad connecting Columbus, Ohio with Wheeling, West Virginia, and eventually, Baltimore, Maryland to say nothing of a stream called Leatherwood Creek, paralleling sometimes within 100 feet of the railroad. On the stream, my grandfather had a gristmill using the old stone burrs and an up and down sawmill, both powered by water wheels. This is partially the setting of the following true story. I never thought to inquire as to the exact date, but I am sure it was sometime in the late 1880's.

My father, Frank, was living there at the time, with a brother-in-law, whose first name was George, who helped run the farm and mills. One morning, Dad heard Uncle George outside his bedroom window shouting, "Frank, come out here, quick! There is an elephant down here in the bottom!"

Now, Dad had always considered Uncle George to be a very level headed and sane man, but the thought crossed his mind and made him wonder if some of Uncle George's marbles had become arranged differently during the night, but to please him, he got up and dressed and went outside to take a look.

Sure enough, up by the highway, about an eighth of a mile away, was an elephant. Now, I doubt if either one had ever seen a live elephant, so what do you do with an elephant?

They put their heads together to decide on what strategy to use. Brave Uncle George suggested they get up around him and see if they could drive the elephant down and into the barnyard. George allowed as to how he would get over the fence and go up through the field and Frank go up the lane and get around him. It seemed like a good idea at the time. I don't know how much protection he thought an old rail would be against an elephant, though.

So, they started to put their strategy into action.

At the time, Shep, the farm dog, elected to go along. I don't know whether he sensed something strange or not, but he did not want to be left out, so he tagged along, which later proved to be a mistake.

Up the lane they started, brave Uncle George over the fence, keeping abreast. They had a small bridge to cross on the way, which turned out to be very lucky.

When they were about ready to fan out and get around the elephant, he suddenly started towards my father at a fast trot. Now, Dad was always a home loving man, but he never felt so great a desire to be at home as at that moment and he never could remember when the lane had ever looked so long. He never stopped to use low or second gear; he just started out in high, but when he heard Uncle George cry, "Run, Frank, run or he will kill you!" he shifted into overdrive.

You would think that would be about all that was humanly possible for one to do, but when he looked back over his shoulder and saw the elephant raise his trunk in the air and trumpet, that's when he became airborne.

Shep's belly was about two inches off the ground and he was doing the best to stay with Dad, letting out little whimpers of fear every time he contacted the ground.

About this time, they were crossing the bridge, but when the elephant came to it, he stopped and gingerly picked his way around the end and eventually back onto the road. Finally, Dad and the elephant ended up in the barnyard.

Now, how do you get an elephant into a barn? Well, it seemed like a good idea to get a half bushel measure and fill it with oats and try to coax him into the barn. Eventually, it worked, but while on his way he spied a feed trough, about one foot high, used to grain the sheep in and to show his accomplishments, he tried to get on it and walk lengthwise. Needless to say, they had plenty of kindling wood for a while.

With all the excitement, Dad and Uncle George had forgotten about old Jack, one of the farm horses, being in the stall. When Jack saw what was coming into the barn, his eyes became about the size of baseballs, and laying back on the halter strap, he let out snorts you wouldn't believe.

When the dust had time to clear away and the family to get their nerves somewhat under control, they noticed an engine on the railroad with one car coming slowly down the track, with a crew looking on both sides of the track, very carefully. Surmising what they were looking for, they waved them down and the elephant's trainer came up very hurriedly and rushed into the barn. With his hook around the elephant's trunk, he led him outside. Then, getting down on his knees, the trainer, very carefully, felt the elephant's legs and whole body to see if he had been injured in any way when he fell off the train. When he was satisfied that everything was alright, he had the elephant entertain them by waking on cross ties to the barn, the ties being laid end to end. They then started up the track to the little village of Salesville, about a mile away, where there was a cattle chute to load cattle into the railroad cars for shipping.

Later, my folks walked down the railroad and found where the car door of the circus train had become opened and he had fallen out on the end opposite his trunk which made quite an impression in the ballast. My sisters would often go down and set down in it and try it on for size. Then, they would go over to the soft, low land to look at the elephant tracks, which looked to be about the size of a nail keg.

So ends my story, except for a few last words about Shep. When he arrived at the house, he went under the house through a hole about two sizes too small and my family didn't get him coaxed out until the next day. They finally decided that it was the dog the elephant was afraid of and wanted to get to Father for protection.

Santa, My Hometown Brother

by Esther Clark Dailey of Las Cruces, New Mexico
born 1948

I am the 12th child, a true coal miner's daughter, of Eugene and Mabel Clark from Sandy Ridge Road in Barnesville, Ohio. I had six brothers and five sisters. Our phone number, a party line of four families, was '265J3'.

Dad worked shifts at Powhatan, Ohio for 30 plus years. He ultimately lost his life because of the mine.

Mom was a seamstress at the Barnesville Manufacturing Company, making pajamas for many years. She made somewhere around 95 cents an hour. She was paid by the pieces she did per hour. Her paycheck stub indicated at that time, Social Security deductions were referred to as "Old Age Benefits."

I was born in 1948, at home, on our kitchen table, with the help of Dr. Stoup and two neighbor ladies, Esther King and Grace Campbell. Hence, I became Esther Grace.

I started my education in 1953, at a one-room schoolhouse called "Stumptown." There were three, including me, in my grade. Six grades were taught by Mrs. Frasier, probably one of the greatest teachers ever. Now, I'm not so sure my brothers would agree as they probably had numerous whippings from her. I recall getting my knuckles cracked, with the ruler, while writing with my left hand. Today, I still use my left hand.

The Clark Clan, top left clockwise: George R., Russell E., Charles P., Bernarde E. (Santa), Elroy L., (Brownie), Leroy H. (Blu), Blanche I., Mable E., Elizabeth L., Clara C., Mamie P., Esther Grace.

When the fourth grade arrived, the country school was shut down and it was off to the big city of Barnesville to continue learning. Lunches in the cafeteria cost 25 cents a day, and they were pretty tasty. On Fridays, I got to eat at Bell's, a little sandwich shop across the street from the school. Again, with my 25 cents, I would get a chopped ham sandwich, ten cents, a bag of chips, five cents, and a cherry cola fountain drink, five cents. That would leave me a nickel for Handy Candy, the penny candy store located at the other end of the block. It was in the front room in a house. Unfortunately I cannot remember the little frail old lady's name that ran the store, but I do remember those penny candies. I really hated to feel rushed if I only had a couple of minutes to decide on my big purchase, before the bell at school would ring telling us that lunch was over. Humm, would it be the red-hot dots, the Neccos, Mary Janes, some red licorice, jumbo pretzel sticks, Chicklets gum, or sugar babies? I would get a bag full for my five cents.

For those of you who don't remember an "apple roll" let me explain. We students would plan to bring an apple from home, and keep it a secret from the teacher. When it was time for a test or something we really weren't too fond of, someone would yell "Apple roll!" All of us that brought an apple would roll it down the aisle to the front of the classroom for the teacher, creating a lot of disruption and laughter. Teacher would get to take all the apples home, thus she wouldn't get upset at us for creating chaos. By the time all was cleaned and we settled down, it would be time for the next class.

Our bus driver was George Finch. Mr. Finch owned and operated the gas station at the end of town. He always gave us a big red net stocking filled with ribbon candy at Christmas, and the last day of school he gave us a huge candy bar. I thought he was rich to do such a nice thing for all of us. I'm certain he was, compared to most of our parents.

I also remember Capteen Creek and Benson Bridge, the ole swimmin' hole, "Watch for those snakes and broken bottles on the bottom," catching lightening bugs by the hundreds and stowing them in a jar or making diamond rings out of the you know what, the bookmobile bringing the library to us, to keep us reading in the summer, how fun, the Leatherwood Drive-in and watching Elvis movies on the big screen, for example, "Love Me Tender." Murphy's five and dime, and saving some of my 25 cents from lunch or candy to buy my mom some "Evening in Paris" perfume for her birthday. How pretty she smelled, at least to me.

The Western Auto store with all those shiny bikes for a Christmas gift for some lucky child. The A and P Grocery store, what a treat to getting to buy potato chips in a big bag.

Having dairy products delivered to the door, that cold chocolate milk on a hot day sure tasted like no other.

Yummy ice cream from the Fairyland on a summer evening. My dad loved "black cows." I think it was the same as a root beer float. Those hot dogs from the Dairy Queen at the top of the hill. Harp's Restaurant on the corner of Chestnut and Main, a favorite lunch hangout for kids.

Paper dolls that we'd play, hour after hour, and have such fun. Cake walks at the country school.

I still visit Barnesville, my hometown, every couple of years or so. Many of my family members remain there to date. The best ever Santa, at least for the past 25 years, lives there. If you see him, tell him "Hello," he's my brother. Bernard E. ("Barney") Clark.

A Cold Weather Rescue

by Gladys M. Zimmerman of Cambridge, Ohio
born in 1930

My family and I lived in a four-room farmhouse at the end of a lane. The lane was one half mile from the main road, where we collected our mail from a rural route carrier, and where my sister and I attended grade school.

During winter months, this one half mile became impassible to any kind of traffic, whether it be automobile, horses, or people. Once the snow started, the drifts became so high and packed from the winds; the only thing to do was find an alternate route to travel. When Dad returned from work, he had to leave his automobile at the schoolhouse and walk home.

Well, he created a path through the woods and down a fence line for the walk, and to make a way for us girls (ages seven and ten) to get to and from school. Back in those days, we didn't have "snow days" or "disaster days." If the main roads were open and the teacher could make it to school, we had school!

One blustery evening on the way home from school, we decided to take a little short-cut from his path; to do so, we had to cross a small water-filled run. A log had fallen across the run and we were sure we could use that log to make our walk home just a little bit closer. It was so-o-o o cold. We needed to get home quickly.

I proceeded to go first, since I was the oldest, and made it just fine; Sister was not so sure-footed and half way across the log, her foot slipped and down she went through a layer of thin ice into the run. I had a terrible time trying to pull her and her book bag out of that hole, but finally succeeded and got her on solid ground.

We still had about a quarter of a mile to go, up hill no less, to get home. She claimed she couldn't move because her snow suit became frozen. I was so frightened I carried her books and my books and pushed her up that hill. I could scarcely get my breath. I was afraid she would freeze to death. Remember, I'm a country girl with very little knowledge about cold weather consequences.

Luckily, Mom was anxiously watching for us and saw the dilemma we were in. She came running to help and literally had to chip ice from Sister's snow suit to get her out of it.

Skunk Cabbage and "Pumpkin" Pie

by Rolland Spring of Roseville, Ohio
born in 1934

My name is Rolland Spring. I was born in 1934 in Hadenville, Ohio to John M. Spring and Mary Faye Spring.

Dad was working in a coal mine in Millfield, Ohio, a little town about fifteen miles north of Hadenville, Ohio. He was laying on the ground working on his car. He got pneumonia and couldn't go to work that day. They had a cave-in at the mine, and about a hundred thirty miners lost their lives. They couldn't get them out, so they sealed the mine. It had to be God that kept him home from work that day. Dad and Mom were both God-fearing people; they loved God.

We moved to Roseville, Ohio on Ramsbottom Road, on a farm two miles east of Roseville, Ohio, about forty miles north of Hadenville, Ohio. I was two years old, my older sister was four years old. Three sisters and two younger brothers were born in the house. Dr. Dozen from Roseville would come to the house to deliver the babies. Our next-door neighbor that lived about a quarter mile away would come to help. We would wake to the sounds of a baby crying. We would think, Oh no, another one. The last two boys was born at Good Samaritan Hospital in Zanesville, Ohio. It's about fifteen miles north of Roseville, Ohio.

When I was four years old, I was playing in the barn. I fell out of the hay mile on the tongue of the hay wagon. That caused me to have a hernia. I had to go to the hospital to get it fixed.

When we would get the earache, Mom would boil skunk cabbage and take a teaspoon and put it in our ear. It worked. It stopped hurting. The skunk cabbage grew in the swamp below the house.

We all had nicknames. Mine was Bud, my younger brother's was Pumpkin. One Thanksgiving, Mom said she was going to make Pumpkin pie; he ran and hid under the bed.

We didn't have electricity. Dad got this Delco system. It was thirty-six volts. It had six six-volt batteries and a one-cylinder gasoline generator. When the batteries got low, we had to start the generator. We had a refrigerator and a wringer washer and light bulbs. Like the electric company, when Mom would wash clothes, we had to run the generator all the time the washer run. We got electricity in 1953 and telephone in 1952.

During the Depression, Dad worked with a team of horses pulling tog out of the woods for two dollars a day, and he had to give his dad half the money because they was his horses.

When I was six years old, I would drive the horses, pulling the hay wagon, loading sheaves of wheat, hauling it to the thrashing machine.

I had a very good childhood, a loving mother and dad. My dad was my best friend. We would work on the farm making hay, cutting corn, etc.

We had three horses, fifteen cows. Dad would play with us in the barn 'til ten to eleven o'clock at night, telling stories about the Bible, after we had our chores done.

We didn't have much money, but we always had plenty to eat, living on the farm. We would butcher two or three pigs and one cow in the winter. My older sister, Edna, at school would trade meat sandwiches for plain mustard sandwiches. We had a meat house out beside the coal house, where we hung the meat. I remember running out to the meat house and breaking off sausage links and turning back in the house.

The railroad tracks run across the county road where we lived on about two miles down the road. Hobos would stop at the house, and Mom would fix them a sack lunch.

We would go over to the railroad tracks and lay pennies on the rail and smash them. We would lay down with our ear on the rails. We would lay there until they blew the whistle.

When we were out in the field working, we could tell when it was lunchtime. Robinson Ramsbottom Pottery Company was a mile up the road. They would blow the whistle at 9:00 AM, 11:30 AM, and at 4:00 PM.

We took old broom handles and found some kind of a little wheel and put it on one end with a nail and push it on the ground.

One time, out in the barn, me and younger brother, George, was fighting over something, and Dad gave us a spanking. We didn't get many spankings, because we were good kids. We would go out behind the barn and smoke corn silk or buglar, when someone would leave it laying around. Mom and Dad didn't smoke or drink or cuss.

We had a coal cook stove in the kitchen, potbelly in the living room, and a grate fire in the back room. We had two bedrooms upstairs, one for the boys and one for girls. Mom and Dad had the one bedroom downstairs.

I had four brothers and four sisters. Our cousin, Paul, stayed with us. In the summer, our uncles and cousins would thumb to our house and stay the summer, help on the farm, or they would stay until we got fighting, and Mom would send them home. We had twin cousins, Paul's brothers, and they would fight all the time with themselves.

We was down in the bottom, below the house, baling hay one day. One of the twins picked up a skunk by the tail and said, "Look at this black and white kitty cat." There was so many staying with us, we had to sleep crossways in bed.

Our outhouse was up on the hill, about a hundred feet from the house. We had a spring out above the barn about six hundred feet from the house. We piped it to the house for water. We didn't need a pump. It ciphered. When Mom washed clothes, we carried water from the creek down over the beside the house, about fifty feet.

We would sleep in the barn in the hay and take feed sacks and tie them together in the apple trees and sleep in them. We was good kids, especially when Mom and Dad went to town.

Alma Grace, doesn't that name chill you to the bones? She was my Uncle Lawrence's daughter. One day, we were fighting, and I was chasing her around the outside of the house. I threw a stick at her, and it went through the big back door glass, breaking it. I got a spanking for that.

One day, we was over at our neighbor's house. Cousin Johnie came by riding on a workhorse. It still had the harness on. I rode over home with him. On the way, Benny Harper came up behind us and blew the horn. The horse took off running. I fell off. My foot caught in the harness, drug my head in the gravel, cutting the side of my head. When the horse stopped, Benny said, "I'll take him to the hospital." When I heard hospital, I took off running all the way home, blood running down the side of my head.

Johnie was Cousin Paul's half-brother. Why Paul stayed with us, his dad died with TB when he was two years old. His mom and my mom was twin sisters. His dad and my dad was brothers.

A Ride with Einstein and Clawed by a Bear

by Jeannine Gaumer of Newcomerstown, Ohio
born 1935

I was born September 23, 1935 in Urbana, Ohio. My father had just completed his education at Princeton, New Jersey, at the seminary where he was ordained a Presbyterian minister. He hadn't been placed at a congregation yet, so we came to live with my mother's parents in Urbana, Ohio.

My favorite story of their stay, while in Princeton, was about a ride with Einstein. He was a professor at that time in Princeton. My mother did some housekeeping for Albert Einstein and his wife. One day, he asked if they had ever seen or been to New York City, and they hadn't, thus, they got a ride into New York City with Mr. and Mrs. Einstein!

When I was about a year old, we moved to Newark, Ohio, my father's first placement with the Presbyterian Church. I was three when we moved to Granville, Ohio for his second placement as a preacher for the Presbyterian. It was here that I was clawed by a bear when I was three and a half.

It happened at the Columbus Zoo. Bears were kept in cages at that time with a bar about two feet high around the cage. I slipped under the bar and reached in to pet a little sun bear who was sitting on his haunch. I petted the top of his head and he didn't like it, so he swatted me with his paw, which took quite a chunk out of my right forearm, and I was bleeding profusely. My mother had left me and my brother, who was five years old, for a moment while she went to check on my baby brother, who had been left sleeping in the car. My, times sure have changed. Today, you would never leave a baby sleeping in the car. If a predator didn't steal your baby, a policeman would be sure to arrest you. I supposed she never dreamed that I would decide to pet a bear!

Our neighbors had a chow dog and to me, that bear looked like a chow dog, and I thought it would be alright to pet him.

Well, my mother's visit to the zoo turned into

anightmare. A towel was wrapped around my arm and I was rushed off to a doctor, where he cleaned and stitched up the wound, which was a mistake. In a day or so, gangrene set in and I ended up in the hospital. Three doctors wanted to amputate my arm, but one doctor said no, and wanted to try and save my arm and he did! No tendons were severed, fortunately, but as I grew, the big scar drew my hand in. My arm looks crippled, but I'm able to use it.

Brother, David, age four and Jeannine Gaumer, age two and a half, in 1938.

I remember my aunt holding my brother up to a window outside of the hospital so he could see me and wave, as children weren't allowed inside to visit. Nowadays, the whole family is allowed in and parents can even stay all night. My brother had a little sailor shirt on with a little whistle in his shirt pocket. That is about all that I remember of that day to visit the zoo.

I was in the third grade when we moved to Newcomerstown, where my father worked with the Presbyterian Church for 17 years. This is when I met a good looking, shy fellow who was 20 years old and I was only 15. At the age of 16 I ran off and got married. I must have broken my parents' hearts, as I know they had hoped I would go to college.

My mother was a school teacher. My oldest brother went to Case Engineering and ended up working at Cape Canaveral. My younger brother went to Miami University and he worked at Goodyear Aerospace in Akron. Even my grandparents went to college in Ada, Ohio in the late 1800's.

As I look back, I realize how foolish I was because this young man had just been released from prison in Chillicothe, where he had served 15 months for assault with a deadly weapon. He was in the military over in Austria. He was a security guard for officers and one night drinking with his buddies, pulled his gun on the MPs. That was the end of his military career. His father was a naval officer and had disowned him. His mother had died when he was five and he had no brothers or sisters.

We were married for 57 years and had nine children, five girls and four boys. Our children ended up being a blessing and joy to my parents.

In 1960 when our sixth child was born, my father and mother left for New York City so he could work with the Fort Washington Presbyterian Church on Manhattan Island. How exciting! They loved it and I was able to make my first trip to the city. I've been there many times and dearly love New York.

My number three brother was born in 1940 and was 20 and went to New York with my parents.

My father only had one good year in New York and contracted myasthenia gravis. He was sick for eight years and died in 1969. My mother moved back here to Newcomerstown in 1977 and she died of pneumonia in 1998. In 1979, we lost our son, who was only 18, with cancer, a brain tumor. My husband died in 2005.

I live here with seven of my children close by. Our firstborn, a daughter, is the only one far away in Wisconsin. My youngest brother is still in New York City and I always look forward to a trip to the big city, to which the Einstein's introduced my parents.

The Worn Out Farmer and the Blizzard

by Dan R. Ischy of Sardis, Ohio
born in 1932

My name is Dan R. Ischy. I am 77 years old. I am a worn-out farmer. I live with my youngest son and my youngest daughter on a 350-acre farm. My wife died of cancer in 1997. I also have an older daughter and son who live away from my home.

My first stories involve memories about encounters with snakes. My wife and I loved to pick wild strawberries. One day we were hunting them, bending over and looking through some berry vines. Usually, wild strawberries grow in shady spots. While we were moving the leaves apart to look for the ruby red berries, I thought I saw something move under the leaves. I alerted my wife, who immediately straightened up and moved away from that spot. I went to our truck parked a short distance away and retrieved an old single shot shotgun I always carried in the truck. After quickly loading the gun, I pulled back the hammer and started again, moving the strawberry leaves in the same spot as before. Sure enough, a big old copperhead struck and clamped on the business end of the shotgun barrel. Needless to say, one less snake! But my wife and I had lost our desire to hunt for more berries that day.

My next story involves my dad. My dad and I were working on a distant, older part of our farm. This part of our farm contained an old abandoned farmhouse. We were moving big flat stones that had been used as stepping stones for a front walk. We lifted one of the bigger stones and under it were two adult copperhead snakes and a lot of baby copperhead snakes. This was the first time I ever saw what the adult snakes did when their young were threatened. The two adult snakes opened their moths and began swallowing all the babies. They were protecting them in the best way they knew how—but there were several snakes that died there that day.

I saw a fight one day between a big blacksnake and a big copperhead snake. They were all tangled up with the blacksnake wrapped around the copperhead. I returned to the scene an hour later. The copperhead snake was dead, and the blacksnake was gone, I assume victorious.

We always enjoyed having blacksnakes stay in our barn and granaries. We valued them as rodent killers. To demonstrate this, I will tell a story I witnessed one day. The ceiling of our milking parlor was covered with white painted aluminum. I was doing the milking one night when all at once, part of the ceiling came falling down. There on the barn floor laid a big blacksnake with a huge rat in his mouth. I left them alone. When I finished up and left the barn, they were still lying where they had fallen. The next morning when I returned to the barn to do the morning chores, I went to look to see what had happened. The rat was still there, but the snake was gone. The rat was too big for the snake to swallow—but he had killed the rat, which was one less rat to get into and eat the grain meant for the cows.

Sometimes the blacksnakes would find their way into the house, where they liked to lay in the cool luxury of the flower beds. When this happened, there was always some flack from the lady folks and many times I can remember carrying them away, back to the barn.

I can remember the big snowstorm on Thanksgiving Day, 1950. Some people measured 43 inches. We lost our electric power. We were essentially marooned. Horses were unable to push through the snow; cows had to be milked by hand. No place to store milk because the milk trucks could not get to the farms to pick up milk. My mother made cottage cheese but soon ran out of storage room for that. We were fortunate enough to have wood heat with plenty of dry wood stored for the winter. We carried well water from a well house for drinking, cooking, and bathing. We had cistern water to carry for watering hogs and chickens. My mother baked bread in our wood stove. We ate home-canned meat and vegetables. Our family was very lucky. We never needed medical care. For the people who did, the neighbors banded together and shoveled a road open.

One day a bulldozer came through and opened a single lane of the main road. We had a neighbor who had a 1941 Dodge one and-a-half ton truck. We loaded 44 ten-gallon cans full of milk and started out at five a.m. to go to the milk company. We had a bad time of it, shoveling through drifted snow. We got back at five a.m. the next day. We bought supplies to bring along back home for us and our neighbors. Those of us who went on this ordeal were very glad when it was over.

On our farm we had several buildings, one of which was called the wood house. In this building we kept our firewood. Some of this wood was hand-split for the cook stove and some was in larger chunks to be used in a stove named a Heatrola. It was my job every morning before I left for school to see to it that there was plenty of both kinds of wood in the house to last my mother all day. I had to walk to school, which was a mile away. When I got home from school, it was my responsibility to have enough hay and straw available from the upstairs lofts to feed the cattle when my dad came in from the fields.

We always ate supper before evening chores. At this time, we could listen to the radio. One of my favorite programs was Tom Mix. His activities included some bang bang shoot 'em up episodes. This always inspired me to make homemade guns, which I carved out of wood. I stored these guns at different locations in the barn so I could have my own shoot 'em up matches after the chores were done.

It was then time to go to the house to do my homework. I would lay behind the cook stove where it was really nice and warm. Many times, my mom had to wake me so I could get up and go to bed. How I would love to go back to those days again.

I have one brother, Tom, and I had a cousin, Bill. Bill's dad died in the war, and Bill came to live with us. I always felt as if Bill was a brother also. We got into mischief sometimes. We had indoor plumbing, but we also had an outhouse at the edge of the garden. This outhouse was always furnished with Sears and Wards catalogs. We boys used the outhouse some when we were outside. We were never sure when it was in use, but we would throw a rock against the side. If you were sitting inside, this made a loud bang close to your ear. One day, my dad was using the outhouse when I threw a rock. Needless to say that ended the rock throwing.

We had dairy cows on our farm that had to be milked twice a day. We had a good cow dog named King. He was a very good friend to me. King and I would bring the cows to the barn to be milked. I would open the gate and if the cows weren't there, I would yell for them. If they still didn't show themselves, I would send King after them. In a little while here they came with King nipping at their heels. King saved me many a step by getting the cows moving to the barn.

We had beef cattle also. We would try to inspect this herd every day to be certain everything was alright. We always took grain along to give them. This would prompt them always to come when we called. One day, there was a calf missing. The mother came to eat grain but soon left again. I followed her and found that the calf had fallen into an old cistern. The cistern had only about a foot of water in it, so there was no danger of the calf drowning. The problem was how to get the 350-pound calf out. I went home and got a tractor with a loader on the front of it. I brought along chains and a ladder. I climbed into the cistern and put two sets of chains around the calf. Then I climbed out of the cistern and hooked the chains to the loader. Luck was with me, and I was able to lift the calf out of the cistern. That was one very glad calf, and she started to eat milk from her mother immediately.

We had a lot of groundhogs on our place before we had so many coyotes. One day it rained all day. About four p.m. it stopped raining and the sun came out. It really became very pleasant. I gook my .22 rifle and went walking on the farm. I managed to kill 12 groundhogs in about two hours' time. A groundhog digs holes in your fields and eats a lot of hay and corn, so this was considered good riddance!

There was always a natural contest between my sons and myself about who was the best shot. One day, my sons and I were working outside the barn. Below the barn we had built a quarter-acre pond. Beyond the pond was a hayfield with some groundhog holes in it. The boys had a high-power rifle with them in case they saw a groundhog. After a short while, a groundhog showed himself on the hillside beyond the pond. The boys took turns shooting and never could make contact. The range was at least 500 feet. Finally, I asked them to let me shoot. I told them I would show them how to do it. Now, there was a high-voltage electric line between me and the groundhog, and none of us could see it. But you guessed it right—I shot that wire right in two. Then I had to explain to the electric man what happened.

Best Years of My Life

by Carolyn E. Smith of Bethesda, Ohio
born 1940

This is a memory that goes back to the year 1955. I grew up in the small village of St. Clairsville, Ohio, which has since become a city. Life was good and school was my favorite time of the year with all the football, basketball games, etc. My parents were expecting a new baby, surprise to them, in my sophomore year. My dad frequently worked away from home and it was while he was away from home that my mom went into labor to deliver my youngest brother. My sister, brother and I stayed with my grandparents and an aunt and uncle who lived right next door to each other.

During this time our school had a "Sweetheart Dance" and I was attending with a young man in my class. My uncle made fun of him because of his big feet; funny how those things stick in your mind. After the dance, Keith brought me home and we stood in the breezeway between the two houses. He asked to "kiss me goodnight." I was so afraid someone would see us, but I let him kiss me goodnight. He left and I went in my grandma's house, went to the bathroom and took a bath and got ready for bed. Then I began the tedious job of brushing my teeth and scrubbing my tongue. It must have taken me a very long time because my grandma said, "What are you doing in there, it's bedtime." I didn't want to tell her that I was so afraid that I'd get pregnant by that "first kiss" I had to scrub and scrub to get it off my mouth. Talk about "young, naive and innocent" and I was 15 years old. Children today know about the birds and the bees so much younger than we did.

In those days girls wore dresses to school and most of them were either homemade or bought out of the Sears or Montgomery Ward catalogs. We had to wear the same dress two days in a row and put on play clothes when we came home. We had one pair of shoes for school, one for play and one for Sunday school, if we were among the fortunate. By the time I entered high school, we were permitted skirts and sweaters and jeans only on pep rally day and that is if you were in the pep band which thankfully I was; I played a clarinet, but played cymbals in the pep band.

Thinking back to bath time, reminds me that we only took baths and shampooed our hair once a week; we "washed off" every other night, but bathing was reserved for Saturday nights.

What amazing memories I have of all those wonderful days of yesterday. Children today grow up so very fast. I feel like they are really missing out on what life is all about, Many of them have lost the innocence of their youth.

I believe those were the best years of my life and I would not trade those times for today with all its modern inventions.

A Home Full of Grandparents

by Shirley Henry of Port Washington, Ohio
born 1936

I grew up in a home unlike most today. In my home I lived with my parents, my grandparents on my father's side, my grandmother on my mother's side, my great grandparents on my father's side and my great grandmother on my mother's side. It surely was a full home and I do mean a home (not just a house.) It was full of love and never once did I regret all of them being there.

One of the first things I was taught, that I believe would be hard to be understood today, was respect for

Four generations on Shirley Henry's mother's side.

others. As we sat down to eat my grandfather was seated at the head of the table. This was a sign in our home of great honor. That honor and respect continued in all decisions and things pertaining to the family. While he listened to his favorite baseball team (the Cleveland Indians) on the radio he was not to be disturbed. Yet when we were snowed in he was the first to challenge me to a game of Canasta. But the one thing, the most important and special to me was the relationship I had with my grandma.

Grandma was a lifeline for me! It was her I could share anything with and was made to feel very special. That relationship with grandmas, I believe, is missing for the most part today. Some grandmas are too busy, some live far away and some are not held in such a high place of honor and respect. It was Grandma that took me on long walks down an old canal to pick Johnny-Jump- Ups, to sit on the porch and just talk, made the greatest date pudding and to really care about what was important to me. And who could put a price tag on the wonderful Christmas Eve's we shared with all the aunts, uncles and cousins. It was my Grandpa's favorite day and he took over all the plans and made it so special to everyone. But looking back the most special event was Grandma's time in the afternoon.

When her door was shut we knew it was her quiet time of prayer and this happened everyday. I feel these prayers still today!

Another thing today's children will never experience, was funeral services that were held in our own living room where the casket sat in our bay window and family and friends came and fellowshipped the good memories we had of that person. When I was about eight I looked in the bedroom door where my great grandparents slept and heard him singing "What a Friend We Have in Jesus" as she died holding his hand. It is such a special memory and one with great significance in my life.

So as a society I believe we miss much by ignoring Grandmas and Grandpas or by leaving to them the responsibilities of raising the children. Grandmas and Grandpas should have that special time to be who they are, not out of the picture or under responsibility that should be on the parents.

Shoeless in the Wheat Bin

by Mary Jane Hill Major of Mantua, Ohio
Born 1931

I was born during the Depression on September 15, 1931 at my Grandmother Griffin's farm in Rinard Mills, Ohio. I think Grandma was born there, as well as all of her ten children and several of her grandchildren.

I have many wonderful memories of the farm. Grandma baked bread and homemade "cow butter." Granddad cured hams and they raised their own pigs. When the time came to butcher, it was an occasion, but lots of work for the adults. And another big day was when the big threshing machine came with neighbor men following. This was neighbors helping neighbors.

Also, ladies came to help with the meals. The table was filled with delicious food. We children had to take our tin plates and eat on the porch. When the wheat was put into the bins we were told not to get in there, but sometimes we took our shoes off and got in anyway. I don't remember if Granddad ever caught us or not.

When I was too small to remember, Mom told me about the time she operated on one of our hens. Each one was precious in those hard times. The hen's craw was so full; Mom took a razorblade and cut it open and cleaned it out, then sewed it with a needle and thread. It lived to lay more eggs.

After this we lived for a time at Granddad Hill's home in their washhouse.

In all of these places we used outhouses and chamber pots. We had catalogues for our toilet paper.

Uncle Wayne and I had to walk over a footbridge to walk to Route 26 and get the school bus to Rinard Mills and to school.

After living here we moved to Brownsville to a house Granddad Hill had built for his mother. Still had an outhouse. One day I was in there and as I tried to get out, our rooster wouldn't let me out so I screamed for Mom and she rescued me.

I went to school there and met my favorite teacher; her name was Helen McHugh. One birthday, she bought me a new pink dress and bows for my hair. I also remember she took me home with her at times.

At this home, our house had a stove in the living room. On Saturday night we brought a washtub in and had our baths.

By the way, Helen McHugh Dye Drake, is still living.

My dad started driving the school bus and we moved to Graysville. Here Dad had a store. Many of the kids who rode the bus came to our house. Mom had a quilting frame set up with a comforter in it and many of the girls helped knot it.

While here, I needed to have my tonsils out, so the doctor who lived down the street, along with a doctor from Woodsfield, took them out on our kitchen table. The doctor who lived in Graysville was R.H. Latta; he also delivered me when I was born. He came up often to check on me after taking my tonsils out and I did fine.

When Dad had to sell the store he got a job with the Buckeye Pipe Line Company and was sent to western Ohio—Bradner; then to Mantua, Ohio where I started high school. In 1945 here, I graduated in 1949, met and married Ben Major, whose Dad also worked for the Buckeye. Ben and I were married one month short of 53 years. We had two sons; Jeffrey Lynn, deceased, and Gregory Allen.

We love coming back to Monroe County since Ben's death in 2002. I don't get there very often. It is still down home to me and I always will love Monroe County where I still have one aunt and many cousins.

Thank you for letting me share my memories.

A Day's Work For a Day's Pay

by Theresa Lemasters of Barnesville, Ohio
born in 1924

Amid today's conveniences and discoveries, I have pleasant thoughts of yesteryear. Growing up in those days has made me a better person.

We didn't have TV games and all the other children's games of today, but we had games Mother Nature provided. In the summer, neighborhood children enjoyed the "old swimming hole" at McMahon's Creek. We fished and caught "crawdads" in the creek. We lifted stones to find snakes.

In the winter, we had fun skating on McMahon Creek. We competed to see who could make the tallest snowman. Snowball games were always a great sport. We looked forward to going into the woods for our Christmas tree and making our own decorations. Never mind if we could not find a pine tree; decorated dead branches made beautiful Christmas trees.

In the spring, we gathered wildflowers and knew their names. It was a delight to carry those bouquets to our teachers. We played "jacks."

In the fall, raking leaves and burying ourselves under mounds of leaves was great fun.

We didn't mind that we had no inside plumbing. In her kitchen, my grandmother had a "hand pump" that provided water from her cistern. Near her sink, Grandmother kept a bucket filled with drinking water from her well. She also used her well to cool the watermelons in the summer.

Everyone had an outside toilet a distance from the house, and that meant shoveling a long snow path. You could tell which families were well off, because they usually had a three-holer instead of a one-holer toilet. Any wallpaper that was left over was saved to paper the toilet. Some used newspaper. We didn't need soft toilet tissue; discarded catalogs did the job.

On wash day, the rinse water was saved to scrub the toilet. You were lucky if the neighborhood boys didn't upset your toilet at Halloween. Once, the boys attached a can filled with urine to the door. Grandfather got the full benefit of that prank!

We had not heard of roller blading, but we had roller skates. Evening fun included wiener roasts and marshmallow toasts. Maybe moms didn't trust the boys; we girls had to be home by nine o'clock.

Homes didn't have many clothes closets in those days; they weren't needed. I remember having play clothes, school clothes, and church clothes—but very few of each. Not having an older sister, I wasn't lucky enough to get hand-me-downs. Dresses and petticoats were made from feed sacks.

Chores had to be done before breakfast—helping in the barn and in the kitchen. No fast foods in the "good old days," but good home cooking on the coal-burning kitchen stove. That kitchen stove also warmed up the kitchen for the Saturday night baths. On cold mornings, we huddled around the pot-bellied stove while dressing for school.

We grew our food supplies. Our mothers and grandmothers canned fruits, vegetables, meats and jellies and jams. Sausages and kraut were preserved in crocks. Folks then knew how to bury apples, carrots, and cabbage to last throughout the winter. Some of us have held onto the blue canning jars, zinc lids, and crocks as cherished reminders of days gone by.

The life of a housewife was not easy. Wash day required the entire day. Starting early in the morning, water was carried from outside to fill the wringer washer and the rinse tubs. First, water had to be heated on the kitchen stove. In lieu of Clorox, white clothes were brightened by boiling. No spray starch in those days; starch was made by boiling a white powder from an "Argo" box. Clothes were line dried in the house in the winter. The house smelled clean from the drying items. The following day was ironing day, using a "sad" iron heated on the kitchen stove.

Homework and reading were done at the kitchen table by the light of a kerosene lamp. One of the daily chores was to clean the chimneys of the kerosene lamps.

Some things don't change. There were homeless people then, too. Those people, commonly known as "bums," traveled around hitching rides on railroad trains. They often knocked at Grandmother's door, asking for food. She gave them sandwiches, made with her home-baked bread and home-canned meat.

Can you imagine life without a few things like TV, automatic washers and dryers, dishwashers, electric sweepers, cell phones, microwave ovens, riding mowers? We had none of these in the good old days, but we had an appreciation of a day's work for a day's pay.

There were fewer lawsuits in those days. A man's word and a handshake were a firm contract. And if you got spanked at school, you could expect the same when you got home. The teacher's word was not disputed. Words like *honesty*, *morals*, and *character* meant more in those days.

P.S. Two spring cleaning chores I dreaded were:

(1) Helping to carry rugs outside and hanging them on the clothesline. We used rug beaters to beat out all the dust. We wore homemade dust bonnets to protect our hair.

(2) Cleaning the bed springs with kerosene. This really caught the dust and perhaps discouraged the bed bugs.

Rain Barrel Candy and a Yard Full of Kids

by I. V. Ankrum of Coshocton, Ohio
born 1924

I was born in the winter of early 1900s, in good old Guernsey County. Looking out my window at the snow and ice on this the 14th of January 2009, it reminds me of the past winters that I have seen. In the earlier days, it often snowed late in September and we didn't see the ground until around April. We never had snow days to call off school, like they have today

For my first four grades of school, I walked a mile and a half to a one room school house which held eight grades and one teacher. My mother would dress us in long-johns underwear, stockings, shoes, overshoes, sweaters, coat, toboggan, scarf and gloves. Making it hard to walk with so many cloths on. But we appreciated the warmth.

Children of today seems to have a bedroom and sometimes a bath of their own. My parents raised ten children in a three room house with a path to where we would set and leaf through the Sears and Roebuck catalog.

We didn't have electric or phone. I was the youngest, so I did get hand-me-downs clothes or Mother would make what was needed. We made up our own toys and games to play.

We always had three meals a day, breakfast, dinner and supper. After supper we would gather around the potbelly wood burning stove, very quietly, while Mother would read to Father and us kids by oil lamp light.

Forakers in the early 1930s. First row: Virgil, Aultman, Irma, Della. Second row: Mary, Lucille, Hazel, Helen. Third row: Vernon, Victor, Marie, Jim.

The older girls would wash the dishes. And sometimes try their hand at making candy. Usually it wouldn't harden like candy is supposed to do. So thinking if gotten cold it would set up quickly, they would place the plate of candy on the ice of a frozed over rain barrel and forget it. Come spring, the ice having melted, Mother would find dishes at the bottom of the rain barrel. She wondered what had happened to them. The rain barrel would have a thorough cleaning before the next rain as we used the water from the barrel for many things.

When I was in the 2nd grade I only weighed 32 pounds. They used to hide me in school instead of the eraser.

In the spring with the melting of snow and the rains, Guernsey County was known for their red mud roads. We were coming home from school and I got stuck in the mud. My sister worked trying to pull me out. Finally she got her arms around my waist and gave a yank, pulling me out of my overshoes, leaving them in the middle of the road. As you probably guessed, they were of no use when we went back to get them.

Mother did the family washing on a wash board. She carried the water from our spring, heating it on the kitchen stove. With such a big family she had an all days washing to do. We often helped with the ironing. We had flatirons which set on the stove until hot, use until cool, change to another hot iron. Those days everything had to be ironed. As of today you don't iron very much.

Us kids couldn't wait until summer, so we could go barefooted. The summers were so hot. When Mother and Dad got up in the mornings, the yard would be full of kids sleeping because it was so hot sleeping in the beds.

My dad would work up the garden plot and us kids would help the plant the garden by dropping seeds, sets potatoes and etc. in rows to be covered. I was always glad when the potatoes growed big enough. Then it was time to bug the potatoes. You got a bucket and a paddle. As you went down the row you would hit the leaves with the paddle, knocking the bugs in the bucket. Don't forget to look under the leaves for bug eggs. Whatever was in the bucket was disposed of later.

My brother and I used to see who could find the most bugs. We often made a game of our chores. Then they weren't so hard to do.

Mother would take us blackberry picking. We always came home with a lot of berries, also many chiggers, which was itchy and very uncomfortable for a few days. But those juicy blackberry pies made up for the discomfort.

It was always interesting to watch my dad take honey from his four beehives. He used a bee smoker and a lace curtain over his face. We would chew the comb like chewing gum. And the honey was so good too.

With the coming of fall, Mother canned everything that she could. We didn't have refrigeration, so my dad would smoke or put down in brine the fall butchering.

Dad also made what was called a tater hole which was a large mound of dirt (soil) with straw on the inside where apples, carrots, turnips, potatoes and etc. was buried for use in the winter.

Bunch and the Eighth Commandment

by Dorothy L. Bussemer of Zanesville, Ohio
born 1921

Today, looking forward to tomorrow when a new President takes over and one of the first challenges he will face is the slide of our country towards depression, this story becomes as real as that time of the first Great Depression. This story is true, and unless God has a very special blessing for our country and our new President works very hard, who knows what a hard working, loving, and intelligent dog might have to resort to breaking the Ten Commandments in order to feed his family. I hope not, but this is one of the stories that, at 87, I can still remember.

This dog, and the lady who came to our door asking if he was the one who stole her chickens and then asking if she and her husband could come and help eat them.

I can only hope it never comes to that again. The courage to live the past should give us the courage to live now and in the future.

If I were Bunch's biographer, I would begin by telling you that he began life on a city landfill. He was the biggest in the litter, and very early in life he began to help his mother in securing food for the rest of the family. Then came the day when a kindly faced man noticed the big black intelligent looking pup and decided he would make a splendid gift for his little niece. The little girl's daddy had died the previous fall, and she had wanted a dog of her own.

Bunch loved his new family, the little girl he belonged to, his new home with a rug of his own to sleep on, and the little girl's mother whom everyone called, Janie.

One thing bothered Bunch, though. Dogs don't go to school to learn lessons, and they don't listen to the radio and read newspapers about what was called the "Great Depression." Yet somehow, Bunch knew something was wrong.

There was very little food in the house. He got his share, even the little girl's milk when her mother wasn't looking.

Bunch knew he had to do something to help. His new family wasn't the smallest pups in the litter; but he was still the man of the family, in his opinion. He began to search the neighborhood for food, and found very little. Nearly everyone was a little hungry in those days.

Then one lucky day he discovered a chicken coop. He slipped in and caught a chicken and carried it home to Janie. Janie had no idea where the chicken came from but she cooked it. Bunch had his share.

From that time, about twice a week he paid a visit to that chicken coop. He got so tired of chicken; but there was nothing else to be had.

Then one day a stranger knocked on Janie's door. When Janie answered the door, the lady asked her if it was her dog that was stealing her chickens. Janie told her it was, but added that she did not know where her dog found the chickens. The lady then asked Janie if she had gas to cook the chickens with. Janie said, "Yes." The lady then asked if she and her husband could come for a meal once in a while as their gas had been shut off. Janie said, "Of Course!" and a lifetime friendship was formed.

Eventually things got better. Janie's new friend found her a job. The little girl was in high school and working part time. There was enough food in the house now, even dog food and a real bone once in a while for Bunch. Bunch enjoyed everything he ate unless it was chicken flavored; he never wanted chicken again in his life.

Oh, and in case you are wondering what happened to Bunch, the only thing he continued to steal was the hearts of people. And the Commandment, "Thou shall not steal," does not apply to stealing the heart of those we love and care for.

Reflections On a Two-room Schoolhouse

by Sally Hale of Stockport, Ohio
born 1946

Having spent 31 years of my life in a classroom educating young students in one grade of their school career, I wish to reflect on my early education in the local two-room schoolhouse.

The first school in what is today Palmer Township, Washington County, Ohio opened in 1804 with eight pupils. One-room schools with varying lengths of the term were held in several locations in the township over the years. The last school to operate in the township is the one I attended. It was a two-room school opened in the early 1930's with no present day amenities.

The last school building is still in use as a township community building. It had two classrooms separated by wooden folding doors. The front of the building had a cloak room and entrance hall for each room, as well as another room called the "music" room, even though not much music took place there. There was a bell tower with a large bell on the roof with the rope hanging down into one of the classrooms.

There was an outdoor pump for drinking water, even though we went through periods of time when the water wasn't potable. At those times, older students would carry water from a neighboring home in a large two-handled cooking pot. Each student was responsible for having his or her own drinking cup which was stored on a shelf in the cloak room. There was a path out the back doors that branched into two to lead to the outhouses.

Heat was provided by a coal heater in each room. These were stoked by one of the older boys. There was a jacket surrounding each so that students could not come in contact with the stove, but the jacket got hot, too. Early on, the floors were oiled. Later, a new varnished floor was laid. Then there was more dust and dirt from the stoves as well as muddy shoes and boots. It didn't get mopped very often.

The school was a part of the Wolf Creek Local School District which in years past had several outlying one-room schools. However, when I attended the district consisted of an elementary and high school in Waterford, an elementary in Watertown, and our little two-room school among the cornfields and farm land.

The teachers were pretty much on their own as to the running of the school. The superintendent of schools was an elderly gentleman who had been in the position for many years. He would periodically show up at the school and converse briefly with the teachers in the front hall. As I remember he was only there a few minutes and never came into the classroom or removed his overcoat in cold weather.

The classrooms were always labeled the "little" room (grades one through four) and the "big" room (grades five through eight) even though they were the same size. Desks were fastened to the floor, each row larger as you moved across the room. Not all students fit the desks very well. Some students had their feet swinging most of the year and others could barely fit between the seat and desk. In that era, it was thought that students must be seated with the light from the windows coming over the left shoulder. Therefore, in the "little" room, the chalkboard was on the wall behind all the students. There was a small square framed board attached to the folding doors, but it didn't have much room for writing. There was a small wobbly table in the back of the room that was utilized when more board space was desired for a given lesson.

Lunch was whatever each student brought in his or her dinner bucket. Sometimes, in nice weather, we'd eat outside on the ground in the shade of one of several large maple trees. Following lunch, it was on to the playground. There was a merry-go-round that got lots of use as well as several see-saws. There never were swings or a slide. Students would bring bats, balls and other things from home. Red rover and tag were popular games in nice weather. In snowy weather there were many games of fox-and-geese, as well as many snow forts constructed.

Supplies were few and far between. The textbooks were always there, but not necessarily up to date or the right number. There was an outdated set of wall maps in the "big" room and usually a globe. I guess the school board furnished the chalk and erasers, which were clapped outside the back door periodically. The only means of duplication was the hectograph pan. The county library system periodically delivered a large denim bag full of books (of their choosing) for us to enjoy for a month or so. They came several times during the year.

There were usually six to eight students in each grade level, sometimes more, sometimes fewer. It must have been easier for the "big" room teacher since those students could work more independently. Subject titles have changed, but we did reading, phonics, arithmetic, writing, history and geography, depending on the grade level. Science and health were never mentioned. Of course, physical education was unstructured on the playground and art usually centered on the holidays.

The high school band director (the only music teacher in the district) came on Friday afternoons for music. This consisted of pushing the piano out into each classroom so he could play and the group could sing. Older students who chose to begin instrumental lessons for later inclusion in the high school band would squeak and squawk for awhile after both rooms had sung. This did happen in the "music" room, but, of course, everyone in the building could hear and usually suffer.

With a late September birthday, I was an eager five-year-old on the school bus with my 4th grade sister to enter first grade. There were no kindergartens. Moms didn't go on the first day and there wasn't a pile of paperwork that had to be done before I got there. I remember my first day vividly as the teacher, new to the area, was getting a class list by asking each student for his or her name. When I gave mine, she asked for my middle name. I knew I could not pronounce "Elizabeth" so my response to her was, "You'll have to ask my sister," who was a few rows away from me.

Since older students were in the classroom, anyone who was a good listener could learn a lot of things before the scheduled year. Older students often helped the teacher with younger ones if they wanted and had the time.

After I finished seventh grade in 1959, the school board decided that our school, with its lack of facilities, had outlived its usefulness, so it was closed. All students were transported to the school in town where they would have eventually gone for high school.

My students always thought I was ancient when I shared about my two-room school experience. However, I feel that I received a good education and it was what helped me to choose my life's career.

The Country Doctor and the Iceball Fight

by Donald W. Fairchild, D.D.S. of Cambridge, Ohio
born in 1923

Dad was a country doctor in the town of Antrim, in Guernsey County, Ohio. It was in Antrim that I have many fond memories and most of all on Grandpa Willis's farm. In fact there are precious memories from O.S.U., service in the Navy in WWII and the Korean conflict and my years of practice as a dentist.

Let me tell you about Dad's office. We lived in the Presbyterian parsonage and Dad's office was in one room of that property.

He was on call twenty-four hours a day. Some days he would be gone all day on house calls. Near by was a barn where a horse was stabled, that he rode in inclimate weather. When roads were improved in the '30s he drove a Model A Ford.

His office was quite simple, with a roll top desk in one corner and an examination table in the other. Two walls were covered with shelves which held medicine of all kinds. There were gallon size bottles of liquid medicine on the floor. In the center of the room was a small pot bellied stove and of course a coal bucket. All medicines were dispensed on the spot since there were no pharmacists for nearly twenty miles. Dispensed *very* cheap – twenty-five and fifty cents.

In these simple surroundings, boils were lanced, burns were treated, broken arms were set, frozen toes were amputated, prenatal exams were performed, and *yes*, clocks and watches were repaired, and a radio was made by my dad who graduated from Starling Love Hospital (OSU) in 1919 with honors of tops in his class.

The standard fee for prenatal exam, delivery, and postnatal care was twenty dollars total. The bill was often paid with farm products or a couple chickens hooked over the horn of his saddle. What a heritage I have and those Depression years!

Dr. Fairchilds Model A on Route 22 before the road was paved in 1930-31. His office is in the background with the entrance by the chair on the porch.

I spent most of the time on Grandpa Willis' farm. He was tall man (six feet, four inches) and Grandma a mere five foot one. Mom was their only child, so when I was born to her, I became Grandpa's special buddy.

When school was dismissed in early May he would be waiting for me in his '28 Chevrolet Coupe. I would give Mom and Dad a big smile and a wave of the hand as we headed for what I considered UTOPIA – Paradise – The Garden of Eden – Adventure Land.

What was the attraction? What did a boy do without T.V., video games, Ipods or computers? What did *we do* without electricity, running water, without playmates, without a radio or A.C.?

I'll tell you: I *lived* every minute of each day. I used my imagination, I explored nature. I learned to appreciate the simple things and developed values that I cling to this day.

I will list a few of the adventures on that farm and conclude with an incident that occurred in grade school in Antrim.

Crawdads in the watering trough
Seining for tadpoles
Jumping in the hay mow
Playing with a copperhead
Lassoing calves (cowboy)
Practicing baseball swing with *stones* and a *stick*
Pig bladder football
Bows and arrows out of limbs
Butchering time – sausage making
Planting my very own garden (gourds)
Cream separating
Day long trip in a road wagon
Accident plowing corn (heroism and tears)
Threshing, shearing sheep
Feather tick beds – Kentucky rifle under the bed
The pump organ
The spring house
Going into the cat business

And *much much* more

* * * *

Scene: Antrim Grade School, Two Rooms. One day in mid winter, at recess, some of us boys were playing Andy Over, three or four on each side of the building. The object was to throw a ball over the building and if you caught it, you would race around to the other side and try to hit one of your opponents. If you hit him he was captured and had to come to your side.

Most of us wore Lindbergh hats which were fashioned after Charles Lindbergh's flying leather helmet. On this day I threw the ball over the school and Thomas Carllisle caught it but when came around the building he threw an *iceball* (frozen snow) which hit me in the head. I became enraged and we started to fight. In the process we wrestled into the basement, full of coal dust.

Our friends yelled, "Fight! Fight!" and the teacher (Craig Titerick) came running to stop the spectacle. Oh-OH-we are in trouble. We will be punished severely! We would not speak to each other, both of us seeing red—eyes aflame with anger.

The wise schoolmaster laid not a hand on either of us. He simply made us sit together the rest of the day and to touch each other until we mutually apologized to the other. Tom's gone now—a good friend. Maybe I'll meet him up there.

Grandpa's Rifle, Once a Year

by Alma Mae Hoopes of Crooksville, Ohio
born 1939

In the 1940's, living on a small farm in Ohio, I was raised to understand that our livelihood came from the land. We canned our own vegetables and fruit. We also prepared our own meat. This was as much a fact of life as children going to the supermarket today. So my story about "Butchering Time" will seem gruesome by today's standards, but to me, at age eight, this was a normal part of growing up. Also, I could be excused from two days of school because it was Butchering Time.

Our two pigs were penned up behind the barn. The pen was made of old dirty fence posts, hewed beams and various lengths of what used to be 8 X 10 inch oak barn planks. It was pieced together with nails and barbed wire like a jigsaw puzzle.

At the front of the pen was a slop trough. We milked our own cows. So, the milk that was left after the cream had been skimmed from the top to make butter and our table scraps were saved in a large bucket. When the bucket was full it was poured into the trough. The two muddy pigs would push, shove, grunt, and get right into the trough feet first.

Grandpa would throw ears of field corn and fodder onto the mud floor of the pen. It would get messy and stink from the mixture of soured milk, spoiled food, and manure.

During the rainy season, the pigs would root and roll in the muddy pen. It was above their knees and each step created a sucking sound. They rooted and dug deeper and deeper until Grandpa would have to reinforce the bottom of the pen so they couldn't escape.

The sour smell and sloppy sight lingers in the back of my mind as the cool days of fall approach, indicating that it is butchering season once again.

Butchering day was an exciting time because neighbors came by to help get the dead pigs hung, gutted, and lowered into scalding water. Then the men would scrape the wiry hair off the skin.

Grandpa only used his small .22 caliber rifle once a year, so when I saw him start out the door with it, I ran to the house and put my head under a pillow. Afterwards, I would run back out to see the pigs dragged into the barn by Bonnie.

Bonnie was our quarter horse; we used her to plow the garden and ride for pleasure. This horse never liked butchering day and would sniff and snort as she was driven towards the pen. Her nostrils flared red when she got a whiff of the dead pigs. The whites of her eyes were enlarged as she approached her load with fear. She pranced frantically as the men struggled to attach the single-tree to a hook that had been plunged through the hock of the pigs' hind legs. The men yelled, "Back Bonnie, whoa Bonnie."

Once hitched-up, she would lunge forward time after time, sweating and prancing, until both pigs were hung by their hind legs from beams in the center of the barn.

When her job was over, Grandpa would take her back to the barn, or as it looked to me, she took him back to the barn. He would take giant steps behind her, trying to keep a tight rein so he wouldn't be dragged to the ground and pulled through the barnyard.

As the men gutted the pigs, the entrails were dropped into large wash tubs. Then the carcasses were left to hang and firm up for a day before we worked the meat.

In the meantime, Grandma and I went to work. We took the entrails and heads into the summer kitchen. There, we cleaned the entrails out to make casings for sausage. After they were cleared, we placed them in salty water and let them stand overnight. The next day we took a dull knife and scraped each entrail, being careful not to tear or poke holes in the long transparent casings. The casings were then placed in clean salt water until we were ready to slip them onto the grinder, which filled the casing as we ground the pork into sausage. The long filled casings were tied into short lengths which made our little pig sausages.

The head was our next project. The ears and tongue were pickled. The brains were soaked in salt water until an outside coating came off. Then they were ready to fry. The rest of the head and other convenient pieces of the pork were used for head cheese. Headcheese is a loaf of jellied and seasoned meat.

Day two was another day I could stay home from school. Grandma and I worked side by side preparing the meat.

The tenderloin was always the first meat cut from the open pit in the carcass. It is the most tender part of a pork loin and is located under the short ribs. This tender strip of round pink meat is about one foot long. We always ate as much tenderloin as we could hold at butchering time. It was served sizzling from the hot iron skillet. Fresh tenderloin needed nothing on it to enhance its taste.

We worked hard, cutting, chopping, and grinding up each pig. Pork chops, sausage, roasts, hams, and fat for lard was processed. There was always a thick layer of fat under the skin that had to be trimmed off the meat to make lard. We cut the fat and fatty skin into one or two inch chunks and put them in an iron kettle. The iron kettle was set-up in the barnyard with a wood fire under it. Slowly, we stirred and rendered the lard from the fat. After all the lard was rendered out, we put the remains into a press and slowly turned a handle, pressing out the rest of the lard and leaving cracklings. The crisp cracklings were a snack much like potato chips are today.

Grandma poured the lard into bread pans. After the lard was firm, she would cut it into one pound loaves, wrap it in wax paper, and store it in the refrigerator. The rest of the lard was poured into a five-gallon can. What wasn't used by spring would get a strong pungent smell. The fresh lard was used in everyday cooking and the making of pies. The really pungent lard would be used to make lye soap.

This mixture of lard and lye made blocks of strong detergent, but not much suds. These hard blocks of soap were shaved off into the laundry tub each Monday: wash day.

The hams were Grandpa's job because he knew how to sugar-cure them. He went about it like a doctor. He filled a large syringe with his "secret solution" and gave the hams shots. He would go through this process for several days. The hams were hung from wooden beams in the cave surrounded by canning jars filled with vegetables and fruit in the back room of our cave. Below the hams was a large bin that held our potatoes.

The cave was dug out from the side of a hill near our driveway. It consisted of two rooms. As we went into the first room, the air was cool and damp. There were shelves on both sides of the entrance for the storage of large bowls and kettles. Both rooms were lit by natural light coming in the through the open doorway. Then directly in front of us was a large wooden door which covered the entrance of the back room. This door had large old hinges. It dragged and skipped across the damp dirt floor as it was forced open. Even in the dead of winter, the back room was dark and cold, but never freezing. I refused to go into this dim, cool, scary room by myself because I had seen spiders and salamanders scurry around the canning jars and in the potato bin.

Grandma and I would go to the cave together and cut slices off the hams for Sunday breakfast.

By spring the hams would be getting a green mold on them. We never minded that because someone told us that it was penicillin and good for us, so we just scraped or washed off the mold and ate the delicious, healthy ham. Some mornings Grandma would fry the ham and then stand at the foot of the stairs and fan the aroma up the stairs by waving a towel. Grandpa and I would awake with the taste of smoked ham already in our mouth. We both scurried down the step for a delicious breakfast of cured ham, fresh eggs, and hot coffee.

In the spring, we would get two more little piglets. Grandpa would repair the pen and I would again look forward to missing a couple days of school at butchering time.

The Rigged Prediction

by Lewis LeMaster of Zanesville, Ohio
born 1950

As the summer days of 1963 waned, I felt little excitement for the upcoming school year. Most of the teachers in Zanesville, Ohio's public schools knew their stuff. But from the naive point of view of a thirteen-year-old, much of the material being taught seemed rather boring and irrelevant. Little did I realize that a special treat awaited me in the eighth grade.

Bill Davis, a U.S. history teacher, was unique, to say the least. He certainly knew American history. In fact, he shared with his students little-known facts about historical figures that almost magically transformed them from musty statues to real human beings, warts and all. Mr. Davis had the entire package: he was a proficient teacher, an excellent entertainer, and an extraordinary comedian. I doubt that anyone ever fell asleep in his class, or even yawned, for that matter.

According to Mr. Davis, many administrators didn't know what to make of him. He just didn't fit the standard description for a teacher of those times. Perhaps even some of them wondered if it was a good thing that the students enjoyed his class so much.

Today there are several sixty-year-olds who probably tell their grandchildren about the U.S. history teacher who, in advance of Election Day, could accurately predict the winner of a presidential contest. In 1959, a few months before the fight for the Presidency between Vice President Nixon and Senator Kennedy had ended, Mr. Davis announced to his classes that long ago, through painstaking research, he had developed a foolproof formula for figuring out who would win the Presidential sweepstakes.

To back his claim, he nailed a picture covered with newspaper onto the wall of his classroom. He then announced that the day after the election, the newspaper would be removed, revealing the winner and proving that his formula was accurate. As a result, the students became extremely interested in the election process, which was unusual for a bunch of thirteen year olds.

The day after the election, the excited students waited with baited breath to see if their teacher was indeed some kind of prophetic genius. As Mr. Davis slowly removed the paper from the picture, the students gasped. To their amazement, hanging on the wall was a portrait of the next President of the United States, John F. Kennedy.

Like many of Mr. Davis's former students, I stayed in touch over the years. One day he shared a secret with me. Listening to the election results back in November of 1959, he had to wait until the wee hours of the morning to learn that Kennedy had won the election by a razor-thin margin. Then, leaving home a little earlier than usual, he went to school, took down the picture of Richard Nixon that had been hanging there for months, and replaced it with that of JFK.

Mr. Davis's stunt, more than anything else, got a bunch of teenagers interested in the political process. That is no small feat. So what if his formula needed a little work?

He's gone now; I miss him each and every day. To me he was the embodiment of what a teacher should be. His students learned the material and had a lot of fun while doing so. In my book, that's the work of a special educator.

Walking the Hollers

by Jean Starr of Millersport, Ohio
born 1938

I remember going to my grandma's house in Oak Hill, Ohio. When I was little, my mom would take me every summer for a week, on her vacation. She worked in a shoe factory.

As far back as I can remember, my older sisters cared for me. We would walk as they called one holler to visit my aunts, and stay overnight, and the next day we would walk another holler to visit uncles, and we would stop along the way to visit Mom's friends. It was so hot. I can remember sinking my feet in the sand, and it would feel so cool. We would just take our time and walk.

I loved to go to my one uncle's house. He had a store, and he would let me make my own ice cream cones, so I always ran to the freezer.

Well, we had our family reunion up at Grandma's old farm house. I was wandering around with my cousin Johnie, and I spied the old freezer out back, so I told Johnie, "Lets go, it's the ice cream." We thought that we would not be spotted. We thought we were sneaking and no one would know. We ran up and quickly raised the lid up, and I screamed and ran faster than I ever ran in my life. Johnie yelled, "It's a big monster out there in the freezer!" My uncles laughed. It was a hog head for making head cheese. I never wanted an ice cream cone again out of that freezer.

I followed my uncle down the field to milk one day. He said, "You want to milk her?"

I said "No." Just then, she had to go, and I never saw so much water in my life. I said, "Does she do that every time you milk her?" He laughed, but I never drank milk there anymore. I told him I only drink milk from the store.

I loved to ride bikes down the old brick road in front of the store with my cousins. I can still smell the country air and feel the early dew. It was wonderful.

When I was six years old I would sneak off and go to the woods, down the road from our house. I would pick wildflowers. I was not allowed to go alone. I saw the boys climb a tree and the other one would throw a rope up to them, and they would swing down, like Tarzan. Also, I climbed the tree. Being so little, I didn't know I had to have the rope, so I just jumped like they did. I broke my arm. Boy was I in trouble. Children's Hospital, Mom called by my Dad to meet us there. I never tried that again.

Then, one day, our neighbor went on vacation. She told me to watch her dog for her. A strange dog went into her yard and was fighting with her dog. I chased him away, but not before he bit me. I was crying, my mom came out and I said that the little dog bit me. She said, "What dog?" It was gone, so back to Children's for 21 rabies shots this time, that was before they did the three in the stomach.

My pets were dogs and cats. I had a cat when I was six years old. I would dress it up like a baby and give him a doll bottle, put him in a buggy, and push him all around the neighborhood and everyone would take pictures. I don't have one, I wish I did. But in my Kodak memory I can still see him frowning at me; I don't think he liked me.

My dad called the Humane Society to come get my dog because she was sick. He said they would make her well, but I was seven years old. I called them, and told them to bring my dog back and the lady said, "Oh, we had to put that dog to sleep." I called my dad a dog killer. I got in trouble two ways this time, for being on the phone, and saying that to my dad.

I rode a train when I was little. My dad was a preacher and he had to preach a young soldier's funeral in Canton, Ohio. I was sitting on the floor of the train playing with puppets with a little girl. I looked up to see a bridge. I asked my mom, "How can this big train go through this little bridge?"

We had an outhouse, and we had a big bad goose. I was very small for my age, and that goose would chase me all the way to the outhouse and I would have to stay in there, and peek through a crack in the wood, and when he'd go away, I'd make a run for the house, but he'd always see me and the race was on. I hated that goose.

Jean Starr, age five.

Haunted house, mine was a Catholic Church and the nuns. Being a daughter to a preacher; I had never seen anything like this. So, one day, my sister and her friend walked me past this church to go to the golf course. All the nuns were out walking, all in black. I ran and cried and told my dad they took me to the haunted house. And I guess he thought it was time to tell me there was other religions out there.

I also have a memory of my dad listening to the Lone Ranger on the radio. My sister and I would go past him and say, "Hi Ho Silver, Away!" And we'd laugh. If he heard us, trouble again.

And yes, we took castor oil, for everything. I'd chase mine with a big spoon of mustard to take the taste away. I hated it.

One day, three girls and I decided to play hooky. One girl heard us planning and said, "If I can't go, I'll tell." So we took her and she had never missed a day of school in her life. We heard this other school was having a ball game, so we wanted to go. We got off our bus at the stop by the store. We went in, took our lunch money, and bought candy and pop, and walked a couple miles to that school to find out there was no game. The game was our school away game, so we had to ride a bus to get to it. As we were walking home, our school janitor was looking for us. When our friend was not in school, she got us caught. So, he loaded us up and took us to school. The principal called our families to come get us as we were not allowed to go to the game. Trouble again.

And then the truant officer came in our room, and wanted to know who the boys are. He said when they see him, they ride their bikes up the railroad track so he can't see them or come get them. One of them was my brother. Trouble again.

Well, now comes the real trouble. My dad and my brother came in from work, told my mom they saw a woman and a man fighting over a gun. She lived on our street. I jumped on my bike, being a busybody, rode up there and told the cops my dad and my brother seen everything. They were dragged into a jury court over murder. She had shot him. My brothers wanted to kill me.

My mom's favorite dish to me was her sauerkraut. She put sugar in it, but I didn't know the secret. So one day she sent me to the store to get sauerkraut. I told the lady I wanted the sweet sauerkraut. She said we don't have that sauerkraut, so I left. My mom had to go back and explain to them.

Party line, yes, we had one. I remember my mom worked, so my sister and I lived on a phone. That was more fun. We found out a girl we didn't like was on the line, so we listened to all her calls and then we would go to tell everything on her and we got caught up on that. Double trouble, for being on the phone and telling rumors.

Best memory, Buckeye Lake Amusement Park, all gone now. Oh what fun the rides: big boat trips up the lake on a riverboat, a boardwalk with fortunetellers, penny arcade, games, guess your weight, guess your age. I had a lot of teddy bears won for me.

My mom's place of work would hold company picnics there. Our whole family would go. It was like a family reunion. We took our kids there when they were small. There was a bar there, where Grand Old Opry stars would come. I sure met a lot of them. I loved Buckeye Lake.

My son has a boat now, and last summer while cruising the lake, he came upon the wood from the old roller coaster in the water. It's still there; it sank with all of our memories on it. That was the good old days. The atmosphere of Buckeye Lake, it was like another world you could escape to. I miss it, I just wish my kids could remember what it was like back then.

One thing to leave you with: back then, if there was as much crime as there is today, we sure didn't know it. That was a time kids could go to the woods, pick wildflowers, break their arms in trees, climb apple trees, pick mulberries, run free in the sun, swim in the creeks, play in deep snows, build snowmen, and sled ride on hillsides.

The school bus driver always had Christmas treats for us, last day of school vacation. For Christmas holiday, he would give us a goody bag, oranges, apples, and candy. We'd go home, drag a tree in, pop corn to string on the tree, get one toy for Christmas, enjoy Christmas plays in church, sing carols up and down the streets. We were happy and we had Christ in Christmas and a baby in the manger. And all memories were made from the good old days.

Tippytoeing in the Olden Days

by Jean Christopher of North Ridgeville, Ohio
born 1926

When our son was little he was always asking about the "olden days." I am not sure just what his thoughts were when he was asking about those olden days, but I wondered if he thought that we fought dragons and rescued fair maidens or drank wine with a bunch of knights at a round table. Since my memory does not go back quite that far, I can't comment on too much of that sort of thing. What I do remember is somewhat less exciting, but visiting two of my aunts down on the farm in Vinton County was always interesting and an experience that I will never forget.

One of my aunts had been married and was divorced. Her name was Emmy. She had assumed the duties of a farm type housewife and did all of the household chores that would normally be expected in that situation. The other aunt, Mary, who was the old maid, took the place of the farmer and raised pigs and milked a few cows and had chickens. This was their source of income and it was meager but adequate to take care of their needs.

There were two things that always took place when I would go there to visit. Aunt Mary always had some little pigs behind the kitchen stove in a box. She would always seem to find a couple that needed more care than their mother could provide, so she would bottle feed them and keep them warm in the kitchen until they were big enough to go back with the other pigs out in the barn.

The other thing that always fascinated me was the old wooden telephone that hung on the wall with a crank on the side. They were on a party line with several other people along the road. They could tell by the number of rings whether the call was for them or for someone else on the line.

One way of keeping up with the news was what was called "eve dropping" on the party line. My aunt Emmy was prone to doing that on a pretty regular basis and it was always funny to see her approach the phone when she was going to pick up the receiver. She would always tippy-toe over to the phone and very gently lift the receiver to listen on someone's conversation. She would cover the transmitter with her hand to try to shut out any outside noise so that no one would know that she was listening. I could never quite figure out the reason for the tippy-toe approach to the phone. I always thought that was sort of a useless step in her method of operation. I guess that since they had no radio at that time, it was probably the best way available for her to keep up with the local news.

I also remember some of the fine food that they would prepare with vegetables and fruit from the farm, but these little incidents were always things that were so interesting to me as a young child when visiting their farm in Southern Ohio.

Confessions of the North Star Boys

by Curtis D. Harper of Byesville, Ohio
born 1939

Our family moved around some when I was in school, but I started to school in first grade at Buffalo. The first day of school I walked home (three blocks) at recess and Mom had to usher me back to school.

That year, we moved to another part of Buffalo, about eight blocks from school. My cousin lived between our house and the school, so about once a week I'd skip school and stop at his house and play with him all day, since he hadn't started to school yet, then walk home with the other kids after school. That lasted until report cards came and Mom found out.

We moved again, during third grade, to what we called the McElwee place. Mr. McElwee lived out our mile-long lane on Rt. 313. He owned our house.

We didn't have running water; just a natural spring. Mom washed clothes on the porch on a wringer washer.

I was 10 years old and had to milk five cows before and after school each day. Mom and Dad ran the cream separator on the back porch.

My oldest sister, Bobbie, and I had to walk across a field that was full of sheep, and down a hollow to our Aunt Angie and Uncle Roy's house, to catch the Buffalo school bus.

Right across the road from their house was where our grandpa, Armstrong Johnson, lived, where he had stuffed animals hanging on the walls. He also had an old Victrola record player and lots of 78 rpm records. I remember listening to Detour, Deck of Cards, Old Shorty, and Wabash Cannonball.

At the McElwee house, we could go just a few feet from our house and pick buckets of blackberries from which Mom and Dad would make blackberry cobbler, then can the rest of the berries.

One day, while Mom and Dad went over to the neighbors, I put my sister up in the sink and cut off some of her hair with scissors. Then I climbed up to the tall cabinets and found some packs of chocolate candy and ate it, only to find about a half hour later that the candy was EX-LAX! Then I ran to the outhouse.

After the 4th grade, we moved out just off Rt. 209 toward Bloomfield, to what we called the Coulter place, and went to Pike School.

In the warm months of school, a lot of kids went to school barefoot.

A couple farmers' sons brought watermelons to school on the bus and sold them for 10 cents apiece.

Dad worked for a farmer who raised pigs and had a huge apple orchard. We kids climbed ladders and picked apples and Mom and Dad ran the sorter and packed the apples.

We had a few cows out there and had a collie dog named Jack. Dad took Jack and had him cow trained to bring in the cows at milking time, by barking at their heels and nipping them. After about a week, the cows got used to Jack and all we had to do was go outside and holler for Jack and we'd see the cows coming towards that barn.

After the sixth grade, when Dad got a job at Republic Steel in Massillon, we moved to a farm just outside Bolivar and attended Bolivar School.

Dad raised pigs and he'd go to the Navarre Nichols Bakery and get some 100 pound sugar sacks full of stale bread and pies and cakes. They'd sort out the pies and cakes for our school lunches and feed the bread to the pigs.

My sister Bobbie and I worked for a potato farmer picking up potatoes for eight cents a crate. After the digger came along and dug up the potatoes, we'd pull a crate between two rows and fill them with potatoes. We made enough to buy our school clothes that summer.

I used to stay with Grandma, Mary Secrest, in the summers when I was younger and she'd let me sleep on her feather-tick mattress. When we stayed at our Grandma and Grandpa Harper's, we got to sleep on a straw tick mattress.

Grandpa Oney Secrest would take me to the Buffalo Red & White Store in his horse and buggy to buy groceries when I was about seven.

Shortly after I started the 9th grade, we moved to Northwestern North Carolina in the mountains, a few miles from West Jefferson. We tenant-farmed and I worked pruning tobacco for 20 cents an hour and we picked bush and pole beans and got paid by the hamper. I helped Dad cut bean poles from mountain laurel bushes. When tobacco was ready to be picked, we'd tie it in bundles and hang them on wood stakes to be cured in the barn before it was ready to be taken to the tobacco auction.

We attended school at Fig, North Carolina, where the grade school was on the lower side of the road, and to get to the high school on the upper side, we had to walk through a tunnel under the main road.

The two main sports at Fig were basketball and horseshoes.

Near the end of my tenth grade we moved back to Ohio where I would finish my schooling at Buffalo in 1957.

Dad and I started digging out a place in the side of the hill on property he bought. We used shovels, picks, and wheelbarrows so he could build a basement house. He and my grandpa Harper laid up the block.

My last two years of school were a treat. Read on:

One day six of us boys picked up a teacher's car, a Nash Metropolitan, and carried it up near the ball diamond under the big pine trees.

One night, late, I was headed home from Buffalo. As I neared the stop sign at Derwent, I noticed one of my pals had turned West on Rt. 313, so I dowsed my lights and followed him up 313, then onto North Star Road to his home. When he pulled over, I turned on my lights and sped by him real fast, throwing dust and gravel everywhere.

One night, four of us were returning home from a Buffalo ball game and one of them told me to see how fast I could go across Derwent railroad tracks. As I went across the tracks at 105 m.p.h., I heard a rumble. When I asked what the noise was, one of them said, "A train behind us!"

There were five of us, called the "North Star Boys." One night, we decided to pull a trick on a couple of miners who would go to Hariett Bar after work and drink 'til real late. We strung hay binder twine across the road from one fence to the other on top of Grant's Hill on North Star Road. About midnight, we seen lights coming up the hill and we spread newspapers across the twine, set fire to it, and ran in the nearby corn field to watch. The driver came around the curve, seen the road all ablaze, slammed on his brakes, then got out and yelled some choice words before he got in his car and drove off.

One night after basketball practice, our coach dropped us off at Rt. 313 and North Star Road. We seen there was nobody home at a nearby house so we put a ladder up to the porch roof and I went up there. Then the others began handing me porch furniture, chairs and a swing. While I was moving things around, they took away the ladder, but I found a high place in the yard to jump down on.

Grandma and Grandpa's house was a place for weekly feasts on Sunday after church for our whole family. Grandpa would go out and kill three or four chickens. Grandma and all the ladies would fix homemade noodles and mashed potatoes on the wood-cook stove. The stove had a reservoir to heat water for washing clothes and stuff. Dad and I would go the Byesville Ice House and get a block of ice, bring it home, put it in a gunny (burlap) sack and smash it up for the ice cream freezer to make ice cream. We grandkids would take turns turning the crank.

Grandpa had a big stump in the feed building behind the house, on where we would crack walnuts and take them in the house for Grandma to make homemade fudge.

Grandma had a refrigerator with the motor on top and she stored crocks of milk in it and skimmed off cream to make butter in the wood churn. She had a gasoline powered washing machine and had to put the exhaust out the window. If we came up the driveway and heard the put-put, we knew it was wash day.

Dad and my uncles, Ray and Eber, showed me how to cut a forked twig from a tree, then tie strips of rubber from an inner tube to it to make a slingshot. Then we took our slingshots and went down the run (creek) and killed frogs and Grandma would fry frog legs.

Grandpa had a pear and cherry orchard between the house and the barn. He planted horseradish and rhubarb along his garden and he had four gooseberry bushes there too.

Nobody ever went home empty handed because they kept a cellar full of canned goods all the time.

Uncle Eber (Bub) used to take me a ride on a sled pulled by a team of oxen. He'd haul trash over the hill on the sled and dump it in a ravine. Then he'd bring firewood back to the house.

I used to like to hear Grandma talk on her crank party-line telephone. If it rang three rings, she'd say, "That's ours."

Those were the good old days.

Eight Children in Two Rooms

by Esther M. Lewis of Zanesville, Ohio
born in 1932

The Bailey family: Helen and Nathaniel. I was borned in a small town called Cutler, Ohio, in January of 1932. It is a small country town, one post office, one grocery store. The larger grocery stores were in Athens, Ohio, Marietta, Ohio, and Parkersburg, West Virginia.

The house I grew up in was a two-room shack. The walls papered with newspapers, Wards catalog. Wooden board floors, scrubbed with bleach to lighten them up some.

My mom and dad—Helen L. Bailey and Nathaniel Bailey—raised eight children in these two rooms. We had kerosene lamps, wood stoves. The children were James Bailey, the oldest; then me, Esther Bailey; Maxine Bailey; Ruth; Yvonnie; Patty; Junior; Danny Bailey. At the time I was borned was after the Great Depression. We were very poor.

We heated the house with a cook iron stove. It burned wood. The stove had four places on top to set pots to cook, a bake oven, and a tank on the back that held and heated water. I never knew there was such a thing as toasters. We toasted our bread in the wood stove oven. We lived on a small ten-acre farm. We had cows, pigs, chickens, guinea hens, no horses. Our cattle for milk, butter, cheese.

My father hunted a lot, and we had wild meat. Groundhog, coon, rabbit, squirrel. I don't know if he hunted in season or not. When there was eight kids to feed, and no work, what was one supposed to do? I can remember hearing my mother and the Jase Mayle neighbors talking about the WPA, which my dad got on after a while. Things were a little better then.

As a kid growing up, we really worked hard. Maxine and I both milked a cow before going to school and also at night after school. When we came home from school, we changed our clothes then went to do our chores. We had no fence around our property, so we watched the cows, feed the hogs, chickens and milk just before dark. We also got wood every night. Then came inside and help finish supper, do dishes, pack lunches. There was not much time to study, because after supper and dishes and lunches for the next day, it was bedtime.

Back then, we had good neighbors. [Ray Mayle?] Our cows would wander on their property, and a lot of nights, we would have to find them to bring them home to milk. We cut wood winter and summer in order to stockpile for the bad weather, rainy or snowing bad. If it wasn't too bad snowing, we cut and sawed and carried up the hill to the house and stacked it. We would go in the woods below the house and saw them down. My brother, Jim, and my dad and Maxine and me. Then we all sawed wood, then split, and carried it up the hill. Sometimes there were trees already down, and we would saw them up. To this day, I didn't know who that woods belong to. We had an old shed my father built to put the cows in for winter and at night.

When we did meals, the food was put on the table in large bowls and then passed around. Mom always made biscuits, bread every meal. On Saturday, she made me make yeast bread. This is what we used for our lunches. It was really a hard life, work, work, work. My mom never had it easy, almost a new child every two years. Along with work, a child to care for. Our bath time was Saturday night in a galvanized tub. After heating water on the old cook stove, strung a curtain across the kitchen, and everyone took baths one at a time.

Then we did get Sunday off from work, because my mom belonged to church, so we rested on Sunday. Every Sunday before church, I would churn butter. Mom would put cream in a half gallon jar, and I'd shake, shake, shake until it came to butter. Then keep putting water in it and working it until the water run clear, add some salt, and that was cow's butter. We also made our cottage cheese. We also did a lot of our food on Saturday for Sunday dinner. We walked two miles to Sunday school and church.

After church and dinner and dishes, play time. Our neighbor girl would go to church with us, and after her dinner, Opel Cunningham would come to our house to play.

Back then, we raised almost everything we ate. We had a big garden every year, picked blackberries, dewberries, black raspberries, and canned them by a hundred quarts or more. We canned green beans in half-gallon jars. We had a place outside where we cold packed our food. We raised green beans, soup beans, potatoes, any kind of food we could raise. If you didn't raise it and prepare for winter, they would be no food. Mom picked wild greens, cold packed them. My father caught a lot of coon, and we cold packed that.

Bailey family in 1972. Front row, left to right: Ruth, Maxine, Patty, Esther. Back row: Jr., Mom, Dad, Jim, Danny.

No, us kids did not get in trouble. My father said, "Keep the kids busy and they won't get in trouble."

We raised several hogs and butchered them. The neighbor men all went to each other's place and help butcher and cut up the meat. Then there was still a lot of work to do, putting up the meat. Back then, no freezers or refrigerators.

My father had this good friend, the Harris. Homer would come and plow our fields and garden for us. My dad and my brother, Jim, planted the corn. All of us helped plant potatoes, beans, and the rest of the garden. In the fall of the year, we banked our potatoes after digging, by making a large hole in the ground and covered with straw and piled dirt over that, and the potatoes kept in there for winter. Hulling the soup beans was a job too. My father trapped too and took the furs and sold them.

Us kids went night hunting with my father, and we would go in the woods and get honey out of trees. Had to do that at night or the bees would sting you. We learned how to dress wild meat, cut it up and soak in salt water. We were raised mostly on wild meat.

We raised our own chickens, had our eggs. On Sunday, we would go out, catch a chicken, chop his head off, and let him flop, flop, flop, then hang him up by the feet and let the blood drain out, then put him in hot water to help take off the feathers, and then singe off the pin feathers, then cut it up and soak in salt water.

My mom could make the best cream pies, crust made with hog lard. On Sunday, our meal was fried chicken, baked beans, mashed potatoes, cream pie or cake, Jello in winter, in summer, green onions, radishes, wilted lettuce. Mostly what we bought was twenty-five pounds sugar, twenty-five pounds flour, salt, baking powder, soda, yeast.

When I was growing up, there was no fans. It sure was hot in the kitchen cooking in summer. We also boiled our white clothes outside in summer and dried them on the clothesline. I washed clothes on a wash board, rub until the knuckles was sore.

After I got in high school, I would go out to work all summer and came back home to go to school. My brother left home before he finished. My father said, "All finish school, then you're on your own. If you make your bed hard, you're the one that will lay in it."

My first paycheck when I worked in Marietta doing housework, taking care of a child, during the summer, was spent on food to take home for the rest of the family, later some clothes for school.

When we were growing up, there was no electric, no phone, but before I left home for good, the power lines came through. No more kerosene lamps, lanterns, flat iron heated on stove to iron with.

Maxine and I went to Columbus that summer to work. My father was also working there. I graduated in 1951. About two years before, that was when we got power. Maxine and I bought Mom a used refrigerator. I think the motor was on top of it. Something was. Now we could have ice-cold water, Jello in summer, and we had a place down by the spring where we kept milk and cream and butter. Now the refrigerator really helped save a lot of trips down the hill to the spring.

We had large barrels behind the house where we caught rainwater. But the drinking water, we carried from the spring. We always had to watch for snakes around the water.

We had no inside toilet. We used a chamber pot inside. Outside, we had outhouse. We had to watch for snakes and bees out there. If there was a bumble bee in there, I'd wait until it came out. No toilet paper. We had old catalog Sears, Wards. Our house walls was papered with newspapers and catalog pages. In later years, we had wallpaper books we would order paper out of.

My father ruled the roost. He made all of us take castor oil, cod liver oil, black draught. I hated all that stuff. If you spit it up, he made us take more.

The Tin Town Arms Race

by Vernon Littleton of Dover, Ohio

born 1933

The area known as "Tin Town" was named for its close proximity to both the Reeves and Greer Steel Mills and also the old American Sheet & Tin Plate. Most of the houses in this 10 to 12 block area were company-owned and afforded reasonable rent for many employees of the

Reeves Steel Mill.

Tin Town was a highly integrated neighborhood consisting of many ethnic groups. Some prejudice existed, but for the most part, the neighbors intermingled and got along very well together. If a problem or fight developed, they could usually work it out without involving the police.

Our home was one of the most popular in the neighborhood, since most of the kids knew they were usually welcome there. We spent many evenings on the front porch swing with Mom telling us ghost stories. On the cool evenings in the fall, she would take us "under the wings" of her knitted shawl, so we could stay warm as she told these scary tales.

We enjoyed many freedoms not available to the young people of today. During the summer months we could play under the streetlights until ten or eleven at night. There were probably less than a dozen cars in all of Tin Town so nobody bothered us as we played Kick the Can, Blind Man's Bluff, Hide and Go Seek or some of the other old-time street games.

After seeing the Robin Hood movie, we would have sword fights with our homemade wooden swords. We often played Cops and Robbers after seeing a gangster movie. There were also many fights between the cowboys and Indians, after the many western movies we saw at the old State Theater.

We made scooters from old roller skates, slingshots and rubber band guns from rubber inner tubes, cork pop guns from window-blind rollers and walking stilts from the old 2x4s we found in the Reeves Steel Mill dump.

Someone got the idea to make a double rubber band gun. Then another made a triple gun and the arms race was on. I think the ultimate achievement was a quad gun as each tried to outdo the other.

As you can see, our many activities didn't cost much and we had enough variety to keep us occupied and out of trouble, most of the time.

The entire area behind our house, extending from Wooster Avenue to the Reeves Mill, served as our playground. A baseball field located near the Reeves Mill was used primarily by the adult leagues. A basketball court, with a combination football-softball field for the kids, was located directly behind our house. Pop built a swing set with chinning bars, a seesaw, and then, when I was about twelve, he added a high jumping pit.

During the summer, we often hiked up the railroad tracks to the Stone Quarry, Elephant Hill and the White Bridge and swam at "Yonko's" and "Bare Ass Beach." These were located just up the river from the Greer Steel Mill. The area always smelled fishy from the accumulation of clamshells opened over the years in a futile attempt to find pearls. Don't ask me how Yonko's got its name, but the other one is rather obvious.

The only time that I can remember Pop giving us a whipping was when he caught us swimming in the river during a thunder and lightning storm. He hurt our feelings more than anything else, since he only used the tip of his belt. But it was a valuable lesson we never forgot.

I learned to swim with a little assistance from the older guys. As I was paddling across the river holding on to a floating log, they caught me out in the middle and showed me how to tread water. When they took the log away I somehow managed to make it back to shore on my own.

We spent a lot of our growing up years along the river where we found a metal boat that had been shot full of holes and sunk in the mud sometime during the 40's. After digging it out of the mud, we managed to patch it up with tar and metal screws. Near the end of WWII, we found a wooden rowboat that had been under water for three or four years. We also fixed it up, and when some of the older guys returned home from the service, they identified it as old "Deadwood," which was a boat they had built from scrap lumber back in the 30's. They thought one of their groups must have sunk it before they left for the service.

We often "borrowed" another boat from the guys across the river. We'd swim across after dark and make a "moonlight requisition" and then a few days later they would recapture it. We continued to steal it back and forth for about two years and it became a big joke since it was "borrowed" so many times that nobody seem to remember who the real owner was. If the truth be known, it was probably stolen from a third party to begin with.

During the summer, my brother and I would often meet Pop after work at the upper end of the street with our wagon. He would pull us home as we shared half a leftover bologna sandwich from his lunch bucket. It's a wonder we never got food poisoning, since the bucket set out in the heat of the steel mill all day.

Summer also brought such events as the ice deliveries, the ragman, the Jewish peddler and street repairs. There was also the occasional hobo looking for a handout, especially back in the late 30's and early 40's.

The iceman would use an ice pick to separate the 300 pound blocks of scored ice into deliverable size chunks of 25, 50 and 100 pounds. We would follow him around the neighborhood picking up ice chips from the back of his truck and on a hot summer day, that was almost as good as ice cream.

The city usually tarred a couple of the Tin Town's streets every summer and we'd follow them around to pick up chunks of fresh hot tar and chew it like gum. From what the medical experts say today, it's a wonder that most of the kids from Tin Town didn't die of cancer.

We also had fun following the Rag Man as he went through the neighborhood repeating his chant, "Raaags, any old raaags today," and then follow up with, "Any old raaags, cans, or bottles today." He had a hanging scale mounted on the back of the truck and everybody complained that his scales were crooked and they were being short weighted. Chances are, they were right.

We always looked forward to the Jewish Peddler who made his rounds once or twice each summer. He carried tapestries, table clothes, fancy pillow covers and a variety of other items. We were not only fascinated by the type of items he sold, but also by his accent, and the fact that he had two thumbs on one hand. The second thumb grew out of the side of his regular thumb, but this never seemed to bother him. After he would show Mom a dozen or so items, she would usually buy one little thing.

The peddler's stops gave the housewives a break from their monotonous routine as they looked at the many items he had to display. Each stop took a great deal of time, but by the end of the day, he had probably made quite a few sales.

Our house was a frequent stop for hobos looking for a handout. We didn't have much but Mom would usually give them a sandwich or bowl of soup. We often wondered why several would pick our house but seldom bothered the neighbors. One day we discovered the marks they would leave on the sidewalk or in the alley. The marks told other hobos that our house was a good place to stop. After that, as soon as one left we'd erase the marks. That seemed to help, and after that, they seemed to bother us less and the neighbors more.

In the days prior to television, we enjoyed the radio as much as TV is enjoyed today. Radio made you visualize the various happening, such as Fibber McGee opening his closet door with everything falling out. Time after time the same old routines would make us laugh. After school we listened to such favorites as The Lone Ranger, Jack Armstrong, Terry and the Pirates, The Mystery Hunters and the Green Hornet. Friday and Saturday evenings featured such favorites as Gang Busters, The Shadow, Lights Out, The Haunted House, Fibber McGee and Molly, Burns and Allen, It Pays to Be Ignorant, Truth or Consequences, The Great Gildersleeve and many others. All you needed for complete enjoyment was a good imagination.

Movies and a fight, all in one night. On Saturday night, before we left for the midnight movie at the State Theater, we'd check out the Red Store (also known as The Bull Pen) for any signs of trouble. This was the local hangout for adults, but kids could also buy pop and candy there. It included a pool room and poker tables along with beer, liquor, soft drinks, soup, sandwiches, candy, and a few grocery items. I don't think they had a liquor license but that never seemed to bother anyone.

Bessie and Flavel lived in an apartment on the second floor at the rear of the store. On more than one occasion, we watched as Bessie, a rather robust woman, would pull Flavel out the front door of the Bull Pen and then drag him home. This usually happened on payday, since that was about the only time that poor old Flavel had enough money to drink or gamble.

We also watched for the Ice Cream Peddler, who used a three wheeled "tri-cycle" with an insulated front compartment to deliver novelty ice-cream items that were packed in dry ice. On several occasions, the group from the "Bull Pen" upset the contents of his tri-cycle on the sidewalk. I always felt sorry for the poor guy as he tried to salvage what little he could out of the mess. I don't know why he didn't avoid the area completely, but I believe, as they would say today, that he was "mentally challenged."

My brother Ed and I each had to scrub one or two linoleum floors to earn our fifty cents for the Saturday night movie. Fifty cents doesn't sound like much today, but at that time, the movie was only 10 or 12 cents, and I believe popcorn, candy bars and pop were five cents each. We could go in as early as 7:00 p.m., watch the featured movie twice, along with a short subject, newsreel, previews of coming attractions, a serial movie episode and finally the midnight movie. This lasted until about 1:00 a.m., after which we would stop at Teddy's Restaurant on the way home for a hamburger or bowl of chili. I think these were 10 cents each and a half pint of chocolate milk was another nickel.

Occasionally, we had a little extra excitement on the way home. Scriven's Tavern was about a half block down the street from Teddy's. Roy Scriven was rather short and overweight, but just as we left Teddy's one night, he was in the process of throwing one of his customers out, even though the guy had a knife. Roy seemed to have the upper hand, but we didn't stay around to find out. Believe me when I say, it didn't take us long to clear out of there.

Another time, a drunk was passed out at one of the street comers near our home. At first we thought he was dead, but when he finally moved we ran home and Mom called the police to see if he was okay. This was even scarier, since it was so late at night.

The State Theater often had apple bobbing or some other contest on Saturday afternoon and would give away two or three bags of groceries on Saturday night. Ed won the groceries the night of a bad snowstorm, so we didn't wait for the show to end. It was really exciting to carry the heavy bags of groceries home through the deep snow, since food was scarce at that time and we knew our parents would be so happy.

In the early 40's, the Harper family was about the

only family in Tin Town without electricity. We thought they were really poor because they used kerosene lamps. Poor or not, Elmer Harper had the largest collection of comic books in the neighborhood.

The late 30's and early 40's was the heyday of comic books, but we thought they had been around forever. In the evenings, several of us would go from house to house trading comics and it seemed like most of the time was spent at Elmer's. By the dim light of a kerosene lamp we would go through his huge collection, trying to read as many as possible before deciding what to trade. I think Elmer must have been the sharpest trader in Tin Town, because he usually got two for one. He would argue that it had a torn cover or it was too old, or some other reason and we were too dumb to realize that the reason he had so many comic books was that he could out talk and out think the rest of us...and we thought he was dumb.

Our parents would send us to bed early on Christmas Eve with nary a sign of Christmas anywhere in the house. Shortly after midnight, Mom and Pop would wake us, and there stood a skinny little Christmas tree all decorated with our few presents underneath. After we opened these, we'd head out to visit a few of our friends, as the lights came on around the neighborhood. In turn, one or two of them would visit our house and after two or three hours of going back and forth, everyone would return home for a few hours sleep.

After dinner on Christmas Day, we'd repeat this procedure, but this time we would stay longer and play with their new games, since we rarely got many of our own.

A typical Christmas for me was usually two or three books. But I do recall one special Christmas when Ed and I received a wooden wagon together and another time, when we got to share a chemistry set. That was about as good as it got. I never had a new bicycle, sled, roller skates or Daisy BB gun like so many of my friends. Mine were always hand-me-downs from my older brothers.

During the war years, Santa Claus would pass out small bags of hard tack candy at the Elk's Lodge. Candy was really scarce during the war years, and it was about the only Christmas candy we would have. The waiting line was usually about two blocks long and after we got our first bag of candy we'd hide it in the bushes, switch clothes and get back in line for a second go round. I think we may have been questioned once or twice, and it never occurred to us that what we were doing was wrong. We didn't seem to realize that if they ran out, some other poor kid wouldn't get any. I guess at that age you don't think of things like that, but when I look back over the years, I just hope I didn't deprive another kid of his Christmas candy.

Struck by Lightning

By Clara Heskett of Bethesda, Ohio
Born 1924

On a rainy Sunday morning in July 1935, on a farm one half mile from Beallsville, Ohio, I was accompanying my older sister, Hilda, and younger brother, Johnnie Dennis, to the pasture to bring the cows into the barn to milk. Johnnie had also brought a horse bridle in case we ran across the old work horse and then we could bring her in as well. Little did we know as we were walking along, so carefree, what was in store for us. An event was about to take place that would change my brother's life and also alter our family life for the next few weeks.

Just as we arrived at the cow pasture it began to rain quite heavily, so we took refuge under a huge maple tree. Johnnie sat down at the trunk of the old maple while Hilda and I chose to stand at the outer edge of the tree. When the rain began to slack, we decided to finish our job and round up the remainder of the cattle. Before Johnnie could move out from under the maple tree, lightening flashed. Hilda and I turned to find smoke rolling up the tree and Johnnie sitting, unresponsive and unconscious. Realizing that he had been struck with lightening we scooped him up and carried him back to the house. Dr. W. S. Burcher was called to his aid. In the meantime, Johnnie was stripped of his wet clothing and put to bed. There were no apparent marks on his body when his clothes were first removed. Within a very short time, however, burns began to appear on his back and arms. (The scars he carried for the rest of his life.) It was later supposed that he had received a glancing blow of lightning when the tree was struck. The horse bridle that he carried at that time had drawn enough of the electricity to cause the damage.

After nearly 48 hours of restless tossing and turning, Johnnie awoke with a terrible headache. He was, at first, curious about what had happened, but soon he didn't need an explanation as the pain from the burns set in. Johnnie was cared for at home instead of going to a hospital, which he would have done today. Johnnie completely recovered from being struck with lightening. He was, however, left with a slight speech impediment, and he only grew a few inches taller than he was on this July day in 1935. Johnnie was 8 years old at the time. I was 10 years of age and my older sister was 14.

Johnnie passed away at 62 years of age in 1990. He began preaching later in life and was still preaching two Sundays a month at the time of his death. His mother passed away at the age of 99 in Jerusalem, Ohio. I am now 85 years of age and my sister, Hilda, is 89. Hilda is in a care center in Woodsfield, Ohio, but I still live in my own home in Bethesda, Ohio.

We will always remember the miraculous way that my brother's life was spared. Everything worked in his favor, the rain in his face as we carried him home, the wool overcoat acting as an insulator and his rubber boots (keeping his feet from being grounded). It all goes to prove that God works in mysterious ways His wonders to perform.

Unique Heritage Lost

by Laverne E. Pickrell of Zanesville, Ohio
born in 1926

Fulda, Ohio, in danger of losing its uniqueness because of "big shovel." Three agencies offer "help," $6,000,000.

Fulda, Ohio is about twenty-five miles northwest of Zanesville, Ohio and about fifty miles east of Columbus, Ohio. Fulda, Ohio's county seat is Caldwell, Ohio, in Noble County

Fulda, Ohio Pioneers. You sometimes hear people talk about the good old days as if they would like to go back to the past and live as the pioneers did. The good old days never existed.

Day after day, the pioneers' life was a life of hardship. The pioneer family depended on their own industry and skill to house, clothe, feed and protect themselves. All the work had to be done by hand. The working day began at dawn and continued right through the evening. Families were large and it was not always easy to provide clothes and meals. While they supplied most of their needs, there were a few items, such as gunpowder and salt that had to be purchased from outside their community.

Salt was important for preserving food. At first the pioneer family used Indian corn and wild meat for food. There were millions of rabbits, raccoons, groundhogs, wild birds, deer, etc. To catch these animals for food and their fur, traps such as deadfalls, snares and deep pits were used.

Sickness was one of the pioneers' worst problems. It was usually many miles to the nearest doctor and such a trip through the woods was dangerous. They relied on home remedies for most of their ills. Most of their home remedies seemed to work. If they became ill with a cold or symptoms of a cold, the patient was given a hot drink. They would dilute whiskey with an equal amount of water. This was homemade whiskey and contained a high amount of alcohol. Then they put a small amount of sugar and cinnamon in the diluted whiskey. This was heated as hot as one could drink it. They gave this hot drink to children, also. The patient was then advised to go to bed and rest.

Another remedy was given for tummy ache. A spoonful of castor oil with a piece of homemade bread to change the terrible taste of castor oil. For a local infection these people would take a small piece of bacon, salted and cured, and put it on the infected area and cover it with a narrow piece of cloth. This salt seemed to cure the infected area. It also lubricated the skin, kept the air off the wound and kept it clean.

They had a remedy for diarrhea, too. The pioneers would dig up blackberry root. They would clean it and cook a tea from it. All food was taken away from the patient and they were given this tea for a day or two. This worked primarily because the dairy products and meats were taken away and a small amount of nourishment came from the warm tea.

These people were not ill very often although the children had childhood illnesses. These pioneers were not ill often because they served regular hot meals three times a day. The meals consisted of "unadulterated" meats, fruits and vegetables. They also served homemade bread, jellies and apple butter along with fresh milk. By working hard in the fresh air they got the necessary exercise. These people retired early and got up early.

The families helped one another. A wonderful community spirit resulted from this practice of working together. Entertainment was always a part of house raisings, log rolling and husking bees. Also this was true at "quilting bees" and butchering day. Great quantities of food was prepared by the pioneer women while their men were busy at their work.

Candles and oil lamps were first used for light. But before a family could begin farming they had to clear the land to build a house and to till the fields. After they raised the food for the summertime, they preserved fruits, vegetables and meats for the winter. Apples, pears and potatoes were stored in a wine cellar since this was the coldest place in the basement. They often had a large barrel of hard cider that had worked off from sweet cider. Friends were served a glass of wine or cider when they visited.

The Fulda, Ohio people were unique. They lived as their ancestors had taught them in Fulda, Germany. The Catholic Church was at the center of the community. The parents belonged to church organizations. The youth had dances every month. The youth from the neighboring communities would attend these social events. The young people in Fulda would also go to the social events of neighboring communities. Once a year they sponsored an all day event. Many people from nearby communities came to the dinners served by these German cooks. In the evening, young people came to dance at the local dance hall. While the young people danced, the parents played bingo in the basement area.

These Fulda people helped each other once a year to butcher the hogs. Ten to twelve families picked a butcher day. Then the men and women went to a specific house early in the morning. Each man had his specific job. Some trimmed hams and shoulders, others ground and seasoned the two kinds of sausage. Many other specific jobs were performed by other men. While the men were working, butchering, the women were expected to prepare many of their favorite dishes. When dinner was ready the men ate alone on this particular day. The women served them the best meal they knew how to prepare. This went on until each family had butchered their hogs and made them ready for smoking and canning. The children enjoyed coming home from school and going out to a big iron container that was hanging over a fire. They liked to fork a piece of cooked heart or liver, salt it and eat if from the open kettle. These were being cooked for a specific kind of sausage. It also contained meat from the jaws and other small pieces of meat.

Another interesting part of living in this German community was helping the adults get some of the small animals used for food supplements. The adult would release a ferret in one of the two openings of the rabbit's dwelling. We children were expected to hold a burlap bag over the opposite hole and catch the rabbit that was scared out by the ferret. The sound of a rabbit running toward the bag that was being held was a frightening but anxious moment. They also made rabbit traps, tempting them with an apple in the trap, and a door would trip catching it live in the box.

The Fulda farmers each had a smokehouse thirty or forty feet from the house. Shortly after butchering, the sausage that had been stuffed into casings and tied in a circle with a few inches of cord, were hung from the ceiling of the smokehouse. Then for a few days the farmers would build and maintain a small fire under the sausage. It was usually made of hickory wood. Then after the hams and shoulders were cured with salt, pepper and saltpeter, they were hung and smoked a few days.

These German farming people could not call a service man if something went wrong and needed repair. They learned to do the repairs themselves. If a water pipe that extended from the house to the hillside developed a leak they would cut a narrow strip of inner tube and wrap and stretch it around the pipe with the leak. Then they would use a thin wire and wire it tight. When the water pipe froze that was exposed across a creek, they would put sufficient fire along the pipe to thaw it. This happened occasionally in the winter. The rest was buried a few inches under the ground.

The Fulda people were bright to exceptional people. They would do things to make life handier and easier for themselves. This hilly country had springs of water on the hillsides. So they would make a small dam at the opening of the spring. They then buried a large metal tank. They knew that if the spring and tank were high enough they would have pressure. So they piped the water to the house and had running water for the faucets in the kitchen and upstairs bathroom. They had enough pressure to flush the commode. But they still had the "outhouse" as a second rest room.

They would build a cistern and catch rainwater to be used for certain purposes. They figured out that rainwater was much softer than spring water. But some of the farmers still carried water from wells, bailing up the water with a bucket. Some did not have bathrooms so they washed with a basin from the kitchen sink and had only the "outhouse" for the restroom.

Adam Nau, featured in this material, had gas wells drilled on his farm. He was smart enough to pipe gas to the small community of Fulda, about a mile away. He put in old style meters and operated the Fulda Gas Company.

It was interesting to see an oil well drilled in. They would hire a driller and when they drilled into the important sand, sometimes at night, the family would watch the "drilling in." Often it was on a hilltop. When the sand was brought up they could tell if it was only slightly oily that it would not be a productive well. It could be very disappointing since the farmer had sold stock in his future well, as well as having his own stake in it.

These people, the first generation born in America, had a fourth grade education in a one-room schoolhouse. They subscribed to farm magazines as the next generation had an eighth grade education. They learned what they could from their "Farm Journal" and "Successful Farming" magazines, besides they had a daily newspaper, published in the county seat at Caldwell. A mailman would drive the country lanes and bring the newspaper along with the daily mail.

The adults got up first in the morning. The man would go to the basement floor and stir up the coal stove fire that had been slacked down for the night. The homes had one register on the second floor so the heat could heat the rest of the house.

The woman of the house would first go to the kitchen and put the coffee on that had been ground in the pantry grinder. The aroma of freshly perked coffee and the smell of a newly fixed fire was what the children experienced before arising in the morning.

The grandfather would sit in the yard and smoke his pipe in the evening. He would sit and study the sky. They knew by watching the sky if it would rain and when it might be nice weather. They needed to know this because each farmer planned his work for the next day.

Each farmer had a few cows for milking. They cooled the milk in milk crocks in cut off barrels. These barrels were put into running water from another spring piped into the basement for this purpose. They separated the cream from the milk with a mechanical separator.

They churned their butter from cream with a churn that had paddles turned by hand. The farmers made cottage cheese and made another cheese from cottage cheese letting it age. Their extra sour cream was sold to the Caldwell, Ohio creamery. At first they drove it to Caldwell. Later a truck came to the farm and picked it up. Later, these people learned how to keep milk sweet and clean and they sold whole milk that was picked up every day.

They raised enough grain to feed a flock of chickens. These produced eggs and frying chickens, as well as stewing chickens. These were cooked with home made noodles. They would sell their extra eggs at the Caldwell, Ohio Creamery once a week, since farmers went to buy sugar, flour, yeast, coffee, etc.

Grandfather Adam Mau.

They mowed and put enough hay in the barn for a herd of eight or nine cows. One steer was raised every year to be butchered in the fall when it got cool enough. But the meat was not to freeze before canning.

Being German farmers, they naturally raised three or four hogs for butchering in the fall. They would build a fire under a large bathtub of water. The hogs were scalded and placed on a large bench. The hairs were easily scraped off then before the hams and shoulders were cut. The farmers saved garbage for the hogs, besides feeding them corn they raised.

They made laundry soap with lye, also for the dishes. The dishwater was poured into large pails for the hogs, along with the garbage. They believed this kept the hogs from having worms.

The church and rectory had to be supported by the parishioners. So they assessed each family $10.00 pew rent besides the regular collection. The school children had to sit in the front seats with the Ursuline Nuns seated just behind them. The adults always sat in their same seat on Sunday morning since they "rented" them. It is interesting to note that the Ursuline Nuns taught the basic "Ten Commandments," a few Bible stories and they disciplined the youth.

A big event for these people was a trip to the "big city," Zanesville, Ohio, to consult with a specialist or to visit an aunt there.

A Fulda, Germany church sent a "GOLD" chalice to the St. Mary's Catholic Church in Fulda, Ohio for their one-hundredth anniversary. The first families to settle at Fulda, Ohio from Fulda, Germany were helped by some German people from western Pennsylvania.

Since the farmers used whiskey for medicine for colds and symptoms of colds, they made their own whiskey. They did not sell the whiskey but used it for medication, their own use and served it to their special friends.

First they had to have a secret room in the farm house. It was illegal to make whiskey and sell it. One farm house had a large walkin wardrobe next to their bathroom. Back of the clothes that hung on a pipe bar was a rope extending out of a small hole in the back wall. The farmer would pull on the rope, thus raising a weight that rested against a large panel along the bathroom wall next to the wardrobe. The weight was mounted at another wall across from the panel in the bathroom. It moved up and freely. After lifting the weight with the rope one could open up a large panel in the bathroom, opening on a hinge-type fitting so well that when it was closed it could not be seen. There was small narrow boards nailed neatly at each place that the panels met each other.

Inside was an attic room, unfinished. Here they had one or two barrels of rye, water and perhaps some sugar. They seemed to know the exact quantities of each ingredient. This was set to work into an alcoholic mash.

At precisely the right time a whiskey still was moved from the secret room and placed on the bathtub. It consisted of a large copper tank set onto a small gas flame. This was cooked at night for two or three nights once a year. The steam would go into a copper tubing that eventually coiled around through cold water. This steam condensed into drops of whiskey of high alcohol. But this liquid was clear in color. So the farmer browned white sugar, stirring constantly. This was added to the whiskey until it was the proper color. They had a tester that tested the alcohol content.

This procedure was never discussed with friends or relatives, nor was it ever discussed in family circles. The whiskey was handled with great care as if it were of great value. They would put it in glass bottles and store it in a secretive place for hot drinks for colds, for their own use and for special friends.

Moving in the Dead of Winter

By Peggy Cunningham of Cumberland, Ohio
Born 1939

Our family, which consisted of Mom; Sarah Eleanor Archer Baker, Dad; William Zueinglius Baker, five kids, which consisted of my three sisters; Phyllis Ann, Mary Frances and Marjorie Lee, my only brother; William

Danny Baker, myself; Peggy Ilean Baker and our grandfather; Henry Clarence Baker, had moved to Noble County in the winter of 1945 as our dad Zue Baker, as he was known, had bought a farm from Mr. Pickenpaugh in the winter of 1944.

With his job as a truck driver he had to wait till January of 1945 to be able to move his family and livestock to the farm in Noble County from the family owned farm at Route 1, Gay, West Virginia. It was located about half way between Spencer and Ripley, West Virginia. Our grandmother had died in February of 1938 and Dad and Mom had to move to Grandfather's farm to take care of him so Grandpa was a member of our family the rest of his life. He always helped our mother by watching over us and teaching us about life. Grandpa was a retired Methodist minister. He shaped our lives as we grew. We loved him dearly.

It was quite an ordeal to move everything in the dead of winter. Dad and Grandpa moved the animals in an old truck that Dad owned. They stopped several times to check on the animals as it was cold weather and it took a little over four hours to arrive to Noble County. This was before the days of the interstate roads. We all arrived safely in Noble County and our mother had to cook our meals on a wood stove as there wasn't any electrical service at the time. That would come a few years later. In West Virginia we had gas wells on the family farm and had free gas to heat the house and to use for gas lights. So this was quite an experience for Mom to use kerosene lights and use the wood cook stove. She had grown up with kerosene lights, but never had to cook on a wood cook stove. She learned real quickly.

The house was huge with four bedrooms upstairs with a large hall way and bathroom, which wasn't in use in the beginning. We had the little house at the end of the path with a sign that said this is it. The attic was very large and it had a large water tank to catch rain water to flush the toilet that wasn't in service yet in the upstairs bathroom. The attic covered all of the upstairs as this was a large house. On the first floor were the pantry that Dad later made into a bathroom, a kitchen, dining room, Mom and Dad's bedroom and two living rooms; one which mom kept only to be used when company came. They were connected with sliding wooden doors and she kept the doors closed except when company came or for special occasions like Christmas or when we had parties.

There was a fireplace with beautiful green inlaid tile with a double mantle in the one we used for everyday and it helped to heat the house. Our mother read many books to us kids in front of the warm cozy fireplace. The house had a large front porch with two swings where Grandpa would sing and tell us stories of his past. There was a smaller screened porch off the kitchen. The basement had five rooms which included the outside mudroom where we hung up our barn clothes after chores were done. A cellar where Dad stored the potatoes and Mom had shelves of canned vegetables and fruits she had canned to feed our family. Also crocks of milk were kept cool for our use and some of the cream was separated to make butter. There was a room with a large fireplace with a huge kettle to heat water. In the winter the kids played in this room and popped popcorn and baked potatoes or parched field corn in the fireplace for a snack. Our mother used it to heat the water for the washing machine before we had a hot water tank. The furnace room, which had a very huge coal furnace that took up most of the room as there were several pipes going to all the rooms for heat. The coal room held a winters worth of coal that Dad and Grandpa hauled and shoveled in before the weather turned cold.

It was a job to heat the house in the wintertime and it kept us busy firing that furnace. Sometimes it would blow the doors open and the pipe off the back of the furnace when the gassy coal would smolder, then ignite and the house would get smoky. Grandpa would have to help get the pipe back on the furnace. This was a dirty job; you would get black from the pipe and smoke. Then Mom would have to open the doors and windows to get rid of the smoke and smell.

We used a tub to take the ashes out of the bottom of the furnace. It took two people to carry them outside to dump them. This was an everyday job in the winter. In the winter Mom put double wool blankets on our beds; they were scratchy, but very warm. Every bed had a large soft feather tick for us to sleep upon. We had several comforts and quilts on our beds. Sometimes Mom heated bricks and wrapped them in towels to tuck in at the foot of the bed to warm us up. In real cold weather this was real nice to hop into bed and feel the warmth.

In the summer we picked blackberries and wild raspberries for Mom to make pies, jams and jellies. We had apple trees in the backyard where we played and ate green apples until they got ripe enough for Mom to make applesauce or pies. We also had an apple orchard down over the hill from the hog barn. Mom made applesauce and pies or cobblers for us all summer and fall. Grandpa and us kids would help pick apples for storage in the cellar until all the apples were gone. In the fall she would cook apple butter outside in the huge copper kettle. Each of us kids got to take a turn stirring the apple butter with the stirrer Grandpa had made for us to use until it was cooked thick and done. We would help Mom wash the jars and lids and then when it was ready we helped her jar it up and wait for it to seal so it could be put into the cellar. We had peach trees and when they were plentiful Mom canned lots of them and made jam and jelly.

In the winter we looked forward to the cookies,

popcorn balls and homemade fudge that Mom made. Grandpa loved the brown sugar fudge and the kids all wanted chocolate fudge or peanut butter fudge. Our mother was a talented cook; she seemed to know how to fix so many good things to eat.

On our farm were several large barns with the biggest one used for horses on one side and cattle on the other side. Each side had a large box stall area to bring in the mares that were ready to foal or the cows that were ready to drop their calves. The cow side had stanchions for the cows to put their heads through and be fastened. They had hay and a box for their ground feed, which they ate as I milked them. When the milk was taken to the house it was strained for the house use or put through a milk separator and the cream was put into a cream can to be sold. The blue milk, as Mom called it, was fed to the pigs in their ground feed, which we call slop.

The barn had a huge hay loft on one side and on the other side the loft was made with space to store machinery. It had a hay fork connected in the middle of the roof of the barn with ropes and pulleys which the horse would be hitched up to pull the hay into the mow. It was very exciting to watch it go up and be tripped and come down into the mow. In the wintertime we all played in the haymow. It was fun to climb up the ladder to get onto the beams and jump down on the loose hay.

Our dad used the next largest barn to house the sheep in the winter. It had a loft for hay, which made it easier to feed the animals in the wintertime. During lambing season; sometimes when a ewe had twins they wouldn't own one of the lambs and Dad would bring it into the house in a box for Mom to feed and keep it warm until it got strong enough to go back to the barn. We always had to watch out for the buck sheep and he would run at you and try to butt you. Dad would watch that he didn't hurt one of the kids. We had a chicken house for the hens that laid eggs, which provided us with many breakfasts. Mom raised baby chicks and when they got big enough in the spring she would sell some for fryers. Sometimes she had to kill, clean and cut the chickens up for the customers. I thought that was a nasty job. I didn't like the smell when you singed the fine hairs over a fire with flames after the chicken had been scalded and the feathers were all removed, Mom didn't seem to mind. Our mother made the best fried chicken in the world.

We had another smaller barn that housed the hogs that Dad raised. It was fun to play with the baby pigs when they were small. We also had pet baby calves and colts. We really enjoyed the baby animals on the farm. We had cats in the barn and always had baby kittens in the spring. Life was exciting on the farm.

We had a double corn crib with a shed between them that we loved to play in as kids. It was fun to climb up there to play. Dad stored a wagon or tractor in between the cribs. In the fall when the weather got cold enough they used this spot when they butchered the hogs. It was a good place to hang the hogs to scald and scrape them. During butchering time the family all came to help. It started early in the morning. Mom would cook a big breakfast of fried potatoes, eggs, biscuits and brown milk gravy. Lots of scalding black coffee for the men and the ladies liked cream in theirs.

Everyone had a job to do; Grandpa sharpened the knives, some of the men would set up saw horses with board to put the hogs on when ready to cup up. Some cut wood to build a fire to heat the water in the drum to scald the hogs. Others fixed up the poles to hang the hogs when the water was ready. Some of the men would go to the barn with Dad's rifle to kill the hogs and stick them to bleed them and help hang them up to dip down into the scalding hot water to remove the hair when they were scraped. The head was removed and cleaned to make mincemeat for pies. The hog was split into and the shoulders, sides, loins and hams were removed. Some had the job of cutting and trimming the meat for sausage to be ground and some cut the hide off and cut the fat off for lard which had to be rendered in the kettle over an open fire. I loved the cracklings; they were so good. Mom made delicious sandwiches of hot shredded chicken, egg salad and peanut butter and jelly and hot coffee at noon to keep the men going to tide them over until they were done and ready for supper.

The women had to clean the guts that were used to stuff sausage. We had an outside kitchen and Aunt Mary would cook the liver and onions out there so it didn't smell up the house. She made the best liver and onions. It was a long busy day and when it ended the hams, shoulders and sides had been salted and put in the smokehouse to be finished when they had cured. Some of the sides had been sliced and fried down to be canned. Some of the sausage was stuffed or had been baked and canned for the winter. Sometimes they would also bake sausage in the crock and the grease over the top would seal it so it could be sliced for sandwiches. When the work was all done the ladies had helped Mom put out a bountiful supper of fresh ham, red eye gravy, mashed potatoes, sweet potatoes, fried cabbage, liver and onions and biscuits with lots of butter and jam. Then for dessert were the wonderful homemade blackberry, cherry, apple and chocolate crème pies and my favorite; graham cracker cream pie.

It was the custom of each family that helped to butcher to take some fresh meat and when they butchered to return the favor. In those days everyone had an ice box as there weren't any refrigerators back then. This way as each family butchered; all the families had fresh meat to eat and when it was all gone you used the canned or cured meat the rest of the winter.

Mom made us biscuits and fresh side of ham for sandwiches and iced sugar cookies in our school lunches; as we didn't have a cafeteria when I started school. We sometimes traded for a baloney sandwich as the other kids in town didn't have hogs for meat. It was a treat for them and us too.

We had made pets out of some of the cows and calves; I wanted a pony so bad that I rode anything that would let me on their back without bucking me off. I had a roan heifer that I had trained to let me ride her like a horse. I was about ten-years-old when our dad bought us a Shetland pony. Dad didn't have a pickup so he took the back seat out of a 1946 Chevy sedan and hauled him home from Zanesville, Ohio in the back seat of the car. His name was Tony and was he ever beautiful. He was black and white and about forty two inches tall. He was so ornery that when he would want to get you off his back he would make his belly tight so that when you put the saddle on his back it made you have to check the girth a bunch of times; as it would be loose when he sucked his belly in. He would wait until he was going up a little hill and get on the top and throw his head down and over you and saddle would go.

All the kids in the neighborhood would come to our house just to ride the pony or to play in the barn and slide down the hay ropes. One time when my mom was going to the store she left the door open on the Jeep while she went back to the house to get the keys. Well while she was gone Tony was in the yard and he climbed into the jeep and she had to get me up to get him out.

Dad built a pond on the farm; this was for extra water for the livestock, but we kids really enjoyed it in the summer as our swimming hole. Grandpa helped Dad to build a raft for us to paddle around the pond. It was such fun to go to the pond for a swim after we had worked in the hayfield all day. Sometimes we rode the ponies right into the water. After we got Tony, Dad bought us four more ponies and all the kids in the neighborhood liked to come ride. Our farm was a gathering place for all our friends. In the wintertime when it snowed Dad would hitch Old Dewey the horse to the sleigh and we had such fun riding in the snow. In the summertime Mom would take us kids all fishing as she loved to fish. My dad wasn't crazy about fishing, however he took us coon hunting and squirrel hunting during the seasons. Our dad taught us all how to shoot a gun the safe and proper safe way and to clean and handle the gun. We were taught to respect a gun and to never point a gun at anyone.

We had a busy wonderful time on the farm. Everyone had responsibility to help look after the livestock and keep them fed and healthy. It kept us busy enough that we didn't have time to get into trouble.

Falling Snakes and Baby Chicks in the Mail

By Bonnie Gross of Coshocton, Ohio
Born 1932

I grew up in an old house atop a hill about one-fourth a mile from the River Road (lover's lane). My parents divorced when I was very young and both remarried. So I got a stepmother, and we hated each other from the beginning.

We got our water from an outdoor pump, used kerosene lamps since we had no electricity, used coal stoves and did laundry by hand. We had 2 washtubs - washed clothes in one, using a washboard and rinsed clothes in the other. I had two younger sisters and it took three of us to wring them out and hang them on the clotheslines. When we did get a washer with a wringer we still had to heat the water on the stove and turn the wringer by hand. Our cook stove was large with a reservoir for heating water and we had two flatirons and one wooden handle. One iron would be heating on the stove and one would be in use. Then we would switch the handle to the other one and we were in business again.

We toasted bread over the stove using a long handled fork. We took our Saturday night baths in one of the tubs behind the stove. I had very long hair, and washing it was a lot of fun! We had eight rooms, five down and three up, a pantry and a long screened-in porch on one side of the house. We had two coal stoves downstairs with a "grille" of some sort in the ceilings- supposed to heat the upstairs. We banked them every night, but the fires always went out and it got very cold upstairs. But we did have a phone, the candlestick kind, and a party line. Eight parties and one was quite a trouble maker. I think she had that phone glued to her ear. There were so many complaints that the phone company tried to give her a private line. I hear she met them at the gate with a gun and wouldn't let them on the property. So they cut the line and she changed her mind.

We had about 120 acres so we raised our own food and my dad was in the butchering business. We girls had plenty of chores. Daily: slop the hogs, gather the eggs (Did you ever try to reach under a setting hen?) and milking cows. Three girls and three cows. I always milked the same one, (Old Jersey) and the barn cats were always waiting for me to squirt milk at them. I probably lost a lot of milk that way. We had a milk separator of some sort and an old wooden butter churn. Later we had a glass churn with a hand turner and we made butter to sell.

In the summer we really had to work! We had an orchard with lots of different fruit trees. There was a small sugar pear tree in the barnyard and I used to climb it and hide until I had eaten my fill. A creek bisected our farm and on the other side there were many kinds of nut trees and a hill covered with wild berries: blueberries, blackberries, elderberries, dewberries, black and red raspberries and perhaps a few others. We had a large garden and canned a lot of food and fruits and made all kinds of jellies and jams. I weeded in the garden, hoed in the potato and corn fields and helped in the wheat field and hay. I remember driving a team of horses pulling a wagon full of hay, and upsetting it. No more driving for me. Then I had to ride the horse that pulled the hay up into the haymow. In the fall we had to help with the butchering. People brought their hogs to be butchered, which we had to chase to the slaughter house. Those hogs could be nasty! Many a time I was the one being chased! And we rendered lard in large vats. I hated to stand and stir the fat. Sometimes when no one was looking I would throw a piece of tenderloin in to cook. The cracklings were good anyway. And the owners usually gave us some sausage. To this day I do not care for sausage.

We had an outhouse up in the orchard, and we had to carry our chamber pot up every morning to empty it. In icy weather or rain that could be downright dangerous! I hated that little job! And we did have some bad weather. As I said, we lived up on top a hill and the lane got very icy in the winter. And we had to walk down to meet the school bus. Sometimes it was so bad the bus driver would call and tell us to meet him up at the top of another hill. So we would cross a little bridge and up the road. We were nearly the first ones picked up, so we had a pretty long ride. We had no snow days then. Instead we went to the boiler room at the school to thaw out before classes.

Winters didn't worry us. We made snow angels, threw snowballs, went sledding - anything we could think of. Indoors we listened to the radio: country music, Inner Sanctum (ooh- that creaking door.) We had an old windup record player, but only two records. "Barney Google" and "That's a lot of bunk." I forgot to say it was a battery operated radio. And I read. Every book I could my hands on: Louisa Alcott, Edgar Burroughs, Craig Kennedy, Zane Grey, Water Babies and Peck's Bad Boys, etc. (Now I work 20 hours a week in a library.) And I still read a lot. We had snowsuits we had to wear to school and I hated them. I found a hollow tree and stuck the snow pants in there and got them out to wear home. That is, until one day they weren't there. Boy was I worried. When I got home my dad was waiting for me, holding them out. I was really scared! I asked him how he found them and he told me he used to hide his saddle in there when he was riding to the one-room school he attended. Anyway, I didn't have to wear them anymore.

Summertime was fun. We ran wild when our work was done. We thought nothing of walking the tracks below our lane two miles to go to a little store to get ice cream. (I forgot to say there was a railroad, right at the foot of our lane, and a river on the other side of the tracks.) And we didn't always stick together. I would walk three or four miles to visit with friends. And I was usually barefoot. We weren't allowed to go down near the river, but who cared? I went anyway. (Found some cute boys fishing.) Got chased a couple of times - once by a goose that chased me over a gate - another time by a Billy goat that put me up a tree. I got pretty good at running.

We weren't indoors much in the summer. Except to do whatever work there was to be done. We girls would fix some sandwiches and we would eat outdoors. We played hopscotch, jacks, tag, hide and seek, etc. There were high banks on both sides of the creek and trees with big vines hanging down, and we would swing across the creek on them. We didn't know they were not attached to the trees. I found a little cave in one of the banks so I decided to explore a little. All I found were some arrowheads. But I knew nothing of their importance. So we tried to make our own bows and arrows. Needless to say, that didn't work. We had better luck when we tried making our own kites. Once in awhile we could actually get one up in the air, but it didn't stay up.

The grown-ups had their own fun too. Once every month or so they would gather at this one house that had a big empty barn for a square dance. My dad played guitar and usually called the dances. I was never any good at that kind of dance, probably because I never really tried. We usually went to town every Saturday night and each of us had a little bit of money. We had three dime stores in town then and we would mostly just go in to look around. We loved to check out the candy section. We also had three movie theaters. Had a big time deciding which picture we would see: I liked Roy Rogers and my sisters liked Gene Autrey. We were told to stay together, but once in awhile we just happened to forget. Thank heavens we were not tattletales. After the movie we would just walk around seeing all the sights and listening to the Salvation Army Band until time to meet our parents. Except for one night. For some reason we were forbidden to go to the Youth Center, so of course we had to go. Dad nearly caught us, so that ended that.

Our county had about eight small schools and nearly each school had its own marching band. We had so many parades and each school band marched. I was a majorette and boy, did I strut my stuff! I remember two parades in particular. First was a Halloween parade. After the parade the costumes were judged. Anyway, I was watching the judging and this Mexican wearing an eye patch kept following me around and putting his arm around me and just being a little too friendly. But I wasn't too worried because I could see the judges keeping an eye on us. Anyway when judging was nearly over, my Mexican admirer took his patch off and rubbed some of the makeup off his face. Would you believe it was my mother? She even got an award because she fooled her own daughter. That caused a lot of laughter. The second parade was our annual Christmas parade. For some reason my dad was late getting there to pick me up, and it was cold, really cold, and I was shivering. The band leader was waiting with me and he took pity on me. He was wearing a long topcoat and he opened it and wrapped it around us. (Couldn't get away with that now.)

Homemade clothes - do I remember them? Oh, yes! We could buy colored and printed feed sacks then. So most of our clothing was made from them. And we did get some hand-me-downs from relatives. I remember getting a dress from a school teacher, which was too big, and I didn't like it, so I took it apart and made it over. Boy, did I get in trouble for that. My great-aunt "Aunt Wye" was quite a good seamstress, and she made us some clothes. I remember a seersucker pinafore, and when tube dresses were the rage she made us each one of them. I really loved both dresses. And for my graduation I had bought some material to make my graduation dress. But when the time came my stepmother refused to let me use our old treadle model sewing machine and she kept the material. That is when my aunt stepped in. She took me to town and bought me a beautiful blue dress, blue sandals (first heels I ever had) and a white hat with a blue veil. (Looked like an upside down flower pot.) But I wore it. And then she decided I needed something done to my hair so she took me to a beauty parlor to get me a permanent. If you have ever seen the movie Bride of Frankenstein you will have an idea of what I went through. I had a contraption on my head with all kinds if wires hooked to another contraption, and it was hot and took so long. Believe it or not - I never had another permanent until about 15 years ago. Once bitten, twice shy.

I really don't know what I would have done without my aunt. I think she was the most memorable person in my life. After her husband died she didn't want to be alone for awhile and they lived in Florida. My dad decided since my grades in school were good and the change wouldn't hurt me, I could go back with her for a couple of months. She kept me on the go. When I wasn't in school we went sight seeing. I saw the Bok Singing Tower, watched them diving for sponges, saw Cuban girls hand rolling cigars, took a ride in a glass-bottom boat, went out on the Million Dollar Pier, went to St. Augustine to see the Fountain of Youth and drank some of the water there. It tasted so good I went back for more. I was enrolled in school there. The kids said I talked too fast and I said they talked too slow. Anyway, it was fun to sit under a palm tree to study. I was there for Halloween and my great-aunt shocked me. I could hardly believe it! She had a harem outfit and let me wear it. And I always thought of her as being old. You live and learn. Then I had to come home.

The War Years. We listened to all the news. We had ration books for tires, gasoline - so many things. Some of us traded stamps with neighbors. We bought ten-cent savings stamps and when we had enough we turned them in for a bond. We were given bags to fill with milkweed and got five-cents for each one we filled. I think they were using milkweed experimentally for parachutes. Anyway, we had milkweed growing all around so we were always out picking it. And we got a new outhouse. Either CCC at WPA built it: a two-seater. How about that! And at one time the CCC was camping on one of our hills. Another time some military unit was there. And we had to stay away.

Snakes we had plenty of. My youngest sister and I were sitting in a porch swing fastened to a big limb on a tree when a snake fell onto the back of the swing exactly between us. We certainly moved fast, upset the swing, and who knows where the snake went. We didn't stay around to find out. One other time I was walking through our cornfield (barefoot, of course) and stepped on a cornstalk. It went one way - I went the other. And we used to play in the haymow until we found ourselves sharing it with a snake.

Other things that scared me were when I was in the field below our house and a man and his dog chased me up a tree. They just sat there waiting for me to come down and I wouldn't. I stayed there until my dad came looking for me. I don't know why he was carrying a rifle or shotgun, but I am glad he was. I never saw him that angry before, but he chased them off in short order, and told that fellow what would happen to him if he ever set foot on our property again. I am glad to say we never saw man or dog again. Another time my dad came home and said he saw a coyote along river road. So that evening about dusk we girls were playing outside and I got the bright idea to yip like I thought a coyote did. So I did and heard two or three yips from down around river road. Talk about three girls fighting to see who gets through the door first.

As soon as I was 16 I started working in the summers. My first job was in a grocery store. That was really something. Everything came in bulk. We weighed out the sugar, flour and such and put it in paper bags. Then my next job was babysitting for a very nice family. They must have felt sorry for me because they asked if I could just move in with them during the week. I don't know what the deal was because all I did was more or less play. Hardly any work at all. Anyway, they had a nephew who came to visit about my age - so they asked him to take me home one Friday night and said there was no hurry. So I'm not sure, but that might have been when I got my first kiss. If it was it was probably his first also. Anyway, it must not have been worth remembering since I'm not certain.

My next job was when I was a senior in school. I worked lunch hour and after school until 10:00. I worked in a truck stop. I was okay making shakes, sundaes and sandwiches, but I hated pumping gas. That's when gas was about four gallons for a dollar. Well, I swore I would never pump gas again. I go to a station now that does it for me.

Now for a few fun things. My youngest sister chased a pretty pussy-cat with a stripe down its back through our orchard. Just when she thought she had it - up came its tail and out came a squirt. She was scrubbed down in tomato juice (good thing we canned plenty) several times. You know that skunk odor is very, very hard to get rid of. On a very cold night I woke up freezing. I reached around to pull the covers to me and felt something big and hairy pressed against my back. I let out a shriek that woke everyone up and I jumped into my sister's bedroom without touching the floor (so my father said.) I guess our big collie dog got cold too. Poor Teddie. That is the only time I remember his ever coming upstairs.

Great grandfather Aron Halt with Patricia, Bonnie and Lois Conley.

I never played hooky, but I was sneaky. The last two years of school my grades were so good I didn't have to take exams; midyear or final, so I was excused from school. (I ended up as valedictorian.) I just did not tell my dad or stepmother. My mother lived near the covered bridge our school bus crossed so I asked the driver to let me off at her house and pick me up to go home. He agreed so I spent the day with her. Yes, we had a covered bridge; a long one. They finally burned it down so as to build a new one.

I don't think I had a favorite teacher. I liked all of them. And I loved school. The night I gave my valedictory speech, I had tears in my eyes. I only wish we had the money for college, but if wishes were horses, etc. I took every math and science class the school taught, the only girl in those classes with about six boys.

Now for some more things that come to mind. We girls would always get the mail from the mailbox at the foot of our lane. Every spring the mailman would leave a note for my dad to be there the next day to pick up the little chicks. That is how we got baby chicks; by mail order. And they were so cute, but so noisy. When they were grown we killed some for us to eat and kept the others for eggs. We laid their neck across a stump and took an axe and chopped their heads off. At least I did until I took a head off and the bird got up and tried to run making weird gurgling sounds. Scared the daylights out of me. And I must not have been too bad because I don't remember getting a spanking.

We girls were always trying something new. We tried to make cigarettes out of dried corn silk and found a package of tobacco in the garage and decided to try it. We were just getting started when our dad came looking for us. He figured our pretty quickly what we were up to, so decided to stop and talk awhile. When we got to the place where we were ready to start heaving he laughed, and told us to spit it out and said he hoped we had learned a lesson. We learned that chewing tobacco made us very, very sick. Another night while we girls were home alone two neighbor boys stopped in. Everything was fine until the older boy began to get too friendly with me and kept it up until I was getting scared. I was standing next to the table and I reached back and got a knife and threw it at him. I pinned him to the door, and then we girls all ran. After they were gone I checked, but no sign of blood anywhere, so I think the knife just went through his shirt sleeve. The next time I saw him he looked healthy enough. But this is one secret we girls kept from my dad forever.

Back to the war years. We tried some of that stuff they sold in place of butter. It looked like lard, tasted like lard and that little orange thing you opened and mixed in was terrible. You couldn't mix it thoroughly. You had orange streaks running through. Ugh! So we went back to our own homemade butter.

We went to Sunday school every week and I was really happy when my great-grandfather would take us. He had an old car with a rumble seat and my sisters were scared to sit back there, but I loved it.

I mentioned our collie dog, but not our house cat. She was a gray soft longhaired cat, Snookie, and she saved our lives. Dad had come in from butchering and hung his overalls behind the kitchen stove to dry. We no sooner got into bed than we heard Snookie making a terrible racket downstairs. When we went down to check we found that the overalls were on fire.

I am the only one left now and all I have are these memories. And lots more that keep coming to mind. I think some things were a lot better then. We seemed to be healthier, needed less to make us happy and we were a lot safer. I think I'll put my memories away now and be happy that I have them.

Boys With Chicken Guts

by David J. Meyer of Zanesville, Ohio
born 1929

Homer and I had heard that by making a "trot-line" we could really clean up on catfish. We wore out the *Outdoor Life* magazine on the material and method of construction. With our hard earned money, we made a 300-foot line with about 50 drop-line hooks and studied the facts of best bait to use. It also stated that best results were at night.

The Muskingum River was calling and Ellis Dam, seven miles up, was calling too. I had use of my dad's kayak-duck-boat, paddle power only, but we were young and strong.

Now, the magazine said the best bait was chicken guts. We were in luck, because Lucas & Allen Grocery, just up the street, had farmers bring live chickens in each Thursday that they slaughtered. We could obtain all the entrails for free. Oh boy, what a gift! My mother let us use three of her quart canning jars that we were to return.

The big catfish adventure was on! Armed with our bait, trot line, and old army wool blankets (sleeping bags), off we went on our bikes to where the boat was tied up. It must have been a sight at nine in the morning seeing two young boys going down Ridge Avenue with fishing poles, camping gear and a wicker basket across the handlebars.

We loaded up the kayak on a hot July day and set off for Ellis Dam, full of how we were going to really clean up on the catfish. It is about a five-hour upstream- paddle to Ellis and when we got there we made a camp. We spent a while studying where to place the trot line and find rocks the right size to hold it on the bottom. We found that it was not easy, with all the dangling hooks, but got the job done.

We had our Spam dinner and were ready to bait up before dark. Now, things got a bit out of hand. It seems strange things had taken place within the jars of chicken entrails that had been lying in the bottom of the boat in the hot sun all day.

When you are around 10 or 11, your mind is full of more important things and it causes brain damage that affects all logic to boys full of adventure. We paddled out and picked up the trot line and laid it across the boat, so one could paddle and the other bait. The baiting job fell to me as Homer's pocketknife was so dull hot butter was a chore. Now, grasping the first jar and removing the lid proved to be very hard and as a last resort I placed it between my knees so I could use both hands on the lid.

You have no idea what a quart of chicken entrails can do after being in the hot sun all day. When the lid popped off, hitting me square in the face, a ten foot column of foul, expanding as it went, chicken bait caused me to holler "Ralph" as I bailed over the side of the boat, somehow not getting a hook in me. Homer looked on in pure surprise, but with presence enough not to allow me in the boat 'till I stripped buck naked.

Needless to say, the other two jars were gently dropped over the side and it took some time before I could tell my mother what happened to them, but she had the grace to see the humor in The Great Adventure.

The Collapse of the Old Covered Bridge

By Ellis B. Bonnell of Lore City, Ohio
Born 1926

There was a covered bridge over Salt Fork Creek, on the road between Old Washington and Winterset in Guernsey County, Ohio. It was a favorite spot for the neighbor boys to gather and loaf in the shady interior. This was in the early 1930s and there was not much traffic.

I lived with my family a half mile south of the bridge. I was probably 10 or 11 years old on this occasion. The road was gravel and it was not unusual for a farm tractor with steel wheels and lugs to travel along the road. On this particular day something unusual did take place. A caterpillar tractor came tracking past the house, pulling two bottom-dump trailers. The one immediately behind the tractor was on steel caterpillar tracks like on the tractor, and the one bringing up the rear had rubber tires.

We could see the bridge from our house and watched, fascinated, as the procession approached the bridge. The tractor disappeared into the gloom of the interior. When the rubber tired trailer, at the back end of the caravan, was about to enter, the whole bridge collapsed.

My dad and I hurried down to the scene of destruction. The driver was unhurt. The floor of the bridge had dropped the 10 feet or so to the level of the creek bank and water level. The sidewalls and roof had fallen to one side.

By the time we got there the operator had unhooked from the trailers. He was able to screw the tractor around and get it to travel up the creek bank to one side of the bridge abutment. The tractor had a winch with a long cable. He got the tractor up onto the road, and using the cable, pulled the trailer with tracks up onto the road. Then he used the cable to pull the rubber-tired trailer across the collapsed bridge. He was in a big hurry to get gone before the authorities could get there. There were no telephones in the area at that time, so he had a good bit of time to make his getaway.

A few curious souls had gathered by the time he got his act together. I never heard whether or not he got arrested.

A temporary bridge was cobbled together as quickly as possible. A new, more permanent, bridge was constructed later on, without a roof.

We neighborhood boys had to do without the sentimental and inviting gloom of the old covered bridge.

Can You Hear Me Now?

by Archie Eugene Thorla of Chandlersville, Ohio
born in 1925

On one of the cell phone commercials there was a man walking and carrying a cell phone and saying, "Can you hear me now?" testing the distance the voice would carry. This could have been a hundred years ago when early telephones were first introduced, although I was not around then. But the service had not progressed and the phrase, "Can you hear me now?" was said quite often. Anything much less would have been two bean cans and a piece of string; however, the distance was greater.

The early telephone was of wood construction, probably designed for a right-handed person, as the crank was on the right side of the case. The left side was the receiver, also designed for a right-handed person, so holding the receiver by the left hand permitted one to write any messages with the right hand on the handy shelf for taking messages. The transmitter was located in the center of this wooden case which protruded out about 12 inches. It was designed to raise or lower for talking as needed, due to height of operator, which usually was standing and not sitting. The telephone was certainly not of a table model and certainly not a portable, but mounted firmly on the outside wall for ease of installing the incoming telephone wire. The telephone would weigh about 30 pounds, which certainly meant it must be mounted securely.

Allow me to describe this device further. I had mentioned about a crank on the right-hand side of the case. Inside the wooden case was a set of five horseshoe magnets. This was for generating an electric current, sending a bell signal to members on this party line or to the central office alerting the one receiving the message, since there was not any electrical power available in homes or elsewhere.

This system was of a local organization in a rural neighborhood. These were rural people and mostly farmers with low incomes that could not afford a system installed by professional technicians. The materials needed were a pole for supporting the insulators and wire. The poles were cut from a farmer's farm, usually locust, because locust had long life. The wire and insulators needed to be purchased, the cost divided by the members of this association. There were generally 10 to 12 members being served by this system.

Antique wall telephone from the early 1900s.

All the labor was furnished by the Association. Post holes needed to be dug, poles installed, brackets attached with the insulators. Next, the wire was attached to the insulators. This line started at the far end of the association and ended at the central office. Each member was responsible for the drop from the main line and entering into the dwelling. This was a one-line installation. The drop line attached to one terminal at the top of the telephone. The other terminal was the ground wire, and this was attached to an iron rod driven into the ground. Thus far, we have a telephone system as humble as it may sound, it did serve a much needed service, as this was the only type of communication except by word of mouth.

Now that we have a system, we must identify each member of the association. A code was devised by turning the crank which generated a current ringing a set of bells at the top of each member's telephone. The I.D. of each member (12 members of the association) was made up of long and short rings. Our I.D. ring was four short rings. Another could be four long rings. The operator, or we called this person Central; this was one long ring, a steady turning of the crank.

As humble as it may sound, we were quite content with the service that we had labored to construct, as it had connected us with the outside world. It was possible by going through the operator (Central) a call could be placed manually to a person in California.

There were many things that it required. Central was on duty 24 hours a day, seven days a week. There were 25 of these associations, which the operator made these connections. At the operator's home, a qualified installer installed a switchboard, and each association's line came into the central office (home). There was a cord that would be inserted by the operator into the line requested to make a complete call.

To make a call, a member would crank one long crank. The operator would answer, "Central," and the member calling would yell, "Central?" The operator would answer, "Yes." "Please get me John

Jones." We did not have a directory and was identified by name only, so of course, the operator was familiar with all residents of the combined system. She would ring the required combination of long and short rings to alert the requested person.

The party line had its advantages and disadvantages. It was a means of the news; we only had a daily newspaper to receive news. When a call was made, it was possible for any or all subscribers to lift the receiver and listen to the conversations. We knew when one was sick, whether they inherited a sum of money, or if a husband had beat his wife or what mother was expecting a baby.

Although the operator (Central) was on duty 24 hours a day and seven days a week, she was on call.

The fees for this service was 65 cents per month, this may seem most modest, but there were some of the members that could not afford the fee. If they did not use the operator's service, they would not be billed for the monthly fee. They could call and visit any one of the association, but were still liable for line maintenance cost.

We did not have the Bell system until 1960, and it was a party line. One subscriber on this line was the County Commissioner, which used the line quite often, and of course, regardless of how important the call, the line was not available; however, should an emergency occur, permission could be requested.

As time progressed we have become privileged to better telephone service. Not only have we better phone service, but many kinds of communications, and to think the service we had was about 50 years ago. We have much to be thankful, may we count our blessings.

The history of this telephone service was experienced by Archie Eugene Thorla from the year 1928 to present.

Grandma and Her Pies

by Rita M. Tipton of Piedmont, Ohio
born 1947

My dad, mother, brother, and myself lived in Woodsfield, Ohio in Monroe County. My dad, Thad Slevin, called Woodsfield the "Valley of Tears."

My grandma lost her husband, Clyde Slevin, in a mine cave in. She remarried Clyde Delong, that owned a shoe repair shop in Woodsfield. Her name was Victoria Delong.

My grandma Delong was a religious, God fearing woman. She would cook a wonderful dinner which always included pie for dessert. In the old days, her pies was tasted by many people all over the county. Grandma baked for the church sale and there was always a pie given to the priest.

My grandma would wash the dishes, I always dried them. I was always anxious to get done because Grandma would sit with us at the kitchen table sipping coffee and we were all eating her wonderful pie.

Grandma told us stories of her life experience. I remember one of her stories that I'll always remember of how strong and wonderful my grandmother was. She sat down and began telling one of her stories.

Grandma said she finished washing dishes when she felt something important or something was happening. She saw two jeweled crowns appear before her; they were shiny and had many jewels and gold on them. Grandma heard a man pounding on the door. She opened it and the man was yelling, "There's a fire at the shoe repair, you had better come." Grandma ran all the way up the street.

Grandma pushed her way through the crowd and said, "Where's my husband and son?"

The people said, "They are in the shop." The policeman tried to hold Grandma back, but she broke through the crowd and ran into the burning building. The place was filled with smoke. Grandma saw her husband and son unconscious on the floor. Grandma was praying to have the strength; she was getting overcome with the smoke.

She suddenly got some strength and dragged my dad and grandpa out of the building. My dad and grandpa's hair was burnt, they were on the ground, and started to come to. They were both okay.

Grandma was crying, she said that God saved them all.

My dad and Grandpa continued to work in the shoe repair shop until the war came. My dad went into the Army in 1941-1945; then, he married my mother in 1945. I was born in 1947.

I really miss my grandma and her pies, but mostly the stories she told me will be in my memory forever. I still visit the "Valley of Tears" where my parents and grandparents are buried in Woodsfield, Ohio.

A Tin Roof at the Olympia

by Betty Arbaugh of Zanesville, Ohio
born 1927

Back in the late 30's it didn't take much to make a child happy. We didn't have much but we always had a good time and was happy with what we had.

Every day we would wait for the ice wagon to come by. The iceman would chip off hunks of ice for me and my friends. We would suck on that ice, with freezing water running down our arms.

When the milkman came in the winter he would leave milk on the porch and the cream would freeze on the top and raise about a half inch above the bottle. I got in trouble for eating the cream off many times.

Whenever the circus came to town there would be a big circus parade down Main Street and everyone would turn out for that. There would be elephants, horses, clowns etc. We really looked forward to that.

Where I lived on Linn Street, there was a large vacant lot close by and the medicine show would come every so often. They would set up a stage and have entertainment and sell medicine in a bottle. That medicine was supposed to cure everything from a fever to a stomachache. They sold it cheap and everyone would grab it up.

When I was small, going to movies was a big treat. There was five theatres to go to: the Weller, Liberty, Grand, Imperial and the Quimby. I got to go for a dime, and popcorn was a nickel a box. You could stay all day as they usually had double features.

When I reached my teen years I was an usher at the Weller and later worked in the box office. We would have standing room only and lines clear to Main Street. Once in a while a big entertainer would come to town and appear at the theatre. That was always exciting.

On Friday and Saturday nights people would all go to town and window shop. They would walk up Main Street then cross the road and come back, stopping to look in all the dress shop windows. You could get a real nice blouse back then for only a dollar and twenty-nine cents.

After walking we would end up down at Katsamp's or the Olympia ice cream parlor. That was a big treat. We would usually end up with a sundae called a Tin Roof. It was covered with peanuts over chocolate and vanilla ice cream.

Before we headed home we would stop at the nut shop on Main Street. It was a very small shop and they sold all kinds of nuts. The shop was busy all the time.

Every Sunday was something to look forward to. My mother always had fried chicken, mashed potatoes and gravy and noodles. For dessert we always had Jell-O with whipped cream. We really looked forward to Sunday dinner. We always had the radio on listening to Guy Lombardo's show. Back then that was the real good music.

Another thing we really enjoyed was listening to the "Hit Parade" on the radio every Saturday night. We would get a bowl of popcorn and sit on the floor in front of the radio and see what songs were going to be number one of the week.

It really didn't take too much to make us happy. No TVs, computers, or any travel. Just a game of Chinese Checkers once in a while, maybe make homemade ice cream, a good show and that was it. I still say those were the good old days.

The Roller Skating Paper Girl and Pal's Funeral

by Floy Jean Pettet Scatterday of Jacobsberg, Ohio
born in 1923

I must have been about nine or ten years old when the opportunity arose for me, a girl, to become a "paper boy." The current carrier was going away to school and had recommended me to the *Zanesville Times-Recorder* as someone who really needed the money. My widowed mother, with four mouths to feed, agreed.

Each day, the mail carrier would drop off a bundle of papers at the post office. I was to deliver them promptly and collect 21 cents every other Friday. Of the 21 cent, I was allowed to keep three cents.

Children of Ray (Dese) and Ruth Pettet: Tom, Floy Jean, Dick.

The route must have been about a three-mile round trip. My only conveyance, other than walking, was roller skating, which worked well going down the hill to East Fultonham. Carrying the skates back up the hill averaged about the weight of the newspapers I delivered.

Some families had dogs, not chained in those days. The dogs did not always care for my presence. Other people who couldn't afford to feed their dogs just let them roam. A big shepherd-collie mix took up residence at our house and survived on ours and neighbors' table scraps. "Pal" became my partner and went with me on the paper route, which was a comfort to my mother.

Pal died just before we moved away from Fultonham (now called "Old Town"). The neighborhood kids attended his "funeral" and we all kept flowers on his grave, mostly dandelions and wildflowers.

One time I saved the pennies I got from my paper route until I had $6.00 to spend for Christmas. I sent it with an order to the Sears-Roebuck Catalogue and bought gifts for my family. Would that $6.00 could bring such joy these days!

The Farmer's College Loan

by Maurice B. Orndorff of Zanesville, Ohio
born in 1917

My grandfather fought in the Civil War. I never saw my grandfather. I was in the WWII in the Pacific, Navy. I was born July 15, 1917. I grew up on an unpaved, unimproved road near Norwich, Ohio on a farm.

We had no telephone, no electricity, no running water. No radio, no T.V. Our source of heat was a coal fired fireplace – no heat upstairs.

I attended a one room, eight grade school. When the unimproved roads became impassible our teacher rode a horse to school. He built an enclosed shed for his horse. My brother and I were the janitors of the school. We had a trap line on the way to school. We caught muskrats, mink and one day a skunk. The teacher sent us home one day when the skunk sprayed us (it was only a mile).

We lived on the border of Salem and Highland Townships. We actually lived in Salem Township, seven miles from the closest high school in Adamsville. As the high school in Norwich, Highland Township was only four and six tenths miles away, our parents asked (petitioned) the Salem school board to transfer into Highland. They obliged. There were no school busses at that time so we walked the four and six tenths miles to Norwich High School.

As Norwich had no gym (only two years of high school), we had to go either to New Concord or Zanesville to practice basketball. As it was impossible for us to go home to eat before practice, the teachers took turns in feeding us at their home before practice. There were no fast food or other restaurants in town. After practice, about 9:00 PM, we walked the distance home in all kinds of weather.

My brother was in the same grade as I was. I was the youngest of six children, five boys and one girl.

Later the roads were improved and school busses picked us up for our last two years of high school at New Concord. We were the first on the bus and the last off – travelling sixteen miles to Bloomfield and Otsego and to New Concord.

When I got to be about fourteen years old I would work for neighboring families in the hay or wheat. The work paid about $1.50 a day. During the Depression work was scarce and pay was very low.

When I finished high school I was able to get a job at the college (Muskingum) part time. The wage was twenty-five cents per hour – labor. We were very glad to get it. It was two years of college and a year of work.

My older brother got me a job at the Ohio Ferro Alloy at Philo, Ohio. I had to pay room and board at a rooming house of a dollar per day. Twenty-five cents off if we missed a meal. The pay at Ohio Ferro was forty cents per hour. I tried to go home on weekends. I was a storekeeper.

My father took out a loan from a neighboring farmer so my brother and I could finish college in 1939.

One incident that got me into trouble when I was about twelve. My oldest brother was working on his Essex and I was poking around, found a screwdriver and wondered if it would work the lock. It did and I locked the transmission on the floor stick shift. We didn't have a key so my three brothers and two passengers had to walk to school. We ended up using a torch to cut the lock off. They walked to school (college) for several days.

After we graduated from college we got jobs at the Columbia Cement where we paid off the farmer's college loan.

Small Girl—Big Memories

by Daphne J. Phillips of New Philadelphia, Ohio
born 1936

When I read your invitation to write about the joys of hometown memories, I was so excited. It occurred to me that I had experienced that joy. I really don't know too much about modern country living; but visiting with grandparents in Gallia County, Ohio, as a child, left me with some wonderful memories that are priceless to me.

Harvesting the hay was one memory; throwing the precious cargo onto the wagon, all the neighborhood men being there to help. And, amidst all the hard work, there would be the anticipation of this wonderful meal prepared by all the women, three tables as I remember. Men ate at the first table, children the second and the women at the last table.

There was always a huge selection of food—the cooks really pulled out all the stops. The freshly killed chickens were so much tastier than we get from today's groceries. Pies and cakes, homemade noodles, lots of mashed potatoes, all the comfort foods that still explain a weight problem today.

Butchering in the fall was another biggie. The slaughter was a memory to forget but all the rest was positive because of all the good meat it provided. Knives were sharpened the day before, and it was the kids' jobs to cut the fat into cubes for the rendering. Then, watching Grandma can the sausage, packing it into the natural gut and then putting it into jars. Later in the year, of course, the joy of eating it.

So many fun times—like being chased by the geese as one tried to carry the filled milk pails into the house or going to bring in the cows (the hillsides being so peaceful as we set out to find them). Or jumping into the wagon full of hay as it sat in the barn, always from the highest rafter we could climb for the big drop, wading in the creek and making toe jam (that means squishing mud up between the toes). Such fun!

Back then, there were some negatives to country living as well as joys—outside privies for example. One didn't waste too much time there when the weather went cooler. And, of course, no phones, no electricity. But somehow the memories were sweeter.

As a little girl, too, I always managed to "forget" my nightie because I knew that Grandma would lend me her long flour sack gown. It smelled so nice and felt so good as we climbed into her Murphy bed. I remember too her always "banking" the fireplace to maintain the heat as long as possible. And, in the summer, I remember sleeping in an upstairs bedroom which had pretty lace curtains that fluttered gently into the room in the early morning. Such peace! Too bad we can't always capture that peace throughout our lives.

And, best of all, there were always a lot of people around. Two five-gallon ice cream makers were hand cranked to fill us all, and we looked forward to the six-layer cakes that accompanied the ice cream, one layer of white and then a layer of pink and repeated until there were six. I wish I could duplicate the taste.

Yes, all of these memories have helped to mold me into what I am today, memories that I wouldn't trade for anything...memories for which I am very grateful. Thanks for letting me share them.

Slip Congestion

By Ellen Mautz of Zanesville, Ohio
Born 1940

"Once upon a time..." Now isn't that how most stories start? When I was growing up there were few cars in the area and even fewer airplanes. We could still play in the street. Kick the Can was one of the games. We could have a game of softball, which included some of the grownups in the empty field or a game of Hide and Seek. It was a time when families sat on the porch or visited with neighbors. Since there was little traffic, it was safe, and parents didn't have to be so fearful of letting the children play outside.

In the fall the children could go trick or treating and be safe, it wasn't necessary to worry about someone putting something in the candy or worry about something happening to them. In the winter when it snowed we could sled ride down the street because cars could not get up the hill. In the summer the school playgrounds were open, with an activity director who had planned activities. At the end of summer there was a program presented for the parents and families.

In the 1940's, radio was the home entertainment center; we would listen until it faded away. We listened to Gunsmoke, The Green Hornet, One Man's Family, Lum and Abner, Amos and Andy, among others. We got a television set in 1953.

We had a wider range of entertainment. We could go to the movies for a quarter. There was the main feature, plus a serial or two called cliff hangers. Someone was always in peril. The movies were a lot different; they were more family oriented. In the evenings the family played board games. Monopoly was not my favorite.

School was a safe place, there were no shootings, bomb threats or major fights and no one ever heard of a cell phone. One of the biggest problems were crinoline slips, they were so full and with all the girls wearing them the school had to ban them; no one could get down the hall because of slip congestion.

We were proud if our mothers made our clothes. My mother made my prom gown. It was white taffeta; all senior girls' gowns were white. After the prom she shortened it to street length. With the extra material she made a jacket for the dress. I wore it graduation night.

Ellen Mautz in her prom gown in 1958.

If we wore blue jeans, BUT NOT TO SCHOOL, they were not full of holes or cuts. Now the holier they are, the happier the individual is and that includes the adults. In some stores they run $200.00 or more. Now if these same individuals were forced to wear them, they would be very upset.

How times have changed, because I guess we could say those really were "The Good Old Days!"

Sunday Made More Sense

by Linda McCahill of New Philadelphia, Ohio
born 1947

My hometown memories are mostly all about changes that have taken place. I can tell you in my 62 years, lots of businesses have gone. Just to name a few, Aberth's Bakery and Goshen Dairy I thought would always be here. They are so missed.

The courthouse no longer has the steps we used to play and sit on. Also, there was an underground restroom next to the steps, one for men and one for women. Our favorite restaurant is gone due to a fire. Other stores in the area, due to the same fire, are gone. Williams' Furniture rebuilt their business and are still here.
The New Philadelphia square has changed so much. My mother and I used to walk uptown all the time and go shopping, then we'd either go to lunch or get ice cream or go to the bakery. My mother is gone and so are all the

places we enjoyed. I was a kid then but those were great memories.

I remember party line phones, sometimes we'd listen when someone else was on the line, even though we didn't know who they were.
We went to the movies every Sunday, it was 15 cents and we'd come home to a dinner my dad would fix. It was always so good.

And I also remember my favorite teacher, Glenna Rimer, in fifth grade. At first, I was scared of her, but then I became very fond of her.

Before we had television, I remember we all sat around and listened to this big radio. There were stories that were on every week. We also had a windup record player, but they didn't look like the records of today. I don't remember what the music was.

I got one spanking in first grade. The reason was, I was always going home, I'd ask to go to the restroom and then I'd go home and my mom always took me back. After the spanking, I didn't do it again. I only lived two blocks away.

I also remember Saturday night baths. I never understood why it had to be on Saturday night. Sunday made more sense but no one ever took one on Sunday.

The wringer washer was fun, my mom used to let me help. Laundry was always done on Monday and in the winter; the clothes got hung up in the house. They were always dry by dinnertime.

These are just a few of my memories and they were good old days. We played outside till dark, and always went sled riding in the winter.

The Ole (Old) Stumptown School (One Room School)

by Blanche Armstrong of New Philadelphia, Ohio
born 1944

I was the eleventh child born in a family of six boys and six girls. We didn't have much of anything growing up in our small town of Barnesville, Ohio, twenty-five miles west of West Virginia.

I attended a one room schoolhouse called Stumptown about six miles from our country home. When I started school, there were six grades. We had six rows of desks with each row per grade. Some rows had one to three students. My row had six (three girls and three boys). The whole school had an enrollment of 20 to 25 kids.

All my siblings attended this school except for the two older ones. When the older ones went there, there were eight grades. I think by 1950 it was only six grades until 1957-when it closed and we all started school in the big city of Barnesville. We didn't have a school bus but was lucky enough to have a neighbor lady drive us to school in her car, sometimes 10 to 12 kids at a time. She was the bus driver.

We never had a playground with swing sets, slides or any other fancy toys to play with, just an old rope swing hanging from a big oak tree. We had to make up our own games. I think the favorite was playing ball with our teacher. Some days we got extra playing time in when there was a tie game.

Other favorite games we all liked to play were Annie Annie Over. In the winter we built snowmen and played Fox and Geese. The fall we all got to rake big piles of leaves. We would hide and jump in them and in the spring you could always find the girls playing house, building our houses out of wood sticks while the boys played Cowboy and Indians. Oh what fun it was!

Our outhouses consisted of one for the girls on one side of the school while the boys had the other side. It got pretty cold in the winter to go outside to use them but we made it through somehow.

Our Christmas Programs were the best. The whole school would put on the huge play for all our parents to come and see. We all helped build the stage and the props we used behind this big curtain. We always had a visit from Santa (mostly my dad) and a gift exchange with a price tag of 25 cents which was hard for most of us getting the 25 cents to spend. But it was fun. Never could figure out how my dad could be Santa and be there too.

Before polio, we all drank water from one dipper, dipping in a bucket of water drawn from the outside pump. We all took turns pumping and carrying it in to the school. After that everyone had to bring their own cup. We had three from our school that got polio.

The bigger boys had to carry coal from the coalhouse to keep the ole potbelly stove which stood in the middle of the school going so we all would stay warm. Sometime the ole stove would get so hot it would turn fire red on the outside, lucky no one got burned.

Life was simple way back then. We never had time to get bored. We always found things to do.

Grandpa Stephen's Last Fall

by Malcolm Kent of Coshocton, Ohio
born 1946

My name is Malcolm, and I was born and raised in a country atmosphere, about seven miles from a small friendly community, nestled in a cradle of hills surrounding the location where the old Erie Canal once saw a bustling trade era, served by way of Canal boats. The name of this town is Coshocton, Ohio, and even today still has an enjoyable visit by thousands of tourists who come to walk the streets of Roscoe Village, just across the river from Coshocton, and to experience for a brief time what folks in the 1800's looked like and how they existed in a very wonderful period of history.

My own boyhood and that of my brother was spent growing up and being nurtured by loving grandparents that taught us values that has served to preserve a deep respect for our forefathers' way of life.

Reproduction of the old horse drawn canal boat in Coshocton, Ohio, a preserved portion of the Erie Canal.

I was born in 1946 and was the younger of two children born to the Kent family. My older brother and I went to live with our grandparents when I was three years old, shortly after our parents separated. We spent our youth in a much simpler era of time that bears little resemblance to life now in 2009.

Children today take for granted the computers, jet airplanes, cell phones and instant everything, but when we were young and full of vigor, our main entertainment was listening to Amos and Andy on the radio and riding our ponies while pretending to be cowboys.

We would, on rare occasions, go into town and visit the movie theater as a special treat. I remember it was one of the very few times we ever got to use an indoor restroom facility.

We did, however, become the first family in our neighborhood to have the privilege of owning a TV set and, needless to say, became the most popular family who received a lot of company on Friday and Saturday nights. Our grandparents, Walter and Dollie, would make popcorn for everyone and, for many months to follow, seemed to be the Country Movie Theatre.

We lived in a two bedroom house with a two bedroom apartment built directly behind the main house where my grandfather Walter's Uncle Ed lived on one side and my grandmother Dolly's father, Stephen, lived on the other.

Uncle Ed was somewhat hard of hearing, so the Cleveland Indian games were always heard by us and even distant neighbors in the summertime, with his radio blaring at full volume.

Grandpa Stephen was a fine Christian man who played the guitar and mouth harp at the same time, belting out Gospel tunes. I always thought it was an interesting contrast with Uncle Ed sitting in his rocking chair, sipping his whiskey and cranking up his radio to drown out Grandpa Stephen, playing "When The Roll Is Called Up Yonder."

I guess this is where my story gets a little bit profound. Grandpa Stephen had epilepsy, which most of the time resulted in seizures that caused him to pass out and take very hard falls, which Uncle Ed had heard hundreds of times over the many years. Also, the little apartment would shake when he hit the floor.

I was a teenager at that time when Grandpa Stephen took ill and became hospitalized. I was very close to this wonderful man and missed him, so I asked my Grandpa Walter to take me to visit him in the hospital. I was deeply saddened that he had passed away only minutes before we arrived.

We returned home and Grandpa Walter and I knocked on Uncle Ed's door to inform him of Stephen's sudden demise. But, quite to Grandpa Walters surprise, Uncle Ed blurted out, "I know Stephen has died tonight," and even told us the exact time of his passing, which was to the very minute it had happened!

Grandpa Walter was shocked beyond belief, as anyone might expect, and exclaimed, "How could you know that?"

Uncle Ed replied, "I heard and felt him fall for the last time."

Life holds many mysteries and that remembrance is one that has stuck with me over the past 62 years.

The Multi-armed Giant

by Martha Lasure of Zanesville, Ohio
born 1936

In the first house that I can remember, we rented a small house that had no running water except in the kitchen sink. The heat was a Franklin Stove in the main room that definitely did not heat the bedrooms.

When I was six years old we were able to rent a much larger house on Larzelere Avenue. In the basement was a huge multi-armed giant. Each late summer, a coal truck came and dumped a load of coal into the basement into a square, fenced in area. Each night my father "banked" the fire in hopes that it would not go out. That meant no heat came upstairs.

Each morning I would stay in bed until I would hear my dad shovel in the coal and stir up the embers. Then I jumped out of bed and dressed for school, standing over the register.

I don't remember being cold at night in spite of the fact that our covers were only quilts sewn by my mother and at quilting parties.

Now we have gas heat and an electric mattress pad. Are we spoiled or what?

Bombs and Spilt Milk

by Erika Strain of Zanesville, Ohio
born in 1936

I do not remember much of my childhood.

I lived in Germany during World War II. One day walking to school with some of my friends—I think we were in the second grade—my shoe came untied. We all stopped so I could tie my shoe. Had we not stopped, I would not be writing this. A small bomb exploded right where we would have been had we continued walking. I'll always remember that.

My mother sent my sister and me to get our milk. Milk was rationed and only small children got any at all. It was in the winter with lots of snow. On our way home I slid and fell. I held on to the milk for dear life. We got it in a milk can and it could have easily spilled. When we got home, my sister yelled, "Erika fell!" My mother was terribly concerned about how much milk I might have lost. I answered her, "None, but my arm hurts." After she realized that I had broken my arm she changed her tune, saying "Why didn't you drop the milk?"

Willie and Joe the Window Pecker

by John W. James, Jr. of New Philadelphia, Ohio
born 1934

When I was a teenager, my buddy and I decided to climb two large trees with pole climbers on our shoes and take two nests of crows with seven baby crows to raise as pets. We had been watching the nests for several weeks. We carried them home, nest and all, about one mile, much to the unhappiness of the mother crows. Two of us each kept one and gave the other five to other friends.

Plaque from Willie's cage.

I named mine "Willie" (after Willie Sutton) and Frank just named his "Joe." I kept Willie in a pen outside or brought him in the house occasionally where he had a favorite chair in the kitchen on which he liked to perch. My mother grew attached to him and when they were outside in the summer while she sat in her lawn chair, he would take her cigarette lighter and fly up to the spouting on the house and deposit it there, much to her dismay. I would get called to get the ladder out to retrieve it.

Willie stayed close by, but one evening he decided to attack the cherries in my neighbor's tree. This wasn't acceptable by the neighbor, so I clipped his wings, after climbing the tree and bringing him home.

Frank and I would ride our bikes to school together and he would tell me on some mornings that he knew that he would be dismissed early and I asked him why. He knew that Joe was following about a block behind, going from tree to tree. Upon arrival at school, Frank and I had some classes together and about third period, Joe would be pecking at the window and seemed to know his schedule and we'd find him doing the same thing at another room. The teacher would say, "Frank, will you please take that crow back home?"

My Willie was with me till my high school graduation day. My hobby was printing pictures and I had negligently not rinsed a photography tray but added water to the tray which had contained dried-up chemicals. Willie decided to bathe in it which I feel caused his demise. Joe was given to a cousin when Frank went into the Air Force.

Spelling Bees and Box Socials

by La Verna Houk of Crooksville, Ohio
born 1906

My name is La Verna Conaway Houk and I will be 103 years old on March 30th. I started school at five years old in 1911 near Crooksville, Ohio.

I did not go to a one-room school, but to a two-room school called Martain, which has been gone for many years. Grades one through three were in the downstairs classroom with one teacher and grades four through eight had one teacher who was my favorite. His name was Joseph Randall and I thought he was an amazing young man since he taught five classes in the same room. He came up with lots of different ways to help us learn.

Each morning he would call the roll and we would recite a Bible verse we had memorized. Some of the boys would repeat "Jesus wept" the shortest verse in the Bible. My class would study our lessons while others were reciting, therefore during that time we had to really concentrate on our own studies. We did learn many things from the older children while listening to them do their schoolwork.

I especially enjoyed the last Friday of the month when we would have a spelling bee with everyone choosing sides. Mr. Randall also would periodically have what he called "Literary Day." Each student was required to recite poetry or sing a song. It was very entertaining and was teaching us many skills at the same time. I still remember some of the pieces I spoke such as "I'm the Little Red

Stamp, I must have the Right of Way." That described the one-cent postage stamp with George Washington's picture on it. At that time you could send a card for one-cent and sending a letter cost two-cents. When I was moved into the upper grades I would play the old pump organ while the children sang.

Sometimes we would have a Box Social. The girls would bring a box of goodies and a boy would buy the box and they would eat it together. One time my older brother unknowingly bought my box and oh, how disappointed he was.

In 1918 or 1919 there was a flu epidemic and many people died. The school was closed down for many weeks, but we would report to an unheated building each Wednesday morning to turn in homework and pick up new assignments. What a job for the teacher.

There wasn't any water at the school so two pupils would take a bucket, walk to the first house closest to the school, which was quite a distance, and carry it back to the school. We each had a folding cup in our desks and would each receive a half cup of water twice a day.

School in the 1900's was quite different than today but we who lived then, enjoyed it. To be a teacher in those years required a lot of patience, planning and making do with whatever was available to teach with.

Sledding Under the Moon

by Jane Ridenbaugn of Warsaw, Ohio
born 1931

When I was growing up in the 1940's, we always had a lot of snow. It came in November and seemed to last till spring. We hardly ever got out of school for snow days and we had to walk if you lived in town.

What I remember best was our sled riding. Every evening after supper, when homework and dishes were done, our parents would let my two older sisters, Helen and Ginny, and me go sled riding. Oh, what fun! There was a Mr. Walker—neighbor—who lived next to us and he had the best hill for sledding. He had a son and daughter at home and he would build us a bonfire to keep warm and his wife gave us hot chocolate. All the older kids from town came out with their sleds. Some were even made from signs big enough for three or four kids to ride. They had the ends turned up and rope through holes in front to steer and pull it back up the hill. I was only about ten or twelve years old but I can still hear us laughing and yelling like it was yesterday.

We went out every night as long as it wasn't snowing or too cold. It was truly a magical time, especially when the moon was out and the stars were overhead. The snow looked like it was glowing.

I am now 77 years old and still remember those days.

The Runaway Pig

by Jean Polen of New Philadelphia, Ohio
born in 1930

When my children were growing up in the 60s, my husband, Kenny, was always throwing parties for our friends and family. He loved having a good time. And we always enjoyed ourselves too. The parties usually went well; but my fondest memory is of the one that went terribly wrong.

It was summer, 1965. Kenny purchased a hog with the intention of having a pig roast. He penned the pig in the kid's playhouse in our backyard.

Kenny and our friend, Chuck Olinger, were getting the fire pit ready, when the kids started squealing, "The pig is loose! The pig is loose!" The pig had escaped from the playhouse!

In those days, our family lived on Second Street in Northeast New Philadelphia. Our house sat on top of the hill. The pig was running up and down the hill, scared for his life.

By this time, a lot of the guests had arrived. They were expecting to see the live hog before the party. Instead, chaos erupted as all the guests, kids and adults, tried to catch the pig.

A family friend, Shirley LaMasters, called the New Philadelphia Police and reported a runaway pig. The officer asked, "Lady, are you pulling my leg? There aren't any pigs in town!" The police came up to check out the situation. I think they just wanted to see if it was a prank call.

Finally, my husband had us all line up on both sides of the driveway. He and Chuck got behind the pig and guided it into the driveway. Then we all herded it into the garage.

Kenny announced to everyone that the pig had lost a little weight, but he would still be good to eat. Then my husband sent all the kids to the store at the bottom of the hill. It was time to kill the pig, and he didn't think the children should see that.

Kenny Polen and Chuck Olinger.

When they got back home, the pig was over the fire pit with an apple in his mouth. It was a happy ending for us, but not so happy for the pig.

Boots, Books and Backpacks

by E. Jane Seeman of New Philadelphia, Ohio
born in 1924

Can you imagine almost 500 children packed into the sanctuary of the First Presbyterian Church on East High Avenue? It was one snowy after-school Friday afternoon for a Children's World Day of Prayer Service. Singing joyfully, the hymns they had learned in weekday classes, the children took part in their very own service.

When the speaker who was coming from a distance had to cancel, a favorite local speaker kept the group alert and interested. It was Lorraine Keplinger, doing a chalk drawing and talk.

While this was the scene upstairs, the floor below gave a person who attempted to pass through an even more amazing sight. It was completely covered with schoolbooks, backpacks and boots. If only a camera had preserved that sight, could you believe what it looked like? Yet, when the service was over, everything was picked up and not one thing was left.

This was a happening, sometime in New Philadelphia, in the nineteen sixties.

The Windshield Turkey

by Melba Carpenter of Barnesville, Ohio
born in 1928

I was born in Noble County in Wayne Township at home. So it's not a hometown story, but country. I lived there before Senaca Lake was made and took a lot of our farmland.

I went to a one room county school called Kennonsburg School. All eight grades were taught by one teacher. Each class had its own area to sit, but when your class was in session it was put on the front row seats. Everyone behaved pretty well because at that time if you got spanked at school you got a worse one when you got home.

Our entertainment at recess and noon was Tag, Red Rover, Base, and sometimes a field trip to the top of Kate Wards Hill. In winter we had a piece of metal tin roofing that we turned up on the end and made a toboggan out of it. I don't remember anyone ever getting hurt with it. It would be outlawed nowadays.

Kennonsburg Country School.

I had two teachers in those eight years, Mr. Brill and Mr. Wilson. They were rotated between two country schools, Kennonsburg and Yoker Valley. Every two years they were switched.

We had outdoor privies and a well for water. One water bucket and one dipper for all to drink from. The way things are today, I wonder how we survived. We weren't taught all the things kids are today, but I still believe that for basics and common sense, I'm about as smart as they are.

Our last day of school in the spring was a big one. Everyone all around brought a large picnic basket of food and kids from other schools played hooky and came to our event. We always had this big meal and then in the evening we put on a three act play which was really a big thing in our community and anyone who had talent for singing or readings also performed.

Most everyone had to walk to school, but in a few of my last years there I was more than a mile away so there was a car that was considered my bus. I think I was in the sixth grade before I had that. When that was started, there was a place we passed that butchered poultry and took them to Pittsburg to sell, and before they were butchered they were let run loose around the place. So one morning as my bus was taking me to school, one of those turkeys flew at the car and came through the windshield and landed on my lap. The turkey survived, but I had glass cuts on my face. I was cleaned up and sent on to school. I had tiny pieces of glass work out of my face for years after that.

When I passed the eighth grade we then had to transfer to Batesville High School. This school averaged between 70 to 80 students that came from about six or seven other country one room grade schools. I graduated with 16 in my class which was a fairly large one at that time.

Two Mistaken Whippings

by Merlin E. Saxton of Coshocton, Ohio
born in 1931

I'm a old man seventy-seven years old. I remember when I was nine or ten, a neighbor friend my age said he had a aunt that lived a couple blocks from our neighborhood that had a cherry tree full of cherries. He was told that he could pick some and sell door to door, so me and him done this.

That night, his aunt told my dad me and him had stoled the cherries. My dad, being a strict disciplinarian, whipped me with a belt, not listening to my explanation that I didn't know he didn't have permission to pick them. He felt bad later when he found out I was telling the truth, twenty-five years later.

I had married and fathered three boys. One passed away young, the other two was eight and four years old. One day a neighbor told me my eight-year-old had pulled up her tomato plants. Like my father, I gave him a whipping, not letting him explain. Later, I found out another boy had pulled them up and my boy was trying to re-plant them. I knew then how my father felt twenty-five years prior.

I lost this boy in 2007 to cancer.

The Model T School Bus

by Ona M. McCarty of Sherrodsville, Ohio
born in 1917

I was born on a farm between two small towns, Sherrodsville with eight grades in school and Leesville with ten grades.

The year I was to start to school (walk to Sherrodsville) they decided to send the ninth grade to Leesville if they could find transportation for them. The road was a dirt road that the wagons made hauling their grain to the mill and there were very few automobiles.

A man in town had a Model T Ford delivery truck. It had a bed and a roof, but open sides. He said he could put boards on each side, a step on the back, and some side curtains to keep the rain out. He thought he could haul 12 or maybe 14. If you lived along the road they would pick you up. There were five of us on the road.

That was great, no walking, only sometimes he would hit a hole or a big stone and a seat would fall down. He would get out and he would cobble it back up and we would all get back in. Our lunch buckets were under the seat.

Sometimes the water would get over the road. He would drive through it until it got too high. If that happened, he would stop at my place and there was a drive we could walk to the railroad and walk up past the water, get on the road again and walk to school. The other ones on the road couldn't get out of their lanes only with a horse, so they didn't go. I was the only little one and the first day I walked with them, I had my dinner eaten when I got to school. I never did that again.

When school was out, we walked back to my place and the bus was waiting and took them back. I walked up the hill to my house. It was approximately two miles to school. When we came home from school, we had to go up a grade on a curve in the road and when it got muddy, that Model T would get stuck. So everyone got out, the big boys would push it over the grade and we would all walk through the mud and get back in. We finally got a little newer bus. We had outside toilets and a pump with a tin cup if you wanted a drink or wash your hands.

When I was starting in 6th grade, Sherrodsville had a high school, so no more bus service. That year the state decided to make a good road, and I had to walk to school, but the road got so muddy while they were working on it, I had to walk the railroad. I had to get across the road to get to the railroad. My dad would lay a board to walk on and pull one behind you to put in front. That night, you used those same boards to get home.

From the 7th grade on, the road was a little better. If you were lucky enough for a car to stop and offer you a ride, you took it. Most days, you never saw a car. Sherrodsville also had outside toilets and a hand pump. I don't know what year they got electricity.

When I was a freshman, we had 12 boys and two girls in our class. When I graduated in 1935, we had 7 boys and one girl, me. We had one typewriter in the office and the Superintendent used it, one finger at a time

I am 92 years old and I live in a brick house in a field beside where I was born.

With all the transportation problems we had, no one ever complained. It made every day interesting.

Santa Claus

by Bernard E. Clark of Barnesville, Ohio
born in 1937

I was born in Bellaire and lived in Neffs for at least four years and my family consisting of my parents and 13 brothers and sisters moved to Barnesville, a small rural town in southeastern Ohio. We moved to a place of around 25 acres. Some of my older brothers and sisters were either married or in the military. Those married moved to other states, some went west to California. My father worked in a local deep coal mine, my mother worked at a sewing factory in the local town. Our dad tried to keep us boys occupied by buying a tractor to do some farming, etc.

Benard Clark "Santa."

I attended grade school at a one room school with one teacher taking care of eight grades. I then attended high school in our nearest town.

Our neighbors up the road had a small farm. Me and my brothers did farm work, helping many of our neighbors do hay, corn, wheat, oats, etc.

I started to take interest in a local neighbor girl. I also started public works, in a town several miles away. A friend got it for me. The neighbor girl and I got married. We were going to go to California, that some of my family which were living there and get a job, but I found employment closer to home, so we stayed in Ohio Valley. I worked in an aluminum plant for around 13 years, then went to a deep mine for around 10 years. In the meantime, my father passed away and my mother passed away. We lived very close to parents and in-laws.

My wife worked in office positions in different factories, etc. We had two sons, Steve and Scott, and one daughter, Sharlein. Our oldest son is married. He and his wife live about eight miles away from us in the same area. We have a granddaughter and grandson. We live in our home place, a farm with our second son. We dairy farmed for around 20 years. Then our son went to public works. Now works for a local mining operation. We no longer dairy. We raise beef cattle, horses, heeler dogs, and border collies.

Our daughter lives in Fort Worth with her husband and his two sons. We visit her and husband every once in a while. She visits here mostly during the pumpkin festival which is held in September and also for the Christmas parade held in December in our town, which I am the Santa Claus for this parade. We take great pleasure in telling you that my wife and I have been married for 52 years.

My brothers and sisters are scattered everywhere. Some live close and the rest live a good piece a way. Some live out of state. We get together once a year for a family reunion of the ones that can make it.

We are members of the Church of Christ which is only a few miles away. Along with our son, daughter-in-law, and grandchildren.

I also have a hobby which I enjoy – horses, working with them, raising, them. I also have a collection of antique Farmall tractors, some of them I have nearly restored. Others I am still working on. I don't get to work on them very much in the summertime, as we put up hay for ourselves and other customers.

This is just a part of our story, but you have to stop somewhere. I hope you like my story.

Red Light, Green Light and Chasing the Goose

by Sue Kaufman of Warsaw, Ohio
born in 1949

I was born in 1949, the fifth of eight children and grew up on a farm in Coshocton County. We amused ourselves with games that we played with each other and the cousins who liked to visit the farm.

One of the games we played on hot summer evenings was "red light, green light." The game started at the back porch where all the kids would line up. A caller would yell "Green light!" and the players start to race around the house. If the caller yelled "Red light!" everyone had to stop where they were. The winner was not only the fastest, but also the one who could sneak in a few extra steps on the red light. If anyone was caught moving on a red light, he or she had to go back to the beginning. When the caller yelled green light, all the kids advanced as fast as they could. The object of the game was to be the first person to touch base, which was the back porch. The winner was the new caller.

An indoor game that we played, during winter holidays, was "school." The students would begin at the top of the stairs. The teacher, usually one of the older children, would ask questions of the students. Anyone who thought they knew the correct answer would raise their hand. The first person to raise their hand would give their answer. If that person was correct, he or she advanced down one step, If that person was wrong, they stayed where they were and someone else was called upon for the answer. After players started to advance, an incorrect answer meant that they would have to back up a step. The student who reached the bottom of the stairway was the winner and the new teacher.

On snowy winter days we would play fox and geese. The game was like tag, except that the players laid out a track by shuffling their feet through the snow. The track started at home and had loops and crossings. The geese started at home and the fox counted to ten and then had to chase the geese until they were caught. No one could leave the track, but could jump from one place to another. The geese tried to get back home where they were safe. A goose that was tagged was the new fox.

The Heavy Bike and the Dented Cans

by Joyce Barnett of Moorpark, California
born in 1939

My dad and mom, Joe and Mildred Kokensparger and us, Joycelyn, Barbara, David and Pamela, lived in the Manor government housing at 163 Indiana Street for about 14 years. That was okay. We had lots of friends that were poor as we were.

We played Red Rover, Red Rover, send this person over, hopscotch, jump rope, marbles, jacks with ball, baseball, hide and seek, paper dolls, had skates with keys, flew kites, played in the warm summer rains. At night as young teenagers we would sit on the steps out front and sing and watch the bats fly around the street lights. When it snowed we built forts, made snowballs. Us kids then always played outside. We moved out when I was 16. I had my first date there with Harry Palmer.

Dad worked at Mosaic Tile for almost 20 years. Never had a car. Wintertimes he rode with friends. He rode a big bicycle to work and later gave that heavy bike to us. We fell a lot with it.

The Manor, government housing, Joyce Barnette's home.

I remember Mom frying bacon for Dad's sandwiches. Couldn't afford for us to eat it too. We would take a piece of bread and dip it into the bacon drippings then pour sugar on it. It was so good. We ate bread with butter and ketchup and bread with miracle whip and butter. Later Dad bought peanut butter. We had it on bread with mayo. "We were moving on up," as the Jeffersons say. I would go out Mondays was wash day, we had soup beans. Every Sunday was fried chicken and mashed potatoes with gravy.

Dad bough this 12 inch TV, used. You put this plastic colored picture on the TV so that the sky was blue, grass was green, watched Howdy Dooty, Roy Rogers, My Three Sons, Lucy, Gene Autry, and others. We were so happy.

Dad would take us grocery shopping in a wagon to Asborne Market on Pine Street. He had his one and only charge account there. Mom would get so mad at him because he would buy their dented food cans too. Said that no one else would buy them. Dad would take Barb and I, when we were six and seven, on a ride on his bicycle through the Woodlawn Cemetery. We loved that. Barb on the front and me on the back.

Our uncle and Aunt Pete and Beulah Swanks used to take us out looking for black walnuts, crab apples, blackberries and mushrooms a lot.

Wash day, all year around we hung out clothes out. We had a wringer washer, with rinse tub. My grandma who lived on a farm in Norwick had a gasoline powered washer on her front porch, later had it converted to an electric one. Also had a hand water pump in her kitchen and outside.

We loved going out to the farm to feed the chickens, pigs, and cows. She had a hand grinder to shuck the corn, a big barn we played in. Grandpa and Grandma Paul and Sara Farus were hard working farmers all their lives.

I used to go the Valley Gem for square dancing. My friend and I were hot and sweaty so we decided to walk home. This was Putnam Avenue. As we got closer to the pottery place, Zanesville or Ohio Pottery, there was a stack of broken pottery. On top of it was this ghost-like figure swaying back and forth. We took off running up toward the lower end of the manor. Looked back, this same ghost-like figure was swaying back and forth on top of someone's car.

I used to babysit for a quarter an hour—at times two and three kids at a time. I would save these quarters and put clothes on layaway when I was 14. Mom and Dad didn't have money to give us. Every Friday Dad would buy us a candy bar. That was it.

I went to see the Elvis Presley movies on Sixth Street. There was a parade one time that had Tab Hunter in it, a movie star. Bob Banfield is from Zanesville, is a news reporter on TV out here for over 20 years.

I went to Wilson's school, Grover Cleveland and the new high school. Walked in the rain, snow, had our leggings and coat and boots on. Take them off in the classroom.

I went steady with Carl Williams in high school, wore his class ring, went to the prom, borrowed a dress from a friend, Roberta Hern. Carl picked me up in his '50 Ford. I had all these cancan slips on, barely fit in his car.

My family moved to a house on Nancy Ave. I worked at a factory that made Voltage Regulators and had large fans at the end of each work station like you would use for a bunch of cows. Rivet machines that the girls would get through their fingers or thumbs. I worked on the Bobbin Grinder which you put spools on, then fill them up with the plastic wire. Was better than the rivet machines. I car-pooled with my friends, and one night they wanted to stop by this nigh club, The Waldorf, on Fifth or Sixth Street. I didn't want to go, because I never go in those places. I went anyway. Sat in a booth watching people. This guy just came over and sat with me, insisted that I go out to eat with him. I did. That is how I met my husband, in of all places, a nightclub where I don't go to. He had just gotten out of the Army. We got married, lived in his grandmother's house on Market Street for a while.

Bob worked at R.C.A. in Cambridge. I still worked at the Voltage Regulator factory. He got laid off. Wanted to move to California where you make more money. Bob bought this old ugly flat gray plain 30-foot trailer for us to take some of our stuff in, plus he sat beds up and had a stove to cook on when we sopped at K.O.A. Campgrounds or rest stops for the kids to get out and play. Stopped at a souvenir shop. Bob found this sticker that said, "57 more payments then it's ours." Put it on the back of the trailer, people would drive by us, just laughing.

Forgot to tell you, Bob had tied our mattress on the front of the trailer. Well, as we were traveling through desert country somewhere, a car pulled along side of us saying, "Your mattress is on fire." People helped Bob get it off, threw it on the ground, started a grass fire. Put that out, that was caused by a cigarette he threw out the window, got into the mattress. Now the trailer looks worse, burnt in the front.

Drove up to an inspection station checking to see if you have any fruit. Inspector wanted to see inside the trailer, opened the door, smoke was pouring out. People from their trailers came running over with their fire extinguishers to help. You guessed it; another cigarette was under the wheel well, which our clothes was in a closet above there. Thank God it was just smoke, otherwise we would have been pulling a trailer that was on fire. Drove a little while longer, then had a flat tire on the trailer.

We stopped in Arizona to visit his Uncle Charles and Aunt Bea. They talked us into living there for a while. We were running low on money. We both got a job at the General Electric plant there. Leased a home for a year. My dad died in Ohio, couldn't afford to go home. We stayed in Arizona for almost two years, got laid off, moved to California where we are now. A "California or Bust" story.

I remember when Mom would be putting this package of yellow stuff on our margarine. At one place we lived they delivered blocks of ice for your refrigerator. Mom never had a toaster, always fixed our toast in the oven, turning it over. That's why today I like crunchy toast.

When World War II was here, food and shoes is stuff was rationed. I have some of those stamps. Then there was the blue stamps you saved from the stores and the S&H green stamps. That was fun. When you had your books filled, you go and cashed them in for dishes, silverware, cook books, etc. I still have some. They illeg on us.

Mosaic Tile would have Bingo games. I won my baseball glove and bat there when I was ten or so.

I will be 70 soon. I do have a lot of memories in Zanesville.

The Cleanest Bathed First

By Freda L. Gaskins of Somerset, Ohio
Born 1930

I was born on April 4, 1930. Dr. Joseph Clouse delivered me to my parents; Charles Henry and Mary Ellen (Nellie) Reichley about 2:30 in the morning. The doctor made house calls in those days. My place of birth was in a bedroom of a small wooden house on what is now called Winegardner Road in Somerset. At the time I was born it was called Pleasantville Road. The road was mud with limestone put on it every now and then. Mostly then.

My choice for getting to school was to ride with my brother Frank in his "Whippet" and be late for school, which I hated, or to walk through the woods to the bus and risk seeing the wandering Gypsies who were common at the time. I was afraid of them because I thought they would steal me for my bright, orange, frilly dress.

We had to wear overshoes, or galoshes as they were called then, to walk to catch the school bus on Route 22, which was about one mile - give or take. When we got off the school bus in Somerset at the square the pavements were dry so we tracked mud on the dry sidewalks all the way to the school, which was Holy Trinity School. And then if we hadn't lost the mud on the way to the school, we tracked it in the hallways of the school.

I suppose our bus driver, Tom Helser, didn't appreciate the mud we left on his bus. There were no assigned seats on the bus back then; at least I don't remember any. Our bus driver owned his own school bus rather than the school district owning it.

I was the middle child of eleven children born to my parents. There were three boys older and three boys younger and two girls older and two girls younger. I always said that I didn't have anyone to play with. My older sisters had each other and my younger sisters had each other and my brothers didn't want a girl around to bother them. We did cut paper dolls out of the Sunday paper. "Tillie the Toiler" was cut out of the comic strip page. Another popular game was marbles - outdoors of course.

We took Saturday night baths because we had to be clean to go to Mass on Sunday morning. The water for the baths in the galvanized tub was pumped from the cistern under the back porch and heated on top of the cook stove on the back porch. The tub was put in the corner of the kitchen and the cleanest child bathed first. When the water was dirty it was changed. Saturday night baths in the old washtub are not my fondest memory, but we had no choice.

Our drinking water had to be carried from the well several yards from the house and was hand-pumped. We had chamber pots but my mother referred to them as "p.t.'s" to avoid saying anything uncivil. We had two chamber pots; one in the upper bedroom area and one for the downstairs bedroom. They were emptied everyday into the outhouse and washed with hot, soapy water. We always had wasps and spiders in the outhouse for company, so the stays were not long ones.

We had a party line phone on the wall in our dining room. I remember my two older sisters racing to get there first to answer it. I am sure that there were times that others listened in to catch up on the news.

We had a wringer washer and every Monday morning the motor on it was started and the loads of clothes were washed. In nice weather, they were hung outside to dry. In rainy weather they were hung on lines in the house. Of course, the water from the cistern had to be heated in a boiler on the gas stove on the back porch. Another memory of the wringer washer was hanging over the tub to "whoop" when our family had whooping cough.

We didn't go to Saturday movies until we were teenagers and then not often. Carpenter's Market in Somerset was then Russell's Theater and movies were ten-cents. Other forms of entertainment included the radio - no TV. There weren't a lot of reasons to go to town except for school and church and the Fourth of July parade.

I don't remember the Depression of the 1930's as such, but we did wear homemade clothes, usually "hand-me-downs." We got one new pair of shoes per year, usually in the fall for school since we went barefoot in the summer. My brother Cecil liked to go barefoot through the cow manure and then would wash his feet by wading through the creek. If our shoes got a hole in the bottom we cut a piece of cardboard the size of the shoe to go inside it.

We had food from our big garden. Mom always canned our vegetables and fruits.

I didn't have a favorite teacher. I liked them all in grade school because I was anxious to learn what they were teaching me.

I remember some pretty bad snowstorms and some pretty powerful thunderstorms. I was scared of lightning. I had wonderful parents and my older brothers and sisters taught me a lot.

Wearing Onion Bags and Dad's Fried Potatoes

by Laura Hidey of New Philadelphia, Ohio
Born 1938

There was 12 kids. I remember when I was four years old Mom had twin boys. I told the doctor to take them home with him. Jerry died; he weighed five pounds. Larry lived; he weighed two pounds.

When I was four, Dad took me out in the field with him and Rudy and Sam to plant potatoes and corn. I planted along side the field and a terrible storm came up and I thought the world was coming to an end.

Rothacher Coal Mine. Laura's Dad at back.

When I started to school I got paddled the first day because I talked back to the teachers.

When I was eight years old we had a bad snowstorm and I cried all day because I couldn't go to school. Dad had to tunnel out to the barn to milk the cow and take care of the chickens and pigs.

One winter, my brother Raymond held me up for a shield and my brother Sam, threw a snowball and hit me in the head.

I had a piece of coal in my head until I was 23.

My brother Fritz tried to teach Mom to drive. She ran the car into the outhouse. He never tried to teach her again.

Mom used to paper with all different kinds of wallpaper and sometimes newspaper, but the walls were clean.

Dad worked in a coal mine.

He told us kids that the biggest watermelon was for a special occasion, but we couldn't wait; we ate it. Boy did we get in trouble.

My two brothers, Rudy and Sam, and I played hooky from school one morning. We had to stay in the house all day. We had to wear onion bags to school. Well, we hid ours at the end of the lane. When we came home and got off the bus, Mom was waiting on us. We got in trouble again.

Dad used to take my brother, Larry, and I berry picking. He had little buckets with handles for us and he took a bucket with water, bread and cheese with us. As soon as we had our buckets full we would have a picnic out by the woods. Boy was that fun.

Out of the 12 of us kids; there is still six left. We didn't have much, but we got along.

Dad made the best fried potatoes in the world. I have tried dozens of times, but I can't make them like his.

My oldest sister, Hazel, had to move in with us. She had nine kids and we all had to do chores. My nephew, Tommy, had to take his turn taking out the chamber pot. Well, he fell down the stairs and made a terrible mess. Nobody liked that mess.

When my niece, Etta, was born I was one year older than her and I threw her on the floor; lucky there was a lot of clothes on the floor.

When we were a little older there must have been eight or 12 of us going Halloweening. My brother, Early, told us there was a ghost out the lane. We said we weren't afraid, but there was a ghost right in front of us. We all tried to get in the front door at the same time. It was a long time before we found out it was him.

Those were the good old days because you could go to anyone's house and eat whatever they had.

Whenever we had a thunderstorm during the night, Mom and Dad would get everyone up and sit downstairs on the couch till it was over so that we were all together.

I had a best friend and we went through all eight grades together. We all went to a one-room schoolhouse for a couple of years. The teacher told me I could ask my brother, Rudy, if I didn't know a word. I did and he threw his change purse at me.

Hiding the Whiskey

By June Gill Hickman of Dover, Ohio
Born 1929

I was born in Pomeroy, Ohio to Otto and Florence Gill in 1929. I was the only one of us eleven kids who was born out of Athens County. We moved a lot. My dad's main job was coal mining, but he also made and sold bootleg whisky for extra money during Prohibition. We lived in the areas around Glouster, Green's Run, Goose Run and Orbeston, except when we lived in Pomeroy for a while.

Dad worked at a coal mine in Millfield, Ohio. He and one of my uncles found out that the 10X, a coal mine in Goose Run, needed men. They went to see about that job and they were lucky that they chose that day to go. There was a big mine explosion in Millfield that very day. If you look it up you will see how many men were killed.

One time the Dry Officers went to the school and questioned my oldest brother about where my dad kept his bootleg, but of course my brother said he didn't know. Sometimes it was kept in the creek close to our house. Sometimes it was hung down the well on ropes, where we got our drinking water.

Mom told me about one time when they heard the Dry Officers were coming. Dad wasn't home, so Mom and my oldest brother, Chuck, busted all the jugs in the creek. I was also told a story about when she was pregnant with my brother Dillon who was later killed in WWII.

I guess my dad needed a drink real bad one Sunday morning. He said, "Seal, if I don't find a drink today I'll swear off of it for life." Mom said she prayed all day that he wouldn't find a drink and he didn't. He never drank again, but he still bootlegged for the extra money it provided.

My Grandpa North was a Pilgrim Holiness preacher. He preached in a church in a hollow called Baily Run. Because of this, we went to church a lot. It was our entertainment too. There used to be a revival, or tent meeting, some place all the time. When we lived in Goose Run, we passed two reservoirs on the way to school or church. One was called Big Resi. The church always baptized people there. It looked just like what you see in the movies.

We didn't live in a bad house. It had five rooms, a front porch, a back porch and a cellar under part of it. We kept milk, canned food, pickles and sauerkraut down in the cellar. Mom made sauerkraut in stone jars. She'd put a plate over the kraut, then a big rock on the plate and then a rag over that. She canned a lot, such as; tomatoes, green beans, apples and berries. Most of it was kept in glass jars with red rubber rings and zinc lids. We sometimes used the red rings to hold up our socks when the elastic gave out. When the jars were emptied, we washed them out and put them upside-down on a fence post until next canning season.

We butchered two hogs every year. The pig pen had a creek running through it for water, but we had to feed those pigs. I hated that job. We kept slop for them, but also had to collect acorns and pull weeds for them. Once in a while they put slack (fine coal) in their pen for some reason. I was always glad when it was time to butcher. We always had people there to help and a lot of food. They killed the pigs, gutted them and dipped them in hot water. Then they scrapped the hair off and cut them up. The kids would get the pig's bladder. We'd clean it up, blow it up and use it as a football. The pork hung in a shanty where it hung for most of the winter. Once something got in the shanty and ate some of the meat. Chuck watched and here there was a knot hole up high and as he watched a big yellow cat stuck its head out of that knot hole. Well, let's just say that was the end of the cat and the knot hole.

With all of us kids, the house was full in the winter. In the spring things got a little roomier though. The boys would clean out the log shanty where we had hung the butchered hogs and would sleep out there until fall. There was a long steep hill behind the shanty. We would ride a wooden homemade sled down that grass hill like you do on snow. It worked on grass, maybe because it had wooden runners. My sister, Sis and me used the pig pen for a playhouse when it was empty. We nailed flour sacks to the walls with the blue sides out. Sometimes some of the boys would help us. Then we had a playhouse for a while.

I wonder why we never saw deer out there back then? The boys did hunt though and Mom cooked the rabbit, squirrel and coon. They caught turtles, but not many fish. When us little kids did fish, we had a straight pin bent and tied to a string. We helped with the garden too. Us little kids had to pick potato bugs off the potato plants all the time: I hated that.

Did I say that our toilet was down over the hill from

the house? It was moved from time to time as it would fill up, but was always in the same approximate area. It wasn't fun making that trip to the toilet in the dark especially in the winter. We kept a chamber pot in the house for at night when we went to bed.

Those might have been the "Good Old Days," but I sure do enjoy my electric washer and dryer, my indoor bathroom, knowing how to drive a car and even the TV sometimes. We were happy then and we are happy now, but back then we had more family time. We visited each other more often. Cousins knew each other then, but now people don't know their extended families. Would I rather be living in the "Good Old Days?" I guess that depends on when you ask me.

Somerset Sledding on Pig Foot Hill

by Jackie Fisher of Somerset, Ohio
born in 1938

I have many memories of growing up in southeast Ohio. Somerset has been my home all of my life. My childhood was spent on West Main Street surrounded by a Sunoco station on my right, Clouse Clinic on my left and Shaheen's pool room across the street. (all of these are gone now)

As a child, I played outside most of the day with the 10 or 12 kids in the neighborhood. (No TV or video games to keep us indoors). We played kick the can, rode our bikes and generally roamed the neighborhood coming inside only to eat meals. We usually stayed out until dark and then spent the evening listening to the radio. In the winter, on snowy days, we passed the time riding our sleds down Pig Foot Hill. If it was icy enough, we could make it clear to the railroad tracks.

Jackie Fisher on her tricycle decorated for Memorial Day in 1941.

Our main treat was Russell's theater. There were three different movies shown every week, most of which were in black & white. It cost 10 cents for the movie and 10 cents for popcorn. The kids would all sit up front and sometimes get pretty rowdy until the manager or usher would come down the aisle with his flashlight and threaten to make us leave.

As teenagers, everyone went to Montell's Snack Bar after school and drank fountain Cokes for a nickel and played the juke box for a dime. If someone was lucky enough to get his or her dad's car, we drove to New Lexington to the skating rink. I also remember hot, steamy Sunday nights traveling to Schmeltzer's Grove in Bremen for square dancing in an open shelter house. We were always so hot after dancing that our clothes were sticking to us and I remember one of the girls took off her wet petticoat and threw it down one of the toilet holes in the out house. How primitive was that?

Most of our shopping was done right in town. During the 40's and 50's, Somerset boasted four grocery stores: Marshall's, Helm's, Bever's and Felt's. Most of these stores would let you charge your groceries until payday. The clerk always slipped a little candy or gum into your grocery bag the day you paid your bill.

There were two schools in Somerset until consolidation in 1960. I attended Holy Trinity and was taught by the Dominican Sisters. One of my memories of the nuns was during the time of our senior class play. I had 3 costume changes and the nun in charge insisted that I bring the outfits in to her so she could see if they were "appropriate." One of the outfits was a full skirt and a red cotton sleeveless blouse. Well, the good sister thought that my bare arms on stage would be a little too risqué. All the girls at that time wore sleeveless blouses, so I didn't see the problem, but there was no chance for rebuttal with the nuns. She promptly took my blouse to the convent and the following day, my red cotton blouse had red satin sleeves sewn on it. I still have those sleeves today tucked away in my scrapbook.

At summer's end, the annual Memorial Day Parade was an exciting event for us kids. We spent hours decorating our bikes and tricycles with red, white & blue crepe paper so we could participate in the parade. It was such a colorful and patriotic tradition that is unfortunately no longer observed. The parade goes on, but decorating bikes with crepe paper has fallen by the wayside.

The Somerset Press was our weekly newspaper. But in a town the size of Somerset, we all knew most of the news via the grapevine before the paper ever arrived...and if there was a death in town, you could be pretty certain it would be someone you knew. I guess that statement would still be true today.

In the late 40's or early 50's, TV finally reached our town. Two of the local businesses displayed a TV in their show windows on Saturday evening to the delight of Somerset citizens who stood for hours watching whatever was showing on the tiny screen. Most of us never dreamed that the day would come when we would have one or more TV sets in our own home.

With the dawn of television, a whole new world opened up. My little brother now sported a raccoon cap and thought he was Davy Crockett, little girls everywhere were wearing Mouseketeer ears and hoping to grow up and look just like Annette Funicello. Teenagers tuned in to watch Dick Clark's American Bandstand. If a singer was featured on bandstand, you knew he would be the new teenage idol.

How fortunate were those of us who grew up in the 40's and 50's. The summer days seemed to last forever and held endless possibilities. There was no need to lock our doors or be fearful of the night and violence was merely a word in the dictionary. Coming of age in southeast Ohio was privilege for which I'll always be grateful.

Old Doc and the Tomato Stakes

By Robert D. Hoskinson of McConnelsville, Ohio
Born 1919

In 1937 I graduated from Doddridge County High School in West Virginia. The first part of June I came to work for six weeks on a farm in Morgan County, Ohio owned by Delbert and Maude Doak.

The farm was located in the corner along Meigs Creek and the Muskingum River. Our wages were $1.00 per day with board and washing. Our day began at 6:00 a.m. and ended after 6:00 p.m. with time for breakfast and dinner, then supper at the end of the day. Mrs. Doak always prepared fine meals.

The Doak home was heated with coal, and oil lamps provided the light. Mr. Doak installed a Delco battery system to generate electricity, which was used for lighting and other purposes at times. There was no rural electricity at this time; the Ohio power plant was built much later. The 12 or 14 head of cows were milked by hand. The milk was separated from the cream, which was shipped and sold.

A tractor provided the power to prepare the soil for the planting of the crops. The tomatoes and cabbage were set out, along with other vegetables. Man power and mule power were used for cultivating the crops. I spent much of my days walking behind a cultivator plow pulled by "Old Doc," a 500-pound mule. He was as smart as he was stubborn. He would knock over the tomato stakes as we plowed, knowing he could rest while I drove the stakes back into the ground. He didn't like to be caught because he knew it meant work. I had to put feed for him in his feed trough in the barn, hide until he came to eat and then catch him. I was not always sure which one of us was the smartest!

Everyday on a truck farm was hurry, as the earlier the produce was ready the higher the prices were when it sold.

On Saturday evenings many folks from the country came to McConnelsville to shop, visit, go to a movie or perhaps enjoy a cold drink. I remember the line of people waiting to get in the Opera House and also the cold root beer we bought for five-cents. I also remember the ice cream wagon with ringing bells making its way along the back streets, selling ice cream in front of homes. Not so many cars back then, but there was a lot of people. Town was a fine place to spend Saturday evenings after a week on the farm.

On Sunday mornings I remember worshiping at the little Presbyterian Church along Route 77 (now Route 60) south of McConnelsville.

May I share an incident I recall? The Doak farm had too many cats. So, Mrs. Doak gave one of her hired hands a dime to get rid of an old cat with several kittens. He placed them in a sack, which was probably made of paper, and threw them into Meigs Creek. The next morning Mrs. Doak opened her back door and there on the porch was the mother cat and all the kittens, ready to greet her! We all had a good laugh. Those were some of the good old days.

Thank God We Lived in the Country

by Winnifred Cunningham of McConnelsville, Ohio
born in 1924

The summer between my junior and senior years in school (1941), I worked for our school bus driver's parents, George and Mate Bowman. They were also the parents of my 7th and 8th grade teacher, "Doc."

One evening, my boyfriend came to see me during the week. I said, "Let's go to Chesterhill to a movie." I said, "Oh, I have a dime," so we went.

He started counting his money; he lacked one penny. Oh! I remembered I'd given my dime to Mom for stamps. You could get three stamps for a dime with a penny left over, but I didn't have that penny.

I worked—cleaned, cooked, and baked—for $2.00 a week. Harold worked for a farmer for $9.00 a week. If they threshed or did extra work, he got $9.50. He was already out of high school.

Oh yes, Harold had a 1930 Model A Ford he'd paid $40 for. Driving 40 miles an hour was fast.

Oh, yes! How well I remember the chamber pots. We never had a bathroom, nor electricity in our home until after World War II. No one ever liked it when it was their turn to empty the thing.

I recall two funny things about chamber pots. My Aunt Genie had a big crockery one that was heavy even when empty. Someway it found its way to our house. One day it was my sister Mildred's turn to empty it. She was going downstairs and she dropped it. She cried, "I couldn't help it! It was heavy!" I had very understanding parents who just said, "Clean up the mess."

Another time, Dad (Clarence Fleming) walked three miles to Bartlett, as he never owned a car, to get the bus to go to Marietta. He'd usually eat a good lunch at the Leader Restaurant at a very reasonable price. Then he always went down on Front Street to Uncle Bill Richardson's Drug Store to get school tablets for us girls. They were shorter than most but with thick sheets of yellow smooth paper. We all were so happy with our new tablets.

That day, Dad bought a new chamber pot and brought it home on the bus. Was he embarrassed? Well everyone needed one since Bartlett didn't have electricity either. But this day we saw him coming home across the bridge carrying a pot.

"Open the lid," he told us. Oh, we all laughed. What a happy surprise: it was full of oranges. What a treat for the whole family!

My neighbor, Mamie Bowman, asked me if I'd like to go to Marietta shopping with her. Oh, yes, I did! I had saved $5.00 from working for-her in-laws and I wanted to buy a new dress and, hopefully, a pair of shoes. When we got to town, I went to J.C. Penney's to look for a dress. Oh! I found a beauty, a pink bemberg dress. I tried it on and it just fit. It was only $2.50, no tax in 1941. I was so happy with my new dress.

Winnifred Fleming Cunningham wearing her pick Bemberg dress with white shoes that cost $5.50 in 1941.

Then I went down on Front Street to Wunder's Shoe Store to look for shoes. There was always a friendly salesman to help you. I told him what I wanted and he brought out just the right thing. It was a pair of white shoes with the toes out and a little broad heel for $3.00. Oh! I'll be back! I went, almost ran, looking for Mamie to borrow the fifty cents from her. I was so excited!

I found her and she gave me the money. I promised her I'd pay her back. Then I went back to get my new shoes.

What a day! I was so excited and happy with my purchases. I had worked for the money that made me feel so good. After I worked another week, I paid Mamie back her money.

I would be a senior in high school that fall. I still get excited thinking about my great purchases and I always felt so dressed up in those clothes.

I am a country girl. Dad only had three acres of ground where our house was. Wolf Creek was on two sides of our place, with a big grist mill and a dam across the road from the house. Milling was Dad's first love, but it was almost obsolete by the time I was very big.

Someone had taught blacksmithing to Dad, so he had a shop down the creek road behind our neighbor's store. It was a good arrangement for both of them, as men would take their horses to be shod to Dad, while they did their grocery shopping in Graham's Store.

When it was time for me to start school in1930, a big yellow school bus picked up four older sisters and me to take us to the brand new brick schoolhouse in Bartlett, three miles away. Our neighbor, Lovell, drove the bus. We had to go over a little run. Sometimes it was full of water or mud and we'd get stuck. Lovell's dad had a pair of mules, so he'd ask Emmett to run up over the hill to tell him of our dilemma. Before long George would come with his mules and pull us out, and we'd be on our way.

One night for some reason I was sleeping on the couch. I laid very quietly because I could hear Mom, Dad, and two big brothers talking very excitedly. "Oh! Graham's Store is on fire!" Later, I asked Mom if I could get a drink of water. "Come right back," she said. Our pump was on the side porch where I could look down at that horrible fire.

Albert had been winding the clock ready to go to their house. He knew it was raining, and suddenly lightning struck a can of kerosene in the back far corner of the basement. When he opened the basement door the flames were so intense that his ankles were burned. They were able to get out the cash register and a few things. The rain came down like a cloudburst. Men from all around came to help. They literally scooped water up off the ground, but to no avail. It was too big a fire. The oldest son, Curtis, picked up the gas pump that had been knocked over and moved it out of the way. Those old gas pumps were tall as you had to pump the gasoline up into them. It said 18 cents a gallon. He tried to move it later, but of course he couldn't budge it.

We lived in the country, but no small towns had fire trucks either. It was 1933. My big brothers, Chester and Max, with Dad's help, brought the forge, anvil and all of Dad's blacksmithing needs and put them under the willow trees across the road from thc housc.

Momma probably wondered, "Now, what are we going to do?" Somehow we'd make do with whatever we had.

Dad always had a big garden, surrounded by a picket fence to keep the chickens, dogs, and whatever out. Inside the picket fence was our big clotheslines and the outhouse. Further out, Dad had a cold frame where he'd start his sweet potato plants.

I had five older sisters. Some of them would have helped Mom prepare hundreds of jars of food for the winter. Even neighbors came and asked Mom to can for them. She had such a big heart that she could never say no.

That neighbor, Thad Roberts, stuttered, so we kids would get him to sing since he could do that without one stutter. I remember helping Dad husk sweet corn for that neighbor so Mom and the girls could can it for them.

Dad went to work for the WPA for very little money, 35 to 50 cents a day perhaps. But it would help to buy the essentials we needed at the neighborhood grocery store.

I'd carry a little basket of eggs down the creek road, then a mile up the hill to Belva Woodburn's new grocery store. It was near our Epworth Methodist Church, and later the Grange Hall. Even if there was just a nickel left over, I'd always take it home.

Our evening snacks were apples or popcorn. Sometimes a big sister would make candy.

We always drank water, milk with our meals. Then I liked buttermilk after someone had churned. We all liked cow butter on Mom's homemade bread.

Momma had such a sweet spirit, so loving and kind, with a heart of gold. Everybody liked "Loie."

She'd cook her good home cooked meals for her big family. I'm number 10 with a younger sister, Mary J. Mom was always in the kitchen. She'd sing as she worked. She'd bake seven loaves of bread twice a week and she never complained about anything. The kitchen was small with one window on each end. She always wore dresses and an apron was a must. She'd pick it up to wipe the perspiration off her face or sometimes fan her face with it.

Mom always made all our clothes. I wore lots of hand-me-downs or made over dresses, but I didn't mind. Were we poor? I suppose everyone would say that we were. We didn't have any money, but no one else did either.

Really we were rich. We had all the vegetables our garden could produce, a truck patch full of sweet corn and potatoes. We were never hungry.

Oh, yes, Dad owned 30 acres up on the Lind Hill.

One day my sister, Margaret, and I were riding a horse across the field, and then we were going down a shortcut to reach the main road. There sat a man up against a tree, maybe "pretending" to be asleep. We went on home and told Dad. The next morning, he walked up on the hill and oh my! His heart sank! Someone had dug all of our sweet potatoes and everyone liked them, especially Dad. We'd counted on them for the winter. I hope they helped someone!

Church was very important to Mom and Dad. We always walked, sometimes twice a day, to church. Our neighbor, Luella, might come and walk with us. A kind neighbor would ask Mom to ride, but we kids and Dad didn't mind walking. We walked everywhere, sometimes barefoot.

When I was big enough to play in the creek below the dam where it was more shallow, my neighbor, Sydnia, would bring an inner tube and we spent hours playing and having fun. One day I was covered with little black bugs. I ran to the house. Dad was sitting in his favorite straight chair beside the cook stove, so he could talk to Mom. I stood before him naked as a jay bird while he cautiously picked blood-sucking leeches off my body.

Another time, I was younger, when Sydnia and I were hunting minnows under the mill in the deep mill pond. I was on the upper side, and Sydnia was nearer the creek. I saw some, leaned over too far, fell in head first, and I couldn't swim. But Sydnia told me to move my arms and legs, so finally I got over to her. I asked her if she'd go with me to tell Mom. I was afraid she'd bawl me out because I'd put on a clean dress. How silly! She was just thankful that I was alright.

My big brother, Chester, did almost drown when he was a teenager. (He's 16 years older than I.) The other boys who were swimming rolled him over a barrel and saved his life.

Dad still ground feed sometimes. I liked to be at the mill with him. He still shod some horses, also. I liked to watch him as he would get the coals red hot, put the shoes in the hot coals. Then he'd take them out and start to shape them with his hammer on the anvil. Then he'd put that shoe into a little tub of water and it would hiss, sizzle and pop as it cooled down. Then back to the fire again to do the same thing over. Then it was time to put the horse's leg between his knees as he'd nail the shoe onto the horse's hoof. About this time Mom would call, "Dinner's ready!" (Never lunch). Dad would invite the horse's owner to eat with us.

Dad was a people person. Back in those days, if a person couldn't pay, Dad shook his hand and said, "Well, pay when you can." Before long they'd be back to make it right with Dad. Those were the days of trusting people, helping or lending to your neighbor, doing a kind deed for whomever had a need, and no one would ever hurt your child.

We didn't lock our doors, but anyone could have got in if we did. But no one would bother our house. I was never afraid of the dark. When I was older, Sydnia and I walked home together on a pitch black night, a mile down that old hill. But I had to walk on down the creek road a short distance to our house after Sydnia was home. I knew where the matches were, so I lit an oil lamp, set it on the dining room table, and went upstairs to bed. I'd usually hear Mom come home as someone stopped to let her out, but Dad would be walking with an old friend, Jot Zumbro, who lived at least two miles further up another road.

Then there were the times that it rained and rained. Dad would say, "Get everything in!" We'd go to gather everything up, the wood and whatever we didn't want to lose, because the creek was coming up. The chickens had to be caught and put in their upstairs. Horses and cows had to be moved to a field far away from the creek. Dad would check the water level every hour and bring the john boat closer and closer to the house, until it would be tied to a porch post.

The water was never in the house while I was at home, but sometimes we could hear it sloshing up under the kitchen floor. There was a crawl space underneath the house for the water to go through. Every one of us has crawled under there at one time or another, just to do it.

When the water went down, oh, what a mess! We wished for a rain to help wash away the mud. Dad would go barefooted to sweep the mud off our walk to the road.

We were a big, loving family. Later when we heard some of the family was coming to visit, we all went to Mom's and Dad's. We enjoyed being together.

Now that I'm 85, I look back and wonder, "How did the city people feed their families when money was scarce?" Some had victory gardens that would help. But for me, thank God we lived in the country!

Streaker on Main Street

by Mildred E. Jackson of Cambridge, Ohio
born in 1928

I don't know if this was my first "trip to town" on my own or not, but my mother told me the story about this one. I can't remember my exact age (probably one and a half or two years old.).

She was preparing to give me a bath after stripping me down to my "birthday suit." That was the pet name for naked. While she was running the water and getting towel, soap, and washcloth ready, I had another idea—I found a door ajar, and when I found myself on our front porch, I proceeded to take a walk. The sun was shining, and conditions were just right!

We lived in a small house about fifty yards from the main street in our town, "The Old National Highway"—Route 40.

Mother searched our home very quickly and came to the conclusion that I had gone out the door, so she ran out to the sidewalk and spotted me. She said she called my name, and when I heard her, my little short legs took off in a run!

When she finally caught up with me, she "swooped" me up, just as I was ready to step off the curb and cross Main Street. Needless to say, I got spanked on the return home. She always said I was probably the "first flasher" our town had ever seen!

The next bath she gave me, she made all of the "preparations" *before* stripping me down and checked the locks on the doors.

I Was a County Line Rambler

by Frances Hill Marks of Orrville, Ohio
born in 1949

I grew up in the 50s and early 60s and, yes, I was a member of a 4-H club called the County Line Ramblers.

We lived near the Guernsey-Tuscarawas county line in southeastern Ohio off of State Route 21. I attended first grade in a one-room schoolhouse for about six months. All eight grades in one room with a pot-bellied stove in the middle of the room, and outside bathrooms. In January 1956 we were consolidated into a new building, Liberty Elementary, with all eight grades, and it seemed huge! I returned there a few years ago and it seemed to have shrunk.

I attended Cambridge High School, riding a bus from 7:00 a.m. till 8:30 a.m. and from 3:20 p.m. to almost 5:00 p.m. daily through the week through some of the most beautiful countryside on back roads and rural farm areas. I passed through this vista in all seasons. This area now is part of Salt Fork Lake Park.

About 1963 there was a lot of talk about a new super highway to be built (Interstate 77). It seemed like a far-fetched dream, because State Route 21 was the main route from north to south and so busy on Friday and Sunday evenings you could hardly get across it. This bottleneck of traffic was mostly caused by families traveling back to West Virginia from northern factory towns for weekend visits. And, of course, many big rigs used the route also.

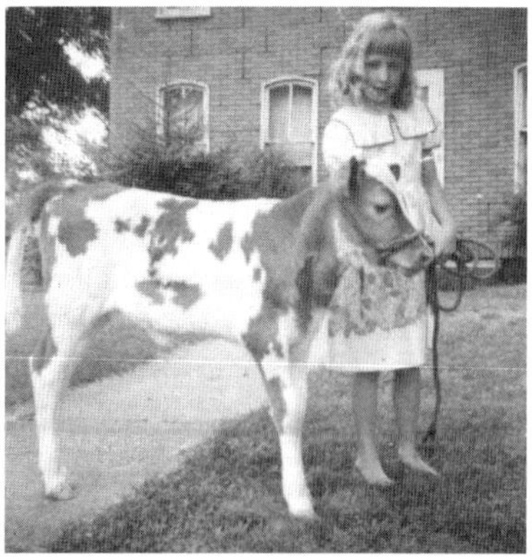
Frances Marks with her 4-H Club project for the Guernsey County Fair in 1959.

A portion of the super highway was completed in 1966, the same year I was a high school junior taking driver's education, a course in which we actually left the classroom in one of two cars, one being a stick-shift, or manual transmission, and one an automatic transmission. What a challenge for me, shifting gears on the hills of

Cambridge! Then one day our class drove onto the new part of the new highway which, unfinished, didn't go far. Our instructor told us to step on the gas! The speed limit was 70 miles per hour. It felt like we were flying. The road was built for speed, but wow, it was hard to go that fast. This has sure changed, now it's hard to slow down to 65.

In this time that I grew up, very rarely did anyone lock their doors. We knew our neighbors, and we trusted them. On Fridays the Omar Bread delivery man came into our home while we were away and left bread on our kitchen counter. On Sundays after church we drove to Kendrick's gas station which was closed on Sundays (as were most stores). On a bench outside was a pile of newspapers, the Akron Beacon Journal, with a rock on top and an empty cigar box. You put your money in the cigar box, lifted the rock and took a paper. Very simple.

When I was five years old, we purchased our first black and white T.V. There was no remote. You had to get up and turn the dial or go outside (in all kinds of weather) and turn the antenna to change channels. We also got a telephone installed at this time and soon after that, we had an inside bathroom. Wow, what progress!

I'm glad I grew up in this era, and some days my heart is back on those country roads riding on a bumpy school bus through a natural wonderland. Yes, I'm proud to have been a County Line Rambler growing up, poor, but rich in spirit.

A Groundhog Named Davy Crockett

By Marcie Welsh Hunter of Zanesville, Ohio
Born 1940

The Welsh family story begins back in the mid-1700's. My grandfather, George Welsh's family, back seven generations, came from Ireland. They settled in Maryland, Cecil County. He married Nancy Cannon and later he enlisted into the Maryland forces during the Revolutionary War. They had 10 children. Later they moved to Pennsylvania and then into Muskingum County where he bought 500 acres. Now on the present road, Welsh Road. The farm house burned a few years ago and the farm has been sold off into a housing develop-ment. They were Presbyterians and they donated the land where the present Muskingum Presbyterian Church now stands. They are all buried in the cemetery beside the church.

My dad, Don H. Welsh, and his father and mother; Charles Herbert and Beulah Vista Hormell Welsh, his sister Margaret Welsh Stahl and his brother Wayne Welsh, lived on the old homestead during the depression. They attended the Muskingum Presbyterian Church during that time. My sisters and myself were all baptized as babies at the church and I attended there in the early 70's.

I remember my dad telling the story about one time they had tore down an old building on the farm and they were burning the old timber. The fire was "red hot" and my dad told his younger brother, seven years his junior, to pick up the nails lying there, "we can still use them." When he picked them up they stuck to his hands, they were so "red hot." My dad got a board thrown at him. What a sense of humor!

Early in the 1940's my dad's parents moved to Zanesville. My grandfather worked for Gardner Real Estate and then later was bailiff of the court where he retired from.

We also moved to Zanesville and lived on Forest Ave. Right across the street was the Euclid Methodist Church. I would walk across the street and climb the steps to go to Sunday school. I remember how big that wood door was and how hard it was to open. 16 years later I would walk down the aisle of that church and get married. My grandparents attended that church until their deaths.

Later we moved to Newark, Ohio and lived on Maple Street. My dad worked on the railroad and was gone a lot. I remember hearing my mom and the neighbors talking about having ''window peekers" in the neighborhood. That scared me a lot. My mom told the story about a black man who sold peanuts and popcorn on the square in downtown Newark. I said to him one Saturday, "why don't you wash that stuff off your face?" he told me, "I've tried and tried, honey, but it won't come off." That scared my mom, but he gave me a free bag of popcorn.

Later we moved into the country about 10 miles from Zanesville in a little town called Stringtown. We lived off the main road down a little steep hill and over a creek. Over a creek - no bridge! We would just drive over it and the cars wheels would just go bump, bump.

We had no modern conveniences; outside plumbing, coal heaters, etc. I remember how scared I was of those coal heaters. When mom would clean them out I was afraid those "clinkers" would catch the house on fire.

You had to be real careful too when you took the trip to the outhouse. We had our own chickens and the rooster was real mean. His name was Jelly and he would chase you and if you weren't careful he'd flop you. He made a delicious Sunday dinner.

One time when we had just gotten some new baby chicks, we went out one morning before our parents were up and brought in 6-8 babies into our bed. They were so cute; little yellow fuzz balls. Well with every "peep, peep" there was a double amount of "poop, poop." Mom was not impressed!

One day my dad's car wasn't working so he was trying to fix it. I was on the porch and for some reason the car back-fired and caught my dad's pants on fire. I remember seeing him rolling around on the ground and finally got the fire out. The place where he worked, National Battery, had a nurse on staff and, she would clean and bandage his legs several times a week. He had blisters from his knees to his ankles. I noticed something different about my dad from that time forward, he was a nicer dad. He always called us "honey" all the time after that. That has always stuck with me.

We moved from that house in 1945 and my parents bought their first house. It was in a town called Shannon. The roads didn't have names back then, but now it's on Shannon Valley Road in Muskingum County about 15 miles from Zanesville, Ohio.

The house had no paint on it and the front porch, instead of glass in the windows, had cheese cloth over them. It looked like an old shack! There was a pitcher pump at the kitchen sink and a fireplace was the only heat and of course the outhouse. There was a small basement, later my dad would dig it out by hand and install a water pump and coal furnace.

I remember how cold that house was with just a fireplace for heat. We started to school that fall at Nashport School. And guess what? They had outhouses too!

We had a large garden every summer and my dad would go up to the neighbors and borrow their work horses and plow and disk the garden. He always let me ride on the back of the horses when he took them home. Later years he would borrow their tractor and he'd let me drive the tractor and finish the disk process.

As kids we loved to play cowboys and Indians. This one time we had made a bow and arrow out of a tree branch. When we shot the arrow, my mom just happened to walk by and the arrow stuck in her head. It stood there for awhile and then slowly dropped. Poor Mom!

My dad was quite an outdoorsman; he fished and hunted all his life. We were real poor and at Christmastime he would sell his animal pelts and mom would go out and buy our Christmas presents. We had fantastic Christmases.

My dad's brother left home at an early age. He went to Nebraska and joined ''The White Horse Troup." They would travel all over the USA and put on shows. They would jump hurdles and ride bulls and do rope tricks etc. The Troup was featured in the August 13, 1945 Life magazine issue. My uncle was in the pictures, but only his family knew who he was. The group also sold programs during their performances of which I have copies. My uncle was known as Nebraska Wayne.

One time he came home for a visit and he took us with him for the day. He needed a haircut. While there, we talked the barbers into cutting our hair. My twin and I had Shirley Temple hair. Barbers had no idea how to cut girls hair back in 1950. My mom was not a happy camper.

We had two very special pets. A groundhog named Davy Crockett and a Cocker Spaniel name Freckles. The groundhog was a baby, but it still could bite. But it didn't take long until he was tame. He lived in the kitchen on the counter; at the end was a cupboard where he could hide. When he got too big my dad made him a little box with a shoot up to the top of the ground. We buried it out behind the garage. Of course he didn't like it and we thought he was a goner. But a few weeks later we found him and became friends again. That little critter loved, Franco American Spaghetti. One morning after we went down to visit him, he tried to follow us back to the house and the dog jumped on him. This time he was a goner! Boo hoo!

One night we woke up and heard these eerie sounds on our bed. The cat had come into our bedroom and had her five babies on our bed. Then one night she came in with her nights catch and we found rabbit parts on our bed the next morning. Messy!

Freckles was a faithful doggie and would sit on the back of the couch and look out the window and wait for us to come home from school, but later he went to doggie heaven.

Of course there was the day mom came running up from the barn yelling, "Big snake in barn, big snake in barn." We went down and sure enough it was a big one. One day my dad stopped at home at lunchtime. When he and his co-worker started toward the house, there lay a big black snake. The co-worker grabbed the snake's tail and whirled it around and snapped off its head. It was the biggest I've ever seen.

We spent a lot of time in the woods; swinging on grapevines and playing hide and seek and riding our bikes. We finally got inside plumbing and hot and cold running water and even automatic heat. We survived the outhouse, radio and even wearing those clothes mom made out of feed sacks. Those were the "Good Olde Days."

1960's Farm Life

by David E. Ball of Roseville, Ohio
born in 1953

I was born in January, 1953. Though not yet 60, I have a few childhood memories. I grew up on the family farm outside Zanesville, Ohio. I lived with two brothers, four sisters, Dad, Mom, and her dad and mom [names not given]. Although we lived much like the Amish, we were Polish.

Grandpa bought this farm, where Mom still lives at age 85, sometime in the late teens or early 20s. He farmed it all his life with horses and horse-drawn equipment. His other main tools were hammer, hand saws, scythe, corn knife, hoe, post-hole digger, and pitchfork. He was flooded out of the Putnam area (south of Zanesville) in the 1913 flood and bought the farm within the next eight or nine years.

Grandma and he had ten daughters and Mom lived on the farm all her life except her time in Oklahoma working on fighter planes during WWII.

Early memories for me include family and noon dinners of chicken, mashed potatoes and gravy, dressing, corn, beans, noodles, dessert, on Sunday after church and Sunday school. With aunts, uncles, cousins, and us we had a crowd. Sunday was a day of rest.

I remember party line phones, polio vaccine on sugar cubes at the local grade school, Friday evening grocery shopping when we also stopped at Burger Chef for a hamburger, fries, and a drink.

We heated the old farmhouse with two stoves that burned wood and coal, but Mom also had a propane cook stove in the kitchen. Mom still has a wringer washer. She never had an automatic one. We have spring water and a concrete block spring house to protect it.

The earliest car I remember Dad driving was a 1953 Chevy. I would love to have it today. When he got a new used car he would just come home from work with it. Most of his cars were large Chevy station wagons for the family.

Summers were spent in the hay field, corn field, garden, fixing fence, hoeing thistle from the pastures, cutting firewood, riding bicycles. We put all our hay up loose, some in the hay mow in the barn, but much on the outside hay stacks. I learned from my grandma and grandpa and became fairly good at building them and putting a good, tight, pointed top on them to keep rain water out. I remember losing one we built too near the county road when someone set it afire.

I learned to milk a cow by hand, make butter, make cottage cheese, can green beans, make cucumber relish, and make homemade lye soap which Mom did to get work clothes clean. We had an outhouse out past the grape arbor and rhubarb but also indoor plumbing. We had apple trees, pear, plum, peach, walnut, hickory, butternut, chestnut, grapes, and raised potatoes, sweet corn, cabbage, squash, cucumbers, beans, tomatoes, eggplant, lettuce, peppers. I also learned how to cut corn with a corn knife and make corn shocks and husk the corn late in the fall. We sometimes planted 200 to 300 pounds of potatoes and had three gardens total.

We met the school bus about a third of a mile from home. It was up a long driveway and over the hill out of sight from home. We missed it a few times and they had to wait for us sometimes.

One of Grandma's sayings was "waste not, want not." We learned to share what we had with anyone and wore some hand-me-down clothes. We learned to appreciate what we had and respect ourselves and others. We went to church every Sunday which helped keep us grounded.

Dad was an infantry sergeant in WWII, but all he ever told us was he walked across Europe. He worked 37 years at Ohio Power Company, 29 years Philo and eight years at Gavin Plant on the Ohio River. He died in 1999.

Some of our daily meals included soup; barley-potato soup, cabbage-potato soup, brown soup with potato, borsht with beets, vegetable-beef soup, and chicken noodle soup. Grandma did much of the cooking as Mom helped outside. Black iron skillets were used for frying chicken, potatoes, hamburger, eggs, etc.

Grandpa had a large horse-drawn sled which he covered with hay and sometimes picked us up from the bus after school in the winter. Our bus driver was Elmer Holbein, one of our neighbors.

We grew up watching Lawrence Welk, Leave It To Beaver, The real McCoys, and other TV shows I can't recall off hand of the 50s and 60s. Bedtime was usually 9 p.m. through the week.

I learned at a young age to harness the work horses and drive them with the hay wagon pulling a hay loader up the wind row of dry hay. I could also back the loaded hay wagon in the barn with horses to unload. I sometimes rode a work horse or occasionally a cow. If they didn't want ridden, they would go under a low hanging tree branch and off I would go.

We sometimes dared to throw rocks at hornet nests in trees. We also sometimes encountered large bumble bees when we gathered eggs in the chicken house. Also, wasps and honey bees and yellow jackets sometimes stung us, as did sweat bees, which hurt for a short while.

We used to find flint arrowheads in the gardens and corn fields on the farm when I was a kid.

Grandpa had a couple of coal mine tunnels in the woods. He used to use and sell some coal from them which was mined by hand by just a few people. I think he had a still in one of them around 1920-1922. He was charged in March, 1922 with possession of materials to make intoxicating liquors and found guilty and charged $200 in court costs.

Back in the late 50s, early 60s we would get snowed in our 1/3 mile driveway. Snow would be on the ground all winter and sometimes drift two to three feet deep. Sometimes we parked at the edge of the county road and walked in and out. Many times we would have to shovel and push to get the car through the snow. A few times the drifts buried the car, and we had to shovel it out.

The hay wagon had a heavy two foot long board on a log chain underneath near the rear wheel. It was attached under the wagon and when we needed a brake for going down steep hills, we put it under the rear tire which rode on it and slid through the field. We then backed up and put it back up under the wagon above the frame.

During early school years, I remember the Ford truck from the Farm Supply Center with a bit of cattle feed, pig feed, or chicken feed. I also remember a bread man and a milk man. We really enjoyed occasional treats of donuts or sweet rolls from the bread man. Also, Mom and Grandma baked cakes and pies and cookies. Grandma's sister visited from New Jersey each summer, and she cooked and baked for us also. She rode the train and we had to pick her up at the train depot in Trinway or Dresden. Later, she rode Greyhound bus, and we would meet her in Zanesville. She would stay about three or four weeks.

David Ball, age 16 in 1969 with corn shucks and black and white dog.

Dillon Dam was built in 1959 to 1960. It is one and-a-half miles from home. We would walk down the creek through our woods to see some of the construction and collect fossils from the large limestone placed near the new highway route 146 along Dillon Lake. We also went to Dillon Lake and caught catfish or carp with our long cane poles.

My earliest cars, many of which I got from my sisters when they got something else, were '64 Nova 4-door, '67 Mustang, '67 firebird, '67 GTO, '67 Camaro, '67 Cutlass. They area all gone now, as things don't last forever.

Also, I remember annual soap box derby races on McIntine Avenue. Also picnics at Dad's parents in Zanesville with his large family of two brothers and five sisters and many kids. Many memories and a lot of good food from those times.

Our childhood transportation was bicycles which we could repair and ride a few miles around the neighborhood on the county roads. We also helped neighbors in their hay fields.

My oldest neighbor is almost 90. He still likes to tell me stories about my Grandpa, who died around 1972. Grandma died in 1968. She had a heart attack the same day Bobby Kennedy got shot, and they died the same day.

Grandpa had a horse named Fred who knew his way home from Zanesville, about seven miles. Before there was much auto traffic, Grandpa would take a load of something to town and visit his sister and drink a glass of wine. He would then visit some friends and drink a little more wine. Then he would get in the wagon, tell Fred to go home, and sleep till they arrived home.

He was about the hardest worker but he took care of his horses. He kept all his fence rows clean with scythe, sickle, and ax. When he needed beef for the family, he would buy a skinny one cheap and fatten it up with all new meat for the family. He didn't speak a lot of English and signed with an "X," but he liked to listen to local news at noon at lunch time and loved the TV shows I mentioned earlier. Also, Wagon Train and Gunsmoke and Beverly Hillbillies.

Those were the good ole days. We would spend hours some Sundays walking in the woods or playing in the creeks. We would pick mushrooms, blackberries, hickory nuts, apples, and etcetera.

Tribute to Grandparents

by Mary L. Touville of Cambridge, Ohio

born 1939

Mary Louise McMurray, maiden name. Borned October 7, 1939. Cambridge, Ohio. Guernsey County. I was borned at my grandparents' home. Cora and Fred Raymond McMurray. My parents were Martha and Clyde McMurray. My brother, Raymond McMurray, was also borned in 1935 at my grandparents' home. He weighed only two pounds. Dr. Camp was the doctor at that time. He made house calls. My brother, being so small, was wrapped in a man's large handkerchief. My grandparents raised us. My granddad on my mother's side of the family was a coal miner.

My brother and I went to school in a one room school. It had grades one through twelve, with only one teacher. Most of the time it was a man teacher. I was able to start school when I was four years old. I had to wear long hair and pigtails. Long, heavy, white stockings and dresses. The thing I can remember best is the Thanksgiving and Christmas programs. That was always a play and food after the programs. At Christmas there was a gift exchange.

When I started the eighth grade, they had closed all the one room county schools and we had to go to Cambridge city schools. We lived 2 1/2 miles from Cambridge, so we had to ride the bus. We rode the bus to the other school also.

We always had to take baths in a tin wash tub until I was around fifteen or sixteen, then we got running water in a bathroom. I didn't have to use the outhouse no more also. We got our first TV when I was sixteen. Before that we would listen to radio on Saturday nights with my grandmother. Some of the programs were, "The Lone Ranger," "The Squeaking Door," "The Phantom," "Dick Tracy" and "Ozzie and Harriet." I know there were others, but I can't remember them.

When I was around five, my grandparents would

take us fishing on Sunday at Sence Lake. My granddad would let us set on the bridge and fish.

While growing up, my grandmother used to put me in the bedroom under the bed whenever I was bad. That was quite often.

My granddad was an auctioneer at the livestock farm about a half a mile from our house. I was allowed to go down on Tuesday, the day of the sale. It was lots of fun.

I can remember the holidays best. Because my grandma would bake for days. When the big day came, my grandparents both would cook a big meal together. I guess my favorite food would have to be homemade ice cream. We kids were allowed to turn the crank until the ice cream was done.

My grandparents had a large garden, and I would help when canning time came.

My grandmother had a treadle sewing machine, and she made all my brothers' and my clothes, until we were teenagers. She also taught me how to sew. She had a wringer washing machine which was in the basement. When I got old enough to help her, we hung the clothes outside on a clothesline in the summertime and in the wintertime, hung them in the basement.

We had three theaters in Cambridge. The Strand, the Liberty, and the State. When we growing up, my brother and I got to go to the theater on Saturdays. Then it cost only twenty-five cents to go in. Candy and pop cost five and ten cents. Strand is the one we went to, because it always had cowboy movies. I loved Roy Rogers and Gene Autry, Cisco kid, Hopalong Cassidy and Lash Larue.

We had a coal furnace and I learned how to fire it when my granddad wasn't home. In the summer, I mowed the yard with an old-fashioned hand pushed lawnmower.

On Saturdays my grandparents took us kids to town. After Grandma took us to the store, we went to the movies. Cambridge had quite a few stores. Here are a few of them. The Courthouse, Library, county sheriff and jail department, city police and jail, train depot, Vance Sporting Goods, Cambridge Iron and Metal, two hospitals, three shoe stores, post-office, Ford car sales, Studebaker car sales, bus station, Benwick Hotel, La Salle Hotel, beauty shops, *Jeffersonian* Newspaper, news stand, Davis Department Store, shoe repairs, Krogers, A&P grocery, five and ten cent store, Jean Frock's women's clothing, Fred Raymond's men's clothing, Central Pharmacy drugstore, Centerfield Gas Station, two hardwares, Coney Island restaurant, Spillman Drugstore, and office and restaurant supplies. Around fifteen bars on Wheeling Avenue and in combined. One named Sara and had a camel out front. I another one was called the Bloody Bucket.

My grandma told me, "If a all black cat crosses in front of you will have bad luck. If you break a mirror, you will have seven years of bad luck. Don't cross under a ladder or you will have bad luck." My grandma believed you could see ghost.

I was around eleven when we had the big snow and ice storm. We go out and help our granddad dig the driveway out and where we would get it down to the main road the snowplow would come through and plow it in again. With the ice on top of the snow, we were able to step off the front porch with our sleds and slide for about a quarter of a mile. We had other big snows, but that is the one I remember the most. The snow would usually start in October and would have it most of the time until March.

I don't know if my grandparents, Cora and Fred McMurray, go under memorable people heading or not. They had three sons. They raised two and one died. After they got married, my granddad took my grandma to live in the country out from Kimbolton. From Kimbolton they had to go by boat to their place. Later in years, my granddad came up to Cambridge and built them a house about 2 1/2 miles from Cambridge. They finished raising their two boys there, and then they raised me and my brother.

My grandma was a homemaker. My granddad, I called him "Pap," was a painter, wallpaper hanger, masonry work, operated a township grader, farmed his land, raised pigs, chickens, gardens, raised beal hound dogs. So that is why I think they are really great people. My granddad died first at eighty-seven, then my grandma died one year to the day my granddad did at seventy-eight. I loved them very much.

The Way to Shaytown

by Alyene Meacham of New Concord, Ohio
born in 1919

I was born in a place called Shaytown in Potter County, Pennsylvania. I don't know long we were there, as we didn't live there long. My mother did not have a doctor, my Aunt May, Dad's sister, was a midwife. I do know I was born with a veil over my face, and they had to take it off as I could have smothered. If they had saved this veil I would have been able to tell the future, at least that's what I was told. My mother told me I had lots of hair down to my ears; she said I had it cut three times before I was three years old.

The way to Shaytown was take Route 17 North Shinglehouse and go about 10 miles and you come to Shaytown Center where you turn at the school house and go up Wild Cat Road about one mile then turn off on a road, don't know as it had a name, but went a short distance and up a hill. The road was bad as the rain and snow had washed the dirt off and there was stones and big holes. Not to far was the house I was born in.

Sharon Center had one store that sold a lot of groceries. It had one gas pump in the front and the oil was kept in a cupboard out back. We got most of the groceries we needed there.

Some people from Oklahoma bought a big farm up the road. They needed someone to work the farm and my dad got the job. So we moved from Shaytown to farther up Wild Cat Road and we worked the farm. They had built a hay barn and three houses plus a corral. They had got wild horses from the west and they had a man who broke them in the corral. They had friends that came and rode them.

Alyene Meacham and daughter, Chery, while her husband was in the Phillipine Islands with the Army.

Our house was built on a raised place so in the winter, we got snow and ice and when we went out of the front door of, we walked across the top of a storage area to get to the [growed?]. In the storage area they kept the plows, hoes and [raeks?][racks?] to use on the farm.

We were right in the Snow Belt so had a lot of it. My dad had bought some paint to paint the walls in the basement. I was probably four or five, and I got into it. He wanted to know who got into the paint, but I said I didn't. He could tell I did as I had paint all over me, so he gave me a spanking. I thought it would hide me, but it wasn't too bad as he told me to never tell a lie again, so I always stop and think.

My dad had a few pigs, horses and chickens. We always planted a big garden, and my mother canned a lot of fruit. When we butchered, she always put meat down in a crock in the basement so we did not have to buy much in groceries. We had vegetables, meat, and my mother did a lot of baking. So we got along fine. My dad worked the farm for four years.

When I was six years of age, I started school down Plank Road in a one room schoolhouse. It was heated with a wood stove and this was also where we got our water. It had outhouses out [illegible], one for boys and one for girls. When you got to school, you went into the coat room. You went into the front which was a small room where you put your wood and dinner bucket. The pump was in this room.

In the winter, someone walked ahead of me so I could get through to get to school. It had only one teacher and she would call the class and the ones in the class left their seats and went down front to a long bench and had their class. When it was done and the teacher would say class dismissed, they would go back to their seats and she would call the next class.

One year at Christmastime they got me a big doll and my sister a smaller one. I took my doll outside and fell on the ice and broke it. My heart was broken, but had to live without it. The next year they bought us both rocking chairs and we loved them. Mine was brown with spindles in the back and under the arms. My sister's was blue. I loved that chair. Then someone too big sat in it and broke the back. It was fixed the best it could be.

I had a black and white cat that was really mine. When I'd take my nap, that cat was my pillow. It would meow until I woke up. I took it with me when I went to my aunt's house. She lived up Belle Run, but my cat went with me.

Deep Snow and a Mile from Home

by Thomas W. (Bill) Reed of Crooksville, Ohio
born 1933

I was born in a small community called Clay Bank, Ohio on April 13, 1933. I got off to a rough start because my mother's breast milk was no good. Luckily, a neighbor lady had a daughter on April 14 and she breast fed both me and her daughter everyday.

Clay Bank no longer exists, but was on old maps of Ohio. When I was six years old, I started to school in Dixie, which was south of Bristol. Later that year I was transferred to Fairview, on Marietta Road. Stanley Allen now lives in this school.

In January of 1943, my father and his brothers went to Detroit and got jobs in the steel mills there, as there was no work in Perry County. With the war going on there was work in the mills. My father came back in March for my mother and us four kids. I was nine years old.

While my father was away I once rode our pony in February, about five miles, to borrow a loaf of bread from my grandmother.

When my father came back and took us back to Detroit, we lived on 1489 Jay Street. This was the colored section of Detroit and we went to an all colored school. There was only five white kids in the whole school. I know all about discrimination, I was there.

Later, in either April or May, in 1943, my father landed a job running a 950 acre farm outside Chelsea, Michigan.

I ended up going to a one room school with only 17 kids, including my sister and two brothers. I was ten years old that summer and was working horses before summer was over.

When I was 11 years, a team of horses ran off with me on a mowing machine and I was almost killed. As a result, a large chunk of meat was cut out of my right knee, clear to the bone. This eventually healed over with scar tissue. I was laid up for weeks.

While living on this farm my father would trap muskrats in the winter. Once when I was with him, running his trap line, the ice gave way and he fell in the lake to his waist. He managed to get out and took off his hip boots and wrang out his socks and finished running his trap line on three different lakes. He made around $500.00 in two weeks in trapping season. This was good money in those days.

In March of 1946, my parents purchased a farm in Perry County, in Bearfield Township, about two miles north of Sayre. They bought it from two bachelor brothers named Harry and Burrel Younkin.

My father's tradition was to always butcher hogs on Thanksgiving. When we butchered on Thanksgiving of 1950, it was snowing and got bad. My dad and mother took our dump truck the next day, and went to New Lexington, to get the sausage ground. This left nine of us kids at home and I was the oldest at 17. It snowed so bad while they were gone, they could only get about a mile from the house. I knew if they couldn't get back, they would try to walk in. After dark, I would step outside and yell for them because I knew that they might get lost in the storm. At midnight, Dad hammered on the door, and I let them in. My mother passed out when the heat hit her. My dad was six foot, two inches tall, and by this time, the snow was up to his waist. He said he had to break a path for Mom and go back and get her as she wanted to rest and he knew she would freeze if they stopped.

We had a big team of Percheron horses, and after about two weeks we hitched them to our old iron wheeled wagon, and went to Street's store in Sayre and get flour, yeast, beans, and whatever else we had to have. The snow was so deep the wheels never turned on the wagon, the bed just drug on the snow, like a sled. Luckily, we had huge horses that could plow through the snow.

We would put a 50 gallon barrel on a sled and go to a pond and break the ice and haul water back to the barn for the other livestock. We were snowed in for about three weeks. Earl Jones, who had a coal mine nearby, brought in a dozer and opened up our road, as he had a powerhouse on our farm that supplied power to the mine. I wonder what this younger generation would do in an event like this.

We had to work all day taking care of the livestock. We had around 15 cows, three horses, about 30 hogs, and a bunch of chickens to feed and water.

When I was in high school I used to run about two miles to catch the high school bus at the old Sayre School. Kids on the bus said that there was ice frozen in my hair in the wintertime.

I have a lot of stories to tell, but will quit for now.

Dreamsville

by Dave Myers of Dover, Ohio
born 1937

Our little community of Maple Grove included a four room, eight grade school building. It is about two miles west of Uhrichsville, Ohio and is located about 150 yards from the panhandle route of the Pennsylvania Railroad. During WWII, we students often watched the trains loaded with equipment (trucks, tanks, jeeps, guns) and passenger trains with troops traveling eastward to embarking ports toward the Western War Theater.

About three miles east of our community was the Dennison Railroad Station. It had been named "Dreamsville" by military personnel, as members of the Salvation Army, Red Cross, various churches and civilian volunteers from surrounding communities met every train, day or night, winter or summer, rain or sunshine and handed out sandwiches, coffee and cookies to the troops. The canteen was in operation during WWI and again from 1940 to 1946 during WWII.

I was in the first or second grade. Our teacher, Mattie Creager and the third and fourth grade teacher, Phyllis McClelland, both volunteered at the canteen and asked us students to bring in playing cards, dominos and other small games which they would hand out to troops at Christmastime. It wasn't much, but we felt proud as we tried to bring a little Christmas cheer to the men traveling to war.

And Doctors Made House Calls!

By Dorothy L. Minger of New Matamoras, Ohio
Born 1925

My mom and dad met when they were teenagers. Dad was good at making sorghum molasses. My mom was helping to carry the cane stocks after they had ground the juice out of the stocks and the juice was poured into a pan over a slow burning fire. When the molasses was done, it was nice and thick, not like the runny kind you buy today. Dad and Mom started dating after one of these cook-offs. Their entertainment was to walk to someone's house on Saturday night, move the furniture and rug out of a room and a few people would play music and they would square dance the night away. Dad did the calling for the dances. In my life I only saw this happen one time at a neighbor's house. It was fun.

When I was a little girl we had snow from the last of November until the next March. It seemed to never stop as we had snow on the ground all winter. You could sled ride anytime. When I was around three-years-old, we lived in Sardis, Ohio. We lived at the foot of the hill from the old well in the middle of the four streets, down from Marv's Place. It was wintertime and my brother was sled riding down the hill. Coming real fast he lost control and flew in the air, came down on a large spike sticking out on the pole; ripped his side wide open and his intestines were coming out. They called for Dr. Little to come from Sistersville, West Virginia. He never gave him anything; sewed him back together and he got along fine. Now days you'd go to the hospital and end up with staph infection.

Teacher, Henry Kreig, inside the Mt. Zion school house in 1910.

We moved to Fly, on top of the hill on Route 800. We had a long hill behind our house. Our house was the old Mt. Zion schoolhouse where my mother had gone to school as a child in the early 1900's. My parents bought and remodeled it for our home in 1929.

I decided to go sled riding one day and thought I could do a belly smacker to get on the sled like my brothers did. Some how I missed most of the sled and the sled runner caught the side of my cheek and scratched a big question mark on my cheek. That stopped me from ever trying that again. A few years later my girlfriend and I decided to start at the top of Fly hill and ride down the highway clear to Route 7. It was a small sled so she sat up to steer with her feet and I hung on to her shoulders, standing up. We didn't get far when an automobile came up behind us and blew the horn. Over in a snowdrift we went, upside down. We got back on the sled and finally got to Route 7 at the bottom of Route 800. We got behind an automobile going back up the hill and held on to the bumper, slipping and sliding, we made it back to the top. The good Lord had to be with us for the things we did and still lived to tell the tale.

Our place was always the community-gathering place. My dad was a mechanic. He always was working on automobiles. There was no electricity out Route 800 in those days. My dad got a generator and batteries and made our electricity. We had lights outside at night and the kids loved to catch the beautiful moths that came to the lights. Dad charged the batteries up so we never were without lights.

I remember lots of little happenings in my lifetime. I remember the 1936 and 1937 floods as if it were yesterday. Also when the Ohio River froze over and you could walk across from Fly to Sistersville. I was in grade school at Fly at the time. Then there was the time a small airplane landed on the river on the West Virginia side. It was taking people for a ride. My brother and I ran all the way down the hill to Fly and crossed the ferryboat. I was waiting to get on the plane and found out I didn't have enough money so some dear, dear lady paid the rest of the money I needed to take a ride. I really enjoyed that ride; landing on the water was fun.

Speaking of the 1936 and 1937 floods, I stood at the first bend going up the hill on Route 800. Houses were floating down the river. All kinds of debris were in the water. The water was halfway up on the bank of the first section of Route 800; clear across to the West Virginia side. Sistersville, West Virginia was covered. The water was going fast and furious down the river with all kinds of drums of stuff being caught by some of the people brave enough to row their skiff out into the river. It was dangerous, but they didn't care. I hope we never have another flood like that as I live just 40-feet from the river's edge today. The 1913 flood was worse, but I didn't see that one, as I wasn't born yet. That one wiped the little town of Cochranville, Ohio right off the map. Cochranville was located half way between Fly and New Matamoras, Ohio. Route 800 was Route 8 in my day.

Then the state decided to put a road right through the middle of our house and we ended up having to move to a farm my dad bought which had nothing but a house, barn, granary, outside privy and water. To get water we had to turn a crank on the well outside; fill the bucket with water and then carry it into the house. There was no gas so we had to burn wood for heat, cook by wood fire and burn oil lamps. We had to carry the chamber pot to the privy house to empty. We didn't have a washer and had to wash on a washboard, rinse, wring and hang clothes out to dry. What a change now from the good old days.

Little by little things changed. Gas lines were run; so then we cooked, heated the house and had gas lights. Wind up phones that you could call and talk to your neighbors; course they all would listen in. Finally electricity came through and we had to have a TV, -a 13-inch black and white, that they could watch wrestling on Saturday night. Neighbors loved to drop by for a cookie and cup of coffee. Everything is different now. People don't take time to visit their neighbors; they all have TV or a computer at home. At nearly 84 years of age, I don't own a computer or a credit card nor do I want either one. I was raised that if you didn't have the cash, you didn't buy it.

When I was young, my mother made my dresses (we didn't wear slacks in those years.) She made them out of feed sacks or material she had gotten from the 5 & 10 in New Matamoras, Ohio. Some of the sacks were pretty. The white ones were used to make our bloomers. Scraps of material were used to make quilts. My mom was a real good seamstress. A few years later my mom sent away to Montgomery Wards and bought me a real pretty blue taffeta dress for 8th grade graduation. The day I was going to wear it, I decided it needed to be pressed. Knowing it all, I thought, I started to press it. I put the iron down on the dress and the whole piece of material shaped like the iron went up in smoke and left a hole in my dress. As luck would have it, my mom very calmly took the one set of ruffles off the sleeves, patched the hole and covered the patch with ruffles in time for me to catch the school bus and no one at school knew what I went through that morning.

Sometime in the 1930's several of us children went to a friend's house to play. We were playing "Run Sheep Run," which was the same as hide and seek. We played until dark. One of the girl's dads came to take us home when it turned dark outside. He drove a car that had running boards on each side of the car. We stood on the running board and held to the inside of the door. When he got to my home, he wasn't slowing down to let me off. Being a child, I was scared I would have to walk back home in the dark so I jumped off rolled down a bank and landed on a pile of stones. One of the stones cut a good size hole in the back of my head. They yelled "Are you ok?" and I said yes and walked across the road to the house. When I got in the door my mom asked what happened. I had blood dripping down both of my shoulders. I told her, so she told dad and he took me out to Trail Run to Yester' s filling station. He bought a bottle of Mercurochrome and poured the entire bottle in the back of my head. That's the only doctoring it had. It got better with no trouble. Somewhere about this same time frame, my friend and I went to round up the cows for milking. When we got them to the gate (the gate was bars you slid back to the side and dropped them to the ground to get out of the pasture) I decided to climb over the top. I caught my heel on the top bar and fell on a pile of rocks. Needless to say, I broke my wrist as the hand and wrist was twisted. My friend ran to the house and told my mom I had broken my arm. When they returned they couldn't find me: I hid. I finally gave up. That time dad had to take me to Dr. Mills to get it set. Dad got me in his Model A Ford and not wanting to take time from his work he swore at me all the way to town. I was a clumsy ox. This hurt me worse than my arm. I was always an accident looking for a place to happen.

Let me tell you about doctors in my day. You could call and the doctor came to your house or you could go to the office in New Matamoras, Ohio, wait you turn (which wasn't a very long wait) and you'd see the doctor, get a couple bags of pills or a shot in the arm and you'd be on your way all for $3.00. He always knew what was wrong and the pills helped, especially his kidney and bladder pills. If you had a cut he would stitch it up right in his office; a broken arm, he would set it, put on a splint and you went home.

Now days you wait a half a day in the emergency room at the hospital and better have good insurance or checkbook. They also had better make some kind of antibiotic for your ailment or you'll get an infection of some kind from just sitting there waiting.

We raised two or three large hogs every year for our main meat for winter. This meant we had to have a butchering day. Our family plus two or three men would come to help. We had to get up early so dad could get the fire started under the drum of water to get it hot enough to scald the hogs. They would shoot the hogs, cut their throat to let them bleed and then douse them (by spring poles) up and down in the hot water until all the bristles would scrape off their skin. They had to gut them, let them hang to cool and then cut the meat into sections. The heads were cleaned and put into a kettle over a fire to cook.

They made different kinds of things with this cooked meat. My brother had to stir this meat so it wouldn't stick. If any liver had been cooked with it he would eat it as soon as it was done. My mother's job was to wash, scrape, turn and scrape the small intestines until they were spotless, as this was the casing used to put the sausage in. I remember watching as mom would stuff sausage; rolling it in circles as it came out of the stuffer in to the casings. The stuffer was also the lard press. They put a lot of fat in a big kettle and melted out the lard, then put it through the press. The cracklings the lard came out of were really good. Of course we always had a big meal for all the workers using the fresh liver and some sausage if it was ready. Everyone took a package of some kind of meat home with them when they left.

My brother made our toy to play with every morning while waiting on the school bus. He took a board about three feet long, nailed a small board at the bottom of it cross ways and called it a hockey stick. We had tin cans so we played tin can hockey. The poor old tin can took a beating back and forth; no one ever won as the bus would come. He also made guns out of wood and cut rubber bands from old inner tubes to shoot with and we'd play war games.

When I was 13-years-old, my mom sent to Montgomery Wards and got me a $3.98 beginners guitar. I taught myself to play it. I would sit on the porch banister, play and sing every evening in the summer until I got pretty good. At 15 I moved to town to do housework and work at the 5 & 10-cent store. My cousin would come by on his bicycle with his guitar; I would hop on with my guitar and we'd go to a friend's house to practice our music. Can you imagine that sight, two people and two guitars on a bicycle going up the street? I continued this until I got married; that's when everything stopped. Life was never the same. My cousin continues to play yet today at 83 years of age.

I never graduated from high school. I attended two years of high school and I hated it. I'd rather have been scrubbing floors. I was scared of teachers and felt very inferior to others, as I was shy. I never seemed to be treated as good as other students in school.

My home-ec teacher would have me help others (as I was taught to cook, sew, etc. at home) and they made the A's and B's and I'd get C's and D's. This really made an impression on me, so I quit school and moved to West Virginia to my aunt's for a week or two- then came home and hid till school was out in the spring. When I turned sixteen it didn't matter as you could get a working permit. I have never felt sorry about quitting, I was just going to be a housewife and mother someday anyway (which I did it all). Today you must finish high school. You can't get a job without a diploma.

I had an aunt living on Leith Run Road for years. I used to go visit her for a few days at a time. You had to walk over a swinging bridge to get to her house. I never saw a snakier place in my life. Everything you would pick up would have snakes under it. One bit my aunt when she stepped off her back porch and she was ill for months.

There was a nice water hole that you could swim in down the stream from the house. I couldn't swim, but I enjoyed wading in the water while I watched the others swim. Up on the hill there was a real nice long grape vine swing that you could swing out on and drop into a pile of leaves. I thought I could do that, so I got hold of the vine; was swinging way out, when my grip was not enough to hold me up and it raked the inside of my hands until they bled, slipping the full length of the vine, but I never let go. I should have known better as I never could hold up my weight enough to play chin-ups. My brothers tried to make a tomboy out of me, but it never happened.

My great aunt Lucy was married young. She was only married a short time when her young husband passed away. She never married again and decided to walk from one relative's house to another relative's house every month: their home was her home. As she got older she got somewhat senile. She would clean out cabinets and arrange them the way she wanted them. She put chairs where she thought they looked best or if the cook stove was on she would adjust the flames to the height she thought they ought to be. When she came to our house, my older brothers would go right behind her and put everything back the way it was. This would go on and on and she never caught on.

One time Aunt Lucy and I walked down Route 800 to the Mehrley Cemetery to put flowers on some of our relative's graves. There was a pasture field all around the fenced in graveyard. While we were there, a big old bull came up and wouldn't let us come back out. He was snorting and pawing the ground, really angry. We were scared and tried to hide behind some of the larger stones. We took a big chance while he was on one side and took off running down through the brush to get to the highway. We finally made it and didn't get hurt. The bull was probably happy we were gone.

My mom told me of the tornado that came through in 1912 and moved the Gravel Hill Baptist Church two-inches off its foundation while church was going on at the time. The church is located a short distance up Route 800 in Fly, Ohio. Mom was 10 years old at the time this happened.

Reaping What You Sow

by Bert Wood of Crossville, Ohio
born 1929

My banking career began at First National Bank in 1952 and lasted until 1975. This was a period of time when banking was considered an honorable profession. When I was a fairly new teller, in the summer of 1952, we had a customer named Happy Powelson, who owned and operated a carnival show that traveled the state during the summers. Each week he would bring in a large bag of money, neatly wrapped and banded. Usually there was several hundred dollars in the bag—mostly ones. The older tellers disliked waiting on Happy partly because of the amount of work and time involved and partly because of his less than attractive appearance. They made him wait while they counted each dollar—sometimes for an hour or more—and always found he had counted his deposit correctly.

The teller line was set up with the most experienced tellers on the front windows and the newer tellers along the side. One day, from my position along the side, I noticed Happy standing in line at a front window. Since I didn't have a customer and hadn't been a teller long enough to become very sophisticated, I asked Happy if I could wait on him. When he set his money bag on the counter, I said, "Happy, I know you're a busy man and an honorable person, so I'll make a deal with you. I'll enter your deposit in your book and set the bag of money under my counter until I can count it. If there's any difference, you'll have to bring it in this afternoon." He said, "You've got a deal." I entered his deposit and he went about his business. Before I could straighten up from putting the bag of money under my counter, here came the short bald-headed vice president and a large woman to back him up. They bombarded me with questions "What did you do? Why didn't you count his deposit?" I explained my deal with Happy, but they were not pleased and warned me that if the deposit was short, it would be coming out of my pay. I asked the lady teller, who had been counting Happy's deposits for years, if he had ever been short? She replied, "Well, no, but that didn't make any difference. He's not to leave your window until the deposit was counted." Until Happy sold the carnival two or three years later, we kept our deal and never had a problem. Although I only saw him occasionally after that, he always made a point to seek me out and speak.

Fast forward a few years when I'm now a junior officer at the bank. One Friday morning, the vault door would not open because another junior officer, who will remain nameless, had set the timers for an extra twelve hours and the vault door would not open until seven o'clock on Friday evening. Friday was payday for GE, Clows, Pretty Products and several other factories. At 9:00 A.M. there would be lines out the front door with people wanting to cash a paycheck—and we had no money! The next few minutes were filled with finger-pointing, pacing and hand wringing. My suggestion to contact the head teller at Coshocton National Bank to borrow money from them, met with objections because CNB would give us the money, but would also call the newspaper (which they did). Finally, that was the only solution on such short notice. CNB agreed to loan us the cash bills, but were short on change and could not spare any coins. Now what to do? Then I remembered, in my many conversations with Happy, he had mentioned that he was a coin collector and that was why his deposits had only been currency. Even though he only had one eye, he spent hours going through bags of coins, looking for rare and unusual finds. When I mentioned that we could see if Happy would loan us coins, management bulked because they were concerned that Happy would remember the long waits in the teller line. I persisted and explained that Happy was my friend and the powers in charge relented and said I could call him. Fortunately, Happy was home. I explained our problem and said we needed five hundred dollars each in halves, quarters and dimes and two hundred dollars each in nickels and pennies. He said, "I'll be right down." Fifteen minutes later, there was a knock on the back door. We opened the door and there was Happy with the trunk lid up on his car. He started handing us bags of coins. Since he wanted to be repaid in coins, I explained, "Happy, there is one problem. I can't repay you until next Tuesday or Wednesday when we get our shipment of coins from Federal Reserve." He replied, "You trusted me, I trust you". We opened on time and the only people who knew of our problem were those who read the daily newspaper. P S. I'm not sure if Happy ever told me his given name, but if he did I've forgotten it.

Mom's Curtains in the Mud Puddle

by Donna Estep of Zanesville, Ohio
born in 1957

My name is Donna Estep. My maiden name is Donna Lynn. I am 51 years old. I went to Monroe Street School and Handcock.

Life back then was way different. We didn't have to lock our doors, and everyone watched out for each other's kids.

I remember when I was eight, me and my cousin wanted to go in the alley to play in this big mud puddle, so I took my mom's plastic curtains down and made us both a two piece suite. We was having so much fun till Mom figured out they were her curtains.

I always looked forward to our Sunday dinners. There always was chicken, mashed potatoes, homemade noodles, and corn. Then afterwards we would go dump picking. I always looked forward to our fireworks. They are on my birthday. I was born on July 4, 1957, and we would always play kickball or baseball in the street. The whole block would play.

The kids we mostly was around was Howard Street, Zane Street, Elm, and Monroe, Hall Avenue. These kids' names were Richard Kinder, Jack Kinder, Sally Kinder. There was Gary Gill, then my first love, Bingie Warden, then there was Linda, PJ Worden, there was Shirley, Deloris, Elkie Smith, the Tiltens and Alexander kids and the McWhorter kids and Davises. These were all like family, and we all took care of each other. We all were like one. Lots of love.

Remembering the Preamble

By Ruby Masterson of Malta, Ohio
born 1912

I remember many things that happened when I was growing up. I will be ninety-seven years old May 28, 2009. I was born in 1912. When people ask me how old I am, I tell them I was born the year the Titanic went down. It sank in April, 1912.

When I was about six years old my father's work was driving a horse drawn hearse for Mr. Hearing, the undertaker of Portersville, Ohio. The year was about 1916 or 1918. One story my father told me, when they drove the horse-drawn hearse to San Toy to get a body, there were several small children in a bed peeping through holes in the comfort at them. San Toy was a coal mining town with a population of two thousand. My father told me many stories, but I remember that one.

Deasy Earles with the horse he drove when he worked at Tiee Plant.

There was a lot of flu cases at that time. My mother, Alice Kirkbride Earles, told me she thought we escaped the flu, for we had eaten a lot of onions that winter.

Later on when I was about ten years old, my father, D.E. Earles, did some farming. He was plowing corn with a one-horse plow. I was riding the horse to guide it. We were under this apple tree. The limbs from the tree drug me off. I grabbed a limb from the tree and held on to it till he came and got me down. I have always remembered that incident of long ago.

I graduated from New Lexington, Ohio High School. I played on the girls' basketball team. I was picked by the coach to play forward on the team from fifty girls who tried out for the team. That made me happy.

My father bought a Victrola for us girls. We kept it playing; often one had to wind it. It had a handle on the side of it. We didn't have a radio, so that's all the music we had. I still have that Victrola and records. It's fun to hear some of those songs again.

Growing up we owned one of those old pump organs. I played it some. I always liked music. Later on in my life I taught myself to play the piano by ear. I play hymns at church often when the regular pianist is absent. Some hymns I play are "Higher Ground," "Just a Closer Walk with Thee," "Because He Lives," "Railway to Heaven," at the Methodist Church at Portersville, Ohio.

I drive my 1968 Ford Mustang sometimes when the weather is nice. I go with others when the weather is cold and bad. I have my driver's license, but I don't drive at night.

When I got married and later on had a baby girl, when I was holding her one day our little dog "Boots" was barking and carrying on. So I put the baby down and looked out the kitchen window and down on the ground below the window was a large copperhead snake. I run to the garage and got a pitchfork. I raised the window and put the pitchfork down through the copperhead snake and killed it. It was a terrifying experience for me I never forgot.

My grandfather, Absolum Kirkbride, a carpenter, made each of his four daughters a set of quilting frames. My mother, Alice Kirkbride Earles, left me her set. Since I don't quilt I gave my set to the McConnelsville Historical Society. The set is over one hundred years old. They are set up with quilts on them for people to see.

My grandfather, when a small boy with his parents, brothers and sisters, went to Kansas in their ox-drawn covered wagon. It was homesteading time. They took the cows along with them to have milk. My great grandfather at night slept under the covered wagon. He had a gun for protection. They stayed there three years.

When I lived at Pennsville, Ohio we kids and others that lived in Penn Township always looked forward to the "Embree Picnic" that was held every year in August. The Embree Picnic was held because of a Mr. Embree that lived in Pennsville, Ohio when he was young. He became a wealthy man in the lumber business. He didn't forget the people he knew when he was young. The Embree Park was made possible by him. He left a money fund for the park's upkeep and also the Embree Picnic held each year in August for people living in Penn Township. They have free ice cream, Crackerjack and lemonade. I attended the Embree Picnic last year, 2008. I didn't see only one girl around my age. Most of the ones I knew long ago are gone now.

When me and my two sisters would go out on dates together, we three girls would sing lots of songs. Our dates enjoyed our singing. One song we always sang a lot was "Carolina Moon," and many other songs that was popular at that time.

When I was in school, our class was told to learn the "Preamble to the Constitution." It seems the teacher always had me to recite things first. I didn't always get them done, but when we were to learn it, I had learned it perfect. He asked ones that knew it to raise their hand. I wanted to say it for I had learned it. So I didn't raise my hand. I made him think I didn't know it. The first thing he said my name, Ruby, I just rattled it off perfect. I surprised him. He didn't know what to say, but he finally said, "Very good."

I can still say the "Preamble to the Constitution." I never forgot it. Word for word.

We were to learn and say the Presidents from George Washington to Abraham Lincoln. I can still say those.

I never forgot them.

When we children were young, I was six years old, we would go and visit my Grandpa and Grandma Kirkbrides. We would travel in a surrey hitched with two horses. We went down through the country. We had to go down a steep hill. When it was rather cold, there was ice on this hill. My father had Mother and all of us get out of the surrey and walk down the road. My father would hold the reins of the horses tight so they wouldn't slip. This road was shady, so the sun didn't get to it to melt the ice. When we returned home, the ice on this hill had melted, so it wasn't any problem. I've always remembered these trips we made.

Picky Chick's Mansion

by Janet Myers of Murrieta, California
born in 1934

My middle name is Yvonne. Eleven days after I was born, the Dionne Quintuplets were born. One was named Yvonne. I always thought it was very clever of my mother to know that event would happen and name me after one of them.

I always felt a certain kinship with them. There were books published about them with many pictures and they were in the newsreels at the movies regularly. So I grew up with them. I even looked like them with very dark hair and eyebrows and, of course, every little girl at that time had her hair fixed like Shirley Temple. But they always seemed to be having more fun than I was, what with all their toys that I lusted over. Of course we were later to learn that they were taken from their parents, dreadfully exploited and raised as though they were a property and not children. For instance, nurses could spank but not hug and kiss. If I had been raised that way, what a difference my memories would have been. Here are some of my favorite:

Waking up on a winter morning and finding it had snowed during the night, transforming the street outside my window into a muffled fairyland with everything all clean and sparkling.

Wading in rain swollen street gutters after a shower and floating boats made of leaves or match boxes.

In the summertime on a hot day, crawling with a book under a bush where it was cool and looking out through the leafy overhang, or climbing into a tree and seeing everything from a different perspective.

Raking and jumping into big piles of leaves and, oh, the smell of them when they were burned in the street.

Sitting on the front porch shelling peas or snapping beans with Mom and enjoying all the wonderful aromas when she did her canning.

Catching lightning bugs and putting them in Mason jars and the odd smell when I would accidentally squash one and the phosphorescence they left on my hands.

The surprise and total joy when my parents bought an entire used set of Nancy Drew books for me when I was about ten.

Learning to knit from the two maiden ladies down the block who ran a boarding house.

Eating the best popcorn of my life when my dad bought me a sack from a street vendor at the courthouse square. His name was "Fats" and he had a sign on his cart that read, "We occupy the entire first floor."

The bliss of buying new school supplies every September—those wonderful fresh new yellow pads and the delicious smell of newly sharpened pencils.

We left the house in the morning and showed up for meals after playing all day outside. Hide and Seek, Mother May I, Tappy on the Ice Box, Red Light-Green Light, jump rope and we had jacks tournaments. We roller skated from morning 'til night. They were the clamp on style of skates and of course, our most treasured possession was the skate key which we wore on a string around our necks. There were favorite places to skate where the cement was smooth and slick with no tree roots growing through and tripping us up. One of those favorite places was the driveway of a Mister Green. His wife was always shooing us away saying, "Mr. Green is very tired and must get some sleep." We obeyed, of course, and wondered just who this Mr. Green was, taking naps in the middle of the day and needing so much sleep. I later learned that Mr. Green was the leader of the CIO labor group before it merged with the AF of L and he worked in Washington, DC. On the rare occasions he was able to come home and get some rest, he always seemed to have kids roller skating in his driveway.

I got a fifteen cent allowance each week when I was old enough to go to the movies with my friends. It got me into the Saturday matinee and an ice cream cone afterwards. Roy Rogers was the matinee idol of choice and I always played him when we played cowboys and Indians. I always made my eyes squinty, trying to look like him and it was really difficult playing that way. But…authentic.

My dad managed a grocery store in the '30s and '40s and I remember during the war the "banana lines" and "cigarette lines" when those hard-to-come-by items were available. Those were the days when the customer was waited on by clerks. When my brother was old enough he became a clerk whether he wanted to or not. I envied him so because I thought it would be great to have that job. Much later I found out that he envied me, too young to work there. He said he had so much trouble when a customer would tell him she wanted a can of peas, a can of peaches, a pound of coffee and a box of Oxydol. He would gather one or two of the items and not remember what the rest were. Then, he said, he got smart. He wrote down all the things the customer needed, would go get them, turn around and not remember which lady he was waiting on.

I finally got to "work" there when I was ten. At Easter time the store sold dyed baby chicks. My job was to fish out the color chick the customer wanted. What fun, sinking my hand into that warm, cheeping, fluffy mass and coming up with the right one.

One year my neighbor, Susan, and I decided to pool our funds and buy one baby chick. We got a purple one and we named it Picky Chick. We made Picky Chick a house out of shoe boxes, from which we cut ends or sides and reassembled to make him a mansion of three rooms. One room had his food and water in jar lids and a kitchen sink from a doll house. Another room had a soft bed, curtains at the window, rugs on the floor and was his bedroom. The third room had shredded newspaper and a dollhouse bathtub and was his loo. We were dismayed that Picky Chick wasn't too picky about where he left his little dollops that were supposed to go in the loo.

He found the kitchen though. He grew to chicken size, losing his purple fluff and growing pretty white feathers, a comb and a crow. At the beginning, Susan and I traded off keeping Picky at our houses every other day. Toward the end Susan's parents got very generous and let me keep him all the time.

When he grew into a nice big bird that wasn't so nice anymore, my parents suggested that he go live with his cousins at a farm. So while I was at school one day, Picky went to the country. I don't even want to think about the coincidence of our having fried chicken that night.

Home Comfort and Thunder Buckets

by Mary M. Smeltzer of McKinney, Texas
born in 1936

I was born on a farm in Muskingum County Ohio in 1936. My dad worked for several different coal mines around the area. My mom was a housewife and worked out in the fields as well as doing all kinds of farm chores. She had two large vegetable gardens where she grew all kinds of veggies to can in glass jars. There were no conveniences like there are today. Life was hard work from sunup to sundown.

Mary Smeltzer's mom, Ann Moidja; stepsister, Martha Moidja and cousin from Cleveland in the 1930s.

Mom cooked and baked on a coal stove (Home Comfort was the name of the stove). It had a reservoir on the side of the stove to heat water for washing dishes and bathing, etc. Also, she would heat the "sad iron" to iron clothes with.

We would bathe in a number three galvanized tin tub that you sat in with your knees almost to your chin, but hey, it got you clean!

Bathrooms, what was that? Well, it was a small building away from your house where you went to do your "business." Others had two holes cut out on a wooden seat. Some had three holes various sizes. Then there was the chamber pot. These were used in the house in case it was too cold to go out or if you needed to go at night. Some were called "thunder buckets," but ours had a fancy name. It was called "Peggy." I don't know why, but that's what we called it. There was always a Sears and Roebuck Catalog or a newspaper that was used for wiping purposes. I know, not very pleasant, huh? Mom would even wallpaper the inside of our outhouse to make it pretty and some paint to brighten it up. Then there were the wasps and spiders we had to be on the lookout for.

We had no telephone service or TV, but we did have a battery powered radio that ran on a six volt car battery. When the battery was dead, Dad would take it 12 miles into town and have it charged. This radio was used mostly to listen to the world news to see what was happening. World War II was going on at this time.

We had an "ice box." That's why a lot of older folks calls the refrigerator an "ice box." It was a wooden cabinet that held a large block of ice that you had to go to the nearest town for. We would put a large tub in the car so when the ice melted during the summer, it wouldn't make a mess in the car. Remember, there was no AC in our cars back then either.

Y'all are probably wondering why no electricity. Well, there was an elderly widow up the road from us who would not let the electric company put any poles on her property, so she kept six families from getting electricity. But after she passed away, her son gave the company permission to put in the electric poles. That was 1945, and the first thing my dad did was go into town and buy a "Crosley Shelvadore" refrigerator. But what was funny, he thought it was an automatic ice maker. He waited and waited for it to make ice cubes. He didn't know you had to put water into the metal ice cube trays.

No running water, so water had to be carried. We had a cistern. A cistern is an artificial reservoir for storing rainwater.

Mom's washing machine was a gasoline powered Maytag wringer. You started the washer like you would start a motorcycle. Mom had two rinse tubs to rinse the clothes. The wringers had two hard rubber rollers to press out the excess water. I had my hand get caught on those rollers while Mom was hanging clothes on the clothesline. She heard me screaming and ran to released the wringer. No broken bones. Just bruised and I was sore for a few days. I was five at the time.

We would butcher a hog in late fall. We would smoke some cuts of meats in the smokehouse, make homemade sausage and can some. Later on we would take our hog into town where they would slaughter the hog and cut up the meats however we wanted, wrapped in freezer paper, and you would rent a freezer from them and whenever you came to town, you would stop and pick up several packages of frozen meats.

We raised our own crops for the farm animals, but Dad also bought feed for the pigs, and these feeds would come in pretty printed feed sacks, which then could be used to make all kinds of clothing, bed sheets, curtains, and etc.

I still own my mom's corn husking peg to shuck corn with. This peg fitted over your hand with a leather and a sharp pointed peg used to tear open the corn from the shucks. The cut corn was cut with a corn knife and put into shocks. A shock is a pile of corn stalks set up in the fields with the butt ends down. It would look like a bunch of Indian teepees in the corn fields.

My dad used a team of horses for a long time to do the farming till the tractors came out and could do the job faster and easier.

We had our own milk cows. Mom made cottage cheese and we churned our own butter and had fresh eggs. Raised our own chickens by hatching baby chicks from eggs.

Our toys were pretend kind or homemade wooden clothespins, not the spring type. Could be a wooden doll or Lincoln Logs. After a storm, I would get a twig and pretend it was my boat and put in the ditch along the country road and just see how far my little boat would go. We did get a store-bought sled using a roofing tin. Was too dangerous, Mom said. We would go to the woods and find a good sized grapevine and swing on those. Now that was fun until they would break.

My favorite place to go as I grew older was the covered bridge where my great grandma lived. It was so peaceful down there. You could hear the birds chirping, water running over the rocks making gurgling sounds in the water. That covered bridge still stands today. A lot of carved initials were also carved inside of those huge hewn logs. I have several pictures of it taken at different years. It still has special memories for me.

We were poor growing up, but we never had to ask for any kind of assistance, never had anything repossessed, and that says a lot about my hard working parents. My hard life growing up made me a better and stronger person, and I can deal with less now, and especially in these times, when people are losing homes and jobs. I can survive, cause I learned way back then how to do without. So I'm content with my life in my old age. This is my story, and it's true.

First in Bath Water and Wonderful Warm Bricks

by Kathryn Weber of Strasburg, Ohio
born 1915

Butchering day was a special day in the life of a farmer. To prepare for it, we made sure we had plenty of wood to heat the water in iron kettles to scald the hogs. The kettles were hung on a pole that was held by two posts ten feet or more apart. A platform on blocks was beside or near the one post. A barrel had one end dug into the ground and the other end tilted onto the platform.

Now that everything is ready, the hogs are shot. A hog hook is placed into the mouth of the dead hog and the hog is put on the platform. His hind end is put into the barrel which has been filled with hot water. You work him back and forth endways until the hair of the hog is loose. When the hair is loose on the hind end, turn the hog around so his head is in the water until the hair is loose. Then the hog is placed on the platform and scraped with a hog scraper until all the hair is removed.

The hog is then put on a hog hanger on the ground close by. The head is cut off, his body cut so the insides can be taken apart. The head is put on the workbench in a shop or building and the ears are cut off, the brains cut out.

The head meat is cooked in a clean kettle. The heart, tongue, jaws, liver, tail, kidneys, are cleaned and then cooked together. The sides are cut up for hams and shoulders. The sausage is made by using the parts cut off from the shoulders and ham. The casing for the sausage is from the intestines. The lard is made from the fat from the sides of the hog. It is a lot of work but everyone works together.

* * * *

We took a bath once a week. It happened on Saturday evening before we went to bed. The wash tub was brought up from the cellar and set in front of the coal stove. The water heated on the stove was poured into the wash tub. In a large family, the smallest child was washed first and the father and mother washed last. I was an only child so I always had nice warm, clean water.

After taking a bath, I usually went to bed. On cold nights, my mother always put a brick warmed on top of the coal stove and then wrapped in newspaper and then wrapped in a cloth before putting the brick into the bed. Oh how good it felt, and it usually stayed warm until morning.

* * * *

I liked to help my mother make soap. We saved the grease when we fried bacon and then used that to make soap. If the grease wasn't white, we heated it and then put it through cheesecloth before making the soap. We used enamel containers in which to pour the heated grease.

The grease had to be not hot and not cold, but just warm. Then we were careful in putting the lye into the grease and used a wooden stick to stir it. It was fun to watch the lard get hard. We cut it into blocks and then took it out of the container. When my mother was young she even made her own lye from wood ashes.

* * * *

I walked to a farm outside of our little town every evening and brought home a quart of milk when I was only five years old. The milk was put into a bucket of water and kept in the basement. We had no icebox ever and I didn't think we needed a refrigerator at the time. We did buy one.

Our first washing machine was oval and made of wood. It had a wringer. The washer rotated up and down. We had two rinse tubs made of enamel. I liked washing with it because I could put the clean clothes in first and put as many washer loads in as I wished using the same water.

The first Christmas I remember was when we had wax candles on the tree. They were only lit when we were in the room where the tree was because the tree might catch on fire. Mother would burn some of the branches on top of the coal stove and the scent was wonderful. I never saw the tree until Christmas morning and I wondered why my dad and mother were not anxious to go downstairs to see if Santa had come. They had stayed up after I went to bed to decorate the tree.

I usually had two presents and was thrilled to get that many. The church usually gave us a sack of candy on the Sunday nearest Christmas. That was something to look forward to. One Christmas I really remember was the Christmas I got a beautiful doll sitting in a rocking chair.

This happened when I was in the first grade. My mother had gone to her sister's farm to help with the butchering. She told me when school was out that I should go to Darrel Richard's house. I played with Darrel all the time and Mrs. Richards would look after me till my mother got home. I did just that.

However, Darrel and I walked to the edge of town and I decided that I would go from there to meet my mother at my aunt's farm. Darrel wouldn't go any further with me so I thought, "O.K. I'll go on by myself."

It was the month of March and the roads were muddy and it was windy. When I got as far as the cemetery I thought, "I didn't realize that the farm was so far away."

I was carrying an umbrella. When I finally arrived at the farm; my umbrella was turned up and my shoes were all muddy. I thought, "They sure will be glad to see me."

Instead, I was met with dismay. My mother went home without me and I was left to stay over night to be sent home the next morning in the farm wagon. I'll never forget that adventure.

Mrs. Richards was so worried about me that she also walked to the farm and came home with my mother.

The Year I Got the Mumps

By Samuel D. Besket of Senecaville, Ohio
Born 1944

Mumps ran wild in school when I was in the 6th grade. When one kid got sick, he passed it around to everyone in the school. I missed two weeks of school, so my older brother brought my lessons home for me. After supper Dad would help me with my lessons.

Mr. Lenoard, my teacher, devoted his life to teaching and all school activities. Mr. Lenoard was a friend of my father. During their younger days they had a men's club that met in the local pool hall. Mr. Lenoard was president and my father was secretary. I don't know what they did, but my mother told me they just sit around a stove and see who can tell the biggest lies. He knew my father quite well.

After I returned to school, I had a lot of catching up to do. Mr. Lenoard gave me extra assignments to help me along. One day, along with my homework, he gave me a note for my father, Sam Senior. Holy cow, nothing good could come out of taking a note home to your parents. I imagined being chained to the kitchen table doing my homework.

When I got home I gave it to Mom since Dad was still at work. To get on Dad's good side, I mowed the lawn and pulled all the nails out of his workbench that I had pounded in.

Dad finally got home from work and after supper Mom gave him the note. I guess she didn't want to upset him before his meal. My father was a very quiet man; seldom did I see him upset. When he did get upset, it was time to clear out.

While he was reading the note, I envisioned all kinds of punishment I would get. Things like cleaning the bricks in the sidewalk, or cleaning the outside toilet, the mother of all cleaning jobs. Dad read the note and just set there and stared holes in the wall. The longer he stared the madder he got. I thought it was best to be quiet, do my homework, and be on my best behavior. As the evening wore on, Dad got back to his old self and nothing was said about the note.

I brushed my teeth, said my prayers and went to bed without being told. The next morning as I was eating my breakfast my Mom let me read the note, which said. "Sam, if you wish Sammy to advance to the 7th grade, please don't help him with his homework. And you might want to consider coming back to the 6th grade." I guess Mr. Lenoard recognized my father's handwriting. Nothing more was said about the note.

Today I am the owner of Dad's workbench. Every time I see the nail holes in it I'm reminded of the note.

The New Years Whistle at the Congo Mine

By Mary Jane Lahmon of Sunbury, Ohio
Born 1941

Our home (with approximately 80 acres) was on the hill directly opposite the hill where the elementary school was located. Our parents were Charles Szakas (1915-1978) born in Congo and Julia Olah Szakas (1917-1984) born near Shawnee. There were six children: Charles Jerald "Jerry" (1939-1999), Mary Jane "Janie" Szakas Lahmon (1941-) now living in Sunbury, Ohio, Robert Eugene (1942-) now living in Moxahala, Ohio, Joseph Delmer (1944-) now living in Aredale, Iowa, John Frances (1946-) now living in Seattle, Washington and Julia Darlene Szakas Decoursey (1948-) now living in Logan, Ohio.

Our grandmother, Mary Szakas, also lived on the hill directly above the slope/entrance to the coal mine. Our home and our grandmother's were demolished at the time a coal company came to strip the valley. To avoid maintaining an access road to the homes, the coal company purchased them and Dad, Mom and Grandmother moved to Drakes.

We also had the coal mine, company store, church, school and a host of residents we considered friends and mentors.

Dad began work at the Congo Mine as a teenager; working in the stables (horses were still in use at the mine). He ended his work there as a night watchman when the mine closed in 1954. A few years after the mine's closing, the old Congo Tipple, which stood so tall in the hollow, burned to the ground. Sparks and flames from the burn ignited on our hill in front of our house, keeping us very busy extinguishing them in the grass as they landed.

Of course to us, Dad's most important job at the mine was when on every New Year's Eve, at 12:00 midnight, he "blew the whistle" to toll in the new year. At any other time, this whistle was used only as an emergency siren alerting the entire town that a disaster had occurred in the mine.

In addition to stocking some grocery items (comparable to a modern-day "convenience store"), the Congo Company Store building also housed the Congo Post Office and the administrative office for the coal mine. The miner's paychecks/vouchers, hourly reports, etc. were handled out of this office.

My memory brings me to three ladies who worked in the store: Joan Jenkins was in the post office and provided service in the store as well, Lou Brown clerked in the store and a Jacqueline, whose last name I can't recall, was the bookkeeper.

I do recall the many mornings when six little Szakas (probably close to the next payday before the big grocery shopping trip to New Lexington or Zanesville) would stop at the company store early in the morning on our way to school, and the ladies would put lunchmeat sandwiches, an apple, orange or banana (our choice) and cookies or a cupcake in a brown bag for each school lunch that day. The lunches were charged to Dad's company store account and, of course, deducted from his pay. We left the store not only with a good lunch for the day, but also with great encouragement and memories of how nice those ladies were to us.

There were also trips to the company store to pick up those things you quickly run out of with a large family: a loaf of bread, milk, etc. And for it to be your turn to walk down our hill, across the mine hollow and up the other hill to the company store was a real treat. For whoever's turn it was, in addition to getting the needed item, was also able to get a special treat for making the trip: an ice cream bar, candy bar, chips, gum or soda (your choice).

Little did I realize at the time, but Jackie, the bookkeeper, was my true inspiration. She was so pretty, dressed so well; I remember telling my parents that when I grew up I wanted an "office job" like Jackie's where I could dress pretty and not have to contend with the dust and dirt inherent with the jobs at the mine. I guess my dream was realized as I retired in 2003 with 41 years of service as office manager and executive assistant to the CEO of the Nationwide Insurance Companies, one of the largest insurance companies in the U.S.A, based in Columbus, Ohio.

As I am involved in my church today, I often reflect on my early religious participation and development. Indeed, the very basis for the on-going faith and beliefs I now have began in the little church in Congo. It was there that I was baptized in 1959. At the time, the services were under the direction of members of the Mennonite faith. The pastor, I remember, was David Helmuth, who married a local girl, Naomi Ketchum. They lived in the house on the curve across from the Kopcho house and next door to the Richard's home. Weekly choir practices were held in that home as well as other fun events for the children of the church.

During my annual involvement today in our church's summer Bible School, I reminisce about the Bible School my brothers, sister and I attended at the Congo Church. In addition to the daily instruction, there was nothing any more fun than the volleyball games that took place on the lawn outside the church on a daily basis. The close of Bible School family picnic was also fun and sometimes found all of us on a picnic-swimming venture at Lake Isabel near Fultonham.

An early photo of Congo Mine. Mary Szakas' (grandmother) house on left hill; Charles Szakas' home is on the hill right above the mine.

We walked (a two-mile-a-day round trip) to the Congo School. The school basically was a two-room schoolhouse with a gym, two outhouses (one for boys and one for girls) and a playground, which consisted of only one big sliding board.

Grades one through four were in one room and the teacher was Beulah Craig. Grades five through eight were in the other room and they were taught by Nina Davis Kaylo, who was also the principal. She also had taught our dad years before us. There is no comparison of today's expectations of requirements for a good education to how we were educated in that little schoolhouse on the hill. Frugality certainly reigned and the budgets were very low (and maybe nonexistent).

Each room had a coal stove that was fueled by the respective teachers. We did have a janitor who, after school hours, would fill the coal buckets for the next day's classes. Water was pumped into a pail and placed in each room. Each student was required to bring their own glass from home; and when they needed a drink, they filled their glass using a dipper from the pail of water. Of course, all lunches were brown-bagged.

Also, when nature called the teachers distributed the requisite toilet paper from a roll to the students. Paper was never left in the outhouses to avoid the possibility of waste and misuse.

If you were fortunate, on Friday afternoons, you might be selected to dust the erasers from the blackboards on a log outside the coal shed. Another reward was to be chosen to ring the big bell for recess, lunch and dismissal. Another treat was when there was an extra nickel, dime or quarter brought from home that allowed you to go down the long steep steps to Stenson's bar at lunch or recess time to purchase a soda, candy bar or chips.

In addition to absorbing the wealth of knowledge that came during class time, there are fond memories of the joy of a good baseball game, playing "Red Rover" in the field, basketball in the gym and the plays and graduation programs held in the gym converted to an auditorium for the special events.

Names of residents I recall during my years in Congo (1940's and 1950's) are: Jones, Baird, Benedict, Bobanich, Parks, Murray, Richards, Wesney, Kopcho, Raskey, Toki, Toth, Ciber, Wilson, Brown, Gaddis, Hinkle, Starling, Stenson, Ferguson, Kanuch, Almashy, Gecsei, Horvath, Vargo, Beddow, Ketchum and Gill. Like the coal mine, company store, school and church, these folks who were there back then are mostly gone. Even most of the homes they lived in, like ours, is gone.

The one remaining Congo constant is the Congo Church that, fortunately, due to the efforts of a great group of people, still calls us to a great homecoming/ reunion every July.

The Morning Train and the Old Back

by Fred D. Turner of New Philadelphia, Ohio
born 1934

I was enrolled in Central Elementary in New Philadelphia, Ohio from 1941 through 1946. At the rear of the school's playground was a railroad track. This railroad ran across the town from Dover, Ohio through to New Philadelphia. This railroad also ran behind my parents' home, about halfway from Dover to New Philadelphia.

Because the steel rails were old and rickety, the train would go very slowly whenever it moved on this track.

In the forties, we had no school buses and our mode of travel was by walking. Somehow, the train schedule was into New Philadelphia about the time school started. My brother and I would hop the freight train and hanging onto a boxcar or a coal hopper car, we would ride to school where we would drop off into the schoolyard.

We didn't do this until we were in the fourth grade, and we could run fast enough to catch and hop the train. It always upset me in the evenings because the train schedule did not operate whenever school was out.

My parents never knew of this dangerous venture that my brother and I did until we both were adults and had children of our own. The railroad cars and tracks were off limits, imposed by my parents, when in my formable grade school years.

This second story occurred on November 20, 1949 as I was dressing for our annual football game with our arch rival, Dover. The Philadelphia-Dover rivalry is the second oldest in the state. Canton McKinley-Massillon being the oldest.

I was a scrub defense end, and dressing next to the star halfback on the team. He was No. 18 and I was No. 17, probably had something to do with the vicinity of our putting on our uniforms together.

Backing up a bit, our star halfback had quit school in the eighth grade, when he turned 16 years of age. In the forties, you could do this if you so desired, and you were through the eighth grade.

After he quit his formal education at age 16, Jim M. joined the U.S. Army. During his Army career he played Army football throughout Europe. Since he was big, strong, and fast, he developed into a star running back for the Army's special service team.

When Jim M. turned 18 years old, he returned home to his family and friends in Roswell, Ohio, a coal mining town located approximately eight miles east of the New Philadelphia school district.

With some recruiting and some encouragement, Jim M. returned to high school and the football team as a freshman in 1948, after his two year Army stint. Jim M. immediately becomes a gridiron star, tearing up the opponents with his power house runs and his tremendous speed. He was an adult playing with kids.

Now we move forward to November 1949, Jim M.'s last game. He is now 20 years old and a sophomore. As I was putting on my uniform, I looked across the bench at a muscular, big, gruff, tough, grizzled individual with a week old beard and I think to myself, this guy is a semi or maybe professional football player. I was only 15 years old with peach fuzz for a beard. Jim M. was 20 years old in his prime of life.

I looked up to Jim M. and thought, I am sure glad he was on my team during the game.

In 1949, the Ohio Athletic Association had a rule, that whenever you turned 21 years old, you could not participate in high school sports. He is now 20 years old.

As we were dressing, into the locker room came the game's official and the Dover's head coach, along with our head football coach. This group of adults approached Jim M. while I stood nearby in amazement, with my mouth hanging open.

Our football coach introduced Jim M. to the game's chief referee who stated to Jim M. that his age of 20 years old was being challenged by Dover's football coach, that perhaps Jim M. was too old to be playing.

The chief referee says to Jim M., "Son, how old are you?" To which the hardened, grizzled, muscular football player snarled, "Twenty."

The referee then asked Jim M., "When is your birthday?"

At this point, Jim M. moves his bearded face into the referee's face and Jim M. again snarls, "Tomorrow."

Since there were no birth certificates available, Jim M. was allowed to play in the upcoming game, in which we defeated Dover behind the running of Jim M., our star running back.

A few weeks after the game, Jim M. quit school and went to work. He was a good worker and became a good citizen of the community.

The Albino Muskrats

By Robert L. Erskine of Cambridge, Ohio
Born 1941

I remember when I was 15 years old, growing up on a farm in southeastern Ohio in 1956. In order to earn some spending money I learned how to trap muskrats in the creek running through our farm. Muskrats dig holes high in the creek bank where they can easily get back and forth from the water to their nice dry den. It's illegal to place a trap in the entrance hole. I had about twelve steel animal traps that I set in the water right outside the muskrat holes. The idea was to stake the end of the trap chain far enough out in the creek so the trapped muskrat would drown in the creek, unable to get up into the hole. If the muskrat was able to get out of the water onto the ground, it would chew its foot off trying to get free.

Trapping took place in the fall season. I waded in the cold creek water in high-top rubber boots, positioning the wooden stake by pounding it in with a mallet underwater, which always resulted in water flying everywhere.

I carried a burlap sack to haul the catch of the day back to the house. My trap line kept me busy every day after I got home from school, skinning the muskrats and scraping off any excess meat or fat from the underneath part of the brownish fur. I stretched the hide and fur over a wooden drying board shaped like a muskrat hide. After the hide dried my father drove me to town to deliver the fur to a dealer who paid me whatever it was worth that season. My earnings depended on the size and quality of the furs.

The most exciting catches I ever made were the three times I trapped albino muskrats from the same hole in the same season. The albino is a freak of nature caused by the absence of pigment in the skin. The county game protector told me a catch of three albino muskrats from the same nest is extremely unusual. He added that finding even one albino of any species is a rare incident in any locality.

When word got out about my unusual catch, the local newspaper wrote an article about me. The best part of the whole experience was when I went to sell those three pure white furs. I earned a lot more money than usual, which I promptly put right back into hunting, fishing and trapping supplies.

Happiness Was Ebert's Ice Cream and Picking the Dump

By Evelyn Krofft of Zanesville, Ohio
Born 1924

It used to be if you wanted to start a conversation, the weather was always a good subject. But not anymore! Standing in line at the Super Market I listened to the people around me. The 'in' conversation went something like this: "Every time I come to the grocery store I can't believe the prices." "You can't trust anyone anymore." "What is this world coming to?" "Our lives seem to be so complicated."

The sad part is there is probably cause for us to give some thought to such statements, but we don't want to get so engrossed with the negative aspects of life that we let them dominate our thinking.

It took me back to a family reunion that happened to be the first time many of us had been together in years. Except for the younger ones we had been reared on the same street (as many families used to be) and as might be expected we talked about what we did to entertain ourselves. Since this was in the 30's, during the big Depression, money was scarce so we made our own entertainment. We played the usual children's games: Hop-Scotch, Hide-and-Seek, played house and dressing up in our parents' old c1othes; but if we were seeking a little adventure that day, we would sit on the steps of the little neighborhood grocery store, ANKNEYS, and wait for the owner's son Ebert to go on a delivery. If we hadn't pestered him too much, and if he were in a good mood that day, he would let us go along. We were not always given that privilege, but it was worth a try.

One day he had a delivery clear across the river on Linden Avenue and he said we could go along. Now our trips were usually just around the block so this was really a long journey for us.

Ebert had converted his Whippet into a delivery car by taking out half of the front seat and all of the back seat, so my cousin Jeanne and I took our places of honor on a couple crates he put where the back seat had been. The biggest problem was trying to stay on the crates when Ebert took a corner too sharp.

All the way over we talked about how hot it was that day. Jeanne would say (loud enough for Ebert to hear) "Ice cream always tastes good on a hot day." That was my cue to say, "Yes, the only way I can really cool off in this heat is with an ice cream cone."

Talk like that usually didn't work, but wonders of wonders, Ebert stopped and bought us an ice cream cone. Guess it sounded good to him too. You see, they didn't sell ice cream in their store. During the Depression in our neighborhood people were lucky to have money for food let alone ice cream. Nothing had ever tasted so good to us! In fact, it was such a momentous occasion that it was still very clear in our memory after all those years.

If that didn't work and if we couldn't think of anything else to do, we'd sit on our front steps and wait for Mr. Waters, the iceman, to deliver ice. When he would go into a house with a block of ice in his gunny sack on his shoulder, we'd hop on the back of his truck, and it was our plan to try to pick up the chips of ice that were scattered around. The trick was to do it before Mr. Waters returned. We could never understand why he got so angry with us when he caught us doing it. I guess that's what made it so exciting.

We also liked to take walks. One trek would take us to Greenwood Cemetery where we would check out the goldfish in the pond, look at the pretty flowers and yes, read the tombstones. You'd be surprised what you can find on tombstones. We even took our lunch when we went out there; and always made sure we had a bag of bread to feed the fish.

On the way home we'd cut through a certain section of the cemetery because there was a huge tombstone with a large ball on top and the name TAYLOR across the front. Now we didn't visit that grave out of respect necessarily, but we knew there were Taylors somewhere in our background so we hung around awhile thinking someone would come by and think we were rich to have relatives who could afford a stone like that.

Some days our walks would take us in another direction to the creek down behind my aunt's house; in fact, WAY down behind my aunt's house (my mother didn't know that either). Of course you don't play in a creek without trying to dam it up. What a joy! If my memory serves me correctly I-70 now runs over our creek bed.

But probably our favorite pastime was to "Pick the Dump." Some of you don't even know what that means and I can't remember why it fascinated us so. In our alley, about one-half block from our house, there was a neighborhood dump. (No trash pick-up in those days.) What treasures we used to find! Old tins and canisters (some I would like to have now), an occasional broken toy (which we'd take home thinking our parents could put it back together for us), old pots and pans, already patched with those round circles that had a screw in the center. We'd pick up a pan; hold it up to the light and say, "Just look at that, only a tiny hole in it and someone is throwing it away. Those people are so wasteful."

Our last piece of "Dump Business" was to fill a box with pieces of colored glass, odd shaped bottles, pretty pictures from catalogs scattered around and then we'd bury it! That was our Buried Treasure.

As we talked about this, we decided that centuries from then, if or when archaeologists unearthed our treasure in that alley behind Eastman Street in Zanesville, Ohio, they would really have a problem figuring out the culture of the civilization that had resided in that area.

After we had buried our treasure, with proper ceremony, we would find a couple good tin cans to stamp on the heels of our shoes and then clomp home in our tin can high heels or sometimes gallop like a horse if we were so inclined that day.

Now don't get me wrong, I wouldn't want to go back in those days for anything because we also remembered having outdoor toilets and getting ready for bed downstairs in front of the open grate and racing up the steps to dive under the covers before we got too cold. But whether it was because there was no TV in those days to tell us that we didn't have all the luxuries that some people were enjoying, or whatever the reason, we didn't give it a thought.

That day at the reunion we laughed and cried as we reminisced about those "good old days" and we all realized that instead of being poor, as some might have labeled us, we were really well off!

In years to come will this generation refer to today as "The Good Old Days?" That may be interesting!

I still talk about the high cost of living, the injustices taking place in the world today and the decline in our moral values, but I hope and pray that we'll always be aware of the fact that as long as we have the love of family and faith in God we are truly blessed!

A man named Manden once said, "The greatest thing a man can do in this world is to make the most possible out of the 'stuff' that has been given him!"

The Tedium of Tobacco Farming

By Vera Earles Evans of Cincinnati, Ohio
Born 1924

My Mother, Alice Kirkbride Earles, was born and raised on a small farm in the gentle, rolling hills of southeastern Ohio. Her parents were Absolem and Hannah Kirkbride and she is one of seven children.

Even though the Kirkbride farm was comparatively small, there was much work to be done and Mother did her share of hard work. Much of the work in the tobacco crop fell to Mother and Uncle Jim, simply because their two older sisters worked away from home quite frequently.

Early spring was a busy time on the Kirkbride farm. First of all it began with Grandpa, Mother, Aunt Mary, Aunt Bessie and Uncle Jim clearing off a patch of new ground which would be used for planting the tobacco. This meant cutting down all the bushes and small undergrowth and piling it all into a huge pile to be burned. One day in particular, Grandpa told Mother and Uncle Jim, after they had worked all morning piling brush, that they could ride the horses back to the barn when they returned to the house at noon for dinner. The horses' names were Pet and Molly, Mother remembers. So at noon, Mother and Uncle Jim were lifted onto the horses by Grandpa, and they started toward the barn. Evidently, Mother in her excitement at being allowed to ride the horse, forgot to guide the animal and the horse walked directly through the sled which Grandpa had been using to haul the brush.

The area to be cleared would probably be an acre or so and after it was all cleared and spaded into workable condition, they would burn the huge brush pile. This was the spot where Grandpa planted the tobacco seed. (A tobacco seed, incidentally, looks quite a lot like a mustard seed.) Grandpa would "tramp" the seed into the ground rather than cover them with dirt.

Then in May, which was the time for the warm spring rains to begin, came the time for the work to really begin with the tobacco. Mother would hear Grandpa in his workshop gathering up boxes and baskets in preparation to go to the tobacco patch and reset the young plants.

So, on such a May morning; Grandpa, Mother, and perhaps Aunt Mary, Aunt Bessie and Uncle Jim; laden with boxes and baskets, would start for the tobacco patch. They gently pulled the fresh, young plants from the moist ground, being sure lots of dirt clung to the roots. Meanwhile, Grandpa would be marking straight rows with what was commonly called a "horse," which was a long wooden pole with a runner on it. In the rows which Grandpa had marked with the "horse" they would use a sharp wooden peg to make holes about eighteen inches apart; place a tobacco plant in each hole and secure them by tamping dirt around the roots.

After the plants had started to take root and grow, Mother and Uncle Jim, along with Grandpa, would have to cultivate the ground. Each would take a row to hoe with Grandpa in the middle row. Because Mother and Uncle Jim were so young they could not hoe quite as fast as their father, so he would help them along by hoeing a few plants on their rows when they were falling behind. Occasionally either Mother or Uncle Jim would accidentally chop off a young plant with their hoe and they would quickly push it back into the ground and heap dirt around it; hoping it would not be detected by Grandpa. However, I suspect it was discovered at a later date when the plants were cultivated the next time.

One day after warm, back-breaking hours of hoeing tobacco; they all sat down under a big shade tree at the edge of the tobacco patch to rest for a few minutes. Far across the valley on the other side of the ridge, Mother could see a great pile of new lumber which was to be used for a new house being built for their neighbors, George and Bertha Martin. Mother saw the lumber with the same eyes as she saw the trees or surrounding countryside. But what she could NOT see that summer day in 1897 was that in a few years that same house would be very important to her. She did not know that summer when she was a girl barely twelve-years-old that in a few short years a young and handsome man named Deasy Earles would leave his home in Ironton, Ohio and come to live with and work for George Martin. She would eventually meet him and they would fall in love and marry on March 25, 1905. They went into housekeeping in the very same house she saw under construction that summer day in 1897.

Probably wedding picture of Absolem Ames Kirkbride and Hannah Parsons.

Along with hoeing and cultivating the tobacco plants, they also had to keep an eye open for the long green tobacco worms. They were striped worms with what looked like little "horns" on their heads. As they hoed the plants, they would pick off any tobacco worms they saw and destroy them. Also the small suckers that developed on the plants had to be picked off and thrown away.

All of these tasks; the hoeing, cultivating, destroying tobacco worms and removing suckers from the plants; were done, not once, not twice, but periodically throughout all of the long hot summer.

One damp, rainy, spring morning Mother remembers in particular, Grandpa was ready to go to the tobacco patch and he was waiting at the fence for Mother, Aunt Mary and Aunt Bessie to go with him. Grandma told him she thought it was too damp and rainy for the girls to go to work in the tobacco field that morning. Mother was clinging to Grandma's skirts, hoping her father would relent and not compel the girls to go with him that day. Finally he consented for Aunt Mary and Aunt Bessie to stay at the house, but he reached across the fence with his long arms, picked up Mother and told her to come along with him. As she walked dutifully, but quietly, along with her father, Mother could hear the bob-whites singing through the early morning mist far across the valley. To this day, whenever she hears the song of the bob-white, it brings back vividly the memory of that morning so long ago when she had to go with her father to the tobacco patch; a task she disliked so thoroughly.

As the long summer drew to a close; a tang of autumn came into the air. The tobacco was then ready to be harvested. Again, as in the growing stages of the tobacco crop, there were several steps to the harvesting. As the autumn days became golden, so did the tobacco leaves which grew closest to the ground. When the lower leaves began to turn yellow that meant they were ready to be stripped from the main stalk. Mother, along with Grandpa, Uncle Jim, Aunt Mary and Aunt Bessie, began the long tedious job of stripping the tobacco leaves and loading them on a sled to be hauled to the barn. After the ripe, yellow leaves were all stripped and hauled to the barn; then came the process of stringing the tobacco leaves on tobacco sticks.

Mother was very adept at this task however much she may have disliked the chore. Mother's uncle, Jim Davis, commented often that the tobacco which she had strung was always done the neatest.

Stringing tobacco is no simple chore. It takes skill as well as a great deal of patience. A tobacco stick is a long, round wooden stick, measuring about four feet long. On one end of the stick a twine string was tied securely. The loose end of the string was threaded through a tobacco needle, which is flat; about six or eight inches long and has a large eye. Then the needle was pushed through two tobacco leaves at a time, with the stems upward, and placed on one side of the tobacco stick. Two more leaves were strung through with the needle and placed on the opposite side of the stick; and so on until the stick was filled with the golden tobacco leaves. It was Mother's great skill at stringing tobacco that every stem was even when she had finished stringing a tobacco stick. Not everyone could string tobacco that neatly. But that is characteristic of Mother's work in everything she did. Once Mother got her wrists so sun burnt while she was stringing tobacco, her Uncle Jim Davis put some limbs with leaves on them on some little bushes over her head for her to have some shade.

As the tobacco sticks were filled, they were hung on racks near the barn. This was only the beginning of the harvesting of the tobacco. The same procedure was repeated with the middle leaves on the tobacco stalk when they began to turn yellow. They too were stripped, hauled to the barn on the sled, strung on the tobacco sticks and placed on the tobacco racks in the same manner as with the ground leaves. Then finally the top leaves were stripped and the same process repeated all over again.

Grandpa always left a few of the choice tobacco plants to go to seed, which he used for planting the following spring. A tobacco plant, before it goes to seed, has a beautiful pink, bushy bloom.

After all the tobacco leaves had been taken to the barn and strung and hung on the racks; then came another important task. The sticks were taken down from the racks and gently placed on the sled, with all the leaves lying flat so as not to crush them, and then hauled to the tobacco house which was some distance from the barn. There would be several sleds full of the strung tobacco. The tobacco house was a simple, plain wooden structure with tiers of racks built in it, beginning at the ceiling. The tobacco sticks were taken from the sled and hung on these racks in the tobacco house.

Grandpa would start a slow burning fire in the long flue underneath the tobacco house and this fire had to be kept burning constantly for two or three weeks until the tobacco was "cured." Some farmers simply "air-cured" their tobacco by letting it hang on the racks in the open air. Grandpa chose to cure his tobacco with smoke. He never himself used tobacco in any form.

Grandpa raised two different kinds of tobacco. One was Harrison tobacco, which has pointed leaves and the other was Burley tobacco, which has a broad, flat leaf.

Although Mother worked in the tobacco field at home from the start to the finish of the crop, she also helped other farmers string tobacco in the autumn. She was paid a mere fifty-cents for every one hundred sticks of tobacco she strung. And the most sticks Mother ever strung in one day was one hundred and fifteen. This amounted to a wage of fifty seven-cents. This is a far cry from today's wages for any job. She strung tobacco for Ferm Fuller and three of her uncles; James Parsons, Charles Christman and Jim Davis. In Mother's sleep she often dreamed of stringing tobacco.

During the time the tobacco was being cured over the slow fire, Mother would also help cut down the bare tobacco stalks in the field and pile them to be burned. Finally the tobacco sticks were taken down from the racks in the tobacco house, re-loaded onto the sled and again returned to the barn. In the barn the tobacco was "bulked." This meant that three tobacco sticks were placed together; the strings were cut and the tobacco rolled into a bulk. Thus, three sticks of strung tobacco were known as a "tobacco bulk."

Now at last, for Mother, the long tedious hours which she had spent in helping to raise and harvest a tobacco crop were over for another year. There was one more step to take and this was Grandpa's job. He would load the tobacco bulks onto the big wagon and take them to market at McConnelsville, Ohio. Tobacco, at that time, sold for approximately six or seven dollars per one hundred pounds. With part of the money which Grandpa received from the tobacco crop, he bought the children their winter shoes.

And oh, what a happy time that was for Mother and the rest of the children to be getting new winter shoes! Before Grandpa left home for McConnelsville, he would measure each child's foot with a stick. In this way he purchased shoes for each child in the proper size. They were shoes made of heavy leather with high laced tops and the children were proud of these shoes as any child today would be of the finest kid leather.

So that is how a tobacco crop was planted, tended and harvested in the long ago days of the 1890's on a small farm in Ohio. Those days are no longer with us, nor will they ever return. But for as long as Mother lived she remembered every detail, every lonely and back-breaking task of raising tobacco on that small Ohio farm so many years ago.

The Talking Box in the Front Room

by Mary Dowell of Nashport, Ohio
born in 1924

I remember the first time I ever heard a radio. It was late 1938. My dad and uncle had gotten some work on a road. The first real work my dad had had for a long time. He came home and told my grandma that my uncle wanted him to bring us girls and Grandma to his house on Saturday night. He told my dad that he had a box in his front room and you could hear people talking in Tennessee. My grandma asked my dad if my uncle had been drinking because we had never heard a radio or knew anything about one.

Dad took us down to my uncle's. It was real cold. They lived on a farm and had a Delco system. My aunt put her two girls, Grandma, and us two girls on the couch, and we had a nice warm blanket and waited for the radio to be turned on. My uncle turned it on. It was the Grand Ole Opry. The first thing we heard was Roy Acuff singing "The Great Speckled Bird." I never hear him singing that yet, but I see my dad, us girls, and Grandma all spellbound. It was so hard to believe. When you was a kid and had never been anywhere. Tennessee might as well been China, because it seemed so far away. My, how times have changed.

When we were growing up, things were real bad. But we didn't know any different, because most everyone was in the same boat. My mother made most all of our clothes. The girls' clothes were mostly from feed sacks, all the sheets and pillow cases. Dish towels were from sugar sacks. I never had bought sheets or slept on one until I got a job in 1952. I got married right after Pearl Harbor. An old lady that lived near by made me a sheet and pillow cases by hand. She didn't have a sewing machine. I was so proud of my new sheets and pillow cases.

When my kids started coming along, I made a lot of their clothes. My little girl had feed sack dresses because you could get some very pretty ones. I had a friend that made quilt tops from the feed sacks. My son never had store bought clothes until he started to school. I made his little pants from the backs of his daddy's wore out pants. Never let anything be thrown away that you could get any good from. Most young ladies now can't sew on a button. We had to learn very young. I guess it was good for me, because now that I can't get around very good, I spend a lot of time doing cross stitch and sewing, and making things put in the time when you are alone and can't get around.

Making Do

by Sara Burkhard Reichart of Zanesville, Ohio
born in 1933

In 1933, fourteen million people were out of work. 233 thousand lost their homes.

In 1933, the year I was born, my parents lost their home on Taylor Street. The bank where they had their loan went under. They lost their home and all the money in the bank. The bank was called State Security, located on Main Street in Zanesville. Mr. Sprangler was the president.

We rented three other homes—Mitchell Avenue, Henry Street, Adamsville Road.

When I was nine years old, my father borrowed money from one of his sisters and made a down payment on a house on Neil Avenue. There was no bathroom, just an outhouse. At night, we had a chamber pot under the bed. No furnace, fireplaces in each room for heat.

We had a building in back. It was called a washhouse. We did laundry in Maytag washer with wringer and two metal rinse tubs. A little potbelly stove to burn coal and keep warm. The two metal rinse tubs were used for our bath, summer in the washhouse and winter in our kitchen, with newspaper pinned to curtains for privacy.

Our mother bought a dress pattern, taught herself to sew, made our dresses for school.

A lot of times, when milkman would come, Mother would say, "Don't leave any milk today. We have no money."

Armco Steel Mill gave each man a plot of ground under the Monroe Street Bridge to plant garden. We canned everything for winter.

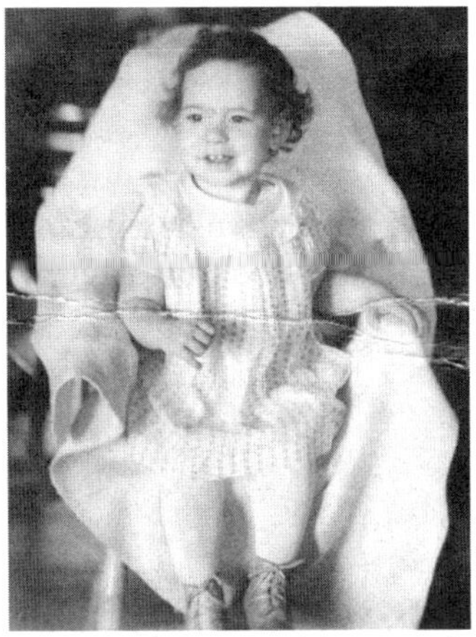

Sara Reichart, age fifteen and one half months, wearing a dress her mother made.

When a young child, around four years old, was helping my dad burn brush in yard on Adamsville Road, bent over to pick up something shiny, dress caught fire. Third degree burns on back, arm, and right hip. In bed with sunlamps on burns trying to dry up burns. They did skin grafting to heal. Took skin from Mother's legs and put on burns.

Early years, Dad would take us to Monroe Street Bridge. He would go on to Armco to work. We would walk to St. Nicholas School, out Monroe Street, Spring Street, Underwood Street, Main Street, and up the hill to school.

When I was about twelve years old, my two older sisters got scarlet fever. Doctor came, put sign on front door (contagious disease). No one allowed in or out. I went to stay with cousins for three weeks.

My first job was at Kresge Five and Ten on Main Street, my tenth grade of school. Worked after school and on Saturday. Made thirty-five cents an hour.

When I graduated, went to work at State and Liberty Theatre. Made fifty cents an hour. 1953, went to work at Hazel Atlas. 1959, bought a Ford Galaxie Convertible.

One more thing. In 1940, we had icebox to keep food cold. On Underwood Street was icehouse. You could buy large square of ice for twenty-five cents.

1942-1944, we had air raids test in school. Everyone crawled under their desks. Also air raid test at home. No lights on, curtains closed.

The Hobos' Mark

by Ruth M. Ward of New Philadelphia, Ohio
born 1923

I was a little girl during the Depression. Many men didn't have jobs and stayed at night at a brickyard close by to stay warm. During the day they walked into our village, knocking on back doors asking for food. My dad always gave them food and a cup of coffee. They used white chalk to mark an X on telephone poles to show where they received food before. There was always an X on the pole in front of our house.

The Equine Hero

by Eva J. Grimes of Byesville, Ohio
born in 1935

I was raised in Noble County and heard many interesting and true happenings from my "Mom Mom." One left a lasting impression on me as a child which involved "Mom Mom" and her horse.

Mom Mom, Minnie Mae Morrison.

As she was riding on this particular day, they approached the area of a bridge. Suddenly without warning the horse stopped dead in its tracks and would not move an inch further.

That day the horse became her hero. The bridge had collapsed and she had been saved from a serious tragedy.

Always Ice Cold

by M. Lorine Medley of Coshocton, Ohio
born in 1940

When I was two years old my parents bought undeveloped property for $50.00, one and half miles from downtown Coshocton and four blocks to the hospital. There was no electric or water, we carry water.

The outhouse was on top of the hill. We used white enamel chamber pots, look like a bucket had a metal handle and a lid on top. It was only used when snow was deep, during the night and illness. Later it had to be empty the next day, carry pot to the outhouse. It was very uncomfortable to sit on, always ice cold and the smell was not pleasant. We did not know about toilets.

Basement of M. Lorine Medley's home where the kitchen and fruit cellar were and coal was stored.

The home place is still in the family and I live in an old two story house for 51 years, two houses over from my old home place.

Skinny Dipping and Mary Ann's Rescue

by Robert A. Miller of Caldwell, Ohio
born in 1929

My story is about skinny dipping. It involves a legendary gossip tale of a strip mine pond. The story goes about mining operation of long past time. Apparently, the bottom of the pit fell through with all of the mining equipment, steam shovels, bulldozers, etc. The remaining space on top of all the equipment, the pit, was full of water of unknown depth.

I was in my teens at the time of this story. My best friend at this time was Dick Rose. Dick's family had a '36 Ford car and Dick had his driver's license and was allowed to use the car on occasion. When he could take the car during the day, we would go out to Coal Ridge for a swim. We never thought of taking swim clothes with us, we just stripped off and jumped in, in our birthday suits.

Even in midsummer, the water was freezing cold, so we didn't stay too long. As far as I know, my father and mother didn't know about these trips. As evidence, I'm still alive at the age of 79.

* * * *

I was out in my backyard working on construction of a raft. I was pretty well done with the work when Dick Rose and his sister showed up to see what I was up to. When they determined that I had built a raft, they immediately started to persuade me to take it down the hill to launch it into Leatherwood Creek. That sounded like an outstanding idea for the fact that Leatherwood was in extremely flood condition.

I mentioned above that Dick's sister was with him. Her name was Mary Ann, she was two or three years younger than Dick and I. She was also quite a "tomboy" and accompanied us on many of our escapades. She was usually welcomed, and, as indicated in the rest of this story, I was sure glad she was there.

They finally convinced me that we should take the raft down the hill and put it in the creek. When the three of us finally got the monster down, we realized the creek was much higher than we expected. In spite of my better judgement, we decided to further this reckless operation. We flipped a coin to see who got the wonderful privilege of riding first. That was me.

When I got on the raft, it felt very good, but that didn't last long. As soon as the raft drifted over to the creek channel, Leatherwood Creek had decided that I had no business being there. The raft did a 180 and dumped me into 20 feet of water with all my clothes on, my boots, long pants, and a jacket (it was early in the spring and rather cold). Dick immediately started yelling, "Save the raft!" I thought that was a bit much when all I was worried about was saving myself. I was rapidly being drawn downstream by the creek's current.

Out of the corner of my eye, I saw Mary Ann running downstream, up on the bank, out of the water. The next thing I was aware of was that Mary Ann had cut down a small tree that fell out over the water. I managed to get myself over to the tree. I was able to get a hand on the tree, and Mary Ann managed to pull me over to get my feet on the ground. Mary Ann had truly saved my life! If she had not succeeded, I surely would have ended in the Gulf of Mexico (down Leatherwood creek to Wills Creek, to the Ohio River, down the Mississippi. Goodbye Bob).

We walked back to Elm Street directly across from Dick's house. His mother would not let me in the house, so I walked back up Woodlawn Avenue to face Mother. She asked where I had been, and I told her that I had fallen into Rose's goldfish pond. I never heard the last of the experience, but I'm sure Mother didn't believe my explanation.

The Found Penny and the Dismantled Tombstones

by Evelyn Wallick of Dover. Ohio
born in 1922

In 1925, a little blonde with one penny was considered pretty lucky and part of the wealthy kids in town. That is how I felt as I was showing my penny to my neighbor, Helen. That's not how I felt when the penny slipped out of my hand and landed in some tall grass next to a telephone pole.

Helen and I got on our hands and knees right then and started looking for the penny. Soon, there were three other neighbor children also on their hands and knees looking in the grass. About that time tears were running down my checks. I was planning to buy a sucker that would last all afternoon.

Just then a tall man came walking down the street and asked what we were doing. After we told him, he asked if he could help. We said, "sure." So he also got on his hands and knees. After a little while, he lifted his hand with a penny and he said, "I just found a penny!" He handed it to me. The tears stopped. We all jumped up and down clapping our hands and screaming with joy. After all these years, I wonder if Jesus had sent us a man with a penny in his pocket.

In the early 20's, we had to find out what to do each day with a neighbor kid, or sit on the front porch to watch the cars go by. On good days we were lucky to see four or five cars. Sometimes, we also saw a horse and buggy. We did a lot of giggling, looking up and down the street.

One day, I was very lucky. The girl across the street told me she heard her father tell her grandpa that a man from our town was hiding his whiskey inside some tombstones. So she got a screwdriver and I got a screwdriver and we headed up town on a hill where there was an old church and cemetery.

Evelyn Gardner Wallick and Faye Gardner Davidson in 1923.

In the cemetery, there were tombstones two feet high made out of four metal pieces that were screwed together. So we spent that afternoon unscrewing the front piece, sticking our hands into the spider webs, then putting it back together and trying the next one. We worked all day on that and went home with sore hands and arms. We didn't find any whiskey and no one found us.

In 1925, there were no trick or treats for Halloween. It was all tricks. In our town, a man who didn't like children lived on the main street in a tall white house with the front door opening into the house. I got some of my friends and we gathered all the tin cans they could find. In those days, our mothers always canned a lot of food in glass jars, so we had a lot of work ahead of us. We all quietly met on the street in front of his house. Then, we very quietly placed the cans against his front door. They went way up, over half of the large door. One of us rang his doorbell. The door opened and there stood the man yelling at the top of his voice. All the tin cans lay around him on the floor. I don't think any of us ran that fast the rest of our lives. That was one of the "Good Old Years."

Mr. Parent Didn't Like Quitters

by Sally Atkinson of Zanesville, Ohio
born in 1948

My name is Sally Jo Atkinson. From 1959 until 1963, I went to school in Chandlersville, Ohio. Those were the happiest years of my school career.

Mr. Ernest Parent was the principal of the school, which also included a high school. He was also my teacher when I was in the eighth grade.

When I was in the seventh grade, I started playing in the junior high band. I had asthma, although it was not serious. Unfortunately, the instrument I chose was the coronet, which was really not suitable for me. In the summer between seventh and eighth grade, I dropped out of band.

During the first week of my eighth grade year, Mr. Parent walked past my desk. He stopped and said, "I heard you quit band." When I replied that I had, he said, "I don't like quitters," and walked away.

Ever since that day, whenever I think of quitting something, I think of Mr. Parent. He will always be one of my favorite teachers.

Revealing Photos in *National Geographic*

by Orville L. Hartline of Leesville, Ohio
born in 1939

Many are the memories of growing up in the 1940's and 50's, and the time spent at my grandmother's farm. My younger brother and I would climb the hills and explore the woods. We would cool off by taking a dip in the stream and spend hours fishing.

When it was raining, and we couldn't play outside, we would look through grandmother's collection of magazines. Our favorite was the *National Geographic*. As young boys, we had a curiosity about girls. The pictures, there in, helped satisfy that curiosity.

The annual, family reunion was an event that all looked forward to...the food we shared, recipes exchanged, and memories revisited. This was also a time of embarrassment for my brother and I. Grandmother had everyone's attention. She took great pride in telling all the relatives how studious my brother and I were in "reading" the *National Geographic* by the hours. The aunts, uncles and older cousins could be heard laughing and chuckling. They weren't as naive as grandmother. We just wanted to disappear.

The Hartline family. Front row:Paul, Orville. Back row: Curtis (dad), Larry, Anna Mae (mom).

Three-county Schooling and an Ornery Spell

by Delbert Snell of Cambridge, Ohio
born 1933

I was born and raised on my father's 123-acre farm located in the northwest corner of Guernsey County, Ohio. To the west was Muskingum County and to the north, Coshocton County.

I started school in the fall of 1939 and was bused to the Otsego local school located in Muskingum County for my first two years. Keep in mind I never moved from the farm until I joined the U.S. Air Force when I was 19 years old.

I don't remember the reason, but it was determined that I should go to Boden, a one room school located in Guernsey County. I was bused about three miles to the school for the next six years, third through eighth grades.

In the spring of 1947, I graduated from the eighth grade and prepared to go to high school, located 14 miles away in Cambridge, the county seat of Guernsey County. However, there was Plainfield High School, just five miles away, located in Coshocton County. My father knew the president of the Plainfield school board and asked him if I could go there. He said as long as I would walk to the bottom of the hill to catch the bus I could attend Plainfield High School.

So for the next four years I would leave my house at the top of the hill and walk one half mile to the bottom of the hill to catch the bus. Halfway down the hill, I crossed from Guernsey County to Muskingum County, then, at the bottom of the hill was Coshocton County.

Although, I never moved, I went to school in three different counties, Muskingum, Guernsey, and Coshocton and the same three counties were involved when I walked a half mile to catch the bus to go to Plainfield High School. I am sure there would not be many, if any, in the whole United States with a similar story.

* * * *

When I was four or five years old and went to church with my parents, many of the ladies would offer me white and or pink lozenges. My mother noticed that I would never take a white one, but always take a pink one. When at home, I would hear my mother tell my dad that she was embarrassed when I refused the white ones. This puzzled my mother for a year or two, and then she finally figured out why I didn't like the white lozenges. When I was a baby I had the colic a lot and my mother gave me peppermint extract many, many times. To this day I don't like anything with a peppermint flavor.

* * * *

My sister was seven years older than I was and we liked to torment each other rather than play together. I was about six or seven years old when this happened. It was a warm summer day and my sister was in the dining room and the door to the back screened in porch was wide open. So, it was easy to hear knocks on the back porch screen door.

It was my turn to have an ornery spell, so I knocked on the screen door and ran around to the front of the house where my sister could not see me when she went to the door. I did this one or two more times and then she realized it was me playing a trick on her. I thought she would not fall for this anymore so I stopped.

A few minutes passed and she heard another knock, so she assumed it was me and she yelled out, "Quit that you silly goose." Then she looked out the open dining room door and to her embarrassment and surprise she saw a stranger, probably a salesman. Then she ran to the back bedroom, where our mom was napping and told her what happened. Mom went to the door and explained to the stranger the reason he was called a "silly goose." Needless to say, my sister was not happy with me.

Moving the Two-Holer

by Fred R. Miller of New Matamoras, Ohio
born in 1923

I am a 1923 model, which means I am almost eighty-six years old young. So I have lived several years in the good old days. When I was five years old, my parents moved about two miles from the house where I was born. We moved everything on a high-wheeled road wagon with a team of horses. That was the beginning of my good old days. It was in August, 1928. No one had ever been in that house for six months, and the grass in the yard was hay.

There were blue plumb trees in the yard. My first job was picking ripe plumbs off the ground, and my mother canned them for winter use. When we went to the little town of New Matamoras for supplies, we went in a horse buggy, or if there was snow, we went in the sled. That was in the wintertime. When the dirt road was dry in the summer, my dad had bought a new Model T Ford in 1925. The cost of it was $420.00.

When I got around ten years old, I started my trapping business. My dad would help me set them. I would tend them every day. A large opossum would bring twenty-five to fifty cents, small ones fifteen to twenty cents. Money was scarce. I saved all the money I got from trapping in the winter. It would add up to fifteen to twenty dollars, but that was pretty good. *No income tax to pay.*

I would work for neighbors' farmers, hoeing corn or raking wheat with a wooden rake, fifty cents a day. Some of the older men would cradle the wheat. They got a dollar a day. Most times, the farmer wouldn't have the money to pay you when you were done. Sometimes it would be almost Christmas when you got paid, but you always got paid. Most of the people were very honest those days.

Now I will include the directions how to build an outhouse in the background. My dad would build it on runners low to the ground, like sled runners, then he would dig a hole just a little smaller than the bottom of the outhouse. Then use a horse to pull it over the hole.

Fred Miller in 1937.

When the time came it needed moved, just dig a new hole about five feet in front of the old two-holer, hitch a horse to it, pull it over the new hole, and you was in business.

That don't go for all, at least one neighbor who tried it. He had a yoke of young oxen, and his seventeen-year-old son decided to move it one day when his dad wasn't home. He hitched the oxen to it, but not too experienced, put the log chain around it too high, and when he started the oxen, he upset the two-holer. Scared the oxen, and they ran off through the woods, completely destroyed the outhouse! Now he was out of business 'til a new one was built.

My aunt and uncle had one of these two-holers and also two teenage girls. When you went to the two-holer at night, there was no electric light. You took the oil lantern. It was a full moon, so the girls went, and when they got inside, they lit the lantern, throwed the match that wasn't out down one of the holes, plenty of paper down there. You guessed it, the two-holer went up in smoke.

Dodie's First Surgery

by Nancy J. Knight Page of Dover, Ohio
born 1931

In the 1930s, few children received an abundance of Christmas gifts. We usually received one or two toys, along with clothes and a bit of candy or nuts.

I was five or six years old, and much to my delight found a new doll under the tree. This doll had hair and eyes that opened and shut.

My joy was short lived, however. My sister Dodie was four years older than I and was a future nurse. A friend was visiting her and together they decided to use my doll as a patient. In the midst of surgery, somehow my doll was split right up the middle. With no expert surgeon to repair the damage, she lay with her body in two equal parts. Through my tears and Mother's hugs, Mary Lee, my oldest sister, told me not to cry.

The next day I was astonished to find that Mary Lee had replaced the doll with another. I never knew where she got the extra money to purchase another doll with hair and eyes that opened and closed, but oh, how I cherished that doll.

The Duck Planting Experiment

By Robert E. Gatten of Tuscarawas, Ohio
Born 1939

As we all know, during the 1940s there was a war going on and everything was rationed. Due to the fact that I was a small boy, I really didn't realize the gravity of certain things. At the time I had a pair of pet ducks that followed me everywhere; they even roosted in an old straw hat that I had.

Meal planning was very creative at best because everything was going into the war effort. One day when I was elsewhere playing, someone in the family got a bright idea and when I came home the family was preparing a meal and the menu was DUCK! Due to the fact my "PETS" were missing, it could only lead to one conclusion.

Picture contributed by Robert Gatten.

After my initial shock that someone could do such a thing and after my mother sat me down and explained things to me; and after my grievous wailing, I put the heads of my ducks in a small box and buried them, hoping that maybe I could grow another pair.

Needless to say, I didn't have an appetite that day and I haven't been interested in any type of duck cuisine since. After growing up a little, I realized that was just the way things were back then and people had to do what they had to do to get by.

It was just that a small boy didn't understand that his choice of pets may not be the best choice if they are part of the food chain.

Some lessons are hard learned, incidentally, my duck planting experiment didn't work.

Junior's Demise and Eloping to Richmond

by Myrna Valentine of Senecaville, Ohio
born in 1940

I was raised on Highland Avenue in Byesville, Ohio, which is no longer there because the interstate came through in the early 60s and took the neighborhood.

We had chamber pots that we used at night, but in the daytime, you went down the hill to the outhouse. Grandpa lived next door to us, and he had a rooster that would chase me and my sister down to the outhouse and flog the door. We would scream and yell for Grandpa to come and get us out. The rooster's name was Junior. Finally we had Sunday dinner, and Junior never bothered us again.

My Aunt Jenny made me and my sister's school clothes, and she got the material from Lewis' Feed Store on 2nd Street in Byesville. The dresses were made from flowered feed sacks, and she put ric-rac buttons on them. That was back in 1946 or 1947.

We had no running water, no bathroom, and our bath was in the kitchen with a big round galvanized tub. Mom would heat water on the stove to fill the tub. Then, my sister and I took turns for the bath, and I might say in the same water.

I remember the big snowstorm in 1950. My Uncle Ray and Aunt Jeanette got married and went to Columbus and was stranded for days up there. My Uncle Chuck had to dig us out where the snow drifted and we couldn't get out our door. There was a path down the middle of the road on Highland Avenue so people could walk to town for groceries.

Dad was a great hunter, and we ate a lot of squirrel and rabbit. That's probably why I am not a big fan of meat today. I remember if he wanted deer, they had to go to Pennsylvania. There was very few deer in Ohio.

Our house was on a hill, so the basement was exposed and had an outside door. After riding our bikes, my sister, Connie, and I were putting our bikes away in the basement. The door was open and there was a snake with its head in the crack of the door. When Connie went into the basement, it bit her on the foot. I ran next door to tell my Aunt Dorothy. She was on a ladder wallpapering and I was yelling that there was a snake in the basement. She said, "Don't get around it," and I told her that it had bit Connie. She almost fell off the ladder. The neighbors called my dad home from work. He worked at Ecko Housewares. He sat Connie on the front porch and took his pocketknife and cut an X on top of her foot, and sucked the blood from her foot. They took a hoe to the snake and cut off its head. No one knew what kind of snake it was, but Dad thought it was a copperhead or a hiss-n-viper.

Our favorite radio program was Inner Sanctum, and us kids would all sit on the floor in front of the big floor-model radio, and we had linoleum floors.

My first kind of date was going to the movie at the Luna Theater with a guy named Charlie. That was in 1953. I know it was a western. Probably Roy Rogers.

In 1955, we had three restaurants downtown where I hung out with my girlfriends, Kay, Mona, and Bernitta. Two of the restaurants stayed open all night—Home Restaurant and Mickey's.

There was a rival between the Byesville guys and the Cambridge guys, and they would go out and drag race. There was a few fights, but in the end, for most of them, they all became friends for a lot of years. I met one of those Cambridge guys in 1955 at the carnival at the Byesville City Park. I dated him until 1957, at which time we eloped to Richmond, Indiana. After three daughters and 52 years, we are still remembering the good old days.

Remembering Milford Elementary School

By Elsie Reinhard of North Royalton, Ohio
Born 1918

On a sultry summer day in the late 1980's, I watched sweating workers raze Milford Elementary School, part of the Cleveland Public Schools. The nearly century old brick building had occupied a large plot between West 46 and West 47 Streets; east and west and Bush and Eichorn Avenues; north and south. A primary building was connected to an upper grade building by a section which housed the business office and the principal's office. A black wrought iron fence surrounded the property.

Milford's kindergarten class of 1924. Elsie Reinhard is in second row, fifth from left.

Memories tugged at my mind. There was Balto, the Siberian husky that bravely led a dogsled team on a mercy trip to Nome, Alaska. In 1925, I guess, there was no other way to get diphtheria vaccine to the sick people in Nome. I remember collecting money so we could bring Balto and his team to live in Cleveland's Brookside Zoo. The pupils helped with their pennies. Later it was so much fun when Balto was brought to Milford School for us to see.

What was elementary school like in the good old days? Until I was in the third grade; getting dressed for that cold school was a challenge. I wore what my mother called a union suit. There was a flap in the back, which unbuttoned for bathroom visits. The suit went to my ankles. The next problem was to pull on long black stocking over the legs.

The school day always started with pupils standing and reciting the Pledge of Allegiance to the 48 star flag standing in the corner. Blackboards covered two sides of the walls. Pictures of Abraham Lincoln and George Washington looked down from the front blackboard. We were taught reading by the look and say method; that is, each child in turn read sentences written on the blackboard. If you were in the back of the class the words were well memorized before your turn. History, geography, arithmetic, grammar and penmanship followed.

The school supplies we brought to school were a Campus tablet and two pencils. We paid two-cents for a pen point to be inserted in a furnished pen holder. We sat at desks fixed to the floor. In the upper right corner of the desk was a hole big enough to receive a small ink bottle. If a pupil spilled ink on the wood floor, it meant an after school session with sandpaper to scrape away the ink stain.

If the principal, Miss Mayers, stopped in, teacher and pupils immediately stood in respect.

My favorite memories of Milford are of the one room library and of my sixth grade teacher, Mrs. Coates, who had a poetry afternoon on Fridays. We were expected to learn and to recite a poem.

There were no movies and no field trips. However, we had special treats such as the visit of Balto and Valentine, Halloween and Christmas parties. Through books, music and examples of teachers, we learned discipline, patriotism, and respect for teachers.

At the close of school we formed neat lines. Miss Dowdell, the second grade teacher; sat at the piano in the hall and played rousing marches to which we left the building. No running and screaming until we were safely away from the building.

Milford's history is part of my family's history. My mother was in the first kindergarten class of 1905. My father graduated in the first eighth grade class. My brother, Leonard Reinhard, and I spent six and a half years as students. I began my teaching career in Milford's primary building. Len went on to spend 35 years as teacher and administrator in the Cleveland Public Schools.

My brother is gone now. Small houses now stand on the plot where once was Milford. But even at age 90 I can still remember the good old days in a very good school.

Party Lines and the Good Lord's Help

by Jeannette Rowlands of Caldwell, Ohio
born in 1933

In the year of 1949 I was 16, pregnant and married. By the time I was 35 years old, I was a widow with eight children. My husband was 45 years old, died of a heart attack.

A couple years later I met a nice man and we married,

but the story was he worked the afternoon shift and didn't get home till around 11:30 at night. So we communicated on the phone a lot, maybe an hour or more every night. We also saw each other on weekends. So it got serious and we married.

But the problem: I was on a party line and all the time because it was late at night and we thought it was private, guess what? My stepmother had been listening in on our conversations. So it goes to say being on a party line was not good, especially when she told me about it later. But she was a good stepmother, so I forgave her.

He has since passed away and also four of my sons, so back in those days, I had bad days and good days, and my children meant the world to me. And only by the good Lord's help did I make it.

Hard Times in Coal Ridge

by Ruth A. Galayda of Olmsted Township, Ohio
born in 1929

My parents were immigrants that came to America from Czechoslovakia. Somehow they both ended up in Ohio and settled in what was then called Laura and later became a town named Coal Ridge (Noble County). They were married there in 1918. They had six children. One child died when he was six—he had pneumonia.

My father worked in the Belle Valley Coal Mine along with most of the other men in town. The mine was not operating enough to make a decent wage, and my parents heard from friends that there were more jobs in Elyria, Ohio. They packed up and went to live there with friends who took them and four children into their home. While they were there, I was born on October 31, 1929, the day the Big Depression started. That ended our stay in Elyria. There were no jobs there either.

Class of 1937. First row seat one; Ruth Mertan Galayda and best friend, Mary.

We went back to Coal Ridge, and Dad went back to the coal mine. I loved Coal Ridge. It was a great place to live.

When I was old enough to go to school, I went to a one-room schoolhouse—one teacher that had to teach about four grades. She was a great teacher, and she handled the children well.

Although we were very poor, I didn't know it. We had a three-room house, kitchen and two bedrooms. We also had a summer kitchen. A coal stove heated our house, no plumbing.

The people in town all helped one another. Many of them had a small farm and were able to have farm animals. This allowed us to have milk, butter and sometimes meat. We did have chickens that supplied us with eggs.

Winters were brutal because we did not have equipment to handle the snow like we have now. But the wonderful summers made up for it. My friends and I always had games to play, even though we just made up a lot of them. We did a lot of berry picking and went fishing to get some catfish for our supper.

When I was seven years old, our life changed forever. I was out in the yard playing, and my mother was talking to a neighbor when I heard her screaming and crying. I heard the coal mine whistle blowing, and I knew something terrible had happened. My father had been killed. He had touched an electrical wire on the car that moved the coal. He was forty-four years old.

Our life changed drastically, and it also changed for everyone living in this wonderful little town. It was 1938, and people had to leave to find jobs in different cities. Some went to Cleveland, Detroit, Pennsylvania and even New York. My two sisters and brother also left. In 1941, my mother decided the family should be together, so we left Coal Ridge for a new life in Cleveland.

World War II started a few months later, and jobs were plentiful when all of the little factories made parts for the war equipment. Now when I think of my life, I think back to the days in Coal Ridge and remember the good times. I see my mother baking bread, sewing clothes, canning fruit and vegetables for winter and taking care of five children.

You have to wonder how they could endure the hardships. I know a lot of people that lived there that do not like to think about that time in their life, but I think it is important to think of it, and I feel lucky to have been part of that era.

Talking to the Operator and Vadah's Gravy

by Betty M. Lyons of Zanesville, Ohio
born 1921

When I was a little girl in a family of eight children, Mother did a lot of canning; it was during the Depression. We would pick berries in gallon buckets along the roadside and in fields. We didn't have berry farms. We got lots of jiggers also.

One of our toys, growing up, was rolling hoops. We would take a metal wheel, also a heavy wire about four feet long, and on one end we would bend it in a half circle and push the wheel. It also was good exercise running after it.

Another one, we would get an old tire, the tires were larger then, one of us would curl up inside the tire and another would roll us around.

I got married in 1937 and was the first one of our family to get a phone. My dad, when he visited us, he would get on the phone and talk to the operators. There wouldn't be anyone to call, but he'd talk to the operators.

It was common back in the pre Depression era to have large families. I grew up in such a family, where I was sixth out of nine children, eight of which survived.

All of the children who could help with the everyday chores, which included cooking, cleaning, gardening and yard work, laundry and babysitting the younger ones. We did get some time for play. We were all close and got along really well most of the time. We would play jokes on each other for harmless entertainment.

When food became too expensive for us, during the Depression, we learned to eat more common things to stretch our food dollars. We butchered our own hogs and chickens and raised our gardens like so many in that day. And if nothing else, we could always have biscuits and gravy. I look back now with fond memories of that delicious food.

One memory stands out. My mother and father left one day with the younger kids. I stayed home with my two older brothers and older sister, whom I adored. Orders were given for Vadah to fix a supper of biscuits and gravy for the four of us. When the time came, we were starved. We were all growing kids and two were boys. They never felt like they ever had enough to eat. As I sat down, eagerly anticipating that hot delicious gravy, piled high on a couple of hot flakey biscuits, my mouth was watering. Out came my sister with the food, but had a bandage on her hand. The gauze had a reddish tint. Somehow, she had cut her hand. One of my older brothers told me that while she had made the gravy, she had dripped her blood into it. The gravy somehow did show a red color. I got sick and couldn't and wouldn't eat it. I couldn't believe it. They were all going to eat it because they were hungry and said they couldn't waste the food in these tough times. So, they sat down to plates piled high and dug in. I was starved, but there was no way I could eat. They happily ate my share, too.

I later found out that my older brothers concocted this story to get a bigger share of food. They had taken red food coloring and bandaged Vadah's hand and put some in the gravy to redden it.

Vadah and I were always close and I never could understand how she could have done this to me, but I guess she was hungry too.

Waiting For Dad

By Joy Russell Gay of Zanesville, Ohio
Born 1926

When I was very young I followed my dad everywhere he went. We sawed wood and fed chickens, especially in the summer and when he was working.

I had a pet chicken named Vesti. It would lay eggs in my hand on command. I had a little car and used to make tunnels in the hillside. Dad always told me if I dig a little more I might get to China. I tried, but never made it. He would laugh.

He always called me Bill; maybe I looked more like a boy than a girl. Margie, my sister, was just a year older than me, but she would rather help Mom.

We used to run the trout line as he called it, a big line across the Muskingum River down by Stone Station. He had a row boat. The boat leaked and I had to bail out the water. I was about six-years-old at that time I think. We had a lot of fun.

He was in World War I and hurt his back. Sometimes he had to just sit in a chair for a long time.

Margie and I played together a lot. Sometimes we would wander off to the crick and go wading. Mom used to come after us, we didn't understand why she was afraid we might drown, and in some places it was real deep. We would come back to the house with her. I don't think we were too bad, but bad enough.

Mom used to boil water on a coal stove to do the washing and rub the clothes on a wash board. It wasn't too bad in the summer, but in the winter she would hang clothes on the line and on the back porch and they would freeze. What a hard life she had, but everyone had it hard; we were all poor. We were happy and had lots of fun.

It wasn't long before Margie went to school. Union Hill School was a one room school house on Union Hill Road. I missed her when she first went. Of course my brother Butch was already in school and they walked to school together.

Ellen Offenbacher and Marion Russell on their wedding day December 11, 1920.

There were three of us until I was eight-years-old and Gerry was born. I was jealous and afraid that I would not get to sit at the table beside my dad, but he said I could. Gerry cried a lot when he was a baby and Mom would rock and walk part of the night. My dad would help too. He used to sing "When a baby gets the colic in the middle of the night, its no place like home." When Gerry got bigger we would help take care of him.

My Dad worked coal mines when he was a teenager. His mom died when he was 13, his dad was already gone, and so brothers and sisters lived together. Dad, his brother-in-law Chase Stone (married to Mom's sister Edna) and two other guys dug out a coal mine in Blue Rock. I don't know how far down it went. It had a tipple that went way up.

Our school, Union Hill, was just up the hill. One day our teacher was sitting in the outhouse, so we climbed out the window and went down to see the coal mine. My dad said, "Come on, Bill, I will take you down." Marge wouldn't go. He lit his carbide light on the cap he wore and we went down. It was a long way and dark and water was dripping from the top. There was a coal car that ran on tracks all the way to the tipple. When we came up, he said, "You better go back to school before you get in trouble. "

In August, 1937, they had the mine all finished. My dad was working on the machine and the flywheel broke and pulled his clothes and him in, killing him. He never got to see the mine working. The other guys didn't do much after that.

I was ten and Gerry was 2 ½. That was a bad time for all of us. It was really hard to realize he was gone. Margie and I always thought he would come back. We used to watch and wait for him.

My mom was a great lady. She never got mad at us and I never heard her say a bad word about anyone. After my Dad was gone she was just lost for awhile. She was so sick after he got killed that I think she almost died too, but she had four kids to take care of and that helped her through the bad times. We had a hard time for a while, but we made it. When she got sick, Marge and I took care of Gerry. Then she got better.

The End with the Eraser

by Roberta L. Keith VanHoughton of Byesville, Ohio
born in 1957

I live in the village of Byesville, Ohio where I was raised by my grandmother, Ada Mae Ables Eubanks (born February 4, 1896); aunt, Ada Mae Eubanks (born May 3, 1920); and uncle, Franklin E. Eubanks (born August 31, 1918).

These are stories that they told me to be remembered from the life in this area.

My grandma had a horse named George and she would hitch him to a buggy to come into Byesville to buy supplies. She lived in a little area outside town called Trail Run. She graduated school with an eighth grade education. She played music by ear and was dedicated to her family.

My uncle left school at age twelve during the Depression to work on a coal truck for twenty-five cents a day. The money was needed to help the family survive. He worked twelve hours shoveling coal on a coal truck and was paid by the day. A pound of bologna was five cents a pound.

My aunt left school also to help with household chores. She washed and ironed clothes. This money also went to the family fund to keep them going during the Depression.

When the soles on their shoes went bad they used old tires for shoe soles. They cut a pencil in half to use for school. They took turns on who would get the end with the eraser.

Quilts were made from old clothes by Great-Grandmother, Hannah Ables, who lived with them. Buttons were saved to reuse before clothes were cut up (I have thirteen quilts as an inheritance...almost one hundred years old).

I have an old fashioned pump organ that they played church hymns on and sang. Going to church was very important. The Bible was the main book to read and learn from.

My uncle said during the Depression they invented Wonder Bread. They "wondered" where the next loaf would come from.

During the war there were "light out" to sirens in case of America being attacked. They had an oil lamp and it had to be turned out (I still have the lamp).

I inherited my great-grandmother's house and live there today. I am the fifth generation to be here.

I am proud to be a resident of the village of Byesville, Ohio and thankful for the values I have been taught by my family. The people here are wonderful. I have been blessed. If this house could talk and I had more room there are so many stories. They live on in my heart and now within the pages of your book.

Lunch for a Quarter and a Two Room School

by Helen Corbett of Newcomerstown, Ohio

There is a few things that happened back between 1944 and 1951. Those days I bought my lunch for twenty-five cents. That got me a sandwich, a candy bar and a bottle of pop.

I went to a two-room school, four grades in each room with a man teacher and a lady teacher. We had busses.

I lived on a big farm. I was the only kid, but I helped my mom and dad work. At age twelve I helped put up hay, drive the tractor and milked cows. We had hogs, chickens, you name it. We did our own butchering for meat. We never went hungry.

Our country roads were bad in winter. My dad would walk eight miles through snow up to his knees. You couldn't drive. My dad had an old 1932 Chevy. You had to use a crank to start it.

At Christmas time I got one doll and maybe a wagon or a trike. We had love and food, so we were happy.

We had good neighbors. Old German couple. They would do anything for you.

This all was in Coshocton and Warsaw, Ohio. My school was in Blissfield, Ohio.

We had an old outhouse. We called it a privy. No toilet paper. You used old catalogues and newspapers to do your job.

Back then my first kiss was at age fifteen, my favorite pet was cats. I still have cats.

We never had no electric till 1954. We had coal stoves to heat and cook on and kerosene lights to get my lessons by. No phones. Battery operated radio. We had an old Delco motor run later on in years to make lights. Then we got electric on.

My grandmother was special to me. She lived just up the road. She made homemade bread, cakes and pies.

All my family is gone now. I have one boy in North Carolina and he is forty-four. I'm now seventy years old and live in Newcomerstown, Ohio.

We had water back on the farm, but when it come to bath time it was a wash pan or a washtub to put your water in. You heated up the reservoir on the old coal stove to have hot water to bathe with. But we always had clean clothes that Mother washed on a washboard, blankets and all. I've seen her knuckles bleed washing blankets.

Yes, we had an old record player you had to wind up. If you wound it up too tight the spring would break.

Later on in years we got a wringer washer. When we got electric in, my mother did make a lot of my clothes.

But those were the days.

Fireworks, Fairs and the Circus

By Marilyn R. Davis of Zanesville, Ohio

Born 1931

Memories as I was growing up (in no particular order.)

A Happy Childhood Home: Dad built a playground for us down below the "hedges." This consisted of a group of trees that lined the back of our lot along with two other lots. Hedge balls would fall from these trees; about four inches in diameter, thus the trees were called "hedges." When I was about ten, we would climb on our next door neighbor's garage roof and climb through these trees, going from tree to tree, without touching the ground, until we came to the vacant lot on the other side of our house.

I remember Dad taking my two brothers and myself up the Licking River to Dillon Falls to swim on a hot summer day.

Marilyn Davis and brothers, Fred (Chub) and Charles (Dink), swimming at Dillon Falls.

Our street was dirt and in the summer the city would put oil on it to keep the dust down. This made it very difficult to cross the street to play with the kids that lived on the other side. You can imagine what our feet and shoes looked like.

Close to the fourth of July, small lean-tos would crop up on the outskirts of town and fire works of all description would be for sale. My favorite were little round black balls about the size of a big marble. You would light their wick and a black oozy thing would curl out from it. Just like squeezing toothpaste from a tube. Sky rockets were also a favorite. They would go high and shower down pretty colored sparks. I had two brothers and they liked the loud firecrackers that you would light and then throw.

Our home was close to the fairgrounds and during fair time, when the garden was plentiful, my Dad would bring me a peck basket with tomatoes, green peppers, cucumbers, etc. to sell to the neighbors on our street. The money I earned was money for the fair and was kept in a glass jar, by my Dad, for me to take to the fair.

In the wintertime, when the snows were right, the city policemen would block off certain streets to be used strictly for sled riding. Wooden horses would be placed at each end of the street and no cars could travel that particular street at that time. Needless to say, streets were selected that had hills.

When I was eight years old I came home from school one day and my Dad told me I had a new baby sister. Wow! I thought that stork must have flown pretty low to drop a new little baby down our chimney! I didn't even know we were expecting a new family member. She was a delight and a pain. She cried a lot and also smiled a lot. I was no longer the baby in the family with two older brothers.

I can remember my Mother taking me for a permanent the first time. The beauty shop was downtown on Main Street; upstairs above a "Five and Dime" store. I sat on a board that was across the chair to make me higher, and then a lot of metal clamps that were attached to electric cords were put on my head. The electric was turned on and I remember my head getting hot, then I had curls!

The downtown stores were open on Saturday nights and everyone came to town. The street corners were always full of people discussing the weather, crops, newest purchases or anything else. Farmers always came to town on Saturday nights so their wives could shop and catch up on the latest news; whether it be gossip or fact.

My parents dealt with a small family owned grocery store on the next block and would pay their bill every two weeks. That was the time my two brothers and I looked forward to because the owner of the store always gave us a big sack of penny candy each time Dad paid the bill.

I remember in the fall when the coal truck would back into our driveway to deliver coal for the winter. They put the chute in a basement window directly into our coal bin. Mom always made sure all windows and doors were shut tight so no coal dust would get into our home. Dad made sure the coal bin was shut tight.

Oh! Springtime! Posters would go up all over the city announcing Barnum and Bailey Circus would be coming to town in May. Our dad always noted the time of arrival and would take us down to the train station to watch the circus unload. Huge elephants walked down a small ramp from a box car. What a sight to see! Also, caged lions were carefully brought from the train. When the train was emptied, a parade would form and go to the fairgrounds. We would get in the car and then Dad would take us to a place on the parade route and park the car along the side of the road so we could watch. The parade would be led by the Ring Master in his red suit with gold braid and a black derby hat on his head. Lions in cages pulled by horses, elephants being prodded by their trainers to keep in line, clowns riding unicycles and brightly dressed performers riding horseback. We waited patiently for the blare of the steam whistles of the calliope (it had the sound of an organ.) The parade soon ended and we drove into the fairgrounds to again see the animals and watch the big tent being raised. Several local teen age boys standing around would be asked to help and to carry water to the animals and help feed them. For this they were rewarded with a free pass to the circus. A "Side Show" also accompanied the circus with freakish animals, maybe a woman with a beard, a two headed snake and a man who could wrap himself up like a pretzel. We were never allowed to spend our money on the "Side Show."

The Fantastic Model B Road Trip

by Doris M. Morrison of Dover, Ohio
Born 1921

I was 26-years-old and never had a car. I lived with my grandparents who could not drive. A man in town had a 1932 Model B Ford with a 1936 V8 motor engine in it. He wanted $100.00 for it; said he hated to sell it to me because it needed so much, but I got it.

My cousin, Ray Stahl, who was in the Navy in New York and kept writing he was homesick, bought a tire off of my uncle, who had a little store in town, and sold it to me for six or seven dollars. His brother, Loy Stahl, a friend of mine, Marylue Stull and I took off to see him. We had a sign on the back of car, said, "To New York or Bust!" When my cousin seen the sign we all cried. He knew the car. We got along fine. Came home and it was so hot, decided to go to Cleveland to Mentor on the lake. My girlfriend and a boy from town who wasn't well, but his mother asked me if he could go too. Got to Mentor and the beach was closed. They thought the sand was causing infrintillis, so we got out the map and took off. We had a Coleman stove, fold up table, charcoal pots and pans. They had little vegetable stands along the road, so we would load up. Ate a lot of jelly and peanut bread. First stop was Brookfield, Ohio; seen a calf who had two heads and a bull with four eyes. Next to Garfield home in Ohio, then Springfield, Illinois to see Lincoln's house and different places about him. To Missouri to see Mark Twain's house and all about him.

Omaha, Nebraska to Boys Town. They took us through; it was really great. Took pictures outside that said Omaha, pop 223844; wonder what it is now. In Iowa we stopped at a little place that said coffee shop. We decided that we was going to have one good meal a day. The manager was a heavyset man. We had eggs, toast and tea. He sat with us and talked all about us. When we went to pay, he said no charge and gave us three candy bars and said, "Be careful, you're good kids." Then we went to Colorado and to Yellowstone Park. We had a little plastic gun in the back window and a policeman took it. We got a big laugh out of that. Seen the beautiful mountains and started down. Had to drive in low because brakes wasn't good. When we got down we went to a filling station and a piece came off of the alternator. The young man said he knew an old man that would weld it. He took us to his place, got him up, and he was mad. Then he took us all around the city, went back and the man had left it outside. He put it on for us and said, "No charge, had a lot of fun with you kids," filled the gas up and said "Good luck." We took Route 39 home and we made it. Over one thousand five hundred miles. The old car was still good. Had it when I got married in 1947. I am 88 years old on May 25th.

Don't Waste...and Thank the Lord

by Ida Miller of Sugarcreek, Ohio
Born 1936

Feed Sacks. Getting into the tough days of living in the 1930's, I remember buying chicken feed in feed sacks that could be washed. We had lots of use for them. There were sacks with monkeys on them. We used those to make hankies…lots, and lots of hankies. No paper tissues were bought at that time.

Nothing was ever wasted in those days. We learned a lot in those days. We learned to be patient with what we had and to thank the Lord for everything we had. We made tea towels, pillowcases, tablecloths, bed sheets, slips, shirts, panties, aprons, dresses and doll clothes. There were feed sacks with roses on them. We took and made a bag big enough to hold one-gallon of shelled popcorn for the teacher for Christmas; it was delicious.

I respect my parents, how they handled these things. It was not going out eating and buying things they didn't need. We had lots of things to do on the farm. We did not have time to be bored. We enjoyed working on the farm. We had eggs to clean, cows to milk, help make hay, getting meals on the table, washing dishes, house cleaning, mowing the yard and also a lot of canning was done. When the blackberries were ripe we all went along to pick blackberries. We canned 100 quarts of blackberries, also applesauce, corn, peaches, cherries, pears, beans, pickles, red beets, vegetable soup, grape juice and meat. When winter came along, canned goods was delicious. Mom also baked a lot of pies, cakes, cookies, bread and rolls. We had a wonderful time.

I came from a family of 12 children: six girls and six boys. I am a twin. My name is Ida and my twin sister's name is Iva. When we were babies, ten months old, my sister, Ada, eight years old, put us in a baby carriage and took us for a ride. Somehow she spilled us out of the carriage. I don't know who cried the most, Ada or the babies, but everything turned out fine. We are still living. We will be 73 in September.

One more thing: when our parents gave us gum, it was a half piece. Today it's one piece or a whole pack. We had to share, but we wanted to make sure to get the biggest piece. But it always turned out fine.

Aunt Anna's Gaslight Predicament

by Beverly Jane Wharton of Barnesville, Ohio
born 1935

I was born in 1935 and everything has changed since then, even the way we build houses. There was no such thing as insulation and plaster-board and we had gas lights.

We lived in a duplex which had been left to my mother and her sister. We lived on one side and my mother's sister, Anna, who didn't get along well with my dad, lived on the other side. She was an old maid, as they called ladies that didn't get married back then.

After their mother died, when my mother was just eight years old, Anna was a good bit older, and after she got a job, took my mother and raised her. She was used to looking after my mother and being in charge, so she interfered sometimes and Daddy said she was bossy.

She had a habit of turning the gas light way down and using it for a night light, you might say. Daddy had warned her many times that she should not do that. Of course she made a point of not listening to anything he said.

My funny story is about when I was a preteen, when our house began to smell of smoke, but no one could see where it was coming from. I was terrified, especially when no one could find out where the smoke was coming from. It was just after the Depression, when we had so little of everything back then, that I immediately started taking all the clothes out of closets and drawers and taking them outside. I was running back and forth and back and forth as fast as my little legs would carry me. My parents and sisters were laughing at me. I was so hurt and then I got mad because they didn't realize the danger. But I wouldn't stop and kept on trying to get everything out of the house.

Stuckey girls: Georgie on left, Beverly and Shirley in 1936.

The fire department was called and they went all over the house and even looked up the fireplaces into the chimneys but no one could find anything.

One of the firemen decided to go around the walls and feel for a hot spot. Low and behold if he didn't solve the mystery. Anna had continued to leave the gas light on low and pushed too close to the wall and the lath wood between the plaster had gotten hotter and hotter, then finally started to smolder and burn. The fireman had to hatchet into the wall and wet it down which caused a lot of water damage inside the house and made a terrible mess, not to mention all that it was going to cost my dad to repair everything. As you might guess, Daddy took the opportunity to give Anna a piece of his mind and it started a Third World War at our house. That episode was a source of big stories that were told and laughed about for the rest of our lives.

Although money was scarce, somehow Daddy used his trade of being a carpenter and also held down a job in the factories, when they were available. We never starved and we had parents that put us first and we knew we were loved.

Most mothers didn't work outside the home and we always knew when we got home from school or outside playing, Mom would be there to tell of the adventures of the day, or the problems we might have had and would tell us how to fix it, while she fixed a cup of cocoa.

Kids grow up so lonesome and mixed up these days. One of the things that I believe causes that, is they don't have Mom at home waiting for them and they have to be afraid of being home alone. If our mom wasn't home, you could go to any neighbors' mom and stay 'til your mom got back.

We didn't have furnaces and we had to go out to the coal house, no matter what the temperature, and bring coal in several times a day...not to mention the trips to the outhouse. Then when summer came, you had to mow the yard with a push mower. Unfortunately, we had some of the steepest banks in town.

It all sounds hard but as I look back, those were the best days of our lives. We caught fireflies and put them in jars and tied the jar to the bicycle handles and said they were our headlights. And then there was the Saturday night trip downtown to a movie or to the ice cream parlor. Everyone else was there and everybody talked to each other and the kids would sit together and laugh and have a good time.

Then Daddy would go down this road outside of town that had big dips in it and it would make us bounce and giggle. Then he would turn around and go home and we would play games or cards 'til it was time for bed, hardly able to wait 'til the next day to go to church and see our friends again, have that big Sunday dinner and go somewhere in the afternoon for a ride to visit friends or family or go to the lake to go swimming in the summer.

I know that we didn't worry about being afraid that someone might kidnap us or hurt us. How sad it makes me to see the things that endanger our little ones now, even many are abused by their own parents.

The 50's were the best time in the world to have grown up. We have lived long enough to see the Industrial Revolution and a Technological Revolution, four or five wars, a man on the moon, and an African America become the President of the United States! What a time to be alive! We have lived to see unbelievable changes.

Pleasant Memories of Close Families

by Marilyn J. Foster of Strasburg, Ohio
born 1930

I grew up in Akron, Ohio. Some of the things I remember while growing up was, first of all, spending a lot of time outside. As a tomboy, I recall skating, riding my bicycle, climbing our backyard cherry tree, jumping rope, and playing jacks.

We lived in a very nice two story, three bedroom, and one bath house and paid all of $28 a month for rent in those Depression days. One time, our landlady came to do some wall papering, and pasted the strips of paper on our ironing board. I decided to have some fun and placed a fake, but very real looking, green snake on the board and gave her quite a scare.

I also remember the neighborhood grocer just a block from our home. He enjoyed deer hunting and brought us venison quite often. That gesture was much appreciated as times were tough, even though my brother and I were not aware of it. We were well taken care of.

My grandparents all lived only 50 miles away and we visited them quite often. Mother's mama and papa lived on a big 160 acre farm out from Wooster. Grandma raised chickens and supplied us with eggs. There was also butter that she churned and potatoes and other vegetables grown in the big garden out back. She and Grandpa also butchered so we had chicken, bacon, sausage, pork, and ham from the little smokehouse. Dad and my two uncles did a lot of hunting on that farm, so we also had rabbit, squirrel, and pheasant for consumption.

Grandma heated huge tubs of water on the old wood stove for doing laundry in the wringer washer. And, of course, on one wall in their kitchen was one of those crank up party line phones.

On one of the hunting trips, my uncle accidentally shot my dad. He had some buckshot in his head and in his leg the rest of his life. It was fortunate that the experience didn't end up a real tragedy.

My other grandparents lived only five miles away in Big Prairie. My dad's mother had been a schoolteacher and my granddad was a banker.

I have fond memories of summertime ice cream socials that I attended with my grandma. They were held out on the lawn of the Methodist Church. Oh, those hot chicken sandwiches and bowls of homemade ice cream were luscious!

As a kid, I fell and broke my right arm while jumping

on the church steps. Then, while visiting my real grandparents, I fell and sprained it very near the time to get the cast off. So, as a result, they had to reset the arm and I had a cast on for so long that I finally learned to write with my left hand, quite awkward!

As a young married woman in the 50's, I remember some very cold and snowy, icy winters. My husband, a Methodist minister, and I lived for a couple of years in a small mining town. We lived in the parsonage, which was quite nice, with six rooms and a *path*. The pipes froze quite often and we had to thaw them out with a blowtorch. The kitchen did present a bit of a problem as it had no counter space and no cupboards. There was a small pitcher pump and a cupboard in a small back room off the kitchen as well as our icebox with the pan underneath which collected the water as the block of ice melted.

I was pregnant with our first child and believe me, I made as few trips as possible to that cold outhouse. To get to it required going down several steps over a small bank in the backyard. I was very grateful for our chamber pot even though I had never seen one before.

My dad liked to fish, so nearly every summer we drove up to a very remote (30 miles from civilization) spot in Canada. There were lots of snakes and bears around, and one night my poor mom was abruptly awakened when a mouse, playing up on the rafters, tumbled down onto her chest.

My younger brother had a scary thing happen. A huge black hairy spider got inside his shirt and down his back. It took us a while to figure out what the yelling and dancing a jig was all about.

While there at the lake, we had no refrigerator, so we had to bury our bacon, butter, etc in a deep hole in the ground. We lost a few items to a dog or scavenger bear that sniffed out our storage place.

In the old cabin was an old crank-up phonograph and over and over we played, "It's a Long Way to Tipperary," etc.

We always had fun picking fresh blueberries up above a hillside on the lake. And those fresh fish out of the lake that my grandmother rolled in cornmeal and cooked in an old iron skillet were oh, so yummy!

Another memory I have of Akron is one year in the 40's, there was a tornado that ripped quite a destructive path through part of town. One family from our church had the entire second floor blown away by the storm. Then in 1951, Ohio had a big ice storm hit. I remember every tree branch, bush, wires, fences, etc were all covered with ice. It was beautiful when the sun shone on all that and it glistened brightly. However, it made for treacherous travel. My husband spent nearly a week in East Liverpool, where he worked before it was safe to drive home.

In my youth, most families lived close to each other. We often were with my cousins, aunts, and uncles out at the farm. All the relatives gathered at Easter, Thanksgiving, and Christmas to enjoy Grandma's homemade noodles, dinner rolls, delicious pies, as well as the churned butter, pickles, whipping cream, and vegetables grown in the garden. Right by the garden was a wonderfully fragrant lilac bush that we all loved to see bloom every spring.

One of my very favorite things to do as a child, and later, a teenager, was to go to church camp in Mt. Vernon every August. It was a ten day camp and we lived in an old army tent that sat on a wooden platform. As a teenage girl, I tended the salad bar in the cafeteria. I met the man I was married to for 54 years there. He was the pianist for the youth meetings and very talented as well as charming and good looking. Both our families took us there from the time we were very young, and we took our four daughters there, as well. It was a great place to meet friends we hadn't seen in a year or two and to make new friends. There was no smoking, drinking, swearing, or any of that, and was like living in a different world for a short time each year. We had such good times, it was always a little sad to see it come to an end.

Grandma Hickey's Skirts and Evelyn's Spring

by Doris Baker of Newcomerstown, Ohio
born in 1935

When I was growing up, my grandmother, Grandma Hickey (short for Hickenbottom), came to live with our family periodically. She lived with each of her eight children for one or two months at a time. She was a great seamstress and would make clothes for me and my three sisters.

We lived on a farm, so we had a good supply of feed sacks. As soon as my dad would bring home the feed, I would go to the granary, where the feed was stored until it was used, to chose which sack I wanted Grandma to use to make a skirt for me.'

One year when we were planning to go to the family reunion, Grandma made a skirt for me and one for my sister, who was next to me in age. It was about 1947, and I was about 12 years old. She also made skirts for three of my cousins—of course of feed sacks too. We all modeled them at the family gathering. You would have thought we were royalty, the way we paraded in those "new" skirts.

As we look back on these days, we realize how little it took to make a young girl happy. The feed sacks were actually just a by-product, but at that time (end of the Great Depression, into WWII a few years after) everyone used every scrap. This taught the young great "life lessons."

Scary Happening for Two Young Kids. This happened in 1941. When I was six and my sister, Evelyn, was three, we went to our uncle's (Howard Naylor) farm. We lived on a farm too, which was about a half mile away. He had apple trees, so our mother, Mabel Lyon, sent us over to his farm to bring some apples home so she could make some applesauce and pies. We took our little wagon and a basket. We picked the apples off the ground and started home.

Along the road going home, we passed a big watering trough. It was a stone hewn out for the water. It measured about two feet by five feet and was three feet deep. It was on our farm, but used by many passers-by. In previous years, it was used by travelers to water their horses. At that time, many people had to stop to add water to their Model T that overheated.

I had the "bright" idea that we needed to wash the apples. So Evelyn and I stopped to wash them. We were fine when we dumped the apples in, but when we tried to get the apples out, Evelyn accidentally tumbled into the water when she reached in. It was over her head and I couldn't pull her out. I started screaming for help, but knew our house was too far from the watering through for our mother to hear. We were also too far from Uncle Howard's to be heard.

I started running for our house. Soon I saw another uncle, Bob Hickenbottom, coming down the road. I quickly told him Evelyn had fallen into the spring. He ran to her rescue. She was gasping for air as he pulled her to safety. I'm not sure who was frightened more, Evelyn or I. Uncle Bob took us home and dried her off.

Then came the time that I had to tell Mom what had happened. She scolded me and reminded me what could have been the result if Uncle Bob had not happened to be coming down the road. To this day we refer to that home as the one "where Evelyn fell into the spring."

Beth's Fire Engine and the Cherry Tree Bell

by Barbara A. Osburn of Zanesville, Ohio
born in 1939

My earliest recollection of life in a small city came when I was about five years old. My family lived on a nice street, lined with trees. Most of the homes were bungalow style. Next door to us was a vacant lot, where my father raised chickens and my two brothers played basketball with the neighbor kids. I don't recall my father having chickens for any length of time, but I do remember one of them following me and pecking at me. I didn't like that much. I was the youngest of four children: two brothers and a sister. I was the baby. My siblings never let me forget it.

Next to the vacant lot was a two-story house which was rare for our street. I can remember one summer day a moving van came and started unloading furniture, etc., to that house. The first thing I saw were two, exactly alike, red fire engines that you pedaled. I became so excited, because I knew there were going to be some kids moving in. We had mostly boys in the neighborhood and I sure was hoping one of those fire engines was for a girl. Alas! Here comes a car pulling into the driveway and guess what? There was a boy and a girl. The girl looked to be about my age and the boy younger. Was I a happy little girl!

I don't remember how I became acquainted, but knowing me, I probably rushed right over and asked if I could ride the fire engine. From that time on, Beth and I became life long friends.

She moved to Cleveland when we were 11 or 12, but we still visited each other. I would spend about 10 days at her house in the summer and she would spend the same at my house. The relationship lasted for over 60 years and many moves, until Beth passed away, living in Kansas.

Another thing I remember, at about the same age, was we had a big front porch on our house and this is where many things took place. I remember my mother sitting on the porch visiting with her best friend, who lived a few houses down the street. I would climb onto her lap and she would rock me and put me to sleep. I don't know if it was the drone of their voices or the creak of the chair, but I do remember going to sleep there. I couldn't tell you what they were talking about. It never interested me. Also, my mother was always kissing my ear. Oh how I hated that!

Now, out front of our house we had a cherry tree. The street was paved and there was a nice sidewalk running all the way down our avenue with a lot of houses. To get to the bus line, you had to walk up to the end of our street, turn right and wait on the corner of the next street. Many people rode the bus back then. Everyone that walked up our street would grab a handful of cherries. My, what a treat. My mother made the best cherry pie in town. I can remember my father sitting on the front porch with a bell he had rigged up to scare off the birds, when they landed in the cherry tree to eat. He would pull a cord and the clanging scared them off. The neighbors all laughed at this, but it worked. He would sit out there for what seemed like hours when he wasn't at work, clanging that bell. When the cherries were ripe for picking, he didn't want to waste any on the birds.

After many years, the cherry tree had to be cut down. I was then a teenager and I kept one of the branches in my bedroom for a long, long time. I hated to see that tree go.

Now I told you as much as I could remember about

the chickens, but my father at some time in my young life also raised rabbits. He built quite a pen in our small backyard and had many, many rabbits. I played with them, but I don't remember exactly how long we had the rabbits or the chickens.

I also remember, two streets over from us, there weren't many house built as yet when I was a youngster, but my father had a huge garden. To me, it was a city block long and wide. I am sure it wasn't, but I do remember the good food that came from it. My mother canned. She canned everything and I remember, after I grew up, the first time I had to buy something at the store in a can, I thought I would die. It sure didn't taste like Mom's home canned food.

Mother liked to go berry picking. She would get all set and made sure I had on long sleeves, long pants, etc., so we wouldn't get jiggers. I didn't much care for that, but again, I liked the pies.

I loved riding my bike and there weren't too many girls in the neighborhood, so I rode a lot with the boys. Sometimes they were nasty, or so I thought at the time, but when I grew up, I still remained friends with some of them. One of them walked me down the aisle at high school graduation and we remained friends.

I remember my father, who was quite the fisherman, had a rowboat and he kept it in our side yard. My two girlfriends and I would get in that boat and sit and play and dream like we were in another world. I also, remember teaching one of my friends, who was older than me, by the way, how to tie her shoes. That had to be a hoot.

We spent a lot of weekends fishing. My mother would pack up a picnic and away we would go. We went all over the state to different parks to fish. I can remember my dad belonging to some kind of fisherman's club and he spent a lot of time in our side yard practicing casting. I fished a little, but I got bored sitting there and being quiet, so Mom and I would go pick wildflowers or hunt for four leaf clovers or read. It was a great life. When all this was taking place, I was the only one left at home. There was such an age difference between me and my siblings. My oldest brother went into the navy when I was a baby, but that is another story.

I can't remember this, but the pictures tell the tale. I dressed myself one summer day and the neighbors took pictures of me and my friend on stilts. My dress was on wrong side out. I believe my dad built the stilts. He was quite an athlete and also loved woodworking. After I grew up, he made me a surfboard and made a pair of water skis as my sister and her husband had a boat and we spent many hours water skiing

My uncle, who was my mother's brother, lived with us when I was a small child. He died when I was fifteen, but he was the apple of my eye. What my parents didn't get for me, my uncle did. He had an office downtown and every Saturday for many summers, when I was a small child, he would work a half a day on Saturday and then he would come home, get me and we would go back to town. First of all he would take me to his office where I was allowed to play on his secretary's typewriter, then we would go to the newsstand and he would buy me comic books or as we called them, "funny books." Wish I had some of those now! Then we would go up the street to this neat little restaurant and we would eat, then he would put me in a cab, tell the cab driver the address and then told him he would recognize the house; it was the one with the mortgage on it. I never quite understood what he meant until years later. Of course, since my uncle never drove and always took cabs, the cab drivers all knew him. I don't know what he did the rest of the time, because he wouldn't come home until real late at night or what I thought was real late.

I had a great childhood. It was during the times when you didn't lock your doors, drugs were never heard of, child abuse wasn't happening...just good old behind smacking if you disobeyed. Also, we called our elders Mr. or Mrs., attended Sunday School and church regularly and enjoyed Sunday dinners with the family and taking rides on Sunday afternoons. A simple life, but good. If my parents weren't rich, I didn't know it. They didn't discuss money matters in front of me. Also, they didn't fight in front of me; if they did, I sure wasn't aware of it. I was a happy little girl.

Now, about my oldest brother. He joined the Navy, as a teenager when I was only a couple of years old. He went off to Japan and was gone a long, long time. When he came home, I had started school, so as soon as he got home, he went right up to that school and took me out of there. He wanted to see his baby sister. I have pictures of me in a sailor suit and hat. I worshiped him. I can also remember, when my parents would get a phone call from him overseas, if I was up the street at the neighbors house, my mom would get out and holler for me that my brother was on the phone and I would run so fast I could have won a marathon. I do remember, when he came home, I brought all the neighborhood kids I could gather up, to come and watch him shave. That was my big brother! Oh yes, the years he was in the Navy, we had a red, white and blue star in the window to let people know we had someone in the service.

At the time I was seven or eight, my father's job took him to Tacoma, Washington. My heart broke. We didn't go with him. I cried myself to sleep many nights. One day, after he had been there several months, he came home on vacation. My parents decided that we would take him back by car. So Mom, Dad, my youngest brother, sister and I got into Dad's old Ford and away we went. That is another whole story, but after we arrived in

Tacoma and went to the hotel where my father was staying (the Fairmont Hotel, with the largest totem pole in the world, beside of it), I thought I had died and gone to heaven. I was allowed to ride up and down the elevator by myself. The hotel owner was acquainted with my father and he had a little girl my age, so he took me home with him to stay overnight with his daughter. I can't even remember her name, but I'm sure I had a great time. I don't remember how long we were in Washington, but I know how hard it was on me, when we had to leave and leave Dad behind. Mom didn't want to move, so after a period of time, Dad quit his job and came back home. That was a happy day for me.

I was also quite a pest. Since my sister was eight years older than me at the time she started dating, I was still a little bratty kid. Boys would come to the house to pick my sister up for a date and, if they were going to stay home, the boyfriend would pay me to stay out of the living room where they were sitting. We didn't have a family room back then and the only way for them to be alone would be for everyone to get out of the living room. Needless to say, I would pester them every time, so I would get a quarter to get lost. Fond memories. Now, I'm not sure where my parents were at this time, but believe me, they were home, maybe on the back porch or backyard.

I cannot remember any bad times during my growing-up years. I feel my childhood was the happiest time of my life, no worries, cares, or heartaches. I spent a lot of time on the porch (with cookies and lemonade) playing with paper dolls and coloring books. What a great time!

Growing up Lutheran, I had to attend two years of catechism before I could join the church. We met every Saturday morning at 9:00 AM. I really hated this, because I liked to sleep in, but I attended every time. After I grew up, I was glad my mother made me do this.

Also, I walked quite a ways to take piano lessons as a child. I didn't keep this up for very long, as I hated to practice and begged my parents to get rid of the piano, which incidentally, they did not do at the time. The piano we had was a player piano and we spent many good times sitting around that piano and pumping the keys to get songs out. I found that to be much more interesting than actually learning to play.

Soon after I started school, new neighbors moved in across the street from us. There was a mom and dad, a son and daughter. The son was the same age as I was and we became friends. I remember one Christmas he and I both got chicken pox a few days before Christmas. We were both pretty sick and I remember I was allowed to get out of bed on Christmas Eve to see the tree. After that, during our convalescence period, he was allowed to come over to my house and play. There we were, pox all over us and in our pajamas, playing on the living room floor. We used to take dominos and make roads and play with cars. Sometimes we used playing cards to make the roads.

When his sister got old enough, she followed me around. No matter what I did or what I got, she had to have the same or do the same. It was very annoying for awhile, until she got big enough that we could really become friends. By that time, boys were yucky, so I didn't play with her brother. I can remember her mother would fix us lunch and we would sit out on her front porch and eat on her little table and chairs. It was always tomato soup. That is when I learned to love tomato soup with milk and lots of butter in it. To this day that is how I eat it.

Another neighbor introduced me to macaroni and cheese. I didn't like it, but because I was invited to eat supper with them, and I was being polite, I continued to eat until I got sick. That was the end of macaroni and cheese. It was many, many years before I could even attempt to eat it. I like it now!

Going backwards, as I said before, my father was a great athlete. He played baseball professionally until he slid in to home base and broke his leg. I believe that was before I was born. Anyway, by the time I was two, I was roller-skating, and wasn't much older than that when I was ice-skating. I remember my good friend Beth and I would roller skate down the middle of our street (in the street) singing, Zippity Do Da. See why my childhood was so happy? All the fun things I got to do. Dad would take me skating after the skating rink in our town opened up. There was a drawing at one time and Dad won a free pair of shoe skates. Of course, he let me get them. I thought I had died and gone to heaven. A brand new pair of shoe skates! Who could ask for anything more?

Now, I must tell you about my first boyfriend. We were in the first grade. When it came time for Valentines Day, it was always a big thing to make a Valentine box at home out of a shoebox. I would decorate it (I'm sure I had help probably from my big sister) then take it to school on Valentines Day along with enough valentines for the whole class. But, my special boy friend, who lived on the next street, would always come after school and bring me a box of candy, of course, heart shaped. He moved to Lancaster when he was very young, but since my mother and his mother were friends and kept in contact, so did he and I. Later on, they moved to Texas. I married, he married. We are still close friends. He now lives in Seattle, but we still keep in contact. When he was going to Texas A&M, he wanted to marry me, but I guess I was too young and that was too far away from my mother and father, and I had a two-year-old at the time. I wonder how many now days keep up with old friends over the years. It seems everyone is so busy doing their own "thing" close friendships aren't a priority.

That is sad. I see friends come and go with the younger generation.

I don't remember too much about World War II, but I vaguely remember ration books. You had to use a ration coupon to buy sugar, if I'm not mistaken. And I remember when oleo first came on the scene, to replace butter. It was white and looked like a bag of lard with a yellow dab in the middle. You had to knead the bag to get the coloring all through, and then you had oleo!

I also remember tax stamps. I spent many hours helping my mother count and sort them for my uncle. They were green and I can remember three-cent stamps. If there were any other denomination, I don't remember. We would put them in stacks and rubber band the stacks. I don't know why, but I helped. Also, during the war, my father was a civil defense person and every so often we had to practice a neighborhood blackout. My dad would go up and down our street to make sure everyone was observing the blackout, no lights on. He wore a patch around his upper arm to identify himself, as a civil defense worker.

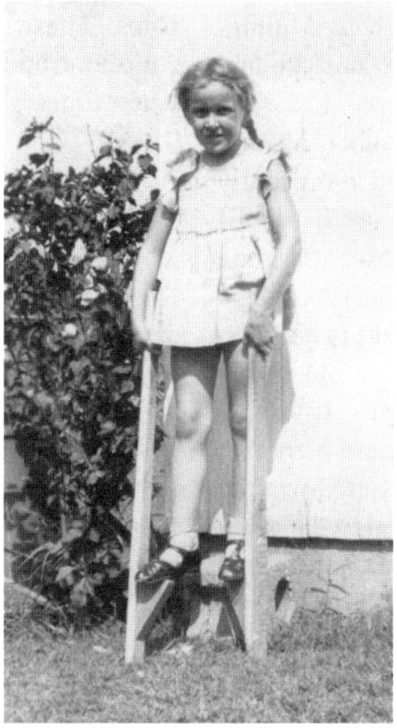

Barbara Osburn with dress on wrong side out walking on stilts.

One thing I can remember as a youngster was how hot the summers could be. Most of the time, especially during the day, I was grateful for the heat, because that meant I could play outside or go swimming. But the hot nights, trying to sleep.... Of course, back then we did not have air conditioning. I can remember times when my window would be open and I would go to the foot of the bed, where my window was located and sleep with my head on the window sill just to get a bit of fresh air. Also, as a child, I had what they called it back then, hay fever. A lot of nights, after a bout of sneezing and blowing my nose, my nose would become stopped up. I would wet a handkerchief and lay across my nose, so I could breath. My mother soon learned that not only was I allergic to ragweed, but I had a feather pillow and I was also allergic to the feathers. I remember a time after I grew up, my future husband brought me a beautiful red rose from his mother's garden. I put it in a vase in my bedroom and you guessed it, I couldn't sleep that night; I was allergic to roses. Needless to say, in my wedding I did not have any roses, as was popular for weddings in the late fifties and early sixties.

As a child, I loved the water. I wasn't afraid of it at all. As a matter of fact, my father took me to an amusement park south of our city, that had a swimming pool with a huge slide and, at two years old, he would sit me on his lap and go down that slide with me and under the water we would go. I loved every minute of it. He taught me to swim, not in that nice clean pool, but in the river. Oh well, it was much cleaner in those days. I grew up loving to swim. I can remember walking a long distance to get to our public swimming pool, but I didn't seem to mind. Even after spending the day swimming and playing in the pool, then I would walk home, which consisted of a very long hill to climb to get home. Didn't mind at all. Of course, I wasn't alone; several of my friends and I would go together. I bet after I arrived home, I had some cookies and lemonade. Can you imagine children today having to walk anywhere?

When I was twelve, my sister got married. Her boyfriend was in the army and when he came home on furlough, they got married. It was a small wedding at our church. The only thing I really remember is, while standing at the altar, my sister dropped one of her gloves and, after they were married, going down the aisle, I had to run up there and retrieve that glove. How embarrassing for me!

I can vaguely remember my older brother getting married. He was married in a funeral home. An aunt and uncle of the gal he married owned the funeral home and that is where they decided to hold the wedding. I do remember my father was still in Tacoma and was to fly in for the wedding. His plane was delayed and he didn't get there until after they said their vows, but at least he made it. My younger brother eloped when he was only 18 or so. I don't remember too much about that time.

After my sister and her husband were married, he was stationed in Colorado. She still lived with us. He called one day and said he was being shipped out to Alaska and would be gone for two years. So right now, my dad packed us all up, mother, father, sister, me, her husband's mom, the mother of one of his buddies, who was stationed with him. Can you imagine driving across the states in a car with six people jammed in there? I know I had a really great time, but couldn't understand why my sister and her husband had a motel room all to themselves, when the rest of us shared. I thought I should be able to stay with them, they had plenty of room.

I could go on forever about my childhood in a small town, but these are some of the highlights and things I remember the most. I know I have been told other things that trigger memories, but these are my most memorable treasures as a child.

Lighting Up Ohio

by L. Ruth Scott of Gnadenhutten, Ohio
born 1927

As a preteen living on a small farm in Ohio in 1940, the excitement was anticipation of the arrival of electricity. The folks had attended the REA (Rural Electrification of America) meetings, had paid the necessary fee for membership, had hired someone to wire the buildings to receive the power. This wiring included the barn, outbuildings and a pole light to light the way at night. REA had planted poles and strung wires to our site and we were ready.

On a Saturday morning in early December, Mother announced that we were going to town. Dad was usually far too busy to go to town, but a younger brother and I went with Mother. As we returned from town, the road came around a hillside that overlooked the farm buildings. Excitedly, Mother said, "Look, the pole light is on!"

When our excitement died down, Mother told us that she had bought a Christmas gift for all of us. It was an electric radio about the size of a shoebox and a contact with the outside world. In 1941 the folks went down the road to visit neighbors as I read and listened to the radio when the announcement came that the Japanese had bombed Pearl Harbor.

Electricity had brought a big change in the family. The bombing of Pearl Harbor brought even bigger changes.

The Tough Thirties

by Richard Baumgardner of Coshocton, Ohio
born in 1932

I was born in a little town of Coshocton, Ohio on October 26, 1932. Times were hard back in the thirties, people out of work, money scarce so as a family we would put in a garden and harvest the produce, can up the tomatoes, carrots, pick blackberries and can make jam and jelly and in the fall, gather all kinds of nuts, walnuts, hickory, hazelnuts, dry them and my mother would make fudge at Christmas with some the nuts. Also, we had a big grape arbor in the backyard. We would pick the grapes and bottle the juice. That was our soda pop in those days. I had the job of putting the caps on the bottles with a lever on it to seal them.

On Sunday evening we would set by the fireplace and listen to the radio to Amos and Andy, Fibber McGee and Molly and Jack Benny. Mom would open up some grape juice and pop some corn grown by my father and that was our enjoyment for the evening. No TV in those days.

I remember Mom's wringer washer. I wanted to help so she let me run some clothes through the wringer. I got my fingers too close to the rollers and they pulled my hand into the wringer. I yelled and Mom hit the pressure release and got my arm out before it broke it. I wasn't hurt but was scared and Mom too.

I remember wearing knicker pants to school with patches on the knees as that was where they would wear first from playing marbles on your knees at recess and putting cardboard in my shoes to cover the holes in the soles. These are just a few of my memories of early childhood and made me more appreciative of little things when times got better.

The Wicked Winter and Naming the Deer

by Dixie Ball Hooper of Dresden, Ohio
born in 1940

The winter of 1944-'45 was by most accounts a wicked one, with low temperatures and lots of snow. So it was in near blizzard conditions when my parents realized it was nearing the time for my first sibling to arrive, and there was no way our old Plymouth could traverse the drifts for three miles to the state highway. They proceeded to bundle up and walk out cross-country on cow paths through the woods, along a ravine, then across a creek and a bottom cornfield to the home of our landlord's family on the highway. Dad walked back home, and a week or so later, the landlord's family brought Mother home with my new little brother.

In the spring, these same dirt roads would bottom out, and the school buses could not travel through the mud, so Dad walked out with me the first mile to the nearest neighbors, and I continued on with the neighbor children to the state highway and back the same way at night.

In the fall of 1950, we moved two miles in the opposite direction to another farm in a different school district.

Summer of No Memories. It had been a late spring in our neck of the woods in 1954. School had already let out for the summer, but there was still little undergrowth in the woods where I walked, scuffing at the green moss along the edge of the creek with my old run-over loafers.

I was in a very sad mood that day. My nine-year-old brother and his friend were allowed to get on their bikes and go to the river to fish. I, on the other hand, though ready to go into high school, was not allowed to leave home. I needed to stay close by in case Mother needed help with my five-year-old sister and two-month-old baby brother.

So here I was on a bright, sunny day with nothing to do but walk through the woods with the lush green grass and the spring wildflowers waving around my feet. The boys would be biking through the covered bridge at Pleasant Valley to fish to their hearts' content, then get an ice cream cone at the general store when they stopped to see the old steam engine snag the mail off the pole as it went by.

Home of Ron Hooper until 1959 which began as a stage coach stop.

Startled, I looked up to see the family of deer are still here. There are five of them now. Three years ago, we saw the first wild deer we had ever seen jump the fence of the cow pasture. My father, who had problems with his eyesight (later diagnosed as macular degeneration), stood with jaw dropped, thinking one of his cows had just jumped the fence, and we all laughed. That year, a new fawn was born, and last spring, they had twins. We still have not seen any others, but it is a big woods. They are wary when they see me, but they don't run far since they see me fairly often in my favorite haunt, and after all, I have given them all names.

Waving goodbye, I walk a way further and come in sight of the old log cabin where the old Runyon brothers live. They came here from Germany, and it is still hard to understand what they say. They come up and help Dad on the farm sometimes, and one time, the younger brother brought a book of pictures back to me, which I had dropped in the woods and thought was lost forever.

A little way further through the woods is the home of the Douglas family. Mrs. Douglas is a very pretty lady, and they have lots of children. One time she brought some very pretty dresses to Mother to use for me. They were made of crepe with tiny covered buttons and intricate beading. My aunt said they were very expensive.

Well, I suppose I have to go back now. The neighbors, who have an orchard, dropped off some apples, and I hope Mom baked a pie. Everything will be the same all summer long, and I will have to go on to high school from another summer with nothing to remember.

Karma. The farmhouse we moved into in 1950 was sixteen rooms. The original half had been a stagecoach stop in the 1800's, built of sandstone blocks with window seats at least eighteen inches deep. An additional eight rooms were added where the owners lived, and the tenants occupied the stone half. There was one water faucet in each side, no central heat or plumbing. A dark cellar under the original section had a corner fireplace, where Indians were supposed to have come in to share the fire as well, and a two-step stone right outside for passengers to climb on and off the stagecoach.

Mother used the cellar to store canned pork, beef, and chicken and every fruit or vegetable available, plus stone jars of green tomato slices or green peppers stuffed with cabbage or sliced cabbage (sauerkraut), all preserved in brine. She did the washing on a washboard with homemade lye soap, which made her hands and arms chafe and blister. By 1956, she finally had a wringer washer.

Entertainment was an old wind-up Victrola with a few "78" records left by a previous occupant (Wreck of the old '97, Grandpa Jones, and Down Yonder), or an old radio we used to listen to "The Shadow Knows" or "Amos N' Andy." In 1958, our older brother bought us a television, and we thought that was the greatest thing ever.

I finished high school living here, and just before I was to be married, the government bought up all the property in the valley to build the Dillon Dam to protect the area down river from torrential flooding. My fiancé and I could have purchased the house and a few acres for five hundred dollars on easement. That sounded like a lot of money in those days, but the sixteen-room historical home would have made a great lodge or bed and breakfast. Even now, fifty years later, my husband says, "Yeah! And who would cook the breakfast?" The buildings were all bulldozed in 1960!

On the east side of the county in the mid 1940's, the family of an eight-year-old boy found themselves with no job and nowhere to live when the landlord sold the house they were living in. Someone mentioned a house in the country, which was empty, so they packed up their few belongings and set off on the fifteen-mile journey. What they found was a small house with no amenities, barely livable, way off the road in a woods. They carried water from the creek and cut fire wood and managed to survive there for three years until a large brick home, which had been a stagecoach stop when it was built in 1833, became available. This house had no central heating either, but had a cistern and a crank telephone, an old Victrola with some records of Wreck of Old '97 and Grandpa Jones to listen to and an old radio to hear "Fibber McGee and Molly" and "Gildersleeve."

They managed to get a cow and a horse and some chickens and raised a garden. When he graduated from high school in 1955, he found a job at a plumbing/electrical company in Zanesville, where my brother was working.

He was still working there in 1958, when I graduated

and went to work there.

A year later, we married and moved to a farm in another part of the county with a house built in 1887, where later this year, we will celebrate our fiftieth anniversary.

Karma!

His home and all the building were bulldozed in the 1960's also when the coal companies began stripping. One of the little towns there was "Young *Hickory*!"

Indian Remedies and Rusted Cars

by Richard Hunt of Byesville, Ohio
born in 1948

Yes, I am sixty years old, and I remember going out in the woods with my parents and grandparents to look for sassafras root. They would collect this root, clean it and boil it to make sassafras tea, and it was very good.

I can also remember my grandparents making their own medicine. I remember the drawing salve; it would pull out a splinter or piece of metal. These were good old remedies. Most of the stuff they made would come from old Indian remedies.

Oh yes, the old player piano, you would put in their rolls and the piano would play them, this was cool.

Remember the cars! When they quit, people would say they are worn out, go get another one and put the old one out by the barn, and there it would rust into the ground.

The Long Path

by Kay M. Spratt of Quaker City, Ohio
born in 1938

Oh yes! The good old days.

Our "pot," AKA The "Thunder Mug" as our family called it for obvious reasons. Our famous white jar with the red and white lid was kept in a little room in the back of the house which we called the wash room. Mom's old washer was there along with the big old galvanized tub we filled with hot water on Saturday night and hoped it was your turn to be first to use it.

We were only allowed to use the pot to do number one. Anything else you had to take the big old light and go out the long path. Of course you guessed it: I always found it necessary to go at night. I would beg and coax my sister to go with me but it was no use. She wouldn't give in. The first thing in the morning who ever used it emptied it. Otherwise my job was to empty it as soon as I got home from school.

We lived beside a family with three boys, one of whom was in my class. The boys had a basketball hoop in their yard where all the boys in the small town of Old Washington, Ohio gathered after school. I used to try to sneak out the path to the outhouse before anyone could to see me, but boys will be boys and they would holler and whistle and ask me what I was doing.

Oh yes, one more thing. Other than the main use, the outhouse is the best place to hide till the supper dishes were washed and dried. I had to get even with my sister somehow for letting me face those spiders alone in the dark.

I wouldn't change a thing; those really were the good old days and some of the best days of my life.

Coon Hunting, Inflated Frogs and Common Sense

by Dick Bare of Mount Perry, Ohio
born in 1927

I was born and raised on a farm near Glenford, Ohio located in Perry County, Hopewell Township. I was born in 1927, August 19th. I still live on the old farm about two hundred yards from the old house where I was born. I grew up working on the farm, where we, as most did, raised sheep, hogs, cows, and chickens and worked the farm with a pair of big workhorses.

I had a good mom and dad, who took me along with a brother and sister to church most every Sunday. I should say Sabbath, as that is what we called it back then.

We worked hard, but we also took time out to enjoy ourselves. Dad was a hunter, and I learned to coon hunt with him at an early age. We killed and ate several kinds of wild game like squirrel, pheasants, rabbits, and quail.

I can remember going to the old general store at Glass Rock and Dad buying a few shells to hunt with. He didn't have enough money to buy them by the box, so the storekeeper would open a box and sell him what he could afford. You learned to be a good shot so you didn't waste shells.

I remember when I was in the first grade, and it was the first night of hunting season. I really wanted to go with Dad, and he wanted me take me, but Mom said I had to go to school the next day and didn't think I should go. Dad and I won out, and I got to go.

Right after dark, we got the old coon hound, walked down the hill to the old covered bridge, crossed through it, then down the creek about a mile to the Huston Woods. We treed and killed a coon, then Dad took off his socks and shoes (We didn't have boots then) and waded across the creek with gun and coon. Then he came back and got me on his back and carried me to the other side.

We walked another mile or so and came to an old gravel road, and there was an old cemetery alongside of the road. I said, "Dad, I know where we are." He said, "I do too, but don't tell Mom." Ha. He didn't want her to know how far we were from home.

We had a fairly large stream of water running through our farm called Jonathan Creek. I remember many evenings, after supper and the chores were done, my brother, Jack, and I would run from the house, cross the road, then into the cow pasture and down to the "crick" to swim and cool off.

By the time we reached the "crick," we had our clothes off and were ready to hit the cool, clear water. We didn't know what a bathing suit was. The water seemed clean to us, and we never heard of pollution back then.

We hunted crawdads, turtles, and frogs while swimming and playing in the water. Did you ever catch a frog, get a straw, stick it in the frog, blow in the straw until the frog was inflated, then turn it back in the water and watch it try to escape? It wasn't easy.

On cold winter nights, our house wasn't too warm. We didn't have a furnace or fireplaces, but we did have something similar to a fireplace that we called grates. We had four in our big house. They didn't put out much heat. You would stand facing the fire, then turn you back to warm your other side. I got up many mornings, and the water would be froze in the bucket.

Bares Covered Bridge over Jonathan Creek taken in 1935.

It was cold going upstairs to bed. Sometimes, Mom would heat a brick on the old wood cook stove, wrap it in some kind of cloth, and we would take it to bed to help keep us warm until we went to sleep.

We didn't have clothes like we do today. If you had two pair of any kind, you were lucky. For boots, we had four-buckle rubber boots that went over your shoes to keep your feet dry. You wore your shoes until they were completely worn out. When your soles of your shoes got holes in them, you cut cardboard or something else and put inside your shoe to cover the hole.

Most every farm had some kind of farm dog. This dog was smart from being with someone most of the time. He was a guard dog, a friend, and knew what was going on. Mom and Dad could tell by his bark at night if he was trying to tell them if any livestock was out or some animals were after the chickens or whatever.

Most farms had orchards with apple, peach, plum, and pear trees. We used them all. It was a treat to go pick a big ripe plum off the tree. To keep apples for winter, Dad would dig a shallow hole on a piece of well-drained yard and lay two or more bushels of apples in it, then cover with a heavy layer of straw. They would keep well way into the winter.

If someone got real sick, you called the doctor, and he would come to your house. Some of those old remedies would still work today if people knew what they were and would use them. There are still many wild roots and greens used today by some of us.

This past spring, I dug some sassafras roots, and my wife, Cree, made sassafras tea. The people years ago said, drink it in the spring, and it purifies your blood.

We picked wild blackberries by the five-gallon bucket full. We ate all we could when they were ripe, and Mom cold-packed the others for winter use. Mom usually had the shelves in the cellar full of meats, vegetables, and fruits.

Back then, when some of us were sick, they said we had the grip. Later they changed that to flu. Now they say we have a virus.

Back then, everyone in the family had to work. The young children usually had to get the wood and/or coal in the house in the evening for the next day. Also kindlin', as there was a fire built in the old cook stove each morning. As you got older, you helped milk the old cows by hand and gather the eggs. There is a lot you can learn from living in the country on a farm. You worked hard and long to make enough to survive and have a happy life. Seems like today, some work to make a lot of money to have a lot of material things and be unhappy.

Many times, I can remember going to church on a Sabbath morning, then coming home and eating dinner. Then in the afternoon, you would sit on the front porch in the old wooden swing and listen to the birds sing or visit with neighbors.

In the winter, when the ice froze five or six inches thick, we would saw the ice in square blocks and haul them to the icehouse, where they were stacked and covered with sawdust, and if you were careful when you took a block out, you would have ice for most of the summer. It was used to make homemade ice cream and keep some food from spoiling.

In the wintertime, at what seemed to be the coldest day of the year, we butchered three or four three-hundred-pound hogs. Dad would be up early to build a big fire outside to heat a fifty-gallon drum of water to scald the hog after he was shot. The neighbors would come and help scrape the hair off and cut the hogs up.

The hams, shoulders, and sides were salted down and wrapped in cloth and hung up in the meat house, where they would keep until way up in the summertime.

The other parts like tenderloin, spare ribs, etc. were cold-packed in jars, where it would keep a long time. Some even pickled the feet, and some had a smokehouse, where parts were cold-packed.

This morning, I got up at 6:30 AM and went and cut two loads of firewood and brought it home to the back yard and stacked and covered it. We heat our home with wood and really like the warm heat we get from it. I've got enough for three years. I thank the good Lord every day that at my age, I can cut wood, hunt, and work like I do. Now I leave you with this question: What ever happened to good old common sense?

Write, call, or come see us.

The Endless Rows in Long Bottom

by Shirley Pfalzgraf of Lewisville, Ohio
born in 1937

This is the story of my beloved mother, Mary L. Truax, of Woodsfield, Ohio, Monroe County, born to Archibald Bohnam and Hannah Catherine Baker Bohnam, January 24, 1900. I know nothing of her parents and childhood, as both my grandparents on both sides, Bohnams and Truaxs had passed away before I was born. In our family history book it writes that Archibald died from drinking, living with a horse, and diphtheria. Hannah died of a blood clot. They had five children, two boys and three girls. My dad's parents, Jacob Truex and Margaret Hendershot Truex, had seven children, five boys and two girls. My dad always spelled his name with an "A" instead of an "E" as his dad's. The only explanation I've ever heard was that he got mad at the rest and started spelling his name "Truax."

On July 22, 1916, Cletis Luthor Truax married Mary at a young age of 16, he being 12 years older. They set up housekeeping in a small house on Home Avenue in Woodsfield. While they lived there, Dad worked in the oil fields. Drilling wells was booming business in Monroe County during that time. They had six children while they lived there, Esther, Doris, Durel (Bus), Paul, Clyde, and Jean, all within less than 8 years.

From there they moved to an old farm house on Dent Ridge, just off Route 800 south of Woodsfield. A story was told by the older ones that there were so many cracks in the walls that when the wind blew, they were so cold. Also, a story was that Mom had a toothache and walked all the way to Woodsfield to the dentist to have it pulled, which was seven miles away. While they lived there, two more children were born, Junior and Charles.

From there they moved to a small farm on Sunfish Creek, owned by the Diehl family of Woodsfield. Dad had gotten hurt working in the oil fields and had an enlarged heart and was unable to work anymore, so they mostly just farmed. There the last three children were born, Judy, Shirley (myself), and Bob. Mom not only raised her 11 children, but also my sister, Doris', two boys, John and Jim. Doris' husband left her and she went to work in Canton while Mom took care of her sons.

During the time we lived there, Mom took in washings and ironings for people to help with finances. This was not an easy task, as we had no electricity and no running water. She did it all on a washboard and hung them to dry outside no matter what the weather. I can remember in the wintertime she would bring Dad's long johns in and stand them in the corner to thaw out.

We had a two holer outhouse that got mighty cold, and you didn't tarry long. And every Saturday night ritual was heating water on a wood stove and putting a wash tub in the corner of the kitchen and all of us taking turns in the same water for our baths. I always wanted to be first.

Now, not all of us were at home at the same time. My older brothers and sisters were off on a life of their own. My oldest sisters were married and having children of their own, and four brothers were in World War II. "Bus" and Clyde were over in Germany; Clyde in the Battle of the Bulge and Paul in the Navy, and Junior just got in the tail end and was still in the States. I can remember when the war was over and Mom running outside yelling, "The war is over, the war is over!" She was so happy. She'd heard it reported on the radio.

Many memories flood my mind as I think of our life there. Since we had no electricity, of course no TV so at night we would gather around a big battery-operated radio and listen to Inner Sanctum, Little Abner, George Burns and Gracie Allen. All the while, Mom sat and crocheted. She was never still. If she wasn't doing laundry, ironing, cleaning, canning, and all her other chores, she was baking bread enough for all of us and helping in the fields.

I remember one real hot day we were hoeing corn in the "Long Bottom," and when I say long, that's what I mean. I was standing, crying, leaning on my hoe and she just said, "You can stand there and cry all day, but you have to hoe your row."

We did everything by hand as we only had two horses, no tractor. We put in hay with a pitchfork and loaded onto a wagon and then up into the barn. Same as when we harvested the corn, cut by hand and then we would all gather around a corn shock and husk it by hand and then into a wagon and shovel into a corn crib.

There were no "snow days" when we went to school. On a good day, we had to walk a mile to catch the school bus and no school bus shanty to wait in. When it was really bad, Dad would harness the horses to a sled and put hay in it and Mom would warm bricks and put at our feet and cover us with a comfort and away we would go to meet the bus at the top of Keylor Hill another mile or so.

I have many memories of growing up at Sunfish Creek. The water would get up high enough that it came near the back of the house. In the summer, Mom would send us to the cave across the road to get a can of something and the little snakes would rear their ugly heads and snap at you. Really made me afraid to go there. In winter we had the hills to sled down and plenty of snow to make snow angels and play fox and geese.

On Christmas Eve, after Dad had cut a tree off the farm, he and Mom would put it up and surprise us on Christmas morning. I don't remember receiving many gifts, maybe a doll tied in the tree and some hard tack candy and some fruit. It was wonderful to get a nice orange. Something we didn't have on a regular basis.

I remember one Christmas I had picked out a really pretty light blue bike at the Western Auto Store in Woodsfield, never thinking beyond my wildest dreams that I would get it. Morning came and no bike, but later when my brother, Junior, and his family came for dinner, he brought my bike. I was so happy. It was our tradition that the older ones came for Christmas dinner. I guess I was a little selfish as I hated it because us "little ones" didn't get to eat till last.

We had no phone and I often wonder, how did we manage? In today's age, even little ones run around with phones on their ears. What if we got sick? There were just home remedies, sassafras, tea, Vicks, castor oil, etc.

When I was 13 or even before, I watched Mom dig a basement by hand to build the house that she helped build on the hill where we moved to about a mile down the road. I don't recall how she acquired this land, but there was over 100 acres. After we moved there, we had electric and we finally got a used black and white TV and later a phone. We never had a car until there because Mom and Dad neither one ever drove or had a driver's license. If we needed anything from town, Dad either walked or some Saturdays we took a taxi in town and while Mom would shop at Yoss' Grocery, she would let us to go the Monroe Theater and watch a western, Gene Autry, Roy Rogers, or Hopalong Cassidy for 10 cents. We were really living it up. Mom would run a bill there and when she paid at the first of the month, he would give us a little brown sack of candy.

We spent a lot of our time in the creek, swimming or with me just playing along the edge, as I was afraid of the water, but the brothers would threaten to throw me in the deep water every once in a while.

We didn't spend much time in the house. Mom wouldn't allow it.

She made most of my clothes by hand out of the flowered chicken feed sacks we used to get. Can you imagine kids wearing that now? I never wore slacks until my sister, Doris, made me a pair out of man's pants that had a patch right in the front. I wore them every day one winter.

Speaking of winter, I remember the bad one of 1950 when we got over three feet of snow. I remember standing at the picture window watching Dad put one foot out of the deep snow and then the other walking to town to get groceries. Back then we didn't have the snow removal or the roads that they do now. We could never make it up our hill and had to walk up it most of the winter.

Dad was a great hunter and trapper, and he instilled this love in the boys. He would shoot rabbits and squirrels and bring them home and Mom would cook them and then brown them in the skillet rolled in flour and Dad thought that squirrel gravy was the best thing he'd ever eaten. I can't eat wild game to this day. I guess I don't have to now.

As we kids grew older and most left home, Mom bought the Allison Restaurant across from the Post Office in town. There was an extra room in back that she and I stayed in while Judy stayed with Dad and cared for his needs and the rest. That building burnt down, what is now Yoss' law office and Auto Parts Store. Later she bought Norris' Restaurant. But there at the first restaurant I met my husband of nearly 53 years. He would come in and pester me while I worked. I watched him load a bus to go to the Army in 1953. He was in the Korean War, but was stationed in Germany. I would work in the restaurant till time to go to school in the morning and when school was out till closing time, around 10:00 p.m. Mom worked from opening till closing seven days a week. Even after I married and we lived here awhile I would help her out. She never tired of cooking in it and no one who ever came in without money left hungry. Seemed as though she wanted to feed the world. What a wonderful cook she was, too.

As her health declined, she had to give up the restaurant but not work. She took elderly people into her home and cared for them. At the young age of 64, she had a massive stroke in Dr. Gillespy's office. They took her to Barnesville Hospital and then released her to home. This was her first trip to the hospital having had all 11 children at home with the help of her sister, Bertha, and sometimes a doctor. My oldest sister, Esther, used to say she would be outside and Mom would call her in and hand her the baby and tell her it was hers to take care of.

We that could took turns caring for her 24 hours a day in a hospital bed, completely paralyzed and being fed through a tube in her nose. She just lived this way from December 2nd to March 27th when she passed away quietly. The sad part about it was she wasn't at the doctor's for herself, but to get medicine for those she was caring for. The story of her life.

The Gruesome Death of Louisa Fox

by Bertha M. Turner of Lebanon, Ohio
born 1914

Today, I hear many of my friends talking about how wonderful the good ole days were and how none of the murder and terrible crimes we see today existed back then. I was born in 1914 near Sewellsville in Belmont County, Ohio, on my parents' farm. My parents were Eldee and Maud Shepherd. Today happens to be January 21 and I remember hearing about a terrible crime being told and retold every night in the living room in front of the fire when I was a little girl. I always remember the date because my mother was born on January 20. On our farm we didn't have radio, television, or even a piano or player so we listened to stories.

Our live-in grandmother, Barbara Alice Calhoun, told us the story of Louisa Fox and we shivered in our nightgowns. I had three sisters and five brothers and I was next to youngest. The story really frightened me. Maybe my grandmother wanted us to fear and be extra careful when we were off the farm.

Bertha Margaret Turner, age four.

Louisa Fox was only thirteen when Tom Carr fell in love with her and wanted to marry her. Tom was twenty-two and both he and Louisa worked as farm hands on a farm near Sewellsville, owned by Mr. and Mrs. Hunter. Supposedly, the Foxes gave permission for their daughter's marriage and then changed their minds when they heard of Tom's bad reputation. Also, Mrs. Hunter urged Louisa to break off the promise to marry and she did.

One cold January night, January 21 to be exact, Tom waited for Louisa to finish milking at the Hunters and walk home to her parents' cabin. Tom waited under an old apple tree, grabbed her, kissed her, and said if he couldn't have her, he would kill her. He cut her throat with a razor while she begged him to stop. He slashed her fourteen times. There was blood everywhere.

Her little brother witnessed the murder and ran home to tell his parents. A group of men scoured the cold countryside looking for Tom who hid out in various places. He cut himself but did not die. He even looked in the window where Louisa's corpse was laid out and later told all of this to the constable.

Finally they caught him and he confessed, was tried in court, and sentenced to death. He was the first man to be legally hung in Belmont County. He wrote a book while he was in jail and said he had killed fourteen other people.

Whenever we heard the story it would stay in our minds for days. When Mother sent me to the spring house to get water after dark, I was always afraid to open the door and go in. Most often I would try to get one of my brothers to go with me.

But, on the other hand, sometimes my brother Bob and I would act out the story of Louisa. I would walk down through our orchard and Bob, carrying a big stick, would jump out of one of Dad's peach trees and shout, "Marry me, Louisa, or else." Grandma would get mad if she heard us playing this game and yet she was the best teller of Louisa Fox stories.

I always thought that this murder took place in the early 1900's because it was so vivid in everyone's memory. Everyone in Belmont County seemed to know the name Louisa Fox. There were even songs about her.

I left Belmont County to go to high school in Newcomerstown in 1928 and forgot about the scary images of Louisa getting killed on her way home from work. Then in 1959 my mother died and I discovered a new fact about Louisa Fox.

Mother had lived with my husband and me in Coshocton, Ohio, since 1941. After her death, I found an old edition of *The Freeport Press* in her sewing basket and read an article about how the notorious Tom Carr killed his thirteen-year-old sweetheart on January 21, 1869! The story was at least fifty years old when I first heard it, but it still had the power to fascinate and frighten.

That bloody story could rival any story on CSI or Criminal Minds today. Human nature just doesn't change and "the good ole days" had their share of criminals and loonies too.

I now live with my daughter in Lebanon, Ohio, but we visit Belmont County on occasion and even drive down the old deserted road to the Shepherd farm where I grew up. The coal company bought it in the 1930's and the house and barns are all gone as well as my eight brothers and sisters. It is as if my family never existed; but I pass on my stories to my children, grandchildren, and great grandchildren.

The First and the Last

by Ed McGlumphy, Sr. of Stone Creek, Ohio
Born in 1931

My first and last spanking was in the seventh grade.

Our old wooden school desk had an inkwell hole on the right top side of the desk with a pencil trough in the middle of the desk.

The girl sitting in front of me had two long, long, long braided pigtails (for that period of time). These pigtails dangled all over the top of my desk. It really annoyed me.

So one day, with a minute before the bell rang, I carefully tied the pigtails through the ink well hole down under the desk top.

The bell rang for lunch. The girl got up, her head jerked back, and she let out a loud scream. Back to my desk came the teacher and said, "Eddie, go to the principal's office, NOW!"

So I did. The principal did not hesitate. He said, "Bend over for one spank with the paddle." Then he said, "Sit on the punishment bench for the lunch period in the hall." He called home and told my parents, and I got another spanking at home.

This was the first and last spanking of my life. It happened in Martins Ferry, Ohio about 1939.

The Roosevelt and Pre Et Silage

by Hillis Mann of Johnston, Ohio
born in 1920

Just a short history: Grew up on a dairy farm, born in 1920 in what was referred to as the Big Depression. Horse-and-buggy days, no electricity, no indoor plumbing. Milked the cow by hand, turned the separator by hand to separate the cream from the whole milk.

Radio: Listened to program "Amos and Andy." Outdoor toilet called an outhouse. Government sponsored program in early 30s, more modern outhouse had a concrete base we called The Roosevelt.

P.W.G. days, government program started and limestone quarry near our farm that was the first ground to treat our dirt roads.

My mother had to wash for a family of five by hand on what they called a scrub board. We didn't get electricity in our area till 1939.

My mother saved her egg money and was able to get a Maytag washing machine powered by a little one-cylinder gas engine in the early 30s. That sure was a wonderful day for Mom.

Now for something on the brighter side. The Plumbly Brothers was operating a dairy farm just east of Somerton, southeastern Belmont County. They had just filled their silo with grass silage a few days before. At that time, grass silage was a fairly new item. They threw down a good size sample so the folks attending the field day they was having could have a looksee. Evret Truex was present; he was quite a comedian, could make a joke out of whatever came his way.

A Dr. So-and-So from Ohio State Agriculture Department was the main speaker for the day. He was on the speaking stump ready to go. Evret had a sample of the light brown colored grass silage in his hand. He got the speaker's attention and said, "I have a question for you."

The speaker swelled up bigger than a toad, ready to drop the whole ball of yarn on this hillbilly way out here in the sticks, "Yes sir, what is your question?"

Evret was looking at the sample in his hand and said, "Has that stuff already been et or is it yet to be et?" Of course, the crowd got a good laugh out of that one.

The Smell of Hay and Lye Soap

by James Bell of West Lafayette, Ohio
born 1923

I was born on Blissfield Route #1 a few minutes after midnight to Bessie Pogue Bell and Clarence Edgar Bell. To start, here is what I know about the Bell family.

Grandpa and Grandmother's home in Zanesville, Ohio.

My great grandfather had four sections of land in Perry County and built the town now called Crooksville. I do not know how many offspring they had, but my grandfather, William James Bell, had a pottery business and must have made a lot of money because he purchased a house on Moxihallie Avenue. I heard he paid over two hundred and thirty-five thousand dollars around 1900. That was a lot of money in those days.

William and Elva Bell had three kids: Clarence William (my dad), Uclidus and Katherine. My mother was a schoolteacher in Akron, Ohio. My dad and Uncle Bill were engineers before the Depression. Dad was the head man with Ohio Power on the Miskgom Power House. I was six and lived in a nice house on Moxihallie. That came to an end. We lost everything. Dad almost lost his mind. He really never got over it.

My mother's mother had a farm where I was born, so we went there to live till I was out of high school at eighteen years. I started first and second grade at Moxihallie Grade School. After we moved, I attended third, fourth and fifth grades at Rock Ridge (this building is still there in the woods), then I went to Blissfield Grade School (I went to reunion in this old brick building).

My dad got jobs surveying and traveled surveying for railroads and dams around Ohio. Sometimes I went with him and Mom. Other times I went to Zanesville and lived with Grandmother Bell and my grandpa that was sick with what they called "dropsy."

Spent one year that I was sorry for (played hooky a lot), but had art class, which I had enjoyed all through my school years.

This forty acre farm was my life. At fourteen we got horses to work and plow fields. Had a big garden that we used to supply food for Mom's relatives. Unbelievable the stuff we growed. We growed four hundred quarts of green beans, some tomatoes, picked cherries, blackberries, and many other types of produce for them. We had lots of apple trees and pear trees too.

The neighbor purchased a full train load of mustang horses that I trained for him. This is another story of later years. I love horse training.

I lived a mile and a quarter from the mailbox. Used horses and Model-T to go places. The road was always bad. Got stuck and had to take a horse to pull the Model-T home.

Missed the smell of hay and the lye soap as you go back to the porch.

We had three cows that I milked, and purchased a sow and twelve pigs (for, you won't believe it, ten dollars).

Talk about poor. A forty-nine pound sack of flour sold for two dollars. Dad cut corn for a month for flour. We got a bull. It was a Holstein pre-born calf. We did not have anything to feed it, so Dad came up with making tea from sweet clover. Unbelievable. It weighed four hundred pounds at a year old.

The pigs growed to herd of one hundred. Always butchered two four hundred pound pigs 'cause Dad and Mom liked pork.

My school years were walking, seven years old, three-fourths of a mile in waist high snow to Rock Ridge. Sixth grade was with one teacher. I remember old poems. Half a league, half a league onward... fourscore and seven, Lincoln address.

We had neighbors a quarter of a mile from us. The only time we saw them was when we went to school with them.

My Uncle Bill gave me Steven's Buckhorn .22 rifle that I shot squirrels and rabbits with for meat. Got good at shooting (in later years shot mule deer and elk in Colorado). I also built my own rifles.

You might like to know we lived in a two story wood house. My dad and Uncle Bill painted it (guess with lead paint). I know there was a lot of red wasps 'cause the next day the house was completely red. They had to scrape and repaint.

Raised a lot of different chickens: Rhode Island Reds, Plymouth Rocks, Banties. The Sunday dinner was delicious. Marble potatoes and peas. I could tell you of the many foods that we enjoyed.

Oh yes, we went to Warsaw High in summer. Walked four miles to see outdoor movies on the streets in Warsaw.

Could tell you many stories of my mom's relatives in Tuscrawas county. Grandpa Pogue ran a brewery in south side New Philla. Had relative that was a mover. His motto was "We can move the earth." Grandmother's brother, Uncle Loid, was the one that got me working in air conditioning and refrigeration with other occupations, plumbing, heating and electrician.

Potato Soup, Snow Cream and Carnivals

by Marilyn Liff of Crooksville, Ohio
born in 1940

Growing up as a child in the 40s was not like today. We had no electric but used kerosene lamps and a wood stove. I remember getting hot water out of the well on the end of the stove to do dishes or wash and standing as close to that old wood stove as possible on cold winter mornings while getting ready for school.

Before going to school there were chores to be done. The chamber pot, or night bucket as we called it, had to be emptied. Going over the hill to the spring to get water, out to the wood pile to bring in wood for the day.

Putting on those thick heavy leggings to go to school. Walking half a mile to catch the bus. Wasn't so bad of a morning, as it was down hill, but after school it was up hill. They didn't cancel school just because of a few inches of snow. I remember walking in snow knee deep and the bus would have chains so it could go.

One time right after getting off the bus, a boy called two of us girls to cross this frozen pond. He went across to show it was safe, so we held hands and about three feet out we went through the ice up to our waist. We got out okay. Believe me, those wet leggings were really heavy and stiff. Need I say we never went on that pond again. I think it took those leggings a week to dry hanging on a nail behind that old wood stove.

I can't remember the exact year, but I believe it was 1950, we had about three feet of snow. I think everything stopped. We were snowed in for a week and ate potato soup. I still like it.

My mom would make snow ice cream for us. I'm sure no one wants to try that today, but it was really good. Treats were rare, as we had no Dairy Queen or store close by, and we had no car, so we had to walk when we did go to the store.

Our clothes were made of feed sacks, Grandma made some really nice dresses. Mom's were not so fancy, you had no trouble telling they came from feed sacks, as they basically still looked like a feed sack. I preferred the dresses Grandma made.

When electricity came to the country, our home got modern. My dad strung wire from room to room. We had a light in each room with a pull string. We got a radio and would listen to Fibber McGee and Molly. Every Saturday night we listened to the Wheeling Jamboree. That was country music. Now that was real music!

We always washed clothes on a wash board, but after the electric we got a wringer washer. I remember my mom had to go to the hospital so I tried to wash clothes. I got something red in the white clothes and everything came out a pretty shade of pink. We wore it anyway.

We hung our clothes out on a line. The smell of those sheets at night was out of this world. They don't smell that good today, not even with fabric softener, which we didn't have then.

I can still smell Mom's homemade bread baking in that old wood stove. Sometimes she would make a pan of cinnamon rolls. I can still taste them.

Of course, we had homemade butter on that homemade bread. I churned the butter in a big old churn. My arms were tired, but the reward was great. I got to drink some of that fresh buttermilk.

The summers were really fun. We had a creek on the farm we played in. We would drink from the creek. It was so cool and tasted so good. Then we would splash around in it, catch crawdads, frogs, and tadpoles. We finally got smart and dammed up a wide spot of the creek. That little pond sure felt good on a hot summer day. Sometimes the cows beat us to the water, but that was okay, they got hot also. We paid them back, as we would break off chunks of their salt blocks and eat it.

During the summer, carnivals came to town. Even when we didn't have money for the rides, it was still fun to watch those that did. The smell of the different foods smelled so good. Our young people today have no idea what a carnival is. They just don't know what they missed.

To my opinion, those were the good old days. Families were closer and did things together and made the best of what they had.

The Dreaded Chore

By Harriett Evans Grimsley of New Caney, Texas
Born 1929

When I was still quite small, my dad and I moved to his parents' farm in Ohio. Everyone had his or her chores to do and as I got older I was assigned some of my own. Most I enjoyed doing; setting the kitchen table for Grandma, sweeping the floor and hanging clothes out on my own special line. But later I was assigned one that I could only call "The Dreaded Chore." I begged and pleaded, but to no avail. This was my duty; to empty the chamber pots!

Ours was not a large farm so there were a few houses near by and in the nearest one lived a large family with rowdy boys. On my early morning trips to the outhouse I would try sneaking across the yard, around the house and scurry along the path to take care of my "dreaded chore" without anyone seeing me. But I just knew the whole world was watching; especially those boys and I could have died. And complaining got me no place with Grandma. She would just laugh and say, "Why, honey, if we all went out of that business, the whole world would stop." Small consolation to a young girl.

Well time passed and the world did not stop, I did not die and those boys got married and moved away as did I later on. Never again did I have to contemplate on that "dreaded chore" or so I thought. Many years later my husband and I were visiting friends and one of those boys and his wife came to see us. The fellows got to talking about those early days where he and I had grown up and the next thing I heard was him telling my husband about the above events. They just laughed and laughed and I was red faced and mortified all over again!

Elvis Skirts and Unsavory Water

by Donna J. Hammer of Roseville, Ohio
born in 1947

I am 61 and I remember when I was very young in the 1950s. My father, Donald J. Wise, was our only parent working outside the home, and money was very tight. There were four of us children, and my mother did a lot of sewing of our clothes for school and for my twin sisters not yet of school age. I remember she made jumpers for my sisters with straps across each shoulder, because they couldn't keep skirts up, and skirts for both my oldest sister and me. To reduce the cost of the material, we would stop at a feed store on Maysville Pike in Zanesville, Ohio. The store was located where the OK Concrete Store was across the street where the CVS Store is now located.

My father would go to the side dock door of the feed store and ask if they had any empty feed sacks for sale. They were floral feed sacks. Material of these designs would probably run three to four dollars a yard now in a fabric store. These sacks would only run my father a few cents apiece and he could get several for just a few dollars. My mother could get a skirt out of

Donna J. Wise Hammer wearing an Elvis skirt in 1957.

each feed sack for my sister, Linda, and me and one each for the twins. We got very excited each time we would stop there because we would think, "Oh boy, we get some new clothes." It felt almost like Christmas all over again.

There was one particular time my father did let my mother buy some material at the store to make us skirts, and it was of Elvis material. My mother made jumpers for Cynthia and Sally (the twins) and a skirt each for me and herself (June E. Wise). My oldest sister, Linda, didn't want one. Her heartthrob was her boyfriend and now husband. I still have a picture of the twins and one of myself in our Elvis skirts from 1957.

My mother washed our precious skirts in an old-time wringer washer. I watched my mother fill the washer each time with clear water but was never around when she emptied it. One day my curiosity got the best of me and when my mother left the room I lowered the hose with the spout on it from the side of the washer and placed it over my mouth so I could have a drink of the nice clear water I had just seen my mother put in the washer just a short time earlier. If I ever had a brain-dead moment when I was young, this had to be one at the top of the list. To my astonishment the dirty wash water came rushing into my mouth and left me spitting and sputtering and making a mess all over the floor.

My mother yelled at me a little, but didn't punish me. Maybe she figured I had punishment enough with the mouthful of dirty wash water.

Then only a short time later my mother made her own mistake with a wringer washer. As she was running the clothes through the wringer, she got her hand too close to the wringer and accidentally ran her hand through; then had to reverse it back out. It must run in the family because my aunt caught her long hair in her wringer. No wonder these washers went out of style. Some people could have mishaps operating them, or they could create a bad taste in your mouth.

These were some of my many memories of a very lean time and happy times like when we used to go to the neighborhood playground and play Red Rover, kick-the-can, and red and green light.

There were sad times too, like when a couple years later my mother miscarried when she had quadruplets.

With all the sad and glad times, my memories of those years are endless. From my favorite pastime of playing with paper dolls, going to the penny candy store when Mom would give us a few pennies or a nickel and coming out with a whole candy sack full, or walking to school every day clear across town. These are only some of my endless memories.

The Doll That Stole My Heart

by Lauretta J. Zesiger of Sugarcreek, Ohio
born in 1926

Like you wanting a story that is touching from days gone by, our minister asked us to write a story about a Christmas past, so now I'm sending it to you. If you like it then I'll send a photo of me holding her. Meaning the doll that stole my heart.

I'm now eighty-three. This is so much of a treat to be a chance to be a part of your book. Wow!

My story was chosen to read to our wonderful congregation that Christmastime.

In the "good old days," giving gifts was much simpler. When I was in the first grade, I stopped and looked in a store window. There was the prettiest doll baby I ever saw. I went home from school and told Mama all about her and how much I liked her. Every day that early December, I would stop and look at her.

Well, one morning she was gone. I just couldn't believe it. I cried all the way to school. My brother kept saying, "Don't cry." My heart was broken so I just had to cry.

Then came Christmas morning. When I jumped out of bed to see what Santa brought me, well, I was amazed. There under the tree was that beautiful doll. I couldn't believe it. My dad said, "Go pick her up, Retta. She needs a hug." I was so happy to have her and she sure got a lot of hugs."

Milk From the Bottom of the Can

By Jim McKay of Zanesville, Ohio
born 1923

Back in September of 1941, I started college at Ohio University in Athens, Ohio. This wasn't very long after the Great Depression and money was hard to come by, so I joined a co-op unit sponsored by the university. This co-op was a group of about thirty-five men that lived in an old hotel building called Palmer Hall. Each student was assigned a job to do for the group. To do my job I was assigned to the breakfast crew. This crew of four or five men was responsible for helping the cook, who was not a student, serve breakfast. We only had two meals a day: morning and night.

We got our milk each morning about 6:00 AM. The milk came in a can about twelve inches in diameter and thirty inches tall. This was in the days before milk was homogenized, so all the cream came to the top of the can. I usually tried to get the job of using a long handled dipper to dip the milk out of the big can and put it in quart pitchers to put on the tables.

Most mornings I would dip some thick cream off the top for a special pitcher for myself and another fellow who liked cream on his cereal like I did. This was thick cream, not good for health, but we did it anyway. By this action I may have helped make some of the first one percent or less butterfat milk from the bottom of the big can.

The second year there, I was assigned to a new job: doing laundry. I never found anything funny about this job. By then most of us were either in the service, or about to be.

The Dive Bombing Crow and American Values

by Jacqueline Lee Smith of Uhrichsville, Ohio
born 1943

Like most children growing up in beautiful Southern Tuscarawas County, Ohio, I never realized how wonderful our little world was. Although our particular geographical area was made up of medium to lower income families we kids in most cases never knew the difference between the two.

Our activities were scheduled around church, family and friends; in that order. Summers were wonderful. My dad and mother both came from large families (18 siblings between the two of them) and had to work hard for what they had. But having a large extended family meant wonderful family reunions always held at the local parks, with good food, lots of hugs, kisses and cheek pinching from aunts and uncles. A baseball game always followed.

Dad planned at least one summer trip for we kids and it usually included my grandmother Cavanaugh Huston and one of her sisters. The memory of one such trip remains very vivid. Dad decided we would go to Myers Lake Amusement Park, which at that time was located in Canton, Ohio. As I recall my mother remained at home with my younger sister and brother. My dad drove and my grandmother and an aunt helped chaperone me and my sister who was three years younger than me. You could always count on laughing, eating and just having a good old time when our family got together. This trip was no exception. After a full day of amusement park activities my grandmother decided before we started the trip home that she would attempt to win a gold fish. She was successful. However, twenty minutes into the trip my aunt began to feel the affects of an upset stomach and in spite of my dad's best efforts he could not pull the car over quickly enough to assist her in avoiding filling the goldfish bowl to capacity. Needless to say the goldfish never made it to Tuscarawas County.

Our family lived in what was called a "double house" but would now be called a duplex located at 1st Street in Dennison. We lived in one side and my paternal grandmother lived in the other. A basement connected the two residences. Directly behind our house was the old Helter & Johnson Feed & Mill. It was a very prosperous business with local farmers buying feed and grain. Sand and gravel was also available for purchase. After hours the owners allowed the neighborhood children to play in a huge pile of sand. It was great. Every Tuesday a company who delivered feed to the mill would arrive in a large truck. My grandmother would give me two dollars and I would purchase enough feed sacks for my grandmother to make several blouses and pillow slips. The feed sacks were soft and were "designed" with different colored flowers. I never realized how much my wardrobe depended on those sacks and I would give anything to have saved one that she had made for me. However they were passed down when out grown!

Our neighborhood held many points of interest for a curious child. Located across the alley from the feed and mill was Grahams Blacksmith Shop. We could go in on any given day and watch the entire process of making horseshoes from start to finish. Sam Graham, whose son George was later to become the Mayor of our Village of Dennison, was operator and owner. He was a colorful character with a dry wit and could be more than a little touchy on a warm day. He was always very kind about allowing us to watch his work from a distance.

We lived just a short walk from the bridge that connected the Village of Dennison and the City of Uhrichsville. Although my parents cautioned me constantly about not being permitted to play under the bridge which provided access to the shores of the Little Stillwater Creek, the instructions went unheeded. Many days were spent fishing, skipping rocks and swinging across the creek on a rope tied to a tree. The rope was a very heavy almost nautical style rope. My memory fails me as to who secured the rope to the tree. The rope provided us with a fun way to cross the creek, almost without incident. The incident that occurred probably provides me with a more vivid memory of the rope than my friends might have. I can't recall whose wedding our family was going to attend. However, I do recall being dressed to the "T' which included a white dress, shoes, socks and white gloves. Of course my grandmother Huston had curled my hair by wrapping it in clothespins while it was wet which meant leaving them in till my hair dried and curled around them. The clothespins were round and wooden not at all similar to the ones you purchase today. When I was dressed my Grandmother instructed me to sit on the front porch and wait for the rest of the family to get dressed and not to get dirty. I knew my friends were down under the bridge swinging on the rope and reasoned to myself that if I just went down to watch I could stay clean. I admit I did struggle back and forth about disobeying my grandmother, but eventually the river won. I made my way down the alley and arrived under the bridge. My friends were amazed to see me all dressed up and of course they challenged me to take a swing on the rope. Although I don't recall how much I resisted, I do remember finally giving in and climbing on the rope white dress and all. I was almost to the muddy shore when, yes, the rope broke. I can still remember the look of horror on the faces of my friends while I struggled to get up the muddy bank. I gathered my pride, and with much dignity and fear, (that was seen by my friends I am certain) I headed for home. Might I take this opportunity to remind you that only ringer washers were in use at our house and everything was hung out to dry.

My Grandmother was looking for me in the backyard and when I saw the look on her face my heart sank deeper than the mud I had sunk into. She told me to go quickly into the house before my father saw me. She was attempting to access the damage when my dad opened the back door. Without a word my grandmother stepped in front of me. My dad was a strict disciplinarian. His face flashed red then white. Grandmother stood her ground. I did not attend the wedding and really dislike wedding ceremonies to this day.

I learned at an early age that our neighborhood was kid friendly and took advantage of getting to know our neighbors. One of our dearest and most kind neighbors was the McCues. "Dinger" as we were permitted to call him was an outdoors man. He scoured the fields of Tuscarawas County hunting arrowheads which were plentiful in our area. He displayed them beautifully on a wall in his home. He was also an avid hunter. I had the thrill of experiencing my first taste of turtle soup, bear, beaver and other such wild game dishes, that Dinger caught and prepared. Louise, Dinger's wife, allowed him to display a beautiful bear rug in their front room. We kids never grew tired of seeing that rug. Dinger was a small man in stature, but taught us kids a lot about life. He worked for the railroad as a crossing guard when the little crossing shacks were placed at railroad crossings. I think everyone knew Dinger. But we were lucky enough to have him as our neighbor. However, there was one member of his "family" that was not as well liked. His name was Jim and he was Dinger's pet crow. We kids were scared to death of him. Only because he would swoop down and deposit an unwanted substance on our heads. He seemed to delight in waiting for me on a school morning when I started the day with freshly shampooed hair and was wearing my Dennison Railroaders Jacket, which was the most expensive piece of clothing in my wardrobe at that time. Watching for Jim was like watching for an airplane diver. He was crafty. We had huge bay windows on all sides of our house. You would think that I could have spotted that black devil on any given day. That's not the way it worked. Just when I thought the coast was clear and would open the door and stepped out from the shelter of the porch roof, there he was. He had perfect aim. If the deposit was not too large I simply wiped it off and continued on to school. If it required more cleaning I had to go back in and make the necessary repairs and was tardy. I would cry all the way to school some days because of that crow. Jim was also a thief. Our home was two stories with the bathroom facing the backyard. The window of the bathroom was off the shower area and had a windowsill large enough to place items on when entering the shower. There were no screens on the window so when open it made the entire bathroom area accessible to the outside elements. My dad always took off his wristwatch and ring and placed them on the open windowsill. The glint of the gold was a real temptation to Jim. A lot of our jewelry and shiny objects went missing during Jim's visits. They were later found in a hollow part of a tree by Dinger. We all had a good laugh over that and were amazed at the collection of neighborhood items Jim had stolen.

Dinger and his wife Louise also had a pet parrot whose name was Polly. The bird could talk and especially loved crackers. I enjoyed coming home from school to the sound of the parrot crying "Polly wants a cracker."

There were four children in our family and my dad worked for the local Evans Clay Pipe Company. Our area was known as the clay center of the world and each summer the industry would sponsor an event for the families who were employed by the clay companies. It was known as "Clay Week." Free tickets were given to the workers. The amount of tickets given to each employee was determined by the number of family members. A carnival would come to town for an entire week. The tickets would provide us kids with free rides, ice cream and hot dogs. We really looked forward to the "Clay Week" event.

The Pennsylvania and B&O Railroads ran tracks through both Dennison and Uhrichsville. Many of our World War II troops who traveled to their destinations were provided with coffee and donuts at the Dennison Depot Canteen. The project was provided by volunteers and many times I am told the soldiers did not even have an opportunity to exit the train, but the train stopped to allow time enough for the volunteers to hand the troops packages through the train windows. The Dennison Depot is an historical site in our village today and is the site of many activities.

I was much to young to have been apart of the canteen activity, however after the death of my maternal grandfather; my grandmother Ross married a gentleman who was employed by the railroad and she received free passes to train destinations such as Columbus, Ohio. She took me along on several such trips. Of course that was a white glove affair for me. I can recall a hat that I also had to wear with a rubber band type strap that was worn under the chin to keep the hat in place. It was very uncomfortable. But the train ride was awesome.

Pauline, pregnant with Jacqueline, and Bill Cavanaugh in 1943.

It seems as though families were much closer when I was a young girl. I was always familiar with all of my cousins and aunts and uncles. Today most of us have become too busy to enjoy extended family activities. My paternal grandmother and my mother were both employed by Twin City Hospital, which is still operating and offering expanded services to our communities. Grandma operated a mangle. It was used to steam press all the sheets and pillow cases needed for patients. There was no air conditioning in the employees work area at that time and grandma earned her money to say the least. My mother was employed in the Dietary Department and walked to and from work each day. Mom was always a petite woman, but that walk to and from work helped her stay that way. During the summer months we all had assigned chores to complete before we were permitted to do any fun activities. With both dad and mom working we kids allowed a lot of flex time between chores. We were never permitted to turn on the television until either mom or dad was home. The idea behind that was so we would not be exposed to the programs that dad thought were to "adult" for us. However, on several occasions we turned on the television not knowing that the "tubes" that were in the television at that time caused the top of the television to stay warm long after it had been turned off. Dad in all his wisdom would simply come in, feel the top of the television and call us all in and inform us that we had to come in from play an hour early because we had watched television sometime during the day. We were amazed that he had found some way of finding out what we thought he would never know. We stopped watching the TV and didn't discover for several years how dad had found out. Once the chores were out of the way we would decide how we could earn our 25-cents, which was the admission fee to the Dennison swimming pool for an all day swim. If I went, my brother and sisters had to go because I was the oldest and responsible for them. Most of the time we earned the money by picking blackberries that was growing in a neighbor's back yard. Unfortunately the neighbor was not so keen on someone else picking her berries so that was not always a solution to obtaining the money.

The summer days never seemed long enough and we stretched each day as long as it would go. We played games such as: Kick the Can, Hide and Go Seek and Red Rover Come Over, knowing that all games came to an end once the street lights came on. No one had to be called home by their parents; at the first flickering of the lights we headed that way.

Of course on some Saturday's all of us headed for the barber shop, "Tom's Barber Shop," to be exact. Tom Lennox, a local barber whose shop was located on the corner of Third Street in Dennison, cut my dad and brother's hair about three times a month and trimmed we girls' bangs about that often as well. It was a family affair. I can remember the exact amount of the cost of trimming our bangs was 50-cents. The reason for my excellent recall of this amount is because my dad gave me fifty cents and told me to take my sister Sandy to Tom's so that he could trim her bangs. My sister wore her long blond hair in braids which were complimented by bangs. After watching Tom trim her bangs on numerous occasions I was certain it looked fairly easy to achieve the desired affect. And besides that money would go along way towards two bags of penny candy. My sister and I both agreed the best location for me to trim her bangs was several houses down from our house that had steps that were hidden by a large flower bush. The house was occupied by Doris Beckett and her mother Mrs. Pittenger. I got the scissors and joined my sister who was patiently waiting for me on the steps. To this day my sister Sandy and I still debate on just how her two pigtails became one that day. But my dad and mom did not debate the punishment in the least bit. My sister survived the haircut and is an active member of her community having served three terms on Dennison Village Council among other accomplishments. I love her and am very proud of her.

We also shared a paper route. Every day after school

we passed The Evening Chronicle, which has been replaced by The Times Reporter. Sandy and I talked dad into letting us take a route that covered a two block area. Most nights after taking the route she and I would lie awake talking about what we would spend our earnings on. Dad had already given us a lecture on how he intended for us to spend it and the two versions were as different as night and day.

Being the oldest in the family was many times a hardship. However it had its rewards also. On many occasions my mom would send me on errands. One errand I really looked forward to was going to Lanning's on the corner of Grant and Third Streets in Dennison. Lanning's sold many things, but the real draw for me was the manner in which you paid for your merchandise.

The accounting department was located on the top floor with merchandise on the middle floor. There were steps leading up to the accounting department which were used by employees only. Your bill would be written up by the sales clerk and your money along with that bill would be placed in a metal cup that was sent to the accounting department by some type of cable. The accounting clerk would than return your receipt and any change due you in metal cup. It was so fascinating to watch the entire process. Although the Lanning Building was later remodeled it was declared an historical landmark. It kept many of its historical distinctions and is utilized as apartments for senior citizens. My father and mother had the distinction of being the first tenants to occupy the building. They lived there for the last five years of their life. This memory really shows my age. Both Dennison and Uhrichsville offered their residents the opportunity to see the latest movies. Dennison was the site of the movie theatre which bore the name of "The Park Theatre." Uhrichsville was the home of the "State Theatre." My uncle, Bob Huston, was the manager of both. To earn extra money for the needs of their growing family, my father and mother cleaned the theatres. Of course we kids shared in the responsibility by picking up all the empty popcorn boxes and candy boxes that were left by the movie attendees and properly disposing of them. We also lifted up each seat so they could be swept under. We were rewarded for our work by being allowed to consume all the left over popcorn in the popping machine. There is some humor to this tale as I later became the Director of the Tuscarawas County Recycling and Litter Prevention Office. A position I held for fourteen years until my retirement.

These are just a few of my childhood memories. The most important memory I have is of my father and mother raising us to love God and live our lives for others. They read their Bibles and tithed to our family church even when money was very tight. I will always cherish the memory of my dad sitting at our big round oak dining room table and after writing out a check to our church, meeting his other responsibilities. My dad was a World War II veteran and instilled in his children respect and love for our country. My parents left us with precious values and memories that we could not and did not understand when were children, but that we now treasure and pass on to our children and grandchildren. Thank you for allowing me to recall these memories and to record them for our children to read and reflect.

Smoke Trails from the Steam Locomotives

by David Staley of Carrollton, Ohio
born 1938

In the 1940's and living in Midvale, Ohio, I walked to and from school. On the walk home in the afternoon, I'd frequently have to wait at the railroad tracks, as the steam locomotive passed by on its way to pick up freight cars at Evans Brick plant. It was exciting watching and hearing that whistle, bell, and seeing that huge machine so close. I wish it was still there for today's children to see.

In the summer, I'd usually walk to the post office to pick up the mail in the afternoon. Taking a short cut across a creek, stones laid on the creek bed to cross on, the locomotive would pass on the elevation above the creek bed, and the engineer would see me and wave. I thought him great, being able to control such a huge wonderful thing.

I would climb to the top of the hill behind our house. From there you could see most of Midvale village and clear down to the river bottoms, where I could see the smoke trails from the engines on the Pennsylvania Railroad.

One day, as I lay there, I felt something scratch my leg. I moved, and it scratched higher up. I looked down at my leg and saw the tail of a snake protruding from my pants leg! I jumped and kicked, and the snake flew out, away went the snake. I don't know which of us was the most scared.

Tinkerbell and the Trains

by Tammy S. Lynn Crom of Zanesville, Ohio
born in 1961

Hello, my name is Tammy Lynn Crom, and I am from Zanes. I was born here and have lived here all my life. I have a lot of memories from a little girl.

When I was seven, I got a dog for Christmas, and Tinkerbell was her name. Everything I did, she did. On every Sunday we would get our bowls and go berry picking along the riverbanks. Tinkerbell went with us so she could run under the trains, well, the train was moving (she always made it). I was so scared, but she made it.

We lived on the side of town that got burnt out then leveled out. Restaurants and hotels and a linen company are there now.

We lived on Elm Street first. It was fun. We were allowed to walk and play all day long. When it was time to go home, we went. I was in the first or second grade.

Then we moved to Zane Street. How we did it. My cousins would help. The little people would pull a Radio Flyer wagon with clothes, and the bigger people would get the bigger stuff.

I have three sisters and one brother. Two brothers have passed away. My mother, she was our backbone of the family. She kept us all together. She was an only parent. She was a very good parent. She lived in Zanes all her life too.

We did not live on Zane Street very long. So we all packed up and moved to Howard Street. We lived there for five years.

That was when all the fun and a lot of memories were made. All my family, cousins, aunts, and uncles lived on that side of town too. My grandma had 18, yes 18, children, so lots of kinfolk.

As the kids we were, we used to go to the Ice House on Underwood Street. We always went to the playground and do what all the kids do. We would stand on the swings, jump off, get bumps and bruises, but had fun doing it.

We knew all the police, and they knew us. We all was good kids.

Well, I have so many memories, I wish I could write them, but my hand is cramping up.

The Twenty-one Foot Telegram

by Paul D. Lacey of Tomball, Texas
born 1947

Hoosiers! What, you might ask, do Hoosiers have to do with Southeastern Ohio? Hoosiers, as you may or may not know is a nickname for folks from Indiana. Hoosiers is also the title of a somewhat renowned basketball movie released in 1986 where a bunch of small town underdog basketball players accomplish the impossible by winning their high school State Basketball Championship. Therein lies the connection to Southeastern Ohio. In 1963-64 the small rural Southeastern Ohio community of Dresden became an example of life imitating art.

Imagine if you will, a small rural town in Southeastern Ohio nestled in the foothills of Muskingum County. A village of 1400. Two stoplights. About the only thing exciting that happens there is the shrill sound of the fire siren alerting the townspeople that a friend, family member or neighbor needs their help.

The autumn leaves are long gone and the bare trees await the first heavy snow. Football season has just ended and basketball is in the air. It's important that football has ended because nearly half of the basketball team is comprised of guys who also play on the football team. The high school at this time has a total of about 115 boys, grades 9 through 12. Total enrollment of 241. Small town America.

The Dresden Jefferson Jayhawks had just experienced one of its best football seasons ever. A record of 8 wins against 2 losses. The basketball team was expected to have an average season. It turned out to be anything but average.

Well into the season the Jayhawks found themselves undefeated at 10-0 when they met their league rivals, Maysville. A very strong team from South Zanesville. The Jayhawks lost 50-52! A heartbreaking loss. The team bounced back and won their next 5 games. This placed them at 15 and 1 as they approached the game with county archrivals Zanesville Rosecrans. A private Catholic school. The Jayhawks experienced their second heart breaking loss of the season 33-35 in an exciting, standing room only game. It was a hard loss occurring only one week before county tournament time.

Again the Jayhawks rallied. Winning both county tournament games, both sectional tournament games, one by only 3 points, and the first of their District tournament games. The team gained more confidence with each win. And, the townspeople started making outfits and signs and banners and caravanned to all of the games. It was the most exciting thing to happen to Dresden since, well, ever! In fact, to get tournament tickets some of the fans were lining up at the school doors the day before they went on sale and slept outside overnight to be at the head of the line.

Next was Zanesville Rosecrans—again. District finals. This time the Jayhawks prevailed 55-33. This victory left no doubt who was the better team.

Next came the Regional tournament. Now, the Dresden Jefferson team was playing in gymnasiums the likes of which they had seen only on TV. The Regionals were held at the Ohio University campus in Athens, Ohio. They won both games, the finals by a score of 55-53.

All of Dresden began to wonder about the possibility of...ah, we don't talk about it!

Next, the state semi-finals to be held in Ohio State University's St. John's arena in Columbus, Ohio. Dresden's gym might hold 400 wild and crazy fans; St. John's capacity exceeded 12,000. The townspeople, as well as the players, were a bit awestruck.

The Jayhawks won their semi-final game 59-49.

Surprising maybe everyone in St. John's arena except the players, coaches and their fans. The fans, the townspeople, were the greatest ever. Even other schools' supporters complimented Dresden fans on their behavior, their enthusiasm, their outfits, and their undying support for their Jayhawks.

Rumor had it that people in Dresden had to draw straws to see who would stay behind to man the telephones at the police station and the fire department. Everyone wanted to be a part of history in the making. Pretty much the entire population of Dresden was in Columbus cheering on the team.

Sign in Dresden Town Park commemorating 1963-64 back-to-back Class "A" State Basketball Championships for Dresden Jefferson Jayhawks.

The final game could not have been more exciting. The teams battled back and forth all game. The Jayhawks were out-manned at least in the height category. Jackson Center had a 6' 5" center that averaged 19 points a game. But the Jayhawks, although a very balanced team, had their own offensive standout in Paul Prince who had led the team in scoring all season.

The Jayhawks had Jackson Center down by 8 points with only two minutes to go. But, Jackson Center rallied and tied the score with 23 seconds remaining. If you're at all familiar with the movie "Hoosiers," then you know the star of the small town team gets the ball in the end with only seconds remaining and fires up a last second shot to win the game. Well, this isn't the movies; it's even better.

The Jayhawks brought the ball in bounds and used up some time. They called time out and set up a play. Sixteen seconds remain. The Jayhawk coaches assumed Jackson Center would try to double team Prince. The play was set for either Jeff Longaberger or Prince. The ball was in bounded, worked around for a few seconds. Somehow Prince broke free to the top of the foul circle. The pass went to Prince; he goes up for the shot with only seconds remaining and...it's...nothing...but ...NET!

The Buzzer sounds: Jayhawks 48, Jackson Center 46. The tiny Podunk town of Dresden Jefferson had done the unthinkable: they became the first town in Muskingum County, class A or B, to win a State Championship.

All season the Jayhawks had beaten the odds. This was way before Al Michaels coined the famous line in the Olympics, "Do you believe in miracles?" But this team, that averaged less than 6' in height, had overcome such odds to get this far; the only description that seemed to apply was "a miracle." But it wasn't; it was destiny. I know, I played on that team. And the next one!

If one wants to discuss miracles, perhaps it was the very next year—1964. After losing Prince and two other seniors from the 1963 team, the Dresden Jayhawks did the truly unthinkable and repeated their Class A State Championship in 1964. Back-to-back State titles! Almost unheard of.

In fact, the last time it had been accomplished was in 1934 and 1935 by the famous Waterloo Wonders. Nearly a 30-year time span. Before that the only other time it had been accomplished in Ohio history was in 1924-25 by Bellpoint (Delaware) Ohio. Both Waterloo and Bellpoint were Class B schools at the time.

The back-to-back titles belie the history and drama surrounding the march to victory during the second season. There were numerous subplots. The head coach, Rich Longaberger, was the assistant coach the previous year. This was his first year as head coach. His brother Jeff was this year's standout offensive player.

The team started off the season once again red hot but had their close calls. Twice during the regular season they upended a very talented and scrappy Frazeysburg team both times by last second shots. Winning each game by two points. They were undefeated again when they met the Maysville squad. Again they suffer defeat 63-42. Again they rally and had only one loss when they meet county rivals Zanesville Rosecrans. Again they lose to the Bishops 48-31. Again they rally and prepare for the tournament season. In fact, for both years they lost during the regular season to the same two teams: Maysville and Rosecrans!

Expectations were high, well, let's say hopeful. Everyone knew the enormous task ahead, but the Jayhawks had been down this road before.

And the fans. The crazy, wild, undeterred fans, the Dresden townspeople. They just knew their Jayhawks could do it again.

The Jayhawks worked their way through the county and sectional tournaments facing Rosecrans in the District semifinal game. This time, however, Rosecrans was ranked number 1 in the state and undefeated at 21-0. The Bishops ran a slowed down offense. The score with about 4 minutes left was 17-17! The Jayhawks held on to win at 26-17.

During the next few games the Jayhawks showed

their mettle. After defeating the No.1 Bishops they beat the No. 10 team in the District finals, and then they defeated another previously unbeaten No.6 ranked team in the Regional finals by a score of 55-53. Next was Mogadore in the state semi-finals. A team that sported a 6' 5", 235 lb. All Ohio center. The Jayhawks led by seven, 51-44 with three minutes to go. Mogadore cut the lead to one but missed a shot with 6 seconds left on the clock. Mogodore got the rebound but Jeff Longaberger stole the ball. Jayhawks win 51-50.

The Jayhawks were in the state finals again for the second year in a row. And, again they were underdogs, a role they had become accustomed to. Their opponents were the No 2 ranked team in the state and 10 point favorites. After all of this, even as defending Champions, Dresden was ranked only at No.7 in the state. That was o.k. They were used to being underdogs and under appreciated, by everyone except their fans. Among other examples of support, nearly the entire town paid 10 cents a person to have their name put on a telegram of support for the team. The telegram was unrolled in the locker room for the players to see prior to taking the floor for the final game. It was 21 feet long!

Apparently the Jayhawks decided the previous year final was too exciting. They played disciplined, tenacious, smart basketball and won by 10 points, 71-61. And, even after winning a second consecutive championship the ultimate snub came when Jeff Longaberger who scored 31 points and pulled down 17 rebounds in the final game was relegated to honorable mention on the UPI all-Ohio team. But, that was o.k. too because history had been made, again. And Dresden feted their heroes with another community celebration.

Anyone who travels our country knows that small towns take great pride in their championship teams often by placing signs of their accomplishments at the town limits, or on the water towers, or in the town square. Dresden is no different. The community has memorialized their champions, along with the coaches, managers and cheerleaders with a prominent sign in a small town park. A fitting gesture I guess. But, it would really be something if there were a way to display that 21-foot long telegram from the community. Coach Longaberger still has it. That would be a fitting gesture.

The movie "Hoosiers" couldn't come close to this. This was more about a small town that became one. This was about the total being greater than the sum of the parts. This was small town America at its best.

These championships were life-changing experiences. Many of the players, who previously had never given college a thought, now realized it might be a possibility.

Both of the head coaches went on to legendary careers as high school coaches. Coach Jack Van Reeth, the 1963 coach, after a few years eventually switched to coaching girls teams. During 1984, 1985, 1986 and 1987 he won 109 straight games and 3 state titles. At one time he was the only Ohio coach to have won state titles in both boys and girls basketball. And, he recently recorded his 800th career win in high school victories. Coach Rich Longaberger, the 1964 coach, had a long and storied career at Dresden. He had an outstanding career record with a plus 70% winning percentage.

Coach Van Reeth is.a member of the Ohio High School Basketball Hall of Fame. This year will mark our 45th anniversary of the championship teams. To date we have been very lucky to have lost only one member of the two teams. We continue to be blessed.

Sleds (and Cow Chips) on a Winter Afternoon

by Linda Burris of Cambridge, Ohio
born 1948

When I was growing up in the late 50s and early 60s, on an afternoon when school was canceled, it would be spent with my sisters outside sled riding on the hills surrounding our home. There was a very steep hill where we either could go down the front or down the side where it wasn't so steep. There was also a long hill where we would trudge up and slide down and eventually have a slick path down that long hill.

The neighborhood children would come to our place to sled ride and other fun things to do in the snow, like follow the leader and of course snowball fights. We would spend all afternoon going from one fun thing to another.

At the bottom of the steep hill was a small creek and when it was ice covered we could go onto the ice and go under the bridge nearby.

It was fun to go down that steep hill, especially if someone was going down on your sled either behind you or laying on your back and going piggyback down the hill.

Sometimes the sled seemed to have a mind of its own and there would be chaos. One of us would fall off the sled or both of us would end up off the sled. Somtimes you would hit a cow chip and go in a different direction than intended and end up in a heap on the snow-covered ground.

It was fun to link our sleds together in a row and try to make it down the long hill and stay linked together and if we didn't stay linked together, we would end up at different spots at the bottom of the hill.

At our ages we didn't even notice the cold. We would be wet from head to toe after an afternoon of sled riding and only stopped either when it was suppertime or it would soon be dark.

When we went inside to get warm. We shed all those wet coats, hats, mittens and jeans and on put on dry clothes and warmed ourselves by our coal stove.

What fun we had on those winter afternoons!

Maytag Years

by Lester Z. Gadd of Newcomerstown, Ohio
born in 1926

I was one of six boys, two girls, and Mother and Dad, all raised in seven-room house and path to a two-hole outside toilet, which was called a privy. We had two pots for night use. We had a fireplace, which we called a grate, and a Home Comfort cook stove was only heat for seven rooms, which wasn't too hot!

Box to heat water with stove was used in two galvanized washtubs and hand wash scrub board. One tub was used on Saturday for our weekly baths. Then in 1932, during the Hoover Depression, Mother scraped up thirty-five dollars, which was a lot of money, to go to C.O. Taylor Hardware to buy a wringer tub type Maytag washing machine, which had a two-cycle engine, which oil was mixed in the gasoline, which was very temperamental to start. It had a foot pedal to pump to start. It had a metal flexible hose for exhaust pipe, which Mother used on screened-in porch in summer and basement in wintertime.

We lived one-quarter mile from Ohio Power Substation and did not get electric 'til 1946. I was one of four brothers who went to World War Two. When I came home in 1946, I was entitled to twenty-six weeks of rocking chair money, so first trip to sign up at Uhrichsville, I got a quarter HP Class motor, fifteen dollars, put on Mother's Maytag. She used fifteen more years.

The Red Topped Boots and the Girl With the Snake

by William M. Shaw of Sarahsville, Ohio
born in 1921

I was born on September 13, 1921 in a farmhouse near Fredericksdale, Noble County, Ohio. Fredericksdale was a small place that included four houses and a country store. There were about twenty other homes located less than a mile from the store that made up the total community. The store included the post office, the barbershop, fuel supply along with groceries, hardware items, dry goods, clothes, shoes and drug store items. It was the social center of the community. The United Brethren Church and the one room school were located about a quarter mile north from the store. You had to cross a stream and railroad track to get to the school and church. The railroad station was located south of the tracks, along this route.

Our house had eight rooms and it was built in the 1880's. It was heated by three fireplaces and a coal burning cook stove. The bedrooms were upstairs and were not heated except on very cold nights when we might put a hot water bottle, a sad iron wrapped in a towel or a half gallon fruit jar filled with hot water between the sheets to remove some of the chill. The bedding consisted of a set of springs, a straw tick, a feather tick, sheets, and as many quilts as needed. There was a chamber pot in those bedrooms in wintertime and it did freeze. The pot had to be taken downstairs in the morning and placed by the fireplace to thaw so it could be emptied. The water supply for the house was a pitcher-pump in the kitchen, which drew water from a 2000-gallon cistern. This was a rather advanced water supply of the time, as most people had to carry water from a spring or well located some distance from the house. Our house was located about a half mile west of the store.

My mom was a schoolteacher and my dad was a World War I veteran and a farmer. Our family included my parents, my younger brother, me and my grandfather. We lived on a 285-acre farm and grew corn, wheat, hay and pasture. Our livestock included beef cattle, sheep, swine, poultry, and a few milk cows. Our power was horses. My chores, in wintertime, included taking care of the horses. We usually had three or four head and they had to be fed and watered each morning and evening. The well we used to water the horses was located near their barn. It was also the source of our drinking water, so I had to bring a three-gallon bucket of water to the house when I fed the horses.

The standard clothing for boys was BVD's, bib overalls and a shirt, work shoes and socks. In colder parts of the year, long underwear, a coat, and overshoes were added. Baths were taken and clothing was changed once a week in wintertime, more often in the summer. The bathtub was a large galvanized laundry tub which was placed in front of the fireplace in the living room. Water was heated on the cook stove in the kitchen and then carried to the tub.

When I was six or seven years old, I saw a picture of a pair of red-topped knee-boots in a magazine and fell in love with them. I am sure I told my parents I wanted those boots more than anything in the world. I got the boots and liked them very much and wore them in the house and outside for several days. Then the trouble began. Whenever it was wet and muddy outside, I was always the one who was asked to do the chores, such as bringing the milk cows from the pasture to the milking barn or to go to the well for a fresh bucket of drinking water. This was my first experience of, "Be careful what you wish for, you may get it."

Most of our food came from the farm. Pork and poultry were the main meat supply. We butchered one 250-pound hog for each member of the family. The hams, shoulders and bacon were salt cured and smoked. They were then placed in a large paper bag along with a little borax to keep the bugs out. The sack was then tied tightly and hung from a nail in the outbuilding. The cured pork supply usually lasted till late summer and we had very little spoilage. Sausage and garden products were canned in quart jars.

Corn meal was a part of our diet. It was used as mush-and-milk, fried mush, corn pone and corn cakes. My dad also used corn meal to make dog feed. He would build an outside fire and use a kettle ring and a 20-gallon kettle. When the water in the kettle started to boil, he would add the corn meal and all the leftover parts from the butchering. It was great dog feed.

The milk cows provided us with milk, cream, butter, cottage cheese, and some cream to sell to the cream station.

The country store was very important to many phases of life in the community. It was our connection to the outside world for our necessities, as well as a few luxuries such as candy, chewing gum, cookies, and yes, chewing tobacco, pipe tobacco and cigarette tobacco to roll your own. The store was heated by a potbellied stove located near the center of the building. Light was provided by two pump-up gasoline lamps which were placed in a hook near the ceiling. In the evening, many of the men of the community would gather to buy a few items, exchange news, tell tall stories and to enjoy snacks such as bologna, long horn cheese or sardines. It was ordered by asking for ten, fifteen or twenty-five cents worth of the product. One day, one of the regulars at the evening gathering asked for a nickel's worth of cheese just to test the storekeeper. It didn't work out that way he thought it would. The storekeeper stepped from behind the counter with the cheese knife in his hand, raised it to the man's face and said, "Smell this."

During a Saturday night in July, an ice cream social was held for all members of the community. The storekeeper would bring packers of ice cream from the produce company and the women would bring cakes. Games were played and a good time was had by all.

The store served as a meeting place for patrons of the local telephone company. They would meet to discuss the condition of the line, buy needed supplies, decide the amount each patron was to pay and plan workdays to repair the line. There were about twenty households on our line. To talk with someone outside our community, we had to go through the central office in Sarahsville.

The railroad that served our community was narrow gauge, only three feet between the rails compared to four-foot, eight and a half inches for a standard gauge track. It was a small train, but it looked big to me. I remember riding the train very few times, but it was exciting. It was our link to the faraway places. Service began in 1883 and continued 'till the late1920's. The train system was known as the OR&W (Ohio River and Western), but it was better known as the BZ&C (Bent, Zigzag & Crooked). The train track ran from Bellaire on the Ohio River to Woodsfield, then Caldwell, and on to Zanesville, a distance of 112 miles. My family only used the train in wintertime when the roads were too muddy to travel in my dad's 1921 model T Ford. My principal use of the railroad was to use the roadbed as a mud-free path to school in the wintertime. The train was a very slow method of transportation, not because it was not capable of high speed, but because it stopped at a station in every small community along the route. There were also flag stations, located about a mile apart in the open country, where you could flag the train to stop and pick you up.

The school was a typical one-room building heated by a potbellied stove located near the center of the room. The girls' desks were on the right side of the room and the boys' on the left. The usual attire for boys was a bib overall, and for the girls, feed-sack dresses. There were shelves at the rear of the room for our lunch pails and the water bucket. Our library was a small wall cabinet, located near the front of the room. I would guess it contained thirty or forty books. I remember two of them: *Tom Sawyer* and *Moby Dick*. There was no artificial light, just the windows. The school site also included two outhouses and a coalhouse. The playground was on the east side of the building and a small stream was on the west side. The public road was in front of the school and railroad track was just past the road. Drinking water came from a spring on the east side of the school or the well at the country store. When a fresh bucket of water was needed, either two girls or two boys were selected to get it. A common tin dipper was used to remove water from the bucket. Some students drank from the dipper and others poured it into personal, collapsible tin cups and drank from the cups. Games included base, blackman, tag, baseball, high jump and long jump. The school day had three break times: a fifteen-minute recess at mid-morning and mid-afternoon and one-hour for lunchtime.

My first school teacher was the teacher who replaced my mother when I came along and put her out of work. I started school in the second grade because my mother had taught me first grade at home. I was six years old. I think the one-room school provided an opportunity for a good education because each of us not only participated in our own learning experience, but also had the opportunity to observe other classes recite many times.

If one started in the first grade, they would have the opportunity to observe eighth graders recite seven times before they were an eighth grader.

One of the older boys was hired to be the janitor for the school. His duties included coming to the building about a half-hour before school time to build a fire in the wintertime and keep it going all day. He also swept the building each day, cleaned the windows once a month and oiled the floor once a year. I think the pay was five dollars a month.

Field trips were a part of the educational experience at the school. We would work to finish our regular classes early on a given day each spring and fall so we could go through the fields and woods of the community to explore the wonders of nature. On one of these trips, a little fourth grade girl captured a small blacksnake and did a show and tell for her fellow students. As she was showing her snake to a seventh grade boy, she made a quick move towards him and he ran with her chasing him all over the hillside.

Spelling contests were sometimes conducted to add a bit of variety to the learning process. Participants would line up across the front of the room and words would be presented to each student. If the word was spelled correctly, the student would hold their place in the line. If incorrect, the student would go to the bottom of the line. On one occasion, a seventh-grade boy had been at the top of the line for several days. Along came the word "sugar." The boy spelled it "suger" and he had to take his place at the bottom of the line. When the students returned to their desks, the boy who spelled the word correctly was sitting at the desk in front of the boy who had missed it. The failed-speller must have felt very frustrated and embarrassed and did a very irrational act by pulling the hair of the boy who beat him. I earned and received my first and only whipping of my school career for this unthinkable act.

This one room school was a good place to begin the educational process. Many of my fellow students became very successful business people. Not many of us are left...only six that I know. I am not sure what one of them did, but one is the retired CEO of an electric power company, another is a retired Oral Surgeon, a retired college professor, a retired school superintendent and the only PhD, and her brother, a professional race horse owner and sulky driver who ran his last race and won in the fall of 2008 at age 89, at Lancaster Ohio.

My high school was at Sarahsville, about a two-mile walk from my home. It was a wooden, four-room building with outdoor plumbing. The gymnasium was located about thirty feet east of the school. During my high school years, the old building was demolished and a new brick building was constructed by WPA. The new building housed both the grade school and the high school. It had indoor plumbing and electricity, provided by a Delco electric generator powered by natural gas. During the construction period, classes were held in small buildings located on the school grounds and in public buildings in Sarahsville. It was a challenging time for both teachers and students. During my last year in school (1937-1938), the grade school I attended was closed and a bus route was established to carry all students from my community to the new school building. I rode to school during my last year. There were about fifteen students in my freshman class and only seven of us graduated. Many good students dropped out due to economic reasons.

Our church was a one-room building with a potbellied stove located near the center of the building. A stage was located at the front for the organist, the choir, and the preacher's lectern. When evening services were held, light was provided by pump-up gasoline lamps. Two were located in the main part of the building, and one in the stage area. The altar was located near the front of the stage. I would guess that about half of the adults in the community attended church regularly and most of the children attended Sunday school. I still have a gold pin I earned for a year of perfect attendance.

During the wintertime, one or two weeks was devoted to evangelistic meetings which were held each evening to give people of the community an opportunity to establish a new relationship with God. Leaders of the church would contact evangelists who would come to the community and stay in the homes of people while they conducted evening worship services. There would be two to four preachers to make up the evangelistic team. Their presentations were very emotional. They would shout, jump up and down, etc. At the end of their presentations, they would invite people to come to the altar to be born again. The group at the altar, with the help of the preachers, would become very emotional, shouting, dancing and crying as they went through whatever experience they were having. I am sure some of the people at the altar were very sincere and perhaps some were not. Similar events occurred each evening for the duration of the services.

One day, two teenage boys who had been attending the meetings were husking corn. When they upset a shock of corn to begin husking, there would often be a family of mice living there. One of the boys said to the other, "I wonder what would happen if we would capture some of these mice and turn them loose at church tonight when all the people are gathered at the altar?" The other boy thought it was a great idea and went to the house and got an empty kitchen matchbox. The boys continued to upset shocks, catch mice, and husk corn 'till the end of the day. By that time, the matchbox was full. They took the box to church that evening and when the altar call was given, they went to the altar with the other people, and when they thought the time was right, released the mice. The shouting, jumping, and dancing reached a tempo never before experienced. It was reported later that everybody at the church got religion that night.

The swimming hole was an important part of our summer activities. The best place to swim was located under and below the bridge located near the country store. Our attire would be called "skinny dipping" today. We would always post a lookout to warn us when anyone was approaching the bridge so we could get under the bridge or muddy the water. One day, the lookout warned us someone was approaching the bridge. It was the little girl who had the snake on the field trip. She was looking straight ahead and walking at a rapid pace as she crossed the bridge. Many other interesting things happened at the swimming hole, but this is one I remember.

Fredericksdale Grade School 1930. Front row, left to right: Laura Bates, Jean Davidson, the girl with the snake, Laverne Carter, Robert Young, James Shaw. Second row: Opal Young, Emma Rose Sutherland, Wava Wentworth, Lillian Wentworth, Lewis Kirkbride, Giman Bates, Walter Young, William Shaw, Wayne Bates, Murl Thomas, our teacher.

The Depression hit Wall Street in 1929, but not 'til 1932 did the full effects reach the country. Most of us were poor in this part of the country, but we didn't know it, so we were used to living without many of the niceties of life. Prices of farm products fell to practically nothing; market hogs were only two or three cents a pound; beef cattle were five or six cents; the market for wool and tobacco was so low many farmers kept their crops for several years, hoping for a better price that never happened in those years. Food was not a problem for the people who lived on the farm. They produced most of their food and had to buy few things such as, sugar, baking powder, salt and pepper. The families that lived in the small villages grew gardens and bartered their labor to farmers for meat and milk. Professionals in the community would barter their services for farm products. One physician, who was a relative, received much of his pay in the form of farm products and baked goods. He never turned anyone away and always accepted what was offered. When he received more than he could use, he would call someone he knew would be glad to come and pick it up.

Debt and sin were very close in the value system of our community. Very few people had savings. One family in the community was reported to have more than ten thousand dollars in the bank and they were perceived as being very rich. Real estate taxes had to be paid by a certain date. Money was scraped together to meet this obligation. I remember one year my dad sold two truckloads of hogs to get the final amount for the taxes. I went with him to the county courthouse on the final day to pay taxes and stood in a long line to make the payment. Many others were in the same shape we were. I remember some food products were distributed to some very poor families by the township trustees. The products included pork shoulders and cheese. The situation at school didn't change very much; a few more patches on the overalls and more scrambled egg sandwiches than at other times. It is difficult to go much farther down the hill when you are at the bottom. I remember one year I wore a hole in the toe of one of my shoes and was embarrassed to wear them to school. My dad told me he only had money for a pair of shoes or a pair of overshoes and since it was wintertime, it would be best to get the overshoes. They would keep my feet dry when I was outside and it was okay to wear the shoes with the hole in the inside. We got the four-buckle overshoes.

There must have been a little surplus cash in 1934, because my grandmother and uncle took me to the Chicago Worlds Fair to experience the Century of Progress event. There were many exciting displays and demonstrations. The ones I remember most concerned automobiles. The Firestone Rubber Company had a small production tire manufacturing line, set up so we could see how a tire was made from start to finish. I visited this display every day I was at the fair. The Chrysler Corporation had just introduced their "Airflow" line of automobiles and was driving them around a track that includes steep hills, rough spots and other challenges. I thought it was the most beautiful automobile I had ever seen, but the design did not catch on and people didn't buy it. Later, it was said the car was many years ahead of its time. My uncle took me to a show in the "Streets of Paris" section of the fair featuring the fan dancer, Sally Rand. Sally used two seven foot ostrich feather fans in her presentation and seemed to be dancing nude, a very exciting experience for this thirteen year old boy. I later learned she was wearing a body stocking. I also learned that about the same time we visited her show, she was hauled to court on an indecency charge. She won the case and returned to her show at the fair. The Superior Court judge who heard the case said, "There is no harm and certainly no injury to public morals when the human body is exposed. Some people would probably want to put pants on a horse." Sally is given credit for making the 1934 Fair a financial success and the fair made Sally a national known figure. My first trip out of Ohio was a trip I remembered for a lifetime.

My maternal grandfather was a rural mail carrier and a person who was always involved in local politics. He never ran for public office, but always had a favorite candidate for township trustee, school board and county offices. In addition to delivering the mail, patrons sometimes left a note in their mailbox asking him to bring a much needed item with him the next day...such as a loaf of bread, a can of baking powder or a pack of tobacco. He did a lot of this sort of thing which was contrary to the rules of the postal service. Because he was a community figure, he had a lot of friends. Because of his political activity, there were some people who didn't like him very much. One of these people filed a complaint with the postal service about his activity and a postal inspector arrived to investigate the complaint. The story is told that the inspector arrived at the post office and requested that he ride along with my grandfather in the buggy as he delivered the mail that day to check the facts. They left the post office and started to deliver the mail and it was common practice that many patrons were at their mailboxes to meet the mailman when he arrived. On three or four occasions, when they met a patron, my grandfather would introduce his guest as an inspector from the United States Postal Service. These patrons were very impressed to meet such an important person and insisted that he have some of their homemade wine. By the time they had finished delivering the mail and were nearing the outskirts of town, my grandfather noticed the inspector had gone to sleep. My grandfather got out of the buggy, wrapped the lines around the whip socket and slapped the horse on his rear quarter. The horse knew his way through town and back to the post office. My grandfather got a good report from the inspector.

Do you remember the little girl with the snake? She graduated from The Ohio State University School of Nursing, spent some time in the Army Cadet Nursing Corps, and later, graduated from The University of Kansas, Nurse Practitioner program. She became one of the first Certified Nurse Practitioners in Ohio. She also caught that boy she was chasing. We were married in March of 1945 and raised four children. All of them were above average.

The Winter Coat Painless Paddling

by Betty Bagent of Zanesville, Ohio
born in 1931

One time when I was seven years old, I got a spanking for eating the icing on a cake. I felt so hurt and felt bad all day. I remember that was the only spanking I got from my mother.

I got one whack from a paddle for turning around and talking at school. I kept my winter coat on, and I never felt a thing.

My favorite teacher was the one that made sure her class learned all of the 50 states and capitols of the U.S. and where they were at on the map.

During the Depression, my dad worked hard on the farm. He got a quart of milk for pay, and he got home and it was sour. Hard times. I remember we lived on another farm, and part of our pay was a ham. We decided to move at the end of the year, so they took the ham back. But the new farm gave us a new ham for coming to work for them.

We went to Buckeye Lake for entertainment in Hebron, Ohio. It was like King's Island today. We made bottled root beer for our pop.

We had a spring house where we kept our butter, cottage cheese, chocolate syrup, milk, and cream for whipping. No icebox or refrigerator. It was all homemade.

Bud, Pete and the Horsefly

by John W. Dodds of Urichsville, Ohio
born in 1925

I was between the ages of 10 or 12 years, and we were very poor. It was during the Depression, and most people didn't have too much money.

One summer, my parents decided that I should go to work for a neighbor lady on her farm. She wanted me to learn to drive a team of oxen, Bud and Pete. This was quite an undertaking for a kid my age. All I had to remember was at the end of the summer I would get a new pair of overalls and a pair of shoes for school.

So, I began the lessons to learn to drive the oxen. It wasn't too hard for me, because I like animals and they like me. As time went on, I learned to hook them to the flat sled and put on their yoke. The hired man, who was working for the lady, and I went up into a wooded area and cut down trees. The lady went along, and she and I used a two-man saw to cut the trees into posts we had split. We then loaded them on to the sled and took them back to the barn. Once we got there, we loaded the posts on to a wagon. The next step was for the hired man and me to take the wagon load over a nearby hill to the

Universal Sewer Pipe Company, where they would be used as mine posts to support the roof of the coal mine. My father was working there at that time.

Another interesting incident with Bud and Pete: We were working in the garden, and I was dragging a harrow behind them and a big horsefly lit on one of them and, of course, it bit him. They took off for the barn, dragging me and the harrow. It got caught in the doorway and thankfully stopped them and me.

Believe me, by the end of that summer, I felt as if I had earned those shoes and overalls! Those were the "good old days," I guess!

The Big Red X and the Easter Basket

By Martha J. Adkins of Chandlersville, Ohio
Born 1936

QUARANTINE! That dreaded big red sign on your door that told the whole world you could not go out and they could not come in. When I was a small child, I remember my brother Tom and I came down with scarlet fever at Easter time. When taken to the doctor, I saw the doctor take his thumbnail and make a big red X across Tom's chest, which turned scarlet and thus the diagnosis that kept us housebound.

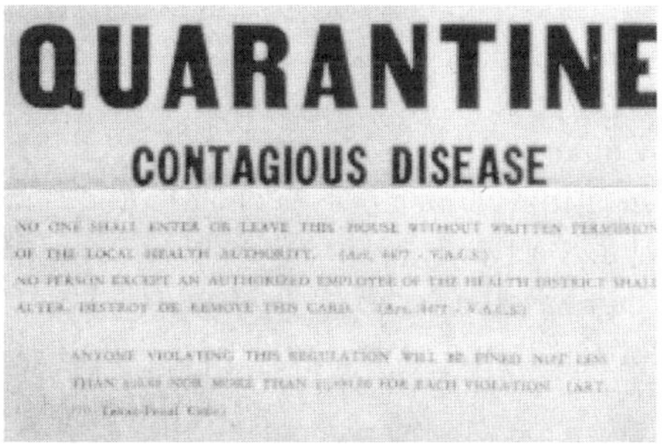

My sisters, Catherine and Edith and another brother, Bob, were taken to my Grandma Herron's to keep them from getting it. At Grandma Herron's, Catherine and Edith got pneumonia, so Bob was taken to Grandma Bliss's house and he came down with the pink eye! All five children now sick with different ailments at three different places.

Since this was Easter time, a kindly neighbor, Mr. Eck, brought Tom and me an Easter basket, something we never had before. It was left at the door since no one was allowed in. Having never had a basket before, I chose a chocolate bunny and ended up with chocolate all over me as it melted from being held too long.

After the end of the scarlet fever, the house had to be fumigated thoroughly with fog from what I'll call little smudge pots before anyone could come back into the house.

While Catherine was at Grandma Herron's, still in bed recovering from pneumonia, she came down with the three-day measles she apparently got from our Uncle Asa. (Everyone thought he was over them enough that no one would get them.) Edith didn't come down with them until she was back home again. Even before all this took place, we kids had the old-fashioned measles. Since we were kept in darkened rooms with very low light so as not to hurt our eyes, Mom read to us from library books to keep us entertained. After the scarlet fever, Dad never let us have library books for the longest time, because he thought we got the scarlet fever from the books Mom had read to us.

Another thing you didn't want to see on your door was a wreath! Also during this era, when someone died, they were most often taken back to the home for friends and neighbors to come calling to pay their respect. A wreath would be hung on the door during that period of time and then the deceased most often would be taken to a church for the final services. If the person owned a business, a wreath would be hung on the door of their business, also.

Haying time in the summer was a good time, most of the time. I say most of the time because after the side-delivery rake made windrows out of the hay, we then used a hay loader to go down the rows which picked up the hay and dropped it onto the wagon. The kid's job was to move the hay around on the wagon so it was evenly loaded. The only problem being it was not only just hay that came down off the hay loader it was also SNAKES which had crawled under the windrowed hay looking for a cool place to stay. There went the fun of the day, as I am not a snake lover. Even though I understand the good they do I just didn't like seeing them come down with hay I was supposed to move.

The hay wagon loaded high was then taken to the barn where we had double haymows, one on each side of the barn's upper story. It also had double openings there where we could push the hay down to the cattle below. We had the hay fork in the center of the loft so that we could divert the hay to either haymow.

The fun part of this was driving the horses (and later tractor) up and back as the hay was pulled to the top before going either direction and then letting the fork back down to grab some more. The worst part was moving the hay around in the haymow to be evenly distributed and creating all that dust.

Another not so fun part of haying is that we had to give up our swing rope that hung from our big maple tree in our front yard because it was the trip rope that dropped the hay once it had been taken to the haymow. A fun part of hay time was going to the creek for a swim at the end of the day to get all the hay chaff off you had collected.

A not so fun part was the annoying sweat bees you always had because they were attracted to perspiration.

You also were hot in the long sleeves you wore to keep as much chaff off you as you could and give the bees less room to land.

A side fun time was playing basketball on the hay loft floor with the basket we had put up on one end. The hay made the floor so slick it was hard to make the basketball maneuvers without sliding. Another not so fun part was having to gather eggs from the nests the chickens made in the haymows. You just knew there would be a SNAKE in there because they liked eggs too. A fun part of haying was after we got the harvest in, we would walk the high beam between the two haymows where the hay fork traveled and then jump off into the fluffy hay. (I wouldn't think of walking that high beam today.)

When you rode a fully loaded hay wagon off the hill down to the barn, if the road was rutted and sloped, you always rode the high side, because you could make a mad leap off if the wagon tipped toward the low side and either upset the load or tipped enough to unload the hay without landing on its side.

Proud To Be A County Girl

by Cora Mellott Tomolonis of Beallsville, Ohio
born 1932

I was born in Monroe County at Cameron, Ohio. I was born to Mary and Dow Mellot in a log cabin up Pain's Run in Adams Township. I attended a two room school in Cameron, until my parents purchased a large farm on top of Pontias Hill outside of Cameron. We moved there when I was 10.

My parents was hard-working farmers with cows, pigs, chickens etc. My parents raised them, and butchered the meat for winter. We had our own eggs.

My mother raised a large garden in the summer so she could can our vegetables for winter; she also canned many jars of fruit, made sauerkraut, salt brine pickles, and stuffed peppers for the long, cold winter months.

In summer, my dad made hay and cut corn and oats for the animals in winter. It was hard, but a very good life.

My father always cut lots of wood and dug coal from his own coal bank for fire in the winter. We had wood and coal heat and kerosene lamps for light.

My sister and I walked to school two-and-a-half miles, but never missed. Sometimes my father would take us down the hill on the sled and horses to the schoolhouse.

For fun, we did a lot of sleigh riding and building snowmen in winter. My mother, in the winter, in the evening, she would bake many doughnuts and homemade candies and lots of cookies. We would have them while we played dominoes or checkers. Sometimes we would listen to the radio after our school work was complete. My mother made sure of that.

We had a very large farmhouse, a long kitchen along the side of the house, a living room, dining room with fireplace, three large bedrooms upstairs, and a small one. Under the living room and dining room was a cold cellar where my mother kept the canned fruit and vegetables and potatoes for winter. Oh yes, we had lots of homemade jellies and jams and homemade ketchup, which I hated. Ketchup wasn't my thing.

My sister was eight years older than me; she had a large rag doll which I loved. She called it E.T.Y. Beck. One day I wanted it. She said, "No!" So I hit her on the belly. I tried to trade her my doll for hers, but she wouldn't. My mother made me sit for one hour on a straight back kitchen chair.

We were raised to appreciate what we had, and not to talk back or mock other people and to respect our elders. My father always asked the blessing before we ate. We attended church, winter and summer, when the weather permitted it. We had a large family, four sisters and three brothers.

I can remember when flour was 80 cents a sack, bread 12 cents a loaf, but we didn't never have to worry about the bread. My mother baked homemade bread every week. I learned many things from my mother and older sister, now then, when I was grown up.

I married and had a family of my own, seven sons and two daughters. One daughter passed away at age 17, one son at birth. I was married 36 years. My husband was sick for 14 years, but I took care of him, then cancer took him. He suffered a long time, but I wouldn't trade my life for nothing.

Now all the children is married. I have four grandsons and three granddaughters. Now I live in Beallsville in a lovely little house and have wonderful landlords that treat me very well, and I respect them for that. I belong to the Beallsville American Legion Auxiliary. Everyone there is friendly and very nice. They hold many events there. It is a beautiful large building on top of the hill; it has a monument and a cannon in the front where they hold Veterans Day services every November 11. They do many things for our school, which is Beallsville Blue Devils.

Well, that's about all about my life. I worked 15 years in Legann sewing factory, Belmont Manufacturing, and Jonathan Logan. But now I live by myself and am very happy and try to be a good friend to everyone.

Grandma's Rooster and the Hearth Knocker

By Louise (Grizzle) Manning of Tampa, Florida
Born in 1938

I remember washing up for school from a wood stove with a water reservoir on the side in Flatwoods, Kentucky, and going to the outhouse with Grandma when she visited, and her yelling, "Heavens to Betsy!" at all the spiders, and walking down the hill to hear "Amos and Andy," "The Creaky Door" after dark, and being afraid to go back home. My brother Ron couldn't listen to the "Lone Ranger" unless he got his firewood all in.

Grandma's rooster wouldn't let me out of the outhouse, and all the other kids were going around the outside of house singing, "I Ain't Gonna Study War No More" after the war, banging on pots and pans.

I was five when I first climbed on a chair and cranked the Victrola and loved to listen to "Don't Fence Me In." My uncle George Grizzle babysat my brother Ron, sister Wilma, and tried to make an electric guitar out of Dad's, and made all the lights go out scaring us all so bad I fell off the chair. In that same house, my dad had gone off to war in World War II, my aunt Clatine and Mom was trying to break wooden matches in between their fingers, and my aunt Lil and I was packing them up and taking them in the yard which was full of leaves. We caught them on fire and Mom yelled, "Run to Grandmas and get a shovel," and running as fast as I could down the path, a blue racer was under a tree and heading down, rolling down, the snake behind me, he decided to go another way. Grandpa brought me back in the old pickup truck. He and an old family friend got it out.

I would cry to go to Grandma's because she always had something good to eat and all my aunts were close in age.

Grandma Grizzle and Mom always had babies close together. Grandma had a dorm-like upstairs, and the older aunts would tell us ghost stories while it was storming, one of which was about a ghost that had lost his big toe. They would tell us younger kids to make sure we didn't have any bobby pins in our hair, or we would surely get struck by lightning.

My maternal grandma Duty put potatoes in the fireplace, and dug them out with the poker. She showed us how to make a bubble blower using an empty thread spool by caking soap on one end and dipping in a cup of water, and blowing. We also learned how to make a Jacob's ladder with twine.

The old home place was on a dirt dusty road. My grandma, Delcie Duty, let my mom visit her cousin down the road, and she had a visitor there who could make the hearth knock. Mom asked her if she could make a box knock; she wanted to take it home to her mom. She got half way home on the lonely dirt road and threw it in the ditch, and ran the rest of the way home. I never knew what to make of this, because my mother was a reserved, quiet Christian until the day she died at 84, and never told a lie all her life. This was probably around 1924.

Ruth, Ron, Wilma, Freda, Louise, Lib, Clotine, Wanda or Eliza Jane sitting.

We were all at Grandma Grizzle's (Mammaw's), and all shared the tub for our weekly bath, and after going to sleep, my brother Ron woke all of us up having an epilepsy seizure which we all called "fits." My aunt Lil woke up so scared, she jumped out of bed and cleared the tub of dirty water with one bound; she was certainly glad she didn't jump into that dirty water.

Bigshot Cussings and the Long Paddle

by Glenn A. Girton of Zanesville, Ohio
born in 1923

Back when I was seven years old, my birthday was July 12, on July 14 my dad died, on July 16 my youngest brother was born. From then on until I was twelve, then I could go to the golf course to caddy. I'd walk five mile around that course for fifty cents. I was a B caddy.

One day I was caddying for the Big 4 which was bigshot lawyers. I couldn't find the ball and they started cussing me, so I just cussed them back. So I caddied until I was sixteen or seventeen, then I went with my brother to haul coal to different people around town. I got me a drivers license.

But when we were not at the golf course, we either played in the woods or went down to the ole swimming hole and skinny dipped. As for windup record player, I still have one today. As for baths, it was behind the cook stove in the kitchen. Us boys would have to bring in the kindling, the coal, the wash water to heat up on the cook stove.

I never talked much to my granddad. Every now and then we (my mom) would harness up the horses and drive about twelve to fifteen miles out to Granddad's. My mother raised all ten kids after my dad passed away, but he gave me a whipping for throwing rocks at my older brother. And when I was in the eighth grade, the principal beat my fanny with a very long paddle, I never have forgotten it. I had it coming because I slapped my English teacher, knocking her across the desk. So I am going to close this now. I know there are more stories to tell.

A Man to Keep Your Eye On

by Russell King of Carrollton, Ohio
born in 1925

I was born in 1925 to a German woman and an English man. That was quite a combination then, after World War I, but they loved each other and that was all that counted. I was born at my grandparents' home and Grandpa was the only one with a job. He worked in a coal mine for 65 years.

I joined the Navy in 1943 when I was 17. The USS Pennsylvania battleship was engaged in 12 major naval battles in the South Pacific and I received the Presidential Unit Citation. Johnny Carson was my division officer, but I never saw him after that.

Russell King.

The Depression never bothered my brother and I, as we didn't know any other way of life. Visiting neighbors and relatives were our enjoyment—which doesn't happen now.

We took a bath in a galvanized tub on the back porch. Water was heated on a cook stove fired with wood or coal. We had no indoor plumbing, and our heat was a pot bellied stove in the living room or a fireplace.

I remember hearing Adolf Hitler's speeches to the German people. My Uncle Edgar was a World War I veteran, and he said, "That is a man to keep your eye on." He was right!

Folks in our community would gather at the Cadiz Square to listen to radio broadcasts. I heard a heavyweight match between Joe Louis and Max Schmelling, which Joe Louis won in the first round by a knockout.

After the Muskingum watershed project started, my dad helped move a cemetery away from the Tappan dam area. The W.P.A. program provided employment, so the economy got a boost at that time.

My brother and I used to take wheels and put them on boards to make scooters—that was fun. Later we took a job hoeing corn for 50 cents a day and bought a new bicycle. We were in seventh heaven.

My kids never believed how far my brother and I walked to school. I took them once by car and now they believe me.

I have a lot more memories, but this is about all you can digest at one time.

A Nineteenth Century Letter

by Virginia Lee Kinney of Pleasant Hill, Ohio
born in 1934

My father's paternal ancestors came to Belmont County, Ohio in 1800. My father's maternal ancestors came to Belmont County, Ohio from Loudoun County, Virginia in 1833.

The enclosed letter written by a Jane M. Smith (whom I do not know) to my husband, Royce B. Kinney's, great grandmother, 12-year-old Amanda Palmer, in Belmont, Belmont Co., Ohio, my husband's ancestor, that was written July 30, 1846 is very interesting.

McArthurstown, Athens Co.
July 30, 1846
My Dear Friend,

I take this opportunity to address a few lines to you, to let you know that I have not forgotten you. We had very disagreeable weather coming here, we started on Tuesday, but as we were heavily loaded and the roads were very bad, we did not get here till the next Monday. I believe there was nothing happened to us while coming here worth putting down on paper.

Now I will try and give you some description of what I have seen and heard [illegible]. I have not seen much of this country yet, but what I have seen I like very well. The people about here are nearly all from the New England States and Yankees. You wished me to tell you what the names of the girls were that I got acquainted with first; they were Mary Ann Keaton and Elizabeth Keaton. I believe they are pretty nice girls.

McArthurstown is about three miles and a half from here. I have been there and got acquainted with some very nice girls there. We had a great many cherrys, there is no other kind about here but morellas. We have a good apple and peach orchard. Some of the peaches are getting ripe now.

There is no Baptists or Friends here, the folks around here are the Methodists or United Brethren. The Methodists have quite a splendid church in McArthurstown. The United Brethren are going to have a camp meeting a few miles from here shortly.

I must not forget to tell you the names of some of the ladys here. I think they are the queerest names I ever heard. Well, there is a [illegible] Langarthe Brown, Cloe

Wolp, Arsula Gibbs, Lois Blashman, [illegible] Andrews, Gabina Chapin. These are just a few of the many queer names I have heard since I came here, but I think they can't be beat, in your neck of woods anyhow.

Amanda, I want you to write just as ever as you receive this and be sure to tell me all the news. I suppose if you went to Miss Bur this summer you have got to be a first rate grammarian by this time, and don't forget to tell me how my [illegible] is getting along with her grammar. By this time, I [illegible] my Burr did not have as many scholars this summer as she had last summer. You remember she promised you and me that she would write us a piece of poetry or prose for a keepsake. I wish if you see her you should please give my respect to her and [illegible] her that I should be happy to receive it now, in the hope of a letter.

When you write, I want you to tell me whether Mary Rogers has gone to [illegible] or not; I would have wrote to her but I didn't know whether she would be at home or not, and also I want you to tell me what the latest fashions are with you.

I had almost forgot to ask you whether you planted that Bachelors [illegible] seed that I gave you and whether it growed or not. If it did I wish you would put a seed or two in your letter, I was so forgetful as to leave all the seed of it I had behind me.

I think I must draw to a close. Remember me to all my old friends and tell them that I should be happy to receive a letter from one or all of them. Tell Josephine and Armind not to forget their old schoolmate. Give my love to Mary Ann, your mother, and the rest. And Tremain.

Learning a Speech by Oil Lamp

by Lucy Busley Burris of Barnesville, Ohio
born in 1918

I was born May 18, 1918, and began school on September, 1924 at Kenwood School, located three miles north of Adena, Ohio, seven miles south of Cadiz, Ohio.

My first teacher was Cora Stephens. She walked several miles to be there. She stayed five years. We had all eight grades in one room with a big round coal stove in center of the room. The eighth grade boys carried the coal in to heat the stove. We had a big water bucket on a shelf in the corner with a dipper. We all drank out of it. We hung our coats and caps on nails in back of the school.

Our school superintendent was D.C. Simpson from Cadiz, Ohio, for we were in Harrison County. The next teacher was Mrs. Stinard for one year. Then George Roth came. He was a wonderful teacher. I learned more the first year he was there than all the other years. I always hated to see the last day of school. He had a way of explaining everything. He would make outlines and explain them very well so you could understand them.

Everyone took homemade bread sandwiches, for there wasn't store bread then or store cakes or cookies. We would have plays at Christmas. The eighth grade boys would build a stage up front. I always had a long speech, so I'd set it by the oil lamp on the table at home and learn it while I washed dishes. No one those days rinsed their dishes.

Left to right: Beatrice Dadd Hendershatt, Sarah Hendershatt Dowdle, Mildred Hendershatt McGlathlin, Lucy Busby Burris.

We never had electric or running water. In 1930, Wonder Bread from Wheeling, West Virginia started to bring bread to Monaco Store in Kenwood. Mr. Monaco owned the store and coal mine where most of the men worked. The bread wasn't sliced yet. It was a while before they done that.

No one had toys to play with, so we played hide and seek, hopscotch, ball, and drop the handkerchief. Great days, great fun.

Pie Crust Ants and Lye Soap

by Barbara Reed of Chandlersville, Ohio
born 1935

On Thanksgiving day, several of the neighbors got together to butcher hogs. They rendered the lard into five gallon tin cans or large stone jars. Crocks or flat pan. *Crocks*. These were to be kept cool so the lard would not get strong in taste.

The can or jar was usually put in the cellar since there was no refrigerator. Hopefully this would last the family to cook and make pie crusts for the whole year.

If you did not get the lid on tight after getting a cup or whatever you needed, tiny red ants would get into the lard and you had to scrim them off the top, as little, tiny red ants were a no-no in your pie crust.

Later in the fall when the lard got a strong taste to it, they used to make lye soap. Lye soap was put in casks to cure for several days and then cut out into chunks. It was used to do laundry and take baths. The soap had a nice, clean smell to it.

But if you made pie crust with the strong lard, it was a taste you wouldn't soon forget.

Backyard Movies in Perry County
by Hazel Deavers of Seffner, Florida
born in 1928

My name is Hazel (Kesler, Speelman) Deavers. I was born on March 14, 1928 in New Lexington, Ohio. My parents were Bert and Bertha Kakensparger Kasler. I was the youngest of three girls. We lived out in the country, Perry County, a few miles from New Lexington, Ohio. It was a small area ten or twelve tile-block houses. The Ludowici Celeadon Tile Plant owned them, and my dad worked there. We were really poor. We didn't have any running water or electric. We carried our drinking water from a spring way down in the woods. We used kerosene lights and dug coal from the clay pits.

We went to school in a one room schoolhouse with six grades in there. We had one teacher. After the sixth grade you were bussed to Junction City, Ohio High School.

The name of our little town was Mainsville. After a few years, the tile plant started making pottery, and my mom got a job there. I still have a few pieces of it.

There wasn't much for us kids who lived there, so on Saturday night we would all get together and walk the country road to Junction City where a man had a projector and a big screen in his yard, and we would sit on the grass and watch the movies. Then we had to walk back home in the dark. It was spooky.

On Sunday, Mom would get us kids ready and we would walk to town and go to the Presbyterian church in New Lexington. One time, all the families got together fixed a picnic brunch and went to Old Man's Cave. I really enjoyed that.

After my two older sisters got married and moved away, I was left with all the chores. By that time, I was riding the school bus to Junction City High school. When I started there, I met a really nice girl. Her name was Harriet Sullivan, and we became really good friends, and we still are. We finally moved into the edge of New Lexington. It was called "Sunnyside" or "Little Italy." Most of the families were Italian. Very nice people lived there. One of the families owned a small grocery store. His name was Tony Market.

Bertha Kasler holding Hazel with Verna on and Irene beside horse.

A few years after we moved into town, I got married to Paul Speelman, and we had a daughter, Pauline. Not long after that, my dad was hit by a car and killed. A couple of years later, Mom went to work at Mt. Carmel Hospital in Columbus. After a few years she passed away. Then I lost my husband and a little after that I lost both my sisters and their husbands. I remarried to Melvin Deavers Jr. His dad had a farm on the Old Somerset Road where he sold fruit and vegetables.

I worked thirty years at Bryant division of Carrier. I retired June 1, 1983 and in 1986 my husband had a stroke and we had to move where it was warmer, so we moved to Florida. I took care of him until August of 1995 when he died. I took him home. He is laid to rest with all his family in the New Lexington, Ohio country. He had been in the Navy.

So here I am in Florida, but my heart is in Perry County, New Lexington, Ohio. Perry County is God's country and my home.

The Sadness of a Two Bath Day
by Ruby G. Swihart of New Philadelphia, Ohio
born 1923

I am 85 years old and I am reflecting on the difference in the use of water when I was a child and now. Saturday was our weekly bath day. Mother, a widow with five children, brought the galvanized tub from the back porch into the dining room, pumped the rainwater from our cistern, from a pump in the kitchen, and heated it on the coal stove. After our baths, one at a time, she dragged it onto the porch and washed the brick wall or irrigated the grape arbor or the flowers. Recycling had no name back then.

We had a half-acre garden about a mile from our house. It was close to the Tuscarawas River. In times of drought, we carried buckets of water from it to irrigate our plants. The nettles always stung us as we made our paths. While the water was free, it was hard work for us.

During the snowy winter months we used a round dishpan or piece of cardboard to slide down the brick hill, a half block from our home. My brother had another plan for frozen water. He and his friends made a fort and the battle was on. We dipped the snowballs in water to make the fight more fierce.

We thought snow ice cream was great. We took clean snow, put sugar and vanilla flavoring on it. Everyone could afford it.

We went swimming or wading in the Tuscarawas River. The daring boys would swing out on a rope hung from a tree, and drop into the water with a yell.

Water, such an important resource.

Two baths, not a week, but on the same day! July 30, 1930 is a day which has remained in my memory, although, at the time, I wasn't aware of the date. This Saturday, Mother brought in the galvanized tub from the back porch, pumped the rainwater from the pump in the kitchen, and heated it on the coal stove. My sister was bathed first. When it was my turn, my brother ran in the front door screaming, "Mom, Mom!" Mom began to scream also and they both ran out the door. As I had never heard my mother raise her voice, I was terrified, but my sister and I ran after them, although we weren't dressed. Down the brick hill to the railroad tracks we ran. My daddy was lying on the ground and Mother kept screaming as she knelt. People I'd never seen before looking on as I tried to understand how Daddy was there on the ground, but he wasn't there.

Our next-door neighbor said I should come with her to her house. She said she would give me a bath. She had a special room and her tub was shiny, white, and huge. More amazing, there were two handles in the wall and hot water and cold poured out. Then she pulled a plug in the bottom of the tub and the water disappeared. Shocked and frightened as I was, the wonder and the beauty of that room, the tub, the miracle of water coming out of the wall, only me using this water, and two baths in one day left memories that are indelibly printed in my mind.

Math, Manners and Morals

by Sue Smith of Somerset, Ohio
born in 1927

I was born, baptized, raised, educated, graduated, worked, married and most probably will be buried in Perry County. I have quite a few memories.

My parents were immigrants from Italy. The tile factory attracted them. They settled on "Sunnyside," (named for Sunny, Italy) a section of town near the fairgrounds in New Lexington. Most of the Italians settled on Sunnyside. It is where I was born. 1927 was the year!

The Depression was in full swing. Yes, we pumped water, shoveled coal, bathed in wash tubs, and walked to school. I attended St. Aloysius Academy, an all girls' school located on a hill above the fairgrounds. It was a convent school with sixty nuns. They taught me math, manners and morals. The school was torn down.

Our teenage years consisted of attending the two local theaters, the New Lex Theater and the Perry Theater. Admission was five cents, bag of popcorn five cents. For ten cents, we were entertained. I played hopscotch, Red Rover, mumbley-peg and marbles.

After graduation, I worked for Ohio Bell Telephone Company. I was a switchboard operator. I wore a headset and connected customers. I was the "Voice with a Smile." Today, I know very little about the technology of communications.

Picnic with the nuns in 1942 at St. Aloysuis Academy.

To get to work in those days, I had to get up the "Straight Hill," and it was straight! Driving back then was a chore for me. You had to be an octopus to drive the standard cars. You had to release your brakes, push in the clutch, shift into gear, press on the gas and zoom up the hill, and pray that no one was ahead of you.

After ten years with "Ma Bell," I met my husband. He brought me to Somerset. We raised five children. Perry County will always be home.

How Blue's West was Won

by Blue Clark of Baynesville, Ohio
born 1939

My name is Blue. I come from big family. My dad and mom, Eugene and Mable Clark, had twelve children; six boys and six girls. We lived on Sandy Ridge Road six miles from Barnesville, Ohio on a little farm.

We all went to a little one-room school, me and my twin brother. Brownie was his name. He had brown eyes and I had blue eyes. That was a nickname. Everyone called us that.

Anyway, my little story. We were the first house in the county to have TV. That was the late 40's or early 50's. A lot of neighbors came to watch TV on Saturday night. That was when I would see the main cowboy throw bullets in the campfire and the crooks that was shooting at him would give up because they thought they were surrounded.

Anyway, I would take bullets to school and mix them in with the coal bucket so when someone would put coal in the potbelly stove they would pop and snap and crack and break the cast iron stove. The kids would jump when the bullets went off and the teacher would say, "Boy, that coal is snappy this year!"

Thank God no one got hurt.

I also tried to burn down the schoolhouse during lunch break.

Strength in Numbers

by Virginia Dittoe of Somerset, Ohio
Born 1931

I was raised on a farm near Somerset, Ohio with 13 brothers and two sisters. The oldest was born in 1925

First family picture in 1947. Back row: Dick, Tom, Al, Margie, Martin, Evie, Harold, Bob. Front row: Don, Bill, Virginia, Dad, Ralph, Mom, Gene, Jimmy, Kenny.

and the youngest in 1948. We were all single births, born at home with the doctor and usually a midwife to assist. There were no pre-natal vitamins, ultrasounds or epidurals and no insurance either. The bill was paid in cash or with a quarter of beef, a ham or chickens (fryers) in the summer. Cloth diapers were used and re-used and babies were breast fed until they were a year old, then placed on cow's milk that was pasteurized.

My mother would bake 13 loaves of bread every other day.

Most meat was raised on the farm and a large garden provided vegetables. Potatoes were a main stay and kept in the cellar in a large bin. Peaches, apples and pears were canned. Blackberries were pickled in the summer and provided jelly and cobbler.

Nine of us attended school, walking a long lane to catch the bus. We took our lunch and the girls would pack them each morning; usually it was a peanut butter sandwich and an apple, and if we were lucky, there was a cookie. Water was free.

The laundry was done once a week. In the late 30's and early 40's the water was carried from a spring and heated in a wash boiler. White clothes, then towels and underwear, colored clothes and then the overalls. There was one tub of hot water with lye soap for washing and one tub of cold water with bluing added for the rinse water. Then they were hung on the line to dry outside in the summer and inside in the winter.

At first we had a wringer washer, then a gasoline engine washer. Sometimes when the gas can was empty we would have to siphon gas from the old truck. One could get dizzy from the gas fumes before they had enough gas siphoned to run the washer. Eventually we got electricity and a new washer: Maytag heavy duty.

A clothesbasket full of shirts dampened down to iron faced us on those days. Before electricity we had to heat heavy irons with detachable wooden handles on the stove and alternate them when they lost their heat.

Needless to say, we had work clothes and clothes for good to wear to church and school. When we needed clothes they were ordered from the Sears Roebuck catalogue or handmade. Sometimes hand-me-downs arrived from cousins or town folk.

During World War II we had ration stamps for meat, gasoline and shoes. Since there were so many of us we would trade the meat stamps for gasoline and shoe stamps.

Our house was heated with coal stoves and kerosene lamps provided light for reading. There was no indoor plumbing. We carried water from the spring and eventually the well. The outhouse and chamber pots were the bathroom.

We survived, and as we grew older, found work. My sisters were the oldest and learned to cook, clean and sew. The oldest would think nothing of catering a wedding reception for two hundred or more, and the second oldest could make and decorate the wedding cake and make the bridesmaids dresses. The older boys learned carpentry and built a dairy barn and a two story chicken house. They later built houses while some learned machine work, masonry and continued farming.

Six of the brother served in the Army. It only seems fitting that the 12th brother graduated from college and became a guidance counselor.

When we get together now and talk about the old days, we didn't know that we were poor, by today's standards, but learned to take each day as it came. Our parents had faith and common sense.

I'm grateful to be alive and able to share these memories.

Homemade Clothes

by Betty Ischy of Lewisville, Ohio
born 1932

I would like to tell you about the homemade clothes our mother made for us.

I am the oldest of five daughters born to our parents, Ernest and Marcella Hoff. We grew up on a farm near Lewisville. Like most farms in the area, our parents raised a variety of crops and animals, plus most of the food for us to eat. Mother made our clothes on a treadle sewing machine from the time we were babies till we finished high school.

Some of the fabric mother used came from the mail order catalogs.

Back then the grain our parents had to buy came in either white cloth bags or print ones. With some soaking, the letters would wash out of the white ones. Mother made our underclothes and things for the home from these.

But to us girls. we looked forward to the print bags which some of the grain came in. We would watch to get more than one with the same print. There was little over one yard of material in each bag.

We also got some print bags from our aunt and uncle because they bought chickenfeed for their chickens.

Mother would sometimes pay a few cents for them or make my aunt something.

She made us some beautiful dresses, skirts and blouses. We also had warm head scarves which she made from a square of fabric, then hemmed it, adding a yarn fringe around the edge. Mother would take an old coat apart, use the wrong side out and make us coats.

I remember one time my sister next to me and I each got a new coat from the catalog. Then after we outgrew them and they looked worn, Mother took them apart and used the wrong side, making my next two sisters two each a new coat.

When there are five girls, you learn to wear hand-me-downs. Mother didn't always have a pattern to make our new clothes, so she made her own by holding up a piece of newspaper to our back, then cutting out the neckline, shoulder width, armpit and waistline.

It was also a good, warm feeling when Mother made us long flannel nightgowns.

I remember the hard work Mother put into making our clothes, and the times we didn't want to stand still while she fitted the outfits on us.

I made my first skirt when I was in the fifth grade. She taught us all to sew.

There was never much money for Christmas gifts, but Mother would always make sure we had something new.

We always had a good outfit for church and our school clothes, so when we got home we had to change into everyday things.

In our days we never heard the word "recycle," but our parents were ahead of their time because we were always finding ways to redo things. We were always taught to make the best of what you have.

My four sisters and I are very thankful for our parents and what we learned from them.

When we all married, we sewed and made clothes for our own children.

Singing on the Stone Step

by June Gilbaugh of Bowerston, Ohio
born in 1923

This is an incident which happened on an almost perfect autumn afternoon upon my returning to the classroom with an excused pass to an outdoor bathroom facility.

On arriving at the entrance of the building, I stopped on the stone step and sang one verse of "Old Black Joe." When I finished, I panicked. How could I enter and face a whole classroom of first through eighth graders?

My wonderful first grade teacher came to the open door and led me back to my seat. Not a word from teacher or student.

I can come to only one conclusion: that teacher knew or sensed this was a rehearsal for days in my future when I would be singing perhaps with a future husband in places as small as one-room schoolhouses or in much larger auditoriums. How right she would be!

Down Home Experiences in Noble County

By Ellen Book Day of Canton, Ohio
Born 1932

My cousin and I lived where there was an outhouse. It was attached to a granary that separated it by large rocks. Well as my cousin was in there, a copperhead snake stuck its head out on a rock. Needless to say, my cousin was out of there very fast.

Oil painting, commissioned by Ellen Day's mother, of covered bridge Ellen grew up beside.

In the late 1940s my mother and I lived in a small house with no electricity. Our enjoyment was listening to our battery radio. When the battery died we were sad. So we would wrap aluminum foil around the ariel get a few more hours listening from it.

When mother worked away, I often stayed with my cousin that I called "Mabel, my other mother" because she was so good to me. Being on a farm she kept the very colorful feed sacks; washed and ironed them and made her daughter and I very pretty skirts. We were so proud of them. Wasn't any Wal-Marts back then.

We all lived around creeks or streams. So when we were in school we were always so excited as they always dismissed school early so we could get safely home before the water rose dangerously high, which happened often.

Another cousin, Freda and I got off the school bus one time and started up the lane to her house. There in middle of lane was a snake all curled up. Due to past experiences, she was scared and froze in place. I walked around the hill (avoiding said snake) to get my uncle to come take care of killing that snake.

My mother and grandparents were probably the most important people in my life, but next to them was cousin Freda that I have mentioned already. She is my sister-in-love. We shared so much in our lives then and now yet. One Halloween we were out to trick or treat at neighbors' homes. Very dark out; no street lights there. So going through the covered bridge there was the most awful pounding on the roof. We were scared too death and ran like crazy. Never found out, but always suspected some neighbor boys. Poor dear Freda has never forgiven me for leaving her behind.

I loved school, but was always cooking up mischief. As class president and near time to graduate, I felt we should have senior take off. That wasn't easy in the boonies. I devised a plan. When the milk truck came and as he delivered upstairs, we would slip out and hide in back of truck knowing he would end up in the little town of Stafford where my boyfriend lived. On the way the driver stopped at a little store and we were very quietly giggling like crazy, as we heard our principle was hunting for us and left word that if we were spotted we better get back to school pronto.

On we went to Stafford and got out of the truck when the coast was clear. Went to my boyfriend's house and talked to his dad. He said Junior had gone to town. I said, "Oh, I was hoping he would deliver us all back home." He told me to go ahead and take the car as it would be okay he was sure. Away we went in his new car. He came to my house that evening and didn't appear to be upset. I knew he wouldn't be as he had tried to date me the last two years. Was a different story after we were married. He always said he should of had me arrested especially since I didn't have a drivers license yet. Even the principle never mentioned the incident.

Was a crazy thing for me to do but makes fun memories.

Wooden Eggs on a Haunted Farm

by Clarence Newcomer of Senecaville, Ohio
born in 1937

My name is Clarence Newcomer. I was born in a log cabin, like George Washington. I lived in cold in the winter and hot in the summer. In the winter, I did not leave water in a glass. It would freeze solid.

In the summer my dad and mother slept downstairs. Us kids slept outside.

In the winter it was bad if you had to go to the outhouse at three or four o'clock in the morning. We had a Sears Catalog for wiping.

We had no TV, no telephone, no refrigerator, no water. We carried water about an eighth of a mile from a spring. That was my brother and my job when we got old enough. Sunday was hard. We had to get at least three tubs up for Monday wash day, plus a couple of buckets.

We had about a half-acre garden. Brother and I would get up at daybreak and start hoeing. My dad was building four rooms on the old log cabin.

I seen this pile of sawdust. It looked like the mash my mother fed the chickens. I got the idea. So I got me a bucket of sawdust, took it out and put it in the trough. I figure if they ate sawdust, they would lay wooden eggs. Not so. I got my butt beat. I was five years old.

One day I broke a lot of limbs down on a tree as to make a slide. Then I got in the tree about 15 feet high. I jumped and came right down through. Then I hit the ground pretty hard. For a couple of days I wasn't feeling too good. Then one day I was hanging upside down holding on by my feet and the limb broke. I came straight down, thought I broke my neck, but didn't.

We had pigs, chickens, and cows. We butchered after New Years. My brother would get the pig bladder and take a straw and blow it up and tie it off. Then let it dry out and it would get like leather and we would kick it around like a football. Most of the toys we had, we made.

After butchering, my job was to smoke the meat about two weeks. Then we cooked the fat in a 20-gallon kettle outside and rendered lard.

I seen around May or June we got a shoulder or a ham. It would be green as grass mold. My mother would wash it off; slice it up fresh ham or shoulder.

My dad got paid every two weeks. He would give me a dollar, and out of that dollar I would get one pound of cashews, four comic books, two hot dogs, and I was set for the day.

I lived in this old log cabin 17 years, and 17 years every night something dragged around in our attic, never miss. We did have electric. My dad had to pay to get it in. Something would turn the light switches off and on. We heard babies crying down in the farm, just screaming their heads off. On hot summer nights we'd see a ball of fire like a tumbleweed. It would be real as fire, but it never caught anything on fire. Never had an answer to anything.

My neighbor had two boys about our age. They had no electric. A lot of times we walked down the road at night and someone would walk right behind us. You could hear their footsteps on the gravel road. I remember one night I was milking the cows. As I went from one cow to the other, something in the hayloft went with me. Hayseed would trickle down on me. I went out that barn like a bullet.

No one every stayed overnight with us. A lot of things went on at that farm.

One day I was helping my mother wash with a wringer washer. Darn if I didn't catch my fingers in those wringers. That was only a few days after my grandmother died. My grandmother set upstairs in her rocking chair and it made the floor squeak. All of a sudden we heard that rocking chair rock. The floor was squeaking. My mother froze. Me too. So then my mother said, "Go up and see." So I went up the stairs as fast as I could and nothing. The rocker wasn't moving. That's why I was home from school. My mother wasn't feeling good, so I stayed home to help her.

When it came to hunting, me and my brother was at our best. We love to hunt so much we hid our guns at night, missed the bus, then we got our guns and hunted all day. Until one day, who did we run into but our dad and my older brother. That ended that. We were off hunting for a week. It was hard not to hunt.

One day my neighbor and I was hunting. I had nine dogs, all good hunters. We came upon this two-gallon can. My dogs kept barking at it, so I picked it up and there was something in it. Something in it all right—a skunk sprayed all over us. I threw up. When we got up to the house, my mother made us take our clothes off outside. What a day. The skunk must have been born in the can and the mother must have kept feeding it and it got too big and couldn't get out.

We had to take Saturday night baths. We had to go to church Sunday morning. The only time we slept in bed in the summer.

The worst snowstorm I ever seen was the 1950 snow; three feet deep. My brother and I could walk right over the fence to go milk the cows. I didn't go to school for three weeks.

On Halloween, we never got any candy. We got shot at and ran off but it was fun.

One day I was down in the woods. There was a bird about 100 yards sitting on a cross-county telephone line. I shot at the bird but hit the line. I didn't tell no one. About two weeks later two men showed up at our house and asked if I had a rifle. I said yes. They asked me to go get it and I did. They asked me to shoot it and I did and ejected the shell. They picked it up and it matched the same firing mark. They were FBI. They said it took them two weeks to find that break. It shut the telephones off in a five mile radius. My dad had to pay a fine.

One time my brother and I were joy riding on country roads. We were getting close to Route 40, and we had to turn around. We turned into a driveway of just new asphalt. Back then it took two or three days for it to dry. We made tire groves three inches deep. People called the state police. We went back down that road flying, cut through woods up on the hill and we watched that police go up and down the road. He never caught us.

When I was 15, my brother was 17. My dad bought a small farm all tractor. We had to haul water for our cows. Our pond would go dry around August. My cousin was at our house and he wanted to drive. Against my better judgement, I let him drive. I told him when we got to the bridge to put his foot on both of the break pedals to stop. What did he do? Got to the bridge and stood up, jammed down on the right break only, threw us right over the bridge, about a 15-foot drop. It mashed that tractor all up. We got a few scrapes and bruises, but we were lucky.

We had five acres of straw to bring in. My dad made us take a one-horse rake and pull that rake around by hand. My brother and cousin pulled and I pushed and then brought it in on a wagon. It took us about 11 hours to do that. We had a horse, but my dad said no horse.

We made a cabin up on the hill. We went up there to sleep, and we had an old wind up record player. We had records a quarter inch thick. We played it loud as we could play it. People heard music half the night, which they did not appreciate.

Those were the good old days and they really were. No one ever asked to get paid for helping. We had a neighbor; he would be down at our house at daybreak, harness up the horse, and go to work.

At 17, I went into the army and that was the end of the good old days.

The White Owl and the New People

by Nancy Egger Rubel of Woodsfield, Ohio
born in 1940

I grew up in the '40s and '50s in Woodsfield, Ohio, the Monroe County seat. Woodsfield has a great old courthouse that dominates the public square. The population of the county at that time was made up of farmers and small family owned businesses. My father's was one of those—L.P. Egger & Son Hardware.

My earliest memory is of my mother taking me "uptown" to the hardware store. I got to try out the new tricycles and make sure they were safe to go to some other youngster.

My Uncle Louis, who was a partner with Dad, was serving in the Army Air Corps during World War II. Since that left Dad shorthanded, my mother was pressed into service helping at the hardware. She did on the job training, learning all the nuts and bolts. One day a gentleman came into the store and seeing only my mother there, seemed reluctant to tell her what he needed. Finally he said, "I'm looking for a 'white owl.'" She evidently figured it out and he went home with his chamber pot (or as some called it, a slop jar).

While my mother was working, I stayed with my maternal grandparents. They lived on Sycamore Street across from the village blacksmith. My grandfather had a drum made for me at the smithy's from some sort of metal. I still have that drum and plan to pass it on to someone in my family someday.

Stores in town were usually open until 5:00 p.m. Monday, Tuesday, Wednesday and Friday, closed Thursday afternoon and open on Saturday until 9:00 p.m. Saturday was a very busy day. That was when everyone came to town and Saturday night was the big night of the week. My mother would drive our car uptown on

Saturday about 5:00 p.m. and park in front of the hardware. (There were no parking meters then.) After we had supper (at home) and my father had gone back to the store, Mom and I would go claim our front row seats in the car and "watch the people go by." (This was a big pastime, no malls, etc.)

There were two movie theaters, the Monroe and Newlife. My father called the Monroe the "shooting gallery." There was always a double feature. One a modern day and the other an oater. Roy Rogers, Gene Autry, Hopalong Cassidy and many more brought the bad guys to justice with their blazing guns. The Newlife was showing somewhat more classic movies, but we certainly had a lot to choose from.

L. P. Egger & Son Hardware "on the Square" in 1960.

When I wanted to go to a show, Dad would give me a quarter. It cost 14 cents to get in, 10 cents for popcorn, and I had a penny left. Saturday matinee was only 10 cents. These prices were good until you reached 12 years old. We all were 11 as long as we could get away with it. The owners of the theater had a daughter who was a year older than me, so she squealed and I had to start paying adult fare.

Everyone over 60 years old remembers the big snow of 1950. I'm sure there have been bigger since, but at that time in our frame of reference, it was the BIGGEST! It started on Thanksgiving Day and when it stopped we had about 36 inches. Dad and I went uptown to watch the trucks being loaded to haul the snow to the fairground where it probably didn't melt until spring. This was being done at night and there were large lights set up in the square to illuminate the work area. Dad said, "You'll probably never see anything like this again," and he was right.

One of the most important events that occurred during the late '50s: Olin Matheson Aluminum came to our county and brought a much needed shot in the arm to our economy. They built a giant plant on the Ohio River near Hannibal. There were numerous new jobs, not to mention new people in our community. They came from all different sections of the country, and no matter how long some have lived here, they are still occasionally described as the "new people." There were some of the new people who were not thrilled with moving to such a rural area. One was heard to remark, "We must still be in the United States; I saw an American flag." The entire area boomed, with new home construction all around. Almost everyone was employed by the plant. If you personally were not, someone in your family probably was. The good times lasted quite a while, but today the boom is over. The facility is still here but has different ownership and limited production. Union troubles and possible mismanagement almost did it in.

The house I grew up in on North Paul Street was one of the older residences in town. Built in the early 1900s, it was large for our family of three. Yes, I was raised an only child, but I never lacked for playmates. Across the street there was Darlene, Rosemary, Johnny, Jimmy and Jack. Two doors down were Jeannie and Dick and on the alley lived Vivian and Norma Jean (they had brothers but all were older). We had quite a neighborhood "gang" in the best sense of the word. We were out early in the morning and played until dark.

I remember one day some of the kids came to the door wanting me to come out and play. Seeing me dressed up, they asked if I was allowed to get dirty. That probably was the result of our mothers saying, "Don't mess up your good clothes."

We had no TV or video games. We made up our own games. On our property was a big, old barn which, I was told, once housed the horses of a previous owner. Next to it was a small buggy barn. Dad went to work and converted it to the perfect playhouse. Nothing fancy, but we loved it. And did we play house! We put on our own plays and dressed up in clothes that a neighbor lady had given us. We were very much in style with hats, high heels and dresses. We even had one of the boys dressed up one day and I've got a picture to prove it. I'll bet Dick has forgotten about that!

The elementary school was two doors away from home, making it very convenient for me to get to class. It was a huge old building that my father had also gone to school in. The restrooms, if you could call them that, were in the basement. They were really just indoor outhouses. There was a new school built at the same location in the early 1950s. Our eighth grade class was the first to graduate from the new building.

We had several churches in Woodsfield, St. Paul's Evangelical and Reformed being one of them. St. Paul's was the church we belonged to. In those years the church was a big part of our lives. We had a fairly large congregation with lots of young families and lots of youngsters. Also a lot of older members. Our Youth Fellowship was well attended and very active in the life of the church. The choir was a big part of my life. I love to sing and play the piano and I know the church helped to instill my appreciation of music. There was a grand old organ in the sanctuary and I had the privilege to play it for Sunday school on several occasions. Several years ago the E&R churches joined with the Disciples of Christ to form the United Church of Christ. So, today it is St. Paul's United Church of Christ. I am very thankful that I was and still am a member of this very special church that meant so much to me growing up.

I have so many wonderful memories about a childhood that was carefree and fun. Sometimes, as I think back to that time, I really hope the kids of today are going to reminisce and say, "We sure had a lot of good times." Somehow I can't imagine them being any better than mine.

Old Spice and a Love Note

by Bessie Fensler of Dover, Ohio
born 1928

From the time I was a very small child, I dreamed of being a teacher. In my estimation, teachers could walk on water, but in 1945 I was only 17 when Bud came along and convinced me he couldn't live without me. He was 36.

I temporarily lost sight of my dream. He was very sweet and very handsome. Nearly all of the young fellows were off fighting the war. We were married within a month and within a year, our little girl was born. She was Betty Lou.

From that day on I was a mother. My life was full. Seven years later, her brother, Bob, was born and then six years later another brother, Bud Jr.

When Buddy was ten, thoughts of teaching resurfaced and I enrolled at Kent State, but before I ever made it to school I discovered I was pregnant. I was 40 years old and Bud was 59.

This time, I had a boy and a girl, Brad and Brooke. Betty Lou was married and Bob was in the military.

My husband guarded those twins with his very life. We never ever left them. We took them everywhere we went. After the twins came, Bud would leave me in bed, get ready for work, and shave and splash Old Spice aftershave on and them come back upstairs and kiss me goodbye and leave me a love note on the table before he went to work.

When he was 65 he retired and I was still young, so he let me go to work driving a school bus.

The twins were in school. I was allowed to store the bus at home so I never had to leave them. They rode with me. Bud Jr. went to Houston to apprentice for an electrician so they were all we had left.

June 15, 1979, Bob came home on Sunday afternoon; he was going to a job in the northern part of the state. He had rigged up a van so he could sleep in it till he got settled. We told him goodbye about 8:30 p.m. and later went to bed.

About 1:00 a.m. Bud got up to go to the bathroom. When he came back to bed he said, "Bob is back, his car is in the driveway." He lay down on the bed, but almost immediately he raised up on his elbow, he sort of fell back down. Within minutes, this was repeated. I said, "Are you alright?" He said, "Yes." But then he did it again and I asked again. He said, "Why do you keep saying that? I'm just trying to turn over, that's all."

Now his speech was slurred. I called 911 and the ambulance was here within ten minutes. They came straight up the stairs and put an oxygen mask on him.

At the hospital when they wanted to get him into a gown we had to hold him up. It was like trying to stand an egg on end. Soon he was in a coma. The doctor said that he had suffered a massive stroke, an aneurysm in the right side of his brain. This was the beginning of a yearlong battle.

My friend Jo Myers, who also drove a bus, said when you need to go, drop those twins off with me and I did. I sat by his bed in case he woke up. Many times, others came in to see him and found me sleeping in the chairs. I was totally exhausted.

The first day after his stroke, I picked the twins up at Jo's and went home. Brad hopped out of the car and started jumping around saying, "Look, Mommy! A firedog, there's a fire dog in the bus."

All doors of the bus were closed and looking out the rear emergency door was the most magnificent Dalmatian, quite large. When I opened the door, she jumped down and went before us to the front door. When I opened the door, she was the first one in just like she had just arrived home. She lay on the carpet in the archway between the kitchen and dining room.

The twins lay on each side of her as though she had been their pet all of their lives. She ate what we ate. I noticed she was blind in her left eye. She never made a sound. When we went upstairs to bed, she went before us, as though she had done this every day of her life. She lay down in the hall between the doors to the twin's rooms.

In the morning, she ate breakfast with us and when we left the house, we left her outside so if her owner came looking for her, he'd find her. At five that evening, when we came home, she met us with wagging tail. Again, she went before us through the door, ate what we ate, and led us up to bed.

I advertised so the owner would know where to find her. Each day was a repeat of the one before.

For 11 days, Daddy remained in a deep coma. I spent my days beside his bed and came home each evening with the twins to find the Dalmatian waiting patiently for us.

When Daddy awoke on the 11th day, his mind was clear, but he was blind in his left eye. He asked me to get a notary so he could take care of his affairs and we did, giving me full power, and then he slept.

Again, I picked up the twins and when we got home, there was no Dalmatian waiting for us. Brad cried, saying, "I should have locked her in the house." We asked around some more, no one around us had any knowledge of a Dalmatian. We never saw her again; it was as though she had never happened.

They never let me bring Bud home; he had to go to a nursing home because he was having frightening seizures. He lived a year and three days, and then one morning, June 18, 1980, his nurse washed his hands and face and told him she was bringing his breakfast. He told his roommate, "I'm going home today, not to the farm, home."

Fifteen minutes later, when the nurse brought his breakfast, she saw a white dove fluttering on the glass door at the end of the hall and when she took his tray in, he had gone home. She asked me to give his Bible to her and I did.

For many mornings after that I woke up each morning to the smell of Old Spice aftershave.

This is not a story. It happened and I don't believe in the supernatural but I believe in Jesus and I believe in miracles.

Showboats and Hobos

By Delma Jackson of Sunbury, Ohio
Born 1943

As a child in the late 1940's and early 1950's, my father worked on construction for Buckeye Power and American Gas and Electric Company, (later AEP). Construction work required moving frequently so I grew up near the Muskingum River and the Ohio River between Steubenville and Middleport.

While living in the Middleport/Pomeroy area, a frequent sight was the showboats traveling up and down the Ohio River. We always knew when they were coming because you could hear the calliope playing and everyone would hurry down to the dock to see the boat and some of the people that were actors on the showboat. It always seemed like a wonderful lifestyle; I suppose like the little boy running away to join the circus.

Riverboat "Joe Cooke" in 1952.

We lived very near the river on Second Street and between us and the river were the railroad tracks. This must have been a travel route for tramps and hobos since we saw a lot of them. My father-in-law from near Bridgeport spent some of his early years as a hobo and told me the difference between a tramp and a hobo was a tramp was basically a beggar whereas a hobo would work for food if asked. Whether or not this is true, I don't know.

At any rate, many times especially during the warmer weather, men would knock on our back screen door and ask for food. My mother was not frightened, so as a result we children weren't either. Only occasionally would the screen door be hooked and I cannot remember any time when Mom refused to give them something to eat. I remember only once when she felt somewhat apprehensive and fed the man to get rid of him. The food was usually a peanut butter and jelly sandwich and maybe some fruit if we had it. There were times when they were asked to maybe weed the garden or rake leaves, and if they did Mom always packed them some food to take with them. We didn't have a lot, but did share as Mom and Dad thought perhaps many of these men were soldiers from WWII that simply had not yet found their place in society.

Growing up in that era was a lot easier and simpler then it is now. I was allowed to roller skate to school in the second grade. The school was about four or five blocks from our house (seemed longer then) and the skates were the kind you put on over your shoes and tightened with a key so when you got to school, you simply took off your skates and still had your shoes on. Heaven help you if you lost your skate key.

I was also allowed to walk by myself to the local library. It was also about four or five blocks. If parents were apprehensive about letting kids "on the street" by themselves, it didn't show. This was our opportunity to be responsible and also learn independence at the same time. On Saturday afternoons my brother, who was two years older, and I were allowed to go the local matinee movie. We always loved the serials such as Superman and Flash Gordon that were on before the main attraction. There were also news reels of the latest news. The price was 14-cents. Again, we went by ourselves with no adults in tow.

In the early 1950's we had a blizzard and a large amount of snowfall that was so deep we could make tunnels in the snow.

I was allowed to occasionally use the telephone which was a switchboard operated system with operator asking, "Number please." My girlfriend's telephone number was "9." Her father was the local funeral director so I don't know if this is why such a low number.

When we moved to Morgan County in the early

1950's we lived out of town and had a party line telephone with a wall crank phone. I remember our number was four short rings. Three short rings belonged to the farmer across the road. Of course you could listen to the other people on the line, but the phone was mounted so high on the wall children couldn't reach it.

Playing outside was what you did unless you were sick or the weather was horrible. We learned to ski on skis made of old barrel staves in the winter and went barefoot in the summer. In the fall we built cabins made of the tomato stakes from the summer garden.

Pal's Bad Idea

by Arlie King of Bowerston, Ohio
born 1930

I live in Bowerston, Ohio, which is a small town of 500 people, if you include dogs and cats. I had a Border Collie dog I called Pal. We would take romps along the Connotton Creek, which bordered our property on the west. We would kick up rabbits. It was fun to see him chase them. One day he came across a skunk, which was not one of his better ideas.

Later in life the Korean War broke out. I remember when I was leaving to go overseas; I gave him a big hug and patted him on his head. He was getting older and I didn't know if we would see each other again. In 1953 my grandmother wrote me and told me he had passed away. I cried, I knew I had lost a dear friend, also a part of me was gone. Of the main people I know is Peter Zontene. We have been friends since the fourth grade. We have been good friends for over 65 years. It has been a great friendship.

After school, when I got home, I had a cow to feed and milk. Then run a paper route and try to play high school basketball if I had any spare time, and do my homework before I went to bed.

I used to listen to Jack Armstrong and Amos and Andy with my grandmother. Radio was a big thing for me for many years. We had a Victrola in our living room, which you would put a round on, then crank it up, and listen to the music. I thought it was great. I had a Bob Burns, Bagooks, which I tried to play, and later on got pretty good at.

In those days we had a wringer washer, a Maytag, once a week that was a chore.

My favorite teacher was my second grade teacher, Mrs. Jane Firebaugh. She had time to listen to your problems and what you were doing in your life at that time in your life. My other favorite teacher was Miss Inez Crawford. She was my junior and senior teacher. She was very strict, but she made learning easy. She took pride in that 80 percent of her 19 also made the honor roll.

We had a building in our town called the "Opera House." Movies were shown on Tuesday and Saturday night. It was ten cents to get in, it always had a good crowd. Now it is a modern library.

When I was young, I used to trap. There were animals to trap on the Connotton Creek, raccoons and muskrats and a very few mink, which I never caught, in the creek.

We had a chicken house, which we had 40 chickens. It was up off the ground about a foot. I used to look under it once a week to see if no animals was trying to get in up through the floor. One day I saw a small trail. I thought it was a rat or weasel. I set a steel trap, buried it in the trail, and covered it up. To my surprise, the next day, I caught a brown male mink. It was the only mink I ever caught. I probably saved the lives of the 40 chickens.

Good Ole Perry County

by Loretta Kay Hillis of Somerset, Ohio
born in 1942

I was born September 13, 1942 in Sayre, Ohio. My parents had another daughter, six years old, and a son two years old. We were all born at home and delivered by Dr. Shaw from New Lexington, Ohio.

Daddy started a new job two months before I was born, July 13, 1942. His job was at Ceramic Supply company (Cesco) in Crookville. Starting pay was fifty cents per hour. He worked this job thirty-three years before retiring from there. He was the financial secretary/treasurer there for most of the time worked.

I had the advantage of getting the childhood diseases at an early age. My sister, being older, would bring them home to me from school. There was no kindergarten when I was young.

Growing up as kids, we had plenty of things to do. We raised cows, chickens, hogs and rabbits. At one time, we had seventy rabbits to feed. We all had jobs to do each day. Slop the hogs, milk the cows, etc.

In the spring, Daddy took us kids mushroom hunting. They were very plentiful then, as there weren't many deer to eat them. If Mom didn't go with us, Daddy always picked a bouquet of woods lilies and purple Proud Williams to take to her.

On Sundays, Daddy always took us to Sunday school and church in Portersville. On Easter, we always got up early and went to sunrise service. This was an Easter tradition.

In May, when the blackberries were ripe, Daddy would hook the wagon to the tractor, and off we'd go to the berry patch. I found a nice patch once and was tramping weeds down to get to it. All at once, I saw a big blacksnake helping himself to the berries. It didn't take me long to get out of that patch. We did not have electricity, so we canned the berries for the winter.

In the summer, we had many gardens, so we were always hoeing the weeds or knocking the potato bugs from the plants. Mom did a lot of canning, so we were always helping her snap beans, etc.

Our Thanksgivings were spent butchering hogs. Daddy was up at the crack of dawn to put a drum of water on the fire so it would boil to scald the hogs. He would kill four to five hogs that day for our family, my grandmother, and my aunt. They would come to our home for dinner. To me, for several years, I thought this was what Thanksgiving was all about.

After letting the meat cure for a few days, we then had to start processing it. We ground our own sausage, had fresh side meat, and Mom would render the lard. This gave us our own cracklins. We would salt and smoke the hams and put in our smokehouse.

Mom was a great cook and baker. She made homemade bread every other day. Her pies, she used the rendered lard for the crust. They were out of this world. She did this on a coal/wood-burning cook stove.

When I was six years old, my family and I was swimming at a place called the Sayre Tile. I was on my way down under the water for the third time when my Uncle John saved me. A couple of years after this, my uncle was fishing at the Sayre Reservoir. He decided he would go swimming. He went in and while swimming, he got cramps and drowned. He was thirty-five years old. After that, I was always afraid of water. We kids would go play in the creek though, just below our home.

I went to school at Sayre Grade School. My dad had gone to the same school. It was a three-room brick building for grades first and second, third and fourth, and seventh and eighth. Seventh and eighth grades were upstairs. The fifth and sixth grade was in a separate building. When I was in the first grade, my teacher was Marsha Woods. I had perfect attendance, and she gave me a pair of yellow socks and a handkerchief.

Just up from Sayre School was a gas station/grocery store, where we could go at lunchtime and buy penny candy. The store was owned and operated by two old maids, Gaye and Verna Hammond.

In the summer, even though we kept quite busy with working in our many gardens, we still had some time to play. Not having much growing up, we used our imaginations. We used branches from bushes to make stick people. We used leaves and thorns to make clothes for our stick people.

We made fake lemonade by putting water in a pail and using the yellow center from a daisy. We would break up the yellow center. We made sandwiches from flat rocks and leaves. We did have a good imagination. When we would get bored doing this, we would go to the creek and catch crawdads.

In the winter, it seemed as though we had snow all winter long. It was sleigh riding in our spare time. We also did a lot of shoveling snow. Our drive was on a slight grade. So we had to shovel to make sure Daddy cold get up it when he came home from work. Once in a while, he had to use chains to get around in the snow. Seems as though there was not equipment then to clear the roads. We never seemed to have many dull moments.

One of the things Mom and we kids would do was go shopping in Zanesville. In order to do this, we would thumb a ride to Crooksville so we could catch the bus to Zanesville and back. No way would you want to do this today!

Once while taking some weeds to the hogs in a wheelbarrow, my sister and I unloaded them with a pitchfork. Afterwards, I wanted to put the fork in the ground. I pulled the fork up with both hands and accidentally ran the fork through one of my toes. My sister pulled the fork out and carried me to the house.

Mom said I'd have to go to the doctor when Daddy got home to get a tetanus shot. Just before time for Daddy to come home, I hid behind a door because I didn't want to go to the doctor. Daddy found me and said I had to go.

I went to the doctor that delivered me as a baby. The doctor gave me the shot, and he gave me the bottle that had the medicine in. He also asked me if I could write my name. I told him I could, so I wrote my name for him. He gave me a dime. I thought I was really rich.

The highlight of Christmastime was Mom and Daddy taking us to the Crooksville Municipal Building to see Santa and get a treat. I would always get to bed early and listen for Santa and sleigh. Was not a big Christmas, like the ones today. I would maybe get a doll and a new outfit that Mom had made. There was always love, and this was more important.

In 1947, I can remember Daddy getting a new tractor, disc, and plow. This was a big deal to us. I still have the tractor, etc. Before, Daddy used our horse to plow and work the gardens ready for planting. As not many people had tractors, they contacted Daddy to do their gardens. He had a list of many that he did each year.

I can remember the flood of 1950. Daddy had taken us kids to an ice cream social in Portersville. While there, a flash flood came up. A neighbor of ours was there, so he said he would take us home. We went through high water, logs on the roads, and debris to get home. We were happy to get home.

We were all three crying when we went in the house. Mom and Daddy did not realize how bad it was, as they were comfortable at home, listening to the Shadow on the battery operated radio, with the kerosene lights on.

The next day, we found out that Daddy's sister's home in Sayre had been flooded. The water was so deep that the refrigerator was laying on its back. The furniture that was salvaged from the water, we stored in our home for a while. This home was later jacked up and moved about a half mile to a higher location.

In the late summer, we would go to our potato patches to dig them and put in our cave for winter. Behind our house, we had a cave that was mostly underground. We also went to apple orchards to get apples to last us through the winter.

The cave is where we kept our canned goods and also crocks of milk, covered with lids. When the cream came to the top, Mom would skim off, and we would churn butter. This was very good on bread that Mom made. She would also make cottage cheese.

Thanksgiving Day butchering. Daddy on tractor and brother standing in 1950.

My sister and I went to school wearing feed sack clothes. We got feed for our animals in the sacks, and Mom made clothes from them. We felt like we were the best-dressed girls in school. Occasionally at Christmas, we would get a boughten dress. We were always in a play at church, so it was very special.

Daddy was a great hunter. He did this for us to have food. He took us kids one night when he went coon hunting. I was crossing a fence and caught my britches. It took me a while to get loose. Occasionally we would go to Grandma and Grandpa's, where the guys would go coon hunting. We would be asleep when Daddy got in from hunting and had to wake up and go home.

In the summer, we would go to the outhouse. In the winter, we used the chamber pot. Once I went outside, and when I stepped up, I looked up, and a big black snake lay up in the rafters. I decided I didn't have to go real bad. If we did go to the outhouse in the winter, we didn't take long to do our job. We also had to do this at school, as we had no indoor plumbing there.

One of the biggest events in our lives was in 1951, when we got electricity. This was a real treat to us. Definitely better than studying with kerosene lights.

In summer, our bath was in a big wash tub. We would fill it up with water and let it sit in the sun during the day to get warm. In the winter, Mom would heat water on the cook stove.

After we got electric, Mom would churn butter. She would sell this by the pound to the men that Daddy worked with. She saved the money from this and bought an electric mixer.

In the summer, we kids had jobs at our neighbors', the old maids. We hoed corn and raked hay with a trip rake, making fifty cents per hour.

Once when my brother and sister were mowing our yard with a reel type mower, my brother cut his hand on the blades. He was pushing the mower up the bank as my sister was pulling it.

One of the treats we had as kids was to go to the picture show with Mom and Daddy. We had to go to New Lexington for these shows. Most of the ones we saw were with Bud Abbott and Lou Costello, Dean Martin and Jerry Lewis, or Ma and Pa Kettle. New Lexington seemed to be far away. While in New Lexington, it was a tradition that we go to Fairmonts Ice Cream place and get an ice cream cone for ten cents.

Mom and Daddy always took us to the McLuney basketball games. The best thing then was the good ole Perry County Basketball Tournaments that were held at the Zanesville Municipal Auditorium. It was always interesting to see who would win, as the winner would go on to Athens to another tournament. The schools back then were McLuney, Somerset, Glenford, Thornville, Moxahala, New Stratsville, Shawnee and Corning.

Sometimes in the summer, living in Sayre, when I didn't have anything to do, I would get up early and ride to Grandma and Grandpa Eveland's with Daddy on his way to work. Grandma would send me to a little store on the corner down from their home to get bread and bologna and some sugar cookies. I really didn't know what boughten bread was, as we were use to homemade bread. Also had boughten milk, and I thought it was very different. Grandma had a crank Victrola, which she let me play it while there.

My grandpa passed away in 1956 and was buried New Year's Day, 1957. After this, I stayed with Grandma during the week and walked to school. I would go home on the weekends to get other clothes. When I'd got home from school, Grandma would say she had a surprise for me. She had made a big bowl of chocolate pudding.

Back years ago, when purchases were made, we

were given tax stamps. Grandma had saved hers. We separated them into the number categories and sent them in to get money. Grandma would get her jewelry out and let me look at it. She gave me some of it, which I still have. She also shared some of her old records, such as Paul Revere's Ride.

Back when my grandparents died, they were shown in the home. I didn't know what it was like to be in a "funeral home." Grandma died in 1958.

My favorite games in school were jump rope and red rover. I made a rope from jar rubbers that Mom could not use for canning. I would fasten them together until I got enough for a rope. Made a great rope, as it had give to it.

When I was a freshman in high school, Daddy had a chance to go to New York City as a past district president of the Eagles. We drove to New Jersey and took the train to New York, as we were told the traffic was terrible. The first cab driver we got in with had the last name of Tracy, which was our last name. We were there a week and got to see some neat sights, but I decided the big city life was not for me. I was ready to go back to Perry County.

When I was in high school in Democracy class, I had an assignment to do. The night before it was due, I had to go somewhere and didn't get it done. I was worried about what to do. I went to school the next day and was thinking about what to do. I went to homeroom for roll call, then on to Democracy class.

I decided to hide in the coat closet in back of the classroom. The doors went clear to the floor. I told some of my classmates what I was doing. At the beginning of class, Mr. Johnson asked where Tracy was. He always called me by my last name. The classmates told him they hadn't a clue as to where I was. I could hardly keep from laughing but needed to keep quiet. He said, "She is really demolishing her grade by not being here."

As soon as class was over, I made sure the teacher was gone. I had study hall next period with the same teacher. I made it look like I was late and just getting to class. He asked me where I had been. I told him I had missed the bus. He asked why I was present for roll call earlier. OOPS! Guess I hadn't thought of that. He made me do a five hundred-word report. This was the last time I skipped class. I don't know if I ever did tell Mom and Daddy!

I can say that in twelve years of school, I only missed twelve and a half days. These were mostly for relatives' funerals.

Many people badmouth Perry County, but I am proud to say I'm glad I was born and raised in good ole Perry County. I have definitely seen a lot of changes over the years. In today's world, I can see that back then, I learned a lot from my parents and was never afraid of hard work like a lot of people today.

One of Daddy's favorite sayings was, "Don't do as I do; do as I say." He also said if I ever got a spanking at school that I would get another when I got home. He never had to do this. I had great respect for my parents. Even though we were not rich while growing up, there was always love. To me, that was far more important.

The Outhouse Snake at Peeper Run School

by Elsie Earles of North Canton, Ohio
born in 1914

I am 94 years old, but I can remember my school days so well. From first grade through eighth grade I went to a one-room schoolhouse called Peeper Run. I walked a half mile and nearly froze my toes by the time I got there.

The janitor was Floyd Timerman and had a fire going in a pot belly stove. We got water from a well and had two outhouses.

My most vivid memory is about a snake on the roof of that outhouse sticking its neck way out. The teacher killed it with a club, but we remained scared for a long time.

For recreation, we had a swing outside on a tree. Also, we square danced to music played on an old record player. The janitor was the caller.

The school house was in a wooded area in Southern Ohio in Morgan County. I remember lots of trees. I took my lunch in a metal box.

This is the way things were way back then.

A Muddy Mistake and Some Very Good Advice

by Don R. McNutt of Blue Rock, Ohio
Born 1924

Spring 1932. I was in the second grade and my cousin, Boyd Reed, was in the first grade at Circle A School, one of several one room, eight grade schools in Brookfield Township, Noble County, Ohio.

Yes, we walked to school and back home, approximately ¾ of a mile every day, sunshine, rain, snow or wind; just like the mail man, only he had an automobile, but used his horse and cart in bad weather.

State Route Ohio 76, now Ohio 83, was being built from Wooster, Ohio south to the Ohio River. The new road was being built higher so it would be above high water when the creeks flooded. To and from school we crossed two creeks that were being covered by new two way concrete bridges that appeared very high. Between the creeks was some high ground that was being hauled away as fill to build a road base. To get the dirt fill, they had a steam shovel to load the dump trucks that hauled and spread on the new road.

School hours were 9:00 a.m. to 4:00 p.m. all eight months, September through April. On the way home we noticed all the workers were gone; good, we'll stop and play on the steam shovel. We were walking on the new road and the mud was ankle deep, very difficult to walk. Finally, we got to the shovel and took turns sitting on the operator's seat and pushing and pulling levers. It was great fun.

When we were ready to leave, I said to Boyd, "From here we'll go up over the hill to the old road where it is not so muddy." We climbed down from the shovel and started up the steep hill. About the second step, my right foot was stuck in the mud. I could not pull it out.

Boyd, on left, Buddy the Angus bull, Richard.

Boyd said, "I'll go get Dad to pull your foot out. If I take a run for it, I can get up the hill." He backed up to get a good start and ran as fast as he could only to go two steps after he passed me. He was stuck, both feet. "What now? I'll unbuckle my four buckle overshoe and get loose so I can go after your dad. I'll go to the new muddy road." Just got started and here came four or five workers to get their lunch buckets out of the shovel. They asked and I told them about the overshoe and that Boyd was stuck in the mud.

They seemed and acted mad. The leader pulled my overshoe out after the second try. He said to another of the men, "Since you have hip boots, you pull Boyd out." By that time Boyd was in over his knees. The worker stepped over to lift Boyd out and as he started to lift he began to sink, so he stopped and pulled up his hip boots. Finally, he was able to get Boyd out, but by then he was in to the top of his hip boots and stuck in the mud.

They told us to get on home, so we started down the new road and along came Franz, my dad's youngest brother, in a four door, green, 1928 Chevrolet with disc wheels. He stopped, picked us up and took us home. I remember how cold my muddy foot was.

The next day or two we heard that it was after dark before the workers got the rescuer dug out of the mud.

Home School—Why? To raise anything successfully, you need good genetics and good environment. For children, the genetics is already completed, but you, the parent, are in charge of the environment. What is a good environment? One that is natural, safe, comfortable and with an animal instinct. Therefore, animals, if permitted, protect, feed, comfort, discipline and love their offspring.

Perhaps discipline and love are the same thing, because you cannot have one without the other. A good environment is where people of all ages live among each other. This lifestyle gives the young, the old and the middle-aged people security and a feeling of being important and useful. They learn to be responsible for themselves and for others and also think and do for themselves.

Day care, pre-kindergarten, kindergarten and pre-school is just the opposite. You are always being told what to do and when to do it, never think for yourself. Therefore, day care and kindergarten children have not had an opportunity to make their own decision about anything. So they lack confidence in anything they think because they have not had an opportunity to discover on their own. An environment with people of all ages permits children to learn from people that know more than they do.

Peer grouping of any age—eight months, eight years, 18 years or 80 years—is a bad environment. Children under school age need no more than one hour per week with their peers; Sunday school, one hour. I have observed seven generations of people and each generation becomes more immature than the previous. Example: presently ages 18-25 have little ability to communicate intelligently with other age groups. Look at their actions during spring break from college. They also lack responsibility. If you have not earned and saved money for a vacation, you do not deserve a vacation.

Ask yourself, when have you been tempted to do wrong things? Were you with your parents or grandparents or your children or grandchildren or your peers? Another question, why should it take 13 years to cover the material in K-12? Home schooling saves taxpayers money.

Green Apples and More

by Doris May Colton of West Lafayette, Ohio
born in 1922

It was summer and my cousin and I were enjoying a few days at our grandma's place in the small village of West Lafayette, Ohio circa 1930s. We were under the old apple tree in her big side yard eating little green apples with a sprinkle of salt. It was the perfect summer's day. I was eight years old, and my cousin was nine at the time.

Now, the following will show you our mindset for what happened later. Our grandfather was a station master for the Pennsylvania Depot just a short walk from his home. My cousin and I would walk up to the depot with one or two pennies to use in the dispenser in the waiting room to get little chocolate squares or Chiclets.

Back to under the old apple tree eating green apples: We watched this man walking up and down the street with a canvas bag over his shoulder going door-to-door leaving something at each porch. Well, our grandparents' house had two porches, and the nice man put something on both of them. Naturally, we just had to look. Oh happy day! It was little squares of chocolate. We then proceeded across the street to the neighbors' porches and helped ourselves to their free little squares of chocolate. Then, we set off back to the old apple tree for a picnic, of sorts, of little green apples and chocolate squares.

Did I mention the name of the little boxes of chocolate was Ex-Lax? It was an advertising campaign for a new product!

At my grandma's, there were no inside facilities; there was a "two-holer" outhouse in the back. Now, picture two little girls, side by side, with basins on their laps going, well…you can paint your own picture!

We recovered quickly, but had no care for chocolate or green apples for some time.

What a thoughtless and foolish way for a company to advertise. In this day and age, one would have smelled a lawsuit in the making.

The Blacksnake and the Machine Washed Dog

by Zelda M. Kinney Clark Stephens of Lewisville, Ohio
born 1935

My name is Zelda Clark Stevens and I lived on Kinney Road in Graysville, Ohio in Monroe County when I was a girl. It was such a nice day and I was fifteen years old and helping my mother in the kitchen. We were going to bake some pies, but when Mother went to get the lard to make the pies, the tin pail was empty, so she told me to go to the cellar and fill up the tin pail. I opened the door to the cellar which was dark and cold (a dug out cellar). And on my head dropped this huge blacksnake. It went from my head to my feet and I was screaming all the time. Needless to say, I had shorts on and a skimpy top. I almost passed out. My mom came running out just as the snake was going out the door. She couldn't get me to go back in the cellar again.

* * * *

I was upstairs in the kitchen doing dishes when the children come in with their dog. I told them to get him out of the house because he smelled and needed a bath.

All of a sudden, I heard the front loading washing machine running, so I went down to check as I hadn't been doing any laundry and saw the dog, Stuffy, going around in the washer! I started screaming and ran and got the dog out. The children came running in and I asked them what they thought they were doing. They could've killed their dog. They said, "But Mom, you said he needed a bath so we thought we would wash him so we could bring him in the house."

The children were Billy Clark, five, Vicky Clark, four, and Shelley, two. Lisa was a baby.

The poor dog was okay, but he wouldn't come close to the washer any more. He was in the washer only about a minute after it filled up and started. Thank God I went down to see who was doing laundry.

Another World Down by the Levee

by Ruth Knowlton Krizan of Lower Salem, Ohio
born in 1927

It is with great joy that I am writing down some of my best memories. I was born December 21, 1927 at 338 Pike Street, Marietta, Ohio at my grandparents' home.

At one time, three of us cousins lived with our grandmother. My mother, aunt, and uncle had left this area looking for work. My parents went to the northern part of Ohio, but my uncle, Charles Henry Hill, Sr., went to Pennsylvania. He worked on a pipeline there. He did this so he could send money home to his mother.

It was bitter cold, and he didn't have decent shoes. He had worn holes in the middle of the soles, and he would get his feet wet. After work each day, he would cut a lot of cardboard to fit his shoes, and as they got wet, he put new ones in. It was in Pennsylvania that he lost a finger while working on the pipeline.

His son and a girl cousin lived at Granny's also. At that time, there was only three cousins, I think! Memories, they flood my mind. My mind works faster than my pen.

My grandfather [Charles William Hill, Bricklayer?] was employed by the City of Marietta. It has been quoted many times how efficient he was at his work. It must have been a record for that time, as some would quote how many he could lay in an hour, while others would quote how many miles of brick he could lay in a day. Brick streets were prominent back then. Pike Street was brick, and so was the levee. Many still are!

Grandfather raised tobacco. He had a very large building, much like a barn. It was open at both ends. At certain times of the year, harvest time, he would hang it so neatly on the inside of the big building in very neat rows. Also twists of tobacco.

Many gentlemen dressed very personable and carried canes. They would point to the leaves of their choice, and Grandfather recorded it. Grampaw's complexion was very similar to his tobacco.

Granny [Mary Ellen Pickens Hill?], however, had reared most of her family by then. She had two sons and two daughters in their teens or early adulthood yet at home. Granny was a laundress, when Grandfather passed away, and she still had children at home and had to finish off paying for their home.

Mary Ellen Pickens Hill.

The home was a grand home, the largest one on Pike Street at the time. The man next door had the second largest. The rest of the homes set very close together, having hardly no side yards.

The yard surrounding Granny's home had three large oak trees on one side of the house. A family of squirrels made their home in them. One side of the house was covered in grapevines. In the front, there was a huge weeping willow tree—a sight to behold. All across the front yard was a hedge.

At the end of the side yard and to the back of the house was a well with a house built around it and a roof over it all and a lid that lifted up so as to access the well. A round log with a chain around it, and on the outside was a handle to wind it down into the well, and by reversing the action, it brought the bucket of water to the top. Good ice cold water.

Granny had chickens at the very back of her property. My grandfather had hollowed out a large sandstone to water them. The stone and size was, as he said, large enough that they couldn't tip their water over.

Granny done all of her laundering on the back porch. She drew all the water by herself and carried it up the back stairs to the back porch stairs, from the bucket to the tubs and copper boilers. She boiled all white clothing. She said it made them whiter. Of course, she had to carry all that water back outside. Then it was rinse water. Granny had something she called bluing. It came in a small bottle. She only used it in the white clothes' rinse water, and she didn't use the whole bottle.

She made her own soap. Under the back porch was an empty space. There she kept a crude wooden thing she called a hopper, into which she would put wood ashes from the fireplace in the house. It was under that porch that the soap was made for her laundries. She took a paring knife and shaved off the soap from the bar, then proceeded to scrub the clothing over a washboard.

Then carried the clean laundry out to a big side yard filled with clotheslines and long poles to boost the long items, such as sheets, up high from the ground. When it was dry, take it all down, and inside, she would lay piece by piece on the table and sprinkle it with lukewarm water and roll it up, then put it back into the basket, then covered it with a towel.

Then came the ironings. She had irons—all iron and some with handles she could take off and on. That way, some could be heating while others were being used.

Grandma's laundry customers knew when to pick them up. Once in a while, the customers would give us grandchildren a penny, and we loved it. It didn't happen every time, but we were always thrilled and thankful.

In the long winter months, sometimes Granny would send one of us children or maybe all of us to the neighbor's house to buy an apple. The neighbor was an attorney and a bachelor. He must have owned an orchard some place, because each one of his rooms filled with apples, all different kinds. Just apples—no furniture.

Granny said, "Mind you don't bring any bad apples. We can't eat rotten." So we went to Mr. Deschler's house and repeated to him Granny's words. He would just smile. Then he selected one for us, and we were homeward bound. Once home, Granny would peel and core the apple, then slice it, and each one of us would get a slice until the apple was gone. Granny kept nothing for herself. That has always been on my mind and bothered me.

In the summer months, I was busy running off to the river, "barefoot" of course. We only wore shoes in the winter. I loved the sand and silt mixture. I could play in it for hours. Granny told us never to go there, that the "bums" would get us, and we would never see home again. My cousins, both older than me, one about three years older, a girl cousin, Margaret L. Smith, the younger cousin than her, a boy cousin, Charles Henry Hill, Jr., and he was only eleven months older than me.

The showboats were on the river (Ohio), also barges and smaller watercraft. I don't know what it was all about, but I knew I loved it. We would go down to the levee and sit for hours watching the activity. The calliope music from the showboats was enticing also, but we could hear them if we were at home too.

When the boats pulled into the levee, they would lower big wooden ramps. The passengers could walk up and down them. I was always overjoyed to see the ladies beautifully dressed and twirling their elegant parasols. The gentlemen dressed just as nicely too. It was good to look at. Sometimes, there was a small high stage that the entertainers performed on. It was all so lovely. Watching the busy activities on the river was like living in another world, at least for the moment.

By the way, the levee was laid up with brick and still is today. I would like to think that my grandfather was part of that work, but I am not quite certain.

My cousins and I would play under the front porch. It was empty except for a Jon boat turned upside down. Some of the best mud pies and chocolates were made there. We used zinc lids from the canning jars for pie and Cokes and acorns from the oak trees, grass and weeds for vegetables and flowers.

Cousin C and I would get into the straight pins in Granny's sewing machine, and we would make paper boats out of newspapers and lay on our tummies on the porch and drop them over the porch into the floodwater. The current carried them away, or they drowned first.

Who Says You Have To Buy 'Em?

by Donald L. Rodabaugh of Coshocton, Ohio
born 1928

Yes, growing up in small town Coshocton, Ohio in the late 1930's and 1940's was good.

We made our own entertainment. Like the time my buddy Dave and I made a cart to push each other around the neighborhood. We built it out of a plank for the bottom and two 2x4's for the axles. We bought cold rolled steel rods from Kagey and Lear Machine Shop to mount whatever kind of wheels we had. This time I had two Red Flyer wagon wheels. Dave had two wagon wheels. Don't know where the other two wheels from our wagons went.

This cart was kinda like a soapbox derby car, only without a body. We bent large heavy nails over the metal rods to secure it to a 2x4 for our axles. We didn't have any 2x4's. So, we went where every kid in the neighborhood went when we needed wood, to the backside of the American Art Works Factory.

This area was fenced in, but not tight. It was hard to get to; we had to cross the top of a very steep, slippery hill behind the factory or go across the bottom of the hill which was usually wet, muddy, and swampy. Some older kids would have had to show us how to get there. We would never have found it by ourselves.

Oh! Did I say we had to wait till the day shift went home for the day? Then, we only had to watch for the night watchman to pass that area. Then we would go in, get a 2x4 each and out and across the back to home.

I lived a block away. Dave lived just across the street from the American Art Works. The company made large tin advertising signs like Coca-Cola, cigarettes, etc. Large signs like four by eight feet.

Anyway, we never considered our 2x4's as stealing. Stealing was like taking something from one of the three ten cent stores on Main Street. There was one kid in the neighborhood who did that. The rest of us knew that wasn't right.

Dave and I made our cart. Ran a bolt down through the front 2x4, tied a rope to each end, to steer, and away we went, taking turns pushing each other all over the neighborhood.

Until one day, we must have had a big disagreement about the cart. I got a saw and sawed the cart in two, right through the middle. My half was the rear half. I carried it home. Now, I didn't have anything.

The next day, Dave came by to show me his new cart. He got another 2x4 and he had two smaller scooter wheels. He had a cart all right, much shorter, but he had a cart. I still didn't have anything.

We made up and were friends for many, many years. I'm 81 years old now. Sadly, Dave passed away a couple years ago.

We used to make other toys and things. Like I think I had the first skateboard in this part of the country. It wasn't called a skateboard then; it was more like a scooter, a plank for the main part. I'd take a steel wheel clamp-on roller skate apart. I'd nail the front half of the skate on one end of the plank and nail the back half of the skate on the other end of the plank. On the front of the plank, I'd nail a wooden apple box. Across the top back edge, nail a smaller wood board for a handle. If I wanted to ride at night, I'd nail a couple of empty soup cans on the front of the box for headlights. Well, they looked like headlights to me.

Another great thing to do with cans was to make horseshoes to wear on our shoes. Take two condensed milk cans, and it seemed everyone used condensed milk at that time. Two small holes were punched in one end to get the milk out, which left a pretty sturdy, empty can. With these we would stomp our heels in to the sides of a can and the can would wrap around our shoe heel and stay on. This was our horseshoes. Then we would run all over the neighborhood on sidewalks or streets with a great clumpity, clumpity, clump. Got five or six kids together and it sounded like a herd of horses. That's what we were doing, riding our horses and slapping our hips to make our horses go faster. It drove the grownups crazy.

One summer when we must have been 11 or 12 years old, my buddy Tom and I spent hours and days adding to the world's atmospheric carbon content, now called air pollution. We made furnaces out of empty one-quart oil cans.

Almost everyone bought their automobile oil in one-quart tin cans then. The tops had triangle shaped openings punched in them to pour the oil out. This made the chimneys for our furnaces. We'd cut a door in the side of the can. Through this door we burnt coal. Everybody had coal in those days. Almost every house in town heated with a coal-burning furnace. Hour after hour, day after day, we lay on our bellies in Tom's backyard and tended our furnaces. One would go in for lunch; the other would tend his fire.

Another thing Tom and I would do was smoke corn silk. We picked the silk when it was green and dried it in old cigar boxes. When it was ready, we'd roll it in newspaper to make cigarettes or cigars. We'd usually smoke it in Tom's detached double garage.

One side had an oil pit built into the floor. That's so men could work on the under side of their cars, like changing oil, etc. It had been boarded over. Someone cut out and put in a trap door and with a small ladder. We kids would go down under and store and smoke our corn silk. The smoke would go up and through the cracks in the boards, but we didn't think about that. We never got caught.

We really lived in Tom's backyard for a few summers. We built racetracks for toy racecars. Every kid in the neighborhood had one. We'd race our bikes around the yard, skidding on the turns, baseball, football; we literally destroyed that back yard. No grass, just dirt and dust.

I ran into Tom's dad one time after I became an adult. Now, their backyard had lush green grass, a brick patio, big sun umbrella and nice outside furniture. I asked Doc why they let us tear up the backyard so badly when we were kids. His answer, with a slight grin, was, "We knew where you guys were." I guess it worked. From my house at that time, from our kitchen window, Mom could see us also.

Then there was skinny-dipping. Some of us tried to see how many places we could skinny dip in. The excuse to go was to go fishing. We'd fish first; if no bites, we'd go swimming.

One favorite place was Mud Port Basin. It had a large flat rock called Carter's Rock, about 2/3 the way down the far side. If anybody else came along we would hear them as they thrashed through the woods.

Mud Port was not too deep and not too much crap on the bottom.

We swam in the Walhonding River, nice slow river. Tuscarawas River; in and out of there one time. It was deep and fast. Muskingum River was too dirty to swim in, didn't even want to eat the fish from there, Wills Creek River right at the little town of Willscreek, right under the bridge.

My buddy for skinny-dipping was Bob. We both had paper routes then. We'd carry our papers very early on Sunday mornings then go fishing. It was usually still dark when we got to the water.

One favorite place was Lake Park. That was the public beach for a fee. Nice sandy beach, pier with tower and two diving boards, and raft. Bob and I would rent a rowboat the night before. Jimmy R., the manager, would tie it up near the dance hall; we'd get it in the morning. We'd usually swim first before fishing, because that place was very public. We'd swim before it got too much daylight. I'll bet nobody else skinny-dipped at lake park.

We tried farm ponds, creeks, while seining for minnows. Y.M.C.A.'s at Zanesville, Newark, New Philly, Canton, East Liverpool, Lima, Tiffin. At the Y's, all men and boys swam naked. Some legitimate places to skinny dip.

Memorable people in my life, Casey Jones I. He was an adult living across the street and down two houses, big, strong, fun guy to be around. One nice summer night, four of us, another neighborhood boy, me, and two good looking girls who lived next door to me. It was after dark, maybe 9:30 or 10:00. We were all sitting on the front steps of the girl's house and all having a good time talking and laughing, not loud enough to bother anyone. Up pulls a police car. Shines a spotlight on us, the one big cop got out, asked our names, where we each lived, looked us over very mean like. He said they got a complaint called in down at the station about some rowdy kids bothering the neighborhood, advised us all to go home. We did. What a bummer.

About three days later, we found out from Casey to my dad, that it was Casey who called the cops. Casey had a cousin who was on the police force at that time. Casey called the station and got ahold of his cousin and told him some kids were just having too much of a good time and could he come by and see what he could do about it. All this time, Casey was sitting on his front porch watching and laughing out loud about spoiling our good time.

We never got mad about it. Casey was a good guy.

Casey had a gasoline bulk delivery business.

Sometimes he would hire me to ride along with him when he would deliver gasoline to farms, throughout the country. He said there were a lot of mean dogs out there. My job was to stand on the truck running board and watch for the dogs to warn him as he filled the farm tanks. I was not to fight the dog, just warn him if I saw any coming. Not a bad job, ride around the country and get paid for it.

Casey would hire me to fill the delivery tanker trucks on real busy days. Like when the price was to go up the next day, he would call all his customers to see if they wanted to be filled up, they would. This was during World War II and gas was rationed and scarce.

One day, when I was about 14 years old, he came to me at home and asked me if I could drive. I said no, I was only 14 and had not even thought about it yet. He said to come on, I need a driver. He had one of his two gas delivery tank trucks and his pickup across the street at his house. He needed both across town to his bulk plant. No other adults around.

He said, "Come on, I'll show you how." We got to his pickup truck, and he said, "Get in behind the wheel, you know how to steer, everyone knows how to steer." He pointed to the floor, "That pedal is the clutch, that pedal is the brake, that's the gas, that is the gear shift, on the floor. Turn the key on, clutch in, press the starter button, give it a little gas, clutch out slowly and you're off. Clutch in, move gearshift up to right, clutch out, more gas, clutch in, gearshift down to right, clutch out, more gas, and you are on your way. Stop at all stop streets and the light at Main Street if it's red. Drive all the way across town in low gear if you don't want to shift gears." He said, "I'll meet you at the bulk plant." He took off in his big truck.

I got there okay, no problems. The pickup jumped some and died when I stopped with the clutch out, but I got there.

Occasionally, he let me drive the pickup around the lot at his bulk plant. No wonder I learned to drive so quickly, when at 15, my dad started to teach me.

Another time I was out with Casey delivering gas to farms in the country. We came up to a car that was pulled off the side of the road. We could see it had a flat tire. Two ladies were standing there looking at it, not knowing what to do next. Casey told them we'd change it for them.

In those days all cars came with a spare tire that fit, car jack, and lug nut wrench. Casey did all the work; I think all I did was hold the lug nuts. They thanked us and drove off.

We got back in the gas truck. Casey looked at me and said, "Don't tell Sue about this." Sue, his wife, might have thought he was having too good a time at his work. I never told.

Another time, several years later, I was mowing yards to earn money. I had a push reel type mower, no engine powered mower in these days. I was struggling to mow a big yard around the corner from my house. It had rained a lot that summer and the grass was high and thick and lush. Push the mower, pull it back, push the mower, pull it back, push again, and pull back. That was the toughest mowing job I ever had. It was going to take me the rest of the summer just to finish this yard.

I had the yard maybe a tenth done when I heard a heavy gas powered reel type motor coming around the house. It was Casey. He had seen me struggling to mow that yard. He drove his pick up truck up to Warsaw about ten miles away and borrowed this gas-powered mower from the Warsaw Cemetery. His father was the cemetery caretaker at that time. This was lucky for me. He mowed that whole yard for me. He wouldn't let me handle that big mower. He said it was too dangerous. It was a brute. I got paid for mowing that yard and Casey wouldn't take the money or even part of it.

He taught me always to help someone that needed help. Don't ask if they need help, just pitch in and help.

There are more Casey stories about gas rationing, my car, and his, a big victory garden during World War II. Casey left an impression on me.

A Few Ideas to Deal With Locusts

by Iva Spires of Zanesville, Ohio
born in 1918

My father's name was Elmer Brown. We lived one mile on Flint Ridge Road from Crooksville, Ohio.

There was flint on our farm, and there had been Indians also. We found parts of arrows, "nothing fancy," while hoeing in the garden. There was a small spring below our house, and we found chippings of arrows there also.

It was around 1928 when we encountered locusts (beetles) the first time. By living out in the country, it was extremely quiet. We woke up one morning and went outside. There were the weirdest sound coming from the forest, just like waves of mooning, then the locusts would come in droves across our huge garden. This went on for days.

Since the forest was close, the locusts didn't do much damage to the shrubbery, because they had the forest to feed on, but they did a lot of damage near the villages. We would pick the locusts off the shrubbery and drop them in water and feed them to the hogs. They loved the locusts. Locusts comes every seventeen years.

When the locusts came again, we lived near a village, so they did a lot more damage. We picked them off the shrubbery and dropped them in water with kerosene added. This killed them. We had a small Chihuahua dog. She ate every one she could catch.

Back to the garden, we had one and a half acres of garden, and we had to throw the flint off the garden to a low spot in the corner by the fence, because it was so difficult to hoe. When hitting the flint, the sparks would fly.

We raised bushels of tomatoes. We did a little different from our neighbors. We started by digging a hole with a post hole digger, then mix rotten manure from the barn and mix it with the dirt. Then we would bury a fence post in the hole and fill with dirt, then plant two tomato plants. When the plant got tall, we tied it to the post.

There were eight in our family, so we canned a hundred quarts of tomatoes every year. When winter came, we would cream the tomatoes and eat with cornbread. We also canned two hundred quarts of sweet apples. We hadn't learned to cold-pack food as yet, so we were fortunate that our father worked at a stoneware pottery.

Andy Brown around 1910.

He brought home two ten-gallon stone jars, and we put corn in the cob in one jar and large cucumbers in the other. We started by filling the jar two-thirds full of water, then add enough salt to float an egg. Then add cooked cucumbers to one jar and cooked corn on the cob to the other. Then they went through the pickling process. When winter came, we would take out what we needed and soak out the salt from the corn, cut off the cob and cook. The cucumbers, we would cut in strips, soak out the salt, add vinegar and sugar and water to make pickles.

With the green beans, we cooked the beans, placed in stoneware jar, added just enough water to cover, using a smaller amount of slat and a little sugar. Then when winter came, and they had went through the pickling process, we were able to cook and eat, but we hadn't used a large amount of salt, therefore, we didn't have to soak out any salt.

Also with green beans, we were able to string them on a string (uncooked) and hang to dry, then store in a cloth bag in a very dry place. Then in winter, they were cooked. They had to be cooked several hours. They were called fodder beans.

As you will notice, when I mention my father, when referred to his mother and father, he said Mother and Father. We were taught to say Moma and Poppa. My mother said Maw and Paw. When young folks went away to college, they came back saying Dad. This made my father very upset. He said it sounded disrespectful.

The lower road, as we called it, was called Snake Holler simply because it followed the creek. There were several young men on that road that did drink heavy, but early in the day, we would hear them singing:

"Show me the way to go home. I'm tired and I want to go to bed. I had a little drink about an hour ago, and it went right to my head." Us children thought they were drunk, but if so, they prob'ly wouldn't be singing.

We had a large pear tree in our far corner of our garden. It had very large pears, "winter pears." That tree has been there ever since I can remember, and it still stands today. I am age ninety, so it is nearly a hundred years old.

Back around 1928, they still were not holding funerals at the funeral home. The corpse were brought back to the house in a casket. There were always a maroon colored veil draped over the door of the casket when it was opened. Two or three of the neighbors would sit up with the corpse at night so the family could sleep. There were no artificial flowers. Teenage girls would stand on each side of the walk holding baskets of flowers when the casket was carried out of the house.

The same thing was true when anyone was sick. The neighbors would sit up with the sick so the family could sleep.

When a young couple got married, in a few days after the wedding, the neighbors would have what the called a "belling." They would wait 'til evening and come near the home and start pounding on old pots and pans and dragging tin cans tied together on the ground and cheering 'til the newlyweds came up with a treat.

My father treated with oranges. There was this young man that my father knew was sweet on my mother, so my father gave him a lemon. Earl said, "I think Elmer gave the sourest orange of the bunch." Since he lived in the country, he prob'ly had never seen a lemon.

We were married May 2, 1938, the very heart of the Depression. My husband was working at a glass factory in Zanesville, Ohio. By late fall, he was out of work, so we were forced to move in with an uncle and baby sit their daughter, because husband and wife worked.

After about a year, he was able to get work on "W.P.A." President Franklin D. Roosevelt started this project called "Work Project Association" to give work for men. There were no modern equipment used, mostly pick and shovel. My husband helped lay brick gutters on both sides of the road in both Woodlawn Cemetery and Greenwood Cemetery in Zanesville, Ohio. They are still there today. He worked for forty-eight dollars per month, but there were still times when he was laid off from this project.

We had a very nice car, but we had to sell it for sixty-five dollars. We kept the money for three months to buy groceries and pay utilities. We were finally able to get a grocery order, and I was able to buy bacon, eggs, canned spaghetti, and canned peaches. All we had before then was potatoes we had raised on a vacant lot.

My mother-in-law wanted to work in the garden. There was no one to watch the baby, so she carried the crib to the garden. She was down pulling weeds when she heard the cat screeching and carrying on. She went to see. There was a black snake crawling up the side of the crib. The cat had hold of the snake's tail, pulling for dear life.

Doctors didn't use to have office hours. They came to the house to visit the sick, either by horseback or horse and buggy. The babies were delivered at home.

Everything was a dark secret. I was in the fifth grade, twelve years old, before I learned where babies came from.

Moving to Cambridge

by Luella Burkhart of Woodsfield, Ohio
born 1942

Dad and Mom, Glen Mayberry and Lorena Burkhardt, got married February 4, 1931. Mom was a schoolteacher in the Miltonsburg, Ohio area. She taught three different one-room schools around Miltonsburg. She taught for five years. The last year she taught they got married.

From February through the end of the school year she lived with her mother and dad. My dad came every weekend to spend with her. At the end of that school year she quit teaching. She moved to their farm with Dad.

Mom used to talk about her teaching years. This one student that she had, she said that when she gave a spelling test and the word "city" was on it, he would spell it "sity." One evening, after school, she made him stay and write "city" 100 times. She said for 99 times he wrote "city," the 100th time, he wrote "sity." She let him go home. After that, when the "city" was on a spelling test, he would write "sity." She said she knew that he knew the correct spelling. She would mark it wrong.

Every summer Max Plumbly and his son went around to all the farms with their thresh machine and threshed the farmers' grain. But before the thresh machine came, the farmers had to cut the grain in the field and store it in the barn.

The thresh machine usually took two or three days at each farm. It would depend on how much grain that there was to thresh out.

Dad had a grain binder. What it did was cut and tied the sheaths of grain and put it on the ground. Then, Dad took his horses and wagon and gathered up the grain sheaths and put them in the barn and wait on the thresh machine. Mom and the kids would shock the bundles of grain; put two sheaths on top to protect the grain from rain if there would happen to rain before Dad could gather it up. The little shocks of grain looked like little huts.

When the thresh machine got to our farm, Max would park it along the side of the back of the barn. All the neighbor men would go help each other. It took a lot of help. The men would push the little bundles of grain out a little door at the top of the barn into the thresh machine below. Someone had to take the string off the bundles before they pushed it into the thresh machine. That was usually the kids' jobs. The bundles of grain would go through the machine. The grain would go into a large bin, the hulls got blown into a pile, and the grain straw would go get baled up into bales of straw.

A baler traveled around with the thresh machine. When the grain bin got full, it would be emptied into sacks. It would be taken to the granary and emptied into bins in the granary. The straw bales got stored in the barn for later use.

All the smaller children just played on those days. We would jump in the pile of hulls. Mom fed the hulls to her chickens. We would jump and play on the stacks of bales of straw.

All the neighbor ladies came and helped my mother cook for all the help. The bigger boys had to help the men. The bigger girls had to help in the kitchen.

In the early 50's the thresh machine got replaced by the grain combine.

Sometimes on a Sunday afternoon, Mom would pack a picnic lunch and we would all go fishing. My uncle, aunt, and two cousins would go with us. My three sisters and I would go fishing in the creek behind the barn. We would cut a limb from the elderberry bush, tie a long string on the end, bend a straight pin into a hook shape, and tie it to the other end of the string. Dig some earthworms and away we would go fishing.

There was one spot in the creek that was deep. There was a lot of little fish in that hole. Sometimes you might get a fish on the hook, but you had to be quick to get the little fish up on the bank, but most of the time the little fish would wiggle off the hook or the hook would straighten out and the fish would slide off. We always went home fishless, but we had a lot of fun.

My cousins had a pet baby raccoon. If we was going to go visit in the evening we would go to the creek and catch some crayfish to take to the baby raccoon. It was really cute. My cousin would put the crayfish in his water bowl. He would stand on his hind legs and eat the crayfish. Raccoons like to fish for their food.

You had to be really careful when trying to catch crayfish. They try to grab you with their claws. We always tried to find little ones, but if not, we would catch the big ones. We would take a stick to catch them. They would grab the stick with their pinchers. Then we would shake it off into a jar.

When the little raccoon got big enough to take care of itself my uncle took him to the woods and let him loose.

We had a beagle dog named "Queen." My little sister and I dressed her up in our doll clothes. She didn't seem to mind, but when we took the clothes off of her she would disappear for a while. I wonder why.

My uncle lived in Quaker City. He kept asking Dad when he was going to give Queen to him. Finally, one day, Dad said he could take her home with him. We was sad to see Queen go to Quaker City. My uncle will take good care of her. He said not to cry, we could come see her anytime we wanted to.

Uncle had her for about three weeks. One day he called and told Dad that Queen had run away. He had taken her to the post office with him and that's when she ran away. He looked all over Quaker for her all day and couldn't find her. This was around 9:00 a.m. Dad and all of us was very sad.

The next morning, around 4:00 a.m., Dad heard a scratching at the front door; he went to see what it was. There sat Queen. She was okay, just tired, cold, and hungry. When she saw Dad she was a really happy little dog. It took her about 19 to 20 hours to get back home. She slept all that day. Uncle told Dad that he wouldn't take her back to Quaker with him because she would just run away again. Maybe next time she wouldn't make it back home.

Every spring, Mother raised baby chicks with a mother hen. Sometimes the mother hens didn't raise enough so Mom would get 25 more baby chicks from the feed mill in town. When the baby chicks would come into the feed mill it was still cold weather. So, to keep the baby chicks warm, Dad took an old washtub, cut a hole in the bottom, put a light bulb through the hole, and turned the tub upside down on bricks. It was high enough from the floor that the baby chicks would go under it. They huddled around the light to keep warm. They looked like a big yellow cotton ball. Mom hoped that she would get five or six hens in the bunch. The rest was roosters. They went for Sunday dinner as soon as they got big enough.

Thanksgiving Day 1950, it started snowing and didn't quit for hours. It snowed all night. The next morning when daylight came, you could see how much snow we got. You couldn't tell where the township road was. It was level from road bank to road bank. It looked like a big white blanket. Wherever you went, you had to shovel your way there and back. The wind blew the paths back shut with snow. A path had to be shoveled for the cattle to get to water.

We were snowed in for days out our township road. My dad made it out the road to check on my grandfather. He lived about a mile out the township road from us. He was okay.

The milk truck couldn't get out our road to pick up our milk. Mom made snow ice cream a lot. We had plenty of snow. What milk we couldn't use, Dad gave it to the pigs.

In the late summer of 1950, Grandma Burkhart came to visit. She lived with my aunt at Miltonsburg. Grandma stayed for a week then she went back home. We were happy to have her come for a visit.

That fall she fell and broke her hip. She never got over it. She passed away in January of 1951. The day of her funeral, that morning, our car wouldn't start. We waited on the milk truck to come pick our milk up. Dad bummed a ride to Barnesville in the back of the milk truck. It was really cold outside and inside the milk truck it was colder. We took a taxicab from Barnesville to Woodsfield. She was at a funeral home in Woodsfield, Ohio. A family member brought us back home after the funeral was out.

Lester and Alice Warwick lived on our road. They both worked in town. They didn't have any animals. They came to visit a lot. They had two girls. Donna was my sister, Jean's, age, Shirley was my age. One evening they came to visit. We talked Dad into letting us ride "Kit," our workhorse. She was the only workhorse that we had. Dad had sold all of his horses after he bought his tractor. She was Dad's favorite horse. He kept her to cultivate Mom's three gardens.

Dad got Kit ready and put us on the horse. Peggy first, she was the littlest, Shirley next, then me. He told us not to go any further than the end of our township road, turn around, and come back. We thought that we was smarter than Dad. As it turned out, we wasn't. We thought that we could go out onto the county road and down a little way, then into the hay field, then back up to the house. It worked for a little while till we went up into the hay field. Kit decided that she wanted some nice green grass. When she put her head down to eat, Shirley and I slid off the side of the horse right into a large mud hole.

When we wasn't back when Dad thought that we should have been, he sent Jean and Donna to look for us. They found us, Peggy still on the horse, the horse eating grass, Shirley and I was looking for her shoe. Shirley had lost her shoe in the mud hole. We never did find that shoe.

When Dad saw us coming, Jean leading Kit, Peggy still on the horse, and the rest of us walking, that cut the visit short, Shirley and I was covered with mud!

Dad sold our farm to Bill and Grace Robb and bought one five miles south of Cambridge, from Al and Helen Kerr. Mr. Kerr had retired from farming and decided to sell his farm and move to Zanesville, Ohio, close to their son.

We was lucky to buy his farm. It was great. The house had a bathroom, water in the house, and gas heat. No more coal and wood to carry in. No more water to carry in the house. The barn had water in it. The cows didn't have to go out in the cold to the creek to get a drink, but Dad put them out for a while in the afternoon so they could get exercise. It was hard on their legs to stand on concrete all day in one place.

We moved to Cambridge in March of 1954. Dad and a neighbor man baled the loose hay from the barn so it could be moved. Dad didn't have a hay baler. He put his hay in loose. A lot of our stuff had already been moved down.

Our last day of school at Baileys Mills was on a Tuesday. That day, Dad and a neighbor moved the cattle, Kit, and all the animals.

When we got home from school, Mom packed up the car and four girls and we left for Cambridge. On the way to the car, I walked through some snow that was still in the yard, thinking to myself, this is probably the last time that I would walk through snow in this yard. We took our stuff that we would need for that night.

On the way to our new house, Mom stopped in Cambridge and got some food for our lunch and to eat when we got there. When we got home, Dad and the neighbor had the milking done, Mom's chickens fed, and was in the house waiting on us. The neighbor had went back to Barnesville.

That night, Mom put mattresses on the floor for us to sleep on. Our beds was still at our old house.

The next morning, Wednesday, we started to our new school, Westland Grade School. This new school was totally different. It had three classrooms; sixth, seventh, and eighth; third, fourth and fifth; and first and second, three teachers, and a gym. This school had a basketball team and cheerleaders. I was in the sixth grade, my older sister, eighth grade, and my little sister in third grade. My sister, Jean, was in the tenth grade. She went to New Concord. In the 60's it was renamed John Glenn High School in honor of the astronaut. He graduated from New Concord High School.

My brother didn't move down with us. He was a senior at Barnesville High School. He stayed with the Shuman family, our neighbors, until he graduated, then he moved to our house. Brother Bill and sister Rita, graduated the same night in 1954, Bill from high school and Rita from Westland eighth grade.

Dad and sister, Jean, went to Barnesville graduation. We rode with a neighbor to graduation. Mom was disappointed that she couldn't go to her only son's high school graduation.

Born at Suppertime

By Mary Cummings of Massilon, Ohio
Born in 1924

Hello, will try to remember some of the funny things in my earlier years, and some that are just so-so.

Was born May 5, 1924 at suppertime (I had missed two meals already) in Belmont, Ohio in Belmont County, and was named Mary Belle. I didn't like my name, so when I was about 18 years old, I changed it to just plain Mary. I thought Mary Belle sounded like a cow. Ha! Ha!

Perhaps I should just say in my childhood, we (my mother and two brothers) lived with our grandparents. One of my memories was the time we all went to church for a revival meeting in a big sled, driven by my Grandpap Thomas, and drawn by two large horses. The sled was filled with straw, and we also had blankets to help keep us warm. When we went into church, maybe there was a little straw on us? Some of the people looked at us and I'm thinking they were saying, "Here comes the farmers."

Of course, I have also had the pleasure of riding to church in a surrey with the fringe on it, buggy, and later my grandpap bought a big red car. Since then, I have ridden in trains and planes.

The dear old coal cooking stove was another story. First, I would have to go upstairs to the corncrib (granary) to get corncobs to help start the fire in the stove the next morning. When I would come down to the door, an old turkey gobbler would be there to flag me all the way to the house and sometimes he would get me. Those claws were really sharp and they really hurt. After the corncob, I would have to go and get some small pieces of wood called kindling. Then I had to fill up the wood box, and next, filling up the coal bucket. After all that, I had to fill the reservoir with water so we would have hot water for the day. Boy, I'm tired, and it isn't suppertime.

In the early summer my older brother Lloyd and I had to hoe corn all day. Of course we had lunch; in those days it was called dinner. Later on in the day we had supper. Back to hoeing the corn, our grandpap would plow in the cornrows of course, with help of a horse. He would plow enough in the morning to keep us busy all afternoon. On some of those afternoons, we would hoe about 20 hills of corn on each end of the rows. Of course, we had to hoe the last four rows all the way across the field, so when Grandpap came back the next morning, he wouldn't know what we had done. Well, the rest of the day, we would go wading in the creek catching tadpoles, little fish, snakes, etc. We knew we shouldn't be doing that, but it was better than hoeing all those rows of corn. We hoed corn until about July 4th, and it was hip high. Wow!

After corn hoeing comes hay season. That means pulling the hay into the barn. I would have to get on one of those sweaty old horses to haul the hay from the wagon to the hayloft until the wagon was empty. Then they would go again to fill that wagon, again and again. After each load, I would go into the house and wash the sweaty old horsehair from me. I really didn't like the job! Yuck!

Lloyd Nichols in knickers, Mary Belle Nichols Cummings,and Elwood Nichols.

The outhouse wasn't all that bad. It was a place where you did all your thinking and planning on what kind of trouble you could get into, when you were relieved of your duty, and got out of that smelly old outhouse and breathed some good old country air. While you were in that beautiful old outhouse, we could look at the good old Sears and Roebuck catalog and plan your next order, but by the time the catalog got to the outhouse, it was too late to order. We also had those old honeybees and wasps that could sting you, and you know where. Ouch! It also provided us our daily streak of exercise to and from the old building, whether the sun was shining, raining, or snowing, you still had to go to the outhouse. God bless the bathrooms we have today. Huh!

Going to school was another one of my good ole days, I think. My brother Lloyd, two years older than me, and I would walk to school every day. It was about 1 ½ miles each way, whether the weather was good or bad, we walked. There were no buses for us.

Now, to get to my pretty wardrobe. I wore dresses made from feed sacks. My mother, Ora, made them and trimmed them with beautiful rick-rack on some of them, others with dainty lace trim and some with cute little ruffles. I looked terrific because I had a different dress for each day of the week. Some of the girls would get together, point their fingers at me, and would giggle, making fun of me. My coats were made from other coats. I guess they looked like Dolly Parton's coat of many colors.

As time went by, things did change for me. In my sophomore year of high school, my mother bought me a beautiful new green Chesterfield coat. Man, that made me look like a million dollars. Also in those days, my brother Lloyd wore knickers until he was through the eighth grade. As a freshman in high school, he wore slacks, not jeans. If jeans had holes in them, they were patched, not like they are today.

I attended Smith Township High School in Centerville, Ohio in Belmont County (there is another Centerville in Ohio) for four wonderful years. I was a very good student, or at least I thought so. I had the honor of being one of the cheerleaders for three years for our basketball team. Maybe I should mention that I had a crush on the center player, (Jr.) on our team. I graduated from Smith Township High School in May, 1942. In September, 1942, I left Belmont County and moved to Stark County and have been here ever since. The rest is another great story. Will never forget those "Good Old Days."

Hip Deep Snow and Low Wages

by Wilma W. Gregg of Zanesville, Ohio
born 1918

I lived on a farm between Philo, Ohio and Stovertown, Ohio, about 30 miles south of Zanesville, Ohio, from 1925 through 1927. I went to a one room school that taught first through eighth grades. There were about 20 to 30 students. We walked about two miles to school through the pastures in snow over hip deep. I remember, at one time, the older boys put a dead skunk in the girls' outhouse and had to stay after school for punishment.

We also had a mail carrier that delivered our mail by horse and buggy.

I remember my grandparents passing away one day and were buried the next because they didn't embalm people then.

In 1935 I worked at the Bloomer Candy Company. I worked 40 hours a week and made $10.00. After I got my social security card in 1936, my pay was $8.88 for 40 hours. I also worked at the A&P Grocery Store for 35 cents per hour. In 1955, I worked at Mercury Match Company and was paid 84 cents per hour. When they went out of business, about 21 years later, I was making $1.77 per hour.

There was three boys and three girls in our family when we lived on the farm. And on Saturdays our parents had two tubs. Dad bathed the boys and Mom bathed the girls.

I remember the radio programs we heard were Amos and Andy, Ma Perkins, Stella Dallas, and Red Skelton shows.

Our mother did our laundry in a tub and wash board. Years later she had a wringer washer, but she also used the wash board. She hung the clothes outside on the clothesline, and many times, I remember the clothes were frozen to the line.

The Non-medical Aroma

by Wanda Rogers of Canton, Ohio
born in 1923

One nice spring morning, I went out with my dog, Pepper, before going to work at the hospital and she went nose to nose with a skunk! Of course the skunk turned around and gave her a full dose of "skunk perfume."

My friend Amanda and I rushed Pepper to the bathtub and gave her a quick bath in tomato juice. We had our white uniforms on and didn't wear gloves when we bathed her. We became immune to the smell.

We went to do our regular duties: Amanda to do EKGs and I to make rounds to check traction setups.

I was on the fifth floor and a nurse and an aide were looking up at the air vents and said, "I smell skunk," and a security guard came around the corner and said, "Phew, I smell skunk." I just stood there, looking innocent.

They soon caught up with me and I was sent home to "take a bath."

I am the 12th child of 13 born into an Amish family. My mother was a short, plump lady, always on the go—cooking, sewing, gardening. On Sunday mornings, she flitted around, making sure the dishes were done, beds made. Then she would rush out the door, tying her bonnet on her head. Father would be waiting impatiently in the buggy saying, "Come on, Mary. We will be late for church."

We went to a regular school in Loogootee, Indiana. We walked about a mile to the bus stop, and then rode the school bus. There was a small store where we waited for the bus. One day we went into the store with some other kids. They had a punchboard there that was popular at the time. You punched a hole in the punchboard that had a little slip of paper that said how much you had to pay. We kids didn't know you had to pay and we didn't have any money. Our father had to come and pay and you can believe that it never happened again.

My sister Martha and I were playing in a field one summer day and didn't know the neighbor had turned a bull loose there. We saw him coming around. Martha was on the plump side. I was a fast runner, but she passed me by getting out of there.

Some mornings my father would make a big skillet of sausage gravy and make biscuits. Then we would all go do our chores before going to school.

I rode in the buggy with my mother when she had errands or to go visiting. I would watch the cars pass us by and wonder what it was like to ride in a car. It looked interesting even though I was young.

My oldest brother, Sam, was 20 years older than me. He got married when he was 19 years old. I always like to tease him, saying, "Sam, you didn't invite me to your wedding." And he would say, "Huh, you weren't even born yet."

Sam was a preacher. One day we were coming back from a wedding and passed by a big patch of watermelons. I said, jokingly, "Sam, let's get us a big, ripe watermelon." Sam answered, without a smile, "Thou shalt not steal!"

I grew up, joined the Mennonite Church. Got a job in a hospital and got a car.

This is about one of my ancestors, John Hawkins and an Indian girl. The year was the early 1800s.

John Henry Hawkins, Simon N. Hawkins, Wesley Morris, Verna and Erna Hawkins, Henry Hakwins seated.

Shadrack and Jane Huggins lived on a ridge in Monogalia County, then Virginia. There was a tribe of Mohawk Indians camped on a creek nearby, could be five miles or more. The Mohawks were a hunting party as there were no Indians in this part of the country. They only traveled or hunted game here.

There was a bunch of renegades came through and picked a fight. Shadrack heard the fight. He had an idea what was taking place, so in a day or two, he went down to see what had happened. On his way down, he saw a very small girl running through the woods. He continued on to the scene and discovered that all the Mohawks had been killed except the little girl he saw in the woods. So he went back and located the girl, ran her down, and took her home with him. He and his wife raised her and gave her the name of Frances, but called her Fanny.

John Hawkins was a neighbor of Shadrack Huggins and he saw Fanny grow up. John was born in 1796. He and his wife, Anna, had 15 children. When Anna passed away, when Fanny became 19 years old, and John was 43 years old they married and had five children.

So John Hawkins was the father of 20 children that he left behind to carry on his name.

Singing to the Chickens

by Ruth Ann Kauffman of Dundee, Ohio
born in 1948

In the 1960s, when I was a young girl, 12 years old, life on the farm was quite different from today's farm or country life. We weren't rich moneywise, but always had plenty to eat, warm clothes, and a good family relationship. Yes, we were rich!

Before going to school, we got up from a warm cozy bed in an unheated upstairs. We often could see our breath. Also, the windows were drafty with little mounds of snow on the windowsills, especially if it was windy, blowing snow. We really were happy to have plastic stapled over our upstairs windows. Of course, now we couldn't see out very well.

With our flannels and socks we raced downstairs where Dad had the wood and coal stoves fired up. He was already outside starting the feeding. Mother and we children went out through the dark to help with chores.

I had one or two cows to sit down beside them and milk one half to one bucket of milk by hand. Often, half a dozen cats would sit patiently behind the cows and us, watching for their drink of milk, which we gave them some in their dish. As soon as we got up they too all got up and meowed all the way to their dish. What a chorus!

Sometimes while milking, we'd squirt milk toward a cat from the cow's teat. The cats soon learned to open their mouth to catch the stream of milk. No wonder they sat watching us.

There often were several calves that we fed milk from a bucket, then later with a milk replacer. We had to be careful, as they gave the bucket a ram with their snout if it got low.

The smell of ensilage with ground grain cow feed on top smelled so good. Later after that was eaten, they were fed hay yet. It smelled so good. The animals were all munching and sounded so contented. We milked a total of 12 cows usually and had several young heifers and calves in barn. They were all bedded with fresh straw, and the barn was quite warm, even in wintertime. Dad often said his feet were warmer in the barn than at the breakfast table. Our kitchen had no basement, and the floors were cold.

After a breakfast of eggs, toast, cereal, milk and cookies, we hustled to get ready for school. I often wondered since, did we smell like the barn? No one ever said anything. We didn't bathe before going to school, but we just washed our face, hands, and arms. Bathing time in winter was only Saturday evenings, necessary or not!

Bathing was another story. A galvanized square tub beside the wood and coal stove on a carpet was our bathtub. We scooped our hot water out of a reservoir (tank) built onto the stove, into the tub, with a bucket of cold water we had pumped from a pitcher pump beside our wash basin in the kitchen, our only source of water in the house. It came from a hand-dug well 30 feet deep, ten feet away from the house. Oh, such good-tasting, fresh, cold water. Spring fed, it almost never went dry. Oh, I've to go get a drink now. It makes me thirsty to think of it.

We also always had a big teakettle of water heating on the stove. We would pour boiling water into a granite, round dishpan, add soap and cold water from the pump until comfortable to wash dishes. We set the dishes into a granite oblong big pan. Then, we'd pour hot water from the teakettle over it to rinse the dishes.

This was all done at a wooden painted dry sink. Later, Mom and Dad bought a used wooden cabinet with countertop (marlite) with a porcelain double sink and ridged porcelain drain boards out from each side of the sink. No running water. We still heated our water, but the drains worked. My, was it fun to do dishes now!

After school, my chores consisted of loading fire wood on a small wagon and pulling it to the porch, unloadeding it in a big walk-in closet beside the stove, then back to the coal house (where we stored our coal) with two coal buckets on the little wagon. I filled those up and pulled it to the steps. Dad or my brother helped me carry those into the same closet.

Meanwhile, Mother emptied the ash trays from the stoves, cleaned up the mess on the floor and fired up the stoves afresh. She started supper. Dad was in the barn doing chores, feeding cattle, and getting the barn cleaned out (of animal manure), etc.

Next I went to carry water (warm water in winter) to the chicken house. I would rinse out the water dish, then add fresh clean water.

Gathering the eggs into the bucket was fun. The nests where the chickens laid their eggs were stuffed with fresh clean straw weekly. Then, we filled their mash hopper with fresh mash from a feed box in the chicken house that Dad kept filled. Also it had ears of dried field corn that we'd knock against some wooden posts to knock off most kernels. The chickens would run to beat each other for the corn. My grandma claimed it makes the chickens scratch the floor to uncover the corn kernels, and that exercise makes big eggs. I don't know about that theory!

Often, I'd sing to the chickens. They would stand, cock their little heads one way, then the other way, look at me and shake their little flabby woddlers together. I though it was amusing. You would get so attached to the chickens, I never wanted to be around come butchering time.

We kept them for laying eggs two years, usually 24 chickens. It did make really good meat to cook for canning broth and chicken boned meat. Mother made the best chicken dressing (stuffing). Also, chicken noodles, etc.

Now the last chore of the evening wasn't much fun, but it had to be done. Either Mom or I had that privilege. Emptying the chamber pot! When really snowy, we first had to shovel a path to the outhouse, carry that odorous (not a good one) vessel to empty it, then pump fresh water from a big old pump outside to rinse it out, pouring the water as far away as possible from the yard. In summertime we went to the outhouse for our potty time, sparing us the job of emptying the pot from the house.

We then went to the barn to help Dad finish the milking. My brother fed the calves, I milked two cows by hand. Occasionally, the cow wasn't so cooperative and would lift her hind leg and nicely step into the bucket of milk. Oh dear! Dad came to the rescue if she didn't kick it away first. What milk was left went into the cat's dish. The bucket had to be washed out before finishing that job. Therefore, those buckets had a few dents. Later, we had stainless steel buckets with a partial cover on them. The cows just kicked them over sometimes, but didn't get a foot inside. But mostly the cows were very nice about it and busy munching hay while we did the milking.

We usually tied their tails up a little with twine connected to the litter carrier track above. That was a container open over the top, hooked on chains running on a track suspended from the barn ceiling. The track went part way around the barn where the cattle were kept. You could let it down to the floor, load the manure into it. When full, you pull the chains to wind it up to the track. Then push it on the track leading outside where the manure spreader was parked. Pull a hanging chain to trip the carrier. It dumped it into the spreader. That was Dad's job.

A few times, Dad had the flu in the winter. Therefore, I and my brother, who was five years younger than me, tried to do the job. We thought that was hard work! Also, doing the feeding, etc. Dad always did.

My dad worked hard, but I had a wonderful dad. I never saw him mad or raise his voice, but he was firm and meant what he said. He had a thin peach tree twig on hooks behind the living room door. He had to use it a few times to break our self wills. I'm thankful now he did. He still loved us and we loved him.

We then, after chores, ate a good hot and hearty supper. Then if we had homework or school lessons to study, we did that. I had honor grades all through school, so hard work didn't hurt me. I still like the satisfaction of accomplishment.

Off to our (in winter) cold beds, we soon warmed up for a good winter sleep.

Very seldom were we sick. To this day (I'm 60), no one in our family had a broken bone or severe sickness.

How wonderfully blessed we were and are. We had a cold house and wore lots of clothes to keep warm. The fire in the stove in the kitchen didn't last all night, so if water was sitting on the round granite hand wash dish, it was frozen ice by morning, as we kept the door shut to the living room. But the living room and Mom and Dad's bedroom part of the house had a basement underneath and also that stove in the living room kept fire all night. The fire box was large. It would take several big chunks of wood plus coal. The kitchen stove had only a very narrow little fire box.

When doing any homework, etc, our pet parakeet (Chipper was often let out of his cage) would love to sit on our pencils, nibble on the erasers, or chomp on our paper corners. He loved to sit on Dad's hand at mealtime to nibble on a piece of buttered bread. He'd fly to the mirror above the wash basin to look in the mirror, then rub his beak on the mirror. Dad's hair was thin over the top. It didn't feel very good when Chipper would sit there and peck at his bald spot. He'd sit on our heads and get tangled in our hair. Then back to his cage he'd go. Sitting there, he'd jabber away besides saying, "Chipper pretty bird!" We really liked him. He died after flying onto a curtain and getting his claws caught and twisted and broke a leg. We buried him in a matches box lined with toilet paper out in the orchard.

We had several cats buried there too. Sometimes it happened in summertime when Dad mowed the hay he mowed into a cat accidentally that was out hiding to catch a field mouse or such, cutting off legs, etc. Oh my, the cat had to be put down. So we buried them there too.

We loved our cats. One kitty was sick. My brother and I gave it Pepto Bismol for its stomach and baby aspirin. It survived to be quite old.

Dad made a livestock rack for on top of my brother's tin toy truck. He had lots of fun stuffing as many cats, usually young ones, into it that he could, their tails sticking out between the slats. Such a sight! Then he'd push or pull them around the barn, letting them out, they ran every which way. But they would come again to play.

Finding a new nest of baby kitties in the hay somewhere was always exciting. But Dad said more cats than cattle is no good. You can believe we hardly ever had any mice or rats around with all the animal feed and grain stored in the barn.

Oh, such was just part of my memories of our childhood, besides good times of wading in the creek, roaming around our rocks and caves instead of canes, playing cowboys and Indians with neighbor children. Good old days!

Feeding the Multitudes and Daily Chores

by Jim and Gwen Young of Somerset, Ohio

Gwen born in 1922 and Jim in 1920

George Gordon Young (1898-1989) was born in Fairfield County. The home site is now part of the Rushcreek Conservancy District and all that remains is a stub of the well casing, covered with rocks. In 1900 his sister Elizabeth Frances was born in the nearby two story Winegardner brick, where the Ralph Young families now reside.

Both children were baptized in Holy Trinity Church in Somerset. When Gordon was quite young the family moved to the Wagner farm north of Somerset and to the adjoining Doctor McKinney farm in 1905. Gordon often said he was "just a little shaver" when he helped drive the cattle from the Fairfield County farm to the Perry County farm.

Double wedding June 17, 1919. Kitty Kullman, flower girl, Joseph J. Kullman, Elizabeth Frances Young, Fr. McKinney, Ida Loretta Sterner, George Gordon Young, Francie Gordon, cousin and flower girl.

Ida Loretta Sterner (1899-1978) married Gordon Young, and his sister Elizabeth married Joseph Kullman in a double wedding ceremony in 1919. Both couples set up housekeeping in the old farm house (which predates 1829) until Aunt Elizabeth and Uncle Joe moved into Somerset.

Ida was well organized: wash on Monday, iron on Tuesday, mend on Wednesday - every little worn spot. Every day; three big meals. "Set the table first," she'd tell me. "When they come in from the field and see the table set, they think the food *is* ready." Next; peel and put the potatoes on, run to the basement for a jar of cold packed beef or out to the smoke house for a link of smoked sausage. She usually had a live-in high school girl to help: a Smith, Hillis, or Egan.

Her first washing machine had a wooden tub with a wooden paddle/agitator in the center driven by a hand operated mechanism connected by a long handle along the side. Someone would pump it up and down like a water pump. Gears meshed with a gear on a horizontal shaft across the top of the machine to another gear on the end of the agitator, which caused it to go back and forth, swishing clothes through water made hot over an outside fire and sudsy by chipping bits of her homemade lye soap from a big bar.

Clothes were hung outside or spread over shrubs to freeze stiff or dry in sun and wind. Her son Jim remembers that red-letter day when the Maytag washing machine arrived, with its gasoline engine, a metal frame and wheels and a wringer you didn't have to turn by hand!

The stiffly starched shirts and rough huck towels were folded or sprinkled and rolled tightly, to be ready for Tuesday - ironing day.

First, a fire had to be built in the kitchen stove to heat the flat irons. Since the stove was heated; might as well bake bread. A table board covered with a blanket and sheet served as an ironing board; to press aprons, blouses, shirts - a long, long day.

Wednesday was mending day. Every little hole in every sock was darned, worn shirt collars were turned and pants were patched. If time allowed and there was a pretty flower printed flour sack to spare, Ida would make an apron on her treadle sewing machine. This apron would be the first apron to protect her housedress. An older second apron would go over this one; to go to the garden or help with the milking. Should someone drive up the driveway, that older apron would be whipped off and hung behind the basement door before she smiled at the guests walking through the gate.

Thursday was reserved for baking all those tasty things she would serve for the weekend guests who might "pop in," or with the "Sunday afternoon" ice cream made in big old freezer Sarah Jane Young had bought at a farm sale. (That freezer is still used on the farm by her great-grandson.) The dining table would be spread with sheets of thin-rolled noodle dough, drying enough to be sliced into narrow strips, and bread would rise in three gallon crockery bowls. Pies, cakes, cookies and next week's supply of granola for the boy's breakfast were baking, while smearcase hung outside under the grape arbor, the whey dripping from a muslin sack into a bucket, which would go to the pigs. Later, Ida would break up the cheese curds and mix them with sweet cream and a handful of salt.

Saturday was busy getting the cream, eggs and butter ready to be sold to the Creamery in town. The money would be used at the L.J. Bever Grocery Store for sugar, raisins, cinnamon, a round of cheese and bananas, if the price was right. Flour was purchased only after their own wheat, corn and buckwheat, milled in Fultonham, was depleted. The square in Somerset was crowded on Saturday evenings when all the farm families came to town and the teenagers walked round and around the square, considering one another. Lucky the boy who had a dime, and could buy two single dip ice cream cones for himself and his girlfriend, at Hatem's Confectionery.

The Sterner families would gather at Grandmother Samantha Decot Sterner's parlor, where "Mandy", short and definitely round, presided. The husbands usually were "having one with the boys" at the bar, or playing euchre in the kitchen. About 9:00 P.M. parents would gather up the children who had fallen asleep on the floor in some untrammeled corner and head for the farm. After all, tomorrow was Mass at Holy Trinity, and milking had to be done early.

In the spring a border had to be hand dug around the garden fence so the sweet peas could get started early, and some onions, radishes and lettuce. Dandelions were considered a necessary spring tonic, wilted with a vinegar\bacon dressing and hard cooked eggs. The roots and flowers were made into dandelion wine. After threat of frost, the real garden was plowed with the horses. There would be peas here too, timed to ripen at the same time little new potatoes could be dug, and served creamed together. Many varieties of beans, beets, salsify, carrots, parsnips, celery, turnips, cabbage and tomatoes flourished in her manure enriched soil. Summer was time for preserving and canning. Many root vegetables were left in the ground to be dug as needed. In the old basement with the hand adzed rafters there were thirty gallon crocks of sauerkraut, shelves of fruits and vegetables, like jewels in the Mason jars. Barrels of cider vinegar and small crocks of eggs preserved in water-glass for the times when the chickens were molting and stopped laying. Sometimes, a pit was dug in the garden, lined with straw and cabbage not stomped into sauerkraut, the apples, turnips and other edible roots were covered with straw and mounded over with dirt, to be opened when the basement supply of foods was depleted in late winter.

Ida used to say she could "feed the multitudes, like Jesus Christ'" and indeed she could, on a moment's notice.

She had often repeated adages: "I feel do-less today." "Offer it up." "It will be a jewel in your crown in heaven." She was big on martyrdom. Ida was always working in motion. If you were sitting still, reading or doing paper work; you weren't working. She and Gordon, an avid reader, had some problems here. I am convinced that the reason all the men in the family took so long in the bathroom was because that was the only place in the house they could read in peace.

During the Depression, Ida's teenaged brothers lived at the farm; working and teasing their young nephews, Jim and John. Fabian, who was sterilizing quart canning crocks in hot water over an open fire, talked Jim into watching them boil; "until they boil down to pints." Austin had the boys help him clear a pasture area of hickory sprouts and rocks. This was Austin's way of repaying Grandfather who had paid a fine the teen had incurred.

Many other relatives found the farm a welcome refuge. Cousin Robert Gordon came for Easter dinner and stayed ten weeks. Uncle Theodore Bishop often came when there was work to be done. He was a tall, raw-boned man who wore a toupee over his bald pate. When dirty work like threshing was to be done he carried the toupee in his pocket.

When the dinner bell called the men from the field, each washed; pumping water from the well into the washbasin and lathering with Ida's bar of lye soap. Once clean, Uncle Theodore retrieved his toupee from the pocket and placed it upon his bald head - not always straight. Then he'd put his chaw of tobacco on a fence post to be retrieved and rechawed after dinner. Ida called Uncle Theodore a "prodigious eater." Often, when the pie came around and he still had a plate piled high with second and third helpings, he'd say, "Better take it now, it might not come around again." Then he'd lift a slice of pie onto the top of the mound on his plate and keep right on devouring! One time John swiped his chaw of tobacco from the fence post and replaced it with a little pile of chicken manure!

Jim (now 89) remembers graduating from "kid" to "crew member" when they needed someone to sit on top of the threshing machine, or separator, to operate the blower, which was a long pipe that would move up and down, or go 45 degrees to the right or left and the straw would blow out on the straw pile. Usually one or two men with pitchforks would move the straw to the outside edge, shaping the pile. You had to be careful not to shoot the stream of straw at the men.

The straw shed was of pole construction, eight to ten feet high, with poles closely placed on top. As the straw piled up, the straw stack was just built up over the top of it. In winter, it made a cozy protected area for the livestock. They could nibble at the straw and get some grain. The straw was pulled from the pile with a straw fork, which was like a pitchfork with tines turned 90 degrees. It was rolled into a doodle and carried in to bed the livestock in the barn. By spring there was a 150 foot circle of tramped down manure and straw to be pitched by hand into a horse-drawn manure spreader and spread over the cropland—a week's work for four or five kids.

Coal Chutes and Burning Leaves

by Joanne Mathias of Dover, Ohio

Having just celebrating my 75th birthday, looking back seems like yesterday. My father passed away at the age of 26 leaving my mother with three children, all under the age of four.

At that time (June of 1936) there was no Social Security and the small amount of aide to dependent children was not adequate enough to support us. My mother moved us into Grandma's house. Mother worked at Uncle Walter Rinehart's grocery store, just a block away from home.

We had no big supermarkets. Mom and pop grocery stores were scattered throughout the town. Some of them would have free delivery. We called our order in and then it would be delivered.

This was a time not long after the Depression and

many people were used to less of everything. I can remember my grandma canning everything in fruit jars and we kept them in the basement "fruit cellar."

Most everyone had a coal furnace. Mr. George Ripple supplied us with coal from his big two ton truck. The coal was emptied into our coal cellar from a big metal chute attached to the back of his tipped truck bed. In the winter, you would see smoke coming from everyone's chimney. Where the soot from the smoke settled on freshly fallen snow, the wind would make it swirl like a whirlpool.

In the fall, everyone would rake their leaves to the side of the road and burn them. Most roads were made of brick then. Not many were paved like they are today. Not everyone had a car back then. Most people walked or rode a bike to where they were going.

We had a refrigerator, but some folks still depended on the iceman to deliver ice. We children would sneak up to the back of the truck to grab a chunk of ice when the iceman disappeared into the house with his big chunk of ice suspended from the big ice tongs.

About everyone had a "victory garden" and would put them up for the winter, meaning they would can the vegetables.

For a time, I went to stay with relatives in Cleveland and went to school there for awhile. The school was Benjamin Franklin School on Spring Road. It was the first school in America that had a garden patch for groups of children. We helped rake and plant and care for the garden and later after school was dismissed for the summer, we went back and each child was given a portion of the harvest.

We didn't have a phone at Grandma's, but in Cleveland, at my Aunt and Uncle's, we had one. I can still remember the number, Florida 5622.

Sometimes we got milk and eggs and live chickens from a nearby farm. Grandma would take the chicken to the coal cellar, chop off its head and hang it by its feet upside down to drain the blood. Later she would douse it up and down in a bucket of boiling water. This allowed her to pick the feathers out faster and cleaner. To this day, I cannot bear the aroma of wonton soup!

Along came the war. We were united! Everyone did their part. At school we would buy stamps each week and stick them in a book. When the book got full, we traded it into a war bond. This was for the war effort.

Because of the war, there were things that we learned to live without. No nylon or silk stockings, silk was used to make parachutes. We saved tin cans. We had to open both ends with a can opener, remove the paper label, and stomp on them to flatten them.

Many things were rationed. Gas, sugar, tires, shoes, and meat were just a few. We had no car, so my mom traded gas and tire coupons for sugar and shoe coupons.

Butter was a premium. We remember getting oleo—a pure white slab with a yellow color packet or color pill that we would knead until it resembled butter.

I remember one embarrassing moment that took place at Second Street School in Dover. I was in the third grade. I asked the teacher if I may be excused to go to the restroom. This was a large room in the basement with about ten stalls back to back. Since there was no rubber for elastic for my panties, we had buttons or string ties instead. Mine was the button variety. I lost a button while unfastening and could not leave and go to class because my pants would fall down. When one toilet flushed, they all flushed automatically and it scared the bijiggers out of me. You can imagine the noise because of the acoustics. I stood there with my panties draped around my ankles, crying. My teacher finally came looking for me and gave me a safety pin.

Mostly as children, we played in our own yards or in our own neighborhoods. We played kick the can and hide and seek. Sometimes we sat on the lawn and would count a certain color of cars as they drove by. We did a lot of pretending in those days and used our imagination. Today everything is in the full color and laid out for them.

We had radio, but no TV. I can hear that creaky door closing on the radio program, called "Inner Sanctum." I could actually see, in my mind, the dust from the Lone Rangers horse as he rode away yelling, "Hi Ho Silver!"

I remember sitting on the front porch waiting for the ice cream man to come. He pedaled a bike with two wheels in front and one in the back. Up front there was a big cooler box full of popsicles and ice cream happy bars.

Another thing I remember is gas station giveaways, dishes tucked into boxes of soap powder, bank night at the movie theaters. A blue light was lit at a street intersection above the traffic light to call the police to the station when a call came in.

People would drive downtown and park their cars and walk home, so that later, they could come back and sit in their cars and watch the people walk down the very busy sidewalks on a Saturday night.

A loaf of bread was a nickel, so was a candy bar and one dip of ice cream. Cigarettes were 18 cents a pack and when you put two dimes in a cigarette vending machine, there would be two pennies inside the cellophane wrapper. Milk was delivered to homes, as was bread and coffee, if you wished.

When you heard a loud voice holler "Rag Man!" you would give your old rags to him and he'd throw them into the back of his old pickup truck. I still don't know what he did with them, except use them for the war effort.

In the warm months you could see children skating on the sidewalks. These skates fit on your shoes and were tightened with a skate key.

In the winter, we ice skated on the canal. The big boys would build a fire in a large oil drum and laid logs near the fire so we could warm our hands and feet. The boys played hockey.

We all read "Funny Books." Spiderman, Superman, and Batman were a few.

During the war, we had blackouts. A siren would alert everyone to pull down their shades and turn out their lights, and outen their fires; anything that an enemy flying over our head could see. A man with an armband came around to make sure that we did what we were supposed to do in this case.

Many women worked at men's jobs during the war. My mom was an inspector on a line that made ammunition buckets at Reeves Mill. This mill previously made spouting and garbage cans.

You could walk down the street and see, in the windows of folks, flags that designated that from that family there were servicemen. A husband or brother or son, there was a star for each one of them.

In those days, doctors made house calls, most babies were born at home. Tonsils were removed in the doctor's office.

When a couple got married, the neighbor kids would gather together and have an old fashioned "belling." The kids would find anything that made a noise, rocks in a can, two lids banged together, anything that made a racket. Then they would sneak up to the house after dark and make lots of noise until the newlyweds acknowledged them. Hopefully, they would hand out candy to us.

Most funerals were held in the deceased's home. A large wreath would be placed on the front door and the body would be in a casket placed in the living room. People would visit at will. As a child, we were told to keep quiet during this time to show respect.

At Halloween, we would dress up mostly like hobos. We would use burned cork to darken our faces. We would wear old tattered clothing. We usually stayed in our own neighborhood. We would knock on the door and the homeowner was expected to guess who we were before handing out the goodies.

The Springhouse Dunking, the Tornado and Romance

by Esther Mae Hufford Conkey Blanks
of Strasburg, Ohio
born 1930

When I was just over four years old, my parents moved from Hamden, Ohio to my mother's parents' farm in Copley, Ohio—not too far from Akron, Ohio. It was a long move back in those days. I really do not remember much about the move except I had to leave my best friend.

We even got into a "big fuss" over some soap flakes my mom gave us to use for snow on whatever we were making in the sandbox. I guess each of us felt the other got more.

It was a small 33 acre farm, but had chickens and cats running around. There were some barns and a long shed. There were a few cows and two work horses. It was a lot more space to play in than I had ever had before.

Not long after we moved, I went into the spring house where there was water in a tank for cooling the milk in the cans until they were picked up each day. The water came down from the back of the farm; was piped into the spring house and also into a tank in the cellar of the house. A pitcher pump was in the kitchen and water could be pumped into a sink there.

I went into the spring house for some reason; I think I must have dropped something into the tank, and so when I reached for it, I fell head first into the tank. Don't ask me how, but I think there was a guardian angel, because I turned myself right side up and got out dripping wet from head-to-toe.

I came to my mom and said, "I drowned in the tank." I didn't realize my mom was soon going to have my brother (those things weren't discussed a lot back then), and that might be why she was so upset when she saw me that way. I do not remember any punishment, but think she dried me up, and we went to bed a while—maybe my scare was enough punishment!

So one afternoon, it was decided I should spend the night with the neighbor girl, who was quite a bit older than I was, but she had some books I just loved to look at—Raggedy Ann and Raggedy Andy. When my dad came after me the next morning, he said there was a surprise for me. Yes, it was a baby brother who had been born right in the farmhouse. The doctor came right to the house. That was in September, 1934.

I had been born in that same room while my mother was visiting her parents back in January of 1930. They said that night was a cold, snowy night and the doctor read poetry while he waited for me to be born.

As my brother, Alvin, got older, he and I played all sorts of imaginary games together—Jack Armstrong and Orphan Annie adventures, taking on characters of all sorts and making the farmyard and the barnyard part of our imaginary life.

When our dad moved some small chicken coops away—likely because of the new brooder house—it left rectangular-shaped areas with no grass, so we decided to play "funeral." I made my brother lie down on the plot and we had a little "service" over him.

When they started having "black-out air raids" due to the war, my dad took training and became an Air Raid Warden. So he got a bicycle to ride when he had to go out checking to see if all lights were out. Thank God we never had any bombs fall on us, and finally the bicycle became our vehicle of travel in our imaginary games.

Esther Blanks' brother, Alvin, and his pet chicken on the back steps of the Copley Farmhouse.

Learning to ride a bike was one of my hard times. I would start at the top of the grade and then fall down when I got to the bottom. It was a man-size boy's bike but I finally learned how [to ride], and it was one of the most favorite things I did.

My dad had bought a brooder house to get some "peeps" and raise more chickens. Later we cleaned it up and it was a delightful "play house" for more imagination.

In our house, we had no bathroom, so on Saturday night we took baths in a big, galvanized, round tub. Water had to be heated on the kitchen range. The kitchen was off-limits for a while, as one after the other took their turns. Being the youngest, I got to be first. Some of the family took "sponge baths" instead of getting in the tub.

One year when our church in Akron, which was about 10 miles away, had Vacation Bible School, I was invited to stay with my best girlfriend from church. Another girl found out and wanted a turn also. So I stayed a week with each one. Their families had nice things and bathrooms in their homes. The second girl I stayed with decided she wanted to come out to our farm and stay overnight. Then she wanted her nightly bath, so we got out the "old tin tub" and she got to take her bath country style. I wonder what she really thought about that experience.

When I was about 11 or 12 years old, my other grandfather got very ill. So my dad went to see him. Whatever he had caused him to die. Our car was an old, maybe 1930 or so, square-shaped Chevy and usually had at least a couple flat tires when we made long trips. So my uncle, who had a new Ford (a 1941 I believe), had my dad drive that up to get our family for the funeral. The trip was about 180 miles and took the greater part of a day when going by car back in those days.

One thing I did not mention, which was a very big part of every summer, was the going to camp meeting starting as a child. That is where I decided to allow Jesus to come into my life. I started going when I was about seven years old; went through the youth plan; was courted by my husband to be there; and we were the Youth Director and Registrar. I am one of the third generations to attend and have three more generations following me. Today I am their historian and have compiled many pages of memorials and memories from over those years.

A turning point in my life. It was 1943. I was 13 years old. It was April. My brother says it was March. Almost 9:15.

Suddenly as we were preparing to go to bed for the night, a storm came up. Rain! Lightning! I decided to leave the bed between two windows and get in my mom's bed. My dad was at work. He was a janitor in the school about half a mile away.

Then like a big BLAST! Windows were breaking, plaster was crumbling, rain was beating in even through some outside walls, doors were coming open that we never used. Lightning flashed and I got a glimpse of my grandmother fighting the window shade at her bedroom window. My brother crawled under the bed!

It lasted maybe 5 minutes. We went downstairs and found my grandpa trying to hold up the refrigerator which a door had pushed off its leveling boards because the wind had pushed open this door we never used. The old wallpaper was hanging in strips all over; windows were broken in every room except the dining room. So that's where we spent the night! The clock had stopped at 9:15 and never ran again.

Grandpa walked up to the school to get my dad. All power was out in the area, but the tornado itself made a path that did not go where the school was. Dad and Grandpa came home when Dad found out what had happened.

The barns were flat. The horses were not hurt as the walls and debris just fell around them. The cows were out of the barn running in the field with the stanchions around their necks. A calf was loose, but they found it and tied it up in the basement of the house (which, by the way, worried me all night—I was afraid it would pull something down and cause further problems).

The corn crib had been shifted, but the bike was still standing up inside. The brooder house had also shifted, but the young chicks were not hurt.

Tornadoes are very strange things! One room had things scattered everywhere, some of it in other rooms, but an Easter lily remained standing in place in the next room without any damage. At the neighbor's house, a board flew through the upstairs window and went down the hall and out another window on the other end of the house.

Some of the neighbor's cattle had to be butchered right away as they had been killed during the tornado, so my dad and grandpa went over there to help them with the butchering.

I don't know if anyone was killed that were in the path of the storm, but our house had so much damage, we bought a small house in the village almost across from the school. We went from 11 rooms to a 5 room house. Our old house was torn down and some of the property where it had been was sold to a man who built a furniture store.

It was a drastic change in our lives. I feared winds for a long time. But I liked the new house and especially the location. I felt more connected to other people

We lost a lot of things—some would have been antiques—stored in a place where rodents and dampness ruined them and some were lost in the storm, but we all survived and still had a good family relationship through it all, even in a three-generation home. We were just happy that we were safe, and we knew God took care of us that night and gave us a new place to live in just a few days!

A true love story. The father of my children passed away suddenly and I was alone. I missed him so much, but had my teaching job and that helped. My children tried to come and see me once in a while. The boys sort of took turns seeing to things that needed cared for. But I was still lonely.

About 2 years later, I decided to go to our school class reunion. I tried to get someone to go with me but without success. I had to drive quite a ways, so I left early and was the first one to get there. Soon another classmate came, but I couldn't recognize him as it had been about 30 years or so since I had seen him. He told me he was Bob Blanks. So we talked and he found out I was a widow.

Our class only had about 55 in it, so we all knew each other, but I had never dated anyone in the class. I had married Jim, from our church. I found out Bob had married right out of high school.

A few months later, on a Saturday afternoon, I found a man standing at my door and remembered seeing him, but thought it must be someone who had asked me to vote for him. He had to tell me he was Bob Blanks. He had called another class member to get my married name and address and decided to come and see me as his wife had passed away with cancer.

Bob and I had a nice visit after coming back from the restaurant. I lived in Dellroy, Ohio and he lived in Akron, Ohio. It was a 50 mile trip each way. He kept coming down to see me about 4 times a week after work. We had a very exciting courtship and my co-workers all said I looked 10 years younger.

My children and his children didn't know what to think. None of his children had ever heard of me and none of mine had ever heard of him. The phones were ringing in California and various parts of Ohio as my 6 children and his 3 kept calling back and forth. My boys accepted Bob pretty fast, but my daughter was reluctant, so I invited her to meet me and have lunch and shared my loneliness and how I felt about the new relationship. She said, "But mom, you were always so level headed!"

Finally we set a date to get married. Bob said he was wearing his truck out driving it so far so often. He had gotten me a diamond. Bob sent his daughters money to fly home for the wedding, and on the way, they said, "Now if we don't like this lady, we WILL stop this wedding one way or other!" Bob took me to see them and I passed inspection!

My son-in-law (Charles Nutt) performed the ceremony and he and my daughter (Beth) sang. A son (Joel) sang. The oldest son (Dan) gave me away. Two sons (Steve and Jesse) were ushers and took pictures. We had invited our classmates and at least 16 came to the wedding. My mother-in-law from my first marriage came and sat in the place of my mother since mine had passed away.

It was near Easter so the church had many Easter lilies. We were married in Akron, OH where my son went to church. My daughter and daughters-in-law took care of a reception afterwards. It was a wonderful day!

Bob was a good husband. We both soon retired and traveled in a camper, then bought a motor home. God was so good to us and gave us 11 and a half wonderful years. Bob got cancer and died before the year was up after the diagnosis. He was a good patient through his illness.

His family are so great to me. They keep in touch. They call, e-mail, send cards and flowers, and say they feel like they have known me all their lives. They say those days Bob and I had were some of the happiest days their dad ever had!

Oil Lamps and a Day Late Newspaper

by Wilma Thompson of Belmont, Ohio
born 1926

I was born May 1, 1926 south of Bethesda, in our farmhouse, daughter of Frank and Mary Schafer. There were five children. Warren Schafer, Margaret Schafer Perkins, and Jack Shafer, they are deceased. My brother Paul Schafer and I are the only ones left. We were poor moneywise, but rich in so many other ways.

Went through the Depression, never went hungry, but how could we when our parents raised a big garden? Mom canned hundreds of fruits and vegetables. Of course, we all helped snap beans, shelled peas etc. Picked blackberries and raspberries and watched for blacksnakes the whole time. We also had a big orchard with apples, pears, and cherry trees.

I remember we had a persimmon tree and my brother Jack would tell me how good they were, then he would give me one that wasn't ripe. Terrible taste, but they were good if they were ripe. Never hear of those trees anymore, but maybe there are some.

I remember the big crocks of sauerkraut in the cellar, keg of cider that would eventually turn to vinegar. There were also bins of apples and potatoes in that dirt floor cellar.

My sister helped Mom in the house, but I was seven years younger than her and I liked to help outdoors. I helped in the hay field. We made hay shocks and built haystacks. No tractors, just the farm horses.

Dad's income was mostly the once a month milk check. Of course we milked cows, cleaned the stables, threw down the hay from the haymow. My two older brothers were still home, so I helped more after they left home. By that time, my brother Paul was big enough to help.

We raised chickens and turkeys so we had our own eggs. Nothing tasted better than my mom's chicken and homemade noodles.

On Saturday, it was a trip to Bethesda or Barnesville for flour, sugar, whatever was needed that we couldn't raise. And we would stop at Woods Dairy in Bethesda and for five cents we got two or three dips of the best ice cream you ever ate.

When it came butchering time, the neighbors came to help, and then Dad and the boys would go help them. We had a smokehouse where Dad seasoned the hams and side meat, then it was hung from the ceiling to keep the four-legged creatures from getting to it. We needed ham slices they would take a sharp butcher knife and cut off what was needed. Sometimes there would be some green mold, but it was cut off and thrown away. Today they would tell us that it would give us food poisoning. Must not have been too unhealthy, as we all lived to be in our 80s, only my brother is 75.

On Saturday evening, Dad would go to the M&K store in Bethesda and get a small basket of bananas for 25 cents. What a treat for us kids! The store wanted to get rid of them before the weekend.

No electricity, no telephone, did all our reading and studying by kerosene lamps. In later years we did get a battery-operated radio, listened to Amos and Andy, Fibber McGee and Molly, Only The Shadow Knows, Jack Benny...those are the ones I remember.

We did get a newspaper, which was always a day late. It came with the daily mail.

We had no inside plumbing, so going down the path in zero weather was something to remember. Every morning the chamber pot was taken out and washed thoroughly. I remember the wash tub baths, but not just on Saturdays, we needed it more often than that.

The E. P. A. would have had us arrested. We had a large coal burning heater in our living room which sat on a big asbestos board, and the mantle behind the stove was protected by a large piece of asbestos.

We had a beautiful collie dog called "Hoover." He was so smart. When he would hear my dad getting up in the morning, he would have the cows at the barn by the time Dad got there. It was a sad time when we had him put to sleep, 18 years old.

We made our own entertainment. Mom played the piano so we sang a lot. We also played a lot of games: dominoes, checkers, cards, etc. We were taught no cheating and no anger when we lost.

We went to the Methodist Church at Mt. Horeb every Sunday where Mom played the old pedal organ. I remember Dad would give us two or three pennies for Sunday school. Across from the church was the one room Mt. Horeb school, which we walked two miles to go to. I went three years there and then my older siblings went to high school so we were transferred to another school and my brother and I could ride the school bus.

Mom had an old wringer washer for years until she bought a Maytag with a gasoline motor, then later, when we moved to Bethesda, and she had an electric motor put on it. She also made lye soap, but I forget how she made it.

When we cleaned the house in the spring everything was taken outdoors. The carpets and feather ticks were thrown over the clothesline and then we kids beat them with a rug beater. We would run in between the feathered tick and one of the others would try to hit that one.

No TV. After Dad would do the plowing, the ground had to be gotten ready for planting, so he had to use a drag and I loved to ride on it. I loved to walk in my bare feet on the soft ground. We liked to ride in the back of the wagon when they hauled in the corn. Then there was threshing time and silo filling time. Neighbors helping neighbors. We kids loved it as we got to go after school wherever they were threshing that day. The men ate first, and then the women and children ate. I can remember when they were at our house. Mom would have our pantry shelves lined with pies. All kinds, but lots of pumpkin.

Mom made all of her clothes and mine and my sister's. She made all the comforters and quilts. She was a beautiful quilter and I still have and use a lot of her quilts.

I got my first store-bought coat when I was a freshman in high school.

The old farmhouse was pretty cold in the winter and there was snow on the windowsills many times.

We had our usual childhood diseases. One year the flu was really bad, but we survived with all the home remedies, especially Watkins Liniment. A Mr. Rine was a salesman for Watkins and Mom got her vanilla and other flavorings from him. I don't remember how often he came, but I remember how nice he was.

I think probably the worst time in our lives was when my two older brothers went to World War II, but they came back safely.

We left the farm in 1944, the same year I graduated from high school. Everything is gone now, the barn fell in years ago and the house later. It was a good life and I thank the good Lord every day for our growing up years and at 82, my mind is still good enough to write this.

I know I missed some things: the old windup Victrola; lying in the yard at night finding the Big Dipper; and catching lightening bugs.

Forgot to mention our refrigeration, which was a spring house down over a little hill from the house. That was where Dad cooled the milk. Ten gallon milk cans, plus our butter and anything that had to be kept cool, was taken down there and we had to go get it for the next meal. There was always an argument between us kids about whose turn it was to go. That spring water was so good.

Mid Century Occupations

by Donald Valentine of Senecaville, Ohio
born in 1937

My name is Don Valentine. I am 71 years old and was born in 1937. I was raised in Cambridge, Ohio in the fairground addition. Listed are some of the fun things we did as kids in the late 40s and early 50s.

Bicycle tag: A group of boys would ride two on a bike, one on the handlebars, and chase each other all over town. You had to tag the boy on the handlebars to make them "it." This game could last for hours.

Running around the block: A group of us would jog around a city block and count the number of times we completed a full round. The boy who completed the most rounds was the winner.

Kick the can: This game consisted of nothing more than kicking a can down the street while running.

Pinning down horns: In the 40s and early 50s most cars had a horn button in the center of the steering wheel. At night we would sneak up to a car and put a matchstick in the crack around the horn. This would hold the button down and the horn would blow until someone removed the matchstick.

Trick or treat was much different in our day. We would knock on the door and the homeowner would ask us in and try to guess who we were. If they guessed, they did not have to give you candy, but they always did. This guessing was possible because we would trick or treat our own neighborhood, and back then everyone knew all the kids in the neighborhood. If no one answered the door, we would soap their windows.

Saturday was a movie day at the Strand Theater. Two cowboy shows and a continuing serial for 11 cents. This was a lot of money for us boys, so we would walk up and down Wheeling Avenue removing pennies from parking meters until we had 11 cents. Money was tight for everyone back then so a lot of people would only place the penny half way in the parking meter, and if a cop came by, he would push it all the way in, but if the penny was still there when they returned, they would remove it.

In the early 50s motorbikes were the newest fad. These bikes were very unreliable and we worked on them every day to keep them running. You had to push them fast to start them. We lived on the south side of town and to get to Wheeling Avenue, there was a long steep hill called 9th Street Hill (now Southgate Bridge). This was our testing grounds for a motorbike. If your bike could climb this hill with you on it, your bike was better than most.

Air raid warning: In the 40s with the war on, I remember when the air raid siren sounded, all lights in the town were turned off. This was so if an enemy bomber was near, they could not locate the town. Each neighborhood had an air raid warden who would walk the streets for violators of the lights out law.

Car washing: To earn spending money in 1950-1951, I washed cars at a service station on Saturdays. A typical carwash consisted of sweeping and cleaning the inside, including emptying the ashtrays, washing the car and under all four fenders, chammy the car and all windows inside and out, painting black tar-like liquid on the tires, running boards, and floor boards. Each car took about one hour. I got paid 50 cents for each car. If I worked fast, I could make $4.50 a day. This would last me all week.

A Nude Sally and the Callaway Band

by Verna Maurer of Bolivar, Ohio
born 1911

Otto Maurer and I were married in August, 1940.

I was working at the telephone office in Bolivar for Emma Thompson, Dorothy Birk's mother. Often, after my shift that ended at 8 p.m., I would go to the Marburger Grocery and Confectionary store. Peg Marburger was a good friend of mine. She came with double dip ice cream cones when I had my accident in 1928.

In 1933, Peg and Ruth Ross planned a trip to Chicago, Illinois. Peg often mentioned to me that I should go with them, but I never took it seriously. One evening, after work, Peg said, "We are leaving in the morning, can't you go?" The wheels in my head began to turn. I went to the telephone office and asked Mrs. Thompson if I could leave for ten days. She said, "Yes, if your dad says so." I went home and asked Mom and Dad, and he said, "If you spend your own money." This was about 9 p.m. by now.

By 4:00 the next morning, I was on my way to Chicago. There was enough money in the house for me. Ruth Ross was driving Marburger's Essex car. Eight hours later, we were in Chicago. Every time we filled the gas tank, we put in a quart of oil in the motor. Ruth went to visit relatives, but spent some days with Peg and I at the fair. Peg and I had a room near the fair area.

Sally Rand, nude with her ostrich feather fan, was a big attraction. The Cab Callaway band was another. This was a trip I will always remember.

At the end of my Bolivar High School junior year, in Bolivar Ohio, 1928, I started working for the American Telephone Company in Bolivar, for Emma Thompson. I lived with my parents, Albert and Edna Zimmerman, in a farm at the edge of Bolivar.

I worked for Emma Thompson for five years, and then received her job. I stayed till 1943.

The Bread Drawer Nap and the Lost Shirley

By Clara C. Shriver of Beallsville, Ohio
Born 1931

My name is Credella Clark Shriver. I was born in Martins Ferry, Ohio on March 19, 1931. I am the third born of 12 children to Eugene and Mabel Clark. My oldest sister, Mamie Paul Lykins, was born December 26, 1923. My older brother, George Robert, was born September 2, 1928.

My earliest memory is when we lived in Barnesville, Ohio on Dutch Ridge, now known as Wiley Avenue. My dad, Eugene, granddad, George W. and my Uncle Earle built our house.

Our closest neighbor was the George Hines family. We kids use to gather at their house to play Hide and Seek. Once I remember going to their shop and locking the door so no one would find me. Then I couldn't get the door unlocked. Eventually my mom heard me crying. They had to remove a window to get me out.

One day a neighborhood girl was at our house visiting. I was playing in the front yard. I don't remember what the conversation was about, but for some reason I called her an "SOB." I had no idea that that was a bad thing to say, but I soon found out. My mother rubbed a bar of yellow Octagon soap in my mouth. I remember sitting on the bank crying and spitting bubbles as my best friend, Beverly Johnson, comforted me. Sadly, before Beverly turned ten, she died of "sleeping sickness."

Florence Wilson lived up the street from us. She would take hollyhocks, a beautiful pink, yellow or red flower, and turn them upside down in a saucer of water. They appeared as though they were pretty fairies dancing in a ball gown.

The Pittman's lived down the street from us. On Sunday they would pick us up to go to church at the West Main Street Church of Christ. The car, as I remember, had isinglass (plastic) windows and snaps to fasten them shut.

My brother Russell was born in Barnesville on June 25th, 1932. My sister Mamie was sent to get the doctor in the middle of the night. Mom said by the time he arrived Russell was born. Dr. Modie cut the cord and charged Dad $35.00. (So I was told.)

My sister Elizabeth was born in Barnesville on June 12th, 1934. She was named after Grandma Hines. In 1934 or 35, when I was three or four, Mamie took me to see the first streamliner train that passed through Barnesville. It was so big, so shiny and so fast. I was impressed!

It was 1935 and times were hard. Dad was unemployed. He would leave on Sunday evening to go to my Grandma Clark's house in West Wheeling, Ohio. He would stay there all week collecting "junk" (anything made of iron, steel, copper or brass) to sell to the local junkyard in order to return home on Friday with groceries that he'd buy from the sell. Sometimes he would bring cream cheese. It was for all of us, but I was certain he bought it especially for me.

My brother Charles Phillip was born in Barnesville, on March 3, 1936. He was the biggest baby for my mom, weighing in at 13 pounds and unknown ounces.

Later that year, we moved to Neffs. My dad, mom and six kids. Dad loaded the bed of the truck with all our belongings. Two big chairs were set on the back to hold all of us kids. I swear we must have looked like the Beverly Hillbillies going down the road.

When I started 1st grade we walked 2.5 miles one way. We would start the year off with a new pair of shoes and they had to last till the end of the year. Summertime we went barefoot.

Mom would make me dresses from her old ones, sometimes with no pattern. (That must have been what is now called re-cycling.)

My mom baked all our bread using 75 pounds of flour every two weeks. Twenty loaves at a time wasn't unusual. She would "air" out the bread drawer, outside, before the next batch would be made.

One particular day my oldest brother, Robert, disappeared. Everyone was hunting for him. My mom grabbed the bread drawer to put it back in the Hoosier cabinet and there he was fast asleep in the opening of the cabinet where the drawer belonged.

Dad bought Mom a beautiful yellow, wood-burning cook stove from Sears & Roebuck store. It had a warming oven on the top and a water reservoir for holding hot water. Oh those modern conveniences! One day, after Dad had fallen behind on the payments, Sears sent a man to pick the stove up. It just happened to be "bread" day for Mom. She told the man, yes, he could take it, but he had to take it right now. He said, "Lady, that stove is red hot. I can't take it now!" Years later, we moved that stove back to Barnesville.

Clark family in 1941. Clara Shriver's oldest sister is missing from picture.

Growing up we learned fast to do as we are told, when we were told to do it. There was no why, or how come, or in a minute. It was NOW! We learned respect for our elders. Yes, Sir, No, Ma'am. Needless to say, Dad didn't "spare the rod." They made us kids what we are today. (Thanks Mom and Dad.)

In 1937 Dad finally landed a good job at the Willow Grove coal mine. Dad had barely left for his shift one afternoon in 1940 when alarms and sirens started blowing. It was a nightmare for everyone waiting the "wait game." The mine had caught on fire; around 70 men lost their lives that day. Dad had many near misses throughout his life of coal mining.

In 1937 or 38, my Granddad Mace bought my sister Liz and me a "Shirley Temple" doll. Oh my, she was beautiful with her red polka dot dress and blond hair. I didn't play with mine much. I kept her in a trunk so she would stay beautiful. My sister on the other hand played with hers constantly. We went to our friend's house to visit and Liz snuck my "Shirley" out of her safe haven and Jim McGuire threw her down the outhouse hole! I was crushed! Devastated! Even now I tell Liz she owes me a Shirley. Today, I'm happy to say I own three old ones and nine new ones. I have many other dolls in my collection. At 78, I'm still a doll lovin' girl!

Sometimes Dad would buy candy and divide it equally between us kids. Not only did we each get the same number of pieces, but the same colors. I wonder if he was trying to tell us that he loved us equally or was it so we wouldn't fuss and argue.

By now my brother Bernard Eugene was born. He came May 19, 1937. Twins, Elroy Leonard and Leroy Howard arrived May 30, 1939. Mable Eunomia entered the family September 15, 1940.

We moved back to Barnesville in 1941. Now there were 10 of us kids. Times were tough so Mom took a job at Hansley's Mill making undergarments for the military. I still have a quilt made by Mom and Dad from some of the same blue and beige material scraps.

Now our home was located below the Lotus Glass Factory. I played with crystal dishes; they were "seconds" that the factory would toss down over the bank. It was like music to our ears when we'd hear them being dumped. Oh mercy, what they would be worth today!

During this time was World War II. The troop trains would pass by our house. The soldiers would ride in box cars, coal cars or passenger trains. They would wave their handkerchiefs and yell to us kids while we were playing. It was a very sad time. When the war ended everybody took the day off work and school for celebrating. People and kids alike were parading in the streets of Barnesville and singing "Hail, Hail, The Gang's all Here." Soldiers were given the respect that they so much deserved. My family is still very much rah, rah for our military. In my immediate family, there were/are 34 relatives that have given service to our country. Something we share with much pride.

My dad's cousin, Jim Gallagher, lived near us. He hired me to run errands for him. A trip to A&P would net me 10-cents. If I ran to Jess Windom's M&K, it was a 5-cent trip. I also carried quarts of milk from Coles Addition for 25 cents a week. I was really raking in the dough, so I thought. At the time, for me it was a lot! Jim would make a ledger entry each time I earned money. When I needed shoes or school supplies, he would calculate my earnings and pay me. I could buy a pair of shoes at Keystone Shoes for $ 1.98. At Murphy's 5 & 10, a tablet cost 5 cents, a penny for a pencil, a box of Crayola crayons would set me back a nickel. We could buy a pound of pretzels for a nickel.

Saturday was the best day of the week. There were two movie houses in town, the State and the Ohio theaters. We couldn't wait to see John Wayne, Roy Rogers or Hopalong Cassidy on the silver screen for a mere 10 cents. Oh what great entertainment!

Two more sisters were born at home. Blanche Clark Armstrong arrived May 2, 1944 at Barnesville Hospital and the last of the bunch, Esther Clark Dailey, aka "Precious," made her debut September 18, 1948. The mold for kids was broken and no more to be had after this one.

Through the years, the hills and valleys, the up and downs, life as it was; there was plenty of love to go around.

Scissors and Floods

by Elva Miller of Sugar Creek, Ohio
born 1934

My Embarrassing Moment. This was in my teenage years, when Mom and I used to go to our monthly sewings, which was for the needy overseas. We made quilts, comforts, and sewed dresses and gowns.

This was one of my first quilts to quilt. I was nervous and didn't know if I could quilt the right way. Anyways, the scissors got scarce on the quilt; no one knew where they got to. Finally, we discovered most of them were on my lap. I think I felt as red as an apple. My sister teased me the rest of her life, when we couldn't find the scissors at home; it was surely on my lap. I am now 74.

The Night before the 1969 Flood. We had picked old fashion, sweet, black cherries during the day in our orchard. Late that evening I cold packed them. Then went with our little children upstairs for bed. Usually we went with them till they slept. So I flopped over the bed with them, and not waking up from my own bed next morning, woke up and looked out the window and all I could see was water and a little of the fence posts sticking out. People thought it couldn't be that I slept through all that thunder and lightning and rain most of the night. The night before, Hubby said we never had such nice corn, looked just like a picture, 24 acres. By the next morning, it was almost history.

Dozens of big carp fish washed out of the creek. Hubby fixed the fence for weeks with hay and crops washed hard against it. But we made it through, and some people brought us some hay and corn, enough to keep the farm going. Also, we had a baby that year and Dad passed away. The year of 1969, I'll never forget.

Chicken Troubles and Magical Electricity

by Marjorie Ott McCune of Newcomerstown, Ohio
born 1927

I am almost 82 years of age and I have seen a lot and have been blessed. I have had seven children, 16 grandchildren, and expecting my ninth great grandchild.

I have a lot of memories. I grew up in the Depression age. My dad didn't have work for many years. He helped my grandpa, Dan Ott, a lot and for that we were supplied meat and milk. We always had butchering. Mom always had a lot of chickens, we ate eggs a lot.

I remember we had a dog that was getting into the chicken yard and killing our chickens. Dad took a dead chicken and tied it around the dog's neck. I don't know whether that ever stopped him or not.

I also remember when I was very young, I would go over to the chicken house and I would have a stick and I would knock the chickens off the roost. I had a lot of fun doing that, until one day I was busy with my pastimes, and all of a sudden I fell a switch on my legs. Dad swiped at me all the way to the house. I never bothered the chickens again.

I remember when the electricity went through, we were so excited. My sister and I had to help Mom clean the lamp chimneys every afternoon, so we could see in the evening and at night. It was almost magical that we could flip a switch and we had light.

Also, I remember my dad finally got a job helping the line go through; his job was helping the men dig holes so they could put the big poles that held the electric line in. Then Dad told us one day, a big pole slipped on them and came down on a young man and killed him. Dad said he heard his death gurgle. It really made us kids sad.

Then, there was the great snow of the 1950's. My husband and I lived in Isleta at the time, and had two small children. We decided we wanted to go up to my mom's, who lived up in Buck Horn. We had an old truck, and I wanted to pick my grandmother up. We did get up to Newcomerstown, but she told us to turn around and go back home. I guess we were young and didn't think it was so bad. So, we went on up, pushing snow all the way up, and we made it. But, we stayed at Mom and Dad's till the snow was pretty well gone. Later, I realized how dangerous that was, especially having two small children with us.

Then, there was the Jack Armstrong radio program, us kids could hardly wait till we got off the bus, rushed into the house, and turned on the radio. We also liked the funnies, especially Red Ryder and Little Beaver.

We lived around the Port Washington area and we were near the Winding Stairs. Dad took us kids along with him and we walked down those stairs. It was fun.

Rocking the Outhouse and Hand-me-downs and Washday

by Clyde D. Patton of Jerusalem, Ohio
born 1936

I had lived on this farm for seventy years. It is about three miles north of Woodsfield, Ohio in Monroe County.

When I was about 12 years old, each weekend I had to help Mom do the wash for our family. We had a wooden tub washing machine that I had to work the power handle back and forward to make the washer work and it also had a hand powered wringer that I had to turn to wring out the wash.

We had an outhouse that my mom built and before that, us boys went out in the yard for the one job, and most of the other, our bathroom trips was done at the barn or over in the woods. The outhouse was built from old lumber that was here on the farm, leftover from other buildings. It was very rough and was covered with tin from an old barn roof.

Us boys had a lot of fun watching for the ladies to go to the tin outhouse so that we could throw rocks at it. Sometimes we heard words that we did not hear too many times before that.

I am 73 years old and I grew up on a farm in Monroe County, near Woodsfield, Ohio. Dad, Charle Patton, and Mom, Hazel Patton, had an 80 acre farm that we lived on. Dad had a few cattle, horse, laying hen, and two hogs for our meat. There was four of us kids: Sue, Carl, Clyde, Clarence. Mom made our clothes out of feed sacks, and that was our underwear and shirts. Pants was made out of whatever she could find to make them out of. At the time, our coats, hats, and mittens were made out of old hand-me-down coats. One of mine was out of the next door neighbor lady's coat and it was as good as if it had been new from a store. I was in the seventh grade before I had clothes from the store. Then I went to work at Grandfather's (Forest Patton) farm and I got $30.00 out of each 500 chickens that they raised and then I got my own clothes.

Free Swimming and Hooky Playing

by Eileen Miller of New Philadelphia, Ohio
born 1929

Oh yes, I remember back to the Depression. We lived in Dover, Ohio. My dad put up billboard ads and was a manager for boxing matches. We lived in Dover in a nice home. Then, the Depression hit. We had to move into a less nice home right by the river.

When the river was ready to overflow, we walked to the riverbank, watching to see if we had to run. As a matter of fact, my brother went into the house through a door in a boat.

We moved to New Philadelphia in a not too nice place. We pulled a wagon up the alley to get free food to eat.

We kids around there would go down to a grassy hill and slide on cardboard down the hill. We also played kick the stick, and one boy got hit in the eye with the stick, and lost the eye.

When it rained we would put on our swimsuits and walk a mile to the park. When the park would let the kids back into the pool, we went in free because we were wet. They thought we had already been in the pool.

When my cousins came to live with us, they used my bed. Guess where I slept—on two chairs pushed together in the front room.

I remember wearing shoes that hurt my feet because they didn't fit well, and wearing clothes that came from the Goodwill store.

We ate a lot of macaroni and hamburger, but we made it through those rough years. Too bad the kids nowadays don't know what it was like having little to go on.

We moved to a better place because Dad got a better job. We moved across from the high school. I disliked school. I would walk in the front door, then go out the back door and play hooky.

I survived those years, married, and had three children. My husband died during the polio time. I remarried and had one more boy, then got a divorce. I have been single ever since.

That is my story. If nothing else, I hope you enjoyed it.

Andy's Momma

by Cicely A. Worthington of Carrollton, Ohio
born in 1926

When I was a schoolgirl in the 1930s in southeastern Ohio, it seemed that Memorial Day was a serious business. You might even call it sacred business.

The town usually awoke to a hot day that promised to get hotter. A day that promised waving flags and solemn speeches. A day that for us kids in Amsterdam Grade School meant a "ransomed" grade card unless we marched the mile hike from the school to the cemetery in the blazing sun to decorate the graves with flowers, with maybe a nickel cone to shorten the long way home. Memorial Day was a day when rusty-boned World War I veterans came out in their ancient uniforms, faces strained with suppressed emotion, to show the town what war was.

As a boy of eleven or twelve my brother had had for several years a special responsibility and he took the charge seriously. Unofficially he was the right hand man of Private Andy Uberti; you might even call him his gun bearer, his "Gunga Din."

How proud my brother was to be "on call" for Andy, as the old man got in line with the other soldiers. On this special day, there was probably many a boy like him who longed for the day when he too might march at the head of a parade, a returned hero waving to an admiring crowd. War seemed an adventure in those days.

Who was Private Uberti? Andy was, as a young man, a naturalized American citizen of Italian birth, inducted into the U.S. Army and sent to fight in Europe in World War I. When he told his story, as he often did as he grew older, he related that as the war went on, the fighting came close to the village where his aged mother still lived. So close, and so long away from his mother, Andy had a great need to see her. He asked permission of his commanding officer to locate and visit his mother. His request was never granted.

Memorial Day for Andy was a day to show loyalty to his adopted country, but it was also a day that brought back sad wartime memories. When inebriated, Andy would relive the lost opportunity to visit his mother, and he would sadly repeat to my brother or to anyone else: "I was ten miles from my village in Italy, only ten miles from my momma, but the boss he no let me go."

Now, in retrospect, I can see us again—just as if caught in time—the band, the soldiers, the kids clutching dead flowers, marching from the Methodist Church on S-Curve, starting through town, passing the war memorial, and all of us sweating and tired, beginning our way up Cemetery Hill.

Already Andy was having problems, and my brother sneaked from his class to help him. As we ascended the steep hill, Andy was breathing hard and as usual by this time, his puttees were unloosening around his ankles, causing the old man to trip now and then. Several times Andy had to drop out of line while my brother rewound his leggings.

Eventually, the band, soldiers and followers reached the summit and the crowd came to solemn rest. As the echo of taps resounded over the valley below, Andy quivered spasmodically and blew into his khaki handkerchief. The volley of shots made us kids cringe, and we held ourselves stiff. Then it was over. We drew a respective sigh of relief. We were released from our bout of patriotism for another year.

Andy, released as well and badly in need of refreshment, wiped his face and handed my brother his gun and his arm. "Johnny" (as Andy misnamed my brother) led the old soldier back down the hill and lunch with the "old boys" at the Veterans Club.

After lunch Andy and his young charge got into Andy's 1929 Modcl T to join a turkey shoot five miles away in a neighboring town. At best, Andy's driving was erratic; with pre-dinner and post-dinner drinks, it was even more so. However, most people in the area knew Andy and his car and gave him wide berth.

The two buddies finally reached the turkey shoot and welcoming friends. When Andy's turn came to shoot, however, even he recognized his aim was off. No problem. My brother's mentor in fishing and hunting, Andy, turned to his young friend and said, "Johnny, you shoot for me."

Ted Worthington at his brother's grave in North Africa in 1943.

I don't know whether this part of the story is true or not, but my brother "claimed" he hit the bull's eye, and the bird was his, and he proudly accepted the applause of the old vets.

Eventually the day waned. And likewise, Andy. He was now completely helpless with the excitement of the day. Someone helped him into his car. Someone else helped my brother tie the legs of the flapping prize he had won and throw the bird into the rumble seat.

Andy got behind the wheel to the squawking noise of an angry turkey, and now, completely out of control, hit the fence behind him and slid into a ditch.

Cursing in two languages, Andy kicked the front fender and left the car lying there. My brother grabbed the turkey. Together they started down the road for home. Rain began to fall. Andy, a bundle of unwrapped leggings and crumpled uniform, wept along with the rain, muttering his old refrain: "My momma, he no let me see my momma. Boy should see momma once more before she die."

Young boy and old man staggered along, each in his own thoughts; probably both were tired and confused. What had happened to a beautiful day? Memorial Day was waving flags and booming guns and proud vets striding in the sun. But it seemed different now. It had ended with a helpless, unhappy, doddering old man.

That day puzzled my brother for a long time. He grew up, and he too went to war, World War II. He fought in North Africa; he experienced the D-Day landing, the Battle of the Bulge, and the push to Berlin. When he finally returned home, he looked up his old fishing buddy. He wanted to tell him something. But while my brother was away, Andy had died. My brother was never able to tell him what he had learned about war.

Now he knew what Andy had known and why Andy cried.

End of the Drought at Walnut Grove

by Rev. Ralph Hollingsworth of Newcomerstown, Ohio
born in 1922

As a boy on the Walnut Grove Farm I experienced the general drought in the middle thirties in southeastern Ohio.

The farm was located on what is Peoli Road between Peoli and Birmingham in northern Guernsey County. It was known as Hollingsworth Ridge during the drought.

I had several tasks and chores to do as we all worked together as families. The number one task was to save water. The wash water was carried to the garden to water the garden plants. I would go to the creek each morning to decide if there was enough water for the farm cattle and sheep.

My dad and uncles would talk about what fields would be used for pasture for a few days. Hay fields were being turned into pasture fields. The men would decide each morning whether to cut a tree or two for the cattle to feed on the leaves. They had the crosscut saw sharpened and ready for the day.

The raising of food was very essential. We chose truck patches in the very low areas where there would be more moisture. We soon learned their location made a big difference.

I also checked the springs on the farm. Some dried up and others didn't. We made wooden frames out of planks and buried them around the springs to collect the small amount of water.

Black potato bugs started to appear on the potatoes. This was a serious problem as they would strip a plant overnight. The plant would then die.

We took containers of drained oil from the Fordson tractor and tapped the plants with small paddles. The bugs would fall into the oil and die. This turned out to be a real chore. It had to be done every day.

There was no fruit on the trees or bushes except elderberries. Patches of elderberry bushes soon became prize possessions. The neighborhood was searched for elderberries just like mushrooms are today. Then the tedious task of cleaning the berries off the stems. Every berry was saved and canned.

A grass fire was a constant concern. No matches were ever carried in the pockets of those who did field work. Sure enough one afternoon, as I got off the school bus, a large field was on fire east of our home on the other side of the creek. The guess was that it was started by a piece of farm machinery becoming too hot for levels of lubrication.

One morning when I went to the creek to check the water level there was a little more water. Enough to make a tiny stream. I stood and looked for a long time. It was like watching a miracle. I realized the water I was looking at came from springs.

Why more?

Of course this was encouraging news for all the family. Real rejoicing on Hollingsworth Ridge. Each morning the stream increased and continued to do so until a rain finally came. But, why more before?

No one ever answered that question for me. Maybe someone who reads this article will have an answer for me.

I realized later that the underground water level under the farm is what saved the water well and certain springs.

The Walnut Grove Farm was richly blessed by Mother Nature even in a drought.

The Blue Chevy Coupe

By Lucille Steel of Dover, Ohio
Born 1934

After some 65 years have passed, the recollections of Grandma and Grandpa and their faded blue Chevy Coupe still provide pleasant memories and a lasting impression on my mind. This late 30's model was a bit rusty, discolored and streaked from age, but the big thing I remember was the marble knob on the steering wheel, which made it possible to turn sharp corners with ease. The coupe was used not only for transportation, but played a part in the financial picture for my grandparents.

My grandparents, Henry and Bertha Maurer, lived on the farm which had been his pioneer grandfather's homestead since the late 1830's. It was rugged, hilly land where they etched out only a meager income. Life was simple, but yet it was good. They ate well from Grandma's productive garden. From the hen house there was chicken for Sunday dinner and eggs every morning for breakfast. Grandma kept busy with canning, preserving and baking. All this was accomplished using the white wood cook stove setting in the corner of her "little kitchen" as she described it.

Grandpa knew farming inside and out. He milked a few cows by hand providing fresh milk for the table. Some was hauled in large milk cans down the road to the cheese house to be made into Swiss cheese. He also slopped a few hogs and pastured a flock of wool-producing sheep. He loved tilling the soil and put in many long hours behind the horses and a plow.

However, Grandma's specialty was tending peeps, feeding chickens and gathering eggs. Each spring they would buy Rhode Island Red peeps to raise and sell as broilers. When the broilers were ready to sell, they needed a way a way to market them. Here is where the old blue coupe came into play.

Early on a summer morning, even though Grandma never had a driver's license, she would back the coupe out of the aged and faded garage across the road and park at the end of the sidewalk in order to get loaded for the trip to Dover fifteen miles away. Grandpa would place a balky chicken crate into the coupe trunk. Using a long wire hook, he would snag the leg of each meaty broiler and place it in the crate until it would hold no more. Grandma would hurry out with a basket heaped high with large brown eggs and lift it into the trunk. It was time to shove off to "peddle their eggs and broilers," as they used to say. The early morning sun was shining and the ride to Dover in the blue coupe was pleasant and enjoyable.

Mast family. Grandfather, Henry A. Mast, holding Lucille Steel and Grandmother holding cousin in 1936.

Usually, our stop was at the western edge of Dover, just off Tuscarawas Avenue. Many Italian families had settled there. Upon our arrival, word spread fast around the neighborhood. Soon the blue coupe was surrounded by apron-clad ladies conversing with each other in their own dialect. Patiently, they waited in line as Grandpa weighed each broiler one by one. Grandma was busy counting eggs into the containers they had brought from their kitchens.

My grandparents had made this trip many times. Their customers knew them and were pleased to have the opportunity to buy farm fresh products at their door.

After the last broiler was sold and the last dozen of eggs purchased, Grandpa closed the trunk and drove to downtown Dover. It was time for lunch. No, we didn't go to a restaurant. Grandma went to the A&P store while Grandpa and I waited in the coupe. She bought a loaf of bread, a pound of sliced bologna, sugared donuts or perhaps a Spanish loaf cake. Quickly, she put together a sandwich for each of us and along with a donut or slice of cake, we enjoyed our meal in the comfort of the blue coupe. I felt loved and secure sitting between Grandma and Grandpa eating a bologna sandwich.

It was time to make our way back to the farm and as we drove along the winding road, I could tell that Grandma and Grandpa were eager to get back to the farm. There was work to be done!

Their lifestyle said something to me. It's important to work hard, earn an honest living and be content with what you have. These are precious memories I will always treasure.

Fond memories of Grandpa and Grandma Mast. A man of integrity, multiple talents, and grandfather to twelve, described my Grandpa Mast, a well respected man in the community. He was a carpenter by trade, who earned the distinction of having built lovely brick homes in the village of Sugarcreek. His faith and trust played an important part in his successful life.

History indicates the Mast immigrants came from the Schwarzenburg community in Canton Bern, Switzerland. They arrived in America on October 8, 1737 on the Charming Nancy of London, having been invited by William Penn. Jacob and Barbara Masht (Mast) settled on land they purchased from the state of Pennsylvania at $3.00 an acre. Their 14 children were born on the farm. A son, Jacob, is our direct line who came to Holmes County in 1812. He was the father of Dr. Abraham, a colorful figure in family history, being a farmer, doctor, minister and father of 18 children.

Grandpa, Henry A. Mast, was born September 30, 1878 into a large family. He grew up in the Walnut Creek area and on December 23, 1900, married Artie Miller. Together they had 4 sons (the oldest being my father) and one daughter.

Grandpa took pride in having built their home. His superb handiwork was evident in the oak woodwork and beautiful floors. In fact, as a child, my dad was in a bit of trouble when he rode a broken trike across the hardwood floor.

Grandpa's leadership in Sugarcreek included among other things, Mast Bros. Planing Mill owned by he and his brother, Abe. At one time he was manager of the Claycraft brickyard. It was once said that Henry Mast was to Sugarcreek what the President is to the country. That is a strong statement!

Music was an important element in the Mast family. In 1917 Grandpa was a member of the Melodious Eight. He played the fiddle and jug in the Mast Family Band. I recall seeing Grandpa's jug used for a doorstop in the living room. Music echoed throughout the Mast home. I treasure having Grandpa's fiddle.

Vivid memories of riding beside Grandpa in his faded purple work car with the gigantic tool chest in the back come to mind. A myriad of drawers held interesting hammers, wrenches, bolts and nuts right at your fingertips!

Grandpa was not a farmer, but occasionally he came to the farm to repair fences. I loved to tag along and "help" him. Just being with him was fun, but I wanted to talk to him. I had loads of questions, but after awhile he didn't answer me. It became a one way conversation. I never could figure that out until I grew older.

Grandpa tended his Jonathan apple trees in the back yard. His grape arbor over the sidewalk yielded blue, red and green grapes in season. He dabbled in peeps and chickens in his temperature controlled incubator and brooder house.

Grandpa had a marvelous bathtub in the house that stood on four legs. It was the neatest thing! Upstairs in the sunroom was a Victrola with a crank that played waltzes and rinky dink music. We grandchildren spent many hours cranking out the music.

Grandpa's hand had been severely injured in a sawing accident. His two middle fingers were cut off at the first knuckle and his little finger was maimed, but still usable. He once told me he had pain until he put the severed fingers in a place I cannot recall.

Another time he was injured with the steam shovel at work and he wanted to see me, but I felt so sorry for him I could only go to the landing in the stairway and he talked to me from upstairs.

I don't remember Grandpa ever wearing a suit coat and tie. That could have been a part of his Mennonite heritage where plain clothing was required.

I recall World War II days when Grandpa listened to the radio and read *LIFE* magazine to keep up on the world news. His youngest son was serving in the military. He had great concern about his son's safety and awaited his return.

Grandpa liked hearing about sports in the area. He and the family enjoyed playing Rook around the kitchen table. We grandchildren played our own game of Smutz, also using the Rook cards.

One Christmas, Grandpa made each family a blackboard. That was a favorite gift.

When the Mast family gathered at Grandpa and Grandma's for a meal, Grandma always believed in having the men eat at the first table. Then the women and children would eat. This was a handed down custom. Another interesting practice was that women in the family were identified by their husband's name before their own. Grandma was known as "Hen-Artie" to her friends and relatives.

After a visit at Grandpa and Grandma's, Grandpa would go to the tall white built-in cupboard, open the door and reach to the shelf and get his candy bag containing malted milk balls. It was always malted milk balls, but I loved 'em!

He and I had this little chant we would say to each other as my parents and I would leave, "Sleep tight, don't let the bed bugs bite!"

Grandpa was a fun loving, positive person who left me with multiplied happy memories, even though he didn't say much while we pounded steeples in the fence.

Mice in a Bucket and a Drunken Rooster

by Amanda Slabaugh of Beach City, Ohio
born 1932

My name is Amanda Slabaugh, I was born and raised on a farm close to Charm, Ohio in Amish country. I am the youngest of ten children. There was a lot of action going on with ten children.

My mom had a stroke and was paralyzed when I was seven years old. Two years later, she died at the age of fifty.

It was hard to grow up without a mom. My dad never got married again. Growing up on a farm, we all learned what hard work was all about. I was fifteen when my dad sold the farm. Then we moved to Charm. We were Amish, but I joined the Mennonites when I was nineteen. We lived there for five years, then my dad sold the house. By then most of my brothers and sisters were married. My dad went to stay with my brother and in 1963 he passed away.

I certainly remember some of the things that happened when I was a child. We had an outhouse, and I hated to go in there. In the summertime there were spiders and wasps in there. In the wintertime it was bitter cold to sit there and do your business.

And yes, I was wearing homemade clothes made out of feed sacks. We were poor and satisfied what we had.

We had a big garden and a lot of fruit trees. It cost very little for groceries. We made our own ice cream, and that was a real treat. Yes, we had two house dogs, but my dad never left me to take one along to bed at night.

When somebody killed a snake, I always liked to take a stick and played with them. Which does sound crazy. I remember one time, I chased a skunk down the road, but I never got sprayed. That was plain luck.

And I loved to sit in the corn crib, trying to catch a mouse. One time, I had three mice in a bucket, but they all died.

I also got into mischief, but my dad never caught me. I loved to go in the chicken house and sit on a stool and watch the chickens eat. Then I would jump up and yell and the chickens would fly all over the place. My brothers would take a rooster and give him a little whiskey. If it was the right amount, the rooster would start to crow. If they gave too much, the rooster would pass out. Two of my sisters were in the orchard picking apples. They wanted to have fun so they stuffed the bottom part of their dresses in their underpants. And then one of the neighbors came walking past. They really hurried to get their dress out. I guess it seemed funny for the neighbor.

This is about my brothers. Sometimes they would take two of the farm cats and tie their tails together. Then they would hang the cats over the clothesline. That really stirred up a fight between the cats.

One more thing. Sometimes a stray dog would come around. If my brothers could catch him, they would tie a tin can on its tail and take a corn cob and dip it in turpentine and rub the dog's rear end with it. The dog just yipped and ran as fast as it could and never came back.

Everything that I wrote is absolutely true. All this happened while we were living on the farm.

My dad's name was Henry Miller. My mom's name, Bena Nisley. I'll list my brothers' and sisters' names in the order they were born. Edna, Roman, John, Ammon, Albert, Mattie, Henry, Lizzie, Ada, and I was the last one.

I got married to Ralph Slabaugh in 1965 and November 6, 1980 he died of a heart attack. My brothers and sisters have all passed away.

Thanks a lot for listening to my stories of things that happened a long time ago. My dad sold the farm in 1947. I was fifteen years old.

Skinny Dipping and Clodhoppers

by James A. Larrick of Cambridge, Ohio
born 1919

When I was growing up in Byesville, Ohio, there were no public pools, so we went swimming in Wills Creek. By the way, we didn't wear bathing suits. We went "skinny dipping."

Wills Creek circled around Byesville, and we had certain places that were good swimming holes. We named the places. The swimming hole where the creek came closest to the train and street car tracks was named The Tile. We had water dammed up there with rocks and put up a rope swing to swing out over the water and jump in.

The next one was Rocky Bottom. At this swimming hole, we could wade out in it. This is where I learned to swim. It was a nice place, because there was a spring that came out from under the rocks. It bubbled all the time, and the water was good to drink.

The most popular swimming hole was called Stony Riffle. It was shallow and kind of sandy underneath. Most everyone went to this one, even adults. So there we had to wear bathing suits.

At some of the swimming holes we made diving boards out of railroad ties and boards.

Once I saved a friend, Waldy, from drowning. We were swimming at The Tile. Everyone would dive in and swim across, about 60 feet, then swim back. Waldy had just learned to swim. Both of us swam across, and I told Waldy he had better rest awhile before swimming back. But he dived in, started swimming, and couldn't make it. I dived in and grabbed him by the hair. He wrapped his arms and legs around me, and we both went under. I managed to get my head above water, got some air, moved forward some, and then under we went again. We kept going this way and finally made it!

We didn't have many store-bought toys, but I remember playing with little iron cars. They were 5 or 6 inches long. My friend, Bob, also had these little cars. He lived about 5 houses up the street from me. At this time the streets were just dirt, not paved. We liked to make roads in the dirt with our iron cars. When it rained, the streets were muddy. We thought it was great fun to push the little cars all the way from his house to my house, making tracks in the mud. We were a muddy mess!

A favorite homemade toy that I always had was a hoop and roller. The hoop was the steel rim of a wooden wagon wheel about 8 inches in diameter and the roller was made from a piece of wire bent with a hook on the end or wood lathe made like a cross. I used the roller to make the hoop roll. It was also fun to play with an old tire, just push it and keep it rolling.

I made stilts to walk around in, airplanes from broomsticks, and swords from lathe sticks. I also made a gun of wood with a spring type clothespin for shooting rubber rings made out of inner tubes from old tires.

My mother used to paper rooms for other people. My job was to get the papering board, ladders, and walking board on my wagon (which I had received for a Christmas present) and to take them to the house of the people that she was papering for.

Spring cleaning was always a big job. All the rugs in the house had to be taken up, taken outside, spread out on the ground, and then beaten with carpet beaters to get out all the dirt.

Washing clothes was a big chore. Rain water from a big barrel at the corner of the house was used. I would carry buckets of water to the tub sitting on a gas stove in the wash house. The wash house was right behind our house. My mother would use Old Settler in the water and skim the dirt off the top of the water to keep the water clear for washing.

I never had a pair of long pants until I was a freshman in high school. I always had to wear knee pants which had an elastic band that could be worn above the knee or worn below the knee. I remember how I hated wearing them above my knees. I would pull them down below my knees as far as I could make them reach. Once I refused to go downtown with Ann, who was living with us at the time, because she wanted me to wear my pants above my knees.

My mother bought me a pair of laced-up to my ankle shoes. I put them on, and my mother said, "Boy, those

Myron, Tracy, Jimmy.

are some clod-hoppers." After hearing this, I went outside, gathered some clumps of dirt from the garden, and proceeded to stomp them all over the sidewalk.

We didn't have running water, but we had a dug well with a pump over it. I remember hunting for the chain at the bottom of the well (when the chain would break and fall to the bottom of the well) using a hook and rope.

We kept a bucket of water with a dipper in it in the house for drinking. I had a habit of wanting a drink of water after going to bed at night, and I wanted fresh water from the well. So, my mother or sister would go downstairs, out to the well, and bring me a fresh drink of water. After about a week of this, my mother said, "If you want a fresh drink of water, get up and go get it." So I did, but that was the last time I ever asked for a drink of fresh water after going to bed.

Mom's Apron and the American Flag

by Dwight Stotts of Zanesville, Ohio
born in 1931

My name is Dwight Stotts. I am from Zanesville, Ohio and this is the way it was growing up in southeastern Ohio for my family and friends.

At the age of six, my parents, five brothers (I being the youngest boy), and my six sisters moved from the country into the city life of Zanesville. Our first home sat on the corner of Luck and Nancy Avenues. We later moved to the west end of town, 161 Brighton Blvd. This home belonged to my grandmother, Addie Jane Stotts. It was an old home, with three rooms on the main level, two bedrooms upstairs and a dirt cellar. Our bathroom had only a commode; baths were taken in a large washtub and we took turns bathing.

Our front yard was small but had a nice sidewalk where the girls, and sometimes us boys, played hopscotch, and a wooden porch swing hung on our front porch. Our back yard was wonderful with a big sugar pear tree at the top of the yard, a garden plot, and plenty of space for Mom to hang the laundry out to dry.

Dad planted tomatoes in his garden so Mom would have them for canning. We enjoyed them all winter as Mom made soups, stews and my favorite, tomato dumplings, for all of us.

Mom always set aside Monday for "wash day." Her clothesline reached from the ole pear tree clear to the bottom of the hill and ended attached to the wood shed on Dad's garage. She always wore her cobbler apron full of wooden clothespins as she hung and pinned the clothes neatly down through the yard.

Of course, Mom always wore an apron wash day or not; it was part of her daily dress. I'm sure with her apron she could wipe her hands free of flour, dab at the miscellaneous tears and wipe smudges of dirt from the faces of 11 children throughout the day.

The woodshed doubled as a make-believe store for my sisters, Ruthie and Wanda, and their friend Jan Covert. Her family owned Covert's Hardware located on West Main Street at the end of the Y Bridge.

At the base of the yard between the woodshed and the alley stood our dad's garage. Dad was a good mechanic and some of his customers were Old Town Cleaners from Maple Avenue and Polks' Junk Yard on the west side of town. He was always busy in the garage. During winter he kept it warm with a potbelly stove which occasionally claimed his eyebrows during lighting!

West of our house down Brighton set Munson Grade School which we all attended. We would run home at lunchtime every day and Mom would have our lunch ready.

Going east on Brighton at the intersection of Brighton and Ridge Avenues sat Fox's Drug Store. They had a wonderful ice cream counter, with small round stools to set on. The pictures that hung on the walls were of yummy sundaes, and all flavors of ice cream cones. There was never enough money for us to get those wonderful looking treats. Sometimes I would have a penny and oh the excitement of buying a penny grab bag to see what treasure waited at the bottom. Sometimes it was even a few pieces of candy! That was a real treat!

Another treat for us was a piece of ice from the ice wagon. Wrapped in a piece of newspaper, it was a real treat.

If you continued walking east on Brighton you would pass some of the most beautiful homes; they were big and I often thought that maybe someday I would buy one of those homes. Now, this is one of Zanesville's historic areas.

At the very end of Brighton, you run right into the Muskingum County Fairgrounds. There stood BIG beautiful iron gates where if you had money, you paid and walked through them fair week. We never had much money for such things, but back then boys would climb the fence along the edge of the fairgrounds, land on the other side running and run for all you had until you were clear of getting caught. My friends, Bob Frye, Mac Smith and I did this each summer and it was a fun time with no serious mischief involved.

Going south of the fairgrounds on Pershing Road

you come to the intersection of Pershing and Pine Street. Here sat Grover Cleveland Junior High School. It was a large old majestic stone and brick structure. Sadly, it was torn down a few years ago to make room for a new, not so majestic, school building. They call it progress! I attended seventh, eighth and ninth grades at Grover Cleveland, walking or riding my bicycle to and from school. It was about one and one half miles each way, and there were no buses for riding; you made it on your own power.

Tenth grade took me into downtown Zanesville to Lash High School on the corners of Shinnick and Fifth Streets. I played as the right guard, right halfback on the football team and being the smallest player, earned the nickname "Peewee." I loved football and had been on a team since eighth grade.

By the middle of my tenth grade year I had begun to work at Prindles Bowling Alley on South Sixth Street. Of course this was a night job, setting pins on the alleys. After work I had the long walk home. Sometimes it would be 1 a.m. before I got home and into bed. It was hard to keep up my grades and work. I was by now buying my own clothes and giving money to Mom when I had extra to help her and Dad out. At this time, I quit school.

I had also been helping my dad with logging in the woods since the age of twelve and education didn't seem as "necessary" as the pay at that time. When I worked with Dad he would put my long black dinner bucket in the seat behind me long ways so my feet would reach the tractor pedals. One day I ran the dozer into a fallen tree loaded with a large hive of bumblebees. What a miserable day that was. I had 22 stings on my head alone, and some were doubled up, I'm sure. When I arrived home, I didn't want Mom to worry so I just told her that I wasn't hungry and went straight up the stairs to bed. I was so sick, I thought sure I would die; maybe it was a wonder I didn't!

In October 1949, I enlisted in the U.S. Army. How well I remember walking to the bus station, stepping up on the bus, saying goodbye to my mother. This was so very hard and tore at my heart because I loved my mother so very much. I was leaving everything that I knew and loved to fight a war that I knew nothing about, but hoping that I was making the right decision. I was to end up serving overseas in Korea and fought in five major battles. I spent 36 months in the army, being honorably discharged in October of 1952. While on that bus ride and while being aboard the ship *General Black*, in route to Korea, I had plenty of time to reflect on life growing up in Zanesville.

I thought about that wonderful old sugar pear tree in the back yard. It had served many purposes over the years. It had given us a wonderful sweet treat every year, and gave my brother Bill and I our first business experience. We had picked pears, filled baskets, and loaded our wagon to the brim to be door to door salesmen. After pulling our wagon the length of Brighton Boulevard and back we hadn't sold one single basket of pears at only five cents per basket. So, being tired and hungry, we just sat ourselves down on some wide porch steps and ate them. I decided right then that I didn't want to be in sales! The tree also provided shade to play in on hot days and switches for bottoms when we needed them.

I thought about the alley at the bottom of our yard and of all of the good times we had playing there. We played kick the-can, marbles, roll the hoop and basketball. One of our favorite games was more-stacks. Someone would lie down on their belly and yell, "More stacks," then someone else would pile on top of them and this would go on until the stack would fall over. And then someone else would take a turn on the bottom of the stack. How much fun that was!

I thought about the squirrel my brother Dale snuck into the house. Mom never allowed any animals in the house; she said their place was outside. But she let Dale keep that squirrel, until one night in his sleep he rolled over on it and come morning the squirrel was stiff. Our beds were pretty full of kids, wasn't much room even for a squirrel!

I remembered hearing Mom yell at us to quit banging the old wooden screen door as we ran in and out of the house. And to quit hitting the house with the front porch swing! I suppose 11 children banging would create quite a racket.

We would lay on our backs out in the yard and search for the big and little dippers in the sky, or watch for a shooting star. To see one of them was always exciting.

I remembered family reunions and the long ride to get to them down in the hills of Morgan County. Kids would be hanging out of every window in the car and singing all the way down. We were so worn out on the way home from playing that we usually slept all the way back to town. One time we were part way home when we realized that we were short one sister. We had gone off and left Peggy Jean in Pennsville at the park. Another family member gathered her up and brought her home.

I thought of holidays, especially Christmas. We would string popcorn for our tree, but as we ate almost as much as we strung, it took quite a while to get it done. We made red and green chains out of strips of paper to decorate our tree too. We only had a very few bulbs. Christmas morning we each got one gift and we would run down the wooden staircase to see what had been placed under the tree for us. We each got a stocking too. These stockings were the real McCoy, not some fancy thing from a department store. No sir, a real wool stocking right out of your drawer. My brother, Ralph, once told me that he was sixteen years old before he realized that hard candy didn't come with fuzz on it! Fuzz or no fuzz, we ate that candy, picking off what we could and knowing it would be a while before there was any more of it. One year I got a wind-up tractor that I had been wanting so badly; first thing my brother Dale wanted to do was show me how to wind it so it could go. He wound it so tight that he broke the spring; I cried and cried. Years later, Dale bought me an iron tractor replica at an auction and gave it to me to replace that one that he had broken when we were just boys. I like to look at it now and let it take me back. It is good to look back and be able to smile and laugh at the things we did and the fun we had growing up together and sharing together.

After I left St. Louis and headed to Washington, I boarded the *General Black*. She carried about 35,000 boys to a stop in Japan and then on to Korea. It took 22 days to make that voyage. I remember many long, cold, wet nights spent in foxholes asking the Lord to get me back to Zanesville, to home, safe. I wanted to find a hometown girl, get married and raise a family there.

And in 1954 I did just that. We had left as boys and those of us who were fortunate enough to return, returned as men. I met and married my wife; this October will mark our 55-year anniversary. Together we have one daughter, two grandchildren and four beautiful great-grandchildren.

God kept his hand on me, my brothers, Jack and Bill, and my great friends, Bob and Mack, while we were serving in Korea and He brought us all back safely to Zanesville, Ohio.

I don't have that house on Brighton Boulevard that I looked at so often as a boy. Instead I built a cozy home on 17 acres outside of the city limits, where I now sit quietly on my porch, looking out across my pond and seeing the reflection of more than just my life. I can see the reflection of the beautiful U.S. flag I hung, waving atop the 30 foot pole across the pond. I am reminded that freedom isn't free, but it was worth the fight.

Corncobs for Company and the Catfish Bite

by Leona M. Wilson of New Philadelphia, Ohio
born in 1943

I was born April 13, 1943 at my grandparents' farm between Stone Creek and Ragersville, Ohio. My grandparents' names were John and Alice Orr. They lived on a big farm. My dad was in the Army when I was born. My grandma and Aunts Betty and Kate helped deliver me. We had a doctor from Ragersville who also helped.

I stayed at my grandparents' until I was five years old. We then moved about four miles down the road where I lived until I was 21 years old.

I got to go to Stone Creek School when I was seven years old. Every year I had measles or chicken pox so I had to stay home. My mom got mad at me because I got sick when we had Farmer's Institute programs at school, which you call PTA today. One year my mom dressed me up like a clown and put rouge and powder so you could not see my measles. My teacher looked at me and sent me and my mom home. Six months later I had chicken pox and put on my mom's makeup so I could go to school and my mom paddled me and sent me to bed for the rest of the day.

We used to use the old chamber pots called combinetts which we had to carry outside in the snow and empty. Wow, those old outhouses were drafty and cold. In the summertime you usually had a blacksnake laying on the seat so you had to be careful where you sat. Wasps made nests inside the toilet paper. We used a lot of Sears, Penny, and Montgomery Ward catalogs plus the newspaper. Saturday you scrubbed the outhouse with old lye soap. I had to shell ears of corn so we could use the corn cobs like toilet paper. We used these when company came.

We only listened to the radio on Saturdays when the farm news was on.

I loved party line phones. I would listen to everyone's call, and then I would tell everyone all the news. Some of the calls were real mushy.

My grandparents had the old crank up phonographs.

I got one spanking at school when I put a tack on a teacher's chair. Mom spanked me four times when the teacher called her.

Saturday night was bath night in the old wash tubs. The water was heated in big wash tubs on an old coal and wood stove in the kitchen.

When the family went fishing and fell out of the boat, a big catfish bit my toes which he thought was fishing worms. I had a sore toe for a week. A neighbor, Clara Dummermuth, wrapped my toes in Mullen plants. It took out the poison and swelling down.

We had a wringer washer that I got my hand caught in. It took all day to wash clothes and hang them on the many clotheslines.

Saturday night movies was Archie Bunker and the fights, then the TV was turned off until next Saturday night.

My mother and the neighbor ladies made our clothes from flowered feed sacks. They made dresses, socks, and panties. If there was enough material left, they made aprons or dust caps. My favorite teachers were Anna Moomaw and Wanda Schlafley. Anna was my grade school teacher and Wanda was my high school teacher.

We had really big deep snows. I had to make tunnels to go to the barn and chicken coops to feed the animals. Milking cows was not my favorite job. The cows always kicked you or swished their tails in your face.

I had a mother snake and a mother skunk chase me from the barn to the house. The faster I ran, they slithered in the grass and ran after me. They stayed on the porch all day.

The neighbor man made me table and chairs and a high chair for my dolls.

All of us neighbor kids went Halloweening and threw corn and upset an old outhouse then we shoved a neighbor boy in the poop because he scared us. The neighbor made us set up his outhouse and clean it.

I took three five-gallon buckets and walked for miles picking blackberries and raspberries for 25 cents a quart. Most of these were sold at general stores in Stone Creek and Ragersville, Ohio. I also picked peaches and sold them for $1.50 for a bushel basket. Strawberries were 15 cents a quart. I picked hickory, black walnuts, and hazelnuts and sold these to Anna Moomaw who took them to Florida.

Leona Wilson's grandparents, John and Alice Orr.

Butchering day started at four a.m. in the morning. I had to carry wood to start the fires. Copper kettles were put on the fire to boil water. I used hog scrapers to take hairs off the hogs. The cows' hide was tanned and clothes were made from this. We made sausage and stuffed it in casings, blood pudding, krepples, and cracklings. The lard was rendered for cooking and baking. The cows' tails was used for oxtail and homemade noodle soup.

I helped plant gardens, make hay by hand; you had to ride the mowing machine, corn picker, corn planter. I helped thresh wheat and oats, shock corn.

Hay was put in the barn by horse and wagon. I would ride the harpoon up in the hay mound then jump off and pull the rope to dump the hay in the mow.

We had a neighbor who had two mules named Jack and Jenny. They would pen them in the barn when they took the truck to town. Jack and Jenny would kick the door open and run down the road and beat them to town.

We also had a red rooster who would flop you and his spurs into your legs. I killed him and my mom made me a peach pie.

My sister and brother got in trouble. They blamed me, so I had to do their chores for a week.

YOUR MEMORIES